THE NORTON READER
Sixteenth Edition

THE NORTON READER
An Anthology of Nonfiction

SIXTEENTH EDITION

MELISSA A. GOLDTHWAITE, *General Editor*
Saint Joseph's University

JOSEPH BIZUP
Boston University

ANNE E. FERNALD
Fordham University

W. W. NORTON & COMPANY
Celebrating a Century of Independent Publishing

W. W. Norton & Company has been independent since its founding in 1923, when William Warder Norton and Mary D. Herter Norton first published lectures delivered at the People's Institute, the adult education division of New York City's Cooper Union. The firm soon expanded its program beyond the Institute, publishing books by celebrated academics from America and abroad. By midcentury, the two major pillars of Norton's publishing program—trade books and college texts—were firmly established. In the 1950s, the Norton family transferred control of the company to its employees, and today—with a staff of five hundred and hundreds of trade, college, and professional titles published each year—W. W. Norton & Company stands as the largest and oldest publishing house owned wholly by its employees.

Editor: Sarah Touborg
Project Editor: Selin Tekgurler
Editorial Assistant: Caroline Fairey Meese
Managing Editor, College: Marian Johnson
Production Manager: Karen Romano
Media Editor: Joy Cranshaw
Media Editorial Assistant: Juliet Godwin
Managing Editor, College Digital Media: Kim Yi
Ebook Producer: Mica Clausen
Marketing Manager, Composition: Michele Dobbins
Design Director: Rubina Yeh
Designer: Juan Paolo Francisco
Director of College Permissions: Megan Schindel
Permissions Clearing: Elizabeth Trammell
Photo Editor: Catherine Abelman
Composition: Westchester Publishing Services
Manufacturing: LSC Communications

Permission to use copyrighted material is included in the credits section of this book, which begins on page 813.

ISBN: 978-1-324-04707-0 (pbk.)

W. W. Norton & Company, Inc., 500 Fifth Avenue, New York, NY 10110
wwnorton.com
W. W. Norton & Company Ltd., 15 Carlisle Street, London W1D 3BS

1 2 3 4 5 6 7 8 9 0

BRIEF CONTENTS

CONTENTS

* *New to this edition*

2. TRADITIONS   64

* *New to this edition*

* *New to this edition*

4. SELF AND SOCIETY   163

* *New to this edition*

* *New to this edition*

* *New to this edition*

* *New to this edition*

* *New to this edition*

* *New to this edition*

* *New to this edition*

10. Nature and the Environment 602

* *New to this edition*

* *New to this edition*

12. LIVING VALUES 719

* *New to this edition*

* *New to this edition*

PREFACE

The Norton Reader began as an attempt to introduce students to the essay as a genre and to create an anthology of excellent nonfiction writing. This new edition continues that tradition, offering a wide selection of essays on a broad range of subjects and including examples of the kinds of writing students are most often assigned, from profiles and arguments to narratives and analyses. With 126 selections in the Full Edition and 77 in the Shorter Edition, *The Norton Reader* offers depth, breadth, and variety for teaching the essay as it has developed over time, including selections from the classic to the contemporary.

As always, *The Norton Reader* has aimed to uphold a tradition of anthologizing excellent prose, starting with Arthur Eastman, the founding editor, who insisted that essays be selected for the quality of their writing. As he put it, "Excellence would be their pillar of smoke by day, of fire by night." With this vision, the original editors of *The Norton Reader* chose classic essays that appealed to modern readers and that are now recognized as comprising the essay canon. We have aimed to continue this practice yet have also adapted the *Reader* to new pedagogies and have updated it by adding new writers whose work appeals to new generations of student readers. We believe that the essays in this volume are well written, focus on topics that matter, and demonstrate what all of us tell our students about good writing.

NEW TO THIS EDITION

- Forty-eight new readings from a diverse array of today's most influential and exciting voices, including Hanif Abdurraqib, Jia Tolentino, Annette Gordon-Reed, Audre Lorde, Michelle Zauner, Emily Wilson, Ibram X. Kendi, Greta Thunberg, Cheryl Strayed, Imani Perry, and many others.

- Four new chapters—"Caring for Self, Caring for Others"; "Body Language"; "Insider Knowledge"; and "Declarations"—will inspire and inform students' reading and writing about issues that matter.

- Refreshed questions at the end of each reading ask students to annotate, consider, and write at the lively intersection of personal writing, civic conversations, and academic ideas. These features help students connect the relevance of their individual experiences to the broader cultural context.

HALLMARK FEATURES OF *THE NORTON READER*

- *The Norton Reader* offers the greatest breadth and depth of any composition reader, with an abundance of contemporary essays anchored by classic and canonical selections. For example, a selection from Tara Westover's best seller, *Educated*, appears alongside Frederick Douglass's "Learning to Read" in the "Education and Learning" chapter. And in "Cultural Critique," James Baldwin's essay "Stranger in the Village" is in conversation with the essay it inspired from Teju Cole, "Black Body."

- Apparatus provides just enough detail—but not so much as to overwhelm the essays themselves. Contextual notes indicate when and where the essay was published; annotations explain unfamiliar persons, events, and concepts; study questions for all essays prompt analysis, discussion, and writing; and biographical information about the authors appears at the end of the book.

- Four expanded indexes organize the readings according to genre, rhetorical mode, date of publication, and additional themes. This feature helps teachers structure courses that meet crucial goals of the WPA Outcomes Statement, which urges that students learn to write in several genres, identify conventions of format and structure, and understand how genres shape reading and writing.

DIGITAL RESOURCES FOR INSTRUCTORS AND STUDENTS

- *The Norton Reader* ebook, now available for both versions of *The Norton Reader*, lets you and your students highlight and annotate within the digital text. Links make it easy to navigate between—and make connections among—the readings. Instructors can embed notes and links for their students to see.

- InQuizitive for Writers supplements *The Norton Reader* with activities to help students learn to edit sentences and work with sources. Question-specific feedback and links to the *Little Seagull Handbook* provide students with extra instruction for these crucial first-year writing skills.

- For instructors, *The Guide to* The Norton Reader includes new sample syllabi, suggested classroom activities, and general advice on planning your course. The *Guide* also includes teaching suggestions and writing assignments to accompany each reading.

- Comprehensive LMS-ready resources provide additional support, including documentation guidelines, model student papers, and customizable grammar and language quizzes.

ACKNOWLEDGMENTS

The editors would like to express appreciation and thanks to the many teachers who provided reviews and invaluable feedback for this edition: Ashley Allee (Louisiana State University, Shreveport), Jennifer Baine (South Arkansas Community College), Marion Bright (Marymount High School), Stacy Brouillette (University of Massachusetts Global), Cleo Cakridas (Quincy College), Virginia Callahan (Niobrara Public High School / Northeast Community College), Frederic Colier (Lehman College), Ashli Cooper (Highland High School), Debra Danielsen (California State University, Fullerton), Bradi Darrah (Indianola High School), Sam Forsythe (El Paso Community College), Denise Gordon (Towson University), Ashley Hogan (Meredith College), Dana Horton (Mercy College), Misti Hughes (Franklin High School), Kathi Johnson (Spartanburg Christian Academy), Melissa Jones (University of Massachusetts Global), Clifton Kaiser (Franklin Road Academy), Heather Kauk (Paola High School), Alissa Keith (University of Lynchburg), Elizabeth Ketner (Colby College), Peter Landino (Terra State Community College), Carol Mitchell (Mercy College), Jennifer Novotney (MMI Preparatory School) Kelli Offenberger (Medina High School), Irene Oujo (Fairleigh Dickinson University), Shelley Palmer (Catawba College), Gina Caponi Parnaby (Marist School), Gavin Paul (Kwantian Polytechnic University), Ruth Prakasam (Suffolk University), Ann Rea (University of Pittsburgh, Johnstown), Evelyn Reynolds (Parkland College), Jayme Ringleb (Meredith College), Joshua Salisbury (United States Military Academy), Danielle Sellers (Trinity Valley School), Eloise Stewart (Fairleigh Dickinson University), Charles Adam Tarlton (Wingate University), Star Taylor (Riverside City College), Vikas Turakhia (Orange High School), Rachel Willis (University of Lynchburg), Chris White (Westland High School), Charles Wuest (Averett University), Cory Youngblood (East Los Angeles College).

We would also like to thank the many teachers who provided input on previous editions: Robin Amaro (Cypress Bay High School), Joseph Berenguel (Asnuntuck Community College), Deborah Bertsch (Columbus State Community College), Paul Bounds (San Jacinto College South), Carla Bradley (Drury University), Mary Dalton (Dreher High School), Gita DasBender (Seton Hall University), Michael DeStefano (Fairfield University), Emily Dial-Driver (Rogers State University), Janet Duckham (Ladue Horton Watkins High School), Michael Duffy (Moorpark College), Christine Ethier (Camden County College– Blackwood Campus), Lori Franklin (Northern New Mexico College), Eva Fritsch (Fontana Unified School District), Jordan Heil (Saint Joseph's University), Danielle Johannsen (University of Minnesota Crookston), Edmund Jones (Seton Hall), Susanna Lankheet (Lake Michigan College), Kevin LaPlante (Walled Lake Northern High School), Jessica Lindberg (Georgia Highlands

College), Martha Michieka (East Tennessee State University), Caitlin Murphy-Grace (Camden County College–Blackwood Campus), Ruth Prakasam (Suffolk University), Lee Romer Kaplan (Solano Community College), Katie Stoynoff (University of Akron), and Cory Youngblood (East Los Angeles College).

We also thank Ira Brodsky for his copyediting; Joel Jordon for his proofreading; Eric B. Chernov for his indexing; and Howard Dinin for his work on the author biographies that appear in the back of the book. At W. W. Norton we thank Editorial Assistant Caroline Fairey Meese for her superb project coordination and editing of our chapter introductions; Karen Romano, Selin Tekgurler, and Rubina Yeh for their expert help with editing, design, and production; Joy Cranshaw, Diane Cipollone, Mica Clausen, and Juliet Godwin for their wonderful work on the website, ebook, and instructor resources; Megan Schindel, Elizabeth Trammell, and Catherine Abelman for their expert permissions work; Debra Morton Hoyt and Jill DeHaan for the new cover design; and our previous editors: Jennifer Bartlett, Carol Hollar-Zwick, Julia Reidhead, Marilyn Moller, and Ariella Foss. We are grateful to the Norton travelers who represent the book on campus so energetically, and to our talented marketers and specialists, Lib Triplett, Elizabeth Pieslor, and Michele Dobbins. A special thanks to our current editor Sarah Touborg, whose kind, savvy, and collaborative spirit helped shape this new edition.

READING *THE* NORTON READER

Reading and the Rhetorical Situation

How do specific people, experiences, and environments help shape identity? How might we live, care for ourselves and others, and communicate in more intentional ways? How do we have true conversations with others, speaking and listening when we hold different beliefs? What are the changes we should advocate for—and why? These are just a few of the questions and issues explored by essays in *The Norton Reader.* Whether you read many or just a few of the selections, we hope that you will find them thought-provoking. We also hope you will use them to inform and improve your own writing; in this anthology, you will find readings that model a wide range of forms and styles from a diverse group of writers.

The pieces collected here come from a variety of publications, from graphic memoirs and daily newspapers to blogs, online magazines, and books. In an anthology like *The Norton Reader*, all of these selections appear in the same format, with the same typeface and layout; most have annotations to explain references and allusions; and all have questions to urge you to think about major issues and themes.

To help in the reading process, we provide information about the context in which the essay first appeared. In some cases, you may wish to go to the original source to learn more about that context, or it may be helpful to research an event that prompted a piece or to learn more about the time in which it was written. We also suggest some ways to read the different kinds of essays included in this anthology. In the next chapter, "Writing with *The Norton Reader*" (pp. xxxvii–lviii), we provide guidance to help you with your own writing. Among the goals of a college anthology like this one is to help make your reading enrich, inspire, and improve your writing.

When you begin reading an essay that your instructor assigns, ask yourself some or all of the following questions. These questions—about audience, author, purpose, and genre—will help you understand the essay, consider its original context, analyze its meaning or effect, recognize its organization and rhetorical strategies, and imagine how you might use similar strategies for your own writing.

WHO IS THE AUDIENCE?

An *audience* consists of those to whom the essay is directed—the people who read the article, listen to the speech, or view the text. The question about audience might be posed in related ways: For whom did the author write?

What readers does the author hope to reach? What readers did the author actually reach? In what ways are you—reading in the present—similar to or different from the author's original audience?

Sometimes the audience is national or international, as in an op-ed for a newspaper like the *Washington Post* or the *New York Times*. Often the audience shares a common interest, as the readers of an environmental magazine or the buyers of books on food or history. To help you understand the original audience for each essay, we provide *contextual notes* at the bottom of the first page of each essay. These notes give information about when and where the essay first appeared and, if it began as a talk, when and where it was delivered and to what audience. As editors, we could swamp you with information about publication and authorship, but we prefer to include more essays and keep contextual information focused on the original audience and publication history—that is, on where the essay appeared, who read it, and (if we know) what reaction it received. For example, Maya Angelou's "Graduation" (pp. 74–83) comes from her autobiography *I Know Why the Caged Bird Sings* (1969); Angelou then continued writing her life story in six sequential volumes, concluding with *Mom & Me & Mom* (2013)—a sequence that testifies to her book's success and its appeal to a wide variety of readers.

In each contextual note, we try to explain a little about the magazines, newspapers, and books that printed these essays—whether it's *MAKE*, a small literary journal published twice a year; the *New York Times Magazine*, a Sunday supplement of the daily newspaper; or *I Know Why the Caged Bird Sings*, a freestanding book.

Although the contextual notes provide some clues about the original audience for each piece, you might also think about yourself and your classmates as the current audience. What has changed since the essay was originally published? What experiences or knowledge do you bring to your reading? Are there ways in which you feel you're not the best audience for a specific essay? Understanding the ways you are or are not the best audience for an essay can help you articulate your response, can enliven class discussions, and can give you ideas for your own writing.

WHO IS THE AUTHOR?

If the audience is those who read the essays, the *author* is the person who writes them. Through their writing, authors introduce themselves to their audiences, revealing personal experiences, preferences, and beliefs that bear on the subject at hand. In "Always Knew I Was Adopted; Just Found Out I'm Gay" (pp. 40–45), the title gives us important facts about the author Sandra Steingraber and her perspective.

Not all authors are as direct as Steingraber. You don't really need to know that Brian Doyle was editor of *Portland Magazine* and the author of several novels to appreciate his meditation on hearts—from those belonging to tiny hummingbirds to huge whales to humans—in "Joyas Voladoras" (pp. 603–5). Nor do you need to know that Florence Williams, author of "ADHD Is Fuel for

Adventure" (pp. 571–79), also wrote a book about breasts. Such biographical facts are interesting but not essential to understanding the essays included.

Because we believe that essayists prefer to introduce themselves and reveal details of personality and experience that they consider most relevant, we do not preface each essay with a biographical note. We think they, as authors, should step forward and we, as editors, should stand back and let them speak. But if you want to learn more about the writer of an essay, you can check the "Author Biographies" at the end of this book. Putting this information at the end of the book gives you a choice. You may already know something about an author and not wish to consult this section, or you may wish to know more about the authors before you read their writing. Or you may just prefer to encounter the authors on their own terms, letting them identify themselves within the essay. Sometimes knowing who authors are and where their voices come from helps readers grasp what they say—but sometimes it doesn't.

WHAT IS THE RHETORICAL CONTEXT AND PURPOSE?

The *rhetorical context*, sometimes called *rhetorical situation* or *rhetorical occasion*, refers to the context—social, political, biographical, historical—in which writing takes place and becomes public. The term *purpose*, in a writing class, refers to the author's goal—whether to inform, to persuade, to entertain, to analyze, or to do something else through the essay. We could also pose these questions: What goals did the writer have in composing and publishing the essay? What effect did the author wish to have on the audience?

For some selections, the rhetorical context is indicated by the *title*. Abraham Lincoln's "Second Inaugural Address" (pp. 685–86) and John F. Kennedy's "Inaugural Address" (pp. 691–94) were speeches that marked the beginning of their terms of office. An inauguration represents a significant moment in a leader's—and the nation's—life. The speech given on such an occasion requires a statement of the president's goals for the next four years. In addition to the title, you can discover more about the rhetorical context of a president's inaugural speech in the *opening paragraphs*. Lincoln, for example, refers back to his first inaugural address and the "impending civil war" (685); then he acknowledges that the war continues and that he prays "this mighty scourge of war may speedily pass away" (686). In the midst of the American Civil War, Lincoln knows that he must, as president, address the political conflict that faces the nation, offer hope for its resolution, and set the moral tone for the aftermath. That's his purpose.

Like the presidential speech, many essays establish the rhetorical context in their opening paragraphs. Editorials and op-eds begin with a *hook*—an opening reference to the issue at hand or the news report under consideration. You might even say that the writer "creates" the rhetorical context and shows us the purpose straightaway. Kwame Anthony Appiah opens his op-ed "Go Ahead, Speak for Yourself" (pp. 164–67), with the lines, "'As a white man,' Joe begins, prefacing an insight, revelation, objection or confirmation he's eager to share—but let's stop him right there. Aside from the fact that he's white, and a man, what's his point?" (164). Readers know that Appiah is writing about speaking as a member of a group, and in the title and opening, he establishes his position right up front (he wants others to speak for themselves rather than use some aspect of their social identity to gain or undermine authority).

If an essay does not establish a rhetorical context in its opening paragraphs, you can find additional information in the *contextual note* (described above) or in the *footnotes* to each essay (described below). For example, the contextual note for "The Declaration of Independence" (pp. 674–80) is:

> On June 11, 1776, Thomas Jefferson was elected by the Second Continental Congress to join John Adams, Benjamin Franklin, Robert Livingston, and Roger Sherman in drafting a declaration of independence. The draft presented to Congress on June 28 was primarily the work of Jefferson. The final version resulted from revisions made to Jefferson's original draft by members of the committee, including Adams and Franklin, and by members of the Continental Congress. (674)

The footnotes (marked with small numerals) give further details about the composition of the Declaration of Independence.

Explanatory footnotes are a common feature of a textbook. When the original authors wrote the footnotes themselves, we indicate that in the contextual note to the text. In Terry Tempest Williams's essay, for example, we state that all notes in this piece were written by the author unless indicated otherwise (648). This tells you that the author wished to cite an expert, add information, or send the reader to another source. In most cases, however, we have written the footnotes to help with difficult words, allusions, and references. We provide information about unfamiliar people, places, works, theories, and so forth that the original audience may have known. For example, for Maya Angelou's "Graduation" (pp. 74–83), we footnote Gabriel Prosser and Nat Turner, but not Abraham Lincoln and Christopher Columbus. Many of Angelou's readers would have known that Prosser and Turner were executed for leading rebellions of enslaved and free Black people in Virginia in the nineteenth century. But because not all readers today know (or remember) this part of American history, we add a footnote.

Although reading the footnotes can facilitate the making of meaning, it can never take the place of reading carefully. Reading is an active process. Experienced readers take responsibility for that action—reading critically, constructing meaning, interpreting what they read. If our footnotes help you read critically, then use them; if they interfere, then just continue reading the main text and skip over them.

Just as authors have a purpose in writing, readers have a purpose for reading. You will read differently depending on your purpose. Are you reading a piece to prepare for classroom discussion? If so, you might consider your position on or experience with the topic being written about. You might assess the author's argument and mark the parts of the essay that seem most and least successful in getting across a point. If your purpose is to gain inspiration as a writer, you might note the stylistic elements (metaphors, similes, varying sentence length, precision of language, and so on) and the rhetorical strategies the writer uses. If you're reading more than one essay on the same topic, you might compare and contrast the authors' positions and approaches. Later in this chapter, we provide sample annotations to model active reading.

WHAT IS THE GENRE AND ITS CONVENTIONS?

Genre is a term used by composition and literature teachers to refer to kinds of writing that have common features and certain conventions of style, presentation, and subject matter. Essay genres include the memoir and the profile, the visual analysis and the op-ed, the literacy narrative and the lyric essay, among others. Genre partially determines the form's content and organization, but it should never do so in a cookie-cutter way.

Conventions are practices or customs commonly used in a genre—like a handshake for a social introduction. Genre and convention are linked concepts, the one implying the other. Articles in a scientific journal (a genre) begin with a title and an abstract (conventions) and include sections about the methodology and the results (also conventions). Op-eds, by convention, begin with a hook; profiles of people or places include a physical description of the subject; literacy narratives include a key episode in the acquisition of reading or writing skills; lyric essays are often written in sections or organized by association rather than by employing explicit transitions. But in reading and writing essays, conventions should not be thought of as rigid rules; rather, they should be seen as guidelines, strategies, or special features.

As you read an essay, think about its form: what it includes, how the writer presents the subject, what features seem distinctive. If you read a pair or group of essays assigned by your teacher, you might ask yourself whether they represent the same genre or are noticeably different. If they are the same, you will recognize similar features; if they are different, you will notice less overlap.

The Norton Reader includes four categories of genres, some of which may overlap:

- **Narrative genres** tell stories. They include personal essays, memoirs, graphic memoirs, and literacy narratives. If you're reading a narrative, note how the author structures the story. Does the narrative begin with a dramatic moment, unfold in chronological order, or have a different structure? What is the balance between scene (putting the reader in the moment) and reflection (making sense of an experience)? What is the effect of the organization the writer chose?

- **Descriptive genres** give details about how a person, place, or thing looks, sounds, and feels, often in a larger framework. These include profiles of people and places, essays about nature and the environment, lyric essays, reportage, and pieces of humor and satire. If you're reading a descriptive genre, note the author's use of language and sensory imagery. What strategies does the writer use to draw the reader in—to make a person, place, or situation come alive for the reader?

- **Analytic genres** examine texts, images, and cultural objects and trends. They include reflection, textual analysis, visual analysis, and cultural analysis. If you're reading an analytical genre, consider the ways that the author looks closely at a text, image, object, or trend and breaks it down into parts in order to understand the whole. What insights does the analysis provide? How does it make you look differently at the subject?

- **Argumentative genres** take positions and use reasons and evidence to support them. These include evaluations and reviews, proposals, op-eds, and speeches. If you're reading an argumentative genre, identify the author's main point, which may come in a thesis statement or may be implied less directly. Once you know the argument, consider the author's support. What evidence does the writer use? Are the sources reputable? Is the reasoning sound? Does the author respond to counterarguments? Is the argument persuasive? Why or why not?

For more detailed information on some of the common genres included in *The Norton Reader* and some features to consider as you read and write, see pp. xl–xlviii.

WHAT ARE RHETORICAL STRATEGIES?

Writers use a range of strategies to develop and organize their material. Here are some of the most common rhetorical strategies:

- **Describing** something or someone appeals to the senses.

- **Narrating** provides an account of actions or events that occur over a period of time.

- **Exemplifying** provides examples to illustrate a claim or idea.

- **Classifying and dividing** groups people or things based on shared qualities.

- **Explaining or analyzing** breaks a process or concept into its component parts.

- **Comparing and contrasting** considers the similarities and differences between or among people, places, things, or ideas.

- **Defining** attempts to give the essential meaning of something.

- **Analyzing cause and effect** considers the reasons something happened (cause) and determines the results (effect).

- **Arguing** makes a claim and provides evidence to support that claim.

Sometimes authors use rhetorical strategies to structure an entire piece. Kathy Fish, for example, uses definition to structure her lyric essay "Collective Nouns for Humans in the Wild" (p. 388). But writers most often use a combination of rhetorical strategies to develop and present their ideas. For example, Maya Angelou in "Graduation" (pp. 74–83) blends narration and description as she tells the story of her graduation from high school. And Frans de Waal uses cause and effect analysis as well as classification, comparison and contrast, description, and narration to make an argument for the presence of animal emotions in "from *Mama's Last Hug*" (pp. 258–64). As you read the essays included in *The Norton Reader*, notice how the writers develop and organize their material—and see if you can get ideas for your own writing. For more details on rhetorical strategies, see pp. xlviii–lii.

STRATEGIES FOR CRITICAL READING

The previous pages gave an overview of different questions to consider when reading, from thinking about the intended audience to recognizing genres and rhetorical strategies. Here we offer some general tips for approaching the reading your instructor assigns.

Preview the essay

Think about the essay's title, read its opening paragraph, and skim the essay to get a sense of its organization and genre. Look at the contextual note on the first page, and try to imagine the experience, issue, or debate that motivated the essayist to write. Previewing is a technique widely used for college reading, but not all writing teachers encourage it. Some teachers explain that it helps readers focus on key issues; others discourage previewing, pointing out that a good essay—like a good novel or movie—can be ruined by knowing the ending. Whether you preview or not might depend on the genre of essay you're reading. While you might want to know an author's argument before reading more carefully, you also might want to allow a personal or lyric essay to unfold—to see where the author takes you.

Annotate in the margin

As you read, note points that seem interesting and important, forecast issues that you think the writer will address, and pose questions of your own. Note the rhetorical strategies and literary features the writer uses. Imagine that you're having a conversation with the author. Respond to their ideas with some of your own. Most essayists want active readers who think about what the essay says, implies, and urges as a personal response or course of action. Similarly, note points that you don't understand or find ambiguous. Use them to energize class discussion. Puzzling over a sentence or a passage with your classmates can lead to crucial points of debate or provide inspiration for your own writing. Here, for example, is a sample annotation of the first nine paragraphs of James Densley and Jillian Peterson's "The Steps We Can Take to Reduce Mass Shootings in America" (pp. 155–58).

On October 1, 2015, after a gunman shot and killed his professor and eight students at Umpqua Community College in Oregon, President Barack Obama, who three years earlier, following the massacre at Sandy Hook elementary school in Connecticut, had failed to force Congress to pass new gun safety laws, stood frustrated at the podium. "Somehow this has become routine. The reporting is routine. My response here at this podium ends up being routine, the conversation in the aftermath of it. . . . We have become numb to this."

"Fail" and "force" stand out to me. Is it the president's job to "force" Congress? Can lawmakers work together?

The repetition of "routine" emphasizes this point.

Fast forward seven years and amid a recent spate of horrific mass shootings—at a Buffalo supermarket, a Texas elementary school, and a Tulsa hospital—it feels like little has changed. In fact, things have gotten worse—mass shootings are more frequent and deadlier than ever.

And we could add many more recent mass shootings to this list.

It's hard not to feel numb. When comparable nations have suffered deadly mass shootings—Australia, Canada, Germany, Great Britain, New Zealand, Switzerland—they respond with new laws curtailing firearm access and they rarely experience another mass shooting. In America, we wait for decisive action that never comes while mass shootings continue unabated.

"Courage" and "conviction" seem to be the counterpart to the earlier "failed" and "force." Here the responsibility lies with lawmakers.

Five years ago, tired of waiting for Congress to act with courage and conviction, we started researching the lives of mass shooters. Our goal was to gather the data that could change the exhausting routine President Obama called out—even if only incrementally, step-by-step. Our findings are outlined in the 2021 book, *The Violence Project: How to Stop a Mass Shooting Epidemic.*

To our genuine surprise, talking to mass shooters in prison and people who knew them, people who planned a shooting but never went through with it, victims' families, shooting survivors, and first responders gave us reason to hope. We learned there are things we can do right here, right now, as <u>individual concerned citizens</u>, to stop a mass shooting before it ever starts.

Here the responsibility to prevent mass shootings shifts to individual citizens.

It begins with a shift in mindset. Mass shooters are not them. They are us—boys and men we know. <u>Our children. Our students. Our colleagues. Our community.</u> This fact may make mass shooters seem harder to stop. The reality is quite the opposite.

The fragments and repetition of "Our" emphasize community responsibility/ relationship.

Half of all mass shooters—and nearly 80% of school mass shooters—communicate intent to do harm ahead of time. They post threats on social media or tell their family and friends in person. This is a crucial opportunity for intervention, but many people don't know <u>what to do with that information or where and how to report it.</u> By training ourselves to say something if we see or hear something that gives us pause, and by lobbying for behavioral intervention and threat assessment teams in our schools and workplaces, communities can proactively respond to these warning signs long before a prospective shooter ever picks up a gun.

It's worth researching more to find out what the best practices for intervention are.

A mass shooting is intended to be the final act of a person who has reached breaking point. <u>No one thinks they'll get away with a mass shooting;</u> mass shootings end one of three ways: with the shooter taking their own life, law enforcement taking it for them, or the perpetrator spending the rest of their life in prison.

This is a good point.

This all means classical deterrence mechanisms like harsh punishment or armed security at the door do little to prevent mass shootings. A suicidal shooter may in fact be drawn to a location if they know someone on site is trained to kill them. Rather than giving desperate people incentive to die, we must give them a reason to live. ●

I want to know more about this. What causes such desperation? What gives people a sense of hope and purpose?

Analyze illustrations

Some of the essays in *The Norton Reader* include illustrations from their original publications. Think about how the essays and the images speak to each other. Consider whether the images enrich, highlight, or possibly challenge the essay. Does the image primarily illustrate the essay, or does it emphasize a feature unexplained by the essayist? Does the image enrich and clarify one aspect of the writing, or does it minimize aspects of the subject, perhaps aspects you find important? What do you see in the images that the essayist discusses or explains? What do you see that the writer overlooks or minimizes? Thinking about images can help you clarify the author's argument or reveal points the author may have missed.

Summarize the essay

Write a summary of the essay. If you're summarizing an argument or analysis, begin by listing its key points and identifying the evidence used in support of each; then try to state briefly, in your own words, the gist, or core, of the essay. The goal is to condense the argument and evidence, while remaining faithful to the author's meaning. If you're summarizing a narrative or descriptive essay, summarize the meaning or effect you think the writer wanted to get across and list the strategies the author used to communicate that meaning or effect to readers. Your summary will be useful when you discuss the essay in class or write about it in a paper.

Keep a reading journal

Use a notebook or an electronic journal for reflections on the essays you read. For each essay, take notes, record your responses, write questions about what puzzles you, and jot down ideas for essays you might want to write. Highlight sentences or passages that you like and might want to use as models for your own writing. You may also want to list questions that the essayist raises and answers, as well as questions that you think the essayist has overlooked.

Use the study questions

Review the questions that follow each essay in *The Norton Reader* and think about the issues—the subject, the structure, or the language—they cover. We include these questions to help you become an active reader, to focus attention on key issues, and to make suggestions for doing or writing something.

- Some questions ask you to locate or mark an essay's structural features, the patterns that undergird and clarify meaning. Narration, description, exposition, persuasion, and argument can follow conventional shapes— but can also distort these shapes—and your ability to recognize these shapes will improve your comprehension.

- Other questions ask you to paraphrase meanings or extend them—that is, to express the meaning in your own words, to provide your own examples, or to reframe points by connecting them to other essays.

- Still other questions ask you to notice special features or conventions that contribute to meaning: the choice of title, the author's voice (or persona), the author's assumptions about audience (and how the author speaks to the audience), and the author's choice of style and forms of expression.

- At least one question, usually the last, asks you to write, to create, or to interact with classmates. Sometimes we ask you to demonstrate comprehension by writing about something from your experience or reading that extends an essay and enforces its argument. Sometimes we invite you to disagree or dissent by writing about something from your experience or knowledge that qualifies the author's argument or calls it into question. We may ask you to compare or contrast two authors' positions—especially when their positions seem opposed. We may ask you to do a project or have a conversation inspired by an essay. Or we may ask you to adapt an essay's rhetorical strategy to a topic of your choice and to make the essay even more your own by basing it on personal experience.

Reread the essay

If possible, read the essay a second time before you discuss it with your peers or write about it. If you're short on time, reread the passages that you annotated. Ask yourself what you see that didn't register on first reading.

Reading need not be only a private activity; it can also become communal and cooperative. Writing down your thoughts or taking part in conversations can clarify your own and others' interpretation of the essays. What interests and motives does each reader bring to a particular essay? What are responsive and responsible readings? Are there irresponsible readings, and how do we decide? All these questions—and others—can emerge as private reading moves into the public arena of the classroom.

Readers write, and writers read. Making meaning by writing is the flip side of making meaning by reading, and we hope to engage you in both processes. But in neither case are meanings passed from hand to hand like nickels, dimes, and quarters. Instead, they are constructed—as a quilt or a house or an institution. We hope that these suggestions for reading will lead you to engaged and fruitful writing.

WRITING WITH *THE NORTON READER*

Writing in Academic Contexts

We hope that the selections in *The Norton Reader*, as well as your class discussions, inspire you to write. Much of the writing you will do in a class will start with an assignment from your instructor. Perhaps you will be asked to respond to some of the essays in *The Norton Reader*—to expand on something a writer has said; to agree, disagree, or both with a claim a writer has made; or to do some research to extend an author's argument and say something new about it. Or you may be assigned a particular genre or kind of writing—a literacy narrative, a profile of a person or place, a visual or textual analysis, or an argumentative paper—and asked to use selections in this book as models of these kinds of writing. We have selected the readings because they are full of important ideas you can react to, either by agreeing or disagreeing, and because the essays represent examples of good writers at their best.

What follows is a brief guide for writing with *The Norton Reader*. We'll look at knowing your purpose, addressing your audience, finding a subject, determining what genre to employ, using rhetorical strategies, and understanding the writing process.

KNOWING YOUR PURPOSE

Your *purpose* is, put simply, the goal for your writing. What do you want to achieve? What points do you want to make? What idea or cause motivates you to write? Anything you can do to sharpen your thinking and infuse your writing with a clear sense of purpose will be for the better: You will find it easier to stay focused and help your readers see your key point and main ideas.

What are some common purposes writers have? For the authors in *The Norton Reader* purposes include informing, persuading, entertaining, and expressing. So, too, your writing will have a primary purpose, usually defined in an assignment by words such as "explain," "describe," "analyze," or "argue." Each is a signal about the purpose for your writing.

For instance, if an assignment asks you to *analyze* the persuasiveness of James Densley and Jillian Peterson's "The Steps We Can Take to Reduce Mass Shootings in America" (pp. 155–58), then your purpose is to explain the claims Densley and Peterson make, examine the evidence they use to support them, discuss points or perspectives they might have included, and develop a thesis about the reasons for the essay's persuasiveness. If an assignment asks you to *argue* for or against their claims about how to reduce mass shootings, then your purpose is to take a side, defending or refuting their claims and using evidence from your own knowledge and from reputable sources to support your argument.

Use these questions to think about your purpose for writing:

- What does the assignment ask you to do? Is the goal to inform readers, entertain them, argue a point, or express an idea or feeling? Beyond a general purpose, what does the assignment require in terms of a specific purpose?

- How does your purpose affect your choice of a subject? What do you know about the subject? How can you find out more about this subject?

- How can you connect to your readers? What will they want or need to know? How do you want them to respond to your writing?

ADDRESSING YOUR AUDIENCE

Just as the authors in *The Norton Reader* aimed their essays at different *audiences*—readers of books, newspapers, magazines, literary journals, and scholarly publications, as well as activists, casual readers, and academics—so you need to imagine your audience as you write. Too wide an audience—"the general public"—and you run the risk of making your essay too diffuse, trying to reach everyone. Too narrow an audience—"my friend Zach"—and you run the risk of being too specific.

How can you imagine an audience of your own? One way is to look around your classroom: That's your immediate audience, the people taking the course with you and your instructor. Another way is to think about your home community: your family, your neighbors, and the people of your town or city. If you're taking an online class, what do you know about your classmates from online discussions or drafts they've shared? Think of your audience as readers like yourself, with some of the same knowledge of the world and some of the same tastes. Consider your audience's range of reference: historical events they have witnessed firsthand, movies and TV shows they know about or have seen, and books they have read or heard of. Think of them as willing to be convinced by whatever you write, but in need of good evidence.

Inevitably, some writers find that imagining an audience composed only of class members seems too restrictive. That's fine; feel free to invoke another audience, say, a group of people who share a certain passion, perhaps for a team, a sport, a game, or a type of music or film. (But remember to consider your instructor, who may need some filling in about the special knowledge you share with your audience.)

Use these questions to guide you in thinking about audience:

- What readers are you hoping to reach?

- What information can you assume your readers know? What information do you need to explain?

■ In what ways will you need to adjust your writing style—the language, tone, sentence structure, complexity, and examples—to meet the needs of your audience?

FINDING A SUBJECT

Like the audience and purpose for your writing, the *subject* of your writing— what you write about—will often be assigned by your instructor. Some assignments are very specific, such as this study question following Stephen King's "On Writing" (pp. 561–62): "Write about a time someone responded to your writing in a way that helped you learn to be a better writer. What kinds of comments and edits did that person make? Why was that response helpful to you?" (563). Other assignments may be more general, such as this writing prompt that follows Scott Russell Sanders's essay about his father and the effects of alcoholism, "Under the Influence" (pp. 16–26): "Drawing on your memories of a family member, write an essay about a problem that person had and its effect on your life" (26). This broader assignment requires you to determine the person you wish to discuss, the problem you wish to analyze, and the larger effect the person and problem had on your life.

Some assignments give you even more leeway in choosing a subject, leaving you with the inevitable question "What should I write about?" In this case, write about what you know or care about, drawing on knowledge you've already gleaned about a subject from personal experience, reading, or research. Your insight does not have to be totally new, but your perspective needs to come from you—a real person writing about a subject that matters.

How do you find what you know or care about? One way is to raise questions about an essay you've read:

■ What is the author's main point? Do you agree or disagree with it?

■ Has the author said enough about the subject? What gaps or omissions do you see, if any?

■ Are the author's examples and evidence convincing? If not, why? Can you provide a more compelling example, additional evidence, or a counterexample?

■ Does this reading speak to another essay in *The Norton Reader*? Can you explain how this reading connects to the other? Do the readings agree or disagree?

■ Is this reading true to your own experience? Has anything like this happened to you, or have you observed anything like this?

You can also choose a subject by reflecting on your own experience:

■ Has someone affected your life in some way—by teaching you, by serving as an example (good or bad), or by changing your attitude?

■ Is there a place that you can describe to others, telling them what makes it unique or special to you?

■ Is there a subject you feel strongly about, something you believe others need to learn about—for example, a program on your campus or in your neighborhood, a controversial item of national significance, or a matter of global importance?

■ Have you had an experience that has taught you something valuable, influenced the way you live, or made you think differently about life, school, work, family, or friends? Readers will be interested in the details of the experience, including how it affected you and what you learned.

DETERMINING A GENRE

Like the purpose, audience, and subject of your writing, the *genre* of your writing may be prescribed in your instructor's assignment. *The Norton Reader* contains a variety of essay genres. What follows is an explanation of narrative, descriptive, analytic, and argumentative genres, as well as the subcategories within them. Please note that although we consider these essay genres separately, they overlap considerably. That is, sometimes arguments include elements of narrative; personal essays usually include reflection; and a memoir might be written in the form of a lyric essay.

Narrative genres

These genres tell a story through *narrative*, using vivid details about people, events, and conflicts or crises. They also reflect on the meaning of the stories, offering the reader an interpretation or explanation of what occurred. Common narrative genres include memoirs, personal essays, and literacy narratives.

Memoir and personal essay   Told from the first-person point of view, the *memoir* is an account of important events or people from an author's life. It includes selected details and descriptions that show how the author feels about and remembers the events or people. Often, memoirs are book-length reflections that span a number of years. *The Norton Reader* includes several selections from longer memoirs: Tara Westover's remembrance of a classroom lecture during her first year of college from *Educated* (pp. 592–94), Maya Angelou's chapter on her high school graduation from *I Know Why the Caged Bird Sings* (pp. 74–83), and Frederick Douglass's "Learning to Read" from *Narrative of the Life of Frederick Douglass, an American Slave, Written by Himself* (pp. 580–84).

Memoirs can also be essay-length reflections on a significant event or person. If you are asked to write a memoir for class, it will likely be one of these shorter pieces, perhaps one in which you narrate an event or series of events that helped shape you or your understanding of yourself.

Another form of autobiographical writing, the *graphic memoir* renders the author's experience in visual and textual form. This form often includes a narrative storyline, dialogue, and drawings that emphasize elements of the story or provide information not directly available in the written narrative. In "Language" (pp. 269–85), Rhea Ewing uses narrative, selections from interviews and interactions, and drawings to reflect on language, gender, and identity. When you read graphic memoirs, and if you choose to create your own, pay close attention to the ways in which images and words are connected—and whether one feature of the text provides information not included elsewhere.

Focusing on a significant personal experience or thematically related experiences, the *personal essay* draws out the meaning as the writer tells the story and reflects on experience. Sometimes a personal essay is called a *memoir* or *autobiographical essay*. Its key features include a dramatic event, a series of moments connected by theme or conflict; vivid details and narration; and an interweaving of narration with reflection on and interpretation of the essayist's experience. For example, in "In the Kitchen" (pp. 185–91), Henry Louis Gates Jr. reflects on the development of his Black identity by considering hair and hair products. He writes, "From Murray's to Duke to Afro Sheen: that was my progression in black consciousness" (189). Many of the personal essays included in *The Norton Reader* show writers making sense of and learning from their experiences or using their experiences to educate and inform others.

Literacy narrative   A subcategory of the personal essay, the *literacy narrative* focuses on learning to read or write. Like other narrative genres, it uses personal experience, requires vivid details, and gives a clear indication of the narrative's significance.

Frederick Douglass's "Learning to Read" (pp. 580–84) is a classic version of the literacy narrative. For Douglass, an enslaved person, reading was forbidden by law, so to learn to read he was "compelled to resort to various stratagems" (580). Douglass's literacy narrative includes rich details about his life as an enslaved person, the strategies he used to acquire literacy, and the essential value that reading held for someone who did not want to remain "*a slave for life*" (581). Other literacy narratives in *The Norton Reader* include Tara Westover's "from *Educated*" (pp. 592–94) and Stephen King's "On Writing" (pp. 561–62), which illustrate with fascinating, sometimes painful, details the meaning of reading, writing, and education in American culture.

Descriptive genres

These genres use *description* to let the reader know how a person, place, or thing looks, sounds, feels, and maybe even smells. But they do more: They give a dominant impression, interpret a person's actions, offer a reflection on the significance of place, or in some other way put the objective details into a larger framework. Descriptive genres in *The Norton Reader* include profiles of people and places, nature and environmental writing, lyric essays, reportage, and humor and satire.

Profile of a person   An in-depth exploration of an individual (or a group of people), the *profile of a person* uses firsthand knowledge, interviews, and research to present its subject. Since readers like to read about interesting subjects, it is sometimes assumed that the person must be interesting beforehand. But really it's the writer who makes the person interesting by discovering special characteristics or qualities through interviews or observation; by finding an interesting angle from which to present the subject; and by including engaging details, anecdotes, or dialogue.

Taté Walker, in "The (Native) American Dream" (pp. 116–22), profiles two Indigenous women who are leaders in teaching others to live more sustainably. Monycka Snowbird raises her own animals and grows her own plants, working with community organizations to educate others on urban food production and Indigenous food systems. Karen Ducheneaux works with her community to build sustainable housing: ecodomes and straw bale buildings powered by renewable resources. Walker quotes these women and emphasizes the ways in which they are both drawing from their traditional roots as Indigenous people. Walker shows both how these women are similar and the different challenges they face with Snowbird living in an urban environment and Ducheneaux living in a rural area.

Profile of a place   Places can also become the focus of a profile. The features of a *profile of a place* involve discovering the special characteristics or qualities of the place; finding an interpretive framework in which to present it; and including engaging details, anecdotes, or dialogue to enliven the essay. Since places can't speak, the essayist must speak for them and make them come alive.

Essayists recreate places through description. Ian Frazier, in "Take the F" (pp. 216–22), uses a subway line (the F Sixth Avenue Local) to locate his Brooklyn neighborhood on the New York City grid, but he also engages the five senses—sight, sound, smell, taste, and touch—to give non–New Yorkers a feel for the place.

E. B. White describes a place far different from Brooklyn, New York. In "Once More to the Lake" (pp. 103–7), he recalls a camp in Maine where he spent time both as a child and as an adult, using lists such as the following one:

> . . . the fade-proof lake, the woods unshatterable, the pasture with the sweetfern and the juniper forever and ever, summer without end; this was the background, and the life along the shore was the design, the cottages with their innocent and tranquil design, their tiny docks with the flagpole and the American flag floating against the white clouds in the blue sky, the little paths over the roots of the trees leading from camp to camp and the paths leading back to the outhouses and the can of lime for sprinkling, and at the souvenir counters at the store the miniature birch-bark canoes and the post cards that showed things looking a little better than they looked. (105)

He also uses comparisons and contrasts to show how this place has changed and how it has remained the same over the decades.

If a profile includes both person and place, as White's essay does, it is what the writer Anne Fadiman calls a "character in context" piece. Many times, we see someone in a characteristic space; the place defines the person, and the person defines the place. Judith Ortiz Cofer's "More Room" (pp. 47–50) shows Cofer's grandmother's house, *la casa de Mamá*. Yet her profile is also about her grandmother, whose "room is the heart of the house" (47). As Cofer describes the changes in the house—and how they came to be—readers learn more about her grandmother.

Nature and environmental writing   This type of writing refers to any composition about nature; it can be a profile of a place or some part of the environment, such as plants or animals. (Think of *nature and environmental writing* as profiling not a person but the desert, a bear, a dragonfly, or a weed.) In "A Wind-Storm in the Forests" (pp. 606–12), John Muir describes winds as "advertisements of all they touch" (611) and shows their effects on trees. In "Joyas Voladoras" (pp. 603–5), Brian Doyle writes about parts of the natural world, but Doyle's purpose is to consider the hearts of birds and mammals and their metaphorical significance, including the human heart with its capacity to be "bruised and scarred, scored and torn, repaired by time and will, patched by force of character" (605).

Much of the writing about nature and the environment in *The Norton Reader* raises questions about science, human nature, and threats to the environment and its inhabitants. Look for them in Terry Tempest Williams's "The Clan of One-Breasted Women" (pp. 648–54), Cormac Cullinan's "If Nature Had Rights" (pp. 631–36), and Greta Thunberg's "There Is Hope" (pp. 666–68).

Lyric essays   Often meditations on topics or ideas, *lyric essays* are like poems: They include close attention to language and frequently use literary elements such as metaphor, simile, repetition, attention to sound, and personification. They may be broken into sections or organized by association rather than logic. Some lyric essayists use nonstandard punctuation or fragments. For example, Kathy Fish often eliminates verbs in her lyric piece "Collective Nouns for Humans in the Wild" (p. 388), helping readers focus on groups of people and the sometimes surprising names associated with them.

Reportage   Although it often includes analysis and evaluation and makes an argument, the primary purpose of *reportage* is to relate information. *The Norton Reader* focuses on reports that inform readers about a particular topic or issue. In "ADHD Is Fuel for Adventure" (pp. 571–79), Florence Williams reports on the ways outdoor and adventure education may help adolescents diagnosed with ADHD.

Humor and satire   Both of these approaches use hyperbole and far-fetched comparisons or descriptions to make a larger point. Sometimes the point of *humor* and *satire* is to show the abuses of a government or political policy, as in the case of Jonathan Swift's "A Modest Proposal" (pp. 423–29), which proposes that the poor sell their children as food to the rich to fix Ireland's depressed economy.

But humor can be used in any genre of writing. Some writers use self-deprecating humor, as Nancy Mairs does in her personal essay "On Being a Cripple" (pp. 312–22), when she describes the serious yet sometimes humorous challenges of living with a disability. She opens her essay by recalling a time when she fell backward in a public restroom, "landing fully clothed on the toilet seat with my legs splayed in front of me: the old beetle-on-its-back routine" (313). Such uses of humor can make a reader more receptive to a writer or speaker, showing that even those addressing serious topics can have a good laugh.

Humor and satire often push the limits of what is acceptable or expected in communication. Since what's funny to one person might be offensive to others, if you use humor in your writing, be aware of potential consequences. Humor can make audiences more receptive to you, but it can also make audiences less receptive if you unintentionally offend someone you're trying to persuade. Of course, satire writers often intentionally ridicule and shame with the purpose of improvement or change. Still, having your teacher, classmates, or friends read drafts of your humorous and satirical writing can help you gauge responses, making sure your humor has the intended effect.

Analytic genres

Genres that engage in *analysis* carefully and methodically examine a text, an image, a cultural object, or a social trend by breaking it into parts, closely reading its components, and noting how the parts work in relation to the whole. In *The Norton Reader*, you will find examples of reflection, textual analysis, visual analysis, and cultural analysis.

Reflection   A form of personal analysis, *reflection* explores the ways in which an experience, practice, idea, or event relates to you and what you can learn from it. Reflection can be done in response to your reading, a past event or series of events, or something you or someone else has done. For example, your teacher might ask you to reflect on your writing process for a specific assignment, to think about what you learned from the process and what you might do differently for the next assignment. Or your teacher might ask you to write a cover letter for a final portfolio of your work for the entire term; in this type of reflection, you might consider why you chose the pieces you did, how you revised those assignments, what you did well, and what you could have done differently. You might also be asked to write a reflection essay on a selection you've read for class and to consider how you made sense of the author's position or ideas in the context of your own experience, ideas, or other reading.

Reflection is also part of writing a personal essay or a literacy narrative, and you will see many examples of reflection in *The Norton Reader*, especially in "Home and Family" and "Education and Learning." In "Under the Influ-ence" (pp. 16–26), Scott Russell Sanders reflects on the effects of having an alcoholic father, "trying to understand the corrosive mixture of helplessness, responsibility, and shame" (17). In "On Being a Cripple" (pp. 312–22), Nancy Mairs reflects on her life with multiple sclerosis. In both examples, the author chooses one aspect of experience and seeks to make sense of it through writ-ing, offering readers an interpretation of that experience.

At times, reflection is also part of writing an argument. In "Be Nice" (pp. 761–63), Matt Dinan reflects on how he perceives himself versus how others see him in terms of "niceness" before moving into a more philosophical argument for being nice. Reflection provides a context for the argument and helps establish the author's purpose and ethos or character.

Textual analysis   Also called *close reading, textual analysis* focuses on written words. It examines words and phrases for explicit and implicit meanings; it looks for similes (comparisons using *like* or *as*) and metaphors (comparisons without explicit connectors) to reveal patterns of association and meaning; and it interprets the whole text on the basis of these methodical, individual observations. The *text* may be anything from the Bible or Koran to poems and novels or ads, billboards, or official memos. In "If Nature Had Rights" (pp. 631–36), Cormac Cullinan considers the importance of close reading and textual analysis in interpreting laws—and creating new ones.

Visual analysis   Like textual analysis, *visual analysis* looks for explicit and implicit meanings; searches for patterns of association; and interprets the whole object based on these methodical, individual observations. Instead of a written text, visual analysis focuses on an image, a photograph, a painting, or another visual. Some visual analyses have as their goal the explanation of the image itself. In "Song Schematics" (pp. 589–91), Michael Hamad creates a visual essay to analyze a sensory process: listening to music. He arranges words and symbols on the page to analyze the process of listening to a Phish song—and his essay invites a visual analysis by readers. In *The Norton Reader* you will find essays that combine textual and visual analysis or that use images to trigger both kinds of analysis. (Watch for essays that include photographs, drawings, graphs, and other visual material.)

Cultural analysis   This genre, called both *cultural analysis* and *cultural cri-tique,* takes an object, trend, fad, or other phenomenon as the subject of its analysis. It uses the strategies of textual and visual analysis described above, adding personal response and research, if desirable, to explain and interpret. Examples of this form predominantly appear in the chapter "Cultural Cri-tique," but they also appear in "Body Language" and "Self and Society."

What kinds of cultural objects and trends do essayists analyze? Almost anything and everything, it seems. Malcolm Gladwell in "Java Man" (pp. 416–22) chooses caffeine as his subject; Margaret Atwood uses the form of a lyric essay to explore "The Female Body" (pp. 265–68); and the scholar Henry

Louis Gates Jr. analyzes hairstyles popular in his youth (pp. 185–91)—how they were created; how movie stars, singers, and Black icons popularized them; and why the styles remain so important for him. Other essayists analyze social practices. For example, in "Go Ahead, Speak for Yourself" (pp. 164–67), Kwame Anthony Appiah critiques the practice of asserting some aspect of one's identity when making an observation or argument.

Argumentative genres

Forms of modern *argument* have their roots in classical Greece and Rome—that is, they go back at least 2,500 years. The Greek philosopher Aristotle held that there were only two essential parts of an argument: (1) the statement of the case and (2) the proof of the case. But he conceded that in practice most orators added two other parts: an introduction and a conclusion.

Roman rhetoricians like Quintilian refined and expanded this simple Aristotelian approach to include five or six parts:

(1) *exordium*: the introduction

(2) *narratio*: the statement or exposition of the case under discussion

(3) *divisio*: the outline of the points or steps in the argument

(4) *confirmatio*: the proof of the case (sometimes called *probatio*)

(5) *confutatio*: the refutation of opposing arguments

(6) *peroratio*: the conclusion

Yet Roman rhetoricians also acknowledged that, for any given argument, orators might want to omit parts. They might, for example, omit *divisio* if the steps of the argument were simple. And orators would often rearrange the parts of their speeches. They might, for instance, refute an opponent's arguments before advancing their own case.

Unless you participate in a debating society, you—like most modern college students—won't see this formal version of classical argument very often. In "The Declaration of Independence" (pp. 674–80), however, Thomas Jefferson used the tactics of classical rhetoric as revived in the eighteenth century. Today, we hear its legacy in public speeches and see traces of it in newspaper editorials. The Greek and Roman philosophers weren't so much prescribing a genre as they were describing common argumentative practices. It makes sense that, if you want to argue your case effectively, you need to introduce it, outline the key points, present your evidence, and refute your opponent's position—the steps they described. You will find these steps in the argumentative genres considered below: evaluations and reviews, proposals, op-eds, and speeches.

Evaluation and review   These genres combine analysis and argument, using clear criteria as the basis for both *evaluation* and *review*. When you write an evaluation, you make and support an argument about quality, whether something is good or bad, effective or ineffective. The criteria the author uses depend on the subject being analyzed. For example, in evaluating a website, you might focus on design and usability. Is it easy to navigate? Do the organization and design fit the content of the site? Are the visuals appropriate to the subject? Reviewing a restaurant, you might consider the quality of the food and service, the value and price, and the atmosphere and décor. In "Be Nice" (pp. 761–63), Matt Dinan uses Aristotle's theories to evaluate "niceness" as a social virtue.

Proposal   Evaluation and review often provide the groundwork for a *proposal*. A proposal includes a clear statement of what is being proposed, a plan for action, and an explanation of desired outcomes. Your instructor may ask you to write a proposal for a long paper or project that you will undertake. If so, you will likely review other essays, books, or articles on your topic before proposing your own project, one that will be different from the literature you've reviewed. Another kind of proposal you might be assigned is to define a problem and its effects and then to propose a workable solution or approach to that problem.

Op-ed   This genre, which is located "opposite" the "editorial" page of a newspaper, focuses on issues of public interest and encourages ordinary citizens to contribute their perspectives, opinions, and arguments to the public debate. *Op-eds* begin with a hook—a link to a recent event or news article that grabs readers' attention. Specific features, or conventions, include a forthright statement of position, evidence in support, often a counterargument or rebuttal of the opposition, and sometimes a formal conclusion. Margaret Renkl's "Christmas Isn't Coming to Death Row" (pp. 752–54) features most of these conventions. Renkl begins by referencing what was at the time of composing a recent execution. Although she considers many arguments for and against the death penalty, she makes her argument clear: that it is not right to take another human's life.

Speech   Because *speeches* derive directly, if also distantly, from the classical tradition of argument, they often show its formal features. Many speechwriters introduce the issue at hand, state their position, offer evidence in support and counterarguments against, and sum up—sometimes with a high rhetorical flourish. These modern tactics are based on the older classical conventions.

Elizabeth Cady Stanton, the nineteenth-century feminist, shows her knowledge of American public oratory in "Declaration of Sentiments and Resolutions" (pp. 680–82). Stanton's declaration, presented at the first US women's rights convention, is modeled on Thomas Jefferson's seminal "The Declaration of Independence" (pp. 674–80). It is no coincidence that these important American speeches and documents use the formal conventions of argument: In so doing, the speakers demonstrate their education, ability, and right to debate the pressing issues of their day.

As you read arguments in various chapters of *The Norton Reader*, consider where and why authors use conventions of argument and where and why they turn to conventions often associated with other genres. In the end, the goal is to make an effective argument, to convince the reader of the validity of your evidence, or to urge the listener to take a prescribed action.

If you have some leeway in choosing the genre you will use, consider which best fits your purpose, audience, and subject:

- What goal do you have for your writing? What genre is most appropriate for that goal?

- Who will read your writing? What genre will best convey the point of your writing to your readers?

- What are you writing about? What genre is suited to your subject?

To gain more understanding of these genres, read plenty of examples, analyze the forms and strategies their authors use, and then try out a genre on your own. There's no better way to understand how a genre works than to try your hand at writing it.

USING RHETORICAL STRATEGIES

As you plan your essay, you will want to think about the *rhetorical strategies* you will use to present your ideas and evidence to readers. These strategies, sometimes called *rhetorical modes* or *techniques*, help a writer organize evidence, arrange facts into a sequence, and provide clusters of information necessary for conveying a purpose or argument. You might choose to *analyze* the cause of an outcome; *compare* one thing to another; *classify* your facts into categories; *define* a key term; *describe* a person, place, or phenomenon; *explain* how a process works; or *narrate* a pertinent event or experience.

Sometimes the writing assignment that your instructor gives will determine the strategy: For example, an assignment to compare Asam Ahmad's "A Note on Call-Out Culture" (pp. 158–60) with his piece "When Calling Out Makes Sense" (pp. 160–61) will require that you use a compare-and-contrast strategy. Your teacher might ask you to *argue* against or for calling someone out in a specific instance. Or you might be asked to *narrate* an experience of calling someone out or being called out.

Many essays use a mix of strategies. You might want to define a key term in an opening paragraph, narrate a story to make a point in the next paragraph, and analyze cause and effect in yet another. Except for very short pieces, most writers use several rhetorical strategies in an essay, choosing the ones that best fit their material.

Following are some rhetorical strategies that you will encounter in *The Norton Reader* and that you will want to use in your own writing.

Describing

When writers *describe* a person, place, or thing, they indicate what it looks like and often how it feels, smells, sounds, or tastes. As a strategy, describing involves showing rather than telling, helping readers see rather than giving them a formal definition, making the subject come alive rather than remaining abstract. When you describe, you want to choose precise verbs, specific nouns, vivid adjectives—unless your subject is dullness itself.

As a writer, you will use description in many kinds of assignments: in profiles of people and places to provide a key to their essence, in visual analysis to reveal the crucial features of a painting or photograph, in cultural critique to highlight the features of the object or phenomenon you will analyze, and in scientific lab reports to give details of an experiment. Almost no essay can be written without at least some description, and many essays rely on this strategy as a fundamental technique. In *The Norton Reader*, you will find description-based study questions in almost every section: "Describe your imagined house in detail," "How would you describe your family, including your chosen family, to someone," "Describe a sports-related tradition and its significance"—these are just a few examples of writing assignments that ask for description.

Narrating

Telling stories may be the most fundamental of all rhetorical strategies. We use *narration* to tell stories about ourselves, about our families, and about friends and neighbors. We tell stories to make a point, to illustrate an argument, to offer evidence or counterevidence, and sometimes even to substitute for an argument. As these uses suggest, narrating appears in many genres: from memoirs and personal essays to op-eds and formal speeches. Narrating is basic to essay writing.

As you plan a segment of narration, think about sequence: the order in which the events occurred (chronological order) or an order in which the events might be most dramatically presented (reverse chronological order or the present moment with flashback). Often, sequential order is easier for the reader to comprehend, but sometimes beginning *in medias res* (in the middle of things) and then flashing back to the beginning creates a more compelling story. Consider incorporating time markers—not only dates but also sequential phrases: *early one evening, later that night, the next morning.* And use transitions and transitional words: *first, then, meanwhile, later, finally.* When you've finished narrating your event or episode, reread it and ask: What have I left out that the reader needs to know? What might I omit because the reader doesn't need to know it?

Exemplifying

This strategy involves a main idea and either an extended example or a series of examples that illustrate—or *exemplify*—that idea. Often, exemplification is combined with other rhetorical modes of development, as in Henry Louis Gates Jr.'s "In the Kitchen" (pp. 185–91). Much of Gates's essay involves narration and description as he reflects on different hairstyles, processes, and products in Black culture. Yet he also provides numerous examples—especially of Black celebrities—to illustrate his ideas.

Classifying and dividing

This strategy involves either *classifying* things by putting them into groups or *dividing* up a large block into smaller units. While this strategy might seem better suited to a biology lab than a writing class, it works well for organizing facts that seem chaotic or for handling big topics that may seem overwhelming. Classifying and dividing allows the writer—and the reader—to get control of a potentially unwieldy topic by breaking it into smaller units of analysis.

You will find that classifying and dividing is helpful in writing all genres of analysis: textual, visual, and cultural. You will also find that it can help in argumentative genres because it enables you, as a writer or speaker, to break down a complex argument into parts or to group pieces of evidence into categories.

Explaining or analyzing a process

With this rhetorical strategy, the writer *explains* how something is done: how to write, how to reduce mass shootings, or how to toss a pizza. Sometimes writers use this strategy in historical essays to show or *analyze* how something was done in the past. Explaining a process can be useful in a range of genres: from a literacy narrative that explains learning to read, to a cultural analysis that offers a method for dealing with harassment, to a reflection that explores a symbolic way to make a religious tradition more inclusive.

To make a process accessible to the reader, you will need to identify the main steps or stages and then explain them in order. Sequence matters. In preparing to write a paragraph explaining a process, it might help to list the steps as a flowchart or recipe—and then turn your list into fully elaborated prose.

Comparing and contrasting

Comparisons look for similarities between things; *contrasts* look for differences. In most uses of this rhetorical strategy, you will want to consider both similarities and differences—that is, you will want to compare *and* contrast. That's because most things worth comparing have commonalities as well as differences. You may end up finding more similarities than differences or vice versa, but when using this strategy, think about both.

Comparing and contrasting may be used for a single paragraph or for an entire essay. It tends to be set up in one of two ways: block or point-by-point. In the block technique, the writer gives all the information about one item and then follows with all the information about the other. Think of it as discussing all about *A*, then all about *B*. Usually, the order of the information is the same for both. In the point-by-point technique, the writer focuses on specific points of comparison, alternating *A*, *B*, *A*, *B* until the points have been covered.

Comparing and contrasting is an excellent strategy to use in writing a report, making an argument in an op-ed, or giving a speech to persuade your audience to take a specific action. You can set forth the pros and cons of different programs, political policies, or courses of action, leading to the recommendation you endorse and believe is most effective.

Defining

This rhetorical strategy involves telling your reader what something is—and what it is not. *Defining* enables you to make sure that both you and your readers understand what you mean by a key term. It may lead to redefining a common term to have a more precise meaning or giving nuance to a term that is commonly used too broadly. Defining and redefining are useful strategies in argumentative writing; they help the audience to reshape their thinking and see a concept in a new light.

This strategy is not as simple as looking up a word in a dictionary, though often that is a good place to begin; you may discover that a word meant something a hundred years ago that it no longer means or that its meaning varies from one context to another. Citing one of these definitions can help in composing your essay. But as a rhetorical strategy, defining may also include giving examples or providing descriptions.

Analyzing cause and effect

Focusing on *causes* helps a writer think about why something happened; focusing on *effects* helps a writer think about what might happen or has happened already. Cause is oriented toward the past; effect looks to the present or future. But you can use this strategy by working in either direction: from present to future or from present to past.

If you were writing about global warming and intending to show its harmful effects, you might lay out your evidence in this sequence:

Cause → leads to → these effects.

If you were writing about a student's actions and trying to identify the pressures that led to those actions, you might reverse the direction:

Effects ← are the result of ← these causes.

Analyzing a cause (or causes) is a crucial strategy for genres such as cultural analysis and op-eds. But you can also use this strategy in a personal essay or reflection, where you might analyze the effects of a childhood experience on your later life, or in a profile of a person, where you might seek the sources (the causes) of the person's adult personality or achievements.

Making an argument

This strategy requires you take a position on—to *make an argument* about—a topic of debate. That is, you need to choose a topic and make a claim with which reasonable people might disagree. Once you take a position on the question or issue at hand, you need to support that position and answer potential objections from those who would disagree with you. Support for an argument can come in many forms—quotations from experts, statistics, facts—but all these forms of evidence must be interpreted, not simply dropped in. Often, after making an argument, a writer proposes a better alternative.

STRATEGIES FOR WRITING

If you were to watch a writer at work, either yourself or someone else, you might see that the task of writing often occurs in stages, which is often referred to as the *writing process*. You generate ideas, write a draft, revise the draft (sometimes once, often many times), edit (make sentence- or word-level changes), and finally, proofread (check to see that the grammar, spelling, and formatting are correct). Along the way, you develop a main point and find examples and evidence to support that point. The next few pages will walk you through these different stages of the writing process.

Generate ideas

For many people, the hardest part of writing is looking at the blank page or empty screen. What can you say? How can you even get started? Sometimes your task is made easier when your instructor gives you a specific assignment, asks a particular question, or uses one of the prompts included in *The Norton Reader*. Here's a prompt for generating ideas that follows Nancy Mairs's "On Being a Cripple" (pp. 312–22):

> Mairs deliberately chooses to call herself a "cripple," and she explains her rationale for doing so. With your classmates, brainstorm a list of other labels or names that groups or individuals familiar to you have chosen for themselves. Select one and discuss the rationale behind the choice and reception following it. (322)

You can generate ideas by examining your own memory for stories you've heard, incidents you've witnessed, or people you've met, or you may need to do some research in order to have enough to say. In addition to brainstorming with classmates, you can use one or more of the following techniques to mine your memory or generate ideas:

- Freewrite for several minutes to discover what you already know and think about a subject.
- Group or cluster related ideas.
- Read some articles about the subject. Take notes on what you read.

- Ask questions about the subject, starting with *who, what, when, why,* and *how.*

Writers develop different ways of finding their material, so experiment with a variety of techniques until you discover one or more that work for you.

Develop a main point or thesis

Most writing you will be assigned in college courses requires a central claim, often called a *thesis.* Most papers contain a thesis statement, often stated in the introduction, that tells readers the main point that will be supported, developed, and extended in the body of the paper.

Sometimes the thesis statement will be an arguable claim supported by evidence, such as William Cronon's claims in "The Trouble with Wilderness" (pp. 637–40) that "wilderness can hardly be the solution to our culture's problematic relationship with the nonhuman world, for wilderness is itself a part of the problem" (637) and that wilderness "is entirely a cultural invention" (637).

At other times, the main point won't be stated so plainly. Instead, it will be implied or evident to the reader, but you won't be trying to argue a claim with evidence. If you're writing a narrative or descriptive piece, for example, you'll have a main point, of course, particularly if you're writing a historical narrative or a profile of a person or place. You will make a claim about the reasons something happened or about the reasons for a person's or place's distinctive characteristics, as Scott Russell Sanders does in "Under the Influence" (pp. 16–26):

> My father drank. He drank as a gut-punched boxer gasps for breath, as a starving dog gobbles food. . . . (16)

Those two sentences, in which Sanders uses similes to describe his father, paint an unflattering picture of his character. The reader can assume that Sanders does not look favorably upon drinking to excess.

Gather evidence

What counts as adequate *evidence* for your claim or thesis? If you're writing an argument, you might use interviews or published studies, facts, and statistics. Quoting authorities on the topic can also lend support to your argument. In other kinds of writing, evidence is drawn more often from personal experience than from secondary sources.

In a literacy narrative, for example, the evidence will be in the examples and details of the story you tell about a formative time in your education. In a profile of a person, the evidence will also take the form of examples—the descriptive details about the person's personality, accomplishments, talents, weaknesses, looks, and behavior; anecdotes or stories about the person's life;

or testimony from people who've observed the person closely. Evidence is also often drawn directly from reading. In a textual analysis, the evidence will be examples that demonstrate the text's structure, style, and language.

Organize your ideas

How you *organize your ideas* in a piece of writing depends to a large extent on your genre and purpose. Chris Wiewiora organizes his descriptive essay "This Is Tossing" (pp. 512–16) chronologically, setting up the goal to toss "11 pies by 11 A.M. One hour" (512). He uses the second person and present tense to heighten the drama and make readers feel like they are a part of the narrative. Rebecca Solnit organizes "How to Be a Writer" (pp. 542–45) in the form of a list. She begins each item on the list in bold text, allowing readers to skim the basic advice but also to read each paragraph for more detailed information.

For many of the essays you write in college—often arguments or analyses, you will use the familiar format of an introduction, body, and conclusion, with separate paragraphs in the body for each major piece of evidence. The introduction often connects your ideas to what your readers already know and seeks to interest them in what you have to say. In the body of an essay, you may want to place your most compelling piece of evidence first, or you may want it to come last to tie matters up for the reader. (But don't hide your best evidence by placing it in the middle.) In the conclusion, you try to wrap things up, finish your line of reasoning, and send your readers off with a final thought.

If you're doing a multimodal project with a mix of text, images, and sound, you'll have additional choices for how to organize your material, but no matter the organization you choose, you'll want to draw readers in, guide them through the material, and leave them with something significant to remember, think about, or act upon.

Write multiple drafts

Experienced writers know they can't do everything at once: find or invent material, assess its usefulness, arrange it in paragraphs, and write it out in well-formed sentences. If you try to produce a piece in one sitting, in a single draft, you are likely to thin out your material, lock yourself into a structure that may not work and that you don't have time to change, and write sentences that won't fully convey your meaning or intention. In the end, writing a few drafts—in short periods spaced over more than a day—will produce a better composition, one that is thoughtful and deserving of a respectable grade. Here are some tips for drafting in stages:

- Start by composing a rough draft or small sections of a draft. Don't feel obliged to start with the introduction and write straight through to the conclusion. If you don't know where to begin, write a section you know you want to include, then move to another. As you compose, you will begin to find out what you mean, what is important to your argument or your story, what is missing, and what needs to be revised. Think of composing a rough draft as a way of discovering what you want to say.

- If you get stuck, try focused freewriting. That is, write all you can in response to a particular idea, not stopping for five minutes. Then read what you've written, looking for your thoughts on the subject. You may have come up with key notions or put yourself in touch with useful ideas.

- If you're writing an argument or analysis, write a single paragraph for each key piece of evidence you have to support your thesis. Later on, you can refine these paragraphs, combining some and breaking up others.

- At any point in this process, print out a clean version of your draft, read it through, and make changes. Add to, subtract from, rearrange, and revise the parts of your essay.

- If you're using sound, photos, drawings, charts, graphs, videos, or other elements, carefully consider the role they play in the composition and what you wish to get across to readers.

Acknowledge the words and ideas of others

Your writing should reflect your own thinking, of course, but you'll often incorporate the ideas and words of others. Synthesizing and citing the work of others will show your readers that you have consulted reputable sources and will make readers more open to your argument. It may help you to think of anything you write as part of a dialogue you are having with other writers and scholars; just be sure to credit the writers and scholars whose words and ideas you borrow or respond to, so your readers can follow the dialogue and know who said what.

When you cite information from another source in your writing, you must credit the source. First, give other authors and other creators credit by acknowledging their work. There are different conventions for citation, depending on discipline. For example, in many English classes, you'll use MLA style. If you cite someone's exact words, put them in quotation marks, or, if you quote more than four lines, indent them without quotation marks. Tell your readers where you got the words by including the author's name in your text and putting the page number of the book or article in parentheses right after the quote. Here is an example of a direct quotation with appropriate MLA citation:

> According to Densley and Peterson, "Half of all mass shooters—and nearly 80% of school mass shooters—communicate intent to do harm ahead of time" (156).

If you paraphrase a source, that is, if you use another person's idea but not the exact words, you still need to cite the source of that idea, even though you have expressed it in your own words. Here is an example of a paraphrase:

> Densley and Peterson, cofounders of the Violence Project, argue that crisis intervention skills and de-escalation techniques can help reduce mass shootings (157).

At the end of your paper on a separate page, list all the sources you have quoted and paraphrased. Many style guides provide directions for formatting source material. The guide used most frequently in English classes is the *MLA Handbook*, published by the Modern Language Association. At the end of each essay, we have included an MLA citation so that you can easily cite the essays you've used in your paper. These citations reflect the 2021 guidelines in the ninth edition of the handbook.

Sometimes writers in a hurry are tempted to absorb others' writing wholesale into their papers. This is *plagiarism*. Plagiarism is unethical because it involves the theft of another writer's words and ideas; in college courses, it is a guarantee of failure when discovered. Avoid plagiarizing at all costs. If you have fallen behind on a writing assignment, tell your instructor. You will often find that teachers will accept a late submission, and even if you are graded down for lateness, that is better than using others' ideas and words without attribution.

Get responses and revise

Although writers can and often do compose and *revise* alone, we all need helpful *responses*, whether from professional editors, teachers, classmates, or friends. Many writing classes encourage that process, teaching students to draft and revise independently but also enabling them to put less-than-final drafts forward for responses from the instructor and fellow students. Examples and arguments that seem clear to the writer may seem forced or exaggerated to another reader. In peer groups, listen to readers who disagree with you, who find your position slanted, overstated, or not fully convincing. Be responsive to their comments and qualify interpretations or further explain points that they do not understand. If you're writing a narrative, you may understand context or know details that won't be clear to readers, so listen to their questions and be willing to add or cut or rearrange parts as needed.

Here are some all-purpose questions that you can use to review a draft on your own or in a peer group. Whether you're talking with classmates face-to-face or responding by writing electronically, the questions should probably be asked in the order below, since they move from larger elements to smaller ones.

Introduction   Treat the introduction as a promise by asking, "Does this essay keep the promises the introduction makes?" If it doesn't, either the introduction or the essay needs to be revised. Try to determine where the problem lies: Is the introduction off track? Do any of the paragraphs wander off topic? Does the introduction promise an organization that isn't followed?

Content   Does this essay include enough material? As you read your own work and that of your classmates, look for examples and details that transmit meaning and engage your interest, understanding, and imagination. Check for adequate and persuasive evidence and multiple illustrative examples that clarify main points. If you or your readers think you need more evidence, examples, or information, revise accordingly.

Evidence and source material   If the paper is an argument or analysis, do you interpret the material clearly and connect examples to the main argument? Your essay, and those you read as a peer reviewer, should specify the meanings of the examples you use; don't expect the examples to speak for themselves. A case in point is the use of quotations. How many are there? How necessary are they? How well are they integrated? What analysis or commentary follows each? Watch for quotations that are simply dropped in, without enough introduction or "placing" so that the reader can understand their significance. Quotations should be well integrated, clearly explaining who is speaking, where the voice is coming from, and what to attend to. If you're writing a narrative or descriptive piece, your evidence and material will come in different forms: vivid details, scenes, and dialogue.

Organization and transitions   Are the main and supporting points of this essay well organized? Writing puts readers in possession of material in a temporal order: That is, readers read from start to finish. Sometimes material that appears near the end of an essay might work better near the beginning; sometimes material that appears near the beginning might better be postponed. Pay attention to transitions between and within paragraphs; if they are unclear, the difficulty may lie in the organization of the material.

Tone   Is the tone of the essay appropriate for its purpose and audience? Whether the tone is lighthearted, serious, reasoned, funny, enraged, thoughtful, or anything else, it needs to be appropriate to the purpose of the essay and sensitive to the expectations of the audience. Be aware of how formal your writing should be and whether contractions, abbreviations, and slang are acceptable.

Sentences   Which sentences unfold smoothly and which sentences might cause readers to stumble? If working in a group, ask your classmates to help you rephrase a sentence or write the thought in new words. Remember, you're trying to reach readers just like your peers, so take their questions and reactions seriously.

Sounds and visuals   It's not just written words that convey meaning. Do the images, videos, or other extratextual elements support the argument, meaning, or effect you wish to get across?

Learning to be a responsive reader of essays in *The Norton Reader* can teach you to respond helpfully to the essays of peer writers in your composition class—and to improve your own. Large and small elements of the composing process are reciprocal. Learn to work back and forth among wholes and parts, sections and paragraphs, introductions and conclusions, words and visuals. As shape and meaning come together, you can begin to refine smaller elements: sentences, phrases, specific words. You can qualify your assertions, complicate your generalizations, and tease out the implications of your examples.

Edit, proofread, and format the final draft

After you have revised the structure of your writing, you should devote time to editing and proofreading. This work is best done after taking time away from your composition and coming to it afresh. You may be tempted to move directly to the proofreading stage, thus shortchanging the larger, more important work described above. So long as the larger elements need repair, it's too soon to work on the smaller ones, so save the tinkering for last. When you're satisfied with the overall shape of your project, turn to the work of tightening your writing by eliminating unnecessary repetition and awkward phrases; and correcting grammar, punctuation, and spelling. Be sure you know what style and format your work should take, be it that of an academic paper with set margins, double-spacing, and a works cited page, or some other format. Ask your instructor if you are unsure about any of these elements or expectations, and make the necessary changes. Then, like other writers, you will need to stop—not because there isn't more to be done but because you have other things to do.

THE NORTON READER
Sixteenth Edition

1 HOME AND FAMILY

Home is the place where, when you have to go there,
They have to take you in.

—ROBERT FROST

Many readers will be familiar with these lines from Robert Frost's poem "The Death of the Hired Man," but some might not know the full narrative of Frost's poem. Silas, "the hired man," had over the years exploited his position working for his employers, coming and going to his own advantage, often leaving his employment when his help was most needed, and then returning when he was near death. Silas had a brother, but he did not return to his biological family when he was about to die. Frost's poem, like the essays here, helps readers consider the nature of home and family. Is there anyone who has "to take you in"?

The writers in this chapter explore an array of experiences and ideas. Joan Didion ponders what it means to return after leaving her family home. Michelle Zauner shows both the comfort and grief evoked by visiting a Korean grocery store after her mother's death. Several writers consider what we inherit from family members: Didion reflects on ways of interacting; Joy Castro on the fear of violence; Diana Abu-Jaber on tastes and preferences; Jason Reynolds on the desire to put family first, even as he seeks to follow his own dreams; and Scott Russell Sanders on tendencies toward addiction.

The relationship between home and family is often complex and shifting. Judith Ortiz Cofer describes her grandparents' home and how when each of their eight children was born, they added on rooms, showing "a house that has grown organically, according to the needs of its inhabitants." After Sandra Steingraber comes out as gay when her children are teens, she and her family plan a new housing arrangement. And Rachel Pieh Jones shows how friends—even those from different cultural and religious backgrounds—can help care for one another and create a mutual sense of belonging.

The readings in this chapter are personal essays, the authors' first-person accounts of their own experiences of home and family. Even though the genre is the same, the strategies—form, tone, organization, focus—that the authors use differ. Leslie Jamison draws from not only personal experience but also literary, historical, and psychological texts as she explores and interrogates what it means to be a stepmother. Kiese Laymon considers how the songs he listens to at night while he's alone in his truck contribute to his own sense of home. Steingraber divides her coming-out essay into ten parts, sharing not only her own story but also the experiences of her partner and a former student. As you read, look for the similarities and differences between how the writers tell their stories of home and family. What similar strategies can you use in your own writing?

After reading these essays, think about the stories you have to tell about your own home or family. How do you define "home"? Is it a particular house, a group of people, a country? Have you ever returned home after a significant time away? Did you see your home or family differently after that absence and return? How do you define "family"? Is it a biological relationship—or more expansive than that? Are there songs or stories that help express your sense of home or family? What trait or behavior of a particular family member most affected you or your relationship with that person? Have you ever been—literally or figuratively—without a home?

JOAN DIDION

On Going Home

I AM HOME for my daughter's first birthday. By "home" I do not mean the house in Los Angeles where my husband and I and the baby live, but the place where my family is, in the Central Valley of California. It is a vital although troublesome distinction. My husband likes my family but is uneasy in their house, because once there I fall into their ways, which are difficult, oblique, deliberately inarticulate, not my husband's ways. We live in dusty houses ("D-U-S-T," he once wrote with his finger on surfaces all over the house, but no one noticed it) filled with mementos quite without value to him (what could the Canton dessert plates mean to him? how could he have known about the assay scales, why should he care if he did know?), and we appear to talk exclusively about people we know who have been committed to mental hospitals, about people we know who have been booked on drunk-driving charges, and about property, particularly about property, land, price per acre and C-2 zoning and assessments and freeway access. My brother does not understand my husband's inability to perceive the advantage in the rather common real-estate transaction known as "sale-leaseback," and my husband in turn does not understand why so many of the people he hears about in my father's house have recently been committed to mental hospitals or booked on drunk-driving charges. Nor does he understand that when we talk about sale-leasebacks and right-of-way condemnations we are talking in code about the things we like best, the yellow fields and the cottonwoods and the rivers rising and falling and the mountain roads closing when the heavy snow comes in. We miss each other's points, have another drink and regard the fire. My brother refers to my husband, in his presence, as "Joan's husband." Marriage is the classic betrayal.

Or perhaps it is not any more. Sometimes I think that those of us who are now in our thirties were born into the last generation to carry the burden of "home," to find in family life the source of all tension and drama. I had by all objective accounts a "normal" and a "happy" family situation, and yet I was almost

From Slouching Towards Bethlehem *(1968), Joan Didion's first work of nonfiction, which includes essays analyzing American culture in the 1960s.*

thirty years old before I could talk to my family on the telephone without crying after I had hung up. We did not fight. Nothing was wrong. And yet some nameless anxiety colored the emotional charges between me and the place that I came from. The question of whether or not you could go home again was a very real part of the sentimental and largely literary baggage with which we left home in the fifties; I suspect that it is irrelevant to the children born of the fragmentation after World War II. A few weeks ago in a San Francisco bar I saw a pretty young girl on crystal[1] take off her clothes and dance for the cash prize in an "amateur-topless" contest. There was no particular sense of moment about this, none of the effect of romantic degradation, of "dark journey," for which my generation strived so assiduously. What sense could that girl possibly make of, say, *Long Day's Journey into Night*?[2] Who is beside the point?

That I am trapped in this particular irrelevancy is never more apparent to me than when I am home. Paralyzed by the neurotic lassitude engendered by meeting one's past at every turn, around every corner, inside every cupboard, I go aimlessly from room to room. I decide to meet it head-on and clean out a drawer, and I spread the contents on the bed. A bathing suit I wore the summer I was seventeen. A letter of rejection from the *Nation,* an aerial photograph of the site for a shopping center my father did not build in 1954. Three teacups hand-painted with cabbage roses and signed "E.M.," my grandmother's initials. There is no final solution for letters of rejection from the *Nation* and teacups hand-painted in 1900. Nor is there any answer to snapshots of one's grandfather as a young man on skis, surveying around Donner Pass in the year 1910. I smooth out the snapshot and look into his face, and do and do not see my own. I close the drawer, and have another cup of coffee with my mother. We get along very well, veterans of a guerrilla war we never understood.

Days pass. I see no one. I come to dread my husband's evening call, not only because he is full of news of what by now seems to me our remote life in Los Angeles, people he has seen, letters which require attention, but because he asks what I have been doing, suggests uneasily that I get out, drive to San Francisco or Berkeley. Instead I drive across the river to a family graveyard. It has been vandalized since my last visit and the monuments are broken, overturned in the dry grass. Because I once saw a rattlesnake in the grass I stay in the car and listen to a country-and-Western station. Later I drive with my father to a ranch he has in the foothills. The man who runs his cattle on it asks us to the roundup, a week from Sunday, and although I know that I will be in Los Angeles I say, in the oblique way my family talks, that I will come. Once home I mention the broken monuments in the graveyard. My mother shrugs.

I go to visit my great-aunts. A few of them think now that I am my cousin,   5
or their daughter who died young. We recall an anecdote about a relative last seen in 1948, and they ask if I still like living in New York City. I have lived in Los Angeles for three years, but I say that I do. The baby is offered a horehound

---

1. Methamphetamine.
2. Tragedy (1956) by playwright Eugene O'Neill (1888–1953) based on the shame and deception that haunted his own family.

drop, and I am slipped a dollar bill "to buy a treat." Questions trail off, answers are abandoned, the baby plays with the dust motes in a shaft of afternoon sun.

It is time for the baby's birthday party: a white cake, strawberry-marsh-mallow ice cream, a bottle of champagne saved from another party. In the evening, after she has gone to sleep, I kneel beside the crib and touch her face, where it is pressed against the slats, with mine. She is an open and trusting child, unprepared for and unaccustomed to the ambushes of family life, and perhaps it is just as well that I can offer her little of that life. I would like to give her more. I would like to promise her that she will grow up with a sense of her cousins and of rivers and of her great-grandmother's teacups, would like to pledge her a picnic on a river with fried chicken and her hair uncombed, would like to give her *home* for her birthday, but we live differently now and I can promise her nothing like that. I give her a xylophone and a sundress from Madeira, and promise to tell her a funny story.

MLA CITATION

Didion, Joan. "On Going Home." *The Norton Reader: An Anthology of Nonfiction*, edited by Melissa A. Goldthwaite et al., 16th ed., W. W. Norton, 2024, pp. 2–4.

QUESTIONS

1. Joan Didion speaks of herself at home as "paralyzed by the neurotic lassitude engendered by meeting one's past at every turn" (paragraph 3). What about the essay helps explain these feelings?

2. Annotate Didion's essay, marking the metaphors she uses to describe the relationship she has with her family (for example, "guerrilla war" in paragraph 3) and the body language she uses to describe interactions with family members (for example, "My mother shrugs" in paragraph 4). Based on your analysis of Didion's use of language, how would you characterize her family relationships?

3. In paragraph 6, Didion says she would like to give her daughter "*home* for her birthday, but we live differently now." In an essay, explain whether or not you think parents today can give their children "home." Include examples to support your argument.

MICHELLE ZAUNER
Crying in H Mart

EVER SINCE MY MOM DIED, I cry in H Mart. For those of you who don't know, H Mart is a supermarket chain that specializes in Asian food. The "H" stands for *han ah reum*, a Korean phrase that roughly translates to "one arm full of groceries." H Mart is where parachute kids[1] go to get the exact brand of instant noodles that reminds them of home. It's where Korean families buy rice cakes to make *tteokguk*, a beef soup that brings in the new year. It's the only place where you can find a giant vat of peeled garlic, because it's the only place that truly understands how much garlic you'll need for the kind of food your people eat. H Mart is freedom from the single-aisle "ethnic" section in regular grocery stores. They don't prop Goya beans next to bottles of sriracha here. Instead, you'll likely find me crying by the *banchan*[2] refrigerators, remembering the taste of my mom's soy-sauce eggs and cold radish soup. Or in the freezer section, holding a stack of dumpling skins, thinking of all the hours that Mom and I spent at the kitchen table folding minced pork and chives into the thin dough. Sobbing near the dry goods, asking myself, "Am I even Korean anymore if there's no one left in my life to call and ask which brand of seaweed we used to buy?"

When I was growing up, with a Caucasian father and a Korean mother, my mom was my access point for our Korean heritage. While she never actually taught me how to cook (Korean people tend to disavow measurements and supply only cryptic instructions along the lines of "add sesame oil until it tastes like Mom's"), she did raise me with a distinctly Korean appetite. This meant an over-the-top appreciation of good food and emotional eating. We were particular about everything: kimchi had to be perfectly sour, *samgyupsal*[3] perfectly crisped; hot food had to be served piping hot or it might as well be inedible. The concept of prepping meals for the week was a ludicrous affront to our life style. We chased our cravings daily. If we wanted the same kimchi stew for three weeks straight, we relished it until a new craving emerged. We ate in accordance with the seasons and holidays. On my birthday, she'd make seaweed soup: a traditional dish for celebrating one's mother that is also what women typically eat after giving birth. When spring arrived and the weather turned, we'd bring our camp stove outdoors and fry up strips of fresh pork belly on the deck. In many ways, food was how my mother expressed her love.

First appeared in the New Yorker *(2018), a weekly magazine of "reportage, commentary, criticism, essays, fiction, satire, cartoons, and poetry," and later (2021) in Michelle Zauner's memoir by the same title about her mother's illness and death and her own Korean identity.*

1. Children sent to live and study abroad without their parents. The term usually refers to Asian children sent to schools in the United States.
2. Side dishes served as a part of Korean meals.
3. Grilled pork belly.

No matter how critical or cruel she seemed—constantly pushing me to be what she felt was the best version of myself—I could always feel her affection radiating from the lunches she packed and the meals she prepared for me just the way I liked them.

I can hardly speak Korean, but in H Mart I feel like I'm fluent. I fondle the produce and say the words aloud—*chamoe* melon, *danmuji*.[4] I fill my shopping cart with every snack that has glossy packaging decorated with a familiar cartoon. I think about the time Mom showed me how to fold the little plastic card that came inside bags of Jolly Pong, how to use it as a spoon to shovel caramel puff rice into my mouth, and how it inevitably fell down my shirt and spread all over the car. I remember the snacks Mom told me she ate when she was a kid and how I tried to imagine her at my age. I wanted to like all the things she did, to embody her completely.

My grief comes in waves and is usually triggered by something arbitrary. I can tell you with a straight face what it was like watching my mom's hair fall out in the bathtub, or about the five weeks I spent sleeping in hospitals, but catch me at H Mart when some kid runs up double-fisting plastic sleeves of *ppeong-twigi* and I'll just lose it. Those little rice-cake Frisbees were my childhood: a happier time, when Mom was there and we'd crunch away on the Styrofoam-like disks after school. Eating them was like splitting a packing peanut that dissolved like sugar on your tongue.

I'll cry when I see a Korean grandmother eating seafood noodles in the food court, discarding shrimp heads and mussel shells onto the lid of her daughter's tin rice bowl. Her gray hair frizzy, cheekbones protruding like the tops of two peaches, tattooed eyebrows rusting as the ink fades out. I'll wonder what my Mom would have looked like in her seventies—if she would have the same perm that every Korean grandma gets as though it were a part of our race's evolution. I'll imagine our arms linked, her tiny frame leaning against mine as we take the escalator up to the food court. The two of us in all black, "New York style," she'd say, her image of New York still rooted in the era of *Breakfast at Tiffany's*.[5] She would carry the quilted-leather Chanel purse that she'd wanted her whole life, instead of the fake ones that she bought on the back streets of Itaewon. Her hands and face would be slightly sticky from QVC anti-aging creams. She'd wear some strange, ultra-high-top sneaker wedges that I'd disagree with. "Michelle, in Korea, every celebrity wears this one." She'd pluck the lint off my coat and pick on me—how my shoulders slumped, how I needed new shoes, how I should really start using that argan-oil treatment she bought me—but we'd be together.

If I'm being honest, there's a lot of anger. I'm angry at this old Korean woman I don't know, that she gets to live and my mother does not, like somehow this stranger's survival is at all related to my loss. Why is she here slurping up spicy

4. Pickled radish.
5. Novella (1958) by Truman Capote (1924–1984) that was the basis for the film (1961) by the same title. The film features Audrey Hepburn (1929–1993) starring as Holly Golightly, who wears oversized sunglasses, a little black dress, and a chignon hairstyle.

jjamppong noodles and my mom isn't? Other people must feel this way. Life is unfair, and sometimes it helps to irrationally blame someone for it.

Sometimes my grief feels as though I've been left alone in a room with no doors. Every time I remember that my mother is dead, it feels like I'm colliding into a wall that won't give. There's no escape, just a hard wall that I keep ramming into over and over, a reminder of the immutable reality that I will never see her again.

H Marts are usually situated far from a city's center. When I lived in Brooklyn, it was an hour-long drive in traffic to Flushing. In Philly, it's about the same to Upper Darby or Elkins Park. H Marts often serve as the center of larger complexes of Asian storefronts, and are surrounded by Asian restaurants that are always better than the ones found closer to town. We're talking Korean restaurants that pack the table so full of *banchan* side dishes that you're forced to play a never-ending game of horizontal Jenga with twenty-plus plates of tiny anchovies, stuffed cucumbers, and pickled everything. This isn't like the sad Asian-fusion joint by your work, where they serve bell peppers in their bibimbap and give you the stink eye when you ask for another round of wilted bean sprouts; this is the real deal.

You'll know that you're headed the right way because there will be signs to mark your path. As you go farther into your pilgrimage, the lettering on the awnings slowly begins to turn into symbols that you may or may not be able to read. This is when my elementary-grade Korean skills are put to the test—how fast can I sound out the vowels while in traffic? I spent more than ten years going to *hangul hakkyo*[6] every Friday, and this is all I have to show for it: I can read the signs for churches in different Asian texts, for an optometrist's office, a bank. A couple more blocks in, and we're in the heart of it. Suddenly, it's like another country. Everyone is Asian, a swarm of different dialects crisscross

6. Korean language school.

like invisible telephone wires, the only English words are "HOT POT" and "LIQUORS," and they're all buried beneath a handful of different characters, with an anime tiger or hot dog dancing next to them.

Inside an H Mart complex, there will be some kind of food court, an appliance shop, and a pharmacy. Usually, there's a beauty counter where you can buy Korean makeup and skin-care products with snail mucin or caviar oil, or a face mask that proudly and vaguely advertises "PLACENTA." (Whose placenta? Who knows?) There will usually be a pseudo-French bakery with weak coffee, bubble tea, and an array of glowing pastries that always look much better than they taste.

Lately, my local H Mart is in Cheltenham, a town northeast of Philadelphia. My routine is to drive in for lunch on the weekends, stock up on groceries for the week, and cook something for dinner with whatever fresh bounty inspired me. The H Mart in Cheltenham has two stories; the grocery is on the first floor and the food court is above it. Upstairs, there is an array of stalls for different kinds of food. One is dedicated to sushi, one is strictly Chinese, and another is for traditional Korean *jjigaes*, bubbling soups served in traditional stone pots called *dolsots*, which act as mini cauldrons to insure that your soup is still bubbling a good ten minutes past arrival. There's a stall for Korean street food, which serves up Korean ramen (which basically just means Shin Cup Noodles with an egg cracked in them); giant steamed dumplings full of pork and glass noodles, housed in a thick, cake-like dough; and *tteokbokki*, chewy, bite-sized cylindrical rice cakes boiled in a stock with fishcakes, red pepper, and *gochujang*, a sweet-and-spicy paste that's one of the three mother sauces used in pretty much all Korean dishes. Last, there's my personal favorite: Korean-Chinese fusion, which serves *tangsuyuk*—a glossy, sweet-and-sour orange pork—seafood noodle soup, fried rice, and *jajangmyeon*.[7]

The food court is the perfect place to people-watch while sucking down salty, fatty, black-bean noodles. I think about my family who lived in Korea, before most of them died, and how Korean-Chinese food was always the first thing we'd eat when my mom and I arrived in Seoul after a fourteen-hour flight from America. Twenty minutes after my aunt would phone in our order, the apartment ringer would buzz "Für Elise"[8] in MIDI, and up would come a helmeted man, fresh off his motorcycle, with a giant steel box. He'd slide open the metal door and deliver heaping bowls of noodles and deep-fried battered pork with its rich sauce on the side. The Saran wrap on top would be concave and sweating. We'd peel it off and dribble black, chunky goodness all over the noodles and pour the shiny, sticky, translucent orange sauce over the pork. We'd sit cross-legged on the cool marble floor, slurping and reaching over one another. My aunts and mom and grandmother would jabber on in Korean, and I would eat and listen, unable to comprehend, bothering my mom every so often to translate.

I wonder how many people at H Mart miss their families. How many are thinking of them as they bring their trays back from the different stalls. Whether they're eating to feel connected, to celebrate these people through food. Which

7. A noodle dish with black-bean sauce.
8. A composition (1810) for piano by Ludwig van Beethoven (1770–1827).

ones weren't able to fly back home this year, or for the past ten years? Which ones are like me, missing the people who are gone from their lives forever?

At one table is a group of young Chinese students, alone without family at schools in America. They have banded together to take the bus forty-five minutes outside the city, into the suburbs of a foreign country, for soup dumplings. At another table, there are three generations of Korean women eating three types of stews: daughter, mom, and grandmother dipping their spoons into each other's *dolsots*, reaching over one another's trays, arms in one another's faces, pinching at their different *banchan* with chopsticks. None of them pay any notice or give second thought to the concept of personal space.

There is a young white man and his family. They giggle together as they butcher the pronunciation of the menu. The son explains to his parents the different dishes they've ordered. Maybe he was stationed in Seoul for military service or taught English abroad. Maybe he's the only one in his family with a passport. Maybe this will be the moment his family decides it's time to travel and discover these things themselves. 15

There is an Asian guy blowing his girlfriend's mind, introducing her to a whole new world of flavors and textures. He shows her how to eat *mul naeng-myeon*, a cold noodle soup that tastes better if you add vinegar and hot mustard first. He tells her about how his parents came to this country, how he'd watch his mom make this dish. When she made it, she didn't add zucchini; she subbed radishes instead. An old man hobbles over to a neighboring table to order the chicken-and-ginseng porridge that he probably eats here every day. Bells go off for people to collect their orders. Women in visors work behind the counters without stopping.

It's a beautiful, holy place. A cafeteria full of people from all over the world who have been displaced in a foreign country, each with a different history. Where did they come from and how far did they travel? Why are they all here? To find the *galangal*[9] no American supermarket stocks to make the Indonesian curry that their father loves? To buy the rice cakes to celebrate Jesa and honor the anniversary of their loved one's passing? To satisfy a craving for *tteokbokki* on a rainy day? Were they moved by a memory of some drunken, late-night snack under a *pojangmacha* tent in Incheon?

We don't talk about it. There's never so much as a knowing look. We sit here in silence, eating our lunch. But I know we are all here for the same reason. We're all searching for a piece of home, or a piece of ourselves. We look for a taste of it in the food we order and the ingredients we buy. Then we separate. We bring the haul back to our dorm rooms or suburban kitchens, and we re-create a dish that couldn't be made without that journey, because what we're looking for isn't accessible at a Trader Joe's. H Mart is where you can find your people under one odorous roof, where you can have faith that you'll find something you can't find anywhere else.

In the H Mart food court, I find myself again, searching for the first chapter of the story that I want to tell about my mother. I am sitting next to a Korean

9. A plant in the ginger family used in cooking and herbal medicine.

mother and her son, who have unknowingly taken the table next to ol' water-
works over here. The kid dutifully gets their silverware from the counter and
places it on paper napkins for the both of them. He's eating fried rice and his
mom has *seolleongtang*, ox-bone soup. He must be in his early twenties, but his
mother is still instructing him on how to eat, just like my mom used to. "Dip
the onion in the paste." "Don't add too much *gochujang* or it'll be too salty."
"Why aren't you eating the mung beans?" Some days, the constant nagging
would annoy me. Woman, let me eat in peace! But, most days, I knew it was the
ultimate display of a Korean woman's tenderness, and I cherished that love.

20   The boy's mom places pieces of beef from her spoon onto his spoon. He is
quiet and looks tired and doesn't talk to her much. I want to tell him how
much I miss my mother. How he should be kind to his mom, remember that
life is fragile and she could be gone at any moment. Tell her to go to the doctor
and make sure there isn't a small tumor growing inside her.

Within the past five years, I lost both my aunt and mother to cancer. So,
when I go to H Mart, I'm not just on the hunt for cuttlefish and three bunches
of scallions for a buck; I'm searching for their memory. I'm collecting the evidence that the Korean half of my identity didn't die when they did. In moments
like this, H Mart is the bridge that guides me away from the memories that
haunt me, of chemo head and skeletal bodies and logging milligrams of hydro-
codone. It reminds me of who they were before: beautiful and full of life, wig-
gling Chang Gu honey-cracker rings on all ten of their fingers, showing me
how to suck a Korean grape from its skin and spit out the seeds.

MLA CITATION

Zauner, Michelle. "Crying in H Mart." *The Norton Reader: An Anthology of
    Nonfiction*, edited by Melissa A. Goldthwaite et al., 16th ed., W. W. Norton,
    2024, pp. 5–10.

QUESTIONS

1. Why does Michelle Zauner cry in H Mart? Is there more than one reason for her
emotion? Cite examples from the essay.

2. Details of food and cooking appear throughout the essay. Mark those passages
and then take a closer look at them. Besides giving us a flavor of Korean food, what
function do these details serve?

3. What foods remind you of home? of a particular person in your family? When
you are away from home or that person, is there a restaurant, grocery store, or type
of food you buy or prepare that brings back memories? Whether through a personal
essay, photo essay, or some other format, introduce the foods that you associate with
home and family to an audience of outsiders.

Jason Reynolds
Between Us: A Reckoning with My Mother

I WAS THIRTEEN when my grandfather's leg was amputated. Above the knee. An infection, they said. Something nasty spreading throughout his body. My mother and I traveled nine hours to South Carolina to ensure the oak tree of our family could sustain after losing a limb. I don't remember the ride to the hospital, or the hospital itself, but I do recall him sleeping flat-backed in bed, post-surgery, and my mother talking to the doctor (or maybe it was the nurse) about the dressing on the wound. A mound of gauze, as if the base of what was left of his leg, now footless and blunt, had been fashioned into a giant Q-tip. My grandfather had been turned into someone else. Someone I would never actually get to know, because he would never leave the hospital again.

I was thirteen when my grandfather's leg was amputated. Above the knee. And thirteen when he died.

His death would mark the end not only of his life, or my mother's tangible relationship with her parents—my grandmother had passed three years prior—but also of our bimonthly journeys to the South. It had become routine for my mother to get off work every other Friday; have my older brother, Allen, and me pack the trunk with duffel bags and a small cooler containing a few aluminum-foiled turkey sandwiches; then give Allen a list of instructions of what not to do while we were gone, though she knew he wouldn't abide by a single word. But I suppose she figured his disobedience in absence was better than his persistent griping, which included tying each word to a disrespectful groan and taking everything in his life out on me by trying to take life out of me. Allen was afflicted with adolescence, and there was just too much ground to cover for my mother to deal with the futility of trying to cure him. Not to mention, at this point, my parents had come undone and she was doing this alone.

In the car, we'd listen to the radio—oldies—and I'd wait for my mother to ask the same question she asked every trip. 5

"How you know these words? You weren't even born when this came out," she'd say. Or, "Boy, what you know about the Temptations?" Or Marvin Gaye. Or Aretha Franklin. As if she hadn't been playing this music each day of my life. Their lyrics seemed to be spackled to the roof of my mouth, sharing space with the emcees of my time, an internal, intergenerational residence and resonance.

We'd pull into rest stops where I'd get peanut M&Ms, or gas stations where we'd load up on six-packs of peanut butter crackers my mother referred to as Nabs, to go with the turkey sandwiches, of course. Sometimes she'd even play a number. Out-of-town lottery felt luckier, she'd say. And whenever she'd get tired, whenever the hypnotic perforated line began to lull her to sleep, she'd crack the window and talk. My mother would sermonize about the importance

Published in the anthology You Are Your Best Thing: Vulnerability, Shame Resilience, and the Black Experience *(2021), edited by Tarana Burke and Brené Brown.*

of dreams and purpose-searching, meditation and energy. She'd say things about how she wanted me to live a grounded life, a centered life, and a life in flight all at the same time. Conversations she felt like she could have only with me—her child, a child—because the bulk of our family saw her crystals and smudging as the antithesis to their conservative views on God.

"Some things are meant to stay between us," she'd say.

My mother would tell me stories about growing up in a no-stoplight town on two hundred acres of land acquired by her great-great-grandfather, who was a freedman. How his chosen name after emancipation was January, and how no one actually knew how he got the land, but everyone believed he somehow inherited it from the family who formerly owned him. He built a house on this acreage, but he only knew of two types of homes—slave quarters and the big house. And to build slave quarters was out of the question. So he built a house resembling the one of the family who had treated him as property. And he tilled the soil and planted vegetables, grew fruit trees. Had hogs and chickens. He got married and raised children. One of those children, John Wesley, would inherit January's green thumb, making him the heir to the land. And as John Wesley grew older he would eventually informally adopt his grandson—my grandfather—whose mother had abandoned him for a life in the North. John Wesley raised my grandfather as his own. Taught him how to reap and sow. Taught him the value of hard work and heredity. Taught him family.

10   When John Wesley died, he left the land and the house in my grandfather's care. And that's where my mother was born and where she'd live until she was ten years old. It's where she learned to snap peas and pick cotton and pluck chickens. It's where she learned, as the middle child, how to take care of her older and younger sisters, the independent and dependable compass of a sometimes wayward siblinghood. Where she, too, would learn family.

That land is the same land my mother and I would pull up to in the middle of the night, the darkness of Carolina a cataract to this country town. But the house wasn't the same house. It had burned down after my mother, aunts, and grandparents packed up and moved to Washington, DC, for more opportunity in 1955. The farm had dried up, and the nation's capital—Chocolate City— was installing a new subway system and needed hands. So life in the country castle was traded for survival in a one-bedroom apartment in the projects.

Once my mother and her sisters were all grown and had children of their own, my grandparents moved back to South Carolina—back home—to their land. My grandfather built a new, smaller house with his hands, and used those same hands to wake up the dirt. Out came the collards, the mustards, the turnips and kale. Out came the watermelon. The cantaloupe. The tomatoes and butter beans. Before Allen was old enough to stay home by himself—and before the divorce—we'd come down every summer as a family, my father taking the wheel, Allen and me in the backseat exchanging elbows. We'd had our first bouts with "everywhere-dust," and our first tastes of squirrel, buckshot still in the meat. We'd gotten to know our cousins, trained our ears to decipher their drawls, and, most important, were introduced to a part of our grandfather we'd never known. We'd only known a city man. But down South, we'd gotten to know a farmer.

A giant who walked the rows, who sprinkled seeds and steered a tractor. A man who smashed melon on the ground and clawed the heart of it with his bare hands and passed it around to my brother and me like Communion host. There was a tenderness to him. A different kind of tenderness but a tenderness all the same. He wasn't one for hugs and kisses but was always sure to thank his children and grandchildren for coming to see him.

"I know y'all busy with your own lives, and you don't have to think about me and your mother down here," he'd say.

"You're my father," my mother would reply. "And you raised us to always put family first."

Then he'd pull a five-dollar bill from his wallet, press it into my palm as if it were a nugget of gold, and say, "Split that with your brother." And when I'd complain about how ridiculous that seemed, seeing as I'd surely blow half of my share on peanut M&Ms on the way home, he'd say, "Don't matter. Y'all brothers. Family."

I was seventeen when my mother was diagnosed with cancer. In her bladder. Caught it early enough, they said. It had eaten away at a part of her before she'd ever told me. But when she did, sitting across from each other at the kitchen table, I could see the bite marks. Could see the fear in her eyes.

"Don't worry," she said. "I'm gonna make it because I need to see you make something of yourself. I ain't going nowhere until then."

So I was thrust into adulthood with a ferocity that seemed unfair and unforgiving. Struggling with college classes, working a boring but paid internship, then going to the hospital to check on my mother, who was in and out of surgery, chemotherapy, and radiation. I don't remember the daily ride to the hospital, and, honestly, I don't remember the hospital either. But I do remember seeing just her head lifted above the horizon line of white sheets. Her skin, ashen and cracked. Tubes. Beeping. And a spot of moisture always in the corners of her eyes. She'd squeeze my hand and nod just enough to let me know she knew I was there.

When I'd leave the hospital, I'd return to my hotbox of a dorm room, where I'd write for hours. Those lyrics I grew up listening to, the rappers and crooners, had somehow, through some backdoor miracle, transmuted into a love of poetry. So every moment I wasn't in class, at work, or in the hospital, I'd be scribbling well-intentioned self-righteousness to be recited aloud at open mics. It became both a thirst and a therapy, on one hand stretching a hole wider, and on the other smearing salve on a wound. I look back now and I wonder how much of it had to do with the weight of family complications, and how much of it was what my brother had—the affliction of adolescence, the natural irritation of growing up, let alone growing up Black. Either way, if it's true that you are what you do most, then over time the writing thing started to crystallize. It started to take hold. And as it did, my mother's cancer started to let go, easing its grip on her life.

I remember the doctor explaining to me the dressing on my mother's wound. There were things in her that had been extracted. Parts of her no longer. She'd been turned into someone else. But she'd made it, which gave me the permission to leave.

I graduated, packed a trash bag with clothes, jumped in a U-Haul with my college roommate, also named Jason, and headed to New York City to chase my dream of being a writer. An unavoidable cliché. I'll spare you the details of the mattress on the floor and the forty-ounce beers for dinner. What's more important to note is that six months into my life in Brooklyn, I'd landed a literary agent, which at the time felt like hitting the numbers. Like my mother always said, sometimes out-of-town lottery feels luckier. But the thing about luck is . . .

I was twenty-two.

I was twenty-two when my mother was admitted to the hospital. Again. This time for vomiting and belly pain. Because of the previous surgeries necessary to remove the cancer, and the constant cutting into her abdomen, an immense amount of scar tissue had formed and had somehow wrapped itself around her small intestine, pinching it, blocking everything from passing through. To correct it meant risking her life. A twelve-hour surgery where any mistake could puncture the intestine and sepsis would bring on an infection she, according to the doctors, wouldn't survive.

I boarded a Greyhound at Port Authority and took the four-and-a-half-hour ride from New York City to DC to ensure the oak tree of this version of our family could sustain after losing bits of its bark. The trip seemed nothing like our rides down South when I was younger. No turkey sandwiches. No M&Ms. No Nabs. Headphones took the place of car speakers blaring Sam Cooke. And there was a man sitting next to me taking up more space than should be legal. More space than Allen ever did. Also, a baby was crying. Also, the bathroom had an encyclopedia of excrement strewn across its surfaces. Someone was sick.

25 There were no stories being told. So I told them to myself. Told myself tales about how I'd willed myself into this position. How I'd bootstrapped and hoofed from city to city, stage to stage, a troubled troubadour who'd taken the hard road and now it was finally paying off. See, while I was going to be with my mother the day before her surgery, I'd never planned to stay. The trip was going to be a down-and-back. A quick turnaround. Because the day of the surgery was also the day I was supposed to sign my first publishing contract. The day my dream was to come true.

I was twenty-two when I met myself.

I don't remember much about the night before. About getting off the bus or who picked me up from the station. I don't even remember how I got to the hospital the next morning. Maybe I rode with her. Maybe my mother was already there and I rode with my aunt. What I do remember is just after the doctors prepped my mother for surgery, just before wheeling her down to the operating room, I was able to stand at her bedside. Her face bare, the gold teardrop earrings she wore every day absent, as was the red lipstick.

"Ma, I want to be here, but today is the day I sign the deal. This is it. What I've been working for. Black boys don't get this kind of shot often. This is my purpose. My dream," I said, salivating at the thought of success. She nodded. Told me to do what I needed to do. I kissed her on her forehead, and was gone.

At twenty-two years old, I left my mother in a potentially fatal surgery so I could do what could've been done a day, a week, even a month later. But I thought about how I'd never seen Black writers growing up, so there couldn't have been many, and if I didn't do it then, they'd retract the opportunity and I'd never get to see who I might become.

Instead, I got to see who I already was.   30

I'm thirty-six now. My mother and I have never talked about the intricacies of that surgery, and whenever I ask about it, she brushes it off. But I know what happened. I know things got shaky, that there were moments when her life teetered. But she made it. Again. And today, as I write this, she turns seventy-five years old. This morning, before sitting at my computer, I called her. We talked about how proud we are of each other, and how our lives together have been nothing short of miraculous. I told her I was working on this essay, and about the shame I carried for over a decade. It sat heavy in me like a dumbbell in my belly, dragged behind me like laces too long. An infection. Something nasty spreading throughout my body.

"That was a long time ago," she said.

"I know, but sometimes I still feel it," I said.

"Baby, you gotta forgive yourself," she said, and went on to talk about how she raised me to go get what I desired. To go be who I wanted to be. To simultaneously live a grounded life, a centered life, and a life in flight. "But above all, I taught you like my daddy taught me—family first."

"Right. And that's the reason I—"   35

"And you've done that, every day since. Why be ashamed of what you've atoned for?" Once again, she was the independent dependable compass pointing true north. And in that moment, this moment, I realized that perhaps I've scratched at the emotional laceration of shame, of selfishness. But if my mother is right, the itching isn't coming from infection anymore, it's coming from the fact I've never removed the dressing from the wound.

"You understand what I'm saying to you, son?" she asked.

"I think so."

"Well, let me make it plain. Some things are meant to stay between us. But this ain't one of them." We talked for a few more minutes between tears and laughter, until finally I had to go.

"Happy birthday, Ma."   40

"Thank you, baby. And thank you for calling me. I know you busy with your own life and you don't have to think about me, so I'm always grateful when you do."

"Of course." I chuckled. "You're my mother."

MLA CITATION

Reynolds, Jason. "Between Us: A Reckoning with My Mother." *The Norton Reader: An Anthology of Nonfiction*, edited by Melissa A. Goldthwaite et al., 16th ed., W. W. Norton, 2024, pp. 11–15.

QUESTIONS

1. Jason Reynolds writes about a decision he made when he was twenty-two that led him to carry shame that "sat heavy . . . like a dumbbell in [his] belly" (paragraph 31) for more than ten years. What was the choice he made? Why was it difficult for him? What did he do to deal with—and seek to let go of—that sense of shame?

2. Annotate the passages in which Reynolds compares and contrasts family car trips to South Carolina with the bus ride he took to Washington, DC, when he went to see his mother who was having surgery. How were these trips similar and different? Why do you think he uses these comparisons and contrasts?

3. Throughout his essay, Reynolds often uses sentence fragments. Mark several places in the essay where he uses fragments and read those passages aloud in the context of the sentence that comes before the fragment and the one that comes after. What is the effect of his use of fragments? Why do you think he uses them?

4. If you had a friend who was struggling with a choice between following personal dreams or putting family first, what advice would you give that person—and why? Is there any part of Reynolds's essay that would inform your thinking? Either write a response to these questions or discuss your ideas with a classmate.

SCOTT RUSSELL SANDERS

Under the Influence

M Y FATHER DRANK. He drank as a gut-punched boxer gasps for breath, as a starving dog gobbles food—compulsively, secretly, in pain and trembling. I use the past tense not because he ever quit drinking but because he quit living. That is how the story ends for my father, age sixty-four, heart bursting, body cooling and forsaken on the linoleum of my brother's trailer. The story continues for my brother, my sister, my mother, and me, and will continue so long as memory holds.

In the perennial present of memory, I slip into the garage or barn to see my father tipping back the flat green bottles of wine, the brown cylinders of whiskey, the cans of beer disguised in paper bags. His Adam's apple bobs, the liquid gurgles, he wipes the sandy-haired back of a hand over his lips, and then, his bloodshot gaze bumping into me, he stashes the bottle or can inside his jacket, under the workbench, between two bales of hay, and we both pretend the moment has not occurred.

"What's up, buddy?" he says, thick-tongued and edgy.

"Sky's up," I answer, playing along.

5   "And don't forget prices," he grumbles. "Prices are always up. And taxes."

Originally published in Harper's Magazine (1989), *an American monthly covering politics, society, culture, and the environment.*

In memory, his white 1951 Pontiac with the stripes down the hood and the Indian head on the snout jounces to a stop in the driveway; or it is the 1956 Ford station wagon, or the 1963 Rambler shaped like a toad, or the sleek 1969 Bonneville that will do 120 miles per hour on straightaways; or it is the robin's-egg blue pickup, new in 1980, battered in 1981, the year of his death. He climbs out, grinning dangerously, unsteady on his legs, and we children interrupt our game of catch, our building of snow forts, our picking of plums, to watch in silence as he weaves past into the house, where he slumps into his overstuffed chair and falls asleep. Shaking her head, our mother stubs out the cigarette he has left smoldering in the ashtray. All evening, until our bedtimes, we tiptoe past him, as past a snoring dragon. Then we curl in our fearful sheets, listening. Eventually he wakes with a grunt, Mother slings accusations at him, he snarls back, she yells, he growls, their voices clashing. Before long, she retreats to their bedroom, sobbing—not from the blows of fists, for he never strikes her, but from the force of words.

Left alone, our father prowls the house, thumping into furniture, rummaging in the kitchen, slamming doors, turning the pages of the newspaper with a savage crackle, muttering back at the late-night drivel from television. The roof might fly off, the walls might buckle from the pressure of his rage. Whatever my brother and sister and mother may be thinking on their own rumpled pillows, I lie there hating him, loving him, fearing him, knowing I have failed him. I tell myself he drinks to ease an ache that gnaws at his belly, an ache I must have caused by disappointing him somehow, a murderous ache I should be able to relieve by doing all my chores, earning A's in school, winning baseball games, fixing the broken washer and the burst pipes, bringing in money to fill his empty wallet. He would not hide the green bottles in his tool box, would not sneak off to the barn with a lump under his coat, would not fall asleep in the daylight, would not roar and fume, would not drink himself to death, if only I were perfect.

I am forty-two as I write these words, and I know full well now that my father was an alcoholic, a man consumed by disease rather than by disappointment. What had seemed to me a private grief is in fact a public scourge. In the United States alone some ten or fifteen million people share his ailment, and behind the doors they slam in fury or disgrace, countless other children tremble. I comfort myself with such knowledge, holding it against the throb of memory like an ice pack against a bruise. There are keener sources of grief: poverty, racism, rape, war. I do not wish to compete for a trophy in suffering. I am only trying to understand the corrosive mixture of helplessness, responsibility, and shame that I learned to feel as the son of an alcoholic. I realize now that I did not cause my father's illness, nor could I have cured it. Yet for all this grown-up knowledge, I am still ten years old, my own son's age, and as that boy I struggle in guilt and confusion to save my father from pain.

Consider a few of our synonyms for *drunk*: tipsy, tight, pickled, soused, and plowed; stoned and stewed, lubricated and inebriated, juiced and sluiced; three sheets to the wind, in your cups, out of your mind, under the table; lit up, tanked up, wiped out; besotted, blotto, bombed, and buzzed; plastered, polluted, putrified; loaded or looped, boozy, woozy, fuddled, or smashed; crocked and shit-faced, corked and pissed, snockered and sloshed.

10   It is a mostly humorous lexicon, as the lore that deals with drunks—in jokes and cartoons, in plays, films, and television skits—is largely comic. Aunt Matilda nips elderberry wine from the sideboard and burps politely during supper. Uncle Fred slouches to the table glassy-eyed, wearing a lamp shade for a hat and murmuring, "Candy is dandy but liquor is quicker." Inspired by cocktails, Mrs. Somebody recounts the events of her day in a fuzzy dialect, while Mr. Somebody nibbles her ear and croons a bawdy song. On the sofa with Boyfriend, Daughter giggles, licking gin from her lips, and loosens the bows in her hair. Junior knocks back some brews with his chums at the Leopard Lounge and stumbles home to the wrong house, wonders foggily why he cannot locate his pajamas, and crawls naked into bed with the ugliest girl in school. The family dog slurps from a neglected martini and wobbles to the nursery, where he vomits in Baby's shoe.

It is all great fun. But if in the audience you notice a few laughing faces turn grim when the drunk lurches on stage, don't be surprised, for these are the children of alcoholics. Over the grinning mask of Dionysus,[1] the leering mask of Bacchus,[2] these children cannot help seeing the bloated features of their own parents. Instead of laughing, they wince, they mourn. Instead of celebrating the drunk as one freed from constraints, they pity him as one enslaved. They refuse to believe *in vino veritas*,[3] having seen their befuddled parents skid away from truth toward folly and oblivion. And so these children bite their lips until the lush staggers into the wings.

— My father, when drunk, was neither funny nor honest; he was pathetic, frightening, deceitful. There seemed to be a leak in him somewhere, and he poured in booze to keep from draining dry. Like a torture victim who refuses to squeal, he would never admit that he had touched a drop, not even in his last year, when he seemed to be dissolving in alcohol before our very eyes. I never knew him to lie about anything, ever, except about this one ruinous fact. Drowsy, clumsy, unable to fix a bicycle tire, throw a baseball, balance a grocery sack, or walk across the room, he was stripped of his true self by drink. In a matter of minutes, the contents of a bottle could transform a brave man into a coward, a buddy into a bully, a gifted athlete and skilled carpenter and shrewd businessman into a bumbler. No dictionary of synonyms for *drunk* would soften the anguish of watching our prince turn into a frog.

Father's drinking became the family secret. While growing up, we children never breathed a word of it beyond the four walls of our house. To this day, my brother and sister rarely mention it, and then only when I press them. I did not confess the ugly, bewildering fact to my wife until his wavering walk and slurred speech forced me to. Recently, on the seventh anniversary of my father's death,

1. Greek name for the god of wine and intoxication.
2. Roman name for the god of wine and intoxication.
3. Latin for "in wine is truth."

I asked my mother if she ever spoke of his drinking to friends. "No, no, never," she replied hastily. "I couldn't bear for anyone to know."

The secret bores under the skin, gets in the blood, into the bone, and stays there. Long after you have supposedly been cured of malaria, the fever can flare up, the tremors can shake you. So it is with the fevers of shame. You swallow the bitter quinine[4] of knowledge, and you learn to feel pity and compassion toward the drinker. Yet the shame lingers in your marrow, and, because of the shame, anger.

For a long stretch of my childhood we lived on a military reservation in Ohio,   15
an arsenal where bombs were stored underground in bunkers, vintage airplanes burst into flames, and unstable artillery shells boomed nightly at the dump. We had the feeling, as children, that we played in a mine field, where a heedless footfall could trigger an explosion. When Father was drinking, the house, too, became a mine field. The least bump could set off either parent.

The more he drank, the more obsessed Mother became with stopping him. She hunted for bottles, counted the cash in his wallet, sniffed at his breath. Without meaning to snoop, we children blundered left and right into damning evidence. On afternoons when he came home from work sober, we flung ourselves at him for hugs, and felt against our ribs the telltale lump in his coat. In the barn we tumbled on the hay and heard beneath our sneakers the crunch of buried glass. We tugged open a drawer in his workbench, looking for screwdrivers or crescent wrenches, and spied a gleaming six-pack among the tools. Playing tag, we darted around the house just in time to see him sway on the rear stoop and heave a finished bottle into the woods. In his good night kiss we smelled the cloying sweetness of Clorets, the mints he chewed to camouflage his dragon's breath.

I can summon up that kiss right now by recalling Theodore Roethke's[5] lines about his own father in "My Papa's Waltz":

> The whiskey on your breath
> Could make a small boy dizzy;
> But I hung on like death:
> Such waltzing was not easy.

Such waltzing was hard, terribly hard, for with a boy's scrawny arms I was trying to hold my tipsy father upright.

For years, the chief source of those incriminating bottles and cans was a grimy store a mile from us, a cinder block place called Sly's, with two gas pumps outside and a moth-eaten dog asleep in the window. A strip of flypaper, speckled the year round with black bodies, coiled in the doorway. Inside, on rusty metal shelves or in wheezing coolers, you could find pop and Popsicles, cigarettes, potato chips, canned soup, raunchy postcards, fishing gear, Twinkies,

4. Drug used to treat malaria, made from the bark of the South American cinchona tree.
5. American poet (1908–1963) whose father also drank a lot.

wine, and beer. When Father drove anywhere on errands, Mother would send us kids along as guards, warning us not to let him out of our sight. And so with one or more of us on board, Father would cruise up to Sly's, pump a dollar's worth of gas or plump the tires with air, and then, telling us to wait in the car, he would head for that fly-spangled doorway.

Dutiful and panicky, we cried, "Let us go in with you!"

20 "No," he answered. "I'll be back in two shakes."

"Please!"

"No!" he roared. "Don't you budge, or I'll jerk a knot in your tails!"

So we stayed put, kicking the seats, while he ducked inside. Often, when he had parked the car at a careless angle, we gazed in through the window and saw Mr. Sly fetching down from a shelf behind the cash register two green pints of Gallo wine. Father swigged one of them right there at the counter, stuffed the other in his pocket, and then out he came, a bulge in his coat, a flustered look on his red face.

Because the Mom and Pop who ran the dump were neighbors of ours, living just down the tar-blistered road, I hated them all the more for poisoning my father. I wanted to sneak in their store and smash the bottles and set fire to the place. I also hated the Gallo brothers, Ernest and Julio, whose jovial faces shone from the labels of their wine, labels I would find, torn and curled, when I burned the trash. I noted the Gallo brothers' address, in California, and I studied the road atlas to see how far that was from Ohio, because I meant to go out there and tell Ernest and Julio what they were doing to my father, and then, if they showed no mercy, I would kill them.

25 While growing up on the back roads and in the country schools and cramped Methodist churches of Ohio and Tennessee, I never heard the word *alcoholism*, never happened across it in books or magazines. In the nearby towns, there were no addiction treatment programs, no community mental health centers, no Alcoholics Anonymous chapters, no therapists. Left alone with our grievous secret, we had no way of understanding Father's drinking except as an act of will, a deliberate folly or cruelty, a moral weakness, a sin. He drank because he chose to, pure and simple. Why our father, so playful and competent and kind when sober, would choose to ruin himself and punish his family, we could not fathom.

Our neighborhood was high on the Bible, and the Bible was hard on drunkards. "Woe to those who are heroes at drinking wine, and valiant men in mixing strong drink," wrote Isaiah. "The priest and the prophet reel with strong drink, they are confused with wine, they err in vision, they stumble in giving judgment. For all tables are full of vomit, no place is without filthiness." We children had seen those fouled tables at the local truck stop where the notorious boozers hung out, our father occasionally among them. "Wine and new wine take away the understanding," declared the prophet Hosea. We had also seen evidence of that in our father, who could multiply seven-digit numbers in his head when sober, but when drunk could not help us with fourth-grade math. Proverbs warned: "Do not look at wine when it is red, when it sparkles in the cup and goes down smoothly. At the last it bites like a serpent, and stings like

an adder. Your eyes will see strange things, and your mind utter perverse things."
Woe, woe.

Dismayingly often, these biblical drunkards stirred up trouble for their own kids. Noah made fresh wine after the flood, drank too much of it, fell asleep without any clothes on, and was glimpsed in the buff by his son Ham, whom Noah promptly cursed. In one passage—it was so shocking we had to read it under our blankets with flashlights—the patriarch Lot fell down drunk and slept with his daughters. The sins of the fathers set their children's teeth on edge.

Our ministers were fond of quoting St. Paul's pronouncement that drunkards would not inherit the kingdom of God. These grave preachers assured us that the wine referred to during the Last Supper was in fact grape juice. Bible and sermons and hymns combined to give us the impression that Moses should have brought down from the mountain another stone tablet, bearing the Eleventh Commandment: Thou shalt not drink.

The scariest and most illuminating Bible story apropos of drunkards was the one about the lunatic and the swine. Matthew, Mark, and Luke each told a version of the tale. We knew it by heart: When Jesus climbed out of his boat one day, this lunatic came charging up from the graveyard, stark naked and filthy, frothing at the mouth, so violent that he broke the strongest chains. Nobody would go near him. Night and day for years this madman had been wailing among the tombs and bruising himself with stones. Jesus took one look at him and said, "Come out of the man, you unclean spirits!" for he could see that the lunatic was possessed by demons. Meanwhile, some hogs were conveniently rooting nearby. "If we have to come out," begged the demons, "at least let us go into those swine." Jesus agreed. The unclean spirits entered the hogs, and the hogs rushed straight off a cliff and plunged into a lake. Hearing the story in Sunday school, my friends thought mainly of the pigs. (How big a splash did they make? Who paid for the lost pork?) But I thought of the redeemed lunatic, who bathed himself and put on clothes and calmly sat at the feet of Jesus, restored—so the Bible said—to "his right mind."

When drunk, our father was clearly in his wrong mind. He became a stranger, as fearful to us as any graveyard lunatic, not quite frothing at the mouth but fierce enough, quick-tempered, explosive; or else he grew maudlin and weepy, which frightened us nearly as much. In my boyhood despair, I reasoned that maybe he wasn't to blame for turning into an ogre. Maybe, like the lunatic, he was possessed by demons. I found support for my theory when I heard liquor referred to as "spirits," when the newspapers reported that somebody had been arrested for "driving under the influence," and when church ladies railed against that "demon drink."

30

If my father was indeed possessed, who would exorcise him? If he was a sinner, who would save him? If he was ill, who would cure him? If he suffered, who would ease his pain? Not ministers or doctors, for we could not bring ourselves to confide in them; not the neighbors, for we pretended they had never seen him drunk; not Mother, who fussed and pleaded but could not budge him; not my brother and sister, who were only kids. That left me. It did not matter that I, too, was only a child, and a bewildered one at that. I could not excuse myself.

On first reading a description of delirium tremens—in a book on alcoholism I smuggled from the library—I thought immediately of the frothing lunatic and the frenzied swine. When I read stories or watched films about grisly meta-morphoses—Dr. Jekyll becoming Mr. Hyde,[6] the mild husband changing into a werewolf, the kindly neighbor taken over by a brutal alien—I could not help seeing my own father's mutation from sober to drunk. Even today, knowing better, I am attracted by the demonic theory of drink, for when I recall my father's transformation, the emergence of his ugly second self, I find it easy to believe in possession by unclean spirits. We never knew which version of Father would come home from work, the true or the tainted, nor could we guess how far down the slope toward cruelty he would slide.

How far a man *could* slide we gauged by observing our back-road neighbors— the out-of-work miners who had dragged their families to our corner of Ohio from the desolate hollows of Appalachia, the tight-fisted farmers, the surly mechanics, the balked and broken men. There was, for example, whiskey-soaked Mr. Jenkins, who beat his wife and kids so hard we could hear their screams from the road. There was Mr. Lavo the wino, who fell asleep smoking time and again, until one night his disgusted wife bundled up the children and went out-side and left him in his easy chair to burn; he awoke on his own, staggered out coughing into the yard, and pounded her flat while the children looked on and the shack turned to ash. There was the truck driver, Mr. Sampson, who tripped over his son's tricycle one night while drunk and got so mad that he jumped into his semi and drove away, shifting through the dozen gears, and never came back. We saw the bruised children of these fathers clump onto our school bus, we saw the abandoned children huddle in the pews at church, we saw the stunned and battered mothers begging for help at our doors.

Our own father never beat us, and I don't think he ever beat Mother, but he threatened often. The Old Testament Yahweh was not more terrible in his wrath. Eyes blazing, voice booming, Father would pull out his belt and swear to give us a whipping, but he never followed through, never needed to, because we could imagine it so vividly. He shoved us, pawed us with the back of his hand, as an irked bear might smack a cub, not to injure, just to clear a space. I can see him grabbing Mother by the hair as she cowers on a chair during a nightly quarrel. He twists her neck back until she gapes up at him, and then he lifts over her skull a glass quart bottle of milk, the milk running down his forearm; and he yells at her, "Say just one more word, one goddamn word, and I'll shut you up!" I fear she will prick him with her sharp tongue, but she is terrified into silence, and so am I, and the leaking bottle quivers in the air, and milk slithers through the red hair of my father's uplifted arm, and the entire scene is there to this moment, the head jerked back, the club raised.

35   When the drink made him weepy, Father would pack a bag and kiss each of us children on the head, and announce from the front door that he was moving out. "Where to?" we demanded, fearful each time that he would leave for good,

6. London physician and his evil alter ego in Robert Louis Stevenson's novella *Strange Case of Dr. Jekyll and Mr. Hyde* (1886).

as Mr. Sampson had roared away for good in his diesel truck. "Someplace where I won't get hounded every minute," Father would answer, his jaw quivering. He stabbed a look at Mother, who might say, "Don't run into the ditch before you get there," or, "Good riddance," and then he would slink away. Mother watched him go with arms crossed over her chest, her face closed like the lid on a box of snakes. We children bawled. Where could he go? To the truck stop, that den of iniquity? To one of those dark, ratty flophouses in town? Would he wind up sleeping under a railroad bridge or on a park bench or in a cardboard box, mummied in rags, like the bums we had seen on our trips to Cleveland and Chicago? We bawled and bawled, wondering if he would ever come back.

He always did come back, a day or a week later, but each time there was a sliver less of him.

In Kafka's[7] *The Metamorphosis*, which opens famously with Gregor Samsa waking up from uneasy dreams to find himself transformed into an insect, Gregor's family keep reassuring themselves that things will be just fine again, "When he comes back to us." Each time alcohol transformed our father, we held out the same hope, that he would really and truly come back to us, our authentic father, the tender and playful and competent man, and then all things would be fine. We had grounds for such hope. After his weepy departures and chapfallen returns, he would sometimes go weeks, even months without drinking. Those were glad times. Joy banged inside my ribs. Every day without the furtive glint of bottles, every meal without a fight, every bedtime without sobs encouraged us to believe that such bliss might go on forever.

Mother was fooled by just such a hope all during the forty-odd years she knew this Greeley Ray Sanders. Soon after she met him in a Chicago delicatessen on the eve of World War II and fell for his butter-melting Mississippi drawl and his wavy red hair, she learned that he drank heavily. But then so did a lot of men. She would soon coax or scold him into breaking the nasty habit. She would point out to him how ugly and foolish it was, this bleary drinking, and then he would quit. He refused to quit during their engagement, however, still refused during the first years of marriage, refused until my sister came along. The shock of fatherhood sobered him, and he remained sober through my birth at the end of the war and right on through until we moved in 1951 to the Ohio arsenal, that paradise of bombs. Like all places that make a business of death, the arsenal had more than its share of alcoholics and drug addicts and other varieties of escape artists. There I turned six and started school and woke into a child's flickering awareness, just in time to see my father begin sneaking swigs in the garage.

He sobered up again for most of a year at the height of the Korean War, to celebrate the birth of my brother. But aside from that dry spell, his only breaks from drinking before I graduated from high school were just long enough to raise and then dash our hopes. Then during the fall of my senior year—the time of the Cuban missile crisis, when it seemed that the nightly explosions at the

7. Franz Kafka (1883–1924), Prague-born novelist and short-story writer.

munitions dump and the nightly rages in our household might spread to engulf the globe—Father collapsed. His liver, kidneys, and heart all conked out. The doctors saved him, but only by a hair. He stayed in the hospital for weeks, going through a withdrawal so terrible that Mother would not let us visit him. If he wanted to kill himself, the doctors solemnly warned him, all he had to do was hit the bottle again. One binge would finish him.

40   Father must have believed them, for he stayed dry the next fifteen years. It was an answer to prayer, Mother said, it was a miracle. I believe it was a reflex of fear, which he sustained over the years through courage and pride. He knew a man could die from drink, for his brother Roscoe had. We children never laid eyes on doomed Uncle Roscoe, but in the stories Mother told us he became a fairy-tale figure, like a boy who took the wrong turning in the woods and was gobbled up by the wolf.

The fifteen-year dry spell came to an end with Father's retirement in the spring of 1978. Like many men, he gave up his identity along with his job. One day he was a boss at the factory, with a brass plate on his door and a reputation to uphold; the next day he was a nobody at home. He and Mother were leaving Ontario, the last of the many places to which his job had carried them, and they were moving to a new house in Mississippi, his childhood stomping grounds. As a boy in Mississippi, Father sold Coca-Cola during dances while the moonshiners peddled their brew in the parking lot; as a young blade, he fought in bars and in the ring, seeking a state Golden Gloves championship; he gambled at poker, hunted pheasants, raced motorcycles and cars, played semiprofessional baseball, and, along with all his buddies—in the Black Cat Saloon, behind the cotton gin, in the woods—he drank. It was a perilous youth to dream of recovering.

After his final day of work, Mother drove on ahead with a car full of begonias and violets, while Father stayed behind to oversee the packing. When the van was loaded, the sweaty movers broke open a six-pack and offered him a beer.

"Let's drink to retirement!" they crowed. "Let's drink to freedom! to fishing! hunting! loafing! Let's drink to a guy who's going home!"

At least I imagine some such words, for that is all I can do, imagine, and I see Father's hand trembling in midair as he thinks about the fifteen sober years and about the doctors' warning, and he tells himself *God damnit, I am a free man*, and *Why can't a free man drink one beer after a lifetime of hard work?* and I see his arm reaching, his fingers closing, the can tilting to his lips. I even supply a label for the beer, a swaggering brand that promises on television to deliver the essence of life. I watch the amber liquid pour down his throat, the alcohol steal into his blood, the key turn in his brain.

45   Soon after my parents moved back to Father's treacherous stomping ground, my wife and I visited them in Mississippi with our five-year-old daughter. Mother had been too distraught to warn me about the return of the demons. So when I climbed out of the car that bright July morning and saw my father napping in the hammock, I felt uneasy, for in all his sober years I had never known him to sleep in daylight. Then he lurched upright, blinked his bloodshot eyes, and greeted us in a syrupy voice. I was hurled back helpless into childhood.

"What's the matter with Papaw?" our daughter asked.

"Nothing," I said. "Nothing!"

Like a child again, I pretended not to see him in his stupor, and behind my phony smile I grieved. On that visit and on the few that remained before his death, once again I found bottles in the workbench, bottles in the woods. Again his hands shook too much for him to run a saw, to make his precious miniature furniture, to drive straight down back roads. Again he wound up in the ditch, in the hospital, in jail, in treatment centers. Again he shouted and wept. Again he lied. "I never touched a drop," he swore. "Your mother's making it up."

I no longer fancied I could reason with the men whose names I found on the bottles—Jim Beam, Jack Daniels—nor did I hope to save my father by burning down a store. I was able now to press the cold statistics about alcoholism against the ache of memory: ten million victims, fifteen million, twenty. And yet, in spite of my age, I reacted in the same blind way as I had in childhood, ignoring biology, forgetting numbers, vainly seeking to erase through my efforts whatever drove him to drink. I worked on their place twelve and sixteen hours a day, in the swelter of Mississippi summers, digging ditches, running electrical wires, planting trees, mowing grass, building sheds, as though what nagged at him was some list of chores, as though by taking his worries on my shoulders I could redeem him. I was flung back into boyhood, acting as though my father would not drink himself to death if only I were perfect.

I failed of perfection; he succeeded in dying. To the end, he considered   50
himself not sick but sinful. "Do you want to kill yourself?" I asked him. "Why not?" he answered. "Why the hell not? What's there to save?" To the end, he would not speak about his feelings, would not or could not give a name to the beast that was devouring him.

In silence, he went rushing off the cliff. Unlike the biblical swine, however, he left behind a few of the demons to haunt his children. Life with him and the loss of him twisted us into shapes that will be familiar to other sons and daughters of alcoholics. My brother became a rebel, my sister retreated into shyness, I played the stalwart and dutiful son who would hold the family together. If my father was unstable, I would be a rock. If he squandered money on drink, I would pinch every penny. If he wept when drunk—and only when drunk—I would not let myself weep at all. If he roared at the Little League umpire for calling my pitches balls, I would throw nothing but strikes. Watching him flounder and rage, I came to dread the loss of control. I would go through life without making anyone mad. I vowed never to put in my mouth or veins any chemical that would banish my everyday self. I would never make a scene, never lash out at the ones I loved, never hurt a soul. Through hard work, relentless work, I would achieve something dazzling—in the classroom, on the basketball floor, in the science lab, in the pages of books—and my achievement would distract the world's eyes from his humiliation. I would become a worthy sacrifice, and the smoke of my burning would please God.

It is far easier to recognize these twists in my character than to undo them. Work has become an addiction for me, as drink was an addiction for my father. Knowing this, my daughter gave me a placard for the wall: WORKAHOLIC. The labor is endless and futile, for I can no more redeem myself through work than I could redeem my father. I still panic in the face of other people's anger, because his drunken temper was so terrible. I shrink from causing sadness or disappointment even to strangers, as though I were still concealing the family shame. I still notice every twitch of emotion in the faces around me, having learned as a child to read the weather in faces, and I blame myself for their least pang of unhappiness or anger. In certain moods I blame myself for everything. Guilt burns like acid in my veins.

I am moved to write these pages now because my own son, at the age of ten, is taking on himself the griefs of the world, and in particular the griefs of his father. He tells me that when I am gripped by sadness he feels responsible; he feels there must be something he can do to spring me from depression, to fix my life. And that crushing sense of responsibility is exactly what I felt at the age of ten in the face of my father's drinking. My son wonders if I, too, am possessed. I write, therefore, to drag into the light what eats at me—the fear, the guilt, the shame—so that my own children may be spared.

I still shy away from nightclubs, from bars, from parties where the solvent is alcohol. My friends puzzle over this, but it is no more peculiar than for a man to shy away from the lions' den after seeing his father torn apart. I took my own first drink at the age of twenty-one, half a glass of burgundy. I knew the odds of my becoming an alcoholic were four times higher than for the sons of nonalcoholic fathers. So I sipped warily.

55   I still do—once a week, perhaps, a glass of wine, a can of beer, nothing stronger, nothing more. I listen for the turning of a key in my brain.

MLA CITATION

Sanders, Scott Russell. "Under the Influence." *The Norton Reader: An Anthology of Nonfiction*, edited by Melissa A. Goldthwaite et al., 16th ed., W. W. Norton, 2024, pp. 16–26.

QUESTIONS

1. Scott Russell Sanders frequently punctuates his memories of his father with information from other sources—dictionaries, medical encyclopedias, poems and short stories, the Bible. Mark those passages in the text. What function do these sources perform? How do they enlarge and enrich Sanders's essay?

2. Why does Sanders conclude his essay with paragraphs 53 to 55? What effect do they create that would be lost without them?

3. Drawing on your memories of a family member, write an essay about a problem that person had and its effect on your life.

JOY CASTRO
Grip

O VER THE CRIB in the tiny apartment, there hung a bullet-holed paper target, the size and dark shape of a man—its heart zone, head zone, perforated where my aim had torn through: 36 little rips, no strays, centered on spots that would make a man die.

Beginner's luck, said the guys at the shooting range, at first. *Little lady*, they'd said, until the silhouette slid back and farther back. They'd cleared their throats, fallen silent.

A bad neighborhood. An infant child. A Ruger GP .357 with speed-loader.[1]

It's not as morbid as it sounds, a target pinned above a crib: the place was small, the walls already plastered full with paintings, sketches, pretty leaves, hand-illuminated psychedelic broadsides of poems by my friends. I masking-taped my paper massacre to the only empty space, a door I'd closed to form a wall.

When my stepfather got out of prison, he tracked my mother down. He found   5
the city where she'd moved. He broke a basement window and crawled in. She never saw his car, halfway up the dark block, stuffed behind a bush.

My mother lived. She wouldn't say what happened in the house that night. Cops came: that's what I know. Silent, she hung a screen between that scene and me. It's what a mother does.

She lived—as lived the violence of our years with him, knifed into us like scrimshaw cut in living bone.

Carved but alive, we learned to hold our breath, dive deep, bare our teeth to what fed us.

When I was 21, my son slept under the outline of what I could do, a death I could hold in my hands.

At the time, I'd have denied its locale any meaning, called its placement   10
coincidence, pointing to walls crowded with other kinds of dreams.

But that dark, torn thing did hang there, its lower edge obscured behind the wooden slats, the flannel duck, the stuffed white bear.

It hung there like a promise, like a headboard, like a *No*, like a terrible poem, like these lines I will never show you, shielding you from the fear I carry— like a sort of oath I swore over your quiet sleep.

First published in the journal Fourth Genre: Explorations in Nonfiction *(2009)*.

1. Ruger GP .357, revolver manufactured by Sturm, Ruger & Company; speed-loader, a device used to reload a revolver rapidly.

MLA CITATION

Castro, Joy. "Grip." *The Norton Reader: An Anthology of Nonfiction*, edited by
    Melissa A. Goldthwaite et al., 16th ed., W. W. Norton, 2024, p. 27.

QUESTIONS

1. Joy Castro opens her essay with an arresting image: a bullet-riddled paper target
pinned over a crib. Why did she decide to hang the target there? How does her explanation evolve between the essay's beginning and end?

2. In her short essay, Castro implies rather than states many details about her life.
Annotate the text, marking the parts that seem most significant. What can you infer
about her family, history, and circumstances?

3. In her final sentence, Castro uses the pronouns "you" and "your" for the first time
in the essay (paragraph 12). Who is the "you" she addresses? How does this shift into
the second person change your understanding and response to the essay? (To spur
your thinking, try imagining the essay without that final sentence.)

4. Castro's essay is only 363 words long, and much of its power derives from its
compactness. Using Castro's essay as a model, write a similarly compact essay
about a meaningful moment from your own life. Write a first draft of at least 1,000
words. Revise it down to 500 words, then to 350 words (about the length of Castro's essay). What changes did you make with each of these revisions? Why?

LESLIE JAMISON
In the Shadow of a Fairy Tale:
On Becoming a Stepmother

WHEN SHE WAS 6, my stepdaughter, Lily, told me that her favorite character in "Cinderella" was the evil stepmother. This
wasn't entirely surprising. During play dates, Lily often liked
to play orphan, writing down long lists of chores: *dichs*
(dishes); *moping* (mopping); *feeding* (the fish). She and a
friend liked to drink something they called pepper water,
which was ordinary tap water they pretended their cruel orphan-handlers had
made undrinkable. Maybe it was thrilling to stage her own mistreatment, to
take power over the situation of powerlessness she had imagined. Maybe she
just liked a virtuous reason to dump water on the floor. When I asked Lily why
Cinderella's stepmother was her favorite character, she leaned close to me and
whispered, like a secret, "I think she looks *good*."

Published in the New York Times Magazine *(2017), a supplement included with the Sunday edition of the* New York Times.

For all her cruelty, the evil stepmother is often the fairy-tale character most defined by imagination and determination, rebelling against the patriarchy with whatever meager tools have been left to her: her magic mirror, her vanity, her pride. She is an artist of cunning and malice, but still—an artist. She isn't simply acted upon; she acts. She just doesn't act the way a mother is supposed to. That's her fuel, and her festering heart.

In many ways, fairy tales—dark and ruthless, often structured by loss— were the stories that most resembled Lily's life. Her mother died just before her 3rd birthday, after a 2½-year struggle with leukemia. Two years later, Lily got a stepmother of her own—not a wicked one, perhaps, but one terrified of being wicked.

I wondered if it was comforting for Lily to hear stories about fairy-tale children who had lost what she had lost—unlike most of the kids at her school, or in her ballet classes, whose mothers were still alive. Or perhaps it brought the stories dangerously near, the fact that she shared so much with them. Maybe it peeled away their protective skins of fantasy, made their pepper water too literal, brought their perils too close. When I read her the old fairy tales about daughters without mothers, I worried that I was pushing on the bruises of her loss. When I read her the old fairy tales about stepmothers, I worried I was reading her an evil version of myself.

I sought these tales avidly when I first became a stepmother. I was hungry   5
for company. I didn't know many stepmothers, and I especially didn't know many stepmothers who had inherited the role as I had inherited it: fully, over-whelmingly, with no other mother in the picture. Our family lived in the after-math of loss, not rupture—death, not divorce. This used to be the normal way of being a stepmother, and the word itself holds grief in its roots. The Old English "steop" means loss, and the etymology paints a bleak portrait: "For stepmoder is selde guod," reads one account from 1290. A text from 1598 says, "With one consent all stepmothers hate their daughters."

The fairy tales are obviously damning: The evil queen from "Snow White" demands the secret murder of her stepdaughter after a magic mirror proclaims her beauty. The stepmother from "Hansel and Gretel" sends her stepchildren into the woods because there isn't enough to eat. Cinderella sits amid her fire-place cinders, sorting peas from lentils, her ash-speckled body appeasing a wicked stepmother who wants to dull her luminosity with soot because she feels threatened by it. It's as if the stepmother relationship inevitably cor-rupts—it is not just an evil woman in the role but a role that turns any woman evil. A "stepmother's blessing" is another name for a hangnail, as if to suggest something that hurts because it isn't properly attached, or something that pre-sents itself as a substitutive love but ends up bringing pain instead.

The evil stepmother casts a long, primal shadow, and three years ago I moved in with that shadow, to a one-bedroom rent-controlled apartment near Gramercy Park. I sought the old stories in order to find company—out of sym-pathy for the stepmothers they vilified—and to resist their narratives, to inoc-ulate myself against the darkness they held.

My relationship with Charles, Lily's father, held the kind of love that fairy tales ask us to believe in: encompassing and surprising, charged by a sense of wonder at the sheer fact of his existence in the world. I uprooted my life for our love, without regret. Our bliss lived in a thousand ordinary moments: a first kiss in the rain, over-easy eggs at a roadside diner in the Catskills, crying with laughter at midnight about some stupid joke he would make during an *American Ninja Warrior* rerun. But our love also—always—held the art and work of parenting, and much of our bliss happened on stolen time: that first kiss while the sitter stayed half an hour late; those diner eggs on a spontaneous road trip possible only because Lily was staying with her grandmother in Memphis; our hands clamped over our mouths during those fits of midnight laughter so we wouldn't wake up Lily in the next room. This felt less like compromise and more like off-roading, a divergence from the scripts I'd always written for what my own life would look like.

I approached the first evening I spent with Lily as a kind of test, though Charles tried to stack the deck in my favor: He decided we would get takeout from the pasta place Lily liked, then spend the evening watching her favorite movie—about two princess sisters, one with a touch that turned everything to ice. That afternoon, I went to find a gift at the Disney Store in Times Square—not only a place I had never been but a place I had never imagined going. I hated the idea of bribing Lily, trading plastic for affection, but I was desperately nervous. Plastic felt like an insurance policy.

10   The clerk looked at me with pity when I asked for the *Frozen* section. I suddenly doubted myself: Was it not a Disney movie? The clerk laughed when I asked the question, then explained: "We just don't have any merchandise left. There's a worldwide shortage."

She was serious. They had nothing. Not even a tiara. Or they had plenty of tiaras, but they weren't the right tiaras. I scanned the shelves around me: Belle stuff, "Sleeping Beauty" stuff, Princess Jasmine stuff. There had to be other movies Lily liked, right? Other princesses? There was a moment when I considered buying something related to *every* princess, just to cover my bases. I had some vague realization that the low-level panic in the back of my throat was the fuel capitalism ran on. On my cellphone, I was on hold with a Toys "R" Us in the Bronx. On my way out, I spotted something shoved into the corner of a shelf. It looked wintry. It had ice-blue cardboard packaging: a sled.

I cannot even tell you my relief. My sense of victory was complete. The sled came with a princess, and also maybe a prince. (A Sami ice harvester, I would learn.) The set came with a reindeer! (Named Sven.) And even a plastic carrot for him to eat. I tucked the box under my arm protectively as I walked to the register. I eyed the other parents around me. Who knew how many of them wanted this box?

I called Charles, triumphant. I told him the whole saga: the clerk's laughter, the *worldwide shortage*, the frantic phone calls, the sudden grace of glimpsing pale-blue cardboard.

"You won!" he said, then paused. I could hear him deciding whether to say something. "The princess," he asked, "what color is her hair?"

I had to check the box. "Brown?" I said. "Sort of reddish?"   15
"You did great," he said after a beat. "You're the best."
But in that beat, I could hear that I had the wrong princess.
Charles wasn't criticizing; he just knew how much a princess could mean.
He had spent the last two years knee-deep in princesses, playing mother and
father at once. The truth of the wrong princess was also the truth of unstable
cause and effect: With parenting, you could do everything you were supposed
to, and it might still backfire, because you lived with a tiny, volatile human
who did not come with any kind of instruction manual. The possibility of failure hung like a low sky, pending weather, over every horizon.

In *The Uses of Enchantment*, the psychoanalyst Bruno Bettelheim makes a
beautiful argument for the kinds of reckoning that fairy tales permit: They allow
children to face primal fears (parental abandonment) and imagine acts of rebellion (defying authority) in a world reassuringly removed from the one they live
in. Enchanted woods and castles are so conspicuously fantastical, their situations so extreme, that children don't need to feel destabilized by their upheavals.
I wondered if that was still true for Lily, whose loss lived more naturally in fairy
tales than other places. It can be a fine line between stories that give our fears a
necessary stage and stories that deepen them—that make us more afraid.

In an 1897 letter to the editor in *Outlook*, a high-circulation turn-of-the-   20
century American lifestyle magazine, one reader laments the effects of reading "Cinderella" to young
children: "The effect or
impression was to put stepmothers on the list of evil
things of life." But in our home,
it was less that "Cinderella" put
stepmothers on an evil list
and more that the story raised
the question—with a kind of
openness that might have
been impossible otherwise—of
whether stepmothers belonged
there. Often, Lily used the figure of a fairy-tale wicked stepmother to distinguish our
relationship from the one we
had just read. "You're not like
her," she would say. Or when it
came to the stepmother she
admired from "Cinderella," she
was generous: "You look better
than her anyway."
     I wondered if claiming
the stepmother as her favor-

ite was another version of playing orphans—a way of claiming the source of fear and taking some control over it. Did she worry I would turn cruel? Did she love me fiercely so I wouldn't? I wondered if it helped her to see us reflected and distorted by a dark mirror, if these more sinister versions of our bond made her feel better about our relationship—or gave her permission to accept what might feel hard about it. I actually found a strange kind of comfort in the nightmare visions of mean stepparents I found in popular media—at least I wasn't cruel like them. It was a kind of ethical schadenfreude.[1]

In many ways, these stories my family inherited mapped imperfectly onto ours. In fairy tales, the father-king was often duped and blind. He had faith in a woman who didn't deserve it. His trust, or his lust, permitted his daughter's mistreatment. Charles was like these fairy-tale fathers in only one way: He trusted me from the beginning. He believed I could be a mother before I believed it. He talked openly about what was hard about parenting, which made it feel more possible to live in love and difficulty—love *as* difficulty. He knew what it meant to wake day after day, choose three possible dresses, pour the cereal, repour the cereal after it spilled, wrestle hair into pigtails, get to school on time, get to pickup on time, steam the broccoli for dinner. He knew how much it meant to learn the difference between the animated ponies with wings and the animated ponies with horns and the animated ponies with both—the alicorns. He knew what it meant to do all that, and then wake up and do it all over again.

My relationship with Lily, too, was not like the story we inherited from fairy tales—a tale of cruelty and rebellion—or even like the story of divorce-era popular media: the child spurning her stepmother, rejecting her in favor of the true mother, the mother of bloodline and womb. Our story was a thousand conversations on the 6 train or at the playground in Madison Square Park. Our story was painting Lily's nails and trying not to smudge her tiny pinkie. Our story was telling her to take deep breaths during tantrums, because I needed to take deep breaths myself. Our story began one night when I felt her small, hot hand reach for mine during her favorite movie, when the Abominable Snowman swirled into view on an icy mountain and almost overwhelmed the humble reindeer.

That first night, when we sang songs at bedtime, she scooted over and patted the comforter, in the same bed where her mother spent afternoons resting during the years of her illness, directly below the hole Charles had made—angrily swinging a toy train into the wall—after a telephone call with an insurance company, a hole now hidden behind an alphabet poster. "You lie here," Lily told me. "You lie in Mommy's spot."

25   If the wicked stepmother feels like a ready-made archetype, then its purest, darkest incarnation is the evil queen from "Snow White." In the Brothers Grimm tale from 1857, she asks a hunter to bring back her stepdaughter's heart. After this attack fails (the hunter has a bleeding heart of his own), the stepmother's aggression takes the form of false generosity. She goes to her stepdaughter in disguise, as an old beggar crone, to offer Snow White objects

1. Joy over another's harm or suffering.

that seem helpful or nourishing: a corset, a comb, an apple. These are objects a mother might give to her daughter—as forms of sustenance, or ways of passing on a female legacy of self-care—but they are actually meant to kill her. They reach Snow White in the folds of her new surrogate family, where the seven dwarves have given her the opportunity to be precisely the kind of "good mother" her stepmother never was. She cooks and cleans and cares for them. Her virtue is manifest in precisely the maternal impulse her stepmother lacks.

The evil stepmother is so integral to our familiar telling of "Snow White" that I was surprised to discover that an earlier version of the story doesn't feature a stepmother at all. In this version, Snow White has no dead mother, only a living mother who wants her dead. This was a pattern of revision for the Brothers Grimm; they transformed several mothers into stepmothers between the first version of their stories, published in 1812, and the final version, published in 1857. The figure of the stepmother effectively became a vessel for the emotional aspects of motherhood that were too ugly to attribute to mothers directly (ambivalence, jealousy, resentment) and those parts of a child's experience of her mother (as cruel, aggressive, withholding) that were too difficult to situate directly in the biological parent-child dynamic. The figure of the stepmother—lean, angular, harsh—was like snake venom drawn from an unacknowledged wound, siphoned out in order to keep the maternal body healthy, preserved as an ideal.

"It is not only a means of preserving an internal all-good mother when the real mother is not all good," Bettelheim argues, "but it also permits anger at this bad 'stepmother' without endangering the good will of the true mother, who is viewed as a different person." The psychologist D. W. Winnicott puts it more simply: "If there are two mothers, a real one who has died, and a stepmother, do you see how easily a child gets relief from tension by having one perfect and the other horrid?" In other words, the shadow figure of the fairy-tale stepmother is a predatory archetype reflecting something true of every mother: the complexity of her feelings toward her child, and a child's feelings toward her.

Even if Lily didn't split her ideas of motherhood into perfect absence and wicked presence, I did—assigning precisely that psychic division of labor. I imagined that her biological mother would have offered everything I couldn't always manage: patience, pleasure, compassion. She would have been *with* Lily in her tantrums. She wouldn't have bribed her with ridiculous amounts of plastic. She wouldn't get so frustrated when bedtime lasted an hour and a half, or else her frustration would have the counterweight of an unconditional love I was still seeking. I knew these self-flagellations were ridiculous—even "real" parents weren't perfect—but they offered a certain easy groove of self-deprecation, comforting in its simplicity. A woman mothering another woman's child, Winnicott observes, "may easily find herself forced by her own imagination into the position of witch rather than fairy godmother."

In a study called "The Poisoned Apple," the psychologist (and stepmother) Elizabeth Church analyzed her interviews with 104 stepmothers through the lens of one particular question: How do these women reckon with the evil archetype they stepped into? "Although their experience was the opposite of the fairy-tale stepmothers," she reported, insofar as "they felt powerless in the very situation where the fairy-tale stepmothers exerted enormous power," they still "tended to identify with the image of the wicked stepmother." She called it their poisoned apple: They felt "wicked" for experiencing feelings of resentment or jealousy, and this fear of their own "wickedness" prompted them to keep these feelings to themselves, which only made them feel more shame for having these feelings in the first place.

30   Folk tales often deploy the stepmother as a token mascot of the dark maternal—a woman rebelling against traditional cultural scripts—but the particular history of the American stepmother is more complicated. As the historian Leslie Lindenauer argues in *I Could Not Call Her Mother: The Stepmother in American Popular Culture, 1750–1960*, the figure of the American stepmother found her origins in the American witch. Lindenauer argues that the 18th-century popular imagination took the same terrible attributes that the Puritans had ascribed to witches—malice, selfishness, coldness, absence of maternal impulse—and started ascribing them to stepmothers instead. "Both were examples of women who, against God and nature, perverted the most essential qualities of the virtuous mother," Lindenauer observes. "Moreover, witches and stepmothers alike were most often accused of harming *other* women's children."

The stepmother became a kind of scapegoat, a new repository for aspects of femininity that felt threatening: female agency, female creativity, female restlessness, maternal ambivalence. By the late 18th century, the stepmother was a stock villain, familiar enough to appear in grammar books. One boy was even injured by his dead stepmother from beyond the grave, when a column above her tombstone fell on his head. The particular villainy of the stepmother—the duplicity of tyranny disguised as care—enabled colonial rhetoric that compared England's rule to "a stepmother's severity," as one 1774 tract put it. In an article that ran in *Ladies' Magazine* in 1773, on the eve of the American Revolution, a stepdaughter laments her fate at the hands of her stepmother: "Instead of the tender maternal affection . . . what do I now see but discontent, ill-nature, and mal-a-pert authority?" The stepmother offers bondage cunningly packaged as devotion.

But the American popular imagination hasn't always understood the stepmother as a wicked woman. If it was true that she was an 18th-century gold digger—a latter-day witch—then it was also true that she was a mid-19th-century saint, happily prostrate to the surge of her own innate maternal impulse. In the Progressive Era, she was proof that being a good mother was less about saintly instincts and more about reason, observation and rational self-improvement. You didn't have to have a biological connection—or even an innate caregiving impulse—you just had to *apply* yourself.

When I interviewed Lindenauer about her research, she told me that she was surprised to discover these vacillations, surprised to find the figure of the virtuous stepmother showing up in the very same women's magazines that had vilified her a few decades earlier. She eventually started to detect a pattern. It seemed as if the stepmother found redemption whenever the nuclear family was under siege: in the immediate aftermath of the Civil War, or when divorce emerged as a social pattern in the early 20th century. The stepmother became a kind of "port in the storm," Lindenauer told me. "It's better to have a stepmother than no mother at all."

The golden era of the American stepmother archetype—the summit of her virtue—was the second half of the 19th century, during and after the Civil War, when sentimental novels and women's magazines were full of saintly stepmothers eager to care for the motherless children who stumbled into their laps. In Charlotte Yonge's 1862 novel, *The Young Step-Mother; or, a Chronicle of Mistakes*, the young stepmother Albinia is portrayed as a woman with a surplus of good will, just waiting for people with needs—read: grief—deep enough to demand the deployment of her excess goodness. Her siblings worry about her marrying a widower with children, afraid she will become a kind of indentured servant, but the novel reassures us that "her energetic spirit and love of children animated her to embrace joyfully the cares which such a choice must impose on her." When her new husband brings her home, he apologizes for what he is asking from her. "As I look at you, and the home to which I have brought you, I feel that I have acted selfishly," he says. But she won't let him apologize. "Work was always what I wished," she replies, "if only I could do anything to lighten your grief and care."

With the children, Albinia says everything right: She is sorry they have her in place of their mother. They can call her Mother, but they don't have to. Although the novel is subtitled *A Chronicle of Mistakes*, Albinia doesn't seem to make many. When I read in the novel's epigraph, "Fail—yet rejoice," it felt like a lie and an impossible imperative at once. In fact, the entire voice of the saintly stepmother felt like an elaborate humblebrag. She knew she would always be second—or third! or fifth! or 10th!—but she didn't care. Not one bit. She just wanted to be useful.

I thought I would be glad to discover these virtuous stepmothers, but instead I found them nearly impossible to accept—much harder to stomach than the wicked stepmothers in fairy tales. My poisoned apple wasn't the wicked stepmother but her archetypal opposite, the saint, whose innate virtue felt like the harshest possible mirror. It would always show me someone more selfless than I was. These stories forgot everything that was structurally difficult about this kind of bond, or else they insisted that virtue would overcome all. This is why fairy tales are more forgiving than sentimental novels: They let darkness into the frame. Finding darkness in another story is so much less lonely than fearing the darkness is yours alone.

I punished myself when I lost patience, when I bribed, when I wanted to flee. I punished myself for resenting Lily when she came into our bed, night after night, which wasn't actually a bed but a futon we pulled out in the living room. Every feeling I had, I wondered: *Would a real mother feel this?* It wasn't the certainty that she wouldn't, but the uncertainty itself: How could I know?

I had imagined that I might feel most like a mother among strangers, who had no reason to believe I wasn't one, but it was actually among strangers that I felt most like a fraud. One day early in our relationship, Lily and I went to a Mister Softee, one of the ice cream trucks parked like land mines all over the city. I asked Lily what she wanted, and she pointed to the double cone of soft serve, the biggest one, covered in rainbow sprinkles. I said, *Great!* I was still at the Disney Store, still thrilled to find the sled set, still ready and willing to pass as mother by whatever means necessary, whatever reindeer necessary, whatever soft-serve necessary.

The double cone was so huge that Lily could barely hold it. Two hands, I would have known to say a few months later, but I didn't know to say it then. I heard a woman behind me ask her friend, "What kind of parent gets her child that much ice cream?" I felt myself go hot with shame. This parent. Which is to say: not a parent at all. I was afraid to turn around. I also wanted to turn around. I wanted to make the stranger feel ashamed, to speak back to the maternal superego she represented, to say: *What kind of mother? A mother trying to replace a dead one.* Instead I grabbed a wad of napkins and offered to carry Lily's cone back to our table so she wouldn't drop it on the way.

As a stepparent, I often felt like an impostor—or else I felt the particular loneliness of dwelling outside the bounds of the most familiar story line. I hadn't been pregnant, given birth, felt my body surge with the hormones of attachment. I woke up every morning to a daughter who called me Mommy but also missed her mother. I often called our situation "singular," but as with so many kinds of singularity, it was a double-edged blade—a source of loneliness and pride at once—and its singularity was also, ultimately, a delusion. "Lots of people are stepparents," my mother told me once, and of course she was right. A Pew Research Center survey found that four in 10 Americans say they have at least one step relationship. Twelve percent of women are stepmothers. I can guarantee you that almost all these women sometimes feel like frauds or failures.

In an essay about stepparents, Winnicott argues for the value of "unsuccess stories." He even imagines the benefits of gathering a group of "unsuccessful stepparents" in a room together. "I think such a meeting might be fruitful," he writes. "It would be composed of ordinary men and women." When I read that passage, it stopped me dead with longing. I wanted to be in that meeting, sitting with those ordinary men and women—hearing about their ice-cream bribes, their everyday impatience, their frustration and felt fraudulence, their desperate sleds.

In the methodology portion of her "Poisoned Apple" study, Church admits that she disclosed to her subjects that she was also a stepmother before interviewing them. After an interview was finished, she sometimes described her own experiences. Many of her subjects confessed that they had told her things during their interviews that they had never told anyone. I could understand that—that they somehow would feel, by virtue of being in the presence of another stepmother, as if they had been granted permission to speak. It was something like the imagined gathering of unsuccessful stepparents, as if they were at an Alcoholics Anonymous meeting in a church basement, taking earned solace in the minor triumphs and frequent failures of their kind: a kind of kin.

The decision to call the stepmother Mother, or the decision not to call her Mother, is often a dramatic hinge in stories about stepmothers, a climactic moment of acceptance or refusal. In a story called "My Step-Mother," published in the *Decatur Republican* in 1870, a young girl regards her new step-mother with skepticism. When her stepmother asks her to play a song on the piano, trying to earn her trust and affection, the girl decides to play "I Sit and Weep by My Mother's Grave." But lo! The stepmother is undeterred. She not only compliments the girl on her moving performance; she shares that she also lost her mother when she was young and also used to love that song. The story ends on a triumphant note, with the daughter finally calling her Mother, an inverted christening—child naming the parent—that inaugurates the "most perfect confidence" that grows between them.

For Lily, calling me Mother wasn't the end of anything. The day after Charles and I married in a Las Vegas wedding chapel—just before midnight on a Saturday, while Lily was having a sleepover with her cousin—Lily asked almost immediately if she could call me Mommy. It was clear she had been waiting to ask. I remember feeling moved, as if we had landed in the credits at the end of a movie, the soundtrack crescendoing all around us.

But we weren't in the credits. We were just getting started. I was terrified. 45
What would happen next? What happened next was pulling into a 7 Eleven for snacks and feeling Lily tug on my sleeve to tell me she had an "adult drink" at the laser-tag birthday party and now felt funny. She didn't want me to tell her dad. It was like the universe had sent its first maternal test. Was she drunk? What should I do? If I was going to let myself be called Mommy, I had to be prepared to deal with the fallout from the laser-tag birthday party. Charles eventually deduced that she had had a few sips of iced tea.

It felt less as if I had "earned" the title of mother—the way it has figured in so many sentimental stories, as a reward for behaving the right way and defying the old archetypes—and more as if I had landed in the 1900 story called "Making Mamma," in which 6-year-old Samantha layers a dressmaker's dummy with old fabric in order to make a surrogate mother for herself. It was as if Lily had bestowed a deep and immediate trust in me—unearned, born of need—and now I had to figure out how to live inside that trust without betraying it.

Once I stepped into the costume of a well-worn cultural archetype, I got used to hearing other people's theories about my life. Everyone had ideas about our family without knowing anything about our family. One woman said our situation was easier than if I had a terrible ex to compete with; another woman said I would be competing with the memory of Lily's perfect biological mother forever. When I wrote about a family vacation for a travel magazine, the editor wanted a bit more pathos: "Has it been bumpy?" she wrote in the margins of my draft. "What are you hoping for from this trip? A tighter family bond? A chance to let go of the sadness? Or . . . ?? Tug at our heartstrings a bit."

I realized that when this editor imagined our family, she envisioned us saturated by sadness, or else contoured by resistance. More than anything, I liked her "Or . . . ??" It rang true. It wasn't that every theory offered by a stranger about our family felt wrong; it was more that most of them felt right, or at least held a grain of truth that resonated. Which felt even more alarming, somehow, to be so knowable to strangers.

But every theory also felt incomplete. There was so much more truth around it, or else something close to its opposite felt true as well. I rarely felt like saying, *No, it's nothing like that*. I usually wanted to say: *Yes, it is like that. And also like this, and like this, and like this.* Sometimes the fact of those assumptions, the way I felt them churning inside everyone we encountered, made stepmotherhood feel like an operating theater full of strangers. I was convinced that I was constantly being dissected for how fully or compassionately I had assumed my maternal role.

50   I only ever found two fairy tales with good stepmothers, and they were both from Iceland. One stars a woman named Himinbjorg, who helps her stepson through his mourning by helping him fulfill the prophecy his mother delivered to him in a dream: that he will free a princess from a spell that had turned her into an ogre. By the time he returns from his mission victorious, the royal court is ready to burn Himinbjorg at the stake, because everyone is convinced that she is responsible for his disappearance. What I read as her selflessness moved me. She is willing to look terrible in order to help her son pursue a necessary freedom. I worried that I cared too much about proving I was a good stepmother, that wanting to seem like a good stepmother might get in the way of actually being a good stepmother. Perhaps I wanted credit for mothering more than I wanted to mother. Himinbjorg, on the other hand, is willing to look like a witch just to help her stepson break the spell he needs to break.

Then there was Hildur. Hildur's husband had vowed never to marry after the death of his first queen, because he was worried that his daughter would be mistreated. "All stepmothers are evil," he tells his brother, "and I don't wish to harm Ingibjorg." He is a fairy-tale king who has already absorbed the wisdom of fairy tales. He knows the deal with stepmoms.

But he falls in love with Hildur anyway. She says she won't marry him, though—not unless he lets her live alone with his daughter for three years before the wedding. Their marriage is made possible by her willingness to invest in a relationship with his daughter that exists apart from him, as its own fierce flame.

The closest thing Lily and I ever had to an Icelandic castle was a series of bathrooms across Lower Manhattan. Bathrooms were the spaces where it was just the two of us: the one with wallpaper made from old newspapers, the one where she insisted that people used to have braids instead of hands, the one at a Subway with a concrete mop sink she loved because it was "cool and simple."

Bathrooms were our space, just as Wednesdays were our day, when I picked her up from school and took her to the Dunkin' Donuts full of cops at Third Avenue and 20th before I rushed her to ballet, got her suited in her rhinestone-studded leotard and knelt before her tights like a supplicant, fitting bobby pins into her bun. At first, I expected an Olympic medal for getting her there only two minutes late. Eventually I realized that I was surrounded by mothers who had done exactly what I'd just done, only they had done it two minutes faster, and their buns were neater. Everything that felt like rocket science to me was just the stuff regular parents did every day of the week.

55   But those afternoons mattered, because they belonged to me and Lily. One day, in a cupcake-shop bathroom in SoHo—a few months before Lily,

Charles and I moved into a new apartment, the first one we would rent together—Lily pointed at the walls: pink and brown, decorated with a lacy pattern. She told me she wanted our new room to look like this. Ours. She had it all planned out. In the new place, Daddy would live in one room, and we would live in the other. Our room would be so dainty, she said. She wasn't even sure boys would be allowed. This was what Hildur knew: We needed something that was only for the two of us.

A few months later, reading Dr. Seuss's *Horton Hatches the Egg* to Lily in that new apartment, I felt my throat constricting. Horton agrees to sit on an egg while Mayzie the bird, a flighty mother, takes a vacation to Palm Beach. Mayzie doesn't come back, but Horton doesn't give up. He sits on a stranger's egg for days, then weeks, then months. "I meant what I said, and I said what I meant," he repeats. "An elephant's faithful, one hundred per cent!"

When the egg finally hatches, the creature that emerges is an elephant-bird: a bright-eyed baby with a small, curled trunk and red-tipped wings. Her tiny trunk made me think of Lily's hand gesticulations—how big and senseless they got, like mine—and how she had started to make to-do lists, as I did, just so she could cross things off. But she also had a poster of the planets in her bedroom, because her mom had loved outer space, and she was proud to say she always had her "nose in a book," just as her grandmother told her that her mother always had. She has two mothers, and she always will.

For me, the stakes of thinking about what it means to be a stepmother don't live in statistical relevance—*slightly more than 10 percent of American women might relate!*—but in the way stepparenting asks us to question our assumptions about the nature of love and the boundaries of family. Family is so much more than biology, and love is so much more than instinct. Love is effort and desire—not a sentimental story line about easy or immediate attachment, but the complicated bliss of joined lives: ham-and-guacamole sandwiches, growing pains at midnight, car seats covered in vomit. It's the days of showing up. The trunks we inherit and the stories we step into, they make their way into us—by womb or shell or presence, by sheer force of will. But what hatches from the egg is hardly ever what we expect: the child that emerges, or the parent that is born. That mother is not a saint. She's not a witch. She's just an ordinary woman. She found a sled one day, after she was told there weren't any left. That was how it began.

MLA CITATION

Jamison, Leslie. "In the Shadow of a Fairy Tale: On Becoming a Stepmother." *The Norton Reader: An Anthology of Nonfiction*, edited by Melissa A. Goldthwaite et al., 16th ed., W. W. Norton, 2024, pp. 28–39.

QUESTIONS

1. Leslie Jamison braids personal experience, textual analysis of fairy tales and other literature, and insight from psychologists and historians to reflect on what it means to be a stepmother. As you read and annotate this essay, mark the passages that seem most important to Jamison's developing sense of what it means to be a

stepmother. What were the most important moments and insights in this essay? Why were they significant?

2. Throughout the essay, Jamison references a plastic sled she bought for her step-daughter. Starting with the introduction of the toy in paragraph 11, trace Jamison's references to the sled. What does it represent or symbolize? Why do you think she keeps returning to that image?

3. In addition to sharing her own experiences, Jamison analyzes several versions of the familiar fairy tale "Snow White" (paragraph 26). Pick a fairy tale that is familiar to you—whether through films or books—and find several versions to compare and contrast. List the major similarities and differences. Why do you think some elements have been changed? Write a new version of your fairy tale, one that makes at least one purposeful change.

SANDRA STEINGRABER
Always Knew I Was Adopted; Just Found Out I'm Gay

A COMING OUT ESSAY IN TEN PARTS

1.

I'M GAY.

Five letters. Two syllables. Is there another declaration in the English language both smaller and bigger than this one?

My 17-year-old son says *mom it's no big deal.* No one, he surmises, should have to "come out." Just be who you are. He says this to me on the porch over plates of pasta, just before we discuss whether or not to walk to Trimmers, at the end of the village, for ice cream. And his words feel to me, even in their wrongness, like rainbow sprinkles on chocolate swirl. Like love.

2.

I'm gay. I'm also 59, a mother of two, a sole breadwinner, and a public health biologist who believes science is a public servant. I fight hard and often against the oil and gas industry. I'm an adoptee without a medical history and a cancer survivor full of scars who undergoes colonoscopies without narcotics, who once stayed up all night to finish a white paper on endocrine-disrupting chemicals before heading to the hospital to have my ovaries removed *because I can sleep under anesthesia.* Six years ago, my husband Jeff suffered a series of unexplained strokes and is disabled. I will always, always care for him. If I'm gay, it's a big deal.

5   My student Mahad texts me. *I'm incredibly proud to see you coming out pub-licly. It's a hard-won right to come out and it takes a lot of courage Sandra and I'm just so happy for you.* These are the words that are helping me write this essay.

Published on Terrain.org *(2019), a place-based online journal that includes literary work as well as articles and community case studies.*

I didn't choose to be gay, but, out of all the possible words I could claim from the sexuality spectrum, I choose the most parsimonious one. It's all I can do for now.

First, a statement of being, like the beginning of a hymn, like the oboe that tunes the orchestra.

I'M

And then the back-of-the-throat, open-mouthed truth.

GAY   10

3.

I didn't *just* find out I'm gay exactly. The finding out began in December 2015 when I left the UN climate talks in Paris and traveled to another conference where I found myself thinking often of a fellow climate activist and trusted friend who had also been in Paris. And when I thought of her, I was overcome with a strange falling feeling. As if I were falling through space outside of my own body. It occurred to me I had a brain tumor. It occurred to me I was falling in love. Once home again, I figured it out. I kept my own counsel.

Until I didn't.

Her response to my confession was a confession of her own.

Thus began a complex process that involved self-discernment, therapy, many long, difficult conversations, but also wonder and awe. This has taken time. The only way I can explain the transformation is via a series of *as ifs*. It's as if I saw the world in black and white and then an unseen molecular signal triggered a cascade of epigenetic changes and, behold, I have color vision. As if color were joy.

It's as if a Rube Goldberg–style chain reaction has been set in motion—a   15
lever is pulled and a ball rolls down a ramp, knocking over an umbrella that spills a bucket that swings a pendulum into a toy car that lights a match that shoots off a rocket that pulls a string that opens a closet door . . . and there she is. A biologist in a closet. She's been there all along. She is me, and I am her, but I am also the careening ball and the tilting bucket and the igniting match.

It's a destabilizing discovery at a time in my life when I value ballast. After some research, I learn that other women in middle age who discover they are gay report similar feelings: *It was like I was watching a movie about myself but unable to control what was unfolding. Everything fell apart.*

Jeff, somehow, feels the truth of my experience and offers kindness and grace. And also grief. Which I share. It's unthinkable that I would scatter this family after so many years of holding us all together. Colleen and Jeff and I meet. We take a long walk together. A plan emerges. Colleen rents a small apartment near our house, and so does Jeff. He and I can take turns spending nights in our house, and the kids can stay put. When Jeff is at the house, I'll stay through the evening to help with dinner and homework and then walk to Colleen's to spend the night. But before this plan can be revealed and phased in, I need to find loving, truthful words that allow me to come out to my kids, who are both in high school. This is a very big deal. Scripts are drafted, rewritten, revised, scrapped, rewritten again.

4.

I always knew I was adopted. In the generation of which I'm part, illegitimacy was shameful and adoption surrounded by silence and deception. Accordingly, I possess a falsified birth certificate that names my adoptive mother and father as having given birth to me in a hospital they've never seen, in a city they have never lived in. It's the only documentation of my birth that I have. Which is to say, in the 1950s and 60s, the disclosure of truth about an adoptee's origins was largely left up to the discretion of one's adoptive parents—if indeed they themselves were provided truthful details by the adoption agency. Although practices varied from state to state, identifying information about one's birth parents was almost always pulled from the public record and sealed.

My parents were progressive for their time. They told my sister and me over and over, starting at an age before memory, that we were adopted. I never didn't know.

20   This is not the case for many other adoptees in my age cohort whose parents chose nondisclosure. But adoption is a secret that wants to come out. Often, adoptees who don't know they are adoptees stumble upon the truth later in life. Based on my conversations with them, these adoptees have a harder time of it. But some also report that the discovery of one's adoption validated a long-standing suspicion, a precognition of difference and unbelonging that lay just under the surface of consciousness. A truth almost, but not quite, in plain sight, that, when revealed, explains a lot. Either way, it's destabilizing, and the whole story of one's identity has to be rewritten, revised, scrapped, rewritten again. Lies have to be unraveled. This is a complex process that requires years.

As for discovering I'm gay: it's *as if* I'm holding in my hands a copy of my original birth certificate. Unsealed at last. This is who I am.

5.

Colleen has always known she is gay. She can't remember a time before this knowledge. She refers to herself as a lesbian now—a word that was not available to her at, say, 16. We are more or less the same age.

Her long-standing self-knowledge does not, however, mean that she came of age within the LGBTQ community or that she was seen, heard, and accepted as a lesbian within her family. Silence, secrecy, and deception were the watchwords. After high school and a first attempt at college, she entered the military—and stayed there, first in the Army and then in the Air Force, at a time when gays and lesbians were barred from serving. Per US Department of Defense Directive 1332.14, January 1981: "Homosexuality is incompatible with military service."

Along the way, she spun stories about imaginary boyfriends. Her date to the military ball was the brother of her then-girlfriend. Like falsified birth certificates that allow adoptees to obtain passports, the presence of an apparent male partner for a lesbian soldier or airman provided cover and the appearance of legitimacy at a time when gay servicemembers could be discharged under other than honorable circumstances if found out. The higher she rose through the ranks, the higher her security clearance and the higher the stakes.

That was a place of shame for me because I knew I was lying. Telling lies is 25
hard. Maintaining those lies is harder. I got good at it, but every lie creates fear
that you will be found out.

Her last two tours of duty were in the White House and in the Pentagon
at a time when the Defense Department was actively gathering data on gays
and lesbians with the explicit intent of pushing back against efforts to lift the
ban, an effort that would eventually result in the equally disastrous Don't Ask
Don't Tell policy in October 1993.

On April 25, 1993, Colleen, still enlisted and carrying a *LIFT THE BAN*
sign, joined the March on Washington for Lesbian, Gay, and Bi Equal Rights
and Liberation, one of the largest protests in American history. It was a daring
choice that came with risk of disclosure, and it was a point of no return.

The March on Washington was huge for me. It was my coming out. The per-
sonnel office in the Pentagon where I then worked was targeting gay and lesbian
servicemembers. I myself was a target. Shortly after the march, I accepted an early
retirement from the Air Force, and when I left that environment, I was done
hiding.

Colleen now organizes Veterans for Climate Justice. It was through our
shared work on climate change that we met. She sees the climate crisis as a
national security crisis. I see it as a public health crisis. We're a good team.

We didn't know that we would fall in love, both of us entering our 60s. 30
Despite our different histories, we are each still discovering our place in the
LGBTQ community.

The first time I lay in her arms, I wept. *I didn't know that things like this*
existed on this planet. Which is the truest thing that I have ever said.

6.

Why I didn't figure this out sooner, reason 1.

My freshman year of college, I made a friend. She was also a biology
major, a year older than I. We studied the intricacies of the Krebs Cycle and
Friedel-Crafts alkylation together, and we shared a love of modernist poetry,
which was rare in the organic chemistry and invertebrate zoology labs.

I do not remember anything leading up to this moment, but during one
late-night study session on my bed, I looked up at her and said *I'm in love*
with you.

She said, in words that I can't recall, that she did not share my feelings and 35
then got up and walked out. I remember her brown hair against her back as she
left the room.

The next day, we both pretended that this never happened. And I was
relieved, so relieved, that she would still be my friend.

7.

Why I didn't figure this out sooner, reason 2.

At the end of my sophomore year of college, I was diagnosed with bladder
cancer. Of all human cancers, it's the one most likely to recur—in 74 percent
of cases it comes back—and so, once diagnosed, a bladder cancer patient leads

a highly medicalized life forevermore. Over the past 40 years, I have logged countless hours in hospitals and procedure rooms, wearing paper gowns, and backless blue cotton gowns, many of those involving my legs up in stirrups.

The medical profession has a name for the fear that is triggered by cancer check-ups. They call it *scanxiety*. Which is clever, but wrong. It's trauma. I cope with medical trauma by disconnecting myself from my body during any sort of medical procedure—like, say, a cystoscope or transvaginal ultrasound—and living inside my head until it's over. I'm good at this, I have a high pain threshold, and I'm also just fucking brave.

40   My case was made complicated by my adoption status and lack of family history to help guide medical decision-making, which meant erring on the side of caution via ordering extra tests. Between 20 and 25—the age where many people focus on sexual discovery—I was living in a different world.

8.

Why I didn't figure this out sooner, reason 3.

My book, *Living Downstream: A Scientist's Personal Investigation of Cancer and the Environment*, is dedicated to Jeannie Marshall, who died before the book was published of a rare spinal cord cancer. She is also a character in the book. A cancer activist trained in engineering, Jeannie was investigating an alleged cancer cluster near her hometown south of Boston, which is how we met, and when she suffered a massive recurrence in 1994, she bequeathed her research materials to me.

We were also lovers of sorts, although I do not disclose this fact in my book, nor did I tell more than a few close friends at the time, nor did she. Jeannie was not out to her (large, Catholic) family, and her identity as a lesbian was mostly a secret that she controlled. She was also partially paralyzed, with a terminal diagnosis, and understandably angry about both. Our relationship was necessarily focused on caregiving. She refused hospice. She died in my arms in the Mass General Hospital and in the presence of a former girlfriend—who was the big love of Jeannie's life and who happened to walk in at just the right moment, for which I will be forever grateful.

At the funeral, I kept our secret. After the funeral, my grief buried it further. Twenty-four years later, I'm revealing it.

9.

45   Mahad Olad is a 21-year-old Somali immigrant from Minneapolis. He's also an American citizen. He's also gay. He is also a student of mine who wrote a paper for my class on the impact of climate change on social conflict in Muslim-dominant nations. Before he came to Ithaca College, he was my daughter's friend from a high school writing workshop at Carleton College. Mahad sometimes stays at our house during school breaks when the dorms are closed.

Two years ago, shortly after the end of the semester, my daughter received a text from Mahad, and she came to me saying *mom I think he's in trouble*.

He was. Having fled in the night from a hotel room in Nairobi, Mahad was at a gated compound at the American Embassy, under the temporary protection of a US counsel. When I got him on the phone, he explained that his family had taken him from Minneapolis to Kenya on false premises. Once there, his mother confronted him with personal essays that he had published in our student newspaper about his intersectional identity as a gay, black immigrant raised in Muslim culture, and she revealed the real purpose of the trip: to deliver him, against his will, to a gay conversion camp run by Somali religious leaders and known for abusive practices.

Throughout the Memorial Day weekend, I worked with our State Department and with Ithaca College to make arrangements to get Mahad out of Kenya and back to campus, with housing, a summer job, and a security detail to keep him safe. All kinds of people collaborated to make this happen. On May 31, 2017, after three days of travel, Mahad arrived at the Ithaca airport, where I found him sleeping on a bench by baggage claim. Since then, he has told the story of his experience to the BBC, the *New York Times*, and has thrown himself into activism. From his own column in the *Ithacan*:

> Similar to the practice of gay conversion therapy in the United States, there are those within the Muslim community who utilize abusive tactics as a way of policing what they consider to be "deviant" behavior. Even though my mother "asked" me to go, I knew that it wasn't really a choice. . . . I know that I want to do everything I can to prevent this from happening to others like me.

I was not out to my students, including Mahad, in 2017. During the long hours I waited for him to arrive back in the United States—and especially during the harrowing moments he was detained by Kenyan security for additional questioning at the airport, and I didn't know if he would be permitted to board the plane or not—I vowed to myself to come out in a more public way. I wanted my LGBTQ students to know they had an ally and mentor. And so here I am.

10.

Today, July 5, is LGBT STEM Day, which intends to showcase and celebrate the lives of LGBTQ+ people in science, technology, engineering, and math around the world. It's also a day to recognize that barriers in STEM to diversity, equality, and inclusion still remain.

And, of course, you want to know the logic behind the date. The numerical translation of July 5 is 705, which in nanometers is the wavelength of the color red, the color of life. And for everyone else in the world, where it's 5 July: 507 is the wavelength of the color green, which is the color of nature.

I'm an adoptee who takes the Darwinian Tree of Life as my personal ancestry. I'm a biologist in love with photosynthesis. It's a good day to say I'm gay.

MLA CITATION

Steingraber, Sandra. "Always Knew I Was Adopted; Just Found Out I'm Gay." *The Norton Reader: An Anthology of Nonfiction*, edited by Melissa A. Goldthwaite et al., 16th ed., W. W. Norton, 2024, pp. 40–45.

Sandra Steingraber with a portrait of biologist Rachel Carson.

QUESTIONS

1. Sandra Steingraber organizes this essay in ten sections. Annotate the essay: In one sentence per section, summarize the main idea of each. How does each section contribute to the overall message of the essay? How do the sections build on each other? How might putting them in a different order change the essay?

2. Steingraber considers many parts of her identity and the roles she plays (mother, scientist, teacher, partner, adoptee, mentor, cancer survivor, and more). Why might it be important for her to discuss these many facets of her identity in an essay about coming out as gay?

3. In paragraph 3, Steingraber's teenage son tells her that *"it's no big deal"* that she's gay and that no one should have to "'come out.'" Why does Steingraber choose to come out publicly?

4. After reading this essay, think about what makes someone part of a family. Marriage? Legal guardianship? Love? How does Steingraber think about her own family? How would you describe your family, including your chosen family, to someone? (If it helps you to visualize it, draw a family portrait or tree that includes the people *you* consider to be family.)

5. In sections 3 and 4, Steingraber includes several *"as if"* statements to explain, through comparison, what learning she was gay felt like. Have you ever come to understand something that was difficult to describe or explain to yourself and others? Write a series of *as if* comparisons to show that new understanding.

JUDITH ORTIZ COFER
More Room

M Y GRANDMOTHER'S HOUSE is like a chambered nautilus; it has many rooms, yet it is not a mansion.[1] Its proportions are small and its design simple. It is a house that has grown organically, according to the needs of its inhabitants. To all of us in the family it is known as *la casa de Mamá*.[2] It is the place of our origin; the stage for our memories and dreams of Island life.

I remember how in my childhood it sat on stilts; this was before it had a downstairs. It rested on its perch like a great blue bird, not a flying sort of bird, more like a nesting hen, but with spread wings. Grandfather had built it soon after their marriage. He was a painter and housebuilder by trade, a poet and meditative man by nature. As each of their eight children were born, new rooms were added. After a few years, the paint did not exactly match, nor the materials, so that there was a chronology to it, like the rings of a tree, and Mamá could tell you the history of each room in her *casa*, and thus the genealogy of the family along with it.

Her room is the heart of the house. Though I have seen it recently, and both woman and room have diminished in size, changed by the new perspective of my eyes, now capable of looking over countertops and tall beds, it is not this picture I carry in my memory of Mamá's *casa*. Instead, I see her room as a queen's chamber where a small woman loomed large, a throne-room with a massive four-poster bed in its center which stood taller than a child's head. It was on this bed where her own children had been born that the smallest grandchildren were allowed to take naps in the afternoons; here too was where Mamá secluded herself to dispense private advice to her daughters, sitting on the edge of the bed, looking down at whoever sat on the rocker where generations of babies had been sung to sleep. To me she looked like a wise empress right out of the fairy tales I was addicted to reading.

Though the room was dominated by the mahogany four-poster, it also contained all of Mamá's symbols of power. On her dresser instead of cosmetics there were jars filled with herbs: *yerba buena, yerba mala*,[3] the making of purgatives and teas to which we were all subjected during childhood crises. She had a steaming cup for anyone who could not, or would not, get up to face life on any given day. If the acrid aftertaste of her cures for malingering did not get you out of bed, then it was time to call *el doctor*.

From Judith Ortiz Cofer's book Silent Dancing: A Partial Remembrance of a Puerto Rican Childhood *(1990), which won the 1991 PEN / Martha Albrand Special Citation for Nonfiction.*

1. A reference to two translations of John 14:2—"In my Father's house are many mansions" (King James Version), and "My father's house has many rooms" (New International Version).
2. Spanish for "Mama's house." All translations that follow are of Spanish words.
3. "Good herbs, bad herbs."

5   And there was the monstrous chifforobe she kept locked with a little golden
key she did not hide. This was a test of her dominion over us; though my cousins
and I wanted a look inside that massive wardrobe more than anything, we never
reached for that little key lying on top of her Bible on the dresser. This was also
where she placed her earrings and rosary at night. God's word was her security
system. This chifforobe was the place where I imagined she kept jewels, satin
slippers, and elegant sequined, silk gowns of heart-breaking fineness. I lusted
after those imaginary costumes. I had heard that Mamá had been a great beauty
in her youth, and the belle of many balls. My cousins had other ideas as to what
she kept in that wooden vault: its secret could be money (Mamá did not hand
cash to strangers, banks were out of the question, so there were stories that her
mattress was stuffed with dollar bills, and that she buried coins in jars in her
garden under rosebushes, or kept them in her inviolate chifforobe); there might
be that legendary gun salvaged from the Spanish-American conflict over the
Island. We went wild over suspected treasures that we made up simply because
children have to fill locked trunks with something wonderful.
        On the wall above the bed hung a heavy silver crucifix. Christ's agonized
head hung directly over Mamá's pillow. I avoided looking at this weapon suspended over where her head would lay; and on the rare occasions when I was
allowed to sleep on that bed, I scooted down to the safe middle of the mattress,
where her body's impression took me in like a mother's lap. Having taken care of
the obligatory religious decoration with a crucifix, Mamá covered the other walls
with objects sent to her over the years by her children in the States. *Los Nueva
Yores*[4] were represented by, among other things, a postcard of Niagara Falls from
her son Hernán, postmarked, Buffalo, NY. In a conspicuous gold frame hung a
large color photograph of her daughter Nena, her husband and their five children
at the entrance to Disneyland in California. From us she had gotten a black lace
fan. Father had brought it to her from a tour of duty with the Navy in Europe (on
Sundays she would remove it from its hook on the wall to fan herself at Sunday
mass). Each year more items were added as the family grew and dispersed, and
every object in the room had a story attached to it, a *cuento*[5] which Mamá would
bestow on anyone who received the privilege of a day alone with her. It was
almost worth pretending to be sick, though the bitter herb purgatives of the body
were a big price to pay for the spirit revivals of her story-telling.
        Mamá slept alone on her large bed, except for the times when a sick grand-
child warranted the privilege, or when a heartbroken daughter came home in need
of more than herbal teas. In the family there is a story about how this came to be.
        When one of the daughters, my mother or one of her sisters, tells the *cuento*
of how Mamá came to own her nights, it is usually preceded by the qualifications that Papá's exile from his wife's room was not a result of animosity between
the couple, but that the act had been Mamá's famous bloodless coup for her
personal freedom. Papá was the benevolent dictator of her body and her life who
had had to be banished from her bed so that Mamá could better serve her fam-

4. "The New Yorkers."
5. "Tale."

ily. Before the telling, we had to agree that the old man was not to blame. We all recognized that in the family Papá was as an *alma de Dios*,[6] a saintly, soft-spoken presence whose main pleasures in life, such as writing poetry and reading the Spanish large-type editions of *Reader's Digest*, always took place outside the vortex of Mamá's crowded realm. It was not his fault, after all, that every year or so he planted a babyseed in Mamá's fertile body, keeping her from leading the active life she needed and desired. He loved her and the babies. Papá composed odes and lyrics to celebrate births and anniversaries and hired musicians to accompany him in singing them to his family and friends at extravagant pigroasts he threw yearly. Mamá and the oldest girls worked for days preparing the food. Papá sat for hours in his painter's shed, also his study and library, composing the songs. At these celebrations he was also known to give long speeches in praise of God, his fecund wife, and his beloved island. As a middle child, my mother remembers these occasions as a time when the women sat in the kitchen and lamented their burdens, while the men feasted out in the patio, their rum-thickened voices rising in song and praise for each other, *compañeros*[7] all.

It was after the birth of her eighth child, after she had lost three at birth or in infancy, that Mamá made her decision. They say that Mamá had had a special way of letting her husband know that they were expecting, one that had begun when, at the beginning of their marriage, he had built her a house too confining for her taste. So, when she discovered her first pregnancy, she supposedly drew plans for another room, which he dutifully executed. Every time a child was due, she would demand, *more space, more space*. Papá acceded to her wishes, child after child, since he had learned early that Mamá's renowned temper was a thing that grew like a monster along with a new belly. In this way Mamá got the house that she wanted, but with each child she lost in heart and energy. She had knowledge of her body and perceived that if she had any more children, her dreams and her plans would have to be permanently forgotten, because she would be a chronically ill woman, like Flora with her twelve children: asthma, no teeth, in bed more than on her feet.

And so, after my youngest uncle was born, she asked Papá to build a large   10
room at the back of the house. He did so in joyful anticipation. Mamá had asked him special things this time: shelves on the walls, a private entrance. He thought that she meant this room to be a nursery where several children could sleep. He thought it was a wonderful idea. He painted it his favorite color, sky blue, and made large windows looking out over a green hill and the church spires beyond. But nothing happened. Mamá's belly did not grow, yet she seemed in a frenzy of activity over the house. Finally, an anxious Papá approached his wife to tell her that the new room was finished and ready to be occupied. And Mamá, they say, replied: "Good, it's for *you*."

And so it was that Mamá discovered the only means of birth control available to a Catholic woman of her time: sacrifice. She gave up the comfort of Papá's sexual love for something she deemed greater: the right to own and

6. Literally, "soul of God"; a thoroughly good person.
7. "Companions."

control her body, so that she might live to meet her grandchildren—me among them—so that she could give more of herself to the ones already there, so that she could be more than a channel for other lives, so that even now that time has robbed her of the elasticity of her body and of her amazing reservoir of energy, she still emanates the kind of joy that can only be achieved by living according to the dictates of one's own heart.

MLA CITATION

Cofer, Judith Ortiz. "More Room." *The Norton Reader: An Anthology of Nonfiction*, edited by Melissa A. Goldthwaite et al., 16th ed., W. W. Norton, 2024, pp. 47–50.

QUESTIONS

1. At the end of the essay, Judith Ortiz Cofer explains in fairly direct terms why her grandmother wanted "more room." Why do you think she uses narration as the primary mode in the rest of the essay? What does she gain by first narrating, then explaining?

2. Cofer uses many similes (comparisons with *like* or *as*) and metaphors (comparisons without specific connectors)—for example, in paragraph 1, she says that her grandmother's house was "like a chambered nautilus" and in paragraph 5 that her grandmother's Bible was "her security system." Annotate the essay, marking all the similes and metaphors you can find. Discuss the use of one or two such comparisons that you find particularly effective.

3. What are the possible meanings of the title?

4. Write about a favorite or mysterious place you remember from childhood.

DIANA ABU-JABER
Lamb Two Ways

EVERY YEAR BETWEEN Halloween and Christmas, my grandmother Grace transforms her apartment into a bakery. Tables and chairs are covered with racks of cooling cookies, eight baking sheets slip in and out of the oven—as tiny as something in a troll's house. The Mixmaster drones. A universe of cookies: chocolate-planted peanut butter; sinus-kicking bourbon balls; leaping reindeer and sugar bells; German press-form cookies from her grandparents' Bavarian village—*Springerle—green wreaths, candy berries; and a challenging, grown-uppy variety named for the uncut dough's sausage shape: Wurstcakes. All part of Grace's arsenal: she's engaged in an internecine war with my father, Bud, over the loyalties of the children. Her Wurstcakes are slim as Communion wafers. Bud dunks them in*

First published in the New Yorker *(2015), a weekly magazine of "reportage, commentary, criticism, essays, fiction, satire, cartoons, and poetry." An extended version of this essay, titled "Crack," appears as the first chapter of Diana Abu-Jaber's memoir* Life Without a Recipe *(2016).*

his demitasse of ahweh[1] *and calls them "Catholic cookies."* Her eyes tighten as she watches him eat.

"Only higher civilizations bake cookies," she says to me, raking fingers through the shrubbery of my hair. "I don't know how you people would cele-brate Christmas if I wasn't around. Run wild like savages."

My parents were married in Gram's church. When the priest presented Dad with a contract to raise his children within the Catholic faith, Dad signed in Arabic. He nudged Gram in the ribs, as if she were in on the joke, and, instead of his name, wrote: *I make no promises.* In my parents' satiny wedding photographs, Grace stared at Bud. *I'm on to you, friend.*

"Never learn how to sew, cook, type, or iron." She bends over the board, passes the hissing iron back and forth, slave rowing a galley ship. "That's how they get you." She pauses long enough to turn that shrewd gaze on me and after a moment I look away. There's cooking, sure, but then there's baking. I learn from Grace that sugar represents a special kind of freedom. It charms almost everyone; it brings love and luck and good favor. Cakes and cookies are exalted—a gift of both labor and sweetness—so good a smart woman is willing to give herself to them.

Adversaries, even enemies, can rely on each other. My father and my grand-   5
mother teach me this by accident. They don't get along and they agree on every-thing. Especially the two essentials:

1. Men are terrible.
2. Save your money (Gram: in bra. Bud: somewhere, preferably not at the horse races).

Also, they both want all the love. As if there is a limited supply and never enough to go around. They wrangle over the children's souls and both set out food for us, bait inside a trap. Bud cooks—earthy, meaty dishes with lemon and oil and onion. Gram is more ruthless—she pries open those foil-lined tins, cookies cov-ered with sugar crystals like crushed rubies, the beckoning finger of vanilla. I think about the story of the witch in her gingerbread house, how she schemed to push Hansel and Gretel into her oven. Gram reads me the story; I sit, rapt, watching her, her sky-blue eyes glittering. *I will fight anyone for you,* she seems to say. Even if it means cooking you and gobbling you up.

Bud doesn't quite grasp the concept of this fight; his wrath is more epi-sodic. Anything that strikes him as American-disrespectful—say, one of us kids gives him the old eye-roll, or an "oh, yuh"—and he'll be shouting the cupboards off the walls. Then he'll storm into the kitchen and fill it with the scent of cauli-flower seething in olive oil and garlic, the bitter, sulfurous ingredients he hacks up when he's in a mood. Stuff that tastes like punishment to an eight-year-old. Most of the time, though, when Grace is around he forgets there's a war on. He argues casually, conversationally, segues into offhanded, cheerful observations and questions: "Why do cookies always come in circles?" Etc. This deepens

---

1. Lebanese and Turkish coffee made with sugar using a traditional Lebanese Rakweh coffeepot.

her rage and despair—he can't even be bothered to remember that they're fighting. So disrespectful!

Grace is vigilant, tallying all those casual betrayals between men and women, as if she were jotting them in a notebook. It's not just Bud, it's all of them. Men as a general category are disappointing and traitorous—in money and family and work and power. Romantic love is another of their snares. "They tell you to wait, wait, wait," she says. "True love will come. True love will make everything so much better. So you wait and wait and wait, and true love turns out to be a nincompoop with a venereal disease."

The insults, the sharp little arrows seem to be everywhere, even in places and moments that seem the most innocent. Gram will take me to see Snow White of the limpid flesh and cretinous voice—and the Prince with the power-ful shoulders who must save her from another woman—an old lady!—and raise the helpless thing, literally, from the dead. After the movie, Gram scowls and mutters, "Flibbertigibbet." Afterward, we go to a café, where they bring us crepes with cherries and whipped cream. "Did you see," she grouses. "Those dwarves, they only wanted her to stay *after* she offered to cook for them."

Only a few of us in the family understand how those crisply divided feelings, love and complaint, float together, united. All grudges are softened by the approach of dinner. Those who labor with Bud in the kitchen are joined in a confederacy—cooking restores us to our senses. During the week, my father works two or more jobs. But Saturday breakfast is a profusion: the sizzling morsels of lamb on the fava beans; diced tomato, celery, and onion on the hummus; tidy, half-fried eggs bundled around their yolks. We hurry to sit and then spend half the meal begging Bud, "Come to the table! Sit down. *Sit.*" Always, he wants to slice one more cucumber.

10   Throughout my childhood, I hear Americans joke about Bud and his harem—his wife and three daughters. He laughs, strong white teeth; he says, "Don't forget my mother-in-law."

Before they'd met, neither Grace nor Bud could have imagined each other, not once in a million years. They came with their ingredients like particles of lost and opposing worlds, the dying old divisions—East and West.

Among my father's library of made-up true stories is a favorite, about meeting his mother-in-law:

Grace was not pleased about her only child falling in with this question-able young man with a mustache. But that was a separate issue from good manners and laying out a nice table for company. At the time, the fanciest dish Grace knew of was shrimp poached in a wine and butter sauce. My father, most recently of the semi-arid village of Yahdoudeh,[2] studied the pale, curling bodies on the plate and saw a combination of cockroach and scorpion; he also deduced that the older lady with the stiff blonde hair and see-through eyes was some sort of *bruja*.[3] He ate only the sweet dinner rolls—which were quite

2. Town in Jordan.
3. Witch.

good—and left the rest untouched. Bud somehow had himself a marvelous time, even with the *bruja*'s blue eye fixed on him. Maybe because of it. Afterward, mortally offended and stiff-backed, Grace scraped shrimp into the garbage, her throat filled with a dark will for revenge.

A few months later, my poor mother, Patty, barely twenty years old, eternal optimist, proposed a do-over: this time in honor of their engagement. Grace decided to pull out all the stops. Telling her version, my grandmother had said, "You know how that is—the more you hate someone the nicer you are to them?" To her, there was nothing better than a glistening, pink ham. In anguish, she slathered it with brown sugar and pineapple slices, voodoo-piercing it with cloves—each a tiny dart.

Dizzy with dismay, my Muslim father stood at the table, staring at the 15 ham—forbidden, "unclean" meat. As soon as Gram saw his expression, she went to the phone book and jotted down the address of the White Castle. She swore she'd had no idea of this dietary restriction. "Who doesn't eat *ham?*" she'd cried twenty years later, still in disbelief. "I was so angry, I was almost laughing."

Bud brought back fries for the table.

You want most what you can't have. Gram would fight him for her daughter, long after the fight was over.

When I am nine, I cook a leg of lamb for my grandmother. A whole leg, just the two of us, but it's important because, in my mind, it's a possible culinary meeting place for him and her. When I suggest it, Gram says *Oh!* She *adores* leg of lamb. She hasn't had it in for_ever_. This is the first dinner I've ever cooked for her. All day I fan away her questions and suggestions. I'm as bossy and kitchen-difficult as my dad. For hours, the big joint burbles in wine and vinegar on top of the stove and fills her apartment with a round, heady scent that makes you weak-kneed. I set the table carefully, with napkins and water glasses. I carve and plate the lamb on top of the stove, then carry it out and place it before her.

She lowers her fork after a few bites, her mouth wilting. "What's wrong?" I'd crushed each garlic clove—a whole head—with salt, pepper, snips of rosemary, and had slipped the paste into slits in the meat, just the way I'd seen my father do. The tender meat breaks into fragments beneath the fork; I could drink the braising sauce with a spoon. "What did I do?"

Gram takes off her glasses and knuckles the corners of her eyes. Finally 20 she says, "I like my lamb *rare*. With mint *jelly*." Her voice is pure pout. She sounds like my four-year-old sister, parked on the top step shouting, "Nobody loves me! You're not the boss of me!" Rummaging through accusations until she finds whatever lines up with the way she feels inside, abandoned in the hard world.

At nine, it's only just beginning to occur to me that I'm on my own here. The adults give you what they can, richer or poorer. Mint jelly! It is accusation and insult. She has detected my father's hand in the sauce. Affronted, I want to slap the table, bluster away, just like my dad does. But how do you argue with mint jelly? I took a risk and failed. It had never occurred to me that tastes and preferences could be so embedded in personality and history.

To me, deliciousness is still a simple matter—I don't have enough experience yet to understand how personal such things are. How you must choose the ingredients and tools slowly, putting together a palate, just as you build a life. Taste is desire, permitted or not, encouraged or not. There is no arguing it away, there is no winner in this fight, no recipe to follow. There is only blind faith and improvisation.

MLA CITATION

Abu-Jaber, Diana. "Lamb Two Ways." *The Norton Reader: An Anthology of Nonfiction*, edited by Melissa A. Goldthwaite et al., 16th ed., W. W. Norton, 2024, pp. 50–54.

QUESTIONS

1. Diana Abu-Jaber shows the *"war"* between her grandmother Grace and her father Bud *"over the loyalties of the children"* (paragraph 1). Although Grace and Bud come from different cultures, they also have some similar personality traits. As you read and annotate the essay, note those traits. What similarities and differences between these two characters figure most prominently in the essay?

2. When telling anecdotes about her relationship with her grandmother, Abu-Jaber references children's stories and fairy tales, such as "Hansel and Gretel" (paragraph 5) and "Snow White" (paragraph 8). What lessons does Grace impart to her granddaughter through her response to these stories?

3. After recounting a failed attempt to please her grandmother by cooking lamb, Abu-Jaber writes, "It had never occurred to me that tastes and preferences could be so embedded in personality and history" (paragraph 21). Have you ever tried to please someone with food that person could not appreciate? Write about the elements of personality and history that shaped that person's preferences.

RACHEL PIEH JONES

A Muslim, a Christian, and a Baby Named "God"

> And sometimes it's the very otherness of a stranger, someone who doesn't belong to our ethnic or ideological or religious group, an otherness that can repel us initially, but which can jerk us out of our habitual selfishness, and give us intonations of that sacred otherness, which is God.
>
> —KAREN ARMSTRONG

HEN GOD AND HIS MOTHER were released from the maternity ward they came directly to my house to use the air conditioner. It was early May and the summer heat that melted lollipops and caused car tires to burst enveloped Djibouti like a

Published in Longreads *(2017), which features and produces "in-depth investigative pieces, profiles, interviews, commentary, book reviews, audio stories, and personal essays."*

wet blanket. Power outages could exceed ten hours a day. Temperatures hadn't peaked yet, 120 degrees would come in August, but the spring humidity without functioning fans during power outages turned everyone into hapless puddles. I prepared a mattress for Amaal and her newborn and prayed the electricity would stay on so she could use the air conditioner and rest, recover.

In 2004 when my family arrived in Djibouti, I needed help minimizing the constant layer of dust; Amaal needed a job. I needed a friend and Amaal, with her quick laugh and cultural insights, became my lifeline. My husband worked at the University of Djibouti and was gone most mornings and afternoons, plus some evenings. We had 4-year-old twins and without Amaal I might have packed our bags and returned to Minnesota out of loneliness and culture shock.

I hired Amaal before she had any children. She wasn't married yet and her phone often rang while she worked, boys calling to see what she was doing on Thursday evening. To see if she wanted to go for a walk down the streets without street lights where young people could clandestinely hold hands or drink beer from glass Coca-Cola bottles. She rarely said yes until Abdi Fatah[1] started calling. He didn't drink alcohol and didn't pressure her into more physical contact than she was comfortable with in this Muslim country. She felt respected. She said yes.

Djibouti is one of the hottest countries in the world, best known to Americans, if at all, as the host of the only US military base in Africa, Camp Lemonnier. Djibouti is also a former French colony, a bastion of peace in a tumultuous region with Yemen across the narrow strait, Eritrea to the west, and Somalia to the east. Djibouti is the main conduit for landlocked Ethiopia's goods, which are hauled by hundreds of trucks snaking every day from the port in Djibouti to Ethiopia's capital, Addis Ababa. And, Djibouti is a Muslim country with a Catholic cathedral, a French Protestant church, and an Ethiopian Orthodox church. From one vantage point near the port, between two *dukaans*[2] selling fresh-squeezed orange juice and rapidly melting ice cream, you can see the white minaret and green-tinted windows of a mosque, the cross on top of the cathedral, and the golden dome of the Orthodox church.

The Quran says, "There is no compulsion in religion," and in Djibouti, this appears to be true. In Djibouti there is also little crossover or intermingling in religion. Djiboutians are Muslims, Ethiopian Orthodox are their specific brand of Orthodox. Other Ethiopians and European, American, and other African expatriates are Catholic or Protestant, or whatever they were when they arrived. And for the most part, they tend to remain in the religious traditions and communities of their forefathers. Each maintains their orthodoxy and orthopraxy, and each calls God by a different name.

This raises questions about the nature of God and the practice of our worship. Is God's name *God*? Dieu? Allah? Ebbe? Waq? How do we approach this entity? On our knees with our foreheads pressed to the ground, years of praying

1. Name has been changed [Author's note].
2. Somali for "shops."

the Islamic *salat*[3] branding us with bruises? Through making the sign of the cross with our right hand, crossing over heart and chest? Through singing songs and raising our hands toward the heavens? Through ritual incense and the mediation of an Orthodox priest? Does our practice make us perfect in the pursuit of knowing and honoring God? Or can God be found outside of ritual and structure and tradition? Can God be found outside the walls of our separate buildings?

I knew Muslims before moving to Djibouti but Amaal became my first close Muslim friend. We laughed at each other's strange habits, like how she slathered her face in green paste made from crushed leaves to dye it whiter and how I brushed my teeth with a green minty paste that frothed and then spit it out. We examined each other's faith, she a Muslim and me a Christian, and how we incorporated it into our daily lives. Amaal told me I had the patience of Job while we waited for our shipped container of supplies to arrive from Dubai and spent months eating from paper plates while sitting on the floor. She told me the Islamic story of this prophet. Job, plagued by the loss of his children and livelihood and suffering from boils. He would pick the maggots that fell out of his boils to the ground and gently replace them on his skin so they wouldn't die, praising Allah for giving him life, even this life of suffering. Amaal had a conflict with a friend and I told her the story of the prophet Joseph from the Bible, how he forgave his eleven brothers who, overcome by jealousy, sold him into slavery.

Amaal taught me how to fold and fry samboosas—dough stuffed with ground beef and onions, folded into a triangle, and fried—and that it was okay to dress like a slob inside the house, but that I needed to put on perfume, makeup, and jewelry to go out in Djibouti, in what Somalis liked to call "the Paris of Somali fashion." No matter that the perfume would soon be overpowered by the sickly sweet stench of constant sweat. No matter that the makeup would melt and clump or that the jewelry would stick to my skin, cheap necklaces leaving green streaks around my neck. Amaal was patient with my languishing language skills and understood me when no one else could. She sometimes translated between me and her elderly relatives, all of us speaking Somali. Amaal had kept me in Djibouti and her friendship helped me stay sane while in Djibouti, so when she asked if she and her newborn could stay with us after the birth, I didn't hesitate.

Water was scarcer than electricity and after giving birth, Amaal wouldn't be able to push a wheelbarrow loaded with 20-liter yellow water jugs from the neighborhood water hose to her house. She could pay a neighbor to do it, she could wait for her husband to come home from work. But she didn't have cash to spare and Abdi Fatah might arrive from work at a time when the water was off, and they would miss their turn at the communal faucet. My house, with a generator and water tank, seemed like a refuge.

10   Her house was the second-to-last at the bottom of a steep and rocky slope. Some expatriates referred to her neighborhood of Balbala as a slum but Amaal would take offense at this term. According to UN-Habitat, a slum is a run-down

3. Muslim ritual prayer performed five times a day.

part of a city with substandard housing, squalor, and lacking in tenure security—inhabitants are transient, rarely staying in one location for long.

Amaal's husband had a good, secure job in the military. She refused to acquiesce to squalor and painted swooping vines and flowers and red curtains on the cement walls of her home. Amaal and her neighbors worked tirelessly against the desert dust to maintain cleanliness. She and Abdi Fatah had their own toilet, though not yet running water. They had electricity, when the electricity was on. They had two rooms and a kitchen. This was not a slum dwelling, it was Djiboutian lower-middle class. It just didn't look like what foreigners expected.

Beyond the front door that Amaal would later paint a bright blue was the cemetery. The unevenly spaced body-sized mounds with no headstones divided her quarter from Cité Barwaaqo, another section of Balbala. She only crossed the cemetery to get to her best friend's house, past goats and kids playing with cars made from milk carton boxes and tin can covers, in the middle of the day, after praying and while whispering "*bismillah al-rahman al-rahiim*" (In the name of Allah, the most gracious, the most merciful). If she returned alive and if no *jinn*[4] had possessed her, then Allah had answered the prayers made in his name, yet again proving to be gracious and merciful.

Beyond the cemetery, the lights visible on clear days, Djibouti's port towered over the Gulf of Tadjoura. Container ships to be unloaded and refueled waited further out at sea, their hulking mass a constant reminder of the world beyond Djibouti. I told Amaal the view from her house was beautiful. She said it was horrifying. I saw water and ships, commerce and travel and development. She saw the cemetery and the aluminum-sided houses, perhaps what UN-Habitat looked at when they labeled her neighborhood a slum.

Amaal's friend in Cité Barwaaqo, Waris, had given birth to a baby girl a few months earlier. Amaal and I paced the hallway of the Dar-Al Hanan maternity hospital while Waris' mother stayed by her laboring daughter. Waris asked for Amaal to come hold her hand but Amaal started to cry from the intensity and terror of labor and retreated to the hallway. She took Waris' phone when it rang and wiped away tears while she answered Waris' husband's inquiries.

Yes, Waris was fine. Yes, it hurt like hell. No, there was no baby yet. No,   15
she didn't want to talk to him.

Later Waris described the pain in vivid detail. Nurses attempting to help laboring mothers pinched their inner thighs, slapped, insulted, and sometimes sat on their bellies while they pushed and women were discouraged from crying out in pain, from revealing weakness. Amaal's takeaway was to stop taking prenatal vitamins.

"They will make the baby too big." She didn't want to push out a big baby and she didn't want to cause a C-section.

"They won't make the baby big," I said. "They will make it healthy."

"My mother-in-law won't allow it."

I convinced Amaal to take the vitamins but she kept them in the refrigerator   20
at my house so her mother-in-law wouldn't discover them and toss the contraband

4. Spirit or demon.

down their hole-in-the-ground toilet. Amaal came to work every day with fresh questions. One day she called me into the bedroom and lifted her dress to show me a rash spreading over her breasts. Another day she asked which sexual positions were least cumbersome during the third trimester. She asked how to help a baby sleep through the night, how to change a diaper, whether or not to give water alongside breast milk. Her mother had died years ago and Amaal started to call me *hooyo* even though I was less than ten years older. Mother.

Three times Amaal called me after midnight and said, breathless, that labor had begun. I drove her and her husband to the French hospital, Bouffard. Because Abdi Fatah was in the military, they were allowed to use this facility. Three times the Djiboutian midwife looked at us with an unspoken question in her eyes. The nervous husband, the concerned foreign friend, and the maybe-laboring mother. Three times she sent us home and told us to come back when Amaal was unable to speak.

When Amaal's labor began in earnest, I was on an airplane returning from a conference in Kenya. My husband picked me up at the airport and drove me directly to the hospital. Soccer games raged in the parking lot over the giant white *X* of the helicopter landing pad. Security guards checked my passport and recognized me from my previous visits with Amaal. I knew my way to the maternity ward; I had paced outside it for hours trying to encourage my own labor a few years earlier.

There was one delivery room and if needed, the cramped exam room could be commandeered, or the floor in the hallway outside the labor room. Amaal shared the room with several other women and they all hoped they would deliver at alternating times so no one would end up on the floor. Despite the frigid air conditioning, Amaal was sweating and instead of breathing through contractions, she cried in a low voice the Djiboutian mourning cry, the sound of both grief and physical pain, "Waaaaywaaaywaaay," and clenched her teeth. Abdi Fatah looked scared and uncomfortable, the only man in the room. His eyes darted from Amaal's face to her stomach and he steadfastly refused to glance at the other women. He asked if he could wait in the hall while I stayed. We prayed for mercy, for miracles, and I wiped Amaal's forehead, whispered that she was beautiful.

Midwives said things like, *If you can't handle the pain then why did you get pregnant in the first place?* They said things like, *This is what you get for messing around.* They said things like, *If you don't hurry up you will have a C-section and then what husband will want you?* I wanted to counter these words, to speak a different reality over Amaal the same way I had needed my husband to tell me I was strong during labor. We could grasp that word, *strong*, and squeeze it dry while our babies turned us inside out.

25

Abdi Fatah returned with a damp towel to cool Amaal's face and kissed her. Her labor progressed slowly and I had to go home to my three children, the youngest, 3 years old, the one born in Djibouti, recovering from chicken pox.

And so I missed the birth of God, hours later and by Cesarean section. In the morning I returned to the hospital to hold the baby and to assuage Amaal's guilt and anger about the vitamins, nervous that she would blame them, or me, for the C-section. Abdi Fatah met me at the gate and took me to her room. He said he didn't care about scars and surgery. He had wanted a girl but now he said he didn't care about girls either. I gave Amaal sliced watermelon and a bag of Coca-Colas and chocolate crème cookies and scooped God into my arms.

"Tell me about his name," I said. Even after five years in Somalia and Djibouti I had never heard this name before.

"God," Amaal said. She pronounced it almost like "goad" with a long *o* sound and a brisk *d*, half-way between a *t* and a *d*. "It means poisonous snake."

"Do you really spell it G-o-d?"

She nodded.

"Do you know what that sounds like in English?"

She nodded. "The French doctor checked on us and read his name off the chart and started laughing. He explained." She said every nurse who came to check on her and saw the chart, laughed. Some bent to kiss God.

Two-and-a-half years earlier I had given birth to the one with chicken pox, at this same hospital. She was born on 9/11 but in 2005, a baby born to a Christian family in a Muslim country with a Somali midwife on an infamous day. I named her Lucy Deeqsan. Deeqsan is a Somali name that means "gift from Allah." In its full meaning, a gift from Allah that is so sufficient I could never ask for anything else.

A few American Christians told me their opinions about this name, which boiled down into, *Anyone who would name their daughter in reference to a pagan god is a heretic.* But Arab Christians used the word Allah for God even before the prophet Mohamed was born. Arab Bibles are filled with the word Allah. If "Dios" can be translated to mean God, if "Dieu" can be translated to mean God, if "Ebbe" can be translated to mean God, these words are simply different jumbles of letters and sounds forced together in an attempt to explain the unexplainable. If "God" is who many people believe God is, neither the concept nor the word can be owned. No religious system, no language can lay claim.

Names can have multiple meanings, multiple narratives. The middle name we chose for our youngest, Deeqsan, could also euphemistically mean "that's enough." And after twins, after giving birth in Djibouti, this baby was our last. *Way noo deeqday,* she was enough for us. So sufficient I could never ask for anything else.

Amaal asked if she and God could stay at my house for the first week or two. Abdi Fatah had to work, he might even be called to Forêt du Day[5] on the other side of Djibouti, in the mountainous Afar region. I had a generator that sometimes functioned, when my husband was home to pull the cord like a lawn mower, and though it never summoned enough power for an air conditioner, in theory it could motivate a ceiling fan. I also had running water.

---

5. One of Djibouti's two protected forest areas.

30

35

"Of course." I promised to visit the hospital every day and on the fourth day, bundled God in a pink baby blanket my mother had shipped from Minnesota as a gift and drove them home.

Amaal and God slept on a thin foam mattress in Lucy Deeqsan's bedroom and Lucy slept with her older sister. The power cut out the first night and the generator didn't work. We lay awake in pools of sweat. In the morning I ate cereal for breakfast and Amaal sent the neighbor boy out for a baguette she could dip in her tea. Amaal invited friends and relatives and in a Djiboutian home after a baby is born, guests flood the rooms. They bring gifts and food and clean the floors and hold the baby. Her friends were shy about coming to an American's house and only Waris visited. I had to teach English at a local women's organization and no one was home to massage Amaal's shoulders or help change God's diapers.

At night, so Amaal could sleep, I rocked God in the wooden Iranian rocking chair I bought at a bazaar while pregnant with Deeqsan. I thought about God and poisonous snakes and the words that divided worlds. Strings of phonetics, scratchings of script, the human desperation to communicate, to name. Words shape the way we see the world. Or does the way we see our world shape the words we use to describe it? Somali has more words related to camels than I will ever be able to learn. English has more nuanced color vocabulary than Somalis deem reasonable. I see the world in rainbows, my Somali friends see the world in relation to camels.

40   When a Djiboutian asks me whether or not I worship Allah, I don't think about the spelling or the sounds or the centuries-ago and still-to-this-day conflicts and crusades. I fill that word up with what I know of our common understanding. We don't agree on all the characteristics of God but we do agree on many. Allah the creator, the ultimate, the most gracious, the giver and taker of life. Yes, when I speak Somali and answer the question, yes, *Allah baan cabuudaa.* When I speak English and then answer the question, yes, I worship God.

When people press and want to know if I am a Muslim or if I have prayed the *salat,* the five-times daily Islamic prayer, I say *no.* When they press deeper and ask if I would like to become a Muslim, I say *no, I love Jesus.* We are not the same, this isn't universalism and I'm not afraid or ashamed of my beliefs that run counter to many of the people I live around. This is acknowledging that while we disagree on concepts of God and in our convictions about things like sin, forgiveness, and the process of redemption, we are people of faith. We can still communicate.

Names tell stories, they hold histories, they convey character and belief and can be unpacked. In the unpacking of Allah or of God, different stories emerge and those stories differ depending upon who is doing the unpacking. As I rock baby God, I think of the stories of the names of my children. One named after her great-grandmother. One named, loosely, after Indiana Jones— or a long-dead Christian preacher, depending on who tells the story of that naming. One named for the country in which she was born. The baby in my arms, named for a snake. Yet none of these names conveys the fullness of that person. Each of these named children must be encountered on their own terms, in relationship, over time.

While living in a Muslim country, I have not changed in my deep convictions about God and about faith but I have witnessed the deep convictions of others about God and faith. We are not the same but that doesn't mean, in an increasingly violent and divided world, that we should join either the jihad or the drones. The differences should not be obstacles but opportunities to engage and discuss and to enter a reconciliation that doesn't insist on uniformity. When a baby is born and his name is God, I fill that word up with the shape of his eyes and the gentle curve of his cheek.

In *The Case for God*, theologian Karen Armstrong writes that God is not the exclusive property of any one tradition. Hard as I tried to make them comfortable, I could not even keep baby God exclusively in my house. I gave Amaal my battery-operated fan. After English class I made *sugo*, a greasy spaghetti sauce, and filled bowls with apple slices and chunks of banana and carried them to her room so she wouldn't have to get up. I held God and washed his white onesie with pink and blue butterflies and bounced him and sang songs.

But eventually Amaal announced that she and God could not recuperate at 45 my home. My isolated, American-culture house was too quiet, too lonely, not any cooler than her own since our generator stubbornly refused to work, and she was taking the baby. If I wanted to hold God, I could find him in Balbala. And so, unable to rest, on the seventh day Amaal and God moved out.

MLA CITATION

Jones, Rachel Pieh. "A Muslim, a Christian, and a Baby Named 'God.'" *The Norton Reader: An Anthology of Nonfiction*, edited by Melissa A. Goldthwaite et al., 16th ed., W. W. Norton, 2024, pp. 54–61.

QUESTIONS

1. An American living in Djibouti, Rachel Pieh Jones describes her friendship with Amaal and how without this friendship Jones "might have packed [her] bags and returned to Minnesota out of loneliness and culture shock" (paragraph 2). As you read the essay, mark the passages that reveal cultural differences. In what ways did Jones and Amaal support one another despite their differences?

2. Jones reflects on the importance of names, naming, and communication. What is necessary for a name to be "unpacked" (paragraph 42), to show the fullness of its meaning?

3. Why did Amaal stay with Jones after God was born? Why did she decide to leave?

4. Have you ever been away from home, living in a new place where you experienced cultural differences? Did you eventually come to feel more at home in that new place? Why or why not? Write about that experience and the people, beliefs, and/or cultural practices that contributed to it.

KIESE LAYMON
Bedtime Songs

I T'S SOMETHING PAST MIDNIGHT in Oxford, Mississippi, and I'm on my way home. Every night I throw on my hoodie, get in my truck, and drive around Lafayette County listening to New York love songs in Mississippi. Tonight, I drove to the Krogers parking lot, the recycling place on Molly Barr, the post office, and I circled the town square four times before heading toward Batesville. I didn't want any food. Didn't have anything to recycle. Wasn't expecting any mail. I still don't drink. I decided to drive because I didn't want to be home. I didn't want to be home because I didn't want to be alone, quiet, still. I'm thankful to have a physical and spiritual place to call home in Mississippi, but there's a loneliness I didn't anticipate when I moved back after living in Poughkeepsie, New York, for fifteen years.

Tonight I need to hear regret. Regret transports me to New York. I'm in Northern Mississippi, but I'm really turning onto Raymond Avenue from Hooker Avenue listening to Kanye's "Spaceship." I'm on I-84 veering onto the Taconic waiting for that part in "Givin Em What They Love," where Prince and Janelle Monáe deftly invent and neglect harmony. I'm sitting in a parking lot behind Jewett House at Vassar College, where I used to teach, listening to J-Live tell me that his art "is destined to be the greatest story ever missed so it's meant to be for whoever's hearing this." I'm listening to "Wax Paper" for the thousandth time, hoping to find one more Easter egg.

And then I'm heading back down Highway 6. Meshell Ndegeocello's version of Force MD's "Tender Love" comes on my raggedy pink iPod. The wandering harmonica, the breathy texture of Ndegeocello's voice, surrender seared in the space between "here" and "I." Surrender is how Beyoncé makes "that I'm not at ease" feel so perfectly out of pocket in "Pray You Catch Me." It's what allows Cassandra Wilson to take her time building syllables and empty space and syllables to "suitcase of memories" in her version of "Time after Time." None of these songs are technically Mississippi songs, but they're all Mississippi songs to me. I really heard them for the first time while living and driving alone in Mississippi these past two years.

I'm too old for bedtime stories, too old to be writing words like these, maybe too old for love songs. But for me, bedtime songs, my body, and my truck are physical links between New York and Mississippi, between a home I was given and a home I made. The music and the movement of my body and the safety of my truck are what I need to make myself sleep and want to wake up. Tonight, for the first time in my life, they remind me that I want to be a tender person much more than I want to be a tender artist. When I pull into my driveway, I want to believe I could have gotten here without all this loneliness, without being forty-

Published in Oxford American *(2019), a quarterly "magazine of the South" affiliated with the University of Central Arkansas.*

four and childless, without all this regretful bedtime music and movement in Mississippi.

I could not.   5

That sentence, or really that sentiment, like the last verse of KRIT's "Drinking Sessions," which I hear sitting in the driveway, is equal parts shameful and revelatory. Like KRIT, I do not understand the difference between extreme sadness and depression, between being lonely and feeling alone, between being afraid to fly and wanting to float, between being good and breathing healthy, between my mama's voice and my daddy's silence, between folks I almost know and friends whose laughs I can imitate.

And most nights, bedtime music is the only thing that gets me close to accepting that lack of understanding. Bedtime music is neither beginning nor end. It's all middle, all terrifying, and all familiar. Maybe that's what home will be until the day I dare to find home in a place not given to me out of economic necessity or bequeathed to me from birth. I think I am ready for that home. I think I am ready to surrender to a soundtrack I've never heard, a soundtrack I only imagine. But right now, I think I am ready to turn this bedtime music off, walk into my house, wash my hands, pray for Grandmama's continued health, and try again tomorrow.

Sometimes bedtime songs, like homes, are sad.

MLA CITATION

Laymon, Kiese. "Bedtime Songs." *The Norton Reader: An Anthology of Nonfiction*, edited by Melissa A. Goldthwaite et al., 16th ed., W. W. Norton, 2024, pp. 62–63.

QUESTIONS

1. Kiese Laymon considers different meanings of home in this short essay. Where does he seem to feel most at home? What kind of home does he hope to find? Mark passages in the essay that support your answer to these questions.

2. What words would you use to characterize the tone or mood of this essay? How does Laymon get that tone across?

3. Listen to some of the songs Laymon mentions. What effect does listening to the songs have? Does it add to your appreciation of the essay? Why?

4. In paragraph 4, Laymon writes that "bedtime songs, my body, and my truck are physical links between New York and Mississippi, between a home I was given and a home I made." Do you have any "bedtime songs" that make you feel less lonely and more at home? Create a playlist or soundtrack of your own.

2 | TRADITIONS

We can either emphasize those aspects of our traditions, religious or secular, that speak of hatred, exclusion, and suspicion *or* work with those that stress the interdependence and equality of all human beings.

—KAREN ARMSTRONG

What we eat and when, what we celebrate and how, whether we believe in and how we name a higher power, how we participate in or care about sports, what values we hold and judge others by—tradition shapes all these practices and more. Like many elements of life and living, traditions are neither a universal positive nor negative. They can strengthen bonds in families and groups, providing a sense of belonging, structure, and security. They can help transfer knowledge, beliefs, and values from elders to new generations. But sometimes following traditions can inhibit critical thinking or even perpetuate violence, justify discrimination and exclusion, or violate human rights. As Karen Armstrong—known for her writing on comparative religion—observes, humans can choose which aspects of tradition to emphasize or follow. We can value and pass on the traditions that help us live in harmony with others, and we can discard or seek to modify those that harm us or others.

The selections included in this chapter consider a range of traditions—some informed by religious beliefs (or a lack thereof); others built around seasons, places, or holidays; and still others created by groups of people and their cultures that have a history of experiencing violence and oppression. These categories, too, overlap through the writers' intersectional identities: Emily Fox Gordon, in "An Atheist's Lament," reflects on her experience of being raised by atheists, celebrating Christian holidays, and becoming aware of the anti-Semitism her Jewish father experienced and that still exists today. Anita Diamant writes about including an orange on the Passover seder plate in order to symbolize "Judaism's ability to adapt and thrive" through inclusion. Teresa Lust in "The Same Old Stuffing" and Annette Gordon-Reed in "On Juneteenth" provide both personal and historical contexts for American holidays and the ways in which they are celebrated.

What individuals and communities dream and hope for and work toward is often influenced by the experiences—both good and bad—that have shaped them and their ancestors. Gordon-Reed, Maya Angelou in "Graduation," and Hanif Abdurraqib in "Blood Summer, In Three Parts" show the ways Black culture has survived and thrived in the face of violent oppression through traditions of resistance, faith, and art. Taté Walker, in "The (Native) American Dream," profiles the work of two Indigenous women who use Native traditions and tribal knowledge to feed and house themselves and their community, educating others in the process. Other pieces included in this chapter (by A. Bartlett Giamatti,

E. B. White, and David Joy) consider the traditions of sports, places, and seasonal rituals linked to hope and positive memories, yet they also include an awareness of the inevitability of change and loss. Many of the essays in this chapter are personal narratives informed by historical research or, at least, an awareness of the past and its effects on the present and future. Together, they encourage readers to reflect on the many ways traditions shape individuals, groups, and societies.

As you read these selections, think about the traditions and histories that have informed your own life and experiences. Which ones have made you feel a sense of belonging or helped create a sense of meaning? Which ones support values you wish to embody and pass on? Are there traditions that have been harmful to you? Are there traditions you participate in that are harmful or exclusionary of others? Are there traditions you think should be revised, updated, or discarded? Are there ways you can, in the words of Karen Armstrong, emphasize aspects of traditions that "stress the interdependence and equality of all human beings"?

Emily Fox Gordon
An Atheist's Lament

MY MOTHER AND FATHER were witty, ambitious people, charter members of the postwar meritocratic elite. His background was Jewish, hers Presbyterian. He came from Philadelphia, where his father sold ladies' underwear, she from Winnetka, Illinois, where her father was a banker. Both my parents were atheists, not the angry, proselytizing kind that prevails in the current moment, but confident and serene. They met at Swarthmore.

I wouldn't call their marriage happy, but it was certainly strong. Especially in its early days, their united differences gave it a kind of hybrid vigor. My father had a clear, powerful mind, a natural gravitas, and a room-filling presence, attributes that took him far. After 15 years of teaching economics at Williams College, he was called to Washington, DC, to serve as an adviser to John F. Kennedy. Later, he was appointed budget director under Lyndon Johnson, and during the Nixon administration he became president of the Brookings Institution. My mother was pretty, clever, and multitalented. She brought her skills as cook, hostess, raconteuse, and thrifty household manager to the joint enterprise of furthering my father's career.

Of my father it could truly be said that he didn't look Jewish. He was tall and fair and spoke without an identifiable accent. In an era when few people were sophisticated about wine, he knew provenances and vintages. When young, he was athletic; as a Rhodes Scholar, he had played lacrosse. He never tried to hide his background, but Jews were rare on the Williams faculty—he was one of

Published in the American Scholar (2020), a magazine published by the Phi Beta Kappa Society.

the first to be hired there—and many people assumed he was as much a WASP as my mother. One who didn't, I later learned, was James Phinney Baxter III, the college president, who referred to my father and his colleague Emile Despres as "those two Jews."

Neither of my parents had grown up in an observant household; neither had been bequeathed belief. The relatives on the Jewish side of my family were resolutely secular. Though my maternal grandparents maintained their membership in the Presbyterian church, they kept their distance from faith. The only outwardly religious relative I recall on either side was my mother's brother Joseph, who was a deacon (or something) in his Minneapolis church. But he was also a Republican, which for my parents put him so far beyond the pale that in all my life I've met him only twice, the second time at my mother's funeral.

5   My parents replaced religion with a belief in reason and beauty. I suppose I shouldn't say "belief," because belief is, or can be, irrational. Perhaps I shouldn't even say "replaced," because that suggests they saw religion as an empty space that needed filling. But neither of my parents arrived at atheism by way of reaction. Instead, it was the frank realization of a secularizing tendency that had worked its way through generations of their respective families.

Atheism united them, but they differed in the backward-looking perspectives that underlay their shared nonbelief. My mother saw religion as a cultural artifact to be preserved by the enlightened generations that had evolved beyond it. My father, a rationalist and a universalist, regarded his Judaism as simply beside the point. Their separate attitudes reflected their personal differences, but also a famous asymmetry between the two religions. Christianity has a lot to preserve. Architecture, sacred art and music, the folk customs that have grown out of it over the centuries: these are just some of the items in the inventory of its great estate. Judaism has its own material culture, of course, but it carries far less baggage than Christianity. In its essence, it's about the word and the book, and is thus more portable.

"When we don't go to church," the old joke goes, "we don't go to the Episcopal church." My parents' versions of disbelief carried different flavors. My mother's was infused with affection and nostalgia, like a delicate tisane, whereas my father's characteristic exasperation gave his dismissiveness a distinctive pungency, like hoppy beer. But once again, the situation was not symmetrical. Belief is commonly considered more essential to Christianity than it is to Judaism. A Christian's sense of identity is tied up in it, or at least that used to be true. But Judaism has no catechism. An unbelieving Jew will remain a Jew by virtue of having been born one. There was nothing my father could do, short of conversion—perhaps not even that—to escape his identity, and much that he did inadvertently reinforced it. His devotion to thinking and reading was itself an element of his Jewishness, or so I later realized. Even though his text was not Torah but John Maynard Keynes, he spent his days in study, and that was a quintessentially Jewish occupation.

*

Except in connection with her duties as president of the local chapter of the League of Women Voters, my mother never attended church, and if there had been a synagogue in Williamstown, my father would never have set foot in it. Likewise, our family never observed the Jewish holidays or lit Sabbath candles. But there the nevers end, because we did celebrate Christmas, which was my mother's production and a major event. We three children sprayed pine cones with gold and silver paint and glued cotton beards on walnuts to make Santas. My mother sat at the piano banging out "It Came Upon a Midnight Clear" and "Hark! The Herald Angels Sing" from the *Fireside Book of Folk Songs* while we sang along full-heartedly. She played hymns as well, including "A Mighty Fortress," that supremely affirmative anthem of Protestantism, suitable for bellowing out at the top of one's lungs. I wonder: How did she expect us to sing that song in a secular spirit? It was like being spoon-fed, then forbidden to swallow.

On the last day of November, she handed out advent calendars. To pry open one stiff little cardboard door each December morning, finding within it the image of a symbolic favor—a glowing star, perhaps, or a rose blooming in snow—was a purer pleasure than unwrapping presents on the 25th, when all the calendar doors hung ajar and only the emptiness of Christmas afternoon awaited us.

At Easter my mother baked a cake in the shape of a lamb, and we children dyed eggs and hunted for jellybeans. I have an early memory of a bunch of daffodils in a glass vase at the center of her holiday dinner table: from my low vantage point their dark swollen stems, diagonally crossed beneath the water line, seemed more to the point than their trumpet-shaped blossoms. Even though we had only a muddled idea of Easter's significance, we understood that for all its bunnies and bonnets, it was not as easily secularized as Christmas. We knew enough to be made uneasy by that holiday's association of Christ's death agonies with the tender renewals of spring.

Beauty was everything to my mother. For my brother and sister and me, Christmas and Easter were occasions of great joy, but she made it clear that we were celebrating these holidays in a purely aesthetic spirit. We were not to believe. Belief was an error, an embarrassment, "tiresome," as she would have put it. She meant her gifts to stay wrapped in memory, not to be ripped open to reveal their meaning. To use them in the service of religious enthusiasm would amount to a kind of desecration, a violation of her canons of taste.

But perversely enough, I wanted to believe, or at least to know what belief meant. I thought I saw shapes moving behind the curtain of ritual, but was never quite able to make them out. For a while at age seven, I attended the local Congregational church by myself, hoping for a revelation. My father rolled his eyes at my folly, but my mother kept a poker face. She knew my interest wouldn't last, and it didn't. I had imagined standing among the adults in the pews, listening, but instead I was immediately placed in Sunday school, where the class collaborated on a mural of Children Around the World, painted in watercolors on brown butcher paper. My inchoate theological questions found no answers.

About my father's background we knew almost nothing. He was too busy marking blue books and running the political campaigns of local Democrats

10

to tell us much; he left these matters to my mother. The only clue he gave us—and I didn't see its cultural significance until much later—was his hobby of pickling Kirby cucumbers from my mother's garden. He kept them soaking in brine in a ceramic vat in the chilly pantry behind our kitchen. We ate a few while they were still half-processed and crisp; the rest stayed submerged until they were authentically limp and semitranslucent when sliced into spears, indistinguishable, I'd later discover, from the pickles served at Katz's in New York.

The little we learned about Jewish culture was conveyed to us not by my father but by our philosemitic and highly literary mother, who read aloud from Leo Rosten's *The Education of H*Y*M*A*N K*A*P*L*A*N*. We all loved those tales of that heroic immigrant from Kiev, enrolled in Mr. Parkhill's class at the American Night Preparatory School for Adults. I don't own the book anymore—it's been 60 years—but I remember by heart two of Hyman Kaplan's devastating bits of doggerel about his classmates:

> Mrs. Moskowitz
> By her it doesnt fits
> A dress—Size 44.

And—a masterpiece of literary economy:

> Bloom, Bloom
> Go out the room!

15   My mother read those lines in a creditable Yiddish accent. We knew they were funny and laughed accordingly, but for us Hyman Kaplan occupied the same faraway fictional universe as Ferdinand the Bull, lying under his cork tree in Seville. If she was using the book to teach us about our paternal heritage, it was a failed lesson, because how could Hyman Kaplan, with his marvelously revealing broken English, bear any relation to our gracefully assimilated father, with his years at Oxford and his knowledge of wine vintages?

I realize now that there was anti-Semitism in the Williamstown of the 1950s, even beyond that of the college president. Jews were not welcome in the Williams College fraternities in those days, and certainly some of the brothers—the ones who urinated out of windows and stuffed cats into washing machines—had just the attitudes one would expect. A certain venerable men's clothing store (which outfitted one of Bing Crosby's sons, newly arrived from California and shivering in a madras jacket) was a bastion of contempt for Jews and Catholics and anyone else not classifiable as WASP. We children were hardly aware of bias against Jews. How could we be, when we hardly knew what it was to be Jewish?

And how was it that we never learned about the death camps? In 1959, we were only 14 years past the liberation of Auschwitz. Our parents and teachers wouldn't have kept it from us deliberately. I suppose one explanation might be that the Holocaust hadn't yet come into full historical focus. Even so, it seems odd that there was nothing in the tone of the time to suggest that the catastrophe had happened at all. The postwar period was a particularly hopeful era, a time when a gifted second-generation Jewish academic like my father could find himself called to Washington by the newly inaugurated president.

*

When I was 12, my family moved to New York City, where my father went to work for the Ford Foundation. We were there for only six months before the call came from Kennedy, but during our Manhattan interval I learned more about the Jewish world. I got to know some of my father's relatives, particularly my great-aunt Helen, who operated a kind of family salon in her small high-rise apartment near Columbus Circle.

At that age, I was hard to have around. It must have come as a guilty relief to my mother to put me on the bus after school and send me to Helen's, where I was fed on demand and made much of by the crew gathered there. I remember some of them, like my great-uncle Abie (who was—exotically enough—a bookie), quite well. Others were elderly second and third cousins whom I could never keep straight. But it hardly mattered which batch of relatives happened to be parked on Helen's couch on any given afternoon; I always got the same wildly enthusiastic reception. Never before had so many faces been thrust into mine; never before had I been so insistently kissed and hugged and taken aside to be quizzed about my life. Such kind people! At that unhappy time in my life, they rescued me. I was a fat, awkward preadolescent, failing in school, so their *kvelling*[1] was necessarily limited in scope. Nevertheless, I was praised for my "charm," my vocabulary, and my hair, which was said to be as full of golden glints as the Breck Girl's.[2] I resisted this attention, squirmed and giggled and tried to edge away as children do when they're fussed over, but even then I knew how much I needed it. The memory of those afternoons at Helen's has warmed me ever since, like a heated stone in my pocket.

And later on—unlike either of my siblings—I married a Jew. My husband's parents were refugees from Hitler's Germany, tense, uncertain people very unlike my own self-assured parents and also quite different from my *haimish*,[3] demonstrative New York relatives. By the time I met them, they were wealthy and well dressed, but still displaced persons, forever carrying with them the troubled air of Europe. From them I gained a new, firsthand understanding of the Holocaust. My husband's father had lost his sister to the camps, and his mother had lost her parents. Both of them came to the United States haunted by grief and terror. They threw themselves into the project of establishing themselves here with an extraordinary energy—as if to save their lives and the lives of all their descendants.

20

1. Yiddish for "feeling or expressing pride in someone else or their accomplishments."
2. One of the teens and young women featured in Breck Shampoo advertisements.
3. Yiddish for "homey, folksy, unpretentious."

Early in my marriage, I attached my filial feelings, which I'd long since with-drawn from my own parents, to my husband's. I loved them for the dangers they had passed;[4] knowing them has made me painfully alert to the anti-Semitism that has been steadily reconstituting itself over the past 60 years. They accepted me in spite of my status as a half Jew, but when I became pregnant, my father-in-law prevailed on me to convert. This was necessary because the Halachic law of descent is matrilineal. It recognizes half Jews whose fathers are Gentiles, but not the half-Jewish children of Gentile mothers.

I had doubts about conversion, but I wanted to please my parents-in-law too much to admit them to myself. They had doubts too, though they hid them. My husband, who at that stage of his life was as impatient with religion as my father had been, wanted no part of the enterprise. Even the rabbi was doubtful. Judaism itself, I couldn't help observing, is deeply ambivalent about conversion. It does not reach out to embrace the convert, but allows itself, rather reluctantly, to be embraced. Why else would the conversion process call for three ritual discourage-ments? Even so, I fulfilled all the rabbi's requirements except for the postpartum ritual bath, the *mikveh*, which I put off for so long that I was embarrassed to return to his office. The conversion failed, but in the end it hardly mattered. My daughter's birth made me a member of the family, if not a member of the Tribe. Since then, I've lived in a Jewish world as a resident alien, a partisan but not a citizen.

*

I'm 72 now, in the midst of one of those reappraisals that seem to be the task of late life. Like my parents, I'm a lifelong atheist. I arrived at disbelief not through an exercise of reason—though I did do that—but because it was passed on to me as a family tradition. That's what made it stick, just as baptism sticks to a Baptist and Zoroastrianism to a Zoroastrian. It's atheism by default, far less confident than my parents' blithe and cheeky version, but seemingly inalien-able. My atheism doesn't mean, however, that I'm done with religion. Is any-one ever? Atheism doesn't eradicate it, only covers it, like a lost city—in my case two lost cities—buried under a mound of earth. I'm no more done with religion than I'm done with my parents, from whom I was estranged all my adult life and who have been dead for decades. Somehow I've managed to preserve inside myself the two religions in which they didn't believe—and in which I don't believe either—and to maintain these negatives in a precarious balance.

Friends have suggested that I make the most of my double heritage. Why not take advantage of the riches of both religions? Why not be both Christian *and* Jew? I know other half Jews who manage to do this, but I find I can't light the menorah even as I decorate the tree. Perhaps it's my mother's aesthetic influence: she wouldn't mix her metaphors that way. But I should give myself credit; in spite of my godless upbringing, I aspire to a certain seriousness about religion. To identify myself as both Christian and Jewish would be to acknowl-

---

4. In William Shakespeare's *Othello, the Moor of Venice* (1603), the titular character says that Desdemona "loved me for the dangers I had passed / and I loved her that she did pity them" (1.3.167–68).

edge that faith is only a set of cultural practices, and even though I don't believe, I want belief to be possible. Because I can't be both; I can only be neither. That's the tribute that my atheism pays to religion.

I must confess that in recent years I've developed a hankering for Chris- 25 tianity that threatens to upset this equilibrium. No doubt it has to do with age and the approach of the end of things. When I lift my eyes to the vaulted ceiling of a cathedral or listen to a Bach cantata, I feel a spiritual dilation. And when I sit at the dinner table of churchgoing friends who say grace, I feel like an anthropologist who has been studying a remote tribe and finds herself unexpectedly included in an arcane rite. I'm agog to observe that my neighbor Dave is talking to God, thanking him for the lasagna were about to eat.

Saying grace amounts only to the perfunctory mumbling of a few words, but the other people at the table would be amazed to know what a storm of contradictory feelings it raises in me. If their heads weren't bowed, they'd see that my eyes have welled up, but also that I'm smirking. My scorn is all too familiar a reaction—it's bred in the bone—but I'm also moved to tears by gratitude. The fact is, I envy Christians. I envy them the consolatory benefits to which their religion entitles them. Fellowship, for example: what would it be like to belong to a community in which everyone accepted me in spite of my sins—not in spite of, because? How would it feel to know that people pray for me?

I envy Christians their holidays, not just Christmas and Easter, but all the obscure feasts, remembrances, and days of repentance that mark the liturgical calendar. For an atheist the year is rather trackless. I envy them the narrative of Christ's birth, death, and resurrection, but more than that, I envy the smaller narratives that religion imposes on every Christian life. How absorbing, how *suspenseful* it would be to move through hours, days, and years with the conviction that what I do matters, that my small choices and responses to contingencies have moral meaning, that they will add up to a whole and that my life will be judged.

I envy these things, but I know quite well that I wouldn't last long as a Christian. Fellowship would soon turn suffocating, and how could I, who can no more pray than fly, pray for the people who pray for me? And while I might long for my life to be shaped by religion, I'm incapable of the belief that is a requirement for that privilege. The best I can do without it is to live by a godless code of ethics, and to accept the discouraging fact that nobody is keeping score.

My understanding of Christianity remains primitive and unevolved. For me, it's a glittering cargo cult, centered on a few remembered tokens, the repository of those transcendent, quasi-mystical sensations that are most intense in childhood. I'm really no more sophisticated about it than I was at age seven, when I presented myself at the Congregational church to be initiated into its mysteries.

On insomniac nights, I bring to mind the folkloric Mexican crèche that it 30 was my job to lay out on a mirrored tray every Christmas Eve. I remember the kneeling kine and the donkey and a cluster of rough-hewn figures representing townspeople, the men with their knees bent in supplication and their arms thrown up in benediction, the women curtseying deeply. I remember the Three Kings, each carrying a rough bundle to represent his gift of gold, frankincense, or myrrh. I remember the out-of-scale heroic angel, half-martial, half-maternal, presiding at the head of the cradle, her great wings unfurled. I can picture the lowered eyes and rosebud mouths of Mary and Joseph. How delicately their faces are painted, eyelashes individually rendered and cheeks glowing as if from within. But the infant Christ himself, lying on a tiny pallet of real straw, is shockingly rudimentary, nothing more than an armless, legless grub.

If I were to take a religious turn, it would be toward Christianity. But strait is the gate and narrow is the way.[5] In order to pass through, I'd have to shrink myself to the size of the child I was before I knew better than to believe. How would I do that, and what would be left of me?

MLA CITATION

Gordon, Emily Fox. "An Atheist's Lament." *The Norton Reader: An Anthology of Nonfiction*, edited by Melissa A. Goldthwaite et al., 16th ed., W. W. Norton, 2024, pp. 65–72.

QUESTIONS

1. What, for Emily Fox Gordon, is the relationship between cultural and religious traditions? What traditions shaped her?

2. Gordon is an atheist and the daughter of atheists. She writes, however, that "atheism doesn't eradicate [religion], only covers it, like a lost city—in my case two lost cities—buried under a mound of earth" (paragraph 23). What does she mean by this metaphor?

3. What relationship do you see between religious and cultural traditions? How have the traditions you experienced as a child shaped you? Are there some traditions you wish to carry into adulthood? Are there any you wish to discard? Why?

ANITA DIAMANT
The Orange on the Seder Plate

EVERY JEWISH FAMILY produces a unique version of the Passover seder—the big ritual meal of traditional foods, served after and amid liturgy, storytelling, and song. We're all surprised at each other's customs: You eat lamb? You don't sing "Chad Gad Ya"?

And yet, virtually every seder does share a few common elements. Matzoh crumbs all over the floor. Wine stains on the tablecloth. A seder plate containing the traditional symbols of the holiday: a roasted shank bone and hardboiled egg, recalling the days of the Temple sacrifices;

Published in Pitching My Tent: On Marriage, Motherhood, Friendship, and Other Leaps of Faith *(2003), Anita Diamant's collection of essays and reflections.*

5. From the Bible verse Matthew 7:14, "Because strait is the gate, and narrow is the way, which leadeth unto life, and few there be that find it."

horseradish and salt water for the bitterness of oppression; parsley for spring; *haroset,* a mixture of wine, nuts, and fruit symbolizing mortar and the heavy labor performed by the Israelite slaves.

And for lots of us, an orange.

The ancient Hebrews who fled into the wilderness didn't know from citrus fruit, and there certainly weren't any Valencias on Grandma's seder plate. Starting in the 1980s, the new holiday symbol has been showing up on an ever-increasing number of Passover tables.

The custom originated with the teacher and writer Susannah Heschel, who   5 first set it out as a symbol of inclusion for lesbian and gay Jews, and in following years for all those who have been marginalized in the Jewish community. Thanks largely to the Internet, Jewish women adopted the fruit as a symbol of their inclusion, and now there are oranges on seder plates all over the world, as well as alternative stories about how they got there in the first place.

Regardless of its genesis, that orange now makes several subtle spiritual and political statements. For one thing, it represents the creative piety of liberal Jews, who honor tradition by adding new elements to the old. The orange also announces that those on the margins have fully arrived as coauthors of Jewish history, as does the presence of another new ritual item, the Miriam's Cup, which acknowledges the role of Moses' sister, the singer-songwriter-prophet, in the story.

The orange is a living part of the ancient pedagogic strategy of Passover. We are commanded to teach our children about the Exodus from Egypt in a manner so vivid that everyone at the table—but especially the kids—remembers (not merely imagines but actually remembers) what it feels like to be a hungry, hunted slave. The seder makes memory manifest, tangible, and solid as Grandpa's kiddush cup.

Just like the shank bone, the orange is there so that someone under the age of thirteen will ask, "What's that thing doing on the seder plate?"

The orange is there so that Mom or Dad can say, "I'm so glad you asked that question. The orange is a symbol of the struggle by Jews who used to be ignored by our tradition—like gays and lesbians, and women, and Jews by choice—to become full partners in religious and community life. The orange is a sign of change, too, because now all kinds of Jews are rabbis and cantors and teachers and leaders. And the orange is a mark of our confidence in the Jewish future, which means that someday maybe you too will bring something new to the seder plate."

The orange on the seder plate is both a playful and a reverent symbol of   10 Judaism's ability to adapt and thrive. It also celebrates the abundant diversity of creation. After all, God, who made the heavens and the earth, and dinosaurs and lemurs and human beings, is clearly a lover of variety and change—not to mention oranges.

MLA CITATION

Diamant, Anita. "The Orange on the Seder Plate." *The Norton Reader: An Anthology of Nonfiction,* edited by Melissa A. Goldthwaite et al., 16th ed., W. W. Norton, 2024, pp. 72–73.

QUESTIONS

1. Why do some Jewish families include an orange on the Passover seder plate? Mark the passages in Anita Diamant's essay that support your answer. Why might other families not include an orange?

2. Diamant writes that an orange on the seder plate "makes several subtle spiritual and political statements" (paragraph 6). What other traditions—or changes to long-held traditions—in your life make such statements? What statements do they make?

3. Is there a tradition you currently follow or have followed that you would like to change? Detail the change you envision as specifically as possible. Can you think of a symbol, object, or practice that would help illustrate that change?

MAYA ANGELOU
Graduation

THE CHILDREN IN STAMPS[1] trembled visibly with anticipation. Some adults were excited too, but to be certain the whole young population had come down with graduation epidemic. Large classes were graduating from both the grammar school and the high school. Even those who were years removed from their own day of glorious release were anxious to help with preparations as a kind of dry run. The junior students who were moving into the vacating classes' chairs were tradition-bound to show their talents for leadership and management. They strutted through the school and around the campus exerting pressure on the lower grades. Their authority was so new that occasionally if they pressed a little too hard it had to be overlooked. After all, next term was coming, and it never hurt a sixth grader to have a play sister in the eighth grade, or a tenth-year student to be able to call a twelfth grader Bubba. So all was endured in a spirit of shared understanding. But the graduating classes themselves were the nobility. Like travelers with exotic destinations on their minds, the graduates were remarkably forgetful. They came to school without their books or tablets or even pencils. Volunteers fell over themselves to secure replacements for the missing equipment. When accepted, the willing workers might or might not be thanked, and it was of no importance to the pregraduation rites. Even teachers were respectful of the now quiet and aging seniors, and tended to speak to them, if not as equals, as beings only slightly lower than themselves. After tests were returned and grades given, the student body,

From I Know Why the Caged Bird Sings (1969), *the first volume of Maya Angelou's autobiography of growing up in a segregated Southern town. After its success, Angelou continued her life story in seven sequential volumes, ending with* Mom & Me & Mom (2013).

1. Town in Arkansas.

which acted like an extended family, knew who did well, who excelled, and what piteous ones had failed.

Unlike the white high school, Lafayette County Training School distinguished itself by having neither lawn, nor hedges, nor tennis court, nor climbing ivy. Its two buildings (main classrooms, the grade school and home economics) were set on a dirt hill with no fence to limit either its boundaries or those of bordering farms. There was a large expanse to the left of the school which was used alternately as a baseball diamond or basketball court. Rusty hoops on swaying poles represented the permanent recreational equipment, although bats and balls could be borrowed from the PE teacher if the borrower was qualified and if the diamond wasn't occupied.

Over this rocky area relieved by a few shady tall persimmon trees the graduating class walked. The girls often held hands and no longer bothered to speak to the lower students. There was a sadness about them, as if this old world was not their home and they were bound for higher ground. The boys, on the other hand, had become more friendly, more outgoing. A decided change from the closed attitude they projected while studying for finals. Now they seemed not ready to give up the old school, the familiar paths and classrooms. Only a small percentage would be continuing on to college—one of the South's A & M (agricultural and mechanical) schools, which trained Negro youths to be carpenters, farmers, handymen, masons, maids, cooks and baby nurses. Their future rode heavily on their shoulders, and blinded them to the collective joy that had pervaded the lives of the boys and girls in the grammar school graduating class.

Parents who could afford it had ordered new shoes and readymade clothes for themselves from Sears and Roebuck or Montgomery Ward. They also engaged the best seamstresses to make the floating graduating dresses and to cut down secondhand pants which would be pressed to a military slickness for the important event.

Oh, it was important, all right. Whitefolks would attend the ceremony, and two or three would speak of God and home, and the Southern way of life, and Mrs. Parsons, the principal's wife, would play the graduation march while the lower-grade graduates paraded down the aisles and took their seats below the platform. The high school seniors would wait in empty classrooms to make their dramatic entrance.

In the Store[2] I was the person of the moment. The birthday girl. The center. Bailey[3] had graduated the year before, although to do so he had had to forfeit all pleasures to make up for his time lost in Baton Rouge.

My class was wearing butter-yellow piqué dresses, and Momma launched out on mine. She smocked the yoke into tiny crisscrossing puckers, then shirred the rest of the bodice. Her dark fingers ducked in and out of the lemony cloth as she embroidered raised daisies around the hem. Before she considered herself finished she had added a crocheted cuff on the puff sleeves, and a pointy crocheted collar.

---

2. Owned by Angelou's grandmother, whom she and her brother called "Momma."
3. Angelou's brother.

I was going to be lovely. A walking model of all the various styles of fine hand sewing and it didn't worry me that I was only twelve years old and merely graduating from the eighth grade. Besides, many teachers in Arkansas Negro schools had only that diploma and were licensed to impart wisdom.

The days had become longer and more noticeable. The faded beige of former times had been replaced with strong and sure colors. I began to see my classmates' clothes, their skin tones, and the dust that waved off pussy willows. Clouds that lazed across the sky were objects of great concern to me. Their shiftier shapes might have held a message that in my new happiness and with a little bit of time I'd soon decipher. During that period I looked at the arch of heaven so religiously my neck kept a steady ache. I had taken to smiling more often, and my jaws hurt from the unaccustomed activity. Between the two physical sore spots, I suppose I could have been uncomfortable, but that was not the case. As a member of the winning team (the graduating class of 1940) I had outdistanced unpleasant sensations by miles. I was headed for the freedom of open fields.

10   Youth and social approval allied themselves with me and we trammeled memories of slights and insults. The wind of our swift passage remodeled my features. Lost tears were pounded to mud and then to dust. Years of withdrawal were brushed aside and left behind, as hanging ropes of parasitic moss.

My work alone had awarded me a top place and I was going to be one of the first called in the graduating ceremonies. On the classroom blackboard, as well as on the bulletin board in the auditorium, there were blue stars and white stars and red stars. No absences, no tardinesses, and my academic work was among the best of the year. I could say the preamble to the Constitution even faster than Bailey. We timed ourselves often: "We the people of the United States in order to form a more perfect union . . ." I had memorized the Presidents of the United States from Washington to Roosevelt in chronological as well as alphabetical order.

My hair pleased me too. Gradually the black mass had lengthened and thickened, so that it kept at last to its braided pattern, and I didn't have to yank my scalp off when I tried to comb it.

Louise and I had rehearsed the exercises until we tired out ourselves. Henry Reed was class valedictorian. He was a small, very black boy with hooded eyes, a long, broad nose and an oddly shaped head. I had admired him for years because each term he and I vied for the best grades in our class. Most often he bested me, but instead of being disappointed I was pleased that we shared top places between us. Like many Southern Black children, he lived with his grandmother, who was as strict as Momma and as kind as she knew how to be. He was courteous, respectful and soft-spoken to elders, but on the playground he chose to play the roughest games. I admired him. Anyone, I reckoned, sufficiently afraid or sufficiently dull could be polite. But to be able to operate at a top level with both adults and children was admirable.

His valedictory speech was entitled "To Be or Not to Be." The rigid tenth-grade teacher had helped him write it. He'd been working on the dramatic stresses for months.

The weeks until graduation were filled with heady activities. A group of small children were to be presented in a play about buttercups and daisies and bunny rabbits. They could be heard throughout the building practicing their hops and their little songs that sounded like silver bells. The older girls (non-graduates, of course) were assigned the task of making refreshments for the night's festivities. A tangy scent of ginger, cinnamon, nutmeg and chocolate wafted around the home economics building as the budding cooks made samples for themselves and their teachers.

In every corner of the workshop, axes and saws split fresh timber as the woodshop boys made sets and stage scenery. Only the graduates were left out of the general bustle. We were free to sit in the library at the back of the building or look in quite detachedly, naturally, on the measures being taken for our event.

Even the minister preached on graduation the Sunday before. His subject was, "Let your light so shine that men will see your good works and praise your Father, Who is in Heaven." Although the sermon was purported to be addressed to us, he used the occasion to speak to backsliders, gamblers and general ne'er-do-wells. But since he had called our names at the beginning of the service we were mollified.

Among Negroes the tradition was to give presents to children going only from one grade to another. How much more important this was when the person was graduating at the top of the class. Uncle Willie and Momma had sent away for a Mickey Mouse watch like Bailey's. Louise gave me four embroidered handkerchiefs. (I gave her crocheted doilies.) Mrs. Sneed, the minister's wife, made me an undershirt to wear for graduation, and nearly every customer gave me a nickel or maybe even a dime with the instruction "Keep on moving to higher ground," or some such encouragement.

Amazingly the great day finally dawned and I was out of bed before I knew it. I threw open the back door to see it more clearly, but Momma said, "Sister, come away from that door and put your robe on."

I hoped the memory of that morning would never leave me. Sunlight was itself young, and the day had none of the insistence maturity would bring it in a few hours. In my robe and barefoot in the backyard, under cover of going to see about my new beans, I gave myself up to the gentle warmth and thanked God that no matter what evil I had done in my life He had allowed me to live to see this day. Somewhere in my fatalism I had expected to die, accidentally, and never have the chance to walk up the stairs in the auditorium and grace-fully receive my hard-earned diploma. Out of God's merciful bosom I had won reprieve.

Bailey came out in his robe and gave me a box wrapped in Christmas paper. He said he had saved his money for months to pay for it. It felt like a box of chocolates, but I knew Bailey wouldn't save money to buy candy when we had all we could want under our noses.

He was as proud of the gift as I. It was a soft-leather-bound copy of a collection of poems by Edgar Allan Poe, or, as Bailey and I called him, "Eap." I turned to "Annabel Lee" and we walked up and down the garden rows, the cool dirt between our toes, reciting the beautifully sad lines.

Momma made a Sunday breakfast although it was only Friday. After we finished the blessing, I opened my eyes to find the watch on my plate. It was a dream of a day. Everything went smoothly and to my credit, I didn't have to be reminded or scolded for anything. Near evening I was too jittery to attend to chores, so Bailey volunteered to do all before his bath.

Days before, we had made a sign for the Store, and as we turned out the lights Momma hung the cardboard over the doorknob. It read clearly: CLOSED. GRADUATION.

25   My dress fitted perfectly and everyone said that I looked like a sunbeam in it. On the hill, going toward the school, Bailey walked behind with Uncle Willie, who muttered, "Go on, Ju." He wanted him to walk ahead with us because it embarrassed him to have to walk so slowly. Bailey said he'd let the ladies walk together, and the men would bring up the rear. We all laughed, nicely.

Little children dashed by out of the dark like fireflies. Their crepe-paper dresses and butterfly wings were not made for running and we heard more than one rip, dryly, and the regretful "uh uh" that followed.

The school blazed without gaiety. The windows seemed cold and unfriendly from the lower hill. A sense of ill-fated timing crept over me, and if Momma hadn't reached for my hand I would have drifted back to Bailey and Uncle Willie, and possibly beyond. She made a few slow jokes about my feet getting cold, and tugged me along to the now-strange building.

Around the front steps, assurance came back. There were my fellow "greats," the graduating class. Hair brushed back, legs oiled, new dresses and pressed pleats, fresh pocket handkerchiefs and little handbags, all homesewn. Oh, we were up to snuff, all right. I joined my comrades and didn't even see my family go in to find seats in the crowded auditorium.

The school band struck up a march and all classes filed in as had been rehearsed. We stood in front of our seats, as assigned, and on a signal from the choir director, we sat. No sooner had this been accomplished than the band started to play the national anthem. We rose again and sang the song, after which we recited the pledge of allegiance. We remained standing for a brief minute before the choir director and the principal signaled to us, rather desperately I thought, to take our seats. The command was so unusual that our carefully rehearsed and smooth-running machine was thrown off. For a full minute we fumbled for our chairs and bumped into each other awkwardly. Habits change or solidify under pressure, so in our state of nervous tension we had been ready to follow our usual assembly pattern: the American national anthem, then the pledge of allegiance, then the song every Black person I knew called the Negro National Anthem. All done in the same key, with the same passion and most often standing on the same foot.

30   Finding my seat at last, I was overcome with a presentiment of worse things to come. Something unrehearsed, unplanned, was going to happen, and we were going to be made to look bad. I distinctly remember being explicit in the choice of pronoun. It was "we," the graduating class, the unit, that concerned me then.

The principal welcomed "parents and friends" and asked the Baptist minister to lead us in prayer. His invocation was brief and punchy, and for a second

I thought we were getting on the high road to right action. When the principal came back to the dais, however, his voice had changed. Sounds always affected me profoundly and the principal's voice was one of my favorites. During assembly it melted and lowed weakly into the audience. It had not been in my plan to listen to him, but my curiosity was piqued and I straightened up to give him my attention.

He was talking about Booker T. Washington, our "late great leader," who said we can be as close as the fingers on the hand, etc. . . . Then he said a few vague things about friendship and the friendship of kindly people to those less fortunate than themselves. With that his voice nearly faded, thin, away. Like a river diminishing to a stream and then to a trickle. But he cleared his throat and said, "Our speaker tonight, who is also our friend, came from Texarkana to deliver the commencement address, but due to the irregularity of the train schedule, he's going to, as they say, 'speak and run.'" He said that we understood and wanted the man to know that we were most grateful for the time he was able to give us and then something about how we were willing always to adjust to another's program, and without more ado—"I give you Mr. Edward Donleavy."

Not one but two white men came through the door off-stage. The shorter one walked to the speaker's platform, and the tall one moved to the center seat and sat down. But that was our principal's seat, and already occupied. The dislodged gentleman bounced around for a long breath or two before the Baptist minister gave him his chair, then with more dignity than the situation deserved, the minister walked off the stage.

Donleavy looked at the audience once (on reflection, I'm sure that he wanted only to reassure himself that we were really there), adjusted his glasses and began to read from a sheaf of papers.

He was glad "to be here and to see the work going on just as it was in the other schools." 35

At the first "Amen" from the audience I willed the offender to immediate death by choking on the word. But Amens and Yes, sirs began to fall around the room like rain through a ragged umbrella.

He told us of the wonderful changes we children in Stamps had in store. The Central School (naturally, the white school was Central) had already been granted improvements that would be in use in the fall. A well-known artist was coming from Little Rock to teach art to them. They were going to have the newest microscopes and chemistry equipment for their laboratory. Mr. Donleavy didn't leave us long in the dark over who made these improvements available to Central High. Nor were we to be ignored in the general betterment scheme he had in mind.

He said that he had pointed out to people at a very high level that one of the first-line football tacklers at Arkansas Agricultural and Mechanical College had graduated from good old Lafayette County Training School. Here fewer Amens were heard. Those few that did break through lay dully in the air with the heaviness of habit.

He went on to praise us. He went on to say how he had bragged that "one of the best basketball players at Fisk sank his first ball right here at Lafayette County Training School."

40   The white kids were going to have a chance to become Galileos and
        Madame Curies and Edisons and Gauguins, and our boys (the girls weren't even
        in on it) would try to be Jesse Owenses and Joe Louises.
            Owens and the Brown Bomber were great heroes in our world, but what
        school official in the white-goddom of Little Rock had the right to decide that
        those two men must be our only heroes? Who decided that for Henry Reed to
        become a scientist he had to work like George Washington Carver, as a boot-
        black, to buy a lousy microscope? Bailey was obviously always going to be too
        small to be an athlete, so which concrete angel glued to what country seat had
        decided that if my brother wanted to become a lawyer he had to first pay pen-
        ance for his skin by picking cotton and hoeing corn and studying correspon-
        dence books at night for twenty years?
            The man's dead words fell like bricks around the auditorium and too
        many settled in my belly. Constrained by hard-learned manners I couldn't
        look behind me, but to my left and right the proud graduating class of 1940
        had dropped their heads. Every girl in my row had found something new to
        do with her handkerchief. Some folded the tiny squares into love knots, some
        into triangles, but most were wadding them, then pressing them flat on their
        yellow laps.
            On the dais, the ancient tragedy was being replayed. Professor Parsons sat,
        a sculptor's reject, rigid. His large, heavy body seemed devoid of will or will-
        ingness, and his eyes said he was no longer with us. The other teachers exam-
        ined the flag (which was draped stage right) or their notes, or the windows which
        opened on our now-famous playing diamond.
            Graduation, the hush-hush magic time of frills and gifts and congratula-
        tions and diplomas, was finished for me before my name was called. The accom-
        plishment was nothing. The meticulous maps, drawn in three colors of ink,
        learning and spelling decasyllabic words, memorizing the whole of *The Rape
        of Lucrece*[4]—it was for nothing. Donleavy had exposed us.
45   We were maids and farmers, handymen and washerwomen, and anything
        higher that we aspired to was farcical and presumptuous.
            Then I wished that Gabriel Prosser and Nat Turner[5] had killed all white-
        folks in their beds and that Abraham Lincoln had been assassinated before the
        signing of the Emancipation Proclamation, and that Harriet Tubman[6] had been
        killed by that blow on her head and Christopher Columbus had drowned in the
        Santa Maria.
            It was awful to be a Negro and have no control over my life. It was brutal
        to be young and already trained to sit quietly and listen to charges brought

4. A 1,855-line narrative poem (1594) by the playwright William Shakespeare (1564–
1616) that recounts the story of the daughter of a Roman prefect. When she was
defiled, she stabbed herself in the presence of her father and her husband.
5. Prosser (c. 1776–1800) and Turner (1800–1831) were executed for leading rebellions
of enslaved and free Black people in Virginia.
6. Black abolitionist (c. 1822–1913) known for her work on the Underground Railroad,
which brought enslaved people to free states through a network of secret routes.

against my color with no chance of defense. We should all be dead. I thought I should like to see us all dead, one on top of the other. A pyramid of flesh with the whitefolks on the bottom, as the broad base, then the Indians with their silly tomahawks and teepees and wigwams and treaties, the Negroes with their mops and recipes and cotton sacks and spirituals sticking out of their mouths. The Dutch children should all stumble in their wooden shoes and break their necks. The French should choke to death on the Louisiana Purchase (1803) while silkworms ate all the Chinese with their stupid pigtails. As a species, we were an abomination. All of us.

Donleavy was running for election, and assured our parents that if he won we could count on having the only colored paved playing field in that part of Arkansas. Also—he never looked up to acknowledge the grunts of acceptance— also, we were bound to get some new equipment for the home economics building and the workshop.

He finished, and since there was no need to give any more than the most perfunctory thank-you's, he nodded to the men on the stage, and the tall white man who was never introduced joined him at the door. They left with the atti- tude that now they were off to something really important. (The graduation ceremonies at Lafayette County Training School had been a mere preliminary.)

The ugliness they left was palpable. An uninvited guest who wouldn't leave.   50 The choir was summoned and sang a modern arrangement of "Onward, Chris- tian Soldiers," with new words pertaining to graduates seeking their place in the world. But it didn't work. Elouise, the daughter of the Baptist minister, recited "Invictus,"[7] and I could have cried at the impertinence of "I am the master of my fate, I am the captain of my soul."

My name had lost its ring of familiarity and I had to be nudged to go and receive my diploma. All my preparations had fled. I neither marched up to the stage like a conquering Amazon, nor did I look in the audience for Bailey's nod of approval. Marguerite Johnson, I heard the name again, my honors were read, there were noises in the audience of appreciation, and I took my place on the stage as rehearsed.

I thought about colors I hated: ecru, puce, lavender, beige and black.

There was shuffling and rustling around me, then Henry Reed was giving his valedictory address, "To Be or Not to Be." Hadn't he heard the whitefolks? We couldn't *be*, so the question was a waste of time. Henry's voice came out clear and strong. I feared to look at him. Hadn't he got the message? There was no "nobler in the mind" for Negroes because the world didn't think we had minds, and they let us know it. "Outrageous fortune"? Now, that was a joke. When the ceremony was over I had to tell Henry Reed some things. That is, if I still cared. Not "rub," Henry, "erase." "Ah, there's the erase." Us.

Henry had been a good student in elocution. His voice rose on tides of promise and fell on waves of warnings. The English teacher had helped him to create a sermon winging through Hamlet's soliloquy. To be a man, a doer, a

7. Inspirational poem (1888) by William Ernest Henley that was once very popular for graduation ceremonies.

builder, a leader, or to be a tool, an unfunny joke, a crusher of funky toadstools. I marveled that Henry could go through with the speech as if we had a choice.

55   I had been listening and silently rebutting each sentence with my eyes closed; then there was a hush, which in an audience warns that something unplanned is happening. I looked up and saw Henry Reed, the conservative, the proper, the A student, turn his back to the audience and turn to us (the proud graduating class of 1940) and sing, nearly speaking,

> "Lift ev'ry voice and sing
> Till earth and heaven ring
> Ring with the harmonies of Liberty . . ."

It was the poem written by James Weldon Johnson. It was the music composed by J. Rosamond Johnson. It was the Negro national anthem. Out of habit we were singing it.

Our mothers and fathers stood in the dark hall and joined the hymn of encouragement. A kindergarten teacher led the small children onto the stage and the buttercups and daisies and bunny rabbits marked time and tried to follow:

> "Stony the road we trod
> Bitter the chastening rod
> Felt in the days when hope, unborn, had died.
> Yet with a steady beat
> Have not our weary feet
> Come to the place for which our fathers sighed?"

Each child I knew had learned that song with his ABC's and along with "Jesus Loves Me This I Know." But I personally had never heard it before. Never heard the words, despite the thousands of times I had sung them. Never thought they had anything to do with me.

On the other hand, the words of Patrick Henry had made such an impression on me that I had been able to stretch myself tall and trembling and say, "I know not what course others may take, but as for me, give me liberty or give me death."

And now I heard, really for the first time:

> "We have come over a way that with tears
> has been watered,
> We have come, treading our path through
> the blood of the slaughtered."

60   While echoes of the song shivered in the air, Henry Reed bowed his head, said "Thank you," and returned to his place in the line. The tears that slipped down many faces were not wiped away in shame.

We were on top again. As always, again. We survived. The depths had been icy and dark, but now a bright sun spoke to our souls. I was no longer simply a member of the proud graduating class of 1940; I was a proud member of the wonderful, beautiful Negro race.

Oh, Black known and unknown poets, how often have your auctioned pains sustained us? Who will compute the lonely nights made less lonely by your songs, or the empty pots made less tragic by your tales?

If we were a people much given to revealing secrets, we might raise monuments and sacrifice to the memories of our poets, but slavery cured us of that weakness. It may be enough, however, to have it said that we survive in exact relationship to the dedication of our poets (include preachers, musicians and blues singers).

MLA CITATION

Angelou, Maya. "Graduation." *The Norton Reader: An Anthology of Nonfiction*, edited by Melissa A. Goldthwaite et al., 16th ed., W. W. Norton, 2024, pp. 74–83.

QUESTIONS

1. Presumably, all of Maya Angelou's readers would have witnessed a graduation ceremony and brought their memories to her essay. As you read, mark the passages where she fulfills the readers' expectations for what a graduation includes. How does she also surprise us with details we may not expect?

2. In paragraph 43, Angelou writes that "the ancient tragedy was being replayed." What does she mean? How does her essay help to resist the tragic script?

3. Write a personal essay about a tradition or an event that you anticipated hopefully but that did not fulfill your expectations, incorporating an explanation of your disappointment into your account, as Angelou does. If you have photos that illustrate your experience or expectations, include those as well.

HANIF ABDURRAQIB
Blood Summer, In Three Parts.

I. A Black Jesus On Stained Glass: 16th Street And The Necessity Of The Black Church

> It is only when we are within the walls of our churches that we are wholly ourselves, that we keep alive a sense of our personalities in relation to the total world in which we live.
>
> —Richard Wright

THE BLACK CHURCHES WHERE I COME FROM ARE still standing. Most of them around my old neighborhood are toying with the idea of collapse, worn down by the type of hard use that only a Black church can endure. The foundations lean from years of the stomp,

Published in Hanif Abdurraqib's They Can't Kill Us Until They Kill Us *(2017), an essay collection on music and culture.*

the clap, the holler. Paint is peeling back from the walls where a picture of Black Jesus hangs, often crooked, but still smiling.

I say this to point out that I don't know what a church on fire looks like. I've never had to walk past what used to be a Black church and see a pile of smoldering bricks, or smell the wood still burning from whatever is left of the old piano. I get to write about the Black church without knowing a neighborhood afraid to go to one.

Like most people, when I think of the 16th Street Baptist Church bombing, I think of Addie Mae Collins, Cynthia Wesley, Carole Robertson, and Denise McNair. I think of the 22 injured, some who never fully recovered from their injuries. I think of Reverend John Cross Jr., who in 2001 recalled how the girls' bodies were found, stacked on top of each other, clinging to each other for dear life.

Though the church holds ceremonies for our dead, no one goes to church to die. I know that which makes the Black church a sacred thing also makes it a thing that is feared. The African Methodist Episcopal Church (AME) was founded by Rev. Richard Allen in 1816 Philadelphia, formed from Black Methodist congregations along the Atlantic, eager for independence from white Methodists. Still, during America's decades of slavery, nothing shook white slave owners more than Black religious meetings. Prayer meetings and religious movements of slaves were closely watched by slave owners, some slaves were whipped if they prayed to Jesus. After emancipation, Black Americans in the South built sanctuaries of their own as a way to find refuge in a country that still didn't feel like the Promised Land. The greatest mission of the Black church, historically, has been to care for the spiritual needs of Black people, with the understanding that since the inception of the American church, the spiritual needs of Black people have been assigned a different tone, a different urgency. It is the difference in looking out on a land that you believe is yours, and a land that you were taken to, forced to build.

5   During the civil rights era, Black churches served as holy ground. A place where Black organizers could meet, strategize, pray, and give thanks. The organization of Black resistance has always sparked white fear, never greater than when violent bigots see a building where Black people are praying to the same God that they do, and doing it with so much fire, so little worry. When a place like this also becomes a base of power for social and political movement, it becomes a target. Taylor Branch, a historian of the Civil Rights Movement, once estimated that from 1954 to 1968, there was a church bombed almost every week. During the freedom summer of 1964, it is estimated that a bombing happened every other day.

The thing that we do on a day like this, where history arrives and reminds us of who it has buried, is that we look back and think about turning points. How a monumental day of violence changed everything that came after it. What hurts me the most is that we don't get to do that here. We do get to mourn Addie Mae, Cynthia, Carole, and Denise in the best way that we can. We do get to reflect on what it means to live in a world where little girls can get dressed up to go to church and not make it out alive. But there isn't the satisfaction of knowing that we live in a world where this could never happen again.

In the mid-'90s, 59 Black churches burned, mostly in the South, leading then-president Bill Clinton to sign the Church Arson Prevention Act. But churches still burned. The Black church was still a target. In the summer of 2015, Dylann Roof walked into the Emanuel African Methodist Episcopal Church in Charleston and unloaded a handgun. In the days following, six Black churches were damaged or destroyed. I imagine this to feel like the whip being taken to the back of any Black community that dares pray to the same Jesus as its white counterparts. When the fear of death is omnipresent, when it has followed you into houses of worship for as long as you've known how to say a prayer, praying becomes an act of immense urgency. To be Black and know how sacred this is, to see a whole history of your sanctuaries burned to the ground, or covered in the blood of your brothers and sisters, it demands you to give yourself over to a loud and eager prayer. One that echoes through an entire week, until you are called back again. The Black church, where we can do this without apology, without the politeness of anxiety. Yes, be loud, and free, and rattle the walls with song. Yes, clap, and stomp, and sweat on whomever you must. Yes, leave baptized and clean. Yes, survive another week and pray for another.

When the 16th Street Baptist Church was rebuilt and reopened in 1964, it did so with a new stained glass window. The Wales Window depicts a Black Christ with his arms outstretched, his right arm pushing away injustice, his left arm extended in an offering of forgiveness. There is a replica of this window in a church near my old neighborhood in Columbus, Ohio. It is said to be inspired by a verse from the gospel of Matthew: "Truly, I say to you, as you did it to one of the least of these my brothers, you did it to me." I think about the image often, though not of the Black Christ. I think about that expectation, to hold off injustice with one arm while still consistently offering forgiveness with the other. I think about how often that is what Blackness in America amounts to. Even when grandmothers are burying their children, and their children's children. What forgiveness looks like when there are still churches being blown apart, still Black bodies who arrived to pray, and ended up murdered.

When the right arm is reaching into a fire to push away decades of injustice that still presents itself, how long before the whole body is engulfed in flames?

I don't know what a community does when it has no more forgiveness left, or when it knows what forgiveness in this age truly means. I don't know how a country can forgive itself for the deaths of those four sweet girls in 1963, just as I don't know how it can forgive itself for the consistent assault on Black sanctuaries ever since. Still, as thankful as I am to come from hands that still reach out for forgiveness, I am even more thankful to come from a people who know the necessity of rebuilding. Who know what a church does, know how to drink all they can from it, and refuse to let it be torn from them.

II. ANOTHER ROPE, A NEWER CITY: THE LEGACY OF IDA B. WELLS AND THE DEATH OF SANDRA BLAND

> Our country's national crime is lynching. It is not the creature
> of an hour, the sudden outburst of uncontrolled fury, or the
> unspeakable brutality of an insane mob.
>
> —IDA B. WELLS

What makes the dead body worthwhile is that it was once living. It is true that in every instance of Black death, we adorn the dead body with its accomplishments. We name the people who loved the person who was once alive. We look for the pictures where they once smiled into the sun, their camera turned on their own face. And we do this, consistently and loudly, because we have to. Because we have seen enough death to know what untruths feed on a body at rest. I say this to illustrate the point that I do not want to talk about Sandra Bland[1] getting her dream job, or the joy that seemed to fill her life before she lost it. I want to speak plainly about the hanging of Black bodies from anything in this country strong enough to hold them. It took three men to remove Ida B. Wells from a train car in 1884, and for his trouble, one of them got her teeth marks in his arm. She should have never been asked to move from her seat to the smoking car of the train and she knew this. She measured the fight and took it on.

This is my favorite story about Ida B. Wells' life. It's the one that will show up first when you click on a *Google* doodle, and I tell it to someone every year on the day of her birth. It makes sense to tell the story every July 16th. I like to think that Ida B. Wells always knew what we see so clearly now. When Black men die, they live on, almost forever. When Black women vanish, they often simply vanish. When enough outlets tell you that your life is an exercise in rehearsing invisibility, when you become invisible, it just seems like you're performing the grand closing act. I admire the work of Ida B. Wells, of course. But more than that, I admire her consistent refusal of silence. It is present in all of us, I believe. But I become most inspired when I see it in Black women. I come from a long line of Black women who spoke, who moved with authority—direct descendants of The School of Wells.

It took two men to arrest Sandra Bland on the side of a road last week. One was holding her firm to the ground while she cried out in pain and, perhaps, fear. We are to believe that she assaulted one of the men, though we do not see it. We so rarely do. We are to believe that Sandra Bland was hanged three days later, though we are not clear on how her body was fixed to a metal bar, or what was used to hang it. But we are to believe that it hanged, nonetheless. We are to believe that this was due to a traffic stop. We are to believe that she was planning a bright future. We are to know that it will not exist.

It is impossible to even mention America's history of lynching without mentioning the woman who fought most fervently to dismantle it at a time when

1. A twenty-eight-year-old Black woman pulled over for a traffic violation in 2015, she was arrested and jailed after an escalating argument with State Trooper Brian Encinia. Three days later, she was found dead in her jail cell. Her death was ruled a suicide.

men were being dragged from their homes and hanged for not paying debts or being too drunk in public places. Or, in other cases, for displeasing law enforcement. There is sacrifice in that. In being a Black woman who fights and is alive at any time in this country's history is a sacrifice. It can still get you a death sentence, though the knife is fashioned differently. When Ida B. Wells couldn't go home to Philadelphia, she fought in Chicago. When the mobs came for her in Chicago, she went to England. And like so many Black women, she fought and lived and loved a family and built a home and wrote and pushed to the front when the front did not want her there. And she did not want to stop the fight until more Black women had room of their own, until Black men stopped being hanged from trees.

But Ida B. Wells died an unceremonious death in 1931 and we are to believe 15 that Sandra Bland hanged from a jail cell on a summer day in 2015. It was the failure of kidneys that took Wells at age 68, not any of the violent mobs, their whetted teeth shining against the moon. I write about Wells today, how much she hated the rope, the Black bodies left hanging in the South. And I write about Sandra Bland today, the all-too-familiar death, the dead body that this country has come to know, the one that we write about even when we are not writing about it. And my hands can't help but shake. I don't know anything more about Sandra Bland than anyone else, other than the fact that I want her life to be one that is not forgotten. I want us to honor the living Black women who fight and I want us to fight for the Black women who no longer have the honor of living. I want us to respect the legacies that were remarkable by virtue of boundary-pushing and I want us to respect the legacies that were remarkable by virtue of being alive and loved. I want these statements to not be "brave," or "unique." I want them to be expected.

III. ON BLACK GRANDMOTHERS AND THE ART OF DYING ON YOUR OWN TERMS

During the time in my life when my grandmother was still living and wholly present, I rarely recall her smelling of anything other than smoke. She smoked More cigarettes, a brand that currently can only be purchased online (and, I'm told, at a few corner stores in the Florida Panhandle). More cigarettes were mostly notable because they used brown paper to wrap the tobacco instead of the traditional white paper that most cigarettes use. My grandmother seemed to always have her thin brown fingers wrapped around a stick of thin brown paper, so often that on some days it seemed like the smoke was rising from her hands all on its own. If she needed to get into her purse for any reason, she often had to sift through a graveyard of emptied red and green packs of cigarettes, cursing under her breath the whole time. The smell of them, though, was distinct. I had no language for it as a child, sitting outside of her room and breathing it in while watching her watch *Supermarket Sweep* in the evening, or watching her watch some soap opera during the summer days when school was out. I found myself not even having language for it as it lingered on my clothing after a good hug. It wasn't until years later, while taking a road trip through the South in my early 20s, that I could name it. In South Carolina, after a hard rain, I walked through an old plantation. And it was the smell descending from the trees after they made room for the storm. A humble attempt at forgiveness.

Almost every Black grandmother I know smokes. I once hugged a friend's grandmother while she was holding a cigarette, and it burned a mark onto my t-shirt. After which she took a long drag, looked me up and down and said, "You gotta watch that, honey." I have known some who put out their cigarettes, look down at them with disgust, and say, "I swear, I'm gonna quit one of these days," which we understand to mean, "I swear, I'm gonna die one of these days." My particular Black generation is the one who, if they are lucky, have two (or more, in some cases) generations of living women that survived despite being pressed up against all manner of relentless tragedy. It's why we laugh at the stories of the grandmother who takes no shit, but we know not to laugh too long. It is the unspoken fear, the unspoken knowledge of what many of these women gave. We know that if the officer's gun didn't kill them, and poverty's hunger didn't kill them, and the violence of marginalized and silenced Black men didn't kill them, there is no measure of swallowed smoke that will shake them free of the earth quickly and easily.

There is pretty much no violence in this country that can be divorced from this country's history. It is an uneasy conversation to approach, especially now, as we are asked to "behave" in the midst of another set of Black bodies left hollow. The Southern Black church has always been a battleground in this history of violence. Most notably, of course, during the Freedom Summer of 1964, but even beyond. The church, if we are to believe that it still exists for this purpose, is a space of ultimate humbling and vulnerability. In the South, the Black church is also a place of fear. To attack the innocent where they feel most secure is cowardly, of course, but it is also a reminder. There is no safety from this. There will be no reprieve from the sickness that spreads and calls people to take up this level of violence. There will be no calm before the storm. There will only be the storm, and then another, louder storm. It will follow you to your homes, press itself between your sleeping children, hang over your shoulders at work, and yes, it will walk into your church, pray to the same God as you do, and then stand up and open fire. There is no way to talk about this without talking about the history of instilling fear in Black people in this country. Without closing our eyes and feeling the warmth from a flaming cross. Or smelling a wet body, limp and descending from a Southern plantation tree.

The weight of this tragedy hung over me on the day after the Charleston shooting. I slept two restless hours in an Ohio hotel, spending most of my time rolling over to scroll through news feeds and news stories. I mostly thought of grandmothers. I thought of the grandmother who told her 5-year-old granddaughter to play dead so that the killer would pass her over. So that she might live long enough to see her name grow fresh in the mouth of someone she loves. It is impossible for me to imagine that this is the world we live in. One where Black girls must learn to play dead before they learn to play the dozens.[2] But it is not impossible for me to imagine what her grandmother has lived through. What she knew that we did not. Survival is truly a language in which the Black matriarch is fluent. Much like this country's violence, there is no survival in this country that can be divorced from this country's history. A grandmother who has maybe stared down death more than once, passing that burden on to the child of her child. I don't know if there is a name for what it is when you are moved to praise something as impossibly sad as this. I don't know if it can be found in a church, even as a little girl is not among the dead inside of it. I imagine that I am writing this because I don't know these answers. I think of this child growing up and knowing what it is to escape death. Wrapping herself in the trauma of that. Knowing at such a young age that to be a Black woman in America is, in a way, to feel like you will survive until you decide to stop surviving.

But, the Black people who pray still must pray. In a good Black church, all   20
manner of sweat, holler, and joy lives in the walls. I'm not sure what it is to set foot in a place of worship where you saw members of your community fighting against an inevitable death. I imagine that to be impossible. I prayed last night in a hotel bathroom. Like many of us, nothing draws me to prayer quicker than desperation. Not knowing what to do with my hands, my heart, or my mind. Sometimes, I don't even know what I'm praying for. Last night, I think I prayed for a Southern Black church that didn't also smell of smoke, of cooked flesh. Where the memories weren't of burial. Where Black children could fall asleep in the front row, their small bodies still, but breathing.

My grandmother began to smoke more as she got older. When she moved to her own apartment, down the street from my childhood house, I'd visit and see empty packs of More cigarettes littering the table. Occasionally, when she'd tell me that she was thinking of quitting, I never knew if she meant the cigarettes. I'm not sure that she ever stopped, though I don't imagine she did. She died in the South, in Alabama. I don't know what smell rises off of the trees there after a storm, but I like to imagine that it's the same smell that is rising in South Carolina today. The way I'd like to imagine it, our grandmothers are with us, even when they're not with us. Teaching us how to pray. Teaching us how to survive.

MLA CITATION

Abdurraqib, Hanif. "Blood Summer, In Three Parts." *The Norton Reader: An Anthology of Nonfiction*, edited by Melissa A. Goldthwaite et al., 16th ed., W. W. Norton, 2024, pp. 83–89.

QUESTIONS

1. As you read "Blood Summer, In Three Parts," note the passages in which Hanif Abdurraqib mentions fire or smoke. Why are the references significant? How are they similar or different? What does smoke represent in this essay?

_____

2. A game of verbal play, in Black culture, that involves exchanging insults.

2. Abdurraqib weaves together several themes in this essay: racist violence, the Black church, Black women, resistance, survival, and prayer. Consider the structure he uses. How does each of the three parts contribute to the message and effect of the essay, developing one or more of the themes?

3. Abdurraqib references many instances of racist violence. Research one of the events he references and its aftermath. What do you think can and should be done to prevent such violence in the future? What successful (or unsuccessful) preventative actions have been taken by lawmakers, protestors, and activists? With your classmates, brainstorm a list of meaningful actions that can be taken in the future.

ANNETTE GORDON-REED
On Juneteenth

I CAN'T LISTEN TO THE SONG "GALVESTON" without thinking about my great-grandparents on my mother's side. That wasn't always true. When I first heard Glen Campbell's version of the song in 1969, I liked it immediately—the plaintive tone, Campbell's guitar, Jimmy Webb's wistful and poignant lyrics about a young man, a soldier in Vietnam thinking about his hometown and the young girl he left behind. There would have been no obvious reason for me to have connected the story told in that record to my great-grandparents, an African-American couple living on a cotton farm outside of Moscow, Texas, during the first two decades of the twentieth century. One of the tests of a great song or poem—any work of art, really—is its capacity to touch different people in different ways across time. That is a cliché, but like all clichés, it contains a basic truth.

My great-grandfather died before I was born. My great-grandmother lived until I was eleven. Though she was sharp-minded up until she drew her final breath, I was too young to see her as the immensely valuable resource she was. She could have told me about her life in Texas from the final two decades of the nineteenth century and into the twentieth—that would have been the very expression of "change over time," the heart of a historian's work. And what she could have told me about the things she had learned from her mother, who had been born in Mississippi, and likely came to Texas some time in the 1860s! Her mother's father, who was of English extraction, owned her and her mother. Either before or after they arrived in Texas, he freed her when she was very young, possibly still an infant. I've grown up to be a historian of slavery, studying the lives of other families through their family stories. I would love to have learned more from my great-grandmother about some of my own family's experiences.

I would also like to have learned more about the everyday life of my great-grandfather, of which I know only snippets—that his daughters called him

Published in On Juneteenth (2021), *a book that weaves together American history, especially Texas history, and family story.*

"Papa," that, according to his niece, his mother looked like "an old Irish woman" (I don't know what that means), that my great-grandmother used to get up before dawn and prepare huge breakfasts that sounded to me more like lunches or dinners. Planting, ploughing, and picking cotton required many calories, and the pork chops, corn bread, and, sometimes, chicken provided much-needed sustenance. My great-grandfather, along with my great-grandmother, were devout Methodists, and their home was the place visiting ministers stayed when they came to preach at the local church.

Because my paternal grandmother died when my father was eleven, and his father died the year before I was born, I had no contact with an older generation from that line to even overhear their talk about times past, let alone ask them about those days. Acquaintances described my paternal grandfather as having had a very dry sense of humor, and my paternal grandmother as very nice and reserved. I know my father's great-grandfather and his brothers, after slavery ended, saved money and in time bought a fairly large amount of land. They, being very tall and big men, made their living felling trees and preparing them for processing and sale—essentially being lumberjacks. That lasted into my father's time, but just one day working on their land when he was a teenager told my father that this hard life was not for him.

Fortunately, merely being in the presence of my grandmother and her sister so often allowed me to learn the broad contours of their lives growing up on a cotton farm with their parents. I learned that my great-grandfather, during some period of the family's lives, would leave home on a seasonal basis and travel to Galveston to work on the wharves. My great-grandparents had three daughters. Their two sons did not survive. To help my great-grandmother and the girls—my grandmother was in the middle—two young men were hired to live on the farm and help out while he was away. Hence my association of the song "Galveston" with my great-grandparents, although the roles were reversed—the man was in Galveston, the woman at her home. I cannot know for certain that my great-grandfather was thinking plaintively and wistfully about my great-grandmother and his daughters, as the young soldier thought of the young woman in his life, though I like to think so. From all I know of them, the family was devoted to one another. It must have been hard, particularly for the girls, to have their father gone for months at a time. But it was for the good of the family.

Why did he go to Galveston? The island, about 140 miles away from the location of his farm, has connections to people of African descent that go back centuries. I doubt that my great-grandfather, though he was literate, knew of or cared anything about Estebanico, who came ashore at, or in the vicinity of, Galveston in the 1500s as likely the first Black person to set foot in the area that would become Texas. That is an interesting detail for a historian but would have no bearing on a decision to go work there. I am certain my great-grandfather would have known of Galveston's other, more important, historical connections to Black people, for those had more immediate relevance to his life.

On June 19, 1865, . . . Gordon Granger, a general in the Army of the United States of America, arrived in Galveston from his post in Louisiana to

5

take command of all the troops in the American army in Texas. The Civil War had been over since April, when the Army of Northern Virginia, headed by General Robert E. Lee, surrendered to General Ulysses S. Grant, commanding general of the Army of the United States. Confederate soldiers in Texas, nevertheless, continued to fight on into May. Indeed, they were victorious in the last battle that took place on Texas soil on May 13, the Battle of Palmito Ranch, near Brownsville, Texas. When it became clear that all other Confederate armies had essentially collapsed—their soldiers were deserting in large numbers—on June 2, 1865, General Kirby Smith, who commanded the Confederate Army of the Trans-Mississippi, surrendered in Galveston to the Army of the United States of America. Texas had become a land in turmoil. Angry Confederate soldiers lashed out after their defeat. Some engaged in rioting and looting. Granger's job was to get to the state, geographically the largest in the Union, impose some degree of order, and announce that all enslaved people were free. He, along with his staff, took up residence in a villa in Galveston. How Granger made the general order known throughout Galveston is disputed. Many histories have Granger reading the Order from the balcony of his quarters. Other accounts say that Granger and soldiers went to strategic places throughout the city and read the Order. In whatever way the news was disseminated, General Order No. 3 had a powerful effect in Texas.

> The people of Texas are informed that, in accordance with a proclamation from the Executive of the United States, all slaves are free. This involves an absolute equality of personal rights and rights of property between former masters and slaves, and the connection heretofore existing between them becomes that between employer and hired labor. The freedmen are advised to remain at their present homes and work for wages. They are informed that they will not be allowed to collect at military posts and that they will not be supported in idleness either there or elsewhere.

This Order was based on the Emancipation Proclamation that President Abraham Lincoln, who had been assassinated the previous April, had issued on New Year's Day, 1863. The Thirteenth Amendment, still in the process of being ratified, provided no basis for it.

Some African Americans in Galveston, and likely other residents, already knew the gist of the general order prior to June 19. Galveston, the largest city in Texas, was a port through which most of the cotton picked and processed in the state was shipped out to the world. Port cities are perfect vehicles for transmission of information to people of all degrees of literacy. Two days before General Granger arrived on the island, Black men working on the wharves began to shout in exaltation. When asked what they were celebrating, they replied, because they were free. The news spread to other towns, but the former slaves had to be very wary of open celebration. While the holiday Juneteenth has grown to be an integral part of life in Texas, celebrated now by Blacks and Whites—and appears on its way to becoming a national holiday[1]—Whites in Texas were incensed by

---

1. On June 17, 2021, President Biden signed Juneteenth National Independence Day into law, making it a federal holiday.

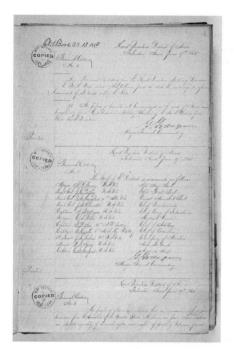

The original General Order No. 3, preserved at the National Archives Building in Washington, DC.

what had transpired, so much so that some reacted violently to Blacks' displays of joy at emancipation. In one town, dozens of newly freed enslaved people were whipped for celebrating. All over the South, but in Texas particularly, Whites unleashed a torrent of violence against the freed men and women—and sometimes, the whites who supported them—that lasted for years.

The language of General Order No. 3 not only announced the end of slavery; it used a concept familiar to Americans from the very beginning, though as we know, it was not carried forward. After stating "all slaves are free," the order continues: "This involves an absolute equality of personal rights and rights of property between former masters and slaves." Language about equality echoed the words of the American Declaration of Independence, "all men are created equal." People have long quibbled about what those words meant to Jefferson personally, as if that actually matters to whether the words are true or not. It does not. But Confederates had explicitly rejected the concept of equality announced in the Declaration, as the vice president of the Confederacy, Alexander Stephens, made clear in March 1861 in his infamous "Cornerstone Speech."

> The new constitution has put at rest, forever, all the agitating questions relating to our peculiar institution African slavery as it exists amongst us the proper status of the negro in our form of civilization. This was the immediate cause of the late rupture and present revolution. Jefferson in his forecast, had anticipated this, as the "rock upon which the old Union would split." He was right. What was conjecture with him, is now a realized fact. But whether he fully comprehended the great truth upon which that rock stood and stands, may be doubted.

Interestingly, this passage concedes that the Framer's compromise over slavery had left matters unclear enough to be the source of "agitating questions." That uncertainty was caused, in part, by the way some members of the founding generation viewed the institution of slavery and people of African descent.

> The prevailing ideas entertained by him [Jefferson] and most of the leading statesmen at the time of the formation of the old constitution, were that the

enslavement of the African was in violation of the laws of nature; that it was wrong in principle, socially, morally, and politically. It was an evil they knew not well how to deal with, but the general opinion of the men of that day was that, somehow or other in the order of Providence, the institution would be evanescent and pass away. . . .

The Framers could reach a compromise over slavery, and allow for the formation of the American Union because Providence, in the form of progress, would solve the problem.

> Those ideas, however, were fundamentally wrong. They rested upon the assumption of the equality of races. This was an error. It was a sandy foundation, and the government built upon it fell when the "storm came and the wind blew." Our new government is founded upon exactly the opposite idea; its foundations are laid, its corner-stone rests, upon the great truth that the negro is not equal to the white man; that slavery subordination to the superior race is his natural and normal condition. This, our new government, is the first, in the history of the world, based upon this great physical, philosophical, and moral truth. . . .

10   That is the basis upon which Texas and other members of the Confederacy had formulated their society. Even before the war, Texas had made this a part of its creed in its own Declaration of Independence that formed the Texas Republic. While it copied the form of the American Declaration, as noted, it left out the language of equality. The general order announced a state of affairs that completely contravened the racial and economic ideals of the Confederacy. Announcing the end of slavery would have been shocking enough. Stating that the former enslaved would now live in Texas on an equal plane of humanity with whites was on a different order of magnitude of shocking. Had the Order said, "Slavery is over. And former slaves will now become the equivalent of peons on the land of whites, with severely diminished to nonexistent legal, social, and political rights"—the state eventually imposed in Texas and throughout the South—the reaction may have been different. But this Order portended much more than that, as Granger's biographer notes.

It was not just the reaction of White Texans that mattered. The idea that the society that oppressed them might be transformed into one based upon equality influenced Black Texans in much the same way that the Declaration of Independence influenced Blacks in the early American Republic. The fear of the Black imagination was strong all throughout slavery. That was one of the reasons free African Americans posed such a problem and was one of the reasons the Texas Constitution prevented the immigration of free Black people into the republic. Seeing that Black people could exist outside of legal slavery put the lie to the idea that Blacks were born to be slaves. Making life as hard as possible for free African Americans, impairing their movement and economic prospects—even if that meant the state would forgo the economic benefits of talented people who wanted to work—was designed to prove that Blacks could not operate outside of slavery.

Race relations entered a new phase a month after Granger departed Galveston in August. Two months after General Order No. 3 was created, the federal agency set up to help the newly freed people in the wake of the change in their status, the Freedmen's Bureau, opened its Texas branch in Galveston. Conceived as part of the United States Army, General Oliver Howard was made commissioner of the Bureau. Howard, the Maine career soldier who would go on to found and serve as the first president of Howard University, appointed Brigadier General Edgar M. Gregory, a New Yorker, as an assistant commissioner to head the Texas branch. Gregory walked into an almost impossible situation. Texas was so large, and violence against the freedmen and hostility toward the American army so great, that it would have taken a far larger number than the men allotted to the Bureau to effectively carry out its mission. By most accounts, Gregory did the best he could for the newly freed African Americans, but he incurred the wrath of Whites for doing so.

Much has been written about the Freedmen's Bureau, a good deal of it falling in line with the Dunning School view of Reconstruction, which condemned as radical and overreaching the idea that freed Blacks should have been treated as if the words about "equality" actually meant something. William A. Dunning, a historian at Columbia University at the turn of the twentieth century, and his followers, praised the efforts to put White southerners back in control of society. It is difficult to read the historiography, old newspaper entries, and letters, and see historians and other observers portray what was happening in this era, the seeming instinctive sympathy for the lost world of White Texans, the intimations of Black inferiority, while presenting an ostensibly neutral and factual narrative. There is no question that the Bureau did not always make the right choices, and that the men who ran it sometimes fell short of the standards of the racial sensibilities of the late twentieth and early twenty-first centuries. For the most part, however, Gregory and other assistant commissioners, with the discipline of soldiers, tried to uphold the Bureau's mandate. They did so in the presence of a hostile group of people who had lost a war and were implacably opposed to the transformation of their economic and social lives, which had been built on chattel slavery.

General Howard, heading a new bureau that was underfunded and poorly staffed, found Texas the most difficult of all the regions under the Bureau's jurisdiction, its White citizens the most resistant to efforts to effect changes in the position of Blacks in the state. Why would White Texans be more obstreperous than other White southerners? It has been suggested that this was because, unlike other Southern states, Texas had not been defeated militarily. They had won the last battle of the Civil War. That the state had been its own Republic, within the living memory of many Texans, also set them apart from the other Confederates. The very thing that has been seen as a source of strength and pride for latter-day Texans, may have fueled a stubbornness that prevented the state from moving ahead at this crucial moment.

One of the Bureau's most important jobs was supervising the contracts of Black workers. Despite General Order No. 3, some enslavers continued to hold Blacks in slavery; making them work for no pay on threats of violence. These were the kinds of situations the Bureau was designed, in part, to fix. Gregory noted, with seeming surprise, that Black Texans, in the face of this hostility, went about the business of making new lives in the state, when they could have,

15

in some places, unleashed carnage on their former enslavers. They, like freed people throughout the South, focused on other things: solemnizing their marriages, keeping away from the violence of Whites, trying to reunite with family members who had been sold during slavery, working, and, very happily, taking advantage of the schools the Bureau created. Adults sat in classrooms with children, all eager to learn to read and write. In the midst of all this, any false step by a Black person, any wrong decision by the Bureau—and there definitely were some—was taken as proof that the whole effort was a grievous mistake.

The overall failure of Reconstruction to fulfill the promise of a South remade with Black southerners participating as equal citizens in the region is well known. But positive things did happen, particularly the building of schools to educate freed Blacks. It was from that area that one of the most influential people in the history of Blacks in Galveston, and in Texas, appeared. His efforts laid the groundwork for my great-grandfather's time in the city. George Ruby, a native New Yorker, who had had an adventuresome life, was put in charge of the Freedmen's Bureau school system. He left that position for a stint as a traveling agent for the Bureau, and returned to Galveston to become a deputy director of customs in 1869. This was before the end of Reconstruction in Texas in 1870, and Blacks were voting and holding office across the state. My own maternal great-great-grandfather registered to vote in 1867. Most important to his career, Ruby became a part of the Union League, an organization started to support the candidacy of Abraham Lincoln. The group helped organize the Republican Party in Texas and sought Black support by championing the rights of Blacks, to the consternation of Whites. His involvement with the League helped him be elected to the Texas State Senate. He also helped organize the Labor Union of Colored Men to get jobs for Black men on Galveston's wharves and to help them keep those jobs.

As his influence waned with the weakening of the Republican Party in Texas, Ruby returned to Louisiana, where he had lived and worked before coming to Texas. He believed that prospects for Blacks were better in that state. Fortunately, he had been a mentor to another Black man, this time a native Texan, who took his place in Galveston politics: Norris Wright Cuney. Cuney was the son of Philip Minor Cuney, a very wealthy White planter and state senator who enslaved over one hundred people on his 2,000-acre plantation. With one of those enslaved people, Adeline Stuart, Cuney had eight children. He eventually freed all of them. The younger Cuney became the head of the Union League in Galveston and was influential in Republican Party politics, though he was never able to win higher-level elective office. While he continued his support for Blacks who worked on the wharves at Galveston, keeping alive a tradition that lasted well into the twentieth century, he angered many of them on occasion when he failed to give sufficient support to strikers. Overall, even as Blacks lost power late in the century, having a person like Cuney in place at least provided a visible reminder that people of color could wield power and influence.

Both Ruby and Cuney were dead before the event that transformed Galveston Island in 1901, the catastrophic hurricane that killed as many as 12,000 people and is still considered the worst natural disaster in the history of the United States. The city was determined to rebuild quickly after the destruction. It did so, in part, by inviting large numbers of immigrants to come to work in the city. In sum, Galveston was, for Texas, progressive and cosmopolitan. Blacks on the island were enormously self-assured, which Whites translated into being "insolent" and "impudent." It was the birthplace of Jack Johnson.[2] I wonder what my great-grandfather made of the place. It would have been enormously different from the society in and around Moscow, deep in East Texas, where one could expect that the traditions and mores laid down in slavery, enforced by the threat and use of vigilante actions, would hold sway. If the promise of Juneteenth lived anywhere in Texas, it was in Galveston.

That sense of promise spread across the state. Black Texans were determined, despite the early intimidating anger of Whites, to celebrate what was initially called Emancipation Day. Most of the first celebrations were in churches, in keeping with the culture of a generally religious people. I also wonder if holding meetings in churches was thought to provide some level of protection in those days. Later, in larger towns, the celebrations migrated to public spaces, though some sort of religious observance might be included in the program. In 1872, in Houston, four Black men, Richard Allen, Richard Brock, Elias Dibble, and Jack Yates, pooled their resources and raised money to buy land in the city for the express purpose of celebrating the holiday, creating Emancipation Park, one of the oldest parks in Texas. It was later taken over by the City of Houston, and in those days of segregation, it was a park for Blacks. Enthusiasm for the celebrations held there, which consisted of speeches, singing, music, waxed and waned over the years, but in the twenty-first century, the renewed interest in Juneteenth spurred the park's revival.

My family went to Houston's Emancipation Park only once, as I recall. All other Juneteenth celebrations were either at my home or at my grandparents' home. The day appeared to me as the first part of a one-two summer punch, June 19 followed closely by July 4—the holiday expressly for Black Texans and the other holiday for all Americans. As far as I knew, Whites did not celebrate Juneteenth during my childhood. But everyone in my area celebrated the Fourth. I do know of the tradition of Blacks celebrating July 5, as a protest to remind people that the ideals of July 4 had not been realized. And I cannot say with any certainty how the people in my family and community viewed the Fourth as a substantive matter—what it was about, how it related to them. It was a holiday, however, a day off to be with relatives and friends. What was not to like? Juneteenth was different. For my great-grandmother, my grandparents, and relatives in their generation, this was the celebration of the freedom of people they had actually known. My great-grandmother's mother had been married three times, outliving all of her husbands. Her last one had been enslaved until the end of the Civil War.

Slavery was just a blink of an eye away from the years my grandparents and their friends were born. Although I was angered by the stories I heard about

2. The first Black world heavyweight boxing champion (1878–1946).

A contemporary Juneteenth celebration in Galveston, Texas.

their lives under Jim Crow, and I had my own issues about the treatment of Blacks in my lifetime, they surely compared life as it was, knowing what it could have been but for the Civil War, the Emancipation Proclamation, and General Order No. 3. Although there was a very long way to go before we had full and equal citizenship, we were able to gather together as a family to celebrate. Family members who were lost, were lost to death, in the way that all families lose people. No one was being sold away.

We children celebrated with the fireworks my grandfather bought—setting off firecrackers and sparklers well into the night. The traditional Juneteenth menu, in addition to usual southern-style cuisine, included red "soda water," as we called it, and barbecued goat. It was a day of excess for me and my friends on the soda water front. Soda was not a part of our daily experience. It was more like a treat. Besides playing in my grandparents' front and back yards, lighting and throwing firecrackers, we spent the day pulling cans and bottles of soda out of large tin buckets filled with ice. I'm not sure why or how the tradition of eating goat started, as it was not common fare in Texas, as far as I knew. Our family, indeed, skipped eating the goat. My mother's stepfather had a small barbecuing business. People would bring meats to him to prepare, and he spent the day before, and a good part of the day of, the holiday fulfilling orders, some of which, undoubtedly, included goat.

As the years passed, another item was added to the menu. My grandmother, who, by the time I knew her, was a housewife, had her own items to make and sell during the holiday: hot tamales. She made them to order throughout the year to raise money to build a new St. Luke's Methodist United

Church, where I had been baptized and where I went as a four-year-old to Miss Ollie's Nursery School, as had my mother. Holidays, Juneteenth included, brought in very large orders. I spent much more time than I wanted in those days sitting with my grandmother, her sister, and my mother, at the kitchen counter and table, preparing dozens of tamales to satisfy her customers and, frankly, to be consumed by our family.

Softening the corn husks in hot water, grinding the pork, beef, or chicken, preparing the masa dough to be spread on the husks, filling the dough with the seasoned meats, and tying the tamales for final preparation—was time-consuming. But it was time spent with people I loved, and who are no longer with me. Like my failure to appreciate what it meant to have a great-grandmother to ask about the past, I didn't know the true value of those moments with the women of my family. Those hours seemed endless to me as a child, but they were actually fleeting. This ritual was fitting, and so very Texan. People of African descent, and to be honest, of some European descent, celebrating the end of slavery in Texas with dishes learned in slavery and a dish favored by ancient Mesoamerican Indians that connected Texas to its Mexican past; so much Texas history brought together for this one special day.

MLA CITATION

Gordon-Reed, Annette. "On Juneteenth." *The Norton Reader: An Anthology of Nonfiction*, edited by Melissa A. Goldthwaite et al., 16th ed., W. W. Norton, 2024, pp. 90–99.

QUESTIONS

1. Annette Gordon-Reed mentions several kinds of traditions in this essay. As you read, mark the places she uses words such as "tradition" and "traditional." What traditions does she describe? Which of these traditions are still practiced today? Which ones have been (or should be) revised or discarded? Explain why.

2. Gordon-Reed combines both American history and her family story in this essay. Why do you think she made that choice rather than focusing on one or the other? In what ways does her inclusion of both family story and the larger historical context contribute to your understanding of Juneteenth?

3. In the years since Juneteenth was declared a federal holiday, what kind of celebrations have you witnessed or been a part of? How do people mark the holiday? How does the national celebration differ from or relate to the celebrations of Black Texans that Gordon-Reed describes?

4. Gordon-Reed recounts the history of Juneteenth, which became a federal holiday in America in 2021 but has been celebrated in some communities for much longer. If you could designate either a federal or state holiday, what would it be and why? How would you like to see people celebrate or mark that holiday? What would be its historical significance? How would you persuade lawmakers to take your proposal seriously?

A. Bartlett Giamatti
The Green Fields of the Mind

I T BREAKS YOUR HEART. It is designed to break your heart. The game begins in the spring, when everything else begins again, and it blossoms in the summer, filling the afternoons and evenings, and then as soon as the chill rains come, it stops and leaves you to face the fall alone. You count on it, rely on it to buffer the passage of time, to keep the memory of sunshine and high skies alive, and then just when the days are all twilight, when you need it most, it stops. Today, October 2, a Sunday of rain and broken branches and leaf-clogged drains and slick streets, it stopped, and summer was gone.

Somehow, the summer seemed to slip by faster this time. Maybe it wasn't this summer, but all the summers that, in this my 40th summer, slipped by so fast. There comes a time when every summer will have something of autumn about it. Whatever the reason, it seemed to me that I was investing more and more in baseball, making the game do more of the work that keeps time fat and slow and lazy. I was counting on the game's deep patterns, three strikes, three outs, three times three innings, and its deepest impulse, to go out and back, to leave and to return home, to set the order of the day and to organize the daylight. I wrote a few things this last summer, this summer that did not last, nothing grand but some things, and yet that work was just camouflage. The real activity was done with the radio—not the all-seeing, all-falsifying television—and was the playing of the game in the only place it will last, the enclosed green field of the mind. There, in that warm, bright place, what the old poet called Mutability[1] does not so quickly come.

But out here, on Sunday, October 2, where it rains all day, Dame Mutability never loses. She was in the crowd at Fenway[2] yesterday, a grey day full of bluster and contradiction, when the Red Sox came up in the last of the ninth trailing Baltimore 8–5, while the Yankees, rain-delayed against Detroit, only needing to win one or have Boston lose one to win it all, sat in New York washing down cold cuts with beer and watching the Boston game. Boston had won two, the Yankees had lost two, and suddenly it seemed as if the whole season might go to the last day, or beyond, except here was Boston losing 8–5, while New York sat in its family room and put its feet up. Lynn,[3] both ankles hurting now as they had in July, hits a single down the right-field line. The crowd stirs. It is on its feet.

First published in the Yale Alumni Magazine and Journal (1977) and on the Yale Alumni Magazine website (2012); it was also included in A Great and Glorious Game: Baseball Writings of A. Bartlett Giamatti (1998). In this essay, A. Bartlett Giamatti describes a game played by the Boston Red Sox and the Baltimore Orioles on October 1, 1977.

1. Dame Mutability, character created by the poet Edmund Spenser and representative of change in one's fortune.
2. Fenway Park, home stadium of the Boston Red Sox.
3. Fred Lynn (b. 1952), outfielder, most notably with the Red Sox.

Hobson, third baseman, former Bear Bryant[4] quarterback, strong, quiet, over 100 RBIs, goes for three breaking balls and is out. The goddess smiles and encourages her agent, a canny journeyman named Nelson Briles.[5]

Now comes a pinch hitter, Bernie Carbo, onetime Rookie of the Year, erratic, quick, a shade too handsome, so laid-back he is always, in his soul, stretched out in the tall grass, one arm under his head, watching the clouds and laughing; now he looks over some low stuff unworthy of him and then, uncoiling, sends one out, straight on a rising line, over the center-field wall, no cheap Fenway shot, but all of it, the physics as elegant as the arc the ball describes.

New England is on its feet, roaring. The summer will not pass. Roaring, they recall the evening, late and cold, in 1975, the sixth game of the World Series, perhaps the greatest baseball game played in the last fifty years, when Carbo, loose and easy, had uncoiled to tie the game that Fisk[6] would win. It is 8–7, one out, and school will never start, rain will never come, sun will warm the back of your neck forever. Now Bailey,[7] picked up from the National League recently, big arms, heavy gut, experienced, new to the league and the club; he fouls off two and then, checking, tentative, a big man off balance, he pops a soft liner to the first baseman. It is suddenly darker and later, and the announcer doing the game coast to coast, a New Yorker who works for a New York television station, sounds relieved. His little world, well-lit, hot-combed, split-second-timed, had no capacity to absorb this much gritty, grainy, contrary reality.

Cox[8] swings a bat, stretches his long arms, bends his back, the rookie from Pawtucket[9] who broke in two weeks earlier with a record six straight hits, the kid drafted ahead of Fred Lynn, rangy, smooth, cool. The count runs two and two, Briles is cagey, nothing too good, and Cox swings, the ball beginning toward the mound and then, in a jaunty, wayward dance, skipping past Briles, feinting to the right, skimming the last of the grass, finding the dirt, moving now like some small, purposeful marine creature negotiating the green deep, easily avoiding the jagged rock of second base, traveling steady and straight now out into the dark, silent recesses of center field.

The aisles are jammed, the place is on its feet, the wrappers, the programs, the Coke cups and peanut shells, the detritus of an afternoon; the anxieties, the things that have to be done tomorrow, the regrets about yesterday, the accumulation of a summer: all forgotten, while hope, the anchor, bites and takes hold where a moment before it seemed we would be swept out with the tide. Rice[10] is up. Rice whom Aaron[11] had said was the only one he'd seen with the ability to

4. Butch Hobson (b. 1951), Red Sox third baseman; Bryant (1913–1983), University of Alabama football coach.

5. Veteran Baltimore Orioles pitcher (1943–2005) in the 1977 game Giamatti describes.

6. Carlton Fisk (b. 1947), catcher for the Red Sox and the Chicago White Sox.

7. Bob Bailey (1942–2018), third baseman for the Red Sox.

8. Ted Cox (1955–2020), shortstop for the Red Sox.

9. Red Sox minor-league team.

10. Jim Rice (b. 1953), Red Sox left fielder.

11. Hank Aaron (1934–2021), right fielder, mostly with the Milwaukee and Atlanta Braves.

break his records. Rice the best clutch hitter on the club, with the best slugging percentage in the league. Rice, so quick and strong he once checked his swing halfway through and snapped the bat in two. Rice the Hammer of God sent to scourge the Yankees, the sound was overwhelming, fathers pounded their sons on the back, cars pulled off the road, households froze, New England exulted in its blessedness, and roared its thanks for all good things, for Rice and for a summer stretching halfway through October. Briles threw, Rice swung, and it was over. One pitch, a fly to center, and it stopped. Summer died in New England and like rain sliding off a roof, the crowd slipped out of Fenway, quickly, with only a steady murmur of concern for the drive ahead remaining of the roar. Mutability had turned the seasons and translated hope to memory once again. And, once again, she had used baseball, our best invention to stay change, to bring change on. That is why it breaks my heart, that game—not because in New York they could win because Boston lost; in that, there is a rough justice, and a reminder to the Yankees of how slight and fragile are the circumstances that exalt one group of human beings over another. It breaks my heart because it was meant to, because it was meant to foster in me again the illusion that there was something abiding, some pattern and some impulse that could come together to make a reality that would resist the corrosion; and because, after it had fostered again that most hungered-for illusion, the game was meant to stop, and betray precisely what it promised.

Of course, there are those who learn after the first few times. They grow out of sports. And there are others who were born with the wisdom to know that nothing lasts. These are the truly tough among us, the ones who can live without illusion, or without even the hope of illusion. I am not that grown-up or up-to-date. I am a simpler creature, tied to more primitive patterns and cycles. I need to think something lasts forever, and it might as well be that state of being that is a game; it might as well be that, in a green field, in the sun.

MLA CITATION

Giamatti, A. Bartlett. "The Green Fields of the Mind." *The Norton Reader: An Anthology of Nonfiction*, edited by Melissa A. Goldthwaite et al., 16th ed., W. W. Norton, 2024, pp. 100–2.

QUESTIONS

1. Throughout his essay, A. Bartlett Giamatti uses both the present tense and the past tense even though he is describing a game that took place the previous day. As you read the essay, mark the places where Giamatti shifts verb tense. Why do you think he made this choice? How would the essay be different if he had chosen to write only in the past tense?

2. In framing his essay, Giamatti reflects on "Mutability" (paragraph 2), how the only thing that is certain is change. How does he connect the themes of baseball, seasons, and change? How does his description of a particular game support or illustrate those themes?

3. Although Giamatti wrote this essay in 1977, many of the images and feelings he describes may seem familiar to contemporary readers. What traditions do you associate with a particular sport or team? Describe a sports-related tradition and its significance in a way that someone unfamiliar with that tradition can understand. If it helps, include a photo or video clip to illustrate.

E. B. WHITE
Once More to the Lake

ONE SUMMER, ALONG ABOUT 1904, my father rented a camp on a lake in Maine and took us all there for the month of August. We all got ringworm from some kittens and had to rub Pond's Extract on our arms and legs night and morning, and my father rolled over in a canoe with all his clothes on; but outside of that the vacation was a success and from then on none of us ever thought there was any place in the world like that lake in Maine. We returned summer after summer—always on August 1st for one month. I have since become a salt-water man, but sometimes in summer there are days when the restlessness of the tides and the fearful cold of the sea water and the incessant wind which blows across the afternoon and into the evening make me wish for the placidity of a lake in the woods. A few weeks ago this feeling got so strong I bought myself a couple of bass hooks and a spinner and returned to the lake where we used to go, for a week's fishing and to revisit old haunts.

I took along my son, who had never had any fresh water up his nose and who had seen lily pads only from train windows. On the journey over to the lake I began to wonder what it would be like. I wondered how time would have marred this unique, this holy spot—the coves and streams, the hills that the sun set behind, the camps and the paths behind the camps. I was sure the tarred road would have found it out and I wondered in what other ways it would be desolated. It is strange how much you can remember about places like that once you allow your mind to return into the grooves which lead back. You remember one thing, and that suddenly reminds you of another thing. I guess I remembered clearest of all the early mornings, when the lake was cool and motionless, remembered how the bedroom smelled of the lumber it was made of and of the wet woods whose scent entered through the screen. The partitions in the camp were thin and did not extend clear to the top of the rooms, and as I was always the first up I would dress softly so as not to wake the others, and sneak out into the sweet outdoors and start out in the canoe, keeping close along the shore in the long shadows of the pines. I remembered being very careful

Originally appeared in "One Man's Meat," E. B. White's column for Harper's Magazine *(1941), an American monthly covering politics, society, culture, and the environment; later included in* One Man's Meat *(1942), a collection of his columns about life on a Maine saltwater farm, and then in* Essays of E. B. White *(1977).*

never to rub my paddle against the gunwale for fear of disturbing the stillness of the cathedral.

The lake had never been what you would call a wild lake. There were cottages sprinkled around the shores, and it was in farming country although the shores of the lake were quite heavily wooded. Some of the cottages were owned by nearby farmers, and you would live at the shore and eat your meals at the farmhouse. That's what our family did. But although it wasn't wild, it was a fairly large and undisturbed lake and there were places in it which, to a child at least, seemed infinitely remote and primeval.

I was right about the tar: it led to within half a mile of the shore. But when I got back there, with my boy, and we settled into a camp near a farmhouse and into the kind of summertime I had known, I could tell that it was going to be pretty much the same as it had been before—I knew it, lying in bed the first morning, smelling the bedroom, and hearing the boy sneak quietly out and go off along the shore in a boat. I began to sustain the illusion that he was I, and therefore, by simple transposition, that I was my father. This sensation persisted, kept cropping up all the time we were there. It was not an entirely new feeling, but in this setting it grew much stronger. I seemed to be living a dual existence. I would be in the middle of some simple act, I would be picking up a bait box or laying down a table fork, or I would be saying something, and suddenly it would be not I but my father who was saying the words or making the gesture. It gave me a creepy sensation.

5   We went fishing the first morning. I felt the same damp moss covering the worms in the bait can, and saw the dragonfly alight on the tip of my rod as it hovered a few inches from the surface of the water. It was the arrival of this fly that convinced me beyond any doubt that everything was as it always had been, that the years were a mirage and there had been no years. The small waves were the same, chucking the rowboat under the chin as we fished at anchor, and the boat was the same boat, the same color green and the ribs broken in the same places, and under the floor-boards the same fresh-water leavings and débris—the dead hellgrammite,[1] the wisps of moss, the rusty discarded fish-hook, the dried blood from yesterday's catch. We stared silently at the tips of our rods, at the dragonflies that came and went. I lowered the tip of mine into the water, tentatively, pensively dislodging the fly, which darted two feet away, poised, darted two feet back, and came to rest again a little farther up the rod. There had been no years between the ducking of this dragonfly and the other one—the one that was part of memory. I looked at the boy, who was silently watching his fly, and it was my hands that held his rod, my eyes watching. I felt dizzy and didn't know which rod I was at the end of.

We caught two bass, hauling them in briskly as though they were mackerel, pulling them over the side of the boat in a businesslike manner without any landing net, and stunning them with a blow on the back of the head. When we got back for a swim before lunch, the lake was exactly where we had left it, the same number of inches from the dock, and there was only the merest suggestion of a

1. Larvae of the dobsonfly.

breeze. This seemed an utterly enchanted sea, this lake you could leave to its own devices for a few hours and come back to, and find that it had not stirred, this constant and trustworthy body of water. In the shallows, the dark, water-soaked sticks and twigs, smooth and old, were undulating in clusters on the bottom against the clean ribbed sand, and the track of the mussel was plain. A school of minnows swam by, each minnow with its small individual shadow, doubling the attendance, so clear and sharp in the sunlight. Some of the other campers were in swimming, along the shore, one of them with a cake of soap, and the water felt thin and clear and unsubstantial. Over the years there had been this person with the cake of soap, this cultist, and here he was. There had been no years.

Up to the farmhouse to dinner through the teeming, dusty field, the road under our sneakers was only a two-track road. The middle track was missing, the one with the marks of the hooves and the splotches of dried, flaky manure. There had always been three tracks to choose from in choosing which track to walk in; now the choice was narrowed down to two. For a moment I missed terribly the middle alternative. But the way led past the tennis court, and something about the way it lay there in the sun reassured me; the tape had loosened along the backline, the alleys were green with plantains and other weeds, and the net (installed in June and removed in September) sagged in the dry noon, and the whole place steamed with midday heat and hunger and emptiness. There was a choice of pie for dessert, and one was blueberry and one was apple, and the waitresses were the same country girls, there having been no passage of time, only the illusion of it as in a dropped curtain—the waitresses were still fifteen; their hair had been washed, that was the only difference—they had been to the movies and seen the pretty girls with the clean hair.

Summertime, oh summertime, pattern of life indelible, the fade-proof lake, the woods unshatterable, the pasture with the sweetfern and the juniper forever and ever, summer without end; this was the background, and the life along the shore was the design, the cottages with their innocent and tranquil design, their tiny docks with the flagpole and the American flag floating against the white clouds in the blue sky, the little paths over the roots of the trees leading from camp to camp and the paths leading back to the outhouses and the can of lime for sprinkling, and at the souvenir counters at the store the miniature birch-bark canoes and the post cards that showed things looking a little better than they looked. This was the American family at play, escaping the city heat, wondering whether the newcomers in the camp at the head of the cove were "common" or "nice," wondering whether it was true that the people who drove up for Sunday dinner at the farmhouse were turned away because there wasn't enough chicken.

It seemed to me, as I kept remembering all this, that those times and those summers had been infinitely precious and worth saving. There had been jollity and peace and goodness. The arriving (at the beginning of August) had been so big a business in itself, at the railway station the farm wagon drawn up, the first smell of the pine-laden air, the first glimpse of the smiling farmer, and the great importance of the trunks and your father's enormous authority in such matters, and the feel of the wagon under you for the long ten-mile haul, and at the top of the last long hill catching the first view of the lake after eleven months of not seeing this cherished body of water. The shouts and cries of the other campers when they saw you, and the trunks to be unpacked, to give up their rich burden. (Arriving was less exciting nowadays, when you sneaked up in your car and parked it under a tree near the camp and took out the bags and in five minutes it was all over, no fuss, no loud wonderful fuss about trunks.)

10 Peace and goodness and jollity. The only thing that was wrong now, really, was the sound of the place, an unfamiliar nervous sound of the outboard motors. This was the note that jarred, the one thing that would sometimes break the illusion and set the years moving. In those other summertimes all motors were inboard; and when they were at a little distance, the noise they made was a sedative, an ingredient of summer sleep. They were one-cylinder and two-cylinder engines, and some were make-and-break and some were jump-spark,[2] but they all made a sleepy sound across the lake. The one-lungers throbbed and fluttered, and the twin-cylinder ones purred and purred, and that was a quiet sound too. But now the campers all had outboards. In the daytime, in the hot mornings, these motors made a petulant, irritable sound; at night, in the still evening when the afterglow lit the water, they whined about one's ears like mosquitoes. My boy loved our rented outboard, and his great desire was to achieve singlehanded mastery over it, and authority, and he soon learned the trick of choking it a little (but not too much), and the adjustment of the needle valve. Watching him I would remember the things you could do with the old one-cylinder engine with the heavy flywheel, how you could have it eating out of your hand if you got really close to it spiritually. Motor boats in those days didn't have clutches, and you would make a landing by shutting off the motor at the proper time and coasting in with a dead rudder. But there was a way of reversing them, if you learned the trick, by cutting the switch and putting it on again exactly on the final dying revolution of the flywheel, so that it would kick back against compression and begin reversing. Approaching a dock in a strong following breeze, it was difficult to slow up sufficiently by the ordinary coasting method, and if a boy felt he had complete mastery over his motor, he was tempted to keep it running beyond its time and then reverse it a few feet from the dock. It took a cool nerve, because if you threw the switch a twentieth of a second too soon you would catch the flywheel when it still had speed enough to go up past center, and the boat would leap ahead, charging bull-fashion at the dock.

We had a good week at the camp. The bass were biting well and the sun shone endlessly, day after day. We would be tired at night and lie down in the accumulated heat of the little bedrooms after the long hot day and the breeze would stir almost imperceptibly outside and the smell of the swamp drift in through the rusty screens. Sleep would come easily and in the morning the red squirrel would be on the roof, tapping out his gay routine. I kept remembering everything, lying in bed in the mornings—the small steamboat that had a long rounded stern like the lip of a Ubangi, and how quietly she ran on the moonlight sails, when the older boys played their mandolins and the girls sang and we ate doughnuts dipped in sugar, and how sweet the music was on the water

2. Methods of ignition timing so that an engine functions properly.

in the shining night, and what it had felt like to think about girls then. After breakfast we would go up to the store and the things were in the same place— the minnows in a bottle, the plugs and spinners disarranged and pawed over by the youngsters from the boys' camp, the fig newtons and the Beeman's gum. Outside, the road was tarred and cars stood in front of the store. Inside, all was just as it had always been, except there was more Coca-Cola and not so much Moxie and root beer and birch beer and sarsaparilla. We would walk out with a bottle of pop apiece and sometimes the pop would backfire up our noses and hurt. We explored the streams, quietly, where the turtles slid off the sunny logs and dug their way into the soft bottom; and we lay on the town wharf and fed worms to the tame bass. Everywhere we went I had trouble making out which was I, the one walking at my side, the one walking in my pants.

One afternoon while we were there at that lake a thunderstorm came up. It was like the revival of an old melodrama that I had seen long ago with child- ish awe. The second-act climax of the drama of the electrical disturbance over a lake in America had not changed in any important respect. This was the big scene, still the big scene. The whole thing was so familiar, the first feeling of oppression and heat and a general air around camp of not wanting to go very far away. In midafternoon (it was all the same) a curious darkening of the sky, and a lull in everything that had made life tick; and then the way the boats suddenly swung the other way at their moorings with the coming of a breeze out of the new quarter, and the premonitory rumble. Then the kettle drum, then the snare, then the bass drum and cymbals, then crackling light against the dark, and the gods grinning and licking their chops in the hills. Afterward the calm, the rain steadily rustling in the calm lake, the return of light and hope and spirits, and the campers running out in joy and relief to go swimming in the rain, their bright cries perpetuating the deathless joke about how they were getting simply drenched, and the children screaming with delight at the new sensation of bathing in the rain, and the joke about getting drenched linking the generations in a strong indestructible chain. And the comedian who waded in carrying an umbrella.

When the others went swimming my son said he was going in too. He pulled his dripping trunks from the line where they had hung all through the shower, and wrung them out. Languidly, and with no thought of going in, I watched him, his hard little body, skinny and bare, saw him wince slightly as he pulled up around his vitals the small, soggy, icy garment. As he buckled the swollen belt suddenly my groin felt the chill of death.

MLA CITATION

White, E. B. "Once More to the Lake." *The Norton Reader: An Anthology of Nonfiction*, edited by Melissa A. Goldthwaite et al., 16th ed., W. W. Norton, 2024, pp. 103–7.

QUESTIONS

1. E. B. White includes many details to describe his impressions of the lake when he went there as a child and when he returns as an adult—for example, about the road, the dragonfly, and the boat's motor. What are some other details, and what do they tell us about what has changed or stayed the same?

2. White's last sentence often surprises readers. Go back through the essay and pick out sections, words, or phrases that prepare for the ending.

3. Write about revisiting a place that has special meaning for you, including details of your early memories and reflections on your more recent visit.

DAVID JOY
Hunting Camp

IN SOUTH CAROLINA, season opens the first week of October. A few die-hards at camp come at the start and stay till the end, but most of us filter in and out whenever time allows. We drive down, go home, work jobs and sneak back on weekends. For three months, life is governed by deer hunting.

Our camp is located in McCormick County. More specifically Plum Branch, a town that is little more than a crossroads. A rutted gravel road cuts between pines to a series of flat-tired, pull-behind campers tarped and covered with tin, a bathhouse, a picnic shelter and a fire pit.

Spread over a few acres, there's Burt and Carole, Zeno and Diana, Billy and Nancy, Florida Joe, Son in Law, Ted, Shady Grady, Jackie, Randall, Jason, Lewis and me. Sometimes Son in Law's son-in-law comes with his son. It's a tongue-twisting maze of names and connections that would be hard to keep straight even if you were there from the beginning.

Most of these men have been coming here since before I was born. They're in their 60s, a few mid-70s, one inching fast for 80. After 45 seasons wandering the same woods, they've come to know the land intimately. They throw around names—the Owl Boxes, the UFO Hole, the Refrigerator Stand—places where they've killed deer for decades. At 34, I'm the youngest one here.

5 Sometimes at night the train goes by, and as the whistle blows the coyotes get to crying and it's about as lonesome a sound as any of us have ever heard. For a few seconds the stories stop, and we turn our ears away from the campfire to listen. The wood crackles and pops, and Florida Joe pokes at the coals with his walking stick.

Sometimes Zeno Ponder passes around a gallon jug of muscadine cordial. The bottle always stops a little longer when it reaches Son in Law. He takes one sip, glances around, sneaks another. Someone gives him hell and everyone

Originally published in Time *(2018), in a special issue on the American South.*

gets to laughing, and, though none of us air a breath of sentimentality, I know it's been a year since any of us felt this good.

Sometimes the South Carolina boys come to visit—Jim, Gary, Mark, Spike and Ugly Buck. Once a season, Jim brings a giant pot of chicken and rice. It's a dish we look forward to same as Florida Joe's cornbread, Son In Law's potatoes and onions or Nancy's cheesecake. We scrape the pot clean and lick our plates knowing every time may be the last because Jim's beat cancer once and has cancer again. Even the toughest men don't last forever.

Two years ago we spread Larry's ashes under the rocks circling the fire. Larry lost one of his legs to a landmine near Ben Luc, pulling patrols along the Mekong River.[1] He had a prosthetic, but that never stopped him from working a climbing stand 20 feet up a pine. It was his liver and heart that failed him. Agent Orange.[2] A large portion of camp served in Vietnam.

Aside from Florida Joe and Billy from Texas, everyone at camp comes from the Blue Ridge Mountains. Jackie's the one first brought me here. He and I ride together from Jackson County, North Carolina. The pine flats of South Carolina are a different landscape altogether from the mountains where we live. This is where the piedmont transitions to sand hills. The sun is relentless and there is seldom a drop of rain. But there are deer here, more than we could ever hope to find back home.

I come from a family of small-game hunters, so it was the men and women at camp who taught me to hunt deer. Jackie Medford showed me how to read sign, scrapes, rubs and licking branches. Last November, Burt Hogsed gave me the tree where I would later kill my biggest deer to date. Zeno Ponder was the one who first handed me a knife and told me where to cut. Any gap that may exist in age is bridged by a deep belief that there is something greater than mere subsistence gained from time afield.

For the most part, ours is a culture on the brink of extinction. Fewer are finding their way into the sport, and every year there is less land to roam. More than just the hunting, though, what we hold on to is a microcosm of what the growing urban-rural divide has erased across much of the rural South. It's that old-time communion that used to be commonplace.

The meals we share are no different than what used to be Sunday suppers. The storytelling around the fire used to be front-porch affairs. The large, extended families that filled church pews, the kinds of families with tongue-twisting mazes of names and connections, don't hold together like they did in the past. Kids move away and seldom return. The fellowship halls where people gathered for reunions are empty. The family graves are grown over with weeds. But there are holdout pockets where story still matters and people are still tied to the land.

At camp we hold on to tradition, and as the moon rises behind the pines, the old men talk and I listen. Deep down I know it won't last, that it can't, so I linger

---

1. Ben Luc, Mekong River: locations of battles and transit routes during the Vietnam War (1954–75).

2. Herbicide used by the American military to clear foliage during the Vietnam War.

on every word. If time favors us all the same, there will come a season when I am alone. Sooner or later, there will come a night when the last of the fire burns out.

MLA CITATION

Joy, David. "Hunting Camp." *The Norton Reader: An Anthology of Nonfiction*, edited by Melissa A. Goldthwaite et al., 16th ed., W. W. Norton, 2024, pp. 108–10.

QUESTIONS

1. Toward the end of his essay, David Joy calls hunting "a culture on the brink of extinction," and then adds: "More than just the hunting, though, what we hold on to is a microcosm of what the growing urban-rural divide has erased across much of the rural South. It's that old-time communion that used to be commonplace" (paragraph 11). What, exactly, is being erased, and what is Joy's attitude toward it? Why does Joy wait until nearly the end of his essay to deliver this observation?

2. Joy's essay is rich with descriptions, histories, and stories. Annotate the essay, marking details that seem especially evocative. How do these details contribute to his essay?

3. What traditions seem most important to hunting camp as Joy describes it? What values do those traditions suggest?

4. Using Joy's essay as a model, write an essay about a place that is meaningful to you and show the traditions that are integral to your experience of that place. Like Joy, try to evoke the feel of your place through concrete description, recollection, and reflection.

TERESA LUST
The Same Old Stuffing

BEFORE YOU SET OUT to revamp your Thanksgiving meal, it pays to consider all the repercussions. Just because the editors of the glossy food magazines have grown weary of the same old turkey and fixings, and even though they are absolutely giddy with excitement over the smoked quail, the spicy black bean stuffing, and the sun-dried tomato and arugula gratin they have in store for this year's feast, it does not mean that everyone will welcome innovation at the Thanksgiving table. Quite the contrary. All some people really want is the tried and true. Some people have grown quite fond of their annual mix of turkey and trimmings, each and every dish, and they do not consider it an onerous task to repeat the meal from one year to the next. They gain comfort from the familiarity

Published in Pass the Polenta: And Other Writings from the Kitchen *(1998), a collection of essays about food and family.*

and the ritual of it all; any tampering with the menu, no matter how minor or well intentioned, only serves to make them feel shortchanged.

This fact my mother discovered to her dismay when she tried out a little something at our own Thanksgiving meal. For years before anyone realized it had become a tradition, she roasted our holiday turkey with two types of stuffing inside it. She filled the bird's main cavity with my paternal grandmother's sage-and-onion dressing. This quintessential American farmhouse preparation was a genuine family heirloom, as Nana had learned to make it at her own mother's side. And for the bird's neck cavity, my mom fixed what you could call an Italian-American hybrid stuffing. Although this filling was not authentically Italian, it was a recipe from my mother's family, and it bespoke her immigrant heritage with its classic Mediterranean combination of sausage, spinach, raisins and nuts.

Then one autumn as the holiday loomed near, my mom found herself contemplating our annual Thanksgiving spread. She saw it suddenly in a new and somewhat bothersome light. What had seemed a skillful act of diplomacy all these years, this bringing together of two family traditions inside one bird, why, it now smacked to her of excess. How the fact had escaped her for so long, she did not know, for she did not go for over-indulgence when it came to family meals. My mother was accommodating, don't misunderstand me. She was a mom who once finished up a marathon session of Dr. Seuss[1] books with a breakfast of green eggs and ham at the behest of her four daughters. Still, she made us eat our peas, and she said things like, "The day your papa starts raising cows that don't come with livers is the day I'll quit serving liver and onions for dinner. Now eat up." Yes, she knew where to draw the line.

What suddenly struck my mother as disturbing was not a matter of gluttony or expense or grams of fat, but of balance. What with the mashed potatoes, the baked yams, the penny rolls, and two types of stuffing, there was altogether too much starch on the plate. Starch, starch, starch. The redundancy of it became an offense that the English teacher in her could no longer abide. Of an instant, the solution became clear: two stuffings were one stuffing too many. One of them would have to go.

So she said to my father, "Jim, which stuffing do you prefer at Thanksgiving?"   5

He replied, "My mother's sage-and-onion dressing, of course. It's the stuffing of my youth. It's the heart of the Thanksgiving meal. By God, it's a national tradition, that stuffing, and I can't even imagine the holiday without it."

This was not the response my mother had in mind. Nana's sage-and-onion dressing had been her candidate for dismissal, because naturally, she preferred her family's stuffing, the one with the Italian touch of sausage, spinach, and raisins. She saw my father's point, though. We celebrated the holiday with his side of the family, and she had them to bear in mind. The children would be too preoccupied with the mashed potatoes to care a whit one way or the other about the stuffing, but her in-laws would feel deprived, no doubt, if Nana's dish didn't grace the table. And she had to admit that the sage-and-onion version

1. Pseudonym of Theodor Seuss Geisel (1904–1991), who wrote children's books such as *Green Eggs and Ham* (1960) and *The Cat in the Hat* (1957).

was more in keeping with the all-American spirit of the holiday. It was more faithful, she assumed, to history. Good heavens, even schoolchildren knew that sage-and-onion dressing appeared on the Pilgrims' rough-hewn banquet table, right alongside the spit-roasted wild turkey, the hearth-braised sweet potatoes, the cranberry sauce, and the pumpkin pie.

I must admit I envisioned such a meal, just as I pictured Miles Standish[2] brandishing a kitchen knife and gallantly carving the turkey roast while he gazed deep into the limpid eyes of Priscilla Mullens.[3] But there is no record of stuffing—sage-and-onion or otherwise—bedecking the table at the Pilgrims' first thanksgiving, which it turns out was not a somber meal, but a frolicsome affair of hunting, games, and wine which lasted three days. For that matter, there isn't even any specific mention of turkeys having been served, though one colonist wrote of an abundance of fowl at the event, and most scholars feel safe in assuming this bounty included a few turkeys. All anyone knows for certain is that the Mayflower folks cooked up five deer, oysters, cod, eel, corn bread, goose, watercress, leeks, berries, and plums. Pumpkins made an appearance, too, but no one bothered to record just how they were cooked. They certainly were not baked in a pie crust, though, for the wheat crop had failed and the ship's supply of flour had long since run out.

The traditional meal as we know it dates back not to the solemn, high-collared Pilgrims, nor even to Colonial times, but to home cooks of the nineteenth century. Not until this era did the idea of an annual day of thanksgiving first take hold. The driving force behind the holiday was New Englander Sarah Josepha Hale (whose legacy also includes the nursery rhyme "Mary Had a Little Lamb"). As editor of the popular magazine Godey's Lady's Book, she promoted the holiday for nearly twenty years within the periodical's pages. She wrote letters annually to the state governors and to the president, and one by one the states gradually took up the idea. Finally, Abraham Lincoln, desperate for any means to promote unity in the war-ravaged country, declared the first national Thanksgiving in 1863.

10   And what did the mistress of the house serve up at this new holiday meal? Her standard company fare for autumn, of course: roast turkey with cranberry sauce, scalloped and mashed potatoes, candied sweet potatoes, braised turnips, creamed onions, cranberry sauce, mince pie, pumpkin pie—the menu has endured remarkably unchanged. And yes, it was standard procedure then to roast the turkey with a stuffing.

The actual practice of filling up a bird's cavity dates back to antiquity; the space made a handy cooking vessel for families who all too often owned only one pot. Recipes have varied over the millennia. The cookbook attributed to the Roman gastronome Apicius gives a formula that includes ground meat, chopped brains, couscous, pine nuts, lovage, and ginger; other than the brains, it sounds like something right out of a trendy contemporary cookbook. English cooks during the Middle Ages favored heavily spiced and honeyed productions based on

2. English military officer (c. 1584–1656) and later captain hired by the Pilgrims.
3. In the poem The Courtship of Miles Standish (1858) by Henry Wadsworth Longfellow, Standish and John Alden vie for the love and attention of Mullens.

pieces of offal that today would make our rarefied stomachs churn. Nineteenth-century American cooks went on stuffing birds, no matter how many pots and pans they had on hand in the kitchen, and recipes much like Nana's sage-and-onion dressing were a beloved part of many an early Thanksgiving repast.

No less dear, though, or popular, or traditional, were a number of other variations. Homemakers in the corn-growing south who went to stuff a turkey favored cornbread in their recipes. Along the eastern seaboard, they tucked in dozens of nectar-sweet shucked oysters, while across the country as far north as the chestnut tree once grew, they featured loads of tender chestnuts in their fillings. And many cooks treasured recipes that called for ground meat, dried fruits, autumn greens, and shelled nuts—the very products of the fall harvest upon which my mother's family recipe was based, so she need not have dismissed her version as unconventional so hastily.

The genteel ladies of the last century would have viewed my mother's dilemma not as a surplus of starch at the meal, but as a paucity of meats. They were impassioned carnivores, these American predecessors of ours, and one meager turkey would have seemed woefully inadequate at a meal showcasing the prodigious bounty of the land. Pull out the stops, Darlene, I can all but hear them tell her. Along with the requisite turkey, they decorated their tables with a chicken pie, a joint of beef, a roast goose, if the budget would allow. Certainly these additional viands would serve to put my mother's menu back on kilter.

I'm sure, too, that at least one of these women would have felt bound by duty to draw my mother aside and whisper that she really ought to call her preparation *dressing* and not *stuffing*. The word "stuffing" has been in use for centuries. Sir Thomas Elyot's *Dictionary* of 1538 uses it as a synonym for "force-meat," defined as "that wherewith any foule is crammed." Sir Thomas obviously wasn't much of a cook, or he would have known that cramming a fowl isn't such a great idea, for the filling expands during the roasting, and it can burst out at the seams if it is packed too tightly. At any rate, all this stuffing and forcing and cramming proved simply too much for the delicate sensibilities of the Victorian age, and the more discreet term "dressing" came into fashion. Today, school-marmish cookbooks often wag a finger and insist that when it is on the inside of the bird it is stuffing, and when it is baked in a separate dish, it's dressing. In reality, this does not play out. If Grandma calls her dish stuffing, then stuffing it is, regardless of its location inside or alongside the bird. Same goes for Aunt Pearl's dressing, no matter where she puts it.

Had my mother sought the counsel of Mrs. Sarah Josepha Hale or her con-   15 temporaries, then, she might have spared herself some anxiety. For although she had resolved herself to her decision, the idea of forgoing her family recipe did not rest easy with her. The days wore on and she grew positively disgruntled. Then one brisk, gray morning with two weeks yet to go before Thanksgiving, she found herself pushing her cart down the butcher's aisle at the supermarket when inspiration struck. Who ever said holiday recipes were for holidays, and holidays only? Who? She need not go without her annual dose of her family's stuffing after all. So she hoisted a fresh turkey into the cart, made a few other spur-of-the-moment additions to her shopping list, and went home and set to work.

She pulled her big frying pan out of the cupboard, set it over a low flame on the stove-top, melted half a stick of butter in it, then crumbled in three-quarters of a pound of bulk pork sausage. After the meat began to brown, she stirred in a diced onion, a couple of cloves of pressed garlic, a few stalks of cutup celery, and a cup or so of sliced button mushrooms. These she let simmer gently until the onions were translucent. She added a large container of the chopped garden spinach she had blanched and frozen last spring, heated it through, then scraped the contents of the pan into a large ceramic bowl. When the mixture cooled to room temperature she sliced a stale loaf of French bread into cubes— enough to make about four cups—then added the bread to the bowl along with a couple of ample handfuls of raisins, sliced almonds, and freshly grated Parmesan cheese—a good half cup of each. She seasoned the stuffing with salt, black pepper, and generous pinches of oregano and rosemary, then drizzled in a glass of white wine. Using her hands, she combined all the ingredients thoroughly, then put a finger to her tongue. A pinch more salt and that would do it. Finally, she spooned the stuffing into the bird, trussed it up, and put it in the oven to roast for the rest of the afternoon.

Incidentally, my mother is quite an accomplished seamstress. She could sew bound buttonholes on a turkey if she wanted to. But she agrees with me that trussing need not be the intricate knit-one-purl-two operation that many cookbooks describe. Such elaborate needlework lingers from the days of the kitchen hearth-fire, when trussing was done to keep the drumsticks and wings from dangling in the flames as the bird turned on a spit. It now functions as a stuffy, old guard test of a cook's dexterity—yes, but can she truss a turkey? By the turn of this century, the massive iron kitchen range had become a standard feature in the American home, and oven roasting rendered unnecessary all the knotting and stitching and battening down. Trussing now primarily serves to keep the stuffing in place, and to give the bird a demure appearance, its ankles politely crossed, when it arrives at the table. Folding back the wings and tying the drumsticks together with kitchen twine usually make for ample treatment.

As my mom put the neck and giblets into a stock-pot on the stove for gravy, she decided a side dish of mashed potatoes would be just the accompaniment to round out the meal. Then she discovered she had a few sweet potatoes in the bin under the kitchen sink, and she thought, now wouldn't those be nice, too, roasted with a little butter, ginger, and brown sugar? And when she remembered the tiny boiling onions that had been rolling around in the refrigerator's bottom drawer, she decided she might as well bake them up au gratin with some bread crumbs and cream.

The turkey spittered and spattered away in the oven, filling every nook in the house with its buttery, winter-holiday scent, and the next thing my mom knew, she was rolling out the crust for a pumpkin pie. My father arrived home from work, draped his overcoat across the banister, and walked into the kitchen just in time to see her plopping the cranberry sauce out of the can. She placed it on the table in a sterling silver dish, its ridged imprints still intact and its jellied body quivering gloriously—God bless those folks at Ocean Spray, they were always a part of our turkey dinners, too. She turned to my father and said, "Dinner's almost ready."

My mom watched as her family gathered around the table and enjoyed a   20
complete turkey feast on that evening in early November. After the meal, my
father stretched back in his chair and folded his hands behind his head. He'd
always thought it a shame, he said, a needless deprivation, that Americans ate
roast turkey only once a year at Thanksgiving. This fine dinner just proved his
point. What a treat, yes, what a treat. But the family's pleasure that night was
merely an added perk for my mother, as she had prepared the meal for herself,
only for herself, and she was feeling deeply satisfied.

When the official holiday finally arrived, my mother made good on her vow
and let Nana's sage-and-onion dressing preside at the evening meal. Out came
the frying pan, and she started to sauté two chopped onions and four thinly
sliced stalks of celery, including the leaves, in a stick of butter. After a moment's
thought, she added two plump cloves of minced garlic to the simmering pan.
She couldn't resist. She knew Nana thought her a bit heavy-handed in the garlic department, but so what, it was her kitchen.

When the vegetables were limp and fragrant, she pulled the pan from the
heat and set it aside to cool. She put the mixture into a bowl along with eight
cups of firm, stale bread cubes, a generous spoonful of dried sage, a healthy
handful of chopped fresh parsley, some salt and pepper, and a pinch of nutmeg. She gave these ingredients a light mixing, drizzled in enough broth to
make the filling hold together when she squeezed a handful of it between her
fingers—three-quarters of a cup, maybe a bit more—then tossed the dressing
together again lightly before she spooned it into the Thanksgiving bird.

That evening Nana arrived with her sweet pickles and her three pies—
apple, pumpkin, mincemeat. Cousins poured into the house toting covered
casserole dishes, an uncle walked through the door, then an aunt. We soon sat
down around two tables to dine, our plates heaped to the angle of repose. Amid
the clanking of cutlery and the giggling and guffawing, and the festive bustle,
my father paused. His fork pierced a juicy slice of dark thigh meat and his knife
was poised in midstroke. He looked down intently and his eyes circled clockwise, studying the contents of his plate. He craned his neck and took an inventory of the platters and bowls laid out on the buffet counter across the room.
"Darlene," he said, "this is some spread we have here, don't get me wrong. But
you know what's missing is that other stuffing you make. The one we had the
other day with the cornucopia of raisins and nuts and such."

My mom nearly dropped her fork. "But you told me you preferred your
mother's dressing."

He looked back down at the turkey and trimmings before him. "Well, yes,   25
but that doesn't mean I don't prefer yours, too. It just doesn't seem like a proper
Thanksgiving without that second stuffing on the table. Don't you agree?"

What he meant, of course, was that my mom's dish had to turn up missing
before he understood just what a part of the celebration it had become. So the
year the turkey had only one stuffing was the year that both recipes became
permanent fixtures on my mother's Thanksgiving menu. When time-honored
traditions get their start while you're not looking, it seems, they need not concern
themselves with balance, or daily nutritional requirements, or even historical

accuracy. For such rituals rise up out of memories, and memories are not subject to hard facts. They are not interested in making room for change.

MLA CITATION

Lust, Teresa. "The Same Old Stuffing." *The Norton Reader: An Anthology of Nonfiction*, edited by Melissa A. Goldthwaite et al., 16th ed., W. W. Norton, 2024, pp. 110–16.

QUESTIONS

1. Teresa Lust includes both family anecdotes and historical research in her essay. As you read the essay, mark the passages that are informed by research. Was there anything about her description of the development of Thanksgiving as a holiday and its traditions that surprised you?

2. In different ways, both Lust and Diana Abu-Jaber, in "Lamb Two Ways" (pp. 50–54), show how families whose members come from different cultural backgrounds either accommodate or resist change, and that change is often represented by food. What similarities and differences do you see between Lust's and Abu-Jaber's essays?

3. Write an essay about a holiday tradition in your family. Use both family anecdotes and historical research. If your essay includes a recipe, consider incorporating it—as Lust does—in narrative form.

TATÉ WALKER
The (Native) American Dream

I N THE MIDST of Colorado Springs' urban sprawl, Monycka Snowbird (Ojibwe) raises fowl, goats, rabbits, and indigenous plants to feed and make household products for her family and neighbors.

About 650 miles north in a sprawling rural landscape on the Cheyenne River reservation in South Dakota, Karen Ducheneaux (Lakota) and her tiospaye[1] are slowly building a series of ecodomes and straw bale buildings powered by solar, wind, and water in an effort to disconnect from pollutants of mind, body, and earth.

The two women represent a growing number of Native people and organizations in the United States both on and off tribal land committed to leading clean, sustainable, and culturally competent lives.

Published in Native Peoples *(2015), a magazine edited by Taté Walker and devoted to "American Indian history, contemporary arts, Native film, theatre, music, culture, Native American recipes, pow-wows & events in North & South America," which was published from 1987 to 2016.*

1. Lakota for "extended family."

The efforts of individuals like these women, in addition to the prevalence of companies specializing in mainstreaming indigenous foods and non-profits committed to building energy efficient and sustainable housing in tribal communities, highlight the popularity and return of such lifestyles.

"Our people had this tiospaye system, where you really made a life with the people you felt close to, and had skills that complemented each other," says Ducheneaux. "We've spent generations at this point getting away from that beautiful system, and we're taught the only way to be successful is to follow the American dream, which is one of autonomy and being paid for your skills." 5

The American dream, Ducheneaux says, doesn't work on the reservation.

"It's not in our nature to turn our back on people who need us," she continues. "Our people without even realizing it sometimes are still living in a tiospaye system, because any success we've had as a people—success in material wealth—is because we can depend on each other."

Studies show food stability, affordability, and access is severely limited for Native communities. According to a report from the USDA's Economic Research Service released in December [2014], just 25.6 percent of all tribal areas were within a mile's distance from a supermarket, compared with 58.8 percent of the total US population.

The latest USDA data also shows 23.5 million people nationwide live in a food desert—that is to say, their access to a grocery store and healthy, affordable food is limited—and more than half of those people are low-income. Many tribal communities and urban areas with high populations of Native people are considered food deserts.

Given the staggering rates of poverty, diseases like diabetes, and unemployment for Natives nationwide—higher for those living on reservations—both 10

Snowbird and Ducheneaux point to the many economic and health benefits of individuals creating their own energies, whether it's food, fuel and power, or social capital.

Returning to traditional roots in a literal sense is also what drives Snowbird, who has lived in Colorado Springs for more than 20 years.

"We as indigenous people have gotten farther away from our traditional food sources than anyone else in this country, and I think that's why we have this sort of swelling epidemic of diabetes and obesity in Indian Country, because we're losing the knowledge of our traditional foods," says Snowbird, 40.

Some 440,000 people live in the Colorado Springs area, and Snowbird works with both Native and non-Native organizations throughout her region to educate and promote the benefits of urban food production, known in some places as backyard or micro farming. She leads educational classes for children and adults, including seed cultivation, plant recognition, harvesting, livestock butchering, and more.

"You can't be sovereign if you can't feed yourself," says Snowbird, borrowing a line from Winona LaDuke (Anishinaabe), an environmental activist and founder of Honor the Earth. "One of the ways colonizers controlled Indian people was to take our food sources away. Let's reclaim our food.

15   "We have to teach our kids it's not just about preserving our cultures and language; it's about restorative stewardship and about knowing where food comes from, who tribally it comes from," Snowbird says. "Indigenous food is medicine. And food brings everyone together."

*

Snowbird learned to appreciate indigenous food systems from her father, who hunted wild game and imparted an appreciation for knowing where your dinner comes from and how to prepare it beyond simply opening a box and heating up the contents.

But being known throughout Colorado Springs as "the Goat Lady" and earning a reputation as a knowledgeable indigenous educator didn't happen until a few years ago, when Snowbird spearheaded a city-wide movement to change and educate people on the local laws of urban food production.

Now Snowbird manages the Colorado Springs Urban Homesteading support group, which boasts roughly 1,200 members. Through that group, Snowbird leads several classes per season on animal husbandry, butchering, and more with her fiery brand of wit and know-how.

Perhaps closer to her heart, however, are the lessons she imparts on the city's urban Native youth. Colorado Springs School District 11, in which Snowbird's two daughters, ages 11 and 13, are enrolled, has the only Title VII Indian Education Program in the city.

"I talk to Title VII kids about what indigenous food is—that it's not just buffalo or corn," she explains. "I try to break it down for them in terms of what they ate at lunch that day, even if it was junk food."   20

Thanks in large part to Snowbird's efforts, the program has several garden beds and a greenhouse growing traditional Native edibles, including Apache brown-striped sunflower seeds, Navajo robin's egg, Pueblo chiles, and more.

"I come in sometimes and kids are bouncing off all the walls," Snowbird says. "But the moment you get their hands in the dirt, it's like all that contact with the earth just calms them."

The children also learn to grow, harvest, and cook with chokecherries, prickly pears, beans, and other local vegetation.

"Starting the kids off with food let's us also discuss Indian issues without putting people on the defensive," Snowbird explains. "It's hard to get mad when you're talking about food."

25   Re-introducing and re-popularizing indigenous foods and traditional cooking, especially among Native youth, will help strengthen Native people and the communities they live in, Snowbird insists.

Snowbird admits maintaining a lifestyle committed to food sovereignty can be hard on her tight budget. However, she says it helps her save and earn money in the long run. Snowbird is able to collect, grow, use, and sell or barter with the milk, eggs, meat, vegetables, cleaning and toiletry items, and other useful goods produced on her property.

"I'm not completely self-sufficient by any means. But urban homesteading—or whatever you want to call it—is about as traditional as you can get," she insists. "It's living off the land within the radius of where you live and knowing the Creator has put what you need right where you are."

*

For outsiders following along on *Facebook* as Ducheneaux and her family transition to living efficiently and sustainably, the process of building an ecodome and maintaining a traditional garden may have seemed as easy as digging a hole.

Except that the hole in question—12 feet across and 4 to 6 feet deep in which the ecodome sits—took three months to dig out back in 2012, thanks to heavy rains and a landscape of gumbo.

30   "It was so much work," Ducheneaux recalls. "We had to move the gumbo out one wheelbarrow at a time."

But the effort, shared by about seven members of Ducheneaux's tiospaye—including her mom, siblings, and their spouses, as well as volunteers—has been well worth it.

On 10 acres of family land on the Cheyenne River reservation, Ducheneaux and her family are creating the Tatanka Wakpala Model Sustainable Community. The family has funded the project with help from Honor the Earth and Bread of Life Church, which donated $4,000 and $2,500 respectively toward the electric power system.

The shell of the small, ecodome home—which the family learned to build via video and trial-by-error—is complete, and a garden featuring plants indigenous to the area produces hundreds of pounds of produce each year.

Considering hers is a reservation located within counties consistently listed as some of the poorest in the nation, and recognizing the tribe suffers from insufficient and inefficient housing where utility bills can reach into the high hundreds or more during the winter months. Ducheneaux hopes her family's model sparks a trend for other tribal members.

"We really believe that even people who aren't eco-friendly will be inspired by our use of wind and solar energy. We put up our own electric system and we'll never have to pay another utility bill," Ducheneaux says.

"We were waiting for the blueprint to drop in our laps. Then we realized no one was going to do it for us, so we said we'd do it ourselves. We'll make mistakes and figure it out."

This year, the goal is to build a round, communal use center out of straw bale and/or tires where things like cooking, bathing, learning, ceremony, or business can be conducted. Ducheneaux hopes the latest building will be complete within the next two years.

"What we have going on out there is a desire to be more self-sufficient. When we sat around talking about this, we asked ourselves, 'What do we need?'" Ducheneaux explains. "We needed to start feeding ourselves and taking responsibility for our own food needs . . . Not just growing food and raising animals, but going back to our Lakota traditions and treating the Earth respectfully by using what it gives us."

*

Living in an urban or reservation setting provides those who want to live sustainably unique challenges, both Snowbird and Ducheneaux say.

40   "One of the challenges is being so far away from everything," Ducheneaux says of rural reservation life. "For a lot of our volunteers, it's eye-opening for them that the hardware store is a one-hour trip just in one direction."

Planning far ahead is key, Ducheneaux says.

Infrastructure, including a severe lack of Internet connectivity, weather, and a disinterested tribal government can also be setbacks, although Ducheneaux notes the latter can benefit sustainability projects due to few, if any, restrictions on things like harvesting rainwater or land use.

For urban Natives, being disconnected from tribal knowledge—for instance, the indigenous names and uses of plants—is a major disadvantage, Snowbird said.

When someone in the community comes forward with that knowledge, it's often exploited for profit, and the people who would benefit most—namely Native youth—are left out.

45   "I always find it surprising how removed from the whole food process people are; they don't know or care where their food comes from," says Snowbird, who harvests edibles on hikes through the mountains or on strolls through downtown. She tries to combat this by giving eggs and other food produced on her property to those who wouldn't—or couldn't—normally buy organic in a supermarket.

"Pretty soon those people are asking me for more eggs and then we're talking about how they can get started with chickens in their backyard or growing herbs on their window sills," Snowbird says, adding those conversations eventually lead to discussions on indigenous issues, regardless of whether the person is Native or not. "We're trying to put the culture back in agriculture."

MLA CITATION

Walker, Taté. "The (Native) American Dream." *The Norton Reader: An Anthology of Nonfiction*, edited by Melissa A. Goldthwaite et al., 16th ed., W. W. Norton, 2024, pp. 116–22.

QUESTIONS

1. Many writers of profiles limit themselves to one subject. Why do you think Taté Walker chose to profile two people who live in different locations?

2. Monycka Snowbird and Karen Ducheneaux draw knowledge from their Native cultures and traditions. Mark the passages that best show Native knowledge and how these women apply that knowledge in their communities. Do you think this knowledge could benefit other communities? If so, how? If not, why?

3. Ducheneaux often mentions a "'tiospaye system,'" a cooperative way of living with those one feels close to and who have complementary skills; she contrasts this way of living with following "'the American dream, which is one of autonomy and being paid for your skills'" (paragraph 5). Look closely at the images included in this profile and then find images that represent the American dream. What do the images in the profile and the ones you chose say about these different approaches to living?

3 CARING FOR SELF, CARING FOR OTHERS

> The most beautiful people we have known are those who have known defeat, known suffering, known struggle, known loss, and have found their way out of the depths. These persons have an appreciation, a sensitivity, and an understanding of life that fills them with compassion, gentleness, and a deep loving concern.
>
> —ELISABETH KÜBLER-ROSS

Call to mind a person who shows compassion and loving concern for others. Do you have a sense of the experiences that helped shape this person? Perhaps, like Ellen Wayland-Smith, who writes in "Natural Magic" about her experience of cancer, the person you know experienced what Wayland-Smith describes as a "radically decentering experience," one that reveals "the self as dependent on some larger unseen thing that humbles by its sheer complexity and magnitude." In other words, people often can become more caring after an earthshaking experience. What acts of self-care or care from others may have helped that person become someone who shows care in turn? Of course, not everyone who experiences suffering becomes more compassionate: Sometimes abused people abuse others; sometimes angry people lash out; sometimes people who need help do not receive that assistance because of systems of inequality beyond their control. The selections in this chapter help us consider diverse ways of caring for ourselves and others through individual acts of care as well as through seeking to prevent violence and to address discrimination and other forms of harm.

Known for her writing about death and grief, Dr. Elisabeth Kübler-Ross explains that working through difficult experiences in life can help people become more compassionate and caring. Several readings in this chapter echo this idea. In "Why We Shouldn't Shield Children from Darkness," Matt de la Peña, through reflecting on his picture books and interactions with children, reminds readers that experiences of loss are as vital to human development as are moments of joy. Cheryl Strayed, who—when she was twenty-two—lost her mother to cancer, gives advice in "The Black Arc of It" to someone seeking to support a grieving loved one. These essays and others show that acts of caring for oneself and caring for others are often connected. For example, seeking help and support from others—as readers see in John Green's "Harvey"—is an act of self-care. Green, too, uses his own experience of suffering with depression to compassionately offer support to others. Even small acts of care—such as the ones that Ross Gay describes in "Tomato on Board"—can set off a volley of joy between oneself and total strangers.

This chapter includes both personal essays and arguments. Using personal essays, some authors show how they practice self-care through spiritual and cultural traditions

(Daisy Hernández), art and time in nature (Ursula Murray Husted), and the search for spaces where they are welcomed (s.e. smith). Other authors make arguments for how to show care in the context of relationships and community. Through relating a personal experience of attending a play and through defining "crip space," smith makes an argument for spaces dedicated to the needs of those with disabilities and shows the importance of design in those spaces: How a space is built can be an act of care or of disregard. James Densley and Jillian Peterson use their research on violence to help others reduce mass shootings, and Asam Ahmad provides guidelines for standing up for oneself or others; he shows that some forms of critique can be invitational and inclusive ("calling in") but also that it sometimes makes sense to "call out" hurtful or discriminatory words, actions, and policies, and, in doing so, to seek accountability.

As you read this chapter, note the different forms of self-care and care for others that the writers portray. Which ones have you experienced or shown? Which ones would you benefit from seeking out or providing to others? Can you think of other ways to work through difficult experiences or to support friends, family, classmates, and members of your community? If that support involves writing, what genres would best help you get across what you're thinking or wish to research?

JOHN GREEN
Harvey

THE MOVIE *HARVEY* stars Jimmy Stewart as Elwood P. Dowd, an alcoholic whose best friend is a six-foot, three-and-a-half-inch-tall invisible white rabbit named Harvey. Josephine Hull won an Oscar for her portrayal of Elwood's sister, Veta, who struggles with whether to commit Elwood to a sanitarium. The film, based on Mary Chase's Pulitzer Prize–winning play of the same name, was an immediate critical and commercial success when it was released in 1950.

But my story of *Harvey* begins in the early winter of 2001, shortly after I suffered what used to be known as a nervous breakdown. I was working for *Booklist* magazine and living on the Near North Side of Chicago in a small apartment that I had until recently shared with a person I'd thought I would marry. At the time, I believed that our breakup had caused my depression, but now I see that my depression at least in part caused the breakup. Regardless, I was alone, in what had been our apartment, surrounded by what had been our things, trying to take care of what had been our cat.

First appeared on the podcast The Anthropocene Reviewed *(2019) in the episode "Veloci-raptors and Harvey" and then included in* The Anthropocene Reviewed: Essays on a Human-Centered Planet *(2021). In both his podcast and in the book, John Green uses the form of the personal essay and a five-star scale to review different aspects of living—from objects to foods, from places to diseases.*

Susan Sontag wrote that "Depression is melancholy minus its charms." For me, living with depression was at once utterly boring and absolutely excruciating. Psychic pain overwhelmed me, consuming my thoughts so thoroughly that I no longer had any thoughts, only pain. In *Darkness Visible*, William Styron's wrenching memoir of depression, he wrote, "What makes the condition intolerable is the foreknowledge that no remedy will come—not in a day, an hour, a month, or a minute. If there is mild relief, one knows that it is only temporary; more pain will follow. It is hopelessness even more than pain that crushes the soul." I find hopelessness to *be* a kind of pain. One of the worst kinds. For me, finding hope is not some philosophical exercise or sentimental notion; it is a prerequisite for my survival.

In the winter of 2001, I had the foreknowledge that no remedy would come, and it was agonizing. I became unable to eat food, so instead I was drinking two two-liter bottles of Sprite per day, which is approximately the right number of calories to consume but not an ideal nutrition strategy.

I remember coming home from work and lying on the peeling linoleum   5
floor of what had been our kitchen, and looking through the Sprite bottle at the green parabolic rectangle of the kitchen window. I watched the bubbles inside the bottle clinging to the bottom, trying to hold on, but inevitably floating up to the top. I thought about how I couldn't think. I felt the pain pressing in on me, like it was an atmosphere. All I wanted was to be separated from the pain, to be free from it.

Eventually, a day came when I could not pick myself up off that linoleum floor, and I spent a very long Sunday thinking about all the ways that the situation might resolve itself. That evening, thank God, I called my parents, and, thank God, they answered.

My parents are busy people with demanding lives who lived fifteen hundred miles away from Chicago. And they were at my apartment within twelve hours of that phone call.

A plan formed quickly. I would leave my job, go home to Florida, get into daily counseling or possibly inpatient treatment. They packed up my apartment. My ex kindly agreed to take the cat. The only thing left was to quit my job.

I loved working at *Booklist*, and I loved my coworkers, but I also knew that my life was in danger. I tearfully told my supervisor that I had to quit, and after giving me a hug as I cried, he told me to talk to the magazine's publisher, Bill Ott.

I thought of Bill as a character out of a noir mystery novel. His incisive wit   10
is both thrilling and intimidating. When I went into his office, he was surrounded by proof pages of the magazine, and he didn't look up until I closed the door. I told him that something was wrong with my head, that I hadn't eaten solid food in a couple of weeks, and that I was quitting to move home to Florida with my parents.

He was silent for a long time after I finished. Bill is a master of pauses. And then at last he said, "Ah, why don't you just go home for a few weeks and see how you feel."

And I said, "But you'll need someone to do my job."

Again, he paused. "Don't take this the wrong way, kid, but I think we'll get by."

At one point that afternoon I started throwing up—excessive Sprite consumption, maybe—and when I came back to my desk to finish packing up my belongings, there was a note from Bill. I still have it. It reads:

> John, I stopped by to say goodbye. Hope all goes well and you're back here in two weeks with an appetite that would put a longshoreman to shame. Now more than ever: Watch Harvey. —Bill

15   For years, Bill had been bothering me to watch *Harvey*, and I steadfastly maintained that black-and-white movies were universally terrible, on account of how the special effects quality is poor and nothing ever happens except people talking.

I was back in Orlando, where I'd grown up. It felt like such a failure to be there, living with my parents, unable to do much of anything. I felt like I was nothing but a burden. My thoughts whorled and swirled. I couldn't ever think straight. I couldn't concentrate enough to read or write. I was in daily therapy, and taking a new medication, but I felt certain it wouldn't work, because I didn't think the problem was chemical. I thought the problem was me, at my core. I was worthless, useless, helpless, hopeless. I was less and less each day.

One night, my parents and I rented *Harvey*. Because it was adapted from a play, *Harvey* is, as I feared, a talky movie. Most of it takes place in only a few locations—the house Elwood P. Dowd shares with his older sister and his niece, the sanitarium where many believe Elwood belongs because his best friend is an invisible rabbit, and the bar where Elwood likes to hang out and drink.

Mary Chase's dialogue is magnificent throughout, but I especially love Elwood's soliloquies. Here is Elwood talking about chatting with strangers at the bar: "They tell me about the big, terrible things they've done and the wonderful things they'll do. Their hopes, and their regrets, and their loves, and their hates. All very large, because nobody ever brings anything small into a bar."

In another scene, Elwood tells his psychiatrist, "I've wrestled with reality for thirty-five years, Doctor, and I'm happy to state I finally won out over it."

20   Elwood is mentally ill. He's not much of a contributor to society. It'd be easy to characterize him as worthless, or hopeless. But he is also extraordinarily kind, even in difficult situations. At one point, his psychiatrist says, "This sister of yours is at the bottom of a conspiracy against you. She's trying to persuade me to lock you up. Today, she had commitment papers drawn up. She has the power of attorney over you." Elwood replies, "My sister did all that in one afternoon. That Veta certainly is a whirlwind, isn't she?"

Despite not being a traditional hero of any kind, Elwood is profoundly heroic. In my favorite line of the movie, he says, "Years ago my mother used to say to me, she'd say . . . 'In this world, you must be oh so smart, or oh so pleasant.' Well, for years I was smart. I recommend pleasant."

In December of 2001, there was perhaps no human alive on Earth who needed to hear those words more than I did.

I don't believe in epiphanies. My blinding-light awakenings always prove fleeting. But I'll tell you this: I have never felt quite as hopeless since watching *Harvey* as I did just before I watched it.

A couple of months after watching *Harvey*, I was able to return to Chicago and to *Booklist*. Although my recovery was halting and often precarious, I got better. It was probably the therapy and the medication, of course, but Elwood played his part. He showed me that you could be crazy and still be human, still be valuable, and still be loved. Elwood offered me a kind of hope that wasn't bullshit, and in doing so helped me to see that hope is the correct response to the strange, often terrifying miracle of consciousness. Hope is not easy or cheap. It is true.

As Emily Dickinson put it,   25

> *"Hope" is the thing with feathers—*
> *That perches in the soul—*
> *And sings the tune without the words—*
> *And never stops—at all—*

I still sometimes stop hearing the tune. I still become enveloped by the abject pain of hopelessness. But hope is singing all the while. It's just that again and again and again, I must relearn how to listen.

I hope you never find yourself on the floor of your kitchen. I hope you never cry in front of your boss desperate with pain. But if you do, I hope they will give you some time off and tell you what Bill told me: Now, more than ever, watch *Harvey*.

I give *Harvey* five stars.

MLA CITATION

Green, John. "*Harvey*." *The Norton Reader: An Anthology of Nonfiction*, edited by Melissa A. Goldthwaite et al., 16th ed., W. W. Norton, 2024, pp. 124–27.

QUESTIONS

1. John Green considers many ways of caring for oneself and caring for others, and he shows that the two acts can be intertwined. As you read his essay, annotate the places where he shows self-care and the places where he shows how others cared for him. What kinds of support did he seek? What kinds of care did others provide?

2. In writing about a film, especially one that many readers have not seen, it is important to give readers enough information to contextualize the film and show how it connects to the larger piece. What kinds of information about *Harvey* does Green provide? Why is that information significant to his essay?

3. Think of a piece of art or literature—such as a film, song, poem, or book—that helped you when you were going through a difficult time. Write a personal review, a letter to a friend, a podcast script, or a short essay that shows why you would recommend that piece to others.

MATT DE LA PEÑA
Why We Shouldn't Shield Children from Darkness

WICE THIS PAST FALL I was left speechless by a child.

The first time happened at an elementary school in Huntington, New York. I was standing on their auditorium stage, in front of a hundred or so students, and after talking to them about books and writing and the power of story, I fielded questions. The first five or six were the usual fare. Where do I get my ideas? How long does it take to write a book? Am I rich? (*Hahahahaha!*) But then a fifth-grade girl wearing bright green glasses stood and asked something different. "If you had the chance to meet an author *you* admire," she said, "what would *you* ask?"

For whatever reason this girl's question, on this morning, cut through any pretense that might ordinarily sneak into an author presentation. The day before, a man in Las Vegas had opened fire on concertgoers from his Mandalay Bay hotel room. Tensions between America and North Korea were reaching a boiling point. Puerto Ricans continued to suffer the nightmarish aftereffects of Hurricane Maria. I studied all the fresh-faced young people staring up at me, trying to square the light of childhood with the darkness in our current world.

All of this, of course, was wildly inappropriate for such a young audience— and had little to do with the question—so I just stood there in awkward silence, the seconds ticking by.

5 Eventually I gave the girl some pre-packaged sound bite about dealing with rejection, or the importance of revision, and then our time was up. But hours later, as I sat in a crowded airport, waiting for a delayed flight, I was still thinking about that girl's question. What *would* I ask an author I admire? Writers like Kate DiCamillo came to mind. Sandra Cisneros. Christopher Paul Curtis.[1]

Now I wanted a do-over.

A thoughtful question like that deserved a more thoughtful response.

Just as my plane reached its cruising altitude, it came to me. If I had the chance to ask Kate DiCamillo anything, it would be this: How honest can an author be with an auditorium full of elementary school kids? How honest should we be with our readers? Is the job of the writer for the very young to tell the truth or preserve innocence?

A few weeks ago, illustrator Loren Long and I learned that a major gatekeeper would not support our forthcoming picture book, *Love*, an exploration of love in a child's life, unless we "softened" a certain illustration. In the scene, a despondent young boy hides beneath a piano with his dog, while his parents argue across the living room. There is an empty Old Fashioned glass resting on top of the piano. The feedback our publisher received was that the moment was a

Originally published in Time *(2018).*

1. DiCamillo (b. 1964), writer best known for her children's books, including *Because of Winn-Dixie*; Cisneros (b. 1954), author of *The House on Mango Street*; Curtis (b. 1953), author of *Bud, not Buddy*.

little too heavy for children. And it might make parents uncomfortable. This discouraging news led me to really examine, maybe for the first time in my career, the purpose of my picture book manuscripts. What was I trying to accomplish with these stories? What thoughts and feelings did I hope to evoke in children?

This particular project began innocently enough. Finding myself overwhelmed by the current divisiveness in our country, I set out to write a comforting poem about love. It was going to be something I could share with my own young daughter as well as every kid I met in every state I visited, red or blue. But when I read over one of the early drafts, something didn't ring true. It was reassuring, uplifting even, but I had failed to acknowledge any notion of adversity.   10

So I started over.

A few weeks into the revision process, my wife and I received some bad news, and my daughter saw my wife openly cry for the first time. This rocked her little world and she began sobbing and clinging to my wife's leg, begging to know what was happening. We settled her down and talked to her and eventually got her ready for bed. And as my wife read her a story about two turtles who stumble across a single hat, I studied my daughter's tear-stained face. I couldn't help thinking a fraction of her innocence had been lost that day. But maybe these minor episodes of loss are just as vital to the well-adjusted child's development as moments of joy. Maybe instead of anxiously trying to protect our children from every little hurt and heartache, our job is to simply support them through such experiences. To talk to them. To hold them.

And maybe this idea also applied to the manuscript I was working on.

Loren and I ultimately fought to keep the "heavy" illustration. Aside from being an essential story beat, there's also the issue of representation. In the book world, we often talk about the power of racial inclusion—and in this respect we're beginning to see a real shift in the field—but many other facets of diversity remain in the shadows. For instance, an uncomfortable number of children out there right now are crouched beneath a metaphorical piano. There's a power to seeing this largely unspoken part of our interior lives represented, too. And for those who've yet to experience that kind of sadness, I can't think of a safer place to explore complex emotions for the first time than inside the pages of a book, while sitting in the lap of a loved one.

We are currently in a golden age of picture books, with a tremendous range to choose from. Some of the best are funny. Or silly. Or informative. Or socially aware. Or just plain reassuring. But I'd like to think there's a place for the emotionally complex picture book, too. Jacqueline Woodson's amazing *Each Kindness* comes to mind, in which the protagonist misses the opportunity to be kind to a classmate. Margaret Wise Brown's *The Dead Bird* is a beautiful exploration of mourning from the point of view of children.   15

Which brings me to the second child who left me speechless last fall.

I was visiting an elementary school in Rome, Georgia, where I read and discussed one of my older books, *Last Stop on Market Street*, as I usually do. But at the end of the presentation I decided, on a whim, to read *Love* to them, too, even though it wasn't out yet. I projected Loren's illustrations as I recited the poem from memory, and after I finished, something remarkable happened.

A boy immediately raised his hand, and I called on him, and he told me in front of the entire group, "When you just read that to us I got this feeling. In my heart. And I thought of my ancestors. Mostly my grandma, though . . . because she always gave us so much love. And she's gone now."

And then he started quietly crying.

And a handful of the teachers started crying, too.

20   I nearly lost it myself. Right there in front of 150 third graders. It took me several minutes to compose myself and thank him for his comment.

On the way back to my hotel, I was still thinking about that boy, and his raw emotional response. I felt so lucky to have been there to witness it. I thought of all the boys growing up in working-class neighborhoods around the country who are terrified to show any emotion. Because that's how I grew up, too—terrified. Yet this young guy was brave enough to raise his hand, in front of everyone, and share how he felt after listening to me read a book. And when he began to cry a few of his classmates patted his little shoulders in a show of support. I don't know if I've ever been so moved inside the walls of a school.

I hope one day I'll have the chance to formally ask Kate DiCamillo my questions about innocence and truth. But I do know this: My experience in Rome, Georgia? *That's* why I write books. Because the little story I'm working on alone in a room, day after day, might one day give some kid out there an opportunity to "feel." And if I'm ever there to see it in person again, next time hopefully I'll be brave enough to let myself cry, too.

MLA CITATION

Peña, Matt de la. "Why We Shouldn't Shield Children from Darkness." *The Norton Reader: An Anthology of Nonfiction*, edited by Melissa A. Goldthwaite et al., 16th ed., W. W. Norton, 2024, pp. 128–30.

QUESTIONS

1. In paragraph 8, Matt de la Peña shares a question he wishes he could ask another writer: "Is the job of the writer for the very young to tell the truth or preserve innocence?" How does he answer his own question in the remainder of his essay? Annotate the essay, marking passages where he considers this question.

2. Did you ever read something that others thought was too sad or otherwise too grown-up for you to read? What was your experience? Would you ever choose to shield children in your care from dark and sad stories?

3. De la Peña writes about visiting elementary schools, something children's book authors often do. Did you ever attend such an assembly? Whether or not an author came to your school, what do you think children learn from meeting writers in person?

4. What book do you remember most from childhood? Did it include pictures or themes that were sad or emotionally complex? Write about the experience of reading or having that book read to you.

CHERYL STRAYED

The Black Arc of It

D
EAR SUGAR,
I'm a thirty-eight-year-old guy and engaged to be married this summer. My fiancée is thirty-five. I don't need romantic advice. I'm writing to you about my fiancée's mother, who passed away from cancer several years before I met her, when my fiancée was twenty-three.

She and her mother were very close. Her death was an awful blow to my fiancée at the time and it still hurts her deeply. It's not like she can't get out of bed or is struggling with depression. She has a great life. One of her friends calls her "joy on wheels" and that's accurate, but I know it isn't the whole story. Her mom's death is always lurking. It comes up on a regular basis. When she cries or talks about how much she misses her mom, I'm supportive, but I usually feel insufficient. I don't know what to say beyond lame things like, "I'm sorry" and "I can imagine how you'd feel" (though I can't because my mom is still alive). She never had much of a relationship with her dad, who left the picture a long time ago, and her sister and her aren't very close, so I can't rely on someone in her family to be there for her. Sometimes I try to cheer her up or try to get her to forget about "the heavy stuff," but that usually backfires and only makes her feel worse.

I don't know how to handle this, Sugar. I feel lame in the face of her grief. I know you lost your mother too. What can you tell me? I want to be a better partner when it comes to handling grief.

Signed,
Bewildered

Dear Bewildered,
Several months after my mother died I found a glass jar of stones tucked in the far reaches of her bedroom closet. I was moving her things out of the house I'd thought of as home, clearing way for the woman with whom my stepfather had suddenly fallen in love. It was a devastating process—more brutal in its ruthless clarity than anything I've ever experienced or hope to again—but when I had that jar of rocks in my hands I felt a kind of elation I cannot describe in any other way except to say that in the cold clunk of its weight I felt ever so fleetingly as if I were holding my mother.

That jar of stones wasn't just any jar of stones. They were rocks my brother and sister and I had given to our mom. Stones we'd found as kids on beaches and trails and the grassy patches on the edges of parking lots and pressed into her hands, our mother's palms the receptacle for every last thing we thought worth saving.   5

First appeared in the Rumpus *(2011), an online literary magazine, where Cheryl Strayed was an advice columnist writing under the pseudonym "Sugar" and later appeared in her collection* Tiny Beautiful Things: Advice on Love and Life from Dear Sugar *(2012).*

I sat down on the bedroom floor and dumped them out, running my fingers over them as if they were the most sacred things on the earth. Most were smooth and black and smaller than a potato chip. *Worry stones* my mother had called them, the sort so pleasing against the palm she claimed they had the power to soothe the mind if you rubbed them right.

What do you do with the rocks you once gave to your dead mother? Where is their rightful place? To whom do they belong? To what are you obligated? Memory? Practicality? Reason? Faith? Do you put them back in the jar and take them with you across the wild and unkempt sorrow of your twenties or do you simply carry them outside and dump them in the yard?

I couldn't know. Knowing was so far away. I could only touch the rocks, hoping to find my mother in them.

Not long before my mother died, I met a woman who'd been attacked by a man as she walked home from a party. By the time I met her she lived in a group home for those with brain injuries. Her own injury was the result of the attack, her head having hit the sidewalk so hard in the course of it that she'd never be the same again. She was incapable of living alone, incapable of so very much, and yet she remembered just enough of her former life as a painter and teacher that she was miserable in the group home and she desperately longed to return to her own house. She refused to accept the explanations given to her as to why she couldn't. She had come to fervently believe that in order to be released she had only to recite the correct combination of numbers to her captors, her caretakers.

10   93480219072, she'd say as they fed her and bathed her and helped her get ready for bed. 6552091783. 4106847508. 05298562347. And on and on in a merciless spiral. But no matter what she said, she would never crack the code. There was no code. There was only the new fact of her life, changed irrevocably.

In the months after my mother died, I thought of this woman an inordinate amount and not only because I was distressed by her suffering. I thought of her because I understood her monumental desire and her groundless faith: I believed that I could crack a code too. That my own irrevocably changed life could be redeemed if only I could find the right combination of things. That in those objects my mother would be given back to me in some indefinable and figurative way that would make it okay for me to live the rest of my life without her.

And so I searched.

I didn't find it in the half empty container of peppermint Tic Tacs that had been in the glove compartment of my mother's car on the day she died or in the fringed moccasins that still stunk precisely of my mother's size six feet a whole year later. I didn't find it in her unfashionably large reading glasses or the gray porcelain horse that had sat on the shelf near her bed. I didn't find it in her pen from the bank with the real hundred-dollar bill shredded up inside or in the butter dish with the white marble ball in its top or in any one of the shirts she'd sewn for herself or for me.

And I didn't find it in those stones either, in spite of my hopes on that sad day. It wasn't anywhere, in anything and it never would be.

15   "It will never be okay," a friend who lost her mom in her teens said to me a couple years ago. "It will never be okay that our mothers are dead."

At the time she said this to me she wasn't yet really my friend. We'd chatted passingly at parties, but this was the first time we were alone together. She was fiftysomething and I was forty. Our moms had been dead for ages. We were both writers with kids of our own now. We had good relationships and fulfilling careers. And yet the unadorned truth of what she'd said—*it will never be okay*—entirely unzipped me.

It will never be okay, and yet there we were, the two of us more than okay, both of us happier and luckier than anyone has a right to be. You could describe either one of us as "joy on wheels," though there isn't one good thing that has happened to either of us that we haven't experienced through the lens of our grief. I'm not talking about weeping and wailing every day (though sometimes we both did that). I'm talking about what goes on inside, the words unspoken, the shaky quake at the body's core. There was no mother at our college graduations. There was no mother at our weddings. There was no mother when we sold our first books. There was no mother when our children were born. There was no mother, ever, at any turn for either one of us in our entire adult lives and there never will be.

The same is true for your fiancée, Bewildered. She is your joy on wheels whose every experience is informed and altered by the fact that she lost the most essential, elemental, primal and central person in her life too soon. I know this without knowing her. It will never be okay that she lost her mother. And the kindest most loving thing you can do for her is to bear witness to that, to muster the strength and courage and humility it takes to accept the enormous reality of its *not okayness* and be okay with it the same way she has to be. Get comfortable being the man who says *oh honey, I'm so sorry for your loss* over and over again.

That's what the people who've consoled me the most deeply in my sorrow have done. They've spoken those words or something like them every time I needed to hear it; they've plainly acknowledged what is invisible to them, but so very real to me. I know saying those cliché and ordinary things makes you feel squirmy and lame. I feel that way too when I say such things to others who have lost someone they loved. We all do. It feels lame because we like to think we can solve things. It feels insufficient because there is nothing we can actually do to change what's horribly true.

But compassion isn't about solutions. It's about giving all the love that you've got.

So give it, sweet pea. It's clear that you've done it already. Your kind letter is proof. But I encourage you to stop being bewildered. Have the guts to feel lame. Say that you're sorry for your lover's loss about three thousand times over the coming years. Ask about her mother sometimes without her prompting. Console her before she asks to be consoled. Honor her mother on your wedding day and in other ways as occasions arise. Your mother-in-law is dead, but she lives like a shadow mother in the woman you love. Make a place for her in your life too.

That's what Mr. Sugar has done for me. That's what some of my friends and even acquaintances have done. It doesn't make it okay, but it makes it better.

Next week it will be twenty years since my mother died. So long I squint every time the thought comes to me. So long that I've finally convinced myself there isn't a code to crack. The search is over. The stones I once gave my mother have scattered, replaced by the stones my children give to me.

I keep the best ones in my pockets. Sometimes there is one so perfect I carry it around for weeks, my hand finding it and finding it, soothing itself along the black arc of it.

Yours,
Sugar

MLA CITATION

Strayed, Cheryl. "The Black Arc of It." *The Norton Reader: An Anthology of Nonfiction*, edited by Melissa A. Goldthwaite et al., 16th ed., W. W. Norton, 2024, pp. 131–34.

QUESTIONS

1. As a reader, what do you expect from an advice column? In what places does Cheryl Strayed, as "Sugar," meet your expectations? In what places does she deviate from those expectations? Annotate the text to show both. Does this piece fit the advice-column genre? Why or why not?

2. Strayed writes quite a bit about the stones she and her siblings gave her mother, so much so that the stones become a symbol (an object that represents something in addition to itself). What do the stones represent in this piece?

3. What advice would you give to "Bewildered" or to someone else who was trying to support a loved one who experienced a painful loss?

DAISY HERNÁNDEZ
Envidia

THEY HAD WARNED ME about the bedsheets.

San Antonio is infamous for high temperatures in the summer, but the dorm rooms at this particular college had some kind of air-conditioning system that cranked nonstop. The combination of the refrigerated air and the windows that had been scaled for decades coated everything in a cold dampness, including the bedsheets and pillowcases and even the twin-sized mattress. I should have been prepared. I wasn't.

I was also not prepared for what would happen in that room during the week I was there to attend a writing workshop. Now that I think about it, though,

Published in Tricycle: The Buddhist Review *(2015), which seeks to provide "a unique and independent public forum for exploring Buddhism, establishing a dialogue between Buddhism and the broader culture, and introducing Buddhist thinking to Western disciplines."*

it makes sense, because dorm rooms are like a monk's room. Or how I imagine a monk's room to be. There's a mattress, a pillow, and a bedsheet. There's the floor and the single light fixture and the walls stripped of color. For teenager and practitioner alike, the room is a blank canvas.

It was the second or third night of the workshop, close to midnight, when I sat on the very cold bed in that dorm room in Texas and realized that I hated at least three of my friends and a woman I knew only marginally.

"Hate" is not the right word. "Hate" is the word I want to use because   5
everyone hates something, like the taste of root beer, for example, or mechanical pencils when the lead jams. There are also the big-world hates we can agree on: genocide, police brutality, high carbon footprints. Hate is, in public at least, accessible and acceptable.

I did not, however, hate three of my friends and the marginal woman. I envied them. I am trying to remember all the reasons now and even who the specific friends were at the time, but the list roughly boiled down to the fact that one friend had a spectacular book deal and another had finished her first book. A third friend was about to marry the love of her life and another had good hair. (I don't mean white folks' hair. I mean thick wavy dark hair that she didn't need to touch in the morning because she woke up looking *that good*.) I hated them all. No, I envied them. I wanted what they had.

The cold bedsheets bit into the back of my thighs while I tossed and turned that night. What makes *envidia*, or envy, so annoying is that it morphs. It looks like hate. It feels like annoyance. It turns into despair. (I'll never get what I want; what's wrong with me? I love my friends, right?) And because envy is hardly ever talked about in public, it is hardly ever an isolated feeling. The moment I recognized envy that night, I felt ashamed.

In the dark, I stared at the unadorned walls, then finally sat up and doubled the flat dorm pillow. If I was going to have an envy attack, I would at least use it as fodder for practicing lovingkindness.[1] I crossed my legs and tucked the pillow-turned-cushion under me. I did a body scan first. The envy was a knob in my solar plexus. A familiar knob. My hopes rose. Maybe it was not envy I was feeling but good old-fashioned depression instead. The moment I brought up the image of one of my friends, though, the knob turned into a knife and sent a stabbing sensation through my chest. Definitely not depression. I tried another round of lovingkindness. *Nada*.

At that point, I had been sitting for a little more than a decade. I considered myself a periphery Buddhist. I had my sangha[2] and I went on silent retreats. I took copious notes at dharma talks. I saw absolutely no conflict between Buddhist teachings and my upbringing in a Cuban-Colombian home where we practiced Catholicism and the Afro-Cuban religion of *Santería*. That night in San Antonio, however, I had to consider the possibility that Buddhism might not help me with envy precisely because I am a Latina, and my family

1. Meditation practice drawn from Buddhism, also known as metta bhavana, that emphasizes love and compassion for self and others.
2. Association or community of fellow spiritual practitioners.

and my culture had raised me to know that envy is not just bad—it's real bad. It's so bad that we have entire cultural practices set up for the sole purpose of keeping envidia out of our lives. Maybe this is what made that night in Texas so painful. I was transgressing a cultural practice dating back hundreds of years. I was courting the demon.

10   For years as a child, I thought all babies were born with white wardrobes and black eyeballs dangling from their shoulders.

The whiteness was consuming. There were the undershirts, the onesies, the beanie hats, the blankets, and the diapers, and in that blinding landscape, every baby had a tiny black eyeball gleaming from her left shoulder. The eyeball—a sphere made of the semiprecious stone jet—was attached to a single red bead and pinned to the baby's onesie with a gold-plated safety pin. Sometimes the black stone had not been shaped into a perfectly round eyeball but into a fist instead, and so the baby had a black fist swaying from her shoulders or hung from a gold necklace and rucked under her onesie.

The babies never touched the amulets but the women did. The mothers and aunties and *comadres*.[3] In New Jersey, the Cuban women cooed at a new baby and asked about feedings, and all the while their anxious fingers pulled at the layers of white blankets and white sweaters until they found the gold-plated safety pin and the eyeball. They smiled and murmured about how good it was that the baby had her *azabache*.[4] No one spoke of the origins of this practice, but the famed Cuban anthropologist Lydia Cabrera attributed it to the religion called Regla de Ochá, or Santería. The azabache, though, is also used in Europe. It's the stone that pilgrims carried for protection on the Camino de Santiago in Spain.

My mother did not care about the origins of the eyeball. A Colombian married to a Cuban, she pinned the azabache to my baby sister because she appreciated hearing that the black eyeball protected infants from the worst evil possible: envy.

Cubans do not believe in emotion as abstraction. When Cubans talk about envy, they talk about bad eyes, or to be exact, "the" bad eye as in *el ojo malo*, the evil eye. Envy, then, is the reason babies get sick for no reason. It's the reason grown women and men lose a job or a lover or even their homes. Envy is not a feeling state; it is an eyeball no one can see. It is the look someone gives you when they want what you have. Babies, being as they are luminous, are especially vulnerable to the evil eye, and in Spanish, because we apparently do not believe that the devil comes in degrees, bad and evil are the same word: *malo*.

15   The irony about the evil eye is that while it lurked everywhere in my childhood, no one admitted to having it. Even now, so many decades later, when I think of asking my mother if she has ever felt envy, my tongue falters. It would be like asking her if she has had sex outside of marriage. A decent woman does

3. Spanish for "godmothers."

4. Jet-stone amulet worn to protect against the evil eye.

not feel envidia. The evil eye is like syphilis or Ebola. It afflicts people who are not us, which is why at the age of 6, I thought envy was someone else's fault, and in my particular case, the fault of Charles Schulz.

In 1950, Schulz started publishing his comic strip *Peanuts*, and to be fair, he probably had no way of anticipating mass consumerism. He probably did not think, while he colored in Snoopy's black nose, that T-shirts and mugs and watches would be produced and sold at high prices based on his drawings. He probably did not think that someone would create a Snoopy telephone. But they did.

The phone, made in 1966, consisted of Snoopy standing upright, smiling and holding the yellow receiver in his right paw, while his bird friend, Woodstock, grinned, a bundle of plastic yellow feathers at his side. The phone's rotary dial sat on a base painted a cherry red.

I was about 6 years old when I saw that telephone in my friend's bedroom and there the problem began. I wanted the Snoopy phone. By this, I don't mean that I hoped Santa would bring me the same phone. I mean that I *needed* to have the Snoopy phone the way my father needed his can of Budweiser and his cigars, the way the old women at the corner store needed their lotto tickets. I could not imagine going on another day of my 6-year-old life without that Snoopy telephone. But, according to my mother, that was exactly what I would have to do, because while my mother had never heard anyone say outright that craving is the root of suffering, she knew that it was and she was no fool. The craving would pass, and my 6-year-old self would get over it.

It's questionable whether I ever did move on (periodically, I eye the Snoopy phones on *eBay*), but I do wonder now if envy helped usher me toward Buddhism. Raised in the Catholic church and on the periphery of the Afro-Cuban religion responsible for the azabaches, I never resonated with the notion of original sin; but craving? I knew craving, and for a long time I knew it as envy. After the Snoopy phone, there were the covered stickerbooks in third grade and the Nike sneakers in high school and the things I envied that I could not name, like the girls whose parents spoke English and people whose bodies weren't pinned to the past by trauma. I wanted it all.

It is possible that Francis Bacon got it right when he said that busy people   20
especially suffer from envy. "A man that is busy, and inquisitive, is commonly envious. . . . For envy is a gadding passion, and walketh the streets, and doth not keep home," he wrote in his essay "Of Envy." When I look back at the short course of my life, I have to admit that I have been roaming the world with a lot of curiosity about how other people live. In fact, in the last couple of years, I have learned that it is even possible to be envious of what I don't want, like a high-profile media job and being pregnant and tote bags that cost two hundred dollars. Spiritual envidia, though, might be the worst, since it's hard to acknowledge—for example, that you are envious of your Zen teacher for waking up at four in the morning to sit and never complaining (at least to you) about her knees when you are sure she is 20 years older than you.

Pema Chödrön's teacher, Chögyam Trungpa Rinpoche,[5] used to say that we failed on the spiritual journey because if we didn't "you would get so obnoxious and uncompassionate about other people." I like this idea. Maybe envy is keeping me on the spiritual journey, on the literal and metaphorical cushion. It's either that or I am the only Latina I know willing to admit that she knows where the ojo malo is located.

That night in San Antonio with the cold bedsheets and the envidia attack, I needed an azabache. That's why I turned to metta. If I could generate lovingkindness for the people I envied, surely it would shift my feelings and thoughts. And it worked. Actually, it began to work after about three nights. For the first two nights in that dorm room, I folded the pillow, sat on it, and brought my cat to mind. The image of her owl-shaped eyes was the equivalent of turning the valve on for metta. I could practically feel the biochemical start of lovingkindness. I got stuck, though, when I transferred it to my friend and her new book deal. Didn't she already have enough good stuff in her life? The thought flared for the first two nights, and on the third, it flared a little less. By the time I left San Antonio, I knew I didn't have a fix for envy. But I did have a way of working with it.

It's strange to compare metta to an amulet, but that is how I think of lovingkindness now. It's a black eyeball pinned to a baby's left shoulder. It's what my mother would gift me if I could ever admit to her the extent of my envidia.

MLA CITATION

Hernández, Daisy. "Envidia." *The Norton Reader: An Anthology of Nonfiction*, edited by Melissa A. Goldthwaite et al., 16th ed., W. W. Norton, 2024, pp. 134–38.

QUESTIONS

1. Daisy Hernández makes a distinction between "hate" and "envy." What is the difference?

2. Hernández writes that she saw no conflict between Buddhist teachings and her upbringing in Catholicism and the Afro-Cuban religion of Santería (paragraph 9). How does she bring different religious, cultural, and spiritual practices together in trying to deal with envy? Cite passages from the essay to support your answer.

3. Hernández focuses on envy as the worst evil in her culture. What was the "worst evil" in the culture in which you grew up? Were there any rituals, amulets, or icons meant to protect people from this evil? Write an essay in which you consider this evil and the safeguards against it.

---

5. Chödrön (b. 1936), American Tibetan Buddhist nun; Rinpoche (1939–1987), meditation expert and teacher of Tibetan Buddhism.

URSULA MURRAY HUSTED
Koan

Published in When Birds Are Near: Dispatches from Contemporary Writers (2020), edited by Susan Fox Rogers.

Nights were spent alone by Lake Wingra listening for Short-eared Owls and whip-poor-wills...

...and days, after and before work, drawing on the University of Wisconsin terrace, watching ducks raise their ducklings and pelicans stopping to rest on their journeys north.

When asleep, I dreamed of flying.

One afternoon, the radio said that the big pelican migration would be coming through Horicon Marsh. I called in sick, something I never did, and drove northeast on US Highway 151.

It was my first true solo expedition.

I waited up all night in the Visitor Center parking lot with my sketchbook ready, too excited to sleep.

MLA CITATION

Husted, Ursula Murray. "Koan." *The Norton Reader: An Anthology of Nonfiction*,
    edited by Melissa A. Goldthwaite et al., 16th ed., W. W. Norton, 2024,
    pp. 139–42.

QUESTIONS

1. Ursula Murray Husted titled this essay "Koan." What is a koan? Why do you think she chose that title for this piece?

2. Throughout this graphic memoir, Husted uses "flight" and "wings" as metaphors, even as she recounts a time when she observed and drew birds. Mark the passages that feature metaphors or similes. Why are they significant?

3. How does the artwork contribute to your understanding of Husted's message? How do the drawings supplement or change what you learn from the written text? Cite examples.

4. For Husted, spending time alone in nature and practicing her art seem to be acts of self-care. How do you practice self-care? Write or draw your response to this question.

Ross Gay
Tomato on Board

WHAT YOU DON'T know until you carry a tomato seedling through the airport and onto a plane is that carrying a tomato seedling through the airport and onto a plane will make people smile at you almost like you're carrying a baby. A quiet baby. I did not know this until today, carrying my little tomato, about three or four inches high in its four-inch plastic starter pot, which my friend Michael gave to me, smirking about how I was going to get it home. Something about this, at first, felt naughty—not comparing a tomato to a baby, but carrying the tomato onto the plane—and so I slid the thing into my bag while going through security, which made them pull the bag for inspection. When the security guy saw it was a tomato he smiled and said, "I don't know how to check that. Have a good day." But I quickly realized that one of its stems (which I almost wrote as "arms") was broken from the jostling, and it only had four of them, so I decided I better just carry it out in the open. And the shower of love began.

It was a shower of love I also felt while carrying a bouquet of lilies through the streets of Rome last summer. People, maybe women especially, maybe women my age-ish and older especially, smiling with approval. A woman in a housedress beating out a rug on a balcony shouted *Bravo!* An older couple holding hands both smiled at me and pulled into each other, knitting their fingers together. My showerers might have been disappointed to know I was not giving the lilies to a sweetheart but to my friends Damiano and Moira, who had translated a few of my poems into Italian and were so kind as to let me

Published in The Book of Delights *(2019), a collection of short personal essays that celebrate the delights in ordinary life.*

stay at their place a few nights while I was passing through. On the way to the vegetarian restaurant Damiano's ex-wife owns with her partner, we walked by what I'm pretty sure Damiano said was the biggest redbud tree in the world. It stretched for yards, lounging periodically onto the mossy earth, its beautiful black bark glistened by the streetlights. Though translation is an act of love, so my showerers needn't be disappointed at all.

Before boarding the final leg of my flight, one of the workers said, "Nice tomato," which I don't think was a come on. And the flight attendant asked about the tomato at least five times, not an exaggeration, every time calling it "my tomato"—*Where's my tomato? How's my tomato? You didn't lose my tomato, did you?* She even directed me to an open seat in the exit row: *Why don't you guys go sit there and stretch out?* I gathered my things and set the li'l guy in the window seat so she could look out. When I got my water I poured some into the li'l guy's soil. When we got bumpy I put my hand on the li'l guy's container, careful not to snap another arm off. And when we landed, and the pilot put the brakes on hard, my arm reflexively went across the seat, holding the li'l guy in place, the way my dad's arm would when he had to brake hard in that car without seatbelts to speak of, in one of my very favorite gestures in the encyclopedia of human gestures.

MLA CITATION

Gay, Ross. "Tomato on Board." *The Norton Reader: An Anthology of Nonfiction*, edited by Melissa A. Goldthwaite et al., 16th ed., W. W. Norton, 2024, pp. 143–44.

QUESTIONS

1. Ross Gay describes a "shower of love" (paragraph 1) from people who observed him carrying a tomato plant on board a plane and a "bouquet of lilies through the streets of Rome" (paragraph 2). Why do you think the people Gay describes responded with affection?

2. Mark the passages where Gay either personifies the tomato plant or compares it to humans. Why do you think he makes connections between the way he cares for the plant and the ways we might treat other humans?

3. Gay writes about a seemingly small thing that gave him and others pleasure. Write a short piece in which you describe a small thing that you consider a delight.

S.E. SMITH

The Beauty of Spaces Created for and by Disabled People

T HE THEATER IS DIM and just warm enough that I don't need my sweater, which I leave draped on the back of my creaky wooden seat. We are hushed, waiting for the lights to come up on the swooping ramp where the dance piece *Descent*, choreographed by Alice Sheppard in collaboration with Laurel Lawson, will be performed. This is one of my favorite parts of any theatrical production, the moment *before*, when anything might happen. Where all the barriers between us have fallen away.

Sheppard and then Lawson roll out, and they begin weaving intricate patterns with their bodies and wheelchairs while the music soars over them, with Michael Maag's lighting and projection weaving around them. The audio describer speaks in a low, rhythmic voice that broadcasts to the whole room, interplaying with the performance and the music.

There is something weighty and sacred here.

It is very rare, as a disabled person, that I have an intense sense of belonging, of being not just tolerated or included in a space but actively owning it; "This space," I whisper to myself, "is for me." Next to me, I sense my friend has the same electrified feeling. This space is for *us*.

I am spellbound. I am also overwhelmed, feeling something swell in my   5
throat as I look out across the crowd, to the wheelchair and scooter users at the front of the raked seating, the ASL interpreter in crisp black next to the stage. Canes dangle from seat backs and a gilded prosthetic leg gleams under the safety lights. A blind woman in the row below me turns a tiny model of the stage over in her hands, tracing her fingers along with it in time to the audio description.

"I really wish I could have crammed all my disabled peeps in there," I say later.

Members of many marginalized groups have this shared experiential touchstone, this sense of unexpected and vivid belonging and an ardent desire to be able to pass this experience along. Some can remember the precise moment when they were in a space inhabited entirely by people like them for the first time. For disabled people, those spaces are often hospitals, group therapy sessions, and other clinical settings. That is often by design; we are kept isolated from one another, as though more than two disabled people in the same room will start a riot or make everyone feel awkward.

The first *social* setting where you come to the giddy understanding that this is a place for disabled people is a momentous one, and one worth lingering over. I cannot remember the first time it happened to me—perhaps a house party in San Francisco or an art show or a meeting of friends at a café. The experiences blend together, creating a sense of crip space, a communal belonging, a deep

Published in Disability Visibility: First-Person Stories from the Twenty-First Century (2020), *edited by Alice Wong.*

rightness that comes from not having to explain or justify your existence. They are resting points, even as they can be energizing and exhilarating.

Crip space is unique, a place where disability is celebrated and embraced—something radical and taboo in many parts of the world and sometimes even for people in those spaces. The idea that we need our own spaces, that we thrive in them, is particularly troubling for identities treated socially as a negative; why would you want to self-segregate with the other cripples? For those newly disabled, crip space may seem intimidating or frightening, with expectations that don't match the reality of experience—someone who has just experienced a tremendous life change is not always ready for disability pride or defiance, needing a kinder, gentler introduction.

10   The creation of spaces explicitly for marginalized people and not for others has been fraught with controversy. Proponents insist they're necessary for people to have intra-community conversations and they create a safe environment for talking through complex issues. They also may say that people find them empowering, especially those who have been cut off from their community.

It isn't that nondisabled people are unwelcome at this dance performance. But the space has not been tailored to their needs and designed to seamlessly accommodate them, and they stand out. The experience pushes the boundaries of their understanding and expectations.

During the Q&A, the dancers roll forward and the ASL interpreter trails them.

"Any questions or comments?" one asks, the interpreter's hands moving swiftly in sync. The audience is momentarily frozen, as all audiences are at this question every time it is asked. The disabled people are still processing. We feel slightly giddy; this is a piece that speaks our common language, silently and beautifully, that reaches the deep parts of us we normally keep buttoned up and hidden away. The nondisabled people are hesitant, nervous, unsure about what to say in response to the work in progress we'd all been invited to witness.

"I liked . . . the ramp," one of the nondisabled people says hesitantly, gesturing at the set.

15   It must have been an unsettling experience, to be invited into our space. To be on the other side of the access divide. To see disabled people spreading their wings and soaring. To see wheelchairs turned into powerful extensions of dancers' bodies, enabling them to do things physically impossible for bipedal people.

Those in positions of power, evidently fearing that people are talking about them behind closed doors, persistently insist on barging into such spaces. They call these spaces divisive, and their organizers are told that they aren't valuing the contributions of allies. These bursts of petty outrage at stumbling upon one of the few places in the world that is not open to them inadvertently highlight exactly why such places are needed.

This is precisely *why* they are needed: as long as claiming our own ground is treated as an act of hostility, we need our ground. We need the sense of community for disabled people created in crip space. Yet, like any ground, it comes with soft spots and pitfalls, a reminder that the landscape is not uniform, can even become treacherous.

Even as some of us find a sense of belonging within these corners of the world carved out for one another, not everyone feels welcome in them; disability is a broad sociocultural identity and experience, and not everyone thinks about disability in the same way. This can be the paradox of crip space: When do we exclude others in our zeal to embrace ourselves, with our refusal to consider the diversity of human experience? How can we cultivate spaces where everyone has that soaring sense of inclusion, where we can have difficult and meaningful conversations?

Crip space is akin to a fragile natural place. It must be protected in order to preserve the delicate things within, while remaining open to change with the seasons and the passage of time. That protection sometimes requires sacrifice or challenge, awkward questions, but that makes it no less vital. Because everyone deserves the shelter and embrace of crip space, to find their people and set down roots in a place they can call home.

After the dance, after the Q&A, after the drinks and snacks in the lobby, we must regretfully disperse back out into the chilly December night. The theater is in the Tenderloin, a community in transition, nudie cuties cheek by jowl with hipster bars, and as we fan out across the sidewalk—stained with bird shit and mysterious sticky substances that cling to wheels and canes—we must return once more into the outside world, beyond crip space. The barriers begin to reappear.   20

A child across the street points at the phalanx of wheelchair users and says, "Look, Mommy!" Two adults stare, surprised when an adult wheelchair user unaccompanied by an attendant, braving the world alone, transfers into his car and slings his wheelchair into the backseat, pulling away from the curb with the quiet hum of an expensive German engine.

At the BART station around the corner, the elevators are, as usual, out of order.

MLA CITATION

smith, s.e. "The Beauty of Spaces Created for and by Disabled People." *The Norton Reader: An Anthology of Nonfiction*, edited by Melissa A. Goldthwaite et al., 16th ed., W. W. Norton, 2024, pp. 145–47.

QUESTIONS

1. What is "crip space"? Annotate the essay, marking the places s.e. smith uses and defines that term. Why are such spaces important?

2. This essay includes discussions of inclusion and exclusion. How do the places smith describes (a performance space, the sidewalk outside the theater, public transportation) and the people in those spaces shape feelings of inclusion and exclusion?

3. Analyze a space with which you are familiar (such as a restaurant, theater, cafeteria, museum, dorm room, classroom, or some other space). Consider the design and decoration of that space; consider who is there and who isn't. Who might feel included in that space? Who might feel excluded? Why?

ELLEN WAYLAND-SMITH
Natural Magic

I.

T O HAVE CANCER is to take an unasked-for trip inside the body, to be forced to see by the stark light of day the body's normally invisible workings. It is to see the self (or a part of the self) lit up on an ultrasound screen, a black mass nestled in the grainy gray flesh of your breast, and know—not in a passing way, but in a fateful, here-to-stay way—that's me. And then you dive in even deeper and understand that the mass exists because of a disorder in your house at the cellular level.

Like rude party guests, your cells have ceased to behave. They do not wait for the proper signal from the host to invite more friends, but multiply with raucous abandon, overrunning the house. They (unlike the rule-abiding hosts) are not bothered by overcrowding. Normal cells are governed by a principle called "contact inhibition": they sense the presence of other cells in the room, and when the room gets too crowded, they politely stop dividing. Cancer cells don't respond to these chemical cues. They fill the rooms to bursting, spilling out the windows, passing out drunk in the back yard.

To know that your life depends on a microscopic dollop of protoplasm and its antics is to see life in a whole new way. The more you think about the complex mechanics of cells and the body, the trillions of tiny signals and movements and chemical shufflings that undergird a single second of a living body's existence, the more improbable your own existence seems. It is a cliché that grave illness and brushes with death tend to heighten humans' sensitivity to the numinous: illness brings us closer to God, or at the very least to a chastened understanding of "what really matters" in life. This is because illness is a radically decentering experience, revealing the self as dependent on some larger unseen thing that humbles by its sheer complexity and magnitude. Call it biological life; the earth's ecosystem; the cosmos; God.

To think of what must happen at a cellular level to allow me each morning to twist my hair into a bun, apply a shade of age-appropriate lipstick, grab my keys and coffee, and head out the door—to glimpse the vast, mysterious architecture that enables and gives its blessing to that self—is to recognize the almost comical contingency of any single life. It is to realize how little in possession of our lives we actually are, how little they belong to us.

II.

5   We secular moderns are ill equipped to deal with this decentering, to make sense of our individual lives as embedded in a larger whole (whether biological

Published in the American Scholar *(2021), a magazine published by the Phi Beta Kappa Society.*

or theological). But for millennia, the self was unintelligible outside of its participation in the cosmos. From ancient Greece up through early modern Western thought, the human body was imagined as a microcosm, replicating in miniature the structure of the universe. No motion of the stars or planets was without its corollary motion in the world of earthly creatures below.

Before it was a disease, *cancer*—from the Greek *karkinos*, or *crab*—was a constellation. Babylonian astronomers, who identified it as early as the second millennium BC as one of a dozen-plus star patterns, used its movements across the night sky to divine the future. The Greeks gave the Babylonian crab a back-story: as Heracles was fighting off the Hydra in one of his 12 labors, Hera sent a giant crab to wrestle him and slow his progress. Heracles, undaunted, crushed the creature easily with his heel. Hera collected the shards of the crab's body and placed them in the night sky, a reward for the poor beast's loyalty.

By the second century AD, Ptolemy had codified the predictive art of star reading in his *Tetrabiblos*, or *Four Books of the Influence of the Stars*. Ptolemy refined the notion of the universe as a series of 10 revolving nested spheres, containing the sun, moon, planets, and stars of the zodiac, with Earth as its fixed center. The Earth itself and everything on it, including the human body, were composed of four elements—earth, water, fire, and air—that in order and balance mirrored the motions of the heavens. Because human, animal, plant, and mineral bodies were created from the same material as astral bodies, they necessarily exerted an influence on one another, creating a web of secret sympathies and correspondences that bound the universe together.

That the sun's motions should influence earthly bodies was evident enough. But the positioning of the moon, planets, stars, and zodiac clusters, though their action might be less directly visible, also affected the wax and wane of Earth's creatures. And Ptolemy wrote that "all the [heavenly bodies'] various influences compounded together," once expertly measured and calculated by the astrologer, could help predict "the destiny and disposition of every human being." This was especially true in matters of health in later centuries, as the four humors composing the human body—blood, phlegm, black bile, and yellow bile—were thought to rise and fall, like the ocean's tides, in response to the distant tug of celestial motions. When the humors in a body became unbalanced, blocked, or thickened, sickness ensued.

Early modern physicians consulted astronomical tables when treating patients. Medical almanacs contained charts for calculating the moon's position as it cycled through the signs of the zodiac, as well as tracking which planet was dominant at each hour of the day and night. When the moon was in its first and third stages, the body's liquids were thought to cluster at the surface of the body like tidal waters, making that a propitious time for blood-letting to drain off polluting humors. To aid in treatment, medical almanacs frequently included an anatomical illustration of the human body, *Homo signorum*, nicknamed by historians Zodiac Man.

Zodiac Man stares out impassively at the viewer in one jewel-colored version, a map of the heavens superimposed on his patient, outstretched body. The figure stands atop two fish representing Pisces, while Leo the lion fills the heart

10

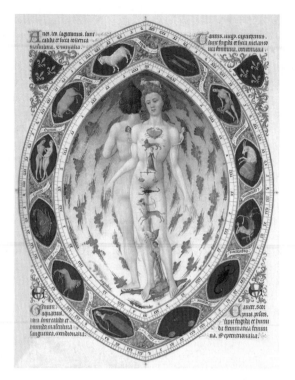

Zodiac Man, an anatomical illustration of the
human body used by early modern physicians.

and chest cavity, and a muscled Taurus sits coiled around his shoulders: to each
body part, its corresponding star cluster. The moon was thought, like a cosmic
magnifying glass, to intensify the power of each zodiac sign, so that the brief
period of their crossing each month was sure to signal a critical phase in any
associated ailment. The careful practitioner who sought to cure a patient of
headaches knew, for example, not to undertake bloodletting when the moon was
in Aries, the constellation responsible for sicknesses of the head.

Once the blood was drawn, the physician carefully examined it for texture, color, smell, and even taste, as a means to further gauge the nature of a
patient's illness. Greasy blood indicated that the liver was failing to concoct
ingested food properly, and an herbal elixir—gathered and compounded when
the heavens were propitiously aligned—might help to right the organ's function. Robert Turner's 1664 plant encyclopedia lists native English plants and
their healing virtues. White maudlyn, a sweet garden herb under the sway of
fiery Jupiter, helped stimulate "cold and weak livers." Water betony, ruled by
cold Saturn, acted as a "good cooler in Burnings and Scaldings," and a paste
made of sheep's dung, hog lard, and leaves of betony mashed in a mortar was
"likewise good to dissolve swellings and hard knobs."

Marsilio Ficino's 1489 *Three Books on Life* gives useful tips on how to augment the body's vitality through medical astrology. "If you want your body . . . to receive power from some member of the cosmos, say from the Sun," he counsels, "seek the things which above all are most Solar among metals and gems, still more among plants, and more yet among animals, especially human beings." Some of the created things with which contact could boost the solar composition of the body: gold, chrysolite, amber, saffron, aloeswood, hawks, swans, and people with blond hair. "The above-mentioned things can be adapted partly to foods, partly to ointments and fumigations, partly to usages and habits," Ficino advises. If you think your liver is failing to do its appointed work of heating the ingested contents of your belly, "draw the power of the liver to the belly both by rubbing and by fomentations made from things which agree with the liver," such as chicory, endive, and pastes concocted from animal livers.

So it was that nothing in the created universe existed in and of and for itself. Leaf and stone, bird and beast, planet and human were not strangers one to the other but secret sharers, speakers of a common cosmic tongue. So it was that the physician, at his patient's side, could taste the stars in a drop of blood.

III.

The English word *zodiac* is derived from the Greek *zoidiakos kyklos*, meaning "circle of little animals." Early modern illustrations of the zodiac look like aerial views of a carousel: a menagerie of sign-creatures—lion, bull, scorpion, fish—wrapped around a sphere. The year that I lived in Florence with my family, on Sunday afternoons in the fall we'd go to the park and hope that the carousel was open. The crispness in the air and the setting November sun were melancholy, so to catch a glimpse of the wheeling carousel, with its string of bright white lights and tinsel music, was like swallowing something warm—a tonic against the encroaching frost, a draught of heat to counterbalance the chill in our cheeks and fingers. My four-year-old would hoist herself up on some slick, colorful beast, and I'd take a seat in one of the gilded coaches painted with curlicues and flowers, my one-year-old perched on my lap, and round we'd go.

Today, as cancer cycles through my body, the memory feels like a talisman, part charm, part warning: tiny spinning animals, earthbound specks of light beneath the darkling sky.

IV.

The hospital where I get my chemo infusions is brand spanking new, bright and white and cheerful in these pre-Covid times. This is encouraging. If my body is bent under the weight of its sickness, the building at least is upright, seemingly immune to the battering of the elements and the wear and tear of time. I grab my café au lait from the kiosk in front of the hospital. The automatic glass doors part before me, and, from behind a modishly curved white desk at the entrance, a young woman smiles expansively and wishes me welcome. I feel as though I could be at a bank or a hotel, which, I suppose, is the point. The modern Western biomedical enterprise is designed to put nature, red in tooth and claw,[1] to rout. That most obscene and inhumane of natural outcomes, death, is an enemy not to be tolerated. We see this in the military vocabulary commonly used to describe cancer treatment itself: it is a "battle," always "valiantly fought," and the patient who "beats" cancer in this zero-sum game is reckoned a "survivor": humans 1, nature 0.

The blood-draw station on the ground floor is my first stop. I wait for the nurse to call my number—0756—then take a seat in the phlebotomist's chair. First the squeak of the rubber strap as she knots it around my bicep, then "make a fist." I wait for what I know will come next. "Good veins," she murmurs from behind her surgical mask, and I feel a blush of idiot pride, as I always do: gold foil star for anatomy. My siphoned blood is whisked offstage for testing, and a specialist trained in the modern art of blood reading will decipher my fate. "Your numbers look good, Ellen," my oncologist, who appears to be no older than 18, will later assure me.

At the blood-draw station, they play ambient music on a loop, the kind that mixes synthesizer panpipes with recorded nature soundscapes: trickling water or wind or birdcalls, sometimes all three. It is music I've heard only in yoga classes or in the massage rooms at boutique spas; it makes me think of warm towels and the sweet smoke of incense. An MRI imaging study, I learn, shows that the brain relaxes its fight-or-flight response when exposed to nature sounds, even recordings of them. Still, I find the music incongruous as I look out at the other patients in the waiting room. We are so many scattered atoms, shuttled one by one through this clean, white biomedical machine. What have we to do with wind and water and birdsong, the bosomy embrace of nature?

After I'm cleared by my oncologist, I head up to the fourth floor and check in. The waiting room crowd here is a little more haggard than that down below: an older man in faded jeans coughs from behind his white protective face mask; a woman in a flowered headscarf pages through *People* magazine. This level is for the Truly III, the transplant and cancer patients. My nurse Michael comes out to get me. He is tousled-blond and chipper, tall and broad shouldered, with gym-perfected pecs and biceps that swell to fill his red scrubs. We chat about small things as he preps my medicines. Did I try the Tylenol and Claritin mix the doctor recommended for postchemo bone pain? Yes, I say, and it doesn't do a damn thing; only Advil helps a little. Michael nods vigorously in agreement. "I'm an Advil fan too," he confesses. As he slides the IV needle into my arm, he apologizes with a wince, mirror neurons at work. "Liiiittle pinch, I'm so sorry."

20   In the infusion room, each patient gets her own mini-cabin, discreetly partitioned. We sit side by side, as if in a movie theater, facing floor-to-ceiling windows that run the length of the building. We each have our own private room with a view. This is a university hospital, and across the street they are

---

1. A phrase depicting the violence of nature from Alfred Lord Tennyson's "*In Memoriam A. H. H.*" (1850), a poem written after the death of Tennyson's friend, Arthur Henry Hallam. The phrase comes from Canto 56: "Who trusted God was love indeed / And love Creation's final law / Tho' Nature, red in tooth and claw / With ravine, shriek'd against his creed."

building a new dormitory for medical students. Beyond the construction is a train track, then the 101 freeway, and beyond that the dusty green foothills of the San Gabriel Mountains. Hawks circle above the palm trees, searching out snakes and mice and rabbits and baby birds, as humans scuttle about on the sidewalks below, noses buried in their phones.

We no longer see the earth as part of us, an entanglement of heart and sinew, bound by the shared tempo of circling blood and circling planets. Rather, we exist in uneasy cohabitation with nature, each carving out its own separate sphere. Nature is ingenious and tries to adapt to our incursions. The hawk learns to hunt and pick across an urban landscape, gorging on human-fed songbirds, a fattened luxury unknown in the wild. It learns to nest in eucalyptus trees, good in a pinch when more hospitable native trees are scarce. As for humans, we take nature in medicinal doses, and always on our own terms, packaged into easily digested health supplements.

V.

In the vegetable kingdom, few plants are more toxic to humans than *Taxus baccata*, the European yew tree. Ingesting even a handful of its evergreen needles can be lethal. They contain compounds, known as taxines, that inhibit calcium and sodium transport in myocardial cells, leading to arrhythmia and then heart failure.

The yew is one of two plant ingredients that the witches in *Macbeth* throw into their maleficent brew: to accompany "root of hemlock digg'd i' the dark," they add "slips of yew, / Silver'd in the moon's eclipse." The animal ingredients the witches harvest for their potion sound even more monstrous to the modern ear. "Fillet of a fenny snake, / In the cauldron boil and bake; / Eye of newt and toe of frog, / Wool of bat and tongue of dog." When Macbeth asks the witches to riddle his future, we are not surprised that his luck turns bad.

But many of these baleful-sounding ingredients would have had a familiar ring to the early modern ear. Herbs and minerals and animal parts were essential to concocting all manner of health-inducing pills, oils, and ointments. Edward Topsell's 1658 *History of Four-Footed Beasts and Serpents* recommends, among "the medicines arising out of the female goat," that "the right eye of a green living Lizard, being taken out, and his head forthwith struck off, and put in a goat's skin, is of great force against . . . Agues," and that a freshly killed adder, "included in a pot with the scrapings of Vines, and therein burnt to ashes," makes an effective paste for soothing boils.

Indeed, so thin was the line separating the medical from the black arts 25 that Robert Turner's herbal manual begins by praising God for enduing "the Plants and Grass of the Field with such salubrious Faculties for our health and preservation" but then quickly turns to warn against their improper use. He speaks ominously of "druids," "heathens," "Medean hags and sorcerers" who forgo the lawful use of God's creatures and, instead, "out of some Diabolical intention, search after the more Magical and occult Vertues of Herbs and Plants to accomplish some wicked end."

There was sinister, demonic magic at work in the witches' brew. But the protoscientific healing arts, freely mixing alchemy, astronomy, and botany, were magic, too, christened "natural magic." Healers worked by trial and error to find the exact combination of herbs and stones and animal parts that would seal the rent in the universe that was a sickly, unbalanced body. The empirical sciences of the 17th century arose not in opposition to natural magic but as its outgrowth. They had their source not in the arid air-castles dreamed up by university philosophers but in the earth-caked grit of the apothecary's lab.

I know about the Janus-faced yew tree, balm or bane depending on its use. Chemists in the 1960s isolated a molecule in yew bark and needles—resulting in paclitaxel, related to but distinct from the lethal compound taxine B—that prevents cell division in tumors. To divide, cells need to be supple and soft, able to split like a hunk of bread dough twisted into two smaller knots. Paclitaxel stiffens the cells' molecular spines; when they go to divide, they splinter apart instead, scattered into lifeless pieces like Hera's crushed crab. Trademarked and lab-produced as Taxol, this tree serum is one of the chemical concoctions that I receive, intravenously, every three weeks.

I have always been bad at numbers. In 11th-grade chemistry, I sat next to another mathematical dunce, a shy, sandy-haired girl named Tina, with whom the teacher paired me up to solve the equations he'd chalked out on the board. "Maybe between the two of you, you'll come up with half the answer," he'd quip. Today, with my unpracticed chemist's eye, I scrutinize the formulas for poison ($C_{33}H_{45}NO_9$) and salve ($C_{47}H_{51}NO_{14}$) respectively; I trace the clusters of their rings and bonds, circles and dashes, with my finger. The skeletal formulae look like miniature constellations, printed in black and white. One arrangement of atoms stops the heart. But scramble the order, add or subtract an electron, and it stalls a tumor. This is a species of combinatory sorcery, mystery at the heart of matter.

After Michael hooks me up, I sit nodding beneath my chemo IV tree, a sac of Taxol hanging from its metal branches like a swollen plastic fruit. I imagine the matter-rich, earthy origins of this elixir—the roughness of scraped brown tree bark and crushed needles, boiled and baked into a clear quintessence—and suddenly, the self-enclosed loop of my body splits open like a vein and floods into the larger wheel of natural life, mixing my blood with its blood, a universal tumble and whirl, the stars in my cells. Slips of yew circling through my tissues, carrying out their chemical magic in the blind heart of my flesh, binding and unbinding, ever-shifting atoms blooming into momentary constellations that (with a dash of luck) will right my body's wobbly universe, at least for a time.

MLA CITATION

Wayland-Smith, Ellen. "Natural Magic." *The Norton Reader: An Anthology of Nonfiction*, edited by Melissa A. Goldthwaite et al., 16th ed., W. W. Norton, 2024, pp. 148–54.

QUESTIONS

1. Ellen Wayland-Smith structures this essay by using sections that discuss not only her own treatments for cancer but also the evolution of modern medicine and how illness was viewed in other times. Annotate each numbered section, summarizing the main point. How do these sections work together to show an individual life "as embedded in a larger whole" (paragraph 5)?

2. Wayland-Smith uses many similes, metaphors, and other kinds of comparisons and contrasts. For example, she compares cancer cells to "rude party guests" (paragraph 2) and compares a particular memory to "a talisman, part charm, part warning" (paragraph 15). Her essay also compares and contrasts different approaches to medicine and treating illness. Which comparisons or contrasts did you find especially effective? Why?

3. Although much of Wayland-Smith's essay shows the move in modern medicine away from "'natural magic'" (paragraph 26), she continues to focus on the natural roots of even some modern treatments, including certain chemotherapies, such as Taxol. Why is that connection important for Wayland-Smith?

4. Consider your own experiences (or the experience of someone you know well) with illnesses and treatments. Can you think of any treatments that could be described as "natural magic"? Give specific examples to illustrate your answer.

JAMES DENSLEY AND JILLIAN PETERSON
The Steps We Can Take to Reduce Mass Shootings in America

ON OCTOBER 1, 2015, after a gunman shot and killed his professor and eight students at Umpqua Community College in Oregon, President Barack Obama, who three years earlier, following the massacre at Sandy Hook elementary school in Connecticut, had failed to force Congress to pass new gun safety laws, stood frustrated at the podium. "Somehow this has become routine. The reporting is routine. My response here at this podium ends up being routine, the conversation in the aftermath of it. . . . We have become numb to this."

Fast forward seven years and amid a recent spate of horrific mass shootings—at a Buffalo supermarket, a Texas elementary school, and a Tulsa hospital[1]—it feels like little has changed. In fact, things have gotten worse—mass shootings are more frequent and deadlier than ever.

Published in Time *(2022) and based on research James Densley and Jillian Peterson did for* The Violence Project: How to Stop a Mass Shooting Epidemic *(2021).*

1. These three mass shootings, during which gunmen killed at least thirty-five people and injured many others, took place between May 14 and June 1, 2022.

A child holds flowers at a memorial dedicated to the victims of a mass shooting.

It's hard not to feel numb. When comparable nations have suffered deadly mass shootings—Australia, Canada, Germany, Great Britain, New Zealand, Switzerland—they respond with new laws curtailing firearm access and they rarely experience another mass shooting. In America, we wait for decisive action that never comes while mass shootings continue unabated.

Five years ago, tired of waiting for Congress to act with courage and conviction, we started researching the lives of mass shooters. Our goal was to gather the data that could change the exhausting routine President Obama called out—even if only incrementally, step-by-step. Our findings are outlined in the 2021 book, *The Violence Project: How to Stop a Mass Shooting Epidemic*.

5   To our genuine surprise, talking to mass shooters in prison and people who knew them, people who planned a shooting but never went through with it, victims' families, shooting survivors, and first responders gave us reason to hope. We learned there are things we can do right here, right now, as individual concerned citizens, to stop a mass shooting before it ever starts.

It begins with a shift in mindset. Mass shooters are not them. They are us—boys and men we know. Our children. Our students. Our colleagues. Our community. This fact may make mass shooters seem harder to stop. The reality is quite the opposite.

Half of all mass shooters—and nearly 80% of school mass shooters—communicate intent to do harm ahead of time. They post threats on social media or tell their family and friends in person. This is a crucial opportunity for intervention, but many people don't know what to do with that information or where and how to report it.[2] By training ourselves to say something if we see or hear something that gives us pause, and by lobbying for behavioral intervention and threat assessment teams in our schools and workplaces, communities can proactively respond to these warning signs long before a prospective shooter ever picks up a gun.

A mass shooting is intended to be the final act of a person who has reached breaking point. No one thinks they'll get away with a mass shooting; mass shootings end one of three ways: with the shooter taking their own life, law enforcement taking it for them, or the perpetrator spending the rest of their life in prison.

This all means classical deterrence mechanisms like harsh punishment or armed security at the door do little to prevent mass shootings. A suicidal shooter may in fact be drawn to a location if they know someone on site is trained to kill them. Rather than giving desperate people incentive to die, we must give them a reason to live.

Like CPR, suicide prevention and crisis intervention are skills anyone can learn—you don't have to be a doctor or psychologist. We've trained thousands of people in verbal and nonverbal de-escalation techniques like active listening and focusing on feelings (not facts) in recent years: police officers, teachers, journalists, college professors, and office workers. Crisis intervention saves lives.

A crisis overwhelms a person's usual coping mechanisms—a person in crisis is like a balloon ready to pop. All we must do is let a bit of the air out. We don't have to completely deflate the balloon, or figure out then and there how and why it got so full, or make sure it can never get inflated again. The goal is not a long-term mental health treatment. Crisis intervention is recognizing when someone is in a crisis and stepping in to help them through that moment.

The problems in the lives of mass shooters feel so massive and overwhelming, but sometimes it's the smallest thing that can get someone through a moment. In a popular TEDx Talk, Aaron Stark describes being diverted from the pathway to violence by a blueberry-peach pie. He was days away from perpetrating a school shooting, but a simple act of kindness, a homemade pie, reminded him that there was still good in the world and saved his life. Likewise, if people can't get their hands on the easiest tools to harm themselves or others, there will be fewer tragedies. Most school shooters get their guns from home, which means parents of school-aged children can prevent death simply by locking up their firearms. Collectively, we all need to be more alert, more compassionate, and in some cases more restrained in order to stop mass shootings. Mass shooters often are inspired by past mass shooters and the notoriety they achieved for their actions. We can counter this by only watching, liking, and sharing media coverage that is solution-focused and that names the real protagonists of these stories: the victims and survivors, communities and first responders. Even in our casual conversations, focus on stories of bravery, strength, and resiliency instead of reveling in scenes of carnage and chaos.

2. Organizations such as Sandy Hook Promise provide training and resources for intervention and reporting.

Mass shootings are not an inevitable fact of American life; they're preventable. But for too long, America has either viewed possible solutions to mass shootings in isolation or created false dichotomies that are pitted against each other, from gun safety measures to mental health treatment. Even when solutions have merit, they are then wrongly dismissed for being imperfect. The reality is that imperfections do not render solutions useless. There is no one solution to this problem. As with Swiss cheese, there are holes—but if you layer the slices, one on top of the other, the holes start to get covered up. Just like we learned in dealing with the COVID-19 pandemic.

And layering imperfect solutions, holistically, is the only way to prevent mass violence.

MLA CITATION

Densley, James, and Jillian Peterson. "The Steps We Can Take to Reduce Mass Shootings in America." *The Norton Reader: An Anthology of Nonfiction*, edited by Melissa A. Goldthwaite et al., 16th ed., W. W. Norton, 2024, pp. 155–58.

QUESTIONS

1. As you read this article, annotate the text, marking the practices that James Densley and Jillian Peterson claim can reduce mass shootings and those practices that they argue do not work. Did any of those claims surprise you? Why?

2. Densley and Peterson write, "Like CPR, suicide prevention and crisis intervention are skills anyone can learn" (paragraph 10). What people, offices, or other resources on your campus provide support for those in crisis or for learning how to respond when you or someone you know needs help? As a class or on your own, brainstorm a list of those resources and when and where to seek assistance.

3. Densley and Peterson write that "layering imperfect solutions, holistically" (paragraph 14) is a way to take action in facing a complex problem. Make a list of three solutions you think will help with the problem of mass shootings and provide support for why you think those solutions are good ones.

ASAM AHMAD

A Note on Call-Out Culture

ALL-OUT CULTURE refers to the tendency among progressives, radicals, activists, and community organizers to publicly name instances or patterns of oppressive behaviour and language use by others. People can be called out for statements and actions that are sexist, racist, ableist, and the list goes on. Because call-

"A Note on Call-Out Culture" (2015) and its follow-up "When Calling Out Makes Sense" (2017) both appeared in Briarpatch Magazine, *a publication that reports on grassroots social movements and seeks to build them.*

outs tend to be public, they can enable a particularly armchair and academic brand of activism: one in which the act of calling out is seen as an end in itself.

What makes call-out culture so toxic is not necessarily its frequency so much as the nature and performance of the call-out itself. Especially in online venues like *Twitter* and *Facebook*, calling someone out isn't just a private interaction between two individuals: it's a public performance where people can demonstrate their wit or how pure their politics are. Indeed, sometimes it can feel like the performance itself is more significant than the content of the call-out. This is why "calling in" has been proposed as an alternative to calling out: calling in means speaking privately with an individual who has done some wrong, in order to address the behaviour without making a spectacle of the address itself.

In the context of call-out culture, it is easy to forget that the individual we are calling out is a human being, and that different human beings in different social locations will be receptive to different strategies for learning and growing. For instance, most call-outs I have witnessed immediately render anyone who has committed a perceived wrong as an outsider to the community. One action becomes a reason to pass judgment on someone's entire being, as if there is no difference between a community member or friend and a random stranger walking down the street (who is of course also someone's friend). Callout culture can end up mirroring what the prison-industrial complex teaches us about crime and punishment: to banish and dispose of individuals rather than to engage with them as people with complicated stories and histories.

It isn't an exaggeration to say that there is a mild totalitarian undercurrent not just in call-out culture but also in how progressive communities police and define the bounds of who's *in* and who's *out*. More often than not, this boundary is constructed through the use of appropriate language and terminology—a language and terminology that are forever shifting and almost impossible to keep up with. In such a context, it is impossible not to fail at least some of the time. And what happens when someone has mastered proficiency in languages of accountability and then learned to justify all of their actions by falling back on that language? How do we hold people to account who are experts at using anti-oppressive language to justify oppressive behaviour? We don't have a word to describe this kind of perverse exercise of power, despite the fact that it occurs on an almost daily basis in progressive circles. Perhaps we could call it *anti-oppressivism*.

Humour often plays a role in call-out culture and by drawing attention to   5
this I am not saying that wit has no place in undermining oppression; humour can be one of the most useful tools available to oppressed people. But when people are reduced to their identities of privilege (as white, cisgender, male, etc.) and mocked as such, it means we're treating each other as if our individual social locations *stand in* for the total systems those parts of our identities represent. Individuals become synonymous with systems of oppression, and this can turn systemic analysis into moral judgment. Too often, when it comes to being called out, narrow definitions of a person's identity count for everything.

No matter the wrong we are naming, there are ways to call people out that do not reduce individuals to agents of social advantage. There are ways of calling people out that are compassionate and creative, and that recognize the whole individual instead of viewing them simply as representations of the systems from which they benefit. Paying attention to these other contexts will mean refusing to unleash all of our very real trauma onto the psyches of those we imagine to only represent the systems that oppress us. Given the nature of online social networks, call-outs are not going away any time soon. But reminding ourselves of what a call-out is meant to accomplish will go a long way toward creating the kinds of substantial, material changes in people's behaviour—and in community dynamics—that we envision and need.

MLA CITATION

Ahmad, Asam. "A Note on Call-Out Culture." *The Norton Reader: An Anthology of Nonfiction,* edited by Melissa A. Goldthwaite et al., 16th ed., W. W. Norton, 2024, pp. 158–60.

When Calling Out Makes Sense

I N 2015, I wrote "A Note on Call-Out Culture" for *Briarpatch Magazine,* and it has since circulated far more widely than I expected and in ways I could not have anticipated.

In the essay, I argued that often in progressive spaces, there is a tendency to view "correct" language and terminology as indications of the integrity of one's politics; that sometimes call-outs can feel performative rather than educational; and that often, the practice of calling people out means reducing individuals to their social locations of privilege, as if that accounts for their oppressive behaviour in all instances. I argued that paying attention to other locations and contexts may help us in better educating each other and holding ourselves accountable without disposing of each other.

While I wrote this critique to help improve how call-outs happen, it has since been mobilized frequently to argue that calling people out is always harmful, and that people should keep all their grievances in the private sphere.

But sometimes the only way we can address harmful behaviours is by publicly naming them, in particular when there is a power imbalance between the people involved and speaking privately cannot rectify the situation.

5   Since power exists on multiple planes, it is not always easy to tell who has more power than you, but class, race, gender, and ability all play a part. "A Note on Call-Out Culture" doesn't distinguish between call-outs that happen among members of the same communities, and those happening between people with different levels of access to power and privilege. But paying attention to this distinction can be crucial in determining how we move forward when being called out.

Discussing the toxic aspects of call-out culture requires acknowledging that some people's anger and rage continues to be considered legitimate and reasonable (white men's, mostly) while our culture teaches us that Black, racialized, and Indigenous people—particularly women—are always already angry and hostile. The question of whose anger counts as legitimate and valid is never just a neutral question; it is informed by what someone looks like, the colour of their skin, their gender, as well as their social standing and location. When thinking about call-out culture or being called out yourself, it is illusory to pretend that everyone's voice is equally heard.

Imagine someone is calling you out. If you benefit or are perceived as benefiting from a privilege that the person calling you out does not have, demanding that the calling out happens privately isn't productive because it maintains your own power. In these instances, I think the most productive way we can respond is by listening, especially in a world that refuses to make space for the anger and rage of Black, racialized, and Indigenous people. This does not mean the culture of outrage that continues to flourish in activist circles does not need to be challenged, but insisting that people from historically marginalized groups only address their grievances politely and privately is another way of insisting that their anger is not legitimate or valid, and should not be heard. As the author A. M. Leibowitz notes: "This is literally what it's like to be part of a marginalized group: politeness is met with a refusal to listen, and anger is met with demands for politeness."

Call-out culture is also often conflated with attempts by survivors of sexual and physical violence to hold their abusers accountable. While my essay was concerned primarily with instances of language and terminology being called out, it has often been used to attempt to shut down conversations around transformative and restorative justice. This is particularly alarming given the endemic nature of sexual violence in our communities.

It is important to note here that there is often a knee-jerk reaction to name many instances of conflict as abuse: the word "abuse" can end up referencing a range of harm, from sexual and physical violence to gaslighting and even straightforward meanness.

But at the same time, we must listen to survivors of sexual and/or physical   10
violence, particularly when they tell us they have not been able to receive accountability through private interactions alone. Survivors publicly naming their abuser are often met with a refusal to listen to their stories, and with tone policing, gaslighting, and/or generally being dismissed. This, despite the fact that survivors going public often do so at an incredible personal cost, and often after years of having tried to privately rectify the situation.

When we insist that all of these conversations must remain in the private sphere, we are insisting that accountability is always a private matter. The history of our movements very clearly shows the opposite is often the case. People continue to take the side of those with more power, more privilege, and more capacity, and often these people are never held accountable for the harm they have caused. This is precisely why call-outs need to happen sometimes.

MLA CITATION

Ahmad, Asam. "When Calling Out Makes Sense." *The Norton Reader: An Anthology of Nonfiction*, edited by Melissa A. Goldthwaite et al., 16th ed., W. W. Norton, 2024, pp. 160–61.

QUESTIONS

1. In these arguments, Asam Ahmad points to both the potential problems with and potential benefits of "call-out culture." Annotate these pieces, marking both the problems and benefits he describes. Do you agree with his argument? Why or why not?

2. What is the difference between "calling out" and "'calling in'" ("A Note on Call-Out Culture," paragraphs 1–2)? When, according to Ahmad, does "calling out" make sense?

3. Ahmad wrote a follow-up to his 2015 piece in part because his initial argument was circulated and used in contexts and for purposes he did not anticipate. Consider the original publication venue *Briarpatch Magazine*. (If you are not familiar with that publication, you can look it up online.) How might Ahmad's original audience overlap with and/or differ from the audience for a textbook? How might the audience affect how his argument is interpreted?

4. Several years have passed since these pieces were published. How have arguments about "call-out culture" (sometimes referred to as "cancel culture") changed in that time?

5. Ahmad writes that "calling out" often happens in online venues ("A Note on Call-Out Culture," paragraph 2). Can you provide examples? Can you cite any specific instances when "calling out" was the best course of action? any instances when "calling in" may have been a better approach? Write a response to these questions, explaining your reasoning and how it connects to Ahmad's argument.

4 SELF AND SOCIETY

No man is an island, entire of itself; every man is a piece of the continent, a part of the main; if a clod be washed away by the sea, Europe is the less, as well as if a promontory were, as well as if a manor of thy friend's or of thine own were; any man's death diminishes me, because I am involved in mankind, and therefore never send to know for whom the bell tolls; it tolls for thee.

—JOHN DONNE

Written almost 400 years ago, while John Donne was in the throes of illness, these words are a quintessential affirmation of our shared humanity. None of us, Donne insists, is autonomous; all of us are part of the greater human whole he terms "mankind." On the other hand, we cannot read Donne's words today without also noticing and questioning how they universalize human experience. In this chapter's terms, while every "self" is necessarily involved in "society," we must also recognize that the nature of this involvement varies with our differences.

Donne considers the relationship between "self" and "society" abstractly; the authors represented in this chapter explore it concretely, through their personal histories and experiences. The chapter begins with two selections that probe the relationship between identity and rhetorical license. In an op-ed, philosopher Kwame Anthony Appiah questions the too-easy way in which speakers can rely on assertions of identity—typically of race or ethnicity, gender or sexual orientation, or social class—to give special weight to their arguments and perspectives. In a longer essay, scholar Rafael Walker asks the reciprocal question: Can people speak or write on subjects that are "outside their own demographics," and if so, should they? Neither writer suggests that our identities are irrelevant to our points of view (how could they be?), but both challenge the notion that identity, in itself, either establishes unassailable rhetorical authority or circumscribes the topics one might address. Framed by this corrective, the chapter offers four groups of readings, each focusing on a different aspect of the self in society.

In the first group, a diverse set of authors considers how we are shaped and sustained by our homes and families, however we understand them. Journalist Jose Antonio Vargas writes of growing up in the United States as an undocumented immigrant, of coming out as a gay man, and of navigating the fear and societal stigma that accompany both identities. Viet Thanh Nguyen reflects on his childhood memories as a refugee, displaced from his home country at the end of the Vietnam War. Henry Louis Gates Jr., one of the United States' most influential public intellectuals, vividly renders his memories of Black barbershops and home hair salons and the familial and social relationships they enable.

Essayist Esmé Weijun Wang explores the intersection of her family's immigrant status and the lurking threat of sexual violence against women.

The chapter continues with two essays examining life choices that run against the grain of societal expectations. Novelist and memoirist Ann Patchett writes of her decision not to have children and of others' responses to it. Joey Franklin, now a university professor, recounts taking a job in a fast-food restaurant, sketches the people he met, and examines the assumptions his decision led others to make about him.

The next pair of readings focuses on place. Ian Frazier offers a rich portrait of Brooklyn, New York, and its people. Poet and author Elizabeth Alexander writes of visiting the Louisiana State Penitentiary (or Angola), of the people she met there, and of the importance of remembering them.

The chapter concludes with two selections that address what is perhaps the most significant factor shaping our social world today: new technologies such as artificial intelligence and robotics and, of course, the internet. Of our interactions with these technologies, sociologist Sherry Turkle asks, "What do we become when we talk to machines?" Journalist Jia Tolentino, writing through the lens of her experiences online, offers a bleak assessment of the profound ways in which the internet has reconfigured our conceptions of self, our relationships to others, and our society.

As you read these pieces, use them to reflect on your own place in society. How would you describe your identity or identities? What social pressures have you faced, and how have you responded to them? Have you ever been judged, stereotyped, or even persecuted because of who you are or who you were perceived to be? What did you do? Have you at any point done so to others? Consider not just your personal experiences but the larger society: What hierarchies of value does society enforce? How are you privileged and constrained by your position in society? How does technology affect your sense of self or mediate your relationships with others? What might you do not just to live in society but to make it better for all?

KWAME ANTHONY APPIAH
Go Ahead, Speak for Yourself

"**A**S A WHITE MAN," JOE BEGINS, prefacing an insight, revelation, objection or confirmation he's eager to share—but let's stop him right there. Aside from the fact that he's white, and a man, what's his point? What does it signify when people use this now ubiquitous formula ("As a such-and-such, I . . .") to affix an identity to an observation?

Typically, it's an assertion of authority: As a member of this or that social group, I have experiences that lend my remarks special weight. The experiences, being representative of that group, might even qualify me to represent

First published as an op-ed in the New York Times *(2018).*

that group. Occasionally, the formula is an avowal of humility. It can be both at once. ("As a working-class woman, I'm struggling to understand Virginia Woolf's blithe assumptions of privilege.") The incantation seems indispensable. But it can also be—to use another much-loved formula—problematic.

The "as a" concept is an inherent feature of identities. For a group label like "white men" to qualify as a social identity, there must be times when the people to whom it applies act as members of that group, and are treated as members of that group. We make lives as men and women, as blacks and whites, as teachers and musicians. Yet the very word "identity" points toward the trouble: It comes from the Latin *idem*, meaning "the same." Because members of a given identity group have experiences that depend on a host of other social factors, they're not the same.

Being a black lesbian, for instance, isn't a matter of simply combining African-American, female and homosexual ways of being in the world; identities interact in complex ways. That's why Kimberlé Crenshaw, a feminist legal theorist and civil-rights activist, introduced the notion of intersectionality, which stresses the complexity with which different forms of subordination relate to one another. Racism can make white men shrink from black men and abuse black women. Homophobia can lead men in South Africa to rape gay women[1] but murder gay men. Sexism in the United States in the 1950s kept middle-class white women at home and sent working-class black women to work for them.

Let's go back to Joe, with his NPR mug and his man bun. (Or are you picturing a "Make America Great Again" tank top and a high-and-tight?)[2] Having an identity doesn't, by itself, authorize you to speak on behalf of everyone of that identity. So it can't really be that he's speaking for all white men. But he can at least speak to what it's like to live as a white man, right?

Not if we take the point about intersectionality. If Joe had grown up in Northern Ireland[3] as a gay white Catholic man, his experiences might be rather different from those of his gay white Protestant male friends there—let alone those of his childhood pen pal, a straight, Cincinnati-raised reform Jew. While identity affects your experiences, there's no guarantee that what you've learned from them is going to be the same as what other people of the same identity have learned.

We've been here before. In the academy during the identity-conscious 1980s, many humanists thought that we'd reached peak "as a." Some worried that the locution had devolved into mere prepositional posturing. The literary theorist Barbara Johnson wrote, "If I tried to 'speak as a lesbian,' wouldn't I be processing my understanding of myself through media-induced images of what

1. Known as "corrective rape" because it is intended to "cure" those subjected to it of their orientations.

2. "Make America Great Again," 2016 presidential campaign slogan of Donald J. Trump (b. 1946), forty-fifth president of the United States; high-and-tight, military-inspired hairstyle.

3. Part of the United Kingdom. In the twentieth century, Northern Ireland suffered decades of conflict between its Protestant-majority and Catholic-minority populations.

5

a lesbian is or through my own idealizations of what a lesbian should be?" In the effort to be "real," she saw something fake. Another prominent theorist, Gayatri Chakravorty Spivak, thought that the "as a" move was "a distancing from oneself," whereby the speaker became a self-appointed representative of an abstraction, some generalized perspective, and suppressed the actual multiplicity of her identities. "One is not just one thing," she observed.

It's because we're not just one thing that, in everyday conversation, "as a" can be useful as a way to spotlight some specific feature of who we are. Comedians do a lot of this sort of identity-cuing. In W. Kamau Bell's[4] recent *Netflix* special, *Private School Negro*, the "as a" cue, explicit or implicit, singles out various of his identities over the course of an hour. Sometimes he's speaking as a parent, who has to go camping because his kids enjoy camping. Sometimes he's speaking as an African-American, who, for ancestral reasons, doesn't see the appeal of camping ("sleeping outdoors on purpose?"). Sometimes—as in a story about having been asked his weight before boarding a small aircraft—he's speaking as "a man, a heterosexual, cisgender Dadman." (Hence: "I have no idea how much I weigh.")

The switch in identities can be the whole point of the joke. Here's Chris Rock,[5] talking about his life in an affluent New Jersey suburb: "As a black man, I'm against the cops, but as a man with property, well, I need the cops. If someone steals something, I can't call the Crips!" Drawing attention to certain identities you have is often a natural way of drawing attention to the contours of your beliefs, values or concerns.

10   But caveat auditor: Let the listener beware. Representing an identity is usually volunteer work, but sometimes the representative is conjured into being. Years ago, a slightly dotty countess I knew in the Hampstead area of London used to point out a leather-jacketed man on a park bench and inform her companions, with a knowing look, "He's the head gay." She was convinced that gays had the equivalent of a pontiff or prime minister who could speak on behalf of all his people.

Because people's experiences vary so much, the "as a" move is always in peril of presumption. When I was a student at the University of Cambridge in the 1970s, gay men were très chic: You couldn't have a serious party without some of us scattered around like throw pillows. Do my experiences entitle me to speak for a queer farmworker who is coming of age in Emmett, Idaho? Nobody appointed me head gay.

If someone is advocating policies for gay men to adopt, or for others to adopt toward gay men, what matters, surely, isn't whether the person is gay but whether the policies are sensible. As a gay man, you could oppose same-sex marriage (it's just submitting to our culture's heteronormativity, and anyway monogamy is a patriarchal invention) or advocate same-sex marriage (it's an affirmation of equal dignity and a way to sustain gay couples). Because members of an identity group won't be identical, your "as a" doesn't settle anything. The same holds for religious, vocational and national identities.

4. American comedian, author, and media personality (b. 1973).
5. American comedian (b. 1965).

And, of course, for racial identities. In the 1990s the black novelist Trey Ellis wrote a screenplay, *The Inkwell*, which drew on his childhood in the milieu of the black bourgeoisie. A white studio head (for whom race presumably eclipsed class) gave it to Matty Rich, a young black director who'd grown up in a New York City housing project. Mr. Rich apparently worried that the script wasn't "black enough" and proposed turning the protagonist's father, a school-teacher, into a garbage man. Suffice to say, it didn't end well. Are we really going to settle these perennial debates over authenticity with a flurry of "as a" arrowheads?

Somehow, we can't stop trying. Ever since Donald Trump eked out his surprising electoral victory, political analysts have been looking for people to speak for the supposedly disgruntled white working-class voters who, switch-ing from their former Democratic allegiances, gave Mr. Trump the edge.

But about a third of working-class whites voted for Hillary Clinton. 15 Nobody explaining why white working-class voters went for Mr. Trump would be speaking for the millions of white working-class voters who didn't. One person could say that she spoke as a white working-class woman in explaining why she voted for Mrs. Clinton just as truthfully as her sister could make the claim in explaining her support for Mr. Trump—each teeing us up to think about how her class and race might figure into the story. No harm in that. Neither one, however, could accurately claim to speak for the white working class. Neither has an exclusive on being representative.

So we might do well to ease up on "as a"—on the urge to underwrite our observations with our identities. "For me," Professor Spivak once tartly remarked, "the question 'Who should speak' is less crucial than 'Who will listen?'"

But tell that to Joe, as he takes a sip of kombucha—or is it Pabst Blue Ribbon?[6] All right, Joe, let's hear what you've got to say. The speaking-as-a con-vention isn't going anywhere; in truth, it often serves a purpose. But here's another phrase you might try on for size: "Speaking for myself . . ."

MLA CITATION

Appiah, Kwame Anthony. "Go Ahead, Speak for Yourself." *The Norton Reader: An Anthology of Nonfiction*, edited by Melissa A. Goldthwaite et al., 16th ed., W. W. Norton, 2024, pp. 164–67.

QUESTIONS

1. In this essay, Kwame Anthony Appiah objects to a common form of argument from authority, in which a speaker or writer prefaces a statement with an assertion of identity: "'as a such-and-such, I . . .'" (paragraph 1). How does this form of argu-ment work, and what are Appiah's objections to it?

---

6. Kombucha, fermented beverage of Chinese origin, today marketed and consumed as a health drink; Pabst Blue Ribbon, American beer traditionally associated with blue-collar workers, later popular with hipsters.

2. Throughout his essay, Appiah returns repeatedly to the example of "Joe" (paragraph 1). What details about "Joe" does Appiah share? How does Appiah use this example to push his readers to examine their own stereotypes and assumptions about identity?

3. In the final paragraph of his essay, just before reiterating the exhortation in his title, Appiah acknowledges, "The speaking-as-a convention isn't going anywhere; in truth, it often serves a purpose" (paragraph 17). What purpose does that convention serve? Why does Appiah offer this concession as he brings his essay to a close?

4. Why is legal scholar Kimberlé Crenshaw's idea of "intersectionality" (paragraph 4) so important to Appiah's argument? In an essay of your own, use this concept to analyze a time in which you used, or heard another speaker using, the "speaking-as-a" convention.

RAFAEL WALKER
Who Gets to Write about Whom?

UNDERSTANDABLY CONCERNED about the problem of cultural appropriation and the pitfalls of deviating from one's "lane," many today—politicians, academics, artists, teenagers—have been contemplating whether it's viable for people to write or talk about others outside their own demographics. Some worry that such a practice enables exploiters to profit from the exploited. (I myself addressed this problem[1] during the fad of Robin DiAngelo's[2] *White Fragility*, when a white woman occupied center stage in conversations about the oppression of black people and reaped a fortune capitalizing on that very oppression.) Others express impatience at the condescending cluelessness of those who, holding court on issues laughably far from their jurisdiction, suck all the oxygen from the room—offending by being not only apart from the afflicted group about whom they opine but also part of the group responsible for the afflictions in the first place.

These complaints are two halves of the same thought, both stemming from the conviction that taking unearned liberties in dealing with other communities causes harm, even exacerbating the issues in need of redress. There is no question that this is a real threat or that such injuries have recurred throughout history, persisting even now.

But is the solution to this predicament, as more and more are suggesting, to forbid people from examining communities to which they don't belong? To

Originally published in the Chronicle of Higher Education *(2022).*

1. See Rafael Walker, "Guilt Lit," the *Point*, September 17, 2020.
2. Professor and consultant (b. 1956) providing anti-racism training to educational institutions, corporations, and other organizations.

pursue this route would be to play what I am calling "body politics," the idea that the body that you inhabit determines what you should and shouldn't say.

I am convinced that playing body politics is deeply wrongheaded—a simplistic, dangerous expedient for a complex problem. To be clear, I'm not offering yet another tired defense of free speech or more centrist handwringing over "cancel culture." My concern is that blanket edicts about who can and should say what may pose a greater hazard than the ills that they were designed to fix.

In a recent controversy, the theology professor Jennifer M. Buck found her   5
book, *Bad and Boujee: Toward a Trap Feminist Theology*, removed from distribution "after," as the *Los Angeles Times* reports, "critics raised concerns about the white author's qualifications to write on the book's stated topics of the 'Black experience, hip-hop music, ethics, and feminism.'"[3] About the only thing that this explanation makes clear is that it remains unclear why, exactly, Buck's book got pulled. Was Buck's expertise the problem, or was it her identity? The apology issued by the publisher, Wipf and Stock, suggests that it was at least partly the latter: "We should have seen numerous red flags, including but not limited to the inappropriateness of a White theologian writing about the experience of Black women."

The ascendancy of body politics has never before now been the goal of marginalized activists and scholars. Far from it. In literary studies, for example, female academics and academics of color felt alienated by the omission of people of their demographics from curricula and scholarship. They sought recognition—to be "seen," as it were—and, given their small numbers within the academy, knew that that would be difficult if their concerns remained important to them alone. A famous example from second-wave feminism[4] illustrates this point vividly. Seeking to justify the fact that her book on "women's" literature excluded nonwhite women, Patricia Meyer Spacks, an eminent white Victorianist, argued that she could write only within her ambit of experience. In response to this specious defense—one rooted in body politics—Alice Walker gamely taunted, "Spacks never lived in 19th-century Yorkshire, so why theorize about the Brontës?"[5]

Walker wrote these words at the end of the 1970s, but plus ça change.[6] While it's difficult to pinpoint the sector of culture responsible for the current obsession with body politics, there's no denying that it peaked during the Black Lives Matter movement, initiated in 2013. A few years afterward, the arts would yield our most salient modern controversy over cultural appropriation. Dana

3. Nathan Solis, "After Publisher Pulls Book by White Professor on 'Trap Feminism,' Founder Speaks Out," the *Los Angeles Times*, April 19, 2022.
4. School of feminist thought dominant from the 1960s through the 1980s.
5. Walker (b. 1944), American author; the Brontës—Charlotte (1816–1855), Emily (1818–1848), and Anne (1820–1849)—English authors and poets.
6. French for "the more things change." The full saying continues *plus c'est la même chose*, "the more they stay the same."

Schutz's painting *Open Casket*, featured at the 2017 Whitney Biennial and itself inspired by BLM, backfired epically. An abstract painting based on the much-circulated newspaper photograph of the open-casket funeral of Emmett Till—a 14-year-old black boy lynched in 1955—*Open Casket* triggered a wave of outrage the likes of which such rarefied venues as the Whitney seldom see.

Schutz professed to have proceeded with good intentions. She imagined herself to be contributing to the larger effort to bring attention to the suffering of black people. "This is about a young boy, and it happened," Schutz told the *New Yorker*. "It's evidence of something that really happened. I wasn't alive then, and it wasn't taught in our history classes."[7]

But many construed Schutz's intended contribution to the black community as an affront to it. And her detractors were angry. The artist Hannah Black, for example, went so far as to demand that the museum not only remove but destroy the painting. The arguments against the work were various, but most concluded that Schutz never should have attempted this piece, or that she could not possibly, by virtue of her being a white woman, do the tragedy justice.

10   It's not my aim to assess the merits of Schutz's artwork or those of other artists embroiled in similar controversies. I'm interested in the question of whether it's possible and ethical to represent or speak about communities of which we are not a part.

Since the most vitriolic debates around this problem have concerned art, it may be helpful to look to art for solutions. Henry James—a male author to whom we owe two of 19th-century literature's most memorable female characters, Olive Chancellor of *The Bostonians* and Isabel Archer of *The Portrait of a Lady*—provided indispensable guidance for fiction writers seeking to range beyond their social vantages. In *The Art of Fiction*, James's famous treatise on the craft, he makes the case that anybody can write well about anything, so long as that person possesses technical mastery and enough experience about their subject to understand it thoroughly.

To leave the matter there, obviously, would more or less foreclose the possibility of artists writing successfully about people and events outside their immediate purviews. But, as always with James, it's more complicated. The amount of experience writers require varies according to the strength of their sensibilities.

By way of illustration, James offers an anecdote about a gifted Englishwoman who excelled in her depiction of a French Protestant youth: "She had got her direct impression, and she turned out her type. She knew what youth was, and what Protestantism; she also had the advantage of having seen what it was to be French, so that she converted these ideas into a concrete image and produced a reality." In drawing her fictional French Protestant, this provincial Englishwoman did not need as much experience of the subject as a real-life French Protestant would have had the advantage of having. Her strong sensibility enabled her to do

7. Calvin Tomkins, "Why Dana Schutz Painted Emmett Till," the *New Yorker*, April 10, 2017.

more with less, for "she was blessed with the faculty which when you give it an inch takes an ell."[8]

The capacity to represent a subject, James intimates, has nothing to do with the body that an artist inhabits; what matters is the experience the artist has and the artist's faculties for digesting that experience. When, in a 1998 interview, Charlie Rose, like so many others at the time, importuned Toni Morrison about body politics, she responded in terms similar to James's, if with more asperity. Asked for the umpteenth time whether she could or would write about white people, Morrison quipped, "It's not a literary question. It has nothing to do with the literary imagination. It's a sociological question that should not be put to me." Earlier in the interview, she apprised Rose, "Anything can happen in art."

If—as James, Morrison, and many others have maintained—anything can   15
happen in art, it seems foolish to suggest that people's bodies determine the limits of their imaginations, and imposing such limits would have a chilling effect on art. From this dictum, it follows that works of art should not be judged by some a priori standard deriving from the accident of the author's birth. If an artwork is counted a failure, it should be counted so on the grounds that the artist failed to translate accurate impressions into resonant forms. Failure, then, becomes a problem either of sensibility or of execution.

After answering the question of whether artists can successfully make art transcending their sociological standpoints, we are left wondering whether they should. Those who play body politics claim that such acts are appropriative and therefore cause harm. But what about a writer who, belonging to one community, helps another by writing about it? Harriet Beecher Stowe's *Uncle Tom's Cabin*,[9] authored by a white woman, is widely thought to have had a hand in turning the nation against slavery. At the same time, Stowe's long-bemoaned maladroitness with her black characters points to deficiencies in sensibility and execution: She didn't understand black people adequately and therefore bungled the attempt to sketch them. Although most probably would agree that the novel's contribution to abolition outweighs the damage done by its caricatures, the caricatures still rankle.

Since *Uncle Tom's Cabin* can't quite settle this ethical dilemma, let's consider another classic American novel engaged in cross-cultural representation. In John Steinbeck's *The Grapes of Wrath*,[10] we have a novel written by a Stanford-educated novelist from an affluent family, about far less-educated farm people forced from their homes into exploitive ranch work. In order to represent his subjects faithfully, as the Steinbeck scholar Robert Demott documents, the novelist conducted extensive research. Not only did he pore over reports from

8. Better known as the modern idiom "Give them an inch and they'll take a mile." An ell is an obsolete unit of measurement.
9. Published in 1852, nine years before the start of the American Civil War (1861–65).
10. Published in 1939.

the Farm Security Administration;[11] he also toured the lodging sites established for the migrant workers and interviewed many of the displaced families. By most critical assessments—my own included—Steinbeck portrays this community with dignity and respect. Perhaps most importantly, the novel brought national attention to the exploitation of migrant workers in California and was cited as an influence by several political figures instrumental in ameliorating working and living conditions at corporate ranches.

The Grapes of Wrath sold dazzlingly—nearly a million copies within the first two years of publication—and scored Steinbeck a lucrative film deal. It won the Pulitzer and was crucial to Steinbeck's winning the Nobel in 1962. Did Steinbeck's successes harm the migrant families about whom he wrote? I would say "yes" if his work had been privileged above works of comparable quality produced by people of that community, as Robin DiAngelo's has been. But, to our knowledge, none of the migrant workers had written a publishable novel on the subject, much less a great one. And both American society and culture seem better for Steinbeck's having written his book.

Body politics, unfortunately, has infiltrated the academy, which should serve—and hitherto has—as society's bulwark against such thinking. Today, scholars in the social sciences and humanities are increasingly discouraged from writing about communities not their own. Men are told that they should let women speak about issues related to women, white scholars that they should keep quiet about communities of color. This is a trend that I resent personally, as a male scholar who has spent his entire career writing about women writers and feminism. I never will be a woman, but does that fact unfit me to conduct research on and teach about women writers? I certainly hope not.

20   Contrary to the argument of many champions of body politics, confining scholars to specialties mirroring their identities risks thwarting, instead of advancing, our attempts at diversity and inclusion. As I have shown elsewhere,[12] failing to encourage minority students to specialize in areas that do not reflect their identity will limit the positions in higher education for which they are qualified and will therefore maintain a structural impediment to diversifying college and university faculties. Widening the pipeline means widening the pool of applicants from underrepresented groups able to fill *all* positions—not just, say, positions in African American or Latinx literature but in medieval and Victorian literature as well.

Beyond these practical considerations, Alice Walker's rejoinder helps to expose body politics for the losing game that it is. It blocks the bridges of empathy we so desperately need. The problems we face compel us to turn not away from but toward one another—with interest, care, and respect. As black epidemiologist Nina Harawa suggests, there is more at risk than simply hurt feelings.

11. Created in 1937 as part of the New Deal to assist farmers during the Great Depression.

12. See Rafael Walker, "The Next Step in Diversifying the Faculty," the *Chronicle of Higher Education*, October 23, 2016.

Condemning body politics in her own field, she issues this admonition to her white colleagues: "If you are not willing to take this risk, you are not allies. You are not serving the communities you study. . . . Well-intentioned or not, you are complicit."

MLA CITATION

Walker, Rafael. "Who Gets to Write about Whom?" *The Norton Reader: An Anthology of Nonfiction*, edited by Melissa A. Goldthwaite et al., 16th ed., W. W. Norton, 2024, pp. 168–73.

QUESTIONS

1. Early in his essay, Rafael Walker remarks, "My concern is that blanket edicts about who can and should say what may pose a greater hazard than the ills that they were designed to fix" (paragraph 4). What, according to Walker, are these "ills," and what is the "greater hazard"?

2. Why does Walker object to what he calls "'body politics,'" the notion that "the body that you inhabit determines what you should and shouldn't say" (paragraph 3)? How do Walker's concerns compare to Kwame Anthony Appiah's perspective in "Go Ahead, Speak for Yourself" (pp. 164–67) on what Appiah calls the "speaking-as-a convention" (paragraph 17)?

3. To support his argument, Walker considers not only contemporary examples (e.g., Jennifer M. Buck's book *Bad and Boujee: Toward a Trap Feminist Theology* and Dana Schutz's painting *Open Casket*) but also several examples from the nineteenth and early twentieth centuries (e.g., the novels of Henry James, John Steinbeck's *The Grapes of Wrath*, and Harriet Beecher Stowe's *Uncle Tom's Cabin*). How does this choice impact your reaction to or analysis of his argument?

4. Consider a work of art or literature that depicts people whose identities differ from that of its creator. Write a letter to the artist or author explaining your reaction to the work.

JOSE ANTONIO VARGAS
My Life as an Undocumented Immigrant

 NE AUGUST MORNING nearly two decades ago, my mother woke me and put me in a cab. She handed me a jacket. "Baka malamig doon" were among the few words she said. ("It might be cold there.") When I arrived at the Philippines' Ninoy Aquino International Airport with her, my aunt, and a family friend, I was introduced to a man I'd never seen. They told me he was my

Published in the New York Times Magazine *(2011), this essay received the June 2011 Sidney Award, which recognizes excellence in socially conscious journalism.*

uncle. He held my hand as I boarded an airplane for the first time. It was 1993, and I was 12.

My mother wanted to give me a better life, so she sent me thousands of miles away to live with her parents in America—my grandfather (Lolo in Tagalog[1]) and grandmother (Lola). After I arrived in Mountain View, Calif., in the San Francisco Bay Area, I entered sixth grade and quickly grew to love my new home, family, and culture. I discovered a passion for language, though it was hard to learn the difference between formal English and American slang. One of my early memories is of a freckled kid in middle school asking me, "What's up?" I replied, "The sky," and he and a couple of other kids laughed. I won the eighth-grade spelling bee by memorizing words I couldn't properly pronounce. (The winning word was "indefatigable.")

One day when I was 16, I rode my bike to the nearby DMV office to get my driver's permit. Some of my friends already had their licenses, so I figured it was time. But when I handed the clerk my green card as proof of US residency, she flipped it around, examining it. "This is fake," she whispered. "Don't come back here again."

Confused and scared, I pedaled home and confronted Lolo. I remember him sitting in the garage, cutting coupons. I dropped my bike and ran over to him, showing him the green card. "Peke ba ito?" I asked in Tagalog. ("Is this fake?") My grandparents were naturalized American citizens—he worked as a security guard, she as a food server—and they had begun supporting my mother and me financially when I was 3, after my father's wandering eye and inability to properly provide for us led to my parents' separation. Lolo was a proud man, and I saw the shame on his face as he told me he purchased the card, along with other fake documents, for me. "Don't show it to other people," he warned.

5   I decided then that I could never give anyone reason to doubt I was an American. I convinced myself that if I worked enough, if I achieved enough, I would be rewarded with citizenship. I felt I could earn it.

I've tried. Over the past 14 years, I've graduated from high school and college and built a career as a journalist, interviewing some of the most famous people in the country. On the surface, I've created a good life. I've lived the American dream.

But I am still an undocumented immigrant. And that means living a different kind of reality. It means going about my day in fear of being found out. It means rarely trusting people, even those closest to me, with who I really am. It means keeping my family photos in a shoebox rather than displaying them on shelves in my home, so friends don't ask about them. It means reluctantly, even painfully, doing things I know are wrong and unlawful. And it has meant relying on a sort of 21st-century underground railroad of supporters, people who took an interest in my future and took risks for me.

Last year I read about four students who walked from Miami to Washington to lobby for the Dream Act, a nearly decade-old immigration bill that would provide a path to legal permanent residency for young people who have been

1. One of two official languages spoken in the Philippines. Its standardized form is Filipino.

educated in this country. At the risk of deportation—the Obama administration has deported almost 800,000 people in the last two years—they are speaking out. Their courage has inspired me.

There are believed to be 11 million undocumented immigrants in the United States. We're not always who you think we are. Some pick your strawberries or care for your children. Some are in high school or college. And some, it turns out, write news articles you might read. I grew up here. This is my home. Yet even though I think of myself as an American and consider America my country, my country doesn't think of me as one of its own.

My first challenge was the language. Though I learned English in the Philip- 10 pines, I wanted to lose my accent. During high school, I spent hours at a time watching television (especially *Frasier*, *Home Improvement*, and reruns of *The Golden Girls*) and movies (from *Goodfellas* to *Anne of Green Gables*), pausing the VHS to try to copy how various characters enunciated their words. At the local library, I read magazines, books, and newspapers—anything to learn how to write better. Kathy Dewar, my high-school English teacher, introduced me to journalism. From the moment I wrote my first article for the student paper, I convinced myself that having my name in print—writing in English, interviewing Americans—validated my presence here.

The debates over "illegal aliens" intensified my anxieties. In 1994, only a year after my flight from the Philippines, Gov. Pete Wilson was re-elected in part because of his support for Proposition 187, which prohibited undocumented immigrants from attending public school and accessing other services. (A federal court later found the law unconstitutional.) After my encounter at the DMV in 1997, I grew more aware of anti-immigrant sentiments and stereotypes: they don't want to assimilate, they are a drain on society. They're not talking about me, I would tell myself. I have something to contribute.

To do that, I had to work—and for that, I needed a Social Security number. Fortunately, my grandfather had already managed to get one for me. Lolo had always taken care of everyone in the family. He and my grandmother emigrated legally in 1984 from Zambales, a province in the Philippines of rice fields and bamboo houses, following Lolo's sister, who married a Filipino-American serving in the American military. She petitioned for her brother and his wife to join her. When they got here, Lolo petitioned for his two children—my mother and her younger brother—to follow them. But instead of mentioning that my mother was a married woman, he listed her as single. Legal residents can't petition for their married children. Besides, Lolo didn't care for my father. He didn't want him coming here too.

But soon Lolo grew nervous that the immigration authorities reviewing the petition would discover my mother was married, thus derailing not only her chances of coming here but those of my uncle as well. So he withdrew her petition. After my uncle came to America legally in 1991, Lolo tried to get my mother here through a tourist visa, but she wasn't able to obtain one. That's when she decided to send me. My mother told me later that she figured she would follow me soon. She never did.

The "uncle" who brought me here turned out to be a coyote, not a relative, my grandfather later explained. Lolo scraped together enough money—I eventually learned it was $4,500, a huge sum for him—to pay him to smuggle me here under a fake name and fake passport. (I never saw the passport again after the flight and have always assumed that the coyote kept it.) After I arrived in America, Lolo obtained a new fake Filipino passport, in my real name this time, adorned with a fake student visa, in addition to the fraudulent green card.

15   Using the fake passport, we went to the local Social Security Administration office and applied for a Social Security number and card. It was, I remember, a quick visit. When the card came in the mail, it had my full, real name, but it also clearly stated: "Valid for work only with INS authorization."

When I began looking for work, a short time after the DMV incident, my grandfather and I took the Social Security card to Kinko's, where he covered the "INS authorization" text with a sliver of white tape. We then made photocopies of the card. At a glance, at least, the copies would look like copies of a regular, unrestricted Social Security card.

Lolo always imagined I would work the kind of low-paying jobs that undocumented people often take. (Once I married an American, he said, I would get my real papers, and everything would be fine.) But even menial jobs require documents, so he and I hoped the doctored card would work for now. The more documents I had, he said, the better.

While in high school, I worked part time at Subway, then at the front desk of the local YMCA, then at a tennis club, until I landed an unpaid internship at the *Mountain View Voice*, my hometown newspaper. First I brought coffee and helped around the office; eventually I began covering city-hall meetings and other assignments for pay.

For more than a decade of getting part-time and full-time jobs, employers have rarely asked to check my original Social Security card. When they did, I showed the photocopied version, which they accepted. Over time, I also began checking the citizenship box on my federal I-9 employment eligibility forms. (Claiming full citizenship was actually easier than declaring permanent resident "green card" status, which would have required me to provide an alien registration number.)

20   This deceit never got easier. The more I did it, the more I felt like an impostor, the more guilt I carried—and the more I worried that I would get caught. But I kept doing it. I needed to live and survive on my own, and I decided this was the way.

Mountain View High School became my second home. I was elected to represent my school at school-board meetings, which gave me the chance to meet and befriend Rich Fischer, the superintendent for our school district. I joined the speech and debate team, acted in school plays, and eventually became co-editor of the *Oracle*, the student newspaper. That drew the attention of my principal, Pat Hyland. "You're at school just as much as I am," she told me. Pat and Rich would soon become mentors, and over time, almost surrogate parents for me.

After a choir rehearsal during my junior year, Jill Denny, the choir director, told me she was considering a Japan trip for our singing group. I told her I couldn't afford it, but she said we'd figure out a way. I hesitated, and then decided to tell her the truth. "It's not really the money," I remember saying. "I don't have the right passport." When she assured me we'd get the proper documents, I finally told her. "I can't get the right passport," I said. "I'm not supposed to be here."

She understood. So the choir toured Hawaii instead, with me in tow. (Mrs. Denny and I spoke a couple of months ago, and she told me she hadn't wanted to leave any student behind.)

Later that school year, my history class watched a documentary on Harvey Milk, the openly gay San Francisco city official who was assassinated. This was 1999, just six months after Matthew Shepard's body was found tied to a fence in Wyoming. During the discussion, I raised my hand and said something like: "I'm sorry Harvey Milk got killed for being gay. . . . I've been meaning to say this. . . . I'm gay."

I hadn't planned on coming out that morning, though I had known that I was gay for several years. With that announcement, I became the only openly gay student at school, and it caused turmoil with my grandparents. Lolo kicked me out of the house for a few weeks. Though we eventually reconciled, I had disappointed him on two fronts. First, as a Catholic, he considered homosexuality a sin and was embarrassed about having "ang apo na bakla" ("a grandson who is gay"). Even worse, I was making matters more difficult for myself, he said. I needed to marry an American woman in order to gain a green card.

Tough as it was, coming out about being gay seemed less daunting than coming out about my legal status. I kept my other secret mostly hidden.

While my classmates awaited their college acceptance letters, I hoped to get a full-time job at the *Mountain View Voice* after graduation. It's not that I didn't want to go to college, but I couldn't apply for state and federal financial aid. Without that, my family couldn't afford to send me.

But when I finally told Pat and Rich about my immigration "problem"—as we called it from then on—they helped me look for a solution. At first, they even wondered if one of them could adopt me and fix the situation that way, but a lawyer Rich consulted told him it wouldn't change my legal status because I was too old. Eventually they connected me to a new scholarship fund for high-potential students who were usually the first in their families to attend college. Most important, the fund was not concerned with immigration status. I was among the first recipients, with the scholarship covering tuition, lodging, books, and other expenses for my studies at San Francisco State University.

As a college freshman, I found a job working part time at the *San Francisco Chronicle*, where I sorted mail and wrote some freelance articles. My ambition was to get a reporting job, so I embarked on a series of internships. First I landed at the *Philadelphia Daily News*, in the summer of 2001, where I covered a drive-by shooting and the wedding of the 76ers star Allen Iverson. Using those articles, I applied to the *Seattle Times* and got an internship for the following summer.

But then my lack of proper documents became a problem again. The *Times's* recruiter, Pat Foote, asked all incoming interns to bring certain paperwork on their first day: a birth certificate, or a passport, or a driver's license plus an original Social Security card. I panicked, thinking my documents wouldn't pass muster. So before starting the job, I called Pat and told her about my legal status. After consulting with management, she called me back with the answer I feared: I couldn't do the internship.

This was devastating. What good was college if I couldn't then pursue the career I wanted? I decided then that if I was to succeed in a profession that is all about truth-telling, I couldn't tell the truth about myself.

After this episode, Jim Strand, the venture capitalist who sponsored my scholarship, offered to pay for an immigration lawyer. Rich and I went to meet her in San Francisco's financial district.

I was hopeful. This was in early 2002, shortly after Senators Orrin Hatch, the Utah Republican, and Dick Durbin, the Illinois Democrat, introduced the Dream Act—Development, Relief, and Education for Alien Minors. It seemed like the legislative version of what I'd told myself: If I work hard and contribute, things will work out.

But the meeting left me crushed. My only solution, the lawyer said, was to go back to the Philippines and accept a 10-year ban before I could apply to return legally.

35   If Rich was discouraged, he hid it well. "Put this problem on a shelf," he told me. "Compartmentalize it. Keep going."

And I did. For the summer of 2003, I applied for internships across the country. Several newspapers, including the *Wall Street Journal*, the *Boston Globe*, and the *Chicago Tribune*, expressed interest. But when the *Washington Post* offered me a spot, I knew where I would go. And this time, I had no intention of acknowledging my "problem."

The *Post* internship posed a tricky obstacle: It required a driver's license. (After my close call at the California DMV, I'd never gotten one.) So I spent an afternoon at the Mountain View Public Library, studying various states' requirements. Oregon was among the most welcoming—and it was just a few hours' drive north.

Again, my support network came through. A friend's father lived in Portland, and he allowed me to use his address as proof of residency. Pat, Rich, and Rich's longtime assistant, Mary Moore, sent letters to me at that address. Rich taught me how to do three-point turns in a parking lot, and a friend accompanied me to Portland.

The license meant everything to me—it would let me drive, fly, and work. But my grandparents worried about the Portland trip and the Washington internship. While Lola offered daily prayers so that I would not get caught, Lolo told me that I was dreaming too big, risking too much.

40   I was determined to pursue my ambitions. I was 22, I told them, responsible for my own actions. But this was different from Lolo's driving a confused teenager to Kinko's. I knew what I was doing now, and I knew it wasn't right. But what was I supposed to do?

I was paying state and federal taxes, but I was using an invalid Social Security card and writing false information on my employment forms. But that seemed better than depending on my grandparents or on Pat, Rich, and Jim—or returning to a country I barely remembered. I convinced myself all would be OK if I lived up to the qualities of a "citizen": hard work, self-reliance, love of my country.

At the DMV in Portland, I arrived with my photocopied Social Security card, my college ID, a pay stub from the *San Francisco Chronicle*, and my proof of state residence—the letters to the Portland address that my support network had sent. It worked. My license, issued in 2003, was set to expire eight years later, on my 30th birthday, on Feb. 3, 2011. I had eight years to succeed professionally, and to hope that some sort of immigration reform would pass in the meantime and allow me to stay.

It seemed like all the time in the world.

My summer in Washington was exhilarating. I was intimidated to be in a major newsroom but was assigned a mentor—Peter Perl, a veteran magazine writer— to help me navigate it. A few weeks into the internship, he printed out one of my articles, about a guy who recovered a long-lost wallet, circled the first two paragraphs, and left it on my desk. "Great eye for details—awesome!" he wrote. Though I didn't know it then, Peter would become one more member of my network.

At the end of the summer, I returned to the *San Francisco Chronicle*. My plan was to finish school—I was now a senior—while I worked for the *Chronicle* as a reporter for the city desk. But when the *Post* beckoned again, offering me a full-time, two-year paid internship that I could start when I graduated in June 2004, it was too tempting to pass up. I moved back to Washington.

About four months into my job as a reporter for the *Post*, I began feeling increasingly paranoid, as if I had "illegal immigrant" tattooed on my forehead— and in Washington, of all places, where the debates over immigration seemed never-ending. I was so eager to prove myself that I feared I was annoying some colleagues and editors—and worried that any one of these professional journalists could discover my secret. The anxiety was nearly paralyzing. I decided I had to tell one of the higher-ups about my situation. I turned to Peter.

By this time, Peter, who still works at the *Post*, had become part of management as the paper's director of newsroom training and professional development. One afternoon in late October, we walked a couple of blocks to Lafayette Square, across from the White House. Over some 20 minutes, sitting on a bench, I told him everything: the Social Security card, the driver's license, Pat and Rich, my family.

Peter was shocked. "I understand you 100 times better now," he said. He told me that I had done the right thing by telling him, and that it was now our shared problem. He said he didn't want to do anything about it just yet. I had just been hired, he said, and I needed to prove myself. "When you've done enough," he said, "we'll tell Don and Len together." (Don Graham is the chairman of the Washington Post Company; Leonard Downie Jr. was then the paper's executive editor.) A month later, I spent my first Thanksgiving in Washington with Peter and his family.

In the five years that followed, I did my best to "do enough." I was promoted to staff writer, reported on video-game culture, wrote a series on Washington's HIV/AIDS epidemic, and covered the role of technology and social media in the 2008 presidential race. I visited the White House, where I interviewed senior aides and covered a state dinner—and gave the Secret Service the Social Security number I obtained with false documents.

50   I did my best to steer clear of reporting on immigration policy but couldn't always avoid it. On two occasions, I wrote about Hillary Clinton's position on driver's licenses for undocumented immigrants. I also wrote an article about Senator Mel Martínez of Florida, then the chairman of the Republican National Committee, who was defending his party's stance toward Latinos after only one Republican presidential candidate—John McCain, the co-author of a failed immigration bill—agreed to participate in a debate sponsored by Univision, the Spanish-language network.

It was an odd sort of dance: I was trying to stand out in a highly competitive newsroom, yet I was terrified that if I stood out too much, I'd invite unwanted scrutiny. I tried to compartmentalize my fears, distract myself by reporting on the lives of other people, but there was no escaping the central conflict in my life. Maintaining a deception for so long distorts your sense of self. You start wondering who you've become, and why.

In April 2008, I was part of a *Post* team that won a Pulitzer Prize for the paper's coverage of the Virginia Tech shootings a year earlier. Lolo died a year earlier, so it was Lola who called me the day of the announcement. The first thing she said was, "Anong mangyayari kung malaman ng mga tao?"

What will happen if people find out?

I couldn't say anything. After we got off the phone, I rushed to the bathroom on the fourth floor of the newsroom, sat down on the toilet, and cried.

55   In the summer of 2009, without ever having had that follow-up talk with top *Post* management, I left the paper and moved to New York to join the *Huffington Post*. I met Arianna Huffington at a Washington Press Club Foundation dinner I was covering for the *Post* two years earlier, and she later recruited me to join her news site. I wanted to learn more about Web publishing, and I thought the new job would provide a useful education.

Still, I was apprehensive about the move: many companies were already using E-Verify, a program set up by the Department of Homeland Security that checks if prospective employees are eligible to work, and I didn't know if my new employer was among them. But I'd been able to get jobs in other newsrooms, I figured, so I filled out the paperwork as usual and succeeded in landing on the payroll.

While I worked at the *Huffington Post*, other opportunities emerged. My HIV/AIDS series became a documentary film called *The Other City*, which opened at the Tribeca Film Festival last year and was broadcast on Showtime. I began writing for magazines and landed a dream assignment: profiling *Facebook*'s Mark Zuckerberg for the *New Yorker*.

The more I achieved, the more scared and depressed I became. I was proud of my work, but there was always a cloud hanging over it, over me. My old eight-year deadline—the expiration of my Oregon driver's license—was approaching.

After slightly less than a year, I decided to leave the *Huffington Post*. In part, this was because I wanted to promote the documentary and write a book about online culture—or so I told my friends. But the real reason was, after so many years of trying to be a part of the system, of focusing all my energy on my professional life, I learned that no amount of professional success would solve my problem or ease the sense of loss and displacement I felt. I lied to a friend about why I couldn't take a weekend trip to Mexico. Another time I concocted an excuse for why I couldn't go on an all-expenses-paid trip to Switzerland. I have been unwilling, for years, to be in a long-term relationship because I never wanted anyone to get too close and ask too many questions. All the while, Lola's question was stuck in my head: What will happen if people find out?

Early this year, just two weeks before my 30th birthday, I won a small   60
reprieve: I obtained a driver's license in the state of Washington. The license is valid until 2016. This offered me five more years of acceptable identification—but also five more years of fear, of lying to people I respect and institutions that trusted me, of running away from who I am.

I'm done running. I'm exhausted. I don't want that life anymore.

So I've decided to come forward, own up to what I've done, and tell my story to the best of my recollection. I've reached out to former bosses and employers and apologized for misleading them—a mix of humiliation and liberation coming with each disclosure. All the people mentioned in this article gave me permission to use their names. I've also talked to family and friends about my situation and am working with legal counsel to review my options. I don't know what the consequences will be of telling my story.

I do know that I am grateful to my grandparents, my Lolo and Lola, for giving me the chance for a better life. I'm also grateful to my other family—the support network I found here in America—for encouraging me to pursue my dreams.

It's been almost 18 years since I've seen my mother. Early on, I was mad at her for putting me in this position, and then mad at myself for being angry and ungrateful. By the time I got to college, we rarely spoke by phone. It became too painful; after a while it was easier to just send money to help support her and my two half-siblings. My sister, almost 2 years old when I left, is almost 20 now. I've never met my 14-year-old brother. I would love to see them.

Not long ago, I called my mother. I wanted to fill the gaps in my memory   65
about that August morning so many years ago. We had never discussed it. Part of me wanted to shove the memory aside, but to write this article and face the facts of my life, I needed more details. Did I cry? Did she? Did we kiss goodbye?

My mother told me I was excited about meeting a stewardess, about getting on a plane. She also reminded me of the one piece of advice she gave me for blending in: If anyone asked why I was coming to America, I should say I was going to Disneyland.

MLA CITATION
Vargas, Jose Antonio. "My Life as an Undocumented Immigrant." *The Norton Reader: An Anthology of Nonfiction*, edited by Melissa A. Goldthwaite et al., 16th ed., W. W. Norton, 2024, pp. 173–81.

QUESTIONS

1. Jose Antonio Vargas describes many of the challenges of living as an undocumented immigrant in America. Which challenges stand out to you? Why?

2. Vargas embraces a broader understanding of family that extends beyond biological kinship. Which people in Vargas's life behaved most like family? How do you understand family?

3. In this essay, Vargas identifies both as an undocumented immigrant and a gay man. How does he portray the relationship between these two aspects of his identity within himself? through the lens of family? of society?

4. Vargas defines what US citizenship means to him: "hard work, self-reliance, love of my country" (paragraph 41). Write an essay in which you reflect on what it means to be a citizen of the country you call home.

VIET THANH NGUYEN
from *The Displaced*

I WAS ONCE A REFUGEE, although no one would mistake me for being a refugee now. Because of this, I insist on being called a refugee, since the temptation to pretend that I am not a refugee is strong. It would be so much easier to call myself an immigrant, to pass myself off as belonging to a category of migratory humanity that is less controversial, less demanding, and less threatening than the refugee.

I was born a citizen and a human being. At four years of age I became something less than human, at least in the eyes of those who do not think of refugees as being human. The month was March, the year 1975, when the northern communist army captured my hometown of Ban Me Thuot in its final invasion of the Republic of Vietnam, a country that no longer exists except in the imagination of its global refugee diaspora of several million people, a country that most of the world remembers as South Vietnam.

Looking back, I remember nothing of the experience that turned me into a refugee. It begins with my mother making a life-and-death decision on her own. My father was in Saigon,[1] and the lines of communication were cut. I do

From The Displaced: Refugee Writers on Refugee Lives *(2018), a collection of seventeen essays written by refugees from Afghanistan, Bosnia, Chile, Ethiopia, Mexico, and other countries.*

1. Capital of the Republic of Vietnam, now Ho Chi Minh City. Hanoi is the capital of contemporary Vietnam.

not remember my mother fleeing our hometown with my ten-year-old brother and me, leaving behind our sixteen-year-old adopted sister to guard the family property. I do not remember my sister, who my parents would not see again for nearly twenty years, who I would not see again for nearly thirty years.

My brother remembers dead paratroopers hanging from the trees on our route, although I do not. I also do not remember whether I walked the entire one hundred eighty-four kilometers to Nha Trang, or whether my mother carried me, or whether we might have managed to get a ride on the cars, trucks, carts, motorbikes, and bicycles crowding the road. Perhaps she does remember but I never asked about the exodus, or about the tens of thousands of civilian refugees and fleeing soldiers, or the desperate scramble to get on a boat in Nha Trang, or some of the soldiers shooting some of the civilians to clear their way to boats, as I would read later in accounts of this time.

I do not remember finding my father in Saigon, or how we waited for another month until the communist army came to the city's borders, or how we tried to get into the airport, and then into the American embassy, and then finally somehow fought our way through the crowds at the docks to reach a boat, or how my father became separated from us but decided to get on a boat by himself anyway, and how my mother decided the same thing, or how we eventually were reunited on a larger ship. I do remember that we were incredibly fortunate, finding our way out of the country, as so many millions did not, and not losing anyone, as so many thousands did. No one, except my sister.

For most of my life, I did remember soldiers on our boat firing onto a smaller boat full of refugees that was trying to approach. But when I mentioned it to my older brother many years later, he said the shooting never happened.

I do not remember many things, and for all those things I do not remember, I am grateful, because the things I do remember hurt me enough. My memory begins after our stops at a chain of American military bases in the Philippines, Guam, and finally Pennsylvania. To leave the refugee camp in Pennsylvania, the Vietnamese refugees needed American sponsors. One sponsor took my parents, another took my brother, a third took me.

For most of my life, I tried not to remember this moment except to note it in a factual way, as something that happened to us but left no damage, but that is not true. As a writer and a father of a son who is four years old, the same age I was when I became a refugee, I have to remember, or sometimes imagine, not just what happened, but what was felt. I have to imagine what it was like for a father and a mother to have their children taken away from them. I have to imagine what it was that I experienced, although I do remember being taken by my sponsor to visit my parents and howling at being taken back.

I remember being reunited with my parents after a few months and the snow and the cold and my mother disappearing from our lives for a period of time I cannot recall and for reasons I could not understand, and knowing vaguely that it had something to do with the trauma of losing her country, her family, her property, her security, maybe her self. In remembering this, I know that I am also foreshadowing the worst of what the future would hold, of what would happen to her in the decades to come. Despite her short absence, or maybe her long one,

I remember enjoying life in Harrisburg, Pennsylvania, because children can enjoy things that adults cannot so long as they can play, and I remember a sofa sitting in our backyard and neighborhood children stealing our Halloween candy and my enraged brother taking me home before venturing out by himself to recover what had been taken from us.

10   I remember moving to San Jose, California, in 1978 and my parents opening the second Vietnamese grocery store in the city and I remember the phone call on Christmas Eve that my brother took, informing him that my parents had been shot in an armed robbery, and I remember that it was not that bad, just flesh wounds, they were back at work not long after, and I remember that the only people who wanted to open businesses in depressed downtown San Jose were the Vietnamese refugees, and I remember walking down the street from my parents' store and seeing a sign in a store window that said ANOTHER AMERICAN DRIVEN OUT OF BUSINESS BY THE VIETNAMESE, and I remember the gunman who followed us to our home and knocked on our door and pointed a gun in all our faces and how my mother saved us by running past him and out onto the sidewalk, but I do not remember the two policemen shot to death in front of my parents' store because I had gone away to college by that time and my parents did not want to call me and worry me.

I remember all these things because if I did not remember them and write them down then perhaps they would all disappear, as all those Vietnamese businesses have vanished, because after they had helped to revitalize the downtown that no one else cared to invest in, the city of San Jose realized that downtown could be so much better than what it was and forced all those businesses to sell their property and if you visit downtown San Jose today you will see a massive, gleaming, new city hall that symbolizes the wealth of a Silicon Valley that had barely begun to exist in 1978 but you will not see my parents' store, which was across the street from the new city hall. What you will see instead is a parking lot with a few cars in it because the city thought that the view of an empty parking lot from the windows and foyer of city hall was more attractive than the view of a mom-and-pop Vietnamese grocery store catering to refugees.

As refugees, not just once but twice, having fled from north to south in 1954 when their country was divided, my parents experienced the usual dilemma of anyone classified as an *other*. The other exists in contradiction, or perhaps in paradox, being either invisible or hypervisible, but rarely just visible. Most of the time we do not see the other or see right through them, whoever the other may be to us, since each of us—even if we are seen as others by some—have our own others. When we do see the other, the other is not truly human to us, by very definition of being an other, but is instead a stereotype, a joke, or a horror. In the case of the Vietnamese refugees in America, we embodied the specter of the Asian come to either serve or to threaten.

Invisible and hypervisible, refugees are ignored and forgotten by those who are not refugees until they turn into a menace. Refugees, like all others, are unseen until they are seen everywhere, threatening to overwhelm our borders, invade our cultures, rape our women, threaten our children, destroy our economies. We who do the ignoring and forgetting oftentimes do not perceive it to be violence, because we do not know we do it. But sometimes we deliberately ignore and forget others. When we do, we are surely aware we are inflicting violence, whether that is on the schoolyard as children or at the level of the nation. When those others fight back by demanding to be seen and heard—as refugees sometimes do—they can appear to us like threatening ghosts whose fates we ourselves have caused and denied. No wonder we do not wish to see them.

MLA CITATION

Nguyen, Viet Thanh. "From *The Displaced.*" *The Norton Reader: An Anthology of Nonfiction*, edited by Melissa A. Goldthwaite et al., 16th ed., W. W. Norton, 2024, pp. 182–85.

QUESTIONS

1. Viet Thanh Nguyen insists on calling himself a refugee even though no one would mistake him for a refugee now (paragraph 1). Why does he make this choice? How might this choice affect how people view other refugees? What parts of the essay inform your answer?

2. Nguyen tells his story through what he remembers, what he does not remember, and what he tries not to remember. Trace Nguyen's use of the word "remember" throughout this essay. Which parts of his experience seem most important for him to remember? Why? How does he emphasize those experiences?

3. Nguyen writes, "I remember all these things because if I did not remember them and write them down then perhaps they would all disappear" (paragraph 11). Is there an important story from your family's history that you want to remember? Interview those family members who would remember the event and write down your own memories. Write an essay that uses your own and your family's memories to reconstruct the details of a significant event.

HENRY LOUIS GATES JR.
In the Kitchen

WE ALWAYS HAD A GAS STOVE IN THE KITCHEN, in our house in Piedmont, West Virginia, where I grew up. Never electric, though using electric became fashionable in Piedmont in the sixties, like using Crest toothpaste rather than Colgate, or watching Huntley and Brinkley rather than Walter Cronkite.[1] But not us: gas, Colgate, and good ole Walter

Originally published in the New Yorker *(1994), a weekly magazine of "reportage, commentary, criticism, essays, fiction, satire, cartoons, and poetry," in advance of the publication of Henry Louis Gates Jr.'s memoir* Colored People *(1994).*

1. Newscasters of the 1960s: Chet Huntley and David Brinkley were on NBC; Cronkite was on CBS.

Cronkite, come what may. We used gas partly out of loyalty to Big Mom, Mama's Mama, because she was mostly blind and still loved to cook, and could feel her way more easily with gas than with electric. But the most important thing about our gas-equipped kitchen was that Mama used to do hair there. The "hot comb" was a fine-toothed iron instrument with a long wooden handle and a pair of iron curlers that opened and closed like scissors. Mama would put it in the gas fire until it glowed. You could smell those prongs heating up.

I liked that smell. Not the smell so much, I guess, as what the smell meant for the shape of my day. There was an intimate warmth in the women's tones as they talked with my Mama, doing their hair. I knew what the women had been through to get their hair ready to be "done," because I would watch Mama do it to herself. How that kink could be transformed through grease and fire into that magnificent head of wavy hair was a miracle to me, and still is.

Mama would wash her hair over the sink, a towel wrapped around her shoulders, wearing just her slip and her white bra. (We had no shower—just a galvanized tub that we stored in the kitchen—until we moved down Rat Tail Road into Doc Wolverton's house, in 1954.) After she dried it, she would grease her scalp thoroughly with blue Bergamot hair grease, which came in a short, fat jar with a picture of a beautiful colored lady on it. It's important to grease your scalp real good, my Mama would explain, to keep from burning yourself. Of course, her hair would return to its natural kink almost as soon as the hot water and shampoo hit it. To me, it was another miracle how hair so "straight" would so quickly become kinky again the second it even approached some water.

My Mama had only a few "clients" whose heads she "did"—did, I think, because she enjoyed it, rather than for the few pennies it brought in. They would sit on one of our red plastic kitchen chairs, the kind with the shiny metal legs, and brace themselves for the process. Mama would stroke that red-hot iron—which by this time had been in the gas fire for half an hour or more—slowly but firmly through their hair, from scalp to strand's end. It made a scorching, crinkly sound, the hot iron did, as it burned its way through kink, leaving in its wake straight strands of hair, standing long and tall but drooping over at the ends, their shape like the top of a heavy willow tree. Slowly, steadily, Mama's hands would transform a round mound of Odetta[2] kink into a darkened swamp of everglades. The Bergamot made the hair shiny; the heat of the hot iron gave it a brownish-red cast. Once all the hair was as straight as God allows kink to get, Mama would take the well-heated curling iron and twirl the straightened strands into more or less loosely wrapped curls. She claimed that she owed her skill as a hairdresser to the strength in her wrists, and as she worked her little finger would poke out, the way it did when she sipped tea. Mama was a southpaw, and wrote upside down and backward to produce the cleanest, roundest letters you've ever seen.

5   The "kitchen" she would all but remove from sight with a handheld pair of shears, bought just for this purpose. Now, the kitchen was the room in which we were sitting—the room where Mama did hair and washed clothes, and where we

2. Odetta Holmes (1930–2008), singer of blues and spirituals in the 1950s and a leading figure in the American folk revival of the 1960s.

all took a bath in that galvanized tub. But the word has another meaning, and the kitchen that I'm speaking of is the very kinky bit of hair at the back of your head, where your neck meets your shirt collar. If there was ever a part of our African past that resisted assimilation, it was the kitchen. No matter how hot the iron, no matter how powerful the chemical, no matter how stringent the mashed-potatoes-and-lye formula of a man's "process," neither God nor woman nor Sammy Davis, Jr.,[3] could straighten the kitchen. The kitchen was permanent, irredeemable, irresistible kink. Unassimilably African. No matter what you did, no matter how hard you tried, you couldn't de-kink a person's kitchen. So you trimmed it off as best you could.

When hair had begun to "turn," as they'd say—to return to its natural kinky glory—it was the kitchen that turned first (the kitchen around the back, and nappy edges at the temples). When the kitchen started creeping up the back of the neck, it was time to get your hair done again.

Sometimes, after dark, a man would come to have his hair done. It was Mr. Charlie Carroll. He was very light-complected and had a ruddy nose—it made me think of Edmund Gwenn, who played Kris Kringle in *Miracle on 34th Street*. At first, Mama did him after my brother, Rocky, and I had gone to sleep. It was only later that we found out that he had come to our house so Mama could iron his hair—not with a hot comb or a curling iron but with our very own Proctor-Silex steam iron. For some reason I never understood, Mr. Charlie would conceal his Frederick Douglass–like[4] mane under a big white Stetson hat. I never saw him take it off except when he came to our house, at night, to have his hair pressed. (Later, Daddy would tell us about Mr. Charlie's most prized piece of knowledge, something that the man would only confide after his hair had been pressed, as a token of intimacy. "Not many people know this," he'd say, in a tone of circumspection, "but George Washington was Abraham Lincoln's daddy." Nodding solemnly, he'd add the clincher: "A white man told me." Though he was in dead earnest, this became a humorous refrain around our house—"a white man told me"—which we used to punctuate especially preposterous assertions.)

My mother examined my daughters' kitchens whenever we went home to visit, in the early eighties. It became a game between us. I had told her not to do it, because I didn't like the politics it suggested—the notion of "good" and "bad" hair. "Good" hair was "straight," "bad" hair kinky. Even in the late sixties, at the height of Black Power, almost nobody could bring themselves to say "bad" for good and "good" for bad. People still said that hair like white people's hair was "good," even if they encapsulated it in a disclaimer, like "what we used to call 'good.'"

Maggie would be seated in her high chair, throwing food this way and that, and Mama would be cooing about how cute it all was, how I used to do just like Maggie was doing, and wondering whether her flinging her food with her left

3. Singer, dancer, and entertainer (1925–1990) with notably "processed" hair.
4. Douglass (1817–1895) was an abolitionist who escaped enslavement. Photographs show him with a lion-like mane of hair.

hand meant that she was going to be left-handed like Mama. When my daughter was just about covered with Chef Boyardee Spaghetti-O's, Mama would seize the opportunity: wiping her clean, she would tilt Maggie's head to one side and reach down the back of her neck. Sometimes Mama would even rub a curl between her fingers, just to make sure that her bifocals had not deceived her. Then she'd sigh with satisfaction and relief: No kink . . . yet. Mama! I'd shout, pretending to be angry. Every once in a while, if no one was looking, I'd peek, too.

10   I say "yet" because most black babies are born with soft, silken hair. But after a few months it begins to turn, as inevitably as do the seasons or the leaves on a tree. People once thought baby oil would stop it. They were wrong.

Everybody I knew as a child wanted to have good hair. You could be as ugly as homemade sin dipped in misery and still be thought attractive if you had good hair. "Jesus moss," the girls at Camp Lee, Virginia, had called Daddy's naturally "good" hair during the war. I know that he played that thick head of hair for all it was worth, too.

My own hair was "not a bad grade," as barbers would tell me when they cut it for the first time. It was like a doctor reporting the results of the first full physical he has given you. Like "You're in good shape" or "Blood pressure's kind of high—better cut down on salt."

I spent most of my childhood and adolescence messing with my hair. I definitely wanted straight hair. Like Pop's. When I was about three, I tried to stick a wad of Bazooka bubble gum to that straight hair of his. I suppose what fixed that memory for me is the spanking I got for doing so: he turned me upside down, holding me by my feet, the better to paddle my behind. Little *nigger*, he had shouted, walloping away. I started to laugh about it two days later, when my behind stopped hurting.

When black people say "straight," of course, they don't usually mean literally straight—they're not describing hair like, say, Peggy Lipton's (she was the white girl on *The Mod Squad*), or like Mary's of Peter, Paul & Mary[5] fame; black people call that "stringy" hair. No, "straight" just means not kinky, no matter what contours the curl may take. I would have done *anything* to have straight hair—and I used to try everything, short of getting a process.[6]

15   Of the wide variety of techniques and methods I came to master in the challenging prestidigitation of the follicle, almost all had two things in common: a heavy grease and the application of pressure. It's not an accident that some of the biggest black-owned companies in the fifties and sixties made hair products. And I tried them all, in search of that certain silken touch, the one that would leave neither the hand nor the pillow sullied by grease.

I always wondered what Frederick Douglass put on *his* hair, or what Phillis Wheatley[7] put on hers. Or why Wheatley has that rag on her head in the little engraving in the frontispiece of her book. One thing is for sure: you can bet that when Phillis Wheatley went to England and saw the Countess of Huntingdon she

---

5. Folk-singing group famous in the 1960s for "Puff the Magic Dragon."

6. Hair-straightening chemical treatment.

7. America's first published Black woman writer (1753–1784).

did not stop by the Queen's coiffeur on her way there. So many black people still get their hair straightened that it's a wonder we don't have a national holiday for Madame C. J. Walker, the woman who invented the process of straightening kinky hair. Call it Jheri-Kurled or call it "relaxed," it's still fried hair.

I used all the greases, from sea-blue Bergamot and creamy vanilla Duke (in its clear jar with the orange-white-and-green label) to the godfather of grease, the formidable Murray's. Now, Murray's was some *serious* grease. Whereas Bergamot was like oily jello, and Duke was viscous and sickly sweet, Murray's was light brown and *hard*. Hard as lard and twice as greasy, Daddy used to say. Murray's came in an orange can with a press-on top. It was so hard that some people would put a match to the can, just to soften the stuff and make it more manageable. Then, in the late sixties, when Afros came into style, I used Afro Sheen. From Murray's to Duke to Afro Sheen: that was my progression in black consciousness.

We used to put hot towels or washrags over our Murray-coated heads, in order to melt the wax into the scalp and the follicles. Unfortunately, the wax also had the habit of running down your neck, ears, and forehead. Not to mention your pillowcase. Another problem was that if you put two palmfuls of Murray's on your head your hair turned white. (Duke did the same thing.) The challenge was to get rid of that white color. Because if you got rid of the white stuff you had a magnificent head of wavy hair. That was the beauty of it: Murray's was so hard that it froze your hair into the wavy style you brushed it into. It looked really good if you wore a part. A lot of guys had parts *cut* into their hair by a barber, either with the clippers or with a straight-edge razor. Especially if you had kinky hair— then you'd generally wear a short razor cut, or what we called a Quo Vadis.

We tried to be as innovative as possible. Everyone knew about using a stocking cap, because your father or your uncle wore one whenever something really big was about to happen, whether sacred or secular: a funeral or a dance, a wedding or a trip in which you confronted official white people. Any time you were trying to look really sharp, you wore a stocking cap in preparation. And if the event was really a big one, you made a new cap. You asked your mother for a pair of her hose, and cut it with scissors about six inches or so from the open end— the end with the elastic that goes up to the top of the thigh. Then you knotted the cut end, and it became a beehive-shaped hat, with an elastic band that you pulled down low on your forehead and down around your neck in the back. To work well, the cap had to fit tightly and snugly, like a press. And it had to fit that tightly because it *was* a press: it pressed your hair with the force of the hose's elastic. If you greased your hair down real good, and left the stocking cap on long enough, voilà: you got a head of pressed-against-the-scalp waves. (You also got a ring around your forehead when you woke up, but it went away.) And then you could enjoy your concrete do. Swore we were bad, too, with all that grease and those flat heads. My brother and I would brush it out a bit in the mornings, so that it looked—well, "natural." Grown men still wear stocking caps—especially older men, who generally keep their stocking caps in their top drawers, along with their cufflinks and their see-through silk socks, their "Maverick" ties, their silk handkerchiefs, and whatever else they prize the most.

20   A Murrayed-down stocking cap was the respectable version of the process, which, by contrast, was most definitely not a cool thing to have unless you
were an entertainer by trade. Zeke and Keith and Poochie and a few other stars
of the high-school basketball team all used to get a process once or twice a year.
It was expensive, and you had to go somewhere like Pittsburgh or DC or
Uniontown—somewhere where there were enough colored people to support a
trade. The guys would disappear, then reappear a day or two later, strutting like
peacocks, their hair burned slightly red from the lye base. They'd also wear
"rags"—cloths or handkerchiefs—around their heads when they slept or played
basketball. Do-rags, they were called. But the result was straight hair, with just a
hint of wave. No curl. Do-it-yourselfers took their chances at home with a concoction of mashed potatoes and lye.

The most famous process of all, however, outside of the process Malcolm X
describes in his "Autobiography," and maybe the process of Sammy Davis, Jr.,
was Nat King Cole's[8] process. Nat King Cole had patent-leather hair. That
man's got the finest process money can buy, or so Daddy said the night we saw
Cole's TV show on NBC. It was November 5, 1956. I remember the date
because everyone came to our house to watch it and to celebrate one of Daddy's
buddies' birthdays. Yeah, Uncle Joe chimed in, they can do shit to his hair that
the average Negro can't even *think* about—secret shit.
        Nat King Cole was *clean*. I've had an ongoing argument with a Nigerian
friend about Nat King Cole for twenty years now. Not about whether he could
sing—any fool knows that he could—but about whether or not he was a handkerchief head for wearing that patent-leather process.
        Sammy Davis, Jr.'s process was the one I detested. It didn't look good on
him. Worse still, he liked to have a fried strand dangling down the middle of his
forehead, so he could shake it out from the crown when he sang. But Nat King
Cole's hair was a thing unto itself, a beautifully sculpted work of art that he and
he alone had the right to wear. The only difference between a process and a
stocking cap, really, was taste; but Nat King Cole, unlike, say, Michael Jackson,
looked *good* in his. His head looked like Valentino's[9] head in the twenties, and
some say it was Valentino the process was imitating. But Nat King Cole wore a
process because it suited his face, his demeanor, his name, his style. He was as
clean as he wanted to be.
        I had forgotten all about that patent-leather look until one day in 1971,
when I was sitting in an Arab restaurant on the island of Zanzibar surrounded
by men in fezzes and white caftans, trying to learn how to eat curried goat
and rice with the fingers of my right hand and feeling two million miles from
home. All of a sudden, an old transistor radio sitting on top of a china cupboard stopped blaring out its Swahili music and started playing "Fly Me to
the Moon," by Nat King Cole. The restaurant's din was not affected at all, but

8. Singer and jazz pianist (1919–1965).
9. Rudolph Valentino (1895–1926), film star known, among other things, for his slicked-
back hair.

in my mind's eye I saw it: the King's magnificent sleek black tiara. I managed, barely, to blink back the tears.

MLA CITATION

Gates, Henry Louis, Jr. "In the Kitchen." *The Norton Reader: An Anthology of Nonfiction*, edited by Melissa A. Goldthwaite et al., 16th ed., W. W. Norton, 2024, pp. 185–91.

QUESTIONS

1. *Kitchen* has two meanings here; write a brief explanation of the significance of both uses of the word in Henry Louis Gates Jr.'s essay.

2. Why do you think Gates alludes to so many celebrities (mostly from the 1950s and 1960s) and brand-name products? Note his preferences and progression. What is the significance of the allusions?

3. Gates observes, "If there was ever a part of our African past that resisted assimilation, it was the kitchen" (paragraph 5). What does *assimilation* mean in the context of this sentence? What do you think it means generally? What does the essay imply about Gates's stance on Black assimilation?

4. Do a project in which you use memories from childhood—including sensory details, popular allusions, and brand-name products—to describe some element of your culture or place in society.

ESMÉ WEIJUN WANG
The Stalker and the Nightgown

I WAS PERHAPS FIFTEEN when the doorbell rang, and because I was preoccupied, my brother, who is four years younger, answered the door. Because I now know that the man who had come to the door was my mother's stalker, I've injected the memory of his arrival at my childhood home with more detail than I actually possess. I remember—or think I remember—that he asked if the Volvo in our driveway was for sale. Never mind that there was no reason to think that the dark green family car would, in fact, be for sale; if it were up for sale, there would be a sign in its window, and it wouldn't be parked in our driveway where no one could see it from the road. But no matter: My brother told the man that he didn't know about the car, but that the man could call our mother, who would be able to tell him. He gave the man our mother's cell phone number, and then the man left.

Originally published in Catapult *(2016), an online magazine that celebrated "stories that explore the space between the lines of our lives, that raise questions rather than give answers."*

What luck on the stalker's part. How could he have known that his gambit would earn him his target's private number? What had he been hoping for when he came to the house, the location of which he knew from following our mother home from work on a forty-five minute drive? Did he expect to find children when he got to the house? What would have happened if I'd answered the door instead, bearing an older and more wary face?

Hours later, with the sky darkening, our mother called the house phone. She calmly told me that she would be returning home with our Uncle Wayne— not a blood relative, but her boss—to pick us up. While we waited for her to come get us, I needed to check that all of the windows were closed and locked. I needed to check that all of the doors were closed and locked. We were not to open the door for anyone until she came to get us.

I don't remember being afraid, though I was old enough to know that something was wrong, and that it was important to obey her in this matter. In about an hour, she arrived with Uncle Wayne. They swept us into the car. For the next few nights, we stayed with my father's sister and her husband, and then we returned home.

*

5   Being the child of Taiwanese immigrants meant that I learned what was normal at my own pace. I didn't realize, for example, that it wasn't typical to wear jeans to bed until I was a teenager; though I'd been on sleepovers since grammar school, the difference between street clothes and sleepwear slipped my notice for years. I conflate the discovery of pajamas with the story of my mother's stalker because in one self-portrait, taken in the months after he came to our home, I am lying in bed, looking into the camera, and I am holding a butcher knife. I'm also wearing a flannel nightgown with lace trim, which means that I must have discovered pajamas by this time.

After the stalker, I slept with a knife by the bed because my mother had begun to sleep with a knife by the bed. My mother bought bulk packages of pepper spray for everyone in the family to use. A new alarm system, installed after my father came home from his business trip and finally learned about the stalker, meant that the windows in our home chirped when opened and closed. Getting some fresh air meant the inevitable, *chirrup*. Closing the same window: *chirrup*. A birdsong, a warning.

I learned that the stalker, after speaking to my brother at our home, began to call my mother, whose tendency has always been to protect her children in all ways—and so I know that the version of events she told me later, at my aunt and uncle's home, is certainly far worse than what actually reached my ears. He'd told her that he *wanted her*. He'd been watching her for months. Now he knew where she and her children lived, and he was going to hurt them—the children—if she didn't give him what he wanted.

I learned later that he had been a gardener for the office building next to hers. Who knew how long he had been watching her, or how long it took for him to work up the nerve to follow her on the long drive home. How long he had waited between following her home and coming to that same house in the middle of the day, or how he'd invented the ruse of asking after the Volvo in the driveway.

I learned these things while my mother told me not to mention any of this to my father, whose business trip to China meant that he would be gone for a while yet longer. She didn't want to worry him, she said. When they spoke, she acted as though nothing was wrong, and my brother and I did the same when we spoke to him on calculated long-distance minutes about school and homework. His absence was normal to us—for years he only flew home on weekends, and for still more years he would be gone for months at a time. Men like Uncle Wayne served as surrogate fathers, and helped my mother deal with things such as the police, who did find the stalker, and gave him a stern talking-to. My mother assured me that the man had been sufficiently frightened by the police; he wouldn't come after us again. I neither believed her nor disbelieved her. I only knew that we would keep going.

The correlation between the stalker and my attachment to that flannel   10
nightgown isn't obvious to me. I'd think that whatever hypervigilance I developed as a teenager would mean an even stronger attachment to sleeping in my street clothes, in case I needed to leap out of bed and run. The butcher knife makes sense to me. The pepper spray that I kept under my pillow makes sense to me. Not the nightgown. I don't know where it came from. I don't know where it went, though I still remember how it felt: soft, but not soft enough to feel easy; warm, but too warm to be of comfort. When I turn to sleepwear now, I tend toward silky, liquid things that don't rub against my skin, although a body is more vulnerable when it's comfortable and unaware—too likely to drowse when it ought to be awake, or sleep too deeply when it should be ready to fight. In adolescence, I made a sartorial concession without ever becoming too relaxed or revealed. A boy I loved told me that I dressed with aggressive modesty.

In graduate school I developed an intense desire to find a nightgown similar to the one I'd had back then. *Etsy*, as it turns out, is flush with frumpy flannel nightgowns; I could have a collection if I so desired, but I bought just one. In those years, I rarely slept in my bedroom, forgoing it and its Ikea bed for the 1970s mustard yellow couch in the living room, where I could watch marathons of *Law and Order: SVU* and *Criminal Minds* until I finally fell asleep.

I'd discovered the latter when I happened upon a 2007 episode called "About Face," which follows the FBI's Behavioral Analysis Unit as they hunt a serial killer who removes his victims' faces. Mandy Patinkin, who left the show after two seasons in 2007, eventually called his role in *Criminal Minds* his "biggest public mistake," saying that he "never thought they were going to kill and rape all [those] women every night, every day, week after week, year after year." Patinkin said about the show, "It was very destructive to my soul and my personality."

But I watched every single episode, hungry. I fell asleep to episodes I'd seen three, four, or five times before. It was hard for me to fall asleep without the sounds of the voices of people killing and being killed and searching for those who had killed before so that they wouldn't kill again.

After the stalker, a few weeks after my mother, brother, and I returned to our home, patrol cars drove by on occasion, and then they stopped coming. My father flew back from China. In our beds, we slept.

MLA CITATION

Wang, Esmé Weijun. "The Stalker and the Nightgown." *The Norton Reader: An Anthology of Nonfiction*, edited by Melissa A. Goldthwaite et al., 16th ed., W. W. Norton, 2024, pp. 191–94.

QUESTIONS

1. Consider the title Esmé Weijun Wang chose for her essay: "The Stalker and the Nightgown." Why does she connect the two things? What does that connection suggest about American society and her place within it as the daughter of Taiwanese immigrants?

2. What is Wang's family like? Annotate her descriptions and explanations within the essay with your observations.

3. The threat of sexual violence against women is a prominent theme in this essay. Annotate the essay to note the ways this theme surfaces. How does Wang treat it? Why, for example, does she find the television shows *Law and Order: SVU* and *Criminal Minds* so captivating?

4. When you think about your own family life, is there an object, person, or event that stands out? Write a reflection in which you explore that memory. Why is it so resonant for you?

ANN PATCHETT
There Are No Children Here

I.

I WAS LATE. My itinerary said the event started at two thirty when in fact it started at two o'clock. I was speaking at an Important Book Festival with an author I admired but had never met, and when I arrived early, or what I thought was early, he was already on the stage chatting away, an empty stool beside him. I ran down the center aisle, apologizing to everyone I passed, and took my place.

"I'm so sorry," I said, by way of introduction.

The author, let's call him Q, could not have been nicer. He was charming, gracious, very tall. He handled the situation easily, and certainly no one in that packed house had been troubled by my absence. Q was that rarest of birds—a commercially successful literary author. I was on tour for my second novel, which

Originally published in Ann Patchett's collection These Precious Days: Essays *(2021).*

would go on to make even less of a ripple than my first, if such a thing were possible.[1] Our books. Q's and mine, had come out around the same time from the same publisher, which is why I was allowed to ride his coattails at the book festival. "We were just talking about what it takes to be a real writer." Q gestured to the audience who had served as his conversational partner in my absence.

I covered my nervousness with enthusiasm. "Terrific!" I said, because truly, who wouldn't want to know? "What does it take to be a real writer?"

"Well, the first thing is, you have to treat writing as your job." Now he was   5
talking to me. "I rent an office. Five days a week I get up and go to work. I put on a jacket, kiss my wife goodbye, and leave the house. I go every day at the same time. I stay a minimum of six hours. Writing is a job, and you have to treat it that way because if it isn't your job, it's your hobby."

"This is wonderful!" I said. "This is why it's so great to listen to writers talk about how they work, because it just goes to show that everyone has their own way." I gave a quick sketch of my life, which included writing in my dining room, in my pajamas, without a schedule. For me, the pleasure of being a writer came from the fact that writing felt nothing like a job. I took my work seriously, but if my grandmother got lonely or needed me to take her to the doctor, or a friend needed a ride to the airport in the middle of the day, I was the person to call. Flexibility was what writers got instead of health insurance.

Q looked at me. He looked at the audience. "You should get an office."

"I live alone."

"It doesn't matter. It's a mindset."

"What else?" I asked. I could barely afford my apartment.   10

"A visual dictionary," he said.

"A what?"

"You can't call yourself a writer if you don't have a visual dictionary."

"Are you serious?"

He was.   15

"I'm a writer, and I have no idea what a visual dictionary is." I was oddly thrilled by this exchange. Our disagreement made a gentle spectacle. No harm done by being late.

He looked at me, puzzled. How could I not know this? He patiently explained that a visual dictionary had pictures of things in which all the parts were labeled—airplanes, human bodies, dogs—so if you were writing a story with, say, a lawn mower in it, you could look up the picture of the lawn mower and reference the parts so that you would come across as someone who really knew his way around a lawn mower. "You might need to know the difference between a Doric column and an Ionic column," he added for good measure.

"To think I've come this far without one."

"You should get one," Q said. "They're great."

I told him I would do exactly that while the audience busily wrote the words   20
visual dictionary on the back of their programs. And then, because we were on a

1. Patchett's first two novels are *The Patron Saint of Liars* (1992) and *Taft* (1994).

stage with time still on the clock, I asked him if there was anything else a person needed in order to be a real writer.

"Children," he said.

"Children," I repeated back, though I hadn't misunderstood him.

He nodded solemnly, for now he was imparting his deepest wisdom. "You can't be a real writer if you don't have children."

"Why not?"

25   "Because until you have children, you don't know what it means to love."

I told him I didn't have children. What I didn't tell him was that I would never have children, and that I had known this for a very long time. I was thirty years old.

"Well—" He stopped. He unfolded his enormous hands. What else could he say?

It struck me very clearly that I could reach into this man's chest and pull out his heart in front of the audience. "Emily Dickinson," I said to him. "Flannery O'Connor, James Baldwin, Eudora Welty, Henry James."

He shook his head sadly. "All I can tell you is that you don't know what's missing until it's there."

30   "And when you wrote your first book?" I asked. I could pull out his heart. I wanted to.

"I wasn't a real writer then," he admitted. "I didn't know."

"We've had a friendly disagreement up until now," I said. I was the new kid, the ingénue. "But I have to tell you, people without children have known love, and we are writers."

A few nervous audience questions popped up after that. They were trying to smooth things over for us, save what could not be saved. When the merciful clock told us our time was up, we walked off the stage in opposite directions and never laid eyes on one another again.

2.

I once got a letter from an editor I'd never met praising me for the work I do on behalf of authors and books and bookstores, the gist of which went something like this: You know how people will say of someone who's selfish and stupid that they should be forcibly sterilized? Well, you do so much good in the world, you should be forcibly impregnated.

35   It took me a minute to realize he meant this as a compliment.

3.

Upon the publication of my first essay collection, *This Is the Story of a Happy Marriage*,[2] I landed a spot on a national radio talk show I'd never been on before. As I sat in the recording studio in Nashville, before we started, the host spoke to me through headphones from another state. She told me how much she liked the book. She reminded me that the interview was taped, and said that if any

2. Published in 2013.

questions made me uncomfortable, all I needed to do was tell her and we could stop. I told her I couldn't imagine what she could ask that would make me uncomfortable, and so we began. She wanted to know how I felt about not having had children.

"I feel fine about it."

"Do you regret your decision?"

"No," I said. "I don't regret it."

"Do you feel that as a woman you were forced to choose between your work as a writer and having children?"   40

"No," I said. "No one forced me to do anything. I just didn't want children."

"Male writers can have children and careers and it isn't as hard for them."

"They probably have wives."

"But is that fair? Your husband is considerably older than you are. Chances are you'll be alone at the end of your life. Don't you worry about that?"

I sat in the booth and stared at the microphone hanging in front of my face.   45
Ben, who owned the studio. Ben, whom I'd known for years, looked up at me through the glass. I was there to talk about a book I'd written, a book that had nothing to do with not having children.

"I brought long-term care insurance," I said.

It wasn't the answer she was looking for. She pressed on, as if my childless life were a matter for investigative reporting. "But doesn't that make you sad? The thought of being old and alone?"

"I don't mind talking about this," I said. "I don't have children. It's not a secret. But I wonder, would you ask Jonathan Franzen[3] the same questions? He doesn't have children."

When the interview aired, all the questions about my childlessness had been edited out.

4·

I like to say that I was raised by nuns. My sister and I were dropped off at the   50
convent in the morning, an hour before school started, and we often stayed an hour after the other children went home because our mother was working. Those were the best parts of the day, when the kids were gone. I liked washing the blackboards and putting books away. We went back to the nuns' private kitchen and the sisters would give us little jobs to do, like folding napkins or putting the silverware into its assigned spots in the silverware drawer. If the nuns were strict during the school day, they struck me as a very comfortable lot once the students had gone. They were considerate to one another, they made jokes. They paid minimal attention to our presence. Most of the time they seemed to forget we were there at all. As long as I asked for nothing, I could spy on them, not by hiding behind a curtain but by being unobtrusive and listening. The nuns worked with children and were happier once those children had gone home. After all, none of them had children of their own. They had made that choice, and from my vantage point, they didn't appear to have any regrets.

3. American essayist and novelist (b. 1959).

People used to ask me if I ever thought about being a nun when I was young, and the answer was no, I always wanted to be a writer. But still, I found certain nonreligious aspects of religious life inspiring.

5.

On book tour in Seattle, a different book tour, yet another book tour, I had lunch with my old friend Debra, whom I hadn't seen in years. Debra and her partner were trying to decide whether to have a child.

"I don't know," she told me. "I'm on the fence. We make lists of all the pros and cons. We go back and forth." Debra was in her early forties but her partner was younger. Her partner would carry the child. "Don't you wrestle with this?" she asked me.

I told her I did not.

55 "But you must have, at some point."

When I was a child, my bed was covered in stuffed animals. I slept with my head propped up on the edge of a giant green frog. My sister wanted only baby dolls, the more realistic the better—dolls whose hinged eyelids came down like shutters when you leaned them back. She practiced changing their empty diapers. She swaddled them and carried them in her arms. Even the memory of those dolls makes me shiver.

"All my life people have been telling me I must want a baby, or that I'm going to want a baby later on." I said. "It's like someone telling me the car keys are in the drawer in the kitchen. 'Go get the car keys out of the drawer.' So I go and I open the drawer and the car keys aren't in there. In fact, nothing's in there. The drawer is empty. I go back and tell them, the keys aren't in the drawer, and this person says to me. 'No, they are, you just need to try harder. Go back and look again.' It doesn't make any sense, but I do it. I go back and look, and the drawer is still empty. People are always telling me I'm wrong. Total strangers have told me that I'm wrong, that I need to go back and check one more time, but there's never anything in the drawer, and there's never going to be anything in the drawer."

My friend thinks about this for a while, and then she nods. "That must be really nice to know," she said.

And I tell her yes, it's wonderful.

6.

60 The day after I saw Debra, I left Seattle and flew to Portland. That's the way book tours work. The woman who picked me up at the airport was a probation officer. She liked books and authors, so she moonlighted as a media escort every now and then when her schedule allowed. After lunch, she took me to the International Rose Test Garden, home to more than ten thousand plants. I don't remember how the subject came up, but as we followed the gravel pathways through the dizzying blossoms, she told me she had always known she didn't want to have children. When she was twenty-five, she decided to have a tubal ligation.

"No one would do it," she said. "Every doctor I went to see told me to wait, that I'd change my mind later on and be sorry for what I'd done. When I pressed them, they said I had to have a psychiatric evaluation, and I did it because I wanted the surgery. And they still wouldn't do it."

"What happened?" I asked. So many roses.

"It took me two years," she said. "But I got it. They think we don't know our own mind when we decide to have an abortion, but we also don't know our own mind when we decide to put ourselves in a position where we'll never have to have an abortion."

"That's because we're fools," I said. "We can't be trusted."

I was still thinking about that woman when I finished the tour a few weeks   65
later and flew home. I was thirty-seven years old and I knew my mind. I told Karl I was going to have a tubal ligation. It would still be another four years before we married.

He shook his head. He told me no.

"A valid opinion," I said, "but they aren't your tubes."

"Never have a surgery you don't need to have," he said to me.

"Having surgery has to be better than taking birth control pills."

"It's not. You've done fine on the pill and you never know when a surgery   70
will go wrong. If nothing's broke, don't fix it."

I thanked him for his input and went to see my gynecologist, who was also a friend. I told her I wanted a tubal ligation.

"No," she said.

"I'm not conducting a poll. I'm asking you to tie my tubes."

"Things can always go wrong, and you're doing well on birth control. If a woman is doing well on birth control, and she goes off it to have a tubal ligation, nine times out of ten she goes back on the pill."

"Even though she can't get pregnant?"   75

My doctor nodded, explaining that the pill had benefits that extended beyond contraception. "Just go home," she told me. You're fine."

I thought about the probation officer back in Portland having this same conversation for two years, having it at twenty-five instead of thirty-seven, and my heart was full of admiration. And exhaustion.

7.

I saw the sister of a friend at a Christmas party. I knew from my friend that her sister had tried to get pregnant for a very long time without success, and that she and her husband were finally able to adopt a child. There she was, a champagne glass in one hand, a beautiful baby girl up against her shoulder. It was Christmas, but this was the reason we were celebrating. I admired the baby. I congratulated her.

"Imagine how selfish a person would have to be to not have a child," she said to me.

8.

80 Karl asked me if I was pregnant.

I laughed and shook my head. "No, why? Do I look pregnant?"

"You do, actually." Because he's a doctor his opinion on such matters carries extra weight.

I was forty years old at the time, and he was fifty-six. I shrugged. "Well, no reason to think so." Was I unnerved? I wasn't sure. I had been fortunate. Birth control, used as directed, had worked my entire life. "I'll keep you posted."

The next day we were in the car. Karl was driving. "If I were pregnant," I said to him, "and there's no reason to think that I am, but if I were, what would you say?"

85 "That it would be your decision."

"I know it would be my decision, but what would you say?"

There was not a beat before his answer, not a flicker of hesitation. "I would say that I'm thrilled. I would say that this is the best thing that could ever happen to us."

I was floored by this answer, and also surprisingly touched. "Really?"

"When a woman tells you she's pregnant, the answer is always 'I'm thrilled,' or you're a complete idiot."

9.

90 I once saw a woman with six small children in a store: a baby strapped to her chest, a child barely walking holding her finger, the other four stair-steps. They hung together, a small flotilla, as she guided them forward. I watched in admiration and something like gratitude. *Thank you for keeping the species alive*, I could have said to her. *You're doing such good work.*

10.

The only time in my life I can remember thinking I might want children, or could imagine possibly wanting them in the future, was when I went to the Todds' house. Dick Todd was the editor for my first two books. He worked at Houghton Mifflin, which was still in Boston then. Dick lived two hours away in the Berkshires and came in to the office once a month, if that. He and his wife Susan lived in an old farmhouse in a wide field. They had raised their three daughters there, Emily, Maisie, and Nell. On several occasions I was invited to their house for the weekend. Emily was in school in Scotland then, Maisie was off at college, and Nell, at least at first, was still in high school. They had a Chesapeake Bay retriever named Coco, who was, according to her vet, the largest dog in Franklin County. Coco slept in the middle of whatever room the people happened to be in. There were always friends coming over, big dinner parties, spectacular Thanksgivings, lots of writers. The dishwasher had been broken for years and they used it as a drying rack after washing the dishes by hand. I was colder in that house than I can ever remember being anywhere else in my life. I slept in Emily's bed upstairs, spreading my coat over the bedspread, and watched the constellation of glow-in-the-dark planets and stars she'd stuck on the sloping ceiling.

Susan and Dick, in their boots and heavy sweaters, would always get around to telling the story of how they'd met and broken up. Dick went off to graduate school at Stanford, and Susan went to New York, where she worked as a copywriter and auditioned for plays. Then Dick showed up again just as Susan was about to go out with some old friends. Dick suggested they get married instead. Not to wait, no reason to wait, they should get married right then. And so they did. Every year they celebrated Wedding Week, because for all their Yankee reserve, theirs was not a love that could be contained by a single day. It was the love, the house, the field, the dog, the dishwasher, the long wooden table in the kitchen, the bowl of apples, the piles and piles of books, the three girls mostly grown and gone, that made me think having children could be okay, as long as they were like the Todd children, by which I mean not around, as long as my life was like the Todds' life.

II.

The kid in the newspaper was named Stevie, and he was eight. I was thirty-nine and lived by myself in a house that I owned. For a short time our local newspaper featured an orphan every week. Later they would transition to adoptable pets, but for a while it was orphans, children you could foster and possibly adopt if everything worked out. The profiles were short, maybe two or three hundred words. This was what I knew: Stevie liked going to school. He made friends easily. He promised he would make his bed every morning. He hoped that if he were very good he could have his own dog, and if he were very, very good, his younger brother could be adopted with him. Stevie was Black. I knew nothing else. The picture of him was a little bigger than a postage stamp. He smiled. I studied his face at my breakfast table until something in me snapped. I paced around my house, carrying the folded newspaper. I had two bedrooms. I had a dog. I had so much more than plenty. In return he would make his bed, try his best in school. That was all he had to bargain with: himself. By the time Karl came for dinner after work I was nearly out of my mind.

"I want to adopt him," I said.

Karl read the profile. He looked at the picture. "You want to be his mother?"   95

"It's not about being his mother. I mean, sure, if I'm his mother that's fine, but it's like seeing a kid waving from the window of a burning house, saying he'll make his bed if someone will come and get him out. I can't leave him there."

"We can do this," Karl said.

We can do this. I started to calm myself because Karl was calm. He was good at making things happen. We could do this. I didn't have to want children in order to want Stevie.

In the morning I called the number in the newspaper. They took down my name and address. They told me they would send the preliminary paperwork. After the paperwork was reviewed, there would be a series of interviews and home visits.

"When do I meet Stevie?" I asked.   100

"Stevie?"

"The boy in the newspaper." I had already told her the reason I was calling.

"Oh, it's not like that," the woman said. "It's a very long process. We put you together with the child who will be your best match."

"So where's Stevie?"

105 She said she wasn't sure. She thought that maybe someone had adopted him.

It was a bait and switch, a well-written story: the bed, the dog, the brother. They knew how to bang on the floor to bring people like me out of the wood-work, people who said they would never come. I wrapped up the conversation. I didn't want a child, I wanted Stevie. It all came down to a single flooding moment of clarity: he wouldn't live with me, but I could now imagine that he was in a solid house with people who loved him. I put him in the safest chamber of my heart, he and his brother in twin beds, the dog asleep in Stevie's arms.

And there they stayed, going with me everywhere until finally I wrote a novel about them called *Run*.[4] Not because I thought it would find them, but because they had become too much for me to carry. I had to write about them so that I could put them down.

12.

André Previn was a pianist, a composer, a conductor. He had four Academy Awards, ten Grammys, five wives, ten children. He was the musical director for several major symphony orchestras. He was the principal conductor for several major symphony orchestras. He wrote film scores, played jazz. He was ninety when he died, or something like that. No one was exactly sure what year he was born, only that his family got out of Berlin ahead of the Nazis.

Sometimes I think about people in terms of units of energy. André Previn must have come into this world with a thousand times more energy than I did, or else he must have marshaled his resources much more effectively. I have just enough energy to write, keep up with the house, be a decent friend, a decent daughter and sister and wife. Part of not wanting children has always been the certainty that I didn't have the energy for it, and so I had to make a choice, the choice between children and writing. The first time it occurred to me that I wouldn't have both, I was still years away from being biologically capable of reproduction. History offers some examples of people who've done a good job with children and writing, I know that, but I wasn't one of those people. I've always known my limitations. I lacked the units of energy, and the energy I had, I wanted to spend on my work. To have a child and neglect her in favor of a novel would be cruel, but to simply skip the child in favor of a novel was to avoid harm altogether.

110 My friend Elizabeth McCracken and I used to talk about this when we were writing our first books. She was twenty-three and I was twenty-six. She had cho-sen writing as well. "Unless," she said, "I fell in love with someone who absolutely wanted to have children and was willing to take half the responsibility. Then I'd think about it, assuming it was clear that he'd be a really great father."

_____

4. Published in 2007.

We were sitting in the Governor Bradford, our favorite bar in Province-town, in the dead of winter. We had the time to imagine and dissect every conceivable scenario for our future, but I couldn't quite envision what she was suggesting: a man who wanted children; a man who wanted to have those children with me; a man who wanted those children with me so much that he would claim half the work, half the love and responsibility, and I would be able to believe that he was telling me the truth, and that the truth wouldn't change a few months in. He would be a wonderful father. He would make sure I still had the time and space to be a writer.

I shook my head. I had never met such a man, nor did I believe in his existence.

"But if you did meet him?" Elizabeth asked. "Would you want to have children?"

I wasn't sure. I think I would have needed to have seen a prototype much earlier in my life so I would know how to recognize him. I certainly wasn't looking.

Years after that conversation, Elizabeth found him, or he found her, and   115
together they had two spectacular children.

Together, together, together.

13.

"Even if you don't want a child," someone said to me once, "you should have one anyway, because later on you'll wish you had one, and then it will be too late."

14.

I don't remember any of my close friends ever asking me when I was going to have children. I suppose by definition of our being close they knew me. But their husbands asked me, or they told me: I needed children. It was important. I sus-pect it had less to do with my best interest and more to do with the fact that I made them nervous walking through the world unencumbered. I was setting a bad example.

People want you to want what they want. If you want the same things they want, then their want is validated. If you don't want the same things, your lack of wanting can, to certain people, come across as judgment. People are forever asking if I'd mind if they ordered a hamburger. "Not unless you force me to eat it," I say. This gets trickier when applied to alcohol. I stopped drinking a long time ago. People feel much more strongly about having a drink than they do about having a burger.

"So then just a glass of champagne."   120
"I don't drink."
"But you'll have champagne for the toast."
I shake my head.
Does my declining a glass of champagne mean that I judge your glass of champagne?
It does not.   125

Does my choice not to have children mean I judge your choices, your children? That I think my life is in some way superior?

It does not.

What it means is that I don't want children. Or a hamburger. Or a gin and tonic. That's all it means.

How I came not to care about other people's opinions is something of a mystery even to me. I was born with a compass. It was the luck of my draw. This compass has been incalculably beneficial for writing—for everything, really—and for that reason I take very good care of it. How do you take care of your internal compass? You don't listen to anyone who tells you to do something as consequential as having a child. Think about that one for a second.

15.

130   After eleven years of dating, Karl and I married. I was forty-one and he was fifty-seven. People said to me, "How wonderful! You can still have a child." These were the same people who had always asked when I was going to have a child, and the news of our late-life legitimacy gave them the excuse to remind us of what we otherwise might have forgotten: reproduction was still biologically possible, or possibly possible. I guess they thought we'd just been waiting for the paperwork to come through.

After Karl and I married and I'd moved into his house, after another year or two elapsed and the clock had run all the way down to midnight, even the most hopeful of bystanders were forced to concede. It was right around that time that I learned a lesson through my own thoughtlessness. Some neighbors who lived a few blocks away had just had their fourth daughter, and when I went to drop off a loaf of pumpkin bread, I met the mother-in-law in the driveway, a woman I knew and liked. "Do you think this is it?" I asked her. "Or do you think they'll have more?"

Inside that house, a woman with three tiny children and a baby in her arms had just come home from the hospital, and I had asked her mother-in-law if there were plans to have more children.

The mother-in-law did her best to hide her dismay at my inquiry, but it was hard. I knew, because I'd been trying to hide my dismay for years. "I wouldn't think of asking them something so personal," she said to me.

Yes, exactly. It was so personal. I might as well have asked, *What do you imagine the outcome of your son's sex life will be in the future?* I was appalled at myself for doing the very thing that had so annoyed me for my entire reproductive life, but the error came with a valuable revelation: I didn't care if they had more children. Of course I didn't care. I was standing in a driveway making the idlest conversation, just as plenty of the people who had asked me when I would get married and when I would have children were making idle conversation. It was nothing but noise, a question for the sake of speaking and not for the sake of inquiry.

135   Some of them cared, but not all of them. I should have realized that earlier.

16.

Throughout my life, the people who held the most urgent opinions on the subject of my childlessness were the members of my immediate family. My mother, my father, my stepfather, my grandmother, all showered me with positive reinforcement when, as a child myself, I said I didn't want children. As I grew up and grew older, they never missed the opportunity to voice their approval. Even my sister, who loved her own children, would at times say to me wearily, "I admire your life choices." Whether this was because the people who knew me best thought I'd be a bad parent, or they wanted the resources I represented for themselves, or they wanted me to know they supported my decision, or they just didn't like children very much—the messiness, noise, trouble—I was never certain, though if I had to guess, the last option seemed the most likely.

17.

Karl's grandfather, Grover VanDevender, worked as a railway conductor on the Southerner. His run was the last leg of the trip—from Meridian, Mississippi, where they lived, to New Orleans. Grover and Karl liked to look at *National Geographic* together and talk about all the places in the world they wanted to go. When Grover died in 1968, he left Karl $2,000 in hopes that he would one day have the kind of great adventure they had dreamed of together. Karl put the money in the bank, and in 1980, when he was thirty-three, he took his five-year-old daughter Josephine trekking in the Himalayas for a month while his wife stayed home with their two-year-old son. For most of the trip, Josephine was carried by a Sherpa in a wicker basket and was fed a diet of chocolate bars and Coca-Cola, which another Sherpa carried in a different basket.

On the trip home, Karl lost Josephine in London Heathrow Airport. He was standing in a ticket line and when he looked down, she was gone. She was missing for over an hour before being found by airport security, asleep in a chair, rolled into a little ball, the kind of ball one might have grown accustomed to after spending a month in a wicker basket.

This story is the centerpiece of the VanDevender family lore, and rightfully so. It's a weird story. Weird and somewhat admirable that Karl would trek to the Himalayas with a five-year-old in honor of his grandfather, weird and less admirable that he left his wife behind to take care of their toddler. But the weirdest and most telling aspect of the story was how the disappearance of Josephine at Heathrow was remembered: the way I always heard it, it was a story about Josephine being irresponsible. Josephine always wandering off. Josephine losing track of time and nearly making them miss their connecting flight home after a month in the Himalayas.

But Josephine was five. She had spent a month subsisting on Coke and chocolate. She had just flown to London from Nepal. The whole thing struck me one day when Josephine and I were together with her own son, who was five at the time.

"That's how old you were when you went to Nepal," I said.

"Yep," she said.

140

"When your father lost you in an airport."

She nodded. Josephine is, among many good things, a good mother and a forgiving daughter. "Crazy, right?"

It is possible to love someone with all your heart and still know your union would never have survived having children together. It was one of the many things that made Karl and me such a good match: I didn't want children and he already had them. I thought it when I caught him pouring half-and-half on the dog's kibble. It was best this way.

18.

Having a dog is not the same thing as having a child.

Writing a book is not the same thing as having a child.

Owning a bookstore is not the same thing as having a child.

Having wonderful stepchildren does not make me a mother.

I know these things to be true, no matter how many times people tell me otherwise.

I am not using the dog or the book or the bookstore or the stepchildren to fill a hole left by not having children, because there is no hole. I can love those people, that dog, those books, for exactly who and what they are.

19.

I was in New York on business and checked in with Marti, who was about to have a baby. She said she and her husband, Barry, were on their way to the hospital and I should come by and hang out. "We can walk the halls," Marti said cheerfully. Marti had a tendency to make difficult things look easy. She was thirty-one and this was her second child.

"Won't you be really busy?" I asked.

"Well, sure, but you're here," she said. "I want to see you."

So I went to the hospital, and her husband and I took turns looping the ward with Marti on our arm. At regular intervals she would stop, take a breath, look up at the ceiling and say, "Okay," then start to walk again. Back in the room, the nurse would check her dilation. Everything was going according to schedule. "Do you want to just stay?" she asked me.

"If you stayed, you could take the pictures," her husband said. They were trying to make me feel welcome, useful, even though it didn't seem like a party I should be crashing at the last minute. On the other hand, I couldn't imagine telling them I had plans. I must have had plans, but I don't remember what they were. I stuck around to see Katherine being born. It wasn't much of a wait. Marti was all business.

That was the one part of the decision not to have children that did in fact make me feel like I missed out. I am deeply moved by what a woman's body is capable of, but just because I could do something didn't mean that I should. Marti and Barry gave me a tremendous gift that day by letting me stay and watch their daughter come into the world. Katherine! From the first minute she was a force every bit as recognizable as her mother. That feeling of life coming

into the room was unlike anything I'd ever experienced before, a flood of joy. I
thought of it ten years later when I climbed into my grandmother's bed and held
her while she died. The light pouring in and the light going out. I never would
have known how close those two things were if it wasn't for Marti and Barry and
Katherine.

20.

My friend Kate and I were talking about childhood, the way writers will. We
are the same age. Our friendship had begun in the years when having children
was no longer on the table.

"I could never do that to someone I loved," I said.

"Do what?"   160

"Childhood."

"Oh, that," she said, nodding. "I get that." Kate didn't have children either.

But the theory doesn't hold up, because my sister's childhood was much
worse than mine, and all she ever wanted was to have children. Children gave
her the chance to give someone else the kind of childhood she'd wanted, and,
in doing so, to find a repository for her enormous love. I, on the other hand,
just wanted to get the hell out of there.

The uncertainty, the complete lack of autonomy or control, leaving places
you never wanted to leave to go to places you never wanted to go, the fear, the
bullying, the helplessness, the awkwardness, the disappointment and shame,
the betrayal by your own body. To have a child required the willful forgetting
of what childhood was actually like; it required you to turn away from the very
real chance that you would do to the person you loved most in the world the
exact same thing that was done to you. No. No, thank you.

21.

For one year of my childhood, we lived in a sprawling condominium complex   165
where I would ride my bike up and down the cul-de-sacs and drives. One day a
car pulled up and the woman inside asked if I babysat. "Sure," I said. It wasn't
true, but I liked the thought of having a job, making money. She wrote down my
phone number and told me where to show up at 6:30 on Saturday night. Then she
drove away.

This was the mid-1970s, the low-water mark of parental oversight. The parents—I can remember nothing about them—said the baby was asleep and they
would be home by midnight. Off they went, I didn't know where. No phone
number was scrawled on a notepad in the kitchen. I was twelve years old, not
that anyone had asked. I was not one of those misleading twelve-year-olds who
could have passed for fifteen. I was a twelve-year-old who could have passed for
nine. When the baby started to cry, I crept up the stairs to his room. I had never
held a baby before, never picked one up. I got him out of the crib. We were both
crying. I called my mother, who came over and stayed with the two of us until
the parents returned. She tended to the baby, who, as it turned out, needed a
great deal of tending.

I was an uncomfortable child, a small adult biding my time. Despite my visible awkwardness with other people's children, I went on to become an extremely popular neighborhood babysitter when we moved again. By nature I am appalled by mess, and people with children lived messy lives. I would put away the books and toys, wash the dishes in the sink, wipe down the counters, run the vacuum. The children in my care were more or less left to their own devices, but they never got hurt and they didn't complain, and the parents came home to a house that bore no resemblance to the house they had left. Looking back, I wonder if they didn't go out to dinner just so I would clean their house for a dollar an hour.

22.

We all think that things are different now, that men and women are different, and the roles we play are different, that society has evolved, that we are safer, wiser, kinder. We look back at the generation before us and the generation before that and wonder, *How did they live?* It's how the next generation will look back at us, shaking their heads at the horror of our ways. Things do change, but in increments too small for us to perceive.

It doesn't matter how old you are. This applies.

23.

170   I met the illustrator Robin Preiss Glasser at the bookstore while she was on tour for the final installment of the Fancy Nancy series. We hit it off, and so Robin, force of nature, force of life, suggested we do a picture book together. While I didn't know a thing about children's literature, Robin was willing to teach me. I was thrilled, not only at her friendship but at the chance to collaborate, to try something new. We made a book together we were both proud of.

But with the book came the book tour. I hadn't been thinking about that part. In my mind I'd only gotten as far as the inherent pleasure of making lambs talk. Now I was supposed to travel the country pitching our book to people who didn't come up to my hip. I was uneasy, but decided to rely on the same strategy that had served me thus far: I would follow Robin's lead. She lived to stand in front of a roomful of children, to make them laugh and teach them something, to stir them up and then settle them down again. (She does this by clapping her hands three times. She tells every group before her talk begins—she will clap three times and they will settle themselves, effectively hypnotizing them into complete submission.) In bookstores, in school gymnasiums, in community centers, we went to meet them, vast seas of squirming bodies decked out in sequins or dirty T-shirts. Armed only with a lamb puppet and a chicken puppet, I tried my best to mimic her charm, but mostly what I did was stand back and watch the children watch her: starstruck and in love. As they lined up with their stacks of tattered Fancy Nancy books and their pristine copy of our book, *Lambslide*,[5] Robin asked them if they liked to get dressed up, and if they liked ice cream. She pulled them into her lap when they came around the table for a picture. She pulled up their shirts and nibbled their stomachs.

5. Published in 2013.

"Are you allowed to do that?" I asked. I wasn't kidding. Was she allowed to touch other people's children?

"Try and stop me," she said, kissing them again.

When a child came to the table crying or about to cry, she would ask if they wanted a butterfly on their hand. Through bleary sobs they would give the slightest hint of a nod, and Robin would take hold of that hand and marvel at it. Then, using a fat permanent marker, she would add a butterfly to the skin, explaining how to do it as she went along, just in case the child had the opportunity to ink up someone else later on. Then the child would stop crying. They'd stare at the butterfly, incredibly pleased, and often climb into Robin's lap for a quick cuddle before moving along. I didn't see this happen once or twice. I saw it day after day, city after city, with approximately every tenth child in every signing line. And every time it happened, the light that is Robin Preiss Glasser glowed brighter.

Had I met Robin early in my life, might that have made the difference? If   175
someone had looked at me like that when I was a child, might I have had children?

No, but it would have come closer to changing my mind than the hypothetical man who might have taken half the responsibility for our hypothetical offspring. Each time we took the stage (or, in many cases, the floor) Robin was astonished by every child restlessly bobbing before us, and when we were done she threw open her arms to welcome them in with no consideration for fear. Every single one of them thrilled her: their beauty, their possibility, their life. Look *at you!* she is saying. *My god, look at you!*

It's the same way she looks at me—me with the books and no children—like not having children was some spectacular idea that I alone came up with. That is, after all, Robin's superpower: to love the person in front of her as she is, to see all the glorious light inside them and reflect it back, everywhere.

MLA CITATION

Patchett, Ann. "There Are No Children Here." *The Norton Reader: An Anthology of Nonfiction*, edited by Melissa A. Goldthwaite et al., 16th ed., W. W. Norton, 2024, pp. 194–209.

QUESTIONS

1. In her essay, Ann Patchett represents herself as certain that she does not want children and comfortable in that certainty. How do others respond to her position? Do people of different genders respond differently? What do these responses suggest about societal expectations for women?

2. In a conversation at a Christmas party, a new adoptive mother comments to Patchett, "'Imagine how selfish a person would have to be to not have a child'" (paragraph 79). Is Patchett's choice selfish? Why or why not? Annotate passages that justify your answer.

3. How does Patchett connect her decision not to have children to her vocation as a writer?

4. Patchett organizes her essay into twenty-three sections or episodes. What is the effect of this structure? How does it facilitate her reflections on her decision not to have children and others' responses to that decision?

5. As Patchett's essay shows, women face strong social pressure to want and have children. Write an essay in which you examine a desire, choice, hope, or aspiration of your own that does not align with others' expectations of you.

JOEY FRANKLIN
Working at Wendy's

I T's 8:45 P.M., and I am standing in front of the counter at Wendy's. It smells of French fries and mop water. In my right hand I hold my résumé. I don't know if I need a résumé to apply for the Wendy's night shift, but I bring it anyway. It anchors me as I drift toward the sixteen-year-old kid behind the counter and ask to speak to his manager.

"One mandarin orange salad?" the boy asks.

"Uh, no. Actually, I'd like to speak to the *manager*." As the cashier retreats to the back of the store, I recognize a large kid with curly hair working the fryer—he used to play football with some of the members of my Boy Scout troop. He looks up at me, and I avert my eyes. Part of me wants to turn around and leave before the manager comes out. A couple in their twenties walks into the restaurant behind me. I step away from the counter and pretend to read the menu, holding my résumé close to my chest. The urge to leave increases. Just then the manager comes out and asks, "You here about the night shift?"

As I hand the manager my résumé, I realize it is a mistake. He doesn't want to know my service experience, or my academic references, or my GPA. All he wants to know is if I can spell my name correctly.

5   "Er, the application is over there," the manager says, handing me back my résumé and pointing to a file folder mounted on the wall next to the counter. I take the application to an empty table in the corner of the restaurant and hunch over it, wishing I had a drink, or a hamburger, or something to put on the table beside me.

The next day I go for an interview with the hiring manager. I sit down at a table in the lobby and answer two questions: "What hours do you want to work?" and "When can you start?"

When he was sixteen, my brother, Josh, got his first job at McDonald's. He lasted two weeks before deciding the greasy uniform and salty mop water weren't worth $5.25 an hour. His manager used to show off rejected applica-

Joey Franklin wrote this essay when he was an English major at Brigham Young University in Provo, Utah. It was published in Twentysomething Essays by Twentysomething Writers *(2006), a collection of writings from the winners of a national contest organized by the publishing company Random House.*

tions to the other employees in the back of the store. Most were high school dropouts looking for spending money, but a few had college degrees. One application was from a doctor who had recently left his practice because he "couldn't handle the mortality rate."

I think about that doctor now as I sit in a small back room at Wendy's. I have just watched thirty minutes of training videos about customer service, floor mopping, heavy lifting, and armed robbery. Chelsea, the training manager, hands me two neatly folded uniforms and a brand-new hat. Holding the hat in my hand, I look out into the kitchen at my new coworkers. At the fryer is the large high school kid I remember from the night before. A skinny brown-haired Asian-looking boy who must be about nineteen years old is washing dishes. Two girls are at the front of the store taking orders, and the manager is on the phone with an angry customer. "Can I do this?" I ask myself, and put on my hat.

Chelsea is pregnant. During our training session, I guess she is about six months along. It turns out she is due in three days. "This is my last week on the day shift," she says. "After the baby is born, I'll be back on nights." This is her first child, she explains, and says she is looking forward to being a mom. She smiles as she pats her stomach and asks about my son.

"Eighteen months," I tell her, "a real handful." I explain that I want to   10
work nights so I can take care of my son during the day while my wife finishes her last semester of college. I ask about the pay, but I already know her answer. "We start at five-seventy-five," she says, "but the night guys get six." I ask her what she thinks about $7. She says she'll see what she can do.

Chelsea trains me on Tuesday and goes into labor on Wednesday. I don't see her again for three weeks.

Kris Livingston's mom ran the register at the Taco Bell on the corner of Lombard Street and Allen Boulevard in a poorer section of Beaverton, Oregon. Her name was Dawn. She was divorced and had three boys. She shared a three-bedroom apartment with another single mom and her own five children. They listened to Snoop Dogg and Ice-T, drank forty-ounce malt liquors, and walked over two miles round-trip every Saturday to watch the neighborhood boys play basketball at Schiffler Park.

On welfare-check days, Dawn went grocery shopping and brought home twelve-packs of Pepsi, stacks of frozen steaks, crinkly bags of potato chips, several gallons of 2 percent milk, and bag after bag of Malt-O-Meal cereal. The week before welfare checks came, they ate eggs and instant ramen—lots of ramen.

Her son Kris was my best friend in sixth grade. We often walked to Taco Bell together to visit his mother. She usually bought us a taco while we sat in a booth in the corner of the store and talked about bicycles, girls, and football. Once, on the way home from visiting his mom, Kris said, "She used to sell drugs, you know. We had plenty of money, and nobody thought she was a bad mom then."

My first night on the job, I work with Dave. He is seventeen years old, five-ten,   15
and keeps his hair short, like a soldier. He goes to an alternative high school if

he wakes up in time and is looking forward to enlisting in the military when he turns eighteen. His dad, who recently remarried and moved, told Dave he would have to find his own place to live. When Dave isn't sleeping on his friends' couches, he lives in his car, a 1982 Volkswagen Rabbit with a hole in the floor just beneath the gas pedal.

Dave works with me a few nights a week and knows the business well. He's quick with a mop, can make all the sandwiches blindfolded, and has the entire computer memorized. When he's not working, he hangs out in the restaurant lobby trying to steal Frosties and old fries when no one is looking. The manager says she will give him food if he needs it and asks that he not steal anymore. "Asking gets you nowhere," he says, and keeps stealing.

Because I live just two blocks from the store, I recognize a disproportionate number of the late-night drive-through customers. Mostly, I see parents of the scouts I work with, or other scout leaders, and occasionally a friend from school. When they pull up to the window and see me in the Wendy's hat and headphones, the following conversation ensues:

"Joey, I didn't know you worked here! How's it going?"

"Good, good. Just flipping burgers."

20   "Hey, you've got to do what you've got to do."

Then I explain the job is temporary, and it's the only job in town that allows me to work at night so I can watch my son during the day while my wife finishes school. I tell them in another month I'll be back in school and working at a better-paying, less humiliating campus job.

One evening a fellow scout leader comes through, and after an exchange similar to the one described above, he says, "Hey, more power to ya. I know a lot of people who think they're above that." He thanks me as I hand him his triple cheeseburger, and he drives around the corner and out of sight.

At 250 pounds, Danny really fills out his uniform. He played varsity football for the local high school, has earned his Eagle Scout award, and knows his way around a car engine. On several occasions he has changed spark plugs, jumped batteries, and even replaced brakes on the cars of fellow employees, usually right in the store parking lot.

Wendy's is the first job Danny has ever had. With six months' experience, he is the senior employee and is being considered for a management position. He brings in about $1,000 a month, much of which he gives to his grandmother. At closing, he always saves the good salads for me and talks the manager into letting me go home early. He likes listening to Metallica, working on his Trans Am, and talking with Tonya, a high school junior who also works at the store.

25   While I'm washing my hands in the bathroom at work, a well-groomed twenty-something man standing at the sink next to me starts a conversation. "Do you like working the night shift?" he asks.

"It's not bad," I say, shaking my wet hands over the sink.

"How long have you worked here?"

"Two weeks."

"Have you ever thought about college?" he asks. I want to tell him I'm in the top 5 percent of students at my college, that I am two semesters away from graduating, and that I'm on my way to grad school to get a PhD in English literature. Instead, I shrug and tell him the same line I tell everyone: "Oh yeah, I'm just working here until my wife finishes." He doesn't believe me. To him, I look like another wasted life, another victim. He thinks I got my girlfriend pregnant, that I never graduated from high school, that I can't do any better than flip burgers at two in the morning. He feels sorry for my kids.

"I only applied here because I knew I would get hired," says Sara the first night I   30
work with her. She is a nineteen-year-old single mother with a sixteen-month-old boy. She is very tall and wears her long brown hair in a ponytail pulled through the hole in the back of her Wendy's hat. I ask her why she needed a job so bad.

"I had to get one," she tells me. "My parole officer said it was the only way to stay out of jail." I start at this and then ask, "Why were you in jail?"

"Drugs," she says, and pauses, testing me. "I was wearing my boyfriend's jacket, and the cops found a heroin pipe in the pocket." I ask how long she was in jail. "One year," she tells me. "I just got out a month ago."

When I was in fifth grade, my dad got a job delivering pizza. As an eleven-year-old, pivoting on that blurry edge between boyhood and adolescence, I found myself bragging to my friends about the prospect of free pizza and then wishing I hadn't told them anything about my father's job. He worked a few nights a week, and when he came home, his uniform smelled like steaming cardboard and burnt cheese, but he always brought home pizza.

Oren is nineteen years old and works at Wendy's to pay for a cell-phone bill and to get out of the house. His parents are devout Mormons and think he is a disgrace to their entire family. He wants to sell marijuana because he believes he can do nothing else. "I don't do anything well," he tells me one night while washing dishes. "I don't know what I want to do with my life." He asks Sara to find some pot for him to sell.

Oren's mother is Japanese, born and raised, and speaks to her children in   35
her native tongue. That means Oren speaks Japanese and has family connections in Japan.

Oren also owns an AK-47 and likes to go up into the canyons and shoot jackrabbits. He showed me a picture once of a rabbit carcass out in the desert, its innards all blown out and dangling for the camera.

Tonight, while working the grill, Danny tells me he has never been on a date. "Girls don't like me," he says as he flips a row of sizzling, square quarter-pound patties. I can tell he believes it. Danny, by his own admission, is the kind of guy whom girls like for support. He is a gentleman, he asks thoughtful questions, and he's always willing to talk. He thinks his weight and his scruff turn girls off. He tells me he is going to ask Tonya to a movie this weekend but isn't sure she'll say yes. Later, Tonya comes into the store, and Danny disappears with her for a few minutes out in the lobby. He comes back with a large smile on his face and says, "I've got a date this weekend, can you work for me?"

I don't like when Dave works the front line with me. I can't make sandwiches very fast yet, and he gets tired of waiting. More than once he pushes me aside to finish an order. If he sees me hesitate on a step, he barks at me, "Red, green, red, green! Ketchup, pickle, tomato, lettuce! Come on, Joe, it's not that hard."

Later, while I'm mopping the floor at closing, Dave comes by and takes the mop from my hand. "Like this," he says, scrubbing the tile vigorously. He thrusts the mop back in my hands and walks away, rolling his eyes.

40   Chelsea is back at work tonight for the first time since having her baby. She appears fairly happy, and I am surprised at how well adjusted she seems to being a working mom. The phone rings several times, and Chelsea takes the calls in her office. She tells me her husband has lots of questions about putting the baby to bed. After the lobby closes, Chelsea disappears into the bathroom for nearly half an hour. This happens every time I work with her. I wonder if she is sick. Then I notice the breast pump in a case on her desk. Another employee tells me Chelsea has been expressing milk in one of the bathroom stalls on her breaks.

Danny and Tonya have been dating for two weeks. He shows up for his shift an hour early to see her before she gets off. They sit in the lobby holding hands and talking for almost the entire hour. When they're not in the store together, she sends text messages to his phone, which I catch him reading while he stands at the grill.

Tonight Danny approaches me while I'm opening boxes of French fries. He wants advice on how to ask Tonya to her junior prom. "I want to do something romantic," he says. I suggest Shakespeare's eighteenth sonnet. He has never heard of it. "'Shall I compare thee to a summer's day . . .'" I recite. "She'll love it." I print off the sonnet at home and bring it to work for him the next day. He writes it in a card and delivers it with flowers. Two weeks later, in a rented tux at Tonya's junior prom, Danny gets his first kiss.

I call my dad tonight. He asks about school, about my son, and about work. I tell him about Wendy's.

"What? Who?" he says.

45   "Me. I got a job at Wendy's." Long pause. "I needed a job I could do at night." More silence. "It's not so bad." Still silence. "I work from nine P.M. to one A.M. a few nights a week."

Just when I think the line must be disconnected, Dad clears his throat and asks, "What happened to your computer job?"

"The guy ran out of work for me."

"Oh." More silence. I imagine he looks around the room to make sure no one is listening before he says, "Wendy's? When did that happen?" I want to tell him that it didn't *happen*, that it wasn't an accident, but I am stuck wondering how to make him understand, and at the same time wondering why I should have to explain anything at all. I wonder what his reaction would be if I had chosen to get more student loans instead of the part-time job. I choose to say nothing. Then I offer him my employee discount on fries next time he is in town. He says he'll take me up on it.

When I come into the store tonight, Dave is talking loudly to some employees gathered in the lobby. I ask what all the laughing is about. They tell me that last night Dave and Oren siphoned all the gas out of Dave's stepmother's four-wheeler, and then they urinated on her car handles.

Everyone dreads working with Chelsea. When she is not in her office counting   50
the till or on the phone with her husband, she sits on the front counter and com-
plains about her mother-in-law. She does very little to help prep the store for closing, and we rarely get out before two A.M.

Tonight she tells me about her mother-in-law's most recent visit. "I cleaned the house for hours before she came," Chelsea says, nursing a Diet Coke. "And the first thing she says when she gets there is how disgusting the place looks. She won't even eat my cooking." According to Chelsea, her mother-in-law has hated her ever since she got engaged. She wouldn't even visit except that Chelsea has a baby now, and the mother-in-law feels obligated. Chelsea's mother-in-law is disappointed that she is still working. "A mother's place is in the home," she says to Chelsea. "Your kids will be ruined."

Tonight Waymon Hamilton comes through the drive-up window with his family. Waymon lives around the corner from me, and his two sons are in my scout troop, but they spend most of their free time traveling around the state playing premier Little League baseball. They order a few value meals, some drinks, and they ask how I'm doing. There is no hint of concern or condolence in their voices, and I appreciate it.

I hand them their food and watch them drive away. Most people know Way-mon the way I know him, as a dedicated father who works hard at a thankless job to provide for his family. His unassuming nature and warm smile are what I see when I think about him. Few people know him as the fleet-footed running back who helped Brigham Young University win Holiday Bowls in 1981 and 1983. Few people know he holds several BYU scoring records, including second place for touchdowns in a season, third in career touchdowns, and fifth for both season and career points scored. I didn't even know he played college football until someone mentioned it at a scout meeting. I once worked all day with Way-mon, putting in a new driveway for a neighbor, and he never mentioned his football days once. He told me about his boys, about teaching public school in California, and about pouring lots of concrete.

After the store closes, I come home, take off my uniform, and climb into bed with my wife. She rolls over, tells me she loves me, and murmurs something about the smell of French fries. I kiss her on the cheek and close my eyes. It is winter, but the house is warm. My son is asleep in the next room. There is food in the fridge, and I have a job that pays an honest wage. In the morning I will make breakfast and send my wife off to school. And then, after the dishes are done, if the weather permits, my son and I will take a walk to the park.

MLA CITATION

Franklin, Joey. "Working at Wendy's." *The Norton Reader: An Anthology of Nonfiction*, edited by Melissa A. Goldthwaite et al., 16th ed., W. W. Norton, 2024, pp. 210–16.

QUESTIONS

1. What is Joey Franklin's attitude toward working at Wendy's? How does he demonstrate it? In answering these questions, look especially at the conclusion of the essay and at the details he chooses about how others respond to him.

2. Franklin describes his coworkers in considerable detail (for example, paragraph 13). What do his descriptions convey about their standing in society?

3. Most of this essay is written in the present tense (with past-tense reflections about former jobs held by family members). What is the effect of Franklin's use of this verb tense? How would the essay differ if he wrote the entire essay in past tense?

4. Write an essay about a job you've held. Use dialogue and details to develop characters.

IAN FRAZIER
Take the F

BROOKLYN, NEW YORK, has the undefined, hard-to-remember shape of a stain. I never know what to tell people when they ask me where in it I live. It sits at the western tip of Long Island at a diagonal that does not conform neatly to the points of the compass. People in Brooklyn do not describe where they live in terms of north or west or south. They refer instead to their neighborhoods and to the nearest subway lines. I live on the edge of Park Slope, a neighborhood by the crest of a low ridge that runs through the borough. Prospect Park is across the street. Airplanes in the landing pattern for LaGuardia Airport sometimes fly right over my building; every few minutes, on certain sunny days, perfectly detailed airplane shadows slide down my building and up the building opposite in a blink. You can see my building from the plane—it's on the left-hand side of Prospect Park, the longer patch of green you cross after the expanse of Green-Wood Cemetery.

First published in the New Yorker *(1995), a weekly magazine of "reportage, commentary, criticism, essays, fiction, satire, cartoons, and poetry," and later included in Ian Frazier's book* Gone to New York: Adventures in the City *(2005).*

We moved to a co-op apartment in a four-story building a week before our daughter was born. She is now six. I grew up in the country and would not have expected ever to live in Brooklyn. My daughter is a city kid, with less sympathy for certain other parts of the country. When we visited Montana, she was disappointed by the scarcity of pizza places. I overheard her explaining—she was three or four then—to a Montana kid about Brooklyn. She said, "In Brooklyn, there is a lot of broken glass, so you have to wear shoes. And, there is good pizza." She is stern in her judgment of pizza. At the very low end of the pizza-ranking scale is some pizza she once had in New Hampshire, a category now called New Hampshire pizza. In the middle is some okay pizza she once had at the Bronx Zoo, which she calls zoo pizza. At the very top is the pizza at the pizza place where the big kids go, about two blocks from our house.

Our subway is the F train. It runs under our building and shakes the floor. The F is generally a reliable train, but one spring as I walked in the park I saw emergency vehicles gathered by a concrete-sheathed hole in the lawn. Firemen lifted a metal lid from the hole and descended into it. After a while, they reappeared, followed by a few people, then dozens of people, then a whole lot of people—passengers from a disabled F train, climbing one at a time out an exit shaft. On the F, I sometimes see large women in straw hats reading a newspaper called the *Caribbean Sunrise*, and Orthodox Jews bent over Talmudic texts[1] in which the footnotes have footnotes, and groups of teenagers wearing identical red bandannas with identical red plastic baby pacifiers in the corners of their mouths, and female couples in porkpie hats, and young men with the silhouettes of the Manhattan skyline razored into their short side hair from one temple around to the other, and Russian-speaking men with thick wrists and big wristwatches, and a hefty, tall woman with long, straight blond hair who hums and closes her eyes and absently practices cello fingerings on the metal subway pole. As I watched the F train passengers emerge among the grass and trees of Prospect Park, the faces were as varied as usual, but the expressions of indignant surprise were all about the same.

Just past my stop, Seventh Avenue, Manhattan-bound F trains rise from underground to cross the Gowanus Canal. The train sounds different—lighter, quieter—in the open air. From the elevated tracks, you can see the roofs of many houses stretching back up the hill to Park Slope, and a bumper crop of rooftop graffiti, and neon signs for Eagle Clothes and Kentile Floors, and flat expanses of factory roofs where seagulls stand on one leg around puddles in the sagging spots. There are fuel-storage tanks surrounded by earthen barriers, and slag piles, and conveyor belts leading down to the oil-slicked waters of the canal. On certain days, the sludge at the bottom of the canal causes it to bubble. Two men fleeing the police jumped in the canal a while ago; one made it across, the other quickly died. When the subway doors open at the Smith–Ninth Street stop, you can see the bay and sometimes smell the ocean breeze. This stretch of elevated is the highest point of the New York subway system. To the south you

1. Rabbinic discussions of law, ethics, philosophy, and history collected in the Talmud, a key text of Judaism.

can see the Verrazano-Narrows Bridge, to the north the World Trade towers. For just a few moments, the Statue of Liberty appears between passing buildings. Pieces of a neighborhood—laundry on clotheslines, a standup swimming pool, a plaster saint, a satellite dish, a rectangle of lawn—slide by like quickly dealt cards. Then the train descends again; growing over the wall just before the tunnel is a wisteria bush, which blooms pale blue every May.

5   I have spent days, weeks on the F train. The trip from Seventh Avenue to midtown Manhattan is long enough so that every ride can produce its own mini-society of riders, its own forty-minute Ship of Fools.[2] Once a woman an arm's length from me on a crowded train pulled a knife on a man who threatened her. I remember the argument and the principals, but mostly I remember the knife—its flat, curved wood-grain handle inlaid with brass fittings at each end, its long, tapered blade. Once a man sang the words of the Lord's Prayer to a mournful, syncopated tune, and he fitted the mood of the morning so exactly that when he asked for money at the end the riders reached for their wallets and purses as if he'd pulled a gun. Once a big white kid with some friends was teasing a small old Hispanic lady, and when he got off the train I looked at him through the window and he slugged it hard next to my face. Once a thin woman and a fat woman sitting side by side had a long and loud conversation about someone they intended to slap silly: "Her butt be in the *hospital*!" "Bring out the ar-*tillery*!" The terminus of the F in Brooklyn is at Coney Island, not far from the beach. At an off hour, I boarded the train and found two or three passengers and, walking around on the floor, a crab. The passengers were looking at the crab. Its legs clicked on the floor like varnished fingernails. It moved in this direction, then that, trying to get comfortable. It backed itself under a seat, against the wall. Then it scooted out just after some new passengers had sat down there, and they really screamed. Passengers at the next stop saw it and laughed. When a boy lifted his foot as if to stomp it, everybody cried, "Noooh!" By the time we reached Jay Street–Borough Hall, there were maybe a dozen of us in the car, all absorbed in watching the crab. The car doors opened and a heavyset woman with good posture entered. She looked at the crab; then, sternly, at all of us. She let a moment pass. Then she demanded, "*Whose* is *that*?" A few stops later, a short man with a mustache took a manila envelope, bent down, scooped the crab into it, closed it, and put it in his coat pocket.

The smells in Brooklyn: coffee, fingernail polish, eucalyptus, the breath from laundry rooms, pot roast, Tater Tots. A woman I know who grew up here says she moved away because she could not stand the smell of cooking food in the hallway of her parents' building. I feel just the opposite. I used to live in a converted factory above an army-navy store, and I like being in a place that smells like people live there. In the mornings, I sometimes wake to the smell of toast, and I still don't know exactly whose toast it is. And I prefer living in a borough of two and a half million inhabitants, the most of any borough in the city. I think of all the

2. Allegory, originally from Plato's *Republic*, depicting a ship with human passengers who are mad, frivolous, or witlessly ignorant of their fate.

rural places, the pine-timbered canyons and within-commuting-distance farm-
land, that we are preserving by not living there. I like the immensities of the
borough, the unrolling miles of Eastern Parkway and Ocean Parkway and Lin-
den Boulevard, and the disheveled outlying parks strewn with tree limbs and
with shards of glass held together by liquor bottle labels, and the tough bridges—
the Williamsburg and the Manhattan—and the gentle Brooklyn Bridge. And I
like the way the people talk; some really do have Brooklyn accents, really do say
"dese" and "dose." A week or two ago, a group of neighbors stood on a street corner watching a peregrine falcon on a building cornice contentedly eating a pigeon
it had caught, and the sunlight came through its tail feathers, and a woman said
to a man, "Look at the tail, it's so ah-range," and the man replied, "Yeah, I soar it."
Like many Americans, I fear living in a nowhere, in a place that is no-place; in
Brooklyn, that doesn't trouble me at all.

Everybody, it seems, is here. At Grand Army Plaza, I have seen traffic tie-ups
caused by Haitians and others rallying in support of President Aristide,[3] and by
St. Patrick's Day parades, and by Jews of the Lubavitcher sect celebrating the
birthday of their Grand Rebbe[4] with a slow procession of ninety-three motor
homes—one for each year of his life. Local taxis have bumper stickers that say
"Allah Is Great"; one of the men who made the bomb that blew up the World
Trade Center used an apartment just a few blocks from me. When an election is
held in Russia, crowds line up to cast ballots at a Russian polling place in Brigh-
ton Beach. A while ago, I volunteer-taught reading at a public elementary school
across the park. One of my students, a girl, was part Puerto Rican, part Greek,
and part Welsh. Her looks were a lively combination, set off by sea-green eyes. I
went to a map store in Manhattan and bought maps of Puerto Rico, Greece, and
Wales to read with her, but they didn't interest her. A teacher at the school was
directing a group of students to set up chairs for a program in the auditorium,
and she said to me, "We have a problem here—each of these kids speaks a different language." She asked the kids to tell me where they were from. One was from
Korea, one from Brazil, one from Poland, one from Guyana, one from Taiwan. In
the program that followed, a chorus of fourth and fifth graders sang "God Bless
America," "You're a Grand Old Flag," and "I'm a Yankee-Doodle Dandy."

People in my neighborhood are mostly white, and middle class or above.
People in neighborhoods nearby are mostly not white, and mostly middle class or
below. Everybody uses Prospect Park. On summer days, the park teems with
sound—the high note is kids screaming in the water sprinklers at the playground,
the midrange is radios and tape players, and the bass is idling or speeding cars.
People bring lawn furniture and badminton nets and coolers, and then they barbecue. Charcoal smoke drifts into the neighborhood. Last year, local residents
upset about the noise and litter and smoke began a campaign to outlaw barbecuing in the park. There was much unfavorable comment about "the barbecuers."
Since most of the barbecuers, as it happens, are black or Hispanic, the phrase

3. Jean-Bertrand Aristide (b. 1953), president of Haiti briefly in 1991 and again from
1994 to 1996 and 2001 to 2004.

4. Menachem Mendel Schneerson (1902–1994).

"Barbecuers Go Home," which someone spray-painted on the asphalt at the Ninth Street entrance to the park, took on a pointed, unkind meaning. But then park officials set up special areas for barbecuing, and the barbecuers complied, and the controversy died down.

Right nearby is a shelter for homeless people. Sometimes people sleep on the benches along the park, sometimes they sleep in the foyer of our building. Once I went downstairs, my heart pounding, to evict a homeless person who I had been told was there. The immediate, unquestioning way she left made me feel bad; later I always said "Hi" to her and gave her a dollar when I ran into her. One night, late, I saw her on the street, and I asked her her last name (by then I already knew her first name) and for a moment she couldn't recall it. At this, she shook her head in mild disbelief.

10   There's a guy I see on a bench along Prospect Park West all the time. Once I walked by carrying my year-old son, and the man said, "Someday he be carrying you." At the local copy shop one afternoon, a crowd was waiting for copies and faxes when a man in a houndstooth fedora came in seeking signatures for a petition to have the homeless shelter shut down. To my surprise, and his, the people in the copy shop instantly turned on him. "I suppose because they're poor they shouldn't even have a place to sleep at night," a woman said as he backed out the door. On the park wall across the street from my building, someone has written in black marker:

COPS PROTECT CITIZENS
WHO PROTECT US FROM COPS.

Sometimes I walk from my building downhill and north, along the Brooklyn waterfront, where cargo ships with scuffed sides and prognathous bows lean overhead. Sometimes I walk by the Brooklyn Navy Yard, its docks now too dormant to attract saboteurs, its long expanses of chain-link fence tangled here and there with the branches of ailanthus trees growing through. Sometimes I head southwest, keeping more or less to the high ground—Bay Ridge—along Fifth Avenue, through Hispanic neighborhoods that stretch in either direction as far as you can see, and then through block after block of Irish. I follow the ridge to its steep descent to the water at the Verrazano Narrows; Fort Hamilton, an army post dating from 1814, is there, and a small Episcopal church called the Church of the Generals. Robert E. Lee once served as a vestryman of this church, and Stonewall Jackson was baptized here. Today the church is in the shade of a forest of high concrete columns supporting an access ramp to the Verrazano-Narrows Bridge.

Sometimes I walk due south, all the way out Coney Island Avenue. In that direction, as you approach the ocean, the sky gets bigger and brighter, and the buildings seem to flatten beneath it. Dry cleaners advertise "Tallis[5] Cleaned Free with Every Purchase Over Fifteen Dollars." Then you start to see occasional lines

5. Jewish prayer shawl.

of graffiti written in Cyrillic.[6] Just past a Cropsey Avenue billboard welcoming
visitors to Coney Island is a bridge over a creek filled nearly to the surface with
metal shopping carts that people have tossed there over the years. A little farther
on, the streets open onto the beach. On a winter afternoon, bundled-up women
sit on the boardwalk on folding chairs around a portable record player outside a
restaurant called Gastronom Moscow. The acres of trash-dotted sand are almost
empty. A bottle of Peter the Great vodka lies on its side, drops of water from its
mouth making a small depression in the sand. A man with trousers rolled up to
his shins moves along the beach, chopping at driftwood with an axe. Another
passerby says, "He's vorking hard, that guy!" The sunset unrolls light along the
storefronts like tape. From the far distance, little holes in the sand at the water's
edge mark the approach of a short man wearing hip boots and earphones and
carrying a long-handled metal detector. Treasure hunters dream of the jewelry
that people must have lost here over the years. Some say that this is the richest
treasure beach in the Northeast. The man stops, runs the metal detector again
over a spot, digs with a clamming shovel, lifts some sand, brushes through it with
a gloved thumb, discards it. He goes on, leaving a trail of holes behind him.

I like to find things myself, and I always try to keep one eye on the ground
as I walk. So far I have found seven dollars (a five and two ones), an earring in
the shape of a strawberry, several personal notes, a matchbook with a 900
number to call to hear "prison sex fantasies," and two spent .25-caliber shells.
Once on Carroll Street, I saw a page of text on the sidewalk, and I bent over to
read it. It was page 191 from a copy of *Anna Karenina*.[7] I read the whole page.
It described Vronsky leaving a gathering and riding off in a carriage. In a great
book, the least fragment is great. I looked up and saw a woman regarding me
closely from a few feet away. "You're reading," she said wonderingly. "From a
distance, I t'ought you were watchin' ants."

My favorite place to walk is the Brooklyn Botanic Garden, not more than fifteen
minutes away. It's the first place I take out-of-towners, who may not associate
Brooklyn with flowers. In the winter, the garden is drab as pocket lint, and you
can practically see all the way through from Flatbush Avenue to Washington Avenue. But then in February or March a few flowerings begin, the snowdrops and
the crocuses, and then the yellow of the daffodils climbs Daffodil Hill, and then
the magnolias—star magnolias, umbrella magnolias, saucer magnolias—go off
all at once, and walking among them is like flying through cumulus clouds. Then
the cherry trees blossom, some a soft and glossy red like makeup, others pink as
a dessert, and crowds fill the paths on weekends and stand in front of the blossoms in their best clothes and have their pictures taken. Security guards tell
people, "No eating, no sitting on the grass—this is a garden, not a park." There
are traffic jams of strollers and kids running loose. One security guard jokes into

6. Alphabet used for Russian and other Slavic languages.
7. Novel by the Russian writer Leo Tolstoy (1828–1910) published in serial installments
between 1873 and 1877.

his radio, "There's a pterodactyl on the overlook!" In the pond in the Japanese Garden, ducks lobby for pieces of bread. A duck quacks, in Brooklynese, "Yeah, yeah, yeah," having heard it all before.

Then the cherry blossoms fall, they turn some paths completely pink next to the grass's green, and the petals dry, and people tread them into a fine pink powder. Kids visit on end-of-school-year field trips, and teachers yell, "Shawon, get back on line!" and boys with long T-shirts printed from neck to knee with an image of Martin Luther King's face run by laughing and swatting at one another. The yellow boxes that photographic film comes in fall on the ground, and here and there an empty bag of Crazy Calypso potato chips. The lilacs bloom, each bush with a scent slightly different from the next, and yellow tulips fill big round planters with color so bright it ascends in a column, like a searchlight beam. The roses open on the trellises in the Rose Garden and attract a lively air traffic of bees, and June wedding parties, brides and grooms and their subsidiaries, adjust themselves minutely for photographers there. A rose called the Royal Gold smells like a new bathing suit and is as yellow.

15   In our building of nine apartments, two people have died and six have been born since we moved in. I like our neighbors—a guy who works for Off-Track Betting, a guy who works for the Department of Correction, a woman who works for Dean Witter, an in flight steward, a salesperson of subsidiary rights at a publishing house, a restaurant manager, two lawyers, a retired machinist, a Lebanese-born woman of ninety-five—as well as any I've ever had. We keep track of the bigger events in the building with the help of Chris, our downstairs neighbor. Chris lives on the ground floor and often has conversations in the hall while her foot props her door open. When our kids are sick, she brings them her kids' videos to watch, and when it rains she gives us rides to school. One year, Chris became pregnant and had to take a blood-thinning medicine and was in and out of the hospital. Finally, she had a healthy baby and came home, but then began to bleed and didn't stop. Her husband brought the baby to us about midnight and took Chris to the nearest emergency room. Early the next morning, the grandmother came and took the baby. Then for two days nobody heard anything. When we knocked on Chris's door we got no answer and when we called we got an answering machine. The whole building was expectant, spooky, quiet. The next morning I left the house and there in the foyer was Chris. She held her husband's arm, and she looked pale, but she was returning from the hospital under her own steam. I hugged her at the door, and it was the whole building hugging her. I walked to the garden seeing glory everywhere. I went to the Rose Garden and took a big Betsy McCall rose to my face and breathed into it as if it were an oxygen mask.

MLA CITATION

Frazier, Ian. "Take the F." *The Norton Reader: An Anthology of Nonfiction*, edited by Melissa A. Goldthwaite et al., 16th ed., W. W. Norton, 2024, pp. 216–22.

QUESTIONS

1. According to Ian Frazier, Brooklynites identify themselves by neighborhood and subway line (paragraph 1). In addition to his subway line, how does Frazier describe where he lives? What techniques help him present his Brooklyn neighborhood to readers who are unfamiliar with the area?

2. Frazier comments that every ride on the F train "can produce its own mini-society of riders" (paragraph 5). What does Frazier's depiction of the subway reveal about New York society more generally?

3. Frazier engages all of the senses—sight, sound, smell, taste, and touch—to portray his Brooklyn home. Choose one example of each that stands out to you. How do these examples create a sense of place?

4. Write an essay about your neighborhood, using techniques identified in questions 1 and 3.

ELIZABETH ALEXANDER
from *The Trayvon Generation*

I AM LOOKING AT A PHOTOGRAPH called *Daddy'O, The Oldest Inmate in Angola State Penitentiary.* A Black man in prison-issue jeans and shirt leans against a tree, his right hand across his heart and his left resting at an angle on his thigh. He looks both calm and distressed, peaceful and haunted. He was seventy-five when the photo was taken by Chandra McCormick, a photographer from New Orleans who along with her husband Keith Calhoun has chronicled Angola prison and its inmates and visitors for many years. They took one iconic photograph of a guard on a horse, surveying the incarcerated men picking cotton in the field, and many other pictures that haunt. *Daddy'O* is the one I return to: his knitted brow, his hand on his heart, the experiences on his face, the stories behind his eyes, and all that they have seen. He served fifteen years in Angola and was then released, spent a few weeks on the outside, and was put in again, where he served time until he died there.[1]

The Louisiana State Penitentiary, known as Angola, sits outside of New Orleans on land the size of the island of Manhattan. It looks today like the plantation it was, with Black men picking cotton, or okra, while white correctional officers ride on horseback to oversee their work. All that is missing in the tableau is the whip. It is both emblem and manifestation of the crisis of mass incarceration in this country and its disproportionate impact on people

From Elizabeth Alexander's book The Trayvon Generation *(2022). All notes in this piece were written by the author unless indicated otherwise.*

1. Chandra McCormick et al., "Louisiana Medley: The Social Justice Photography of Chandra McCormick and Keith Calhoun," Artist Talk, Harvard Art Museums, November 6, 2019, video, https://youtu.be/a4iSAwjBtnw.

of color, inside and outside the prisons and the neighborhoods and communities they draw from. Incarcerated people are too often forgotten, sent away and out of sight, far from people who love them, with tremendous obstacles to strong relationships.

The extraordinary documentary *Time*, by Garrett Bradley, follows the Rob and Sibil Fox Richardson family through the years of their teenaged courtship, the birth of six sons, and Rob's robbery conviction, sixty-year sentence, incarceration at Angola, and eventual release. The title is apt: the film, which is in large part compiled of home video that Fox recorded and preserved, gives a strange and surreal sense of how time spools both quickly and interminably across the family-defining years of Rob's incarceration. Fox will not let her family unravel, and holding Rob both in the present and in the light of memory when he is locked away is her achievement and what the film bears witness to and allows viewers to see and share.

Angola houses the largest population of lifers on planet Earth, and by many estimates, at least 90 percent of those incarcerated will die there.[2] I planned a trip there with a group of colleagues doing philanthropic work in New Orleans because to understand the City of New Orleans we needed to include and see this place that cages upwards of six thousand people, most of whom hail from Orleans or Jefferson Parish. Here or not here, they are here.

5   We were interested in the *Angolite*, the George Polk Award-winning prison newsmagazine, and the radio station, and the famous hospice. I wanted to learn more about the many musicians who served significant time there: Lead Belly, two of the Neville Brothers, James Booker.[3] Musicologists John and Alan Lomax believed that because of the intense isolation and privation at prisons like Angola and Mississippi's Parchman Farm, also a former plantation, certain powerful forms of Black music developed and were sustained within their walls.

The second-oldest Neville brother, Charles, served five years in Angola in the early 1960s for possession of two marijuana joints. When he got out, he sang and recorded with his brothers songs like "Angola Bound" that were created inside the prison. Angola has drawn attention from many other artists. Deborah Luster is a white photographer who, after the murder of her mother, sought to explore and reconcile her feelings by photographing a wide range of people in Angola. She published it in the book *One Big Self: Prisoners of Louisiana*, which she made with the late poet C. D. Wright.[4]

The prisoners brought what they could to their portrait sessions—what they owned, what they could borrow—to shape the message they wanted to send out through the image. Luster creates these portraits as tintypes, a beautiful and

2. James Ridgeway, "God's Own Warden," *Mother Jones*, July/August 2011, https://www.motherjones.com/politics/2011/07/burl-cain-angola-prison/.

3. Lead Belly, stage name of blues singer Huddie William Ledbetter (1888–1949); Neville Brothers, family rhythm-and-blues group; Booker (1939–1983), rhythm-and-blues keyboard player [Editor's note].

4. Deborah Luster and C. D. Wright, *One Big Self: Prisoners of Louisiana* (Santa Fe, NM: Twin Palms Publishing, 2003).

anachronistic form that creates a single image. The effect is one of suspended time. On the reverse, Luster engraves names, birthdates, birthplaces, nicknames, how many children they might have, hobbies, interests, aspirations, and dreams. She also includes their Department of Corrections ID numbers, where they are incarcerated, the length of sentence, their assigned jobs within the prison system—such as chair factory, work field, or metal fab. Luster then gave those photographed their portraits, a moment of ownership over their own image and a meaningful way to connect with loved ones on the outside.

"I returned twenty-five thousand prints to inmates," Luster says. "They made themselves so vulnerable for me, and it's not often that you have an encounter like that. I know a lot of it was that they were actually posing for the people that they loved—their husbands, their wives, their children." She continues,

> There was a woman who asked to be photographed. She said, "I've been here fifteen years. I'm down for ninety-nine years. I have nineteen children. My children haven't spoken to me since I came to prison. Perhaps if I had some photographs I could send them, it would soften their hearts to me." A few months later, she said, "Four of my children came to visit me. The baby came and he's now nineteen. He was five years old when I came to prison."[5]

The photographs capture the sitters with the formality of remembrance, some of the millions of not-dead separated from society. If we forget them, we will not understand who, in total, we are.

Picking cotton is the first rotation men do when they are brought into   10
Angola, for which they earn between four and forty cents an hour.[6] The prisoners are almost exclusively Black. The guards are almost exclusively white. I read on the wall in the small entry museum that in 1835 Black women prisoners were there because they resisted the conditions of slavery.

Some of those men—not men, those fifteen-year-olds—were not in prison for life without parole because of rape or premeditated murder but some for "reckless eyeballing."

"Reckless eyeballing" is a concept most infamous for its use by pre–civil rights courts to punish and imprison Black men for looking at white women.[7] However, it is still used for any form of gaze deemed "aggressive" or "inappropriate," especially when a Black person looks a white person with power directly in the eye. Black incarcerated men are frequently thrown into solitary confinement for making direct eye contact with their white guards.

---

5. The Kitchen Sisters, "After Mother's Murder, Artist Photographs Prisoners," *All Things Considered*, June 30, 2010, NPR, https://www.npr.org/2010/06/30/128212442/after-mothers-murder-artist-photographs-prisoners.

6. Katie Rose Quandr and James Ridgeway, "At Angola Prison, Getting Sick Can Be a Death Sentence," *In These Times*, December 2016, https://www.inthetimes.com/features/angola-prison-healthcare-abuse-investigation.html.

7. See, for example, Mary Frances Berry, "'Reckless Eyeballing': The Matt Ingram Case and the Denial of African American Sexual Freedom," the *Journal of African American History* 93, no. 2 (2008): 223–34.

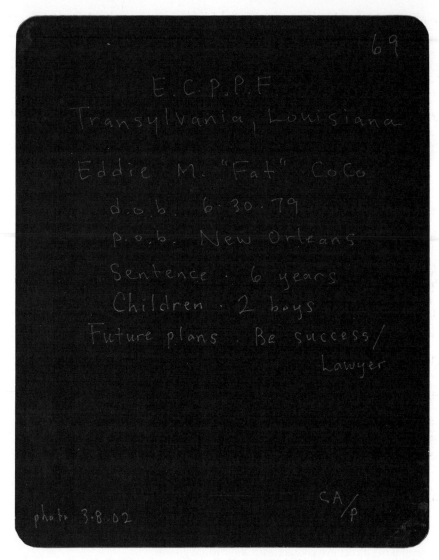

Deborah Luster's *Eddie M. "Fat" Coco Jr., Transylvania, Louisiana* (March 8, 2002).

Deborah Luster's *Eddie M. "Fat" Coco Jr., Transylvania, Louisiana* (March 8, 2002).

There is a membership golf course on the property for people outside the prison. From the restaurant and the golf course you can view the infamous Camp J, where men are kept in solitary confinement. I asked the warden if we might drive by Camp J, and the warden told us no.

There is entertainment at the prison provided for outsiders, including a famous rodeo.

We did not see the rodeo.

We did not see Camp J.

15

We did not see the camels that are kept on the property for the nativity scene that is assembled every year on the golf course.

We did visit a writing and meditation group that was called a "compassion group." In the group we heard men speak about meditating, about understanding why people have pain, understanding who they are, learning to be reflective. The sessions last eight weeks and an inmate can attend once in his entire time in the prison, eight weeks in literally a lifetime in the case of most of the men in the room.

One man, perhaps thirty-five, told us he had been sentenced to life when he was fifteen.

20   The writing group was all Black men. The teacher was a white woman who created a literal, physical circle in which the men talked about themselves and their lives in response to a reading. The stated goal of the group, according to the warden, was "to make the men calm."

At least 90 percent of the men imprisoned there will die there. As a guest, I stood outside the circle, but as I listened I could not help but move in because the human force drew me in and it felt wrong to stand outside. One of the men, who had been in prison since he was a teenager, said, "We dress our ideas in clothes to make the abstract visible." The phrase arrested me. I thought about my own career as a professor and about the thin line that separated some of the young men I have taught from these young men. If any student of mine spoke these words I would have leaned closer, been drawn in by the image, and asked to understand more.

This life is the only life. There is no liberation in the by-and-by.

The warden and I both cried when we left the writing group.

We then asked to see the hospice that has been praised in more than one film. Hospice provides a way to leave this earth with dignity. What does it mean to have a hospice for a population when fifteen-year-olds have been sentenced to life without parole, which is to say to die there?

25   What does it mean to a middle-aged person condemned while still a teenager to die in prison to have eight weeks out of his entire life in a mindfulness group?

I want to tell you about Herman Wallace. He was convicted of armed robbery and sent to Angola in 1971. Once there he established the Angola chapter of the Black Panther Party[8] with Ronald Ailsworth, Albert Woodfox, and Gerald Bryant after receiving permission from the Panther central office in Oakland. The Angola Panthers organized to improve conditions at the prison, which made them targets of the administration.

In 1972 a white prison guard named Brent Miller was murdered inside Angola. By 1974 Wallace and Woodfox were convicted for the murder, with no physical evidence linking them to the scene of the crime. After the murder Wallace, Woodfox, and Robert King were put in solitary, where they were held for more than forty years—the longest period anyone has been held in solitary confinement in American history—until their release was secured.

8. Left-wing political organization embracing armed self-defense and Black Power that was founded in Oakland, California, in 1966 [Editor's note].

jackie sumell's *Herman Wallace's Conference Room* (2008).

Artist jackie sumell learned of Wallace's story in 2001 and shortly thereafter wrote to him, commencing a twelve-year friendship during which they exchanged over three hundred letters and many phone calls. While at Stanford as an MFA student, sumell received the assignment of asking a professor to describe their most exorbitant dream home, in order to study spatial relationships. "I struggled to balance the futility of my assignment—which reinforced the power dynamics of wealth, race, and privilege—with the stark reality of Herman's condition," she wrote in an artist statement later. So she turned to Herman, rather than a Stanford professor, and asked the seemingly simple question:

> What kind of house does a man who has lived in a six-foot-by-nine-foot box for almost thirty years dream of?

Over the ensuing weeks and months, he imagined and described to her a house meticulously designed, with a black panther on the bottom of the swimming pool, photographs of Black heroes, a bar with martini glasses. It had a library with books about Black liberation and an iconic seventies fur throw across the end of the bed.

She designed and drew the house he visioned, and then made a maquette of it, and then began to create architectural renderings, down to every detail. Through their letters and her practice of and faith in the power of what art can do, they activated the power of his imagination and creativity to vision his freedom and future, even when his release was not remotely likely.

While she was working on the house, his conviction was overturned. Herman Wallace was released from prison. He visited with sumell, and his family, and celebrated his freedom.

He died three days later.

sumell finished *Herman's House* as a moveable work of art and has toured it in art spaces around the country. She continues to keep Herman's legacy alive through the *Solitary Gardens* project, where solitary confinement cells are turned into equally sized garden beds. Incarcerated prisoners in solitary confinement design the gardens' plant life and tend to them in collaboration with those on the outside.

It started with a question to a man who lived forty-one years in solitary confinement for a crime he did not commit.

35   Before I saw Angola prison myself, and walked where the thousands and thousands of human beings whose lives have been affected by it lived, these artists showed me so. More of us can know because the art sees for us and carries traces of the lives of the human beings who are remembered by their loved ones and whom we cannot turn away from.

What do you picture when you picture your home?

MLA CITATION

Alexander, Elizabeth. "From *The Trayvon Generation*." *The Norton Reader: An Anthology of Nonfiction*, edited by Melissa A. Goldthwaite et al., 16th ed., W. W. Norton, 2024, pp. 223–30.

QUESTIONS

1. In this essay, Elizabeth Alexander insists on the importance of seeing and remembering those imprisoned at Angola. How does this insistence fuel her essay?

2. What connections does Alexander perceive between slavery and the prison system? How does she explore these connections in her essay?

3. Alexander weaves together the stories of Angola prisoners and the artists who photographed them or created artworks inspired by them. Why do you think she adopted this dual focus?

4. In her final paragraphs, Alexander considers artist jackie sumell's work *Herman's House*, a scale model of a house envisioned by Herman Wallace, who was held in solitary confinement for over forty years for allegedly participating in the murder of a guard. In her closing sentence, Alexander asks her reader, "What do you picture when you picture your home?" (paragraph 36). Write a letter to Alexander answering this question. In your letter, describe your imagined house in detail and explain why its design is meaningful to you.

SHERRY TURKLE

The End of Forgetting

> *There are some people who have tried to make friends . . . but*
> *they've fallen through so badly that they give up. So when they*
> *hear this idea about robots being made to be companions, well,*
> *it's not going to be like a human and have its own mind to walk*
> *away or ever leave you or anything like that.*
>
> —A SIXTEEN-YEAR-OLD GIRL, CONSIDERING
> THE IDEA OF A MORE SOPHISTICATED SIRI

THOREAU TALKS OF THREE CHAIRS and I think about a fourth.[1] Thoreau says that for the most expansive conversations, the deepest ones, he brought his guests out into nature—he calls it his withdrawing room, his "best room." For me, the fourth chair defines a philosophical space. Thoreau could go into nature, but now, we contemplate both nature and a second nature of our own making, the world of the artificial and virtual. There, we meet machines that present themselves as open for conversation. The fourth chair raises the question: Who do we become when we talk to machines?

Some talking machines have modest ambitions—such as putting you through the paces of a job interview. But others aspire to far more. Most of these are just now coming on the scene: "caring robots" that will tend to our children and elders if we ourselves don't have the time, patience, or resources; automated psychotherapy programs that will substitute for humans in conversation. These present us with something new.

It may not feel new. All day every day, we connect with witty apps, we type our information into dialogue programs, and we get information from personal digital assistants. We are comfortable talking at machines and through machines. Now we are asked to join a new kind of conversation, one that promises "empathic" connections.

Machines have none to offer, and yet we persist in the desire for companionship and even communion with the inanimate. Has the simulation of empathy become empathy enough? The simulation of communion, communion enough?

The fourth chair defines a space that Thoreau could not have seen. It is our nick of time.   5

What do we forget when we talk to machines—and what can we remember?

From Sherry Turkle's book Reclaiming Conversation: The Power of Talk in a Digital Age *(2015). Turkle is a renowned authority on the psychological, interpersonal, and social effects of computers and communication technologies. This version of the essay is abridged.*

1. Reference to *Walden* (1854), by American transcendentalist Henry David Thoreau (1817–1862), from which Turkle takes the epigraph of her book: "I had three chairs in my house; one for solitude, two for friendship, three for society."

"A Computer Beautiful Enough
That a Soul Would Want to Live in It"

In the early 1980s, I interviewed one of Marvin Minsky's young students who told me that, as he saw it, his hero, Minsky, one of the founders of artificial intelligence (AI), was "trying to create a computer beautiful enough that a soul would want to live in it."

That image has stayed with me for more than thirty years.

In the AI world, things have gone from mythic to prosaic. Today, children grow up with robotic pets and digital dolls. They think it natural to chat with their phones. We are at what I have called a "robotic moment," not because of the merits of the machines we've built but because of our eagerness for their company. Even before we make the robots, we remake ourselves as people ready to be their companions.

For a long time, putting hope in robots has expressed an enduring technological optimism, a belief that as things go wrong, science will go right. In a complicated world, what robots promise has always seemed like calling in the cavalry. Robots save lives in war zones; they can function in space and in the sea—indeed, anywhere that humans would be in danger. They perform medical procedures that humans cannot do; they have revolutionized design and manufacturing.

But robots get us to hope for more. Not only for the feats of the cavalry, but for simple salvations. What are the simple salvations? These are the hopes that robots will be our companions. That taking care of us will be their jobs. That we will take comfort in their company and conversation. This is a station on our voyage of forgetting.

What do we forget when we talk to machines? We forget what is special about being human. We forget what it means to have authentic conversation. Machines are programmed to have conversations "as if" they understood what the conversation is about. So when we talk to them, we, too, are reduced and confined to the "as if."

Simple Salvations

Over the decades, I have heard the hopes for robot companionship grow stronger, even though most people don't have experience with an embodied robot companion at all but rather with something like Siri, Apple's digital assistant, where the conversation is most likely to be "locate a restaurant" or "locate a friend."

But even telling Siri to "locate a friend" moves quickly to the fantasy of finding a friend in Siri. People tell me that they look forward to the time, not too far down the road, when Siri or one of her near cousins will be something like a best friend, but in some ways better: one you can always talk to, one that will never be angry, one you can never disappoint.

And, indeed, Apple's first television advertising campaign for Siri introduced "her" not as a feature, a convenient way of getting information, but as a companion. It featured a group of movie stars—Zooey Deschanel, Samuel L. Jackson, John Malkovich—who put Siri in the role of confidante. Deschanel, playing the ditzy ingénue, discusses the weather, and how she doesn't want to wear shoes or clean house on a rainy day. She just wants to dance and have tomato soup. Siri plays the role of the best friend who "gets her." Jackson has a conversation with Siri that is laced with double meanings about a hot date: A lady friend is coming over and Jackson is cooking gazpacho and risotto. It's fun to joke with his sidekick Siri about his plans for seduction. Malkovich, sitting in a deep leather chair in a room with heavy wall moldings and drapes—it might be an apartment in Paris or Barcelona—talks seriously with Siri about the meaning of life. He likes it that Siri has a sense of humor.

In all of this, we are being schooled in how to have conversations with a machine that may approximate banter but doesn't understand our meaning at all; in these conversations, we're doing all the work but we don't mind.

I was on a radio show about Siri with a panel of engineers and social scientists. The topic turned to how much people like to talk to Siri, part of the general phenomenon that people feel uninhibited when they talk to a machine. They like the feeling of no judgment. One of the social scientists on the program suggested that soon a souped-up and somewhat smoothed-out Siri could serve as a psychiatrist.

It didn't seem to bother him that Siri, in the role of psychiatrist, would be counseling people about their lives without having lived one. If Siri could *behave* like a psychiatrist, he said, it could be a psychiatrist. If no one minded the difference between the as if and the real thing, let the machine take the place of the person. This is the pragmatism of the robotic moment.

But the suggestions of a robotic friend or therapist—the simple salvations of the robotic moment—are not so simple at all.

Because for all that they are programmed to pretend, machines that talk   20
to us as though they care about us don't know the arc of a human life. When we speak to them of our human problems of love and loss, or the pleasures of tomato soup and dancing barefoot on a rainy day, they can deliver only performances of empathy and connection.

What an artificial intelligence *can* know is your schedule, the literal content of your email, your preferences in film, TV, and food. If you wear body-sensing technologies, an AI can know what emotionally activates you because it may infer this from physiological markers. But it won't understand what any of these things *mean* to you.

But the meaning of things is just what we want our machines to understand. And we are willing to fuel the fantasy that they do.

VULNERABILITY GAMES

We have been playing vulnerability games with artificial intelligence for a very long time, since before programs were anywhere near as sophisticated as they are now. In the 1960s, a computer program called ELIZA, written by MIT's Joseph Weizenbaum, adopted the "mirroring" style of a Rogerian psychotherapist. So, if you typed, "Why do I hate my mother?" ELIZA might respond, "I hear you saying that you hate your mother." This program was effective—at least for a short while—in creating the illusion of intelligent listening. And there is this: *We want to talk to machines even when we know they do not deserve our confidences. I call this the "ELIZA effect."*

Weizenbaum was shocked that people (for example, his secretary and graduate students) who knew the limits of ELIZA's ability to know and understand nevertheless wanted to be alone with the program in order to confide in it. ELIZA demonstrated that almost universally, people project human attributes onto programs that present as humanlike, an effect that is magnified when they are with robots called "sociable" machines—machines that do such things as track your motion, make eye contact, and remember your name. Then people feel in the presence of a knowing other that cares about them. A young man, twenty-six, talks with a robot named Kismet that makes eye contact, reads facial expressions, and vocalizes with the cadences of human speech. The man finds Kismet so supportive that he speaks with it about the ups and downs of his day.

25   Machines with voices have particular power to make us feel understood. Children first learn to know their mothers by recognizing their voices, even while still in the womb. During our evolution, the only speech we heard was the speech of other humans. Now, with the development of sophisticated artificial speech, we are the first humans asked to distinguish human from non-human speech. Neurologically, we are not set up to do this job. Since human beings have for so long—say, 200,000 years—heard only human voices, it takes serious mental effort to distinguish human speech from the machine-generated kind. To our brains, speaking is something that people do.

And machines with humanlike faces have particular power as well.

In humans, the shape of a smile or a frown releases chemicals that affect our mental state. Our mirror neurons fire both when we act and when we observe others acting. *We feel what we see on the face of another.* An expressive robot face can have this impact on us. The philosopher Emmanuel Lévinas writes that the presence of a face initiates the human ethical compact. The face communicates, "Thou shalt not kill me." We are bound by the face even before we know what stands behind it, even before we might learn it is the face of a machine that cannot be killed. And the robot's face certainly announces, for Lévinas, "Thou shalt not abandon me"—again, an ethical and emotional compact that captures us but has no meaning when we feel it for a machine.

An expressive machine face—on a robot or on a screen-based computer program—puts us on a landscape where we seek recognition and feel we can get it. We are in fact triggered to seek empathy from an object that has none to give.

I worked at the MIT Artificial Intelligence Laboratory as people met the sociable, emotive robot Kismet for the first time. What Kismet actually said had no meaning, but the sound came out warm or inquiring or concerned.

30   Sometimes Kismet's visitors felt the robot had recognized them and had "heard" their story. When things worked perfectly from a technical stand-

point, they experienced what felt like an empathic connection. This convincing imitation of understanding is impressive and can be a lot of fun if you think of these encounters as theater. But I saw children look to Kismet for a friend in the real. I saw children hope for the robot's recognition, and sometimes become bereft when there was nothing nourishing on offer.

Estelle, twelve, comes to Kismet wanting a conversation. She is lonely, her parents are divorced; her time with Kismet makes her feel special. Here is a robot who will listen just to her. On the day of Estelle's visit, she is engaged by Kismet's changing facial expressions, but Kismet is not at its vocal best. At the end of a disappointing session, Estelle and the small team of researchers who have been working with her go back to the room where we interview children before and after they meet the robots. Estelle begins to eat the juice, crackers, and cookies we have left out as snacks. And she does not stop, not until we ask her to please leave some food for the other children. Then she stops, but only briefly. She begins to eat again, hurriedly, as we wait for the car service that will take her back to her after-school program.

Estelle tells us why she is upset: Kismet does not like her. The robot began to talk with her and then turned away. We explain that this is not the case. The problem had been technical. Estelle is not convinced. From her point of view, she has failed on her most important day. As Estelle leaves, she takes four boxes of cookies from the supply closet and stuffs them into her backpack. We do not stop her. Exhausted, my team reconvenes at a nearby coffee shop to ask ourselves a hard question: Can a broken robot break a child?

We would not be concerned with the ethics of having a child play with a buggy copy of Microsoft Word or a torn Raggedy Ann doll. A word-processing program is there to do an instrumental thing. If it does worse than usual on a particular day, well, that leads to frustration but no more. But a program that encourages you to connect with it—this is a different matter.

How is a broken Kismet different from a broken doll? A doll encourages children to project their own stories and their own agendas onto a passive object. But children see sociable robots as "alive enough" to have their own agendas. Children attach to them not with the psychology of projection but with the psychology of relational engagement, more in the way they attach to people.

If a little girl is feeling guilty for breaking her mother's crystal, she may punish a row of Barbie dolls, putting the dolls into detention as a way of working through her own feelings. The dolls are material for what the child needs to accomplish emotionally. That is how the psychology of projection works: It enables the working through of the child's feelings. But the sociable robot presents itself as having a mind of its own. As the child sees it, if this robot turns away, it wanted to. That's why children consider winning the heart of a sociable robot to be a personal achievement. You've gotten something lovable to love you. Again, children interact with sociable robots, not with the psychology of projection but with engagement. They react as though they face another person. There is room for new hurt.

Estelle responded to this emotionally charged situation with depression and a search for comfort food. Other children who faced a disappointing con-

versation with Kismet responded with aggression. When Kismet began an animated conversation that Edward, six, could not understand, he shoved objects
into Kismet's mouth—a metal pin, a pencil, a toy caterpillar—things Edward
found in the robotics laboratory. But at no point did Edward disengage from
Kismet. He would not give up his chance for Kismet's recognition.

The important question here is not about the risks of broken robots.
Rather, we should ask, "Emotionally, what positive thing would we have given
to these children if the robots had been in top form?" Why do we propose
machine companionship to children in the first place? For a lonely child, a
conversational robot is a guarantee against rejection, a place to entrust confidences. But what children really need is not the guarantee that an inanimate
object will simulate acceptance. They need relationships that will teach them
real mutuality, caring, and empathy.

So, the problem doesn't start when the machine breaks down. Children
are not well served even when the robots are working perfectly. In the case of
a robot babysitter, you already have a problem when you have to explain to a
child why there isn't a person available for the job.

TREATING MACHINES AS PEOPLE; TREATING PEOPLE AS MACHINES

In all of this, an irony emerges: Even as we treat machines as if they were
almost human, we develop habits that have us treating human beings as
almost-machines. To take a simple example, we regularly put people "on pause"
in the middle of a conversation in order to check our phones. And when we
talk to people who are not paying attention to us, it is a kind of preparation for
talking to uncomprehending machines. When people give us less, talking to
machines doesn't seem as much of a downgrade.

40   At a panel on "cyberetiquette," I was onstage with a technology reporter
and two "advice and manners" columnists. There was general agreement among
the panelists on most matters: No texting at family dinners. No texting at restaurants. Don't bring your laptop to your children's sporting events, no matter
how tempting.

And then came this question from the audience: A woman said that as a
working mother she had very little time to talk to her friends, to email, to text, to
keep up. "Actually," she confessed, "the only time I have is at night, after I'm off
work and before I go home, when I go family shopping at Trader Joe's. But the
cashier, the guy at the checkout counter, he wants to talk. I just want to be on
my phone, into my texts and *Facebook*. Do I have the right to just ignore him?"
The two manners experts went first. Each said a version of the same thing: The
man who does the checkout has a job to do. The woman who asked the question
has a right to privacy and to her texting as he provides his service.

I listened uncomfortably. I thought of all the years I went shopping with my
grandmother as I grew up and all the relationships she had with tradespeople at
every store: the baker, the fishmonger, the fruit man, the grocery man (for this is
what we called them). These days, we all know that the job the man at the check-

out counter does could be done by a machine. In fact, down the street at another supermarket, it is done by a machine that automatically scans your groceries. And so I shared this thought: Until a machine replaces the man, surely he summons in us the recognition and respect you show a person. Sharing a few words at the checkout may make this man feel that in his job, this job that *could* be done by a machine, he is still seen as a human being.

This was not what the audience and my fellow panelists wanted to hear. As I took stock of their cool reaction to what I said, I saw a new symmetry: We want more from technology and less from each other. What once would have seemed like "friendly service" at a community market had become an inconvenience that keeps us from our phones.

It used to be that we imagined our mobile phones were there so that we could talk to each other. Now we want our mobile phones to talk to us. That's what the new commercials for Siri are really about: fantasies of these new conversations and a kind of tutelage in what they might sound like. We are at a moment of temptation, ready to turn to machines for companionship even as we seem pained or inconvenienced to engage with each other in settings as simple as a grocery store. We want technology to step up as we ask people to step back.

People are lonely and fear intimacy, and robots seem ready to hand. *And we are ready for their company if we forget what intimacy is.* And having nothing to forget, our children learn new rules for when it is appropriate to talk to a machine. 45

Stephanie is forty, a real estate agent in Rhode Island. Her ten-year-old daughter, Tara, is a perfectionist, always the "good girl," sensitive to any suggestion of criticism. Recently, she has begun to talk to Siri. It is not surprising that children like to talk to Siri. There is just enough inventiveness in Siri's responses to make children feel that someone might be listening. And if children are afraid of judgment, Siri is safe. So Tara expresses anger to Siri that she doesn't show to her parents or friends—with them she plays the part of a "perfect child." Stephanie overhears her daughter yelling at Siri and says, "She vents to Siri. She starts to talk but then becomes enraged."

Stephanie wonders if this is "perhaps a good thing, certainly a more honest conversation" than Tara is having with others in her life. It's a thought worth looking at more closely. It is surely positive for Tara to discover feelings that she censors for other audiences. But talking to Siri leaves Tara vulnerable. She may get the idea that her feelings are something that people cannot handle. She may persist in her current idea that pretend perfection is all other people want from her or can accept from her. Instead of learning that people can value how she really feels, Tara is learning that it is easier not to deal with people at all.

If Tara can "be herself" only with a robot, she may grow up believing that only an object can tolerate her truth. What Tara is doing is not "training" for relating to people. For that, Tara needs to learn that you can attach to people with trust, make some mistakes, and risk open conversations. Her talks with the inanimate are taking her in another direction: to a world without risk and without caring.

• • •

FROM BETTER THAN NOTHING TO BETTER THAN ANYTHING

The bonds of attachment and the expression of emotion are one for the child. When children talk with people, they come to recognize, over time, how vocal inflection, facial expression, and bodily movement flow together. Seamlessly. Fluidly. And they learn how human emotions play in layers, again seamlessly and fluidly.

50   Children need to learn what complex human feelings and human ambivalence look like. And they need other people to respond to their own expressions of that complexity. These are the most precious things that people give to children in conversation as they grow up. No robot has these things to teach.

These are the things that we forget when we think about children spending any significant amount of time talking with machines, looking into robotic faces, trusting in their care. Why would we play with fire when it comes to such delicate matters?

But we do. It's part of a general progression that I've called "from better than nothing to better than anything." We begin with resignation, with the idea that machine companionship is better than nothing, as in "there are no people for these jobs." From there, we exalt the possibilities of what simulation can offer until, in time, we start to talk as though what we will get from the artificial may actually be better than what life could ever provide. Child-care workers might be abusive. Nurses or well-meaning mothers might make mistakes. Children say that a robotic dog like the AIBO pet will never get sick, and can be turned off when you want to put your attention elsewhere. And, crucially, it will never die. Grown-ups have similar feelings. A robot dog, says an older woman, "won't die suddenly, abandon you, and make you very sad."

In our new culture of connection, we are lonely but afraid of intimacy. Fantasies of "conversation" with artificial beings solve a dilemma. They propose the illusion of companionship without the demands of friendship. They allow us to imagine a friction-free version of friendship. One whose demands are in our control, perhaps literally.

I've said that part of what makes our new technologies of connection so seductive is that they respond to our fantasies, our wishes, that we will always be heard, that we can put our attention wherever we want it to be, and that we will never have to be alone. And, of course, they respond to an implied fourth fantasy: that we will never have to be bored.

55   When people voice these fantasies, they are also describing, often without realizing it, a relationship with a robot. The robot would always be at attention, and it would be tolerant of wherever your attention might take you. It certainly wouldn't mind if you interrupted your conversation to answer a text or take a call. And it would never abandon you, although there is the question of whether it was ever really there in the first place. As for boredom, well, it would do its best to make boredom, for you, a thing of the past.

If, like Tara, we choose to share our frustrations with robot friends because we don't want to upset our human friends with who we really are and what we're really feeling, the meaning of human friendship will change. It may become the place you go for small talk. You'd be afraid that people would be tired out by big talk. This means that there won't be any more big talk because robots won't understand it.

Yet so many people talk to me about their hope that someday, not too far down the road, an advanced version of Siri will be like a best friend. One who will listen when others won't. I believe this wish reflects a painful truth I've learned in my years of research: The feeling that "no one is listening to me" plays a large part in our relationships with technology. That's why it is so appealing to have a *Facebook* page or a *Twitter* feed—so many automatic listeners. And that feeling that "no one is listening to me" makes us want to spend time with machines that seem to care about us. We are willing to take their performances of caring and conversation at "interface value."

When roboticists show videos of people happy to engage with sociable robots, the tendency is to show them off as moments of exalted play. It is as though a small triumph is presented: We did it! We got a person to talk happily with a machine! *But this is an experiment in which people are the "reengineered" experimental subjects.* We are learning how to take as-if conversations with a machine seriously. Our "performative" conversations begin to change what we think of as conversation.

We practice something new. But we are the ones who are changing. Do we like what we are changing into? Do we want to get better at it?

TURNING OURSELVES INTO SPECTATORS

In the course of my research, there was one robotic moment that I have never forgotten because it changed my mind.

I had been bringing robots designed as companions for the elderly into nursing homes and to elderly people living on their own. I wanted to explore the possibilities. One day I saw an older woman who had lost a child talking to a robot in the shape of a baby seal. It seemed to be looking in her eyes. It seemed to be following the conversation. It comforted her. Many people on my research team and who worked at the nursing home thought this was amazing.

This woman was trying to make sense of her loss with a machine that put on a good show. And we're vulnerable: People experience even pretend empathy as the real thing. But robots can't empathize. They don't face death or know life. So when this woman took comfort in her robot companion, I didn't find it amazing. I felt we had abandoned this woman. Being part of this scene was one of the most wrenching moments in my then fifteen years of research on sociable robotics.

For me, it was a turning point: I felt the enthusiasm of my team and of the staff and the attendants. There were so many people there to help, but we all stood back, a room of spectators now, only there to hope that an elder would

60

bond with a machine. It seemed that we all had a stake in outsourcing the thing we do best—understanding each other, taking care of each other.

That day in the nursing home, I was troubled by how we allowed ourselves to be sidelined, turned into spectators by a robot that understood nothing. That day didn't reflect poorly on the robot. It reflected poorly on us and how we think about older people when they try to tell the stories of their lives. Over the past decades, when the idea of older people and robots has come up, the emphasis has been on whether the older person will talk to the robot. Will the robot facilitate their talking? Will the robot be persuasive enough to do that?

65   But when you think about the moment of life we are considering, it is not just that older people are supposed to be talking. *Younger people are supposed to be listening.* This is the compact between generations. I was once told that some older cultures have a saying: When a young person misbehaves, it means that "they had no one to tell them the old stories." When we celebrate robot listeners that cannot listen, we show too little interest in what our elders have to say. We build machines that guarantee that human stories will fall upon deaf ears.

There are so many wonderful things that robots can do to help the elderly—all those things that put the robot in the role of the cavalry. Robots can help older people (or the ill or homebound) feel greater independence by reaching for cans of soup or articles of clothing on high shelves; robots can help shaky hands cook. Robots can help to lower an unsteady body onto a bed. Robots can help locate a mislaid pair of glasses. All of these things seem so much for the good. Some argue that a robot chatting with an older person is also unequivocally for the good. But here, I think we need to carefully consider the human specificity of conversation and emotional care.

Sociable robots act as evocative objects—objects that cause us to reflect on ourselves and our deepest values. We are in the domain of that fourth chair where we consider nature—our natures and the second natures we have built. Here, talking with machines forces the question: What is the value of an interaction that contains no shared experience of life and contributes nothing to a shared store of human meaning—and indeed may devalue it? This is not a question with a ready answer. But this is a question worth asking and returning to.

It is not easy to have this kind of conversation once we start to take the idea of robotic companionship seriously. Once we assume it as the new normal, this conversation begins to disappear.

Right now we work on the premise that putting in a robot to do a job is always better than nothing. The premise is flawed. If you have a problem with care and companionship and you try to solve it with a robot, you may not try to solve it with your friends, your family, and your community.

70   The as-if self of a robot calling forth the as-if self of a person performing for it—this is not helpful for children as they grow up. It is not helpful for adults as they try to live authentically.

And to say that it is just the thing for older people who are at that point where they are often trying to make sense of their lives is demeaning. They, of all people, should be given occasions to talk about their real lives, filled with real losses and real loves, to someone who knows what those things are.

MLA CITATION

Turkle, Sherry. "The End of Forgetting." *The Norton Reader: An Anthology of Nonfiction*, edited by Melissa A. Goldthwaite et al., 16th ed., W. W. Norton, 2024, pp. 231–40.

QUESTIONS

1. This essay, from Sherry Turkle's book *Reclaiming Conversation*, considers the ways in which the advent of "talking machines" is changing the nature and meaning of "conversation." What do we traditionally understand conversation to be? How, according to Turkle, is that understanding changing? What is her attitude toward these changes? What is yours?

2. In her first sentence, Turkle alludes to the epigraph to her book about her three chairs, which she takes from the nineteenth-century American writer Henry David Thoreau. How, according to Turkle, have new technologies changed our conceptions of self ("solitude"), of relationships ("friendship"), and of society?

3. Turkle breaks her essay into short sections, each organized around a story of individual people's interactions with a computer program, talking machine, or robot. Why do you think Turkle uses this structure? How does it contribute to the essay's argument and effect?

4. For one day, document all the times you talk to a machine: programs, apps, devices, terminals, computers, robots, chatbots, and so on. Note the time, duration, and nature of each interaction. Drawing on these notes, write an essay about your own "conversations" with machines.

JIA TOLENTINO
The I in the Internet

IN THE BEGINNING the internet seemed good. "I was in love with the internet the first time I used it at my dad's office and thought it was the ULTIMATE COOL," I wrote, when I was ten, on an *Angelfire* subpage titled "The Story of How Jia Got Her Web Addiction." In a text box superimposed on a hideous violet background, I continued:

> But that was in third grade and all I was doing was going to Beanie Baby sites. Having an old, icky bicky computer at home, we didn't have the Internet. Even *AOL* seemed like a far-off dream. Then we got a new top-o'-the-line computer in spring break '99, and of course it came with all that demo stuff. So I finally had *AOL* and I was completely amazed at the marvel of having a profile and chatting and IMS!!

Originally published in Jia Tolentino's book Trick Mirror: Reflections on Self-Delusion *(2019). This version of the essay is abridged.*

Then, I wrote, I discovered personal webpages. ("I was astonished!") I learned HTML and "little Javascript trickies." I built my own site on the beginner-hosting site *Expage*, choosing pastel colors and then switching to a "starry night theme." Then I ran out of space, so I "decided to move to *Angelfire*. Wow." I learned how to make my own graphics. "This was all in the course of four months," I wrote, marveling at how quickly my ten-year-old internet citizenry was evolving. I had recently revisited the sites that had once inspired me, and realized "how much of an idiot I was to be wowed by *that*."

• • •

In 1999, it felt different to spend all day on the internet. This was true for everyone, not just for ten-year-olds: this was the *You've Got Mail*[1] era, when it seemed that the very worst thing that could happen online was that you might fall in love with your business rival. Throughout the eighties and nineties, people had been gathering on the internet in open forums, drawn, like butterflies, to the puddles and blossoms of other people's curiosity and expertise. Self-regulated newsgroups like *Usenet* cultivated lively and relatively civil discussion about space exploration, meteorology, recipes, rare albums. Users gave advice, answered questions, made friendships, and wondered what this new internet would become.

Because there were so few search engines and no centralized social platforms, discovery on the early internet took place mainly in private, and pleasure existed as its own solitary reward. A 1995 book called *You Can Surf the Net!* listed sites where you could read movie reviews or learn about martial arts. It urged readers to follow basic etiquette (don't use all caps; don't waste other people's expensive bandwidth with overly long posts) and encouraged them to feel comfortable in this new world ("Don't worry," the author advised. "You have to *really* mess up to get flamed."). Around this time, *GeoCities* began offering personal website hosting for dads who wanted to put up their own golfing sites or kids who built glittery, blinking shrines to Tolkien or Ricky Martin or unicorns, most capped off with a primitive guest book and a green-and-black visitor counter. *GeoCities*, like the internet itself, was clumsy, ugly, only half functional, and organized into neighborhoods: /area51/ was for sci-fi, /westhollywood/ for LGBTQ life, /enchantedforest/ for children, /petsburgh/ for pets. If you left *GeoCities*, you could walk around other streets in this ever-expanding village of curiosities. You could stroll through *Expage* or *Angelfire*, as I did, and pause on the thoroughfare where the tiny cartoon hamsters danced. There was an emergent aesthetic—blinking text, crude animation. If you found something you liked, if you wanted to spend more time in any of these neighborhoods, you could build your own house from HTML frames and start decorating.

5   This period of the internet has been labeled Web 1.0—a name that works backward from the term Web 2.0, which was coined by the writer and user-experience designer Darcy DiNucci in an article called "Fragmented Future," published in 1999. "The Web we know now," she wrote, "which loads into a

1. Romantic-comedy film from 1998 starring Meg Ryan and Tom Hanks.

browser window in essentially static screenfuls, is only an embryo of the Web to come. The first glimmerings of Web 2.0 are beginning to appear. . . . The Web will be understood not as screenfuls of texts and graphics but as a transport mechanism, the ether through which interactivity happens." On Web 2.0, the structures would be dynamic, she predicted: instead of houses, websites would be portals, through which an ever-changing stream of activity—status updates, photos—could be displayed. What you did on the internet would become intertwined with what everyone else did, and the things other people liked would become the things that you would see. Web 2.0 platforms like *Blogger* and *Myspace* made it possible for people who had merely been taking in the sights to start generating their own personalized and constantly changing scenery. As more people began to register their existence digitally, a pastime turned into an imperative: you had to register yourself digitally to exist.

• • •

As with the transition between Web 1.0 and Web 2.0, the curdling of the social internet happened slowly and then all at once. The tipping point, I'd guess, was around 2012. People were losing excitement about the internet, starting to articulate a set of new truisms. *Facebook* had become tedious, trivial, exhausting. *Instagram* seemed better, but would soon reveal its underlying function as a three-ring circus of happiness and popularity and success. *Twitter*, for all its discursive promise, was where everyone tweeted complaints at airlines and bitched about articles that had been commissioned to make people bitch. The dream of a better, truer self on the internet was slipping away. Where we had once been free to be ourselves online, we were now *chained* to ourselves online, and this made us self-conscious. Platforms that promised connection began inducing mass alienation. The freedom promised by the internet started to seem like something whose greatest potential lay in the realm of misuse.

Even as we became increasingly sad and ugly on the internet, the mirage of the better online self continued to glimmer. As a medium, the internet is defined by a built-in performance incentive. In real life, you can walk around living life and be visible to other people. But you can't just walk around and be visible on the internet—for anyone to see you, you have to *act*. You have to communicate in order to maintain an internet presence. And, because the internet's central platforms are built around personal profiles, it can seem—first at a mechanical level, and later on as an encoded instinct—like the main purpose of this communication is to make yourself look good. Online reward mechanisms beg to substitute for offline ones, and then overtake them. This is why everyone tries to look so hot and well-traveled on *Instagram*; this is why everyone seems so smug and triumphant on *Facebook*; this is why, on *Twitter*, making a righteous political statement has come to seem, for many people, like a political good in itself.

This practice is often called "virtue signaling," a term most often used by conservatives criticizing the left. But virtue signaling is a bipartisan, even apolitical action. *Twitter* is overrun with dramatic pledges of allegiance to the Second Amendment that function as intra-right virtue signaling, and it can be something like virtue signaling when people post the suicide hotline after a celebrity death.

Few of us are totally immune to the practice, as it intersects with a real desire for political integrity. Posting photos from a protest against border family separation, as I did while writing this, is a microscopically meaningful action, an expression of genuine principle, and also, inescapably, some sort of attempt to signal that I am good.

Taken to its extreme, virtue signaling has driven people on the left to some truly unhinged behavior. A legendary case occurred in June 2016, after a two-year-old was killed at a Disney resort—dragged off by an alligator while playing in a no-swimming-allowed lagoon. A woman, who had accumulated ten thousand *Twitter* followers with her posts about social justice, saw an opportunity and tweeted, magnificently, "I'm so finished with white men's entitlement lately that I'm really not sad about a 2yo being eaten by a gator because his daddy ignored signs." (She was then pilloried by people who chose to demonstrate their own moral superiority through mockery—as I am doing here, too.) A similar tweet made the rounds in early 2018 after a sweet story went viral: a large white seabird named Nigel had died next to the concrete decoy bird to whom he had devoted himself for years. An outraged writer tweeted, "Even concrete birds do not owe you affection, Nigel," and wrote a long *Facebook* post arguing that Nigel's courtship of the fake bird exemplified . . . *rape culture.* "I'm available to write the feminist perspective on Nigel the gannet's non-tragic death should anyone wish to pay me," she added, underneath the original tweet, which received more than a thousand likes. These deranged takes, and their unnerving proximity to online monetization, are case studies in the way that our world—digitally mediated, utterly consumed by capitalism—makes communication about morality very easy but makes actual moral living very hard. You don't end up using a news story about a dead toddler as a peg for white entitlement without a society in which the discourse of righteousness occupies far more public attention than the conditions that necessitate righteousness in the first place.

10   On the right, the online performance of political identity has been even wilder. In 2017, the social-media-savvy youth conservative group Turning Point USA staged a protest at Kent State University featuring a student who put on a diaper to demonstrate that "safe spaces were for babies." (It went viral, as intended, but not in the way TPUSA wanted—the protest was uniformly roasted, with one *Twitter* user slapping the logo of the porn site *Brazzers* on a photo of the diaper boy, and the Kent State TPUSA campus coordinator resigned.) It has also been infinitely more consequential, beginning in 2014, with a campaign that became a template for right-wing internet-political action, when a large group of young misogynists came together in the event now known as Gamergate.

The issue at hand was, ostensibly, a female game designer perceived to be sleeping with a journalist for favorable coverage. She, along with a set of feminist game critics and writers, received an onslaught of rape threats, death threats, and other forms of harassment, all concealed under the banner of free speech and "ethics in games journalism." The Gamergaters—estimated by

Deadspin[2] to number around ten thousand people—would mostly deny this harassment, either parroting in bad faith or fooling themselves into believing the argument that Gamergate was actually about noble ideals. Gawker Media, *Deadspin*'s parent company, itself became a target, in part because of its own aggressive disdain toward the Gamergaters: the company lost seven figures in revenue after its advertisers were brought into the maelstrom.

In 2016, a similar fiasco made national news in Pizzagate, after a few rabid internet denizens decided they'd found coded messages about child sex slavery in the advertising of a pizza shop associated with Hillary Clinton's[3] campaign. This theory was disseminated all over the far-right internet, leading to an extended attack on DC's Comet Ping Pong pizzeria and everyone associated with the restaurant—all in the name of combating pedophilia—that culminated in a man walking into Comet Ping Pong and firing a gun. (Later on, the same faction would jump to the defense of Roy Moore, the Republican nominee for the Senate who was accused of sexually assaulting teenagers.) The over-woke left could only dream of this ability to weaponize a sense of righteousness. Even the militant antifascist movement, known as antifa, is routinely disowned by liberal centrists, despite the fact that the antifa movement is rooted in a long European tradition of Nazi resistance rather than a nascent constellation of radically paranoid message boards and *YouTube* channels. The worldview of the Gamergaters and Pizzagaters was actualized and to a large extent vindicated in the 2016 election—an event that strongly suggested that the worst things about the internet were now *determining*, rather than reflecting, the worst things about offline life.

Mass media always determines the shape of politics and culture. The Bush era is inextricable from the failures of cable news; the executive overreaches of the Obama years were obscured by the internet's magnification of personality and performance; Trump's rise to power is inseparable from the existence of social networks that must continually aggravate their users in order to continue making money. But lately I've been wondering how everything got so *intimately* terrible, and why, exactly, we keep playing along. How did a huge number of people begin spending the bulk of our disappearing free time in an openly torturous environment? How did the internet get so bad, so confining, so inescapably personal, so politically determinative—and why are all those questions asking the same thing?

I'll admit that I'm not sure that this inquiry is even productive. The internet reminds us on a daily basis that it is not at all rewarding to become aware of problems that you have no reasonable hope of solving. And, more important, the internet already is what it is. It has already become the central organ of contemporary life. It has already rewired the brains of its users, returning us to a state of primitive hyperawareness and distraction while overloading us with much more sensory input than was ever possible in primitive times. It

2. Sports blog founded in 2005 and now owned by G/O Media.
3. First female candidate (b. 1947) from a major political party to run for president of the United States.

has already built an ecosystem that runs on exploiting attention and monetizing the self. Even if you avoid the internet completely—my partner does: he thought #tbt[4] meant "truth be told" for ages—you still live in the world that this internet has created, a world in which selfhood has become capitalism's last natural resource, a world whose terms are set by centralized platforms that have deliberately established themselves as near-impossible to regulate or control.

15   The internet is also in large part inextricable from life's pleasures: our friends, our families, our communities, our pursuits of happiness, and— sometimes, if we're lucky—our work. In part out of a desire to preserve what's worthwhile from the decay that surrounds it, I've been thinking about five intersecting problems: first, how the internet is built to distend our sense of identity; second, how it encourages us to overvalue our opinions; third, how it maximizes our sense of opposition; fourth, how it cheapens our understanding of solidarity; and, finally, how it destroys our sense of scale.

In 1959, the sociologist Erving Goffman laid out a theory of identity that revolved around playacting. In every human interaction, he wrote in *The Presentation of Self in Everyday Life*, a person must put on a sort of performance, create an impression for an audience. The performance might be calculated, as with the man at a job interview who's practiced every answer; it might be unconscious, as with the man who's gone on so many interviews that he naturally performs as expected; it might be automatic, as with the man who creates the correct impression primarily because he is an upper-middle-class white man with an MBA. A performer might be fully taken in by his own performance—he might actually believe that his biggest flaw is "perfectionism"—or he might know that his act is a sham. But no matter what, he's performing. Even if he stops *trying* to perform, he still has an audience, his actions still create an effect. "All the world is not, of course, a stage,[5] but the crucial ways in which it isn't are not easy to specify," Goffman wrote.

          To communicate an identity requires some degree of self-delusion. A performer, in order to be convincing, must conceal "the discreditable facts that he has had to learn about the performance; in everyday terms, there will be things he knows, or has known, that he will not be able to tell himself." The interviewee, for example, avoids thinking about the fact that his biggest flaw actually involves drinking at the office. A friend sitting across from you at dinner, called to play therapist for your trivial romantic hang-ups, has to pretend to herself that she wouldn't rather just go home and get in bed to read Barbara Pym.[6] No audience has to be physically present for a performer to engage in this sort of selective concealment: a woman, home alone for the weekend, might scrub the baseboards and watch nature documentaries even though she'd rather trash the place, buy

4. Hashtag meaning "throwback Thursday."
5. Allusion to lines from William Shakespeare's *As You Like It*: "All the world's a stage, / And all the men and women merely players" (2.7.139–40).
6. English comic novelist (1913–1980).

an eight ball, and have a *Craigslist* orgy. People often make faces, in private, in front of bathroom mirrors, to convince themselves of their own attractiveness. The "lively belief that an unseen audience is present," Goffman writes, can have a significant effect.

Offline, there are forms of relief built into this process. Audiences change over—the performance you stage at a job interview is different from the one you stage at a restaurant later for a friend's birthday, which is different from the one you stage for a partner at home. At home, you might feel as if you could stop performing altogether; within Goffman's dramaturgical framework, you might feel as if you had made it backstage. Goffman observed that we need both an audience to witness our performances as well as a backstage area where we can relax, often in the company of "teammates" who had been performing alongside us. Think of coworkers at the bar after they've delivered a big sales pitch, or a bride and groom in their hotel room after the wedding reception: everyone may still be performing, but they *feel* at ease, unguarded, alone. Ideally, the outside audience has believed the prior performance. The wedding guests think they've actually just seen a pair of flawless, blissful newlyweds, and the potential backers think they've met a group of geniuses who are going to make everyone very rich. "But this imputation—this self—is a product of a scene that comes off, and is not a cause of it," Goffman writes. The self is not a fixed, organic thing, but a dramatic effect that emerges from a performance. This effect can be believed or disbelieved at will.

Online—assuming you buy this framework—the system metastasizes into a wreck. The presentation of self in everyday internet still corresponds to Goffman's playacting metaphor: there are stages, there is an audience. But the internet adds a host of other, nightmarish metaphorical structures: the mirror, the echo, the panopticon.[7] As we move about the internet, our personal data is tracked, recorded, and resold by a series of corporations—a regime of involuntary technological surveillance, which subconsciously decreases our resistance to the practice of *voluntary* self-surveillance on social media. If we think about buying something, it follows us around everywhere. We can, and probably do, limit our online activity to websites that further reinforce our own sense of identity, each of us reading things written for people just like us. On social media platforms, everything we see corresponds to our conscious choices and algorithmically guided preferences, and all news and culture and interpersonal interaction are filtered through the home base of the profile. The everyday madness perpetuated by the internet is the madness of this architecture, which positions personal identity as the center of the universe. It's as if we've been placed on a lookout that oversees the entire world and given a pair of binoculars that makes everything look like our own reflection. Through social media, many people have quickly come to view all new information as a sort of direct commentary on *who they are.*

7. A circular prison imagined by utilitarian philosopher Jeremy Bentham (1748–1832) with a guard tower at the center and cells around the periphery, allowing a guard to potentially observe every prisoner while prisoners cannot tell if they are being observed at any given time.

• • •

20   The first time I was ever paid to publish anything, it was 2013, the end of the blog era. Trying to make a living as a writer with the internet as a standing precondition of my livelihood has given me some professional motivation to stay active on social media, making my work and personality and face and political leanings and dog photos into a continually updated record that anyone can see. In doing this, I have sometimes felt the same sort of unease that washed over me when I was a cheerleader and learned how to convincingly fake happiness at football games—the feeling of acting as if conditions are fun and normal and worthwhile in the hopes that they will just magically become so. To try to write online, more specifically, is to operate on a set of assumptions that are already dubious when limited to writers and even more questionable when turned into a categorical imperative for everyone on the internet: the assumption that speech has an impact, that it's something like action; the assumption that it's fine or helpful or even *ideal* to be constantly writing down what you think.

    I have benefited, I mean, from the internet's unhealthy focus on opinion. This focus is rooted in the way the internet generally minimizes the need for physical action: you don't have to do much of anything but sit behind a screen to live an acceptable, possibly valorized, twenty-first-century life. The internet can feel like an astonishingly direct line to reality—click if you want something and it'll show up at your door two hours later; a series of tweets goes viral after a tragedy and soon there's a nationwide high school walkout—but it can also feel like a shunt diverting our energy *away* from action, leaving the real-world sphere to the people who already control it, keeping us busy figuring out the precisely correct way of explaining our lives. In the run-up to the 2016 election and increasingly so afterward, I started to feel that there was almost nothing I could do about ninety-five percent of the things I cared about other than form an opinion—and that the conditions that allowed me to live in mild everyday hysterics about an unlimited supply of terrible information were related to the conditions that were, at the same time, consolidating power, sucking wealth upward, far outside my grasp.

    I don't mean to be naïvely fatalistic, to act like *nothing* can be done about *anything*. People are making the world better through concrete footwork every day. (Not me—I'm too busy sitting in front of the internet!) But their time and labor, too, has been devalued and stolen by the voracious form of capitalism that drives the internet, and which the internet drives in turn. There is less time these days for anything other than economic survival. The internet has moved seamlessly into the interstices of this situation, redistributing our minimum of free time into unsatisfying micro-installments, spread throughout the day. In the absence of time to physically and politically engage with our community the way many of us want to, the internet provides a cheap substitute: it gives us brief moments of pleasure and connection, tied up in the opportunity to constantly listen and speak. Under these circumstances, opinion stops being a first step toward something and starts seeming like an end in itself.

I started thinking about this when I was working as an editor at *Jezebel*,[8] in 2014. I spent a lot of the day reading headlines on women's websites, most of which had by then adopted a feminist slant. In this realm, speech was constantly framed as a sort of intensely satisfying action: you'd get headlines like "Miley Cyrus Spoke Out about Gender Fluidity on Snapchat and It Was Everything" or "Amy Schumer's Speech about Body Confidence at the Women's Magazine Awards Ceremony Will Have You in Tears." Forming an opinion was also framed as a sort of action: blog posts offered people guidance on how to feel about online controversies or particular scenes on TV. Even identity itself seemed to take on these valences. Merely to exist as a feminist was to be doing some important work. These ideas have intensified and gotten more complicated in the Trump era, in which, on the one hand, people like me are busy expressing anguish online and mostly affecting nothing, and on the other, more actual and rapid change has come from the internet than ever before. In the turbulence that followed the Harvey Weinstein[9] revelations, women's speech swayed public opinion and led directly to change. People with power were forced to reckon with their ethics; harassers and abusers were pushed out of their jobs. But even in this narrative, the importance of action was subtly elided. People wrote about women "speaking out" with prayerful reverence, as if speech itself could bring women freedom—as if better policies and economic redistribution and true investment from men weren't necessary, too.

Goffman observes the difference between doing something and *expressing* the doing of something, between feeling something and conveying a feeling. "The representation of an activity will vary in some degree from the activity itself and therefore inevitably misrepresent it," Goffman writes. (Take the experience of enjoying a sunset versus the experience of communicating to an audience that you're enjoying a sunset, for example.) The internet is engineered for this sort of misrepresentation; it's designed to encourage us to create certain impressions rather than allowing these impressions to arise "as an incidental by-product of [our] activity." This is why, with the internet, it's so easy to stop trying to be decent, or reasonable, or politically engaged—and start trying merely to *seem* so.

• • •

In April 2017, the *Times* brought a millennial writer named Bari Weiss onto its opinion section as both a writer and an editor. Weiss had graduated from Columbia, and had worked as an editor at *Tablet* and then at the *Wall Street Journal*. She leaned conservative, with a Zionist[10] streak. At Columbia, she

25

8. Web journal founded in 2007 focusing on politics, fashion, and entertainment from a feminist perspective.

9. American film producer (b. 1952). The revelation of his many sexual assaults on women precipitated the #MeToo movement in 2017.

10. *Tablet*, online journal founded in 2009 focusing on Jewish issues; *Wall Street Journal*, major American newspaper known for its conservative editorial orientation; Zionist, a proponent of Zionism, which is historically a nationalist movement calling for a

had cofounded a group called Columbians for Academic Freedom, hoping to pressure the university into punishing a pro-Palestinian professor who had made her feel "intimidated," she told NPR in 2005.

At the *Times*, Weiss immediately began launching columns from a rhetorical and political standpoint of high-strung defensiveness, disguised with a veneer of levelheaded nonchalance. "Victimhood, in the intersectional way of seeing the world, is akin to sainthood; power and privilege are profane," she wrote—a bit of elegant phrasing in a piece that warned the public of the rampant anti-Semitism evinced, apparently, by a minor activist clusterfuck, in which the organizers of the Chicago Dyke March banned Star of David flags. She wrote a column slamming the organizers of the Women's March[11] over a few social media posts expressing support for Assata Shakur and Louis Farrakhan.[12] This, she argued, was troubling evidence that progressives, just like conservatives, were unable to police their internal hate. (Both-sides arguments like this are always appealing to people who wish to seem both contrarian and intellectually superior; this particular one required ignoring the fact that liberals remained obsessed with "civility" while the Republican president was actively endorsing violence at every turn. Later on, when *Tablet* published an investigation into the Women's March organizers who maintained disconcerting ties to the Nation of Islam, these organizers were criticized by liberals, who truly do not lack the self-policing instinct; in large part because the left does take hate seriously, the Women's March effectively splintered into two groups.) Often, Weiss's columns featured aggrieved predictions of how her bold, independent thinking would make her opponents go crazy and attack her. "I will inevitably get called a racist," she proclaimed in one column, titled "Three Cheers for Cultural Appropriation." "I'll be accused of siding with the alt-right or tarred as Islamophobic," she wrote in another column. Well, sure.

Though Weiss often argued that people should get more comfortable with those who offended or disagreed with them, she seemed mostly unable to take her own advice. During the Winter Olympics in 2018, she watched the figure skater Mirai Nagasu land a triple axel—the first American woman to do so in Olympic competition—and tweeted, in a very funny attempt at a compliment, "Immigrants: they get the job done." Because Nagasu was actually born in California, Weiss was immediately shouted down. This is what happens online when you do something offensive: when I worked at *Jezebel*, people shouted me down on *Twitter* about five times a year over things I had written or edited, and sometimes outlets published pieces about our mistakes. This was often

---

Jewish state in Israel/Palestine and today is associated with support for Israel as a Jewish state and homeland.

11. Protest march in Washington, DC, and other cities on January 17, 2017, the day after Donald J. Trump's inauguration as forty-fifth president of the United States.

12. Shakur (b. 1947), American Black Liberation Army member convicted of murdering a New Jersey state trooper; Farrakhan (b. 1933), anti-Semitic Black nationalist and head of the Nation of Islam.

overwhelming and unpleasant, but it was always useful. Weiss, for her part, tweeted that the people calling her racist tweet racist were a "sign of civilization's end." A couple of weeks later, she wrote a column called "We're All Fascists Now," arguing that angry liberals were creating a "moral flattening of the earth." At times it seems that Weiss's main strategy is to make an argument that's bad enough to attract criticism, and then to cherry-pick the worst of that criticism into the foundation for another bad argument. Her worldview requires the specter of a vast, angry, inferior mob.

It's of course true that there are vast, angry mobs on the internet. Jon Ronson wrote the book *So You've Been Publicly Shamed* about this in 2015. "We became keenly watchful for transgressions," he writes, describing the state of *Twitter* around 2012. "After a while it wasn't just transgressions we were keenly watchful for. It was misspeakings. Fury at the terribleness of other people had started to consume us a lot. . . . In fact, it felt weird and empty when there *wasn't* anyone to be furious about. The days between shamings felt like days picking at fingernails, treading water." Web 2.0 had curdled; its organizing principle was shifting. The early internet had been constructed around lines of affinity, and whatever good spaces remain on the internet are still the product of affinity and openness. But when the internet moved to an organizing principle of *opposition*, much of what had formerly been surprising and rewarding and curious became tedious, noxious, and grim.

• • •

Many Gamergaters cut their expressive teeth on *4chan*, a message board that adopted as one of its mottos the phrase "There are no girls on the internet." "This rule does not mean what you think it means," wrote one *4chan* poster, who went, as most of them did, by the username Anonymous. "In real life, people like you for being a girl. They want to fuck you, so they pay attention to you and they pretend what you have to say is interesting, or that you are smart or clever. On the Internet, we don't have the chance to fuck you. This means the advantage of being a 'girl' does not exist. You don't get a bonus to conversation just because I'd like to put my cock in you." He explained that women could get their unfair social advantage back by posting photos of their tits on the message board: "This is, and should be, degrading for you."

Here was the opposition principle in action. Through identifying the effects   30
of women's systemic objectification as some sort of vagina-supremacist witchcraft, the men that congregated on *4chan* gained an identity, and a useful common enemy. Many of these men *had*, likely, experienced consequences related to the "liberal intellectual conformity" that is popular feminism: as the sexual marketplace began to equalize, they suddenly found themselves unable to obtain sex by default. Rather than work toward other forms of self-actualization—or attempt to make themselves genuinely desirable, in the same way that women have been socialized to do at great expense and with great sincerity for all time—they established a group identity that centered on anti-woman virulence, on telling women who happened to stumble across *4chan* that "the only interesting thing about you is your naked body. tl;dr: tits or GET THE FUCK OUT."

In the same way that it behooved these trolls to credit women with a maximum of power that they did not actually possess, it sometimes behooved women, on the internet, to do the same when they spoke about trolls. At some points while I worked at *Jezebel*, it would have been easy to enter into one of these situations myself. Let's say a bunch of trolls sent me threatening emails—an experience that wasn't exactly common, as I have been "lucky," but wasn't rare enough to surprise me. The economy of online attention would suggest that I write a column about those trolls, quote their emails, talk about how the experience of being threatened constitutes a definitive situation of being a woman in the world. (It would be acceptable for me to do this *even though* I have never been hacked or swatted[13] or Gamergated, never had to move out of my house to a secure location, as so many other women have.) My column about trolling would, of course, attract an influx of trolling. Then, having proven my point, maybe I'd go on TV and talk about the situation, and then I would get trolled even more, and then I could go on defining myself in reference to trolls forever, positioning them as inexorable and monstrous, and they would return the favor in the interest of their own ideological advancement, and this whole situation could continue until we all died.

The political philosopher Sally Scholz separates solidarity into three categories. There's social solidarity, which is based on common experience; civic solidarity, which is based on moral obligation to a community; and political solidarity, which is based on a shared commitment to a cause. These forms of solidarity overlap, but they're distinct from one another. What's political, in other words, doesn't also have to be personal, at least not in the sense of first-hand experience. You don't need to step in shit to understand what stepping in shit feels like. You don't need to have directly suffered at the hands of some injustice in order to be invested in bringing that injustice to an end.

But the internet brings the "I" into everything. The internet can make it seem that supporting someone means literally sharing in their experience—that solidarity is a matter of *identity* rather than politics or morality, and that it's best established at a point of maximum mutual vulnerability in everyday life. Under these terms, instead of expressing morally obvious solidarity with the struggle of black Americans under the police state or the plight of fat women who must roam the earth to purchase stylish and thoughtful clothing, the internet would encourage me to express solidarity through inserting my own identity. *Of course* I support the black struggle because *I*, myself, as a woman of Asian heritage, have *personally* been injured by white supremacy. (In fact, as an Asian woman, part of a minority group often deemed white-adjacent, I have benefited from American anti-blackness on just as many occasions.) *Of course* I understand the difficulty of shopping as a woman who is overlooked by the fashion industry because *I*, myself, have *also* somehow been

13. A form of harassment or intimidation in which police or authorities are called to a location under false pretenses (usually that a horrible crime has occurred).

marginalized by this industry. This framework, which centers the self in an expression of support for others, is not ideal.

The phenomenon in which people take more comfort in a sense of injury than a sense of freedom governs many situations where people are objectively *not* being victimized on a systematic basis. For example, men's rights activists have developed a sense of solidarity around the absurd claim that men are second-class citizens. White nationalists have brought white people together through the idea that white people are endangered, specifically white men—this at a time when 91 percent of *Fortune* 500 CEOs are white men, when white people make up 90 percent of elected American officials and an overwhelming majority of top decision-makers in music, publishing, television, movies, and sports.

Conversely, and crucially, the dynamic also applies in situations where   35
claims of vulnerability are legitimate and historically entrenched. The greatest moments of feminist solidarity in recent years have stemmed not from an affirmative vision but from articulating extreme versions of the low common denominator of male slight. These moments have been world-altering: #YesAllWomen, in 2014, was the response to Elliot Rodger's Isla Vista massacre, in which he killed six people and wounded fourteen in an attempt to exact revenge on women for rejecting him. Women responded to this story with a sense of nauseating recognition: mass violence is nearly always linked to violence toward women, and for women it is something approaching a universal experience to have placated a man out of the real fear that he will hurt you. In turn, some men responded with the entirely unnecessary reminder that "not all men" are like that. (I was once hit with "not all men" right after a stranger yelled something obscene at me; the guy I was with noted my displeasure and helpfully reminded me that not all men are jerks.) Women began posting stories on *Twitter* and *Facebook* with #YesAllWomen to make an obvious but important point: not all men have made women fearful, but yes, all women have experienced fear because of men. #MeToo, in 2017, came in the weeks following the Harvey Weinstein revelations, as the floodgates opened and story after story after story rolled out about the subjugation women had experienced at the hands of powerful men. Against the normal forms of disbelief and rejection these stories meet with—it can't possibly be *that* bad; something about *her* telling *that* story seems suspicious—women anchored one another, establishing the breadth and inescapability of male abuse of power through speaking simultaneously and adding #MeToo.

• • •

What's amazing is that things like hashtag design—these essentially ad hoc experiments in digital architecture—have shaped so much of our political discourse. Our world would be different if Anonymous hadn't been the default username on *4chan*, or if every social media platform didn't center on the personal profile, or if *YouTube* algorithms didn't show viewers increasingly extreme content to retain their attention, or if hashtags and retweets simply didn't exist. It's because of the hashtag, the retweet, and the profile that solidarity on the internet gets inextricably tangled up with visibility, identity, and self-promotion. It's telling that the most mainstream gestures of solidarity are pure representation, like viral reposts or avatar photos with cause-related filters, and meanwhile the *actual* mechanisms through which political solidarity is enacted, like strikes and boycotts, still exist on the fringe. The extremes of performative solidarity are all transparently embarrassing: a Christian internet personality urging other conservatives to tell Starbucks baristas that their name is "Merry Christmas," or Nev Schulman from the TV show *Catfish* taking a selfie with a hand over his heart in an elevator and captioning it "A real man shows his strength through patience and honor. This elevator is abuse free." (Schulman punched a girl in college.) The demonstrative celebration of black women on social media—white people tweeting "black women will save America" after elections, or Mark Ruffalo[14] tweeting that he said a prayer and God answered as a black woman—often hints at a bizarre need on the part of white people to personally participate in an ideology of equality that ostensibly requires them to chill out. At one point in *The Presentation of Self*, Goffman writes that the audience's way of shaping a role for the performer can become more elaborate than the performance itself. This is what the online expression of solidarity sometimes feels like—a manner of listening so extreme and performative that it often turns into the show.

The final, and possibly most psychologically destructive, distortion of the social internet is its distortion of scale. This is not an accident but an essential design feature: social media was constructed around the idea that a thing is important insofar as it is important to you. In an early internal memo about the creation of *Facebook*'s News Feed, Mark Zuckerberg observed, already beyond parody, "A squirrel dying in front of your house may be more relevant to your interests right now than people dying in Africa." The idea was that social media would give us a fine-tuned sort of control over what we looked at. What resulted was a situation where we—first as individuals, and then inevitably as a collective—are essentially unable to exercise control at all. *Facebook*'s goal of showing people only what they were interested in seeing resulted, within a decade, in the effective end of shared civic reality. And this choice, combined with the company's financial incentive to continually trigger heightened emotional responses in its users, ultimately solidified the current norm in news media consumption: today we mostly consume news that corresponds with our ideological alignment, which has been fine-tuned to make us feel self-righteous and also mad.

• • •

Like many among us, I have become acutely conscious of the way my brain degrades when I strap it in to receive the full barrage of the internet—these unlimited channels, all constantly reloading with new information: births, deaths, boasts, bombings, jokes, job announcements, ads, warnings, complaints, confessions, and political disasters blitzing our frayed neurons in huge

14. American actor and producer (b. 1967).

waves of information that pummel us and then are instantly replaced. This is an awful way to live, and it is wearing us down quickly.

• • •

But the worse the internet gets, the more we appear to crave it—the more it gains the power to shape our instincts and desires. To guard against this, I give myself arbitrary boundaries—no *Instagram* stories, no app notifications—and rely on apps that shut down my *Twitter* and *Instagram* accounts after forty-five minutes of daily use. And still, on occasion, I'll disable my social media blockers, and I'll sit there like a rat pressing the lever, like a woman repeatedly hitting myself on the forehead with a hammer, masturbating through the nightmare until I finally catch the gasoline whiff of a good meme. The internet is still so young that it's easy to retain some subconscious hope that it all might still add up to something. We remember that at one point this all felt like butterflies and puddles and blossoms, and we sit patiently in our festering inferno, waiting for the internet to turn around and surprise us and get good again. But it won't. The internet is governed by incentives that make it impossible to be a full person while interacting with it. In the future, we will inevitably be cheapened. Less and less of us will be left, not just as individuals but also as community members, as a collective of people facing various catastrophes. Distraction is a "life-and-death matter," Jenny Odell writes in *How to Do Nothing.* "A social body that can't concentrate or communicate with itself is like a person who can't think and act."

• • •

What could put an end to the worst of the internet? Social and economic collapse would do it, or perhaps a series of antitrust cases followed by a package of hard regulatory legislation that would somehow also dismantle the internet's fundamental profit model. At this point it's clear that collapse will almost definitely come first. Barring that, we've got nothing except our small attempts to retain our humanity, to act on a model of actual selfhood, one that embraces culpability, inconsistency, and insignificance. We would have to think very carefully about what we're getting from the internet, and how much we're giving it in return. We'd have to care less about our identities, to be deeply skeptical of our own unbearable opinions, to be careful about when opposition serves us, to be properly ashamed when we can't express solidarity without putting ourselves first. The alternative is unspeakable. But you know that—it's already here.

40

MLA CITATION

Tolentino, Jia. "The I in the Internet." *The Norton Reader: An Anthology of Nonfiction,* edited by Melissa A. Goldthwaite et al., 16th ed., W. W. Norton, 2024, pp. 241–55.

QUESTIONS

1. Consider Jia Tolentino's title "The I in the Internet." What different types of *I*'s (and eyes) does she write about? How are they connected?

2. Tolentino's essay is both an account of her own experience with the internet and an analysis of "five intersecting problems" with it (paragraph 15). What persona does Tolentino project in her essay? Does this persona incline you to be more or less persuaded by her arguments?

3. Over the course of her essay, Tolentino refers to many other sources, including the 1995 book *You Can Surf the Net!* (paragraph 4), sociologist Erving Goffman's 1959 book *The Presentation of Self in Everyday Life* (paragraphs 16–19, 24, and 36), various writings by the journalist Bari Weiss (paragraphs 25–27), and the work of political philosopher Sally Scholz (paragraph 32). Annotate the essay, noting how she uses these and other sources to advance her own argument.

4. Tolentino ends her essay on a bleak note, suggesting that there is little we can do to resist the internet's detrimental effects on our humanity (paragraphs 39–40). Do you share her perspective? Why or why not?

5. Over the course of her essay, Tolentino makes a number of general assertions about the internet and its effects. For example: "Through social media, many people have quickly come to view all new information as a sort of direct commentary on *who they are*" (paragraph 19); "With the internet, it's so easy to stop trying to be decent, or reasonable, or politically engaged—and start trying merely to *seem* so" (paragraph 24); "The early internet had been constructed around lines of affinity. . . . But when the internet moved to an organizing principle of *opposition*, much of what had formerly been surprising and rewarding and curious became tedious, noxious, and grim" (paragraph 28); and "This is what the online expression of solidarity sometimes feels like—a manner of listening so extreme and performative that it often turns into the show" (paragraph 36). Document your engagement with the internet over the course of a single day. Then, in an essay or multimedia project, test one of Tolentino's statements against your own experience.

5 BODY LANGUAGE

We show our emotions, but we talk about our feelings.
—FRANS DE WAAL

According to primatologist and ethologist Frans de Waal, our bodies show emotion through "facial expression, skin color, vocal timbre, gestures, odor," and more. At times, our bodies communicate things beyond our conscious awareness. Yet there are also times when we need to talk or write to communicate feelings and ideas that will not be accessible to others unless we do so. The authors in this chapter consider bodies and language in several ways: reflecting on the language people use to identify their own bodies; using observations and looking for patterns to make meaning; and critiquing judgments and assumptions about bodies, especially when those judgments and assumptions are harmful to individuals and groups. The authors represented in this chapter, too, often consider the ways bodies, language, and categorizations (such as race, gender, age, ability, class, and other categories) intersect and communicate in complex ways.

In making a distinction between emotions and feelings, de Waal wants readers to understand the importance of holistic observation, of pattern recognition, and of scientific study of emotions and behaviors. While de Waal's research is primarily related to non-human animals, he also sees connections between animal and human emotions and behaviors. In "Seeing Each Other," social psychologist Jennifer L. Eberhardt, too, takes a scientific approach, using studies and field experiments, to deepen understandings of "identity, power, and privilege" and "the many ways the brain can be altered by experience." She considers the "challenges of cross-racial identification" and its implications for crime, surveillance, and policing.

As Claudia Rankine reminds readers in the selection from her book *Citizen*, "the body has memory. The physical carriage hauls more than its weight." That weight can be the burden of stereotypes, unrealistic expectations, false assumptions, limiting beliefs, racist profiling, or even physical violence, as Garnette Cadogan explores in his essay about walking while Black. One way of coming to terms with such burdens is to choose the words—adjectives, nouns, and pronouns—that best describe personal experience: Nancy Mairs chooses the term "cripple"; June Eric-Udorie describes the freedom she experienced in accepting herself as "disabled" rather than seeing herself as broken and in need of healing; Amy Sequenzia, who communicates through typing, takes pride in her "loud hands"; and Rhea Ewing reflects on the process of choosing one's own pronouns—and how that process can be influenced by conversation, observation, fear, support, and acceptance. As Roxane Gay observes, however, even personal feelings and terms can be complicated; she describes a mix of self-love and self-hatred, as well as mixed feelings about weight-loss surgery, in a culture that makes living in certain bodies—termed "fat" and "unruly"—difficult. In "The Female Body," Margaret Atwood shows the complicated relationship between a sense of self and a gendered body as a topic. In her playful lyric essay, she writes a cultural critique of the ways the female body is objectified.

As you read the selections in this chapter, consider your own bodily experience as well as how you view and respond to others. How does it feel to be you, to live in your body? Are there labels you choose for yourself, ones you reject? How do you use your body to communicate? Do you see yourself differently depending on where you are and who else is there? In "How It Feels to Be Colored Me," Zora Neale Hurston uses similes and metaphors to describe her experience. She writes, "Among the thousand white persons, I am a dark rock surged upon, and overswept, but through it all, I remain myself." What similes and metaphors help communicate your experience? In what ways can you be more open to observing and listening to others, especially those whose bodies and experiences differ significantly from your own?

FRANS DE WAAL
from *Mama's Last Hug*

W ATCHING BEHAVIOR COMES NATURALLY TO ME, so much so that I may be overdoing it. I didn't realize this until I came home one day to tell my mother about a scene on a regional bus. I must have been twelve. A boy and girl had been kissing in the gross way that I couldn't relate to but that is typical of teenagers, with open mouths moistly clamped onto each other. This by itself was nothing special, but then I noticed the girl afterward chewing gum, whereas before the kiss I had seen only the boy chewing. I was puzzled but figured it out—it was like the law of communicating vessels. When I told my mom, however, she was less than thrilled. With a troubled expression, she told me to stop paying such close attention to people, saying it was not a very nice thing to do.

Observation is now my profession. But don't expect me to notice the color of a dress or whether a man wears a hairpiece—those things don't interest me in the least. Instead, I focus on emotional expressions, body language, and social dynamics. These are so similar between humans and other primates that my skill applies equally to both, although my work mostly concerns the latter. As a student, I had an office overlooking a zoo colony of chimpanzees, and as a scientist at the Yerkes National Primate Research Center, near Atlanta, Georgia, I have had a similar situation for the last twenty-five years. My chimps live outdoors at a field station and occasionally get into upheavals that cause such a ruckus that we

Published as the prologue to Frans de Waal's book Mama's Last Hug: Animal Emotions and What They Tell Us about Ourselves *(2019), which explores the capacity of animals to experience emotion.*

rush to the window to take in the spectacle. What most people will see as a chaotic melee of twenty hairy beasts running about hollering and screaming is in
fact a highly ordered society. We recognize every ape by face, even just by voice,
and know what to expect. Without pattern recognition, observation remains
unfocused and random. It would be like watching a sport that you've never played
and don't know much about. You basically see nothing. This is why I can't stand
American television coverage of international soccer matches: most sports narra-
tors came late to the game and fail to grasp its fundamental strategies. They have
eyes for the ball only and keep on blabbing during the most pivotal moments.
This is what happens when we lack pattern recognition.

Looking beyond the central scene is key. If one male chimpanzee intimi-
dates another by throwing rocks or charging closely past the other, you need to
deliberately take your eyes off them to check the periphery, where new developments arise. I call it holistic observation: considering the wider context. That
the threatened male's best buddy is asleep in a corner doesn't mean we can
ignore him. As soon as he wakes up and walks toward the scene, the whole
colony knows things are about to change. A female gives a loud hoot to announce
the move, while mothers press their youngest offspring close.

And after the commotion has died down, you don't just turn away. You keep
your eyes on the main actors—they aren't finished yet. Of the thousands of reconciliations I've witnessed, one of the first took me by surprise. Shortly after a
confrontation, two male rivals walked upright, on two legs, toward each other,
fully pilo-erect—meaning their hair was standing on end, making them look
twice their regular size. Their eye contact looked so fierce, I expected a revival of
the hostilities. But when they got close to each other, one of them suddenly
turned around and presented his behind. The other responded by grooming
closely around the anus of the
first male, uttering loud lip-
smacks and tooth-clacks to indicate his dedication to the task.
Since the first male wanted to
do the same, they ended up in
an awkward 69 position, which
allowed each of them to groom
the other's behind at the same
time. Soon thereafter they
relaxed and turned around to
groom each other's faces. Peace
was restored.

The initial grooming location may seem odd, but remember that English (as well as many
other languages) has expressions
such as *brown-nosing* and *ass-
licking*. I'm sure there is a good
reason. Among humans, intense

5

Illustration by Frans de Waal.

fear may cause vomiting and diarrhea—we say we "crap our pants" when we're frightened. That's also a common occurrence in apes, minus the pants. Bodily exits yield critical information. Long after a skirmish has ended, you may see a male chimpanzee casually stroll to the precise location in the grass where his rival had been sitting, only to bend down and take a sniff. Although vision is about as dominant a sense in chimpanzees as it is in us, smell remains critically important. In our species, too, as covert filming has demonstrated, after we shake hands with another person, especially someone of the same sex, we often scent our own hand. We lift it casually close to our face to gather a chemical whiff that informs us about the other's disposition. We do so unconsciously, as we do so many things that resemble the behavior of other primates. Nevertheless, we like to see ourselves as rational actors who know what we're doing, while we depict other species as automatons. It's really not that simple.

We are constantly in touch with our feelings, but the tricky part is that our emotions and our feelings are not the same. We tend to conflate them, but feelings are internal subjective states that, strictly speaking, are known only to those who have them. I know my own feelings, but I don't know yours, except for what you tell me about them. We communicate about our feelings by language. Emotions, on the other hand, are bodily and mental states—from anger and fear to sexual desire and affection and seeking the upper hand—that drive behavior. Triggered by certain stimuli and accompanied by behavioral changes, emotions are detectable on the outside in facial expression, skin color, vocal timbre, gestures, odor, and so on. Only when the person experiencing these changes becomes aware of them do they become feelings, which are conscious experiences. We show our emotions, but we talk about our feelings.

Take reconciliation, or a friendly reunion following a confrontation. Reconciliation is a measurable emotional interaction: to detect it, all you, as an observer, need is some patience to see what happens between former antagonists. But the feelings that accompany a reconciliation—contrition, forgiveness, relief—are knowable only to those who experience them. You may suspect that others have the same feelings as you, but you can't be sure even with respect to members of your own species. Someone may claim they have forgiven another person, for example, but can we trust this information? All too often, despite what they have told us, they bring up the affront in question on the first occasion that arises. We know our own inner states imperfectly and often mislead both ourselves and those around us. We're masters of fake happiness, suppressed fear, and misguided love. This is why I'm pleased to work with nonlinguistic creatures. I'm forced to guess their feelings, but at least they never lead me astray by what they tell me about themselves.

The study of human psychology usually relies on the use of questionnaires, which are heavy on self-reported feelings and light on actual behavior. But I favor the reverse. We need more observations of actual human social affairs. As a simple example, let me take you to a large conference in Italy, which I attended many years ago as a budding scientist. Being there to speak about how primates resolve conflicts, I hadn't expected to see a perfect human example on display. A certain scientist was acting up in a way that I had never seen before and rarely have since. It must have been the combination of him being famous and being a native English speaker. At international meetings, Americans and Brits often mistake the extraordinary privilege of being able to speak in their mother tongue for intellectual superiority. Because no one is going to disagree with them in broken English, they are rarely disabused of this notion.

There was a whole program of lectures, and after every one, our famous English-speaking scientist jumped out of his seat in the front row to help us understand the work. Just as one Italian speaker finished presenting her work, for example, and even as the applause for her lingered, this scientist rose from his seat, climbed to the podium, took the speaker's mike, and literally said, "What she actually meant to say . . ." I don't remember the topic anymore, but the Italian speaker pulled a face. It was hard to miss this man's cockiness and disrespect for her—nowadays we'd call it "mansplaining."

Most of the audience members had been listening through a translation   10
service—in fact, their delayed linguistic connection may have helped them see through his behavior, in the same way that we're better at reading body language in a televised debate when the sound is turned off. They began to hiss and boo.

The expression of surprise on the face of our famous scientist showed how much he had misjudged the reception of his power grab. Until then, he'd thought it was going swimmingly. Flustered and perhaps humiliated, he hastily stepped down from the podium.

I kept my eyes on him and on the Italian speaker as they sat in the audience. Within fifteen minutes, he approached her and offered her his translation device, since she didn't have one. She politely accepted (perhaps without actually needing one), which counts as an implicit peace offer. I say "implicit" because there were no signs that they mentioned the previous awkward moment. Humans often signal good intentions after a confrontation (a smile, a compliment) and leave it at that. I couldn't follow what they were saying, but a third party told me that after all lectures were over, the scientist approached the speaker a second time and literally told her, "I have made a complete ass of myself." This admirable bit of self-knowledge came close to an explicit reconciliation.

Despite the ubiquity of human conflict resolution, and its fascinating unfolding at the conference, my own lecture got a mixed reception. I had only just begun my studies, and science was not yet ready for the idea that other species perform reconciliations. I don't think anyone doubted my observations—I provided lots of data and photographs to make my case—but they simply didn't know what to make of them. At the time, theories about animal conflict focused on winning and losing. Winning is good, losing is bad, and all that matters is who gets the resources. In the 1970s, science viewed animals as Hobbesian:[1] violent, competitive, selfish, and never genuinely kind. My emphasis on peacemaking made no sense. In addition, the term sounded emotional, which was

---

1. Allusion to English political philosopher Thomas Hobbes (1588–1679) and his book *Leviathan* (1651), which details his contract theory. Hobbes argued that those living within the state of nature, rather than being governed by social contracts, would be selfish and have "nasty, brutish and short" lives.

not well regarded. Some colleagues took a patronizing approach, explaining that I had fallen for a romantic notion that didn't belong in science. I was still very young, and they lectured me that everything in nature revolves around survival and reproduction, and that no organism will get very far with peace-making. Compromise is for the weak. Even if chimps showed such behavior, they said, it's doubtful they actually needed it. And surely no other species ever did the same. I was studying a fluke.

Several decades and hundreds of studies later, we know that reconciliation is in fact common and widespread. It occurs in all social mammals, from rats and dolphins to wolves and elephants, and also in birds. The behavior serves relationship repair, so much so that if nowadays we discovered a social mammal that *didn't* reconcile after fights, we'd be surprised. We'd wonder how they kept their society together. But at the time I didn't know this and politely listened to all the free advice. It didn't change my mind, though, because for me observation trumps any theory. What animals do in real life always has priority over preconceived notions about how they ought to behave. When you are a born observer, this is what you get: an inductive approach to science.

15   Similarly, if you observe, as Charles Darwin famously did in *The Expression of the Emotions in Man and Animals*, that other primates employ human-like facial expressions in emotionally charged situations, you cannot get around similarities in their inner lives. They bare their teeth in a grin, they produce hoarse chuckling sounds when tickled, and they pout their lips when frustrated. This automatically becomes the starting point of your theories. You may hold whatever view you like about animal emotions or the absence thereof, but you will have to come up with a framework in which it makes sense that humans and other primates communicate their reactions and intentions via the same facial musculature. Darwin naturally did so by assuming emotional continuity between humans and other species.

Nevertheless, there is a world of difference between behavior that expresses emotions and the conscious or unconscious experience of those states. Anyone who claims to know what animals feel doesn't have science on their side. It remains conjecture. This is not necessarily bad, and I'm all for *assuming* that species related to us have related feelings, but we should not overlook the leap of faith that it asks us to take. Even when I tell you that *Mama's Last Hug* was an embrace between an old chimpanzee and an old professor a few days before her death, I cannot include her feelings in my description. The familiar behavior as well as its poignant context do suggest them, yet they remain inaccessible. This uncertainty has always vexed students of the emotions and is the reason the field is often considered murky and messy.

Science doesn't like imprecision, which is why, when it comes to animal emotions, it is often at odds with the views of the general public. Ask the man or woman in the street if animals have emotions, and they will say "of course." They know their pet dogs and cats have all sorts of emotions, and by extension they grant them to other animals as well. But ask professors at a university the same question, and many will scratch their heads, look bewildered, and ask what exactly you mean. How do you even *define* emotions? They may follow B. F. Skinner, the

American behaviorist who promoted a mechanistic view of animals, by dismissing emotions as "excellent examples of the fictional causes to which we commonly attribute behavior." True, it is nowadays hard to find a scientist who outright denies animal emotions, but many are uncomfortable talking about them.

Readers who feel insulted on behalf of animals by those who doubt their emotional lives should keep in mind that without the scrutiny typical of science, we'd still believe the earth is flat or that maggots spontaneously crawl out of rotting meat. Science is at its best when it questions common preconceptions. And even though I disagree with the skeptical view of animal emotions, I also feel that just affirming their existence is like saying that the sky is blue. It doesn't get us very far. We need to know more. What kind of emotions? How are they felt? What purpose do they serve? Is the fear presumably felt by a fish the same as that felt by a horse? Impressions are not enough to answer such questions. Look how we study the inner life of our own species. We bring human subjects into a room where they watch videos or play games while strapped to equipment that measures their heart rate, galvanic skin response, facial muscle contractions, and so on. We also scan their brains. For other species, we need to take the same close-up look.

I love to follow wild primates around, and over the years I've visited a great many field sites in far corners of the earth, but there's a limit to what I or anyone else can learn from this. One of the most emotional moments I ever witnessed was when wild chimpanzees high above me suddenly burst out in bloodcurdling screams and hoots. Chimps are among the noisiest animals in the world, and my heart stood still not knowing the cause of the commotion. As it turns out, they had captured a hapless monkey and were leaving little doubt about how much they prized its meat. While I watched the apes cluster around the possessor of the carcass and feast, I wondered if he shared it with them because he had more than enough to eat and didn't care or because he wanted to get rid of all those beggars, who couldn't stop whining while gingerly touching every morsel he brought to his mouth. Or perhaps, as a third possibility, his sharing was altruistic, based on how much he knew the others wanted a piece. There is no way to know for sure from watching alone. We'd need to change the hunger state of the meat owner or make it harder for the others to beg. Would he still be as generous? Only a controlled experiment would allow us to get at the motives behind his behavior.

This has worked extremely well in studies on intelligence. Today we dare speak of animal mental life only after a century of experiments on symbolic communication, mirror self-recognition, tool use, planning for the future, and adoption of another's viewpoint. These studies have blown big drafty holes in the wall that supposedly separates humans from the rest of the animal kingdom. We can expect the same to happen with respect to the emotions, but only if we adopt a systematic approach. Ideally, we'd use findings from both the lab and the field, putting them together as different pieces of the same puzzle.

Emotions may be slippery, but they are also by far the most salient aspect of our lives. They give meaning to everything. In experiments, people remember emotionally charged pictures and stories far better than neutral ones. We like

20

to describe almost everything we have done or are about to do in emotional terms. A wedding is romantic or festive, a funeral is full of tears, and a sports match may be great fun or a disappointment depending on its outcome.

We have the same bias when it comes to animals. An Internet video of a wild capuchin monkey cracking nuts with stones will get far fewer hits than one of a buffalo herd driving lions away from a calf: the ungulates take the predators on their horns, while the calf frees itself from their claws. Both videos are impressive and interesting, but only the second one pulls at our heartstrings. We identify with the calf, hear its bleating, and are delighted by the reunion with its mother. We conveniently forget that for the lions there is nothing happy about this outcome.

That's another thing about the emotions: they make us take sides.

Not only are we keenly interested in emotions; they structure our societies to a degree that we rarely acknowledge. Why would politicians seek higher office if not for the hunger for power that marks all primates? Why would you worry about your family if not for the emotional ties that bind parents and offspring? Why did we abolish slavery and child labor if not for human decency grounded in social connectedness and empathy? To explain his opposition to slavery, Abraham Lincoln specifically mentioned the pitiful sight of chained slaves he had encountered on trips through the South. Our judicial systems channel feelings of bitterness and revenge into just punishment, and our health care systems have their roots in compassion. Hospitals (from the Latin *hospitālis*, or "hospitable") started out as religious charities run by nuns and only much later became secular institutions operated by professionals. In fact, all our most cherished institutions and accomplishments are tightly interwoven with human emotions and would not exist without them.

25   This realization makes me look at animal emotions in a different light, not as a topic to contemplate by itself but as capable of shedding light on our very existence, our goals and dreams, and our highly structured societies. Given my specialization, I naturally pay most attention to our fellow primates, but not because I believe their emotions are inherently more worthy of attention. Primates do express them more similarly to us, but emotions are everywhere in the animal kingdom, from fish to birds to insects and even in brainy mollusks such as the octopus.

I will only rarely refer to other species as "other animals" or "nonhuman animals." For simplicity's sake, I will mostly call them just "animals," even though for me, as a biologist, nothing is more self-evident than that we are part of the same kingdom. We *are* animals. Since I don't look at our own species as emotionally much different from other mammals, and in fact would be hard-pressed to pinpoint uniquely human emotions, we had better pay careful attention to the emotional background we share with our fellow travelers on this planet.

MLA CITATION

Waal, Frans de. "From *Mama's Last Hug.*" *The Norton Reader: An Anthology of Nonfiction,* edited by Melissa A. Goldthwaite et al., 16th ed., W. W. Norton, 2024, pp. 258–64.

QUESTIONS

1. Frans de Waal observes conflict and reconciliation between humans and also between nonhuman primates. What do you gain from reading about examples of both? Does it change your perspective on animal emotions? on reconciliation between humans?

2. Mark the places in the essay where de Waal discusses the difference between feelings and emotions. What is the distinction he makes between them? Why is it important?

3. On your own or with classmates, brainstorm a list of reasons why it might be important to observe and study nonhuman animal emotions. How might the knowledge gained from such observations and studies affect or inform human choices and behavior? What benefits might such studies have for animals? What potential do they have to impact human-animal relationships, such as with pets, livestock, or wildlife?

MARGARET ATWOOD
The Female Body

> "... entirely devoted to the subject of 'The Female Body.' Knowing how well you have written on this topic ... this capacious topic ..."
> —LETTER FROM *Michigan Quarterly Review*

I.

I AGREE, IT'S A HOT TOPIC. But only one? Look around, there's a wide range. Take my own, for instance.

I get up in the morning. My topic feels like hell. I sprinkle it with water, brush parts of it, rub it with towels, powder it, add lubricant. I dump in the fuel and away goes my topic, my topical topic, my controversial topic, my capacious topic, my limping topic, my nearsighted topic, my topic with back problems, my badly-behaved topic, my vulgar topic, my outrageous topic, my aging topic, my topic that is out of the question and anyway still can't spell, in its oversized coat and worn winter boots, scuttling along the sidewalk as if it were flesh and blood, hunting for what's out there, an avocado, an alderman, an adjective, hungry as ever.

This essay was originally published in a 1990 special issue of the Michigan Quarterly Review, *a print journal of essays, poetry, and short stories. The issue was entirely devoted to the female body.*

2.

The basic Female Body comes with the following accessories: garter belt, pan tigirdle, crinoline, camisole, bustle, brassiere, stomacher, chemise, virgin zone, spike heels, nose ring, veil, kid gloves, fish-net stockings, fichu, bandeau, Merry Widow, weepers, chokers, barrettes, bangles, beads, lorgnette, feather boa, basic black, compact, Lycra stretch one-piece with modesty panel, designer peignoir, flannel nightie, lace teddy, bed, head.

3.

The Female Body is made of transparent plastic and lights up when you plug it in. You press a button to illuminate the different systems. The Circulatory System is red, for the heart and arteries, purple for the veins; the Respiratory System is blue; the Lymphatic System is yellow; the Digestive System is green, with liver and kidneys in aqua. The nerves are done in orange and the brain is pink. The skeleton, as you might expect, is white.

5   The Reproductive System is optional, and can be removed. It comes with or without a miniature embryo. Parental judgment can thereby be exercised. We do not wish to frighten or offend.

4.

He said, I won't have one of those things in the house. It gives a young girl a false notion of beauty, not to mention anatomy. If a real woman was built like that she'd fall on her face.

She said, If we don't let her have one like all the other girls she'll feel singled out. It'll become an issue. She'll long for one and she'll long to turn into one. Repression breeds sublimation. You know that.

He said, It's not just the pointy plastic tits, it's the wardrobes. The wardrobes and that stupid male doll, what's his name, the one with the underwear glued on.

She said, Better to get it over with when she's young. He said, All right but don't let me see it.

10 She came whizzing down the stairs, thrown like a dart. She was stark naked. Her hair had been chopped off, her head was turned back to front, she was missing some toes and she'd been tattooed all over her body with purple ink, in a scrollwork design. She hit the potted azalea, trembled there for a moment like a botched angel, and fell.

He said, I guess we're safe.

5.

The Female Body has many uses. It's been used as a door-knocker, a bottle-opener, as a clock with a ticking belly, as something to hold up lampshades, as a nutcracker, just squeeze the brass legs together and out comes your nut. It bears torches, lifts victorious wreaths, grows copper wings and raises aloft a ring of neon stars; whole buildings rest on its marble heads.

It sells cars, beer, shaving lotion, cigarettes, hard liquor; it sells diet plans and diamonds, and desire in tiny crystal bottles. Is this the face that launched a thousand products? You bet it is, but don't get any funny big ideas, honey, that smile is a dime a dozen.

It does not merely sell, it is sold. Money flows into this country or that country, flies in, practically crawls in, suitful after suitful, lured by all those hairless pre-teen legs. Listen, you want to reduce the national debt, don't you? Aren't you patriotic? That's the spirit. That's my girl.

She's a natural resource, a renewable one luckily, because those things wear out   15
so quickly. They don't make 'em like they used to. Shoddy goods.

6.

One and one equals another one. Pleasure in the female is not a requirement. Pair-bonding is stronger in geese. We're not talking about love, we're talking about biology. That's how we all got here, daughter.

Snails do it differently. They're hermaphrodites, and work in three's.

7.

Each female body contains a female brain. Handy. Makes things work. Stick pins in it and you get amazing results. Old popular songs. Short circuits. Bad dreams.

Anyway: each of these brains has two halves. They're joined together by a thick cord; neural pathways flow from one to the other, sparkles of electric information washing to and fro. Like light on waves. Like a conversation. How does a woman know? She listens. She listens in.

The male brain, now, that's a different matter. Only a thin connection. Space   20
over here, time over there, music and arithmetic in their own sealed compart-ments. The right brain doesn't know what the left brain is doing. Good for aiming though, for hitting the target when you pull the trigger. What's the tar-get? Who's the target? Who cares? What matters is hitting it. That's the male brain for you. Objective.

This is why men are so sad, why they feel so cut off, why they think of themselves as orphans cast adrift, footloose and stringless in the deep void. What void? she asks. What are you talking about? The void of the Universe, he says, and she says Oh and looks out the window and tries to get a handle on it, but it's no use, there's too much going on, too many rustlings in the leaves, too many voices, so she says, Would you like a cheese sandwich, a piece of cake, a cup of tea? And he grinds his teeth because she doesn't understand, and wanders off, not just alone but Alone, lost in the dark, lost in the skull, searching for the other half, the twin who could complete him.

Then it comes to him: he's lost the Female Body! Look, it shines in the gloom, far ahead, a vision of wholeness, ripeness, like a giant melon, like an apple, like a metaphor for *breast* in a bad sex novel; it shines like a balloon, like a foggy noon, a watery moon, shimmering in its egg of light.

Catch it. Put it in a pumpkin, in a high tower, in a compound, in a chamber, in a house, in a room. Quick, stick a leash on it, a lock, a chain, some pain, settle it down, so it can never get away from you again.

MLA CITATION

Atwood, Margaret. "The Female Body." *The Norton Reader: An Anthology of Nonfiction*, edited by Melissa A. Goldthwaite et al., 16th ed., W. W. Norton, 2024, pp. 265–68.

QUESTIONS

1. Although Margaret Atwood describes her own body in this essay (especially paragraph 2), she describes herself as an object, rather than a subject. What difference does that change make?

2. In section 5, Atwood lists a range of objects made in the shape of women's bodies. What does she suggest these objects connote about women and how society views women's bodies?

3. Although this essay neither makes an explicit argument nor has a thesis statement, it does have a definite point of view. What is the implicit argument of Atwood's piece?

4. This essay is written in sections, and the tone, approach, and method shift from section to section. Annotate the essay, marking the approach used in each section. What is the overall effect of this abundance?

5. In section 2, Atwood writes that the "basic Female Body comes with the following accessories" (paragraph 3). Look closely at the list she provides. Which ones are familiar to you? Which words did you need to look up? What do these items suggest about societal expectations for women? What accessory would you like to see on this list? Why?

RHEA EWING
Language

A chapter from Rhea Ewing's Fine: A Comic about Gender (2022), *a graphic nonfiction book about gender expression based on both interviews and personal reflection.*

Rhea, 2011

Rhea, 2011

I was at a small after-party for a Minneapolis indie comic expo. It was here I connected with Kai, whom I would later interview for this project.

Oh man, look at all these cool people!

Kai is friendly and warm, which helped break past my nerves. After our introductions, Kai asked me something I'd never been asked before:

Hi Rhea, it's good to see you again!

How was the show for you?

By the way, I meant to ask this earlier...

It was great, thanks!

What's your preferred pronoun?

It was like someone had seen me for the first time.

Of course, I had no good immediate answer.

um...

The etiquette of talking about pronouns has changed since then.

I guess "she" is

usually okay...

The word "preferred" is usually dropped from the conversation, as it makes trans people's pronouns seem optional in a way that is not true for most of us.

But I don't... prefer it. I...

But for me, at the time, the idea that I could have a **preference** in how I was referred to by others was a revelation.

I guess I don't know.

The question made me feel like a mask had been taken off.

Leaving me free to examine whatever was beneath it.

I'm not arguing for a return to this language, just noting that I found it personally useful at the time.

Some people I spoke to were very relaxed about pronouns (an attitude I envied).

Jamie, 2013

I let people use the pronouns they feel fit me, and "him, he, his" is what everyone uses.

Semantics is something I don't worry that much about.
I am me. The pronouns someone uses when they refer to me do not change my inner truth.

CON SCHEDULE

But for others, hearing the correct pronoun is vital to feeling seen and accepted.

Valerie, 2012

My younger sister, she's been really supportive.

That's been good.

My parents aren't the most accepting ever.

Like they'll get my pronouns right, then correct themselves with the wrong one, and then I'll correct them.

She- no he.

He

him

his

SON

Really is annoying!

Do you think they'll get it eventually?

"Eventually" needs to hurry up and get here!

JAC, 2013

Ignacio, 2013

When I first came out as trans, I wanted to go by "he" and "she," switching back and forth, in the same sentence even.

But that was severely difficult for people to do, and they always chose "she." They would never go back and forth.

So then I used "he," and it was really good in the beginning because it really pinpointed to people that I was trans identified.

...But after a while it really didn't feel like me.

1. Reference to the song "Say My Name," included on the album *The Writing's on the Wall* (1999) by Destiny's Child.

Rhea, 2013

After a lot of (too much?) thought, I decided to try going by they/them pronouns. I liked that most people are already familiar with singular they. Most of us already use singular they (whether we admit to it or not) in both casual speech and writing. It was a relatively convenient choice.

My trial period was limited to certain people and geographic locations. I had a map in my head of where it felt safe to use each set of pronouns. Where I did and did not want to be seen a certain way.

Rhea, 2018

Now I use they/them pronouns all the time, everywhere.

Part of it was that it was starting to seem kind of silly to be closeted when I've, like, spoken about my gender identity in radio interviews about my art.

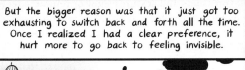

But the bigger reason was that it just got too exhausting to switch back and forth all the time. Once I realized I had a clear preference, it hurt more to go back to feeling invisible.

I would constantly imagine the worst-case scenarios if I was outed.

Rejection. Violence. Ridicule.

A constant nightmare.

Being out was so freeing. Instead of hiding and constantly imagining the worst, I could wait and see what actually did and didn't happen.

Thanks for trusting me!

My kid is trans. Will you talk to them?

...

Delusional

Woah

?

Eh.

I could trust that I was being seen and accepted (or not) for who I actually am.

This isn't the case for everyone, but for me this was the best solution!

MLA CITATION

Ewing, Rhea. "Language." *The Norton Reader: An Anthology of Nonfiction*, edited
    by Melissa A. Goldthwaite et al., 16th ed., W. W. Norton, 2024, pp. 269–85.

QUESTIONS

1. Rhea Ewing shows their personal process of thinking through and choosing pronouns. They also include excerpts from interviews with others. How do Ewing's
interviews and interactions shape Ewing's own process? Why is it important to talk
with other people about their choices and experiences?

2. In graphic essays, the drawings provide information that cannot be accessed fully
through the words alone. As you read and analyze this essay, look at the ways Ewing
shows body language. How do the expressions and gestures show or reinforce feelings and emotions? Choose a few panels in which Ewing shows emotion particularly well. What parts of the drawing communicate emotion? What other information
do you gain from the drawings that helps you understand the text more fully?

3. Ewing provides several reasons why a person might use different pronouns in
different contexts. What are some of those reasons? Are there other reasons you
could add?

4. Ewing provides three tips for "getting used to friends' new pronouns" (p. 282).
Analyze the structure of those panels and how Ewing provides those tips. Think of
some advice or tips (on a topic important to you) that you think would be helpful
to others or that show others how to practice love or respect in an unfamiliar way.
Create a piece that includes those tips along with graphics and perhaps even sound
(a comic, a video, photos, or some mix of images and words).

ZORA NEALE HURSTON
How It Feels to Be Colored Me

I AM COLORED but I offer nothing in the way of extenuating circumstances
except the fact that I am the only Negro in the United States whose
grandfather on the mother's side was not an Indian chief.

I remember the very day that I became colored. Up to my thirteenth
year I lived in the little Negro town of Eatonville, Florida. It is exclusively a colored town. The only white people I knew passed through the
town going to or coming from Orlando. The native whites rode dusty horses,
the Northern tourists chugged down the sandy village road in automobiles. The

Originally published in the political magazine World Tomorrow *(1928), just as Zora Neale
Hurston was graduating from Barnard College; collected and reprinted in* I Love Myself
When I Am Laughing . . . and Then Again When I Am Looking Mean and Impressive
(1973), a volume of Hurston's writings edited by Alice Walker.

town knew the Southerners and never stopped cane chewing[1] when they passed. But the Northerners were something else again. They were peered at cautiously from behind curtains by the timid. The more venturesome would come out on the porch to watch them go past and got just as much pleasure out of the tourists as the tourists got out of the village.

The front porch might seem a daring place for the rest of the town, but it was a gallery seat for me. My favorite place was atop the gate-post. Proscenium box for a born first-nighter. Not only did I enjoy the show, but I didn't mind the actors knowing that I liked it. I usually spoke to them in passing. I'd wave at them and when they returned my salute, I would say something like this: "Howdy-do-well-I-thank-you-where-you-goin'?" Usually automobile or the horse paused at this, and after a queer exchange of compliments, I would probably "go a piece of the way" with them, as we say in farthest Florida. If one of my family happened to come to the front in time to see me, of course negotiations would be rudely broken off. But even so, it is clear that I was the first "welcome-to-our-state" Floridian, and I hope the Miami Chamber of Commerce will please take notice.

During this period, white people differed from colored to me only in that they rode through town and never lived there. They liked to hear me "speak pieces" and sing and wanted to see me dance the parse-me-la, and gave me generously of their small silver for doing these things, which seemed strange to me for I wanted to do them so much that I needed bribing to stop. Only they didn't know it. The colored people gave no dimes. They deplored any joyful tendencies in me, but I was their Zora nevertheless. I belonged to them, to the nearby hotels, to the county—everybody's Zora.

But changes came in the family when I was thirteen, and I was sent to   5
school in Jacksonville. I left Eatonville, the town of the oleanders,[2] as Zora. When I disembarked from the river-boat at Jacksonville, she was no more. It seemed that I had suffered a sea change. I was not Zora of Orange County any more, I was now a little colored girl. I found it out in certain ways. In my heart as well as in the mirror, I became a fast brown—warranted not to rub nor run.

But I am not tragically colored. There is no great sorrow dammed up in my soul, nor lurking behind my eyes. I do not mind at all. I do not belong to the sobbing school of Negrohood who hold that nature somehow has given them a lowdown dirty deal and whose feelings are all hurt about it. Even in the helter-skelter skirmish that is my life, I have seen that the world is to the strong regardless of a little pigmentation more or less. No, I do not weep at the world—I am too busy sharpening my oyster knife.[3]

Someone is always at my elbow reminding me that I am the granddaughter of slaves. It fails to register depression with me. Slavery is sixty years in the past. The operation was successful and the patient is doing well, thank you.

1. Chewing sugarcane.
2. Fragrant tropical flowers common in the South.
3. A play on the popular expression "The world is my oyster."

The terrible struggle[4] that made me an American out of a potential slave said "On the line!" The Reconstruction said "Get set!"; and the generation before said "Go!" I am off to a flying start and I must not halt in the stretch to look behind and weep. Slavery is the price I paid for civilization, and the choice was not with me. It is a bully adventure and worth all that I have paid through my ancestors for it. No one on earth ever had a greater chance for glory. The world to be won and nothing to be lost. It is thrilling to think—to know that for any act of mine, I shall get twice as much praise or twice as much blame. It is quite exciting to hold the center of the national stage, with the spectators not knowing whether to laugh or to weep.

The position of my white neighbor is much more difficult. No brown specter pulls up a chair beside me when I sit down to eat. No dark ghost thrusts its leg against mine in bed. The game of keeping what one has is never so exciting as the game of getting.

I do not always feel colored. Even now I often achieve the unconscious Zora of Eatonville before the Hegira.[5] I feel most colored when I am thrown against a sharp white background.

10   For instance at Barnard. "Beside the waters of the Hudson"[6] I feel my race. Among the thousand white persons, I am a dark rock surged upon, and overswept, but through it all, I remain myself. When covered by the waters, I am; and the ebb but reveals me again.

Sometimes it is the other way around. A white person is set down in our midst, but the contrast is just as sharp for me. For instance, when I sit in the drafty basement that is The New World Cabaret with a white person, my color comes. We enter chatting about any little nothing that we have in common and are seated by the jazz waiters. In the abrupt way that jazz orchestras have, this one plunges into a number. It loses no time in circumlocutions, but gets right down to business. It constricts the thorax and splits the heart with its tempo and narcotic harmonies. This orchestra grows rambunctious, rears on its hind legs and attacks the tonal veil with primitive fury, rending it, clawing it until it breaks through to the jungle beyond. I follow those heathen—follow them exultingly. I dance wildly inside myself; I yell within, I whoop; I shake my assegai[7] above my head, I hurl it true to the mark *yeeeeooww*! I am in the jungle and living in the jungle way. My face is painted red and yellow and my body is painted blue. My pulse is throbbing like a war drum. I want to slaughter something— give pain, give death to what, I do not know. But the piece ends. The men of

4. The Civil War. Reconstruction was the period immediately following the war. One of its effects was that northern educators came South to teach those newly freed from slavery.

5. Journey undertaken away from a dangerous situation into a more highly desirable one (literally, the flight of Muhammad from Mecca in 622 CE).

6. Barnard, a women's college in New York City, is located near the Hudson River; the quote is a reference to Psalm 137: "by the waters of Babylon."

7. South African hunting spear.

the orchestra wipe their lips and rest their fingers. I creep back slowly to the veneer we call civilization with the last tone and find the white friend sitting motionless in his seat, smoking calmly.

"Good music they have here," he remarks, drumming the table with his fingertips.

Music. The great blobs of purple and red emotion have not touched him. He has only heard what I felt. He is far away and I see him but dimly across the ocean and the continent that have fallen between us. He is so pale with his whiteness then and I am *so* colored.

At certain times I have no race, I am *me*. When I set my hat at a certain angle and saunter down Seventh Avenue, Harlem City, feeling as snooty as the lions in front of the Forty-Second Street Library, for instance. So far as my feelings are concerned, Peggy Hopkins Joyce on the Boule Mich[8] with her gorgeous raiment, stately carriage, knees knocking together in a most aristocratic manner, has nothing on me. The cosmic Zora emerges. I belong to no race nor time. I am the eternal feminine with its string of beads.

I have no separate feeling about being an American citizen and colored. I am merely a fragment of the Great Soul that surges within the boundaries. My country, right or wrong. 15

Sometimes, I feel discriminated against, but it does not make me angry. It merely astonishes me. How *can* any deny themselves the pleasure of my company? It's beyond me.

But in the main, I feel like a brown bag of miscellany propped against a wall. Against a wall in company with other bags, white, red and yellow. Pour out the contents, and there is discovered a jumble of small things priceless and worthless. A first-water diamond, an empty spool, bits of broken glass, lengths of string, a key to a door long since crumbled away, a rusty knife-blade, old shoes saved for a road that never was and never will be, a nail bent under the weight of things too heavy for any nail, a dried flower or two still a little fragrant. In your hand is the brown bag. On the ground before you is the jumble it held—so much like the jumble in the bags, could they be emptied, that all might be dumped in a single heap and the bags refilled without altering the content of any greatly. A bit of colored glass more or less would not matter. Perhaps that is how the Great Stuffer of Bags filled them in the first place— who knows?

MLA CITATION

Hurston, Zora Neale. "How It Feels to Be Colored Me." *The Norton Reader: An Anthology of Nonfiction*, edited by Melissa A. Goldthwaite et al., 16th ed., W. W. Norton, 2024, pp. 286–89.

8. Joyce (1893–1957), American beauty and fashion-setter of the 1920s; Boule Mich, Boulevard Saint-Michel, a fashionable Parisian street.

QUESTIONS

1. From the beginning, Zora Neale Hurston startles us. "I remember the very day that I became colored" (paragraph 2). Why does Hurston insist that one *becomes* colored? What happened on that day to make her so?

2. Each section of Hurston's essay explores a different possible identity, some based on skin color, others emphasizing history, culture, or gender. As you read, annotate the essay, marking the different ways she explains her sense of self. What does Hurston accomplish by such an approach?

3. The final paragraph introduces a key simile: "like a brown bag of miscellany propped against a wall" (paragraph 17). How does Hurston develop this simile? What does she mean by it?

4. Like Nancy Mairs in "On Being a Cripple" (pp. 312–22), Hurston chooses a label, "colored me," to explore questions of personal identity. Compare Hurston's use of "colored" with Mairs's use of "cripple."

CLAUDIA RANKINE
from *Citizen*

H ENNESSY YOUNGMAN aka Jayson Musson,[1] whose *Art Thoughtz* take the form of tutorials on *YouTube*, educates viewers on contemporary art issues. In one of his many videos, he addresses how to become a successful black artist, wryly suggesting black people's anger is marketable. He advises black artists to cultivate "an angry nigger exterior" by watching, among other things, the Rodney King video[2] while working.

Youngman's suggestions are meant to expose expectations for blackness as well as to underscore the difficulty inherent in any attempt by black artists to metabolize real rage. The commodified anger his video advocates rests lightly on the surface for spectacle's sake. It can be engaged or played like the race card and is tied solely to the performance of blackness and not to the emotional state of particular individuals in particular situations.

On the bridge between this sellable anger and "the artist" resides, at times, an actual anger. Youngman in his video doesn't address this type of anger: the anger built up through experience and the quotidian struggles against dehuman-

From Claudia Rankine's Citizen: An American Lyric *(2014), a genre-challenging book of poetry and prose that powerfully interrogates the contours of race in contemporary America.*

1. Artist, performer, and YouTuber (b. 1977). Youngman is a persona Musson adopts in his internet videos.
2. In 1991, four Los Angeles police officers were videoed beating King, a Black man, during his arrest. The officers were charged with using excessive force, but the lack of any guilty verdicts precipitated the 1992 Los Angeles riots.

ization every brown or black person lives simply because of skin color. This other kind of anger in time can prevent, rather than sponsor, the production of anything except loneliness.

You begin to think, maybe erroneously, that this other kind of anger is really a type of knowledge: the type that both clarifies and disappoints. It responds to insult and attempted erasure simply by asserting presence, and the energy required to present, to react, to assert is accompanied by visceral disappointment: a disappointment in the sense that no amount of visibility will alter the ways in which one is perceived.

Recognition of this lack might break you apart. Or recognition might illuminate the erasure the attempted erasure triggers. Whether such discerning creates a healthier, if more isolated, self, you can't know. In any case, Youngman doesn't speak to this kind of anger. He doesn't say that witnessing the expression of this more ordinary and daily anger might make the witness believe that a person is "insane."

And insane is what you think, one Sunday afternoon, drinking an Arnold Palmer,[3] watching the 2009 Women's US Open[4] semifinal, when brought to full attention by the suddenly explosive behavior of Serena Williams. Serena in HD before your eyes becomes overcome by a rage you recognize and have been taught to hold at a distance for your own good. Serena's behavior, on this particular Sunday afternoon, suggests that all the injustice she has played through all the years of her illustrious career flashes before her and she decides finally to respond to all of it with a string of invectives. Nothing, not even the repetition of negations ("no, no, no") she employed in a similar situation years before as a younger player at the 2004 US Open, prepares you for this. Oh my God, she's gone crazy, you say to no one.

What does a victorious or defeated black woman's body in a historically white space look like? Serena and her big sister Venus Williams brought to mind Zora Neale Hurston's[5] "I feel most colored when I am thrown against a sharp white background." This appropriated line, stenciled on canvas by Glenn Ligon,[6] who used plastic letter stencils, smudging oil sticks, and graphite to transform the words into abstractions, seemed to be ad copy for some aspect of life for all black bodies.

Hurston's statement has been played out on the big screen by Serena and Venus: they win sometimes, they lose sometimes, they've been injured, they've been happy, they've been sad, ignored, booed mightily, they've been cheered, and through it all and evident to all were those people who are enraged they are there at all—graphite against a sharp white background.

3. Named for the professional golfer, a beverage that is half iced tea and half lemonade.

4. One of the four Grand Slam professional tennis tournaments.

5. Major Black novelist, folklorist, and anthropologist (1891–1960); see "How It Feels to Be Colored Me" (pp. 286–89).

6. American painter, sculptor, and visual artist (b. 1960) who often integrates references to other artists, writers, and cultural figures into his work.

For years you attribute to Serena Williams a kind of resilience appropriate only for those who exist in celluloid. Neither her father nor her mother nor her sister nor Jehovah her God nor NIKE camp[7] could shield her ultimately from people who felt her black body didn't belong on their court, in their world. From the start many made it clear Serena would have done better struggling to survive in the two-dimensionality of a Millet[8] painting, rather than on their tennis court—better to put all that strength to work in their fantasy of her working the land, rather than be caught up in the turbulence of our ancient dramas, like a ship fighting a storm in a Turner[9] seascape.

10   The most notorious of Serena's detractors takes the form of Mariana Alves, the distinguished tennis chair umpire. In 2004 Alves was excused from officiating any more matches on the final day of the US Open after she made five bad calls against Serena in her quarterfinal matchup against fellow American Jennifer Capriati. The serves and returns Alves called out were landing, stunningly unreturned by Capriati, inside the lines, no discerning eyesight needed. Commentators, spectators, television viewers, line judges, everyone could see the balls were good, everyone, apparently, except Alves. No one could understand what was happening. Serena, in her denim skirt, black sneaker boots, and dark mascara, began wagging her finger and saying "no, no, no," as if by negating the moment she could propel us back into a legible world. Tennis superstar John McEnroe,[10] given his own keen eye for injustice during his professional career, was shocked that Serena was able to hold it together after losing the match.

Though no one was saying anything explicitly about Serena's black body, you are not the only viewer who thought it was getting in the way of Alves's sight line. One commentator said he hoped he wasn't being unkind when he stated, "Capriati wins it with the help of the umpires and the lines judges." A year later that match would be credited for demonstrating the need for the speedy installation of Hawk-Eye, the line-calling technology that took the seeing away from the beholder. Now the umpire's call can be challenged by a replay; however, back then after the match Serena said, "I'm very angry and bitter right now. I felt cheated. Shall I go on? I just feel robbed."

And though you felt outrage for Serena after that 2004 US Open, as the years go by, she seems to put Alves, and a lengthening list of other curious calls and oversights, against both her and her sister, behind her as they happen.

Yes, and the body has memory. The physical carriage hauls more than its weight. The body is the threshold across which each objectionable call passes into consciousness—all the unintimidated, unblinking, and unflappable resil-

7. Richard Williams (b. 1942), Serena and Venus's father, also served as their coach; he and their mother Oracene Williams (b. 1952) raised their daughters as Jehovah's Witnesses; the Nike shoe and apparel company sponsors camps for a variety of sports.

8. Jean-François Millet (1814–1875), French realist painter.

9. J. M. W. Turner (1775–1851), English Romantic painter. The reference is to his 1840 painting *The Slave Ship*.

10. American tennis player (b. 1959), with the most combined singles and doubles championships, known for his heated arguments with referees.

ience does not erase the moments lived through, even as we are eternally stupid or everlastingly optimistic, so ready to be inside, among, a part of the games.

And here Serena is, five years after Alves, back at the US Open, again in a semifinal match, this time against Belgium's Kim Clijsters. Serena is not playing well and loses the first set. In response she smashes her racket on the court. Now McEnroe isn't stunned by her ability to hold herself together and is moved to say, "That's as angry as I've ever seen her." The umpire gives her a warning; another violation will mean a point penalty.

She is in the second set at the critical moment of 5–6 in Clijsters's favor, serving to stay in the match, at match point. The line judge employed by the US Open to watch Serena's body, its every move, says Serena stepped on the line while serving. What? (The Hawk-Eye cameras don't cover the feet, only the ball, apparently.) What! Are you serious? She is serious; she has seen a foot fault, one no one else is able to locate despite the numerous replays. "No foot fault, you definitely do not see a foot fault there," says McEnroe. "That's overofficiating for certain," says another commentator. Even the ESPN tennis commentator, who seems predictable in her readiness to find fault with the Williams sisters, says, "Her foot fault call was way off." Yes, and even if there had been a foot fault, despite the rule, they are rarely ever called at critical moments in a Grand Slam match because "You don't make a call," tennis official Carol Cox says, "that can decide a match unless it's flagrant."

As you look at the affable Kim Clijsters, you try to entertain the thought that this scenario could have played itself out the other way. And as Serena turns to the lineswoman and says, "I swear to God I'm fucking going to take this fucking ball and shove it down your fucking throat, you hear that? I swear to God!" As offensive as her outburst is, it is difficult not to applaud her for reacting immediately to being thrown against a sharp white background. It is difficult not to applaud her for existing in the moment, for fighting crazily against the so-called wrongness of her body's positioning at the service line.

She says in 2009, belatedly, the words that should have been said to the umpire in 2004, the words that might have snapped Alves back into focus, a focus that would have acknowledged what actually was happening on the court. Now Serena's reaction is read as insane. And her punishment for this moment of manumission is the threatened point penalty resulting in the loss of the match, an $82,500 fine, plus a two-year probationary period by the Grand Slam Committee.

Perhaps the committee's decision is only about context, though context is not meaning. It is a public event being watched in homes across the world. In any case, it is difficult not to think that if Serena lost context by abandoning all rules of civility, it could be because her body, trapped in a racial imaginary, trapped in disbelief—code for being black in America—is being governed not by the tennis match she is participating in but by a collapsed relationship that had promised to play by the rules. Perhaps this is how racism feels no matter the context—randomly the rules everyone else gets to play by no longer apply to you, and to call this out by calling out "I swear to God!" is to be called insane, crass, crazy. Bad sportsmanship.

15

Two years later, September 11, 2011, Serena is playing the Australian Sam Stosur in the US Open final. She is expected to win, having just beaten the number-one player, the Dane Caroline Wozniacki, in the semifinal the night before. Some speculate Serena especially wants to win this Grand Slam because it is the tenth anniversary of the attack on the Twin Towers. It's believed that by winning she will prove her red-blooded American patriotism and will once and for all become beloved by the tennis world (think Arthur Ashe[11] after his death). All the bad calls, the boos, the criticisms that she has made ugly the game of tennis—through her looks as well as her behavior—that entire cluster of betrayals will be wiped clean with this win.

20   One imagines her wanting to say what her sister would say a year later after being diagnosed with Sjögren's syndrome[12] and losing her match to shouts of "Let's go, Venus!" in Arthur Ashe Stadium: "I know this is not proper tennis etiquette, but this is the first time I've ever played here that the crowd has been behind me like that. Today I felt American, you know, for the first time at the US Open. So I've waited my whole career to have this moment and here it is."

It is all too exhausting and Serena's exhaustion shows in her playing: she is losing, a set and a game down. Yes, and finally she hits a great shot, a big forehand, and before the ball is safely past Sam Stosur's hitting zone, Serena yells, "Come on!" thinking she has hit an irretrievable winner. The umpire, Eva Asderaki, rules correctly that Serena, by shouting, interfered with Stosur's concentration. Subsequently, a ball that Stosur seemingly would not have been able to return becomes Stosur's point. Serena's reply is to ask the umpire if she is trying to screw her again. She remembers the umpire doing this to her before. As a viewer, you too, along with John McEnroe, begin to wonder if this is the same umpire from 2004 or 2009. It isn't—in 2004 it was Mariana Alves and in 2009 it was Sharon Wright; however, the use of the word "again" by Serena returns her viewers to other times calling her body out.

Again Serena's frustrations, her disappointments, exist within a system you understand not to try to understand in any fair-minded way because to do so is to understand the erasure of the self as systemic, as ordinary. For Serena, the daily diminishment is a low flame, a constant drip. Every look, every comment, every bad call blossoms out of history, through her, onto you. To understand is to see Serena as hemmed in as any other black body thrown against our American background. "Aren't you the one that screwed me over last time here?" she asks umpire Asderaki. "Yeah, you are. Don't look at me. Really, don't even look at me. Don't look my way. Don't look my way," she repeats, because it is that simple.

Yes, and who can turn away? Serena is not running out of breath. Despite all her understanding, she continues to serve up aces while smashing rackets and fraying hems. In the 2012 Olympics she brought home two of the three

11. Black professional tennis player (1943–1993) who became a public-health advocate after contracting HIV. He was awarded the Presidential Medal of Freedom shortly after his death.

12. Autoimmune disorder.

gold medals the Americans would win in tennis. After her three-second cele-
bratory dance on center court at the All England Club,[13] the American media
reported, "And there was Serena . . . Crip-Walking[14] all over the most lily-white
place in the world. . . . You couldn't help but shake your head. . . . What Serena did was akin to cracking a tasteless, X-rated joke inside a church. . . . What
she did was immature and classless."

Before making the video *How to Be a Successful Black Artist*, Hennessy
Youngman uploaded to *YouTube*, *How to Be a Successful Artist*. While putting
forward the argument that one needs to be white to be truly successful, he adds,
in an aside, that this might not work for blacks because if "a nigger paints a
flower it becomes a slavery flower, flower de *Amistad*,"[15] thereby intimating that
any relationship between the white viewer and the black artist immediately
becomes one between white persons and black property, which was the legal
state of things once upon a time, as Patricia Williams[16] has pointed out in *The
Alchemy of Race and Rights*: "The cold game of equality staring makes me feel
like a thin sheet of glass. . . . I could force my presence, the real me contained
in those eyes, upon them, but I would be smashed in the process."

Interviewed by the Brit Piers Morgan after her 2012 Olympic victory, Ser-   25
ena is informed by Morgan that he was planning on calling her victory dance
"the Serena Shuffle"; however, he has learned from the American press that it
is a Crip Walk, a gangster dance. Serena responds incredulously by asking if
she looks like a gangster to him. Yes, he answers. All in a day's fun, perhaps,
and in spite and despite it all, Serena Williams blossoms again into Serena Williams. When asked if she is confident she can win her upcoming matches, her
answer remains, "At the end of the day, I am very happy with me and I'm very
happy with my results."

Serena would go on to win every match she played between the US Open
and the year-end 2012 championship tournament, and because tennis is a
game of adjustments, she would do this without any reaction to a number of
questionable calls. More than one commentator would remark on her ability to
hold it together during these matches. She is a woman in love, one suggests.
She has grown up, another decides, as if responding to the injustice of racism
is childish and her previous demonstration of emotion was free-floating and
detached from any external actions by others. Some others theorize she is
developing the admirable "calm and measured logic" of an Arthur Ashe, who
the sportswriter Bruce Jenkins felt was "dignified" and "courageous" in his ability to confront injustice without making a scene. Jenkins, perhaps inspired by

13. Located in London, home of the Wimbledon Championships, a Grand Slam
tournament.

14. Dance style originally associated with the Crips, a predominantly Black gang based
in southern California.

15. American ship that transported African people captured to be enslaved. Those
people mutinied on July 2, 1839.

16. American legal scholar (b. 1951) known for her writings on race and the law.

Serena's new comportment, felt moved to argue that her continued boycott of Indian Wells[17] in 2013, where she felt traumatized by the aggression of racist slurs hurled at her in 2001, was lacking in "dignity" and "integrity" and demonstrated "only stubbornness and a grudge." (Serena lifted her boycott in 2015, and Venus lifted hers in 2016.)

Watching this newly contained Serena, you begin to wonder if she finally has given up wanting better from her peers or if she too has come across Hennessy's *Art Thoughtz* and is channeling his assertion that the less that is communicated the better. Be ambiguous. This type of ambiguity could also be diagnosed as dissociation and would support Serena's claim that she has had to split herself off from herself and create different personae.

Now that there is no calling out of injustice, no yelling, no cursing, no finger wagging or head shaking, the media decides to take up the mantle when on December 12, 2012, two weeks after Serena is named WTA Player of the Year, the Dane Caroline Wozniacki, a former number-one player, imitates Serena by stuffing towels in her top and shorts, all in good fun, at an exhibition match. Racist? CNN wants to know if outrage is the proper response.

It's then that Hennessy's suggestions about "how to be a successful artist" return to you: be ambiguous, be white. Wozniacki, it becomes clear, has finally enacted what was desired by many of Serena's detractors, consciously or unconsciously, the moment the Compton[18] girl first stepped on court. Wozniacki (though there are a number of ways to interpret her actions—playful mocking of a peer, imitation of the mimicking antics of the tennis player known as the joker, Novak Djokovic) finally gives the people what they have wanted all along by embodying Serena's attributes while leaving Serena's "angry nigger exterior" behind. At last, in this real, and unreal, moment, we have Wozniacki's image of smiling blond goodness posing as the best female tennis player of all time.

MLA CITATION

Rankine, Claudia. "From *Citizen*." *The Norton Reader: An Anthology of Nonfiction*, edited by Melissa A. Goldthwaite et al., 16th ed., W. W. Norton, 2024, pp. 290–96.

QUESTIONS

1. Claudia Rankine asks, "What does a victorious or defeated black woman's body in a historically white space look like?" (paragraph 7). Her answer is Serena (and Venus) Williams. How, according to Rankine, has Serena Williams's race affected the way she has been treated as a professional athlete in a traditionally "white" sport?

2. Although Serena Williams is Rankine's main subject, she frames her essay by beginning and ending with the *YouTube* persona Hennessy Youngman, whose videos

---

17. Held in Indian Wells, California, a Premier Mandatory tournament on the women's professional tennis tour from 2009 to 2020, now a WTA 1000 tournament.

18. Serena Williams's birthplace, a city south of Los Angeles, California.

"are meant to expose expectations for blackness as well as to underscore the difficulty inherent in any attempt by black artists to metabolize real rage" (paragraph 2). How is this framing important to Rankine's discussion of Williams? How would the essay read differently if it began at paragraph 6 (as does a version excerpted in the online magazine *Slate*)?

3. Throughout her essay, Rankine deliberately and prominently uses the second-person pronouns "you" and "yours." What is the effect of this choice?

4. Write an essay about a time you were treated unfairly. What was the situation? How did you react? If you could go back and do things differently, would you? If so, how? If not, why not?

5. Many others in addition to Rankine have written about Serena Williams. Rankine herself has written about Williams elsewhere. Find some of these other articles and essays, comparing and contrasting one or more of them with Rankine's. If there are images included, consider those, too.

GARNETTE CADOGAN
Black and Blue

> "My only sin is my skin. What did I do, to be so black and blue?"
> —FATS WALLER, "(What Did I Do to Be So) Black and Blue?"

> "Manhattan's streets I saunter'd, pondering."
> —WALT WHITMAN, "Manhattan's Streets I Saunter'd, Pondering"

MY LOVE FOR WALKING started in childhood, out of necessity. No thanks to a stepfather with heavy hands, I found every reason to stay away from home and was usually out—at some friend's house or at a street party where no minor should be—until it was too late to get public transportation. So I walked.

The streets of Kingston, Jamaica, in the 1980s were often terrifying—you could, for instance, get killed if a political henchman thought you came from the wrong neighborhood, or even if you wore the wrong color. Wearing orange showed affiliation with one political party and green with the other, and if you were neutral or traveling far from home you chose your colors well. The wrong color in the wrong neighborhood could mean your last day. No wonder, then, that my friends and the rare nocturnal passerby declared me crazy for my long late-night treks that traversed warring political zones. (And sometimes I did pretend to be crazy, shouting non sequiturs when I passed through especially

First published in Freeman's *under the title "Walking While Black" (2015) and included in the essay collection* The Fire This Time: A New Generation Speaks about Race *(2016), edited by Jesmyn Ward.*

dangerous spots, such as the place where thieves hid on the banks of a storm drain. Predators would ignore or laugh at the kid in his school uniform speaking nonsense.)

I made friends with strangers and went from being a very shy and awkward kid to being an extroverted, awkward one. The beggar, the vendor, the poor laborer—those were experienced wanderers, and they became my nighttime instructors; they knew the streets and delivered lessons on how to navigate and enjoy them. I imagined myself as a Jamaican Tom Sawyer,[1] one moment sauntering down the streets to pick low-hanging mangoes that I could reach from the sidewalk, another moment hanging outside a street party with battling sound systems, each armed with speakers piled to create skyscrapers of heavy bass. These streets weren't frightening. They were full of adventure when they weren't serene. There I'd join forces with a band of merry walkers, who'd miss the last bus by mere minutes, our feet still moving as we put out our thumbs to hitchhike to spots nearer home, making jokes as vehicle after vehicle raced past us. Or I'd get lost in Mittyesque[2] moments, my young mind imagining alternate futures. The streets had their own safety: Unlike at home, there I could be myself without fear of bodily harm. Walking became so regular and familiar that the way home became home.

The streets had their rules, and I loved the challenge of trying to master them. I learned how to be alert to surrounding dangers and nearby delights, and prided myself on recognizing telling details that my peers missed. Kingston was a map of complex, and often bizarre, cultural and political and social activity, and I appointed myself its nighttime cartographer. I'd know how to navigate away from a predatory pace, and to speed up to chat when the cadence of a gait announced friendliness. It was almost always men I saw. A lone woman walking in the middle of the night was as common a sight as Sasquatch;[3] moonlight pedestrianism was too dangerous for her. Sometimes at night as I made my way down from hills above Kingston, I'd have the impression that the city was set on "pause" or in extreme slow motion, as though as I descended I was cutting across Jamaica's deep social divisions. I'd make my way briskly past the mansions in the hills overlooking the city, now transformed into a carpet of dotted lights under a curtain of stars, saunter by middle-class subdivisions hidden behind high walls crowned with barbed wire, and zigzagged through neighborhoods of zinc and wooden shacks crammed together and leaning like a tight-knit group of limbo dancers. With my descent came an increase in the vibrancy of street life—except when it didn't; some poor neighborhoods had both the violent gunfights and the eerily deserted streets of the cinematic Wild West. I knew well enough to avoid those even at high noon.

1. A character in several novels by Mark Twain (1835–1910) who is an adolescent boy characterized by his boisterousness and fertile imagination.
2. Walter Mitty, a character from "The Secret Life of Walter Mitty" (1939) by James Thurber, is a timid man given to heroic fantasies and daydreams.
3. A mythical ape-like creature, the subject of repeated "sightings" in North America.

I'd begun hoofing it after dark when I was ten years old. By thirteen I was   5
rarely home before midnight, and some nights found me racing against dawn.
My mother would often complain, "Mek yuh love street suh? Yuh born a hospital; yuh neva born a street." ("Why do you love the streets so much? You were
born in a hospital, not in the streets.")

I left Jamaica in 1996 to attend college in New Orleans, a city I'd heard called
"the northernmost Caribbean city." I wanted to discover—on foot, of course—
what was Caribbean and what was American about it. Stately mansions on oak-
lined streets with streetcars clanging by, and brightly colored houses that made
entire blocks look festive; people in resplendent costumes dancing to funky
brass bands in the middle of the street; cuisine—and aromas—that mashed up
culinary traditions from Africa, Europe, Asia, and the American South; and a
juxtaposition of worlds old and new, odd and familiar: Who wouldn't want to
explore this?

On my first day in the city, I went walking for a few hours to get a feel for
the place and to buy supplies to transform my dormitory room from a prison
bunker into a welcoming space. When some university staff members found
out what I'd been up to, they warned me to restrict my walking to the places
recommended as safe to tourists and the parents of freshmen. They trotted out
statistics about New Orleans' crime rate. But Kingston's crime rate dwarfed
those numbers, and I decided to ignore these well-meant cautions. A city was
waiting to be discovered, and I wouldn't let inconvenient facts get in the way.
These American criminals are nothing on Kingston's, I thought. They're no real
threat to me.

What no one had told me was that I was the one who would be considered
a threat.

Within days I noticed that many people on the street seemed apprehensive of me: Some gave me a circumspect glance as they approached, and then
crossed the street; others, ahead, would glance behind, register my presence,
and then speed up; older white women clutched their bags; young white men
nervously greeted me, as if exchanging a salutation for their safety: "What's up,
bro?" On one occasion, less than a month after my arrival, I tried to help a man
whose wheelchair was stuck in the middle of a crosswalk; he threatened to shoot
me in the face, then asked a white pedestrian for help.

I wasn't prepared for any of this. I had come from a majority-black country   10
in which no one was wary of me because of my skin color. Now I wasn't sure who
was afraid of me. I was especially unprepared for the cops. They regularly stopped
and bullied me, asking questions that took my guilt for granted. I'd never received
what many of my African-American friends call "The Talk": No parents had told
me how to behave when I was stopped by the police, how to be as polite and cooperative as possible, no matter what they said or did to me. So I had to cobble
together my own rules of engagement. Thicken my Jamaican accent. Quickly
mention my college. "Accidentally" pull out my college identification card when
asked for my driver's license.

My survival tactics began well before I left my dorm. I got out of the shower with the police in my head, assembling a cop-proof wardrobe. Light colored oxford shirt. V-neck sweater. Khaki pants. Chukkas. Sweatshirt or T-shirt with my university insignia. When I walked I regularly had my identity challenged, but I also found ways to assert it. (So I'd dress Ivy League style, but would, later on, add my Jamaican pedigree by wearing Clarks Desert Boots, the footwear of choice of Jamaican street culture.) Yet the all-American sartorial choice of white T-shirt and jeans, which many police officers see as the uniform of black troublemakers, was off-limits to me—at least, if I wanted to have the freedom of movement I desired.

In this city of exuberant streets, walking became a complex and often oppressive negotiation. I would see a white woman walking towards me at night and cross the street to reassure her that she was safe. I would forget something at home but not immediately turn around if someone was behind me, because I discovered that a sudden backtrack could cause alarm. (I had a cardinal rule: Keep a wide perimeter from people who might consider me a danger. If not, danger might visit me.) New Orleans suddenly felt more dangerous than Jamaica. The sidewalk was a minefield, and every hesitation and self-censored compensation reduced my dignity. Despite my best efforts, the streets never felt comfortably safe. Even a simple salutation was suspect.

One night, returning to the house that, eight years after my arrival, I thought I'd earned the right to call my home, I waved to a cop driving by. Moments later, I was against his car in handcuffs. When I later asked him— sheepishly, of course; any other way would have asked for bruises—why he had detained me, he said my greeting had aroused his suspicion. "No one waves to the police," he explained. When I told friends of his response, it was my behavior, not his, that they saw as absurd. "Now why would you do a dumb thing like that?" said one. "You know better than to make nice with police."

A few days after I left on a visit to Kingston, Hurricane Katrina[4] slashed and pummeled New Orleans. I'd gone not because of the storm but because my adoptive grandmother, Pearl, was dying of cancer. I hadn't wandered those streets in eight years, since my last visit, and I returned to them now mostly at night, the time I found best for thinking, praying, crying. I walked to feel less alienated—from myself, struggling with the pain of seeing my grandmother terminally ill; from my home in New Orleans, underwater and seemingly abandoned; from my home country, which now, precisely because of its childhood familiarity, felt foreign to me. I was surprised by how familiar those streets felt. Here was the corner where the fragrance of jerk chicken greeted me, along with the warm tenor and peace-and-love message of Half Pint's[5] "Greetings," broadcast from a small but powerful speaker to at least a half-mile radius. It was as if I had walked into 1986, down to the soundtrack. And there was the wall of the neighborhood shop, adorned with the Rastafarian colors red, gold, and green

4. Category 5 hurricane that devasted New Orleans in 2005.
5. Jamaican singer (b. 1961), born Lindon Andrew Roberts.

along with images of local and international heroes Bob Marley, Marcus Garvey, and Haile Selassie.[6] The crew of boys leaning against it and joshing each other were recognizable; different faces, similar stories. I was astonished at how safe the streets felt to me, once again one black body among many, no longer having to anticipate the many ways my presence might instill fear and how to offer some reassuring body language. Passing police cars were once again merely passing police cars. Jamaican police could be pretty brutal, but they didn't notice me the way American police did. I could be invisible in Jamaica in a way I can't be invisible in the United States.

Walking had returned to me a greater set of possibilities. And why walk, if   15
not to create a new set of possibilities? Following serendipity, I added new routes to the mental maps I had made from constant walking in that city from childhood to young adulthood, traced variations on the old pathways. Serendipity, a mentor once told me, is a secular way of speaking of grace; it's unearned favor. Seen theologically, then, walking is an act of faith. Walking is, after all, interrupted falling. We see, we listen, we speak, and we trust that each step we take won't be our last, but will lead us into a richer understanding of the self and the world.

In Jamaica, I felt once again as if the only identity that mattered was my own, not the constricted one that others had constructed for me. I strolled into my better self. I said, along with Kierkegaard,[7] "I have walked myself into my best thoughts."

When I tried to return to New Orleans from Jamaica a month later, there were no flights. I thought about flying to Texas so I could make my way back to my neighborhood as soon as it opened for reoccupancy, but my adoptive aunt, Maxine, who hated the idea of me returning to a hurricane zone before the end of hurricane season, persuaded me to come to stay in New York City instead. (To strengthen her case she sent me an article about Texans who were buying up guns because they were afraid of the influx of black people from New Orleans.)

This wasn't a hard sell: I wanted to be in a place where I could travel by foot and, more crucially, continue to reap the solace of walking at night. And I was eager to follow in the steps of the essayists, poets, and novelists who'd wandered that great city before me—Walt Whitman, Herman Melville, Alfred Kazin, Elizabeth Hardwick. I had visited the city before, but each trip had felt like a tour in a sports car. I welcomed the chance to stroll. I wanted to walk alongside Whitman's ghost and "descend to the pavements, merge with the crowd, and gaze with them." So I left Kingston, the popular Jamaican farewell echoing in my mind: "Walk good!" *Be safe on your journey*, in other words, *and all the best in your endeavors.*

---

6. Rastafari, religion and political movement arising in Jamaica in the 1930s; Marley (1945–1981), Jamaican musician and Rastafarian regarded as a national hero; Garvey (1887–1940), Jamaican-born leader of the Pan-African movement, which asserted the unity of all peoples of African descent; Selassie (1892–1975), emperor of Ethiopia revered as a prophet or the messiah in Rastafari.

7. Søren Kierkegaard (1813–1855), Danish philosopher and theologian.

I arrived in New York City, ready to lose myself in Whitman's "Manhattan crowds, with their turbulent musical chorus!"[8] I marveled at what Jane Jacobs praised as "the ballet of the good city sidewalk"[9] in her old neighborhood, the West Village. I walked up past midtown skyscrapers, releasing their energy as lively people onto the streets, and on into the Upper West Side, with its regal Beaux Arts[10] apartment buildings, stylish residents, and buzzing streets. Onward into Washington Heights, the sidewalks spilled over with an ebullient mix of young and old Jewish and Dominican-American residents, past leafy Inwood, with parks whose grades rose to reveal beautiful views of the Hudson River, up to my home in Kingsbridge in the Bronx, with its rows of brick bungalows and apartment buildings nearby Broadway's bustling sidewalks and the peaceful expanse of Van Cortlandt Park. I went to Jackson Heights in Queens to take in people socializing around garden courtyards in Urdu, Korean, Spanish, Russian, and Hindi. And when I wanted a taste of home, I headed to Brooklyn, in Crown Heights, for Jamaican food and music and humor mixed in with the flavor of New York City. The city was my playground.

20   I explored the city with friends and then with a woman I'd begun dating. She walked around endlessly with me, taking in New York City's many pleasures. Coffee shops open until predawn; verdant parks with nooks aplenty; food and music from across the globe; quirky neighborhoods with quirkier residents. My impressions of the city took shape during my walks with her.

As with the relationship, those first few months of urban exploration were all romance. The city was beguiling, exhilarating, vibrant. But it wasn't long before reality reminded me I wasn't invulnerable, especially when I walked alone.

One night in the East Village, I was running to dinner when a white man in front of me turned and punched me in the chest with such force that I thought my ribs had braided around my spine. I assumed he was drunk or had mistaken me for an old enemy, but found out soon enough that he'd merely assumed I was a criminal because of my race. When he discovered I wasn't what he imagined, he went on to tell me that his assault was my own fault for running up behind him. I blew off this incident as an aberration, but the mutual distrust between me and the police was impossible to ignore. It felt elemental. They'd enter a subway platform; I'd notice them. (And I'd notice all the other black men registering their presence as well, while just about everyone else remained oblivious to them.) They'd glare. I'd get nervous and glance. They'd observe me steadily. I'd get uneasy. I'd observe them back, worrying that I looked suspicious. Their suspicions would increase. We'd continue the silent, uneasy dialogue until the subway arrived and separated us at last.

I returned to the old rules I'd set for myself in New Orleans, with elaboration. No running, especially at night; no sudden movements; no hoodies; no objects—especially shiny ones—in hand; no waiting for friends on street cor-

8. From American poet Walt Whitman's poem "Give Me the Splendid Silent Sun" (1867).
9. From writer and activist Jacobs's book *The Death and Life of Great American Cities* (1961).
10. Style of architecture influential in the late nineteenth century.

ners, lest I be mistaken for a drug dealer; no standing near a corner on the cell phone (same reason). As comfort set in, inevitably I began to break some of those rules, until a night encounter sent me zealously back to them, me having learned that anything less than vigilance was carelessness.

After a sumptuous Italian dinner and drinks with friends, I was jogging to the subway at Columbus Circle—I was running late to meet another set of friends at a concert downtown. I heard someone shouting and I looked up to see a police officer approaching with his gun trained on me. "Against the car!" In no time, half a dozen cops were upon me, chucking me against the car and tightly handcuffing me. "Why were you running?" "Where are you going?" "Where are you coming from?" "I said, why were you running?!" Since I couldn't answer everyone at once, I decided to respond first to the one who looked most likely to hit me. I was surrounded by a swarm and tried to focus on just one without inadvertently aggravating the others.

It didn't work. As I answered that one, the others got frustrated that I wasn't answering them fast enough and barked at me. One of them, digging through my already-emptied pockets, asked if I had any weapons, the question more an accusation. Another badgered me about where I was coming from, as if on the fifteenth round I'd decide to tell him the truth he imagined. Though I kept saying—calmly, of course, which meant trying to manage a tone that ignored my racing heart and their spittle-filled shouts in my face—that I had just left friends two blocks down the road, who were all still there and could vouch for me, to meet other friends whose text messages on my phone could verify that, yes, sir, yes, officer, of course, officer, it made no difference.

For a black man, to assert your dignity before the police was to risk assault. In fact, the dignity of black people meant less to them, which was why I always felt safer being stopped in front of white witnesses than black witnesses. The cops had less regard for the witness and entreaties of black onlookers, whereas the concern of white witnesses usually registered on them. A black witness asking a question or politely raising an objection could quickly become a fellow detainee. Deference to the police, then, was sine qua non for a safe encounter.

The cops ignored my explanations and my suggestions and continued to snarl at me. All except one of them, a captain. He put his hand on my back, and said to no one in particular, "If he was running for a long time he would have been sweating." He then instructed that the cuffs be removed. He told me that a black man had stabbed someone earlier two or three blocks away and they were searching for him. I noted that I had no blood on me and had told his fellow officers where I'd been and how to check my alibi—unaware that it was even an alibi, as no one had told me why I was being held, and of course, I hadn't dared ask. From what I'd seen, anything beyond passivity would be interpreted as aggression.

The police captain said I could go. None of the cops who detained me thought an apology was necessary. Like the thug who punched me in the East Village, they seemed to think it was my own fault for running.

Humiliated, I tried not to make eye contact with the onlookers on the sidewalk, and I was reluctant to pass them to be on my way. The captain, maybe noticing my shame, offered to give me a ride to the subway station. When he dropped me off and I thanked him for his help, he said, "It's because you were polite that we let you go. If you were acting up it would have been different." I nodded and said nothing.

30   I realized that what I least liked about walking in New York City wasn't merely having to learn new rules of navigation and socialization—every city has its own. It was the arbitrariness of the circumstances that required them, an arbitrariness that made me feel like a child again, that infantilized me. When we first learn to walk, the world around us threatens to crash into us. Every step is risky. We train ourselves to walk without crashing by being attentive to our movements, and extra-attentive to the world around us. As adults we walk without thinking, really. But as a black adult I am often returned to that moment in childhood when I'm just learning to walk. I am once again on high alert, vigilant.

    Some days, when I am fed up with being considered a trouble-maker upon sight, I joke that the last time a cop was happy to see a black male walking was when that male was a baby taking his first steps. On many walks, I ask white friends to accompany me, just to avoid being treated like a threat. Walks in New York City, that is; in New Orleans, a white woman in my company some-times attracted more hostility. (And it is not lost on me that my woman friends are those who best understand my plight; they have developed their own vigi-lance in an environment where they are constantly treated as targets of sexual attention.) Much of my walking is as my friend Rebecca once described it: A pantomime undertaken to avoid the choreography of criminality.

Walking while black[11] restricts the experience of walking, renders inaccessible the classic Romantic[12] experience of walking alone. It forces me to be in con-stant relationship with others, unable to join the New York flaneurs[13] I had read about and hoped to join. Instead of meandering aimlessly in the footsteps of Whitman, Melville, Kazin, and Vivian Gornick,[14] more often, I felt that I was tiptoeing in Baldwin's—the Baldwin who wrote, way back in 1960, "Rare, indeed, is the Harlem citizen, from the most circumspect church member to the most shiftless adolescent, who does not have a long tale to tell of police incompetence, injustice, or brutality. I myself have witnessed and endured it more than once."[15]

    Walking as a black man has made me feel simultaneously more removed from the city, in my awareness that I am perceived as suspect, and more closely connected to it, in the full attentiveness demanded by my vigilance. It has made

11. A play on "driving while Black," which refers to the racial profiling of drivers by police.

12. Nineteenth-century literary, artistic, musical, and intellectual movement empha-sizing emotion, individual subjectivity, and the imagination.

13. From the French *flâneur*, meaning "idler" or "stroller."

14. Authors and essayists Herman Melville (1819–1891), Alfred Kazin (1915–1998), and Gornick (b. 1935) have all written about walking in New York City.

15. From James Baldwin's essay "Fifth Avenue, Uptown" (1960).

me walk more purposefully in the city, becoming part of its flow, rather than observing, standing apart.

But it also means that I'm still trying to arrive in a city that isn't quite mine. One definition of home is that it's somewhere we can most be ourselves. And when are we more ourselves but when walking, that natural state in which we repeat one of the first actions we learned? Walking—the simple, monotonous act of placing one foot before the other to prevent falling—turns out not to be so simple if you're black. Walking alone has been anything but monotonous for me; monotony is a luxury.

A foot leaves, a foot lands, and our longing gives it momentum from rest   35
to rest. We long to look, to think, to talk, to get away. But more than anything else, we long to be free. We want the freedom and pleasure of walking without fear—without others' fear—wherever we choose. I've lived in New York City for almost a decade and have not stopped walking its fascinating streets. And I have not stopped longing to find the solace that I found as a kid on the streets of Kingston. Much as coming to know New York City's streets has made it closer to home to me, the city also withholds itself from me via those very streets. I walk them, alternately invisible and too prominent. So I walk caught between memory and forgetting, between memory and forgiveness.

MLA CITATION

Cadogan, Garnette. "Black and Blue." *The Norton Reader: An Anthology of Nonfiction*, edited by Melissa A. Goldthwaite et al., 16th ed., W. W. Norton, 2024, pp. 297–305.

QUESTIONS

1. In his essay, Garnette Cadogan recounts and reflects on his encounters with the police as a Black man walking in three cities: Kingston, then New Orleans, then New York. How do the police perceive Black men? How does Cadogan perceive himself? What do Cadogan's experiences in these cities have in common? How do they differ?

2. This essay was originally titled "Walking While Black" but was later retitled "Black and Blue." How does this change shift the focus of the essay?

3. Writing of his early excursions in Kingston, Cadogan portrays himself as an astute observer and analyst: "I learned how to be alert to surrounding dangers and nearby delights, and prided myself on recognizing telling details that my peers missed" (paragraph 4). What does this characterization of his boyhood imply about his purpose as an author?

4. As you read and annotate this essay, note the steps Cadogan takes to mitigate the perception that he is a threat. What are some of the things he tries? Why? How successful are his efforts? Note, too, the ways he feels threatened. What is the relationship between fear and freedom? When walking in public, are you more likely to feel fear or to be feared? Why?

JENNIFER L. EBERHARDT
Seeing Each Other

I SPENT THE FIRST TWELVE YEARS of my life in Cleveland, Ohio, in an all-black world. My family, my neighbors, my teachers, my classmates, my friends—every person I had any meaningful contact with until that point was black. So when my parents announced we were moving to a nearly all-white suburb called Beachwood, I was excited about living in a bigger house but worried about how I would be greeted by my new middle school classmates.

I worried they would make fun of me—my brown skin, my wiry hair, my large dark eyes. I worried about my way of speaking—my cadence, my word choice, my voice.

Yet when I arrived that fall, white students went out of their way to welcome me. They introduced themselves. They invited me to eat with them at lunch. They showed me around the school and loaded me up with details on the dizzying array of activities now open to me. It was what my parents had always dreamed of. I could sing in the choir or act in a play. I could study sign language or learn gymnastics. I could try out for the volleyball team or run for a seat on the student council.

My classmates seemed genuinely interested in helping me transition to this new place. I was grateful, and yet I struggled to make new friends. I'd call students by the wrong name, walk past a classmate in the hall without speaking, fail to remember the girl I'd shared a lunch table with in the cafeteria the day before. They didn't seem to hold it against me. They understood that I was meeting people every day and it was a lot to take in. But I knew there was something more going on. Every day I was confronted with a mass of white faces that I could not distinguish from one another. I didn't know how to do it or even where to start.

5   I'd had no practice recognizing white faces. They all looked alike to me. I could describe in detail the face of the black woman I happened to pass in a shopping mall. But I could not pick out from a crowd the white girl who sat next to me in English class every day.

I found myself constantly seduced by the easiest way to sort people. I would hold on to the fact that the girl in the red sweater said this and the girl in the gray sweatshirt said that. This helped me to track a conversation in the moment, but I would be at a loss again the very next day.

I tried training myself to pay attention to features that I'd never needed to notice in my black neighborhood—eye color, various shades of blond hair, freckles. I tried remembering the most distinctive feature about each person I encountered. But all the faces would ultimately blend together again in my mind.

Published as the first chapter of Jennifer L. Eberhardt's book Biased: Uncovering the Hidden Prejudice That Shapes What We See, Think, and Do *(2019). Eberhardt is a social psychologist and Stanford professor who studies racial perception, racial bias, and race and crime.*

As time went on, I worried that my new friends would begin to drift away. Who would want to be friends with a girl who had to be reminded to whom she was talking from one day to the next?

Stripped of this most basic skill, I became a different person in my new neighborhood—awkward, uncertain, hesitant, withdrawn. I was afraid of making a mistake, of embarrassing myself or hurting the feelings of people I'd grown to like.

By springtime, whenever I saw girls whispering among themselves, I'd wonder whether their patience was finally wearing thin. *Are they talking about me?* I'd sidle over to try to join the conversation, but they'd fall silent whenever I showed up.

I was relieved when one of the popular girls invited me to lunch at a restaurant one weekend. When I walked in, she was sitting at a table with a group of girls I didn't recognize, until they all yelled out, "Happy birthday!" I scanned their faces and realized that these were the classmates I'd seen whispering in the hall, planning a surprise party for the new girl who still hadn't managed to get their names right.

They'd brought gifts that reflected touchstones in their lives, including albums by musicians I'd never heard of: Bruce Springsteen, Billy Joel. I was moved beyond words by the gesture; no one had ever planned a surprise party for me. But when we finished the cake, hugged good-bye, and parted ways, I still was not confident I could tell those faces apart.

The irony of that school year always troubled me. I worried about being ostracized because I wasn't one of them. But I was the one stumbling over our racial differences. They wanted to connect, and so did I. But I had suddenly acquired a deficiency that they were not aware of and that I did not understand.

Decades later, I would realize that I was not alone.

THE SCIENCE OF RECOGNITION

For nearly fifty years, scientists have been documenting the fact that people are much better at recognizing faces of their own race than faces of other races—a finding dubbed the "other-race effect."

It's a universal phenomenon, and it shows up in different racial groups across the United States and in countries all over the world. It appears early and intensifies over time. By the time babies are three months old, their brains react more strongly to faces of their own race than to faces of people unlike them. That race-selective response only grows stronger as children move into adolescence, which suggests it is driven, in part, by the circumstances of our lives.

We learn what's important—the faces we see every day—and over time our brain builds a preference for those faces, at the expense of skills needed to recognize others less relevant. That experience-driven evolution of face perception skills remodels our brains so they can operate more efficiently.

Scientists see the other-race effect as a sign that our perceptive powers are shaped by what we see. That cringe-worthy expression *"They all look alike"* has long been considered the province of the bigot. But it is actually a function of biology and exposure. Our brains are better at processing faces that evoke a sense of familiarity.

I'd struggled to recognize my white classmates' faces because black faces were all I'd been routinely exposed to in the twelve years before I moved to the suburbs. My adolescent brain took some time to catch up to the new world I was navigating, but I would soon develop new skills to function in that world.

20   Race is not a pure dividing line. Children who are adopted by parents of a different race do not exhibit the classic other-race effect. For example, researchers in Belgium found that white children were better at recognizing white faces than Asian faces. But Chinese and Vietnamese children who'd been adopted by white families were equally good at recognizing white and Asian faces.

Age and familiarity with various age-groups can also be factors. In England, a study of primary school teachers found that they were better at recognizing the faces of random eight- to eleven-year-olds than were college students who spent most of their time around other college students. And scientists in Italy found that maternity-ward nurses were better at telling infants apart by looking at their faces than were people from other professions—a proficiency that helps to ensure "mix-ups don't happen in the nursery," the researchers suggest.

Our experiences in the world seep into our brain over time, and without our awareness they conspire to reshape the workings of our mind.

IMAGING RACE

I couldn't have known back in middle school that my own brain development played a part in my struggle to connect. But I was convinced that skin color had a role in the dislocation I felt. That's ultimately what drew me to the field of social psychology. It offered the perspective I needed to address a question fundamental to my own adolescent experience: *How does race shape who we are and how we experience the world?* That question is the starting point of bigger questions about identity, power, and privilege that have molded our country and roiled the world for centuries.

Today, I am a professor and a researcher at Stanford University, a campus nestled in Silicon Valley, the heart of the start-up economy and a magnet for bright, energetic young people eager to tap the rich vein of technology for scientific solutions to social problems. When I arrived at Stanford, I was enticed by the tools of neuroscience research and began exploring the ways that race might influence basic brain functioning.

25   The brain is not a hardwired machine. It's a malleable organ that responds to the environments we are placed in and the challenges we face. This view of the brain runs counter to what most of us learned in science class. In fact, the whole idea of neuroplasticity runs counter to what scientists believed to be true about the brain for centuries. Only fairly recent advances in neuroscience have allowed us to peek inside the brain and track its adaptation over time. Slowly, we're beginning to understand the many ways the brain can be altered by experience.

For example, in the last several decades, we have learned that when someone becomes blind, the occipital lobe, typically dedicated to processing visual stimuli, can dedicate itself instead to processing other types of stimuli, including sound and touch. When someone has a stroke, they might be able to learn to speak again, despite massive damage to specific areas of the temporal lobe that are dedicated to processing language. We don't know yet the extent of this neuroplasticity. And some of the most intriguing lessons come not only from studying damaged brains but also from watching people with normal brain function acquire unusual skills.

Research has shown that something as simple as driving a taxi can offer lessons in how basic practice and repetition can retrain our brains to function differently. In 2000, not long after I arrived at Stanford, a team led by Professor Eleanor Maguire published a paper that caused quite a stir in the neuroscience community. They'd scanned the brains of London cabdrivers in an effort to examine how the hippocampus—a horseshoe-shaped structure in the medial temporal lobe—might grow in response to demands placed upon it by the taxing experience of driving through the London city streets day in and day out.

Maguire's team found that the brains of taxicab drivers—who had by necessity learned the structural layout of more than twenty-five thousand London streets—showed significant differences in the hippocampus, the part of the brain that plays a critical role in spatial memory and navigation. The taxi drivers' navigational expertise was associated with increased gray matter. They had enlarged posterior hippocampal regions, in comparison with a control group of people who didn't drive cabs for a living. In fact, the longer the drivers had been on the job and the more experience they had, the larger their posterior hippocampus.

I found this all remarkable because it seemed to show not only how powerful our experiences must be to fundamentally change our brain but also how swiftly the transformation can take place. In the case of the taxi drivers, developing a deep structural knowledge of their environment forced a striking structural change in their brains. And that change happened not over hundreds of thousands of years but within a few years of an individual's life. Individual expertise, as it turns out, has its own neurobiological signature.

That revelation led me to pose another question, driven by both scientific curiosity and personal memories of my own adolescent lapse: *Because our experiences in the world are reflected in our brains, might our expertise in recognizing faces of our own race—and failing to recognize those of others—display its own neurobiological signature as well?*

Neuroscientists were initially skeptical about the prospect of race having an influence on something as basic, ancient, and important as how faces register in our brains. The act of perceiving faces is both critical and complicated, which may be why the task is distributed across multiple areas of the occipitotemporal region, stretching across two of four major lobes of the brain. The superior temporal sulcus—a trench-like structure in the temporal lobe that's vital to social competence—helps us to read the many different expressions that can suddenly emerge on someone's face, signaling us to approach, to smile, to share, to flee, or to quickly arm ourselves. A region known as the fusiform face area, buried deep near the base of the brain, helps us distinguish the familiar from the unfamiliar, friend from foe.

The fusiform face area, known as the FFA, is widely thought to be both primitive and fundamental to our survival as a species. Affiliation is a basic human need. Without the ability to track the identity of those around us, we are left alone, vulnerable, and exposed.

The FFA has been studied extensively, yet despite decades of research there had been little attention paid to whether race might influence FFA functioning. From the narrow perspective of brain science, the primary function of the FFA is to detect faces. Race, most scientists felt, should have nothing to do with that.

Against that backdrop, I began working with a team of Stanford neuroscientists who specialized in human memory to look further into the matter. Together, we recruited dozens of white and black volunteers and subjected them to functional magnetic resonance imaging (fMRI) scans that allowed us to track the blood flow changes in the brain that illustrate neural activity.

35   As is common, our study participants had giant coils wrapped around their heads to transmit the images. We slid them into a tube-like scanner (a giant magnet, actually) and showed them a series of faces of black and white strangers. We monitored the process from a control room nearby, taking whole-brain pictures as each face appeared before their eyes. The stronger their response to a face, the more oxygen flooded the targeted part of their brain and the brighter our measuring sensors shined.

By tracking the activation of the FFA over multiple displays of strangers' faces, we found that the FFA was responding more vigorously to faces that were the same race as the study participant. That finding held true for both the black and the white people we scanned. We also found that the more dramatic the FFA response to a specific face, the more likely the study participants were able to recognize that stranger's face when they were shown the photograph again later, outside the scanner.

Ours was the first neuroimaging study to demonstrate that there is a neural component to the same-race advantage in the face-recognition process. It offered support for the emerging notion that the brain tunes itself to our experiences as we move through life. And we learned that race can serve as a powerful interpretive lens in that tuning process. Race, as it turns out, could exert influence over one of the brain's most basic functions. The FFA, with its bright colors on our imaging scans, provided us with a clear picture of how in- and out-group distinctions—set in motion by our relationship to the world around us—are mapped onto the inner workings of our brains.

THE PURSE SNATCHERS

Call it scientific progress or streetwise knowledge. But what it took me decades to learn about the role of race in face recognition turned out to be common knowledge among an opportunistic band of young men on a crime spree in Oakland.

It was 2014 and I had just begun analyzing racial disparities in policing with the Oakland Police Department when the story made its rounds: Despite a substantial decline in crime across the city, the shopping district in Chinatown had registered an alarming rise in strong-arm robberies. Apparently, black teenage boys were roaming the streets, snatching the purses of middle-aged Asian women.

The police developed leads, made arrests, and even recovered some stolen property. But the cases fell apart before the suspects could be prosecuted, because even if a victim had seen the robber's face as he grabbed her purse and ran, none of the women could pick the culprits out of a police lineup.

"We would make stops on the suspect," recalled Captain LeRonne Armstrong from the police department. "Yet the victim could not ID. Absent the ID, you couldn't charge the case. This made it impossible to prosecute."

As the young men began to figure out that Asian women couldn't tell them apart, it turned into a license to steal, Armstrong explained to me years later, after some of the crimes were solved and the robbers who were bound for jail had confessed the details. "When we'd ask, 'Why'd you focus in on this particular woman?' they'd say to us very openly, 'The Asian people can't ID. They just can't tell brothers apart.' They'd tell us, 'Like, this is our dream. That's why we go.'"

There was a clear pattern to whom the teens targeted and where and how they struck. They focused on a neighborhood crowded with female, middle-aged Chinese shoppers. They approached from behind, grabbed the purses, and fled, so the victim didn't have much time to study their faces. And sure enough, Armstrong said, in nearly 80 percent of the cases tracked by Oakland police, the Asian victims could not identify the young men who robbed them. Black women, on the other hand, could identify black robbery suspects at a much higher rate, even after a mere glance.

The challenges of cross-racial identification are as well known to law enforcement officials as they are to scientists. Research and real-life experience have shown that the chance of false alarms—of identifying someone as the culprit who is not—goes way up when the suspect is of a different race from the victim. That's the practical fallout of the other-race effect.

Oakland investigators worked to minimize the possibility of misidentification. They followed scientific guidelines on how to construct and use lineups with textbook precision. They even tried offering the victims training, directing them "to focus on anything at all that was distinctive," Armstrong told me. *Was his skin dark or light? Did he have gold teeth? Was his hair in dreadlocks or braids?* "We needed them to move beyond the generic 'male black' description." But for the most part, the Asian women couldn't move beyond it. Even with all the training, they were still unable to distinguish one black teenager's face from another.

Ultimately, what did help put an end to the crime spree was technology. When cameras were placed outside the businesses that lined the busy streets of Chinatown, the risks of being caught suddenly shot up. The camera could capture what the women could not. The boys knew the jig was up.

Captain Armstrong's description of the situation led me to recall my own as a newcomer to Beachwood. I too tried the "remember what's distinctive" strategy. I failed and the Asian women failed, despite our strong desire to get it right. Yet the women's inability to remember those black male faces went beyond awkward moments and insecurities about conversations held in hushed tones. Their inability to remember those faces stymied the police and spread fear across the Chinatown community for months and months before the cameras were installed. These teenagers could rob them at will—even in broad daylight. They needed no mask. Their face was their mask.

MLA CITATION

Eberhardt, Jennifer L. "Seeing Each Other." *The Norton Reader: An Anthology of Nonfiction*, edited by Melissa A. Goldthwaite et al., 16th ed., W. W. Norton, 2024, pp. 306–12.

QUESTIONS

1. Jennifer L. Eberhardt's chapter explains the "other-race effect" for a general readership. What is this effect, and how does Eberhardt present it so that nonscientists can understand it? Mark the passages that support your answers.

2. Eberhardt introduces her chapter by recounting her own struggles as a Black child to identify her white classmates after transferring to a middle school. How does this anecdote complicate conventional assumptions about racial bias? Why might Eberhardt have chosen to open her chapter with it?

3. One of Eberhardt's research interests is the connection between race and crime, and in the final section of her chapter she presents an episode that touches on this theme, telling of "black teenage boys" (paragraph 39) who deliberately targeted Asian women for robberies because such women would struggle to identify them. Analyze Eberhardt's account of this episode and reflect on its significance. Why might she have chosen to end her chapter with it? What inferences can we draw (and not draw) from it? What are its practical implications for such issues as public safety, policing, or the administration of criminal justice? Discuss your answers with your classmates.

NANCY MAIRS
On Being a Cripple

> To escape is nothing. Not to escape is nothing.
> —LOUISE BOGAN

THE OTHER DAY I was thinking of writing an essay on being a cripple. I was thinking hard in one of the stalls of the women's room in my office building, as I was shoving my shirt into my jeans and tugging up my zipper. Preoccupied, I flushed, picked up my book bag, took my cane down from the hook, and unlatched the door. So many movements unbalanced me, and as I pulled the door open I fell over backward, landing fully clothed on the toilet seat with my

From Plaintext *(1986), Nancy Mairs's book of personal essays about life with multiple sclerosis.*

legs splayed in front of me: the old beetle-on-its-back routine. Saturday after-noon, the building deserted, I was free to laugh aloud as I wriggled back to my feet, my voice bouncing off the yellowish tiles from all directions. Had anyone been there with me, I'd have been still and faint and hot with chagrin. I decided that it was high time to write the essay.

First, the matter of semantics. I am a cripple. I choose this word to name me. I choose from among several possibilities, the most common of which are "handi-capped" and "disabled." I made the choice a number of years ago, without think-ing, unaware of my motives for doing so. Even now, I'm not sure what those motives are, but I recognize that they are complex and not entirely flattering. People—crippled or not—wince at the word "cripple," as they do not at "handi-capped" or "disabled." Perhaps I want them to wince. I want them to see me as a tough customer, one to whom the fates/gods/viruses have not been kind, but who can face the brutal truth of her existence squarely. As a cripple, I swagger.

But, to be fair to myself, a certain amount of honesty underlies my choice. "Cripple" seems to me a clean word, straightforward and precise. It has an hon-orable history, having made its first appearance in the Lindisfarne Gospel[1] in the tenth century. As a lover of words, I like the accuracy with which it describes my condition: I have lost the full use of my limbs. "Disabled," by contrast, sug-gests any incapacity, physical or mental. And I certainly don't like "handi-capped," which implies that I have deliberately been put at a disadvantage, by whom I can't imagine (my God is not a Handicapper General), in order to equal-ize chances in the great race of life. These words seem to me to be moving away from my condition, to be widening the gap between word and reality. Most remote is the recently coined euphemism "differently abled," which partakes of the same semantic hopefulness that transformed countries from "undevel-oped" to "underdeveloped," then to "less developed," and finally to "develop-ing" nations. People have continued to starve in those countries during the shift. Some realities do not obey the dictates of language.

Mine is one of them. Whatever you call me, I remain crippled. But I don't care what you call me, so long as it isn't "differently abled," which strikes me as pure verbal garbage designed, by its ability to describe anyone, to describe no one. I subscribe to George Orwell's thesis that "the slovenliness of our language makes it easier for us to have foolish thoughts."[2] And I refuse to participate in the degeneration of the language to the extent that I deny that I have lost any-thing in the course of this calamitous disease; I refuse to pretend that the only differences between you and me are the various ordinary ones that distinguish any one person from another. But call me "disabled" or "handicapped" if you like. I have long since grown accustomed to them; and if they are vague, at least they hint at the truth. Moreover, I use them myself. Society is no readier to accept crippledness than to accept death, war, sex, sweat, or wrinkles. I would

1. Illustrated manuscript of the four gospels of the New Testament (c. 700 CE) done by Irish monks. English commentaries were added in the tenth century.
2. Quotation from "Politics and the English Language" (1946) by Orwell (1903–1950), British essayist and novelist; see pp. 340–50.

never refer to another person as a cripple. It is the word I use to name only myself.

5   I haven't always been crippled, a fact for which I am soundly grateful. To be whole of limb is, I know from experience, infinitely more pleasant and useful than to be crippled; and if that knowledge leaves one open to bitterness at my loss, the physical soundness I once enjoyed (though I did not enjoy it half enough) is well worth the occasional stab of regret. Though never any good at sports, I was a normally active child and young adult. I climbed trees, played hopscotch, jumped rope, skated, swam, rode my bicycle, sailed. I despised team sports, spending some of the wretchedest afternoons of my life, sweaty and humiliated, behind a field-hockey stick and under a basketball hoop. I tramped alone for miles along the bridle paths that webbed the woods behind the house I grew up in. I swayed through countless dim hours in the arms of one man or another under the scattered shot of light from mirrored balls, and gyrated through countless more as Tab Hunter and Johnny Mathis[3] gave way to the Rolling Stones, Creedence Clearwater Revival, Cream. I walked down the aisle. I pushed baby carriages, changed tires in the rain, marched for peace.

When I was twenty-eight I started to trip and drop things. What at first seemed my natural clumsiness soon became too pronounced to shrug off. I consulted a neurologist, who told me that I had a brain tumor. A battery of tests, increasingly disagreeable, revealed no tumor. About a year and a half later I developed a blurred spot in one eye. I had, at last, the episodes "disseminated in space and time" requisite for a diagnosis: multiple sclerosis. I have never been sorry for the doctor's initial misdiagnosis, however. For almost a week, until the negative results of the tests were in, I thought that I was going to die right away. Every day for the past nearly ten years, then, has been a kind of gift. I accept all gifts.

Multiple sclerosis is a chronic degenerative disease of the central nervous system, in which the myelin that sheathes the nerves is somehow eaten away and scar tissue forms in its place, interrupting the nerves' signals. During its course, which is unpredictable and uncontrollable, one may lose vision, hearing, speech, the ability to walk, control of bladder and/or bowels, strength in any or all extremities, sensitivity to touch, vibration, and/or pain, potency, coordination of movements—the list of possibilities is lengthy and, yes, horrifying. One may also lose one's sense of humor. That's the easiest to lose and the hardest to survive without.

In the past ten years, I have sustained some of these losses. Characteristic of MS are sudden attacks, called exacerbations, followed by remissions, and these I have not had. Instead, my disease has been slowly progressive. My left leg is now so weak that I walk with the aid of a brace and a cane; and for distances I use an Amigo, a variation on the electric wheelchair that looks rather like an electrified kiddie car. I no longer have much use of my left hand. Now my right side is weakening as well. I still have the blurred spot in my right eye. Overall, though, I've been lucky so far. My world has, of necessity, been cir-

---

3. Hunter (1931–2018), American actor and singer popular in the 1960s; Mathis (b. 1935), American singer popular in the 1950s and 1960s and well known for his love ballads.

cumscribed by my losses, but the terrain left me has been ample enough for me to continue many of the activities that absorb me: writing, teaching, raising children and cats and plants and snakes, reading, speaking publicly about MS and depression, even playing bridge with people patient and honorable enough to let me scatter cards every which way without sneaking a peek.

Lest I begin to sound like Pollyanna, however, let me say that I don't like having MS. I hate it. My life holds realities—harsh ones, some of them—that no right-minded human being ought to accept without grumbling. One of them is fatigue. I know of no one with MS who does not complain of bone-weariness; in a disease that presents an astonishing variety of symptoms, fatigue seems to be a common factor. I wake up in the morning feeling the way most people do at the end of a bad day, and I take it from there. As a result, I spend a lot of time *in extremis*[4] and, impatient with limitation, I tend to ignore my fatigue until my body breaks down in some way and forces rest. Then I miss picnics, dinner parties, poetry readings, the brief visits of old friends from out of town. The offspring of a puritanical tradition of exceptional venerability, I cannot view these lapses without shame. My life often seems a series of small failures to do as I ought.

I lead, on the whole, an ordinary life, probably rather like the one I would have led had I not had MS. I am lucky that my predilections were already solitary, sedentary, and bookish—unlike the world-famous French cellist I have read about, or the young woman I talked with one long afternoon who wanted only to be a jockey. I had just begun graduate school when I found out something was wrong with me, and I have remained, interminably, a graduate student. Perhaps I would not have if I'd thought I had the stamina to return to a full-time job as a technical editor; but I've enjoyed my studies.

In addition to studying, I teach writing courses. I also teach medical students how to give neurological examinations. I pick up freelance editing jobs here and there. I have raised a foster son and sent him into the world, where he has made me two grandbabies, and I am still escorting my daughter and son through adolescence. I go to Mass every Saturday. I am a superb, if messy, cook. I am also an enthusiastic laundress, capable of sorting a hamper full of clothes into five subtly differentiated piles, but a terrible housekeeper. I can do italic writing and, in an emergency, bathe an oil-soaked cat. I play a fiendish game of Scrabble. When I have the time and the money, I like to sit on my front steps with my husband, drinking Amaretto and smoking a cigar, as we imagine our counterparts in Leningrad and make sure that the sun gets down once more behind the sharp childish scrawl of the Tucson Mountains.

This lively plenty has its bleak complement, of course, in all the things I can no longer do. I will never run again, except in dreams, and one day I may have to write that I will never walk again. I like to go camping, but I can't follow George and the children along the trails that wander out of a campsite through the desert or into the mountains. In fact, even on the level I've learned

10

4. Latin for "in the last straits." Here it means "at the limits of endurance."

never to check the weather or try to hold a coherent conversation: I need all my attention for my wayward feet. Of late, I have begun to catch myself wondering how people can propel themselves without canes. With only one usable hand, I have to select my clothing with care not so much for style as for ease of ingress and egress, and even so, dressing can be laborious. I can no longer do fine stitchery, pick up babies, play the piano, braid my hair. I am immobilized by acute attacks of depression, which may or may not be physiologically related to MS but are certainly its logical concomitant.

These two elements, the plenty and the privation, are never pure, nor are the delight and wretchedness that accompany them. Almost every pickle that I get into as a result of my weakness and clumsiness—and I get into plenty—is funny as well as maddening and sometimes painful. I recall one May afternoon when a friend and I were going out for a drink after finishing up at school. As we were climbing into opposite sides of my car, chatting, I tripped and fell, flat and hard, onto the asphalt parking lot, my abrupt departure interrupting him in mid-sentence. "Where'd you go?" he called as he came around the back of the car to find me hauling myself up by the door frame. "Are you all right?" Yes, I told him, I was fine, just a bit rattly, and we drove off to find a shady patio and some beer. When I got home an hour or so later, my daughter greeted me with "What have you done to yourself?" I looked down. One elbow of my white turtleneck with the green froggies, one knee of my white trousers, one white kneesock were blood-soaked. We peeled off the clothes and inspected the damage, which was nasty enough but not alarming. That part wasn't funny: The abrasions took a long time to heal, and one got a little infected. Even so, when I think of my friend talking earnestly, suddenly, to the hot thin air while I dropped from his view as though through a trap door, I find the image as silly as something from a Marx Brothers movie.

I may find it easier than other cripples to amuse myself because I live propped by the acceptance and the assistance and, sometimes, the amusement of those around me. Grocery clerks tear my checks out of my checkbook for me, and sales clerks find chairs to put into dressing rooms when I want to try on clothes. The people I work with make sure I teach at times when I am least likely to be fatigued, in places I can get to, with the materials I need. My students, with one anonymous exception (in an end-of-the-semester evaluation), have been unperturbed by my disability. Some even like it. One was immensely cheered by the information that I paint my own fingernails; she decided, she told me, that if I could go to such trouble over fine details, she could keep on writing essays. I suppose I became some sort of bright-fingered muse. She wrote good essays, too.

15   The most important struts in the framework of my existence, of course, are my husband and children. Dismayingly few marriages survive the MS test, and why should they? Most twenty-two- and nineteen-year-olds, like George and me, can vow in clear conscience, after a childhood of chicken pox and summer colds, to keep one another in sickness and in health so long as they both shall live. Not many are equipped for catastrophe: the dismay, the depression, the extra work, the boredom that a degenerative disease can insinuate into a rela-

tionship. And our society, with its emphasis on fun and its association of fun with physical performance, offers little encouragement for a whole spouse to stay with a crippled partner. Children experience similar stresses when faced with a crippled parent, and they are more helpless, since parents and children can't usually get divorced. They hate, of course, to be different from their peers, and the child whose mother is tacking down the aisle of a school auditorium packed with proud parents like a Cape Cod dinghy in a stiff breeze jolly well stands out in a crowd. Deprived of legal divorce, the child can at least deny the mother's disability, even her existence, forgetting to tell her about recitals and PTA meetings, refusing to accompany her to stores or church or the movies, never inviting friends to the house. Many do.

But I've been limping along for ten years now, and so far George and the children are still at my left elbow, holding tight. Anne and Matthew vacuum floors and dust furniture and haul trash and rake up dog droppings and button my cuffs and bake lasagna and Toll House cookies with just enough grumbling so I know that they don't have brain fever. And far from hiding me, they're forever dragging me by racks of fancy clothes or through teeming school corridors, or welcoming gaggles of friends while I'm wandering through the house in Anne's filmy pink babydoll pajamas. George generally calls before he brings someone home, but he does just as many dumb thankless chores as the children. And they all yell at me, laugh at some of my jokes, write me funny letters when we're apart—in short, treat me as an ordinary human being for whom they have some use. I think they like me. Unless they're faking. . . .

Faking. There's the rub. Tugging at the fringes of my consciousness always is the terror that people are kind to me only because I'm a cripple. My mother almost shattered me once, with that instinct mothers have—blind, I think, in this case, but unerring nonetheless—for striking blows along the fault-lines of their children's hearts, by telling me, in an attack on my selfishness, "We all have to make allowances for you, of course, because of the way you are." From the distance of a couple of years, I have to admit that I haven't any idea just what she meant, and I'm not sure that she knew either. She was awfully angry. But at the time, as the words thudded home, I felt my worst fear, suddenly realized. I could bear being called selfish: I am. But I couldn't bear the corroboration that those around me were doing in fact what I'd always suspected them of doing, professing fondness while silently putting up with me because of the way I am. A cripple. I've been a little cracked ever since.

Along with this fear that people are secretly accepting shoddy goods comes a relentless pressure to please—to prove myself worth the burdens I impose, I guess, or to build a substantial account of goodwill against which I may write drafts in times of need. Part of the pressure arises from social expectations. In our society, anyone who deviates from the norm had better find some way to compensate. Like fat people, who are expected to be jolly, cripples must bear their lot meekly and cheerfully. A grumpy cripple isn't playing by the rules. And much of the pressure is self-generated. Early on I vowed that, if I had to have MS, by God I was going to do it well. This is a class act, ladies and gentlemen. No tears, no recriminations, no faintheartedness.

One way and another, then, I wind up feeling like Tiny Tim,[5] peering over the edge of the table at the Christmas goose, waving my crutch, piping down God's blessing on us all. Only sometimes I don't want to play Tiny Tim. I'd rather be Caliban,[6] a most scurvy monster. Fortunately, at home no one much cares whether I'm a good cripple or a bad cripple as long as I make vichyssoise with fair regularity. One evening several years ago, Anne was reading at the dining-room table while I cooked dinner. As I opened a can of tomatoes, the can slipped in my left hand and juice spattered me and the counter with bloody spots. Fatigued and infuriated, I bellowed, "I'm so sick of being crippled!" Anne glanced at me over the top of her book. "There now," she said, "do you feel better?" "Yes," I said, "yes, I do." She went back to her reading. I felt better. That's about all the attention my scurviness ever gets.

20   Because I hate being crippled, I sometimes hate myself for being a cripple. Over the years I have come to expect—even accept—attacks of violent self-loathing. Luckily, in general our society no longer connects deformity and disease directly with evil (though a charismatic once told me that I have MS because a devil is in me) and so I'm allowed to move largely at will, even among small children. But I'm not sure that this revision of attitude has been particularly helpful. Physical imperfection, even freed of moral disapprobation, still defies and violates the ideal, especially for women, whose confinement in their bodies as objects of desire is far from over. Each age, of course, has its ideal, and I doubt that ours is any better or worse than any other. Today's ideal woman, who lives on the glossy pages of dozens of magazines, seems to be between the ages of eighteen and twenty-five; her hair has body, her teeth flash white, her breath smells minty, her underarms are dry; she has a career but is still a fabulous cook, especially of meals that take less than twenty minutes to prepare; she does not ordinarily appear to have a husband or children; she is trim and deeply tanned; she jogs, swims, plays tennis, rides a bicycle, sails, but does not bowl; she travels widely, even to out-of-the-way places like Finland and Samoa, always in the company of the ideal man, who possesses a nearly identical set of characteristics. There are a few exceptions. Though usually white and often blonde, she may be black, Hispanic, Asian, or Native American, so long as she is unusually sleek. She may be old, provided she is selling a laxative or is Lauren Bacall. If she is selling a detergent, she may be married and have a flock of strikingly messy children. But she is never a cripple.

Like many women I know, I have always had an uneasy relationship with my body. I was not a popular child, largely, I think now, because I was peculiar: intelligent, intense, moody, shy, given to unexpected actions and inexplicable notions and emotions. But as I entered adolescence, I believed myself unpopular because I was homely: my breasts too flat, my mouth too wide, my hips too narrow, my clothing never quite right in fit or style. I was not, in fact, particularly ugly, old photographs inform me, though I was well off the ideal;

5. Disabled, sickly young boy saved by Ebenezer Scrooge's generosity in Charles Dickens's novel *A Christmas Carol* (1843).
6. Son of the witch Sycorax in William Shakespeare's play *The Tempest* (c. 1611).

but I carried this sense of self-alienation with me into adulthood, where it regenerated in response to the depredations of MS. Even with my brace I walk with a limp so pronounced that, seeing myself on the videotape of a television program on the disabled, I couldn't believe that anything but an inchworm could make progress humping along like that. My shoulders droop and my pelvis thrusts forward as I try to balance myself upright, throwing my frame into a bony S. As a result of contractures, one shoulder is higher than the other and I carry one arm bent in front of me, the fingers curled into a claw. My left arm and leg have wasted into pipe-stems, and I try always to keep them covered. When I think about how my body must look to others, especially to men, to whom I have been trained to display myself, I feel ludicrous, even loathsome.

At my age, however, I don't spend much time thinking about my appearance. The burning egocentricity of adolescence, which assures one that all the world is looking all the time, has passed, thank God, and I'm generally too caught up in what I'm doing to step back, as I used to, and watch myself as though upon a stage. I'm also too old to believe in the accuracy of self-image. I know that I'm not a hideous crone, that in fact, when I'm rested, well dressed, and well made up, I look fine. The self-loathing I feel is neither physically nor intellectually substantial. What I hate is not me but a disease.

I am not a disease.

And a disease is not—at least not singlehandedly—going to determine who I am, though at first it seemed to be going to. Adjusting to a chronic incurable illness, I have moved through a process similar to that outlined by Elisabeth Kübler-Ross in *On Death and Dying*.[7] The major difference—and it is far more significant than most people recognize—is that I can't be sure of the outcome, as the terminally ill cancer patient can. Research studies indicate that, with proper medical care, I may achieve a "normal" life span. And in our society, with its vision of death as the ultimate evil, worse even than decrepitude, the response to such news is, "Oh well, at least you're not going to *die*." Are there worse things than dying? I think that there may be.

I think of two women I know, both with MS, both enough older than I to have served me as models. One took to her bed several years ago and has been there ever since. Although she can sit in a high-backed wheelchair, because she is incontinent she refuses to go out at all, even though incontinence pants, which are readily available at any pharmacy, could protect her from embarrassment. Instead, she stays at home and insists that her husband, a small quiet man, a retired civil servant, stay there with her except for a quick weekly foray to the supermarket. The other woman, whose illness was diagnosed when she was eighteen, a nursing student engaged to a young doctor, finished her training, married her doctor, accompanied him to Germany when he was in the service, bore three sons and a daughter, now grown and gone. When she can, she travels with her husband; she plays bridge, embroiders, swims regularly; she

25

7. An influential 1969 book by Swiss American psychiatrist Kübler-Ross positing five stages of grief.

works, like me, as a symptomatic-patient instructor of medical students in neurology. Guess which woman I hope to be.

At the beginning, I thought about having MS almost incessantly. And because of the unpredictable course of the disease, my thoughts were always terrified. Each night I'd get into bed wondering whether I'd get out again the next morning, whether I'd be able to see, to speak, to hold a pen between my fingers. Knowing that the day might come when I'd be physically incapable of killing myself, I thought perhaps I ought to do so right away, while I still had the strength. Gradually I came to understand that the Nancy who might one day lie inert under a bedsheet, arms and legs paralyzed, unable to feed or bathe herself, unable to reach out for a gun, a bottle of pills, was not the Nancy I was at present, and that I could not presume to make decisions for that future Nancy, who might well not want in the least to die. Now the only provision I've made for the future Nancy is that when the time comes—and it is likely to come in the form of pneumonia, friend to the weak and the old—I am not to be treated with machines and medications. If she is unable to communicate by then, I hope she will be satisfied with these terms.

Thinking all the time about having MS grew tiresome and intrusive, especially in the large and tragic mode in which I was accustomed to considering my plight. Months and even years went by without catastrophe (at least without one related to MS), and really I was awfully busy, what with George and children and snakes and students and poems, and I hadn't the time, let alone the inclination, to devote myself to being a disease. Too, the richer my life became, the funnier it seemed, as though there were some connection between largesse and laughter, and so my tragic stance began to waver until, even with the aid of a brace and a cane, I couldn't hold it for very long at a time.

After several years I was satisfied with my adjustment. I had suffered my grief and fury and terror, I thought, but now I was at ease with my lot. Then one summer day I set out with George and the children across the desert for a vacation in California. Part way to Yuma I became aware that my right leg felt funny. "I think I've had an exacerbation," I told George. "What shall we do?" he asked. "I think we'd better get the hell to California," I said, "because I don't know whether I'll ever make it again." So we went on to San Diego and then to Orange, up the Pacific Coast Highway to Santa Cruz, across to Yosemite, down to Sequoia and Joshua Tree, and so back over the desert to home. It was a fine two-week trip, filled with friends and fair weather, and I wouldn't have missed it for the world, though I did in fact make it back to California two years later. Nor would there have been any point in missing it, since in MS, once the symptoms have appeared, the neurological damage has been done, and there's no way to predict or prevent that damage.

The incident spoiled my self-satisfaction, however. It renewed my grief and fury and terror, and I learned that one never finishes adjusting to MS. I don't know now why I thought one would. One does not, after all, finish adjusting to life, and MS is simply a fact of my life—not my favorite fact, of course—but as ordinary as my nose and my tropical fish and my yellow Mazda station wagon. It may at any time get worse, but no amount of worry or anticipation can prepare me for a new loss. My life is a lesson in losses. I learn one at a time.

And I had best be patient in the learning, since I'll have to do it like it or not. As any rock fan knows, you can't always get what you want. Particularly when you have MS. You can't, for example, get cured. In recent years researchers and the organizations that fund research have started to pay MS some attention even though it isn't fatal; perhaps they have begun to see that life is something other than a quantitative phenomenon, that one may be very much alive for a very long time in a life that isn't worth living. The researchers have made some progress toward understanding the mechanism of the disease: It may well be an autoimmune reaction triggered by a slow-acting virus. But they are nowhere near its prevention, control, or cure. And most of us want to be cured. Some, unable to accept incurability, grasp at one treatment after another, no matter how bizarre: megavitamin therapy, gluten-free diet, injections of cobra venom, hypothermal suits, lymphocytopheresis, hyperbaric chambers. Many treatments are probably harmless enough, but none are curative.

The absence of a cure often makes MS patients bitter toward their doctors. Doctors are, after all, the priests of modern society, the new shamans, whose business is to heal, and many an MS patient roves from one to another, searching for the "good" doctor who will make him well. Doctors too think of themselves as healers, and for this reason many have trouble dealing with MS patients, whose disease in its intransigence defeats their aims and mocks their skills. Too few doctors, it is true, treat their patients as whole human beings, but the reverse is also true. I have always tried to be gentle with my doctors, who often have more at stake in terms of ego than I do. I may be frustrated, maddened, depressed by the incurability of my disease, but I am not diminished by it, and they are. When I push myself up from my seat in the waiting room and stumble toward them, I incarnate the limitation of their powers. The least I can do is refuse to press on their tenderest spots.

This gentleness is part of the reason that I'm not sorry to be a cripple. I didn't have it before. Perhaps I'd have developed it anyway—how could I know such a thing?—and I wish I had more of it, but I'm glad of what I have. It has opened and enriched my life enormously, this sense that my frailty and need must be mirrored in others, that in searching for and shaping a stable core in a life wrenched by change and loss, change and loss, I must recognize the same process, under individual conditions, in the lives around me. I do not deprecate such knowledge, however I've come by it.

All the same, if a cure were found, would I take it? In a minute. I may be a cripple, but I'm only occasionally a loony and never a saint. Anyway, in my brand of theology God doesn't give bonus points for a limp. I'd take a cure; I just don't need one. A friend who also has MS startled me once by asking, "Do you ever say to yourself, 'Why me, Lord?'" "No, Michael, I don't," I told him, "because whenever I try, the only response I can think of is 'Why not?'" If I could make a cosmic deal, who would I put in my place? What in my life would

I give up in exchange for sound limbs and a thrilling rush of energy? No one. Nothing. I might as well do the job myself. Now that I'm getting the hang of it.

MLA CITATION

Mairs, Nancy. "On Being a Cripple." *The Norton Reader: An Anthology of Nonfiction,* edited by Melissa A. Goldthwaite et al., 16th ed., W. W. Norton, 2024, pp. 312–22.

QUESTIONS

1. How does Nancy Mairs organize her essay? What connects the different parts to each other?

2. What stereotypes of people with disabilities does Mairs expect us to believe in? How does she set out to counter them?

3. Mairs writes, "Like many women I know, I have always had an uneasy relationship with my body" (paragraph 21). Annotate the essay, marking the places where Mairs considers the factors that shape her relationship with her body. In what ways do disease, age, gender, and other factors intersect in this essay?

4. Mairs deliberately chooses to call herself a "cripple," and she explains her rationale for doing so. With your classmates, brainstorm a list of other labels or names that groups or individuals familiar to you have chosen for themselves. Select one and discuss the rationale behind the choice and the reception following it.

JUNE ERIC-UDORIE
When You Are Waiting to Be Healed

T HE HEAT OF THE AUDITORIUM made my head ring, and my dress felt like it was gripping tightly onto my skin. Around me were black folk, littered in every corner of the church auditorium, their bodies pressed closely together. From afar, their bodies seemed to blend, making it hard to tell just how many people sat in each pew. It was not unusual at this time of year to have a sudden influx of new faces. The Sunday before Christmas, we celebrated Thanksgiving, where families wore matching ankara[1] and lace and the children danced in front of the entire church, their bodies sticky with sweat as they made moves that matched the deafening sound of the drums. Beside me, my grandmother was

This essay first appeared in Catapult *(2016), an online magazine that celebrated "stories that explore the space between the lines of our lives, that raise questions rather than give answers," and was later published in* Disability Visibility: First-Person Stories from the Twenty-First Century *(2020), edited by Alice Wong.*

1. Fabrics with traditional African designs, colors, and symbols.

dancing, hips swaying to the rhythms of the talking drum, her smile wide enough to expose the stark contrast between her pearl-white teeth and the dark opening between them.

I wanted to dance, too: free my limbs; take off my shoes and place them underneath the pew in front of me; join the raucous congregation, their voices gradually rising above the instruments as they sang, *Come and join me, sing hallelujah*. But I was fifteen years old, an awkward teenage girl, and my body felt like an alien shell. I was about to leave the auditorium and head to the bathroom—a last-ditch attempt to remove myself from the noisy congregation that resembled a bustling marketplace—when the pastor instructed the band to stop. He looked toward the church and announced that it was time for communion, and my grandmother grabbed my arm. There was no escape.

A deacon handed me a little plastic cup containing fruit wine. On top was a thin wafer of bread, the sign of the cross imprinted in the middle. "Dip the bread in the wine and place the communion on your eyes," my grandmother said. "If you *really* believe, if you really pray and cry out, then God will heal you."

I sighed, took a deep breath as my insides coiled from shame, and did as I was told. The words came out as a breathy whisper: *Pretty women wonder where my secret lies.*[2] Maya Angelou comforted me as I placed wafers soaked in wine over my eyelids, a corner of my heart still aching for a miracle. I had done this many times, and each time there was no result. I had stopped believing that God could even work miracles. But that Sunday, my bones became feeble, as if the very thing that held them together had dissipated, and I asked God for a miracle.

For a huge part of my childhood, I felt like I was a piece of clockwork waiting to be fixed. The feelings started early, with the numerous appointments to eye specialists with my mother, trying to see if there was a way to cure my dancing eyes. "It is incurable," the doctor would say, and when we got home my mother would wail, even though that doctor, like many other doctors, simply confirmed what she was told when I was born on that rainy Thursday in 1998. 5

*

I was born with congenital idiopathic nystagmus. The American Nystagmus Network defines nystagmus as a "complex condition where the eyes move involuntarily in a small, repeated back-and-forth motion," making it hard to see clearly. Nystagmus is believed to affect between one in one thousand and one in two thousand people. Nystagmus affects people in different ways, but it does lead to reduced vision. It can be caused by "a problem with the way the eye sends messages back to the brain or how certain parts of the brain make sense of this information." Sometimes it is linked to other inherited neurological conditions or other health problems like albinism or Down syndrome. On some occasions, like mine, it can be entirely random.

2. The opening line of the poem "Phenomenal Woman" (1978) by Maya Angelou (1928–2014).

When I was in first grade, a boy at school called me a witch because I could not make my eyes swivel to the left when he asked me to. I went to the bathroom, sat on the toilet seat, and cried, tears soaking my yellow school uniform shirt, stopping only to breathe or listen to the soft whistling of the wind between the trees. That was the moment in which I learned that there was something permanently wrong with me. I was not a piece of clockwork waiting to be fixed. I had lost too many pieces and would never be fixed.

At home, conversations about my nystagmus were sparse, except when discussed as a thing that God would "deliver me" from. I received conflicting messages: God does not make mistakes; everything God creates is perfect; God corrects the things that are imperfect. With these messages, my nystagmus became a huge source of shame. I was praying a lot, asking God to heal me so that I could have some sort of normality. When it looked like healing was not going to happen, I worked on compromises instead. I wanted to know what it was like to be able to see clearly for one day, to not trip up the stairs because I missed a step. When that didn't happen, I asked for less time: twelve hours, thirty minutes, ten seconds. None of my prayers were answered.

In 2012, an ophthalmologist at a hospital in Oxford, England, asked if I'd considered registering as partially sighted. I was stunned. The implication—the idea that *I* could have a disability—was so momentous that I didn't say anything for a while. I was learning to navigate the world as a young black woman, and I did not feel I had the right to claim a disability. For fourteen years, my nystagmus was a thing I was waiting to be healed from, while I also knew deep down that it was a permanent state. When you are waiting to be healed, you reject a lasting condition; the idea that I could be disabled felt like I was ignoring the magic of an all-powerful god and settling for less—the conclusions of mere mortals.

10   Saying that I had a disability felt like I was adding ink to a penciled truth. The label "disabled" was not one that I felt I could claim as my own; it was not rightfully mine. I had grown up surrounded by people who undermined the severity of my disability, and so for me to claim the label, when I didn't feel "disabled enough," felt disingenuous. I was black, female, young, Nigerian, British—but I was *not* disabled. Claiming that label felt like lauding myself with an extra unnecessary burden.

It took me a few moments before I managed to pull myself together and told him I would talk to my mom. On the way back to school, I called my ma and told her what the doctor had said.

"He wants me to register as partially sighted." There was silence, and then my mother hung up. We never brought it up again.

*

When I stepped onto the train platform in Bath, England, all I felt was dread and fear. The fear I felt was so raw, it seemed to scratch at the surface of my skin and uncover the truth that lay underneath. Bath was mysteriously quiet. It was too early on a Saturday morning, and I could almost taste the freshness of the air against my lips. The sky was a translucent blue, and the clouds seemed to stretch on for perpetuity. It was roughly a month after my seventeenth birthday and the first time I had gone anywhere on my own. I was nearing adulthood, and it felt important for me to try and confront my fears of being independent.

Now I knew the truth. I was a disabled black girl. The truth, for many years, sat at the entrance of my throat—a lump so large that I could start breathing and living in my body only when I was finally able to swallow and accept it. That unusually warm English summer, I sat in a café in Bath, alone. I had gone there on my own. I had asked for help when I was lost, and when the person started pointing to things I could not see, I did not nod and pretend I understood. I said, "I have a visual disability," proclaiming what had been the truth since the day I was born.

That unusually warm English summer, I knew that the most important   15
thing I had to learn—before I turned eighteen in June the next year—was to not be ashamed of who I was. The embarrassment I felt every time I missed a step, every time a friend pulled me back because I hadn't seen a car coming, was a thing I had to let go. I had to practice forgiving myself.

I took a deep breath and—alongside the oxygen and the carbon dioxide—I exhaled tidbits of the intense shame and fear that I had carried as an extra weight on my backbone. It was not huge, a trip to Bath, but it was important because throughout my teenage years, I had never been given the opportunity to learn to live with my disability and move through the world on my own terms. Everybody else around me was scared that something bad would happen. But nothing had happened, and I felt like a winner, sitting in that café and staring into the green park of nothingness.

I've been living in London for just over two weeks. The city is vast, and the people walk too quickly. You can hear the birds only if you wake up early enough, that time of the day where the sky still seems to exist in between morning and night and it's unclear exactly what time it is. This is how it is on Sunday mornings when I am walking to church, and the very city that never stops moving seems to pause a bit. When I walk into that church service, I am not the believer that I used to be. I sing over the sound of the drums, and I smile when I see other children in the congregation dancing with too much energy. I come to church happy in the body I exist in; I come to church knowing that I am not a mistake waiting to be fixed. I do not come to church with a heart that is begging for the most special part of me to change. I come to church happy and whole. I come to church free.

MLA CITATION

Eric-Udorie, June. "When You Are Waiting to Be Healed." *The Norton Reader: An Anthology of Nonfiction*, edited by Melissa A. Goldthwaite et al., 16th ed., W. W. Norton, 2024, pp. 322–25.

QUESTIONS

1. When an ophthalmologist first suggests that June Eric-Udorie register as partially sighted, she has difficulty accepting the label "disabled." Why? Why does she later choose that word to describe herself?

2. Annotate the essay, marking the places where Eric-Udorie describes embodied experience (the experience of living in a particular body), whether her own or those of others. In what ways do her observations change over the course of the essay?

3. Eric-Udorie describes a change in how she came to view herself as a person with a disability. She went from feeling like "a piece of clockwork waiting to be fixed" (paragraph 5) to feeling "happy and whole" (paragraph 17). Have you ever experienced a change in your feelings about yourself? Are there similes that help describe your feelings? Write down a few. Which one comes closest to describing how you once felt or feel now?

ROXANE GAY
What Fullness Is

T HE FIRST WEIGHT-LOSS SURGERY was performed during the 10th century, on D. Sancho, the king of León, Spain. He was so fat that he lost his throne, so he was taken to Córdoba, where a doctor sewed his lips shut. Only able to drink through a straw, the former king lost enough weight after a time to return home and reclaim his kingdom.

The notion that thinness—and the attempt to force the fat body toward a state of culturally mandated discipline—begets great rewards is centuries old.

Modern weight-loss surgery began in the 1950s, when surgeons employing various techniques caused their patients fairly distressing problems, like severe diarrhea, dehydration, kidney stones, gallstones, and even death—but, generally, the patients lost weight. Surgeons have since refined their techniques, using a range of restriction or malabsorption methods to force the human body to lose weight. They have tried wiring patients' jaws shut to force weight loss through liquid diets. They have stapled stomachs into smaller pouches to restrict caloric intake. They have developed gastric bands and balloons to restrict the amount of food that can enter the stomach. But it was the first laparoscopic gastric bypass—in which the gastrointestinal tract is routed around a person's stomach—performed in 1994, that enabled bariatric surgery to go more mainstream by way of minimal invasion.

Some of these interventions have succeeded for people, and some have failed, because not even surgical intervention can overcome the reasons why many people gain and then struggle to lose weight. Some bodies and minds simply cannot be brought to heel.

5   I capitulated to a procedure after more than 15 years of resistance and had a sleeve gastrectomy at the UCLA Ronald Reagan Hospital in January 2018. I told only a few people; I did not tell my family. I felt—in equal parts—hope, defeat, frustration, and disgust.

Originally published in 2018 on the social journalism and blog site Medium.

The first time I contemplated weight-loss surgery, it was at the bidding of my parents. My father and I went to an orientation seminar at the Cleveland Clinic[1] and learned about gastric bypass. There were graphic, deeply disturbing videos and a question-and-answer session. I submitted myself to a clinical assessment about the problem of my body. It wasn't the right time, I decided. I could be better, eat less, move more.

And over the next several years, I certainly tried to, intermittently or constantly, depending on how you look at it. I continued a near-lifetime of disordered eating, and restriction, and overeating. Sometimes I was motivated enough to work out. Sometimes I wasn't. Mostly I was overwhelmed by inertia. I had a desire to lose weight but an inability—or, perhaps, unwillingness—to force myself toward the deprivation required for the significant weight loss the world told me I needed.

The truth is that my desire for weight loss has long been about satisfying other people more than myself, finding a way to fit more peacefully into a world that is not at all interested in accommodating a body like mine. And the dominant cultural attitude toward fatness is that the fat body is a medical problem, a drain on society, an aesthetic blight. As a fat person, I am supposed to want to lose weight. I am supposed to be working on the problem of my body. I am supposed to apply discipline to physical unruliness. I'm not supposed to be fine with my body. I am not supposed to yearn, simply, for people to let me be, to see me, accept me, and treat me with dignity exactly as I am.

I am, however, sometimes fine with my body. I am fine with my curves, the solidity of me. I am strong and tall. I enjoy the way I take up space, that I have presence. I have someone who appreciates my body and only hates everything I must deal with by virtue of living in this world in this body.

Sometimes I hate my body, the unruliness of it. I hate all my limitations. I hate my lack of discipline. I hate how my unhappiness is never enough to truly motivate me to regain control of myself, once and for all. I hate the way I hunger but never find satisfaction. I want and want and want but never allow myself to reach for what I truly want, leaving that want raging desperately beneath the surface of my skin.

And the moment I step outside the safety of my home, I hate how visible I am, how people treat me, how they stare and comment both loudly and under their breath, how rude children remind me I'm fat and their rude parents say nothing, how I have to think and overthink where I go and how I will fit into any given space. I do not know how to carry myself with confidence when I go out into the world. Any sense of self I have is often shattered within minutes, and then I am all insecurities and fears, wishing myself into a more socially acceptable form.

And given my career trajectory, there are pictures and videos of me everywhere. I hate these images, cringe when I see them, and then hate myself for cringing, for not seeing myself with kindness. Trolls make memes of my pictures and post them to internet message boards with cruel captions. They tweet these

10

1. Major hospital and medical-research center in Ohio.

memes at me. They remind me, every chance they get, that I am fat: more than, but less than. Every single day, I am confronted by how people really see me. I am confronted by the fact that no matter what I achieve, I will always be fat first. I will always have this weakness; it will always be easily exploited.

If you're not one statistic, though, you're another. According to the American Society for Bariatric and Metabolic Surgery, 216,000 people received a bariatric procedure in 2016. Doctors tout weight-loss surgery as the gold standard for weight loss, though a relatively small number of the estimated one-third of Americans who are considered obese actually get the surgery.

Many doctors have used that exact phrase with me—"the gold standard"—over the years. They told me that this surgery will save my life, and that if I didn't get the surgery, I wouldn't live until 40. When I turned 40, they told me that if I didn't get the surgery, I wouldn't live until 50.

15   This surgery is touted as the only real option for the morbidly and supermorbidly obese. It is not a question of if a fat person will get weight-loss surgery, but when.

Of course, weight-loss surgery is extraordinarily expensive, and many insurance policies will not cover it. The out-of-pocket cost in the United States is high enough that many people travel to Mexico and Malaysia to get it for a fraction of the cost. My insurance company will cover weight-loss surgery—but only after you've gone through six months of medically supervised weight loss; you have to prove that you deserve to have yourself cut open.

Given my schedule, this six-month waiting period was a requirement I was never going to be able to meet, so I ended up paying for the surgery out of pocket. I suppose I should be grateful that I could afford to do so, but mostly, I'm bitter. The expense was breathtaking.

If there is a silver lining, the expense also removed a lot of bureaucratic red tape. I was able to schedule my surgery and address all the presurgical requirements with relative ease once the surgeon realized he didn't have to deal with an insurance company. Health care is as wantonly susceptible to the ills of capitalism as everything else.

After more than 15 years of refusing it, I made the decision to get weight-loss surgery on an ordinary day. At home in Lafayette, Indiana, a young man yelled at me to move my fat black ass while I was crossing a grocery store parking lot to my car. It was the last straw.

20   I tried to hold my head high, shuffled as quickly as I could, put my groceries in my car, and sat behind the steering wheel. I sat there, shaking, wishing I could have been as quick in that moment to put him in his place as I would have been online. I wanted to call someone for comfort, but I was at a silent impasse with the only person to whom I could talk. Instead, I pressed my head against the steering wheel and sobbed. When I collected myself, I drove home and went to bed. I hoped I might not wake up, but I did.

The most common weight-loss procedures today are the gastric bypass and the gastric sleeve. These procedures are usually done laparoscopically in a matter of hours, with the patient under general anesthesia. In gastric bypass, the stomach is reduced, creating a small pouch, which is then connected farther down the small intestine. Sleeve gastrectomy is slightly less drastic and the more common procedure performed. The stomach size is reduced and reshaped into a slender tube, restricting how much a person can eat. In these procedures, patients also lose their appetites as a result of reduced ghrelin, a hormone that stimulates appetite.

In both procedures, the patient's anatomy is irreversibly changed, and they lose a significant amount of weight quickly. Both procedures result in malnutrition, requiring patients to take multivitamins and other supplements for the rest of their lives. Other risks and complications include hair loss, ulcers, leaks, gastric bleeding, bowel obstruction, gallstones, and dehydration. These are all fairly horrifying risks, but (the medical establishment has decided) they are less horrifying than the medical risks of fatness. People who choose weight-loss surgery trade one kind of health for another.

After such drastic weight loss, many patients need expensive, extensive plastic surgery to deal with the excess skin. The TLC network even has a show—spun off from *My 600-Lb Life*—called *Skin Tight*, about people who have lost a significant amount of weight and want to get skin-removal surgery, altering their anatomy once again.

And with the growing popularity of bariatric surgery, an entire industry has risen around it—supplements, special foods, dishware, and more. There are online forums, *YouTube* channels, bariatric eating blogs, and other such communities. Where there is money to be made, capitalism finds a way.

The morning after I decided to get weight-loss surgery, I called a local bariatric surgeon and made an appointment for a consultation. A few hours later, the program administrator called me back and told me I would need to lose 75 pounds before they would even consider operating on me. I immediately felt hopeless: If I could lose 75 pounds on my own, I wouldn't be considering surgery. The surgeon, the coordinator told me, was involved in some kind of study and only wanted good outcomes; he did not inspire me with confidence. I was told to watch some online videos about the surgery and fill out a lot of paperwork and then we could get started. 25

After a few days of allowing myself to wallow in defeat, I got a recommendation from a friend and found an excellent surgeon in Los Angeles (where I also live) who did inspire with me confidence. This surgeon was very frank; I just stared and nodded. He told me at our first appointment in December that surgery was my best option. He remarked that it was good that I carried most of my weight in my lower body, because it would be easier for him to do the surgery. I was an unruly body for him to fix, nothing less, nothing more. He asked me to try losing some weight before the surgery to reduce the size of my liver, but he wasn't too prickly or unrealistic about it. Just don't gain any more weight, he said.

I looked at my work calendar for 2018 and realized I had a small window within which to do this surgery and recover. Before I lost my nerve, I rescheduled the two events I had in January and told my doctor I wasn't going to be able to wait six weeks before flying again post-surgery, as recommended. In a matter of hours, I was scheduled for surgery in early January.

I was then weighed and measured. I had blood drawn and an EKG and an echocardiogram performed. I attended a three-hour workshop where I learned more about the surgery, how to prepare, what the initial weeks and after the surgery would be like, and so on. A nutritionist cautioned us not to visit online forums about bariatric surgery, and I heeded her advice (until I didn't). I received a binder full of information, much of it rather starkly depressing about the "lifestyle changes" that would be demanded of me both before and after the surgery. I bought vitamins and whey protein and tried to wrap my mind around the vastly different way I'd have to be eating in just a few weeks. I saw a psychologist who would determine if I was emotionally prepared for the surgery. After 45 minutes, she determined that I was and charged me $300 for the consultation.

During every part of the preoperative process, I doled out obscene sums of money to a range of medical providers. And every night, I stared at the ceiling, wondering if I would actually go through with it. I chastised myself for allowing myself to get to this point, for lacking the discipline to lose weight by any other means.

30   I had made a drastic decision to change my body, but I did not suddenly develop a healthier relationship toward food. In the weeks leading up to my surgery, I tried to eat all the foods I thought that I was probably never going to be able to eat again, paying particular and loving attention to fried foods and soda. A few nights before surgery, friends and I went to my favorite steakhouse, and I enjoyed a Caesar salad and a finely marbled rib eye with mashed potatoes and green beans almondine and butter cake with fresh whipped cream and gin and tonics with a splash of grenadine. I savored every single bite, often with my eyes closed. I mourned what I was losing, or what I thought I was losing.

The morning of the surgery, I went to the hospital, checked in, and was weighed and escorted to a long row of hospital beds just waiting for patients who would submit themselves to surgical blades for one reason or another. I was hungry and thirsty and nervous. I told the friend accompanying me that the gown the hospital provided probably wouldn't fit me, and she said that couldn't possibly happen, given the nature of my impending procedure. I was right: The gown was indeed too small, and, at six in the morning, I was too tired and too defeated to even laugh or feel any kind of satisfaction for understanding just how shortsighted this world is when it comes to different kinds of bodies.

As I do whenever I'm going under general anesthesia, I told the anesthesiologist to give me extra, because I've seen the movie *Awake*.[2] I was wracked with guilt about not telling my family, and then worried that I was probably going to die and my parents would find out in such a terrible way. As I worried, I was strapped to the operating table, and then, mercifully, I lost consciousness. I don't remember anything about the surgery, and I'm thankful for that because it means that the drugs worked. When I woke up, a nurse was peering at me and then broke into a smile. She said, "I know who you are! My girlfriend

2. A 2007 thriller whose plot hinges on a heart-surgery patient remaining conscious while under anesthesia.

and I love your books." I was still pretty out of it, so I muttered, "Please don't tell the internet I'm here."

I care too much what people think. I hate that about myself. Before and after my surgery, I worried what people would think if and when they found out. Each time I went to the doctor's office, I prayed no one would recognize me, and rarely were those prayers answered. I'm just a writer, but I am recognized in public with alarming frequency. "What are you doing here?" a fan asked one afternoon as I walked into the UCLA Medical Center, and I smiled and said, "Routine checkup."

I worried that people would think I betrayed fat positivity,[3] something I do very much believe in even if I can't always believe in it for myself. I worried that everyone who responded so generously to my memoir, *Hunger*, would feel betrayed. I worried I would be seen as betraying myself. I worried I would be seen as taking the easy way out, even though nothing about any of this has been easy, not one thing. I worried.

The surgeon made five neat incisions across my torso and stitched them   35
from the inside so I would eventually have minimal scarring. As I came to my senses, I felt each of those incisions, throbbing gently, reminding me that something invasive had happened to my body. The worst part of the first few hours after the surgery was that I couldn't drink anything until the following morning: I had a brand-new stomach, and a whole lot of stitches holding that brand-new stomach together, so it was best to leave this newly delicate anatomy alone.

As the hours wore on, I felt desiccated. I wanted water more than I have ever wanted anything in my life. I could satisfy myself only with a tiny sponge dipped in ice to dab on my lips and tongue. When no one was looking, I took tiny sips of the melted water pooling at the bottom of my Styrofoam cup—I did.

The hospital buzzed around me. Nurses doted on me. My surgeon stopped by and told me everything had gone well. My liver was nice and small, he said with a smile, and commended me for losing weight before the procedure. I felt a swell of pride and then hated myself for that swell, for being so pedestrian as to take pleasure in the sort of validation that goes against so much of what I believe about how bodies should be allowed to be.

There was a TV, but I couldn't bother to focus on it. I was on excellent pain medication that I controlled with a little remote, so it was all very pleasant, less the torment of the desert of my mouth. The woman next door also had weight-loss surgery, and she talked loudly about how she was a changed woman. It was like she was trying to prove she deserved the surgery, that she was a better woman now. It was aggravating because I did not feel at all changed; I did not have a new outlook on life.

Every few hours, I got up and walked around so as to avoid blood clots. I dozed. I chatted drowsily with loved ones watching over me. Eventually, I passed out, all praise to Dilaudid. Late the next afternoon, I went home, where I could have only water, clear broth, Gatorade, and sugar-free Jell-O for three days.

---

3. The fat acceptance movement, which arose in the 1960s, resists the stigmatization of fat people and promotes positive attitudes toward fatness.

40   For the two weeks after that, I could have only liquids like more Gatorade, juices, soups, thinned yogurt. From weeks two to four, I could eat only soft foods. My new diet was as horrible and boring and bland as you might imagine, but it was also manageable. Anything is manageable if it isn't forever.

Slowly, I started coming to terms with how quickly my relationship to food was changing and how disordered my relationship to food had been and for so long. I had to think—carefully—about what I ate and how. I became full after only a few bites. I had to think about protein and making sure I was getting enough. (I never did, because I'm a very picky eater and the protein shakes made me gag.) I wasn't hungry, but I was starving.

That incident in the parking lot was also an accumulation of frustrations and heartache I no longer wanted to carry—doctors not taking me seriously and always trying to "treat" my weight before anything else, never fitting in spaces I wanted to be in, the obsessive rituals I developed around deciding if and how I could go out in public, feeling unfit and hating exercise because everything was so arduous, having such limited fashion options, the familial concern that was a yoke I couldn't ever get out from under, the societal concern that was a yoke I couldn't ever get out from under, the nagging worry that my weight would eventually come between me and the one person in my life who has never made me feel anything but good in my body, the nagging worry that, eventually, my luck would run out and all the terrible things that doctors had long been warning me about would come to pass.

I had to face the extent of my unhappiness and how much of that unhappiness was connected to my body. I had to accept that I could change my fat body faster than this culture will change how it views, treats, and accommodates fat bodies. And I had to do so while recognizing that losing weight wasn't actually going to make me happier—which may have been the bitterest part of all.

That's how I found myself going back to therapy after nearly a decade away—a decade of telling myself that I was fine and fixed and emotionally whole. The nutritionist affiliated with my surgeon gave me a recommendation, and I made an appointment. Within the first five minutes, I knew it wasn't going to work: She stared at me for long, intensely awkward lengths of time. At the beginning of the session, she was simply silent, and I was not at all sure what I was supposed to do with that silence.

45   After two sessions, I decided to try someone else. He was a brash, handsome older man who got under my skin, forcing me to face uncomfortable truths, forcing me to get comfortable with feeling my feelings—something I've avoided for most of my life. At some point during many of our sessions, he says, "You're mad at me," and I pretend I am not and he knows I am lying, and onward we go, doing the necessary work of breaking me down so that, someday, I might build myself back up again.

The dominant narrative around weight-loss surgery is that it changes your life and makes everything better. It's a lovely fantasy that, by cutting yourself open and having parts of yourself removed, everything that weighed you down will be lifted. But it is only a fantasy.

People who have weight-loss surgery are more likely to commit suicide. Many married people get divorced after the surgery because their spouses cannot cope with the changes, so much so that "bariatric divorce" is a thing. The psychologist I saw for my presurgical evaluation warned that the first year is really difficult, and many patients end up suffering from depression and regretting the surgery. The second year is better, she said, trying to reassure me after my face fell. And she was right: I am depressed and miserable. I am cold all the time and exhausted because I'm only eating between 1,200 and 1,500 calories.[4] I am filled with regrets because everything has changed, but everything is exactly the same.

I am losing a significant amount of weight very quickly—that's what the scale shows, on those rare occasions when I am not too afraid to get on the scale, terrified I've done all this, spent all this money, only to not lose weight. My clothes are looser. My shoes are inexplicably loose. My ring is loose. I fit into my car in a way I never have. I fit into chairs better. I fit everywhere better, and it's still so early.

But I can't believe that I am losing weight, despite all this evidence. I've told my person—more than once that someone is messing with me, sabotaging my sanity by adjusting my seat in the car, stretching out my clothes and shoes to trick me. I am assured such is not the case, that my body is actually changing. For a few moments, I am quieted, and then the doubt creeps back in.

When I look in the mirror, I see no difference—none at all. No one, save for a couple people, has openly acknowledged any weight loss, if they've even noticed, which is a relief and a frustration and a reminder of just how much weight I have to lose. I don't want any weight loss to be acknowledged (or, worse, celebrated), but I also very much do.   50

I've replaced one set of anxieties with another. I worry I'm eating too much and stretching my new stomach (something I was warned about, repeatedly and vigorously). I have brief moments where I allow myself to imagine hiking Runyon Canyon[5] or wearing a fabulous outfit because it is available in my size or going to see a musical without making special arrangements . . . and then I tell myself to get ahold of myself. I tell myself not to want. I tell myself that I've failed to discipline my body before and I will probably fail this time, too. I tell myself these things because I've carried this weight for almost 30 years and it is terrifying to face who I could be without it.

I had weight-loss surgery, but I am still the same person who went under the knife. I still have that yawning cavern inside of me that I want to fill with food, only now I cannot fill it with food. I'm rarely hungry, but I am ravenous. Want continues to rage desperately beneath the surface of my skin. I turned to food when I was sad and happy and lonely and scared and anxious. I turned to food, and away from everything else; it was my comfort and my friend. Food

4. The US Department of Agriculture (USDA) estimates in a 2020 report, to be updated in 2025, that women need to consume 1,600–2,400 calories per day.

5. A park in Los Angeles, California.

helped me survive something I did not think I would survive. Food numbed the uncomfortable feelings I very much did not want to feel.

And then, that comfort was gone. I've lost the best friend I never had the courage to acknowledge but who was my constant, loyal companion nonetheless. I am left holding the shattered pieces of whatever has been left behind, trying to assemble them into something new, something that serves me better.

The forced restriction brought about by the surgery is maddening. Yes, I eat, but I physically cannot overeat. At restaurants, waitstaff interrogate me about all the food I leave on my plate. At home, I eat sad, tiny portions (or, given what I used to eat, what feel like tiny portions). After a few bites of anything, the discomfort begins, and then that discomfort evolves into pain.

55   Sometimes, when I am feeling rebellious, I try to ignore that pain and try to surrender to my desire to eat with abandon. My body reminds me that rebellion will not be tolerated. For the first time in as long as I can remember, I am empty, but I know what fullness is, and I hate this knowing.

MLA CITATION

Gay, Roxane. "What Fullness Is." *The Norton Reader: An Anthology of Nonfiction*, edited by Melissa A. Goldthwaite et al., 16th ed., W. W. Norton, 2024, pp. 326–34.

QUESTIONS

1. In her essay, Roxane Gay takes the occasion of her weight-loss surgery to examine "the dominant cultural attitude toward fatness" (paragraph 8) as well as her complex feelings about her own weight and body. Annotate the essay, marking the passages in which she reflects on cultural attitudes toward fatness and her own feelings about her body. Where do those attitudes overlap? Where do they diverge? Why?

2. What role does race play in Gay's essay?

3. Gay's relationship to food changed as a result of her weight-loss surgery. What was it before her surgery, and what is it after? What does Gay mean when she writes, "I'm rarely hungry, but I am ravenous" (paragraph 52)? Consider her title and concluding sentence: "For the first time in as long as I can remember, I am empty, but I know what fullness is, and I hate this knowing" (paragraph 55). What is this "fullness," and why does she hate knowing it?

4. In this essay, Gay explores her ambivalence about her weight-loss surgery and its consequences. Using Gay's essay as a model, write an essay about a major decision you have made about which you have mixed or complex feelings.

AMY SEQUENZIA
Loud Hands: I Speak Up with My Fingers

I HAVE LOUD HANDS. I must, since I use my hands to communicate. I type what I want to say.

But that's not the only reason why I have loud hands. It is because I finally learned that I cannot be silenced, I will not be silenced.

Being a non-speaking autistic once meant, to me, accepting what people decided I wanted, felt, thought.

It is the way many autistic people are treated. In my case, it got to a point where people said I did not feel pain. After a burning accident, with second-degree burns on my arm, some people decided that I wasn't feeling anything, that I should go on with my day as they had planned it. The same thing happened after I broke my nose. Nobody thought or bothered to ask me how I felt. They silenced my hands, and because my face doesn't always show my emotions, they silenced my voice.

I am autistic. For too long this statement, so real and true, was something I was told to be sorry about. I was expected to be grateful that people pitied me; that they were forgiving of the "weird" ways I behaved; that they would make decisions for me because I did "not understand anything." The word "proud" was not expected to accompany the word "autistic." So I kept my hands quiet.

I use my very loud hands today to say: I am a proud autistic woman.

Loud hands can have many meanings. It has, in my life. It meant, when I was young, to learn how to type. I had not been successful in using sign language. Typing helped me be able to choose my favorite food, my favorite color. It also allowed me to tell my parents things that, up to that point, I could only get out through crying, smiling, or screaming.

I had found a voice but it wasn't my voice. My parents believed in me but they were alone. I looked, and still do, very disabled. I also have other disabilities. The things I was typing then were not what I felt. Instead I was trying to apologize for being me. I was accepting the assumptions about myself that were the assumptions of many, if not most, neurotypical people. I was typing what I thought to be the truth about myself. I was ashamed of being autistic, like most people believed autistic kids, and all autistics, should be. I was seen, and saw myself, as a burden and an "unfortunate event."

Because of my other disabilities I was not able to communicate for a long time. I was having too many seizures and spent many days in hospitals. After that I was numb from the medication. Between the terror in my brain and all the medications trials I lost some years of learning how to speak up. I wasn't strong enough. It took a long while for me to relearn too many lost skills. When I started typing again I began to feel like I deserved to be heard.

It has been a long and slow process. My self-esteem has been severely damaged by years of listening to people talking about me in front of me, calling me

Originally published in the anthology Loud Hands: Autistic People, Speaking (2012). *Amy Sequenzia is a nonspeaking Autistic activist, writer, and poet.*

names, labeling me "severe" and "retarded," even saying I did not have human dignity (I heard about that later, not as it was said).

Despite this sad reality, I would no longer have "quiet hands." It all started with small poems. I was speaking up about my life and some people started to pay attention.

Typing about my life was not easy. Through poems, I began to show how similar in our dreams and expectations of being heard and respected we all are, autistic and neurotypical alike. I will call this phase the second step in my loud hands process. At this time, I also became aware of other autistics who were also speaking up for the right to be respected, the right to be heard. They were, and still are, an inspiration.

I like to think that my coming out with autistic pride helped me gather the support from some neurotypical friends. This is very important to me because I need a lot of help with everything I do. They respect me, understand my difficulties and allow me to be myself. Having these friends' support allows me to continue to type my thoughts. Their help with my safety and general care allows me to focus on speaking out. If I had to focus on things like, for example, eating without making a mess, this would take a lot of energy from me (besides, the cerebral palsy interferes with my coordination). I prefer to use my energy on things I believe are more important to my life, and things that I can try to change and have a greater impact.

But my process wasn't finished. To have really loud hands I needed to speak out and state it clear that I am autistic and proud of it. I had to overcome the anxiety of exposing myself and the echo of old voices in my head, the voices of teachers and "experts" who said so many times that I was nothing.

15   So I started by typing letters on disabilities advocacy; I went places and challenged people's misconceptions about me; I wrote an essay. The final phase of my process: I now have loud hands.

But being proud of being autistic is not enough to end stereotypes. We are part of a large spectrum and each one of us has very specific challenges. The many labels given to us by neurotypical "experts" make our struggles towards inclusion more difficult.

Autistics with a "high functioning" label might also have hidden disabilities that make others deny the accommodations necessary for them to thrive. They are expected to overcome their autistic related anxieties and fit in, "get over it."

Autistics with the label "low functioning" are not expected to succeed, ever. Unless, maybe, after many years, they can look and act a little more like a "normal" person. They are the "hopeless" ones, the ones who need to be "fixed." Their stories become "tragedies" and their real self, ignored. Most neurotypical people refuse or never think about trying to understand their language or allow them to express themselves. They are segregated, bullied, pitied but never heard, never listened to. There is still very little interest in trying new approaches to address the usually extreme anxiety and sensory issues that are manifested in what is, again, labeled "odd behavior." The favorite approach still is to "fix" the autistic, children and adults. The children might be lucky with a sensible early intervention that values who they are and makes sure their abilities are valued too. The adults are usually ignored, isolated from community living or, almost always, treated like children, chastised for their "wrong behavior."

Non-speaking autistics are also labeled "low functioning." That's me. There still is a misconception that if you don't speak you can't understand, think or even hear. People talk about you, not to you; they ask questions not to you, but direct the conversation towards a third person, even when you can communicate through signs or other augmentative communication devices; or they talk to you by yelling, as if a loud voice will make us "understand better."

Despite many non-speaking autistics coming out as self-advocates, there still is great bias and suspicion about their abilities. In some cases, these autistic individuals communicate through facilitated communication (FC)—I am one of them. Because of many years of being labeled "low functioning," "severe," "difficult," and despite a very complete set of guidelines intended to assure the FC user authorship, we are often looked at with suspicion, as frauds. The fact that many have been validated in several studies and others now type independently is conveniently ignored. 20

Is it because of the way we look? Is it because some of us need breaks to recharge, calm down or just do a little flapping between lines? We still want to be respected as we are, with the whole set of things we do to manage better our responses to outside stimuli. Even though we might have found a way to communicate and show expressive intelligence, we still have to fight for the right to be ourselves.

I personally can tell that it is very frustrating when I am so misunderstood. When I decide to type, it can take days or even weeks for me to finish an essay. Then I have to review it, line by line. I need breaks, my arms get stiff. If I have a bad seizure, I might need more than a day to recover. But sometimes I type quickly and without breaks. Every time, I get very tired from the brainwork, trying to organize thoughts in an intelligible way. And then, when I meet people, I might be completely overwhelmed and unable to type or focus on anything. That's when I most need to do the things I do to be able to focus again. Or I need to be left alone. It is also when I am dismissed as "too severe." It is as if I am only worthy if I behave in a certain way that the neurotypicals find acceptable.

Hidden abilities created the myth of "low functioning" autistics, like hidden disabilities created the myth of "high functioning" autistics. It doesn't really matter to our lives and how we live what label we are given. We still fight misconceptions, from all sides. It seems that the great majority of neurotypicals want us to be more like them, talk like them, and not do things, when we speak, that they don't do when they speak. That's one important reason for the neurodiversity movement. That's why having loud hands is so imperative. We are who we are and we are not ashamed of it.

When I started typing essays and reading articles by other autistic self-advocates, I saw that we all want the same things, no matter where in the spectrum or where in our personal lives we find ourselves. We want to be respected for who we are, autistics that flap, spin, twirl, fidget; autistics that communicate not only by talking but by any other way; we want to be included for the things we can do, the way we can do these things; we want to be supported so we can be ourselves and reach our potential, at our own time and in our own terms.

25   We have loud hands and we want to be heard.

MLA CITATION

Sequenzia, Amy. "Loud Hands: I Speak Up with My Fingers." *The Norton Reader: An Anthology of Nonfiction*, edited by Melissa A. Goldthwaite et al., 16th ed., W. W. Norton, 2024, pp. 335–38.

QUESTIONS

1. Amy Sequenzia tells an empowering story of having been silenced and then learning how to speak for herself. Describe a time when you felt silenced. How did you learn to find your voice?

2. Describe some of the challenges Sequenzia faced—and still faces—in expressing herself. How do these challenges—and her pride in communicating despite them—affect your sense of the importance of writing?

3. Although we use our hands to make noise, many people do not think of hands as "loud." Annotate the essay, marking the passages in which Sequenzia refers to "loud" hands. What reasons does she offer for calling her hands (and sometimes other people's hands) "loud"?

4. Sequenzia writes about those who understand and believe in her and those who misunderstand her. In writing or in a discussion with your classmates, explain the difference that friends and allies make in your life, especially when navigating a space, experience, or social expectation you find challenging.

6 Language and Community

> If there's a book that you want to read, but it hasn't been written yet, then you must write it.
>
> —Toni Morrison

Living in the everyday stress of school, you may find it challenging to remember why writing matters, and why it matters to write with precision and care. The tools that we use to write—not computers and pens, but words, language, grammar, and rhetoric—are the object of study for the ten authors in this chapter. They show us how to write what has yet to be written, and they alert us to the dangers of the written word improperly deployed. These essays are both serious and comic—often in the same piece. They remind us of the power we have when we decide to speak for ourselves and the power we concede when we let others speak for us. Equally importantly, these authors think about and demonstrate in their own writing how language—a word, a story, an entire spoken or written language—works to create and strengthen the bonds of community.

Here you will find advice for how to write, how to advocate for yourself, how to preserve languages that those in power do not want you to speak, how to think about swearing, and why you might want to look for new ways to express yourself. At the same time, these essays go well beyond tips and tricks: They show you the stakes of writing, and, in several cases, describe the jobs of people who devote their lives to caring about words. In a chapter that begins with dying metaphors and ends with dead memes, there is immense vitality, urgency, and momentum.

This chapter opens with George Orwell's classic 1946 essay "Politics and the English Language." In it, he rails against propaganda and advocates for clear, direct prose. Reacting against the political obfuscations of the Cold War, Orwell identifies a range of bad habits in political writing that persist to this day. You can read Orwell just for advice, but if you step back and imagine the greater dangers that he sees in a world that fails to take language seriously and fails to recognize the growth of misstatements, inaccuracies, and propaganda, you may find reason to renew your commitment to becoming a better reader and writer. Several authors in this chapter, including Gloria Anzaldúa and Ngũgĩ wa Thiong'o, describe the importance of exploring their heritage language at home in a world where English dominates. For Joan Naviyuk Kane, the call to preserve a language is even stronger, as she labors to preserve Inupiaq, the endangered Indigenous language that her ancestors were once prohibited from speaking. This, too, is an important part of coming into your own voice as a writer whether your language is Spanish, Gĩkũyũ, Inupiaq, or another of the thousands of spoken and written languages and dialects across the world. These essays help us understand the value of being multilingual and the losses that come when speaking one's own language is prohibited. Molly McCully Brown offers a reflection on how language around her disability has followed her throughout life and begins to imagine a more empowering idea of language to understand and describe disability. Kory Stamper and John McWhorter show us how complicated a single word can be, even a simple verb like "take" or a common swear word, such as "shit." Kathy Fish's essay on collective nouns—a familiar quirk of the English language—ends with a devastating twist, while David Shields's hilarious exploration of the many clichés of sports writing is, as he might say, a slam dunk. Finally, we move from words to memes with Lauren Michele Jackson's thoughtful analysis of why some memes barely last a day, while others keep coming around again and again. It's a brilliant new way to think about what might end up enduring from the ephemeral world of internet culture.

As you read and respond to these essays, think not only about *how* to make your writing better but also *why*: what is at stake in what you're arguing and why it matters for people to understand you, your perspective, and the context from which you write. These essays will give you new ways to think about the many communities to which you belong, as well as tools for using language to explain who you are and to understand others in turn. Whether humorous or profane, sincere or sharp, sure or questioning, these essays will both challenge and accompany you in the process of becoming a better writer.

GEORGE ORWELL

Politics and the English Language

MOST PEOPLE WHO BOTHER with the matter at all would admit that the English language is in a bad way, but it is generally assumed that we cannot by conscious action do anything about it. Our civilization is decadent and our language—so the argument runs—must inevitably share in the general collapse. It follows that any struggle against the abuse of language is a sentimental archaism, like preferring candles to electric light or hansom cabs to aeroplanes. Underneath this lies the half-conscious belief that language is a natural growth and not an instrument which we shape for our own purposes.

Now, it is clear that the decline of a language must ultimately have political and economic causes: it is not due simply to the bad influence of this or that individual writer. But an effect can become a cause, reinforcing the original cause and producing the same effect in an intensified form, and so on indefinitely. A man may take to drink because he feels himself to be a failure, and then fail all the more completely because he drinks. It is rather the same thing that is happening to the English language. It becomes ugly and inaccurate

From Shooting an Elephant and Other Essays *(1950), a collection of George Orwell's best-known essays. "Politics and the English Language" is one of the most famous modern arguments for a clear, unadorned writing style. All notes in this piece were written by the author unless indicated otherwise.*

because our thoughts are foolish, but the slovenliness of our language makes it easier for us to have foolish thoughts. The point is that the process is reversible. Modern English, especially written English, is full of bad habits which spread by imitation and which can be avoided if one is willing to take the necessary trouble. If one gets rid of these habits one can think more clearly, and to think clearly is a necessary first step towards political regeneration: so that the fight against bad English is not frivolous and is not the exclusive concern of professional writers. I will come back to this presently, and I hope that by that time the meaning of what I have said here will have become clearer. Meanwhile, here are five specimens of the English language as it is now habitually written.

These five passages have not been picked out because they are especially bad—I could have quoted far worse if I had chosen—but because they illustrate various of the mental vices from which we now suffer. They are a little below the average, but are fairly representative samples. I number them so that I can refer back to them when necessary:

"(1) I am not, indeed, sure whether it is not true to say that the Milton who once seemed not unlike a seventeenth-century Shelley had not become, out of an experience ever more bitter in each year, more alien [*sic*] to the founder of that Jesuit sect which nothing could induce him to tolerate."

—PROFESSOR HAROLD LASKI (*ESSAY IN FREEDOM OF EXPRESSION*).

"(2) Above all, we cannot play ducks and drakes with a native battery of idioms which prescribes such egregious collocations of vocables as the Basic *put up with* for *tolerate* or *put at a loss* for *bewilder*."

—PROFESSOR LANCELOT HOGBEN (*INTERGLOSSA*).

"(3) On the one side we have the free personality: by definition it is not neurotic, for it has neither conflict nor dream. Its desires, such as they are, are transparent, for they are just what institutional approval keeps in the forefront of consciousness; another institutional pattern would alter their number and intensity; there is little in them that is natural, irreducible, or culturally dangerous. But *on the other side*, the social bond itself is nothing but the mutual reflection of these self-secure integrities. Recall the definition of love. Is not this the very picture of a small academic? Where is there a place in this hall of mirrors for either personality or fraternity?"

—ESSAY ON PSYCHOLOGY IN *POLITICS* (NEW YORK).

"(4) All the 'best people' from the gentlemen's clubs, and all the frantic fascist captains, united in common hatred of Socialism and bestial horror of the rising tide of the mass revolutionary movement, have turned to acts of provocation, to foul incendiarism, to medieval legends of poisoned wells, to legalize their own destruction of proletarian organizations, and rouse the agitated petty-bourgeoisie to chauvinistic fervour on behalf of the fight against the revolutionary way out of the crisis."

—COMMUNIST PAMPHLET.

"(5) If a new spirit *is* to be infused into this old country, there is one thorny and contentious reform which must be tackled, and that is the humanization and galvanization of the B.B.C. Timidity here will bespeak cancer and atrophy of the soul. The heart of Britain may be sound and of strong beat, for instance, but the British lion's roar at present is like that of Bottom in Shakespeare's *Midsummer Night's Dream*—as gentle as any sucking dove. A virile new Britain cannot continue indefinitely to be traduced in the eyes or rather ears, of the world by the effete languors of Langham Place, brazenly masquerading as 'standard English.' When the Voice of Britain is heard at nine o'clock, better far and infinitely less ludicrous to hear aitches honestly dropped than the present priggish, inflated, inhibited, school-ma'amish arch braying of blameless bashful mewing maidens!"

—LETTER IN *TRIBUNE*.

Each of these passages has faults of its own, but, quite apart from avoidable ugliness, two qualities are common to all of them. The first is staleness of imagery; the other is lack of precision. The writer either has a meaning and cannot express it, or he inadvertently says something else, or he is almost indifferent as to whether his words mean anything or not. This mixture of vagueness and sheer incompetence is the most marked characteristic of modern English prose, and especially of any kind of political writing. As soon as certain topics are raised, the concrete melts into the abstract and no one seems able to think of turns of speech that are not hackneyed: prose consists less and less of *words* chosen for the sake of their meaning, and more and more of *phrases* tacked together like the sections of a prefabricated henhouse. I list below, with notes and examples, various of the tricks by means of which the work of prose-construction is habitually dodged:

DYING METAPHORS

5   A newly invented metaphor assists thought by evoking a visual image, while on the other hand a metaphor which is technically "dead" (e.g. *iron resolution*) has in effect reverted to being an ordinary word and can generally be used without loss of vividness. But in between these two classes there is a huge dump of worn-out metaphors which have lost all evocative power and are merely used because they save people the trouble of inventing phrases for themselves. Examples are: *Ring the changes on, take up the cudgels for, toe the line, ride roughshod over, stand shoulder to shoulder with, play into the hands of, no axe to grind, grist to the mill, fishing in troubled waters, on the order of the day, Achilles' heel, swan song, hotbed.* Many of these are used without knowledge of their meaning (what is a "rift," for instance?), and incompatible metaphors are frequently mixed, a sure sign that the writer is not interested in what he is saying. Some metaphors now current have been twisted out of their original meaning without those who use them even being aware of the fact. For example, *toe the line* is sometimes written *tow the line*. Another example is *the hammer and the anvil*, now always used with the implication that the anvil gets the worst of it. In real life it is always the anvil that breaks the hammer, never the other way about: a writer who stopped to think what he was saying would be aware of this, and would avoid perverting the original phrase.

Operators or Verbal False Limbs

These save the trouble of picking out appropriate verbs and nouns, and at the same time pad each sentence with extra syllables which give it an appearance of symmetry. Characteristic phrases are: *render inoperative, militate against, make contact with, be subjected to, give rise to, give grounds for, have the effect of, play a leading part (role) in, make itself felt, take effect, exhibit a tendency to, serve the purpose of, etc., etc.* The keynote is the elimination of simple verbs. Instead of being a single word, such as *break, stop, spoil, mend, kill,* a verb becomes a *phrase,* made up of a noun or adjective tacked on to some general-purposes verb such as *prove, serve, form, play, render.* In addition, the passive voice is wherever possible used in preference to the active, and noun constructions are used instead of gerunds (*by examination of* instead of *by examining*). The range of verbs is further cut down by means of the *-ize* and *de-* formation, and the banal statements are given an appearance of profundity by means of the *not un-* formation. Simple conjunctions and prepositions are replaced by such phrases as *with respect to, having regard to, the fact that, by dint of, in view of, in the interests of, on the hypothesis that;* and the ends of sentences are saved from anticlimax by such resounding commonplaces as *greatly to be desired, cannot be left out of account, a development to be expected in the near future, deserving of serious consideration, brought to a satisfactory conclusion,* and so on and so forth.

Pretentious Diction

Words like *phenomenon, element, individual* (as noun), *objective, categorical, effective, virtual, basic, primary, promote, constitute, exhibit, exploit, utilize, eliminate, liquidate,* are used to dress up simple statements and give an air of scientific impartiality to biased judgments. Adjectives like *epoch-making, epic, historic, unforgettable, triumphant, age-old, inevitable, inexorable, veritable,* are used to dignify the sordid processes of international politics, while writing that aims at glorifying war usually takes on an archaic colour, its characteristic words being: *realm, throne, chariot, mailed fist, trident, sword, shield, buckler, banner, jackboot, clarion.* Foreign words and expressions such as *cul de sac, ancien régime, deus ex machina, mutatis mutandis, status quo, gleichschaltung, weltanschauung,* are used to give an air of culture and elegance. Except for the useful abbreviations *i.e., e.g.,* and *etc.,* there is no real need for any of the hundreds of foreign phrases now current in English. Bad writers, and especially scientific, political and sociological writers, are nearly always haunted by the notion that Latin or Greek words are grander than Saxon ones, and unnecessary words like *expedite, ameliorate, predict, extraneous, deracinated, clandestine, subaqueous* and hundreds of others constantly gain ground from their Anglo-Saxon opposite numbers.[1] The jargon

1. An interesting illustration of this is the way in which the English flower names which were in use till very recently are being ousted by Greek ones, *snapdragon* becoming *antirrhinum, forget-me-not* becoming *myosotis,* etc. It is hard to see any practical reason for this change of fashion: it is probably due to an instinctive turning-away from the more homely word and a vague feeling that the Greek word is scientific.

peculiar to Marxist writing (*hyena, hangman, cannibal, petty bourgeois, these gentry, lackey, flunkey, mad dog, White Guard,* etc.) consists largely of words and phrases translated from Russian, German or French; but the normal way of coining a new word is to use a Latin or Greek root with the appropriate affix and, where necessary, the *-ize* formation. It is often easier to make up words of this kind (*deregionalize, impermissible, extramarital, nonfragmentatory* and so forth) than to think up the English words that will cover one's meaning. The result, in general, is an increase in slovenliness and vagueness.

MEANINGLESS WORDS

In certain kinds of writing, particularly in art criticism and literary criticism, it is normal to come across long passages which are almost completely lacking in meaning.[2] Words like *romantic, plastic, values, human, dead, sentimental, natural, vitality,* as used in art criticism, are strictly meaningless in the sense that they not only do not point to any discoverable object, but are hardly ever expected to do so by the reader. When one critic writes, "The outstanding feature of Mr. X's work is its living quality," while another writes, "The immediately striking thing about Mr. X's work is its peculiar deadness," the reader accepts this as a simple difference of opinion. If words like *black* and *white* were involved, instead of the jargon words *dead* and *living,* he would see at once that language was being used in an improper way. Many political words are similarly abused. The word *Fascism* has now no meaning except in so far as it signifies "something not desirable." The words *democracy, socialism, freedom, patriotic, realistic, justice,* have each of them several different meanings which cannot be reconciled with one another. In the case of a word like *democracy,* not only is there no agreed definition, but the attempt to make one is resisted from all sides. It is almost universally felt that when we call a country democratic we are praising it: consequently the defenders of every kind of régime claim that it is a democracy, and fear that they might have to stop using the word if it were tied down to any one meaning. Words of this kind are often used in a consciously dishonest way. That is, the person who uses them has his own private definition, but allows his hearer to think he means something quite different. Statements like *Marshal Pétain was a true patriot, The Soviet Press is the freest in the world, The Catholic Church is opposed to persecution,* are almost always made with intent to deceive. Other words used in variable meanings, in most cases more or less dishonestly, are: *class, totalitarian, science, progressive, reactionary, bourgeois, equality.*

Now that I have made this catalogue of swindles and perversions, let me give another example of the kind of writing that they lead to. This time it must of its nature be an imaginary one. I am going to translate a passage of good

2. Example: "Comfort's catholicity of perception and image, strangely Whitmanesque in range, almost the exact opposite in aesthetic compulsion, continues to evoke that trembling atmospheric accumulative hinting at a cruel, an inexorably serene timelessness. . . . Wrey Gardiner scores by aiming at simple bull's-eyes with precision. Only they are not so simple, and through this contented sadness runs more than the surface bittersweet of resignation" (*Poetry Quarterly*).

English into modern English of the worst sort. Here is a well-known verse from *Ecclesiastes*:

> "I returned and saw under the sun, that the race is not to the swift, nor the battle to the strong, neither yet bread to the wise, nor yet riches to men of understanding, nor yet favour to men of skill; but time and chance happeneth to them all."

Here it is in modern English: 10

> "Objective consideration of contemporary phenomena compels the conclusion that success or failure in competitive activities exhibits no tendency to be commensurate with innate capacity, but that a considerable element of the unpredictable must invariably be taken into account."

This is a parody, but not a very gross one. Exhibit (3), above, for instance, contains several patches of the same kind of English. It will be seen that I have not made a full translation. The beginning and ending of the sentence follow the original meaning fairly closely, but in the middle the concrete illustrations— race, battle, bread—dissolve into the vague phrase "success or failure in competitive activities." This had to be so, because no modern writer of the kind I am discussing—no one capable of using phrases like "objective consideration of contemporary phenomena"—would ever tabulate his thoughts in that precise and detailed way. The whole tendency of modern prose is away from concreteness. Now analyse these two sentences a little more closely. The first contains forty-nine words but only sixty syllables, and all its words are those of everyday life. The second contains thirty-eight words of ninety syllables: eighteen of its words are from Latin roots, and one from Greek. The first sentence contains six vivid images, and only one phrase ("time and chance") that could be called vague. The second contains not a single fresh, arresting phrase, and in spite of its ninety syllables it gives only a shortened version of the meaning contained in the first. Yet without a doubt it is the second kind of sentence that is gaining ground in modern English. I do not want to exaggerate. This kind of writing is not yet universal, and outcrops of simplicity will occur here and there in the worst-written page. Still, if you or I were told to write a few lines on the uncertainty of human fortunes, we should probably come much nearer to my imaginary sentence than to the one from *Ecclesiastes*.

As I have tried to show, modern writing at its worst does not consist in picking out words for the sake of their meaning and inventing images in order to make the meaning clearer. It consists in gumming together long strips of words which have already been set in order by someone else, and making the results presentable by sheer humbug. The attraction of this way of writing is that it is easy. It is easier—even quicker, once you have the habit—to say *In my opinion it is a not unjustifiable assumption that* than to say *I think*. If you use ready-made phrases, you not only don't have to hunt about for words; you also don't have to bother with the rhythms of your sentences, since these phrases are generally so arranged as to be more or less euphonious. When you are composing in a hurry—when you are dictating to a stenographer, for instance, or making a public speech—it is natural to fall into a pretentious, Latinized style. Tags like *a consideration which we should do well to bear in mind* or *a conclusion to which all of us would readily assent* will save many a sentence from coming down with a bump. By using stale metaphors, similes and idioms, you save much mental effort, at the cost of leaving your meaning vague, not only for your reader but for yourself. This is the significance of mixed metaphors. The sole aim of a metaphor is to call up a visual image. When these images clash—as in *The Fascist octopus has sung its swan song, the jackboot is thrown into the melting pot*—it can be taken as certain that the writer is not seeing a mental image of the objects he is naming; in other words he is not really thinking. Look again at the examples I gave at the beginning of this essay. Professor Laski (1) uses five negatives in fifty-three words. One of these is superfluous, making nonsense of the whole passage, and in addition there is the slip *alien* for akin, making further nonsense, and several avoidable pieces of clumsiness which increase the general vagueness. Professor Hogben (2) plays ducks and drakes with a battery which is able to write prescriptions, and, while disapproving of the everyday phrase *put up with*, is unwilling to look *egregious* up in the dictionary and see what it means. (3), if one takes an uncharitable attitude towards it, is simply meaningless: probably one could work out its intended meaning by reading the whole of the article in which it occurs. In (4), the writer knows more or less what he wants to say, but an accumulation of stale phrases chokes him like tea leaves blocking a sink. In (5), words and meaning have almost parted company. People who write in this manner usually have a general emotional meaning—they dislike one thing and want to express solidarity with another—but they are not interested in the detail of what they are saying. A scrupulous writer, in every sentence that he writes, will ask himself at least four questions, thus: What am I trying to say? What words will express it? What image or idiom will make it clearer? Is this image fresh enough to have an effect? And he will probably ask himself two more: Could I put it more shortly? Have I said anything that is avoidably ugly? But you are not obliged to go to all this trouble. You can shirk it by simply throwing your mind open and letting the ready-made phrases come crowding in. They will construct your sentences for you—even think your thoughts for you, to a certain extent—and at need they will perform the important service of partially concealing your meaning even from yourself. It is at this point that the special connection between politics and the debasement of language becomes clear.

In our time it is broadly true that political writing is bad writing. Where it is not true, it will generally be found that the writer is some kind of rebel, expressing his private opinions and not a "party line." Orthodoxy, of whatever colour, seems to demand a lifeless, imitative style. The political dialects to be found in pamphlets, leading articles, manifestos, White Papers and the speeches of under-secretaries do, of course, vary from party to party, but they are all alike in that one almost never finds in them a fresh, vivid, homemade turn of speech. When one watches some tired hack on the platform mechanically repeating the familiar phrases—*bestial atrocities, iron heel, blood-stained tyranny, free peoples of the world, stand shoulder to shoulder*—one often has a curious feeling that one is not watching a live human being but some kind of dummy: a feeling which suddenly becomes stronger at moments when the light catches the speaker's spectacles and turns them into blank discs which seem to have no eyes behind them. And this is not altogether fanciful. A speaker who uses that kind of phraseology has gone some distance towards turning himself into a machine. The appropriate noises are coming out of his larynx, but his brain is not involved as it would be if he were choosing his words for himself. If the speech he is making is one that he is accustomed to make over and over again, he may be almost unconscious of what he is saying, as one is when one utters the responses in church. And this reduced state of consciousness, if not indispensable, is at any rate favourable to political conformity.

In our time, political speech and writing are largely the defence of the indefensible. Things like the continuance of British rule in India, the Russian purges and deportations, the dropping of the atom bombs on Japan, can indeed be defended, but only by arguments which are too brutal for most people to face, and which do not square with the professed aims of political parties. Thus political language has to consist largely of euphemism, question-begging and sheer cloudy vagueness. Defenceless villages are bombarded from the air, the inhabitants driven out into the countryside, the cattle machine-gunned, the huts set on fire with incendiary bullets: this is called *pacification*. Millions of peasants are robbed of their farms and sent trudging along the roads with no more than they can carry: this is called *transfer of population* or *rectification of frontiers*. People are imprisoned for years without trial, or shot in the back of the neck or sent to die of scurvy in Arctic lumber camps: this is called *elimination of unreliable elements*. Such phraseology is needed if one wants to name things without calling up mental pictures of them. Consider for instance some comfortable English professor defending Russian totalitarianism. He cannot say outright, "I believe in killing off your opponents when you can get good results by doing so." Probably, therefore, he will say something like this:

"While freely conceding that the Soviet régime exhibits certain features   15
which the humanitarian may be inclined to deplore, we must, I think, agree that a certain curtailment of the right to political opposition is an unavoidable concomitant of transitional periods, and that the rigors which the Russian people have been called upon to undergo have been amply justified in the sphere of concrete achievement."

The inflated style is itself a kind of euphemism. A mass of Latin words falls upon the facts like soft snow, blurring the outlines and covering up all the details. The great enemy of clear language is insincerity. When there is a gap between one's real and one's declared aims, one turns as it were instinctively to long words and exhausted idioms, like a cuttlefish squirting out ink. In our age there is no such thing as "keeping out of politics." All issues are political issues, and politics itself is a mass of lies, evasions, folly, hatred and schizophrenia. When the general atmosphere is bad, language must suffer. I should expect to find—this is a guess which I have not sufficient knowledge to verify—that the German, Russian and Italian languages have all deteriorated in the last ten or fifteen years, as a result of dictatorship.

But if thought corrupts language, language can also corrupt thought. A bad usage can spread by tradition and imitation, even among people who should and do know better. The debased language that I have been discussing is in some ways very convenient. Phrases like *a not unjustifiable assumption, leaves much to be desired, would serve no good purpose, a consideration which we should do well to bear in mind*, are a continuous temptation, a packet of aspirins always at one's elbow. Look back through this essay, and for certain you will find that I have again and again committed the very faults I am protesting against. By this morning's post I have received a pamphlet dealing with conditions in Germany. The author tells me that he "felt impelled" to write it. I open it at random, and here is almost the first sentence that I see: "(The Allies) have an opportunity not only of achieving a radical transformation of Germany's social and political structure in such a way as to avoid a nationalistic reaction in Germany itself, but at the same time of laying the foundations of a co-operative and unified Europe." You see, he "feels impelled" to write—feels, presumably, that he has something new to say—and yet his words, like cavalry horses answering the bugle, group themselves automatically into the familiar dreary pattern. This invasion of one's mind by ready-made phrases (*lay the foundations, achieve a radical transformation*) can only be prevented if one is constantly on guard against them, and every such phrase anaesthetizes a portion of one's brain.

I said earlier that the decadence of our language is probably curable. Those who deny this would argue, if they produced an argument at all, that language merely reflects existing social conditions, and that we cannot influence its development by any direct tinkering with words and constructions. So far as the general tone or spirit of a language goes, this may be true, but it is not true in detail. Silly words and expressions have often disappeared, not through any evolutionary process but owing to the conscious action of a minority. Two recent examples were *explore every avenue* and *leave no stone unturned*, which were killed by the jeers of a few journalists. There is a long list of flyblown metaphors which could similarly be got rid of if enough people would interest themselves in the job; and it should also be possible to laugh the *not un-* formation out of existence,[3] to reduce the amount of Latin and Greek in the average sentence, to drive out foreign phrases and strayed scientific words, and, in general, to make pretentiousness unfashionable. But all these are minor points. The defence of the English language implies more than this, and perhaps it is best to start by saying what it does *not* imply.

To begin with it has nothing to do with archaism, with the salvaging of obsolete words and turns of speech, or with the setting up of a "standard English" which must never be departed from. On the contrary, it is especially concerned with the scrapping of every word or idiom which has outworn its usefulness. It has nothing to do with correct grammar and syntax, which are of no importance so long as one makes one's meaning clear, or with the avoidance of Americanisms, or with having what is called a "good prose style." On

---

3. One can cure oneself of the *not un-* formation by memorizing this sentence: *A not unblack dog was chasing a not unsmall rabbit across a not ungreen field.*

the other hand it is not concerned with fake simplicity and the attempt to make written English colloquial. Nor does it even imply in every case preferring the Saxon word to the Latin one, though it does imply using the fewest and shortest words that will cover one's meaning. What is above all needed is to let the meaning choose the word, and not the other way about. In prose, the worst thing one can do with words is to surrender to them. When you think of a concrete object, you think wordlessly, and then, if you want to describe the thing you have been visualizing you probably hunt about till you find the exact words that seem to fit. When you think of something abstract you are more inclined to use words from the start, and unless you make a conscious effort to prevent it, the existing dialect will come rushing in and do the job for you, at the expense of blurring or even changing your meaning. Probably it is better to put off using words as long as possible and get one's meaning as clear as one can through pictures or sensations. Afterwards one can choose—not simply *accept*—the phrases that will best cover the meaning, and then switch round and decide what impression one's words are likely to make on another person. This last effort of the mind cuts out all stale or mixed images, all prefabricated phrases, needless repetitions, and humbug and vagueness generally. But one can often be in doubt about the effect of a word or a phrase, and one needs rules that one can rely on when instinct fails. I think the following rules will cover most cases:

(i) Never use a metaphor, simile or other figure of speech which you are used to seeing in print.

(ii) Never use a long word where a short one will do.

(iii) If it is possible to cut a word out, always cut it out.

(iv) Never use the passive where you can use the active.

(v) Never use a foreign phrase, a scientific word or a jargon word if you can think of an everyday English equivalent.

(vi) Break any of these rules sooner than say anything outright barbarous.

These rules sound elementary, and so they are, but they demand a deep change of attitude in anyone who has grown used to writing in the style now fashionable. One could keep all of them and still write bad English, but one could not write the kind of stuff that I quoted in those five specimens at the beginning of this article.

I have not here been considering the literary use of language, but merely language as an instrument for expressing and not for concealing or preventing thought. Stuart Chase[4] and others have come near to claiming that all abstract words are meaningless, and have used this as a pretext for advocating a kind of political quietism. Since you don't know what Fascism is, how can you struggle

20

4. Chase (in *The Tyranny of Words* [1938] and *The Power of Words* [1954]) and S. I. Hayakawa (in *Language in Action* [1939]) popularized the semantic theories of Alfred Koryzbski [Editor's note].

against Fascism? One need not swallow such absurdities as this, but one ought to recognize that the present political chaos is connected with the decay of language, and that one can probably bring about some improvement by starting at the verbal end. If you simplify your English, you are freed from the worst follies of orthodoxy. You cannot speak any of the necessary dialects, and when you make a stupid remark its stupidity will be obvious, even to yourself. Political language—and with variations this is true of all political parties, from Conservatives to Anarchists—is designed to make lies sound truthful and murder respectable, and to give an appearance of solidity to pure wind. One cannot change this all in a moment, but one can at least change one's own habits, and from time to time one can even, if one jeers loudly enough, send some worn-out and useless phrase—some *jackboot, Achilles' heel, hotbed, melting pot, acid test, veritable inferno* or other lump of verbal refuse—into the dustbin where it belongs.

MLA CITATION

Orwell, George. "Politics and the English Language." *The Norton Reader: An Anthology of Nonfiction*, edited by Melissa A. Goldthwaite et al., 16th ed., W. W. Norton, 2024, pp. 340–50.

Questions

1. State George Orwell's main point as precisely as possible.

2. What kinds of prose does Orwell analyze in this essay? Look, in particular, at the passages he quotes in paragraph 3. Annotate these passages. What kinds of writing are they, and where would you find their contemporary equivalents?

3. Apply Orwell's rule iv, "Never use the passive where you can use the active" (paragraph 19), to paragraph 14 of his essay. What happens when you change his passive constructions to active? Has Orwell forgotten rule iv or is he covered by rule vi, "Break any of these rules sooner than say anything outright barbarous" (paragraph 19)?

4. Orwell wrote this essay in 1946. Choose at least two examples of political discourse from current media and discuss, in an essay, the extent to which Orwell's analysis of the language of politics still applies today. Which features that he singles out for criticism appear most frequently in the examples you chose?

GLORIA ANZALDÚA
How to Tame a Wild Tongue

E'RE GOING TO have to control your tongue," the dentist says, pulling out all the metal from my mouth. Silver bits plop and tinkle into the basin. My mouth is a motherlode. The dentist is cleaning out my roots. I get a whiff of the stench when I gasp. "I can't cap that tooth yet, you're still draining," he says.

"We're going to have to do something about your tongue," I hear the anger rising in his voice. My tongue keeps pushing out the wads of cotton, pushing back the drills, the long thin needles. "I've never seen anything as strong or as stubborn," he says. And I think, how do you tame a wild tongue, train it to be quiet, how do you bridle and saddle it? How do you make it lie down?

> "Who is to say that robbing a people of
> its language is less violent than war?"
>
> —RAY GWYN SMITH[1]

I remember being caught speaking Spanish at recess—that was good for three licks on the knuckles with a sharp ruler. I remember being sent to the corner of the classroom for "talking back" to the Anglo teacher when all I was trying to do was tell her how to pronounce my name. "If you want to be American, speak 'American.' If you don't like it, go back to Mexico where you belong."

"I want you to speak English. *Pa'hallar buen trabajo tienes que saber hablar el inglés bien. Qué vale toda tu educación si todavía hablas inglés con un* 'accent,'" my mother would say, mortified that I spoke English like a Mexican. At Pan American University, I and all Chicano students were required to take two speech classes. Their purpose: to get rid of our accents.   5

Attacks on one's form of expression with the intent to censor are a violation of the First Amendment. *El Anglo con cara de inocente nos arrancó la lengua.* Wild tongues can't be tamed, they can only be cut out.

OVERCOMING THE TRADITION OF SILENCE

> *Ahogadas, escupimos el oscuro.*
> *Peleando con nuestra propia sombra*
> *el silencio nos sepulta.*

En boca cerrada no entran moscas. "Flies don't enter a closed mouth" is a saying I kept hearing when I was a child. *Ser habladora* was to be a gossip and

From Borderlands / La Frontera: The New Mestiza *(1987), a collection of experimental essays and memoirs that combine English, Spanish, and Chicano Spanish. All notes in this piece were written by the author. The author has asked that no translations of Spanish or Chicano Spanish be added.*

1. Ray Gwyn Smith, *Moorland Is Cold Country*, unpublished book.

a liar, to talk too much. *Muchachitas bien criadas*, well-bred girls don't answer back. *Es una falta de respeto* to talk back to one's mother or father. I remember one of the sins I'd recite to the priest in the confession box the few times I went to confession: talking back to my mother, *hablar pa' 'trás, repelar. Hocicona, repelona, chismosa*, having a big mouth, questioning, carrying tales are all signs of being *mal criada*. In my culture they are all words that are derogatory if applied to women—I've never heard them applied to men.

The first time I heard two women, a Puerto Rican and a Cuban, say the word "*nosotras*," I was shocked. I had not known the word existed. Chicanas use *nosotros* whether we're male or female. We are robbed of our female being by the masculine plural. Language is a male discourse.

> And our tongues have become
> dry the wilderness has
> dried out our tongues and
> we have forgotten speech.
> —IRENA KLEPFISZ[2]

Even our own people, other Spanish speakers *nos quieren poner candados en la boca*. They would hold us back with their bag of *reglas de academia*.

Oyé como ladra: el lenguaje de la frontera

> *Quien tiene boca se equivoca.*
> —MEXICAN SAYING

10   "*Pocho*, cultural traitor, you're speaking the oppressor's language by speaking English, you're ruining the Spanish language," I have been accused by various Latinos and Latinas. Chicano Spanish is considered by the purist and by most Latinos deficient, a mutilation of Spanish.

But Chicano Spanish is a border tongue which developed naturally. Change, *evolución, enriquecimiento de palabras nuevas por invención o adopción* have created variants of Chicano Spanish, *un nuevo lenguaje. Un lenguaje que corresponde a un modo de vivir.* Chicano Spanish is not incorrect, it is a living language.

For a people who are neither Spanish nor live in a country in which Spanish is the first language; for a people who live in a country in which English is the reigning tongue but who are not Anglo; for a people who cannot entirely identify with either standard (formal, Castilian) Spanish nor standard English, what recourse is left to them but to create their own language? A language which they can connect their identity to, one capable of communicating the realities and values true to themselves—a language with terms that are neither *español ni inglés*, but both. We speak a patois, a forked tongue, a variation of two languages.

2. Irena Klepfisz, "*Di rayze aheym* / The Journey Home," in *The Tribe of Dina: A Jewish Women's Anthology*, Melanie Kaye/Kantrowitz and Irena Klepfisz, eds. (Montpelier, VT: Sinister Wisdom Books, 1986), 49.

Chicano Spanish sprang out of the Chicanos' need to identify ourselves as a distinct people. We needed a language with which we could communicate with ourselves, a secret language. For some of us, language is a homeland closer than the Southwest—for many Chicanos today live in the Midwest and the East. And because we are a complex, heterogeneous people, we speak many languages. Some of the languages we speak are:

1. Standard English
2. Working class and slang English
3. Standard Spanish
4. Standard Mexican Spanish
5. North Mexican Spanish dialect
6. Chicano Spanish (Texas, New Mexico, Arizona and California have regional variations)
7. Tex-Mex
8. *Pachuco* (called *caló*)

My "home" tongues are the languages I speak with my sister and brothers, with my friends. They are the last five listed, with 6 and 7 being closest to my heart. From school, the media and job situations, I've picked up standard and working class English. From Mamagrande Locha and from reading Spanish and Mexican literature, I've picked up Standard Spanish and Standard Mexican Spanish. From *los recién llegados*, Mexican immigrants, and *braceros*, I learned the North Mexican dialect. With Mexicans I'll try to speak either Standard Mexican Spanish or the North Mexican dialect. From my parents and Chicanos living in the Valley, I picked up Chicano Texas Spanish, and I speak it with my mom, younger brother (who married a Mexican and who rarely mixes Spanish with English), aunts and older relatives.

With Chicanas from *Nuevo México* or *Arizona* I will speak Chicano Spanish   15 a little, but often they don't understand what I'm saying. With most California Chicanas I speak entirely in English (unless I forget). When I first moved to San Francisco, I'd rattle off something in Spanish, unintentionally embarrassing them. Often it is only with another Chicana *tejana* that I can talk freely.

Words distorted by English are known as anglicisms or *pochismos*. The *pocho* is an anglicized Mexican or American of Mexican origin who speaks Spanish with an accent characteristic of North Americans and who distorts and reconstructs the language according to the influence of English.[3] Tex-Mex, or Spanglish, comes most naturally to me. I may switch back and forth from English to Spanish in the same sentence or in the same word. With my sister and my brother Nune and with Chicano *tejano* contemporaries I speak in Tex-Mex.

From kids and people my own age I picked up *Pachuco*. *Pachuco* (the language of the zoot suiters) is a language of rebellion, both against Standard Spanish and Standard English. It is a secret language. Adults of the culture and

3. R. C. Ortega, *Dialectología Del Barrio*, trans. Hortencia S. Alwan (Los Angeles, CA: R. C. Ortega Publisher & Bookseller, 1977), 132.

outsiders cannot understand it. It is made up of slang words from both English and Spanish. *Ruca* means girl or woman, *vato* means guy or dude, *chale* means no, *simón* means yes, *churo* is sure, talk is *periquiar, pigionear* means petting, *que gacho* means how nerdy, *ponte águila* means watch out, death is called *la pelona*. Through lack of practice and not having others who can speak it, I've lost most of the *Pachuco* tongue.

CHICANO SPANISH

Chicanos, after 250 years of Spanish/Anglo colonization, have developed significant differences in the Spanish we speak. We collapse two adjacent vowels into a single syllable and sometimes shift the stress in certain words such as *maíz/maiz, cohete/cuete*. We leave out certain consonants when they appear between vowels: *lado/lao, mojado/mojao*. Chicanos from South Texas pronounced *f* as *j* as in *jue (fue)*. Chicanos use "archaisms," words that are no longer in the Spanish language, words that have been evolved out. We say *semos, truje, haiga, ansina*, and *naiden*. We retain the "archaic" *j*, as in *jalar*, that derives from an earlier *h* (the French *halar* or the Germanic *halon* which was lost to standard Spanish in the 16th century), but which is still found in several regional dialects such as the one spoken in South Texas. (Due to geography, Chicanos from the Valley of South Texas were cut off linguistically from other Spanish speakers. We tend to use words that the Spaniards brought over from Medieval Spain. The majority of the Spanish colonizers in Mexico and the Southwest came from Extremadura—Hernán Cortés was one of them—and Andalucía. Andalucians pronounce *ll* like a *y*, and their *d*'s tend to be absorbed by adjacent vowels: *tirado* becomes *tirao*. They brought *el lenguaje popular, dialectos y regionalismos.*[4])

Chicanos and other Spanish speakers also shift *ll* to *y* and *z* to *s*.[5] We leave out initial syllables, saying *tar* for *estar, toy* for *estoy, hora* for *ahora* (*cubanos* and *puertorriqueños* also leave out initial letters of some words). We also leave out the final syllable such as *pa* for *para*. The intervocalic *y*, the *ll* as in *tortilla, ella, botella*, gets replaced by *tortia* or *tortiya, ea, botea*. We add an additional syllable at the beginning of certain words: *atocar* for *tocar, agastar* for *gastar*. Sometimes we'll say *lavaste las vacijas*, other times *lavates* (substituting the *ates* verb endings for the *aste*).

20   We use anglicisms, words borrowed from English: *bola* from ball, *carpeta* from carpet, *máchina de lavar* (instead of *lavadora*) from washing machine. Tex-Mex argot, created by adding a Spanish sound at the beginning or end of an English word such as *cookiar* for cook, *watchar* for watch, *parkiar* for park, and *rapiar* for rape, is the result of the pressures on Spanish speakers to adapt to English.

4. Eduardo Hernandéz-Chávez, Andrew D. Cohen, and Anthony F. Beltramo, *El Lenguaje de los Chicanos: Regional and Social Characteristics of Language Used by Mexican Americans* (Arlington, VA: Center for Applied Linguistics, 1975), 39.

5. Hernandéz-Chávez, xvii.

We don't use the word *vosotros/as* or its accompanying verb form. We don't say *claro* (to mean yes), *imagínate*, or *me emociona*, unless we picked up Spanish from Latinas, out of a book, or in a classroom. Other Spanish-speaking groups are going through the same, or similar, development in their Spanish.

Linguistic Terrorism

> *Deslenguadas. Somos los del español deficiente.* We are your linguistic night-mare, your linguistic aberration, your linguistic *mestisaje*, the subject of your *burla*. Because we speak with tongues of fire we are culturally crucified. Racially, culturally and linguistically *somos huérfanos*—we speak an orphan tongue.

Chicanas who grew up speaking Chicano Spanish have internalized the belief that we speak poor Spanish. It is illegitimate, a bastard language. And because we internalize how our language has been used against us by the dominant culture, we use our language differences against each other.

Chicana feminists often skirt around each other with suspicion and hesitation. For the longest time I couldn't figure it out. Then it dawned on me. To be close to another Chicana is like looking into the mirror. We are afraid of what we'll see there. *Pena.* Shame. Low estimation of self. In childhood we are told that our language is wrong. Repeated attacks on our native tongue diminish our sense of self. The attacks continue throughout our lives.

Chicanas feel uncomfortable talking in Spanish to Latinas, afraid of their censure. Their language was not outlawed in their countries. They had a whole lifetime of being immersed in their native tongue; generations, centuries in which Spanish was a first language, taught in school, heard on radio and TV, and read in the newspaper.

If a person, Chicana or Latina, has a low estimation of my native tongue,   25
she also has a low estimation of me. Often with *mexicanas y latinas* we'll speak English as a neutral language. Even among Chicanas we tend to speak English at parties or conferences. Yet, at the same time, we're afraid the other will think we're *agringadas* because we don't speak Chicano Spanish. We oppress each other trying to out-Chicano each other, vying to be the "real" Chicanas, to speak like Chicanos. There is no one Chicano language just as there is no one Chicano experience. A monolingual Chicana whose first language is English or Spanish is just as much a Chicana as one who speaks several variants of Spanish. A Chicana from Michigan or Chicago or Detroit is just as much a Chicana as one from the Southwest. Chicano Spanish is as diverse linguistically as it is regionally.

By the end of this century, Spanish speakers will comprise the biggest minority group in the US, a country where students in high schools and colleges are encouraged to take French classes because French is considered more "cultured." But for a language to remain alive it must be used.[6] By the end of

---

6. Irena Klepfisz, "Secular Jewish Identity: Yidishkayt in America," in *The Tribe of Dina*, Kaye/Kantrowitz and Klepfisz, eds., 43.

this century English, and not Spanish, will be the mother tongue of most Chicanos and Latinos.

So, if you want to really hurt me, talk badly about my language. Ethnic identity is twin skin to linguistic identity—I am my language. Until I can take pride in my language, I cannot take pride in myself. Until I can accept as legitimate Chicano Texas Spanish, Tex-Mex and all the other languages I speak, I cannot accept the legitimacy of myself. Until I am free to write bilingually and to switch codes without having always to translate, while I still have to speak English or Spanish when I would rather speak Spanglish, and as long as I have to accommodate the English speakers rather than having them accommodate me, my tongue will be illegitimate.

I will no longer be made to feel ashamed of existing. I will have my voice: Indian, Spanish, white. I will have my serpent's tongue—my woman's voice, my sexual voice, my poet's voice. I will overcome the tradition of silence.

> My fingers
> move sly against your palm
> Like women everywhere, we speak in code. . . .
> —MELANIE KAYE/KANTROWITZ[7]

"Vistas," corridos, y comida: My Native Tongue

In the 1960s, I read my first Chicano novel. It was *City of Night* by John Rechy, a gay Texan, son of a Scottish father and a Mexican mother. For days I walked around in stunned amazement that a Chicano could write and could get published. When I read *I Am Joaquín*[8] I was surprised to see a bilingual book by a Chicano in print. When I saw poetry written in Tex-Mex for the first time, a feeling of pure joy flashed through me. I felt like we really existed as a people. In 1971, when I started teaching High School English to Chicano students, I tried to supplement the required texts with works by Chicanos, only to be reprimanded and forbidden to do so by the principal. He claimed that I was supposed to teach "American" and English literature. At the risk of being fired, I swore my students to secrecy and slipped in Chicano short stories, poems, a play. In graduate school, while working toward a PhD, I had to "argue" with one advisor after the other, semester after semester, before I was allowed to make Chicano literature an area of focus.

30   Even before I read books by Chicanos or Mexicans, it was the Mexican movies I saw at the drive-in—the Thursday night special of $1.00 a carload—that gave me a sense of belonging. "*Vámonos a las vistas*," my mother would call out and we'd all—grandmother, brothers, sister and cousins—squeeze into the car. We'd wolf down cheese and bologna white bread sandwiches while watching

7. Melanie Kaye/Kantrowitz, "Sign," in *We Speak in Code: Poems and Other Writings* (Pittsburgh, PA: Motheroot Publications, Inc., 1980), 85.

8. Rodolfo Gonzales, *I Am Joaquín / Yo Soy Joaquín* (New York, NY: Bantam Books, 1972). It was first published in 1967.

Pedro Infante in melodramatic tear-jerkers like *Nosotros los pobres*, the first "real" Mexican movie (that was not an imitation of European movies). I remember seeing *Cuando los hijos se van* and surmising that all Mexican movies played up the love a mother has for her children and what ungrateful sons and daughters suffer when they are not devoted to their mothers. I remember the singing-type "westerns" of Jorge Negrete and Miguel Aceves Mejía. When watching Mexican movies, I felt a sense of homecoming as well as alienation. People who were to amount to something didn't go to Mexican movies, or *bailes* or tune their radios to *bolero*, *rancherita*, and *corrido* music.

The whole time I was growing up, there was *norteño* music sometimes called North Mexican border music, or Tex-Mex music, or Chicano music, or *cantina* (bar) music. I grew up listening to *conjuntos*, three- or four-piece bands made up of folk musicians playing guitar, *bajo sexto*, drums and button accordion, which Chicanos had borrowed from the German immigrants who had come to Central Texas and Mexico to farm and build breweries. In the Rio Grande Valley, Steve Jordan and Little Joe Hernández were popular, and Flaco Jiménez was the accordion king. The rhythms of Tex-Mex music are those of the polka, also adapted from the Germans, who in turn had borrowed the polka from the Czechs and Bohemians.

I remember the hot, sultry evenings when *corridos*—songs of love and death on the Texas-Mexican borderlands—reverberated out of cheap amplifiers from the local *cantinas* and wafted in through my bedroom window.

Corridos first became widely used along the South Texas / Mexican border during the early conflict between Chicanos and Anglos. The *corridos* are usually about Mexican heroes who do valiant deeds against the Anglo oppressors. Pancho Villa's song, "*La cucaracha*," is the most famous one. *Corridos* of John F. Kennedy and his death are still very popular in the Valley. Older Chicanos remember Lydia Mendoza, one of the great border *corrido* singers who was called *la Gloria de Tejas*. Her "*El tango negro*," sung during the Great Depression, made her a singer of the people. The everpresent *corridos* narrated one hundred years of border history, bringing news of events as well as entertaining. These folk musicians and folk songs are our chief cultural mythmakers, and they made our hard lives seem bearable.

I grew up feeling ambivalent about our music. Country-western and rock-and-roll had more status. In the 50s and 60s, for the slightly educated and *agringado* Chicanos, there existed a sense of shame at being caught listening to our music. Yet I couldn't stop my feet from thumping to the music, could not stop humming the words, nor hide from myself the exhilaration I felt when I heard it.

There are more subtle ways that we internalize identification, especially in the forms of images and emotions. For me food and certain smells are tied to my identity, to my homeland. Woodsmoke curling up to an immense blue sky; woodsmoke perfuming my grandmother's clothes, her skin. The stench of cow manure and the yellow patches on the ground; the crack of a .22 rifle and the reek of cordite. Homemade white cheese sizzling in a pan, melting inside a folded *tortilla*. My sister Hilda's hot, spicy *menudo, chile colorado* making it deep red, pieces of *panza* and hominy floating on top. My brother Carito barbecuing *fajitas* in the backyard. Even now and 3,000 miles away, I can see my mother spicing the ground beef, pork and venison with *chile*. My mouth salivates at the thought of the hot steaming *tamales* I would be eating if I were home.

Si le preguntas a mi mamá, "¿Qué eres?"

> "Identity is the essential core of who
> we are as individuals, the conscious
> experience of the self inside."
> —Kaufman[9]

Nosotros los Chicanos straddle the borderlands. On one side of us, we are constantly exposed to the Spanish of the Mexicans; on the other side we hear the Anglos' incessant clamoring so that we forget our language. Among ourselves we don't say *nosotros los americanos, o nosotros los españoles, o nosotros los hispanos*. We say *nosotros los mexicanos* (by *mexicanos* we do not mean citizens of Mexico; we do not mean a national identity, but a racial one). We distinguish between *mexicanos del otro lado* and *mexicanos de este lado*. Deep in our hearts we believe that being Mexican has nothing to do with which country one lives in. Being Mexican is a state of soul—not one of mind, not one of citizenship. Neither eagle nor serpent, but both. And like the ocean, neither animal respects borders.

> *Dime con quien andas y te diré quien eres.*
> (Tell me who your friends are and I'll tell you who you are.)
> —Mexican saying

Si le preguntas a mi mamá, "¿Qué eres?" te dirá, "Soy mexicana." My brothers and sister say the same. I sometimes will answer *"soy mexicana"* and at others will say *"soy Chicana" o "soy tejana."* But I identified as *"Raza"* before I ever identified as *"mexicana"* or "Chicana."

As a culture, we call ourselves Spanish when referring to ourselves as a linguistic group and when copping out. It is then that we forget our predominant Indian genes. We are 70 to 80% Indian.[10] We call ourselves Hispanic[11] or Spanish-American or Latin American or Latin when linking ourselves to other Spanish-speaking peoples of the Western hemisphere and when copping out.

---

9. Gershen Kaufman, *Shame: The Power of Caring* (Cambridge, MA: Shenkman Books, 1980), 68.

10. John R. Chávez, *The Lost Land: The Chicano Image of the Southwest* (Albuquerque: U of New Mexico P, 1984), 88–90.

11. "Hispanic" is derived from *Hispanis* (*España*, a name given to the Iberian Peninsula in ancient times when it was a part of the Roman Empire) and is a term designated by the US government to make it easier to handle us on paper.

We call ourselves Mexican-American[12] to signify we are neither Mexican nor American, but more the noun "American" than the adjective "Mexican" (and when copping out).

Chicanos and other people of color suffer economically for not acculturating. This voluntary (yet forced) alienation makes for psychological conflict, a kind of dual identity—we don't identify with the Anglo-American cultural values and we don't totally identify with the Mexican cultural values. We are a synergy of two cultures with various degrees of Mexicanness or Angloness. I have so internalized the borderland conflict that sometimes I feel like one cancels out the other and we are zero, nothing, no one. *A veces no soy nada ni nadie. Pero hasta cuando no lo soy, lo soy.*

When not copping out, when we know we are more than nothing, we call ourselves Mexican, referring to race and ancestry; *mestizo* when affirming both our Indian and Spanish (but we hardly ever own our Black ancestry); Chicano when referring to a politically aware people born and/or raised in the US, *Raza* when referring to Chicanos; *tejanos* when we are Chicanos from Texas.   40

Chicanos did not know we were a people until 1965 when Cesar Chavez and the farmworkers united and *I Am Joaquín* was published and *la Raza Unida* party was formed in Texas. With that recognition, we became a distinct people. Something momentous happened to the Chicano soul—we became aware of our reality and acquired a name and a language (Chicano Spanish) that reflected that reality. Now that we had a name, some of the fragmented pieces began to fall together—who we were, what we were, how we had evolved. We began to get glimpses of what we might eventually become.

Yet the struggle of identities continues, the struggle of borders is our reality still. One day the inner struggle will cease and a true integration take place. In the meantime, *tenémos que hacer la lucha. ¿Quién está protegiendo los ranchos de mi gente? ¿Quién está tratando de cerrar la fisura entre la india y el blanco en nuestra sangre? El Chicano, si, el Chicano que anda como un ladrón en su propia casa.*

Los Chicanos, how patient we seem, how very patient. There is the quiet of the Indian about us.[13] We know how to survive. When other races have given up their tongue, we've kept ours. We know what it is to live under the hammer blow of the dominant *norteamericano* culture. But more than we count the blows, we count the days the weeks the years the centuries the eons until the white laws and commerce and customs will rot in the deserts they've created, lie bleached. *Humildes* yet proud, *quietos* yet wild, *nosotros los mexicanos-Chicanos* will walk by the crumbling ashes as we go about our business. Stubborn, persevering, impenetrable as stone, yet possessing a malleability that renders us unbreakable, we, the *mestizas* and *mestizos*, will remain.

12. In 1848 the Treaty of Guadalupe Hidalgo created the Mexican-American.

13. Anglos, in order to alleviate their guilt for dispossessing the Chicano, stressed the Spanish part of us and perpetrated the myth of the Spanish Southwest. We have accepted the fiction that we are Hispanic, that is Spanish, in order to accommodate ourselves to the dominant culture and its abhorrence of Indians. Chávez, 88–91.

QUESTIONS

1. Gloria Anzaldúa includes many Spanish words and phrases, some of which she explains, others which she leaves untranslated. Why do you think she does this? What different responses might bilingual versus English-only readers have to her writing?

2. The essay begins with an example of Anzaldúa's "untamed tongue." What meanings, many metaphoric, does Anzaldúa give for "tongue" or "wild tongue"? How does the essay develop these meanings?

3. Anzaldúa speaks of Chicano Spanish as a "living language" (paragraph 11). What does she mean by this, and what examples does she give of how it lives and breathes? What goes into making sure a language stays alive?

4. If you speak or write more than one language, or come from a community that uses expressions that you believe to be unique or uncommon, write an essay in which you incorporate that language and/or alternate it with English. Think about the ways that Anzaldúa uses both English and Spanish.

Ngũgĩ wa Thiong'o
Decolonizing the Mind

I WAS BORN into a large peasant family: father, four wives and about twenty-eight children. I also belonged, as we all did in those days, to a wider extended family and to the community as a whole.

   We spoke Gĩkũyũ[1] as we worked in the fields. We spoke Gĩkũyũ in and outside the home. I can vividly recall those evenings of storytelling around the fireside. It was mostly the grown-ups telling the children but everybody was interested and involved. We children would re-tell the stories the following day to other children who worked in the fields picking the pyrethrum[2] flowers, tea-leaves or coffee beans of our European and African landlords.

Published in Decolonizing the Mind: The Politics of Language in African Literature (1986), *an essay collection that Ngũgĩ wa Thiong'o describes as his "farewell to English as a vehicle for any of [his] writings." The Kenyan novelist, playwright, and social critic has been a pioneer of African literature and a critic of colonialism. Although his first novels were composed in English, Ngũgĩ now writes in Gĩkũyũ, often translating his own work into English.*

1. Language spoken by the Gĩkũyũ (or Kikuyu) people, the majority of Kenyans.
2. Type of chrysanthemum often used as an insecticide or for medicinal purposes.

The stories, with mostly animals as the main characters, were all told in Gĩkũyũ. Hare, being small, weak but full of innovative wit and cunning, was our hero. We identified with him as he struggled against the brutes of prey like lion, leopard, hyena. His victories were our victories and we learned that the apparently weak can outwit the strong. We followed the animals in their struggle against hostile nature—drought, rain, sun, wind—a confrontation often forcing them to search for forms of co-operation. But we were also interested in their struggles amongst themselves, and particularly between the beasts and the victims of prey. These twin struggles, against nature and other animals, reflected real-life struggles in the human world.

Not that we neglected stories with human beings as the main characters. There were two types of characters in such human-centered narratives: the species of truly human beings with qualities of courage, kindness, mercy, hatred of evil, concern for others; and a man-eat-man two-mouthed species with qualities of greed, selfishness, individualism and hatred of what was good for the larger co-operative community. Co-operation as the ultimate good in a community was a constant theme. It could unite human beings with animals against ogres and beasts of prey, as in the story of how dove, after being fed with castor-oil seeds, was sent to fetch a smith working far away from home and whose pregnant wife was being threatened by these man-eating two-mouthed ogres.

There were good and bad story-tellers. A good one could tell the same story   5
over and over again, and it would always be fresh to us, the listeners. He or she could tell a story told by someone else and make it more alive and dramatic. The differences really were in the use of words and images and the inflection of voices to effect different tones.

We therefore learned to value words for their meaning and nuances. Language was not a mere string of words. It had a suggestive power well beyond the immediate and lexical meaning. Our appreciation of the suggestive magical power of language was reinforced by the games we played with words through riddles, proverbs, transpositions of syllables, or through nonsensical but musically arranged words. So we learned the music of our language on top of the content. The language, through images and symbols, gave us a view of the world, but it had a beauty of its own. The home and the field were then our pre-primary school but what is important, for this discussion, is that the language of our evening teach-ins, and the language of our immediate and wider community, and the language of our work in the fields were one.

And then I went to school, a colonial school, and this harmony was broken. The language of my education was no longer the language of my culture. I first went to Kamaandura, missionary run, and then to another called Maanguuũ run by nationalists grouped around the Gĩkũyũ Independent and Karinga Schools Association. Our language of education was still Gĩkũyũ. The very first time I was ever given an ovation for my writing was over a composition in Gĩkũyũ. So for my first four years there was still harmony between the language of my formal education and that of the Limuru peasant community.

It was after the declaration of a state of emergency over Kenya in 1952 that all the schools run by patriotic nationalists were taken over by the colonial regime and were placed under District Education Boards chaired by Englishmen. English became the language of my formal education. In Kenya, English became more than a language: it was *the* language, and all the others had to bow before it in deference.

Thus one of the most humiliating experiences was to be caught speaking Gĩkũyũ in the vicinity of the school. The culprit was given corporal punishment—three to five strokes of the cane on bare buttocks—or was made to carry a metal plate around the neck with inscriptions such as I AM STUPID or I AM A DONKEY. Sometimes the culprits were fined money they could hardly afford. And how did the teachers catch the culprits? A button was initially given to one pupil who was supposed to hand it over to whoever was caught speaking his mother tongue. Whoever had the button at the end of the day would sing who had given it to him and the ensuing process would bring out all the culprits of the day. Thus children were turned into witch-hunters and in the process were being taught the lucrative value of being a traitor to one's immediate community.

10   The attitude to English was the exact opposite: any achievement in spoken or written English was highly rewarded; prizes, prestige, applause; the ticket to higher realms. English became the measure of intelligence and ability in the arts, the sciences, and all the other branches of learning. English became *the* main determinant of a child's progress up the ladder of formal education.

As you may know, the colonial system of education in addition to its apartheid racial demarcation had the structure of a pyramid: a broad primary base, a narrowing secondary middle, and an even narrower university apex. Selections from primary into secondary were through an examination, in my time called Kenya African Preliminary Examination, in which one had to pass six subjects ranging from Maths to Nature Study and Kiswahili.[3] All the papers were written in English. Nobody could pass the exam who failed the English language paper no matter how brilliantly he had done in the other subjects. I remember one boy in my class of 1954 who had distinctions in all subjects except English, which he had failed. He was made to fail the entire exam. He went on to become a turn boy[4] in a bus company. I who had only passes but a credit in English got a place at the Alliance High School, one of the most elitist institutions for Africans in colonial Kenya. The requirements for a place at the University, Makerere University College, were broadly the same: nobody could go on to wear the undergraduate red gown, no matter how brilliantly they had performed in all the other subjects unless they had a credit—not even a simple pass!—in English. Thus the most coveted place in the pyramid and in the system was only available to the holder of an English language credit card. English was the official vehicle and the magic formula to colonial elitedom.

Literary education was now determined by the dominant language while also reinforcing that dominance. Orature (oral literature) in Kenyan languages stopped. In primary school I now read simplified Dickens and Stevenson along-

3. Swahili, a major East African language.
4. Someone who brings in customers; a tout.

side Rider Haggard. Jim Hawkins, Oliver Twist, Tom Brown[5]—not Hare, Leopard and Lion—were now my daily companions in the world of imagination. In secondary school, Scott and G. B. Shaw vied with more Rider Haggard, John Buchan, Alan Paton, Captain W. E. Johns.[6] At Makerere I read English: from Chaucer to T. S. Eliot with a touch of Grahame Greene.[7]

Thus language and literature were taking us further and further from ourselves to other selves, from our world to other worlds.

What was the colonial system doing to us Kenyan children? What were the consequences of, on the one hand, this systematic suppression of our languages and the literature they carried, and on the other the elevation of English and the literature it carried? To answer those questions, let me first examine the relationship of language to human experience, human culture, and the human perception of reality.

Language, any language, has a dual character: it is both a means of communication and a carrier of culture. Take English. It is spoken in Britain and in Sweden and Denmark. But for Swedish and Danish people English is only a means of communication with non-Scandinavians. It is not a carrier of their culture. For the British, and particularly the English, it is additionally, and inseparably from its use as a tool of communication, a carrier of their culture and history. Or take Swahili in East and Central Africa. It is widely used as a means of communication across many nationalities. But it is not the carrier of a culture and history of many of those nationalities. However in parts of Kenya and Tanzania, and particularly in Zanzibar,[8] Swahili is inseparably both a means of communication and a carrier of the culture of those people to whom it is a mother-tongue.   15

Language as communication has three aspects or elements. There is first what Karl Marx[9] once called the language of real life, the element basic to the whole notion of language, its origins and development: that is, the relations people enter into with one another in the labor process, the links they necessarily establish among themselves in the act of a people, a community of human beings, producing wealth or means of life like food, clothing, houses. A human

---

5. Charles Dickens (1812–1870), British novelist, author of *Oliver Twist*; Robert Louis Stevenson (1850–1894), Scottish novelist, creator of Jim Hawkins in *Treasure Island*; H. Rider Haggard (1856–1925), British adventure novelist; Brown, chief character in *Tom Brown's Schooldays* in the novel by Thomas Hughes.

6. Sir Walter Scott (1771–1832), Scottish poet and novelist; George Bernard Shaw (1856–1950), Irish-born playwright; Buchan (1875–1940), Scottish adventure novelist, author of *The Thirty-Nine Steps*, and also governor general of Canada; Paton (1903–1988), South African novelist; Johns (1893–1968), British writer famous for the Biggles stories for boys.

7. Geoffrey Chaucer (c. 1343–1400), English poet, author of *The Canterbury Tales*; Eliot (1888–1965), American-born English poet; Greene (1904–1991), British novelist.

8. Island off the east coast of Africa; part of Tanzania since 1964.

9. German political philosopher (1818–1883).

community really starts its historical being as a community of co-operation in production through the division of labor; the simplest is between man, woman and child within a household; the more complex divisions are between branches of production such as those who are sole hunters, sole gatherers of fruits or sole workers in metal. Then there are the most complex divisions such as those in modern factories where a single product, say a shirt or a shoe, is the result of many hands and minds. Production is co-operation, is communication, is language, is expression of a relation between human beings and it is specifically human.

The second aspect of language as communication is speech and it imitates the language of real life, that is communication in production. The verbal signposts both reflect and aid communication or the relation established between human beings in the production of their means of life. Language as a system of verbal signposts makes that production possible. The spoken word is to relations between human beings what the hand is to the relations between human beings and nature. The hand through tools mediates between human beings and nature and forms the language of real life: spoken words mediate between human beings and form the language of speech.

The third aspect is the written signs. The written word imitates the spoken. Where the first two aspects of language as communication through the hand and the spoken word historically evolved more or less simultaneously, the written aspect is a much later historical development. Writing is representation of sounds with visual symbols, from the simplest knot among shepherds to tell the number in a herd or the hieroglyphics among the Agĩkũyũ gicaandi[10] singers and poets of Kenya, to the most complicated and different letter and picture writing systems of the world today.

In most societies the written and the spoken languages are the same, in that they represent each other: what is on paper can be read to another person and be received as that language, which the recipient has grown up speaking. In such a society there is broad harmony for a child between the three aspects of language as communication. His interaction with nature and with other men is expressed in written and spoken symbols or signs which are both a result of that double interaction and a reflection of it. The association of the child's sensibility is with the language of his experience of life.

20   But there is more to it: communication between human beings is also the basis and process of evolving culture. In doing similar kinds of things and actions over and over again under similar circumstances, similar even in their mutability, certain patterns, moves, rhythms, habits, attitudes, experiences and knowledge emerge. Those experiences are handed over to the next generation and become the inherited basis for their further actions on nature and on themselves. There is a gradual accumulation of values which in time become almost self-evident truths governing their conception of what is right and wrong, good and bad, beautiful and ugly, courageous and cowardly, generous and mean in their internal and external relations. Over a time this becomes a way of life

10. Agĩkũyũ, another term for Gĩkũyũ; gicaandi, a particular Kenyan song genre.

distinguishable from other ways of life. They develop a distinctive culture and history. Culture embodies those moral, ethical and aesthetic values, the set of spiritual eyeglasses, through which they come to view themselves and their place in the universe. Values are the basis of a people's identity, their sense of particularity as members of the human race. All this is carried by language. Language as culture is the collective memory bank of a people's experience in history. Culture is almost indistinguishable from the language that makes possible its genesis, growth, banking, articulation and indeed its transmission from one generation to the next.

Language as culture also has three important aspects. Culture is a product of the history which it in turn reflects. Culture in other words is a product and a reflection of human beings communicating with one another in the very struggle to create wealth and to control it. But culture does not merely reflect that history, or rather it does so by actually forming images or pictures of the world of nature and nurture. Thus the second aspect of language as culture is as an image-forming agent in the mind of a child. Our whole conception of ourselves as a people, individually and collectively, is based on those pictures and images which may or may not correctly correspond to the actual reality of the struggles with nature and nurture which produced them in the first place. But our capacity to confront the world creatively is dependent on how those images correspond or not to that reality, how they distort or clarify the reality of our struggles. Language as culture is thus mediating between me and my own self; between my own self and other selves; between me and nature. Language is mediating in my very being. And this brings us to the third aspect of language as culture. Culture transmits or imparts those images of the world and reality through the spoken and the written language, that is through a specific language. In other words, the capacity to speak, the capacity to order sounds in a manner that makes for mutual comprehension between human beings is universal. This is the universality of language, a quality specific to human beings. It corresponds to the universality of the struggle against nature and that between human beings. But the particularity of the sounds, the words, the word order into phrases and sentences, and the specific manner, or laws, of their ordering is what distinguishes one language from another. Thus a specific culture is not transmitted through language in its universality but in its particularity as the language of a specific community with a specific history. Written literature and orature are the main means by which a particular language transmits the images of the world contained in the culture it carries.

Language as communication and as culture are then products of each other. Communication creates culture: culture is a means of communication. Language carries culture, and culture carries, particularly through orature and literature, the entire body of values by which we come to perceive ourselves and our place in the world. How people perceive themselves affects how they look at their culture, at their politics and at the social production of wealth, at their entire relationship to nature and to other beings. Language is thus inseparable from ourselves as a community of human beings with a specific form and character, a specific history, a specific relationship to the world.

So what was the colonialist imposition of a foreign language doing to us children?

The real aim of colonialism was to control the people's wealth: what they produced, how they produced it, and how it was distributed; to control, in other words, the entire realm of the language of real life. Colonialism imposed its control of the social production of wealth through military conquest and subsequent political dictatorship. But its most important area of domination was the mental universe of the colonized, the control, through culture, of how people perceived themselves and their relationship to the world. Economic and political control can never be complete or effective without mental control. To control a people's culture is to control their tools of self-definition in relationship to others.

25   For colonialism this involved two aspects of the same process: the destruction or the deliberate undervaluing of a people's culture, their art, dances, religions, history, geography, education, orature and literature, and the conscious elevation of the language of the colonizer. The domination of a people's language by the languages of the colonizing nations was crucial to the domination of the mental universe of the colonized.

Take language as communication. Imposing a foreign language, and suppressing the native languages as spoken and written, were already breaking the harmony previously existing between the African child and the three aspects of language. Since the new language as a means of communication was a product of and was reflecting the "real language of life" elsewhere, it could never as spoken or written properly reflect or imitate the real life of that community. This may in part explain why technology always appears to us as slightly external, *their* product and not *ours*. The word "missile" used to hold an alien faraway sound until I recently learnt its equivalent in Gĩkũyũ, *ngurukuhĩ*, and it made me apprehend it differently. Learning, for a colonial child, became a cerebral activity and not an emotionally felt experience.

But since the new, imposed languages could never completely break the native languages as spoken, their most effective area of domination was the third aspect of language as communication, the written. The language of an African child's formal education was foreign. The language of the books he read was foreign. The language of his conceptualization was foreign. Thought, in him, took the visible form of a foreign language. So the written language of a child's upbringing in the school (even his spoken language within the school compound) became divorced from his spoken language at home. There was often not the slightest relationship between the child's written world, which was also the language of his schooling, and the world of his immediate environment in the family and the community. For a colonial child, the harmony existing between the three aspects of language as communication was irrevocably broken. This resulted in the disassociation of the sensibility[11] of that child from his natural and social environment, what we might call colonial alienation. The alienation became reinforced in the teaching of history, geography, music, where bourgeois Europe was always the center of the universe.

11. Echo of T. S. Eliot's famous phrase "dissociation of sensibility," a break from the past, when thought and feeling were unified.

The disassociation, divorce, or alienation from the immediate environment becomes clearer when you look at colonial language as a carrier of culture.

Since culture is a product of the history of a people which it in turn reflects, the child was now being exposed exclusively to a culture that was a product of a world external to himself. He was being made to stand outside himself to look at himself. *Catching Them Young* is the title of a book on racism, class, sex, and politics in children's literature by Bob Dixon. "Catching them young" as an aim was even more true of a colonial child. The images of his world and his place in it implanted in a child take years to eradicate, if they ever can be.

Since culture does not just reflect the world in images but actually, through those images, conditions a child to see that world a certain way, the colonial child was made to see the world and where he stands in it as seen and defined by or reflected in the culture of the language of imposition. 30

And since those images are mostly passed on through orature and literature it meant the child would now only see the world as seen in the literature of his language of adoption. From the point of view of alienation, that is of seeing oneself from outside oneself as if one was another self, it does not matter that the imported literature carried the great humanist tradition of the best Shakespeare, Goethe, Balzac, Tolstoy, Gorky, Brecht, Sholokhov,[12] Dickens. The location of this great mirror of imagination was necessarily Europe and its history and culture and the rest of the universe was seen from that center.

But obviously it was worse when the colonial child was exposed to images of his world as mirrored in the written languages of his colonizer. Where his own native languages were associated in his impressionable mind with low status, humiliation, corporal punishment, slow-footed intelligence and ability or downright stupidity, non-intelligibility and barbarism, this was reinforced by the world he met in the works of such geniuses of racism as a Rider Haggard or a Nicholas Monsarrat;[13] not to mention the pronouncement of some of the giants of western intellectual and political establishment, such as Hume (". . . The negro is naturally inferior to the whites. . . ."), Thomas Jefferson (". . . The blacks . . . are inferior to the whites on the endowments of both body and mind. . . ."), or Hegel[14] with his Africa comparable to a land of childhood still enveloped in the dark mantle of the night as far as the development of self-conscious history was concerned. Hegel's statement that there was nothing harmonious with humanity to be found in the African character is representative of the racist images of Africans

12. William Shakespeare (1564–1616), English playwright; Johann Wolfgang von Goethe (1749–1832), German novelist and playwright; Honoré de Balzac (1799–1850), French novelist; Leo (Count Lev Nikolayevich) Tolstoy (1828–1910), Russian novelist; Maxim Gorky (1868–1936), Russian dramatist; Bertolt Brecht (1898–1956), German dramatist; Mikhail Aleksandrovich Sholokhov (1905–1984), Russian novelist.

13. *The Tribe That Lost Its Head* (1956) was this British novelist's (1910–1979) satirical look at British colonialism and the African independence movement.

14. David Hume (1711–1776), Scottish Enlightenment philosopher and historian; Jefferson (1743–1826), third US president, 1801–9; Georg Wilhelm Friedrich Hegel (1770–1831), German philosopher.

and Africa such a colonial child was bound to encounter in the literature of the
colonial languages. The results could be disastrous.

MLA CITATION

Ngũgĩ wa Thiong'o. "Decolonizing the Mind." *The Norton Reader: An Anthology of
Nonfiction*, edited by Melissa A. Goldthwaite et al., 16th ed., W. W. Norton,
2024, pp. 360–68.

QUESTIONS

1. The last paragraphs of Ngũgĩ wa Thiong'o's essay contain the names of many
classic and contemporary European writers. Why do you think he chose to include
them? Can you relate their inclusion to the way Ngũgĩ presents himself in this essay?

2. What literary writers did you read in school? What values were your teachers
(or school) imparting in selecting those writers in particular?

3. Ngũgĩ experienced a particularly stark contrast between the values contained
within the oral stories of his family and the written English of school. Annotate
where he describes and contrasts these values and discuss the different systems.
Have you noticed differences between what your extended family values and what
your schools seem to want you to value?

4. When this essay was published in 1986, the idea of "decolonizing" the mind,
rather than territory, was relatively new. What does it mean to decolonize a mind?
Find and read a current article about mental decolonization. Compare Ngũgĩ's
goals and his use of the term with how that article uses it.

JOHN McWHORTER
Profanity and Shit

• • •

FROM THE BOWELS OF HISTORY

SOME WILL TELL YOU that the journey started belowdecks. One
deathless tale has it that *shit* started as an acronym—*ship high in
transit*—supposedly marked on bags of manure when transported
by sea in some unspecified earlier era. This time differed from
ours in that certain locales apparently needed to have dung
imported, and the issue was keeping the manure dry. If it was

From Nine Nasty Words: English in the Gutter: Then, Now, and Forever *(2021). John
McWhorter is a professor of linguistics, a podcaster, and an opinion columnist for the* New York
Times. *All notes in this piece were written by the author unless indicated otherwise. This version
of the essay is abridged.*

packed down deep in the hull, then got wet, decomposition created methane gas, which, if meeting the lantern of an unwary sailor sneaking down at night to get a peek at the shitbags, could blow the boat to pieces.

This story neglects how far back words tend to go, and it's easy to disprove. *Shit* is alive and well in Old English, before 1000 CE, long before a sentence like "ship high in transit" would even have been possible, because among other things, *transit* had yet to enter the language. Then also, *shit* is one kitten in a litter of equivalent words in other Germanic languages, like it in shape and meaning. That is, some single word in an ancestor tongue, spoken around twenty-five hundred years ago around what would become Denmark, before English existed, birthed descendants all over northern and western Europe: *schijt* in Dutch; *skit* in Swedish; *Scheisse* in German. In those languages, the acronym "ship high in transit" would look nothing like *s-h-i-t*.

Perhaps they took on *shit* the way English later took on *sushi*? It seems doubtful. All the words, including ours, emerged long before there even existed English sailors, much less one warning his mates about exploding bags of manure. Equally doubtful is that those hypothetical sailors would start using such an acronym. Presumably they, too, already had a name for the stuff.

And finally we must revisit the question: Who would have been seeking and purchasing bags of crap by the bushel and why? Yes, in the nineteenth century, guano boats furnished western Europe and the United States with bird and bat poop from South America, uniquely nutrient-rich and handy as fertilizer, for a spell. But this was long, long after we have solid evidence that the word *shit* had already existed essentially forever.

*

The real origin story has its charms, although a less dramatic one than the one about shit boats. English ultimately traces back to a language spoken by people living in what is now Ukraine, who almost certainly used a word *skei* that meant "cut off" or "slice." Over the millennia, some of their descendants settled in England, with *skei* having morphed to *scit*. But in Old English, its meaning had drifted into a particular kind of cutting off. Likely some people along the way started referring to defecation as going to "cut one off" or the like—the expression *to pinch a loaf* is unavoidable as a comparison. *Sc-* soon became *sh-*, and so just as a *scip* was our *ship*, *scit* is, um, yeah.

Talk about six degrees—you never know which words will be related, both within and between languages. The ancient *skei* spread to hundreds of languages both westward in Europe and eastward into Asia, emerging with different shapes and meanings in all of them. In Greek, *skei* transformed in ways that make sense to us as variants on "cut off," such as *schism* and *schizoid* that refer to division, that which has been cut asunder. Latin was more creative: *skei* became *sci*—or, with the verbal ending that had emerged in it, *scire*, a word you might recognize from high school Latin as simply the respectable word for "to know."

Careful study shows that this, too, was related to the original meaning. The idea was that to know is to slice matters, make careful distinctions, the way philosophers such as Plato and Aristotle so exhaustively laid out their assumptions when attempting an argument. President Andrew Johnson of all people once laid out this classical sense of "knowing" beautifully, saying that he wished he had become a scholar because "it would have satisfied my desire to analyze things, to examine them in separate periods and then unite them again to view them as a whole."

English inherited *scire* by borrowing from Latin in the word *science*. This means that *shit* and *science* are brother words despite their starkly opposite demeanors. *Conscience*, too, as a combination of *con* "with" and *science*, is a sibling of a word that in English means "feces." Or, in my favorite example, *nice* traces back to Latin *nescius*, as in *ne* "not" and *scius* being a form of our friend *scire* and meaning "knowing." The way words alter and pivot through time never fails to astonish me; . . . to us, *nice* means "blandly pleasing" but *nescius* meant "ignorant." Here's the genealogy: if you're ignorant you're weak; if you're weak you're fussy; if you're fussy you're dainty; if you're dainty you're precise and proper; if you're precise and proper you are rated as agreeable. At least this is how English evolved over almost a thousand years as *nice* went from dum-dum to your dependably inoffensive cousin Roberta. But this means that *shit* and *nice* were once related as closely as the Winklevoss brothers are depicted in *The Social Network*.[1] Think of *nescius* meaning "not shit," and you pretty much get *nice*.

PLOWED UNDER

In Old and Middle English, *shit* was used as freely as *poop* is today. It seemed absurd, when most people lived on the land, to be coy about something one's animals did daily, and that one did oneself about as frequently, and with less privacy than people would later. Ancient and medieval English speakers felt about *shit* roughly the way American Anglophones now feel about *damn*— roughly, "What's the big deal?"

10   The sea change from the free writing of "shitte" to the word not appearing in the *Webster's New World Dictionary* as late as 1970 began after the Reformation. Protestantism stressed an inwardly focused quest to demonstrate one's faith in Jesus via the avoidance of sin. To the extent that the body itself was classified as waywardly inclined, as an undependable "flesh" resisting the discipline of the mind, words and expressions suggesting transgression acquired a new sense of threat.

Then also, from the sixteenth century on in England, people experienced ever greater degrees of what we know as privacy. Mercantile prosperity, plus innovations in heating technology, allowed many bigger houses with more rooms. This encouraged a sense that certain things were private rather than public matters. As late as the 1400s, the nobleman feeling the call of nature would take care of his needs off in a corner of the stairwell. He wouldn't take his daughter on his shoulders to watch him do it, nor did anyone normally chat

---

1. Film (2010) depicting the origins of *Facebook* with a focus on Mark Zuckerberg wresting control from the Winklevoss twins, Cameron and Tyler, who are depicted as indistinguishable [Editor's note].

him up while he was in the act, but the private privy, the private bedroom, the eclipse of times when all saw one another naked on a regular basis and children were accustomed to listening to and even watching their parents have sex, all reinforced a sense that bodily matters were to be kept to yourself. Religious convictions as well as architectural innovations now made possible this reticence.

Anthropology teaches us that there are no human societies in which feces is not considered repulsive, so it is predictable that starting in the 1500s, *shit* would be classified as profane in the sense of *damn* and *hell*. In the 1630s, the Latin term *feces* crept in as a polite alternative (*excrement* first referring to any old substance seeping out of the body). We see the artfully euphemistic nature of *feces* in its Latin meaning of "dregs," like those of wine at the bottom of a barrel full of it. That rather deftly nails things without getting too specific.

Shit was from then on a "bad" word, and that evaluation carried over the Atlantic. In the early twentieth century, Edna St. Vincent Millay and her sister were bedazzled by the atmosphere of Greenwich Village, where, as the *Masses* cartoonist Art Young described, a woman could say *damn* without being looked at askance. Edna's sister late in her life recalled, "So we sat darning socks on Waverly Place and practiced the use of profanity as we stitched. Needle in, shit. Needle out, piss. Needle in, fuck. Needle out, cunt." This teaches us that in some contexts ordinary people were using the word *shit* all the time. But we can only know it now by eavesdropping, such as perusing their graffiti. Lexicographer Allen Walker Read did just this in the late 1920s, uncovering latrine poetry such as the flinty "Roses are red, violets are blue, I took a shit, and so did you," or this one of 1928 from the Yellowstone Park campground, delicately straddling the tautological and the haikuesque:

> This Shithouse stinks like shit
> Because it is so shitty

• • •

I'd bet quite a lot that the first *shit* on film was made the year before at that same Hal Roach studio, an early Laurel and Hardy romp. But it's an accident we aren't supposed to catch. In 1929, with sound having come to film only a year or two before, actors trained in silents were still getting used to the fact that anything they said would be recorded and heard. As character actor Edgar Kennedy plays his usual frustrated melonhead, now trying to get out of a crowded car, he unmistakably grunts under his breath, "Oh, shit!"

• • •

THE GRAMMAR THEY DON'T TELL YOU ABOUT

In any case, as a verb, *shit* has a quirk: What exactly is the past tense form, would you say? The Middle English form was *shote*, but that's clearly lost today. One is tempted to substitute *shitted*, but it doesn't feel quite right. What

15

likely comes to mind is *shat*, but that also always feels arch, "not real," and in a way it isn't. The change from *shote* to *shat* was modeled on how we put *sit* in the past tense: *sit*, *sat*, and so *shit*, *shat*. However, this only happened about two hundred years ago and seems to have been intended with precisely the air of play that we feel in it today.

The truth is that *shit* is a defective verb. It has no unironic, vanilla past tense form that doesn't make you giggle a bit, which is why some readers are surely thinking that the real past tense form is "took a shit"!

Nevertheless, what this little word lacks in tense marking it more than makes up for in how multifarious it has been otherwise. It has come to mean so very much more than, well, a stool, and far beyond the extended meaning of "stuff" (*Get your shit out of my room*).

Let's start with an analogy. The multifarious array of flora and fauna in this world emerged via step-by-step evolutionary pathways that we can schematize as a family tree. In the same way, the full efflorescence of what *shit* can mean is so vast that it can seem a kind of chaos. Yet the bloom actually lends itself to, of all things, an elegant analysis, whereby a humble word accreted a magnificent but systematic cobble of meanings.

Linguists have a way of charting evolutions of this kind; it is a common process, hardly limited to peculiar, notorious, or salacious words. It's all about metaphorical extensions, and a prototypical example is the word *back*. You likely think first of your own back. Yes—that indeed is where it all began, the original, core meaning. But one of the foundations of the human language faculty is metaphor, and a word like *back* cannot just sit with that single meaning when it is so handy as a way of conveying others. *Back* flowered into what we could treat as three main directions.

20   First, it came to refer to not just the anatomical but to position—since your back is behind you, it was natural to refer to things as being in back, in the back of, even when no human body's back was involved. This positional usage led, through further metaphor, to referring to past time. If the past is behind us, then we might also say that something happened three years *back*, that we wish we could go *back* in time.

Back also became a way to reference support for someone or something. To have someone's back means that you are literally behind them to block them from falling down in some way. There is a short step to speaking of *backing* someone up, and then *backing* up an argument—and just think how far we have come, from the area below your shoulder blades to "You've got to back that up—I need facts!"

The third direction goes even further—just what is "back" about *back* in *The cat came back*? The idea is that someone has started out, and then turned backward, thus coming back. Hence to give something *back* is to reverse its original direction—i.e., back to you. This all means that *back in an hour* silently references what you can get talked about behind or stabbed in.

This diagram shows the true family relationship of *back* in a way that a list can only approximate:

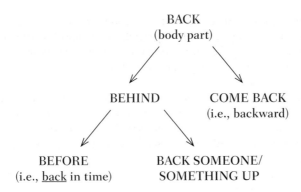

THE REAL SHIT

Shit lends itself to equivalent treatment, and yields a diagram much richer, almost as if bearing out the nature of a word that can refer to fertilizer (sometimes so enthusiastically that you need a surplus supply shipped in, kept nice and dry above the waterline!). We get four metaphorical directions that explain pretty much all the ways we use the word in everyday language.

Extension 1—Feces Is Unwelcome

The metaphorical meaning closest to the root connotation of *feces* is that of the unwelcome, given the noxious nature of the substance. Hence the idea of haranguing someone as giving them shit. When I was in college, one of the managers in a dining hall I worked in was a brilliantined fellow with a pencil mustache (a look that was already obsolete by the 1980s) and a keening, petulant voice, given to complaining, "Everybody shits on me!"[2] But the man is relevant to us in that the expression he was so fond of embodied this metaphorical usage of shit as a burden, an insult.

Extension 2—Feces Is Real

But then, in a fashion few of us would think of immediately but makes a certain sense, we also associate shit with authenticity, with "the real." That babies, the most unfiltered form of humanity, have no control over it is part of where this sentiment comes from. Too, there is its universality despite its lowliness—it serves as a kind of demotic unifier, revealing the mundane in any individual regardless of exterior accoutrement or achievement.

Hence the expression that someone very good at something is "the shit," as in not some amateur but the real thing. That expression seems to have started with Black Americans—I first caught it in the 1980s from Black American persons—but not only has it jumped over the past few decades into general parlance, but this idea of shit as "real" was mainstream long before, in the expression "the real shit." Why is this how we designate the best music, the most potent hashish, or whatever someone has locked away for special occasions?

2. One worker was known for a rather deft imitation of this man.*
* It was me.

Note also the related usage, where someone who is knowledgeable about something "really knows their shit." Try translating these usages into any other language and get a sense of how odd they are despite how familiar we are with them. Yet they cohere as linked to a matter of essence.

So cozily has this extension of the meaning settled into English that it has become, of all things, a new pronoun of sorts. We get our shit together: note the parallel with "get our*selves* together"—we use *shit* to refer to that most authentic of the authentic, the self. In a sense we refer to our shit as the essence of ourselves, that which we, to set our lives on the right path, must get together, gather, make right.

30 That usage pops up in other ways—*Watch out with that; it'll fuck your shit up* does not refer to *shit* as in stuff. That drug will not merely disorganize your nightstand drawer but harm you at your personal core. As I write this, a few nights ago I saw two guys walking down the street, one of whom seemed somewhat into his cups. When he tripped stepping up onto a curb, the friend said, "Watch your shit!" This clearly referred neither to the man's possessions nor his bowels—it meant simply "Watch your*self*."

• • •

Shit provides us with an alternate-world table of reflexive pronouns that convey both person and number—like vanilla ones—but also an attitude toward the person or thing in question, conveying lowdown, unfiltered honesty (your shit). *Get your shit together* implies a sense of the self without illusions or proprieties. Your goals, your sense of whether they will be achieved, your relationships, warts and all, your temper, your wardrobe choices, your pits, all of it—your *shit*, man. And yes, it does work even when the evaluator is as biased as your own self, as in *I finally got my shit together, man!*

So—book English:

myself	ourselves
yourself	yourselves
himself, herself, itself	themselves

Real English:

NEUTRAL:		WARMLY FORTHRIGHT:	
myself	ourselves	my shit	our shit
yourself	yourselves	your shit	your (pl.) shit
himself, herself, itself	themselves	his shit, her shit	their shit
itself		its shit	

This is, I must note, our first slice into what will be a whole new schema of how pronouns work in the "authentic" English we hear, know, and use. Profanity affords us a window into English as she is truly spoke: stay tuned.

Extension 3—Feces Is Lowly

Meanwhile, the most prolific branch of the basic meaning is the one that chan-   35
nels the sense of shit, in its ickiness, as referring to denigration and belittlement. The most immediate offshoots are our designating something as "like shit" (*He dances like shit*), referring to someone as a shit, and using *shit* as an adjective either in the form *shitty* or even as the bare word itself, as in living *a shit life* (this is more popular in the United Kingdom than in the United States, where we would usually say *a shitty life*).

However, the extensions via denigration go far beyond these intuitive usages. Think of a typical American English sentence like *I don't put up with that shit.* We certainly intend no literal reference to shit; rather, we aim to convey a dismissive attitude toward whatever is at issue. *I can't stand that shit. That shit looks like it's seventy years old! I've seen that shit since last year, and I know it when I see it.* What *that shit* means is just "that." It's a way of saying *that* with an air of vulgar dismissal.

In other words, *that shit* is a pronoun—a naive documenter of English, possibly even having already noted the independent word *shit* itself, would hear "that shit" as nothing but a pronoun people use when vaguely peeved. Or, really, just when speaking casually without even being especially peeved, depending on whom it is. The pronominal essence becomes clear, even if misleadingly in the technical sense, in a sentence like *Shit ain't right.* It's short for "That shit ain't right," yes. But, wow, when in rapid speech *shit* is pronounced without *that* in this way, we are tantalizingly close to a mere *it*—"It ain't right"—as if *shit* shortened to *it* amid the hustle. The Martian observer might mistakenly think that in an earlier English, there was no *it*, but only the longer form *shit*—that *he, she,* and *it* came from *he, she,* and *shit!*

Extension 3.1—Lowly Means Humble   But this branch sprouts more meanings in mushroomlike fashion. We get into extensions of extensions, even. If feces is about the lowly, then a natural association is humility, and here is where we come to *shit* meaning one's possessions. The idea that what one packs when moving is one's "shit" makes perfect sense when we know that word's meanings ooch bit by bit via visceral sentiment.

The "stuff" usage stems from the fact that the way we use language means commanding what a linguist calls softeners, which start with expressions like *sort of* and *kind of* and "type thing," and, yes, *like: I thought it was sort of the first time anyone had come out and told her that,* we say. The *sort of* is a hedge that allows us to not seem too prosecutorial in pointing that out, especially if we thought she needed to be told. But softening permeates real-life expression far beyond isolatable bits like *sort of.* It's time to leave a party, but really, you can't just say, "I am leaving." Rather, you say—and actually *must* say, on the pain of seeming chilly and abrupt—"I'm gonna head out." There are two soft-eners here—both the just-one-of-the-gang *gonna* instead of *going to*, and espe-cially *head out*, which is how American Anglophones depart from a social gathering in a nondisruptive way. "I'm going to let you go," we say to bring a phone call to an end, when the other person gave no indication of wanting to stop talking. Propriety doesn't allow the straightforward "I'm going to hang up now"—it would convey displeasure, just as if you "ended" an interview rather than "wrapping it up."

40   *I need somewhere to put my shit* conveys the same nuance—it may seem "vulgar," but to refer to your "things" sounds a little metallic in a colloquial situ-ation. You could say "stuff," too—something shaggy, *humble*, that is—but *shit* is even more so. *Six months and he still hasn't gotten his shit out of here*—someone could say this, David Mamet *American Buffalo*–style, of a loved one, or dude to dude. The "shit" has a leveling function—we all have junk like our underwear, phone chargers, and deodorant.

The humility extension yields yet another grade A usage, in the eternal and ubiquitous *and shit*, or really *'n' shit*. So easy to dismiss as a random vul-garity, *and shit* actually harbors a certain subtlety, due to the logical lines via which the word has evolved. A ways back, people were wearing T-shirts that read, "I is a college student." Ha ha—they present themselves as educated but can't conjugate the verb *to be*, or don't know that Black English is not consid-ered formal language. Around then, a pal of mine found especially funny another T-shirt: "I am a college student. And shit." He loved it because "and shit" seemed incongruous with higher education, but *technically* . . .

Technically, if someone said that, it would make a certain sense. State straight out "I am a college student" and it conveys a certain aggression, an arrogance, given the status associated with the position. One might also express that one is happy to be in college because of assorted implications, such as upward mobility and spending time with other students and all they have to offer, or even enjoying the fact that you are one of the only members of your family who has had the opportunity.

But who has the time to say all that? A fleet, vivid expression can do the heavy lifting for you. A handy one would be "and stuff"—as in, we all inhabit this context and are aware of all that goes along with being a college student, i.e., that stuff. But here is where the softening comes in. One wishes not only to call on that shared knowledge but also to convey that one does not feel superior in being connected to it.

What better way to convey that humility, with *shit* already referring to one's physical rubbish not to mention one's very self (recall: *get my shit together*), than with substituting "and shit" for the older "and stuff" (much older—*and stuff* goes back to when English was still spelled funny). *I'm a college student and all of that, well, shit you know that I don't need to specify, and I don't mean to sound too high-and-mighty but, well, I'll get a better job than someone who isn't a college student and . . . aw shucks, y'know . . . shit.*

45   One must, as a mensch, strike a humble pose.

Extension 3.2—Lowly Means Fake   Then *shit* is also fake, as we reflect in phrases like *don't shit me*. But as ordinary as that expression is, it's based on another metaphor of a metaphor: that one way of being lesser is to be inauthentic. Thus also the noun version, where we talk of someone telling you "some shit"—*He gave me some shit about it being illegal to make a left turn at that intersection.* The wondrous thing about this branch is that it means that *shit* lends itself to metaphorization as both real (*he's the shit*) and unreal (*don't give me that shit*). Language can be that way, such that *literally* is used to mean both "by the letter" and the opposite concept of "figuratively," à la *I was literally boiling to death* when you, of course, were not.

Extension 3.3—Lowly Means Worthless   We use *shit* in a way that channels that something lowly is of little value, is a nullity. *It's shit* would be the most basic expression, followed by *I don't give a shit*.[3] Or *I got shit*—imagine an adult, potty-mouthed Charlie Brown, who got a handful of rocks while trick-or-treating, saying that rather than the neutral "I got a rock"—and also the way we use *for shit* as in *he can't run for shit* or *these shoes don't fit for shit*.

But an alternate magic happens on this branch, where speakers quietly reinterpret a chunk of language and yank it into new functions that would make no sense if the original one hadn't reigned before. The denigration-is-worthlessness metaphor first creates the intuitive *dumb as shit, pale as shit, mean as shit*. Those mean "very dumb," "very pale," "very mean," so possibly we will start using *as shit* to mean *very* even with positive matters.

So, if you can say *poor as shit* to mean impoverished, then it can feel right to say *rich as shit* to mean loaded, *happy as shit* to mean elated. There is no literal application here, naturally. But if we use *as shit* as an intensifier of lousy things, hardly thinking of the literal meaning of *shit* at all, then after a while we can wrap our heads around expressions like judging someone as "hot as shit."

Extension 4—Feces Is Intense

This last extension stems from the same kind of reinterpretation as the one that yields that magnificently senseless *happy / rich / hot as shit*. Why is it that we can say, "If you see one of those bastards, run like shit"? Or "If it overheats, fan it like shit till I get back with some water"? What do the negative associations of feces have to do with an intense and effective action?

50

---

3. Or the more graphic *I don't give two shits*. On that, linguists, proclaiming that there is no such thing as "wrong language," are often asked if there's anything people say that irritates them. I must admit that this one does rub me the wrong way—for my taste, too graphic for how often some people use it. I don't wish to have that image summoned under anything less than the most urgent of circumstances. I'm quite aware that legions would disagree, do not hear the expression as sensually repellent, and think I should just get over it. And they are right—or I have no way of telling them they aren't that I could confidently back up with pure logic, which teaches us that judgmental attitudes about language are always arbitrary.

Here, the issue is substitution, of a kind that makes sense only in light of previous circumstances. We can also use *like hell* in this function—*run like hell; fan it like hell*. Hell is an extreme setting, singular and feared, so it's hardly bizarre that it becomes a way of expressing extremity. . . . But then, colorful expressions have a way of fading in power. Yesterday's *inde-goddamn-pendent* is today's *inde-fuckin'-pendent*, yesterday's *I don't give a damn* is today's *I don't give a shit* (but please, not two), or even more currently *I don't give a fuck*.

In the same way, yesterday's *run like hell* becomes today's *run like shit* out of a sense that a fresher cuss was needed to get the heat across. Any literal meaning is irrelevant. What mattered was slipping in a word of equal power. These days, *run like fuck* is just as good if not better, despite making not a bit more sense.

As such, our grimy little word lends itself to a diagram like the one for boring *back*, as in:

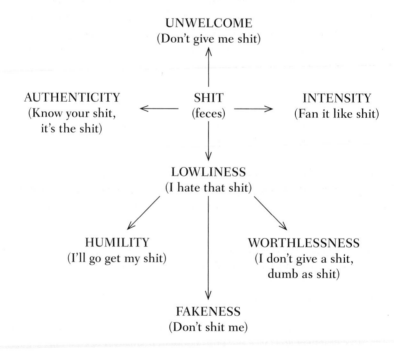

Who knew this was what *shit* is all about? One might adjudge the true nature of this word as *the shit* indeed. Curse words are not just vulgar and thoughtless. They morph and meander and slip according to predictable, and even elegant, contours of cognitive associations. A final metaphor, perhaps: *shit* is elegant!

• • •

MLA CITATION

McWhorter, John. "Profanity and Shit." *The Norton Reader: An Anthology of Nonfiction*, edited by Melissa A. Goldthwaite et al., 16th ed., W. W. Norton, 2024, pp. 368–78.

QUESTIONS

1. How does knowing more about a word's history, etymology, and usage change your sense of the word?

2. For a day, notice every time you hear someone use the word *shit*. Catalog how they use it. Where do the usages fit in John McWhorter's grammar? Can you find any new usages?

3. What is your family's attitude to *shit* and other so-called nasty words? Reflect, in a personal essay (in written, audio, or video format), on your family's attitude to swear words in the context of McWhorter's description of how these words work. How does the taboo on cursing show up in your family?

4. Look up *shit* in the *Oxford English Dictionary*, studying both the etymology and some of the history of the word. Follow a set of family connections different from McWhorter's and give a short account of what you find.

MOLLY McCULLY BROWN
Something's Wrong with Me

THE EARLIEST LEXICON I remember having available to define myself is a medical glossary of defect and attempted repair: *ruptured amniotic sac, neurological disorder, increased spasticity, impaired fine-motor control, dorsal rhizotomy, cartilage disintegration, orthopedic surgeon, orthotics, plaster molding, gait monitoring and maintenance, physical therapy, magnetic resonance imaging, double upright KFOs*. Find all cross-listed under deformity; deficiency; disability.

By kindergarten, I could tell you, in the Donald Duck voice I spoke with because I couldn't really clear my throat: *I have cerebral palsy, which is a little like a stroke that happens when you're born*. There is probably not a single other sentence I have uttered more frequently in all my years of being alive. It appears in every facet of my life, addressed at one time or another to nearly every stranger and acquaintance and friend. To the potential employer: *I have cerebral palsy, which is a little like a stroke that happens when you're born*. To the handsome, confused guy across the table in the coffee shop: *I have cerebral palsy, which is a little like . . .* To the college girl in the grocery store aisle who looks shiftily at the

First appeared in the *Rumpus* (2014), an online literary magazine, and then in Molly McCully Brown's 2020 collection of essays Places I've Taken My Body.

adapted Segway that I sometimes use to get around, the man behind me in line at the ATM who asks why I'm in a wheelchair, the mother and her little boy, the older woman coming out of church who sees my cane and my weird walk and says, *You're too beautiful to be disabled, what happened to you!?*

I have cerebral palsy . . .

One day I report an interaction like this, and a friend's surprise at a stranger's forwardness, to my father on the phone. I say: *I had to tell her this happens to me all the time.* He corrects me, out of what impulse I'm not completely sure: *Well, not all the time, but sometimes* . . . I don't remember if I force the issue, but it's true—all the time. At least once almost every time I leave my house. This is not an exaggeration.

*

5   There is a strange kind of security about having something so immutable at the center of yourself. Once, I was interviewed briefly for a local news segment about new adaptive technology. The caption underneath me while I spoke read: *Molly Brown: physically disabled.* It's hard to argue with this. Whatever ontological unease I feel, however ethereal my thoughts become, the truth of my body is literal and absolute, like an anchor pulling me back to the world.

And that other essential, persistent refrain is as important as ever, however often I repeat it. I am lucky—lucky to be alive, to be as mobile and unscarred as I am, to be as independent as I am capable of being. I am lucky to have been born to smart, devoted parents, to have received an extraordinary education, to be able to articulate my life and my body. I am lucky that it is possible for me to stand up, both literally and figuratively, for myself and others like me when it's called for. I am lucky for a million other reasons that I am not listing here.

*

But can I admit something unflattering and exhausted and ungenerous?

I'm so tired of talking about disability. I'm tired of talking about its place in culture and politics. I'm tired of talking about my body and other people's bodies, and of feeling like leaving my house in the morning is a political act. I'm tired of, whatever I write and whatever I'm thinking, feeling disability bang around at the back of my brain and insist on a presence in everything. Get out. Leave me alone. Get out. Get out.

I spent nearly the entire day yesterday sitting in front of this computer trying not to write this essay—which I feel like I've written a thousand versions of before—negotiating out loud with the thick, warm air: I will write about anything else, anything at all. There's a whole world out there, and I spent my week imagining women slowly losing their minds trapped in a hospital. Couldn't there be something else in my writing mind? Last week, when a woman in the Thai restaurant where I was picking up takeout looked at my Segway and, not knowing any better, asked me if I wouldn't rather just walk, I almost said, *You bitch!* just so I wouldn't have to say, *Actually, I have cerebral palsy* . . .

10   I'm tired of feeling left out of every conversation about femininity, and every conversation about feminism, like I can't ever find another voice in the

chorus like mine, an experience that matches my own. Trying to explain this to a good friend who's recently started blogging for a feminist website, I say: nobody anywhere in the media looked anything like me when I was growing up. Nobody on television, or on any magazine cover, or in any book. Even in counterculture I couldn't find a model.

I'm not alone in feeling the impact of that silence, that lack. Introducing a recent report on disability representation in the media, Ford Foundation senior fellow Judith E. Heumann writes:

> Growing up, I rarely, if ever, saw anyone with a disability on television or in movies. If disabled people were shown at all, they were portrayed as villains to be reviled . . . or as objects of pity for charitable causes such as the Jerry Lewis Telethon and on numerous soap operas where "good" or beloved characters were apt to be miraculously cured of their disability. Without question, there was nobody I could look to and say, "There's a positive, high-achieving disabled person like me," and certainly no one I could look to as a role model who reflected my actual lived experience.

According to the Centers for Disease Control and Prevention, one out of every four Americans has a disability, but Heumann notes in her report that only 2.1 percent of primetime broadcast TV series regulars—a total of sixteen characters—have disabilities. In the one hundred top grossing movies of the last ten years, only 2.5 percent of characters are depicted with disabilities. Those numbers grow even more dismal and damaging if you're a disabled woman, or person of color, looking to see yourself reflected in the media around you.

The consequences of this lack of representation aren't merely intellectual or theoretical. As I aged out of childhood, nothing in my world made any room for me, warned me, or prepared me, for the life I'd have to lead. Nothing offered any advice: Here's how your disability can co-exist with your gender, your sexuality, your politics, your ambition. Here's how to talk about it to bosses and lovers, here's how not to let it get so big it drowns out everything else about you. I had to make it all up as I went along.

The ugliest, most selfish part of me is tired of feeling responsible for the chasm I feel—like somehow I have to end it, change it, fill it up.

*

The other night, I put on a nice dress and went to a bar I don't usually frequent, but that I knew was accessible. I parked my Segway against the back wall and chose a table close enough that I could see it, but far enough away that it wasn't obviously mine. I sat in the semi-dark and drank a bourbon and enjoyed the thought that, looking at me, nobody would know, that sitting at the table right now I could be any pretty young woman with a book in a bar. For all they knew, I could go dance. I could get up and walk right out of there, painless and fluid and unremarkable. I wouldn't need to field a single comment or question, or get a single sorry look.

This lasted a few minutes, and then I felt guilty as hell for trying to crawl 15 out of my own skin.

Later, I put off sending the email in which I have to write and tell the woman interviewing me for a job on Tuesday that I'm in a wheelchair. I worry about the mother who emailed me about tutoring her daughter in SAT prep, and then just stopped writing after I revealed I use one. Who knows what happened, but . . .

*

I've been seeing someone very casually for a little while, and while he's made it clear he's interested, it's also clear that he's more than a little uncomfortable with his relationship to my body: He looks down at the floor when I walk around my apartment, is reluctant to go out together in public. When we're lying on my bed and his hand finds the small snarl of scar tissue on my lower back, he flinches, pulls away. He doesn't touch me anywhere near there again.

One night, before he comes over, I catch myself wondering whether I ought to put cover-up on the bruises that dot my legs and feet from the fall I took the previous night, and trying to imagine how I can stand up as little as possible once he arrives: *If I've already poured our drinks, then* . . . It's more than wanting to be pretty, than putting on mascara or a dress that makes me look skinnier. In all of this, I'm trying to play-act not just a different body, but a different life in which this history of damage isn't mine and, on a night when he's more uncomfortable than usual, I don't need to worry that I might fall down the concrete stairs ahead of him because my pride won't let me take his arm.

And here, again, my privilege rises to the surface: My daily life is manageable enough that I have time to meditate on the cultural position of disability. When I need a night off from my body I can go to a bar and sidle away from myself, pretend to be a different kind of woman with a different existence. I can blend in, pass. And, however complicated it has been—will be—there have been people who've loved me, found me beautiful, become comfortable beside me. When I really remember all this, it is enough to begin to soothe the tired, freaked-out, fucked-up part of me that's been screaming for a break.

*

20   The truth is, mostly, I don't want a different life or even a different body. I've brokered peace with my hair, my spade-like nails, my ghostly pale skin. My neck is my mother's neck, my face is my father's face. And this body, as complicated as it is, gave me rapt attention. It gave me empathy and maturity. It gave me discipline and poetry, and enough hurt and strangeness to really need it. And I wouldn't trade away anything that might take with it the way I fill up when I read Emily Dickinson. *After great pain, a formal feeling comes* . . .

The truth is I want the same thing so many activists work for. I want a different, better world than the one I came of age in. Each child with a disability will always know too early the dictionary of defects and treatments essential to her life. But I want for them all to have, too, another language with which to talk about their bodies and their lives: one of pride and complexity, intimacy and particularity, survival and triumph. I want them all to know that there are other bodies that look and move like theirs, bodies that aren't lying in hospital beds or aging bitterly in the corners of rooms, and I want them to have easy access to voices that will comfort and console and instruct them and welcome their presence in the chorus. I don't want them to go it alone. I want them to believe in the possibility of love, and adventure, and beauty, and a whole complete life, however trite that all sounds. And there are people out there working to make this possible, people who know the only corrective to absence, stereotyping, and silence comes when we raise our voices.

To help realize the world I want, I have to write, I have to talk. Language is my medium. It is the thing that has borne me up and out of every valley, the thing that has tied me to other people and made my life large. Often, it's the only thing I really believe in.

*

So I stop fighting with the air and write this essay. I tell the woman who's interviewing me next week what to expect. I gather myself and put my hands in my hair, lean close to that guy I'm seeing and say: *Listen, you can tell me if you're feeling uncomfortable and we'll talk about it, you can ask questions if you have them, you can take your time getting to know me, but you can't push me away like that because you're freaking out about the wheelchair. I'm done with the part of my life where I feel ashamed of myself and of my body. I'm not about to go back there, okay? That's the deal.*

And, when I'm ready, I stand up from the table in that bar. I stumble a little and stomp over to the wall. Outside, some guy at one of the tables stops me. *Hey, what's the deal with the Segway?* In a lot of ways, I'm better at this than anything else, meant for this sentence and the conversation it starts: *Hi, I use it instead of a wheelchair; I have cerebral palsy, which is . . .*

MLA CITATION

Brown, Molly McCully. "Something's Wrong with Me." *The Norton Reader: An Anthology of Nonfiction*, edited by Melissa A. Goldthwaite et al., 16th ed., W. W. Norton, 2024, pp. 379–83.

QUESTIONS

1. Molly McCully Brown's disability is only partially apparent to strangers. How does that affect how others think about her and her disability? How does it affect how she sees herself?

2. Annotate each time Brown repeats a variation of the sentence "*I have cerebral palsy, which is a little like a stroke that happens when you're born*" (paragraph 2). How does the sentence, and her attitude to it, change over the course of the essay?

3. Is there something about yourself that people consistently notice when they meet you that you wish they didn't? What is it? What does it say about you? What do you wish they knew about you instead? How do you wish they could think of that aspect of you differently?

4. In paragraph 21, Brown expresses a desire for "another language . . . of pride and complexity, intimacy and particularity, survival and triumph" for children growing up with a disability. How does Brown imagine and create that language in this essay?

5. Interview a group of people. Ask them to introduce themselves by name and one key fact. Then ask them to explain why they chose that fact and to reflect on the significance of it. What does it communicate about them, their history, and their sense of belonging? Compile your findings into a project.

JOAN NAVIYUK KANE
Passing through Danger

I T'S NICE TO IMPART a piece of good news. On the phone, I'm telling my mother about our King Island dictionary, which we've almost finished digitizing.

"But," my twelve-year-old son interjects, "we were getting kicked out of Mom's office building, they almost didn't let us in on the last day! I have to fix the page order and put it in a PDF again."

It's 9 P.M. in Cambridge, Massachusetts, and my younger son, who turned ten last month, is finishing a bowl of rice on the living room floor of our apartment. I've called my parents in Anchorage, in part to check on them, in part so my mom can ask the boys when they're going to bed, in part so the boys can thank her for the letters they received (in which she asked my younger son, "Why do you stay up so long?").

And I called in part to ask my mother about Inupiaq etymology. King Island is where our family is from. When I moved to Cambridge to take a year-long fellowship at the Radcliffe Institute, one of my projects—one I hoped to share with my sons—was completing a dictionary of the dialect we grew up speaking. I'm trying to find a word for *pandemic*. The etymology in English is muddied, and semantic vagueness troubles me. I see people using a cognate—*sikpin?*—for "Are you sick?" and it doesn't seem right. I find words in other dialects that don't seem to have affinity with words in the King Island dialect.

5   I ask my mom about the prefix *nan-*. It seems to have to do with avoidance, precarity, suffering, speaking ill, inflicting pain. *Nanaagaa*: she/he is avoiding it. *Naniiklaa*: she/he is complaining about her/him. *Naniagna.tuq*: a precipitous place is frightening. *Naniaqtuna*: I feel terror in a precarious place. *Nanituq*: she/he is sick. *Nanitkia*: she/he beat her/him. *Naniirvik*: hospital, sanatorium. *Nanirun* translates to "epidemic" in most Inupiaq dialects. My mother's explanation is characteristically direct: "It's something that makes you suffer. *Nanirun.*"

I tell my mom that my older son and I have been experiencing a lot of déjà vu. Tonight he helped me make an eggplant and potato curry with ingredients

Originally published on April 3, 2020, as part of the Yale Review's *"Pandemic Files": essays, fiction, and poetry responding to the crisis caused by COVID-19.*

from a combination of sources—none of them a grocery store. He was eager to mince garlic once we'd trimmed spots of rot; he watched me peel a ginger root before taking on the task himself. When he tastes it, then asks if we can make it again tomorrow without the eggplant, I stop and tell him I feel like we've had this conversation before.

"But I've never been brave or hungry enough to try eggplant until tonight," he answers.

Déjà vu, I explain. "Like when I hear Brahms," he says.

"Like my dreams when I wake up in the morning," says his younger brother.

Our phone calls with my mother punctuate the days now. My sons record 10 words in our dialect and learn to make sentences. They ask her questions. We don't speak of the future, and I don't want to ask too much about her mother—orphaned in the 1918 flu pandemic. My grandmother's parents and three siblings were all killed by the flu at Qawairaq (Mary's Igloo) on the Seward Peninsula, where, according to ethnohistorians, the mortality rate was 54 percent. I don't ask about the baby boy who died, according to church records, at the orphanage where my grandmother and her two sisters were raised through early childhood.

Instead, we talk about things she might remember from her visits to Harvard Square twenty, twenty-five years ago, when I was an undergraduate and she was the proud mother of the first Inupiaq bound to take a degree at Harvard College. We tell her about the empty streets of Cambridge and Boston. Of the boys sharing one scooter, using the bike lanes to get around now that there's no traffic. We report on the birds and blooms we catalogue on our daily walks.

I tell her about the Inuit-related books I've managed to read lately. I spare her the details of the essay I am trying to write, the one I need to step away from in order to sleep. I tell her how I spend hours teaching my younger son long division. Helping the boys with Spanish, Mandarin, social studies, and a dozen other subjects. I say we're playing violin duets and flute trios together.

The essay I started to write reads as a complaint, a summary of injustices, a preparation for worse to come. I think of the federal termination of the Mashpee Wampanoag tribe's claims to sovereign land that has just happened in the past few days, the government taking their land out of trust. I think of the eighty-one ventilators the Indian Health Service is said to have for all of us beneficiaries of the system.

I hope my parents stay home. I hope people stay away from them. We're so far, with no way of returning to Alaska and no place to stay even if we did. My sons like it here in Massachusetts, though they dream of moving to Abu Dhabi, to Japan, of a couple of years in the EU.

In recent weeks, we've all stopped saying things like "Remember when we 15 had a house?" "I miss having a yard." My sons now say, "I miss my friends." I ask which friends, in Alaska or Cambridge. "All of them," they say. Cambridge is empty. Our building is almost vacant. We're stuck here for now.

We departed Alaska for Massachusetts last August, several weeks ahead of schedule. Wells Fargo had begun posting notices on our family home that the bank would soon be boarding up the doors and windows. A judge had ordered me to stop paying the mortgage (which I'd qualified for as a tribally enrolled homebuyer), determining it was my ex-husband's responsibility. He hadn't paid for more than eight months.

My sons and I spent most of the spring and summer emptying out the house, sorting our belongings into one of three piles: ship, share, sell. I can't remember what we did with the N95 respirator masks. They had become a necessity in our final weeks, as we ferried boxes to the post office, brought bin after bin to relatives or Goodwill. I confer with my sons: they tell me we tossed the masks into the garbage before boarding our redeye to Seattle.

Anchorage's hospitals had been handing out the masks to patients as a matter of public health. Air quality in much of Alaska had been deemed hazardous for most of the summer, as six hundred wildfires burned areas roughly equal in size to the state of Connecticut. Millions of acres of the state's trees were dead from an infestation of invasive spruce-bark beetles; the invasion had spread as decades of dramatically rising temperatures expanded their habitat. Forests stood tinder-dry after prolonged drought. Many months in 2018 and 2019 saw the hottest days in the history of recorded subarctic and arctic temperatures; Anchorage had a newsworthy stretch of 90-degree days in early July.

The state was ill prepared to contain these wildfires—some caused by humans, some sparked by lightning, more prevalent in the intensifying storms of the arctic and subarctic—having never invested much in training or educat-

The Swan Lake Fire near Anchorage, Alaska, in 2019.

ing its population. Much of Alaska continues to do without running water, roads, and communications networks.

In Anchorage—a racist, violent city already in financial crisis due to Alaska's dependence on petroleum and colonial economic policies, compounded by a massive 7.1 earthquake in November 2018—office buildings, schools, homes, and hospitals lacked air filtration systems that could make the air safe enough to breathe. It was a relief to dump those masks in the trash on our way out: reminders of the multiple traumas we were leaving. 20

We left a place that was not healthy. We adapted. We adjusted our expectations of time, space, and one another.

Have the governments imposed upon my family—municipal, state, and federal—ever responded constructively to disasters? Or have they only perpetuated them, protracted them? How much trust could I have?

When I wake my older son, he asks if he can read the news before he reads a book. I consent. I wish I knew how other single mothers cope right now with schools shut, childcare programs on hiatus, and the libraries, bookstores, and playgrounds closed to everyone. I've found little relief between cooking, cleaning, corresponding with students and my bosses at two different universities. I can't bring myself to respond to most emails and texts. I call my parents. I wish I could tell my sons something certain.

I consider the stretch ahead: how much closer we might grow, how clear our boundaries might become. We're fortunate to weather this here. We read. I write much less than I hope to. I wonder when things will change. I wonder if things have ever stopped changing for my family—for my mother, my sons. For my community. I think about our changing, living language, too. What do I convey to my children?

Naguasautuq: it got better? *Itqiitigaaŋa*: it makes me uneasy. *Agulaq*: it is the distance between things. 25

MLA CITATION

Kane, Joan Naviyuk. "Passing through Danger." *The Norton Reader: An Anthology of Nonfiction*, edited by Melissa A. Goldthwaite et al., 16th ed., W. W. Norton, 2024, pp. 384–87.

QUESTIONS

1. According to Joan Naviyuk Kane, why is it important to preserve Inupiaq? What is gained when people work to preserve an Indigenous language?

2. Throughout the essay, Kane wrestles with the ways she is trying to balance being present with her awareness of past injustice and her fears of an uncertain future. How does the project of creating a dictionary connect to these complicated feelings?

3. Look at the list of words with the prefix *naŋ-* (paragraph 5). Choose a word connected to something important to you—a joyful or frightening event or

phenomenon—and make a list of words connected to it. What does this constellation of words evoke for you? Write, film, or draw your response to this experience.

4. Interview one of your grandparents or a person of their generation about words and expressions they once used—or still do—that few people use today. Is working to preserve those ways of speaking important to them? Share your findings with your classmates.

KATHY FISH
Collective Nouns for Humans in the Wild

 GROUP OF GRANDMOTHERS is a *tapestry*. A group of toddlers, a *jubilance* (see also: a *bewailing*). A group of librarians is an *enlightenment*. A group of visual artists is a *bioluminescence*. A group of short story writers is a *Flannery*. A group of musicians is—a *band*.

A *resplendence* of poets.

A *beacon* of scientists.

A *raft* of social workers.

5   A group of first responders is a *valiance*. A group of peaceful protestors is a *dream*. A group of special education teachers is a *transcendence*. A group of neonatal ICU nurses is a *divinity*. A group of hospice workers, a *grace*.

Humans in the wild, gathered and feeling good, previously an *exhilaration*, now: *a target*.

A *target* of concert-goers.

A *target* of movie-goers.

A *target* of dancers.

10   A group of schoolchildren is a *target*.

Originally published in the Jellyfish Review *(2017), an online journal that publishes "beautiful things with stings."*

MLA CITATION

Fish, Kathy. "Collective Nouns for Humans in the Wild." *The Norton Reader: An Anthology of Nonfiction*, edited by Melissa A. Goldthwaite et al., 16th ed., W. W. Norton, 2024, p. 388.

Questions

1. In this essay, Kathy Fish takes the oddity of collective nouns and plays with them for dramatic effect. Now that you know the impact of the conclusion, look back at the essay itself: Are there other places where the author helps prepare you for the seriousness with which she ends? Annotate the words or sentences you find.

2. Find a list of collective nouns online. Look at them and discuss which ones are the most interesting, apt, poetic, and surprising.

3. Choose a linguistic phenomenon of your own—collective nouns or, perhaps, texting abbreviations, phrasal verbs, or clichés—and following Fish's model, write a very brief essay that starts off as a catalogue, then takes a more serious turn.

Kory Stamper
Capturing "Take" for the Dictionary

I T WAS 2001, three years into my tenure as a writer and editor of dictionaries at Merriam-Webster. There were about 20 of us lexicographers working on revising the *Collegiate Dictionary* for its eleventh edition. We had just finished the letter S.

By the time that last batch of defining and its citations—snippets of words used in context—for S had been signed back in on the production spreadsheet, the editors were not just pleased; we were giddy. You'd go to the sign-out sheet, see that we're into T, and make some little ritual obeisance to the moment: a fist pump, a sigh of relief and a heavenward glance, a little "oh yeah" and a tiny dance restricted to your shoulders (you *are* at work, after all). Sadly, lexicographers are not suited to survive extended periods of giddiness. In the face of such woozy delight, the chances are good that you will do something rash and brainless.

Unfortunately, my rash brainlessness was obscured from me. I signed out the next batch in T and grabbed the printouts of the entries I'd be revising for that batch along with the boxes—*two boxes!*—of citations for the batch. While flipping through the galley pages, I realized that my batch—the entire thing—was just one word: "take." *Hmm*, I thought, *that's curious.*

Lexicography, like most professions, offers its devotees some benchmarks by which you can measure your sad little existence, and one is the size of the

This essay was first published in Slate, *an online magazine that covers culture, politics, and current affairs, in 2017.*

words you are allowed to handle. Most people assume that long words or rare words are the hardest to define because they are often the hardest to spell, say, and remember. The truth is, those are usually a snap. "Schadenfreude" may be difficult to spell, but it's a cinch to define, because all the uses of it are very, very semantically and syntactically clear. It's always a noun, and it's often glossed, because even though it's now an English word, it's one of those delectable German compounds we love to slurp into English.

5   Generally speaking, the smaller and more commonly used the word is, the more difficult it is to define. Words like "but," "as," and "for" have plenty of uses that are syntactically similar but not identical. Verbs like "go" and "do" and "make" (and, yes, "take") don't just have semantically oozy uses that require careful definition but semantically drippy uses as well. "Let's do dinner" and "let's do laundry" are identical syntactically but feature very different semantic meanings of "do." And how do you describe what the word "how" is doing in this sentence?

It's not just semantic fiddliness that causes lexicographical pain. Some words, like "the" and "a," are so small that we barely think of them as words. Most of the publicly available databases that we use for citational spackling don't even index some of these words, let alone let you search for them—for entirely practical reasons. A search for "the" in our in-house citation database returns over 1 million hits, which sends the lexicographer into fits of audible swearing, then weeping.

To keep the lexicographers from crying and disturbing the people around them, sometimes these small words are pulled from the regular batches and are given to more senior editors for handling. They require the balance of concision, grammatical prowess, speed, and fortitude usually found in wiser and more experienced editors.

I didn't know any of that at the time, of course, because I was not a wise or more experienced editor. I was hapless and dumb, but dutifully so: Grabbing a fistful of index cards from one of the two boxes, I began sorting the cards into piles by part of speech. This is the first job you must do as a lexicographer dealing with paper, because those citations aren't sorted for you. I figured that "take" wasn't going to be too terrible in this respect: There's just a verb and a noun to contend with. When those piles were two-and-a-half inches high and began cascading onto my desk, I decided to dump the rest of the citations into my pencil drawer and stack my citations in the now-empty boxes.

Sorting citations by their part of speech is usually simple. Most words entered in the dictionary only have one part of speech, and if they have more than one, the parts of speech are usually easy to distinguish between—the noun "blemish" and the verb "blemish," for example, or the noun "courtesy" and the adjective "courtesy." By the time you've hit *T* on a major dictionary overhaul like a new edition of the *Collegiate*, you can sort citations by part of speech in your sleep. For a normal-sized word like "blemish," it's a matter of minutes.

10   Five hours in, I had finished sorting the first box of citations for "take."

It is unfortunate that the entries that take up most of the lexicographer's time are often the entries that no one looks at. We used to be able to kid ourselves while tromping through "get" that someone, somewhere, at some point in time, was going to look up the word, read sense 11c ("hear"), and say to themselves, "Yes, *finally*, now I understand what 'Did you get that?' means. Thanks, Merriam-Webster!" Sometimes, in the delirium that sets in at the end of a project when you are proofreading pronunciations in 6-point type for eight hours a day, a little corner of your mind wanders off to daydream about how perhaps your careful revision of "get" will somehow end with your winning the lottery, bringing about world peace, and finally becoming the best dancer in the room.

But nowadays, thanks to the marvels of the internet, we know exactly what sorts of words people look up regularly. They generally don't look up long, hard-to-spell words—no "rhadamanthine" or "vecturist" unless the Scripps National Spelling Bee is on TV. They tend to look up words in the middle of the road. Some of the all-time top lookups at Merriam-Webster are "paradigm," "disposition," "ubiquitous," and "esoteric," words that are used fairly regularly but also in contexts that don't tell the reader much about what they mean.

This also means that the smallest words, like "but" and "as" and "make," are not looked up either. Most native English speakers know how to navigate the collocative waters of "make" or don't need to figure out what exactly "as" means in the sentence "You are as dull as a mud turtle." They recognize that it marks comparison, somehow, and that's it. But that's not good enough for lexicography.

It is also a perverse irony that the entries that end up taking the most lexicographical time are usually fairly fixed. Steve Kleinedler, the executive editor of *The American Heritage Dictionary*, notes that one of his editors overhauled 50 or 60 of the most basic English verbs back in the first decade of the 21st century. "Because he did that, they don't really need to be done again anytime soon. That was probably the first time they'd been done in 40 years." This isn't dereliction on *The American Heritage Dictionary*'s part: These words don't make quick semantic shifts. "Adding new idioms to these entries: easy-peasy," Steve says. "But in terms of overhauling 'take' or 'bring' or 'go,' if you do it once every 50 years, you're probably set."

The citations sorted, I decided to tackle the verb first. The entry for the verb is far longer than the entry for the noun: 107 distinct senses, subsenses, and defined phrases. And, perhaps hidden in all those cards, a few senses or idioms to add.

When one works with paper citations, the unit of work measurement is the pile. Every citation gets sorted into a pile that represents the current definitions for the word, and new piles for potential new definitions. I looked at the galleys, then my desk, and began methodically moving everything on my desk that I could—date stamp, desk calendar, coffee—to the bookshelf behind me.

My first citation read, "She was taken aback." I exhaled in relief: This is simple. I scanned the galley and found the appropriate definition—"to catch or come upon in a particular situation or action" (sense 3b)—and began my pile. The next handful of citations were similarly dispatched—a pile for sense 2, a pile for sense 1a, a pile for sense 7d—and I began to relax. In spite of its size, this is no different from any other batch, I reasoned. I am going to whip through this, and then I am going to take a two-week vacation, visit my local library, and *go outside.*

Fate, now duly tempted, intervened. My next cit read, "Reason has taken a back seat to sentiment." I confidently flipped it onto the pile with "taken aback" and then reconsidered. This use of "take" didn't really mean "to catch or come upon in a particular situation or action," did it? I tried substitution: Reason did not catch or come upon a backseat. No: Reason was made secondary to sentiment. I scanned the galleys and saw nothing that matched, then put the citation in a "new sense" pile. But before I could grab the next citation, I thought, "Unless . . ."

When a lexicographer says "unless . . ." in the middle of defining, you should turn out the lights and go home, first making sure you've left them a supply of water and enough nonperishable food to last several days. "Unless . . ." almost always marks the beginning of a wild lexical goose chase.

20   There is a reality to what words mean that is amplified when you're dealing with the little words. The meaning of a word depends on its context, but if the context changes, so does the meaning of the word. The meaning of "take" in "take a back seat" changes depending on the whole context: "There's no room up front, so you have to take a back seat" has a different meaning from "reason takes a back seat to sentiment." This second use is an idiom, which means it gets defined as a phrase at the end of the entry. I started a new pile.

My rhythm had been thrown off, but upon reading the next citation, I was confident I'd regain momentum: ". . . take a shit." Profanity and a clear, fixed idiom that will need its own definition at the end of the entry—yes, I can do this.

Only "take a shit" is not a fixed idiom like "take a back seat" is. You can also take a crap. Or a walk, or a breather, or a nap, or a break. I scanned the galleys, flipping from page to page. "To undertake and make, do, or perform," sense 17a. I considered. I tried substitution with hysterical results: "to undertake and make a shit," "to undertake a shit," "to undertake and do a shit," "to undertake and perform a shit." This got me thinking, which is always dangerous. Can one "perform" or "do" a nap? Does one "undertake and make" a breather? Maybe that's 17b, "to participate in." But my sprachgefühl, my internal feeling for English and how it worked, screeched: "participate" implies that the thing being participated in has an originating point outside the speaker. So you take (participate in) a meeting, or you take (participate in) a class on French philosophy. I tentatively placed the citation in the pile for 17a, then spent the next five minutes writing each sense number and definition down on a sticky note and affixing it to the top citation of each pile. My note for sense 17a included the parenthetical "(Refine/revise def? Make/do/perform?)."

I sat back and berated myself a bit. I have redefined "Monophysite" and "Nestorianism"; I can swear in a dozen languages; I am not a moron. This should be easy. My next citation read, ". . . arrived 20 minutes late, give or take."

What? This isn't a verbal use! How did this get in here? I took a pinched-lip look around my cubicle for the guilty party—someone has been in here futzing with my citations!—then realized I was the guilty party. Clearly, I needed to refile this. But where? After five minutes of staring at the citation, I took the well-trod path of least resistance and decided that maybe it's adverbial ("eh, close enough"). Yes, I'll just put this citation . . . in the nonexistent spot for adverbial uses of "take," because there are no adverbial uses of "take." My teeth began to hurt.

I placed the citation in a far corner of my desk, which I mentally labeled "Which Will Be Dealt With in Two or Three Days."   25

Next: ". . . this will only take about a week." My brain saw "take about" and spat out "phrasal verb." Phrasal verbs are two- or three-word phrases that are made up of a verb and a preposition or adverb (or both), that function like a verb, and whose meaning cannot be figured out from the meanings of each individual constituent. "Look down on" in "He looked down on lexicography as a career" is a phrasal verb. The whole phrase functions as a verb, and "look down on" here does not mean that the anonymous He was physically towering over lexicography as a career and staring down at it, but rather that he thought lexicography as a career was unimportant or not worth his respect. Phrasal verbs tend to be completely invisible to a native speaker of English, which is why I was so very proud of spotting one at first glance. I created a new pile for the phrasal verb "take about," and then my sprachgefühl found its voice: "That's not a phrasal verb."

I squeezed my eyes shut and silently asked the cosmos to send the office up in a fireball right now. After a moment, I realized that my sprachgefühl had picked loose a bit of information that fell neatly to the bottom of my brainpan: The "about" is entirely optional. Try it: "This will only take a week" and "this will only take about a week" mean almost the same thing. The pivot point for meaning is not "take" but "about," which means that this use of "take" is a straightforward transitive use. I flipped the card onto the pile for sense 10e(2), "to use up (as space or time)."

It had been an hour, and I had gotten through perhaps 20 citations. I sifted all my "Done" piles into one and grabbed a ruler. The pile of handled citations was a quarter-inch thick. Then I measured the cit boxes. Each was full. Each was 16 inches long.

Over the next two weeks, the tensile strength of my last nerve was tested by "take." My working definition of "desk" expanded as I ran out of flat spaces to stack citations. Piles appeared on the top of my monitor, in my pencil drawer, filed between rows on my keyboard, teetering on the top of the cubicle wall, shuffled onto the top of the CPU under my desk. Still I didn't have enough space: I began to carefully, carefully put piles of citations on the floor. My cubicle looked as if it had hosted the world's neatest ticker-tape parade.

When dealing with entries of this size, you will inevitably hit the Wall. If   30
you run, or have tried to run, then you are familiar with the Wall. It's the point in a run when you are pushed (or pushing) beyond your physical endurance. Your focus pulls inward on your searing lungs, your aching calves, that hitch in your right hip that is probably because you didn't stretch but might just be a precursor to your lower body literally (sense 2: figuratively) exploding from the

effort you are putting forth. The ground has tilted upward; your feet are made of concrete and are 50 times bigger than you thought; your neck begins to bow because even the effort of holding your fat melon upright is too much. You are not euphoric, or Zen, or any of the other things that *Runner's World* magazine makes running look like. You are at the Wall, where you are nothing but a loose collection of human limits.

I hit my human limits about three-quarters of the way through the verb "take." As I looked at a citation for "took first things first," I felt myself slowly unspooling into idiocy. I knew the glyphs before me had to be words, because my job was all about words, and I knew they had to be English, because my job was all about English. But knowing something doesn't make it true. *This was all garbage*, I thought, and as I felt my brain slip sideways, and the yawing ache open up in my gut, one thought flitted across my mind before I slammed head-long into the lexicographer's equivalent of the Wall: "Oh my God, I'm going to die at my desk like in that urban legend, and they will find my body under an avalanche of 'take.'"

That night over dinner, my husband asked if I was OK. I looked up at him, utterly lost. "I don't think I speak English anymore." He looked mildly alarmed; he only speaks English. "You're probably just stressed," he said. "But what does that even mean?" I whined. "Just thinking about what it means makes my brain itch!" He went back to looking mildly alarmed.

It took me three more days to finish sorting the citations for the verb "take." I was ecstatic—yes, I had done it!—and then immediately depressed: Shit, I still had to actually do the defining work on "take," and I still had the noun to go! Lucky for me, I had decided to use the sticky notes to make changes to existing entries. "Make, do, or undertake" didn't end up getting a revision in the end, but a rough handful of senses needed expanding or fixing; one definition meant to cover uses like "she took the sea air for her health" had been unfortunately phrased "to expose oneself to (as sun or air) for pleasure or physical benefit," which I hurriedly changed to "to put oneself into (as sun, air, or water) for pleasure or physical benefit" so as not to encourage medicinal flashing.

On the floor were my piles for citations that I needed to mentally squint at a bit more and piles of citations for new senses of "take." It was late in the afternoon, the sun slicing gold along the wall. Before I took care of those, I decided to reward myself by answering the email correspondence I had let accumulate while I had been ears-deep in "take." I'd start afresh in the morning.

35   The next morning, I came into work and discovered that the overnight cleaning crew had decided to move all the piles I had left on the floor, dumping them into a cascade of paper on my chair. It was a cinematic moment: I dropped my bag and stared open-mouthed at the blank spaces where 20 or so piles of citations used to sit. As my sinuses prickled, I realized, almost too late, that I was about to cry, and if I cried, I would most certainly make noise. I left my bag in the middle of the floor and went to the ladies', where I leaned against the paper towel dispenser and wondered if it was too late to go back to the

bakery where I had once worked and have indignant people throw cakes at my head again.

Lexicography is a steady plod in one direction: onward. I was doing no good standing there with my head on the cool plastic. Besides, a few of my colleagues were waiting for me to move so they could dry their hands. I re-sorted the tidy stack the cleaning crew left and papered every flat surface within five feet of my cubicle with "DO NOT MOVE MY PAPERS!!! KLS!!!!" I sat grimly in my chair and decided that a little fun was in order: It was time to stamp the covered citations and file them away.

When you're done working on an entry, the paper citations get put in one of three places: the "Used" group, which are the citations used as evidence for every existing definition in the entry; the "New" group, which holds the citations for each new sense you draft; and the "Rejected" group, which holds the citations for any use whose meaning isn't covered by the existing entry or by a newly proposed definition. Used and new citations are stamped by the editor who worked on the entry to mark that they were used for a particular book. When the whole floor was consumed with a defining project, you'd occasionally hear a sudden rhythmic thumping, like someone tapping their toe in miniature. It was an editor stamping citations.

I took out my customized date stamp and began marking the covered cits, pile by pile, as used. After the first handful, I stamped a little more exuberantly, and my cubemate hemmed in irritation. No matter. I had no punching bag to pummel; I had no nuclear device to detonate. But I had a date stamp, and by the power vested in me by Samuel Johnson and Noah Webster,[1] I was going to put this goddamned verb to bed.

MLA CITATION

Stamper, Kory. "Capturing 'Take' for the Dictionary." *The Norton Reader: An Anthology of Nonfiction*, edited by Melissa A. Goldthwaite et al., 16th ed., W. W. Norton, 2024, pp. 389–95.

QUESTIONS

1. Kory Stamper writes about the ups and downs of finally getting to the letter *T* in the dictionary. Describe a time when you experienced a similar roller coaster of accomplishment and recognition of how far you had yet to go.

2. Look up the word *take* in *The Merriam-Webster Dictionary*. Read the whole definition. Knowing what you know now about how a lexicographer works, what surprises you most about this definition?

---

1. Johnson (1709–1784), British writer and lexicographer whose *Dictionary of the English Language* (1755) was the first English dictionary; Webster (1758–1843), American lexicographer and spelling reformer, wrote the first American dictionary of the English language in 1828.

3. Annotate the moments in which Stamper writes about procrastinating (see, for example, paragraph 25). What kind of procrastinator is she? How do her habits of procrastination compare with yours?

4. Read Joan Naviyuk Kane's "Passing through Danger" (pp. 384–87). How do the challenges of capturing a word differ between a single-language dictionary and a bilingual one?

DAVID SHIELDS

Words Can't Begin to Describe What I'm Feeling

I 'LL BE HONEST WITH YOU: I'm here to tell you: The big key is: The bottom line is:

There's no question about it. There's no doubt about it. You got that right. I couldn't agree with you more. Obviously, the statistics speak for themselves.

He's a highly touted freshman. Last week was his coming-out party. He has all the makings of a great one. He has unlimited potential. He's a can't-miss prospect. You'll be hearing a lot from him. He can play at the next level. He can play on Sundays. He's got his whole future ahead of him. He's a youngster who bears watching. He's being groomed for a future starting job. The team is really high on him. He's going to set the world on fire. He's a rookie phenom.

He moves well for a big man. He's sneaky-fast. He has lightning-fast reflexes. He has great lateral mobility. He can pick 'em up and put 'em down. He has speed *and* quickness. He's a cutter and a slasher. He has speed to burn. He's fleet-footed. He's a speed merchant. He can fly. You can't teach speed.

5   He's a unique physical specimen. He has a low center of gravity. He plays bigger than his size. He's built like a brick outhouse. He's a stud. He's a warrior. He's a bulldog. He has a linebacker mentality. He's fearless. He's a physical player. He's an impact player.

He's a tough, hard-nosed player. He's their spark plug. He's their role player. He understands his role on this team. He lets the game come to him. He's the consummate team player. He's an unselfish player. He's a real throwback. He plays with a lot of emotion. He has a passion for the game. He always gives 110 percent. He plays for the name on the front of the jersey, not the name on the back of it.

He's their playmaker. He's their field general. He's their floor general. He's a good table-setter. He's the glue that holds this team together. He makes the players around him better. He's a stand-up guy. The team looks to him for leadership. He's a leader on this team. He's a leader on and off the field.

Originally published in Verbatim: The Language Quarterly *(2003) and reprinted in David Shields's book* Other People: Takes and Mistakes *(2017), this piece is as much about language as it is about sports.*

He's a true professional. He's a professional hitter. He just goes out there and gets the job done. I was just doing my job. I was just hoping I could make a contribution in whatever way they needed me.

He's some kind of player. He's the real deal. He's legit. He can flat-out play. He's as good a player as there is in this league. He's one of the best in the business. He's a franchise player. Players like that don't come along very often. He's in a league of his own. He's a future Hall of Famer. He's a first-ballot lock. You can't say enough about him.

He's got ice water running through his veins. He's got the guts of a burglar. He thrives under pressure. He always comes through in the clutch. He always comes through at crunch time. He's their go-to guy when the game's on the line. He's money. He can carry the team on his shoulders. He can take them to the promised land.

He's shooting well from downtown. He's making a living behind the arc. He's getting some good open looks. He's shooting the lights out. He's in a zone. He's feeling it. He's in a groove. He's lighting it up. He's on fire. He's hot. He's locked in. He's unconscious.

He blew 'em away.

They pay him to make those catches. That pass was very catchable. He's usually a sure-handed receiver. He usually makes that catch. He heard footsteps. He's become a little gun-shy. He's got all the skills—he just needs to put them together. He needs to bulk up in the off-season. He needs to elevate his game. He's playing out of position. He lacks the killer instinct.

He's only played sparingly this season. He's the subject of trade rumors. He's being shopped around. He's on the trading block. He's bounced around a lot. He's a journeyman. He's the player to be named later. He's lost a step. He's their elder statesman. He has a new lease on life. I just want to give something back to the community. He's a great role model. He's a winner in the bigger game of life. I just want to be able to take care of myself and my family.

He doesn't have that good fastball today. He's getting by with breaking stuff. He took something off that pitch. He's getting shelled. He's getting rocked. They're teeing off on him. Stick a fork in him—he's done. They need to pull the plug. He hits the showers. Today I didn't have my plus-stuff. Regardless of what kind of stuff you have on a given day, you just try to go out there and pitch to the best of your ability and give your team an opportunity to win.

He got hung out to dry on that play. That was blown coverage. That was a missed assignment. They're playing in the shadow of their goalposts. He couldn't turn the corner. They're looking at third down and forever. They have to establish the running game. They have to air it out more. They have to take care of the football. That missed extra point could come back to haunt them. You gotta hit the holes they make for you. You gotta follow your blockers out there. He's been quiet so far—they need to get him some more carries in the second half. This is their deepest penetration of the half. They've got to punch it in from here. They can't cough it up here. They need to just go out and make football plays.

He has all the time in the world. He has all day back there. He has all kinds of time. He has an eternity. He threw into double coverage. He threw up a prayer. He'd like to have that one back.

We just couldn't execute. We weren't able to sustain anything. They got us out of our game plan early. They took us completely out of our rhythm.

We got beat like a gong. They beat us like a drum. They outplayed us. We ran into a buzz saw. Turnovers absolutely killed us. We didn't get any calls. Sometimes this game just comes down to the way the ball bounces. We didn't get any breaks. They were the better team today. Give them credit. We just didn't get the job done. We weren't mentally prepared. For some reason they've just got our number. We didn't come to play. They stepped up and made football plays. Football players make football plays. They wanted it more than we did. This was a wake-up call. I tip my hat to them. We beat ourselves. We only have to look in the mirror. I don't want to point any fingers. We came up a little short. We had our chances. They outplayed us in every phase of the game. They just made the big plays and we didn't. We dug ourselves a deep hole. We have to put this loss behind us. It's going to be a long plane ride home.

20   The coach is on the hot seat. His head is on the chopping block. Unfortunately, there are days like this. We're in the business of winning. It's the nature of this business. It's time to move on. We have to look forward. We need a change of direction. We need a clean slate. We need someone who can take us to the next level.

I feel the time has come for new leadership of this ball club. Everyone has to be held accountable. It's all about winning and losing. I take the blame. I'm not going to stand up here and make excuses. Obviously, I'm disappointed things didn't work out. This is my responsibility and I feel badly I haven't been able to get us where we should be. I want to thank our great fans. I'm looking forward to the next chapter in my life. First I'm going to spend more time with my family.

I'm excited about this opportunity. I'm looking forward to the challenge. I have high expectations for this team. This franchise has a great winning tradition. We've got a good solid foundation to build on. We're going to right the ship. We're going to get things turned around. This is a great sports town.

They stumbled coming out of the gate. They got off on the wrong foot. They're finally showing signs of life. They need a late surge. It's been an up-and-down season. It's a marathon, not a sprint.

This team is starting to make some noise. They've finally gotten off the schneid. The players have bought into the system. He's got them headed in the right direction. He's a players' coach. He's more of a people person than an X's and O's guy. These guys have been busting their tails for him. He gets the most out of his players. They've turned the corner. They've raised the bar. They've gotten over the hump. They're loaded this year. They're stacked. They have a strong supporting cast. There's no I in "team." They've added a new wrinkle to their offense. They're finally getting the respect they deserve. They're for real. They're here to stay. They're playing with newfound confidence. They've got great team chemistry. This team is like a family. Everything's clicking. We're starting to gel. Everybody's on the same page. We're hitting on all cylinders now. Everybody's contributing.

We've got the league's best offense against the league's best defense— something's gotta give. We've got an intriguing matchup. This is a pivotal game. This game is for the bragging rights. These teams flat don't like each other. There's no love lost between these two teams. There's bad blood between these two teams. It's gonna be a war out there. When these two teams get together, you really *can* throw out their records.

You have to respect their athleticism. You have to respect their quickness. They have tremendous leaping ability. They can put up big numbers. They do a great job defensively. They play tough *D*.

They're feeling each other out. Here's the payoff pitch. He chased a bad pitch. Tough to lay off that pitch. Three up, three down. This is shaping up to be a real pitchers' duel. That ball should be playable. It's a can of corn. The ball took a bad hop. Strike-'im-out, throw-'im-out double play. Inning over. He got a good jump. That brings the tying run to the plate. He hits 'em where they ain't. He's a long-ball threat. He hit a solo shot back in the fifth. He's seeing the ball real well. He wears them out. He made good contact. He hit that ball squarely. He hit that ball on the sweet spot. He knocked the cover off the ball. In any other ballpark, that's a home run. Chicks dig the long ball. He's sitting dead red. He got all of it. He went yard. He hit it into the cheap seats. He flat jacked it. He went deep. He went downtown. Going, going, gone. It's outta here. See ya later. Goodbye, baseball. Kiss it goodbye. Aloha means goodbye.

It's been all theirs to this point. It's theirs to lose. They're not playing to win—they're playing not to lose. They're putting the ball in the deep freeze. They've gone four corners. Now's the time to run some clock.

Looks like we've got some extracurricular activity going on out there. Let's hope cooler heads prevail. They're mucking it up in the corner. He stood him up on the blue line. That's gotta hurt. He was mugged. He's gonna feel that one on Monday. Looks like we've got a player shaken up. Looks like he got his bell rung. That hit really cleaned his clock. He ran into a brick wall. He was literally run over by a freight train. He was blindsided. He's slow getting up. He was really clotheslined. They can ill afford to lose him. Their locker room must look like a MASH unit. X-rays are inconclusive. He left the field under his own power. We hate to speculate on the nature of the injury.

There's a flag on the play. It depends on where they spot it. Terrible call, terrible call. We got hosed. We got jobbed. We got robbed. Highway robbery. We knew it was going to be tough going up against the other team—I didn't know we were going to have to play the guys in the striped shirts as well. They're the best refs money can buy. The refs should just let them play. Bad calls even out over the course of a season.

It ain't over till it's over. As Yogi said, it ain't over till it's over. It ain't over till the fat lady sings. They won't go quietly. We've still got plenty of football left. No need to panic—there's plenty of time left.

You can feel the momentum shifting. Big Mo. They're going for the jugular. They can smell blood in the water. They're within striking distance. *Now* we've got a football game. It's a whole new ball game. This team shows a lot of character. This team shows a lot of poise. This team shows a lot of resiliency. This team shows a lot of heart.

It all started out with good field position. They've marched down the field. That was a goal-scorer's goal. He lit the lamp. He went high to the top shelf. He put the biscuit in the basket. He found the twine. He went upstairs. He nailed the buzzer-beater. She really stuck the landing. He hit pay dirt. Nothing but net. This should be a chip shot for him. The kick splits the uprights.

What an incredible turnaround.

35 We found a way to win. A win is a win. It wasn't pretty, but we'll take it. I'm really proud of the way our guys hung in there. This is always a tough place to play. We're just glad to get out of here with a *W*. We're happy we could pull this one out at the end. They're tough competitors. They gave us all we could handle. They're a class act. Give them a lot of credit. I tip my hat to them. There are no easy games in this league. The game was a lot closer than the final score indicates. They weren't going to come in here and just lie down for us. We're going to use this as a building block. We'll use this win as a stepping-stone to the next level.

What a difference a week makes.

We were really on our game. We took them out of their game. We really came to play. We brought our A game. We knew what we had to do and went out and did it. We answered the call. This team has finally learned how to win. It was a total team effort. Obviously, this was a great win for us. It was a big win for us. We came to play. We stuck to the game plan. We wanted to make a statement. We sent a message. We came through when it counted. We're going to savor the victory tonight, then tomorrow morning we'll start looking at film.

The only thing that matters in the Stanley Cup playoffs is the man between the pipes. You can't win an NBA championship without a dominant big man. You can't win in the NFL without establishing the run. Offense puts fannies in the seats—defense wins championships. You've got to have pitching if you're going to make it through the postseason.

We just need to go out there and take care of business. It all just comes down to execution. You can't leave anything on the table. We have to go out and leave it all on the ice. We need to bring it. We need to dig deeper than we've ever dug before. We just gotta go out tomorrow and have fun.

40 They've battled back from the brink of elimination. They're down but not out. They're in a must-win situation. They need a win to stave off elimination. Lose and go home. Go big or go home. There's no tomorrow. I know it's a cliché, but we just have to take it one game at a time.

We gotta stick to the basics. We need to remember what got us here. You gotta dance with who brung you. This is it. This is for all the marbles.

They need to keep up their intensity. They have to stay focused. They have to get after it. They have to rise to the occasion. They've got tremendous mental toughness. They're a blue-collar team. They're overachievers. They've come out of nowhere. They're a real "Cinderella" story. They have to stay hungry. They're loaded for bear.

The city has rallied around this team. We've got die-hard fans. We feed off the energy of our fans. Our fans are our twelfth man. We've got the greatest fans in the world.

We're happy to be in the postseason and now we want to go out there and do some damage. We're capable of going deep in the postseason. We're not just happy to be here. This team has a chance to do something special. Hopefully, we can steal one on the road. In the playoffs, anything can happen.

Game time.   45

The fans are on their feet. This crowd is going wild. This place is a madhouse. This place is pandemonium. You can feel the electricity. Ya gotta love these fans. Ya gotta love this game.

MLA CITATION

Shields, David. "Words Can't Begin to Describe What I'm Feeling." *The Norton Reader: An Anthology of Nonfiction*, edited by Melissa A. Goldthwaite et al., 16th ed., W. W. Norton, 2024, pp. 396–401.

QUESTIONS

1. The journal in which this piece of writing originally appeared, *Verbatim: The Language Quarterly*, has the tagline "Language and linguistics for the layperson since 1974." What is David Shields showing us about the nature of language with this montage of sports clichés? What makes a cliché a cliché?

2. Consider the piece as a whole: How is it organized paragraph by paragraph? What, in terms of genre, would you call it? An essay? A short story? Something else? Annotate as you read and mark passages that you feel back up your characterization of the piece.

3. Listen carefully to a conversation about a subject that interests you and note when the speakers use clichés. Do they help or hinder the speakers in communicating their meaning?

4. Swap papers with another student. Mark any sentences in your partner's paper that contain clichés. Swap back and revise to eliminate the clichés in your own paper that your partner marked.

LAUREN MICHELE JACKSON
A Unified Theory of Meme Death

EMES AREN'T BUILT TO LAST. This is an accepted fact of online life. Some of our most beloved cultural objects are not only ephemeral but transmitted around the world at high speed before the close of business. Memes sprout from the ether (or so it seems). They charm and amuse us. They sicken and annoy us. They bore us. They linger for a while on *Facebook* and then they die—or rather retreat back into the cybernetic ooze unless called upon again.

The constancy of this narrative may be observed in any number of internet memes in recent memory, from the incredibly short-lived (Damn Daniel, Dat Boi, Salt Bae, queer Babadook) to the ones seemingly too perfect to ever perish like Harambe the gorilla[1] and Crying Jordan. The recent "Disloyal Man Walking With His Girlfriend and Looking Amazed at Another Seductive Girl," the title of the stock image shot by photographer Antonio Guillem, just made the rounds a few months ago.

At a glance—even from a digital native—meme death seems like a much less mysterious phenomenon than meme birth. While tracing the origin of any individual meme requires a separate trip down the rabbit hole, it makes sense to assume that memes die because people get tired of them. Even as a concept such as "average attention span" is not incredibly useful to psychologists who study attention (different tasks require different attention strategies), there's a general assumption that this number is shrinking. "Everybody knows" a generation raised on feeds and apps must have focus issues, and that assessment isn't totally false. Our devices are "engineered to chip away at [our] concentration" in what's called the "attention economy," writes Bianca Bosker in the *Atlantic*, and apps such as *Twitter* keep us anxious for the next big thing in news, pop culture, or memes. Our overextended attention leads to an obvious explanation for meme death: We are so overstimulated that what brings us joy cannot even hold our focus for long. But is that really why memes die?

In 2012, the third and final meeting of ROFLCon, a biennial convention on internet memes hosted by the Massachusetts Institute of Technology, anticipated a shift in the formal qualities of meme culture, ushered in by social-media sites like *Facebook* and *Twitter*. Indeed, this was the tail end of an era, one defined by the once-ubiquitous image-macro template as applied to subgenres like Advice Animals, LOLcats, and Doge. At the conference, *4chan*[2] founder Christopher "moot" Poole was "wistfully nostalgic for the slower-speed good ol'

Published in the Atlantic *(2017), a magazine covering literature, culture, and politics. Lauren Michele Jackson writes widely about issues of race, culture, and technology.*

1. Gorilla at the Cincinnati Zoo who, in 2016, was shot and killed after a child fell into his enclosure.

2. Website for sharing anonymously posted images.

days," *Wired*'s Brian Barrett reported, fearful that memes gone "mainstream" would betray the niche communities that considered memes a kind of intellectual property all their own.

"These days, memes spread faster and wider than ever, with social net-   5
works acting as the fuel for mass distribution," *Wired*'s Andy Baio wrote that same year. "As internet usage shifts from desktops and laptops to mobile devices and tablets, the ability to mutate memes in a meaningful way becomes harder." Both Poole and Baio suggest that memes lose something essential—whether a close-knit humor or the opportunity to add a unique, creative contribution— when they are enjoyed by a larger community. Social networks, some feared, would drive memes to extinction. But Chris Torres, the creator of Nyan cat, anticipated that the break from the old-school would be a good thing. "The internet doesn't really need to have its hand held anymore with websites that choose memes for them," he told the *Daily Dot*'s Fernando Alfonso III in 2014. "As long as there is creativity in this world then they are never going away. This may just be the calm before the storm of amazing new material."

And in 2017, it's clear that the doomsday crew vastly underestimated internet users' creativity. Increased mobility and access across platforms and communities has brought to the surface some of the funniest and weirdest content the web has ever known. Contrary to what Poole and Baio implied, weird humor and memes are hardly the exclusive domain of Redditors[3] or the mostly white tech bros who populated ROFLCon. Today, many of the internet's favorite memes come from fringe or ostracized communities—often from black communities, for whom oddball humor has long been an art form.

While internet memes categorically remain alive and well, individual memes *do* seem to die off faster than in Poole's "good ol' days." They just don't last like they used to: Compare the lifespans of say, Bad Luck Brian to Arthur's clenched fist or confused Mr. Krabs. But if overexposure is partially to blame for their demise, it certainly doesn't tell the whole story. Nor can it alone account for the varied lifespans amongst concurrent memes. Crying Jordan lasted years; did Damn Daniel even last two weeks? Salt Bae took over social media in January 2017, but was quickly overshadowed by gifs of Drew Scanlon ("white guy blinking") and rapper Conceited ("black guy duck face"), which lasted throughout the spring.

Why do some memes last longer than others? Are they just funnier? *Better*? And if so, what makes a meme better? The answer lies not in traditional memetics, but in the study of jokes.

Though he has yet to return to the subject in earnest since 1976's *The Selfish Gene*, Richard Dawkins[4] remains a specter over discussions of internet memes. The study, in which Dawkins extends evolutionary theory to cultural development, has been elaborated upon as well as critiqued in the three decades since its publication, spawning the field of memetics and drawing ire from neurologists

3. Users of the popular thread-based website *Reddit*.
4. English evolutionary biologist and writer (b. 1941) known for championing atheism.

and anthropologists alike. In *The Selfish Gene* and in memetics at large, "memes" are components of culture that survive, propagate, and/or die off just like genes do. Memetics in general is uninterested in *why* these components survive, or the contexts that allow them to do so—and much as individual persons are considered unwitting actors within the gene pool at large, so too are our intentions deemed irrelevant when it comes to the transmission of culture.

10   On the scientific side, researchers such as the behavioral scientists Carsta Simon and William M. Baum worry that the scientific rigor implied by "memes as genes" has yet to be met by actual memetics research. Anthropologists and sociologists "charge that memetics sees 'culture' as a series of discrete individual units, and that it blurs the lines between metaphor and biology," wrote the Fordham University researcher Alice Marwick in 2013. And, as I've written, thinking of memes solely in this way tends to "relegate agency to the memes themselves" as if they are not subject to human innovation, creation, and responses. Memetics, more interested in the movement of memes than their content, may be helpful in tracking or predicting meme lifespans, but cannot fully account for how human participation factors in.

The weakness of the memes-as-genes theory becomes more apparent in an online context. By Dawkins's deliberately capacious definition, the word "meme" may apply to sayings, bass lines, accents, clothing, myths, and body modification. In this vein, a meme in terms of digital culture could mean a viral hashtag like #tbt, tweet threading as a form of storytelling, or netspeak. However, memes as they're popularly discussed nowadays often index something much more specific—a phrase or set of text, often coupled with an image, that follows a certain format within which user adjustments can be made before being redistributed to amuse others. Also known as: a joke.

Jokes are more than funny business and, in fact, laughter (even in acronym form) is not the standard for defining what is or is not a joke. We often laugh at things that are not jokes (like wipeouts); and jokes do not always elicit laughter (like a bad wedding toast). That memes employ humorous devices does not de facto render them jokes. But as it so happens, memes and jokes do share several formal qualities. And looking at memes as jokes may also help answer why some memes dry up, and why and when others return.

"Only when it comes to jokes is the idea of 'meaning' so often vehemently denied," Elise Kramer, an anthropologist currently at the University of Illinois, wrote in a 2011 study of online rape jokes. "Poems, paintings, photographs, songs, and so on are all seen as having meaning 'beneath' the aesthetic surface, and the relationship between the message and the medium is often the focus of appreciation." Kramer's point is not that jokes cannot be explicated or unpacked, but rather that jokes—and memes, I'll add—uniquely and deliberately make depth inconsequential to their appreciation. As displayed by recent gaffes like Bill Maher's "house nigger" joke[5] and Tina Fey's "let them eat cake"

5. In 2017, while interviewing Senator Ben Sasse of Nebraska, Maher (b. 1956), a comedian and talk-show host known for his provocative political commentary, ironically referred to himself with this epithet. He later apologized.

A statue of Harambe, the gorilla, was positioned across from the *Charging Bull* on Wall Street as a commentary on corporate greed.

sketch,[6] comedy remains the most resilient place for ethically dodgy art. Reading "too much" into jokes is frowned upon and offended audiences are often told "it's not that deep."

Memes are viewed the same way, even by those who write about them. There's an obligatory defense embedded in most meme coverage, as if writers sense they must keep the analysis at a minimum lest they spoil the fun. In a love letter to Doge, Adrian Chen[7] wondered if "by writing it I played a crucial role" in guiding the meme toward obsolescence, "proving once again that writing about internet culture is basically inseparable from ruining internet culture." Last summer, while declaring Harambe too dark to be corporatized and therefore too weird to die, *New York Magazine*'s Brian Feldman admitted "there are other ways to end the Harambe meme. Like writing a think piece about it." A month later the *Guardian*'s Elena Cresci repeated the line like gospel: "When it comes to memes, there's a rule: It is dead as soon as the think pieces come out." She even likens memes to jokes directly, asserting that "when memes go mainstream it means they're not funny anymore. Memes are just

6. Fey (b. 1970), American comedian, writer, and actress, appeared on *Saturday Night Live*'s comedic news broadcast *Weekend Update* to offer a controversial response to white nationalist demonstrations in Charlottesville, Virginia, in 2017.

7. American journalist (b. 1984) and writer for the *New Yorker*.

in-jokes between people on the internet, and everyone knows jokes are much less funny one you've explained them."

15   This evaluation shows another way memes and jokes are similar: Both are, returning to Kramer, "aesthetic forms where felicity (i.e., 'getting' it) is seen as an instantaneous process." Unlike a painting, novel, or even a rousing *Twitter* thread which one is expected to "savor" like "a good meal," the person who does not get the joke or meme immediately is considered a lost cause. "The person who spends too much time mulling over a joke is accused of ruining it," Kramer writes. Tech reporters included, apparently.

But a commonly held accusation doesn't equal truth. We might observe a correlation between a summer of Harambe think pieces and its decline not long after, or blame the *New Yorker* for making Crying Jordan uncool, but it's worth noting that such pieces exist *because* their subject matter has reached a certain critical mass that makes them worth writing about. (With all due respect, I don't believe *New York Magazine*, the *New Yorker*, or even the *Atlantic* is propelling memes into zeitgeist.) "Mainstream" doesn't exactly signal the death knell, either. The "white guy blinking" gif continues to make the rounds when called upon— following the season finale of *Game of Thrones*, for example—and the line "ain't nobody got time for that," from a popular 2012 meme, met hearty laughter and applause when I attended Disney's *Aladdin*, the musical, this fall. Some memes "die" and come back again, some surge and then are all but obsolete. Applying theories on the joke might help explain why.

Because of the shared attributes between jokes and memes, research on jokes can provide a template for how to study memes as both creative and formulaic. That includes finally finding a satisfactory answer to how and why memes "die." In a 2015 thesis, Ashley Dainas argues that what folklorists call the "joke cycle" is "the best analogue to internet memes." The joke cycle describes the kinds of commonplace, well-circulated jokes that become known to mass culture at large, such as lightbulb jokes or dead-baby jokes. Unlike other jokes that are highly specific—an inside joke between two friends, for example—these jokes have a mass appeal that compels them to be shared and adjusted enough to stay fresh without losing the source frame. These jokes evolve in stages, from joke to anti-joke, and will retreat over time only to resurge again later, even a whole generation later.

Viewing jokes as cultural artifacts, researchers aren't just concerned with plotting a joke's life cycle but also the social contexts that make the public latch onto a specific joke during a certain time. Lightbulb jokes, for example, arose as a type of ethnic joke in the '60s and "had swept the country" by the late '70s, wrote the late folklorist Alan Dundes. The joke, with its theme of sexual impotence (something/one is inevitably getting screwed), was "a metaphor which lends itself easily to minority groups seeking power." It was one means to thinly veil prejudices, using the joke as an outlet for anxieties about the civil-rights legislation achieved in the '60s, and carried out in the '70s and beyond. Hence most lightbulb jokes, even when they don't cross ethnic or racial lines, tend to be a comment on some social, cultural, or economic position—"How many sorority girls does it take to change a light-bulb?" et al.

Dead-baby jokes became popular in around the same period, a time marked not only by racial upheaval but gendered, domestic changes alongside second-wave feminism: increased access to contraception, sex education in school, women forestalling or even forfeiting motherhood in favor of financial independence. While determining exact causal relationships is a sticky matter, Dundes advised, "folklore is always a reflection of the age in which it flour-ishes . . . whether we like it or not."

And so too memes. Like jokes, memes are often asserted to be hollow, [20] devoid of depth, but it would be foolish to believe that. Memes capture and maintain people's attention in a given moment because something about that moment provides a context that makes that meme attractive. This might pro-vide a more satisfying, but also more expansive, answer than simple boredom for why memes fall out of immediate favor. The context that makes a meme, once gone, breaks it. New contexts warrant new memes.

The 2016 US election season and aftermath brought into focus how memes become political symbols, from Pepe the Frog to protest signs. In Pepe's case, the otherwise chill and harmless character created by artist Matt Furie in the early 2000s was on the decline until he got a new context when the alt-right reappropriated him leading into the election. Pepe was resur-rected from obscurity when internet culture found a new need for the car-toon's special brand of male millennial grotesquerie.

Memes don't just arise out of atmospheric necessity but disappear as well. The same election season effectively killed off Crying Jordan, when perhaps the idea of loss suddenly became too poignant, too meaningful for the disem-bodied head of a crying black figure to read as playful. Memes catch on when we need them most and retreat when they are no longer attuned to public sentiment.

Ultimately, fans and founders of the old-school meme-distribution meth-ods aren't entirely wrong. Flash-in-the-pan memes like Dat Boi are limited by a format that restricts the meme's ability to evolve to the next creative iteration of itself. Dat Boi—which didn't have much going on beneath the surface weirdness of a unicycling frog—could mutate no further, got stale, and trailed off without the chance to become cyclical (the irony) in a way that would allow it to last beyond its moment. Harambe, for all its weirdness, could not survive much beyond the life of the news story that spawned it. (In the meantime, as a friend points out, the Cincinnati Zoo has been working overtime with PR for nine-month-old hippo Fiona,[8] who's since become something of an internet sensation herself.)

The "expanding brain" meme, however, continues to chug along for the greater portion of 2017. The meme, which mocks the infinite levels of intel-lectual one-upmanship common to any and all online discussions, is exactly

8. Nile hippopotamus born at the Cincinnati Zoo on January 24, 2017, six weeks prematurely.

what's called for in this post-truth moment where everyone is a pundit. I fore-see this one sticking around for a long while yet. Meanwhile, it's easy to see why a festive meme like "couples costume idea" would come and go in accor-dance with the month of October.

25   As Dundes cautioned with jokes, we should not be too confident in claim-ing cause and effect between memes and their present contexts. Time and distance can assist us in evaluating why some memes ignited our feed, why some burned out quickly, and why others stuck around. The answers to these questions are not so random, but suggestive of the cultural, political, and eco-nomic times we live in. Provided we actually remember the memes.

"The World Wide Web has become the international barometer of current events," the music librarian Carl Rahkonen wrote back in 2000. "The life of a joke cycle will never be the same as it was before the internet." No kidding. The pace of life online tests the durability of culture like nothing else before, but it is still ultimately *culture*. The memes we forget say as much about us as the memes that hold our attention—for however long that is. We create and pass on the things that call to our current experiences and situations. Memes are us.

MLA CITATION

Jackson, Lauren Michele. "A Unified Theory of Meme Death." *The Norton Reader: An Anthology of Nonfiction*, edited by Melissa A. Goldthwaite et al., 16th ed., W. W. Norton, 2024, pp. 402–8.

QUESTIONS

1. Consider Lauren Michele Jackson's title "A Unified Theory of Meme Death." It plays on a term from physics, "unified field theory," first used by Albert Einstein to refer to a single theory that would reconcile the theories of relativity and electro-magnetism. Why might Jackson have chosen a title that invokes the hard sciences? What is "meme death," and why does she choose it as her topic? What does she mean by "theory," and what specifically is she endeavoring to "unify"?

2. Jackson rejects Richard Dawkins's notion that cultural "memes" are like biologi-cal "genes" and argues instead that memes are more like jokes. What are her objec-tions to Dawkins's metaphor, and why does she think memes are better understood by analogy to jokes?

3. In addition to writing about technology, Jackson is also a scholar of Black cul-ture. How does race or ethnicity play into her understanding of memes?

4. In a project of your own, apply Jackson's "theory" to analyze the birth, life, and death of a particular meme with which you are familiar.

7 CULTURAL CRITIQUE

> Culture makes people understand each other better. And if they
> understand each other better in their soul, it is easier to over-
> come the economic and political barriers. But first they have to
> understand that their neighbour is, in the end, just like them,
> with the same problems, the same questions.
>
> —PAULO COELHO

While the oldest uses of "culture" are associated with agriculture, the word has, over the past several centuries, come to refer more broadly to the assemblage of traditions, customs, and practices that define and enable our social lives. A shared culture, in this sense, is what knits a group of individuals into a community or a people. The word can also refer to a given people's creative life, along with its products. The word "critique" can sometimes mean mere complaint, but it is better understood to mean probing analysis and judgment—often as a prelude to change. A cultural critique, then, is a clear-eyed assessment of some aspect of culture—or of a culture—in an effort to arrive at some empowering revelation about it. This chapter's essays, while varying in topic, scope, and style, all undertake this sort of intellectual work.

Some of the essays explore the cultural meanings and associations of particular objects or artifacts. Malcolm Gladwell, in "Java Man," considers our love of coffee and what that reveals about our society's character. Jessica Grose, in "What It Means to Raise an American Girl Now," ponders the implications of American Girl dolls and the values they embody for young girls growing up in our time. Sometimes these meanings and associations can be disturbing. Eula Biss, in her lyric essay "Time and Distance Overcome," illuminates an unsettling correlation between the proliferation of telephone poles, which were rapidly erected in the decades after Alexander Graham Bell invented the telephone in 1876, and their use in lynchings. Nora Ephron, in "The Boston Photographs," reflects on the decision of several newspapers to publish explicit photographs of a woman and child falling from a burning building.

Other essays in the chapter examine not particular objects but values, beliefs, attitudes, and political positions that might otherwise seem natural or obvious. Tim Kreider, in "The 'Busy' Trap," disarmingly scrutinizes the frenetic pace at which most of us live our lives and the underlying crisis of meaning it evinces. Jonathan Swift, in his scathing satire "A Modest Proposal," condemns the blithe disregard of the elite in eighteenth-century Ireland for the rampant poverty in their midst.

The chapter concludes with a cluster of essays on the embodiment and experiences of Black men. J. Drew Lanham, in "Red-headed Love Child," considers how race, place, and history intersect to shape his sense of identity and position in society during his bird-ing trip in Nebraska. James Baldwin, in his iconic 1953 essay "Stranger in the Village," moves from an account of his experience as a Black man living in a small Swiss village to a profound reflection on the dynamics of race in mid-twentieth-century America. Teju Cole, in "Black Body," examines the experience of visiting that same village sixty years later through the lens of Baldwin's essay and interprets Baldwin's essay through the lens of his own experience in turn.

A challenge every writer faces when engaging in cultural critique is the challenge of scale: that is, the challenge of showing how concrete objects, events, and experiences are connected to larger norms, values, beliefs, and patterns. In the different ways they lever-age carefully detailed observations into more general insights, the writers in this chapter have much to teach us about meeting this challenge. As you read their essays (and as you write your own), use them as Cole uses Baldwin's "Stranger in the Village": as occasions and models for interpreting and assessing the cultures in which you participate, for recog-nizing your own positions within them, and for exercising your power to change them.

EULA BISS
Time and Distance Overcome

"F WHAT USE is such an invention?" the *New York World* asked shortly after Alexander Graham Bell first demonstrated his telephone in 1876. The world was not waiting for the telephone.

Bell's financial backers asked him not to work on his new invention because it seemed too dubious an investment. The idea on which the telephone depended—the idea that every home in the country could be connected by a vast network of wires suspended from poles set an average of one hundred feet apart—seemed far more unlikely than the idea that the human voice could be transmitted through a wire.

Even now it is an impossible idea, that we are all connected, all of us.

"At the present time we have a perfect network of gas pipes and water pipes throughout our large cities," Bell wrote to his business partners in defense of his idea. "We have main pipes laid under the streets communicating by side pipes with the various dwellings. . . . In a similar manner it is conceivable that cables of telephone wires could be laid under ground, or suspended overhead, communicating by branch wires with private dwellings, counting houses, shops, manufactories, etc., uniting them through the main cable."

From Notes from No Man's Land: American Essays (2009), *Eula Biss's collection of writings on race relations in America.*

Imagine the mind that could imagine this. That could see us joined by one 5
branching cable. This was the mind of a man who wanted to invent, more than
the telephone, a machine that would allow the deaf to hear.

For a short time the telephone was little more than a novelty. For twenty-five
cents you could see it demonstrated by Bell himself, in a church, along with
singing and recitations by local talent. From some distance away, Bell would
receive a call from "the invisible Mr. Watson."[1] Then the telephone became a
plaything of the rich. A Boston banker paid for a private line between his office
and his home so that he could let his family know exactly when he would be
home for dinner.

Mark Twain[2] was among the first Americans to own a telephone, but he wasn't
completely taken with the device. "The human voice carries entirely too far as
it is," he remarked.

By 1889, the *New York Times* was reporting a "War on Telephone Poles."
Wherever telephone companies were erecting poles, home owners and business
owners were sawing them down or defending their sidewalks with rifles.

Property owners in Red Bank, New Jersey, threatened to tar and feather the
workers putting up telephone poles. A judge granted a group of home owners an
injunction to prevent the telephone company from erecting any new poles.
Another judge found that a man who had cut down a pole because it was "obnoxious" was not guilty of malicious mischief.

Telephone poles, newspaper editorials complained, were an urban blight. The 10
poles carried a wire for each telephone—sometimes hundreds of wires. And in
some places there were also telegraph wires, power lines, and trolley cables.
The sky was netted with wires.

The war on telephone poles was fueled, in part, by that terribly American concern for private property, and a reluctance to surrender it for a shared utility.
And then there was a fierce sense of aesthetics, an obsession with purity, a
dislike for the way the poles and wires marred a landscape that those other new
inventions, skyscrapers and barbed wire, were just beginning to complicate. And
then perhaps there was also a fear that distance, as it had always been known
and measured, was collapsing.

The city council in Sioux Falls, South Dakota, ordered policemen to cut down
all the telephone poles in town. And the mayor of Oshkosh, Wisconsin, ordered

1. Thomas Watson (1854–1934), engineer and assistant to Bell. His name became the
first words ever spoken on a telephone: "Mr. Watson, come here—I want to see you."
2. Pen name of Samuel Clemens (1835–1910), American novelist, journalist, and
humorist.

the police chief and the fire department to chop down the telephone poles there. Only one pole was chopped down before the telephone men climbed all the poles along the line, preventing any more chopping. Soon, Bell Telephone Company began stationing a man at the top of each pole as soon as it had been set, until enough poles had been set to string a wire between them, at which point it became a misdemeanor to interfere with the poles. Even so, a constable cut down two poles holding forty or fifty wires. And a home owner sawed down a recently wired pole, then fled from police. The owner of a cannery ordered his workers to throw dirt back into the hole the telephone company was digging in front of his building. His men threw the dirt back in as fast as the telephone workers could dig it out. Then he sent out a team with a load of stones to dump into the hole. Eventually, the pole was erected on the other side of the street.

Despite the war on telephone poles, it would take only four years after Bell's first public demonstration of the telephone for every town of more than ten thousand people to be wired, although many towns were wired only to themselves. By the turn of the century, there were more telephones than bathtubs in America.

"Time and dist. overcome," read an early advertisement for the telephone. Rutherford B. Hayes[3] pronounced the installation of a telephone in the White House "one of the greatest events since creation." The telephone, Thomas Edison declared, "annihilated time and space, and brought the human family in closer touch."

15   In 1898, in Lake Cormorant, Mississippi, a black man was hanged from a telephone pole. And in Weir City, Kansas. And in Brookhaven, Mississippi. And in Tulsa, Oklahoma, where the hanged man was riddled with bullets. In Danville, Illinois, a black man's throat was slit, and his dead body was strung up on a telephone pole. Two black men were hanged from a telephone pole in Lewisburg, West Virginia. And two in Hempstead, Texas, where one man was dragged out of the courtroom by a mob, and another was dragged out of jail.

A black man was hanged from a telephone pole in Belleville, Illinois, where a fire was set at the base of the pole and the man was cut down half-alive, covered in coal oil, and burned. While his body was burning the mob beat it with clubs and cut it to pieces.

Lynching, the first scholar of the subject determined, is an American invention. Lynching from bridges, from arches, from trees standing alone in fields, from trees in front of the county courthouse, from trees used as public billboards, from trees barely able to support the weight of a man, from telephone poles,

---

3. Nineteenth president of the United States (1822–1893) who served from 1877 to 1881.

from streetlamps, and from poles erected solely for that purpose. From the middle of the nineteenth century to the middle of the twentieth century, black men were lynched for crimes real and imagined, for whistles, for rumors, for "disputing with a white man," for "unpopularity," for "asking a white woman in marriage," for "peeping in a window."

The children's game of telephone depends on the fact that a message passed quietly from one ear to another to another will get distorted at some point along the line.

More than two hundred antilynching bills were introduced to the US Congress during the twentieth century, but none were passed. Seven presidents lobbied for antilynching legislation, and the House of Representatives passed three separate measures, each of which was blocked by the Senate.

In Pine Bluff, Arkansas, a black man charged with kicking a white girl was hanged from a telephone pole. In Longview, Texas, a black man accused of attacking a white woman was hanged from a telephone pole. In Greenville, Mississippi, a black man accused of attacking a white telephone operator was hanged from a telephone pole. "The negro only asked time to pray." In Purcell, Oklahoma, a black man accused of attacking a white woman was tied to a telephone pole and burned. "Men and women in automobiles stood up to watch him die." 20

The poles, of course, were not to blame. It was only coincidence that they became convenient as gallows, because they were tall and straight, with a crossbar, and because they stood in public places. And it was only coincidence that the telephone poles so closely resembled crucifixes.

Early telephone calls were full of noise. "Such a jangle of meaningless noises had never been heard by human ears," Herbert Casson wrote in his 1910 *History of the Telephone*. "There were spluttering and bubbling, jerking and rasping, whistling and screaming."

In Shreveport, Lousiana, a black man charged with attacking a white girl was hanged from a telephone pole. "A knife was left sticking in the body." In Cumming, Georgia, a black man accused of assaulting a white girl was shot repeatedly, then hanged from a telephone pole. In Waco, Texas, a black man convicted of killing a white woman was taken from the courtroom by a mob and burned, then his charred body was hanged from a telephone pole.

A postcard was made from the photo of a burned man hanging from a telephone pole in Texas, his legs broken off below the knee and his arms curled up and blackened. Postcards of lynchings were sent out as greetings and warnings until 1908, when the postmaster general declared them unmailable. "This is the barbecue we had last night," reads one.

25   "If we are to die," W. E. B. DuBois[4] wrote in 1911, "in God's name let us perish
      like men and not like bales of hay." And "if we must die," Claude McKay[5] wrote
      ten years later, "let it not be like hogs."

      In Pittsburg, Kansas, a black man was hanged from a telephone pole, cut
      down, burned, shot, and stoned with bricks. "At first the negro was defiant,"
      the *New York Times* reported, "but just before he was hanged he begged hard
      for his life."

      In the photographs, the bodies of the men lynched from telephone poles are
      silhouetted against the sky. Sometimes two men to a pole, hanging above the
      buildings of a town. Sometimes three. They hang like flags in still air.

      In Cumberland, Maryland, a mob used a telephone pole as a battering ram to
      break into the jail where a black man charged with the murder of a policeman
      was being held. They kicked him to death, then fired twenty shots into his
      head. They wanted to burn his body, but a minister asked them not to.

      The lynchings happened everywhere, in all but four states. From shortly before
      the invention of the telephone to long after the first transatlantic call. More in
      the South, and more in rural areas. In the cities and in the North, there were
      race riots.

30   Riots in Cincinnati, New Orleans, Memphis, New York, Atlanta, Philadelphia,
      Houston . . .

      During the race riots that destroyed the black section of Springfield, Ohio, a
      black man was shot and hanged from a telephone pole.

      During the race riots that set fire to East St. Louis and forced five hundred
      black people to flee their homes, a black man was hanged from a telephone
      pole. The rope broke and his body fell into the gutter. "Negros are lying in the
      gutters every few feet in some places," read the newspaper account.

      In 1921, the year before Bell died, four companies of the National Guard were
      called out to end a race war in Tulsa that began when a white woman accused
      a black man of rape. Bell had lived to complete the first call from New York to
      San Francisco, which required 14,000 miles of copper wire and 130,000 tele-
      phone poles.

      My grandfather was a lineman. He broke his back when a telephone pole fell.
      "Smashed him onto the road," my father says.

      4. American historian and writer (1868–1963).
      5. Jamaican American writer (1889–1948).

When I was young, I believed that the arc and swoop of telephone wires along 35
the roadways was beautiful. I believed that the telephone poles, with their
transformers catching the evening sun, were glorious. I believed my father when
he said, "My dad could raise a pole by himself." And I believed that the telephone itself was a miracle.

Now, I tell my sister, these poles, these wires, do not look the same to me.
Nothing is innocent, my sister reminds me. But nothing, I would like to think,
remains unrepentant.

One summer, heavy rains fell in Nebraska and some green telephone poles
grew small leafy branches.

ON "TIME AND DISTANCE OVERCOME"[6]

I began my research for this essay by searching for every instance of the phrase
"telephone pole" in the *New York Times* from 1880 to 1920, which resulted in
370 articles. I was planning to write an essay about telephone poles and telephones, not lynchings, but after reading an article headlined "Colored Scoun-
drel Lynched," and then another headlined "Mississippi Negro Lynched," and
then another headlined "Texas Negro Lynched," I searched for every instance of
the word "lynched" in the *New York Times* from 1880 to 1920, which resulted in
2,354 articles.

   I refer, in this essay, to the first scholar of lynching, meaning James E. Cut-
ler, author of the 1905 book *Lynch-Law*, in which he writes, on the first page,
"Lynching is a criminal practice which is peculiar to the United States." This
is debatable, of course, and very possibly not true, but there is good evidence
that the Italian Antonio Meucci invented a telephone years before Bell began
working on his device, so as long as we are going to lay claim to one invention,
we might as well take responsibility for the other.

   Bell would say, late in his life: "Recognition for my work with the deaf has 40
always been more pleasing than the recognition of my work with the telephone."
His own hearing was failing by the time he placed the first cross-country call,
from New York to his old friend Thomas Watson in San Francisco, and what
he said to Watson then was an echo of the first sentence he ever spoke into his
invention, a famous and possibly mythical sentence that is now remembered in
several slightly different versions, one being, "Mr. Watson, come here—I want
you," and another being, "Mr. Watson, come here—I need you!"

MLA CITATION

Biss, Eula. "Time and Distance Overcome." *The Norton Reader: An Anthology of
    Nonfiction*, edited by Melissa A. Goldthwaite et al., 16th ed., W. W. Norton,
    2024, pp. 410–15.

6. At the end of her book, Biss provides background information for each of her essays,
including how she arrived at the topic and the research involved.

QUESTIONS

1. Eula Biss focuses on the historical coincidence of the installation of telephone poles and the lynching of Black people. Annotate all the ways that Biss connects these topics and discuss the merits of the juxtaposition. How does she make the coincidence into something meaningful?

2. Consider Biss's style and form. How would you describe her sentences? Biss notes that even into the early twentieth century, postcards of lynchings were sent through the mail (paragraph 24). How are her paragraphs like postcards? How is her essay organized? What is its arc?

3. Following Biss's model (paragraphs 38–40), write an author's note for an old research paper. In your note, describe how the paper changed as you did your research.

4. In her essay, Biss connects a transformative new communication technology—the telephone and its supporting infrastructure—to a profound evil: the widespread lynching of Black people in the late nineteenth and early twentieth centuries. Using Biss's essay as a model, do a project of your own that similarly explores the associations between a communication technology with which you are familiar (e.g., smartphones, texting, various types of social media) and some social, cultural, or political issue.

MALCOLM GLADWELL
Java Man

THE ORIGINAL COCA-COLA was a late nineteenth-century concoction known as Pemberton's French Wine Coca, a mixture of alcohol, the caffeine-rich kola nut, and coca, the raw ingredient of cocaine. In the face of social pressure, first the wine and then the coca were removed, leaving the more banal modern beverage in its place: carbonated, caffeinated sugar water with less kick to it than a cup of coffee. But is that the way we think of Coke? Not at all. In the nineteen-thirties, a commercial artist named Haddon Sundblom had the bright idea of posing a portly retired friend of his in a red Santa Claus suit with a Coke in his hand, and plastering the image on billboards and advertisements across the country. Coke, magically, was reborn as caffeine for children, caffeine without any of the weighty adult connotations of coffee and tea. It was—as the ads with Sundblom's Santa put it—"the pause that refreshes." It added life. It could teach the world to sing.

One of the things that have always made drugs so powerful is their cultural adaptability, their way of acquiring meanings beyond their pharmacology. We

First published in the New Yorker *(2001), a weekly magazine of "reportage, commentary, criticism, essay, fiction, satire, cartoons, and poetry," to which Malcolm Gladwell has been a regular contributor.*

think of marijuana, for example, as a drug of lethargy, of disaffection. But in Colombia, the historian David T. Courtwright points out in *Forces of Habit*, "peasants boast that cannabis helps them to *quita el cansancio* or reduce fatigue; increase their *fuerza* and *ánimo*, force and spirit; and become *incansable*, tireless." In Germany right after the Second World War, cigarettes briefly and suddenly became the equivalent of crack cocaine.[1] "Up to a point, the majority of the habitual smokers preferred to do without food even under extreme conditions of nutrition rather than to forgo tobacco," according to one account of the period. "Many housewives . . . bartered fat and sugar for cigarettes." Even a drug as demonized as opium has been seen in a more favorable light. In the eighteen-thirties, Franklin Delano Roosevelt's grandfather Warren Delano II made the family fortune exporting the drug to China, and Delano was able to sugar-coat his activities so plausibly that no one ever accused his grandson of being the scion of a drug lord. And yet, as Bennett Alan Weinberg and Bonnie K. Bealer remind us in their marvellous book *The World of Caffeine*, there is no drug quite as effortlessly adaptable as caffeine, the Zelig[2] of chemical stimulants.

At one moment, in one form, it is the drug of choice of café intellectuals and artists; in another, of housewives; in another, of Zen monks; and, in yet another, of children enthralled by a fat man who slides down chimneys. King Gustav III, who ruled Sweden in the latter half of the eighteenth century, was so convinced of the particular perils of coffee over all other forms of caffeine that he devised an elaborate experiment. A convicted murderer was sentenced to drink cup after cup of coffee until he died, with another murderer sentenced to a lifetime of tea drinking, as a control. (Unfortunately, the two doctors in charge of the study died before anyone else did; then Gustav was murdered; and finally the tea drinker died, at eighty-three, of old age—leaving the original murderer alone with his espresso, and leaving coffee's supposed toxicity in some doubt.) Later, the various forms of caffeine began to be divided up along sociological lines. Wolfgang Schivelbusch, in his book *Tastes of Paradise*, argues that, in the eighteenth century, coffee symbolized the rising middle classes, whereas its great caffeinated rival in those years—cocoa, or, as it was known at the time, chocolate—was the drink of the aristocracy. "Goethe,[3] who used art as a means to lift himself out of his middle class background into the aristocracy, and who as a member of a courtly society maintained a sense of aristocratic calm even in the midst of immense productivity, made a cult of chocolate, and avoided coffee," Schivelbusch writes. "Balzac,[4] who despite his sentimental allegiance to the monarchy, lived and labored for the literary mar-

---

1. The spread of this smokeable form of cocaine in the 1980s and 1990s provoked much social and political anxiety, leading to such measures as harsh prison sentences for the drug's possession or use.

2. Title character in a 1983 Woody Allen film whose appearance changes to match his company and context.

3. Johann Wolfgang von Goethe (1749–1832), German poet, author, and intellectual.

4. Honoré de Balzac (1799–1850), French novelist.

ketplace and for it alone, became one of the most excessive coffee-drinkers in history. Here we see two fundamentally different working styles and means of stimulation—fundamentally different psychologies and physiologies." Today, of course, the chief cultural distinction is between coffee and tea, which, according to a list drawn up by Weinberg and Bealer, have come to represent almost entirely opposite sensibilities:

Coffee Aspect	Tea Aspect
Male	Female
Boisterous	Decorous
Indulgence	Temperance
Hardheaded	Romantic
Topology	Geometry
Heidegger	Carnap
Beethoven	Mozart
Libertarian	Statist
Promiscuous	Pure

That the American Revolution began with the symbolic rejection of tea in Boston Harbor, in other words, makes perfect sense. Real revolutionaries would naturally prefer coffee. By contrast, the freedom fighters of Canada, a hundred years later, were most definitely tea drinkers. And where was Canada's autonomy won? Not on the blood-soaked fields of Lexington and Concord but in the genteel drawing rooms of Westminster, over a nice cup of Darjeeling and small, triangular cucumber sandwiches.

5   All this is a bit puzzling. We don't fetishize the difference between salmon eaters and tuna eaters, or people who like their eggs sunny-side up and those who like them scrambled. So why invest so much importance in the way people prefer their caffeine? A cup of coffee has somewhere between a hundred and two hundred and fifty milligrams; black tea brewed for four minutes has between forty and a hundred milligrams. But the disparity disappears if you consider that many tea drinkers drink from a pot, and have more than one cup. Caffeine is caffeine. "The more it is pondered," Weinberg and Bealer write, "the more paradoxical this duality within the culture of caffeine appears. After all, both coffee and tea are aromatic infusions of vegetable matter, served hot or cold in similar quantities; both are often mixed with cream or sugar; both are universally available in virtually any grocery or restaurant in civilized society; and both contain the identical psychoactive alkaloid stimulant, caffeine."

It would seem to make more sense to draw distinctions based on the way caffeine is metabolized rather than on the way it is served. Caffeine, whether it is in coffee or tea or a soft drink, moves easily from the stomach and intestines into the bloodstream, and from there to the organs, and before long has penetrated almost every cell of the body. This is the reason that caffeine is such a wonderful stimulant. Most substances can't cross the blood-brain barrier, which is the body's defensive mechanism, preventing viruses or toxins from entering the central nervous system. Caffeine does so easily. Within an hour or so, it reaches its peak concentration in the brain, and there it does a number of things—principally, blocking the action of adenosine, the neuromodulator that makes you sleepy, lowers your blood pressure, and slows down your heartbeat. Then, as quickly as it builds up in your brain and tissues, caffeine is gone—which is why it's so safe. (Caffeine in ordinary quantities has never been conclusively linked to serious illness.)

But how quickly it washes away differs dramatically from person to person. A two-hundred-pound man who drinks a cup of coffee with a hundred milligrams of caffeine will have a maximum caffeine concentration of one milligram per kilogram of body weight. A hundred-pound woman having the same cup of coffee will reach a caffeine concentration of two milligrams per kilogram of body weight, or twice as high. In addition, when women are on the Pill, the rate at which they clear caffeine from their bodies slows considerably. (Some of the side effects experienced by women on the Pill may in fact be caffeine jitters caused by their sudden inability to tolerate as much coffee as they could before.) Pregnancy reduces a woman's ability to process caffeine still further. The half-life of caffeine in an adult is roughly three and a half hours. In a pregnant woman, it's eighteen hours. (Even a four-month-old child processes caffeine more efficiently.) An average man and woman sitting down for a cup of coffee are thus not pharmaceutical equals: in effect, the woman is under the influence of a vastly more powerful drug. Given these differences, you'd think that, instead of contrasting the caffeine cultures of tea and coffee, we'd contrast the caffeine cultures of men and women.

But we don't, and with good reason. To parse caffeine along gender lines does not do justice to its capacity to insinuate itself into every aspect of our lives, not merely to influence culture but even to create it. Take coffee's reputation as the "thinker's" drink. This dates from eighteenth-century Europe, where coffeehouses played a major role in the egalitarian, inclusionary spirit that was then sweeping the continent. They sprang up first in London, so alarming Charles II that in 1676 he tried to ban them. It didn't work. By 1700, there were hundreds of coffeehouses in London, their subversive spirit best captured by a couplet from a comedy of the period: "In a coffeehouse just now among the rabble I bluntly asked, which is the treason table." The movement then spread to Paris, and by the end of the eighteenth century coffeehouses numbered in the hundreds—most famously the Café de la Régence, near the Palais Royal, which counted among its customers Robespierre, Napoleon, Voltaire, Victor Hugo, Théophile Gautier, Rousseau, and the Duke of Richelieu.[5] Previously, when men had gathered together to talk in public places, they had done so in bars, which drew from specific socioeconomic niches and, because of the alcohol they served, created a specific kind of talk. The new coffeehouses, by contrast, drew from many different classes and trades, and they served a stimulant, not

5. French politicians, authors, or nobility.

a depressant. "It is not extravagant to claim that it was in these gathering spots that the art of conversation became the basis of a new literary style and that a new ideal of general education in letters was born," Weinberg and Bealer write.

It is worth noting, as well, that in the original coffeehouses nearly everyone smoked, and nicotine also has a distinctive physiological effect. It moderates mood and extends attention, and, more important, it doubles the rate of caffeine metabolism: it allows you to drink twice as much coffee as you could otherwise. In other words, the original coffeehouse was a place where men of all types could sit all day; the tobacco they smoked made it possible to drink coffee all day; and the coffee they drank inspired them to talk all day. Out of this came the Enlightenment. (The next time we so perfectly married pharmacology and place, we got Joan Baez.[6])

10   In time, caffeine moved from the café to the home. In America, coffee triumphed because of the country's proximity to the new Caribbean and Latin American coffee plantations, and the fact that throughout the nineteenth century duties were negligible. Beginning in the eighteen-twenties, Courtwright tells us, Brazil "unleashed a flood of slave-produced coffee. American per capita consumption, three pounds per year in 1830, rose to eight pounds by 1859."

What this flood of caffeine did, according to Weinberg and Bealer, was to abet the process of industrialization—to help "large numbers of people to coordinate their work schedules by giving them the energy to start work at a given time and continue it as long as necessary." Until the eighteenth century, it must be remembered, many Westerners drank beer almost continuously, even beginning their day with something called "beer soup." (Bealer and Weinberg helpfully provide the following eighteenth-century German recipe: "Heat the beer in a saucepan; in a separate small pot beat a couple of eggs. Add a chunk of butter to the hot beer. Stir in some cool beer to cool it, then pour over the eggs. Add a bit of salt, and finally mix all the ingredients together, whisking it well to keep it from curdling.") Now they began each day with a strong cup of coffee. One way to explain the industrial revolution is as the inevitable consequence of a world where people suddenly preferred being jittery to being drunk. In the modern world, there was no other way to keep up. That's what Edison[7] meant when he said that genius was ninety-nine per cent perspiration and one per cent inspiration. In the old paradigm, working with your mind had been associated with leisure. It was only the poor who worked hard. (The quintessential preindustrial narrative of inspiration belonged to Archimedes,[8] who made his discovery, let's not forget, while taking a bath.) But Edison was saying that the old class distinctions no longer held true—that in the industrialized world there was as much toil associated with the life of the mind as there had once been with the travails of the body.

In the twentieth century, the professions transformed themselves accordingly: medicine turned the residency process into an ordeal of sleeplessness,

6. American folksinger and political activist (b. 1941).
7. Thomas Alva Edison (1847–1931), American inventor.
8. Greek mathematician and inventor (c. 287 BCE–c. 212 BCE).

the legal profession borrowed a page from the manufacturing floor and made its practitioners fill out time cards like union men. Intellectual heroics became a matter of endurance. "The pace of computation was hectic," James Gleick writes of the Manhattan Project[9] in *Genius*, his biography of the physicist Richard Feynman. "Feynman's day began at 8:30 and ended fifteen hours later. Sometimes he could not leave the computing center at all. He worked through for thirty-one hours once and the next day found that an error minutes after he went to bed had stalled the whole team. The routine allowed just a few breaks." Did Feynman's achievements reflect a greater natural talent than his less productive forebears had? Or did he just drink a lot more coffee? Paul Hoffman, in *The Man Who Loved Only Numbers*, writes of the legendary twentieth-century mathematician Paul Erdős that "he put in nineteen-hour days, keeping himself fortified with 10 to 20 milligrams of Benzedrine or Ritalin, strong espresso and caffeine tablets. 'A mathematician,' Erdős was fond of saying, 'is a machine for turning coffee into theorems.'" Once, a friend bet Erdős five hundred dollars that he could not quit amphetamines for a month. Erdős took the bet and won, but, during his time of abstinence, he found himself incapable of doing any serious work. "You've set mathematics back a month," he told his friend when he collected, and immediately returned to his pills.

Erdős's unadulterated self was less real and less familiar to him than his adulterated self, and that is a condition that holds, more or less, for the rest of society as well. Part of what it means to be human in the modern age is that we have come to construct our emotional and cognitive states not merely from the inside out—with thought and intention—but from the outside in, with chemical additives. The modern personality is, in this sense, a synthetic creation: skillfully regulated and medicated and dosed with caffeine so that we can always be awake and alert and focussed when we need to be. On a bet, no doubt, we could walk away from caffeine if we had to. But what would be the point? The lawyers wouldn't make their billable hours. The young doctors would fall behind in their training. The physicists might still be stuck out in the New Mexico desert. We'd set the world back a month.

That the modern personality is synthetic is, of course, a disquieting notion. When we talk of synthetic personality—or of constructing new selves through chemical means—we think of hard drugs, not caffeine. Timothy Leary used to make such claims about LSD, and the reason his revolution never took flight was that most of us found the concept of tuning in, turning on, and dropping out to be a bit creepy. Here was this shaman, this visionary—and yet, if his consciousness was so great, why was he so intent on altering it? More important, what exactly were we supposed to be tuning in to? We were given hints, with psychedelic colors and deep readings of "Lucy in the Sky with Diamonds,"[10] but that was never enough. If we are to re-create ourselves, we would like to know what we will become.

9. Project that built the atomic bomb.
10. A 1967 song by the Beatles.

15   Caffeine is the best and most useful of our drugs because in every one of its forms it can answer that question precisely. It is a stimulant that blocks the action of adenosine, and comes in a multitude of guises, each with a ready-made story attached, a mixture of history and superstition and whimsy which infuses the daily ritual of adenosine blocking with meaning and purpose. Put caffeine in a red can and it becomes refreshing fun. Brew it in a teapot and it becomes romantic and decorous. Extract it from little brown beans and, magically, it is hardheaded and potent. "There was a little known Russian émigré, Trotsky[11] by name, who during World War I was in the habit of playing chess in Vienna's Café Central every evening," Bealer and Weinberg write, in one of the book's many fascinating café yarns:

> A typical Russian refugee, who talked too much but seemed utterly harmless, indeed, a pathetic figure in the eyes of the Viennese. One day in 1917 an official of the Austrian Foreign Ministry rushed into the minister's room, panting and excited, and told his chief, "Your excellency . . . Your excellency . . . Revolution has broken out in Russia." The minister, less excitable and less credulous than his official, rejected such a wild claim and retorted calmly, "Go away . . . Russia is not a land where revolutions break out. Besides, who on earth would make a revolution in Russia? Perhaps Herr Trotsky from the Café Central?"

The minister should have known better. Give a man enough coffee and he's capable of anything.

MLA CITATION

Gladwell, Malcolm. "Java Man." *The Norton Reader: An Anthology of Nonfiction*, edited by Melissa A. Goldthwaite et al., 16th ed., W. W. Norton, 2024, pp. 416–22.

QUESTIONS

1. How serious do you think Malcolm Gladwell is when he says that we're all drugged on caffeine? How can you tell? Annotate moments in the essay that reveal his tone or perspective.

2. Gladwell creates a binary between coffee and tea. Describe another binary between two closely similar forms—such as seashore vs. mountains; Coke vs. Pepsi; skis vs. snowboards. How do binaries work? What limitations do you see in the binary you created or in Gladwell's?

3. Gladwell offers several hypotheses for caffeine's success as the drug of choice for the modern world. Which one do you find most persuasive, and why?

4. Write a description of some of the rituals that you or someone you know indulges in with coffee or tea.

---

11. Leon Trotsky (1879–1940), Marxist intellectual and a leader of the Russian Revolution of 1917.

JONATHAN SWIFT

A Modest Proposal

FOR PREVENTING THE CHILDREN OF POOR PEOPLE IN IRELAND FROM BEING A BURDEN TO THEIR PARENTS OR COUNTRY, AND FOR MAKING THEM BENEFICIAL TO THE PUBLIC

I T IS A MELANCHOLY OBJECT to those who walk through this great town[1] or travel in the country, when they see the streets, the roads, and cabin doors, crowded with beggars of the female-sex, followed by three, four, or six children, all in rags and importuning every passenger for an alms. These mothers, instead of being able to work for their honest livelihood, are forced to employ all their time in strolling to beg sustenance for their help-less infants, who, as they grow up, either turn thieves for want of work, or leave their dear native country to fight for the Pretender in Spain, or sell them-selves to the Barbadoes.[2]

I think it is agreed by all parties that this prodigious number of children in the arms, or on the backs, or at the heels of their mothers, and frequently of their fathers, is in the present deplorable state of the kingdom a very great addi-tional grievance; and therefore whoever could find out a fair, cheap, and easy method of making these children sound, useful members of the commonwealth would deserve so well of the public as to have his statue set up for a preserver of the nation.

But my intention is very far from being confined to provide only for the children of professed beggars; it is of a much greater extent, and shall take in the whole number of infants at a certain age who are born of parents in effect as little able to support them as those who demand our charity in the streets.

As to my own part, having turned my thoughts for many years upon this important subject, and maturely weighed the several schemes of other projectors,[3] I have always found them grossly mistaken in their computation. It is true, a child just dropped from its dam may be supported by her milk for a solar year, with little other nourishment; at most not above the value of two shillings,[4] which the mother may certainly get, or the value in scraps, by her

Printed in 1729 as a pamphlet, a form commonly used for political debate in the eighteenth century.

1. Dublin.

2. The Pretender, James Francis Edward Stuart (1688–1766), was a claimant to the English throne. He was barred from succession after his father, King James II, was deposed in a Protestant revolution; thereafter, many Irish Catholics joined the Pre-tender in his exile in France and Spain and in his unsuccessful attempts at counter-revolution. Many poor Irish people sought to escape poverty by emigrating to the Barbados and other western English colonies, paying for transport by binding them-selves to work for a landowner there for a period of years.

3. People with projects; schemers.

4. A shilling was worth one-twentieth of a pound.

lawful occupation of begging; and it is exactly at one year old that I propose to provide for them in such a manner as instead of being a charge upon their parents or the parish, or wanting food and raiment for the rest of their lives, they shall on the contrary contribute to the feeding, and partly to the clothing, of many thousands.

There is likewise another great advantage in my scheme, that it will prevent those voluntary abortions, and that horrid practice of women murdering their bastard children, alas, too frequent among us, sacrificing the poor innocent babes, I doubt, more to avoid the expense than the shame, which would move tears and pity in the most savage and inhuman breast.

The number of souls in this kingdom being usually reckoned one million and a half, of these I calculate there may be about two hundred thousand couples whose wives are breeders; from which number I subtract thirty thousand couples who are able to maintain their own children, although I apprehend there cannot be so many under the present distresses of the kingdom; but this being granted, there will remain an hundred and seventy thousand breeders. I again subtract fifty thousand for those women who miscarry, or whose children die by accident or disease within the year. There only remain an hundred and twenty thousand children of poor parents annually born. The question therefore is, how this number shall be reared and provided for, which, as I have already said, under the present situation of affairs, is utterly impossible by all the methods hitherto proposed. For we can neither employ them in handicraft or agriculture; we neither build houses (I mean in the country) nor cultivate land. They can very seldom pick up a livelihood by stealing till they arrive at six years old, except where they are of towardly parts;[5] although I confess they learn the rudiments much earlier, during which time they can however be looked upon only as probationers, as I have been informed by a principal gentleman in the county of Cavan, who protested to me that he never knew above one or two instances under the age of six, even in a part of the kingdom so renowned for the quickest proficiency in that art.

I am assured by our merchants that a boy or a girl before twelve years old is no salable commodity; and even when they come to this age they will not yield above three pounds, or three pounds and half a crown[6] at most on the Exchange; which cannot turn to account either to the parents or the kingdom, the charge of nutriment and rags having been at least four times that value.

I shall now therefore humbly propose my own thoughts, which I hope will not be liable to the least objection.

I have been assured by a very knowing American of my acquaintance in London, that a young healthy child well nursed is at a year old a most delicious, nourishing, and wholesome food, whether stewed, roasted, baked, or boiled; and I make no doubt that it will equally serve in a fricassee or a ragout.

I do therefore humbly offer it to public consideration that of the hundred and twenty thousand children, already computed, twenty thousand may be

5. Promising abilities.

6. One crown was worth one-quarter of a pound.

reserved for breed, whereof only one fourth part to be males, which is more than we allow to sheep, black cattle, or swine; and my reason is that these children are seldom the fruits of marriage, a circumstance not much regarded by our savages, therefore one male will be sufficient to serve four females. That the remaining hundred thousand may at a year old be offered in sale to the persons of quality and fortune through the kingdom, always advising the mother to let them suck plentifully in the last month, so as to render them plump and fat for a good table. A child will make two dishes at an entertainment for friends; and when the family dines alone, the fore or hind quarter will make a reasonable dish, and seasoned with a little pepper or salt will be very good boiled on the fourth day, especially in winter.

I have reckoned upon a medium that a child just born will weigh twelve pounds, and in a solar year if tolerably nursed increaseth to twenty-eight pounds.

I grant this food will be somewhat dear, and therefore very proper for landlords, who, as they have already devoured most of the parents, seem to have the best title to the children.

Infant's flesh will be in season throughout the year, but more plentiful in March, and a little before and after. For we are told by a grave author, an eminent French physician,[7] that fish being a prolific diet, there are more children born in Roman Catholic countries about nine months after Lent than at any other season; therefore, reckoning a year after Lent, the markets will be more glutted than usual, because the number of popish infants is at least three to one in this kingdom; and therefore it will have one other collateral advantage, by lessening the number of Papists among us.[8]

I have already computed the charge of nursing a beggar's child (in which list I reckon all cottagers, laborers, and four fifths of the farmers) to be about two shillings per annum, rags included; and I believe no gentleman would repine to give ten shillings for the carcass of a good fat child, which, as I have said, will make four dishes of excellent nutritive meat, when he hath only some particular friend or his own family to dine with him. Thus the squire will learn to be a good landlord, and grow popular among the tenants; the mother will have eight shillings net profit, and be fit for work till she produces another child.

Those who are more thrifty (as I must confess the times require) may flay the carcass; the skin of which artificially[9] dressed will make admirable gloves for ladies, and summer boots for fine gentlemen.   15

As to our city of Dublin, shambles[10] may be appointed for this purpose in the most convenient parts of it, and butchers we may be assured will not be wanting; although I rather recommend buying the children alive, and dressing them hot from the knife as we do roasting pigs.

---

7. François Rabelais (1483–1553), comic writer.
8. The speaker is addressing Protestant Anglo-Irish people, who were the chief landowners and administrators, and his views of Catholicism in Ireland and abroad echo theirs.
9. Skillfully.
10. Slaughterhouses.

A very worthy person, a true lover of his country, and whose virtues I highly esteem, was lately pleased in discoursing on this matter to offer a refinement upon my scheme. He said that many gentlemen of this kingdom, having of late destroyed their deer, he conceived that the want of venison might be well supplied by the bodies of young lads and maidens, not exceeding fourteen years of age nor under twelve, so great a number of both sexes in every county being now ready to starve for want of work and service; and these to be disposed of by their parents, if alive, or otherwise by their nearest relations. But with due deference to so excellent a friend and so deserving a patriot, I cannot be altogether in his sentiments; for as to the males, my American acquaintance assured me from frequent experience that their flesh was generally tough and lean, like that of our schoolboys, by continual exercise, and their taste disagreeable; and to fatten them would not answer the charge. Then as to the females, it would, I think with humble submission, be a loss to the public, because they soon would become breeders themselves: and besides, it is not improbable that some scrupulous people might be apt to censure such a practice (although indeed very unjustly) as a little bordering upon cruelty; which, I confess, hath always been with me the strongest objection against any project, how well soever intended.

But in order to justify my friend, he confessed that this expedient was put into his head by the famous Psalmanazar, a native of the island Formosa,[11] who came from thence to London above twenty years ago, and in conversation told my friend that in his country when any young person happened to be put to death, the executioner sold the carcass to persons of quality as a prime dainty; and that in his time the body of a plump girl of fifteen, who was crucified for an attempt to poison the emperor, was sold to his Imperial Majesty's prime minister of state, and other great mandarins of the court, in joints from the gibbet, at four hundred crowns. Neither indeed can I deny that if the same use were made of several plump young girls in this town, who without one single groat[12] to their fortunes cannot stir abroad without a chair,[13] and appear at the playhouse and assemblies in foreign fineries which they never will pay for, the kingdom would not be the worse.

Some persons of a desponding spirit are in great concern about that vast number of poor people who are aged, diseased, or maimed, and I have been desired to employ my thoughts what course may be taken to ease the nation of so grievous an encumbrance. But I am not in the least pain upon that matter, because it is very well known that they are every day dying and rotting by cold and famine, and filth and vermin, as fast as can be reasonably expected. And as to the younger laborers, they are now in almost as hopeful a condition. They cannot get work, and consequently pine away for want of nourishment to a degree that if at any time they are accidentally hired to common labor, they

11. Actually a Frenchman, George Psalmanazar (1679–1763) had passed himself off as from Formosa (now Taiwan) and had written a fictitious book about his "homeland," with descriptions of human sacrifice and cannibalism.

12. Coin worth about four English pennies.

13. Sedan chair, used for carrying a person of importance.

have not strength to perform it; and thus the country and themselves are happily delivered from the evils to come.

I have too long digressed, and therefore shall return to my subject. I think   20
the advantages by the proposal which I have made are obvious and many, as well as of the highest importance.

For first, as I have already observed, it would greatly lessen the number of Papists, with whom we are yearly overrun, being the principal breeders of the nation as well as our most dangerous enemies; and who stay at home on purpose to deliver the kingdom to the Pretender, hoping to take their advantage by the absence of so many good Protestants, who have chosen rather to leave their country than to stay at home and pay tithes against their conscience to an Episcopal curate.

Secondly, the poorer tenants will have something valuable of their own, which by law may be made liable to distress,[14] and help to pay their landlord's rent, their corn and cattle being already seized and money a thing unknown.

Thirdly, whereas the maintenance of an hundred thousand children, from two years old and upwards, cannot be computed at less than ten shillings a piece per annum, the nation's stock will be thereby increased fifty thousand pounds per annum, besides the profit of a new dish introduced to the tables of all gentlemen of fortune in the kingdom who have any refinement in taste. And the money will circulate among ourselves, the goods being entirely of our own growth and manufacture.

Fourthly, the constant breeders, besides the gain of eight shillings sterling per annum by the sale of their children, will be rid of the charge of maintaining them after the first year.

Fifthly, this food would likewise bring great custom to taverns, where the   25
vintners will certainly be so prudent as to procure the best receipts for dressing it to perfection, and consequently have their houses frequented by all the fine gentlemen, who justly value themselves upon their knowledge in good eating; and a skillful cook, who understands how to oblige his guests, will contrive to make it as expensive as they please.

Sixthly, this would be a great inducement to marriage, which all wise nations have either encouraged by rewards or enforced by laws and penalties. It would increase the care and tenderness of mothers toward their children, when they were sure of a settlement for life to the poor babes, provided in some sort by the public, to their annual profit instead of expense. We should see an honest emulation among the married women, which of them could bring the fattest child to the market. Men would become as fond of their wives during the time of their pregnancy as they are now of their mares in foal, their cows in calf, or sows when they are ready to farrow; nor offer to beat or kick them (as is too frequent a practice) for fear of a miscarriage.

Many other advantages might be enumerated. For instance, the addition of some thousand carcasses in our exportation of barreled beef, the propagation of swine's flesh, and improvement in the art of making good bacon, so much

14. Seizure for the payment of debts.

wanted among us by the great destruction of pigs, too frequent at our tables, which are no way comparable in taste or magnificence to a well-grown, fat, yearling child, which roasted whole will make a considerable figure at a lord mayor's feast or any other public entertainment. But this and many others I omit, being studious of brevity.

Supposing that one thousand families in this city would be constant customers for infants' flesh, besides others who might have it at merry meetings, particularly weddings and christenings, I compute that Dublin would take off annually about twenty thousand carcasses, and the rest of the kingdom (where probably they will be sold somewhat cheaper) the remaining eighty thousand.

I can think of no one objection that will possibly be raised against this proposal, unless it should be urged that the number of people will be thereby much lessened in the kingdom. This I freely own, and it was indeed one principal design in offering it to the world. I desire the reader will observe, that I calculate my remedy for this one individual kingdom of Ireland and for no other that ever was, is, or I think ever can be upon earth. Therefore let no man talk to me of other expedients: of taxing our absentees at five shillings a pound: of using neither clothes nor household furniture except what is of our own growth and manufacture: of utterly rejecting the materials and instruments that promote foreign luxury: of curing the expensiveness of pride, vanity, idleness, and gaming in our women: of introducing a vein of parsimony, prudence, and temperance: of learning to love our country, in the want of which we differ even from Laplanders and the inhabitants of Topinamboo:[15] of quitting our animosities and factions, nor acting any longer like the Jews, who were murdering one another at the very moment their city was taken:[16] of being a little cautious not to sell our country and conscience for nothing: of teaching landlords to have at least one degree of mercy toward their tenants: lastly, of putting a spirit of honesty, industry, and skill into our shopkeepers; who, if a resolution could now be taken to buy only our native goods, would immediately unite to cheat and exact upon us in the price, the measure, and the goodness, nor could ever yet be brought to make one fair proposal of just dealing, though often and earnestly invited to it.[17]

30   Therefore I repeat, let no man talk to me of these and the like expedients, till he hath at least some glimpse of hope that there will ever be some hearty and sincere attempt to put them in practice.

But as to myself, having been wearied out for many years with offering vain, idle, visionary thoughts, and at length utterly despairing of success, I fortunately fell upon this proposal, which, as it is wholly new, so it hath something solid and real, of no expense and little trouble, full in our own power, and whereby

15. District in Brazil.

16. Reference to the siege of Jerusalem by the Romans in 70 CE during which, according to the Roman historian Flavius Josephus, the city's residents resorted to infighting and even cannibalism.

17. Swift himself had made these proposals seriously in various previous works, but to no avail.

we can incur no danger in disobliging England. For this kind of commodity will not bear exportation, the flesh being of too tender a consistence to admit a long continuance in salt, although perhaps I could name a country[18] which would be glad to eat up our whole nation without it.

After all, I am not so violently bent upon my own opinion as to reject any offer proposed by wise men, which shall be found equally innocent, cheap, easy, and effectual. But before something of that kind shall be advanced in contradiction to my scheme, and offering a better, I desire the author or authors will be pleased maturely to consider two points. First, as things now stand, how they will be able to find food and raiment for an hundred thousand useless mouths and backs. And secondly, there being a round million of creatures in human figure throughout this kingdom, whose sole subsistence put into a common stock would leave them in debt two millions of pounds sterling, adding those who are beggars by profession to the bulk of farmers, cottagers, and laborers, with their wives and children who are beggars in effect; I desire those politicians who dislike my overture, and may perhaps be so bold to attempt an answer, that they will first ask the parents of these mortals whether they would not at this day think it a great happiness to have been sold for food at a year old in the manner I prescribe, and thereby have avoided such a perpetual scene of misfortunes as they have since gone through by the oppression of landlords, the impossibility of paying rent without money or trade, the want of common sustenance, with neither house nor clothes to cover them from the inclemencies of the weather, and the most inevitable prospect of entailing the like or greater miseries upon their breed forever.

I profess, in the sincerity of my heart, that I have not the least personal interest in endeavoring to promote this necessary work, having no other motive than the public good of my country, by advancing our trade, providing for infants, relieving the poor, and giving some pleasure to the rich. I have no children by which I can propose to get a single penny; the youngest being nine years old, and my wife past childbearing.

MLA CITATION

Swift, Jonathan. "A Modest Proposal." *The Norton Reader: An Anthology of Nonfiction*, edited by Melissa A. Goldthwaite et al., 16th ed., W. W. Norton, 2024, pp. 423–29.

QUESTIONS

1. Identify examples of the reasonable voice of Jonathan Swift's authorial persona, such as the title of the essay itself.

2. Look, in particular, at instances in which Swift's authorial persona proposes shocking things. How does the style of "A Modest Proposal" affect its content?

---

18. England.

3. Verbal irony consists of saying one thing and meaning another. At what point in this essay do you begin to suspect that Swift is using irony? What additional evidence of irony can you find?

4. Do some background reading on the historical relationship between England and Ireland and the religious conflicts between Catholics and Protestants in the seventeenth and eighteenth centuries. Did this exercise change your response to Swift's essay? If so, how?

5. Write a "modest proposal" of your own in the manner of Swift to remedy a real problem; that is, propose an outrageous remedy in a reasonable voice.

TIM KREIDER
The "Busy" Trap

IF YOU LIVE IN AMERICA in the 21st century you've probably had to listen to a lot of people tell you how busy they are. It's become the default response when you ask anyone how they're doing: "Busy!" "So busy." "*Crazy* busy." It is, pretty obviously, a boast disguised as a complaint. And the stock response is a kind of congratulation: "That's a good problem to have," or "Better than the opposite."

Notice it isn't generally people pulling back-to-back shifts in the ICU or commuting by bus to three minimum-wage jobs who tell you how busy they are; what those people are is not busy but *tired. Exhausted. Dead on their feet.* It's almost always people whose lamented busyness is purely self-imposed: work and obligations they've taken on voluntarily, classes and activities they've "encouraged" their kids to participate in. They're busy because of their own ambition or drive or anxiety, because they're addicted to busyness and dread what they might have to face in its absence.

Almost everyone I know is busy. They feel anxious and guilty when they aren't either working or doing something to promote their work. They schedule in time with friends the way students with 4.0 GPA's make sure to sign up for community service because it looks good on their college applications. I recently wrote a friend to ask if he wanted to do something this week, and he answered that he didn't have a lot of time but if something was going on to let him know and maybe he could ditch work for a few hours. I wanted to clarify that my question had not been a preliminary heads-up to some future invitation; this *was* the invitation. But his busyness was like some vast churning noise through which he was shouting out at me, and I gave up trying to shout back over it.

Even *children* are busy now, scheduled down to the half-hour with classes and extracurricular activities. They come home at the end of the day as tired as grown-ups. I was a member of the latchkey generation and had three hours

Written as part of a series on anxiety in the New York Times *opinion pages (2012). Tim Kreider is a cartoonist and essayist.*

of totally unstructured, largely unsupervised time every afternoon, time I used to do everything from surfing the *World Book Encyclopedia*[1] to making animated films to getting together with friends in the woods to chuck dirt clods directly into one another's eyes, all of which provided me with important skills and insights that remain valuable to this day. Those free hours became the model for how I wanted to live the rest of my life.

The present hysteria is not a necessary or inevitable condition of life; it's something we've chosen, if only by our acquiescence to it. Not long ago I Skyped with a friend who was driven out of the city by high rent and now has an artist's residency in a small town in the south of France. She described herself as happy and relaxed for the first time in years. She still gets her work done, but it doesn't consume her entire day and brain. She says it feels like college—she has a big circle of friends who all go out to the café together every night. She has a boyfriend again. (She once ruefully summarized dating in New York: "Everyone's too busy and everyone thinks they can do better.") What she had mistakenly assumed was her personality—driven, cranky, anxious and sad— turned out to be a deformative effect of her environment. It's not as if any of us wants to live like this, any more than any one person wants to be part of a traffic jam or stadium trampling or the hierarchy of cruelty in high school— it's something we collectively force one another to do.

5

1. First published in 1917 and popular until the 1990s, this encyclopedia for school-children provided information in accessible language and included many illustrations.

Busyness serves as a kind of existential reassurance, a hedge against emptiness; obviously your life cannot possibly be silly or trivial or meaningless if you are so busy, completely booked, in demand every hour of the day. I once knew a woman who interned at a magazine where she wasn't allowed to take lunch hours out, lest she be urgently needed for some reason. This was an entertainment magazine whose raison d'être[2] was obviated when "menu" buttons appeared on remotes, so it's hard to see this pretense of indispensability as anything other than a form of institutional self-delusion. More and more people in this country no longer make or do anything tangible; if your job wasn't performed by a cat or a boa constrictor in a Richard Scarry[3] book I'm not sure I believe it's necessary. I can't help but wonder whether all this histrionic exhaustion isn't a way of covering up the fact that most of what we do doesn't matter.

I am not busy. I am the laziest ambitious person I know. Like most writers, I feel like a reprobate who does not deserve to live on any day that I do not write, but I also feel that four or five hours is enough to earn my stay on the planet for one more day. On the best ordinary days of my life, I write in the morning, go for a long bike ride and run errands in the afternoon, and in the evening I see friends, read or watch a movie. This, it seems to me, is a sane and pleasant pace for a day. And if you call me up and ask whether I won't maybe blow off work and check out the new American Wing at the Met or ogle girls in Central Park or just drink chilled pink minty cocktails all day long, I will say, what time?

But just in the last few months, I've insidiously started, because of professional obligations, to become busy. For the first time I was able to tell people, with a straight face, that I was "too busy" to do this or that thing they wanted me to do. I could see why people enjoy this complaint; it makes you feel important, sought-after and put-upon. Except that I hate actually being busy. Every morning my inbox was full of e-mails asking me to do things I did not want to do or presenting me with problems that I now had to solve. It got more and more intolerable until finally I fled town to the Undisclosed Location from which I'm writing this.

Here I am largely unmolested by obligations. There is no TV. To check e-mail I have to drive to the library. I go a week at a time without seeing anyone I know. I've remembered about buttercups, stink bugs and the stars. I read. And I'm finally getting some real writing done for the first time in months. It's hard to find anything to say about life without immersing yourself in the world, but it's also just about impossible to figure out what it might be, or how best to say it, without getting the hell out of it again.

10   Idleness is not just a vacation, an indulgence or a vice; it is as indispensable to the brain as vitamin D is to the body, and deprived of it we suffer a mental affliction as disfiguring as rickets. The space and quiet that idleness provides is a necessary condition for standing back from life and seeing it whole,

2. French for "reason for being."
3. Children's book writer and illustrator (1919–1994) whose books used animals—cats, rats, rabbits, and pigs—and sometimes worms for characters.

for making unexpected connections and waiting for the wild summer lightning strikes of inspiration—it is, paradoxically, necessary to getting any work done. "Idle dreaming is often of the essence of what we do," wrote Thomas Pynchon[4] in his essay on sloth. Archimedes' "Eureka" in the bath, Newton's apple, Jekyll & Hyde and the benzene ring:[5] history is full of stories of inspirations that come in idle moments and dreams. It almost makes you wonder whether loafers, goldbricks and no-accounts aren't responsible for more of the world's great ideas, inventions and masterpieces than the hardworking.

"The goal of the future is full unemployment, so we can play. That's why we have to destroy the present politico-economic system." This may sound like the pronouncement of some bong-smoking anarchist, but it was actually Arthur C. Clarke,[6] who found time between scuba diving and pinball games to write *Childhood's End* and think up communications satellites. My old colleague Ted Rall[7] recently wrote a column proposing that we divorce income from work and give each citizen a guaranteed paycheck, which sounds like the kind of lunatic notion that'll be considered a basic human right in about a century, like abolition, universal suffrage and eight-hour workdays. The Puritans turned work into a virtue, evidently forgetting that God invented it as a punishment.

Perhaps the world would soon slide to ruin if everyone behaved as I do. But I would suggest that an ideal human life lies somewhere between my own defiant indolence and the rest of the world's endless frenetic hustle. My role is just to be a bad influence, the kid standing outside the classroom window making faces at you at your desk, urging you to just this once make some excuse and get out of there, come outside and play. My own resolute idleness has mostly been a luxury rather than a virtue, but I did make a conscious decision, a long time ago, to choose time over money, since I've always understood that the best investment of my limited time on earth was to spend it with people I love. I suppose it's possible I'll lie on my deathbed regretting that I didn't work harder and say everything I had to say, but I think what I'll really wish is that I could have one more beer with Chris, another long talk with Megan, one last good hard laugh with Boyd. Life is too short to be busy.

MLA CITATION

Kreider, Tim. "The 'Busy' Trap." *The Norton Reader: An Anthology of Nonfiction*, edited by Melissa A. Goldthwaite et al., 16th ed., W. W. Norton, 2024, pp. 430–33.

4. American novelist (b. 1937).

5. Discoveries—Archimedes's method for calculating the volume of an object with an irregular shape, Isaac Newton's discovery of the principle of gravity, Robert Louis Stevenson's dream that led to his famous novel *Strange Case of Dr. Jekyll and Mr. Hyde*, and Friedrich August Kekulé's reverie of a snake with its tail in its mouth, which shares a shape with a benzene ring—that connect moments of daydreaming with originality, invention, and productivity.

6. British science and science-fiction writer, inventor, and TV host (1917–2008) best known for coauthoring the screenplay for *2001: A Space Odyssey*.

7. American columnist and political cartoonist (b. 1963).

QUESTIONS

1. Tim Kreider writes against the American penchant for "busyness" and in favor of idleness. What reasons does he give for each of these views?

2. Both Kreider, in paragraph 10, and Malcolm Gladwell, in "Java Man" (pp. 416–22, paragraph 11), contrast the contemporary obsession with busyness with the legend of Archimedes's eureka moment in the bathtub. What does that story mean for each essay? What stories about discovery do you cherish, and what do they reveal about your beliefs about idleness and busyness?

3. "The 'Busy' Trap" is what is known as a *familiar essay*—that is, an essay on an everyday topic whose author relies on personal anecdote and reflection, coupled with a conversational style, to establish a distinctive voice and build rapport with readers. Annotate instances of anecdote and reflection in Kreider's essay. What techniques does he use to create a conversational style? Why do you think he chose to write a familiar essay rather than a more formal argument or a traditional opinion piece?

4. In his essay, Kreider counters conventional wisdom by criticizing a seeming virtue (busyness) and celebrating a seeming vice (idleness). Using Kreider's essay as a model, write an essay in which you argue for the reversal or inversion of the accepted hierarchy between a pair of values, emotions, qualities, or concepts.

NORA EPHRON
The Boston Photographs

"I MADE ALL KINDS OF PICTURES because I thought it would be a good rescue shot over the ladder . . . never dreamed it would be anything else. . . . I kept having to move around because of the light set. The sky was bright and they were in deep shadow. I was making pictures with a motor drive and he, the fire fighter, was reaching up and, I don't know, everything started falling. I followed the girl down taking pictures . . . I made three or four frames. I realized what was going on and I completely turned around, because I didn't want to see her hit."

You probably saw the photographs. In most newspapers, there were three of them. The first showed some people on a fire escape—a fireman, a woman and a child. The fireman had a nice strong jaw and looked very brave. The woman was holding the child. Smoke was pouring from the building behind them. A rescue ladder was approaching, just a few feet away, and the fireman had one arm around the woman and one arm reaching out toward the ladder. The second picture showed the fire escape slipping off the building. The child had fallen on the escape and seemed about to slide off the edge. The woman was grasping desperately at the legs of the fireman, who had managed to grab

Nora Ephron wrote this essay as a columnist on media for Esquire *(1975). It later appeared in her collection* Scribble, Scribble: Notes on the Media *(1978).*

the ladder. The third picture showed the woman and child in midair, falling to the ground. Their arms and legs were outstretched, horribly distended. A potted plant was falling too. The caption said that the woman, Diana Bryant, nineteen, died in the fall. The child landed on the woman's body and lived.

The pictures were taken by Stanley Forman, thirty, of the *Boston Herald American*. He used a motor-driven Nikon F set at 1/250, f 5.6–8. Because of the motor, the camera can click off three frames a second. More than four hundred newspapers in the United States alone carried the photographs; the tear sheets from overseas are still coming in. The *New York Times* ran them on the first page of its second section; a paper in south Georgia gave them nineteen columns; the *Chicago Tribune*, the *Washington Post* and the *Washington Star* filled almost half their front pages, the *Star* under a somewhat redundant headline that read: SENSATIONAL PHOTOS OF RESCUE ATTEMPT THAT FAILED.

The photographs are indeed sensational. They are pictures of death in action, of that split second when luck runs out, and it is impossible to look at them without feeling their extraordinary impact and remembering, in an almost subconscious way, the morbid fantasy of falling, falling off a building, falling to one's death. Beyond that, the pictures are classics, old-fashioned but perfect examples of photojournalism at its most spectacular. They're throwbacks, really, fire pictures, 1930s tabloid shots; at the same time they're technically superb and thoroughly modern—the sequence could not have been taken at all until the development of the motor-driven camera some sixteen years ago.

Most newspaper editors anticipate some reader reaction to photographs like   5
Forman's; even so, the response around the country was enormous, and almost all of it was negative. I have read hundreds of the letters that were printed in letters-to-the-editor sections, and they repeat the same points. "Invading the privacy of death." "Cheap sensationalism." "I thought I was reading the *National Enquirer*." "Assigning the agony of a human being in terror of imminent death to the status of a side-show act." "A tawdry way to sell newspapers." The *Seattle Times* received sixty letters and calls; its managing editor even got a couple of them at home. A reader wrote the *Philadelphia Inquirer*: "*Jaws* and *Towering Inferno* are playing downtown; don't take business away from people who pay good money to advertise in your own paper." Another reader wrote the *Chicago Sun-Times*: "I shall try to hide my disappointment that Miss Bryant wasn't wearing a skirt when she fell to her death. You could have had some award-winning photographs of her underpants as her skirt billowed over her head, you voyeurs." Several newspaper editors wrote columns defending the pictures: Thomas Keevil of the *Costa Mesa* (California) *Daily Pilot* printed a ballot for readers to vote on whether they would have printed the pictures; Marshall L. Stone of Maine's *Bangor Daily News*, which refused to print the famous assassination picture of the Vietcong prisoner in Saigon, claimed that the Boston pictures showed the dangers of fire escapes and raised questions about slumlords. (The burning building was a five-story brick apartment house on Marlborough Street in the Back Bay section of Boston.)

For the last five years, the *Washington Post* has employed various journalists as ombudsmen, whose job is to monitor the paper on behalf of the public.

The *Post*'s current ombudsman is Charles Seib, former managing editor of the *Washington Star*; the day the Boston photographs appeared, the paper received over seventy calls in protest. As Seib later wrote in a column about the pictures, it was "the largest reaction to a published item that I have experienced in eight months as the *Post*'s ombudsman. . . .

"In the *Post*'s newsroom, on the other hand, I found no doubts, no second thoughts . . . the question was not whether they should be printed but how they should be displayed. When I talked to editors . . . they used words like 'interesting' and 'riveting' and 'gripping' to describe them. The pictures told something about life in the ghetto, they said (although the neighborhood where the

tragedy occurred is not a ghetto, I am told). They dramatized the need to check on the safety of fire escapes. They dramatically conveyed something that had happened, and that is the business we're in. They were news. . . .

"Was publication of that [third] picture a bow to the same taste for the morbidly sensational that makes gold mines of disaster movies? Most papers will not print the picture of a dead body except in the most unusual circumstances. Does the fact that the final picture was taken a millisecond before the young woman died make a difference? Most papers will not print a picture of a bare female breast. Is that a more inappropriate subject for display than the picture of a human being's last agonized instant of life?" Seib offered no answers to

the questions he raised, but he went on to say that although as an editor he
would probably have run the pictures, as a reader he was "revolted by them."

In conclusion, Seib wrote: "Any editor who decided to print those pictures
without giving at least a moment's thought to what purpose they served and what
their effect was likely to be on the reader should ask another question: Have I
become so preoccupied with manufacturing a product according to professional
traditions and standards that I have forgotten about the consumer, the reader?"

10   It should be clear that the phone calls and letters and Seib's own reaction
were occasioned by one factor alone: the death of the woman. Obviously, had

she survived the fall, no one would have protested; the pictures would have had a completely different impact. Equally obviously, had the child died as well— or instead—Seib would undoubtedly have received ten times the phone calls he did. In each case, the pictures would have been exactly the same—only the captions, and thus the responses, would have been different.

But the questions Seib raises are worth discussing—though not exactly for the reasons he mentions. For it may be that the real lesson of the Boston photographs is not the danger that editors will be forgetful of reader reaction, but that they will continue to censor pictures of death precisely because of that reaction. The protests Seib fielded were really a variation on an old theme—and we saw plenty of it during the Nixon-Agnew years—the "Why doesn't the press print the good news?" argument. In this case, of course, the objections were all dressed up and cleverly disguised as righteous indignation about the privacy of death. This is a form of puritanism that is often justifiable; just as often it is merely puritanical.

Seib takes it for granted that the widespread though fairly recent newspaper policy against printing pictures of dead bodies is a sound one; I don't know that it makes any sense at all. I recognize that printing pictures of corpses raises all sorts of problems about taste and titillation and sensationalism; the fact is, however, that people die. Death happens to be one of life's main events. And it is irresponsible—and more than that, inaccurate—for newspapers to fail to show it, or to show it only when an astonishing set of photos comes in over the Associated Press wire. Most papers covering fatal automobile accidents will print pictures of mangled cars. But the significance of fatal automobile accidents is not that a great deal of steel is twisted but that people die. Why not show it? That's what accidents are about. Throughout the Vietnam war, editors were reluctant to print atrocity pictures. Why *not* print them? That's what that war was about. Murder victims are almost never photographed; they are granted their privacy. But their relatives are relentlessly pictured on their way in and out of hospitals and morgues and funerals.

I'm not advocating that newspapers print these things in order to teach their readers a lesson. The *Post* editors justified their printing of the Boston pictures with several arguments in that direction; every one of them is irrelevant. The pictures don't show anything about slum life; the incident could have happened anywhere, and it did. It is extremely unlikely that anyone who saw them rushed out and had his fire escape strengthened. And the pictures were not news—at least they were not national news. It is not news in Washington, or New York, or Los Angeles that a woman was killed in a Boston fire. The only newsworthy thing about the pictures is that they were taken. They deserve to be printed because they are great pictures, breathtaking pictures of something that happened. That they disturb readers is exactly as it should be: that's why photojournalism is often more powerful than written journalism.

MLA CITATION

Ephron, Nora. "The Boston Photographs." *The Norton Reader: An Anthology of Nonfiction*, edited by Melissa A. Goldthwaite et al., 16th ed., W. W. Norton, 2024, pp. 434–39.

QUESTIONS

1. Why does Nora Ephron begin with the words of the photographer Stanley Forman? What information—as well as perspective—does her opening paragraph convey?

2. What was the public reaction to the publication of the Boston photographs? What reasons did newspeople give for printing them? How does Ephron arrange these responses?

3. In her conclusion, Ephron declares the *Washington Post*'s justifications for publishing the Boston photographs "irrelevant" and then states her own perspective: "They deserve to be printed because they are great pictures, breathtaking pictures of something that happened. That they disturb readers is exactly as it should be: that's why photojournalism is often more powerful than written journalism" (paragraph 13). How would you respond to her defense of the photographs' publication? to her perspective on the power of photographic over written journalism?

4. Find a startling photographic image that recently appeared in print or online, and write an argument for or against its publication. Should there be limits on which images get published? If so, how should society decide what those limits should be?

JESSICA GROSE
What It Means to Raise an American Girl Now

O NE OF THE IMAGES that has stuck with me from the pandemic's[1] early days is the doll hospital my daughters made from cardboard boxes. Not long after their world was locked down, my children's American Girl dolls were afflicted with an unnamed illness and put to bed for weeks. My own girls, who were 7 and 3 at the time, took their self-appointed jobs as doll nurses very seriously, and would frequently check on their patients, keeping me and my husband apprised of their progress.

There was a reason my kids chose their American Girl dolls and not their Barbies or LOL Surprise! dolls for this scenario: American Girls look more like actual girls than a lot of popular dolls do, and the form of realistic play that they facilitate is a healthy way of processing stress. Psychologists say that building a story around an upsetting event can help kids regain a sense of control.

For the uninitiated, some American Girl dolls have elaborate, historically informed backstories, which are described in a series of books. (The American Girl company also sells unnamed, customizable dolls for the modern era whose

First published in the online newsletter of the New York Times *in 2022 and published in the print edition two days later.*

1. COVID-19, a respiratory disease, emerged in China in late 2019 and became a global pandemic by the spring of 2020, prompting stay-at-home orders and other forms of enforced isolation across the world.

stories are unwritten.) Kit Kittredge, for example, is an aspiring journalist living through the Great Depression. Her tagline is "weather hard times with grit and gratitude." But when I asked my younger daughter recently what she likes about Kit, she didn't say anything about her plucky perseverance. She matter-of-factly said, "Kit looks like me and her eyes close so she can go to sleep."

I was an American Girl devotee when I was their age. There were only three of them when they hit the market in 1986 (before the company became a Mattel subsidiary): Samantha Parkington, Kirsten Larson and Molly McIntire.[2] I had Samantha, who was born at the end of the Gilded Age and then orphaned, living through the start of the Progressive Era[3] with her well-to-do Grandmary. While I admit that I was initially drawn to Samantha's outfits (her fur hat and

2. The Kirsten Larson doll represents a mid-nineteenth-century Swedish immigrant to the United States; the Molly McIntire doll represents a Scottish American girl growing up in Illinois in the 1940s.

3. The Gilded Age, a period in US history from the 1870s to the beginning of the twentieth century characterized by rapid industrial growth, political corruption, and wide

plaid cape were to die for), I enjoyed the books too. Samantha is headstrong, often pushing back against her grandmother's admonitions to be more ladylike.

5   American Girls representing other eras, ethnicities and parts of our country have been added over the years: There's Nanea Mitchell, who lived through the attack on Pearl Harbor; Addy Walker, who escaped slavery in North Carolina; and Josefina Montoya, who lives in New Mexico when it's still part of Mexico.[4] What all their stories have in common, as Amy Schiller explained in the *Atlantic* in 2013,[5] is that they interface with the issues of their time. In one book, the wealthy Samantha gives a speech in front of her school about the horrors of child labor. "The book is a bravura effort at teaching young girls about class privilege, speaking truth to power and engaging with controversial social policy, all based on empathetic encounters with people whose life experiences differ from [their] own," Schiller wrote.

Their stories have something else in common. They highlight a cultural narrative of continual progress for girls and women. When I played with the dolls in the late 1980s and early '90s, the prevailing message I absorbed was that girls could do anything and be anything—girl power![6]—and we would soon see Grandmary's antiquated lectures in the rearview. That narrative was always a fantasy, and very obviously not as true for everyone. (The cheapest doll-and-book set cost $74 in 1990, underscoring how out of reach the fantasy, and the dolls, were and are for many kids.) But for me, the message was still something hopeful to cling to.

I've been thinking a lot about what it means to raise an American girl in this moment, when continual progress—for my daughters, for all girls—doesn't feel inevitable. Their right to bodily autonomy is more conditional. The backlash against not conforming to gendered ideals seems more virulent than in recent memory. American children are growing up at a moment when, seemingly, we can't even have a wholesome Independence Day celebration without mass casualties.[7] How do I introduce my daughters to the reality of a world like this without making them despair?

REMIXING THE AMERICAN GIRL

Maybe part of the answer is telling the truth in all its absurd failure and glory. Several brilliant American Girl doll meme accounts on *Instagram* have done just that. They've made me laugh and, even though they're laced with dark irony,

disparities in wealth; the Progressive Era, a period of political and social reform running from the late nineteenth century to World War I.

4. Mexico ceded the area that would become New Mexico, the forty-seventh US state, to the United States at the end of the Mexican-American War (1846–48).

5. Amy Schiller, "American Girls Aren't Radical Anymore," the *Atlantic*, April 23, 2013 [Author's note].

6. Slogan from the 1990s attributed to the punk band Bikini Kill and then adopted by the Spice Girls, a British girl group [Editor's note]; "History of the '90's: Looking Back at the Girl Power Phenomenon," *Global News*, September 18, 2019 [Author's note].

7. On July 4, 2022, a mass shooter killed seven people and injured many more during an Independence Day celebration in Highland Park, Illinois.

they still retain some of the plucky hopefulness of Kit and Samantha. These accounts take photos of the American Girls and put them in ridiculous situations for a doll. Many of their posts portray the dolls witnessing random historical moments—like when Dan Quayle misspelled the word "potato"[8]—with their blank yet slightly knowing half-smiles dominating the images.

Some of the memes from an account called @hellicity_merriman start with the prompt, "We need an American Girl doll who . . ." My favorite silly example: "we need an american girl doll who eats cheese out of the bag with her hand." (Deal with it, Grandmary!)

Other examples of these sharp memes are more politically resonant. A meme account whose *Instagram* handle is a bawdy play on "Kit Kittredge" posted a viral image after *Roe v. Wade* fell,[9] highlighting the states where the Nixon-era[10] American Girl doll Julie may have had more access to abortion in 1974 than we do today.

Lydia Burns, who is 24 and runs that account, told me that when she was a girl growing up in Kentucky, American Girl dolls were considered edgy, and some people at her church boycotted them. In 2005, conservative groups were upset because the American Girl brand supported a charity called Girls Inc., which the American Family Association[11] claimed was "a pro-abortion, pro-lesbian advocacy group." Burns said her mother is a feminist who stuck by the American Girl dolls and allowed her daughter to continue playing with them despite the blowback. The books and the dolls, Burns said, "exposed me to ideas of girls who don't look like me, and a set of history" that involved cultural and political conflict, offering perspectives she wasn't necessarily getting at school.

On a certain level, what these adult creators are doing is the same thing my kids were doing with their doll hospital: working through the distressing news of the day with their doll icons. This is something enthusiasts have always done with American Girl dolls, said Nina Diamond, a professor emerita in the department of marketing at DePaul University and the lead author of a 2009 paper in the *Journal of Marketing* titled "American Girl and the Brand Gestalt: Closing the Loop on Sociocultural Branding Research." In it, she and her co-authors wrote:

> Meanings associated with these iconic brands serve to eliminate felt tensions between societal ideals and people's day-to-day experiences, and they address the anxieties of a nation through myths or stories that affect the way people think about themselves and their lives.

8. During a 1992 school visit, US Vice President James Danforth Quayle "corrected" a student's spelling of *potato* to *potatoe*.

9. *Roe v. Wade*, a 1973 Supreme Court decision legalizing abortion in the United States, was overturned by the subsequent decision *Dobbs v. Jackson Women's Health Organization* in 2022.

10. Richard Milhous Nixon (1913–1994), thirty-seventh president of the United States, served from 1969 until his resignation in 1974.

11. A fundamentalist Christian advocacy group.

Diamond describes American Girl as one of the most successful "open source" brands,[12] meaning that all of its constituents—kids, their parents, journalists, cultural commentators—are contributing to and remixing the American Girls' meaning in the world. And, by extension, adding a small piece to the image—and aspiration—that actual American girls and women have of ourselves.

Tara Strauch, an associate professor of history at Centre College, taught a class where she had students look at the dolls as a "vehicle for teaching" and consuming "historical narratives." Strauch told me that one of the students' projects was to create their own historical doll's story. One student created an American Girl doll who lived through 9/11 while also figuring out her sexuality. "Those of us who grew up with them are still trying to use them to understand the world, putting our thoughts and ideals into their mouths in fun and subversive" ways, Strauch told me.

15   Memes aren't a replacement for actual advocacy or action. They're an escape that makes me feel a little better about raising my kids at a time that can often feel anti-girl, anti-woman and even anti-humanity. Burns doesn't just run an American Girl *Instagram* account, she also works with student organizers to create real-world change. The two women who run @hellicity_merriman met working in politics. These women, all of whom are in their 20s, are communicating that even when life feels apocalyptic, both laughter and change are possible. As my colleague Valeriya Safronova put it in an article about these memes:[13]

> Each image imagines the American Girl dolls surviving highly stressful, sometimes catastrophic events. Within the world of these memes, there is nothing the world won't throw at an American Girl doll, and there is nothing she can't do. She, a representation of the childhoods of countless girls, can succeed where others have failed.

There's a can-do attitude to the memes, one that I already see in my older daughter. She's only 9, and any time she learns something awful about the world she responds with outrage and a desire to change it, urgently. When she saw a magazine headline about the rapid decline of bee populations due to climate change, she earnestly exclaimed, "We need to save all the bees!"

I want her to bottle that energy and keep it with her, at least in some small way, even as she becomes increasingly aware of the flawed world around her as she grows. She's a few years away from marching on the National Mall,[14] but she's learning that progress doesn't happen without effort and determination, and that's a message any American girl should know by heart. The world can

---

12. The analogy is to "open-source" software, for which modifiable source code is freely available online.

13. Valeriya Safronova, "American Girl Doll Jokes Are All the Rage," the *New York Times*, June 23, 2022, updated July 13, 2022 [Author's note].

14. A park in Washington, DC, containing and bordered by national monuments and museums, that has been the site of several important protests and marches, including the 1963 March on Washington and the 2004 March for Women's Lives.

be a bleak place, and every story doesn't have a happy ending, but my daughters' American Girl dolls eventually left their cardboard hospital and made a full recovery. We need an American girl who helps save the bees, and maybe it will be my kid.

MLA CITATION

Grose, Jessica. "What It Means to Raise an American Girl Now." *The Norton Reader: An Anthology of Nonfiction*, edited by Melissa A. Goldthwaite et al., 16th ed., W. W. Norton, 2024, pp. 440–45.

Questions

1. What values, according to Jessica Grose, do American Girl dolls embody? How, as material and cultural artifacts—in their physical attributes, their stories, their marketing and branding—do American Girl dolls transmit these values?

2. After lamenting that we live in a time "when continual progress—for my daughters, for all girls—doesn't feel inevitable," Grose wonders, "How do I introduce my daughters to the reality of a world like this without making them despair?" (paragraph 7). She then looks to the meme culture surrounding American Girl dolls as a possible answer. What is it about this culture that Grose finds so appealing and empowering?

3. Grose recognizes that because of their cost, American Girl dolls were not available to everyone: "The cheapest doll-and-book set cost $74 in 1990, underscoring how out of reach the fantasy, and the dolls, were and are for many kids" (paragraph 6). Nevertheless, she also notes that for her, "the message was still something hopeful to cling to" (paragraph 6). Annotate the essay to note places where Grose acknowledges issues of social class. How does she navigate these issues?

4. Consider an iconic brand from your own childhood that continues to be meaningful to you or that helped shape your understanding of the world. Using Grose's essay as a model, do a project that links that brand's presence in your childhood to your life and values today.

J. Drew Lanham
Red-headed Love Child

"DADDY! DADDY! DADDY!" Someone was trying to get my attention, but as far as I knew my legitimate spawn were more than a thousand miles away in South Carolina. Here I was, in the middle of God-knows-where, Nebraska, and standing not ten feet away was a little blue-eyed boy with curly red hair claiming me

Published in When Birds Are Near: Dispatches from Contemporary Writers (2020), edited by Susan Fox Rogers.

as something I wasn't. I froze in the midst of a difficult decision, choosing between Wrigley's Big Red and Juicy Fruit chewing gum. Now there was a different dilemma beyond spicy-sweet or fruity deliciousness. For a moment I was cornered by a three-foot-tall child whose blue eyes could've been left behind by the glaciers that once covered this part of the world. Maybe three or four years old at most, the cherub stood there, confident of the candy aisle proclamation that I was the one so designated to pick him up, squeeze him tight, and twirl him around in some sort of joyous father-son reunion.

Of course, I had no intention of getting anywhere near this toddler. A big black man picking up a Caucasian kid in what seemed the ivory center of the lily-white Corn Husker State would've likely resulted in sirens wailing and the deployment of local, state, and federal authorities—or so I thought. But in spite of the instinct telling me to put as much distance between the red-haired boy and myself as quickly as possible, I stood there, staring back; my brown eyes met his blue ones. There was something about him that was, well, different. Maybe it was the red 'fro. Maybe it was his not-so-white skin.

Soon, a rather attractive auburn-haired white woman found her child in the middle of making a connection with a man of color. I suspect it was not a first for either of them. She grabbed the toddler. "He's not your Daddy! I—I'm sorry sir." With that and a few more hastily constructed words of apology, embarrassment, and anger thrown in for added effect, they both went on to buy whatever convenient thing they were in a convenience store to buy. I chose Big Red. At that moment, spice seemed the way to go.

Back in the rental car that had pushed across a good deal of central Nebraska, I retold the story to my travel buddies, Matt and Steve. They found the event that had occurred on a gasoline fill-up at first unbelievable and then unbelievably funny. The happening provided some comic relief as the miles wore on. I speculated about what trashy television show I'd end up on in twenty years with some burly biracial Cornhusker man claiming a life less fulfilled without me. Steve and Matt promised that "what happened in Nebraska would stay in Nebraska!"[1]

5 It wasn't my first birding trip out west, but it might become my most memorable if random children kept stepping forward to claim me as their father. The curly coif and the not-so-pale skin pointed to the boy's other half being of a darker hue. Given that I'd only seen one black person since I'd been in Nebraska, I began to recalculate my thumbnail homogenous analysis of the state.

Ask 100 people anything about Nebraska, and you'll get "corn" somewhere in the first three words of their response. If you'd asked me about Nebraska just a few weeks before my first trip there, my answer may have been more complex and included something about prairie birds, the famed college football team in Lincoln—and corn. And so when I landed in Grand Island, Nebraska, a place probably not otherwise noteworthy for much more than being smack in the middle of Nebraska corn country, I knew that we were there for more than grain. We'd journeyed out in the last days of March to witness the tail end of

1. Allusion to "What happens here, stays here," the slogan for Las Vegas from 2003 to 2020.

one of the great ornithological wonders in North America: the northward migration of Sandhill Cranes along the Platte River.

For probably 10,000 years or more, the tall, steel-gray birds have thrown their unmusically beautiful calls across the shallow floodplain that is now in the heart of America's corn and burger-producing bread-basket. I'd seen Sandhill Cranes before, but in Grand Island, they did not seem to occur singly anywhere. As we scouted on that first day for cranes, it became apparent that even at the waning end of the migration *rare* was not an accurate descriptor for the undulating ribbons of birds that cruised the skies, circled on rising thermals, and dropped like paratroopers into stubble-riddled cornfields lying brown and rich with river-run soil. In the air they were gracefully buoyant and powerful fliers. On the ground they were just as stately—walking, stalking, dancing, and prancing as crane-kind does. When you are surrounded by cranes it is easy to understand how the family of birds have generated awe and worship around the world. As the day closed we watched the evening roosting ritual as a half dozen here, twenty or more there, flew out of the setting sun like legions of phoenix to roost on the sandbars in the shallows of the Platte. By dusky dark there were thousands of long-necked, long-legged silhouettes gathered together and calling in the most pleasingly discordant chorus. It was a sound etched deep in my soul.

I recalled the crane music, the soft rush of the river's flow, and the calling of frogs as I fell asleep that night.

We wrapped up our crane filming job the next day and headed north towards South Dakota for a date with Greater Prairie-Chickens. As we sped along highways, my initial impression of Nebraska catering to corn was borne out. The landscape was like rough five-o'clock shadow with the stubble evidence of the combine's shaving the previous season. Soon the next season's planting would go in, and green fingers of the grass that would become agricultural gold would spring up in the no-plow rows. But for now, I was tiring of the sameness. Cranes were beginning to become an afterthought when the miles mercifully scrunched the foreverness of flat fields into rolling hills covered with grass and occasional stands of pine forest. In between the rises, there were crevices and draws that pulled water into small ponds and larger lakes that were dotted with ducks. Big cottonwood trees stood here and there, testament to wetness lying not so far beneath the sand.

We'd entered the Sandhills;[2] ancient high dunes still bore the evidence of wagon travel in the visible parallel ruts that stretched across the arid expanses. Every now and again, some small town would pop up. With a sign declaring populations in the tens or maybe hundreds at most, the apparent requisites for civilization included a grain elevator, a church, and maybe a gas station. The town where my biracial would-be love child and I were reunited was a metropolis compared to anything else we saw out there. Outside of the towns lay a landscape that felt wild and sometimes foreboding. The dunes went on and on.

10

2. At about 19,300 square miles, this region is among the world's largest expanses of grass-stabilized sand dunes.

Other than the barbed-wire fences festooned with old tires, there was little else indicative of human presence.

We saw American White Pelicans soaring like pale pterodactyls over the duck-dotted potholes and counted Swainson's Hawks like mile markers sitting tall on every other telephone pole. Nebraska sits on top of the Ogallala Aquifer, an enormous underground lake that slakes the thirst of much of the Midwest and its never-ending (and unsustainable) desire for water to keep the breadbasket productive. There were birds everywhere, but our target wouldn't be so easy to spot from roadside voyeuring. We'd have to rise early and seduce the presence of our targets in silence.

Prairie-chickens, in one form or another, ranged across almost two-thirds of the eastern and midwestern US in the not-too-distant past. With various regions possessing their own uniquely adapted species, "chicken" numbers have declined dramatically as prairie habitats have been plowed under or overgrazed.

We were lucky enough to be in a place where the birds could still be found with patience and a bit of luck. What we wanted was more than a look, though. We were there to see Greater Prairie-Chickens dance in a millennia-old ritual that made sure more prairie-chickens would be conceived and hatched to keep the prairie pulse pumping. To see the dance required a predawn hike across the sandy terrain and whispered silence in a blind built by the federal wildlife folks for the purpose of chicken-spying.

As much as birders depend on their eyes, many of us would be blind without our ears. The morning of our rendezvous, the ceaseless prairie winds vibrated with northern leopard frogs snoring and chuckling from the draws, pheasant cocks crowing, and American Bitterns pumping as the stars dimmed in the coming dawn. It was more dream than real. Only a few days before, I'd been in the spring-greening forests of the South Carolina piedmont and now I was in a world so different that it seemed otherworldly. Here, the grasses were the old growth. Underfoot and all around me, life abounded in the rolling hills and wetlands in a diversity that was almost uncountable. Maybe it was just the wind that drew the tears from my eyes. Maybe it was the privilege of the place that made me choke back the joyful weeping. Though I'd never set foot in this place, I felt a part of it—rooted deep like the grasses in the sand.

15   Being in the midst of it all was like having a Muse[3] sing the sweetest lullaby. Once in the blind, I closed my eyes—not to sleep, but to somehow soak it all in: the sounds, smells, and sights. I prayed to some force beyond me in thanks for all I had seen and the chickens I could not see. And then *wooooooooooom*—from somewhere out there a low moan floated in on the wind. It came again, *wooooooooooooooom wooooooooooom*; gentle and ghastly—*wooooooooooooom wooooooooooooom*—prairie-chickens!

Our attention focused on the lek, a sandy dance floor the chickens had cleared and displayed on for generations. With the blind not more than a few

3. A divine source of literary, artistic, and intellectual inspiration in Greek mythology.

feet from it, we had a front-row seat. The "wooming" had stopped when something suddenly appeared center stage! Squinting hard to somehow squeeze light onto the subject, I made out the form of a plump fowl that, yes, looked chicken-like. It was my first Greater Prairie-Chicken.

There was nothing particularly spectacular about it. In size and character, it did look like a small brown-speckled hen. The bird pecked around a bit and was soon joined by another. Once the second chicken flew in, any resemblance to what farm folks back home call "yard birds" disappeared. The two birds faced off on opposite ends of the oval dancing ground, plumage puffed out with two tufts of feathers standing out like horns on their heads. They fanned out their tails like miniature strutting turkey-gobblers. Two tangerine-colored sacs swelled up like small balloons on the sides of their necks. Their oversized eyebrows flamed yellow in the freshly risen sun. The puffing and fanning soon became a dance; a twirling, foot-stamping, wing-dragging dance daring the other bird to do something more.

As daylight finally broke, a crowd had gathered around the stage. We weren't the only watchers. A half dozen hens and a few other cocks had sneaked in to see the show. The peekaboo was serious business for the chickens—a matter of life and death. The ladies would ultimately choose a dancer to mate with and produce the next generation of *Tympanuchus cupido*—little drumming lovers. The usually secretive males took few risks in combat, since bluffs were the way evolution made sure the species didn't cut off its nose to spite its face. The greater risk came in the exposure to predators that were probably also watching. Bout after bout of display and occasional contact continued for hours, and then, just as suddenly as it began, it ended. The birds left as they'd entered.

We had our show on film, and I had the thrill of a birding lifetime. Pheasants crowed, frogs chuckled, and the bittern boomed beyond the dawn clock it usually punched.

Birds connect me to strange places in ways that make me feel at home. Try as I might to explain it to those who've never lost the hours watching feathered life go about its business in some coastal bay marsh or mountain cove forest, it's a hard point to press home. Home is indeed where the heart is. For me, that means that I can find comfort in piedmont old fields and new sunrises on prairie sweeps. Southwestern deserts and south Texas palm groves feel more familiar than not.

I consider myself a migratory creature, traveling back and forth across the country to find birds and the wild places they live. Places like the rolling Nebraska Sandhills, the sky islands of southeast Arizona, the cold running streams of Yosemite, the flat-topped buttes of Montana, the Texas Big Bend, and the Kansas tallgrass comprise the many places "out west" where I've been to see birds. They are like many of the places I go to see birds anywhere in the world: far off the beaten path and mostly populated by white people. In my crisscrossing and wild wandering I seldom find other black birders. In some ways I used to see myself as a pioneer of sorts, a first among the throngs of

20

seekers in far-flung places wandering underneath big skies or witnessing wind-swept vistas.

After our chicken and crane odyssey Matt, Steve, and I took the long way back to our airport in Grand Island. We found an out-of-the-way wildlife refuge called Fort Niobrara. We drove through a loose herd of bison with Afro-headed bulls standing taller than the car. In the visitor's center I found a revelation that dispelled any notions I had about being the first black man to venture into northern Nebraska. Along with a giant stuffed bison that made me feel tiny, there was a historical display with grainy depictions of soldiers. I looked closer, thinking at first the old photograph was simply casting shadows on the faces of the regiment. But then the words brought the truth home. These were black men! Sent to the far ends of the late nineteenth- and early twentieth-century western frontier to hold the line and press the manifest destiny of a growing nation, black American military men, the famed Buffalo Soldiers,[4] had been here long before I was anyone's thought.

More than 100 years ago, black men of the US Army's Ninth and Tenth Cavalry and Twenty-Fourth and Twenty-Fifth Infantry[5] followed orders and endured the extremes of heat, cold, dust, mud, insects, and disease that often plague the out-of-the-way places I go by choice to find birds. In between the daily tasks of surviving rampant racism from the US Army, skirmishes with American Indians fighting (rightfully) to hold onto homelands, and incursions from Mexican patriots (trying to understandably reclaim lost homeland),[6] I'm sure there wasn't much time for the leisure of watching birds or rising at dawn to witness a prairie ritual. But then again, this Nebraska trip was breaking brain barriers I'd long held as dogma. Maybe I was giving these brave men short shrift.

I'd like to think that all of us, regardless of circumstance, find some way to appreciate the wonders of the world around us. Maybe on an evening watch, a blue-coated[7] black looked skyward during his to-and-from march, his ears catching the trumpeting calls of uncountable numbers of Sandhill Cranes coming in to rest on the sandbars of the shallow North Platte. Maybe the trumpeting chorus makes low pay and lack of respect fade for just a moment as the sun glances off broad gray wings. Perhaps a brown-faced horseman, the son of a slave now free, wears knee boots dusty from the trail and a broad-brimmed hat slouched low over tired eyes. He sits tired but tall in his McClellan saddle[8] after a patrol through the Sandhills. As the troop pauses to let tired mounts

4. Manifest destiny, a term dating from 1845 for the belief that the United States was destined to expand to the Pacific Ocean; Buffalo Soldiers, so called for their characteristic buffalo-hide coats and robes.

5. Army regiments comprising Black soldiers led by predominantly white officers.

6. The Mexican-American War (1846–48) ensued after the US annexation of Texas from Mexico in 1845.

7. Reference to the US Army's blue uniforms.

8. Style of saddle developed by US Army Captain George B. McClellan and adopted by the US Army in 1855.

rest and drink from a pothole pond, he ponders the spectacle of a snipe climbing high and twittering to the heavens one minute and plummeting to the ground the next. Maybe there were a few opportunities for duck dinners to break the monotony of beans and bread. A two-lined phalanx of free black men on bay mounts must have been impressive, winding their way across rolling grassland, the eerie cries of Long-billed Curlews and the sweet songs of Western Meadowlarks pacing creaking saddle leather and jingling bridle rings. A bold pair of acrobatic Scissor-tailed Flycatchers takes advantage of the bounty of bugs kicked up by the horses' hooves, and a trooper marvels at the boldness and grace of the long-tailed birds.

Black people, or people of any color, surely could not have ignored the beauty of towering sequoias or the breathtaking beauty of sunrises and sunsets painting the Rocky Mountains and Great Plains. No, I don't have any café au lait love children in the Sandhills of Nebraska or anywhere else for that matter. The blue-eyed boy was mistaken in that matter. But then, maybe there's more to what the little one saw than I give him credit for. Perhaps somewhere in the colorful memory of that curly-haired boy, there's a Buffalo Soldier who fathered a memory we all need to claim. 25

MLA CITATION

Lanham, J. Drew. "Red-headed Love Child." *The Norton Reader: An Anthology of Nonfiction*, edited by Melissa A. Goldthwaite et al., 16th ed., W. W. Norton, 2024, pp. 445–51.

QUESTIONS

1. Consider the themes of race, identity, place, and history in this essay. How does J. Drew Lanham initially understand his relationship to the people and places of Nebraska, and how does his encounter with the Buffalo Soldiers exhibit at the visitor's center of the Fort Niobrara National Wildlife Refuge (paragraph 22) change that conception?

2. Lanham's title "Red-headed Love Child" refers not to what might seem to be his essay's main topics—the birds Lanham and his companions observed on their trip or the history of the Buffalo Soldiers—but to a boy he describes encountering in his first few paragraphs. Why might Lanham have chosen this title? How does the title shape your understanding of the essay?

3. Lanham presents himself as both an expert and a novice. What techniques or devices does he use to balance these two roles? Annotate moments in the essay that shape his characterization of himself as well as the reader's idea of him.

4. Plan a visit to a place with which you are unfamiliar (your destination need not be remote; it just needs to be new to you) and record your preconceptions. Then go. Record your experiences, attending not just to the items on your itinerary but also to any chance encounters or surprises. How did your visit change your understanding of your destination? of yourself?

JAMES BALDWIN
Stranger in the Village

ROM ALL AVAILABLE EVIDENCE no black man had ever set foot in this tiny Swiss village before I came. I was told before arriving that I would probably be a "sight" for the village; I took this to mean that people of my complexion were rarely seen in Switzerland, and also that city people are always something of a "sight" outside of the city. It did not occur to me—possibly because I am an American—that there could be people anywhere who had never seen a Negro.

It is a fact that cannot be explained on the basis of the inaccessibility of the village. The village is very high, but it is only four hours from Milan and three hours from Lausanne. It is true that it is virtually unknown. Few people making plans for a holiday would elect to come here. On the other hand, the villagers are able, presumably, to come and go as they please—which they do: to another town at the foot of the mountain, with a population of approximately five thousand, the nearest place to see a movie or go to the bank. In the village there is no movie house, no bank, no library, no theater; very few radios, one jeep, one station wagon; and at the moment, one typewriter, mine, an invention which the woman next door to me here had never seen. There are about six hundred people living here, all Catholic—I conclude this from the fact that the Catholic church is open all year round, whereas the Protestant chapel, set off on a hill a little removed from the village, is open only in the summertime when the tourists arrive. There are four or five hotels, all closed now, and four or five *bistros*, of which, however, only two do any business during the winter. These two do not do a great deal, for life in the village seems to end around nine or ten o'clock. There are a few stores, butcher, baker, *épicerie*,[1] a hardware store, and a money-changer—who cannot change travelers' checks, but must send them down to the bank, an operation which takes two or three days. There is something called the *Ballet Haus*, closed in the winter and used for God knows what, certainly not ballet, during the summer. There seems to be only one schoolhouse in the village, and this for the quite young children; I suppose this to mean that their older brothers and sisters at some point descend from these mountains in order to complete their education—possibly, again, to the town just below. The landscape is absolutely forbidding, mountains towering on all four sides, ice and snow as far as the eye can reach. In this white wilderness, men and women and children move all day, carrying washing, wood, buckets of milk or water, sometimes skiing on Sunday afternoons. All week long boys and young men are to be seen shoveling snow off the rooftops, or dragging wood down from the forest in sleds.

First published in Harper's Magazine *(1953) and then included in* Notes of a Native Son *(1955), James Baldwin's collection of essays that describes and analyzes the experience of being Black in America and Europe.*

1. French for "grocery shop."

The village's only real attraction, which explains the tourist season, is the hot spring water. A disquietingly high proportion of these tourists are cripples, or semi-cripples, who come year after year—from other parts of Switzerland, usually—to take the waters. This lends the village, at the height of the season, a rather terrifying air of sanctity, as though it were a lesser Lourdes.[2] There is often something beautiful, there is always something awful, in the spectacle of a person who has lost one of his faculties, a faculty he never questioned until it was gone, and who struggles to recover it. Yet people remain people, on crutches or indeed on deathbeds; and wherever I passed, the first summer I was here, among the native villagers or among the lame, a wind passed with me—of astonishment, curiosity, amusement, and outrage. That first summer I stayed two weeks and never intended to return. But I did return in the winter, to work; the village offers, obviously, no distractions whatever and has the further advantage of being extremely cheap. Now it is winter again, a year later, and I am here again. Everyone in the village knows my name, though they scarcely ever use it, knows that I come from America—though, this, apparently, they will never really believe: black men come from Africa—and everyone knows that I am the friend of the son of a woman who was born here, and that I am staying in their chalet. But I remain as much a stranger today as I was the first day I arrived, and the children shout *Neger! Neger!* as I walk along the streets.

It must be admitted that in the beginning I was far too shocked to have any real reaction. In so far as I reacted at all, I reacted by trying to be pleasant—it being a great part of the American Negro's education (long before he goes to school) that he must make people "like" him. This smile-and-the-world-smiles-with-you routine worked about as well in this situation as it had in the situation for which it was designed, which is to say that it did not work at all. No one, after all, can be liked whose human weight and complexity cannot be, or has not been, admitted. My smile was simply another unheard-of phenomenon which allowed them to see my teeth—they did not, really, see my smile and I began to think that, should I take to snarling, no one would notice any difference. All of the physical characteristics of the Negro which had caused me, in America, a very different and almost forgotten pain were nothing less than miraculous—or infernal—in the eyes of the village people. Some thought my hair was the color of tar, that it had the texture of wire, or the texture of cotton. It was jocularly suggested that I might let it all grow long and make myself a winter coat. If I sat in the sun for more than five minutes some daring creature was certain to come along and gingerly put his fingers on my hair, as though he were afraid of an electric shock, or put his hand on my hand, astonished that the color did not rub off. In all of this, in which it must be conceded there was the charm of genuine wonder and in which there was certainly no element of intentional unkindness, there was yet no suggestion that I was human: I was simply a living wonder.

I knew that they did not mean to be unkind, and I know it now; it is necessary, nevertheless, for me to repeat this to myself each time that I walk out of

5

2. Site of visions of the Virgin Mary and now a prominent pilgrimage destination.

the chalet. The children who shout *Neger!* have no way of knowing the echoes this sound raises in me. They are brimming with good humor and the more daring swell with pride when I stop to speak with them. Just the same, there are days when I cannot pause and smile, when I have no heart to play with them; when, indeed, I mutter sourly to myself, exactly as I muttered on the streets of a city these children have never seen, when I was no bigger than these children are now: *Your* mother *was a nigger.* Joyce is right about history being a nightmare[3]—but it may be the nightmare from which no one *can* awaken. People are trapped in history and history is trapped in them.

There is a custom in the village—I am told it is repeated in many villages— of "buying" African natives for the purpose of converting them to Christianity. There stands in the church all year round a small box with a slot for money, decorated with a black figurine, and into this box the villagers drop their francs. During the *carnaval* which precedes Lent, two village children have their faces blackened—out of which bloodless darkness their blue eyes shine like ice—and fantastic horsehair wigs are placed on their blond heads; thus disguised, they solicit among the villagers for money for the missionaries in Africa. Between the box in the church and the blackened children, the village "bought" last year six or eight African natives. This was reported to me with pride by the wife of one of the *bistro* owners and I was careful to express astonishment and plea- sure at the solicitude shown by the village for the souls of black folks. The *bis- tro* owner's wife beamed with a pleasure far more genuine than my own and seemed to feel that I might now breathe more easily concerning the souls of at least six of my kinsmen.

I tried not to think of these so lately baptized kinsmen, of the price paid for them, or the peculiar price they themselves would pay, and said nothing about my father, who having taken his own conversion too literally never, at bottom, forgave the white world (which he described as heathen) for having saddled him with a Christ in whom, to judge at least from their treatment of him, they themselves no longer believed. I thought of white men arriving for the first time in an African village, strangers there, as I am a stranger here, and tried to imagine the astounded populace touching their hair and marvel- ing at the color of their skin. But there is a great difference between being the first white man to be seen by Africans and being the first black man to be seen by whites. The white man takes the astonishment as tribute, for he arrives to conquer and to convert the natives, whose inferiority in relation to himself is not even to be questioned; whereas I, without a thought of conquest, find myself among a people whose culture controls me, has even, in a sense, created me, people who have cost me more in anguish and rage than they will ever know, who yet do not even know of my existence. The astonishment with which I might have greeted them, should they have stumbled into my African village a few hundred years ago, might have rejoiced their hearts. But the astonishment with which they greet me today can only poison mine.

3. James Joyce (1882–1941), Irish novelist; Stephen Dedalus, a character in Joyce's novel *Ulysses* (1992), says, "History is a nightmare from which I am trying to escape."

And this is so despite everything I may do to feel differently, despite my friendly conversations with the *bistro* owner's wife, despite their three-year-old son who has at last become my friend, despite the *saluts* and *bonsoirs*[4] which I exchange with people as I walk, despite the fact that I know that no individual can be taken to task for what history is doing, or has done. I say that the culture of these people controls me—but they can scarcely be held responsible for European culture. America comes out of Europe, but these people have never seen America, nor have most of them seen more of Europe than the hamlet at the foot of their mountain. Yet they move with an authority which I shall never have; and they regard me, quite rightly, not only as a stranger in their village but as a suspect latecomer, bearing no credentials, to everything they have—however unconsciously—inherited.

For this village, even were it incomparably more remote and incredibly more primitive, is the West, the West onto which I have been so strangely grafted. These people cannot be, from the point of view of power, strangers anywhere in the world; they have made the modern world, in effect, even if they do not know it. The most illiterate among them is related, in a way that I am not, to Dante, Shakespeare, Michelangelo, Aeschylus, Da Vinci, Rembrandt, and Racine; the cathedral at Chartres says something to them which it cannot say to me, as indeed would New York's Empire State Building, should anyone here ever see it. Out of their hymns and dances come Beethoven and Bach. Go back a few centuries and they are in their full glory—but I am in Africa, watching the conquerors arrive.

The rage of the disesteemed is personally fruitless, but it is also absolutely inevitable; this rage, so generally discounted, so little understood even among the people whose daily bread it is, is one of the things that makes history. Rage can only with difficulty, and never entirely, be brought under the domination of the intelligence and is therefore not susceptible to any arguments whatever. This is a fact which ordinary representatives of the *Herrenvolk*,[5] having never felt this rage and being unable to imagine, quite fail to understand. Also, rage cannot be hidden, it can only be dissembled. This dissembling deludes the thoughtless, and strengthens rage and adds, to rage, contempt. There are, no doubt, as many ways of coping with the resulting complex of tensions as there are black men in the world, but no black man can hope ever to be entirely liberated from this internal warfare—rage, dissembling, and contempt having inevitably accompanied his first realization of the power of white men. What is crucial here is that, since white men represent in the black man's world so heavy a weight, white men have for black men a reality which is far from being reciprocal; and hence all black men have toward all white men an attitude which is designed, really, either to rob the white man of the jewel of his naïveté, or else to make it cost him dear.

The black man insists, by whatever means he finds at his disposal, that the white man cease to regard him as an exotic rarity and recognize him as a human being. This is a very charged and difficult moment, for there is a great

4. French for "hellos" and "good evenings."
5. German for "master race."

deal of will power involved in the white man's naïveté. Most people are not naturally reflective any more than they are naturally malicious, and the white man
prefers to keep the black man at a certain human remove because it is easier
for him thus to preserve his simplicity and avoid being called to account for
crimes committed by his forefathers, or his neighbors. He is inescapably aware,
nevertheless, that he is in a better position in the world than black men are,
nor can he quite put to death the suspicion that he is hated by black men therefore. He does not wish to be hated, neither does he wish to change places, and
at this point in his uneasiness he can scarcely avoid having recourse to those
legends which white men have created about black men, the most usual effect
of which is that the white man finds himself enmeshed, so to speak, in his own
language which describes hell, as well as the attributes which lead one to hell,
as being as black as night.

Every legend, moreover, contains its residuum of truth, and the root function of language is to control the universe by describing it. It is of quite considerable significance that black men remain, in the imagination, and in
overwhelming numbers in fact, beyond the disciplines of salvation; and this
despite the fact that the West has been "buying" African natives for centuries.
There is, I should hazard, an instantaneous necessity to be divorced from this
so visibly unsaved stranger, in whose heart, moreover, one cannot guess what
dreams of vengeance are being nourished; and, at the same time, there are few
things on earth more attractive than the idea of the unspeakable liberty which
is allowed the unredeemed. When, beneath the black mask, a human being
begins to make himself felt one cannot escape a certain awful wonder as to
what kind of human being it is. What one's imagination makes of other people
is dictated, of course, by the laws of one's own personality and it is one of the
ironies of black-white relations that, by means of what the white man imagines
the black man to be, the black man is enabled to know who the white man is.

I have said, for example, that I am as much a stranger in this village today
as I was the first summer I arrived, but this is not quite true. The villagers wonder less about the texture of my hair than they did then, and wonder rather
more about me. And the fact that their wonder now exists on another level is
reflected in their attitudes and in their eyes. There are the children who make
those delightful, hilarious, sometimes astonishingly grave overtures of friendship in the unpredictable fashion of children; other children, having been taught
that the devil is a black man, scream in genuine anguish as I approach. Some
of the older women never pass without a friendly greeting, never pass, indeed,
if it seems that they will be able to engage me in conversation; other women
look down or look away or rather contemptuously smirk. Some of the men drink
with me and suggest that I learn how to ski—partly, I gather, because they cannot imagine what I would look like on skis—and want to know if I am married,
and ask questions about my *métier*.[6] But some of the men have accused *le sale
nègre*[7]—behind my back—of stealing wood and there is already in the eyes of

6. French for "occupation" or "profession."
7. French slur for "the dirty Negro."

some of them that peculiar, intent, paranoiac malevolence which one some-times surprises in the eyes of American white men when, out walking with their Sunday girl, they see a Negro male approach.

There is a dreadful abyss between the streets of this village and the streets of the city in which I was born, between the children who shout *Neger!* today and those who shouted *Nigger!* yesterday—the abyss is experience, the Ameri-can experience. The syllable hurled behind me today expresses, above all, won-der: I am a stranger here. But I am not a stranger in America and the same syllable riding on the American air expresses the war my presence has occa-sioned in the American soul.

For this village brings home to me this fact: that there was a day, and not 15 really a very distant day, when Americans were scarcely Americans at all but discontented Europeans, facing a great unconquered continent and strolling, say, into a marketplace and seeing black men for the first time. The shock this spectacle afforded is suggested, surely, by the promptness with which they decided that these black men were not really men but cattle. It is true that the necessity on the part of the settlers of the New World of reconciling their moral assumptions with the fact—and the necessity—of slavery enhanced immensely the charm of this idea, and it is also true that this idea expresses, with a truly American bluntness, the attitude which to varying extents all masters have had toward all slaves.

But between all former slaves and slave-owners and the drama which begins for Americans over three hundred years ago at Jamestown,[8] there are at least two differences to be observed. The American Negro slave could not suppose, for one thing, as slaves in past epochs had supposed and often done, that he would ever be able to wrest the power from his master's hands. This was a sup-position which the modern era, which was to bring about such vast changes in the aims and dimensions of power, put to death; it only begins, in unprece-dented fashion, and with dreadful implications, to be resurrected today. But even had this supposition persisted with undiminished force, the American Negro slave could not have used it to lend his condition dignity, for the reason that this supposition rests on another: that the slave in exile yet remains related to his past, has some means—if only in memory—of revering and sustaining the forms of his former life, is able, in short, to maintain his identity.

This was not the case with the American Negro slave. He is unique among the black men of the world in that his past was taken from him, almost liter-ally, at one blow. One wonders what on earth the first slave found to say to the first dark child he bore. I am told that there are Haitians able to trace their ancestry back to African kings, but any American Negro wishing to go back so far will find his journey through time abruptly arrested by the signature on the bill of sale which served as the entrance paper for his ancestor. At the time— to say nothing of the circumstances—of the enslavement of the captive black man who was to become the American Negro, there was not the remotest pos-sibility that he would ever take power from his master's hands. There was no

8. Founded in 1607, the first lasting English settlement in North America.

reason to suppose that his situation would ever change, nor was there, shortly, anything to indicate that his situation had ever been different. It was his necessity, in the words of E. Franklin Frazier,[9] to find a "motive for living under American culture or die." The identity of the American Negro comes out of this extreme situation, and the evolution of this identity was a source of the most intolerable anxiety in the minds and the lives of his masters.

For the history of the American Negro is unique also in this: that the question of his humanity, and of his rights therefore as a human being, became a burning one for several generations of Americans, so burning a question that it ultimately became one of those used to divide the nation. It is out of this argument that the venom of the epithet *Nigger!* is derived. It is an argument which Europe has never had, and hence Europe quite sincerely fails to understand how or why the argument arose in the first place, why its effects are frequently disastrous and always so unpredictable, why it refuses until today to be entirely settled. Europe's black possessions remained—and do remain—in Europe's colonies, at which remove they represented no threat whatever to European identity. If they posed any problem at all for the European conscience it was a problem which remained comfortingly abstract: in effect, the black man, as a *man* did not exist for Europe. But in America, even as a slave, he was an inescapable part of the general social fabric and no American could escape having an attitude toward him. Americans attempt until today to make an abstraction of the Negro, but the very nature of these abstractions reveals the tremendous effects the presence of the Negro has had on the American character.

When one considers the history of the Negro in America it is of the greatest importance to recognize that the moral beliefs of a person, or a people, are never really as tenuous as life—which is not moral—very often causes them to appear; these create for them a frame of reference and a necessary hope, the hope being that when life has done its worst they will be enabled to rise above themselves and to triumph over life. Life would scarcely be bearable if this hope did not exist. Again, even when the worst has been said, to betray a belief is not by any means to have put oneself beyond its power; the betrayal of a belief is not the same thing as ceasing to believe. If this were not so there would be no moral standards in the world at all. Yet one must also recognize that morality is based on ideas and that all ideas are dangerous—dangerous because ideas can only lead to action and where the action leads no man can say. And dangerous in this respect: that confronted with the impossibility of remaining faithful to one's beliefs, and the equal impossibility of becoming free of them, one can be driven to the most inhuman excesses. The ideas on which American beliefs are based are not, though Americans often seem to think so, ideas which originated in America. They came out of Europe. And the establishment of democracy on the American continent was scarcely as radical a break with the past as was the necessity, which Americans faced, of broadening this concept to include black men.

20   This was, literally, a hard necessity. It was impossible, for one thing, for Americans to abandon their beliefs, not only because these beliefs alone

9. Black sociologist (1894–1962).

seemed able to justify the sacrifices they had endured and the blood that they had spilled, but also because these beliefs afforded them their only bulwark against a moral chaos as absolute as the physical chaos of the continent it was their destiny to conquer. But in the situation in which Americans found themselves, these beliefs threatened an idea which, whether or not one likes to think so, is the very warp and woof of the heritage of the West, the idea of white supremacy.

Americans have made themselves notorious by the shrillness and the brutality with which they have insisted on this idea, but they did not invent it; and it has escaped the world's notice that those very excesses of which Americans have been guilty imply a certain, unprecedented uneasiness over the idea's life and power, if not, indeed, the idea's validity. The idea of white supremacy rests simply on the fact that white men are the creators of civilization (the present civilization, which is the only one that matters; all previous civilizations are simply "contributions" to our own) and are therefore civilization's guardians and defenders. Thus it was impossible for Americans to accept the black man as one of themselves, for to do so was to jeopardize their status as white men. But not so to accept him was to deny his human reality, his human weight and complexity, and the strain of denying the overwhelmingly undeniable forced Americans into rationalizations so fantastic that they approached the pathological.

At the root of the American Negro problem is the necessity of the American white man to find a way of living with the Negro in order to be able to live with himself. And the history of this problem can be reduced to the means used by Americans—lynch law and law, segregation and legal acceptance, terrorization and concession—either to come to terms with this necessity, or to find a way around it, or (most usually) to find a way of doing both these things at once. The resulting spectacle, at once foolish and dreadful, led someone to make the quite accurate observation that "the Negro-in-America is a form of insanity which overtakes white men."

In this long battle, a battle by no means finished, the unforeseeable effects of which will be felt by many future generations, the white man's motive was the protection of his identity; the black man was motivated by the need to establish an identity. And despite the terrorization which the Negro in America endured and endures sporadically until today, despite the cruel and totally inescapable ambivalence of his status in his country, the battle for his identity has long ago been won. He is not a visitor to the West, but a citizen there, an American; as American as the Americans who despise him, the Americans who fear him, the Americans who love him—the Americans who became less than themselves, or rose to be greater than themselves by virtue of the fact that the challenge he represented was inescapable. He is perhaps the only black man in the world whose relationship to white men is more terrible, more subtle, and more meaningful than the relationship of bitter possessed to uncertain possessors. His survival depended, and his development depends, on his ability to turn his peculiar status in the Western world to his own advantage and, it may be, to the very great advantage of that world. It remains for him to fashion out of his experience that which will give him sustenance, and a voice.

The cathedral at Chartres, I have said, says something to the people of this village which it cannot say to me; but it is important to understand that this cathedral says something to me which it cannot say to them. Perhaps they are struck by the power of the spires, the glory of the windows; but they have known God, after all, longer than I have known him, and in a different way, and I am terrified by the slippery bottomless well to be found in the crypt, down which heretics were hurled to death, and by the obscene, inescapable gargoyles jutting out of the stone and seeming to say that God and the devil can never be divorced. I doubt that the villagers think of the devil when they face a cathedral because they have never been identified with the devil. But I must accept the status which myth, if nothing else, gives me in the West before I can hope to change the myth.

25   Yet, if the American Negro has arrived at his identity by virtue of the absoluteness of his estrangement from his past, American white men still nourish the illusion that there is some means of recovering the European innocence, of returning to a state in which black men do not exist. This is one of the greatest errors Americans can make. The identity they fought so hard to protect has, by virtue of that battle, undergone a change: Americans are as unlike any other white people in the world as it is possible to be. I do not think, for example, that it is too much to suggest that the American vision of the world—which allows so little reality, generally speaking, for any of the darker forces in human life, which tends until today to paint moral issues in glaring black and white—owes a great deal to the battle waged by Americans to maintain between themselves and black men a human separation which could not be bridged. It is only now beginning to be borne in on us—very faintly, it must be admitted, very slowly, and very much against our will—that this vision of the world is dangerously inaccurate, and perfectly useless. For it protects our moral high-mindedness at the terrible expense of weakening our grasp of reality. People who shut their eyes to reality simply invite their own destruction, and anyone who insists on remaining in a state of innocence long after that innocence is dead turns himself into a monster.

The time has come to realize that the interracial drama acted out on the American continent has not only created a new black man, it has created a new white man, too. No road whatever will lead Americans back to the simplicity of this European village where white men still have the luxury of looking on me as a stranger. I am not, really, a stranger any longer for any American alive. One of the things that distinguishes Americans from other people is that no other people has ever been so deeply involved in the lives of black men, and vice versa. This fact faced, with all its implications, it can be seen that the history of the American Negro problem is not merely shameful, it is also something of an achievement. For even when the worst has been said, it must also be added that the perpetual challenge posed by this problem was always, somehow, perpetually met. It is precisely this black-white experience which may prove of indispensable value to us in the world we face today. This world is white no longer, and it will never be white again.

MLA CITATION

Baldwin, James. "Stranger in the Village." *The Norton Reader: An Anthology of Nonfiction*, edited by Melissa A. Goldthwaite et al., 16th ed., W. W. Norton, 2024, pp. 452–60.

QUESTIONS

1. James Baldwin was an American, but he lived for many years in France. Consider the role of geography in this essay. How does Baldwin use his experience in the Swiss village to comment on America?

2. Trace the use of the word "stranger" over the course of the essay. How does Baldwin's use of the word evolve as the essay develops?

3. Baldwin writes that "by means of what the white man imagines the black man to be, the black man is enabled to know who the white man is" (paragraph 12). What does Baldwin mean by this statement, and why is this insight important to his essay?

4. Of Baldwin's essay, Teju Cole in "Black Body" (pp. 461–70) observes: "The part of the essay that focuses on the Swiss village is both bemused and sorrowful. . . . But, later in the essay, when he writes about race in America, he is not at all bemused. He is angry and prophetic, writing with a hard clarity and carried along by a precipitous eloquence" (paragraph 3). Where in Baldwin's essay does this transition occur? Can you identify or annotate examples of the stylistic qualities Cole notes?

5. The cultural critic and historian Sharifa Rhodes-Pitts, as quoted by Cole, notes that one of Baldwin's characteristic techniques as a writer is to start with an experience and then, in cinematic fashion, "'zoom out to a wide view while the lens remains focused on a point in the distance'" (paragraph 9). Annotate moments in Baldwin's essay that demonstrate this technique. Then apply it in a project or essay of your own: Narrate a lived experience and then "zoom out" to view it in a wider social, cultural, or historical context.

TEJU COLE
Black Body

T HEN THE BUS began driving into clouds, and between one cloud and the next we caught glimpses of the town below. It was suppertime and the town was a constellation of yellow points. We arrived thirty minutes after leaving that town, which was called Leuk. The train to Leuk had come in from Visp, the train from Visp had come from Bern, and the train before that was from Zürich, from which I had started out in the afternoon. Three trains, a bus, and a short stroll, all of it through beautiful country, and then we reached

First published in the New Yorker *(2014) as "Black Body: Rereading James Baldwin's 'Stranger in the Village.'" Reprinted in Teju Cole's collection* Known and Strange Things *(2016).*

Leukerbad, Switzerland.

Leukerbad[1] in darkness. So Leukerbad, not far in terms of absolute distance, was not all that easy to get to. August 2, 2014: it was James Baldwin's birthday. Were he alive, he would be turning ninety. He is one of those people just on the cusp of escaping the contemporary and slipping into the historical—John Coltrane would have turned eighty-eight in the same year; Martin Luther King, Jr.,[2] would have turned eighty-five—people who could still be with us but who feel, at times, very far away, as though they lived centuries ago.

James Baldwin left Paris and came to Leukerbad for the first time in 1951. His lover Lucien Happersberger's family had a chalet in a village up in the mountains. And so Baldwin, who was depressed and distracted at the time, went, and the village (which is also called Loèche-les-Bains) proved to be a refuge for him. His first trip was in the summer, and lasted two weeks. Then he returned, to his own surprise, for two more winters. His first novel, *Go Tell It on the Mountain*, found its final form here. He had struggled with the book for eight years, and he finally finished it in this unlikely retreat. He wrote something else, too, an essay called "Stranger in the Village"; it was this essay, even more than the novel, that brought me to Leukerbad.

"Stranger in the Village" first appeared in *Harper's Magazine* in 1953, and then in the essay collection *Notes of a Native Son* in 1955. It recounts the expe-

1. Swiss town about which James Baldwin writes in "Stranger in the Village"; see pp. 452–60.
2. Coltrane (1926–1967), American jazz saxophonist; King (1929–1968), American civil rights leader.

rience of being black in an all-white village. It begins with a sense of an extreme journey, like Charles Darwin's in the Galápagos or Tété-Michel Kpomassie's in Greenland.[3] But then it opens out into other concerns and into a different voice, swiveling to look at the American racial situation in the 1950s. The part of the essay that focuses on the Swiss village is both bemused and sorrowful. Baldwin is alert to the absurdity of being a writer from New York who is considered in some way inferior by Swiss villagers, many of whom have never traveled. But, later in the essay, when he writes about race in America, he is not at all bemused. He is angry and prophetic, writing with a hard clarity and carried along by a precipitous eloquence.

I took a room at the Hotel Mercure Bristol the night I arrived. I opened the windows to a dark view in which nothing was visible, but I knew that in the darkness loomed the Daubenhorn mountain. I ran a hot bath and lay neck-deep in the water with my old paperback copy of *Notes of a Native Son*. The tinny sound from my laptop was Bessie Smith singing "I'm Wild About That Thing," a filthy blues number and a masterpiece of plausible deniability: "Don't hold it, baby, when I cry / Give me every bit of it, else I'll die." She could be singing about a trombone. And it was there in the bath, with his words and her voice, that I had my body-double moment: here I was in Leukerbad, with Bessie Smith singing across the years from 1929; and I am black like him; and I am slender; and have a gap in my front teeth; and am not especially tall (no, write it: short); and am cool on the page and animated in person, except when it is the other way around; and I was once a fervid teenage preacher (Baldwin: "Nothing that has happened to me since equals the power and the glory that I sometimes felt when, in the middle of a sermon, I knew that I was somehow, by some miracle, really carrying, as they said, 'the Word'—when the church and I were one"); and I, too, left the church; and I call New York home even when not living there; and feel myself in all places, from New York City to rural Switzerland, the custodian of a black body, and have to find the language for all of what that means to me and to the people who look at me. The ancestor had briefly taken possession of the descendant. It was a moment of identification. In that Swiss village in the days that followed, that moment guided me.

"From all available evidence no black man had ever set foot in this tiny Swiss village before I came," Baldwin wrote. But the village has grown considerably since his visits, more than sixty years ago. They've seen blacks now; I wasn't a remarkable sight. There were a few glances at the hotel when I was checking in, and in the fine restaurant just up the road; there are always glances. There are glances in Zürich, where I spent the summer, and there are glances in New York City, which has been my home for fourteen years. There are glances all over Europe and in India, and anywhere I go outside Africa. The test is how long the glances last, whether they become stares, with what intent they occur,

3. Darwin (1809–1882), an English naturalist, visited the Galápagos Islands during the second expeditionary voyage of the HMS *Beagle* (1831–36); Kpomassie (b. 1941), born in Togo, spent more than a decade working his way from Africa, through Europe, to Greenland.

whether they contain any degree of hostility or mockery, and to what extent connections, money, or mode of dress shield me in these situations. To be a stranger is to be looked at, but to be black is to be looked at especially. ("The children shout *Neger! Neger!* as I walk along the streets.") Leukerbad has changed, but in which way? There were, in fact, no bands of children on the street, and few children anywhere at all. Presumably the children of Leukerbad, like children the world over, were indoors, frowning over computer games, checking *Facebook*, or watching music videos. Perhaps some of the older folks I saw in the streets were once the very children who had been so surprised by the sight of Baldwin, and about whom, in the essay, he struggles to take a reasonable tone: "In all of this, in which it must be conceded that there was the charm of genuine wonder and in which there was certainly no element of intentional unkindness, there was yet no suggestion that I was human: I was simply a living wonder." But now the children or grandchildren of those children are connected to the world in a different way. Maybe some xenophobia or racism is part of their lives, but part of their lives, too, are Beyoncé, Drake, and Meek Mill, the music I hear pulsing from Swiss clubs on Friday nights.

Baldwin had to bring his records with him in the fifties, like a secret stash of medicine, and he had to haul his phonograph up to Leukerbad, so that the sound of the American blues could keep him connected to a Harlem[4] of the spirit. I listened to some of the same music while I was there, as a way of being with him: Bessie Smith singing "I Need a Little Sugar in My Bowl" ("I need a little sugar in my bowl / I need a little hot dog on my roll"), Fats Waller singing "Your Feet's Too Big." I listened to my own playlist as well: Bettye Swann, Billie Holiday, Jean Wells, *Coltrane Plays the Blues*, the Physics, Childish Gambino. The music you travel with helps you to create your own internal weather. But the world participates, too: when I sat down to lunch at the Römerhof restaurant one afternoon—that day, all the customers and staff were white—the music playing overhead was Whitney Houston's "I Wanna Dance with Somebody." History is now and black America.

At dinner, at a pizzeria, a table of British tourists stared at me. But the waitress was part black, and at the hotel one of the staff members at the spa was an older black man. "People are trapped in history, and history is trapped in them," Baldwin wrote. But it is also true that the little pieces of history move around at tremendous speed, settling with a not-always-clear logic, and rarely settling for long. And perhaps more interesting than my not being the only black person in the village is the plain fact that many of the other people I saw were also foreigners. This was the biggest change of all. If, back then, the village had a pious and convalescent air about it, the feel of "a lesser Lourdes," it is much busier now, packed with visitors from other parts of Switzerland, and from Germany, France, Italy, and all over Europe, Asia, and the Americas. It has become the most popular thermal resort in the Alps. The municipal baths are full. There are hotels on every street, at every price point, and there are

---

4. Neighborhood in New York City and a historical center of Black culture.

restaurants and luxury-goods shops. If you wish to buy an eye-wateringly costly watch at 4,600 feet above sea level, it is now possible to do so.

The better hotels have their own thermal pools. At the Hotel Mercure Bristol, I took an elevator down to the spa and sat in the dry sauna. A few minutes later, I slipped into the pool and floated outside in the warm water. Others were there, but not many. A light rain fell. We were ringed by mountains and held in the immortal blue.

In her brilliant *Harlem Is Nowhere*, Sharifa Rhodes-Pitts writes, "In almost every essay James Baldwin wrote about Harlem, there is a moment when he commits a literary sleight-of-hand so particular that, if he'd been an athlete, sportscasters would have codified the maneuver and named it 'the Jimmy.' I think of it in cinematic terms, because its effect reminds me of a technique wherein camera operators pan out by starting with a light shot and then zoom out to a wide view while the lens remains focused on a point in the distance." This move Rhodes-Pitts describes, this sudden widening of focus, is present even in his essays that are not about Harlem. In "Stranger in the Village," there's a passage about seven pages in where one can feel the rhetoric revving up, as Baldwin prepares to leave behind the calm, fabular atmosphere of the opening section. Of the villagers, he writes:

> These people cannot be, from the point of view of power, strangers anywhere in the world; they have made the modern world, in effect, even if they do not know it. The most illiterate among them is related, in a way I am not, to Dante, Shakespeare, Michelangelo, Aeschylus, Da Vinci, Rembrandt, and Racine; the cathedral at Chartres says something to them which it cannot say to me, as indeed would New York's Empire State Building, should anyone here ever see it. Out of their hymns and dances come Beethoven and Bach. Go back a few centuries and they are in their full glory—but I am in Africa, watching the conquerors arrive.

What is this list about? Does it truly bother Baldwin that the people of Leukerbad are related, through some faint familiarity, to Chartres? That some distant genetic thread links them to the Beethoven string quartets? After all, as he argues later in the essay, no one can deny the impact "the presence of the Negro has had on the American character." He understands the truth and the art in Bessie Smith's work. He does not, and cannot—I want to believe—rate the blues below Bach. But there was a certain narrowness in received ideas of black culture in the 1950s. In the time since then, there has been enough black cultural achievement from which to compile an all-star team: there's been Coltrane and Monk and Miles, and Ella and Billie and Aretha. Toni Morrison, Wole Soyinka, and Derek Walcott happened, as have Audre Lorde, and Chinua Achebe, and Bob Marley. The body was not abandoned for the mind's sake: Alvin Ailey, Arthur Ashe, and Michael Jordan happened, too. The source of jazz and the blues also gave the world hip-hop, Afrobeat, dancehall, and house. And, yes, by the time James Baldwin died, in 1987, he, too, was recognized as an all-star.

Thinking further about the cathedral at Chartres, about the greatness of that achievement and about how, in his view, it included blacks only in the negative, as

10

devils, Baldwin writes that "the American Negro has arrived at his identity by virtue of the absoluteness of his estrangement from his past." But the distant African past has also become much more available than it was in 1953. It would not occur to me to think that, centuries ago, I was "in Africa, watching the conquerors arrive." But I suspect that for Baldwin this is, in part, a piece of oratory, a grim cadence on which to end a paragraph. In "A Question of Identity" (another essay collected in Notes of a Native Son), he writes, "The truth about that past is not that it is too brief, or too superficial, but only that we, having turned our faces so resolutely away from it, have never demanded from it what it has to give." The fourteenth-century court artists of Ife[5] made bronze sculptures using a complicated casting process lost to Europe since antiquity, and which was not rediscovered there until the Renaissance. Ife sculptures are equal to the works of Ghiberti or Donatello. From their precision and formal sumptuousness we can extrapolate the contours of a great monarchy, a network of sophisticated ateliers, and a cosmopolitan world of trade and knowledge. And it was not only Ife. All of West Africa was a cultural ferment. From the egalitarian government of the Igbo to the goldwork of the Ashanti courts, the brass sculpture of Benin, the military achievement of the Mandinka Empire[6] and the musical virtuosi who praised those war heroes, this was a region of the world too deeply invested in art and life to simply be reduced to a caricature of "watching the conquerors arrive." We know better now. We know it with a stack of corroborating scholarship and we know it implicitly, so that even making a list of the accomplishments feels faintly tedious, and is helpful mainly as a counter to Eurocentrism.

There's no world in which I would surrender the intimidating beauty of Yoruba-language poetry for, say, Shakespeare's sonnets, or one in which I'd prefer chamber orchestras playing baroque music to the koras[7] of Mali. I'm happy to own all of it. This carefree confidence is, in part, the gift of time. It is a dividend of the struggle of people from earlier generations. I feel little alienation in museums, full though they are of other people's ancestors. But this question of filiation tormented Baldwin. He was sensitive to what was great in world art, and sensitive to his own sense of exclusion from it. He made a similar list in the title essay of Notes of a Native Son (one begins to feel that lists like this had been flung at him during arguments): "In some subtle way, in a really profound way, I brought to Shakespeare, Bach, Rembrandt, to the stones of Paris, to the Cathedral at Chartres, and the Empire State Building a special attitude. These were not really my creations, they did not contain my history; I might search them in vain forever for any reflection of myself. I was an interloper; this was

5. Yoruba city that by the eleventh century was the capital of an extensive kingdom.

6. Igbo, a people inhabiting southeastern Nigeria; Ashanti, a people inhabiting southern Ghana and a West African empire originating in the late seventeenth century; Benin, a West African kingdom from the thirteenth through the nineteenth centuries; Mandinka Empire, also Wassoulou Empire, created through military conquest in the late nineteenth century.

7. Twenty-one-stringed musical instruments.

not my heritage." The lines throb with sadness. What he loves does not love him in return.

This is where I part ways with Baldwin. I disagree not with his particular sorrow but with the self-abnegation that pinned him to it. Bach, so profoundly human, is my heritage. I am not an interloper when I look at a Rembrandt portrait. I care for them more than some white people do, just as some white people care more for aspects of African art than I do. I can oppose white supremacy and still rejoice in Gothic architecture. In this, I stand with Ralph Ellison:[8] "The values of my own people are neither 'white' nor 'black,' they are American. Nor can I see how they could be anything else, since we are people who are involved in the texture of the American experience." And yet I (born in the United States more than half a century after Baldwin) continue to understand, because I have experienced in my own body the undimmed fury he felt about racism. In his writing there is a hunger for life, for all of it, and a strong wish to not be accounted nothing (a mere nigger, a mere *neger*) when he knows himself to be so much. And this "so much" is neither a matter of ego about his writing nor an anxiety about his fame in New York or in Paris. It is about the incontestable fundamentals of a person: pleasure, sorrow, love, humor, and grief, and the complexity of the interior landscape that sustains those feelings. Baldwin was astonished that anyone anywhere should question these fundamentals—thereby burdening him with the supreme waste of time that is racism—let alone so many people in so many places. This unflagging ability to be shocked rises like steam off his written pages. "The rage of the disesteemed is personally fruitless," he writes, "but it is also absolutely inevitable."

Leukerbad gave Baldwin a way to think about white supremacy[9] from its first principles. It was as though he found it in its simplest form there. The men who suggested that he learn to ski so that they might mock him, the villagers who accused him behind his back of being a firewood thief, the ones who wished to touch his hair and suggested that he grow it out and make himself a winter coat, and the children who, "having been taught that the devil is a black man, scream[ed] in genuine anguish" as he approached: Baldwin saw these as prototypes (preserved like coelacanths) of attitudes that had evolved into the more intimate, intricate, familiar, and obscene American forms of white supremacy that he already knew so well.

It is a beautiful village. I liked the mountain air. But when I returned to my room from the thermal baths, or from strolling in the streets with my camera, I read the news online. There I found an unending sequence of crises: in the Middle East, in Africa, in Russia, and everywhere else, really. Pain was general. But within that larger distress was a set of linked stories, and thinking about "Stranger in the Village," thinking with its help, was like injecting a contrast dye into my encounter with the news. The American police continued

8. American novelist (1914–1994), author of *Invisible Man* (1952).

9. Ideology asserting the superiority of white people that has its origins in seventeenth-century European race theory and anthropology.

shooting unarmed black men, or killing them in other ways. The protests that followed, in black communities, were countered with violence by a police force that is becoming indistinguishable from an invading army. People began to see a connection between the various events: the shootings, the fatal choke hold,[10] the stories of who was not given lifesaving medication. And black communities were flooded with outrage and grief.

15   In all of this, a smaller, much less significant story (but one that nevertheless signified), caught my attention. The mayor of New York and his police chief have a public-policy obsession with cleaning, with cleansing, and they decided that arresting members of the dance troupes that perform in moving subway cars was one of the ways to clean up the city.[11] I read the excuses for this becoming a priority: some people feared being seriously injured by an errant kick (it has not happened, but they sure feared it), some people considered the dancing a nuisance, some policymakers believed that going after misdemeanors is a way of preempting major crimes. And so, to combat this menace of dancers, the police moved in. They began chasing, and harassing, and handcuffing. The "problem" was dancers, and the dancers were, for the most part, black boys. The newspapers took the same tone as the government: a sniffy dismissal of the performers. And yet these same dancers are a bright spark in the day, a moment of unregulated beauty, artists with talents unimaginable to their audience. What kind of thinking would consider their abolition an improvement in city life? No one considers Halloween trick-or-treaters a public menace. There's no law enforcement against people selling Girl Scout cookies or against Jehovah's Witnesses.[12] But the black body comes prejudged, and as a result it is placed in needless jeopardy. To be black is to bear the brunt of selective enforcement of the law, and to inhabit a psychic unsteadiness in which there is no guarantee of personal safety. You are a black body first, before you are a kid walking down the street or a Harvard professor who has misplaced his keys.[13]

          William Hazlitt,[14] in an 1821 essay entitled "The Indian Jugglers," wrote words that I think of when I see a great athlete or dancer: "Man, thou art a wonderful animal, and thy ways past finding out! Thou canst do strange things, but thou turnest them to little account!—To conceive of this effort of extraor-

10. In 2014, Eric Garner, a Black man, died after being subjected to a choke hold by a New York City police officer.

11. Bill de Blasio (b. 1961), mayor of New York City (2014–21); William Bratton (b. 1947), New York City police commissioner (1994–96 and 2014–16). Bratton embraced the "broken windows theory" of policing, which emphasizes the aggressive policing of minor crimes as a way of preventing more serious crime.

12. Girl Scouts, an organization that has traditionally raised money by selling cookies door-to-door; Jehovah's Witnesses, a Christian denomination known for door-to-door evangelization.

13. In 2012, Trayvon Martin, an unarmed Black teenager, was shot by George Zimmerman, who claimed he was acting in self-defense; in 2009, Black professor Henry Louis Gates Jr. was arrested at his home in Cambridge, Massachusetts, after a neighbor called the police to report that his home was being broken into.

14. English critic and essayist (1778–1830).

dinary dexterity distracts the imagination and makes admiration breathless."
In the presence of the admirable, some are breathless not with admiration but
with rage. They object to the presence of the black body (an unarmed boy in a
street, a man buying a toy, a dancer in the subway, a bystander) as much as
they object to the presence of the black mind. And simultaneous with these
erasures is the unending collection of profit from black labor and black innovation. Throughout the culture, there are imitations of the gait, bearing, and
dress of the black body, a vampiric "everything but the burden" co-option of
black life.

Leukerbad is ringed by mountains: the Daubenhorn, the Torrenthorn, the
Rinderhorn. A high mountain pass called the Gemmi, another 2,800 feet above
the village, connects the canton of Valais with the Bernese Oberland. Through
this landscape—craggy, bare in places and verdant elsewhere, a textbook instance
of the sublime—one moves as though through a dream. The Gemmi Pass is
famous for good reason, and Goethe was once there, as were Byron, Twain, and
Picasso.[15] The pass is mentioned in a Sherlock Holmes adventure, when Holmes
crosses it on his way to the fateful meeting with Professor Moriarty at Reichen-
bach Falls.[16] There was bad weather the day I went up, rain and fog, but that was
good luck, as it meant I was alone on the trails. While there, I remembered a
story that Lucien Happersberger told about Baldwin going out on a hike in these
mountains. Baldwin had lost his footing during the ascent, and the situation was
precarious for a moment. But Happersberger, who was an experienced climber,
reached out a hand, and Baldwin was saved. It was out of this frightening
moment, this appealingly biblical moment, that Baldwin got the title for the book
he had been struggling to write: *Go Tell It on the Mountain*.

If Leukerbad was his mountain pulpit, the United States was his audience.
The remote village gave him a sharper view of what things looked like back
home. He was a stranger in Leukerbad, Baldwin wrote, but there was no possibility for blacks to be strangers in the United States, or for whites to achieve
the fantasy of an all-white America purged of blacks. This fantasy about the
disposability of black life is a constant in American history. It takes a while to
understand that this disposability continues. It takes whites a while to understand it; it takes nonblack people of color a while to understand it; and it takes
some blacks, whether they've always lived in the United States or are latecom-
ers like myself, weaned elsewhere on other struggles, a while to understand it.
American racism has many moving parts, and has had enough centuries in
which to evolve an impressive camouflage. It can hoard its malice in great stillness for a long time, all the while pretending to look the other way. Like
misogyny, it is atmospheric. You don't see it at first. But understanding comes.

15. Johann Wolfgang von Goethe (1749–1832), German poet, author, and intellectual;
Lord Byron (1788–1824), English Romantic poet; Mark Twain, pen name of Samuel
Clemens (1835–1910), American novelist, journalist, and humorist; Pablo Picasso
(1881–1973), Spanish modernist painter.
16. See the short story "The Final Problem" (1893) by Sir Arthur Conan Doyle.

"People who shut their eyes to reality simply invite their own destruction, and anyone who insists on remaining in a state of innocence long after that innocence is dead turns himself into a monster." The news of the day (old news, but raw as a fresh wound) is that black American life is disposable from the point of view of policing, sentencing, economic policy, and countless terrifying forms of disregard. There is a vivid performance of innocence, but there's no actual innocence left. The moral ledger remains so far in the negative that we can't even get started on the question of reparations. Baldwin wrote "Stranger in the Village" more than sixty years ago. Now what?

MLA CITATION

Cole, Teju. "Black Body." *The Norton Reader: An Anthology of Nonfiction*, edited by Melissa A. Goldthwaite et al., 16th ed., W. W. Norton, 2024, pp. 461–70.

QUESTIONS

1. When it was first published in the *New Yorker*, Teju Cole's essay was subtitled "Rereading James Baldwin's 'Stranger in the Village.'" How does Cole "reread" James Baldwin's classic essay "Stranger in the Village" (pp. 452–60)? How does his experience as "the custodian of a black body" (paragraph 4) compare with Baldwin's? What does Cole's engagement with Baldwin allow him to recognize or understand that he might not have otherwise?

2. Cole is troubled by Baldwin's stance toward what has traditionally been called European or Western culture, writing "This is where I part ways with Baldwin" (paragraph 12). What about Baldwin's stance troubles Cole? What stance does he adopt instead?

3. Cole's many references to music form a kind of "soundtrack" to his essay. How does he mix periods and musical genres? What role does this soundtrack play in his essay?

4. Cole ends his essay with a question: "Now what?" (paragraph 19). Why might he have chosen to conclude this way?

5. Using Cole's essay as a model, write an essay of your own in which you use an interpretation of one of the essays in this chapter of *The Norton Reader* to examine an aspect of your identity and relationship to some element of society.

8 INSIDER KNOWLEDGE

Specialists can find the most incredibly hidden things.
—ANNIE DILLARD

Michel de Montaigne, the sixteenth-century French philosopher who gave the genre of the essay its name, called his writings *essais*, meaning that they were trials or attempts, always provisional. In the tradition of Montaigne, the essay demands no special expertise from its writers and presumes none from its readers. It thus differs from such specialized forms as the research report or scientific article, which are produced by experts for experts. This is not to deny the value of specialized knowledge: Montaigne read widely and was familiar with the ways of the world, and his insights depend not just on his experience but also on the depth and breadth of his learning. Indeed, there is a particular kind of insight that is available only to experts.

The selections in this chapter, written by specialists or by journalists who rely on them, all endeavor to open to a general readership various sorts of insider knowledge and the insights, questions, and even problems arising from it. The chapter begins with a group of essays focused on science and medicine. In "Sex, Drugs, Disasters, and the Extinction of Dinosaurs," evolutionary biologist and paleontologist Stephen Jay Gould offers a lively introduction to the scientific method and its explanatory power. In "When Doctors Make Mistakes," surgeon Atul Gawande reflects on the fallibility of physicians and its implications. In "The Woman in the Photograph," journalist Rebecca Skloot ponders the ethics and economics of medical research. The cluster concludes with "On Going Viral," a wide-ranging reflection on this commonplace metaphor, by microbiologist and virologist Joseph Osmundson.

The chapter then turns to a pair of essays that explore the kind of practical knowledge acquired and honed through work. Chris Wiewiora's "This Is Tossing" explains the intricacies of tossing the perfect pizza while Mike Rose's "Blue-Collar Brilliance" is a touching rumination on the nature of intelligence and the often-unacknowledged intellectual dimensions of physical work.

In "The Secret Reason Hazing Continues," journalist Alexandra Robbins relies on extensive personal interviews and scholarly research to interrogate the persistence of hazing in Greek student life.

The chapter concludes with three essays on practice. Classicist Emily Wilson, in "A Translator's Reckoning with Women of the *Odyssey*," explains her approach to translating Homer's *Odyssey*. Art critic Philip Kennicott, in "How to View Art: Be Dead Serious about It, but Don't Expect Too Much," offers a primer on visiting museums. Essayist Rebecca Solnit offers her advice to us all in "How to Be a Writer."

As you read these selections, attend not just to their content but to how their "insider" writers communicate it. What special insights do they deliver? What "hidden things" do they illuminate? What personas do they project? What techniques do they use not just to make their knowledge accessible but to interest you and convey its import? Finally, consider the kinds of insider knowledge you possess and how you can share it with others. After all, we're all specialists in something.

STEPHEN JAY GOULD

Sex, Drugs, Disasters, and the Extinction of Dinosaurs

CIENCE, IN ITS MOST FUNDAMENTAL DEFINITION, is a fruitful mode of inquiry, not a list of enticing conclusions. The conclusions are the consequence, not the essence.

My greatest unhappiness with most popular presentations of science concerns their failure to separate fascinating claims from the methods that scientists use to establish the facts of nature. Journalists, and the public, thrive on controversial and stunning statements. But science is, basically, a way of knowing—in P. B. Medawar's[1] apt words, "the art of the soluble." If the growing corps of popular science writers would focus on *how* scientists develop and defend those fascinating claims, they would make their greatest possible contribution to public understanding.

Consider three ideas, proposed in perfect seriousness to explain that greatest of all titillating puzzles—the extinction of dinosaurs. Since these three notions invoke the primally fascinating themes of our culture—sex, drugs, and violence—they surely reside in the category of fascinating claims. I want to show why two of them rank as silly speculation, while the other represents science at its grandest and most useful.

Science works with testable proposals. If, after much compilation and scrutiny of data, new information continues to affirm a hypothesis, we may accept it provisionally and gain confidence as further evidence mounts. We can never be completely sure that a hypothesis is right, though we may be able to show with confidence that it is wrong. The best scientific hypotheses are also generous and expansive: they suggest extensions and implications that enlighten related, and even far distant, subjects. Simply consider how the idea of evolution has influenced virtually every intellectual field.

5   Useless speculation, on the other hand, is restrictive. It generates no testable hypothesis, and offers no way to obtain potentially refuting evidence. Please note that I am not speaking of truth or falsity. The speculation may

---

Originally published in Discover *(1984), a monthly magazine reporting on "science, medicine, technology, and the world around us"; reprinted in Stephen Jay Gould's collection of essays* The Flamingo's Smile: Reflections in Natural History *(1985).*

1. British biologist and pioneer in the science of organ transplants (1915–1987).

well be true; still, if it provides, in principle, no material for affirmation or rejection, we can make nothing of it. It must simply stand forever as an intriguing idea. Useless speculation turns in on itself and leads nowhere; good science, containing both seeds for its potential refutation and implications for more and different testable knowledge, reaches out. But, enough preaching. Let's move on to dinosaurs, and the three proposals for their extinction.

1. Sex: Testes function only in a narrow range of temperature (those of mammals hang externally in a scrotal sac because internal body temperatures are too high for their proper function). A worldwide rise in temperature at the close of the Cretaceous period caused the testes of dinosaurs to stop functioning and led to their extinction by sterilization of males.

2. Drugs: Angiosperms (flowering plants) first evolved toward the end of the dinosaurs' reign. Many of these plants contain psychoactive agents, avoided by mammals today as a result of their bitter taste. Dinosaurs had neither means to taste the bitterness nor livers effective enough to detoxify the substances. They died of massive overdoses.

3. Disasters: A large comet or asteroid struck the earth some 65 million years ago, lofting a cloud of dust into the sky and blocking sunlight, thereby suppressing photosynthesis and so drastically lowering world temperatures that dinosaurs and hosts of other creatures became extinct.

Before analyzing these three tantalizing statements, we must establish a basic ground rule often violated in proposals for the dinosaurs' demise. *There is no separate problem of the extinction of dinosaurs.* Too often we divorce specific events from their wider contexts and systems of cause and effect. The fundamental fact of dinosaur extinction is its synchrony with the demise of so many other groups across a wide range of habitats, from terrestrial to marine.

The history of life has been punctuated by brief episodes of mass extinction. A recent analysis by University of Chicago paleontologists Jack Sepkoski and Dave Raup, based on the best and most exhaustive tabulation of data ever assembled, shows clearly that five episodes of mass dying stand well above the "background" extinctions of normal times (when we consider all mass extinctions, large and small, they seem to fall in a regular 26-million-year cycle. . . .). The Cretaceous debacle, occurring 65 million years ago and separating the Mesozoic and Cenozoic eras[2] of our geological time scale, ranks prominently among the five. Nearly all the marine plankton (single-celled floating creatures) died with geological suddenness; among marine invertebrates, nearly 15 percent of all families perished, including many previously dominant groups, especially the ammonites (relatives of squids in coiled shells). On land, the dinosaurs disappeared after more than 100 million years of unchallenged domination.

In this context, speculations limited to dinosaurs alone ignore the larger phenomenon. We need a coordinated explanation for a system of events that includes the extinction of dinosaurs as one component. Thus it makes little

---

2. Mesozoic era, 252.5 to 66 million years ago; Cenozoic era, 65.5 million years ago to the present day.

sense, though it may fuel our desire to view mammals as inevitable inheritors of the earth, to guess that dinosaurs died because small mammals ate their eggs (a perennial favorite among untestable speculations). It seems most unlikely that some disaster peculiar to dinosaurs befell these massive beasts—and that the debacle happened to strike just when one of history's five great dyings had enveloped the earth for completely different reasons.

The testicular theory, an old favorite from the 1940s, had its root in an interesting and thoroughly respectable study of temperature tolerances in the American alligator, published in the staid *Bulletin of the American Museum of Natural History* in 1946 by three experts on living and fossil reptiles—E. H. Colbert, my own first teacher in paleontology; R. B. Cowles; and C. M. Bogert.

The first sentence of their summary reveals a purpose beyond alligators: "This report describes an attempt to infer the reactions of extinct reptiles, especially the dinosaurs, to high temperatures as based upon reactions observed in the modern alligator." They studied, by rectal thermometry, the body temperatures of alligators under changing conditions of heating and cooling. (Well, let's face it, you wouldn't want to try sticking a thermometer under a 'gator's tongue.) The predictions under test go way back to an old theory first stated by Galileo[3] in the 1630s—the unequal scaling of surfaces and volumes. As an animal, or any object, grows (provided its shape doesn't change), surface areas must increase more slowly than volumes—since surfaces get larger as length squared, while volumes increase much more rapidly, as length cubed. Therefore, small animals have high ratios of surface to volume, while large animals cover themselves with relatively little surface.

10   Among cold-blooded animals lacking any physiological mechanism for keeping their temperatures constant, small creatures have a hell of a time keeping warm—because they lose so much heat through their relatively large surfaces. On the other hand, large animals, with their relatively small surfaces, may lose heat so slowly that, once warm, they may maintain effectively constant temperatures against ordinary fluctuations of climate. (In fact, the resolution of the "hot-blooded dinosaur" controversy that burned so brightly a few years back may simply be that, while large dinosaurs possessed no physiological mechanism for constant temperature, and were not therefore warm-blooded in the technical sense, their large size and relatively small surface area kept them warm.)

Colbert, Cowles, and Bogert compared the warming rates of small and large alligators. As predicted, the small fellows heated up (and cooled down) more quickly. When exposed to a warm sun, a tiny 50-gram (1.76-ounce) alligator heated up one degree Celsius every minute and a half, while a large alligator, 260 times bigger at 13,000 grams (28.7 pounds), took seven and a half minutes to gain a degree. Extrapolating up to an adult 10-ton dinosaur, they concluded that a one-degree rise in body temperature would take eighty-six hours. If large animals absorb heat so slowly (through their relatively small surfaces), they will also be unable to shed any excess heat gained when temperatures rise above a favorable level.

3. Galileo Galilei (1564–1642), Italian astronomer and mathematician.

The authors then guessed that large dinosaurs lived at or near their optimum temperatures; Cowles suggested that a rise in global temperatures just before the Cretaceous extinction caused the dinosaurs to heat up beyond their optimal tolerance—and, being so large, they couldn't shed the unwanted heat. (In a most unusual statement within a scientific paper, Colbert and Bogert then explicitly disavowed this speculative extension of their empirical work on alligators.) Cowles conceded that this excess heat probably wasn't enough to kill or even to enervate the great beasts, but since testes often function only within a narrow range of temperature, he proposed that this global rise might have sterilized all the males, causing extinction by natural contraception.

The overdose theory has recently been supported by UCLA psychiatrist Ronald K. Siegel. Siegel has gathered, he claims, more than 2,000 records of animals who, when given access, administer various drugs to themselves— from a mere swig of alcohol to massive doses of the big H. Elephants will swill the equivalent of twenty beers at a time, but do not like alcohol in concentrations greater than 7 percent. In a silly bit of anthropocentric speculation, Siegel states that "elephants drink, perhaps, to forget . . . the anxiety produced by shrinking rangeland and the competition for food."

Since fertile imaginations can apply almost any hot idea to the extinction of dinosaurs, Siegel found a way. Flowering plants did not evolve until late in the dinosaurs' reign. These plants also produced an array of aromatic, amino-acid-based alkaloids—the major group of psychoactive agents. Most mammals are "smart" enough to avoid these potential poisons. The alkaloids simply don't taste good (they are bitter); in any case, we mammals have livers happily supplied with the capacity to detoxify them. But, Siegel speculates, perhaps dinosaurs could neither taste the bitterness nor detoxify the substances once ingested. He recently told members of the American Psychological Association: "I'm not suggesting that all dinosaurs OD'd on plant drugs, but it certainly was a factor." He also argued that death by overdose may help explain why so many dinosaur fossils are found in contorted positions. (Do not go gentle into that good night.)[4]

Extraterrestrial catastrophes have long pedigrees in the popular literature of extinction, but the subject exploded again in 1979, after a long lull, when the father-son, physicist-geologist team of Luis and Walter Alvarez proposed that an asteroid, some 10 km in diameter, struck the earth 65 million years ago (comets, rather than asteroids, have since gained favor. . . . Good science is self-corrective).

The force of such a collision would be immense, greater by far than the megatonnage of all the world's nuclear weapons. . . . In trying to reconstruct a scenario that would explain the simultaneous dying of dinosaurs on land and so many creatures in the sea, the Alvarezes proposed that a gigantic dust cloud, generated by particles blown aloft in the impact, would so darken the earth that photosynthesis would cease and temperatures drop precipitously. (Rage, rage against the dying of the light.)[5] The single-celled photosynthetic

4. First line of a villanelle (1951) by Welsh poet Dylan Thomas (1914–1953).
5. Third line of Thomas's villanelle.

oceanic plankton, with life cycles measured in weeks, would perish outright, but land plants might survive through the dormancy of their seeds (land plants were not much affected by the Cretaceous extinction, and any adequate theory must account for the curious pattern of differential survival). Dinosaurs would die by starvation and freezing; small, warm-blooded mammals, with more modest requirements for food and better regulation of body temperature, would squeak through. "Let the bastards freeze in the dark," as bumper stickers of our chauvinistic neighbors in sunbelt states proclaimed several years ago during the Northeast's winter oil crisis.

All three theories, testicular malfunction, psychoactive overdosing, and asteroidal zapping, grab our attention mightily. As pure phenomenology, they rank about equally high on any hit parade of primal fascination. Yet one represents expansive science, the others restrictive and untestable speculation. The proper criterion lies in evidence and methodology; we must probe behind the superficial fascination of particular claims.

How could we possibly decide whether the hypothesis of testicular frying is right or wrong? We would have to know things that the fossil record cannot provide. What temperatures were optimal for dinosaurs? Could they avoid the absorption of excess heat by staying in the shade, or in caves? At what temperatures did their testicles cease to function? Were late Cretaceous climates ever warm enough to drive the internal temperatures of dinosaurs close to this ceiling? Testicles simply don't fossilize, and how could we infer their temperature tolerances even if they did? In short, Cowles's hypothesis is only an intriguing speculation leading nowhere. The most damning statement against it appeared right in the conclusion of Colbert, Cowles, and Bogert's paper, when they admitted: "It is difficult to advance any definite arguments against this hypothesis." My statement may seem paradoxical—isn't a hypothesis really good if you can't devise any arguments against it? Quite the contrary. It is simply untestable and unusable.[6]

Siegel's overdosing has even less going for it. At least Cowles extrapolated his conclusion from some good data on alligators. And he didn't completely violate the primary guideline of siting dinosaur extinction in the context of a general mass dying—for rise in temperature could be the root cause of a general catastrophe, zapping dinosaurs by testicular malfunction and different groups for other reasons. But Siegel's speculation cannot touch the extinction of ammonites or oceanic plankton (diatoms make their own food with good sweet sunlight; they don't OD on the chemicals of terrestrial plants). It is simply a gratuitous, attention-grabbing guess. It cannot be tested, for how can we know what dinosaurs tasted and what their livers could do? Livers don't fossilize any better than testicles.

20   The hypothesis doesn't even make any sense in its own context. Angiosperms were in full flower ten million years before dinosaurs went the way of all flesh.[7]

6. Principle of falsifiability, most notably articulated by the philosopher Karl Popper (1902–1994).

7. Quotation from 3 Kings 2:2 (Douay-Rheims Bible) and title of a novel by Samuel Butler (1835–1902).

Why did it take so long? As for the pains of a chemical death recorded in contortions of fossils, I regret to say (or rather I'm pleased to note for the dinosaurs' sake) that Siegel's knowledge of geology must be a bit deficient: muscles contract after death and geological strata rise and fall with motions of the earth's crust after burial—more than enough reason to distort a fossil's pristine appearance.

The impact story, on the other hand, has a sound basis in evidence. It can be tested, extended, refined and, if wrong, disproved. The Alvarezes did not just construct an arresting guess for public consumption. They proposed their hypothesis after laborious geochemical studies with Frank Asaro and Helen Michael had revealed a massive increase of iridium in rocks deposited right at the time of extinction. Iridium, a rare metal of the platinum group, is virtually absent from indigenous rocks of the earth's crust; most of our iridium arrives on extraterrestrial objects that strike the earth.

The Alvarez hypothesis bore immediate fruit. Based originally on evidence from two European localities, it led geochemists throughout the world to examine other sediments of the same age. They found abnormally high amounts of iridium everywhere—from continental rocks of the western United States to deep sea cores from the South Atlantic.

Cowles proposed his testicular hypothesis in the mid-1940s. Where has it gone since then? Absolutely nowhere, because scientists can do nothing with it. The hypothesis must stand as a curious appendage to a solid study of alligators. Siegel's overdose scenario will also win a few press notices and fade into oblivion. The Alvarezes' asteroid falls into a different category altogether, and much of the popular commentary has missed this essential distinction by focusing on the impact and its attendant results, and forgetting what really matters to a scientist—the iridium. If you talk just about asteroids, dust, and darkness, you tell stories no better, and no more entertaining than fried testicles or terminal trips. It is the iridium—the source of testable evidence—that counts and forges the crucial distinction between speculation and science.

The proof, to twist a phrase, lies in the doing. Cowles's hypothesis has generated nothing in thirty-five years. Since its proposal in 1979, the Alvarez hypothesis has spawned hundreds of studies, a major conference, and attendant publications. Geologists are fired up. They are looking for iridium at all other extinction boundaries. Every week exposes a new wrinkle in the scientific press. Further evidence that the Cretaceous iridium represents extraterrestrial impact and not indigenous volcanism continues to accumulate. As I revise this essay in November 1984 (this paragraph will be out of date when the book is published), new data include chemical "signatures" of other isotopes indicating unearthly provenance, glass spherules of a size and sort produced by impact and not by volcanic eruptions, and high-pressure varieties of silica formed (so far as we know) only under the tremendous shock of impact.

My point is simply this: Whatever the eventual outcome (I suspect it will   25 be positive), the Alvarez hypothesis is exciting, fruitful science because it generates tests, provides us with things to do, and expands outward. We are having fun, battling back and forth, moving toward a resolution, and extending the hypothesis beyond its original scope. . . .

As just one example of the unexpected, distant cross-fertilization that good science engenders, the Alvarez hypothesis made a major contribution to a theme that has riveted public attention in the past few months—so-called nuclear winter. . . . In a speech delivered in April 1982, Luis Alvarez calculated the energy that a ten-kilometer asteroid would release on impact. He compared such an explosion with a full nuclear exchange and implied that all-out atomic war might unleash similar consequences.

This theme of impact leading to massive dust clouds and falling temperatures formed an important input to the decision of Carl Sagan[8] and a group of colleagues to model the climatic consequences of nuclear holocaust. Full nuclear exchange would probably generate the same kind of dust cloud and darkening that may have wiped out the dinosaurs. Temperatures would drop precipitously and agriculture might become impossible. Avoidance of nuclear war is fundamentally an ethical and political imperative, but we must know the factual consequences to make firm judgments. I am heartened by a final link across disciplines and deep concerns—another criterion, by the way, of science at its best:[9] A recognition of the very phenomenon that made our evolution possible by exterminating the previously dominant dinosaurs and clearing a way for the evolution of large mammals, including us, might actually help to save us from joining those magnificent beasts in contorted poses among the strata of the earth.

MLA CITATION

Gould, Stephen Jay. "Sex, Drugs, Disasters, and the Extinction of Dinosaurs." *The Norton Reader: An Anthology of Nonfiction*, edited by Melissa A. Goldthwaite et al., 16th ed., W. W. Norton, 2024, pp. 472–78.

QUESTIONS

1. How, according to Stephen Jay Gould, does good science differ from "silly speculation" (paragraph 3)?

2. What, for Gould, distinguishes "science at its best" (paragraph 27) from merely good science?

3. Gould considers three explanations for the extinction of the dinosaurs, what he calls the "testicular theory" (paragraphs 8–12), the "overdose theory" (paragraphs 13–14), and the "asteroidal zapping" theory (paragraphs 15–16). How does his writing style communicate his attitude toward each of them?

4. Gould criticizes science journalists for focusing on science's conclusions rather than its methods. Consider, in an essay or project, the helpful and harmful effects of science journalism for the public's perception of the work of scientists.

---

8. American scientist and writer (1934–1996) who hosted and produced the popular TV series *Cosmos* (1980).

9. This quirky connection so tickles my fancy that I break my own strict rule about eliminating redundancies from these essays and end both this and the next piece with this prod to thought and action [Author's note].

ATUL GAWANDE
When Doctors Make Mistakes
I—CRASH VICTIM

A T 2 A.M. ON A CRISP FRIDAY IN WINTER, I was in sterile gloves and gown, pulling a teenage knifing victim's abdomen open, when my pager sounded. "Code Trauma, three minutes," the operating-room nurse said, reading aloud from my pager display. This meant that an ambulance would be bringing another trauma patient to the hospital momentarily, and, as the surgical resident on duty for emergencies, I would have to be present for the patient's arrival. I stepped back from the table and took off my gown. Two other surgeons were working on the knifing victim: Michael Ball, the attending (the staff surgeon in charge of the case), and David Hernandez, the chief resident (a general surgeon in his last of five years of training). Ordinarily, these two would have come later to help with the trauma, but were stuck here. Ball, a dry, imperturbable forty-two-year-old Texan, looked over to me as I headed for the door. "If you run into any trouble, you call, and one of us will peel away," he said.

I did run into trouble. In telling this story, I have had to change significant details about what happened (including the names of the participants and aspects of my role), but I have tried to stay as close to the actual events as I could while protecting the patient, myself, and the rest of the staff. The way that things go wrong in medicine is normally unseen and, consequently, often misunderstood. Mistakes do happen. We think of them as aberrant; they are anything but.

The emergency room was one floor up, and, taking the stairs two at a time, I arrived just as the emergency medical technicians wheeled in a woman who appeared to be in her thirties and to weigh more than two hundred pounds. She lay motionless on a hard orange plastic spinal board—eyes closed, skin pale, blood running out of her nose. A nurse directed the crew into Trauma Bay 1, an examination room outfitted like an O.R., with green tiles on the wall, monitoring devices, and space for portable X-ray equipment. We lifted her onto the bed and then went to work. One nurse began cutting off the woman's clothes. Another took vital signs. A third inserted a large-bore intravenous line into her right arm. A surgical intern put a Foley catheter[1] into her bladder. The emergency-medicine attending was Samuel Johns, a gaunt, Ichabod Crane–like[2] man in his fifties. He was standing to one side with his arms crossed, observing, which was a sign that I could go ahead and take charge.

First published in the New Yorker *(1999), a weekly magazine of "reportage, commentary, criticism, essays, fiction, satire, cartoons, and poetry," and then in Atul Gawande's first book* Complications: A Surgeon's Notes on an Imperfect Science *(2002). Gawande is a surgeon at Boston's Brigham and Women's Hospital.*

1. Thin tube inserted into the bladder to drain urine.
2. Fictional hero of Washington Irving's "Legend of Sleepy Hollow" (1802) who was described as having a lanky frame.

If you're in a hospital, most of the "moment to moment" doctoring you get is from residents—physicians receiving specialty training and a small income in exchange for their labor. Our responsibilities depend on our level of training, but we're never entirely on our own: there's always an attending, who oversees our decisions. That night, since Johns was the attending and was responsible for the patient's immediate management, I took my lead from him. But he wasn't a surgeon, and so he relied on me for surgical expertise.

5   "What's the story?" I asked.

An E.M.T. rattled off the details: "Unidentified white female unrestrained driver in high-speed rollover. Ejected from the car. Found unresponsive to pain. Pulse a hundred, B.P. a hundred over sixty, breathing at thirty on her own . . ."

As he spoke, I began examining her. The first step in caring for a trauma patient is always the same. It doesn't matter if a person has been shot eleven times or crushed by a truck or burned in a kitchen fire. The first thing you do is make sure that the patient can breathe without difficulty. This woman's breaths were shallow and rapid. An oximeter, by means of a sensor placed on her finger, measured the oxygen saturation of her blood. The "O_2 sat" is normally more than ninety-five percent for a patient breathing room air. The woman was wearing a face mask with oxygen turned up full blast, and her sat was only ninety percent.

"She's not oxygenating well," I announced in the flattened-out, wake-me-up-when-something-interesting-happens tone that all surgeons have acquired by about three months into residency. With my fingers, I verified that there wasn't any object in her mouth that would obstruct her airway; with a stethoscope, I confirmed that neither lung had collapsed. I got hold of a bag mask, pressed its clear facepiece over her nose and mouth, and squeezed the bellows, a kind of balloon with a one-way valve, shooting a litre of air into her with each compression. After a minute or so, her oxygen came up to a comfortable ninety-eight percent. She obviously needed our help with breathing. "Let's tube her," I said. That meant putting a tube down through her vocal cords and into her trachea, which would insure a clear airway and allow for mechanical ventilation.

Johns, the attending, wanted to do the intubation. He picked up a Mac 3 laryngoscope, a standard but fairly primitive-looking L-shaped metal instrument for prying open the mouth and throat, and slipped the shoehornlike blade deep into her mouth and down to her larynx. Then he yanked the handle up toward the ceiling to pull her tongue out of the way, open her mouth and throat, and reveal the vocal cords, which sit like fleshy tent flaps at the entrance to the trachea. The patient didn't wince or gag: she was still out cold.

10   "Suction!" he called. "I can't see a thing."

He sucked out about a cup of blood and clot. Then he picked up the endotracheal tube—a clear rubber pipe about the diameter of an index finger and three times as long—and tried to guide it between her cords. After a minute, her sat started to fall.

"You're down to seventy percent," a nurse announced.

Johns kept struggling with the tube, trying to push it in, but it banged vainly against the cords. The patient's lips began to turn blue.

"Sixty percent," the nurse said.

Johns pulled everything out of the patient's mouth and fitted the bag mask   15
back on. The oximeter's luminescent-green readout hovered at sixty for a
moment and then rose steadily, to ninety-seven percent. After a few minutes,
he took the mask off and again tried to get the tube in. There was more blood,
and there may have been some swelling, too: all the poking down the throat
was probably not helping. The sat fell to sixty percent. He pulled out and
bagged her until she returned to ninety-five percent.

When you're having trouble getting the tube in, the next step is to get specialized expertise. "Let's call anesthesia," I said, and Johns agreed. In the
meantime, I continued to follow the standard trauma protocol: completing the
examination and ordering fluids, lab tests, and X-rays. Maybe five minutes passed
as I worked.

The patient's sats drifted down to ninety-two percent—not a dramatic
change but definitely not normal for a patient who is being manually ventilated. I checked to see if the sensor had slipped off her finger. It hadn't. "Is the
oxygen up full blast?" I asked a nurse.

"It's up all the way," she said.

I listened again to the patient's lungs—no collapse. "We've got to get her
tubed," Johns said. He took off the oxygen mask and tried again.

Somewhere in my mind, I must have been aware of the possibility that her   20
airway was shutting down because of vocal-cord swelling or blood. If it was,
and we were unable to get a tube in, then the only chance she'd have to survive
would be an emergency tracheostomy: cutting a hole in her neck and inserting
a breathing tube into her trachea. Another attempt to intubate her might even
trigger a spasm of the cords and a sudden closure of the airway—which is
exactly what did happen.

If I had actually thought this far along, I would have recognized how ill-
prepared I was to do an emergency "trache." Of the people in the room, it's true,
I had the most experience doing tracheostomies, but that wasn't saying much. I
had been the assistant surgeon in only about half a dozen, and all but one of them
had been non-emergency cases, employing techniques that were not designed for
speed. The exception was a practice emergency trache I had done on a goat. I
should have immediately called Dr. Ball for backup. I should have got the trache
equipment out—lighting, suction, sterile instruments—just in case. Instead of
hurrying the effort to get the patient intubated because of a mild drop in saturation, I should have asked Johns to wait until I had help nearby. I might even have
recognized that she was already losing her airway. Then I could have grabbed a
knife and started cutting her a tracheostomy while things were still relatively
stable and I had time to proceed slowly. But for whatever reasons—hubris,
inattention, wishful thinking, hesitation, or the uncertainty of the moment—I
let the opportunity pass.

Johns hunched over the patient, intently trying to insert the tube through
her vocal cords. When her sat once again dropped into the sixties, he stopped
and put the mask back on. We stared at the monitor. The numbers weren't
coming up. Her lips were still blue. Johns squeezed the bellows harder to blow
more oxygen in.

"I'm getting resistance," he said.

The realization crept over me: this was a disaster. "Damn it, we've lost her airway," I said. "Trache kit! Light! Somebody call down to O.R. 25 and get Ball up here!"

25   People were suddenly scurrying everywhere. I tried to proceed deliberately, and not let panic take hold. I told the surgical intern to get a sterile gown and gloves on. I took a bactericidal solution off a shelf and dumped a whole bottle of yellow-brown liquid on the patient's neck. A nurse unwrapped the tracheostomy kit—a sterilized set of drapes and instruments. I pulled on a gown and a new pair of gloves while trying to think through the steps. This is simple, really, I tried to tell myself. At the base of the thyroid cartilage, the Adam's apple, is a little gap in which you find a thin, fibrous covering called the cricothyroid membrane. Cut through that and—voilà! You're in the trachea. You slip through the hole a four-inch plastic tube shaped like a plumber's elbow joint, hook it up to oxygen and a ventilator, and she's all set. Anyway, that was the theory.

I threw some drapes over her body, leaving the neck exposed. It looked as thick as a tree. I felt for the bony prominence of the thyroid cartilage. But I couldn't feel anything through the rolls of fat. I was beset by uncertainty— where should I cut? should I make a horizontal or a vertical incision?—and I hated myself for it. Surgeons never dithered, and I was dithering.

"I need better light," I said.

Someone was sent out to look for one.

"Did anyone get Ball?" I asked. It wasn't exactly an inspiring question.

30   "He's on his way," a nurse said.

There wasn't time to wait. Four minutes without oxygen would lead to permanent brain damage, if not death. Finally, I took the scalpel and cut. I just cut. I made a three-inch left-to-right swipe across the middle of the neck, following the procedure I'd learned for elective cases. I figured that if I worked through the fat I might be able to find the membrane in the wound. Dissecting down with scissors while the intern held the wound open with retractors, I hit a vein. It didn't let loose a lot of blood, but there was enough to fill the wound: I couldn't see anything. The intern put a finger on the bleeder. I called for suction. But the suction wasn't working; the tube was clogged with the clot from the intubation efforts.

"Somebody get some new tubing," I said. "And where's the light?"

Finally, an orderly wheeled in a tall overhead light, plugged it in, and flipped on the switch. It was still too dim; I could have done better with a flashlight.

I wiped up the blood with gauze, then felt around in the wound with my fingertips. This time, I thought I could feel the hard ridges of the thyroid cartilage and, below it, the slight gap of the cricothyroid membrane, though I couldn't be sure. I held my place with my left hand.

35   James O'Connor, a silver-haired, seen-it-all anesthesiologist, came into the room. Johns gave him a quick rundown on the patient and let him take over bagging her.

Holding the scalpel in my right hand like a pen, I stuck the blade down into the wound at the spot where I thought the thyroid cartilage was. With small, sharp strokes—working blindly, because of the blood and the poor light—I cut down through the overlying fat and tissue until I felt the blade scrape against the almost bony cartilage. I searched with the tip of the knife, walking it along until I felt it reach a gap. I hoped it was the cricothyroid membrane, and pressed down firmly. Then I felt the tissue suddenly give, and I cut an inch-long opening.

When I put my index finger into it, it felt as if I were prying open the jaws of a stiff clothespin. Inside, I thought I felt open space. But where were the sounds of moving air that I expected? Was this deep enough? Was I even in the right place?

"I think I'm in," I said, to reassure myself as much as anyone else.

"I hope so," O'Connor said. "She doesn't have much longer."

I took the tracheostomy tube and tried to fit it in, but something seemed to be blocking it. I twisted it and turned it, and finally jammed it in. Just then, Ball, the surgical attending, arrived. He rushed up to the bed and leaned over for a look. "Did you get it?" he asked. I said that I thought so. The bag mask was plugged onto the open end of the trache tube. But when the bellows were compressed the air just gurgled out of the wound. Ball quickly put on gloves and a gown.

"How long has she been without an airway?" he asked.

"I don't know. Three minutes."

Ball's face hardened as he registered that he had about a minute in which to turn things around. He took my place and summarily pulled out the trache tube. "God, what a mess," he said. "I can't see a thing in this wound. I don't even know if you're in the right place. Can we get better light and suction?" New suction tubing was found and handed to him. He quickly cleaned up the wound and went to work.

The patient's sat had dropped so low that the oximeter couldn't detect it anymore. Her heart rate began slowing down—first to the sixties and then to the forties. Then she lost her pulse entirely. I put my hands together on her chest, locked my elbows, leaned over her, and started doing chest compressions.

Ball looked up from the patient and turned to O'Connor. "I'm not going to get her an airway in time," he said. "You're going to have to try from above." Essentially, he was admitting my failure. Trying an oral intubation again was pointless—just something to do instead of watching her die. I was stricken, and concentrated on doing chest compressions, not looking at anyone. It was over, I thought.

And then, amazingly, O'Connor: "I'm in." He had managed to slip a pediatric-size endotracheal tube through the vocal cords. In thirty seconds, with oxygen being manually ventilated through the tube, her heart was back, racing at a hundred and twenty beats a minute. Her sat registered at sixty and then climbed. Another thirty seconds and it was at ninety-seven percent. All the people in the room exhaled, as if they, too, had been denied their breath. Ball and I said little except to confer about the next steps for her. Then he went back downstairs to finish working on the stab-wound patient still in the O.R.

We eventually identified the woman, whom I'll call Louise Williams; she was thirty-four years old and lived alone in a nearby suburb. Her alcohol level

on arrival had been three times the legal limit, and had probably contributed
to her unconsciousness. She had a concussion, several lacerations, and significant soft-tissue damage. But X-rays and scans revealed no other injuries from
the crash. That night, Ball and Hernandez brought her to the O.R. to fit her
with a proper tracheostomy. When Ball came out and talked to family members, he told them of the dire condition she was in when she arrived, the difficulties "we" had had getting access to her airway, the disturbingly long period
of time that she had gone without oxygen, and thus his uncertainty about how
much brain function she still possessed. They listened without protest; there
was nothing for them to do but wait.

II—THE BANALITY OF ERROR

To much of the public—and certainly to lawyers and the media—medical error
is a problem of bad physicians. Consider some other surgical mishaps. In one, a
general surgeon left a large metal instrument in a patient's abdomen, where it
tore through the bowel and the wall of the bladder. In another, a cancer surgeon
biopsied the wrong part of a woman's breast and thereby delayed her diagnosis
of cancer for months. A cardiac surgeon skipped a small but key step during a
heart-valve operation, thereby killing the patient. A surgeon saw a man racked
with abdominal pain in the emergency room and, without taking a C.T. scan,
assumed that the man had a kidney stone; eighteen hours later, a scan showed a
rupturing abdominal aortic aneurysm, and the patient died not long afterward.

How could anyone who makes a mistake of that magnitude be allowed to
practice medicine? We call such doctors "incompetent," "unethical," and "negligent." We want to see them punished. And so we've wound up with the public
system we have for dealing with error: malpractice lawsuits, media scandal,
suspensions, firings.

50   There is, however, a central truth in medicine that complicates this tidy
vision of misdeeds and misdoers: *All* doctors make terrible mistakes. Consider
the cases I've just described. I gathered them simply by asking respected surgeons I know—surgeons at top medical schools—to tell me about mistakes they
had made just in the past year. Every one of them had a story to tell.

In 1991, the *New England Journal of Medicine* published a series of landmark papers from a project known as the Harvard Medical Practice Study—a
review of more than thirty thousand hospital admissions in New York State. The
study found that nearly four percent of hospital patients suffered complications
from treatment which prolonged their hospital stay or resulted in disability or
death, and that two-thirds of such complications were due to errors in care. One
in four, or one percent of admissions, involved actual negligence. It was estimated that, nationwide, a hundred and twenty thousand patients die each year
at least partly as a result of errors in care. And subsequent investigations around
the country have confirmed the ubiquity of error. In one small study of how clinicians perform when patients have a sudden cardiac arrest, twenty-seven of
thirty clinicians made an error in using the defibrillator; they may have charged

it incorrectly or lost valuable time trying to figure out how to work a particular model. According to a 1995 study, mistakes in administering drugs—giving the wrong drug or the wrong dose, say—occur, on the average, about once for every hospital admission, mostly without ill effects, but one percent of the time with serious consequences.

If error were due to a subset of dangerous doctors, you might expect malpractice cases to be concentrated among a small group, but in fact they follow a uniform, bell-shaped distribution. Most surgeons are sued at least once in the course of their careers. Studies of specific types of error, too, have found that repeat offenders are not the problem. The fact is that virtually everyone who cares for hospital patients will make serious mistakes, and even commit acts of negligence, every year. For this reason, doctors are seldom outraged when the press reports yet another medical horror story. They usually have a different reaction: *That could be me*. The important question isn't how to keep bad physicians from harming patients; it's how to keep good physicians from harming patients.

Medical-malpractice suits are a remarkably ineffective remedy. Troyen Brennan, a Harvard professor of law and public health, points out that research has consistently failed to find evidence that litigation reduces medical-error rates. In part, this may be because the weapon is so imprecise. Brennan led several studies following up on the patients in the Harvard Medical Practice Study. He found that fewer than two percent of the patients who had received substandard care ever filed suit. Conversely, only a small minority among the patients who did sue had in fact been the victims of negligent care. And a patient's likelihood of winning a suit depended primarily on how poor his or her outcome was, regardless of whether that outcome was caused by disease or unavoidable risks of care.

The deeper problem with medical-malpractice suits, however, is that by demonizing errors they prevent doctors from acknowledging and discussing them publicly. The tort system makes adversaries of patient and physician, and pushes each to offer a heavily slanted version of events. When things go wrong, it's almost impossible for a physician to talk to a patient honestly about mistakes. Hospital lawyers warn doctors that, although they must, of course, tell patients about complications that occur, they are never to intimate that they were at fault, lest the "confession" wind up in court as damning evidence in a black-and-white morality tale. At most, a doctor might say, "I'm sorry that things didn't go as well as we had hoped."

There is one place, however, where doctors can talk candidly about their mistakes, if not with patients, then at least with one another. It is called the Morbidity and Mortality Conference—or, more simply, M. & M.—and it takes place, usually once a week, at nearly every academic hospital in the country. This institution survives because laws protecting its proceedings from legal discovery have stayed on the books in most states, despite frequent challenges. Surgeons, in particular, take the M. & M. seriously. Here they can gather behind closed doors to review the mistakes, complications, and deaths that occurred on their watch, determine responsibility, and figure out what to do differently next time.

55

III—SHOW AND TELL

At my hospital, we convene every Tuesday at five o'clock in a steep, plush amphitheatre lined with oil portraits of the great doctors whose achievements we're meant to live up to. All surgeons are expected to attend, from the interns to the chairman of surgery; we're also joined by medical students doing their surgery "rotation." An M. & M. can include almost a hundred people. We file in, pick up a photocopied list of cases to be discussed, and take our seats. The front row is occupied by the most senior surgeons: terse, serious men, now out of their scrubs and in dark suits, lined up like a panel of senators at a hearing. The chairman is a leonine presence in the seat closest to the plain wooden podium from which each case is presented. In the next few rows are the remaining surgical attendings; these tend to be younger, and several of them are women. The chief residents have put on long white coats and usually sit in the side rows. I join the mass of other residents, all of us in short white coats and green scrub pants, occupying the back rows.

For each case, the chief resident from the relevant service—cardiac, vascular, trauma, and so on—gathers the information, takes the podium, and tells the story. Here's a partial list of cases from a typical week (with a few changes to protect confidentiality): a sixty-eight-year-old man who bled to death after heart-valve surgery; a forty-seven-year-old woman who had to have a reoperation because of infection following an arterial bypass done in her left leg; a forty-four-year-old woman who had to have bile drained from her abdomen after gall-bladder surgery; three patients who had to have reoperations for bleeding following surgery; a sixty-three-year-old man who had a cardiac arrest following heart-bypass surgery; a sixty-six-year-old woman whose sutures suddenly gave way in an abdominal wound and nearly allowed her intestines to spill out. Ms. Williams's case, my failed tracheostomy, was just one case on a list like this. David Hernandez, the chief trauma resident, had subsequently reviewed the records and spoken to me and others involved. When the time came, it was he who stood up front and described what had happened.

Hernandez is a tall, rollicking, good old boy who can tell a yarn, but M. & M. presentations are bloodless and compact. He said something like: "This was a thirty-four-year-old female unrestrained driver in a high-speed rollover. The patient apparently had stable vitals at the scene but was unresponsive, and brought in by ambulance unintubated. She was G.C.S. 7 on arrival." G.C.S. stands for the Glasgow Coma Scale, which rates the severity of head injuries, from three to fifteen. G.C.S. 7 is in the comatose range. "Attempts to intubate were made without success in the E.R. and may have contributed to airway closure. A cricothyroidotomy[3] was attempted without success."

These presentations can be awkward. The chief residents, not the attendings, determine which cases to report. That keeps the attendings honest—no one can cover up mistakes—but it puts the chief residents, who are, after all, underlings, in a delicate position. The successful M. & M. presentation inevi-

3. Incision through the cricothyroid membrane to secure a patient's airway during an emergency, described in paragraphs 31 to 46.

tably involves a certain elision of detail and a lot of passive verbs. No one screws up a cricothyroidotomy. Instead, "a cricothyroidotomy was attempted without success." The message, however, was not lost on anyone.

Hernandez continued, "The patient arrested and required cardiac compressions. Anesthesia was then able to place a pediatric E.T. tube and the patient recovered stable vitals. The tracheostomy was then completed in the O.R." ₆₀

So Louise Williams had been deprived of oxygen long enough to go into cardiac arrest, and everyone knew that meant she could easily have suffered a disabling stroke or been left a vegetable. Hernandez concluded with the fortunate aftermath: "Her workup was negative for permanent cerebral damage or other major injuries. The tracheostomy was removed on Day 2. She was discharged to home in good condition on Day 3." To the family's great relief, and mine, she had woken up in the morning a bit woozy but hungry, alert, and mentally intact. In a few weeks, the episode would heal to a scar.

But not before someone was called to account. A front-row voice immediately thundered, "What do you mean, 'A cricothyroidotomy was attempted without success?'" I sank into my seat, my face hot.

"This was my case," Dr. Ball volunteered from the front row. It is how every attending begins, and that little phrase contains a world of surgical culture. For all the talk in business schools and in corporate America about the virtues of "flat organizations," surgeons maintain an old-fashioned sense of hierarchy. When things go wrong, the attending is expected to take full responsibility. It makes no difference whether it was the resident's hand that slipped and lacerated an aorta; it doesn't matter whether the attending was at home in bed when a nurse gave a wrong dose of medication. At the M. & M., the burden of responsibility falls on the attending.

Ball went on to describe the emergency attending's failure to intubate Williams and his own failure to be at her bedside when things got out of control. He described the bad lighting and her extremely thick neck, and was careful to make those sound not like excuses but merely like complicating factors. Some attendings shook their heads in sympathy. A couple of them asked questions to clarify certain details. Throughout, Ball's tone was objective, detached. He had the air of a CNN newscaster describing unrest in Kuala Lumpur.[4]

As always, the chairman, responsible for the over-all quality of our surgery ₆₅ service, asked the final question. What, he wanted to know, would Ball have done differently? Well, Ball replied, it didn't take long to get the stab-wound patient under control in the O.R., so he probably should have sent Hernandez up to the E.R. at that point or let Hernandez close the abdomen while he himself came up. People nodded. Lesson learned. Next case.

At no point during the M. & M. did anyone question why I had not called for help sooner or why I had not had the skill and knowledge that Williams needed. This is not to say that my actions were seen as acceptable. Rather, in the hierarchy, addressing my errors was Ball's role. The day after the disaster, Ball had caught me in the hall and taken me aside. His voice was more wounded

4. Capital of Malaysia hit by political and economic crises in the late 1990s.

than angry as he went through my specific failures. First, he explained, in an emergency tracheostomy it might have been better to do a vertical neck incision; that would have kept me out of the blood vessels, which run up and down— something I should have known at least from my reading. I might have had a much easier time getting her an airway then, he said. Second, and worse to him than mere ignorance, he didn't understand why I hadn't called him when there were clear signs of airway trouble developing. I offered no excuses. I promised to be better prepared for such cases and to be quicker to ask for help.

Even after Ball had gone down the fluorescent-lit hallway, I felt a sense of shame like a burning ulcer. This was not guilt: guilt is what you feel when you have done something wrong. What I felt was shame: *I* was what was wrong. And yet I also knew that a surgeon can take such feelings too far. It is one thing to be aware of one's limitations. It is another to be plagued by self-doubt. One surgeon with a national reputation told me about an abdominal operation in which he had lost control of bleeding while he was removing what turned out to be a benign tumor and the patient had died. "It was a clean kill," he said. Afterward, he could barely bring himself to operate. When he did operate, he became tentative and indecisive. The case affected his performance for months.

Even worse than losing self-confidence, though, is reacting defensively. There are surgeons who will see faults everywhere except in themselves. They have no questions and no fears about their abilities. As a result, they learn nothing from their mistakes and know nothing of their limitations. As one surgeon told me, it is a rare but alarming thing to meet a surgeon without fear. "If you're not a little afraid when you operate," he said, "you're bound to do a patient a grave disservice."

The atmosphere at the M. & M. is meant to discourage both attitudes— self-doubt and denial—for the M. & M. is a cultural ritual that inculcates in surgeons a "correct" view of mistakes. "What would you do differently?" a chairman asks concerning cases of avoidable complications. "Nothing" is seldom an acceptable answer.

70   In its way, the M. & M. is an impressively sophisticated and human institution. Unlike the courts or the media, it recognizes that human error is generally not something that can be deterred by punishment. The M. & M. sees avoiding error as largely a matter of will—of staying sufficiently informed and alert to anticipate the myriad ways that things can go wrong and then trying to head off each potential problem before it happens. Why do things go wrong? Because, doctors say, making them go right is hard stuff. It isn't damnable that an error occurs, but there is some shame to it. In fact, the M. & M.'s ethos can seem paradoxical. On the one hand, it reinforces the very American idea that error is intolerable. On the other hand, the very existence of the M. & M., its place on the weekly schedule, amounts to an acknowledgment that mistakes are an inevitable part of medicine.

But why do they happen so often? Lucian Leape, medicine's leading expert on error, points out that many other industries—whether the task is manufacturing semiconductors or serving customers at the Ritz-Carlton—simply wouldn't countenance error rates like those in hospitals. The aviation industry has reduced the frequency of operational errors to one in a hundred thousand flights, and most of those errors have no harmful consequences. The buzz-word at General Electric these days is "Six Sigma," meaning that its goal is to make product defects so rare that in statistical terms they are more than six standard deviations away from being a matter of chance—almost a one-in-a-million occurrence.

Of course, patients are far more complicated and idiosyncratic than air-planes, and medicine isn't a matter of delivering a fixed product or even a cata-logue of products; it may well be more complex than just about any other field of human endeavor. Yet everything we've learned in the past two decades—from cognitive psychology, from "human factors" engineering, from studies of disasters like Three Mile Island and Bhopal[5]—has yielded the same insights: not only do all human beings err but they err frequently and in predictable, patterned ways. And systems that do not adjust for these realities can end up exacerbating rather than eliminating error.

The British psychologist James Reason argues, in his book *Human Error*, that our propensity for certain types of error is the price we pay for the brain's remarkable ability to think and act intuitively—to sift quickly through the sen-sory information that constantly bombards us without wasting time trying to work through every situation anew. Thus systems that rely on human perfection present what Reason calls "latent errors"—errors waiting to happen. Medicine teems with examples. Take writing out a prescription, a rote procedure that relies on memory and attention, which we know are unreliable. Inevitably, a physician will sometimes specify the wrong dose or the wrong drug. Even when the pre-scription is written correctly, there's a risk that it will be misread. (Computerized ordering systems can almost eliminate errors of this kind, but only a small minority of hospitals have adopted them.) Medical equipment, which manufac-turers often build without human operators in mind, is another area rife with latent errors: one reason physicians are bound to have problems when they use cardiac defibrillators is that the devices have no standard design. You can also make the case that onerous workloads, chaotic environments, and inadequate team communication all represent latent errors in the system.

James Reason makes another important observation: disasters do not sim-ply occur; they evolve. In complex systems, a single failure rarely leads to harm. Human beings are impressively good at adjusting when an error becomes apparent, and systems often have built-in defenses. For example, pharmacists and nurses routinely check and counter-check physicians' orders. But errors do not always become apparent, and backup systems themselves often fail as a result of latent errors. A pharmacist forgets to check one of a thousand pre-scriptions. A machine's alarm bell malfunctions. The one attending trauma

---

5. In 1979, there was a partial meltdown of a pressurized water reactor at Three Mile Island Nuclear Generating Station near Harrisburg, Pennsylvania; the Bhopal gas disaster occurred in December 1984 at the Union Carbide pesticide plant in Bhopal, Madhya Pradesh, India, exposing 500,000 people to dangerous chemicals.

surgeon available gets stuck in the operating room. When things go wrong, it is usually because a series of failures conspire to produce disaster.

75   The M. & M. takes none of this into account. For that reason, many experts see it as a rather shabby approach to analyzing error and improving performance in medicine. It isn't enough to ask what a clinician could or should have done differently so that he and others may learn for next time. The doctor is often only the final actor in a chain of events that set him or her up to fail. Error experts, therefore, believe that it's the process, not the individuals in it, which requires closer examination and correction. In a sense, they want to industrialize medicine. And they can already claim one success story: the specialty of anesthesiology, which has adopted their precepts and seen extraordinary results.

IV—NEARLY PERFECT

At the center of the emblem of the American Society of Anesthesiologists is a single word: "Vigilance." When you put a patient to sleep under general anesthesia, you assume almost complete control of the patient's body. The body is paralyzed, the brain rendered unconscious, and machines are hooked up to control breathing, heart rate, blood pressure—all the vital functions. Given the complexity of the machinery and of the human body, there are a seemingly infinite number of ways in which things can go wrong, even in minor surgery. And yet anesthesiologists have found that if problems are detected they can usually be solved. In the nineteen-forties, there was only one death resulting from anesthesia in every twenty-five hundred operations, and between the nineteen-sixties and the nineteen-eighties the rate had stabilized at one or two in every ten thousand operations.

But Ellison (Jeep) Pierce had always regarded even that rate as unconscionable. From the time he began practicing, in 1960, as a young anesthesiologist out of North Carolina and the University of Pennsylvania, he had maintained a case file of details from all the deadly anesthetic accidents he had come across or participated in. But it was one case in particular that galvanized him. Friends of his had taken their eighteen-year-old daughter to the hospital to have her wisdom teeth pulled, under general anesthesia. The anesthesiologist inserted the breathing tube into her esophagus instead of her trachea, which is a relatively common mishap, and then failed to spot the error, which is not. Deprived of oxygen, she died within minutes. Pierce knew that a one-in-ten-thousand death rate, given that anesthesia was administered in the United States an estimated thirty-five million times each year, meant thirty-five hundred avoidable deaths like that one.

In 1982, Pierce was elected vice-president of the American Society of Anesthesiologists and got an opportunity to do something about the death rate. The same year, ABC's 20/20 aired an exposé that caused a considerable stir in his profession. The segment began, "If you are going to go into anesthesia, you are going on a long trip, and you should not do it if you can avoid it in any way. General anesthesia [is] safe most of the time, but there are dangers from human error, carelessness, and a critical shortage of anesthesiologists.

This year, six thousand patients will die or suffer brain damage." The program presented several terrifying cases from around the country. Between the small crisis that the show created and the sharp increases in physicians' malpractice-insurance premiums at that time, Pierce was able to mobilize the Society of Anesthesiologists around the problem of error.

He turned for ideas not to a physician but to an engineer named Jeffrey Cooper, the lead author of a ground-breaking 1978 paper entitled "Preventable Anesthesia Mishaps: A Study of Human Factors." An unassuming, fastidious man, Cooper had been hired in 1972, when he was twenty-six years old, by the Massachusetts General Hospital bioengineering unit, to work on developing machines for anesthesiology researchers. He gravitated toward the operating room, however, and spent hours there observing the anesthesiologists, and one of the first things he noticed was how poorly the anesthesia machines were designed. For example, a clockwise turn of a dial decreased the concentration of potent anesthetics in about half the machines but increased the concentration in the other half. He decided to borrow a technique called "critical incident analysis"—which had been used since the nineteen-fifties to analyze mishaps in aviation—in an effort to learn how equipment might be contributing to errors in anesthesia. The technique is built around carefully conducted interviews, designed to capture as much detail as possible about dangerous incidents: how specific accidents evolved and what factors contributed to them. This information is then used to look for patterns among different cases.

Getting open, honest reporting is crucial. The Federal Aviation Administration has a formalized system for analyzing and reporting dangerous aviation incidents, and its enormous success in improving airline safety rests on two cornerstones. Pilots who report an incident within ten days have automatic immunity from punishment, and the reports go to a neutral, outside agency, NASA, which has no interest in using the information against individual pilots. For Jeffrey Cooper, it was probably an advantage that he was an engineer, and not a physician, so that anesthesiologists regarded him as a discreet, unthreatening interviewer.

The result was the first in-depth, scientific look at errors in medicine. His detailed analysis of three hundred and fifty-nine errors provided a view of the profession unlike anything that had been seen before. Contrary to the prevailing assumption that the start of anesthesia ("takeoff") was the most dangerous part, anesthesiologists learned that incidents tended to occur in the middle of anesthesia, when vigilance waned. The most common kind of incident involved errors in maintaining the patient's breathing, and these were usually the result of an undetected disconnection or misconnection of the breathing tubing, mistakes in managing the airway, or mistakes in using the anesthesia machine. Just as important, Cooper enumerated a list of contributory factors, including inadequate experience, inadequate familiarity with equipment, poor communication among team members, haste, inattention, and fatigue.

The study provoked widespread debate among anesthesiologists, but there was no concerted effort to solve the problems until Jeep Pierce came along. Through the anesthesiology society at first, and then through a foundation

80

that he started, Pierce directed funding into research on how to reduce the problems Cooper had identified, sponsored an international conference to gather ideas from around the world, and brought anesthesia-machine designers into safety discussions.

It all worked. Hours for anesthesiology residents were shortened. Manufacturers began redesigning their machines with fallible human beings in mind. Dials were standardized to turn in a uniform direction; locks were put in to prevent accidental administration of more than one anesthetic gas; controls were changed so that oxygen delivery could not be turned down to zero.

Where errors could not be eliminated directly, anesthesiologists began looking for reliable means of detecting them earlier. For example, because the trachea and the esophagus are so close together, it is almost inevitable that an anesthesiologist will sometimes put the breathing tube down the wrong pipe. Anesthesiologists had always checked for this by listening with a stethoscope for breath sounds over both lungs. But Cooper had turned up a surprising number of mishaps—like the one that befell the daughter of Pierce's friends—involving undetected esophageal intubations. Something more effective was needed. In fact, monitors that could detect this kind of error had been available for years, but, in part because of their expense, relatively few anesthesiologists used them. One type of monitor could verify that the tube was in the trachea by detecting carbon dioxide being exhaled from the lungs. Another type, the pulse oximeter, tracked blood-oxygen levels, thereby providing an early warning that something was wrong with the patient's breathing system. Prodded by Pierce and others, the anesthesiology society made the use of both types of monitor for every patient receiving general anesthesia an official standard. Today, anesthesia deaths from misconnecting the breathing system or intubating the esophagus rather than the trachea are virtually unknown. In a decade, the over-all death rate dropped to just one in more than two hundred thousand cases—less than a twentieth of what it had been.

85   And the reformers have not stopped there. David Gaba, a professor of anesthesiology at Stanford, has focused on improving human performance. In aviation, he points out, pilot experience is recognized to be invaluable but insufficient: pilots seldom have direct experience with serious plane malfunction anymore. They are therefore required to undergo yearly training in crisis simulators. Why not doctors, too?

Gaba, a physician with training in engineering, led in the design of an anesthesia-simulation system known as the Eagle Patient Simulator. It is a life-size, computer-driven mannequin that is capable of amazingly realistic behavior. It has a circulation, a heartbeat, and lungs that take in oxygen and expire carbon dioxide. If you inject drugs into it or administer inhaled anesthetics, it will detect the type and amount, and its heart rate, its blood pressure, and its oxygen levels will respond appropriately. The "patient" can be made to develop airway swelling, bleeding, and heart disturbances. The mannequin is laid on an operating table in a simulation room equipped exactly like the real thing. Here both residents and experienced attending physicians learn to perform effectively in all kinds of dangerous, and sometimes freak, scenarios: an anesthesia-machine malfunction, a power outage, a patient who goes into cardiac arrest during surgery, and even a cesarean-section patient whose airway shuts down and who requires an emergency tracheostomy.

Though anesthesiology has unquestionably taken the lead in analyzing and trying to remedy "systems" failures, there are signs of change in other quarters. The American Medical Association, for example, set up its National Patient Safety Foundation in 1997 and asked Cooper and Pierce to serve on the board of directors. The foundation is funding research, sponsoring conferences, and attempting to develop new standards for hospital drug-ordering systems that could substantially reduce medication mistakes—the single most common type of medical error.

Even in surgery there have been some encouraging developments. For instance, operating on the wrong knee or foot or other body part of a patient has been a recurrent, if rare, mistake. A typical response has been to fire the surgeon. Recently, however, hospitals and surgeons have begun to recognize that the body's bilateral symmetry makes these errors predictable. Last year, the American Academy of Orthopedic Surgeons endorsed a simple way of preventing them: make it standard practice for surgeons to initial, with a marker, the body part to be cut before the patient comes to surgery.

The Northern New England Cardiovascular Disease Study Group, based at Dartmouth, is another success story. Though the group doesn't conduct the sort of in-depth investigation of mishaps that Jeffrey Cooper pioneered, it has shown what can be done simply through statistical monitoring. Six hospitals belong to this consortium, which tracks deaths and complications (such as wound infections, uncontrolled bleeding, and stroke) arising from heart surgery and tries to identify various risk factors. Its researchers found, for example, that there were relatively high death rates among patients who developed anemia after bypass surgery, and that anemia developed most often in small patients. The fluid used to "prime" the heart-lung machine caused the anemia, because it diluted a patient's blood, so the smaller the patient (and his or her blood supply) the greater the effect. Members of the consortium now have several promising solutions to the problem. Another study found that a group at one hospital had made mistakes in "handoffs"—say, in passing preoperative lab results to the people in the operating room. The study group solved the problem by developing a pilot's checklist for all patients coming to the O.R. These efforts have introduced a greater degree of standardization, and so reduced the death rate in those six hospitals from four percent to three percent between 1991 and 1996. That meant two hundred and ninety-three fewer deaths. But the Northern New England cardiac group, even with its narrow focus and techniques, remains an exception; hard information about how things go wrong is still scarce. There is a hodgepodge of evidence that latent errors and systemic factors may contribute to surgical errors: the lack of standardized protocols, the surgeon's inexperience, the hospital's inexperience, inadequately designed technology and techniques, thin staffing, poor teamwork, time of day, the effects of managed care and corporate medicine, and so on and so on. But which are the major risk factors? We still don't know. Surgery, like most of medicine, awaits its Jeff Cooper.

V—GETTING IT RIGHT

90   It was a routine gallbladder operation, on a routine day: on the operating table
was a mother in her forties, her body covered by blue paper drapes except for
her round, antiseptic-coated belly. The gallbladder is a floppy, finger-length sac
of bile like a deflated olive-green balloon tucked under the liver, and when
gallstones form, as this patient had learned, they can cause excruciating bouts
of pain. Once we removed her gallbladder, the pain would stop.

There are risks to this surgery, but they used to be much greater. Just a
decade ago, surgeons had to make a six-inch abdominal incision that left
patients in the hospital for the better part of a week just recovering from the
wound. Today, we've learned to take out gallbladders with a minute camera
and instruments that we manipulate through tiny incisions. The operation,
often done as day surgery, is known as laparoscopic cholecystectomy, or "lap
chole." Half a million Americans a year now have their gallbladders removed
this way; at my hospital alone, we do several hundred lap choles annually.

When the attending gave me the go-ahead, I cut a discreet inch-long semi-
circle in the wink of skin just above the belly button. I dissected through fat
and fascia until I was inside the abdomen, and dropped into place a "port," a
half-inch-wide sheath for slipping instruments in and out. We hooked gas tubing up to a side vent on the port, and carbon dioxide poured in, inflating the
abdomen until it was distended like a tire. I inserted the miniature camera. On
a video monitor a few feet away, the woman's intestines blinked into view. With
the abdomen inflated, I had room to move the camera, and I swung it around to
look at the liver. The gallbladder could be seen poking out from under the edge.

We put in three more ports through even tinier incisions, spaced apart to
complete the four corners of a square. Through the ports on his side, the
attending put in two long "graspers," like small-scale versions of the device that
a department-store clerk might use to get a hat off the top shelf. Watching the
screen as he maneuvered them, he reached under the edge of the liver, clamped
onto the gallbladder, and pulled it up into view. We were set to proceed.

Removing the gallbladder is fairly straightforward. You sever it from its stalk
and from its blood supply, and pull the rubbery sac out of the abdomen through
the incision near the belly button. You let the carbon dioxide out of the belly,
pull out the ports, put a few stitches in the tiny incisions, slap some Band-Aids
on top, and you're done. There's one looming danger, though: the stalk of the
gallbladder is a branch off the liver's only conduit for sending bile to the intestines for the digestion of fats. And if you accidentally injure this main bile duct,
the bile backs up and starts to destroy the liver. Between ten and twenty percent
of the patients to whom this happens will die. Those who survive often have
permanent liver damage and can go on to require liver transplantation. According to a standard textbook, "injuries to the main bile duct are nearly always the
result of misadventure during operation and are therefore a serious reproach to
the surgical profession." It is a true surgical error, and, like any surgical team
doing a lap chole, we were intent on avoiding this mistake.

Using a dissecting instrument, I carefully stripped off the fibrous white tissue and yellow fat overlying and concealing the base of the gallbladder. Now we could see its broad neck and the short stretch where it narrowed down to a duct—a tube no thicker than a strand of spaghetti peeking out from the surrounding tissue, but magnified on the screen to the size of major plumbing. Then, just to be absolutely sure we were looking at the gallbladder duct and not the main bile duct, I stripped away some more of the surrounding tissue. The attending and I stopped at this point, as we always do, and discussed the anatomy. The neck of the gallbladder led straight into the tube we were eying. So it had to be the right duct. We had exposed a good length of it without a sign of the main bile duct. Everything looked perfect, we agreed. "Go for it," the attending said.

I slipped in the clip applier, an instrument that squeezes V-shaped metal clips onto whatever you put in its jaws. I got the jaws around the duct and was about to fire when my eye caught, on the screen, a little globule of fat lying on top of the duct. That wasn't necessarily anything unusual, but somehow it didn't look right. With the tip of the clip applier, I tried to flick it aside, but, instead of a little globule, a whole layer of thin unseen tissue came up, and, underneath, we saw that the duct had a fork in it. My stomach dropped. If not for that little extra fastidiousness, I would have clipped off the main bile duct.

Here was the paradox of error in medicine. With meticulous technique and assiduous effort to insure that they have correctly identified the anatomy, surgeons need never cut the main bile duct. It is a paradigm of an avoidable error. At the same time, studies show that even highly experienced surgeons inflict this terrible injury about once in every two hundred lap choles. To put it another way, I may have averted disaster this time, but a statistician would say that, no matter how hard I tried, I was almost certain to make this error at least once in the course of my career.

But the story doesn't have to end here, as the cognitive psychologists and industrial-error experts have demonstrated. Given the results they've achieved in anesthesiology, it's clear that we can make dramatic improvements by going after the process, not the people. But there are distinct limitations to the industrial cure, however necessary its emphasis on systems and structures. It would be deadly for us, the individual actors, to give up our belief in human perfectibility. The statistics may say that someday I will sever someone's main bile duct, but each time I go into a gallbladder operation I believe that with enough will and effort I can beat the odds. This isn't just professional vanity. It's a necessary part of good medicine, even in superbly "optimized" systems. Operations like that lap chole have taught me how easily error can occur, but they've also showed me something else: effort does matter; diligence and attention to the minutest details can save you.

This may explain why many doctors take exception to talk of "systems problems," "continuous quality improvement," and "process reëngineering." It is the dry language of structures, not people. I'm no exception: something in me, too, demands an acknowledgment of my autonomy, which is also to say my ultimate culpability. Go back to that Friday night in the E.R., to the moment when I stood, knife in hand, over Louise Williams, her lips blue, her throat a swollen, bloody, and suddenly closed passage. A systems engineer might have proposed some useful changes. Perhaps a backup suction device should always be at hand, and better light more easily available. Perhaps the institution could have trained me better for such crises, could have required me to have operated on a few more goats. Perhaps emergency tracheostomies are so difficult under any circumstances that an automated device could have been designed to do a better job. But the could-haves are infinite, aren't they? Maybe Williams could have worn her seat belt, or had one less beer that night. We could call any or all of these factors latent errors, accidents waiting to happen.

100   But although they put the odds against me, it wasn't as if I had no chance of succeeding. Good doctoring is all about making the most of the hand you're dealt, and I failed to do so. The indisputable fact was that I hadn't called for help when I could have, and when I plunged the knife into her neck and made my horizontal slash my best was not good enough. It was just luck, hers and mine, that Dr. O'Connor somehow got a breathing tube into her in time.

There are all sorts of reasons that it would be wrong to take my license away or to take me to court. These reasons do not absolve me. Whatever the limits of the M. & M., its fierce ethic of personal responsibility for errors is a formidable virtue. No matter what measures are taken, medicine will sometimes falter, and it isn't reasonable to ask that it achieve perfection. What's reasonable is to ask that medicine never cease to aim for it.

MLA CITATION

Gawande, Atul. "When Doctors Make Mistakes." *The Norton Reader: An Anthology of Nonfiction*, edited by Melissa A. Goldthwaite et al., 16th ed., W. W. Norton, 2024, pp. 479–96.

QUESTIONS

1. Atul Gawande states flatly, "*All* doctors make terrible mistakes" (paragraph 50). He proceeds to analyze why. What are the main reasons he offers?

2. In section IV, "Nearly Perfect," Gawande discusses attempts by different medical groups to eliminate or reduce error. Annotate the essay, marking and responding to these examples. What approaches have been effective? What are the limits of these approaches?

3. Although it incorporates significant research, this essay is also a personal narrative. Gawande both begins and ends his essay by narrating a specific experience of his in the operating room. How are these examples similar? How are they different? How does the rhetorical purpose of these anecdotes change as Gawande moves through his discussion of medical error?

4. Write an essay about a time when you made a serious error. Try, like Gawande, to incorporate the research or advice of others who might help you understand the reasons for your error.

REBECCA SKLOOT
The Woman in the Photograph

THERE'S A PHOTO ON MY WALL of a woman I've never met, its left corner torn and patched together with tape. She looks straight into the camera and smiles, hands on hips, dress suit neatly pressed, lips painted deep red. It's the late 1940s and she hasn't yet reached the age of thirty. Her light brown skin is smooth, her eyes still young and playful, oblivious to the tumor growing inside her—a tumor that would leave her five children motherless and change the future of medicine. Beneath the photo, a caption says her name is "Henrietta Lacks, Helen Lane or Helen Larson."

No one knows who took that picture, but it's appeared hundreds of times in magazines and science textbooks, on blogs and laboratory walls. She's usually identified as Helen Lane, but often she has no name at all. She's simply called HeLa, the code name given to the world's first immortal human cells—*her* cells, cut from her cervix just months before she died.

Her real name is Henrietta Lacks.

From The Immortal Life of Henrietta Lacks (2010), *which recounts how cancer cells taken from Henrietta Lacks in 1951 without her consent became the dominant human cell line ("HeLa") used in medical and scientific research. In 2023, the Lacks family reached a settlement with one biotechnology company that has long profited from the cell line.*

I've spent years staring at that photo, wondering what kind of life she led, what happened to her children, and what she'd think about cells from her cervix living on forever—bought, sold, packaged, and shipped by the trillions to laboratories around the world. I've tried to imagine how she'd feel knowing that her cells went up in the first space missions to see what would happen to human cells in zero gravity,[1] or that they helped with some of the most important advances in medicine: the polio vaccine, chemotherapy, cloning, gene mapping, in vitro fertilization. I'm pretty sure that she—like most of us— would be shocked to hear that there are trillions more of her cells growing in laboratories now than there ever were in her body.

5   There's no way of knowing exactly how many of Henrietta's cells are alive today. One scientist estimates that if you could pile all HeLa cells ever grown onto a scale, they'd weigh more than 50 million metric tons—an inconceivable number, given that an individual cell weighs almost nothing. Another scientist calculated that if you could lay all HeLa cells ever grown end-to-end, they'd wrap around the Earth at least three times, spanning more than 350 million feet. In her prime, Henrietta herself stood only a bit over five feet tall.

I first learned about HeLa cells and the woman behind them in 1988, thirty-seven years after her death, when I was sixteen and sitting in a community college biology class. My instructor, Donald Defler, a gnomish balding man, paced at the front of the lecture hall and flipped on an overhead projector. He pointed to two diagrams that appeared on the wall behind him. They were schematics of the cell reproduction cycle, but to me they just looked like a neon-colored mess of arrows, squares, and circles with words I didn't understand, like "MPF Triggering a Chain Reaction of Protein Activations."

I was a kid who'd failed freshman year at the regular public high school because she never showed up. I'd transferred to an alternative school that offered dream studies instead of biology, so I was taking Defler's class for high-school credit, which meant that I was sitting in a college lecture hall at sixteen with words like *mitosis* and *kinase inhibitors* flying around. I was completely lost.

"Do we have to memorize everything on those diagrams?" one student yelled.

Yes, Defler said, we had to memorize the diagrams, and yes, they'd be on the test, but that didn't matter right then. What he wanted us to understand was that cells are amazing things: There are about one hundred trillion of them in our bodies, each so small that several thousand could fit on the period at the end of this sentence. They make up all our tissues—muscle, bone, blood—which in turn make up our organs.

10   Under the microscope, a cell looks a lot like a fried egg: It has a white (the *cytoplasm*) that's full of water and proteins to keep it fed, and a yolk (the *nucleus*) that holds all the genetic information that makes you you. The cytoplasm buzzes like a New York City street. It's crammed full of molecules and vessels endlessly shuttling enzymes and sugars from one part of the cell to

1. In 1960, a year before Yuri Gagarin became the first person to enter outer space, a sample of HeLa cells was placed on the Russian *Korabl-Sputnik 2* satellite.

another, pumping water, nutrients, and oxygen in and out of the cell. All the while, little cytoplasmic factories work 24/7, cranking out sugars, fats, proteins, and energy to keep the whole thing running and feed the nucleus—the brains of the operation. Inside every nucleus within each cell in your body, there's an identical copy of your entire genome. That genome tells cells when to grow and divide and makes sure they do their jobs, whether that's controlling your heartbeat or helping your brain understand the words on this page.

Defler paced the front of the classroom telling us how mitosis—the process of cell division—makes it possible for embryos to grow into babies, and for our bodies to create new cells for healing wounds or replenishing blood we've lost. It was beautiful, he said, like a perfectly choreographed dance.

All it takes is one small mistake anywhere in the division process for cells to start growing out of control, he told us. Just *one* enzyme misfiring, just one wrong protein activation, and you could have cancer. Mitosis goes haywire, which is how it spreads.

"We learned that by studying cancer cells in culture," Defler said. He grinned and spun to face the board, where he wrote two words in enormous print: HENRIETTA LACKS.

Henrietta died in 1951 from a vicious case of cervical cancer, he told us. But before she died, a surgeon took samples of her tumor and put them in a petri dish. Scientists had been trying to keep human cells alive in culture for decades, but they all eventually died. Henrietta's were different: they reproduced an entire generation every twenty-four hours, and they never stopped. They became the first immortal human cells ever grown in a laboratory.

"Henrietta's cells have now been living outside her body far longer than   15
they ever lived inside it," Defler said. If we went to almost any cell culture lab in the world and opened its freezers, he told us, we'd probably find millions—if not billions—of Henrietta's cells in small vials on ice.

Her cells were part of research into the genes that cause cancer and those that suppress it; they helped develop drugs for treating herpes, leukemia, influenza, hemophilia, and Parkinson's disease; and they've been used to study lactose digestion, sexually transmitted diseases, appendicitis, human longevity, mosquito mating, and the negative cellular effects of working in sewers. Their chromosomes and proteins have been studied with such detail and precision that scientists know their every quirk. Like guinea pigs and mice, Henrietta's cells have become the standard laboratory workhorse.

"HeLa cells were one of the most important things that happened to medicine in the last hundred years," Defler said.

Then, matter-of-factly, almost as an afterthought, he said, "She was a black woman." He erased her name in one fast swipe and blew the chalk from his hands. Class was over.

As the other students filed out of the room, I sat thinking, *That's it? That's all we get? There has to be more to the story.*

I followed Defler to his office.   20

"Where was she from?" I asked. "Did she know how important her cells were? Did she have any children?"

"I wish I could tell you," he said, "but no one knows anything about her."

After class, I ran home and threw myself onto my bed with my biology textbook. I looked up "cell culture" in the index, and there she was, a small parenthetical:

> In culture, cancer cells can go on dividing indefinitely, if they have a continual supply of nutrients, and thus are said to be "immortal." A striking example is a cell line that has been reproducing in culture since 1951. (Cells of this line are called HeLa cells because their original source was a tumor removed from a woman named Henrietta Lacks.)

That was it. I looked up HeLa in my parents' encyclopedia, then my dictionary: No Henrietta.

As I graduated from high school and worked my way through college toward a biology degree, HeLa cells were omnipresent. I heard about them in histology, neurology, pathology; I used them in experiments on how neighboring cells communicate. But after Mr. Defler, no one mentioned Henrietta.

25   When I got my first computer in the mid-nineties and started using the Internet, I searched for information about her, but found only confused snippets: most sites said her name was Helen Lane; some said she died in the thirties; others said the forties, fifties, or even sixties. Some said ovarian cancer killed her, others said breast or cervical cancer.

Eventually I tracked down a few magazine articles about her from the seventies. *Ebony* quoted Henrietta's husband saying, "All I remember is that she had this disease, and right after she died they called me in the office wanting to get my permission to take a sample of some kind. I decided not to let them." *Jet* said the family was angry—angry that Henrietta's cells were being sold for twenty-five dollars a vial, and angry that articles had been published about the cells without their knowledge. It said, "Pounding in the back of their heads was a gnawing feeling that science and the press had taken advantage of them."

The articles all ran photos of Henrietta's family: her oldest son sitting at his dining room table in Baltimore, looking at a genetics textbook. Her middle son in military uniform, smiling and holding a baby. But one picture stood out more than any other: in it, Henrietta's daughter, Deborah Lacks, is surrounded by family, everyone smiling, arms around each other, eyes bright and excited. Except Deborah. She stands in the foreground looking alone, almost as if someone pasted her into the photo after the fact. She's twenty-six years old and beautiful, with short brown hair and catlike eyes. But those eyes glare at the camera, hard and serious. The caption said the family had found out just a few months earlier that Henrietta's cells were still alive, yet at that point she'd been dead for twenty-five years.

All of the stories mentioned that scientists had begun doing research on Henrietta's children, but the Lackses didn't seem to know what that research was for. They said they were being tested to see if they had the cancer that killed Henrietta, but according to the reporters, scientists were studying the Lacks family to learn more about Henrietta's cells. The stories quoted her son

Lawrence, who wanted to know if the immortality of his mother's cells meant that he might live forever too. But one member of the family remained voiceless: Henrietta's daughter, Deborah.

As I worked my way through graduate school studying writing, I became fixated on the idea of someday telling Henrietta's story. At one point I even called directory assistance in Baltimore looking for Henrietta's husband, David Lacks, but he wasn't listed. I had the idea that I'd write a book that was a biography of both the cells and the woman they came from—someone's daughter, wife, and mother.

I couldn't have imagined it then, but that phone call would mark the begin-   30
ning of a decadelong adventure through scientific laboratories, hospitals, and mental institutions, with a cast of characters that would include Nobel laureates, grocery store clerks, convicted felons, and a professional con artist. While trying to make sense of the history of cell culture and the complicated ethical debate surrounding the use of human tissues in research, I'd be accused of conspiracy and slammed into a wall both physically and metaphorically, and I'd eventually find myself on the receiving end of something that looked a lot like an exorcism. I did eventually meet Deborah, who would turn out to be one of the strongest and most resilient women I'd ever known. We'd form a deep personal bond, and slowly, without realizing it, I'd become a character in her story, and she in mine.

Deborah and I came from very different cultures: I grew up white and agnostic in the Pacific Northwest, my roots half New York Jew and half Midwestern Protestant; Deborah was a deeply religious black Christian from the South. I tended to leave the room when religion came up in conversation because it made me uncomfortable; Deborah's family tended toward preaching, faith healings, and sometimes voodoo. She grew up in a black neighborhood that was one of the poorest and most dangerous in the country; I grew up in a safe, quiet middle-class neighborhood in a predominantly white city and went to high school with a total of two black students. I was a science journalist who referred to all things supernatural as "woo-woo stuff"; Deborah believed Henrietta's spirit lived on in her cells, controlling the life of anyone who crossed its path. Including me.

"How else do you explain why your science teacher knew her real name when everyone else called her Helen Lane?" Deborah would say. "She was trying to get your attention." This thinking would apply to everything in my life: when I married while writing this book, it was because Henrietta wanted someone to take care of me while I worked. When I divorced, it was because she'd decided he was getting in the way of the book. When an editor who insisted I take the Lacks family out of the book was injured in a mysterious accident, Deborah said that's what happens when you piss Henrietta off.

The Lackses challenged everything I thought I knew about faith, science, journalism, and race. Ultimately, this [story] is the result. It's not only the story of HeLa cells and Henrietta Lacks, but of Henrietta's family—particularly Deborah—and their lifelong struggle to make peace with the existence of those cells, and the science that made them possible.

MLA CITATION

Skloot, Rebecca. "The Woman in the Photograph." *The Norton Reader: An Anthology of Nonfiction*, edited by Melissa A. Goldthwaite et al., 16th ed., W. W. Norton, 2024, pp. 497–501.

QUESTIONS

1. Was the surgeon who first cultivated Henrietta Lacks's cells for research justified in doing so? Why or why not?

2. Rebecca Skloot writes, "As I worked my way through graduate school studying writing, I became fixated on the idea of someday telling Henrietta's story" (paragraph 29). Why does Skloot find Henrietta Lacks's story so compelling?

3. This essay is the prologue to Skloot's book *The Immortal Life of Henrietta Lacks*. Why does Skloot dwell so extensively on her own story in the essay?

4. Write the story of a research project of your own. What or who motivated you to undertake the project? How did you go about your research? What obstacles did you encounter? What discoveries did you make? Looking back on the process, what did you learn about yourself as a researcher or as a person?

JOSEPH OSMUNDSON
On Going Viral

START WITH A VIRUS. In 2020, as economies worldwide shut down to limit the spread of COVID-19, we all stayed home and stared at our screens. We saw—on our screens—something happening to the sky, to the planet. Air pollution gone in Wuhan, China; water turbidity lower in Ahmedabad, India; mountains visible on the horizon from a smog-free Los Angeles in the United States. With people inside, animals returned: coyotes in San Francisco; ducks in Vegas; goats in Wales.

"We are the virus," came the memes on *Twitter*, "the earth is better without us." Nature is healing.

My response to this metaphor—"we are the virus"—is to ask what, in this imagining, is a virus and who, in this metaphor, are we. What stories does our culture tell about viruses, and how do these stories construct understanding of our bodies, our health, our neighbors, our lovers? In this viral story—*We Are the Virus*—humans have exploited the earth, emptying out and using up its resources, expanding and reproducing beyond the capacity of the earth, our host, and now the earth, our host, is slowly dying. Just like a virus, which uses our body, leaves us dying, emptied out of ourselves.

Originally published in Joseph Osmundson's book Virology: Essays for the Living, the Dead, and the Small Things in Between *(2022).*

This is one viral story: consumption, illness, death.

And isn't this a true story? Just like Ebola or HIV might do, we're ruining   5
the planet—our host—to replicate ourselves or our culture or to maximize our
wealth. Others were quick to label this thinking ecofascist—using climate
change or the earth's perceived needs as a way to eliminate "unneeded" human
beings as if too many people were the problem. There's a pretty obvious way to
fix the problem of too many humans and it's called genocide. But what's being
produced isn't too many humans, it's too many humans with extreme, obscene
wealth; maybe *they* are the virus, or capitalism itself. Couldn't *that* be true?

This viral story—even if it is true—is not without consequence. In this
story of capitalism or racism as a virus, we are naming a virus as a thing of
excessive self-interest, a thing that will overwhelm the whole, a thing that will
kill, a thing *against* life itself. What would that mean for a person living with
HIV or a person living with CMV[1] or a person living with herpes, which is to
say any person living on this living planet?

In this metaphor, there is a single viral story, and it is one of excess leading to death. This may indeed be one viral story. But applying it broadly to the
larger cultural notion of not a virus but The Virus, we quickly find that the
center will not hold.[2]

All viral stories fall apart if we just consider them enough; there are viruses
that consume and kill, but there are many, many more viruses that do not.

And you know by now that this has to do with the molecular life of the
virus. There is no perfect virus; there are RNA viruses and DNA[3] viruses;
there are enveloped and nonenveloped viruses; and each virus has a different
protein on its surface that allows it to kiss up on and interact with and maybe
even get inside a different type of cell. Some viruses come for a few days,
others for a lifetime. All of this is determined—in large part—by the molecular biology of the virus, a particular type of story, but one we too rarely tell.

"Of course," wrote Susan Sontag, "one cannot think without metaphors,"   10
which she defined, based on Aristotle, as "saying a thing is or is like something-
it-is-not."[4] "We are the virus" is therefore a metaphor, calling one thing another.
Language is metaphorical in this way, where words stand in for the things they
represent. "Table," the word, is not a table; the word conjures the table and, in
a way, becomes it.

Microbiology is a real world, microbes are real, material things, but they
are not like a table. When we say "bacterium" or when we say "virus," the word
conjures the invisible material, things too small for *us* to see. Say "*Staphylococcus*" and "table" to a person on the street and ask what image each word
conjures. A table is a goddamned table! If *Staph* means anything at all, it's a

---

1. Cytomegalovirus.

2. Allusion to "The Second Coming" by Irish poet William Butler Yeats (1865–1939):
"Things fall apart; the centre cannot hold."

3. Ribonucleic acid and deoxyribonucleic acid, molecules that carry genetic information.

4. From *Illness as Metaphor; and AIDS and Its Metaphors* (1989) by American writer
and filmmaker Sontag (1933–2004).

wound, an infection, not a bacterium. But *Staphylococcus aureus* lives on the skin or in the nose of between 30 and 50 percent of the healthy population without ever causing an infection, producing a wound. What is *Staph* then? The very language of microbes is built from metaphor; this looks like a crown, *corona*; this looks like an envelope, *env*; this looks like a spike, the spike protein now, *S*; these bacteria look like a bunch of grapes under a microscope, and so *staphylo-*, ancient Greek for that fruit still attached to its vine, nothing, or everything, to do with a wound, depending on how you look.

Yet, when it comes to health, Sontag demands that we remove metaphors from our thinking, our language, entirely. "But the metaphors cannot be distanced by just abstaining from them. They have to be exposed, criticized, belabored, used up." When looking at microbes, metaphors are so baked into our language that I think it is impossible to use them up. They will always exist; it becomes our imperative to choose metaphors and stories that have the capacity to not harm but heal.

HIV is a virus, a material thing. Functionally, while HIV might not be exactly the same sequence as it was in 1981, it's largely the same virus: the same genes in the same order that bind to the same cells that replicate in the same way and to the same effect. What HIV means now is not the same thing it meant in 1981 or 1987 or 1997 or 2007.[5]

Viral stories will change, their centers will not hold.

15   One way to use up harmful metaphors of The Virus is to ask if they are true to begin with. But a true metaphor can still do harm. HIV does kill, but it is not the most typical virus. COVID-19 kills. Influenza killed my friend Sarah. But viruses exist all around us, always. Most of them do us no harm. To generalize, to make metaphors and narratives, from the *only* deadly exceptions as opposed to the benign rule is just one lazy way to not quite tell the full truth. If these stories—I will start telling some of them now—are almost-true but harmful, we must tell also the more common, or more careful, or more loving stories, the metaphors, that describe the world we live in *and* the one we want to build.

Lose someone to a virus. On February 11, 2009, while working in my lab studying phage, I got a phone call from a college acquaintance I didn't keep in good touch with. Worry, immediately. Why was she calling at 11 A.M. on a workday when we hadn't spoken in years? I stood up and walked to the lab's stockroom, the one place in the open-floor workspace with a hint of privacy that didn't also have a toilet in it. It was a small room, maybe 8 feet by 8 feet, with metal shelving units built against the wall, stacked with boxes full of petri dishes and pipette tips and filter units for sterilizing buffers. I took the call as I rushed into the room to make sure it wouldn't go to voicemail. I sat down on a large box shoved up against the shelves.

5. In 1981, the US Centers for Disease Control and Prevention acknowledged the disease now called AIDS (this acronym was adopted in 1982); in 1987, the NAMES Project Memorial Quilt, or AIDS Quilt, was displayed on the National Mall, Washington, DC; in 1997, new HIV infections reached a global peak; in 2007, the World Health Organization published its most recent revision of its scheme for classifying HIV infections.

"Sarah died last night." She was crying.

I called Andrei immediately. He worked just one floor below. "Come to the stockroom. The Darst lab stockroom." In 2 minutes he was there, hugging me.

"Honey, what happened?" It was the first death of a close friend. How could I even explain?

Sarah Tilman was one of my best friends from college. Only weeks before,   20 I'd taken a cheap bus down to Washington, DC, to visit her. I stayed on her couch. Both biology majors with French minors, she now taught bio at a public high school and I was starting my PhD, a couple years in. We'd been study buddies but quickly became friends. I had a crush on her, of course, but it never amounted to much. She was from Minneapolis; her dad was an ecology professor. She'd sold her car because, after moving from Minnesota, she found she didn't need it out east. She taught high school because she loved kids; she was part of the Washington DC Teacher Corps because she thought Teach For America sucked—they just have a bunch of idiot kids working there, they teach for two years, all first-year teachers suck, and then they go off to work in policy or whatever. Sarah was in it for the long haul, 10 years at least, because she became better and could give more to her kids.

Those are facts about my friend, who died. I'd tell you, but I forgot her favorite color. Excuse me a second. I have to get a glass of water.

Two months later, I sat across the table from a lawyer in the Starbucks near my lab. She asked questions about Sarah. Was she thinking about grad school? Yes. How long did she plan to continue teaching? At least two or three more years, she was deciding between grad school in education and in biology. Sarah shouldn't have died. This lawyer, hair tied up, dressed in a dark gray suit, was here to determine how much her life was worth. I hated her, but smiled at her and pretended everything was fine. Just a normal meeting in a normal Starbucks on a normal Wednesday afternoon. When I'd visited Sarah just weeks before she died, we'd had a big debrief about her next steps. This lawyer needed to know that information so she could plug it into a formula about future earnings and decide how much the doctors who led to her death needed to pay her family. I saw the spreadsheet in her head, the numbers ticking off, what my friend had become: money.

Sarah died of flu. Two weeks before, we went out drinking. As a teacher, she was worried about the winter virus season, so we used Emergen-C powder as a mixer, just powder and vodka and ice. We knew to mix the powder in first before cooling the drink on ice because the powder would be less soluble in cold water; we'd learned that together. We were with another friend—I don't remember, now, who. The three of us, 27 years old, children really, drinking vodka and Emergen-C before going out dancing at a gay bar.

She died of a virus. Influenza A. The virus had infected cells in her heart, which it occasionally does, but the hospital had failed to recognize a severe dip in her blood pressure. They sent her home. Hours later, feeling ill again, she called an ambulance. When she stood up to walk out of her home, her blood pressure dangerously low, she had a heart attack. They never could restart her virus-laden heart. She died.

25   In a classroom, in 2004, I'd sat next to Sarah and learned about influenza, how it's a virus with eight separate RNA molecules, viral chromosomes in a way. We learned, too, about how these eight molecules and the fact that flu infected swine and birds and us and could swap these eight molecules around made it a high-risk virus for becoming a respiratory pandemic, killing millions, just like in 1918.[6]

It didn't take a pandemic for Sarah to die. She died a viral death. My grief was too much to bear.

At her funeral, everyone spoke of heaven and seeing her again, but I didn't believe in that, and I don't think Sarah did either. I remember thinking to myself that it had never been as hard to not believe as it was just then. I remember thinking you can't just believe when you want to, you had to believe all the time, and I knew I wasn't capable of that. I'd tried. I was sitting in a church crying. She had an open casket but I couldn't look at her body, dead. I knew my goodbye to her was final. But looking back now, I feel like I say goodbye each time I remember her, and then remember, again, that she's not here.

In my email, from the lawyer, with the subject line "Tilman case":

> I just wanted to let you know that this case settled on Friday, so there will be no trial appearance asked of you. I think that ——— and ——— Tilman were pleased overall with how things went, and felt a sense of closure. They are wonderful people. Thank you very much for your assistance, and your willingness to meet with me and talk about Sarah, it was definitely helpful.
> Wishing you all the best in the future!
>
> Regards,

I know what viruses can do. A virus killed one of my best friends. But to stay mad at the virus is to stay mad at the world. She died because doctors didn't care for her well enough. Care could have saved her. It should have. It is care we need in this viral world.

30   I think I'm writing so much about the lawyer because if I even tried to describe what she looked like, Sarah, I would remember that I'd never see her again. The lawyer was tall and thin with dark hair; she had thin eyebrows and kind eyes, which—I think—she practiced. Sarah was short and rail thin, she had brown hair that she sometimes straightened but that naturally curled. Her smile, when she was smiling, crept up one side of her face more than the other, just slightly, which is how you knew she hadn't practiced it, it was real, and there she was, smiling at you.

Conjure a virus. Just years before we first saw a virus on an electron microscope, author Zora Neale Hurston wrote one down. Janie, somewhere near the

---

6. The 1918 influenza pandemic is estimated to have caused between 50 and 100 million deaths.

end of *Their Eyes Were Watching God*,[7] having left one husband and buried another, is something-like-happy with her third husband, Tea Cake. They live out on the muck farming when a storm hits, a hurricane, and everything is mud and everything else is water. In the chaos of the storm, Tea Cake is bitten by a rabid dog. When the storm finally goes, rabies makes the chaos of the storm physical in the body of Tea Cake:

"Tea Cake was lying with his eyes closed and Janie hoped he was asleep. He wasn't. A great fear had took hold of him. What was this thing that set his brains afire and grabbed at his throat with iron fingers? Where did it come from and why did it hang around him?"

"Tea Cake had two bad attacks that night. Janie saw a changing look come in his face. Tea Cake was gone. Something else was looking out of his face."

Rabies, a virus, is taking Tea Cake away from Janie. But it's not just killing him. Before he dies, the rabies is turning him into something he isn't. Even while he's alive, he's gone, his body no longer under his control.

Rabies is a single-stranded RNA virus that infects muscle cells and neurons, the cells used to send information in, to, and from our brains. This is why rabies take us away before we die: once it arrives in our brains, it kills our neurons. And which neurons it kills might not be random either; evolution appears to have favored rabies viruses that specifically kill regions of the brain resulting in aggressive behavior and fear of nothing except water. It's from the salivary glands that the virus must find its next host, through a bite. Aggressive behavior and not swallowing anything, not even spit, probably helps the virus move on.

Janie is protective of Tea Cake, even in this state: "Folks would do such mean things to her Tea Cake if they saw him in such a fix. Treat Tea Cake like he was some mad dog when nobody in the world had more kindness about them."

But the virus had its own story to write, written there in its RNA genome: "Tea Cake couldn't come back to himself until he had got rid of that mad dog that was in him and he couldn't get rid of the dog and live. He had to die to get rid of the dog."

These days, and even then, rabies doesn't have to kill. It's not the only version of this story. The doctor that Janie sees after the hurricane tells her that another version of everything was possible: "Some shots right after it happened would have fixed him right up," he says. Rabies rarely kills now; we can vaccinate after an animal bite right up until the moment when the virus reaches the brain, where it will do its worst damage. Rabies is still out there, in the world, and it probably always will be because of its presence and spread in animals. But through science and medicine, we can insist that it doesn't have the final say.

This is one viral fear that we have, being taken over, losing ourselves, effectively becoming a *zombie*. Something in us eating our brain but letting us live. Something taking over our brain and telling us to *chase! run! bite!* but absolutely not, ever, to drink. "And she was beginning to feel fear," Hurston wrote of Janie,

7. Hurston (1891–1960), major Black novelist, folklorist, and anthropologist; *Their Eyes Were Watching God*, Hurston's novel that was published in 1937.

"of this strange thing in Tea Cake's body." This *strange thing*, this nightmare, this virus, turning us into something like itself: not living but not yet dead.

40   Imagine going viral. See, viruses can mean so many things, and here the excess of the virus is not to be feared but longed for. Susan Sontag wrote that "one set of messages of the society we live in is: Consume. Grow. Do what you want. Amuse yourselves." In late capitalism, we exchange our labor for money, and that money for things and experiences. "The very working of this economic system," she wrote, "which has bestowed these unprecedented liberties, most cherished in the form of physical mobility and material prosperity, depends on encouraging people to defy limits."

This desire she names for growth, consumption, for never-enough, is central to the viral metaphors we use. Some viruses have the ability to replicate within hours, infecting one cell, then a hundred, then a thousand, so difficult for the fully living to achieve. This exponential growth, too, is seen in the ability of information to flow via the Internet: if one person shares a video, and then three people share that video, and then each one of those people who receive it has three people share that video in turn, you can reach an unprecedented number of eyes and minds in an astonishingly short time.

The use of viral metaphors to describe information flow through culture likely begins, in the modern era, with Richard Dawkins defining a *meme* in his book *The Selfish Gene*.[8] Dawkins's project is both revolutionary and deeply troubling; he is applying the laws of Darwin[9] (survival of the fittest[10]) not to the level of individual organisms like you or me, but to our genetic units, to the genes we carry. It's our genes that "want" to survive and multiply. We, as living, thinking people, are helpless carriers of the true tyrants of evolutionary need: our DNA. That Dawkins would end up being so shitty and racist is not surprising to me; social Darwinism is an extension of Darwin's theory of survival of the fittest into social structures: poor people are less good and deserve to die. Dawkins applies survival of the fittest to the most microscopic level, social Darwinists to the most macro biological level: culture. Both overextend the metaphor beyond the possibility of something-like truth and into the realm of overt, measurable, too-flat-to-be-true harm.

Dawkins's ideas do hold some water in some cases (sequences related to viruses are the most likely to evolve "selfishly," as he argues). All these cis white men! In their imaginations, the possibility that life could be collective, communal, isn't real. The metaphor is always individualistic, always selfish, always a brutal war for limited resources, the options being death alone or survival alone. Of course, there are many ways in which evolution does indeed

8. Dawkins, English evolutionary biologist and writer (b. 1941) known for championing atheism; *The Selfish Gene*, Dawkins's book that was published in 1976.

9. Charles Darwin (1809–1882), English naturalist who, in *On the Origin of Species* (1859), identified natural selection as the cause of biological evolution.

10. The phrase "survival of the fittest" was first used not by Darwin but by the English biologist and sociologist Herbert Spencer (1820–1903) in his *Principles of Biology* (1864).

act on organisms (and even communities) as opposed to genes alone. In his work, though, he defines a meme: a piece of information that flows through culture. Ideas or performances can evolve over time a lot like life: replication and mutation, competition and variation. And the best memes will travel the farthest the fastest, through competition, the survival of the clickiest (sorry).

Viruses—and going viral—promise us just exactly what COVID-19 demonstrated in early 2019: exponential growth seemingly without limit. Living organisms follow rules of replication and reproduction, where one becomes two becomes four becomes eight; viruses know no such laws.

On *Twitter*, one can have only 2,000 (or even 200) followers and write 45 that perfect tweet. A writer I used to date told me, one night, that he knew for a fact that people in the Kardashian family read his *Twitter* feed, and one day, maybe, they'd re-tweet him, and from there . . . I didn't get a clear sense of what he thought would happen next.

Leave Britney Alone! and Charley bit my finger! and David after Dentist! and hashtag FreeBritney! and Antoine Dodson! Dodson went viral for a local news clip recorded the day after his sister was nearly raped in the home they shared. It was full of Black queer anger and resilience, It went viral. Within weeks, he had a song on iTunes, appearances on NBC, a merchandise line, and a website. He endorsed a sex offender tracker app. His goal was to raise enough money to get his family a home in a safer neighborhood. Within a few months, his family was able to move. Within two years, he was working on a *Beverly Hillbillies*–type[11] reality show about his family's attempted move to Los Angeles, which never materialized. In 2018, he posted a *YouTube* video using catchphrases from his video to promote his business in real estate. CelebrityNetWorth.com, in 2020, listed his net worth as $100,000, which is less than half the median home cost in Huntsville, Alabama, where he now lives.

Of course there are exceptions, artists savvy and talented enough to use virality to create a lasting creative platform and not just 15 nanoseconds of fame. Lil Nas X[12] is my favorite; his TikToks are hilarious, his music catchy, his celebrity joyous. His trolling of folks who told him he was going to hell with his "Montero" video? I mean, we don't deserve him.

Lil Nas X, though, is the anomaly. That so many stories of viral success end with a family-sit-com return to life-as-before doesn't seem to deter our collective desire for this type of attention. I work on it constantly, but I feel it in myself, too. We may want to go viral for the right reasons—for an essay, not a banana peel nosedive on camera—but we want to go viral nonetheless. The viral story: break the rules of life, spread everywhere faster than we can even imagine. For so many of us, like Dodson, like many folks I grew up with back home, the options for escaping one's hellish predicament seem so limited; going viral might be a lottery you know you're certain to lose sooner or later, but at least you're holding, in your hand, a piece of paper that could turn itself into a ticket out.

11. American sitcom (1962–71) about a family from the Ozarks who discover oil on their property, become rich, and move to Beverly Hills.
12. American rapper (b. 1999).

Going viral also allows the possibility of building one's celebrity (and therefore earning ability) outside of traditional media. One doesn't need to be the child of an actor to have access to media industry insiders—agents and casting agents. One doesn't have to be cast in a VH1 reality show. One just needs an *Instagram* or *Twitter* or *Twitch* or *TikTok* or whatever will come next. The raced, classed, gendered aspects of this are obvious. Many minoritized people have gone viral, and some have used that virality to build a lasting career. Writer Kiese Laymon dedicated his first book to "the Internet" after a viral essay on Gawker.com helped him sell thousands of copies with no support from his small press. He'd spent years being ignored by mainstream publishing who didn't think his stories would sell to their imagined readers. The Internet—virality—showed that he had readers, that he could sell books to people publishing didn't think *read*. With virality offering novel pathways to creative success, especially to queer people and people of color, no wonder it's also derided, mocked, called immature, pathological, superficial.

50   If going viral (or playing a professional sport, or taking on hundreds of thousands of dollars of college debt) is needed to be able to have the resources to live a good life, there is a problem not with our desire for virality, but in the circumstances of our everyday lives, of the cultural body we make up. What's wrong with our everyday lives to create this need? We too often lack resources, financial stability, healthcare independent of our work, the right to work, the right, too, to leisure and making and consuming art. Kiese Laymon calls this having healthy choices and second chances, and we all deserve both. Who has access to either depends on gender and sexuality and race and class and geography and so much more. Here again the metaphor of the virus is pointing to the wrong harm. Going viral isn't pathological, nor is our desire for virality. Our culture—where so many live so close to death on a daily basis—profoundly is.

And yet this desire, this obsession, can drive us mad, even as we blame ourselves for not surviving well enough in a death-making world.

Watch a virus. In the popular (but not very good) American film *I Am Legend*, Will Smith plays the sexiest ever virologist living in the aftermath of a deadly viral pandemic. In his basement lab, he searches for a cure. He does clinical trials on lab rats. On the radio, he calls out for other survivors. At night the zombies come out, called Darkseekers, to hunt for uninfected flesh. The virus, originally rolled out as a vaccine-like cure for cancer, killed most of humanity and turned most of the rest against itself. This, like in most zombie movies, is a death worse than death, a never-ending death, a death wherein we feast on the living, whether we once loved them or not. This viral story, this metaphor (the virus turning us into something we're not, the virus turning us into an image of itself, always hungry for a new host) is an extension of the rabies viral stories like Hurston's.

The film also uses one of the most common viral stories; in a flashback to the initial viral crisis, with a cancer vaccine mutating and killing those never vaccinated, Will Smith's wife asks him, "Did it jump? Is it airborne?" Once the virus is airborne, invisible but everywhere, nothing can stop it. Never mind that many viruses already are airborne, or travel by air, including rhinoviruses, measles, influenza, and yes, coronaviruses, too. "Did it jump?" Can the virus jump from body to body through the air, no physical connection? What then? What now?

I'm a virologist (sort of) and I have a dog (unlike Smith's German shepherd, Max is 15 pounds and afraid of plastic bags blowing in the wind). In the world of *I Am Legend*, as in the postapocalypse of *The Road* or *The Walking Dead*, I would have been sure not to survive the mass death, even if by my own hand. I'm not the type of virologist who would watch his family die and stick around looking for the cure. I would just choose to die, too.

In this story, in this viral metaphor, the virus itself stands in for the hubris of humanity. It comes from an attempt to subvert nature, to cure cancer by using a virus. The virus is there to show us nature will always win; it's human-made but—like nature itself—cannot be controlled. "God didn't do this!" Will Smith screams at the first human he meets in years. "We did!"   55

For centuries, syphilis did what we now imagine rabies to do. Because tertiary syphilis infects and kills cells in the human brain, it can affect behavior and mood. It can turn us into a living non-self. In the twentieth century, antibiotics intervened. Then viruses filled that void. From Hurston's very real rabies to Will Smith's imagined Krippin virus, the human horror is becoming a shell, a body without a brain. Viruses are our tool to tell stories of this horror.

I watched my grandfather die, a shell of himself, barely able to speak, not able to walk. He couldn't remember who I was. Why don't we tell of this essential human fear—losing our minds but not our bodies—with the stories we have, the true ones, about the people who we've lost this way? For one thing, unlike Will Smith, my grandpa couldn't take off his shirt and do L-sit pull-ups on camera. Dementia doesn't make you chase down folks, although it can make you bite. It may be partially genetic, but it isn't infectious—unless you mean its mad cow cousin. Viruses have become a way of telling the story of lost cognitive ability while actually looking away from the vast majority of lives we lose this way. We seem not to deem most of the people dementia happens to worthy of telling stories about. No heroes to be found there. No saving the world, no fixing it, no six-packed scientists, fighting the very thing that might kill them.

In the original book *I Am Legend* by Richard Matheson, the zombies are not made by viral infection but by infection with a bacterium. In the years between the book (1954) and the movie (2007), we witnessed HIV and Ebola and SARS. Rabies, the actual virus that makes us zombie-like for a time before we die, has faded from our collective consciousness. Here in America, it is extremely rare in humans. The real virus has been replaced by a metaphorical one, a virus that can do anything, the idea of a virus. Even in that horrible year, 2020, what we imagined was worse than the worst nature can do.

MLA CITATION

Osmundson, Joseph. "On Going Viral." *The Norton Reader: An Anthology of Nonfiction*, edited by Melissa A. Goldthwaite et al., 16th ed., W. W. Norton, 2024, pp. 502–11.

QUESTIONS

1. In this essay, Joseph Osmundson ponders different meanings of the metaphor or story of "The Virus" (paragraph 7). What are these different meanings? He is particularly interested in how these metaphors and stories break down: "All viral stories fall apart if we just consider them enough" (paragraph 8). How do the metaphors and stories Osmundson considers fall apart?

2. Osmundson divides his essay into five sections. Note their different topics, themes, arguments, and stylistic registers. How do these sections progress from one to the next? What connects them? Annotate the essay, noting turning points in his style and argument.

3. How would you characterize Osmundson's voice in this essay? How is it informed by his expertise as a virologist?

4. Osmundson criticizes social Darwinism, the "extension of Darwin's theory of survival of the fittest into social structures," for stretching this "metaphor beyond the possibility of something-like truth and into the realm of overt, measurable, too-flat-to-be-true harm" (paragraph 42). What does Osmundson mean by this statement? What alternative conception of culture and society does he offer?

5. We are all experts in something. Using Osmundson's essay as a model, do a project in which you use your own expertise in some area to interpret a personal experience, social phenomenon, or event.

CHRIS WIEWIORA
This Is Tossing

I T'S 10 A.M. An hour before Lazy Moon Pizzeria opens. You have an hour—this hour—to toss. You're supposed to have 11 pies by 11 A.M. One hour.

You have always failed to have 11 by 11. Sometimes you fail because you went to bed after midnight or didn't have a bowl of cereal in the morning or you tear a pie and then you're already down one and you don't believe you can ever be anywhere near perfect. On those days, the store manager comes over and inspects your not-yet-full pie rack and shakes his head. More often, you fail because the manager didn't turn on the doughpress, so you have to wait for it to warm up; or he didn't pull a tray of dough from the fridge, so all the doughballs are still frozen; or one of the two ovens wasn't turned on, so you'll be slower without being able to cook two pies at once. On those days you shake your head and maybe swear a bit, cursing the situation more than the manager, because you already feel like a failure before you've

Published in MAKE (2013), *a Chicago-based literary magazine that is "chock full of fiction, poetry, essays, art, and review." Chris Wiewiora's essay appeared in an issue devoted to architecture.*

even started. Either way, this everyday failure to meet a near impossible expectation weighs down on you. If you could do 11 by 11—just once—you feel like you would truly be a professional, albeit a professional pizza tosser, and it would prove that what you do in this restaurant matters.

But instead of focusing on all that, focus on what you can do: try to go to bed early the night before, in the morning eat a bowl of cereal with your coffee, and on the way to work take it easy, drive nice and easy—not slow or fast, but easy—because 11 by 11 is hard, almost impossible, and you don't need to think about that when you open the door to the restaurant's *err-err* electronic buzzer.

And today when you walk in, in between the *err-err*, the music blasting through the restaurant's sound system is good; some simple drum beats, a bass line thumping in your throat, and guitar riffs with a hook. Bluesy rock 'n' roll. You bounce your foot as you put on your apron and clock in a few minutes early.

You wash your hands humming the Happy Birthday song to yourself. It's   5
not your birthday, or anyone's birthday that you know of, but you're supposed to wash your hands for approximately 20 seconds. There's a laminated paper above all the hand-washing sinks that says to sing the ABCs, but you don't want to feel like some kid who doesn't know how to do his job.

Today, and all days that you toss, you're tucked behind the counter by the door, where you will welcome customers when they come in. But for now you should focus on tossing. You take a look at the clock. It blinks 9:59 A.M. You have an hour.

You check that the doughpress is on; it ticks like a coffeemaker's hotplate. The temperature knob is set right. And (yes!) there's a tray of dough already out. You're ready. Here goes.

The dough has risen a little, each bag forming a sliced-off cone, a plateau. You take the spray bottle of extra virgin olive oil and squirt twice on a hubcap-size round plate that you call the swivel plate because it's set on a swivel arm attached to the dough press. You spread the oil on the swivel plate with your bare hands, glossing the surface as well as your skin.

You pick up a bag of dough, feeling its weight settle in your palm. You know it's at least three point five pounds, no more than three point seven five. And out of the plastic, the dough feels like condensed flesh, like a too-heavy breast. You can't help that that's what you think of when you take the mound of dough in your hands and place it nippleside up on the swivel plate.

You push the cone down into itself to form a thick circle. You keep push-   10
ing with the palm of your hand around and around the circle to even it out, so the circle of dough will fit in the space the swivel plate will swivel under. Above is a heated plate that will come down and sandwich the dough.

You swivel the swivel plate, lining it up with the hotplate, and take hold of a lever in front of you and pull down with both hands. You don't press down so hard that the dough spills out of the circumference, but also not so lightly that the dough only warms on the outside while the core is still cold. You count six "Mississippi's" as the dough flattens and warms and expands into a bigger and bigger and bigger and bigger and bigger and bigger circle.

You pull up the handle, swivel out that swivel plate, take the edge of the dough in your hand, flip it over like a pancake, swivel the swivel plate back into its space and pull down on the handle, letting the hotplate press down again. You repeat until the fourth flip, when you *really* press down, spilling the dough out the sides. You lift up the handle and again swivel out the swivel plate, but now you lift the dough up and off the swivel plate altogether, placing it onto a tray called a sheetpan.

This circle of dough is called a patout, because before the dough press—and you can imagine how hard it was to do this—tossers would have to physically push down on the cold dough and shape it with force. No more than six patouts stack each tray, because more than that squishes them with their own weight. When you have filled two trays they go one above the other on a rack-cart that you wheel under a stainless steel counter.

At the counter, you burrito-roll each patout off the tray and unfurl it. There are two plastic containers: one with bright yellow grains like sand (but it's cornmeal), and another filled with fluffy flour. For now, it's only flour you need. You take a handful and spread it on the stainless steel counter, powdering the olive-oil-slick dough. Along the edge of the floured patout, you press into the dough with your fingers in a 180-degree arc, forming a crust on half of one side and then the other. And so, one by one, your stack of patouts is floured up.

15   Behind you is the pie rack where large wooden paddles called peels rest after they've pulled pies out of the oven to cool. On top of the pie rack is a square peel without a handle. Next to the floury counter is another counter where this particular peel goes. On it, you will sprinkle—just sprinkle—a little bit of cornmeal so that when the big thirty-inch "skin" of the pie is laid on top and the sauce is ladled onto the skin—when that is all done you can easily shake the pie off the peel, leaving it in the oven to bake.

Now, you set your stance. Lower body: legs under your shoulders and knees bent, with your weight up on your forefoot, your heels hardly touching the linoleum floor. Upper body: torso taut but elastic, because you know that you will be twisting back and forth. Then with your hands straight out, fingers together like you're about to go swimming and thumbs tucked in so they don't pierce the dough, you're ready.

You lightly pinch the first patout. The flour makes taking the patout off the stack feel like a silky turn of a page. You lay the patout over your other hand and, it's odd, but initially you slap the dough back and forth with your hands. It begins in your wrists, the dough not only slapping but also rotating between your palms in a figure eight, an infinity symbol, an hourglass.

If someone looked closely they would see that in front of your chest, your right middle finger briefly touches your left middle finger. Then your right hand slides from your left middle finger toward your left inner elbow, while your left forearm remains straight. From above, when your two middle fingers touch, your arms will look like an equilateral triangle with one side always collapsing toward its opposite corner, pivoting back and forth, back and forth.

It's confusing. But you've done this so much by now that you just feel it. As you go on, your hands slap the dough in a curvy crisscross motion, making it turn, making it stretch into a larger circle. A circle big enough now to toss.

And this is what a tosser does. (Yes, you will sauce the skin of dough, and   20
put the pie in the oven, and set the timer for 3 minutes, maybe 30 seconds more or less depending on how cool or hot the ovens are that day. And after the pies have cooled, you'll cut some of them into halves and quarters, while leaving a few pies whole.) But what really defines you as a tosser is not the patouts or the flouring or the cutting, but the tossing. It sounds so simple, but you're a tosser because you toss. And this, this is it:

You drape the dough over your left forearm like a dishrag. No, not a dishrag. That's too much like a waiter. And you're so much more than that. You think, How many people in the world know how to do something so particular?

You're not even in the restaurant when you toss. You're elsewhere. It's you and the dough, like matador and bull. You can imagine that flap of dough like a cape. And since you imagine the dough to be a cape, you can imagine the rest of it all as sport, too. And the dough hangs down, slung low, where your right hand cups the heaviest, lowest edge. Your left hand will spring up and out, and your entire left arm will straighten as your shoulder locks, then your elbow, then your wrist, so that your arm shoots out like a discus thrower's.

But before that, your body winds up by corkscrewing down: your left arm lurches to your hips and curls behind your back, your torso twists, and you're crunched down with so much potential energy that when you come up, it all goes into your right hand, which whisks the dough off your wrist like it's a Frisbee. And if you snapped a picture of this moment, your left hand would be turning over, palm-side up, opening. That same swimming hand that slapped the dough now ready to receive it when it comes back like a boomerang. That dough spinning, spinning, spinning in the air, its beauty summed up by little kids who come to the counter to watch. You know they want to ask you how you do it, but instead of asking, maybe because you're an adult, they point and then explain to you, or the parent holding them up, or especially a younger sibling: "It's magic!"

You know exactly what these kids mean, because every time you are here under the dough, you remember back—way back—to kindergarten. When you were out on the playground for recess, away from the dull pounding of the fluorescent lights. The best days of recess were when you all played parachute with the extraordinarily large multicolored nylon circle. You and all the rest of the kids got hold of a spot and, together, lifted the parachute up and then down, trapping air under it, like catching a big empty cloud. But what you really loved was when everyone lifted the parachute up again, releasing the air, and before the parachute floated down, one by one, you all got a turn to run under its stained-glass canopy.

You come out of the zone. You glance at the clock. Its red block numbers   25
blink 10:55. You're on your last pie. The others are on the rack, cut, and logged in. And this one will only take 3 minutes in the oven. It doesn't take you longer than 2 minutes and change to toss and sauce a pie. You've almost played a perfect game. 11 by 11. One hour. Just one more.

And you take this last circle of dough, slap it back and forth, and wind up and toss it so that the dough nearly brushes one bulb of the draped Christmas tree lights strung from the ceiling tiles. And as you're under the dough—for a second you feel trapped, because you realize after this you can't ever be better— you wish you could be back in school, having fun like a kid again with no expectation of something perfect never being better. But you're here, on this last pie, with your left arm open and ready and waiting as it spins and spins and spins above you, about to come down.

MLA CITATION

Wiewiora, Chris. "This Is Tossing." *The Norton Reader: An Anthology of Nonfiction*, edited by Melissa A. Goldthwaite et al., 16th ed., W. W. Norton, 2024, pp. 512–16.

QUESTIONS

1. Chris Wiewiora uses sensory language—specifically sight, sound, and touch—to help readers imaginatively experience the process of tossing pizza dough. Locate places in the essay where his use of sensory language helps you imagine this process clearly.

2. Wiewiora uses the second-person point of view ("you") and present tense. Why do you think he uses that perspective and verb tense? How do these choices affect your reading of the essay?

3. Write an essay in which you guide readers through a process, teaching them to do something that may be unfamiliar to them. Like Wiewiora, use sensory language, the second-person point of view, and present tense.

MIKE ROSE
Blue-Collar Brilliance

M Y MOTHER, ROSE MERAGLIO ROSE (Rosie), shaped her adult identity as a waitress in coffee shops and family restaurants. When I was growing up in Los Angeles during the 1950s, my father and I would occasionally hang out at the restaurant until her shift ended, and then we'd ride the bus home with her. Sometimes she worked the register and the counter, and we sat there; when she waited booths and tables, we found a booth in the back where the waitresses took their breaks.

There wasn't much for a child to do at the restaurant, and so as the hours stretched out, I watched the cooks and waitresses and listened to what they said. At mealtimes, the pace of the kitchen staff and the din from customers picked

Published in the American Scholar *(2009), a magazine published by the Phi Beta Kappa society. In this essay, as in much of his other work, Mike Rose approaches his arguments about class, education, and literacy through his personal experience and family history.*

up. Weaving in and out around the room, waitresses warned *behind you* in impassive but urgent voices. Standing at the service window facing the kitchen, they called out abbreviated orders. *Fry four on two,* my mother would say as she clipped a check onto the metal wheel. Her tables were *deuces, four-tops,* or *six-tops,* according to their size; seating areas also were nicknamed. The *racetrack,* for instance, was the fast-turnover front section. Lingo conferred authority and signaled know-how.

Rosie took customers' orders, pencil poised over pad, while fielding questions about the food. She walked full tilt through the room with plates stretching up her left arm and two cups of coffee somehow cradled in her right hand. She stood at a table or booth and removed a plate for this person, another for that person, then another, remembering who had the hamburger, who had the fried shrimp, almost always getting it right. She would haggle with the cook about a returned order and rush by us, saying, *He gave me lip, but I got him.* She'd take a minute to flop down in the booth next to my father. *I'm all in,* she'd say, and whisper something about a customer. Gripping the outer edge of the table with one hand, she'd watch the room and note, in the flow of our conversation, who needed a refill, whose order was taking longer to prepare than it should, who was finishing up.

I couldn't have put it in words when I was growing up, but what I observed in my mother's restaurant defined the world of adults, a place where competence was synonymous with physical work. I've since studied the working habits of blue-collar workers and have come to understand how much my mother's kind of work demands of both body and brain. A waitress acquires knowledge and intuition about the ways and the rhythms of the restaurant business. Waiting on seven to nine tables, each with two to six customers, Rosie devised memory strategies so that she could remember who ordered what. And because she knew the average time it took to prepare different dishes, she could monitor an order that was taking too long at the service station.

Like anyone who is effective at physical work, my mother learned *to work*   5
smart, as she put it, *to make every move count.* She'd sequence and group tasks: What could she do first, then second, then third as she circled through her station? What tasks could be clustered? She did everything on the fly, and when problems arose—technical or human—she solved them within the flow of work, while taking into account the emotional state of her co-workers. Was the manager in a good mood? Did the cook wake up on the wrong side of the bed? If so, how could she make an extra request or effectively return an order?

And then, of course, there were the customers who entered the restaurant with all sorts of needs, from physiological ones, including the emotions that accompany hunger, to a sometimes complicated desire for human contact. Her tip depended on how well she responded to these needs, and so she became adept at reading social cues and managing feelings, both the customers' and her own. No wonder, then, that Rosie was intrigued by psychology. The restaurant became the place where she studied human behavior, puzzling over the problems of her regular customers and refining her ability to deal with people in a difficult world. She took pride in *being among the public,* she'd say. *There isn't a day that goes by in the restaurant that you don't learn something.*

Rosie solved technical and human problems on the fly.

My mother quit school in the seventh grade to help raise her brothers and sisters. Some of those siblings made it through high school, and some dropped out to find work in railroad yards, factories, or restaurants. My father finished a grade or two in primary school in Italy and never darkened the schoolhouse door again. I didn't do well in school either. By high school I had accumulated a spotty academic record and many hours of hazy disaffection. I spent a few years on the vocational track, but in my senior year I was inspired by my English teacher and managed to squeak into a small college on probation.

My freshman year was academically bumpy, but gradually I began to see formal education as a means of fulfillment and as a road toward making a living. I studied the humanities and later the social and psychological sciences and taught for 10 years in a range of situations—elementary school, adult education courses, tutoring centers, a program for Vietnam veterans[1] who wanted to go to

1. American veterans of a twenty-two-year (1954–75) conflict between South Vietnam, which was allied with the United States, and communist North Vietnam.

college. Those students had socioeconomic and educational backgrounds similar to mine. Then I went back to graduate school to study education and cognitive psychology[2] and eventually became a faculty member in a school of education.

Intelligence is closely associated with formal education—the type of schooling a person has, how much and how long—and most people seem to move comfortably from that notion to a belief that work requiring less schooling requires less intelligence. These assumptions run through our cultural history, from the post—Revolutionary War period, when mechanics were characterized by political rivals as illiterate and therefore incapable of participating in government, until today. More than once I've heard a manager label his workers as "a bunch of dummies." Generalizations about intelligence, work, and social class deeply affect our assumptions about ourselves and each other, guiding the ways we use our minds to learn, build knowledge, solve problems, and make our way through the world.

Although writers and scholars have often looked at the working class, they have generally focused on the values such workers exhibit rather than on the thought their work requires—a subtle but pervasive omission. Our cultural iconography promotes the muscled arm, sleeve rolled tight against biceps, but no brightness behind the eye, no image that links hand and brain.   10

One of my mother's brothers, Joe Meraglio, left school in the ninth grade to work for the Pennsylvania Railroad.[3] From there he joined the Navy, returned to the railroad, which was already in decline, and eventually joined his older brother at General Motors[4] where, over a 33-year career, he moved from working on the assembly line to supervising the paint-and-body department. When I was a young man, Joe took me on a tour of the factory. The floor was loud—in some places deafening—and when I turned a corner or opened a door, the smell of chemicals knocked my head back. The work was repetitive and taxing, and the pace was inhuman.

Still, for Joe the shop floor provided what school did not; it was *like schooling*, he said, a place where *you're constantly learning*. Joe learned the most efficient way to use his body by acquiring a set of routines that were quick and preserved energy. Otherwise he would never have survived on the line.

As a foreman, Joe constantly faced new problems and became a consummate multi-tasker, evaluating a flurry of demands quickly, parceling out physical and mental resources, keeping a number of ongoing events in his mind, returning to whatever task had been interrupted, and maintaining a cool head under the pressure of grueling production schedules. In the midst of all this, Joe learned more and more about the auto industry, the technological and social dynamics of the shop floor, the machinery and production processes, and the

2. Branch of psychology concerned with such subjects as perception, memory, thinking, and learning.

3. Railroad (1846–1968) that extended from the mid-Atlantic region of the United States to the Midwest.

4. American company that for much of the twentieth century was the world's largest automaker.

basics of paint chemistry and of plating and baking. With further promotions, he not only solved problems but also began to find problems to solve: Joe initiated the redesign of the nozzle on a paint sprayer, thereby eliminating costly and unhealthy overspray. And he found a way to reduce energy costs on the baking ovens without affecting the quality of the paint. He lacked formal knowledge of how the machines under his supervision worked, but he had direct experience with them, hands-on knowledge, and was savvy about their quirks and operational capabilities. He could experiment with them.

In addition, Joe learned about budgets and management. Coming off the line as he did, he had a perspective of workers' needs and management's demands, and this led him to think of ways to improve efficiency on the line while relieving some of the stress on the assemblers. He had each worker in a unit learn his or her co-workers' jobs so they could rotate across stations to relieve some of the monotony. He believed that rotation would allow assemblers to get longer and more frequent breaks. It was an easy sell to the people on the line. The union, however, had to approve any modification in job duties, and the managers were wary of the change. Joe had to argue his case on a number of fronts, providing him a kind of rhetorical education.

15   Eight years ago I began a study of the thought processes involved in work like that of my mother and uncle. I catalogued the cognitive demands of a range of blue-collar and service jobs, from waitressing and hair styling to plumbing and welding. To gain a sense of how knowledge and skill develop, I observed experts as well as novices. From the details of this close examination, I tried to fashion what I called "cognitive biographies" of blue-collar workers. Biographical accounts of the lives of scientists, lawyers, entrepreneurs, and other professionals are rich with detail about the intellectual dimension of their work. But the life stories of working-class people are few and are typically accounts of hardship and courage or the achievements wrought by hard work.

Our culture—in Cartesian[5] fashion—separates the body from the mind, so that, for example, we assume that the use of a tool does not involve abstraction. We reinforce this notion by defining intelligence solely on grades in school and numbers on IQ tests.[6] And we employ social biases pertaining to a person's place on the occupational ladder. The distinctions among blue, pink, and white collars carry with them attributions of character, motivation, and intelligence. Although we rightly acknowledge and amply compensate the play of mind in white-collar and professional work, we diminish or erase it in considerations about other endeavors—physical and service work particularly. We also often ignore the experience of everyday work in administrative deliberations and policymaking.

But here's what we find when we get in close. The plumber seeking leverage in order to work in tight quarters and the hair stylist adroitly handling scis-

5. Recalling the dualist philosophy of René Descartes (1596–1650), French scientist, mathematician, and philosopher.
6. Tests that give a numerical measure of intelligence, the intelligence quotient.

With an eighth-grade education, Joe (hands together) advanced to supervisor of a General Motors paint-and-body department.

sors and comb manage their bodies strategically. Though work-related actions become routine with experience, they were learned at some point through observation, trial and error, and, often, physical or verbal assistance from a co-worker or trainer. I've frequently observed novices talking to themselves as they take on a task, or shaking their head or hand as if to erase an attempt before trying again. In fact, our traditional notions of routine performance could keep us from appreciating the many instances within routine where quick decisions and adjustments are made. I'm struck by the thinking-in-motion that some work requires, by all the mental activity that can be involved in simply getting from one place to another: the waitress rushing back through her station to the kitchen or the foreman walking the line.

The use of tools requires the studied refinement of stance, grip, balance, and fine-motor skills. But manipulating tools is intimately tied to knowledge of what a particular instrument can do in a particular situation and do better than other similar tools. A worker must also know the characteristics of the material one is engaging—how it reacts to various cutting or compressing devices, to degrees of heat, or to lines of force. Some of these things demand judgment, the weighing of options, the consideration of multiple variables, and, occasionally, the creative use of a tool in an unexpected way.

In manipulating material, the worker becomes attuned to aspects of the environment, a training or disciplining of perception that both enhances knowledge and informs perception. Carpenters have an eye for length, line, and angle; mechanics troubleshoot by listening; hair stylists are attuned to shape, texture, and motion. Sensory data merge with concept, as when an auto mechanic relies on sound, vibration, and even smell to understand what cannot be observed.

20   Planning and problem solving have been studied since the earliest days of modern cognitive psychology and are considered core elements in Western definitions of intelligence. To work is to solve problems. The big difference between the psychologist's laboratory and the workplace is that in the former the problems are isolated and in the latter they are embedded in the real-time flow of work with all its messiness and social complexity.

Much of physical work is social and interactive. Movers determining how to get an electric range down a flight of stairs require coordination, negotiation, planning, and the establishing of incremental goals. Words, gestures, and sometimes a quick pencil sketch are involved, if only to get the rhythm right. How important it is, then, to consider the social and communicative dimension of physical work, for it provides the medium for so much of work's intelligence.

Given the ridicule heaped on blue-collar speech, it might seem odd to value its cognitive content. Yet, the flow of talk at work provides the channel for organizing and distributing tasks, for troubleshooting and problem solving, for learning new information and revising old. A significant amount of teaching, often informal and indirect, takes place at work. Joe Meraglio saw that much of his job as a supervisor involved instruction. In some service occupations, language and communication are central: observing and interpreting behavior and expression, inferring mood and motive, taking on the perspective of others, responding appropriately to social cues, and knowing when you're understood. A good hair stylist, for instance, has the ability to convert vague requests (*I want something light and summery*) into an appropriate cut through questions, pictures, and hand gestures.

Verbal and mathematical skills drive measures of intelligence in the Western Hemisphere, and many of the kinds of work I studied are thought to require relatively little proficiency in either. Compared to certain kinds of white-collar occupations, that's true. But written symbols flow through physical work.

Numbers are rife in most workplaces: on tools and gauges, as measurements, as indicators of pressure or concentration or temperature, as guides to sequence, on ingredient labels, on lists and spreadsheets, as markers of quantity and price. Certain jobs require workers to make, check, and verify calculations, and to collect and interpret data. Basic math can be involved, and some workers develop a good sense of numbers and patterns. Consider, as well, what might be called material mathematics: mathematical functions embodied in materials and actions, as when a carpenter builds a cabinet or a flight of stairs. A simple mathematical act can extend quickly beyond itself. Measuring, for example, can involve more than recording the dimensions of an object. As I watched a cabinetmaker measure a long strip of wood, he read a number off the tape out loud, looked back over his shoulder to the kitchen wall, turned back to his task, took another measurement, and paused for a moment in thought. He was solving a problem involving the molding, and the measurement was important to his deliberation about structure and appearance.

In the blue-collar workplace, directions, plans, and reference books rely   25
on illustrations, some representational and others, like blueprints, that require training to interpret. Esoteric symbols—visual jargon—depict switches and receptacles, pipe fittings, or types of welds. Workers themselves often make sketches on the job. I frequently observed them grab a pencil to sketch something on a scrap of paper or on a piece of the material they were installing.

Though many kinds of physical work don't require a high literacy level, more reading occurs in the blue-collar workplace than is generally thought, from manuals and catalogues to work orders and invoices, to lists, labels, and forms. With routine tasks, for example, reading is integral to understanding production quotas, learning how to use an instrument, or applying a product. Written notes can initiate action, as in restaurant orders or reports of machine malfunction, or they can serve as memory aids.

True, many uses of writing are abbreviated, routine, and repetitive, and they infrequently require interpretation or analysis. But analytic moments can be part of routine activities, and seemingly basic reading and writing can be cognitively rich. Because workplace language is used in the flow of other activities, we can overlook the remarkable coordination of words, numbers, and drawings required to initiate and direct action.

If we believe everyday work to be mindless, then that will affect the work we create in the future. When we devalue the full range of everyday cognition, we offer limited educational opportunities and fail to make fresh and meaningful instructional connections among disparate kinds of skill and knowledge. If we think that whole categories of people—identified by class or occupation—are not that bright, then we reinforce social separations and cripple our ability to talk across cultural divides.

Affirmation of diverse intelligence is not a retreat to a softhearted definition of the mind. To acknowledge a broader range of intellectual capacity is to take seriously the concept of cognitive variability, to appreciate in all the Rosies and Joes the thought that drives their accomplishments and defines who they are. This is a model of the mind that is worthy of a democratic society.

MLA CITATION

Rose, Mike. "Blue-Collar Brilliance." *The Norton Reader: An Anthology of Nonfiction*, edited by Melissa A. Goldthwaite et al., 16th ed., W. W. Norton, 2024, pp. 516–23.

QUESTIONS

1. In his closing paragraph, Mike Rose asserts that the expanded understanding of intelligence for which he is arguing suggests "a model of the mind that is worthy of a democratic society" (paragraph 29). What are the social or political implications of this connection between mind and democracy?

2. Rose's essay was originally subtitled "Questioning Assumptions about Intelligence, Work, and Social Class." What assumptions is Rose questioning, either directly or indirectly?

3. Rose introduces his general argument with detailed accounts of the work lives of two family members: his mother and his uncle. Why do you think he makes this choice?

4. Rose describes himself as writing "'cognitive biographies' of blue-collar workers" (paragraph 15). Drawing as Rose does on interviews and careful observation, write a cognitive biography of someone you know.

ALEXANDRA ROBBINS
The Secret Reason Hazing Continues

H AZING, AS PRACTICED in most places, is wrong, it is unethical, it is dangerous, and it is a crime in 44 states and Washington, DC. Yet 73 percent of Greeks are hazed, according to the most recent large-scale hazing study. Binghamton University was so plagued by hazing complaints in 2012, including allegations that fraternity brothers were waterboarding pledges, that the school's former assistant director of Greek life told the *New York Times*, "My entire tenure from start to finish, I was scared to death that someone was going to die."[1] Sure enough, in 2017, freshman pledge Conor Donnelly fell to his death while trying to climb a balcony at an Alpha Sigma Phi party. (Investigators ruled that while hazing was not involved, alcohol was a factor in his death.)

Between 2010 and 2017, at least 17 pledges died from hazing by university-recognized fraternities and at least two more in underground or local fraternities, according to hazing expert Hank Nuwer's extensive research.[2] The most frequently reported hazing behaviors among college students involve alcohol consumption, humiliation, isolation, sleep deprivation, and sex acts, a recent Association for the Study of Higher Education report revealed. . . .

College hazing began in the early 1800s as a way for sophomores to needle freshmen. Fraternity hazing increased in the late 1860s with the return of students who learned hazing practices when they fought in the Civil War. Hazing "was conducted to impress the new members with the honor being

From Alexandra Robbins's book Fraternity: An Inside Look at a Year of College Boys Becoming Men *(2019). As a journalist, Robbins relies extensively on news sources and personal interviews. The reading as presented here does not reproduce her notes documenting personal interviews; however, it does reproduce her notes documenting quotations and expert and scholarly sources on which she relies. All notes in this piece were written by the author.*

1. Peter Appleborne, "At a Campus Scarred by Hazing, Cries for Help," *New York Times*, September 18, 2012.

2. https://www.hanknuwer.com/hazing-deaths.

conferred upon them in their initiation into the brotherhood," historian Nicholas Syrett noted. "It was also designed to recoup the masculinity and authority of the upperclassmen, who had been groveling before freshmen in their attempts to get them to pick their fraternity over others." Post-World War II, hazing grew more extreme and dangerous, and more likely to involve alcohol.

Twenty-first-century fraternity hazing is "even more brutal than before," said Susan Lipkins, a psychologist who runs InsideHazing.com. The media shows us only what Lipkins called "the tip of the iceberg"[3] of fraternity hazing traditions, the more sensational incidents: Wilmington College Gamma Phi Betas either watched or participated as members blindfolded pledges, told them to strip, stuffed their mouths with Limburger cheese, and whipped them so violently that doctors had to remove a 19-year-old's injured testicle. Hofstra University Sigma Pis allegedly poured ghost pepper hot sauce on pledges' genitals and goaded pledges to vomit on one another. At the University of Tennessee, a Pi Kappa Alpha nearly died of alcohol poisoning because brothers were butt-chugging (funneling alcohol through a rubber tube inserted in their rectums). Washington and Lee University's Phi Kappa Psi used a stun gun on a pledge.

There's a little-known reason that hazing continues, despite laws criminalizing the behavior, more public fraternity crackdowns, and social media tools that make hazing easier to catch and prove. It's a reason that members of several fraternities confirmed to me. It's also why Sam (a pseudonym), an adult who was formerly one of the highest-ranking national officers of a fraternity whose hazing killed a member, continues to defend the practice.

In 2018, four members of the Baruch College chapter of Pi Delta Psi, all from Queens, New York, were convicted on felony charges of voluntary manslaughter in the death of freshman Michael Deng. The Pi Delta Psi fraternity, found guilty on a felony count of involuntary manslaughter, was fined and banned from Pennsylvania, where the incident took place, for 10 years. During a retreat in the Poconos, fraternity brothers blindfolded Deng, forced him to walk across an icy path carrying a 30-pound backpack filled with sand, and repeatedly "speared" him, plowing headfirst into him and slamming him to the ground. Deng died from a resulting brain injury.[4]

The national office of Deng's fraternity was quick to distance itself from the chapter with a statement claiming the brothers "violated the values and rules of our organization, including our strict no-hazing policy."[5] But it turned out that the ritual that killed the freshman was a common fraternity tradition that was

5

3. Lipkins, interview with the author.

4. See, for example, "Ex-Frat Officer Testifies against Brothers in Pledge's Death," Associated Press State and Local, December 1, 2015; "Frat Member Charged with Murder in Pledge's 2013 Death Breaks Down in Tears at Arraignment," *New York Daily News*, October 23, 2015; Jay Caspian Kang, "What a Fraternity Hazing Death Revealed about the Painful Search for an Asian-American Identity," *New York Times Magazine*, August 9, 2017.

5. Jamie Altman, "5 Pi Delta Psi Fraternity Members Could Face Third-Degree Murder Charges," *USA Today College*, September 15, 2015.

very much intertwined with the "values and rules" the national office publicly accused the chapter of violating. The problem, Sam claimed, was in the execution, not the concept.

All chapters of Pi Delta Psi, an Asian American fraternity, have a "standardized education," or pledge program, during which brothers learn Asian American cultural history, Sam said. Each pledge also had to keep a handwritten pledge book containing the fraternity's mission statement, a list of brothers and their backgrounds, and the pledge's reflections on the process. (At the time I interviewed Sam, most of these pledge practices were suspended.) While pledge books aren't uncommon among other fraternities, Pi Delta Psi expected pledges to memorize not only the information but also the page and line numbers where that information could be found.

Pi Delta Psi used pledge books, which many groups consider hazing, to give pledges a sense of early Chinese immigrants' experiences at the detention center on San Francisco's Angel Island. Sam explained that Angel Island officers repeatedly quizzed immigrants on minute details about family members living in the United States. "How many cobblestones were in front of their house? When was their neighbor's daughter born? The relatives of detained immigrants started sneaking books of answers into the detention center, which immigrants memorized cover to cover because they knew the smallest slipup could be reason for them to be sent back," he said. "The entire experience during our pledge process was designed to humble the new member and make him appreciate the progress of civil rights since that time."

10   The fraternity used similar reasoning to rationalize the initiation ritual that chapters called the Gauntlet, or Bamboo Ceiling, which was intended to reflect the discrimination experienced by past generations of Asian Americans. Sam said the ritual was supposed to go like this: To symbolize the immigrant's difficult attempt to reunite with his family in the United States, the pledge was blindfolded outside at night with only the voice of his Big Brother to guide him. As he tried to walk toward his Big, other brothers pushed him to the ground and held him down while shouting racial slurs at him and yelling at him to go back to his country. "The point is that you struggle to get back up to get to your Big Brother, like previous [Asian American] generations faced a lot of adversity, and to see if you have the resilience to overcome the adversity. Then, at the very end, when it looks like the pledge is completely physically and emotionally depleted, the other brothers help him up and carry him to his Big Brother to show that you can overcome but you have to ask for help."

At Baruch, Sam said, the chapter took the ritual too far. They did it on icy ground rather than grass, and they battered Deng instead of pushing him down. "The point is to get them tired, not to physically assault them," he said. One of the defendants told police that Deng was singled out for harsher treatment because he "wasn't going with the flow, which pissed off the brothers."

The Gauntlet was hazing, Sam admitted. And even though the ritual killed a member, Sam, who, as an adult national fraternity officer, had power and authority over more than 1,000 undergraduates, defended hazing. "Hazing works," he told me. "Hazing creates an unusually strong bond between people who weather tough times together, and the toughness also creates the illusion of reaching a worthwhile goal. It increases the value of the letters because you've undergone such a hard process of obtaining them."

Thus, one of the major reasons fraternity hazing persists: It appears that a number of the involved adults and alumni *want* it to. And it didn't help optics when the Fraternity and Sorority Political Action Committee (FSPAC)— which raises money for federal office candidates who "champion Greek issues," according to its website—reportedly tried to stall legislation intended to curb hazing. In 2013, media outlets reported that FSPAC had played a part in persuading US representative Frederica Wilson, a Florida Democrat who called herself the "Haze Buster," not to introduce her federal anti-hazing bill.

With this kind of pressure, it's no surprise that 95 percent of hazed students don't report the hazing. According to the Novak Institute on Hazing at the University of Kentucky, 37 percent of surveyed students said they did not report it because they didn't want to get the group in trouble, while 42 percent were afraid other group members might retaliate or ostracize them. The real surprise is that 25 percent of hazed students believed that coaches and advisors knew the hazing was happening and, worse, reported that alumni were physically present in at least a quarter of hazing incidents.

Some brothers told me that even as some fraternity-affiliated adults loudly condemn hazing in public, in private they tell students to do it anyway. A recent Maryland fraternity brother told me that alumni and chapter advisors are anti-hazing "on paper." But "even they secretly want hazing to continue. A lot of alumni say, 'You should haze.' They come back, tell us their ridiculous stories, and flex and sound cool. Then they get hammered with all the college kids and drive away."   15

Brothers described how some older members' attitudes help convince young pledges that they want to be hazed, or that the activities aren't technically hazing. Pledges might not know the difference; research shows that nine out of ten college students who are hazed don't actually believe they were hazed. A New York City freshman told me his chapter didn't haze and then described forced-drinking events that clearly constituted hazing.

Why might alumni and older members want hazing to continue? Many of them harbor a genuine belief that it is their responsibility to make their pledges into "better" men. They see hazing as necessary tough love, "designed to knock you down to build you up as a man," a southern sophomore explained. Others take comfort in the tradition; if the fraternity remains the same, the experience of being a member remains an unbroken line that continued under their watch and will continue, unchanging, into the future. They see themselves as stewards of the institution. Still others are convinced their lifelong friendships with pledge brothers formed precisely because they faced adverse conditions together. They want new members to have these relationships, too.

A Virginia fraternity alum said his chapter's older members were "pro-hazing, pro-drinking, anti-change. This is understandable. What they went through with their elders was objectively worse than what we went through, and yet they came through and were very good friends. The conclusion they drew from it, and the conclusion nearly all such groups draw, is that 'it worked, we came together, we're close now, and there's nothing wrong with it.'"

When he and other members of his class tried to reform their chapter's hazing practices, older members constantly pushed back. "It wears you down, it indoctrinates you. And some of us, myself included, were turning into what we'd tried to avoid becoming. When I was 19, I knew the emotional abuse was harmful, immoral, and should be abolished. When I was 21, I didn't have it in me to care anymore because I'd been called a whiny bitch for years."

*

20   Pat, a recent grad from Nevada, was his chapter's pledge master his senior year. "Hazing serves a point. Everything's supposed to be done for a reason. There's no reason to dump an ice bucket on a kid while he's sleeping," he said. That's easy to say but hard to justify. A northern brother told me that every hazing tradition "is attached to the morality" of a fraternity value, but then he couldn't remember the lesson he was supposed to have learned when he and his pledge brothers had to eat live goldfish.

Pat's strategy was to use hazing to, in his view, fix individuals' character flaws. When he saw a few pledges picking on another pledge, he made them walk around with their target all day (while Snapchatting him proof) to get to know the student better. He told freshmen he believed were "full of themselves" to dress in humiliating costumes, like girls' cheerleading uniforms. He ordered "loudmouth" pledges not to speak, and quiet pledges to get girls' numbers. He sent what he called the "bookish" pledges to mandatory gym hours with athletes and told the athletes to sit next to the bookish pledges in class. "Some quiet pledges needed to break out of their shell, and some people needed to be taught they weren't the best person in the world," he told me.

Pat learned these strategies from the older brothers who had hazed him. They demanded that he chug a beer in five seconds or he'd have to chug another. When he did, spiking the cup like a football, the pledge master ordered him to chug a mixture of whiskey, hot sauce, and tobacco "if you think you're so good at drinking." He did, and projectile-vomited. "I'm glad that happened to me. It taught me a lesson," Pat said. "I thought I was all that. I learned not to open my mouth and not to be a jerk. I learned to respect my superiors." Three years later, though, he was arrested for assaulting an adult.

Pat insisted that the word *hazing* gives what should be acceptable rituals a negative connotation. "A lot of hazing is essentially team building with alcohol," he said. "If you called it brotherhood building or character building, people would see it differently."

Pledges endure the mistreatment for many reasons. Jake convinced himself that if older brothers had participated in a hazing activity, then it must be okay. And perhaps more students are willing to be hazed, and hazed hard, because the stakes of acceptance seem higher than in the years before social media. The "I'm in, you're out" dichotomy has never been as stark as it is now. Many kids believe that, as the recent Maryland alum told me, "Hazing is a necessary evil everyone goes through because they want so badly to be part of the culture. There's a big fear of missing out. Now that everything's showcased—you see on *Facebook* everyone's at parties and you're not—there's a big pressure to be included."

There's another, more basic human instinct that could help explain why   25 hazing continues, why otherwise nice people participate in it, and why it's so hard to curtail: Hazing can be viewed as a means of group survival.[6] People generally want to believe they are decent citizens who make good decisions. So when they do something stupid or cruel, they feel uncomfortable afterward when they try to reconcile their behavior with their image of themselves. Social psychologists call this tension or anxiety "cognitive dissonance."[7] Cognitive dissonance theory suggests that because we want our behavior to be consistent with our beliefs, we try to minimize that discomfort. One way to do that is to change our beliefs so that the behavior makes sense to us.

In 1959, researchers decided to test how cognitive dissonance applies to groups. They hypothesized that people who undergo a humiliating initiation to get into a group will rationalize their behavior afterward by concluding that the group must be worth the pain of getting in, or else they wouldn't have degraded themselves. To get into a group that held discussions on the psychology of sex, the researchers had college women read embarrassing or obscene words such as *fuck*, *cock*, and *screw*—remember, this was the 1950s—and sexually graphic passages. The group discussion they participated in afterward was designed to be "one of the most worthless and uninteresting discussions imaginable" about secondary sex behavior in animals. The researchers found that the initiates who read the most embarrassing material were most likely to believe the group was valuable.[8] In the 1960s, different researchers took the experiment further. Instead of asking students to read sexual material, they gave them electric shocks, ranging from weak to powerful. Sure enough, the more painful the shocks, the more a student later convinced herself of the value of a similarly worthless group.[9]

This is what happens during and after hazing, social psychologists say. Pledges convince themselves that their fraternity membership was worth the suffering by coming up with rationales ("This fraternity is awesome"; "Our pledge class bonded"; "Everyone else had to do it"). By the time they've been initiated, former hazees are persuaded that membership justifies not only the hazing they endured but also the hazing they might inflict on the next pledges. Hazing leads "future society members to find the group more attractive and worthwhile," Robert Cialdini wrote in his excellent book *Influence*. "The more effort that goes into a commitment, the greater is its ability to influence the attitudes of the person who made it. . . . As long as it is the case that people like and believe in what they have struggled to get, these groups will continue

6. Robert B. Cialdini, *Influence: The Psychology of Persuasion*, rev. ed. (New York: Collins, 2007).

7. Leon Festinger and James M. Carlsmith, "Cognitive Consequences of Forced Compliance," *Journal of Abnormal and Social Psychology* 58, no. 2 (1959).

8. Elliot Aronson and Judson Mills, "The Effect of Severity of Initiation on Liking for a Group," *Journal of Abnormal and Social Psychology* 59, no. 2 (1959).

9. Cialdini.

to arrange effortful and troublesome initiation rites. The loyalty and dedication of those who emerge will increase to a great degree the chances of group cohesiveness and survival."[10]

For alumni, if the hazing continues, the unchanging tradition psychologically validates that their own experiences were acceptable. "Hazing has become the central tenet of fraternal culture, I don't deny that," Sam said. "It's just human nature. Something will be worth more to you if you invest more time and effort into it. If we're just given something, no matter how valuable it actually is, we're going to value it less if it's just handed to us."

This may be why hazing rituals have names such as the Gauntlet. For 2017 Penn State pledge Timothy Piazza, who died following this tradition, the Gauntlet was an obstacle course of drinking stations where pledges had to quickly consume various kinds of alcohol. Many brothers want pledges to feel that they are completing a quest to get into the club, that not just anyone is worthy, that the letters of the fraternity must be earned, that membership is an exclusive privilege reserved only for those who work for it.

30   One of the problems with this mentality is the idea that by joining something larger than they are, these young students believe they must subordinate themselves to it. In some cases, they are made to feel that they should prioritize the image of the fraternity over the well-being of a brother. On too many occasions, fraternity members have tried to cover up or ignore a pledge's injury, presumably because they wanted to protect the fraternity. In 2016, for example, Towson University Tau Kappa Epsilons made a 19-year-old pledge eat cat food and drink what was apparently vinegar and pickle juice, burning his esophagus and causing him to vomit blood. They reportedly bullied him into delaying medical treatment so the fraternity wouldn't "get into trouble." He was eventually hospitalized with significant damage to his esophagus, tongue, intestinal lining, and stomach.[11]

At Penn State, Piazza's turn through the Gauntlet, a Beta Theta Pi chapter hazing tradition, led him to drink what prosecutors called a "life-threatening"[12] amount of alcohol: 18 drinks in 82 minutes. His subsequent drunken falls injured his brain and ruptured his spleen. Rather than getting him the medical attention he needed, fraternity brothers left him lying there for 12 hours— and a brother directed the pledge master to "make sure the pledges keep quiet about last night."[13]

When Michael Deng lay dying after the Pi Delta Psi Gauntlet, fraternity brothers waited two hours to take him to the hospital. The fraternity's 28-year-old national president reportedly instructed the brothers to dispose of any fraternity

10. Ibid.

11. Petula Dvorak, "Time to Dismantle Fraternities and the Sexism, Rape Culture, and Binge Drinking They Encourage," *Washington Post*, September 15, 2016; "Towson University Suspends Fraternity amid Hazing Allegations," WBAL-TV, April 7, 2016.

12. Sarah Maslin, "19 and Coming into His Own, until a Fatal Night of Hazing," *New York Times*, May 21, 2017.

13. Sam Ruland, "Messages from the Night of Bid Acceptance to the Days Following Piazza's Death," *Daily Collegian*, May 9, 2017.

items in the rental house. One of the defendants testified that the fraternity encouraged pledges to lie to police. He also said the fraternity had a "special email address" for brothers to inform fraternity leaders if a pledge had suffered a hazing injury, so the organization could come up with an excuse.[14]

Even if some adults who run a fraternity's national headquarters truly do want hazing to stop, they likely aren't deploying the manpower necessary to enforce their own rules. So impressionable kids are pledging allegiance to a group that is mainly supervised by other impressionable kids. The Baruch College Pi Delta Psi chapter president testified that he "did not have the authority" to stop the Gauntlet ritual that killed Deng,[15] but that another brother, the "pledge educator," did.[16]

Piazza's mother told the *Today* show that she wasn't concerned when Piazza said he wanted to join a fraternity because she had read that Beta Theta Pi was a "non-hazing, non-alcohol fraternity."[17] But between 2010 and the time Piazza pledged, major hazing incidents occurred in at least 23 Beta chapters across the country—and those are just the instances in which chapters were caught and the media found out about them. That means that about 16 percent of Beta Theta Pi's approximately 144 chapters (as of 2017, the year Piazza pledged) were caught hazing.

Then again, fraternities could argue the flip side: 84 percent of Beta chapters did not conduct major hazing (or were not caught). Sam explained a national officer perspective: "It's very difficult to have complete oversight even if you have a seasoned National Board. Accidents and perversion do happen. Is that worth it in the end? If 70 to 80 percent of the process is going right, you're positively impacting people's lives, you're producing leaders, is the good that you do as an organization worth the minority of instances where there's humiliation, mission creep, mental or physical harm coming to these very young college students, even death? And if the answer is no, then how much do we have to minimize risk to be worth it? Those are the fundamental questions I ask myself that I don't know the answers to. Those answers will produce the answer to whether Greek life can justify its own existence."

One of the most common fraternity hazing techniques is "planned failure." Planned failure involves "near-impossible tasks where failure is punished with hazing," according to a 2016 article by University of California–Santa Barbara professor Aldo Cimino.[18] Even in some chapters that don't haze, brothers try to scare pledges into worrying that they will fail to be good enough to be initiated.

35

14. Chris Pleasance, "President of New York Fraternity Where Pledge Died during Hazing Reveals the Rituals Were Encouraged and Members Would Cook Up Excuses if Someone Got Hurt," *Daily Mail*, December 1, 2015.

15. Ibid.

16. See, for example, Tracy Connor, "Student Tried to Cover Up Frat Link in Fatal Hazing: Cops," NBC News, November 2, 2015.

17. "Hazing in America," *Today*, NBC, September 18, 2017.

18. Aldo Cimino, "Fraternity Hazing and the Process of Planned Failure," *Journal of American Studies* 52, no. 1 (2016).

Some chapters set up pledges to fail because they want them to believe that their activity—5:45 A.M. jogs, calisthenics, a buffet of gross food—isn't so much hazing as a punishment tailored to their individual pledge class because they made a mistake.[19] The pledges don't know they would have had to complete these tasks anyway. They don't know the brothers often manufacture reasons, as Daniel did when he barged into the basement and yelled at Jake's pledge class, "You guys don't know how badly you fucked up! You have just opened the gates of hell!"

Members also might use this technique to avoid personal responsibility for the hazing. "If hazees believe that they can avoid some hazing, but continually fail to meet the conditions for doing so, they may blame themselves or 'the rules,' rather than the hazers. This is especially so if the rules of hazing are seen as pre-dating the hazers, who are themselves bound by tradition," Cimino wrote.[20]

And that's the crux of the issue: tradition. The perceived weight of tradition is an authority unto itself. If the boys believe that the good of the group overrides the comfort of the individual, they might feel more invested in show-ing respect for the traditions that govern the group. "The things we did were traditions that came down. They told us, 'It happened to us,' so we did it to pledges below us, and the people above us did it to us because it happened to them," said the Maryland alum. "Hazing only exists because it always existed. It proves that tradition is like the worst thing that's ever happened. People are sold on it. This is the way it's always been, so that has to be the way it is now."

40   Yet many fraternity chapters, such as Oliver's, do not haze. Brothers who told me their chapter runs only nonhazing pledge activities or non-humiliating team-building exercises believe their brotherly bonds are just as strong as or stronger than the bonds within chapters that haze.

Some of the nonhazing pledge activities brothers described include taking weekly classes about fraternity history and traditions; organizing a community service project; completing assignments related to setting goals for themselves in college and beyond; taking classes on how to write a résumé; and learning etiquette. "We learned how to be a gentleman, how to be appropriate around women. I thought it was amazing that finally someone was teaching me proper etiquette. Like if you're walking down the street with a woman, you walk between them and traffic, to protect them from danger. Wait until the woman sits before you do. How to introduce someone. I thought that stuff was fun," a New Jersey junior said. "We were shown what was good to wear, where your tie should line up, where to put a tie clip, how to match things, cuff links. Inter-esting things improving people's behavior that I'll never forget."

A Pennsylvania chapter requires its pledges to join at least one other campus organization. A New York chapter has its pledges cook and serve a three-course dinner for brothers' girlfriends. A Virginia chapter puts pledges in charge of a major annual philanthropy event, which "involved us dividing up tasks based on our strengths, meeting with local business owners, and actually running the

19. Ibid.
20. Ibid.

event," a brother said. "While some of these assignments were stressful, they emphasized the importance of teamwork. We were never allowed to leave someone behind or let someone do all the work. It really pulled us together as a family, and we learned a lot about each other's strengths and weaknesses."

An upstate New York chapter consisting mostly of engineering students combines education and team-building projects. Pledges have weekly quizzes and discussions about assigned reading from the fraternity's education guide (about leadership, ethics, etc.). They plan a fun residential community event for students who live nearby, a community service event (such as a park cleanup), and a brotherhood event (usually nonalcoholic, such as a campus-wide game of Capture the Flag).

The pledges also participate in strictly nonalcoholic one-to-one class bonding events with older classes of brothers to get to know them better; shadow brothers to learn how they handle their duties, like manning the door at a party; and handcraft a gift for the brotherhood. Usually the gift involves building furniture from scratch or buying furniture and painting it. Handmade gifts have included a bench, large coffee table, TV stand, and foldable beer pong table. "Our secret to success was a strict adherence to our belief that all people are worthy of respect, including candidates. It seems impossible to respect someone and want them to become your brother and at the same time pressure them to do things that are against their health or better judgment," a recent grad said. "Coming into a fraternity where it feels like everyone is on your side and wants to see you be successful is a powerful thing. It creates strong relationships from the get-go and perpetuates a positive environment. Alumni felt the same way; they always praised us for continuing the mission of the chapter."

When Ben founded his South Carolina chapter, on a campus where other fraternities hazed, he filled the pledge period with what he called "shared experiences." He regularly sent the pledges to study hall together, told them to attend a "pledge breakfast" once or twice a week, and put them in charge of organizing tailgates, a major affair. "That can be an adverse situation sometimes because they have to come together and delegate responsibilities," he said. "I found I didn't have to get them into line, put 10 bottles of liquor in front of them, and say, 'You have to drink this' because we don't know what else to do."

Ben assigned pledges these nonhazing tasks because he believed the process taught them to work together, rely on one another, and hold themselves and their pledge brothers accountable, "which in turn begins to build a healthy foundation for trust, friendship, and ultimately brotherhood," he said. "They learn to work with the fraternity brothers, which is 'managing up,' in a sense," pitching the fraternity treasurer for event funds and approaching brothers to access tents, banners, and music equipment.

Brothers and pledges together went on weekend excursions to the mountains and day trips to Six Flags. "We had 12 brothers drive the pledges somewhere to do social activities as a group," Ben said. "We focused on having shared experiences any way we could get them. A lot of that comes from having a fraternity house where they can come over after class or just be around each other.

There's not a super formula to it. It doesn't take a lot for people to become friends. That was the premise I began with when thinking of ways to bring 50 fraternity brothers and 20 pledges together, and it worked."

MLA CITATION

Robbins, Alexandra. "The Secret Reason Hazing Continues." *The Norton Reader: An Anthology of Nonfiction*, edited by Melissa A. Goldthwaite et al., 16th ed., W. W. Norton, 2024, pp. 524–34.

QUESTIONS

1. Writing as a journalist, Alexandra Robbins endeavors to explain the reasons hazing in fraternities persists. What are these reasons? Do you find them valid? Why or why not? Annotate the essay, tracking your response as the essay progresses.

2. Robbins identifies several of her sources by their first names. What is the effect of this decision? One of her sources, Sam, defends the practice of hazing. Why does she give him so much attention? What do you think of Sam?

3. In the final section of her piece, Robbins notes that many fraternities do not haze but rely on "nonhazing pledge activities or non-humiliating team-building exercises" to foster "brotherly bonds" (paragraph 40). Do you think the activities and exercises she offers as examples would be effective? Have you seen or heard of any of them implemented on campus? Is it reasonable to suggest that they could replace the practice of hazing? Why or why not?

4. Identify a social or cultural practice on your campus or in your community that is widely regarded as harmful but nevertheless persists. Interview several people who engage in or are affected by that practice to understand the reasons for its persistence and ongoing arguments against it. Then propose a positive alternative in an essay or project.

EMILY WILSON
A Translator's Reckoning with the Women of the Odyssey

SINCE I COMPLETED MY TRANSLATION of the *Odyssey*, which is the first published version of Homer's epic in English translated by a woman, readers have often assumed that I must sympathize above all with the story's female characters. I am asked, in particular, about my interpretation of Penelope, Odysseus' faithful wife. Penelope spends twenty years in tearful isolation, waiting for her man to come home

Originally published in the New Yorker *(2017), a weekly magazine of "reportage, commentary, criticism, essays, fiction, satire, cartoons, and poetry." Emily Wilson's translation of Homer's* Odyssey *was published by W. W. Norton in 2017.*

from war—and also, as it happens, from the cave and bed of two beautiful goddesses—while caring for her son and warding off the advances of her abusive suitors. At the same time, she manages to fool the suitors with her sneaky trick of weaving by day and unpicking her work at night, telling them that she can never marry until her project is finished. Moreover, she successfully needles her husband by pretending to have moved the bed that he constructed out of a still-living olive tree, a reminder that she has the power to hurt him by sleeping with another man. She's canny, she's strong-willed, she has grit, she has a vivid imagination, she's loyal, she's a competent, mostly single mother who shows deep love for her difficult, moody son, and she keeps a big and complex household running for two decades. You have to love her for all these things, and I do.

But many students, scholars, and general readers want even more from this literary character: they want her to fit the ideal of an empowered woman. It is comforting to subscribe to the notion—as Daniel Mendelsohn[1] does in his recently published memoir, *An Odyssey*, and as Robert Fagles[2] does, in his translation of the poem—that the marriage between Odysseus and Penelope is a partnership of intellectual equals, based on true love and a shared outlook on life. Odysseus speaks, in Homer's poem, of the ideal of like-mindedness (*homophrosyne*) in marriage. It is not usually mentioned that he brings it up only when talking to an impressionable teen-age girl, Nausicaa, whom he avoids telling that he's married, and whom he has a strong ulterior motive for buttering up since his life depends on her help. (We should know by now that powerful older men do not always tell young women the truth.) Moreover, the sentimentalized reading of Penelope erases some facts about her social position that the original poem makes very clear.

Whereas Odysseus has many choices, many identities, many places to go and people to be and to see, Penelope has only one choice, and it is defined exclusively by her marital status: she can wait for Odysseus, or marry someone else—and even this very limited choice is not open forever, since the abusive suitors can eventually force her hand. In Mary Beard's[3] forthcoming pamphlet, *Women and Power*, she writes about a scene in the *Odyssey* that she calls Western literature's "first recorded example of a man telling a woman to 'shut up'"—Telemachus telling Penelope, in Book One, to be silent after she asks the poet performing in her palace to sing a different tune.

The silencing of female voices, and the dangers of female agency, are central problems in the poem. Penelope's strictly constrained position is presented in some ways as necessary, since élite wives who act more freely may do scary things—like the half-divine Helen,[4] who abandons her husband for another

---

1. American critic, essayist, and translator (b. 1960).

2. American scholar, poet, and translator (1933–2008).

3. English classicist (b. 1955).

4. The daughter of Zeus and Leda born after Zeus's seduction (or rape) of Leda while in the form of a swan. Helen leaves her husband Menelaus for Paris (or is abducted by him), inaugurating the decade-long Trojan war.

Philipp Veit's *Athena Visiting Penelope at the Loom* (1833–36).

man, or her sister Clytemnestra,[5] who helps her lover murder her husband. In Ithaca, Odysseus owns the house, the weapons, the wealth, the slaves, the farm, the orchard, and the seat in the council of men; Penelope does not even fully share the marriage bed, which her husband calls "my bed." Penelope is, like her husband, highly intelligent; but her intelligence, evoked by her standard epithet, *periphron*, "circumspect," suggests caution and risk aversion. Her keen mind is not liberating; it keeps her stuck. By contrast, Odysseus' intelligence is defined as an ability to find a fix for any situation: he is *polymechanos*, the guy with a solution for everything, and an iron will. The poem sets up a sharp distinction between Odysseus' fantasy and Penelope's realism. He believes that, after twenty years away from home, he can return to being exactly the man he used to be, while she knows that, no matter how strong or smart or faithful she is, she can never be the same. In one of the most upsetting and beautiful passages of the poem, Penelope cries so desperately that her very being seems to dissolve. In my translation, it reads:

> Her face was melting, like the snow that Zephyr
> scatters across the mountain peaks; then Eurus
> thaws it, and as it melts, the rivers swell
> and flow again. So were her lovely cheeks
> dissolved in tears.

5. Married to Agamemnon, leader of the Greeks during the Trojan war. While he is away, she becomes involved with Aegisthus, her cousin by marriage.

Other translations of this passage say that her tears "melted" or "streamed"   5
down her cheeks, or that (in the English cliché) her "heart" melted. But Homer's original text says that her *chros*—her "skin" or "flesh"—melted, and that
her cheeks themselves dissolved (*teketo kala pareia*). Penelope experiences her
marriage in terms of grief, abandonment, and the loss of identity—a loss that,
disturbingly, Homer presents as a necessary and natural process, like the coming of spring on the mountain. In translating this passage, I wanted to bring
out both the beauty and the precision of the imagery, and the horror—a common, relatable horror—of being a woman who experiences her attachment to
her husband as the destruction of her self. I wanted the reader of my English
to feel as I do in reading the Greek: for Penelope, and with her pain, rather
than prettifying or trivializing her grief.

All this may make Penelope seem like an innocent victim, but she is also
a woman of privilege, who colludes in, indeed insists on, the silencing of more
vulnerable women. Penelope clutches desperately at whatever shards of autonomy are available in her husband's house. After Odysseus slaughters her suitors, he tells Telemachus to kill the female slaves who have slept with them.
Contemporary translators and commentators often present the massacre of
these women as if it were quite ordinary, and entirely justified. The murdered
slaves are routinely described in contemporary American English translations
as "disobedient maids," and are labelled as "sluts" or "whores"—a level of verbal abuse that finds absolutely no analogue in the Greek. The killing of these
abused slaves (who are usually referred to, euphemistically, as "servants" or
"maids") is often described as if it were unquestionably ethical. The study
guide SparkNotes describes these women as "disloyal women servants" who
must be "executed," while CliffsNotes calls them "maidservants" who were
"disloyal," and claims that their murder has a "macabre beauty." In the poem's
original language, Telemachus refers to them only with *hai*, the feminine
article—"those female people who . . . slept beside the suitors." In my translation, I call them "these girls," and hope to convey the scene in both its grue-
some inhumanity and its pathos: "their heads all in a row, / were strung up
with the noose around their necks / to make their death an agony. They gasped,
/ feet twitching for a while, but not for long."

There is a vision of empowered femininity in the *Odyssey*, but it is conveyed
not in the mortal world but in that of the gods. The poem's plot is, of course,
engineered by the wonderfully gender-fluid goddess Athena, who protects and
saves her favorite human from the Sirens, goddesses and female monsters who
try to entrap him or transform him or hide him or devour him or swallow him
up, with their dangerous feminine wiles. The divine Calypso, Aphrodite, and
Circe provide passionate models of female power—idealized fantasies of how
much agency mortal women might have, if only social circumstances were completely different. I read Homer's great poem as a complex and truthful articulation of gender dynamics that continue to haunt us. The *Odyssey* traces deep
male fears about female power, and it shows the terrible damage done to women,
and perhaps also to men, by the androcentric social structures that keep us
silent and constrained. Birds in Homer are the ultimate image of speech and of

freedom. Athena repeatedly transforms herself into a bird of prey, whooshing up to the rooftops or surfing across the waves of the sea. The silenced slave girls are "like doves or thrushes," caught in a hunter's net. Penelope, meanwhile, is like a "pale gray nightingale" who "sits among the leaves / that crowd the trees." She can't fly, but her warbling amounts to a "symphony of sound."

MLA CITATION

Wilson, Emily. "A Translator's Reckoning with the Women of the *Odyssey*." *The Norton Reader: An Anthology of Nonfiction*, edited by Melissa A. Goldthwaite et al., 16th ed., W. W. Norton, 2024, pp. 534–38.

QUESTIONS

1. In the first paragraph of her essay, Emily Wilson suggests that the act of "translation" necessarily involves "interpretation." What does she mean? What did Wilson want to accomplish with her translation of the *Odyssey*? What does she imply about previous translations?

2. Why is it significant that her translation "is the first published version of Homer's epic in English translated by a woman" (paragraph 1)? What does Wilson uncover in her translation of Homer's Greek that previous translations fail to?

3. If you are multilingual, compare a short poem or passage that has been translated from a language you know into English or vice versa. Write about the choices made by the translator and consider whether the translation is a faithful rendering of the original poem or passage. If you are not multilingual, compare two English translations of a poem or passage written in another language. Write a comparison of the two versions.

PHILIP KENNICOTT

How to View Art: Be Dead Serious about It, but Don't Expect Too Much

1. TAKE TIME

THE BIGGEST CHALLENGE when visiting an art museum is to disengage from our distracted selves. The pervasive, relentless, all-consuming power of time is the enemy. If you are thinking about where you have to be next, what you have left undone, what you could be doing instead of standing in front of art, there is no hope that anything significant will happen. But to disengage from time

Published in the Washington Post *(2014), where Philip Kennicott is an art and architecture critic.*

has become extraordinarily complicated. We are addicted to devices that remind us of the presence of time, cellphones and watches among them, but cameras too, because the camera has become a crutch to memory, and memory is our only defense against the loss of time.

The raging debate today about whether to allow the taking of pictures inside the museum usually hinges on whether the act of photographing is intrusive or disruptive to other visitors; more important, the act is fundamentally disruptive to the photographer's experience of art, which is always fleeting. So leave all your devices behind. And never, ever make plans for what to do later in a museum; if you overhear people making plans for supper, drinks or when to relieve the baby sitter, give them a sharp, baleful look.

Some practical advice: If you go an hour before closing time, you won't have to worry about what time it is. Just wait until the guards kick you out. Also: If you have only an hour, visit only one room. Anything that makes you feel rushed, or compelled to move quickly, will reengage you with the sense of busy-ness that defines ordinary life. This is another reason that entrance fees are so pernicious: They make visitors mentally "meter" the experience, straining to get the most out of it, and thus re inscribe it in the workaday world where time is money, and money is everything.

2. Seek Silence

Always avoid noise, because noise isn't just distracting, it makes us hate other people. If you're thinking about the mind-numbing banality of the person next to you, there's little hope that you will be receptive to art. In a museum, imagine that you have a magnetic repulsion to everyone else. Move toward empty space. Indulge your misanthropy.

That's not always easy. Too many museums have become exceptionally noisy, and in some cases that's by design. When it comes to science and history museums, noise is often equated with visitor engagement, a sign that people are enjoying the experience. In art museums, noise isn't just a question of bad manners but a result of the celebrity status of certain artworks, such as the *Mona Lisa*, which attracts vast and inevitably tumultuous throngs of visitors to the Louvre. But any picture that attracts hordes of people has long since died, a victim of its own renown, its aura dissipated, its meaning lost in heaps of platitudes and cant. Say a prayer for its soul and move on.

Seek, rather, some quiet corner of the museum full of things no one else seems to care about. Art that is generally regarded as insipid (19th-century American genre paintings) or hermetic (religious icons from the Byzantine world) is likely to feel very lonely, and its loneliness will make it generous. It may be poor, but it will offer you everything it has.

3. Study Up

One of the most deceptive promises made by our stewards of culture over the past half century is: You don't need to know anything to enjoy art. This is true only in the most limited sense. Yes, art can speak to us even in our ignorance.

But there's a far more powerful truth: Our response to art is directly proportional to our knowledge of it. In this sense, art is the opposite of popular entertainment, which becomes more insipid with greater familiarity.

So study up. Even 10 minutes on *Wikipedia* can help orient you and fundamentally transform the experience. Better yet, read the old cranks of art history, especially the ones who knew how to write and have now become unfashionable (Kenneth Clark, Ernst Gombrich[1]). When visiting special exhibitions, always read the catalogue, or at least the main catalogue essay. If you can't afford the catalogue, read it in the gift shop.

Rules for the gift shop: Never buy anything that isn't a book; never "save time" for the gift shop because this will make you think about time; never take children, because they will associate art with commerce.

10   Many museums have public education programs, including tours through the galleries with trained docents. Always shadow a docent tour before joining one. If the guide spends all his or her time asking questions rather than explaining art and imparting knowledge, do not waste your time. These faux-Socratic dialogues are premised on the fallacy that all opinions about art are equally valid and that learning from authority is somehow oppressive. You wouldn't learn to ski from someone who professed indifference to form and technique, so don't waste your time with educators who indulge the time-wasting sham of endless questions about what you are feeling and thinking.

4. ENGAGE MEMORY

The experience of art is ephemeral, and on one level we have to accept that. But beyond the subjective experience, art is also something to be studied and debated. Unfortunately, unlike most things we study and debate, art is difficult to summarize and describe. Without a verbal description of what you have seen, you may feel as if nothing happened during your visit. You may even feel you can't remember anything about it, as if it was just a wash of images with nothing to hold on to.

But even if the actual experience of art is difficult to retain and remember, the names of the artists, the countries in which they worked, the years they lived and were active, and a host of other things are easily committed to memory. Some museum educators, who know these things, will tell you this kind of detail doesn't matter; they are lying. Always try to remember the name of and at least one work by an artist whom you didn't know before walking into the museum.

When trying to remember individual art works, make an effort to give yourself a verbal description of them. Perhaps write it in a notebook. The process of giving a verbal description will make details of the work more tangible, and will force you to look more deeply and confront your own entrenched blindness toward art. If your description feels clichéd, then go back again and again until you have said something that seems more substantial. If all else fails, simply

1. Clark (1903–1983), British author and former director of the National Gallery in London; Gombrich (1909–2001), art historian and author of *The Story of Art* (1950).

commit the visual details of the work to memory, its subject matter, or general color scheme, or surface texture. Turn away from the work and try to remember it; turn back and check your mental image against the work itself. This isn't fun. In fact, it can be exhausting. That means you're making progress in the fight against oblivion.

5. Accept Contradiction

Art must have some utopian ambition, must seek to make the world better, must engage with injustice and misery; art has no other mission than to express visual ideas in its own self-sufficient language. As one art lover supposedly said to another: Monet, Manet,[2] both are correct.

Susan Sontag[3] once argued "against interpretation" and in favor of a more immediate, more sensual, more purely subjective response to art; but others argue, just as validly, that art is part of culture and embodies a wide range of cultural meanings and that our job is to ferret them out. Again, both are correct.

15

The experience of art always enmires us in contradictions. I loathe figurative contemporary art except when I don't; ditto on abstraction. When looking at a painting, it's often useful to try believing two wildly contradictory things: That it is just an object, and an everyday sort of object; and that it is a phenomenally radical expression of human subjectivity. Both are correct.

Art is inspiring and depressing, it excites and enervates us, it makes us more generous and more selfish. A love-hate relationship with an artist, or a great work of art, is often the most intense and lasting of all relationships. After years of spending time in art museums, I've come to accept that I believe wildly contradictory and incompatible things about art. The usual cliché about this realization would be that by forcing us to confront contradiction, art makes us more human. But never trust anyone who says that last part: "art makes us more human." That's meaningless.

Rather, by forcing us to confront contradiction, art makes us ridiculous, exposes our pathetic attempts to make sense of experience, reveals the fault lines of our incredibly faulty knowledge of ourselves and the world. It is nasty, dangerous stuff, and not to be trifled with.

Some practical advice: If you feel better about yourself when you leave a museum, you're probably doing it all wrong.

MLA CITATION

Kennicott, Philip. "How to View Art: Be Dead Serious about It, but Don't Expect Too Much." *The Norton Reader: An Anthology of Nonfiction*, edited by Melissa A. Goldthwaite et al., 16th ed., W. W. Norton, 2024, pp. 538–41.

2. Oscar-Claude Monet (1840–1926), French impressionist painter; Édouard Manet (1832–1883), early modern French painter known for bridging realist and impressionist art movements.

3. American filmmaker and author of fiction, nonfiction, and plays (1933–2004).

QUESTIONS

1. Philip Kennicott regards the art museum as a place that should stand apart from, and in opposition to, what he calls our "workaday world where time is money, and money is everything" (paragraph 3). According to Kennicott, what contemporary conditions, attitudes, beliefs, or habits of mind impair our ability to properly view art?

2. Kennicott uses the form of a list to guide readers in how to view art. Which of his five directives do you think is most important? least important? Is there anything you would add to his list?

3. Kennicott suggests that art should unsettle us: "If you feel better about yourself when you leave a museum, you're probably doing it all wrong" (paragraph 19). Do you agree? Why or why not? How important is enjoyment to the appreciation of art?

4. Visit an art museum on your campus or in your community and follow Kennicott's advice. Write a letter to Kennicott describing and reflecting on your experience. How did following his advice shape your experience?

REBECCA SOLNIT
How to Be a Writer

1) **WRITE. THERE IS NO SUBSTITUTE.** Write what you most passionately want to write, not blogs, posts, tweets or all the disposable bubblewrap in which modern life is cushioned. But start small: write a good sentence, then a good paragraph, and don't be dreaming about writing the great American novel or what you'll wear at the awards ceremony because that's not what writing's about or how you get there from here. The road is made entirely out of words. Write a lot. Maybe at the outset you'll be like a toddler—the terrible twos are partly about being frustrated because you're smarter than your motor skills or your mouth, you want to color the picture, ask for the toy, and you're bumbling, incoherent and no one gets it, but it's not only time that gets the kid onward to more sophistication and skill, it's effort and practice. Write bad stuff because the road to good writing is made out of words and not all of them are well-arranged words.

2) **Remember that writing is not typing.** Thinking, researching, contemplating, outlining, composing in your head and in sketches, maybe some typing, with revisions as you go, and then more revisions, deletions, emendations, additions, reflections, setting aside and returning afresh, because a good writer is always a good editor of his or her own work. Typing is this little transaction in the middle of two vast thoughtful processes. There is such a thing as too much revision—I've seen things that were amazing in the 17th version get flattened out in the 23rd—but nothing is born perfect. Well, some things almost are, but they're freaks. And you might get those magical perfect passages if you write a

Originally published at Literary Hub *(lithub.com) in 2016. Rebecca Solnit is a San Francisco–based writer, historian, and activist.*

lot, including all the stuff that isn't magic that has to be cut, rethought, revised, fact-checked, and cleaned up.

3) Read. And don't read. Read good writing, and don't live in the present. Live in the deep past, with the language of the Koran or the Mabinogion or Mother Goose or Dickens or Dickinson or Baldwin or whatever speaks to you deeply. Literature is not high school and it's not actually necessary to know what everyone around you is wearing, in terms of style, and being influenced by people who are being published in this very moment is going to make you look just like them, which is probably not a good long-term goal for being yourself or making a meaningful contribution. At any point in history there is a great tide of writers of similar tone, they wash in, they wash out, the strange starfish stay behind, and the conches. Check out the bestseller list for April 1935 or August 1978 if you don't believe me. Originality is partly a matter of having your own influences: read evolutionary biology textbooks or the Old Testament, find your metaphors where no one's looking, don't belong. Or belong to the other world that is not quite this one, the world from which you send back your messages. Imagine Herman Melville in workshop in 1849 being told by all his peers that he needed to cut all those informative digressions and really his big whale book was kind of dull and why did it take him so long to get to the point. And actually it was a quiet failure at the time. So was pretty much everything Thoreau published, and Emily Dickinson published only a handful of poems in her lifetime but wrote thousands.

4) Listen. Don't listen. Feedback is great, from your editor, your agent, your readers, your friends, your classmates, but there are times when you know exactly what you're doing and why and obeying them means being out of tune with yourself. Listen to your own feedback and remember that you move forward through mistakes and stumbles and flawed but aspiring work, not perfect pirouettes performed in the small space in which you initially stood. Listen to what makes your hair stand on end, your heart melt, and your eyes go wide, what stops you in your tracks and makes you want to live, wherever it comes from, and hope that your writing can do all those things for other people. Write for other people, but don't listen to them too much.

5) Find a vocation. Talent is overrated, and it is usually conflated with nice   5
style. Passion, vocation, vision, and dedication are rarer, and they will get you through the rough spots in your style when your style won't give you a reason to get up in the morning and stare at the manuscript for the hundredth day in a row or even give you a compelling subject to write about. If you're not passionate about writing and about the world and the things in it you're writing about, then why are you writing? It starts with passion even before it starts with words. You want to read people who are wise, deep, wild, kind, committed, insightful, attentive; you want to be those people. I am all for style, but only in service of vision.

6) Time. It takes time. This means that you need to find that time. Don't be too social. Live below your means and keep the means modest (people with trust funds and other cushions: I'm not talking to you, though money makes many, many things easy, and often, vocation and passion harder). You probably have to do something else for a living at the outset or all along, but don't develop expensive habits or consuming hobbies. I knew a waitress once who thought fate was keeping her from her painting but taste was: if she'd given up always being the person who turned going out for a burrito into ordering the expensive wine at the bistro she would've had one more free day a week for art.

7) **Facts.** Always get them right. The wrong information about a bumblebee in a poem is annoying enough, but inaccuracy in nonfiction is a cardinal sin. No one will trust you if you get your facts wrong, and if you're writing about living or recently alive people or politics you absolutely must not misrepresent. (Ask yourself this: do I like it when people lie about me?) No matter what you're writing about, you have an obligation to get it right, for the people you're writing about, for the readers, and for the record. It's why I always tell students that it's a slippery slope from the things your stepfather didn't actually do to the weapons of mass destruction Iraq didn't actually have.[1] If you want to write about a stepfather who did things your stepfather didn't, or repeat conversations you don't actually remember with any detail, at least label your product accurately. Fiction operates under different rules but it often has facts in it too, and your credibility rests on their accuracy. (If you want to make up facts, like that Emily Brontë was nine feet tall and had wings but everyone in that Victorian era was too proper to mention it, remember to get the details about her cobbler and the kind of hat in fashion at the time right, and maybe put a little cameo at her throat seven and a half feet above the earth.)

8) **Joy.** Writing is facing your deepest fears and all your failures, including how hard it is to write a lot of the time and how much you loathe what you've just written and that you're the person who just committed those flawed sentences (many a writer, and God, I know I'm one, has worried about dying before the really crappy version is revised so that posterity will never know how awful it was). When it totally sucks, pause, look out the window (there should always be a window) and say, I'm doing exactly what I want to be doing. I am hanging out with the English language (or the Spanish or the Korean). I get to use the word turquoise or melting or supernova right now if I want. I'm with Shelley, who says that poets are the unacknowledged legislators of the universe, and I am not fracking or selling useless things to lonely seniors or otherwise abusing my humanity. Find pleasure and joy. Maybe even make lists of joys for emergencies. When all else fails, put on the gospel song "Steal My Joy"—refrain is "Ain't gonna let nobody steal my joy." Nobody, not even yourself.

But it's not about the joy, it's about the work, and there has to be some kind of joy in the work, some kind from among the many kinds, including the joy of hard truths told honestly. Carpenters don't say, I'm just not feeling it

1. President George W. Bush justified starting the Second Iraq War in 2003 on the claim that Iraq was developing these weapons. This claim turned out to be false.

today, or I don't give a damn about this staircase and whether people fall through it; how you feel is something that you cannot take too seriously on your way to doing something, and doing something is a means of not being stuck in how you feel. That is, there's a kind of introspection that's wallowing and being stuck, and there's a kind that gets beyond that into something more interesting and then maybe takes you out into the world or into the place where deepest interior and cosmological phenomena are at last talking to each other. I've written stuff amidst hideous suffering, and it was a way not to be so stuck in the hideous suffering, though it was hard, but also, hard is not impossible, and I didn't sign up with the expectation that it would be easy.

9) **What we call success is very nice and comes with useful byproducts, but success is not love,** or at least it is at best the result of love of the work and not of you, so don't confuse the two. Cultivating love for others and maybe receiving some for yourself is another job and an important one. The process of making art is the process of becoming a person with agency, with independent thought, a producer of meaning rather than a consumer of meanings that may be at odds with your soul, your destiny, your humanity, so there's another kind of success in becoming conscious that matters and that is up to you and nobody else and within your reach.

10

10) **It's all really up to you,** but you already knew that and knew everything else you need to know somewhere underneath the noise and the bustle and the anxiety and the outside instructions, including these ones.

MLA CITATION

Solnit, Rebecca. "How to Be a Writer." *The Norton Reader: An Anthology of Nonfiction*, edited by Melissa A. Goldthwaite et al., 16th ed., W. W. Norton, 2024, pp. 542–45.

QUESTIONS

1. Rebecca Solnit's first rule for writing is "Write": a clue that this how-to essay is a little offbeat. Which of her rules took you most by surprise? Which are you going to try out for yourself?

2. Study the numbered items in Solnit's list. What internal organization and logic stand behind this list?

3. In paragraph 3, Solnit recommends reading things that are old, unpopular, and out of the way. Do you have cultural texts (books, movies, or music) that you love that most people have not heard of or don't often engage with now? How do those items shape your outlook? Why are the statements in this order?

4. Pick an activity in which you are skilled and write your own "How to be a ____" guide for novices. Following Solnit's example, experiment with mixing seriousness and humor.

9 EDUCATION AND LEARNING

> The best thing for being sad . . . is to learn something. That's
> the only thing that never fails.
>
> —T. H. WHITE

In T. H. White's 1958 novel *The Once and Future King*, the wizard Merlyn counsels a young King Arthur to turn from his sadness and focus on learning. There is great value in Merlyn's advice—a life committed to learning and education can lift us out of our day-to-day worries—but this advice doesn't account for the complexities of the modern system of education. Learning and school go hand in hand, but that partnership is not without tension. Institutions of education involve schools, both welcoming and inhospitable; teachers, both good and bad; peers, both generous and cruel; and us, at times eager to learn, at times too sad, distracted, or uninterested to fully participate in the opportunity to learn. Sometimes the educational system is the perfect setting for learning; sometimes learning happens despite it. The essays in this chapter explore some of the many aspects of education (the school system, teachers, and all the structures and processes to promote learning) and learning itself (the process of coming to know for yourself), which will help you consider a multitude of ways to think about the value of your own education.

In "The Sanctuary of School," Lynda Barry describes being neglected at home but finding solace in the classroom. Victoria Chang recalls in "Dear Teacher" the respite she found in a teacher who taught Chang to love poetry, even as she felt isolated as one of the only Chinese students in her school. Sometimes teachers and mentors teach us most when they are not gentle or encouraging, but blunt in their judgments of what we still need to learn. Horror writer Stephen King looks at the lessons in writing he got from an experienced editor. In "Me Talk Pretty One Day," David Sedaris offers a comic picture of the challenges of learning a new language as an adult and pokes fun at a mocking teacher.

Technological innovations, such as artificial intelligence, assignment software, and remote classrooms, challenge and transform how we think about learning. In "Look Up from Your Screen," Nicholas Tampio grounds his argument against more screen time in schools in experience as well as philosophical and neuroscientific research. Taking a different approach, journalist Florence Williams investigates the benefits of adventure-based education for a specific group of students—those diagnosed with ADHD—and considers the historically important role of exploration and adventure in benefiting humanity. Both invite us to resist the seductions of technology and engage in real-world, full-body learning experiences.

Many of the essays in this chapter tell the story of a deep, personal drive to learn. Frederick Douglass, who was born enslaved, helps readers reflect on history and how access to an education was not always freely given. He tells, in first person, how others both aided and sought to prevent his literacy. Douglass's narrative illustrates how some individuals have fought to learn despite prohibitions against learning; his narrative encourages readers to think about who has access to what kind of education. In a different story of overcoming, Native American writer Elissa Washuta contrasts the lessons of her schoolbooks with what she learned reading on her own in the library, celebrating the magical ways that storybooks helped her persist. Michael Hamad invents a new way to understand music, turning from theory to drawing to represent how songs make him think and feel. Tara Westover, who didn't attend school until college, discovers the inadequacy of her homeschooling and the subsequent gaps left in her knowledge, even as she remains certain of the good intentions of her father. These essays confirm that the innate human drive to learn is more powerful than we often recognize.

Despite varying privileges and disparities, all students face challenges. In "College Pressures," William Zinsser considers the anxieties and fears expressed by students at Yale in the 1970s. He categorizes four kinds of pressures college students face—economic, parental, peer, and self-induced. Although his essay was published nearly fifty years ago, you might recognize similar problems. Sungjoo Yoon, who wrote his essay while still in high school, describes the unnerving and complicated ways that external politics invade the classroom when school boards decide to ban books. His essay "I'm a High School Junior. Let's Talk about *Huckleberry Finn* and *Mockingbird*" will help you refine your sense of what happens when learning is at odds with the system of education. In what ways have the pressures described in these essays changed, intensified, or resolved?

As you read and then turn to writing about learning and education, consider your own definitions of these terms. What does it mean, to you, to be educated? What technologies and pedagogies have aided your learning? What formative people have shifted your relationship to learning, for better or worse? What pressures do you face as a student? Do you see any potential solutions in these essays that might ease those pressures? What form will allow you to get across your points about education most effectively? What stories will you tell about your own educational experience?

LYNDA BARRY

The Sanctuary of School

I WAS 7 YEARS OLD the first time I snuck out of the house in the dark. It was winter and my parents had been fighting all night. They were short on money and long on relatives who kept "temporarily" moving into our house because they had nowhere else to go.

My brother and I were used to giving up our bedroom. We slept on the couch, something we actually liked because it put us that much closer to the light of our lives, our television.

Published in the New York Times *(1992). Lynda Barry is a cartoonist and author.*

At night when everyone was asleep, we lay on our pillows watching it with the sound off. We watched Steve Allen's[1] mouth moving. We watched Johnny Carson's[2] mouth moving. We watched movies filled with gangsters shooting machine guns into packed rooms, dying soldiers hurling a last grenade and beautiful women crying at windows. Then the sign-off finally came and we tried to sleep.

The morning I snuck out, I woke up filled with a panic about needing to get to school. The sun wasn't quite up yet but my anxiety was so fierce that I just got dressed, walked quietly across the kitchen and let myself out the back door.

5   It was quiet outside. Stars were still out. Nothing moved and no one was in the street. It was as if someone had turned the sound off on the world.

I walked the alley, breaking thin ice over the puddles with my shoes. I didn't know why I was walking to school in the dark. I didn't think about it. All I knew was a feeling of panic, like the panic that strikes kids when they realize they are lost.

A Dark Outline

That feeling eased the moment I turned the corner and saw the dark outline of my school at the top of the hill. My school was made up of about 15 nondescript portable classrooms set down on a fenced concrete lot in a rundown Seattle neighborhood, but it had the most beautiful view of the Cascade Mountains. You could see them from anywhere on the playfield and you could see them from the windows of my classroom—Room 2.

I walked over to the monkey bars and hooked my arms around the cold metal. I stood for a long time just looking across Rainier Valley. The sky was beginning to whiten and I could hear a few birds.

Easy to Slip Away

In a perfect world my absence at home would not have gone unnoticed. I would have had two parents in a panic to locate me, instead of two parents in a panic to locate an answer to the hard question of survival during a deep financial and emotional crisis.

10   But in an overcrowded and unhappy home, it's incredibly easy for any child to slip away. The high levels of frustration, depression and anger in my house made my brother and me invisible. We were children with the sound turned off. And for us, as for the steadily increasing number of neglected children in this country, the only place where we could count on being noticed was at school.

"Hey there, young lady. Did you forget to go home last night?" It was Mr. Gunderson, our janitor, whom we all loved. He was nice and he was funny and he was old with white hair, thick glasses and an unbelievable number of keys. I could hear them jingling as he walked across the playfield. I felt incredibly happy to see him.

1. Host of *The Tonight Show*, 1954–56.
2. Host of *The Tonight Show Starring Johnny Carson*, 1962–92.

He let me push his wheeled garbage can between the different portables as he unlocked each room. He let me turn on the lights and raise the window shades and I saw my school slowly come to life. I saw Mrs. Holman, our school secretary, walk into the office without her orange lipstick on yet. She waved.

I saw the fifth-grade teacher, Mr. Cunningham, walking under the breezeway eating a hard roll. He waved.

And I saw my teacher, Mrs. Claire LeSane, walking toward us in a red coat and calling my name in a very happy and surprised way, and suddenly my throat got tight and my eyes stung and I ran toward her crying. It was something that surprised us both.

It's only thinking about it now, 28 years later, that I realize I was crying from relief. I was with my teacher, and in a while I was going to sit at my desk, with my crayons and pencils and books and classmates all around me, and for the next six hours I was going to enjoy a thoroughly secure, warm and stable world. It was a world I absolutely relied on. Without it, I don't know where I would have gone that morning. 15

Mrs. LeSane asked me what was wrong and when I said "Nothing," she seemingly left it at that. But she asked me if I would carry her purse for her, an honor above all honors, and she asked if I wanted to come into Room 2 early and paint.

PAINTING'S POWER

She believed in the natural healing power of painting and drawing for troubled children. In the back of her room there was always a drawing table and an easel with plenty of supplies, and sometimes during the day she would come up to you for what seemed like no good reason and quietly ask if you wanted to go to the back table and "make some pictures for Mrs. LeSane." We all had a chance at it—to sit apart from the class for a while to paint, draw and silently work out impossible problems on 11×17 sheets of newsprint.

Drawing came to mean everything to me. At the back table in Room 2, I learned to build myself a life preserver that I could carry into my home.

We all know that a good education system saves lives, but the people of this country are still told that cutting the budget for public schools is necessary, that poor salaries for teachers are all we can manage and that art, music and all creative activities must be the first to go when times are lean.

NO BABY-SITTING

Before- and after-school programs are cut and we are told that public schools are not made for baby-sitting children. If parents are neglectful temporarily or permanently, for whatever reason, it's certainly sad, but their unlucky children must fend for themselves. Or slip through the cracks. Or wander in a dark night alone. 20

We are told in a thousand ways that not only are public schools not important, but that the children who attend them, the children who need them most, are not important either. We leave them to learn from the blind eye of a

television, or to the mercy of "a thousand points of light"[3] that can be as far away as stars.

I was lucky. I had Mrs. LeSane. I had Mr. Gunderson. I had an abundance of art supplies. And I had a particular brand of neglect in my home that allowed me to slip away and get to them. But what about the rest of the kids who weren't as lucky? What happened to them?

By the time the bell rang that morning I had finished my drawing and Mrs. LeSane pinned it up on the special bulletin board she reserved for drawings from the back table. It was the same picture I always drew—a sun in the corner of a blue sky over a nice house with flowers all around it.

Mrs. LeSane asked us to please stand, face the flag, place our right hands over our hearts and say the Pledge of Allegiance. Children across the country do it faithfully. I wonder now when the country will face its children and say a pledge right back.

MLA CITATION

Barry, Lynda. "The Sanctuary of School." *The Norton Reader: An Anthology of Nonfiction*, edited by Melissa A. Goldthwaite et al., 16th ed., W. W. Norton, 2024, pp. 547–50.

QUESTIONS

1. How does Lynda Barry's school experience contrast with her home life? What specifically makes school a "sanctuary"?

---

3. Metaphor for private philanthropy and volunteer service implicitly in contrast to government-run social programs; popularized by former US president George H. W. Bush.

2. In paragraphs 19 to 21, Barry calls for better funding for public schools. Imagine that Barry has received an unrestricted $500,000 grant to improve her elementary school. How do you think she would spend it?

3. Barry is best known as a cartoonist. Describe the drawing that accompanies this essay to someone who has never seen it. How does the drawing comment on and enhance your understanding of the essay?

4. Building on your own experience, write an argument about how we might improve our schools.

VICTORIA CHANG
Dear Teacher

D EAR TEACHER,
The tall, handsome boy who was reading my poem aloud in front of the class had stopped cold, turned around, and begun whispering to you. The rooms in the windowless high school always seemed too bright, as if they knew they were about to lose to darkness.

You called me up to your desk. I hated getting up and walking around in class. I was unremarkable and strange. I was remarkably Chinese. I was so Chinese that I didn't know that I shouldn't have written a poem about contemplating suicide for a class assignment.

I was so Chinese that I didn't know that an American teacher might see this as a problem. At the same time, though, I had no idea what being Chinese meant. I had no idea what being American meant. I was here and nowhere. I could still hate something I didn't understand. I could still be something I didn't know.

You couldn't help me. I needed to be in a different country, where people looked like me, even a different state, like California. Where people didn't ignore me. Where people, when they did see me, didn't pull their eyes out thin and laugh. But that wasn't going to happen. And I couldn't see outside the funhouse mirror of my life.

The racist act is not always the most harmful. It's the surprise of it, the fraught waiting, each moment like a small trip wire. You never know when you might confront it, so to survive, you live your life in stillness, in self-perpetuated invisibility. And then there's the aftermath of shame.   5

Dear Teacher, you read us so many poems, so much Shakespeare, had us memorize so many poems, that I never became American, but I became a writer.

> Because I could not stop for Death—
> He kindly stopped for me—

Originally appeared in Victoria Chang's Dear Memory: Letters on Writing, Silence, and Grief (2021), a collection of essays in the form of letters.

The carriage held but just Ourselves—
And Immortality.[1]

These words have passed through my brain almost daily. How you loved Dickinson. I remember your frilly old-fashioned powder blue blouses, tucked into tight pencil skirts, your gray hair, small wire spectacles, nylons, and little flats, how you pranced in front of the classroom reciting:

I'm Nobody! Who are you?
Are you—Nobody—too?
Then there's a pair of us!
Don't tell! they'd advertise—you know! . . . [2]

I don't know how much of Dickinson or Shakespeare or Keats stuck in my teenage mind, but to learn from you that writing was a possibility, not as a career, but simply as a way to move into and out of pain, was the real gift.

I'm not sure if you are still alive and, if you are, you probably don't remember me, but that chasm between us was filled with poetry instead of misunderstanding. Instead of silence. When you shared poems with me, you were filling the space between us with language.

10   I didn't know what was happening at the time, but I see it now. The language of poetry reminded me to stay alive. It reminded me that, when it felt like I had nothing, I was nothing, I still had words. I could ride language as if on horseback, and it could take me anywhere, including more deeply into myself.

I don't remember what I told you when you called me up to the front of the classroom and whispered in my ear. I'm sure my face was expressionless and burning. But I remember how your hair curled at the bottom, as if shaped by a roller, how you smelled like perfume and joy. I still remember the way your eyes looked desperate and worried, their insistence that I step out of something. You weren't satisfied with my silence.

I remember nodding as if I was fine. I *was* fine. I had language. And it would be the one thing that would keep returning, like light. Language felt like wanting to drown but being able to experience drowning by standing on a pier.

MLA CITATION

Chang, Victoria. "Dear Teacher." *The Norton Reader: An Anthology of Nonfiction*, edited by Melissa A. Goldthwaite et al., 16th ed., W. W. Norton, 2024, pp. 551–52.

QUESTIONS

1. In paragraph 2, Victoria Chang describes herself as "unremarkable and strange." What do you think she means by that phrase? How can a person be at once unremarkable and strange? What made her feel that way?

---

1. First stanza of a poem (1863) by Emily Dickinson (1830–1886).
2. First stanza of a poem (1891) by Dickinson.

2. Chang's teacher helps her by inviting her to share in a love of poetry, not by addressing either her feelings of isolation or the racism she experiences. How does Chang describe the difference that made to her? Think back on a time when a teacher helped you through a personally hard time.

3. Look up one of the two Emily Dickinson poems that Chang quotes. Study it and write about what connects that poem, thematically or otherwise, to Chang's mood and situation as a student.

4. Following Chang's model, write an essay in the form of a letter to a person who impacted your life or mattered to you without knowing it.

SUNGJOO YOON
I'm a High School Junior. Let's Talk about Huckleberry Finn *and* Mockingbird.

IN LATE 2020, when the Burbank Unified School District removed five classic novels from mandatory reading lists in my city's classrooms, I started a petition to protest the decision. The petition, which is still open, has more than 5,000 signatures.

I was a sophomore at Burbank High School at the time and had read four of the five books in school—*Adventures of Huckleberry Finn* by Mark Twain, *Roll of Thunder, Hear My Cry* by Mildred D. Taylor, *To Kill a Mockingbird* by Harper Lee and *The Cay* by Theodore Taylor. The fifth, *Of Mice and Men* by John Steinbeck, I read on my own a few years earlier.

The books were being removed from the core curriculum, according to Matt Hill, the superintendent of the Burbank Unified district, after complaints from students and parents that the depictions of racism and language in these works—particularly the use of the N-word—caused harm to Black students.

My position was this: I acknowledged that Black students were being marginalized in our classrooms (I was sympathetic, too; I am all too familiar with the demeaning nature of racism)—but did not think that it was the fault of these books or their content. I believed, and still believe, that the solution was not to remove the books but to add books written by people of color and to better train teachers to teach these books sensitively to students.

As the petition attracted signatures, I spoke at several school board meetings on the issue. I recall one meeting in particular. I had prepared to talk about how these novels helped shape me both as a student and as a human being. I spoke briefly about how reading the story of a Black family in the Deep South in *Roll of Thunder, Hear My Cry*, under the guidance of a caring teacher, had moved me to tears and to a commitment to learn more about the resilience and resistance of the people upon whose backs this country was built. I explained how these class experiences helped move me and some fellow students from

5

Originally published as an op-ed in the New York Times *(2022).*

complacent private citizens to people who today are deeply involved in the fight for social justice.

There was more I could have said: How Atticus Finch's defense of Tom Robinson in *To Kill a Mockingbird* taught me the danger of complacency; how the unlikely friendships of Huckleberry Finn and Jim in *Adventures of Huckleberry Finn* or Phillip Enright and Timothy in *The Cay* taught me that love transcends any and all differences.

But standing on the boardroom floor as comments from others in the meeting began, I witnessed the public forum—made up mostly of parents, administrators and educators—devolve into tribalist dissension. The meeting quickly became a two-sided shouting match pitting supposed "freedoms" against purported "justice." There was plenty of arguing but little or no meaningful discussion on why those novels were in question or what students would lose or gain by a ban against them.

At that moment, I had a long-overdue realization: How we as Americans approach restrictions on literature curriculums is not only flawed but also wholly reactionary. My experience at that meeting and others convinced me that the problem is not *that* we disagree but *how*. We need to shift focus away from reflexive outrage about restrictions and bans and toward actual discussions of the merits and drawbacks of the individual books.

Nearly a year and a half later, the Burbank book restriction is still in place, and more have been approved in schools and school districts across the country. A report from PEN America[1] this month found that 86 school districts in the United States have banned 1,586 books in the past year. From the Tennessee school board that decided *Maus*, Art Spiegelman's graphic novel about the Holocaust, could no longer be taught, to the Oklahoma State Legislature's proposed law giving a parent of any student the power to enforce bans on books "of a sexual nature," to the sweeping removal of 130 books with sexual themes from school shelves at the request of a Texas superintendent, one element unites all the conflicts around these bans—a political and ideological partisanship that buys more into contemporary culture wars than into our students' education.

One fact often overlooked in these disputes is that both conservatives and   10
liberals engage in book banning and removal when it suits their political goals. Burbank is a liberal stronghold where the majority of voters in the last five presidential elections cast ballots for Democrats; Granbury, the district in Texas that removed the 130 books this year for "pervasively vulgar" content or "pornography"—in what many believe is code speak to conceal prejudice against those who identify as LGBTQ—is a conservative stronghold that voted Republican in those same five elections.

Americans, conditioned to resist violations of our "freedom" at every turn, tend to reflexively reject any literary censorship. But we often forget that these types of book bans aren't instituting a nationalized book burning or punishments for reading the books; rather, they are often decisions about whether certain groups of children are emotionally or developmentally ready for certain books. The truth is that all schools have curriculums and that deciding what is included and what is not is a crucial responsibility that involves subjective decisions about what is best for students. And I do want to give this notion some deference.

When I was 10, I found myself voraciously reading all things related to World War II; along that path, I picked up a copy of Iris Chang's 1997 book, *The Rape of Nanking*. Two chapters in, as the executions of innocent children my age were described in detail, I learned that the contents of the historical account were just about as discomforting as the title itself. Terrified and upset, I put the book down and stored it deep in my closet.

Did my aversion to that book negate the severity of the war crimes that occurred on the Sino-Japanese front? Absolutely not. But did it show that I was probably too young to read it? Yes. Both principles can be simultaneously true: Certain books can be important to society while being upsetting or harmful to a child. We can and ought to reject the false binary being sold to us today, because

---

1. A nonprofit organization founded in 1922 to defend and celebrate free expression in the United States and worldwide through the advancement of literature and human rights.

there *is* some value in restricting curriculum to children when those decisions are informed by a knowledge of the books and the capacities of the students.

I hope that the adults who make the decisions about our schools and our educations and those who fuel the public arguments over them can put an end to their hyperpartisanship and help us to begin rigorous conversations about the content and value of the books themselves.

15   Because at that meeting I never did get to say my piece about what those other books had done for me.

MLA CITATION

Yoon, Sungjoo. "I'm a High School Junior. Let's Talk about *Huckleberry Finn* and *Mockingbird*." *The Norton Reader: An Anthology of Nonfiction*, edited by Melissa A. Goldthwaite et al., 16th ed., W. W. Norton, 2024, pp. 553–56.

QUESTIONS

1. Go back through the essay and annotate each instance of censorship Sungjoo Yoon mentions. Fill out your annotations with a sentence or two on the text that was banned or on the community that banned it. How does this help you understand the decision to ban each book? Do you agree with the decision?

2. Yoon describes his frustration with adults who underestimate young people and try to control what they read while noting the necessity of determining a curriculum. What role, if any, should adults have in guiding younger people toward certain books or away from others?

3. In paragraphs 6 and 15, Yoon alludes to what he wishes he had been able to say at a school board meeting. Drawing on the rest of the essay, what do you think he would have said, given the chance?

4. Yoon's argument insists that two things can be true at once: that books can be upsetting and unsuitable for readers of a certain age, and that banning them is wrong (paragraph 13). Write an essay in response to this complexity: To what extent do you agree with the compromises Yoon proposes?

DAVID SEDARIS
Me Talk Pretty One Day

A T THE AGE OF FORTY-ONE, I am returning to school and have to think of myself as what my French textbook calls "a true debutant." After paying my tuition, I was issued a student ID, which allows me a discounted entry fee at movie theaters, puppet shows, and Festyland, a far-flung amusement park that advertises with billboards picturing a cartoon stegosaurus sitting in a canoe and eating what appears to be a ham sandwich.

I've moved to Paris with hopes of learning the language. My school is an easy ten-minute walk from my apartment, and on the first day of class I arrived early, watching as the returning students greeted one another in the school lobby. Vacations were recounted, and questions were raised concerning mutual friends with names like Kang and Vlatnya. Regardless of their nationalities, everyone spoke in what sounded to me like excellent French. Some accents were better than others, but the students exhibited an ease and confidence I found intimidating. As an added discomfort, they were all young, attractive, and well dressed, causing me to feel not unlike Pa Kettle[1] trapped backstage after a fashion show.

The first day of class was nerve-racking because I knew I'd be expected to perform. That's the way they do it here—it's everybody into the language pool, sink or swim. The teacher marched in, deeply tanned from a recent vacation, and proceeded to rattle off a series of administrative announcements. I've spent quite a few summers in Normandy, and I took a monthlong French class before leaving New York. I'm not completely in the dark, yet I understood only half of what this woman was saying.

"If you have not *meimslsxp* or *lgpdmurct* by this time, then you should not be in this room. Has everyone *apzkiubjxow*? Everyone? Good, we shall begin." She spread out her lesson plan and sighed, saying, "All right, then, who knows the alphabet?"

It was startling because (a) I hadn't been asked that question in a while and (b) I realized, while laughing, that I myself did not know the alphabet. They're the same letters, but in France they're pronounced differently. I know the shape of the alphabet but had no idea what it actually sounded like.

"Ahh." The teacher went to the board and sketched the letter *a*. "Do we have anyone in the room whose first name commences with an *ahh*?"

Two Polish Annas raised their hands, and the teacher instructed them to present themselves by stating their names, nationalities, occupations, and a brief list of things they liked and disliked in this world. The first Anna hailed from an industrial town outside of Warsaw and had front teeth the size of

5

Originally appeared in Esquire, *March 1999, and later reprinted as the title essay of David Sedaris's collection in 2000.*

1. A comic character from a series of films in the 1940s and 1950s about an old-fashioned, middle-aged couple struggling to keep up with modern fashion and technology.

tombstones. She worked as a seamstress, enjoyed quiet times with friends, and hated the mosquito.

"Oh, really," the teacher said. "How very interesting. I thought that everyone loved the mosquito, but here, in front of all the world, you claim to detest him. How is it that we've been blessed with someone as unique and original as you? Tell us, please."

The seamstress did not understand what was being said but knew that this was an occasion for shame. Her rabbity mouth huffed for breath, and she stared down at her lap as though the appropriate comeback were stitched somewhere alongside the zipper of her slacks.

10   The second Anna learned from the first and claimed to love sunshine and detest lies. It sounded like a translation of one of those Playmate of the Month data sheets, the answers always written in the same loopy handwriting: "Turnons: Mom's famous five-alarm chili! Turnoffs: insecurity and guys who come on too strong!!!!"

The two Polish Annas surely had clear notions of what they loved and hated, but like the rest of us, they were limited in terms of vocabulary, and this made them appear less than sophisticated. The teacher forged on, and we learned that Carlos, the Argentine bandonion[2] player, loved wine, music, and, in his words, "making sex with the womens of the world." Next came a beautiful young Yugoslav who identified herself as an optimist, saying that she loved everything that life had to offer.

The teacher licked her lips, revealing a hint of the sauce-box we would later come to know. She crouched low for her attack, placed her hands on the young woman's desk, and leaned close, saying, "Oh yeah? And do you love your little war?"

While the optimist struggled to defend herself, I scrambled to think of an answer to what had obviously become a trick question. How often is one asked what he loves in this world? More to the point, how often is one asked and then publicly ridiculed for his answer? I recalled my mother, flushed with wine, pounding the tabletop late one night, saying, "Love? I love a good steak cooked rare. I love my cat, and I love . . ." My sisters and I leaned forward, waiting to hear our names. "Tums," our mother said. "I love Tums."

The teacher killed some time accusing the Yugoslavian girl of masterminding a program of genocide, and I jotted frantic notes in the margins of my pad. While I can honestly say that I love leafing through medical textbooks devoted to severe dermatological conditions, the hobby is beyond the reach of my French vocabulary, and acting it out would only have invited controversy.

15   When called upon, I delivered an effortless list of things that I detest: blood sausage, intestinal pâtés, brain pudding. I'd learned these words the hard way. Having given it some thought, I then declared my love for IBM typewriters, the French word for *bruise*, and my electric floor waxer. It was a short list, but still I managed to mispronounce *IBM* and assign the wrong gender to both the

2. *Bandoneón* in Spanish; a concertina, similar to an accordion. The instrument is central to the tango music of Argentina and Uruguay.

floor waxer and the typewriter. The teacher's reaction led me to believe that these mistakes were capital crimes in the country of France.

"Were you always this *palicmkrexis?*" she asked. "Even a *fiuscrzsa ticiwelmun* knows that a typewriter is feminine."

I absorbed as much of her abuse as I could understand, thinking—but not saying—that I find it ridiculous to assign a gender to an inanimate object incapable of disrobing and making an occasional fool of itself. Why refer to Lady Crack Pipe or Good Sir Dishrag when these things could never live up to all that their sex implied?

The teacher proceeded to belittle everyone from German Eva, who hated laziness, to Japanese Yukari, who loved paintbrushes and soap. Italian, Thai, Dutch, Korean, and Chinese—we all left class foolishly believing that the worst was over. She'd shaken us up a little, but surely that was just an act designed to weed out the deadweight. We didn't know it then, but the coming months would teach us what it was like to spend time in the presence of a wild animal, something completely unpredictable. Her temperament was not based on a series of good and bad days but, rather, good and bad moments. We soon learned to dodge chalk and protect our heads and stomachs whenever she approached us with a question. She hadn't yet punched anyone, but it seemed wise to protect ourselves against the inevitable.

Though we were forbidden to speak anything but French, the teacher would occasionally use us to practice any of her five fluent languages.

"I hate you," she said to me one afternoon. Her English was flawless. "I really, really hate you." Call me sensitive, but I couldn't help but take it personally.

After being singled out as a lazy *kfdtinvfm*, I took to spending four hours a night on my homework, putting in even more time whenever we were assigned an essay. I suppose I could have gotten by with less, but I was determined to create some sort of identity for myself: David the hard worker, David the cut-up. We'd have one of those "complete this sentence" exercises, and I'd fool with the thing for hours, invariably settling on something like "A quick run around the lake? I'd love to! Just give me a moment while I strap on my wooden leg." The teacher, through word and action, conveyed the message that if this was my idea of an identity, she wanted nothing to do with it.

My fear and discomfort crept beyond the borders of the classroom and accompanied me out onto the wide boulevards. Stopping for a coffee, asking directions, depositing money in my bank account: these things were out of the question, as they involved having to speak. Before beginning school, there'd been no shutting me up, but now I was convinced that everything I said was wrong. When the phone rang, I ignored it. If someone asked me a question, I pretended to be deaf. I knew my fear was getting the best of me when I started wondering why they don't sell cuts of meat in vending machines.

My only comfort was the knowledge that I was not alone. Huddled in the hallways and making the most of our pathetic French, my fellow students and I engaged in the sort of conversation commonly overheard in refugee camps.

"Sometime me cry alone at night."

20

25   "That be common for I, also, but be more strong, you. Much work and
someday you talk pretty. People start love you soon. Maybe tomorrow, okay."
          Unlike the French class I had taken in New York, here there was no sense
of competition. When the teacher poked a shy Korean in the eyelid with a freshly
sharpened pencil, we took no comfort in the fact that, unlike Hyeyoon Cho, we
all knew the irregular past tense of the verb *to defeat*. In all fairness, the teacher
hadn't meant to stab the girl, but neither did she spend much time apologizing,
saying only, "Well, you should have been *vkkdyo* more *kdeynfulh*."
          Over time it became impossible to believe that any of us would ever improve.
Fall arrived and it rained every day, meaning we would now be scolded for the
water dripping from our coats and umbrellas. It was mid-October when the
teacher singled me out, saying, "Every day spent with you is like having a cesarean section." And it struck me that, for the first time since arriving in France,
I could understand every word that someone was saying.
          Understanding doesn't mean that you can suddenly speak the language.
Far from it. It's a small step, nothing more, yet its rewards are intoxicating and
deceptive. The teacher continued her diatribe and I settled back, bathing in
the subtle beauty of each new curse and insult.
          "You exhaust me with your foolishness and reward my efforts with noth-
ing but pain, do you understand me?"
30   The world opened up, and it was with great joy that I responded, "I know
the thing that you speak exact now. Talk me more, you, plus, please, plus."

MLA CITATION

Sedaris, David. "Me Talk Pretty One Day." *The Norton Reader: An Anthology of
    Nonfiction*, edited by Melissa A. Goldthwaite et al., 16th ed., W. W. Norton,
    2024, pp. 557–60.

QUESTIONS

1. In the hands of another writer, this French teacher might be called abusive and
cruel. How does David Sedaris make her funny? Point to one or two specific places
in the text where he makes his humorous intent clear.

2. Sedaris prints a string of unpronounceable nonsense letters to mark the spots
where he doesn't understand. Tara Westover calls these "black-hole words" in "From
Educated" (pp. 592–94, paragraph 8). Describe in your own terms the experience
of being completely unable to understand what someone is saying. How does your
mind fill in gaps in your understanding?

3. Do a project (a paper, short video, or podcast) that gives an account of the humorous struggles involved in learning a new language.

STEPHEN KING
On Writing

ARDLY A WEEK after being sprung from detention hall, I was once more invited to step down to the principal's office. I went with a sinking heart, wondering what new shit I'd stepped in.

It wasn't Mr. Higgins who wanted to see me, at least; this time the school guidance counselor had issued the summons. There had been discussions about me, he said, and how to turn my "restless pen" into more constructive channels. He had enquired of John Gould, editor of Lisbon's weekly newspaper, and had discovered Gould had an opening for a sports reporter. While the school couldn't *insist* that I take this job, everyone in the front office felt it would be a good idea. *Do it or die*, the G.C.'s eyes suggested. Maybe that was just paranoia, but even now, almost forty years later, I don't think so.

I groaned inside. I was shut of[1] *Dave's Rag*, almost shut of *The Drum*, and now here was the Lisbon *Weekly Enterprise*. Instead of being haunted by waters, like Norman Maclean in *A River Runs through It*,[2] I was as a teenager haunted by newspapers. Still, what could I do? I rechecked the look in the guidance counselor's eyes and said I would be delighted to interview for the job.

Gould—not the well-known New England humorist or the novelist who wrote *The Greenleaf Fires* but a relation of both, I think—greeted me warily but with some interest. We would try each other out, he said, if that suited me.

Now that I was away from the administrative offices of Lisbon High, I felt able to muster a little honesty. I told Mr. Gould that I didn't know much about sports. Gould said, "These are games people understand when they're watching them drunk in bars. You'll learn if you try."   5

He gave me a huge roll of yellow paper on which to type my copy—I think I still have it somewhere—and promised me a wage of half a cent a word. It was the first time someone had promised me wages for writing.

The first two pieces I turned in had to do with a basketball game in which an LHS player broke the school scoring record. One was a straight piece of reporting. The other was a sidebar about Robert Ransom's record-breaking performance. I brought both to Gould the day after the game so he'd have them for Friday, which was when the paper came out. He read the game piece, made two minor corrections, and spiked it.[3] Then he started in on the feature piece with a large black pen.

From On Writing: A Memoir of the Craft *(2000). Stephen King is primarily known for his horror and suspense novels and stories.*

1. Slang for "no longer being involved in."

2. Story collection (1976) that includes the often-quoted words "I am haunted by waters."

3. Journalistic slang for "withholding publication," often out of fear that the story cannot be sufficiently verified.

I took my fair share of English Lit classes in my two remaining years at Lisbon, and my fair share of composition, fiction, and poetry classes in college, but John Gould taught me more than any of them, and in no more than ten minutes. I wish I still had the piece—it deserves to be framed, editorial corrections and all—but I can remember pretty well how it went and how it looked after Gould had combed through it with that black pen of his. Here's an example:

> Last night, in the ~~well-loved~~ gymnasium of Lisbon
> High School, partisans and Jay Hills fans alike were
> stunned by an athletic performance unequalled in
> school history. Bob Ransom, ~~known as "Bullet" Bob~~
> ~~for both his size and accuracy,~~ scored thirty-seven
> points. Yes, you heard me right. ~~Plus~~ he did it with
> grace, speed . . . and with an odd courtesy as well,
> committing only two personal fouls in his ~~knight-like~~
> quest for a record which has eluded Lisbon ~~thinclads~~ *players*
> since ~~the years of Korea~~ *1953.* . . .

Gould stopped at "the years of Korea" and looked up at me. "What year was the last record made?" he asked.

10   Luckily, I had my notes. "1953," I said. Gould grunted and went back to work. When he finished marking my copy in the manner indicated above, he looked up and saw something on my face. I think he must have mistaken it for horror. It wasn't; it was pure revelation. Why, I wondered, didn't English teachers ever do this? It was like the Visible Man Old Raw Diehl had on his desk in the biology room.

"I only took out the bad parts, you know," Gould said. "Most of it's pretty good."

"I know," I said, meaning both things: yes, most of it was good—okay anyway, serviceable—and yes, he had only taken out the bad parts. "I won't do it again."

He laughed. "If that's true, you'll never have to work for a living. You can do *this* instead. Do I have to explain any of these marks?"

"No," I said.

15   "When you write a story, you're telling yourself the story," he said. "When you rewrite, your main job is taking out all the things that are *not* the story."

Gould said something else that was interesting on the day I turned in my first two pieces: write with the door closed, rewrite with the door open. Your stuff starts out being just for you, in other words, but then it goes out. Once you know what the story is and get it right—as right as you can, anyway—it belongs to anyone who wants to read it. Or criticize it. If you're very lucky (this is my idea, not John Gould's, but I believe he would have subscribed to the notion), more will want to do the former than the latter.

MLA CITATION

King, Stephen. "On Writing." *The Norton Reader: An Anthology of Nonfiction*, edited by Melissa A. Goldthwaite et al., 16th ed., W. W. Norton, 2024, pp. 561–62.

QUESTIONS

1. Stephen King provides an example of the way his editor marked up his work. What rationale can you provide for the edits? Would you have made different choices if you were the editor? Why?

2. King uses dialogue and description to help characterize his editor. In which parts of the text do you get the best sense of who John Gould is? Why are those parts effective?

3. King writes about learning from an editor. What or who has most helped you become a stronger writer? What has it been like for you to learn to appreciate and incorporate criticism from a coach, teacher, or mentor?

4. Write about a time someone responded to your writing in a way that helped you learn to be a better writer. What kinds of comments and edits did that person make? Why was that response helpful to you?

NICHOLAS TAMPIO

Look Up from Your Screen

A ROOSTER CROWS and awakens my family at the farm where we are staying for a long weekend. The air is crisp, and stars twinkle in the sky as the Sun rises over the hill. We walk to the barn, where horses, cows, chickens, pigs, dogs and cats vie for our attention. We wash and replenish water bowls, and carry hay to the cows and horses. The kids collect eggs for breakfast.

The wind carries the smells of winter turning to spring. The mud wraps around our boots as we step in puddles. When we enter a stall, the pigs bump into us; when we look at the sheep, they cower together in a corner. We are learning about the urban watershed, where eggs and beef come from, and how barns were built in the 19th century with wood cauls rather than metal nails. We experience the smells of the barn, the texture of the ladder, the feel of the shovels, the vibration when the pigs grunt, the taste of fresh eggs, and the camaraderie with the farmers.

As a parent, it is obvious that children learn more when they engage their entire body in a meaningful experience than when they sit at a computer. If you doubt this, just observe children watching an activity on a screen and then doing the same activity for themselves. They are much more engaged riding a

Published in Aeon (2018), *a digital magazine "committed to big ideas, serious enquiry and a humane worldview." All notes in this piece were written by the author unless indicated otherwise.*

horse than watching a video about it, playing a sport with their whole bodies rather than a simulated version of it in an online game.

Today, however, many powerful people are pushing for children to spend more time in front of computer screens, not less. Philanthropists such as Bill Gates and Mark Zuckerberg have contributed millions of dollars to "personal learning," a term that describes children working by themselves on computers, and Laurene Powell Jobs has bankrolled the XQ Super School project to use technology to "transcend the confines of traditional teaching methodologies."[1] Policymakers such as the US Secretary of Education Betsy DeVos call personalized learning "one of the most promising developments in K–12 education,"[2] and Rhode Island has announced a statewide personalized learning push for all public school students.[3] Think tanks such as the Brookings Institution recommend that Latin-American countries build "massive e-learning hubs that reach millions."[4] School administrators tout the advantages of giving all students, including those at kindergarten, personal computers.

5   Many adults appreciate the power of computers and the internet, and think that children should have access to them as soon as possible. Yet screen learning displaces other, more tactile ways to discover the world. Human beings learn with their eyes, yes, but also their ears, nose, mouth, skin, heart, hands, feet. The more time kids spend on computers, the less time they have to go on field trips, build model airplanes, have recess, hold a book in their hands, or talk with teachers and friends. In the 21st century, schools should not get with the times, as it were, and place children on computers for even more of their days. Instead, schools should provide children with rich experiences that engage their entire bodies.

To better understand why so many people embrace screen learning, we can turn to a classic of 20th-century French philosophy: Maurice Merleau-Ponty's *Phenomenology of Perception* (1945).[5]

According to Merleau-Ponty, European philosophy has long prioritized "seeing" over "doing" as a path to understanding. Plato, René Descartes, John Locke,

---

1. "XQ: The Super School Project," Emerson Collective, accessed June 25, 2019, https://www.emersoncollective.com/xq-the-super-school-project/.

2. Alyson Klein, "Betsy DeVos: Many Students Aren't Being Prepared for the Careers of Tomorrow," *Education Week - Politics K–12*, accessed June 25, 2019, http://blogs.edweek .org/edweek/campaign-k-12/2017/11/betsy_devos_jobs_future_choice_florida.html?cmp =SOC-SHR-FB.

3. Benjamin Herold, "Rhode Island Announces Statewide K–12 Personalized Learning Push," *Education Week - Digital Education*, accessed June 25, 2019, https://blogs .edweek.org/edweek/DigitalEducation/2017/02/rhode_island_personalized_learning .html?cmp=SOC-SHR-FB.

4. Rebecca Winthrop and Adam Barton, "Innovation to Leapfrog Educational Progress in Latin America," *Brookings* (blog), March 22, 2018, https://www.brookings.edu /research/innovation-to-leapfrog-educational-progress-in-latin-america/.

5. Phenomenology is a branch of philosophy devoted to the study of consciousness and experience [Editor's note]; Maurice Merleau-Ponty, *Phenomenology of Perception*, trans. Donald Landes (New York: Routledge, 2013).

David Hume, Immanuel Kant: each, in different ways, posits a gap between the mind and the world, the subject and the object, the thinking self and physical things. Philosophers take for granted that the mind sees things from a distance. When Descartes announced "I think therefore I am," he was positing a fundamental gulf between the thinking self and the physical body. Despite the novelty of digital media, Merleau-Ponty would contend that Western thought has long assumed that the mind, not the body, is the site of thinking and learning.

According to Merleau-Ponty, however, "consciousness is originally not an 'I think that,' but rather an 'I can.'"[6] In other words, human thinking emerges out of lived experience, and what we can do with our bodies profoundly shapes what philosophers think or scientists discover. "The entire universe of science is constructed upon the lived world," he wrote.[7] *Phenomenology of Perception* aimed to help readers better appreciate the connection between the lived world and consciousness.

Philosophers are in the habit of saying that we "have" a body. But as Merleau-Ponty points out: "I am not in front of my body, I am in my body, or rather I am my body."[8] This simple correction carries important implications about learning. What does it mean to say that I am my body?

The mind is not somehow outside of time and space. Instead, the body thinks, feels, desires, hurts, has a history, and looks ahead. Merleau-Ponty invented the term "intentional arc" to describe how consciousness connects "our past, our future, our human milieu, our physical situation, our ideological situation, and our moral situation."[9] He makes readers attend to the countless aspects of the world that permeate our thinking.

Merleau-Ponty challenges us to stop believing that the human mind transcends the rest of nature. Humans are thinking animals whose thinking is always infused with our animality. As the cognitive scientist Alan Jasanoff explains in a recent *Aeon* essay, it is even misleading to idealize the brain independent of the rest of the viscera.[10] The learning process happens when an embodied mind "gears" into the world.

Take the example of dancing. From a Cartesian perspective, the mind moves the body like a puppeteer pulls strings to move a puppet. To learn to dance, in this paradigm, a person needs to memorize a sequence of steps. For Merleau-Ponty, on the contrary, the way to learn to dance is to move one's physical body in space: "in order for the new dance to integrate particular elements of general motricity, it must first have received, so to speak, a motor consecration."[11]

6. Merleau-Ponty, 139.

7. Merleau-Ponty, lxxii.

8. Merleau-Ponty, 151.

9. Merleau-Ponty, xli.

10. Alan Jasanoff, "We Are More than Our Brains: On Neuroscience and Being Human," *Aeon*, accessed June 25, 2019, https://aeon.co/essays/we-are-more-than-our-brains-on -neuroscience-and-being-human.

11. Merleau-Ponty, 144.

The mind does not reflect and make a conscious decision before the body moves; the body "catches" the movement.

Philosophers have long attributed a spectatorial stance to the mind, when in fact the body participates in the world. It is common sense that the head is the "seat of thought," but "the principal regions of my body are consecrated to actions," and the "parts of my body participate in their value."[12] People learn, think and value with every part of their bodies, and our bodies know things that we can never fully articulate in words.

Surely, one could reply, this might be true for physical activities such as dancing but does not apply to all intellectual pursuits. Merleau-Ponty would respond: "The body is our general means of having a world."[13] Everything we learn, think or know emanates from our body. It is by walking through a meadow, hiking beside a river, and boating down a lake that we are able to appreciate the science of geography.[14] It is by talking with other people and learning their stories that we can appreciate literature. Buying food for our family infuses us with a conviction that we need to learn mathematics. We cannot always trace the route from experience to knowledge, from a childhood activity to adult insight. But there is no way for us to learn that bypasses the body: "the body is our anchorage in a world."[15]

Merleau-Ponty would not be surprised if people showed him students learning on a screen. Students can project themselves into the world that they see on a screen, just as many people are capable of thinking abstractly. As long as children have had some exposure to the world and other people, they should be able to make some sense of what they see on screens.[16]

Still, Merleau-Ponty gives us reasons to resist the trend towards computer-based education. Proponents of personalized learning point to the advantages of having kids on computers for much of the school day, including students working at their own pace to meet learning objectives. However, from a phenomenological perspective, it is not clear why students will want to do this for very long when the experience is so removed from their flesh-and-blood lives. Teachers and parents will have to use incentives, threats and medication to make children sit at computers for long stretches of time when children want to run, play, paint, eat, sing, compete and laugh. To put it bluntly: advocates of screen learning sometimes seem to forget that children are young animals that want to move in the world, not watch it from a distance.

At the farm, my children learned from being around the animals, trees, pastures, streams, stars and other physical objects. Things became more real, more immediate, than they would have been if a screen had mediated them. However, the experience was as deep as it was because of the relationships we formed with our hosts. The farmers would hold my children when placing them on horses or look them in the eye when explaining how to move sheep from

12. Merleau-Ponty, 147.
13. Merleau-Ponty, 147.
14. Merleau-Ponty, lxxii.
15. Merleau-Ponty, 146.
16. On the word "projection," see Merleau-Ponty, 115.

one stall to the next. Our children had fun with their children while playing by the stream at dusk before dinner. When we drove away from the farm, my young son had tears in his eyes; he didn't want to leave his new friends.

For proponents such as DeVos, computer-based education empowers students to work independently at their own pace, including at home rather than in brick-and-mortar public schools. Based on my experience at the farm, however, I would argue that this highlights one of the problems of screen learning: it does not easily enable children to form human relationships that are crucial to a satisfying educational experience.

In his important book *Face-to-Face Diplomacy: Social Neuroscience and International Relations* (2018), Marcus Holmes explains the science that justifies this intuition.[17] Drawing upon research in philosophy of mind, cognitive science and social neuroscience, Holmes argues that physical copresence is essential to generate trust and empathy among human beings. Though his research addresses the puzzle of why diplomats insist on meeting face-to-face for important discussions, his work also explains the science of why people find it more satisfying to meet in person than to communicate by screens.

According to Holmes, diplomats insist on meeting in person with their colleagues. Good negotiators have a "feel for the game" that works only when they share drinks, go on walks, shake hands, or have private conversations with their peers.[18] Diplomats know that they need to embrace, breathe the same air, and look each other in the eye if they are going to arrive at optimal outcomes.

Holmes draws upon neuroscience to explain why face-to-face meetings, as a rule, achieve better results. Researchers such as the neuroscientist Marco Lacoboni at the University of California, Los Angeles have diagrammed the "mirroring system" that enables human beings to understand each other's intentions. Within the brain, there are mirror neurons that fire when we do an action or when we see another person doing the action. Folk psychology holds that when we see another person, we think for a moment before deciding how to react. According to the new "simulation theory," we actually feel what the other person feels as mirror neurons fire in just the same manner as if the experience was happening to us. The mirroring system "enables advanced neural synchronization between individuals."[19]

Communicating in person enables people to "pick up micro-changes in facial expressions" and detect other people's sincerity.[20] Neuroscience shows that humans do a good job of reading other people's minds. People often deceive one another, but meeting face-to-face aids the detection of deceit. In games, people are more likely to trust one another when they play in person rather than when they play online. Likewise, there is greater rapport and "coupling" when

20

17. Marcus Holmes, *Face-to-Face Diplomacy: Social Neuroscience and International Relations* (Cambridge, United Kingdom; New York: Cambridge University Press, 2018).
18. Holmes, 8.
19. Holmes, 6.
20. Holmes, 6.

people get together in the flesh:[21] "Put simply, face-to-face interaction is an unrivaled mechanism for intention understanding."[22]

To what extent can new technology replicate face-to-face interactions? Holmes acknowledges that writing, calling or video-chatting often works fine for many forms of communication but insists that people must meet in the flesh to achieve a high degree of trust or social bonding. Citing the sociologist Randall Collins at the University of Pennsylvania, Holmes explains that people want to be in the physical presence of other people to generate emotional energy, "a feeling of confidence, elation, strength, enthusiasm, and initiative in taking action."[23] Communicating via email or the internet makes it harder to read another's body language or perceive what is happening in the background as the other person talks into the computer's camera. Communicating from a distance does "not provide the same physical and emotional connection" as bodily co-participation.[24]

We can transfer insights about social neuroscience from international relations theory to education theory. Placing children in front of screens enables them to access information, meet people around the world, play games, read things, purchase things and so forth that would otherwise be inaccessible. But as an "interaction ritual," screen learning generates less emotional energy than sharing a physical space with other teachers and students. Students looking at a screen will not trust, or care about, their teachers or students to the same degree. People might speak their mind more freely when there aren't the same visual cues to hold their tongues, but this also means that people are more likely to be uninhibited and antagonistic.[25] People will not have the same investment in an online education community.

A screen cannot provide the same emotional resonance as staying at a farm, participating in its rhythms, and forming bonds with the other people. Educators should be considering how to provide such opportunities to more students, including those whose parents do not have the time and resources to plan such trips themselves.

For many young people, digital media, even when used appropriately, can make education and community life worse. Digital media is a mixed blessing, at best, and many young people would prefer to spend less time on screens. At some level, most of us already know this. When private schools advertise, the images are often of kids doing physical activities or hanging out with a group of friends. People are fighting common sense, philosophy and science when they argue for children to spend more time on screens.

One could reasonably reply that many young people enjoy being on screens, and gain efficacy by being on the internet. This is the claim of the report "Children's Rights in the Digital Age" (2014), made by a team of Australian

21. Holmes, 40.

22. Holmes, 5.

23. Holmes, 263.

24. Holmes, 264.

25. Lynne Wainfan and Paul K. Davis, *Challenges in Virtual Collaboration*, Product Page, 2004, https://www.rand.org/pubs/monographs/MG273.html.

researchers partnering with the United Nations Children's Fund (UNICEF).[26] The researchers interviewed children around the world and used their words and examples to conclude: "Hearing the sentiments of children in eight different languages allows one truth to sound loud and clear: we need to take the necessary steps to ensure that all children can reap the opportunities of digital access."

The report describes the real benefits that children accrue from spending time on digital media. Children can gain access to information, get faster service delivery, express themselves artistically and politically, have fun, and make and maintain friendships with others around the world. The report acknowledges the dangers of digital media, including exposure to violent and pornographic images, excessive use, and data-privacy concerns. But it argues that the "risk narrative" is overstated. If children and their caregivers are responsible, it maintains, then they will likely reap the benefits of online access.

In a remarkable epilogue, however, the report quotes young people from around the world answering the question of what would happen if digital media disappeared. Here are a few of the responses from teenagers in different counties: "I'd spend more time doing things outside, not watching TV or my phone or anything, I'd find more productive things to do" (Australia). "If I don't have any digital media then I would read story books" (Thailand). "It would not do any harm. In the end we are not hard-wired to digital media. We are not controlled by digital media" (Turkey). "It would make other people more confident to be able to talk to other people face to face, not over the internet, actually be able to have conversations with them" (Australia). "People would learn to live with other things, using other ways" (Brazil). "At first it would be very hard just to get used to it, but since everyone would not have it, everyone would get over it. It'd be better as well 'cause everyone would be able to talk more, to work harder for friendship" (Australia).[27]

If the move to digital learning continues, children will spend much, if not 30 most, of their waking hours in front of screens. They will use apps before they go to school, spend their days in front of computers, do their homework online, and then entertain themselves with digital media. Children are losing opportunities to experience the world in all its richness. The gestalt of a farm transcends what pixels and speakers can convey. Screens drain the vitality from many educational experiences that could be better done in the flesh. This drift toward screen learning is only inevitable if people do nothing to stop it. So let's stop it.

BIBLIOGRAPHY

Herold, Benjamin. "Rhode Island Announces Statewide K–12 Personalized Learning Push." *Education Week - Digital Education.* Accessed June 25, 2019. https://

26. Amanda Third et al., "Children's Rights in the Digital Age: A Download from Children around the World" (Young and Well Cooperative Research Centre, 2014), https://www.unicef.org/publications/index_76268.html.
27. Third et al., 76–77.

blogs.edweek.org/edweek/DigitalEducation/2017/02/rhode_island_personalized
learning.html?cmp=SOC-SHR-FB.

Holmes, Marcus. *Face-to-Face Diplomacy: Social Neuroscience and International Relations*. Cambridge, United Kingdom; New York: Cambridge University Press, 2018.

Jasanoff, Alan. "We Are More than Our Brains: On Neuroscience and Being Human." *Aeon*. Accessed April 2, 2019. https://aeon.co/essays/we-are-more-than-our-brains-on-neuroscience-and-being-human.

Klein, Alyson. "Betsy DeVos: Many Students Aren't Being Prepared for the Careers of Tomorrow." *Education Week - Politics K–12*. Accessed June 25, 2019. http://blogs.edweek.org/edweek/campaign-k-12/2017/11/betsy_devos_jobs_future_choice_florida.html?cmp=SOC-SHR-FB.

Merleau-Ponty, Maurice. *Phenomenology of Perception*. Translated by Donald Landes. New York: Routledge, 2013.

Third, Amanda, et al. "Children's Rights in the Digital Age: A Download from Children around the World." Young and Well Cooperative Research Centre, 2014. https://www.unicef.org/publications/index_76268.html.

Wainfan, Lynne, and Paul K. Davis. *Challenges in Virtual Collaboration: Videoconferencing, Audioconferencing, and Computer-Mediated Communications*. Product Page. Santa Monica, CA: RAND Corporation, 2004. https://www.rand.org/pubs/monographs/MG273.html.

Winthrop, Rebecca, and Adam Barton. "Innovation to Leapfrog Educational Progress in Latin America." *Brookings* (blog), March 22, 2018. https://www.brookings.edu/research/innovation-to-leapfrog-educational-progress-in-latin-america/.

"XQ: The Super School Project." Emerson Collective. Accessed June 25, 2019. https://www.emersoncollective.com/xq-the-super-school-project/.

MLA CITATION

Tampio, Nicholas. "Look Up from Your Screen." *The Norton Reader: An Anthology of Nonfiction*, edited by Melissa A. Goldthwaite et al., 16th ed., W. W. Norton, 2024, pp. 563–70.

QUESTIONS

1. Nicholas Tampio quotes philosophers, scientists, and proponents of education to make the argument that education is better suited to in-the-flesh interactions than screen learning. He also draws from his own experience of spending time on a farm with his children. Which sources helped you understand his argument best? Why?

2. Find and read one of the sources that Tampio cites. Go back to the part of his essay where he references it and write an annotation or two to explain how the source informs the argument.

3. Tampio and Florence Williams, in "ADHD Is Fuel for Adventure" (pp. 571–79), both make an argument for more physical, in-person, and outdoor education. How are their arguments similar? How are they different?

4. Consider the place of both "screen learning" and "more tactile ways to discover the world" (paragraph 5) in your own educational experience. Write about a valuable

educational experience you've had—whether it involves screens or field trips or sports—and why it was successful.

5. Go twenty-four hours without a screen (outside of school and work obligations). Make a project—an essay, drawing, or voice memo—about the experience.

FLORENCE WILLIAMS
ADHD Is Fuel for Adventure

BY SECOND GRADE, it was clear that while Zack Smith could sit in a chair, he had no intention of staying in it. He was disruptive in class, spoke in a loud voice, and had a hard time taking turns with others. His parents fed him a series of medications for attention-deficit hyperactivity disorder, or ADHD, many of which didn't work. Zack, who attended school in West Hartford, Connecticut, was placed in special classrooms where he showed a propensity for lashing out. Twice suspended, he was miserable. He didn't seem to care about anything at school. When his parents realized that his path would likely lead to worse trouble, they pulled the ripcord on eighth grade.

Where Zack eventually landed is clinging spread-eagle to an east-facing slab of quartzite in the West Virginia panhandle. His chin-length, strawberry blond hair curls out beneath a Minion-yellow helmet. A harness cinches his T-shirt—the sleeves of which have been ripped off—obscuring the *Call of Duty: Advanced Warfare* lettering.

"I have a wedgie!" he bellows out from 20 feet up.

Belaying him is another 14-year-old—pale, earnest Daniel. Earlier in the day, Daniel asked, "Do I have to belay? I'm only 95 pounds." Both kids still look a little apprehensive, but there's no question that they are paying full attention to the wall of rock and to the rope that unites them. Yesterday beneath a picnic awning in a campground near Seneca Rocks, they and 12 other scrappy teens from the Academy at SOAR learned how to tie figure-eights and Prusiks, the knots that would safeguard their lives, under the tutelage of trip leader Joseph Geier, the academy's director, and seven other energetic field instructors mostly in their twenties. The students' ages span five years, but in the spectrum of puberty, the younger kids look like they could be the square roots of the biggest ones. Zack occupies an awkward middle ground, lanky and knock-kneed, with a surprisingly deep voice and a crooked smile.

He gradually moves his right foot to a new nub and pulls himself higher. 5
He scrabbles upward, finally victoriously slapping a carabiner on the top rope before rappelling down. "Oh man, my arms hurt," he says at the bottom, his pale cheeks flushed from sun and exertion. Daniel accidentally steps on the

Originally published in Outside *(2016), a revised and extended version of this piece is included in Florence Williams's book* The Nature Fix: Why Nature Makes Us Happier, Healthier, and More Creative *(2017).*

climbing rope and, per the rules, has to kiss it. This happens so often that no one remarks on it. For a moment both boys cheer on Tim, a small boy from the DC area with bright eyes behind eyeglasses so thick they look like safety gear. The aspirational name tape on the back of his helmet reads T Bone Sizzler. A group chant begins: "Go, Tim, go—oh, go Tim!"

Before enrolling in this adventure-based boarding school for grades seven through twelve, Zack, like a lot of these students, had already spent some summers at SOAR's Balsam, North Carolina, camp or its programs in California, Florida, and Wyoming for kids of both sexes with ADHD, dyslexia, and other learning disabilities. SOAR's founding principle—radical several decades ago and still surprisingly underappreciated—was that kids with attention deficits thrive in the outdoors. Since then ADHD diagnoses have exploded—11 percent of American kids are now said to have it—while recess, PE, and access to nature have shriveled miserably.

Zack's first SOAR summer involved a three-week stint of horse-packing in the Wind River Range. Before the trip, he says, he would have preferred to stay home and play video games. "I hated nature," as he puts it. But something clicked under the wide Wyoming skies. He found he was able to focus on tasks; he was making friends and feeling less terrible about himself. Zack turned his restlessness into a craving for adventure—which is perhaps what it was meant to be all along.

It's one thing to let kids unplug and run loose in the woods in summer, but shifting the whole academic year outside—SOAR students alternate two weeks on the forested campus in North Carolina and two weeks in the field—reflects either parental desperation, intrepid educational insight, or a combination of the two. Zack's backstory is a common one, especially among boys, who are diagnosed at more than twice the rate of girls. History is full of examples of restless youths who went on to become celebrated iconoclasts, like wilderness advocate John Muir, who spent his early childhood sneaking out at night, dangling from the windowsill by his fingertips, and scaling treacherous seaside cliffs in Dunbar, Scotland. Frederick Law Olmsted, who would later change the torso of Manhattan and influence scores of other cities with his park designs, hated school. His tolerant headmaster would let him roam the countryside instead. Ansel Adams's[1] parents plucked their fidgety boy out of class, gave him a Brownie box camera, and took him on a grand tour of Yosemite. It was unschooling, California style.

Olmsted, looking back on his life, identified the problem as the stifling classroom, not troublesome boys. "A boy," he wrote, "who would not in any weather & under all ordinary circumstances, rather take a walk of ten to twelve miles some time in the course of every day than stay quietly about a house all day, must be suffering from disease or a defective education."

10   The Academy at SOAR—which became accredited three years ago—is determined to find a better way. The school has just 32 students, 26 of them

---

1. American environmentalist and landscape photographer (1902–1984).

boys, divided into four mixed-age houses. Each kid has an individualized curriculum, and the student-teacher ratio is five to one. Tuition is a steep $49,500 per year, on par with other boarding schools, although you won't find a Hogwartsian dining hall or stacks of leather-bound books. The school still covers the required academics, as well as basic life skills like cooking, but finds that the kids pay more attention to a history lesson while standing in the middle of a battlefield or a geology lecture while camping on a monocline.

"We started from scratch," says SOAR's executive director John Willson, who began working there as a camp counselor in 1991. "We're not reinventing the wheel—we threw out the wheel." The school's founders didn't have any particular allegiance to adventure sports; they just found that climbing, backpacking, and canoeing were a magic fit for these kids, at these ages, when their neurons are exploding in a million directions. "When you're on a rock ledge," Willson says, "there's a sweet spot of arousal and stress that opens you up for adaptive learning. You find new ways of solving problems."

Some of the teens who arrive at SOAR are still putting their clothes on backward, not uncommon among kids with ADHD. They forget to eat or they can't stop. They lash out in anger, and they're easily frustrated. Symptoms tend to express themselves differently in boys and girls. The classic symptoms in boys, which are better understood, are hyperactivity, impulsivity, and distractibility; girls tend to show less of the hyperactivity, which makes the condition harder to spot. We all fall somewhere on the continuum of these traits, but people with more extreme symptoms appear to have different chemistry in the parts of their brains that govern reward, movement, and attention. They may have trouble listening or sitting still, and they get distracted by external stimuli. They can be hyper-focused, but they also get bored easily, so they tend to be risk takers, looking for charged activities that help flood their brains with feel-good neurotransmitters like dopamine and norepinephrine, which otherwise get gummed up in the ADHD brain. Kids with the condition are more likely to suffer head injuries, accidentally ingest poisons, and take street drugs.

With all these liabilities, you might think such heritable traits would diminish in humans over time; that's the way Darwin awards work. The fact that they remain so common, though, means that these same characteristics must have once conferred tremendous advantages on individuals and ultimately on the human race.

It's worth taking a look into the brains of kids like Zack, because not only do kids with ADHD need exploration, but exploration needs them. Zack and his tethered band of misfits might look like merry miscreants, but they hold clues to the adventure impulses lurking in all of us, impulses that are increasingly at risk in a world moving indoors—onto screens and away from nature. Attentional mutants everywhere have saved the human species, and they may yet spare us the death of adventure.

The human brain evolved outside, in a world filled with interesting things, but 15 not an overwhelming number of interesting things. Everything in a child's world was nameable: foods, creatures, the stars. We were supposed to notice passing distractions; if we didn't, we could get eaten. But we also needed a certain amount of stick-to-itiveness so that we could build tools, stalk game, raise babies, and plan big. Evolution favored early humans who could both stay on task and switch tasks when needed, and our prefrontal cortex evolved to let us master the ability. In fact, how nimbly we allocate our attention may be one of humanity's greatest and most distinctive skills, argues neuroscientist Daniel Levitin of McGill University.

Most humans had brains that craved novelty and wanted to explore—to a degree. This worked out for us. As Levitin writes in *The Organized Mind*, our species expanded into more habitats than any creature the earth had ever seen, to the point where humans plus our livestock and pets now account for 98 percent of the planet's terrestrial vertebrates. But evolution also favored variability, and some of us pushed exploration more than others.

Wondering if we have a specific adventure gene, researchers have looked at the DNA of humans in the farthest reaches of the globe—the descendants of people who kept moving until there was no place else to go. One mutation kept popping up: a variant called 7R on the DRD4 gene that helps regulate how signals from dopamine are processed. People with 7R are more likely to take financial risks and to travel and try new things, probably as a way to juice up their stingy dopamine delivery. Long story short, this gene mutation, which affects roughly 20 percent of today's global population, does indeed cluster in

places like Siberia, Tierra del Fuego, and Australia, where humans had migrated over the longest routes.

It turns out that the gene also clusters in people who have ADHD. It would be too easy to say that any one gene or set of genes explains the human capacity to explore or explains ADHD, since both are determined by numerous genetic and environmental factors. And not all kids with ADHD like risk taking. But to Dale Archer, a Lake Charles, Louisiana, psychiatrist and author of *The ADHD Advantage*, the link makes sense. Once upon a time, the dominant traits of ADHD were highly adaptive. They were—and still can be—gifts that enable rapid interpretation of sensory data, thinking on your feet, curiosity, and creative restlessness. "The thing with the ADHDer is that we get bored easily but we do great in a crisis, we can function really well," says Archer, a surf kayaker, solo sailor, and cyclist who shares the diagnosis with his adult son. According to him and others in the learning-differences community, Napoleon probably had ADHD (along with some other issues) and so did Captain James Cook, Ernest Shackleton, Thomas Edison, and Eleanor Roosevelt.

If you take a typical ADHD kid, layer on some experience and maturity, tamp down the impulsive bits, and add some goal aspirations and a keen ability to plan and dream, you end up with a high-adrenaline achiever like alpinist Conrad Anker or adventurer Sir Richard Branson, both of whom believe they have the condition. They are comfortable in extreme environments, enlivened by risk, able to thrive on the unknown. When Branson dropped out of school at age 16 to start his first company, he says, "The headmaster told me that I would either end up in prison or become a millionaire." Since then he has scored two first-ever transoceanic ballooning records, received eight helicopter rescues, and founded the Virgin Group.

20 "I am hyper situationally aware," says Anker. "It was a trainwreck in second grade—every input received my attention. When I'm alpine climbing, that keeps me alive." Anker can nimbly process snow conditions, incoming weather, and rope integrity to make quick decisions. His brain likes intense environments, he says, but too much pointless stimulation, like on a busy city street, drives him bananas. Precision wingsuit flier Jeb Corliss was diagnosed with ADHD when he was ten. "My sisters are normal people. I'm hyper, yeah, big deal," he says. "I believe that a lot of people are like that, and they use it to their advantage." Corliss says flying through the air is when he feels calm and peaceful.

As a laconic, impulsive, and depressed teen in northeast Ohio, Matt Rutherford landed in juvenile detention five times for petty crimes and in rehab twice. Some 15 years later, he became the first sailor to circumnavigate the Americas alone. During his 308 days at sea, his secondhand 27-foot boat started falling apart under him. It caught on fire, he lost his water supply, his fuel bladder sprang a leak, and, just past French Guiana, he nearly smacked into a freighter. "The more challenging it is," he says, "the happier I am. The more rocks, the more ice, the better."

In fact, ADHD traits are so common among modern-day alpinists, rock climbers, BASE jumpers, snowboarders, and other extreme athletes that the observation raises several important questions: If adventure sports are such a great fit for people with ADHD, why aren't more doctors, schools, and families boosting participation? And, as kids are asked to sit still for longer periods of time indoors and given more medications to help them do it, what is the fate of the next generation of adventurers? Does the mass medicalization of ADHD mean the human species has reached peak exploration?

If you're the sort of person who eats chaos for breakfast, sitting in school all day may well suck out your soul. But with the rise of industrialism, educators thought all kids should be in standardized classrooms. "ADHD got its start 150 years ago when compulsory education got started," says Stephen Hinshaw, a psychologist at the University of California at Berkeley. "In that sense, you could say it's partially a social construct. If you look at the symptoms of ADHD, maybe they're not really symptoms anymore if you get in the right profession or the right ecological niche. We've learned some of this by looking at extreme athletes, who have found that niche."

But school often isn't it. To oversimplify, it's like taking kids who are genetically meant to be hunters and gatherers and making them tend crops instead. Not only will they feel bored and inadequate, but the constrained setting will actually make their symptoms worse. For kids like Zack, school feels stifling and rule bound. They act up. They may get moved into even more restrictive environments, sometimes with chain-link fences, guards, and neurotropic meds that go beyond ADHD to deal with the ensuing anxiety, depression, and aggression. Sometimes they end up in trouble or, as Zack feared might happen to him, get "gooned" in the middle of the night by burly strangers intent on packing him off to a residential therapeutic program that looks like Outward Bound in the brochure but ends up feeling like a gulag.

Interestingly, researchers have observed similar patterns in lab rats—who, 25 let's face it, suffer the ultimate cosmic gooning. When Jaak Panksepp, a neuroscientist at Washington State University, restricted the play of young rats, their frontal lobes (which control executive function) failed to grow normally. "We had the insight that if animals don't play, if there are not sufficient spaces for them to engage, they develop play hunger," says Panksepp. "They have impulse-control problems and eventually problems with social interactions."

Panksepp points out that while common stimulant medications for ADHD like Ritalin and Adderall may improve attention skills and academic performance in many kids, they do so at the cost of reducing the playfulness urge— at least temporarily. "We know these are anti-play drugs in animals," he says. "That is clear and unambiguous." The bigger question is whether the drugs— and all the enforced sedentary behavior—squeeze the adventure impulse out of kids in the longer term. Psychologists tend to disagree on this point, but the truth is, no one really knows. It's not a boutique question. Of the 6.4 million diagnosed kids in America, about half are taking prescription stimulants, an increase of 28 percent since 2007.

For athletes like Corliss and swimmer Michael Phelps, who has also been diagnosed with ADHD, the sport itself becomes their medication, filling their brains with endorphins and endocannabinoids. But for every hour that a drug is supplying a kid's fix, that's an hour a potential explorer is not looking longingly out the window plotting escape. Of course, some kids, Hinshaw points out, need medication even to make big plans, not to mention learn algebra. Other families, he notes, are seeing the value in medication holidays, allowing kids to come off their drugs on weekends and during summers.

At SOAR, many students arrive on meds, and many stay on them. At all times, the instructors have locked and sealed messenger bags full of pharmaceuticals strapped to their torsos like baby marsupials. Though Willson emphasizes that SOAR is not a way to get kids off ADHD meds, some do find that they can taper off. Zack's parents said they're planning to toss his during his holiday break, and they expect to lower the dose of his stimulant as well. "The changes in him have been nothing short of miraculous," says his mother, Marlene De Pecol. "Now he's just happy."

Taking meds didn't seem to alter the daring trajectory of solo sailor Rutherford. He took multiple pills for six years until he was 16, when, like Zack, he managed to find a place more compatible with his brain's wiring—the Eagle Rock School in Estes Park, Colorado, an adventure-based boarding school funded by the American Honda Education Corporation. Anker, meanwhile, says it's possible he wouldn't be making first ascents today if he'd taken Ritalin through his teenage years. His parents encouraged him to go outside instead. Climbing developed his technical mastery while helping him sit still when he needed to. It also likely helped his prefrontal cortex mature.

30   The senior Ankers were ahead of the curve, or perhaps about 10,000 years behind the curve, depending on how you look at it.

The fact is, all human children learn by exploration, and we are tying their shoelaces together—not just with medication, but through over-structured, overmanaged classrooms and sports teams, less freedom to roam, and ever more dazzling indoor seductions. Modern life has made all of us distractible and overwhelmed. As McGill's Levitin explains, the average American owns and must keep track of thousands of times more possessions than the average hunter-gatherer. Each of us, one 2013 study projected, consumes 74 gigabytes daily. Teens now interact with screens more than six and a half hours per day, and that's not including time at school, according to Common Sense Media, a nonprofit that helps parents make smart technology choices. "The digital age is profoundly narrowing our horizons and our creativity, not to mention our bodies and physiological capabilities," says environmental photographer James Balog, even as his hard-won chronicles of a changing planet are delivered to millions digitally. Yet Balog, who says he has mild ADHD, can hardly get his eighth-grade daughter off her phone. "These are hours not being spent outside," he says. "It kills me."

The news isn't all bad. While per capita visits to natural areas are down, participation by young people in a number of adventure sports like snowboarding and rock climbing is up. Solid research continues to make the case that kids benefit from time outside and regular exercise, and some schools are getting the message by instituting early-morning programs. More psychiatrists are also prescribing exercise for kids with ADHD. But the National Institute of Mental Health makes no mention of physical activity as a treatment option on its extensive website.

The radio silence on exercise is surprising, because studies consistently show that aerobic activity targets the same attentional networks that ADHD medication does. While fitness improves learning in both kids and adults, it's adolescents like Zack—whose prefrontal cortex is in the very midst of laying down a lifetime of hardware—who seem to benefit the most. John Green, a biobehavioral psychologist at the University of Vermont, and graduate student Meghan Eddy exercised some adult and juvenile rats and then tasked them with learning how to find food in a maze. The young rats who exercised bested the non-exercisers and did as well as rats on Ritalin. It seemed the playful and exploratory adolescent years exist to boost learning in mammals, just as SOAR's Willson intuited. Or, as Green more formally puts it, "The adolescent prefrontal cortex is ready to be molded by environmental experience."

So there you have it: the time is now. There's a limited window to best launch these kids and, perhaps in so doing, safeguard a future of innovative exploration by the very young people who are wired to do it better than anybody else.

The ADHD population is an advance guard. If they can recognize how to better adapt their environments for their brains, there's hope for the rest of us. 35

After many years languishing in the Formica-filled classrooms of West Hartford, Zack Smith is ready. He and his pals gather around the fire pit back at camp, bellies full of hamburgers and pickles. It's very dark out. Tomorrow all 14 boys will make the four pitches up the South Peak at Seneca Rocks. A couple of days after that, they'll backpack across the Dolly Sods Wilderness Area, and then they'll visit Stonewall Jackson's grave and read poetry written by the general's sister-in-law. For now, they're tired if not exactly mellow.

Zack's job for the day is Captain Planet, meaning he's the mighty taker-out of trash. Another kid named Max is Scribe. At 16, Max is an expeller of colossal farts, and proud of it. "I don't do anything halfway in the outdoors," he says. He shared with me on the trail that he is also an expert squirrel hunter, climber, and river runner. When he is done with school, he intends to find a job guiding. Now, beturbaned in a purple bandana, he opens the group journal and prepares to record notes on the day's events under the narrow red beam of a headlamp.

Zack is lying on his back and looking up at the stars. He is impressed. "We don't have these at home," he says.

MLA CITATION

Williams, Florence. "ADHD Is Fuel for Adventure." *The Norton Reader: An Anthology of Nonfiction*, edited by Melissa A. Goldthwaite et al., 16th ed., W. W. Norton, 2024, pp. 571–79.

QUESTIONS

1. Florence Williams argues that there may be an advantage to ADHD. What positive qualities does she associate with ADHD?

2. What aspects of the Academy at SOAR seem most educationally sound to you? Are there any downsides you see to this type of education? Are there aspects of outdoor education that should be incorporated into more traditional classrooms?

3. Research a diagnosed learning disability—such as dyscalculia, dysgraphia, or dyslexia. What kinds of activities and educational settings would be most beneficial to those with the learning disability you researched? Make a list of specific activities that could be beneficial. Be creative, thinking beyond activities usually done in traditional classroom spaces.

FREDERICK DOUGLASS

Learning to Read

I LIVED IN MASTER HUGH'S FAMILY about seven years.[1] During this time, I succeeded in learning to read and write. In accomplishing this, I was compelled to resort to various stratagems. I had no regular teacher. My mistress, who had kindly commenced to instruct me, had, in compliance with the advice and direction of her husband, not only ceased to instruct, but had set her face against my being instructed by any one else. It is due, however, to my mistress to say of her, that she did not adopt this course of treatment immediately. She at first lacked the depravity indispensable to shutting me up in mental darkness. It was at least necessary for her to have some training in the exercise of irresponsible power, to make her equal to the task of treating me as though I were a brute.

My mistress was, as I have said, a kind and tender-hearted woman; and in the simplicity of her soul she commenced, when I first went to live with her, to treat me as she supposed one human being ought to treat another. In entering upon the duties of a slaveholder, she did not seem to perceive that I sustained to her the relation of a mere chattel, and that for her to treat me as a human being was not only wrong, but dangerously so. Slavery proved as injurious to her as it did to me. When I went there, she was a pious, warm, and tender-hearted woman. There was no sorrow or suffering for which she had not a tear. She had bread for the hungry, clothes for the naked, and comfort for every mourner that came within her reach. Slavery soon proved its ability to divest her of these heavenly qualities. Under its influence, the tender heart became stone, and the lamblike disposition gave way to one of tigerlike fierceness. The first step in her downward course was in her ceasing to instruct me. She now commenced to practise her husband's precepts. She finally became even more violent in her opposition than her husband himself. She was not satisfied with simply doing as well as he had commanded; she seemed anxious to do better.

From Frederick Douglass's autobiography Narrative of the Life of Frederick Douglass, an American Slave, Written by Himself *(1845).*

1. In Baltimore, Maryland.

Nothing seemed to make her more angry than to see me with a newspaper. She seemed to think that here lay the danger. I have had her rush at me with a face made all up of fury, and snatch from me a newspaper, in a manner that fully revealed her apprehension. She was an apt woman; and a little experience soon demonstrated, to her satisfaction, that education and slavery were incompatible with each other.

From this time I was most narrowly watched. If I was in a separate room any considerable length of time, I was sure to be suspected of having a book, and was at once called to give an account of myself. All this, however, was too late. The first step had been taken. Mistress, in teaching me the alphabet, had given me the *inch*, and no precaution could prevent me from taking the *ell*.[2]

The plan which I adopted, and the one by which I was most successful, was that of making friends of all the little white boys whom I met in the street. As many of these as I could, I converted into teachers. With their kindly aid, obtained at different times and in different places, I finally succeeded in learning to read. When I was sent of errands, I always took my book with me, and by going one part of my errand quickly, I found time to get a lesson before my return. I used also to carry bread with me, enough of which was always in the house, and to which I was always welcome; for I was much better off in this regard than many of the poor white children in our neighborhood. This bread I used to bestow upon the hungry little urchins, who, in return, would give me that more valuable bread of knowledge. I am strongly tempted to give the names of two or three of those little boys, as a testimonial of the gratitude and affection I bear them; but prudence forbids;—not that it would injure me, but it might embarrass them; for it is almost an unpardonable offence to teach slaves to read in this Christian country. It is enough to say of the dear little fellows, that they lived on Philpot Street, very near Durgin and Bailey's ship-yard. I used to talk this matter of slavery over with them. I would sometimes say to them, I wished I could be as free as they would be when they got to be men. "You will be free as soon as you are twenty-one, *but I am a slave for life!* Have not I as good a right to be free as you have?" These words used to trouble them; they would express for me the liveliest sympathy, and console me with the hope that something would occur by which I might be free.

I was now about twelve years old, and the thought of being *a slave for life*   5 began to bear heavily upon my heart. Just about this time, I got hold of a book entitled *The Columbian Orator*.[3] Every opportunity I got, I used to read this book. Among much of other interesting matter, I found in it a dialogue between a master and his slave. The slave was represented as having run away from his master three times. The dialogue represented the conversation which took place between them, when the slave was retaken the third time. In this dialogue, the whole argument in behalf of slavery was brought forward by the master, all of which was disposed of by the slave. The slave was made to say some very smart

2. Once a unit of measurement equal to forty-five inches. The saying is proverbial.
3. Popular collection of poems, dialogues, plays, and speeches.

as well as impressive things in reply to his master—things which had the desired though unexpected effect; for the conversation resulted in the voluntary emancipation of the slave on the part of the master.

In the same book, I met with one of Sheridan's[4] mighty speeches on and in behalf of Catholic emancipation. These were choice documents to me. I read them over and over again with unabated interest. They gave tongue to interesting thoughts of my own soul, which had frequently flashed through my mind, and died away for want of utterance. The moral which I gained from the dialogue was the power of truth over the conscience of even a slaveholder. What I got from Sheridan was a bold denunciation of slavery, and a powerful vindication of human rights. The reading of these documents enabled me to utter my thoughts, and to meet the arguments brought forward to sustain slavery; but while they relieved me of one difficulty, they brought on another even more painful than the one of which I was relieved. The more I read, the more I was led to abhor and detest my enslavers. I could regard them in no other light than a band of successful robbers, who had left their homes, and gone to Africa, and stolen us from our homes, and in a strange land reduced us to slavery. I loathed them as being the meanest as well as the most wicked of men. As I read and contemplated the subject, behold! that very discontentment which Master Hugh had predicted would follow my learning to read had already come, to torment and sting my soul to unutterable anguish. As I writhed under it, I would at times feel that learning to read had been a curse rather than a blessing. It had given me a view of my wretched condition, without the remedy. It opened my eyes to the horrible pit, but to no ladder upon which to get out. In moments of agony, I envied my fellow-slaves for their stupidity. I have often wished myself a beast. I preferred the condition of the meanest reptile to my own. Any thing, no matter what, to get rid of thinking! It was this everlasting thinking of my condition that tormented me. There was no getting rid of it. It was pressed upon me by every object within sight or hearing, animate or inanimate. The silver trump of freedom had roused my soul to eternal wakefulness. Freedom now appeared, to disappear no more forever. It was heard in every sound, and seen in every thing. It was ever present to torment me with a sense of my wretched condition. I saw nothing without seeing it, I heard nothing without hearing it, and felt nothing without feeling it. It looked from every star, it smiled in every calm, breathed in every wind, and moved in every storm.

I often found myself regretting my own existence, and wishing myself dead; and but for the hope of being free, I have no doubt but that I should have killed myself, or done something for which I should have been killed. While in this state of mind, I was eager to hear any one speak of slavery. I was a ready listener. Every little while, I could hear something about the abolitionists. It was some time before I found what the word meant. It was always used in such connections as to make it an interesting word to me. If a slave ran away and

---

4. Richard Brinsley Sheridan (1751–1816), Irish dramatist and political leader. The speech, arguing for the abolition of laws denying Roman Catholics in Great Britain and Ireland civil and political liberties, was actually made by the Irish patriot Arthur O'Connor.

succeeded in getting clear, or if a slave killed his master, set fire to a barn, or did any thing very wrong in the mind of a slaveholder, it was spoken of as the fruit of *abolition*. Hearing the word in this connection very often, I set about learning what it meant. The dictionary afforded me little or no help. I found it was "the act of abolishing"; but then I did not know what was to be abolished. Here I was perplexed. I did not dare to ask any one about its meaning, for I was satisfied that it was something they wanted me to know very little about. After a patient waiting, I got one of our city papers, containing an account of the number of petitions from the north, praying for the abolition of slavery in the District of Columbia, and of the slave trade between the States. From this time I understood the words *abolition* and *abolitionist*, and always drew near when that word was spoken, expecting to hear something of importance to myself and fellow-slaves. The light broke in upon me by degrees. I went one day down on the wharf of Mr. Waters; and seeing two Irishmen unloading a scow of stone, I went, unasked, and helped them. When we had finished, one of them came to me and asked me if I were a slave. I told him I was. He asked, "Are ye a slave for life?" I told him that I was. The good Irishman seemed to be deeply affected by the statement. He said to the other that it was a pity so fine a little fellow as myself should be a slave for life. He said it was a shame to hold me. They both advised me to run away to the north; that I should find friends there, and that I should be free. I pretended not to be interested in what they said, and treated them as if I did not understand them; for I feared they might be treacherous. White men have been known to encourage slaves to escape, and then, to get the reward, catch them and return them to their masters. I was afraid that these seemingly good men might use me so; but I nevertheless remembered their advice, and from that time I resolved to run away. I looked forward to a time at which it would be safe for me to escape. I was too young to think of doing so immediately; besides, I wished to learn how to write, as I might have occasion to write my own pass. I consoled myself with the hope that I should one day find a good chance. Meanwhile, I would learn to write.

The idea as to how I might learn to write was suggested to me by being in Durgin and Bailey's ship-yard, and frequently seeing the ship carpenters, after hewing, and getting a piece of timber ready for use, write on the timber the name of that part of the ship for which it was intended. When a piece of timber was intended for the larboard side, it would be marked thus—"L." When a piece was for the starboard side, it would be marked thus—"S." A piece for the larboard side forward, would be marked thus—"L. F." When a piece was for starboard side forward, it would be marked thus—"S. F." For larboard aft, it would be marked thus—"L. A." For starboard aft, it would be marked thus—"S. A." I soon learned the names of these letters, and for what they were intended when placed upon a piece of timber in the shipyard. I immediately commenced copying them, and in a short time was able to make the four letters named. After that, when I met with any boy who I knew could write, I would tell him I could write as well as he. The next word would be, "I don't believe you. Let me see you try it." I would then make the letters which I had been so fortunate as to learn, and ask him to beat that. In this way I got a good many lessons in writing, which it is quite possible I should never have gotten in any other way. During this time, my copy-book was the board fence, brick wall, and pavement; my pen and ink was a lump of chalk. With these, I learned mainly how to write. I then commenced and continued copying the Italics in Webster's Spelling Book,[5] until I could make them all without looking on the book. By this time, my little Master Thomas had gone to school, and learned how to write, and had written over a number of copy-books. These had been brought home, and shown to some of our near neighbors, and then laid aside. My mistress used to go to class meeting at the Wilk Street meetinghouse every Monday afternoon, and leave me to take care of the house. When left thus, I used to spend the time in writing in the spaces left in Master Thomas's copy-book, copying what he had written. I continued to do this until I could write a hand very similar to that of Master Thomas. Thus, after a long, tedious effort for years, I finally succeeded in learning how to write.

MLA CITATION

Douglass, Frederick. "Learning to Read." *The Norton Reader: An Anthology of Nonfiction*, edited by Melissa A. Goldthwaite et al., 16th ed., W. W. Norton, 2024, pp. 580–84.

QUESTIONS

1. Enslaved people were prohibited from learning to read and write. How does this prohibition drive Frederick Douglass? How does it affect those around him? Annotate the moments when Douglass and others around him act with an awareness that they are acting against the rules of the time.

2. Douglass's story might today be called a *literacy narrative*—an account of how someone learns to read and write. What are the key features of this narrative? What obstacles did Douglass face? How did he overcome them? Who and what helped him?

3. In paragraph 7, Douglass describes his perplexity in understanding the connotation of *abolition* because the dictionary did not connect it to the abolition of slavery. Why do you think the dictionary at the time excluded this context? Have you ever been frustrated by incomplete information in a dictionary or thesaurus? How do you usually discover the meaning of unfamiliar words or words in new contexts?

4. Write your own literacy narrative—an account of how you learned to read and write.

---

5. *The American Spelling Book* (1783) by Noah Webster (1758–1843), American lexicographer.

ELISSA WASHUTA
Picture Books as Doors to Other Worlds

M Y CATHOLIC PICTURE BOOKS made me think heaven was a town built on a layer of stratocumulus clouds, which disappointed me, because I wanted a heaven like the garden on the other side of the door in Alice's wonderland. I considered myself the true owner of the library's copy of Disney's *Alice in Wonderland*, nesting in its puffy white VHS case until I could bring it home again. I studied Alice as she crept through the black woods and sat in disoriented defeat among the mome raths. I watched her shrink and grow. I was looking for the garden, too. Our lawn violets never spoke. There had to be a door somewhere, but I couldn't even find a rabbit hole to fall down. In the woods, I turned over rocks, looking for the underworld, always fearing I'd find a nest of snakes instead.

Once I could read, I worked through the book enough times to memorize parts. Maybe my woods were already wonderland. Maybe my cat would dissolve into a hanging grin. At school, when boys played games that ended with the loser having to kiss me without my invitation, I understood I was stuck somewhere, like Alice: "There were doors all the way down the hall, but they were all locked, and when Alice had been all the way down one side and up the other, trying every door, she walked sadly down the middle, wondering how she was ever to get out again."

In the Disney adaptation, Alice faces only one door. It is locked, and has a talking face. "You did give me quite a turn!" the door puns, and makes sure we get the joke: "Rather good, what? Doorknob, turn?" Alice peers through the keyhole mouth at the garden. In my recollection of the movie, the viewer sees what she sees. I can picture it: fountains, hedges, rosebushes, topiaries.

But I imagined the image. Alice doesn't look through a door-portal until the film is nearly over. She's been crying in the woods, singing to the creatures gathered to gawk at her pain, saying to herself, "It would be so nice if something would make sense for a change!" when the Cheshire Cat, a puff of purple around a crescent moon of teeth, tells her there's a way out. He makes a door appear in a tree trunk. Alice steps in to meet the tyrant queen in her garden. I should have seen this as a cautionary tale: the girl thinks she's looking for something that makes sense, but the deeper she pushes, the closer she gets to the seat of senseless violence in the world.

*

Early colonizers of the Americas believed the devil lived here, having been banished from Europe through religious effort. Europeans believed Native peoples worshipped gods that served Satan. Sixteenth-century Spanish colonizers executed a Guachichil woman whose people resisted conquest. She lived in a place

5

From Elissa Washuta's 2021 essay collection White Magic *and published in the* Paris Review. *Washuta is a member of the Cowlitz Indian Tribe. Her book explores how mainstream white culture has appropriated Native ideas of ritual, spirituality, and magic.*

occupied by Tlaxcalan and Tarascan converts to Christianity, and she tried to persuade them to rebel against Spanish rule by threatening them with black magic. The Spanish, fearing a loss of control, charged her with witchcraft and killed her immediately. Alison Games recounts this in *Witchcraft in Early North America*, writing that "witches were not only rebels against godly order (as they were throughout Europe), but also armed rebels bent on overthrowing established governments." Revolts were blamed on the devil. The settlers became obsessed with witches.

But I didn't know about any of this when I was four, as my parents read to me from my favorite picture books, Patricia Coombs's Dorrie the Little Witch series. Every book begins the same: "This is Dorrie. She is a witch. A little witch." Some arrangement of introductory details follows: her room is messy, her socks mismatched. She has a cat named Gink and a mother known as the Big Witch. Dorrie strives and fails to be good; the Big Witch is important and busy. Left alone to figure out how to behave, Dorrie often ends up in the secret room where her mother makes magic. She fumbles with spells, coming up with her own elixirs after failing to find them in the Big Witch's book of magic.

I don't know whether I understood that world to be pretend. My mother was a big witch, too: important, a role model, and a healer, in a way, a nurse with national recognition and local renown. But I was left alone only when I wanted to be. It was my mother and father who read me the books.

I mixed every liquid hair product in my parents' bathroom cabinet, hoping to come up with the spell Dorrie sought to ease the constriction of adult reality's force upon the glittering cloud of childhood. I held out hope for finding a book of magic that might have what I needed.

My schoolbooks held only dead ends: a rule for every known thing, and every thing was a known thing, except for the things the church knew to be unknown, like the mechanism God uses to turn bread into his body or what that even means since the Communion host doesn't seem like anything but an unusual cracker melting on the tongue.

10   But there was something existing in my house—not a being like God or Satan, but something potent and present as a gas. In the hallway, surrounded by the bedroom and bathroom doors, I felt I wasn't alone. Belief in ghosts seemed to fall under superstition, which was sinful as a subcategory of idolatry, so I didn't let myself think of the women in the large old photo hanging in our house's hallway as anything but ink on framed paper. The standing woman smiled and the sitting woman did not. Their hair was gathered tight behind their heads and their skin was cloaked in black cloth. My mom said they were my great-grandmother and great-great-grandmother, granddaughter and daughter of Tumulth, but this was impossible. I had never smiled at anyone as if my eyes were jaws and I had never sat with my sadness as if it were a second nervous system. They wore black, like witches, but they couldn't be, because all witches were white.

They knew something, though.

I decided to read every book in the library, looking for instructions I could use. The books I found weren't about witches—they were about otherworld travelers. In *The Castle in the Attic*, by Elizabeth Winthrop, a boy uses a magic token to turn people into miniatures who can pass through a toy castle into another world. Lynne Reid Banks wrote about similar magic five years earlier in *The Indian in the Cupboard*, but I didn't take to that book, probably not because it features a white boy who plays God with a tiny Iroquois man—I was used to that—but because I wanted to travel to the otherworlds, not have their residents come to me.

In Anne Lindbergh's *Travel Far, Pay No Fare*, two children use a magic bookmark to go into the worlds of books. Inside one, a woman says, "Houses aren't the only things with windows. Time and space may well have them too." I collected library bookmarks and tried every one, hoping to travel across the threshold of the page. I even made my own, carefully lettered with the words from the book: "Travel far, / Pay no fare, / Let a story / Take you there!"

I couldn't get it to work, so I reread the book periodically, looking for a missed step in the instructions. I found my answer in *A Wrinkle in Time*, by Madeleine L'Engle. The journey between worlds was a tesseract, travel in the fifth dimension, possible only by the thoroughly initiated, which I was not. "Playing with time and space is a dangerous game," says the protagonist's father. "It's a frightening as well as an exciting thing to discover that matter and energy are the same thing, that size is an illusion, and that time is a material substance. We can know this, but it's far more than we can understand with our puny little brains."

All these books illuminated small pieces of the same set of principles. There were too many connections for the magic not to be real. The books never taught me to travel to other worlds, so I began to wonder whether I could manipulate this one.

15

*

I think dreams are riddles because they need to be solved. I am sure dreams are enigmas because they really can't be. After I read *The Battle for the Castle*, Winthrop's sequel to *The Castle in the Attic*, in which the hero and his friend defend their castle from attack by large rats, I began dreaming I was in a besieged castle. I never dream I'm naked, flying, or falling. In my nightmares, I don't have long before the people outside the walls come to kill me.

*

I was prepared to see books as riddles long before high school teachers taught me the mode of literary study I'd have to unlearn, searching texts for the single correct interpretation coded in symbols and subtext. In one of my favorite childhood books, there really was a solution. *The Eleventh Hour: A Curious Mystery* is a picture book by Graeme Base in which an elephant named Horace throws a party for his eleventh birthday. He invites ten animal friends to his house, plans eleven games, and prepares a feast to be served at eleven o'clock. But the guests arrive to the banquet hall to find the food already eaten. Readers are tasked with identifying the thief using "a little close observation and some simple deduction." The solution is in a sealed section at the book's end, following a warning: "Do not turn this page until you have tried your hardest to unravel the Mystery—for the getting of wisdom is no match for the thrill of the chase, and those who choose the longer road shall reap their reward!"

Clues are encoded in basic cryptography in every illustration: WATCH THE CLOCKS lettered into the wrought iron of the property's entry gate, RED HERRING spelled out on fallen tennis balls, PUT NO TRUST IN HIDDEN CODES AND MESSAGES decoded from symbols substituted for letters, a verse visible when the book is held up to a mirror: "Yea, all who seek take heed forsooth—For everyone has told the truth!" Technically, that is factual. But someone is lying, of course, by omission.

The Eleventh Hour, I Spy, Where's Waldo?, Magic Eye: I wanted all books to make me feel the way these did when my whole body and brain lurched with the click of visual recognition. I still do. I want the whole world to make me feel it.

MLA CITATION

Washuta, Elissa. "Picture Books as Doors to Other Worlds." *The Norton Reader: An Anthology of Nonfiction*, edited by Melissa A. Goldthwaite et al., 16th ed., W. W. Norton, 2024, pp. 585–88.

QUESTIONS

1. Elissa Washuta plays with multiple meanings of the word "witch" and asks us to keep track of the way that word's value changes across contexts. Mark each time she uses the word and annotate it, explaining its meaning in that specific context. Where is it good to be a witch? scary? Where is Washuta's value for witches at odds with the people around her?

2. As a Native American who was raised Catholic, Washuta grew up with conflicting messages on spirituality and magic. How did children's books help her make sense of her sometimes-clashing traditions?

3. Washuta likes the idea of books as riddles (paragraphs 16 and 17). What do you think she means by this? How does her delight in riddles contrast with the way her teachers expect her to interpret books?

4. Write about a magical book that mattered to you when you were young. What did you think about that book's description of magic then, and how has your sense of magic changed now?

MICHAEL HAMAD
Song Schematics

A S A KID, I saw random shapes in my head when I listened to music. They were mostly large, abstract geometric patterns, usually either blue or yellow in color, that floated around and interacted with some unseen gravitational force; other times I saw things that looked like gears or pulleys. Last year, after two decades of studying music theory, I stumbled into this weird visual language to explain what I hear. I call these drawings "schematics" because (as far as I can tell) they look like wiring diagrams.

My schematics are all drawn in real time (though I'll go back and add details, fix bad handwriting, and so on). They're also proportional. This one, of Phish playing "Chalk Dust Torture" in Camden, New Jersey, is roughly fourteen minutes long, so if you look at the exact center of the schematic, you're seeing what happens at minute seven. Creating these schematics is a form of meditation; when I'm drawing, I'm hearing the music, but I'm also thinking about other stuff: family, work, whatever. I think about my bad posture and the thickness of writing utensils. Sometimes I'll hear music that's not coming through my headphones. That's a strange feeling. Other times I'll listen to one piece of music and look at a schematic of something else, and I'll hear both. Mostly, though, I watch random ideas surface and disappear, and then I return directly to the music.

If you make music theory something fascinating to look at, will more people become interested in learning about it? I hope so. I've done more than a hundred of these in less than a year. Improvisational rock—the Grateful Dead, Phish, Umphrey's McGee—works best, but I want to see what a Katy Perry song looks like, or *Revolver*.[1] There's work to be done.

Printed in the music issue of the Believer *(2014), "a magazine of interviews, essays, and reviews" published by McSweeney's.*

1. Grateful Dead, rock band formed in 1965; Phish, rock band formed in 1983; Umphrey's McGee, rock band formed in 1997; Perry (b. 1984), American singer-songwriter; *Revolver*, Beatles album released in 1966.

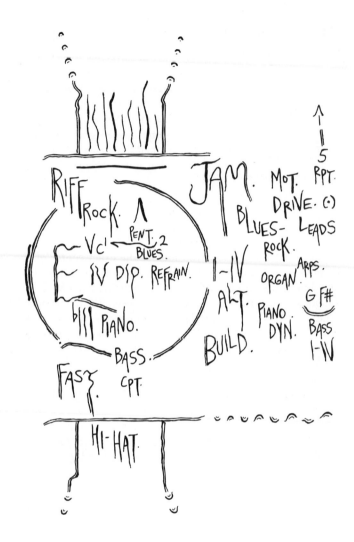

GENERAL

ARROWS = *tendencies, directions, or leanings in the music*

(.) = *major structural moments in the piece (to my ears)*

KEY = *tonal center, indicated by a capital letter (E, G, etc.)*

MODE = *the pitch collection used within a certain key*

I, II, III, ETC. = *harmonic function, or the gravity of certain chords next to each other within a certain key*

PENT = *a pentatonic (five-note) pitch collection or melody*

BLUES-ROCK = *improvisation using the blues-rock collection of pitches*

PROG = *the existence of a chord progression (it doesn't mean "progressive rock")*

VC = *verse/chorus (1, 2, etc.); vocals are present*

ARPS = *arpeggios (instrument is usually indicated)*

MOT = *a recurring motif or melodic fragment*

^5, ^7, ETC. = *indication that a certain scale degree within the key is being emphasized melodically*

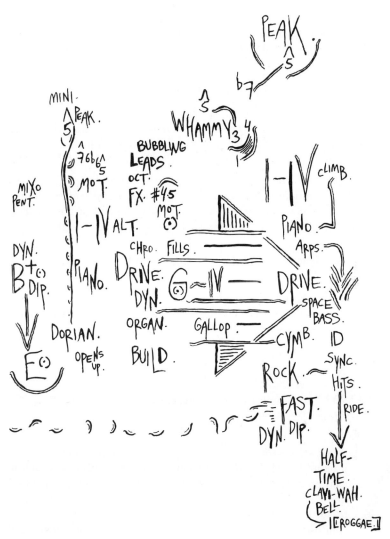

DYNAMICS

DYN DIP = "*dynamic dip*" *or a drop in volume or intensity*
BUILD = *a gradual increase in dynamics or intensity*
DRIVE = *maintaining a pretty much full-throttle dynamics/intensity level*
GALLOP = *DRIVE on acid (you'll know it when you hear it)*
PEAK = *you'll know it when you hear it*

PERCUSSION

FILLS = *the drummer plays outside the usual beat, adding intensity*

HITS = *two or more players lock together on a rhythmic or melodic riff*
SYNC HITS = *two or more instruments cooperate in some syncopated fashion*

TONE/COLOR

OCT = *the guitarist is playing in octaves*
FX = *the guitarist hits some sort of effects pedal*

MLA CITATION

Hamad, Michael. "Song Schematics." *The Norton Reader: An Anthology of Nonfiction*, edited by Melissa A. Goldthwaite et al., 16th ed., W. W. Norton, 2024, pp. 589–91.

QUESTIONS

1. Annotate Michael Hamad's annotations of his schematics. Look up the definition of some of his musical terminology and explain it more fully; annotate the schematics themselves by translating the terms as well as the size and the emphasis he gives them.

2. Hamad's system is unique to him, and he finds it more useful than traditional music theory. Have you ever developed your own system for solving a problem or explaining something? How do you think such personal systems might help us learn?

3. Pick a song you really love and listen to it intently. What do you do when you listen, and how does the way you listen compare with Hamad's technique?

4. Choose a favorite song and represent it in another medium, following the model of Hamad's song schematics· Draw it, write about it, use your imagination. Then describe what this experience taught you about the song and what you hope it helps others to notice.

TARA WESTOVER
from *Educated*

AMERICAN HISTORY was held in an auditorium named for the prophet Joseph Smith.[1] I'd thought American history would be easy because Dad had taught us about the Founding Fathers—I knew all about Washington, Jefferson, Madison. But the professor barely mentioned them at all, and instead talked about "philosophical underpinnings" and the writings of Cicero and Hume,[2] names I'd never heard.

In the first lecture, we were told that the next class would begin with a quiz on the readings. For two days I tried to wrestle meaning from the textbook's

From Educated *(2018), Tara Westover's memoir about growing up in a Mormon survivalist family, having her first classroom experience when she enrolled at Brigham Young University at the age of seventeen, and going on to earn a PhD from Cambridge University.*

1. Founder of Mormonism (1805–1844).
2. Marcus Tullius Cicero (106–43 BCE), Roman orator, philosopher, politician, and lawyer; David Hume (1711–1776), Scottish Enlightenment philosopher and historian.

dense passages, but terms like "civic humanism" and "the Scottish Enlightenment" dotted the page like black holes, sucking all the other words into them. I took the quiz and missed every question.

That failure sat uneasily in my mind. It was the first indication of whether I would be okay, whether whatever I had in my head by way of *education* was enough. After the quiz, the answer seemed clear: it was not enough. On realizing this, I might have resented my upbringing but I didn't. My loyalty to my father had increased in proportion to the miles between us. On the mountain, I could rebel. But here, in this loud, bright place, surrounded by gentiles disguised as saints, I clung to every truth, every doctrine he had given me. Doctors were Sons of Perdition. Homeschooling was a commandment from the Lord.

Failing a quiz did nothing to undermine my new devotion to an old creed, but a lecture on Western art did.

The classroom was bright when I arrived, the morning sun pouring in warmly through a high wall of windows. I chose a seat next to a girl in a high-necked blouse. Her name was Vanessa. "We should stick together," she said. "I think we're the only freshmen in the whole class." 5

The lecture began when an old man with small eyes and a sharp nose shut tered the windows. He flipped a switch and a slide projector filled the room with white light. The image was of a painting. The professor discussed the composition, the brushstrokes, the history. Then he moved to the next painting, and the next and the next.

Then the projector showed a peculiar image, of a man in a faded hat and overcoat. Behind him loomed a concrete wall. He held a small paper near his face but he wasn't looking at it. He was looking at us.

I opened the picture book I'd purchased for the class so I could take a closer look. Something was written under the image in italics but I couldn't understand it. It had one of those black-hole words, right in the middle, devouring the rest. I'd seen other students ask questions, so I raised my hand.

The professor called on me, and I read the sentence aloud. When I came to the word, I paused. "I don't know this word," I said. "What does it mean?"

There was silence. Not a hush, not a muting of the noise, but utter, almost violent silence. No papers shuffled, no pencils scratched. 10

The professor's lips tightened. "Thanks for *that*," he said, then returned to his notes.

I scarcely moved for the rest of the lecture. I stared at my shoes, wondering what had happened, and why, whenever I looked up, there was always someone staring at me as if I was a freak. Of course I *was* a freak, and I knew it, but I didn't understand how *they* knew it.

When the bell rang, Vanessa shoved her notebook into her pack. Then she paused and said, "You shouldn't make fun of that. It's not a joke." She walked away before I could reply.

I stayed in my seat until everyone had gone, pretending the zipper on my coat was stuck so I could avoid looking anyone in the eye. Then I went straight to the computer lab to look up the word "Holocaust."

15   I don't know how long I sat there reading about it, but at some point I'd read enough. I leaned back and stared at the ceiling. I suppose I was in shock, but whether it was the shock of learning about something horrific, or the shock of learning about my own ignorance, I'm not sure. I do remember imagining for a moment, not the camps, not the pits or chambers of gas, but my mother's face. A wave of emotion took me, a feeling so intense, so unfamiliar, I wasn't sure what it was. It made me want to shout at her, at my own mother, and that frightened me.

I searched my memories. In some ways the word "Holocaust" wasn't wholly unfamiliar. Perhaps Mother *had* taught me about it, when we were picking rose-hips or tincturing hawthorn. I did seem to have a vague knowledge that Jews had been killed somewhere, long ago. But I'd thought it was a small conflict, like the Boston Massacre, which Dad talked about a lot, in which half a dozen people had been martyred by a tyrannical government. To have misunderstood it on this scale—five versus six million—seemed impossible.

I found Vanessa before the next lecture and apologized for the joke. I didn't explain, because I couldn't explain. I just said I was sorry and that I wouldn't do it again. To keep that promise, I didn't raise my hand for the rest of the semester.

MLA CITATION

Westover, Tara. "From *Educated*." *The Norton Reader: An Anthology of Nonfiction*, edited by Melissa A. Goldthwaite et al., 16th ed., W. W. Norton, 2024, pp. 592–94.

QUESTIONS

1. Tara Westover recounts an experience that revealed her lack of knowledge about history. How did her professor respond to her question about the Holocaust? What other ways might he have responded?

2. Westover describes reading terms that seem "like black holes, sucking all the other words into them" (paragraph 2). Have there been any "black-hole" words for you in reading for your classes? What do you do when you encounter a word or term you don't understand?

3. Most people have had the experience of being confused or realizing they don't know something that others seem to know or understand. Write about an experience you or someone you know has had in recognizing the limits of personal knowledge.

WILLIAM ZINSSER
College Pressures

Dear Carlos: I desperately need a dean's excuse for my chem midterm which will begin in about 1 hour. All I can say is that I totally blew it this week. I've fallen incredibly, inconceivably behind.

Carlos: Help! I'm anxious to hear from you. I'll be in my room and won't leave it until I hear from you. Tomorrow is the last day for . . .

Carlos: I left town because I started bugging out again. I stayed up all night to finish a take-home make-up exam & am typing it to hand in on the 10th. It was due on the 5th. PS I'm going to the dentist. Pain is pretty bad.

Carlos: Probably by Friday I'll be able to get back to my studies. Right now I'm going to take a long walk. This whole thing has taken a lot out of me.

Carlos: I'm really up the proverbial creek. The problem is I really *bombed* the history final. Since I need that course for my major I . . .

Carlos: Here follows a tale of woe. I went home this weekend, had to help my Mom, & caught a fever so didn't have much time to study. My professor . . .

Carlos: Aargh! Trouble. Nothing original but everything's piling up at once. To be brief, my job interview . . .

Hey Carlos, good news! I've got mononucleosis.

Who are these wretched supplicants, scribbling notes so laden with anxiety, seeking such miracles of postponement and balm? They are men and women who belong to Branford College, one of the twelve residential colleges at Yale University, and the messages are just a few of the hundreds that they left for their dean, Carlos Hortas—often slipped under his door at 4 A.M.—last year.

But students like the ones who wrote those notes can also be found on campuses from coast to coast—especially in New England and at many other private colleges across the country that have high academic standards and highly motivated students. Nobody could doubt that the notes are real. In their urgency and their gallows humor they are authentic voices of a generation that is panicky to succeed.

My own connection with the message writers is that I am master of Branford College. I live in its Gothic quadrangle and know the students well. (We have 485 of them.) I am privy to their hopes and fears—and also to their stereo music and their piercing cries in the dead of night ("Does anybody *ca-a-are*?"). If they went to Carlos to ask how to get through tomorrow, they come to me to ask how to get through the rest of their lives.

Mainly I try to remind them that the road ahead is a long one and that it will have more unexpected turns than they think. There will be plenty of time to change jobs, change careers, change whole attitudes and approaches. They

Written when William Zinsser was head of a residential college at Yale University and published in a small-circulation bimonthly magazine about rural life, Blair and Ketchum's Country Journal *(1979), which has since ceased publication.*

don't want to hear such liberating news. They want a map—right now—that they can follow unswervingly to career security, financial security, Social Security and, presumably, a prepaid grave.

5   What I wish for all students is some release from the clammy grip of the future. I wish them a chance to savor each segment of their education as an experience in itself and not as a grim preparation for the next step. I wish them the right to experiment, to trip and fall, to learn that defeat is as instructive as victory and is not the end of the world.

My wish, of course, is naive. One of the few rights that America does not proclaim is the right to fail. Achievement is the national god, venerated in our media—the million-dollar athlete, the wealthy executive—and glorified in our praise of possessions. In the presence of such a potent state religion, the young are growing up old.

I see four kinds of pressure working on college students today: economic pressure, parental pressure, peer pressure, and self-induced pressure. It is easy to look around for villains—to blame the colleges for charging too much money, the professors for assigning too much work, the parents for pushing their children too far, the students for driving themselves too hard. But there are no villains; only victims.

"In the late 1960s," one dean told me, "the typical question that I got from students was 'Why is there so much suffering in the world?' or 'How can I make a contribution?' Today it's 'Do you think it would look better for getting into law school if I did a double major in history and political science, or just majored in one of them?'" Many other deans confirmed this pattern. One said: "They're trying to find an edge—the intangible something that will look better on paper if two students are about equal."

Note the emphasis on looking better. The transcript has become a sacred document, the passport to security. How one appears on paper is more important than how one appears in person. A is for Admirable and B is for Borderline, even though, in Yale's official system of grading, A means "excellent" and B means "very good." Today, looking very good is no longer good enough, especially for students who hope to go on to law school or medical school. They know that entrance into the better schools will be an entrance into the better law firms and better medical practices where they will make a lot of money. They also know that the odds are harsh. Yale Law School, for instance, matriculates 170 students from an applicant pool of 3,700; Harvard enrolls 550 from a pool of 7,000.

10   It's all very well for those of us who write letters of recommendation for our students to stress the qualities of humanity that will make them good lawyers or doctors. And it's nice to think that admission officers are really reading our letters and looking for the extra dimension of commitment or concern. Still, it would be hard for a student not to visualize these officers shuffling so many transcripts studded with As that they regard a B as positively shameful.

The pressure is almost as heavy on students who just want to graduate and get a job. Long gone are the days of the "gentleman's C," when students journeyed through college with a certain relaxation, sampling a wide variety of courses—music, art, philosophy, classics, anthropology, poetry, religion—that would send them out as liberally educated men and women. If I were an employer I would rather employ graduates who have this range and curiosity than those who narrowly pursued safe subjects and high grades. I know countless students whose inquiring minds exhilarate me. I like to hear the play of their ideas. I don't know if they are getting As or Cs, and I don't care. I also like them as people. The country needs them, and they will find satisfying jobs. I tell them to relax. They can't.

Nor can I blame them. They live in a brutal economy. Tuition, room, and board at most private colleges now comes to at least $7,000, not counting books and fees. This might seem to suggest that the colleges are getting rich. But they are equally battered by inflation. Tuition covers only 60 percent of what it costs to educate a student, and ordinarily the remainder comes from what colleges receive in endowments, grants, and gifts. Now the remainder keeps being swallowed by the cruel costs—higher every year—of just opening the doors. Heating oil is up. Insurance is up. Postage is up. Health-premium costs are up. Everything is up. Deficits are up. We are witnessing in America the creation of a brotherhood of paupers—colleges, parents, and students, joined by the common bond of debt.

Today it is not unusual for a student, even if he works part time at college and full time during the summer, to accrue $5,000 in loans after four years— loans that he must start to repay within one year after graduation. Exhorted at commencement to go forth into the world, he is already behind as he goes forth. How could he not feel under pressure throughout college to prepare for this day of reckoning? I have used "he," incidentally, only for brevity. Women at Yale are under no less pressure to justify their expensive education to themselves, their parents, and society. In fact, they are probably under more pressure. For although they leave college superbly equipped to bring fresh leadership to traditionally male jobs, society hasn't yet caught up with this fact.

Along with economic pressure goes parental pressure. Inevitably, the two are deeply intertwined.

I see many students taking pre-medical courses with joyless tenacity. They   15
go off to their labs as if they were going to the dentist. It saddens me because I know them in other corners of their life as cheerful people.

"Do you want to go to medical school?" I ask them.

"I guess so," they say, without conviction, or "Not really."

"Then why are you going?"

"Well, my parents want me to be a doctor. They're paying all this money and . . ."

Poor students, poor parents. They are caught in one of the oldest webs of   20
love and duty and guilt. The parents mean well; they are trying to steer their sons and daughters toward a secure future. But the sons and daughters want to major in history or classics or philosophy—subjects with no "practical" value. Where's the payoff on the humanities? It's not easy to persuade such loving parents that the humanities do indeed pay off. The intellectual faculties developed

by studying subjects like history and classics—an ability to synthesize and relate, to weigh cause and effect, to see events in perspective—are just the faculties that make creative leaders in business or almost any general field. Still, many fathers would rather put their money on courses that point toward a specific profession—courses that are pre-law, pre-medical, pre-business, or, as I sometimes heard it put, "pre-rich."

But the pressure on students is severe. They are truly torn. One part of them feels obligated to fulfill their parents' expectations; after all, their parents are older and presumably wiser. Another part tells them that the expectations that are right for their parents are not right for them.

I know a student who wants to be an artist. She is very obviously an artist and will be a good one—she has already had several modest local exhibits. Meanwhile she is growing as a well-rounded person and taking humanistic subjects that will enrich the inner resources out of which her art will grow. But her father is strongly opposed. He thinks that an artist is a "dumb" thing to be. The student vacillates and tries to please everybody. She keeps up with her art somewhat furtively and takes some of the "dumb" courses her father wants her to take—at least they are dumb courses for her. She is a free spirit on a campus of tense students—no small achievement in itself—and she deserves to follow her muse.

Peer pressure and self-induced pressure are also intertwined, and they begin almost at the beginning of freshman year.

"I had a freshman student I'll call Linda," one dean told me, "who came in and said she was under terrible pressure because her roommate, Barbara, was much brighter and studied all the time. I couldn't tell her that Barbara had come in two hours earlier to say the same thing about Linda."

25   The story is almost funny—except that it's not. It's symptomatic of all the pressures put together. When every student thinks every other student is working harder and doing better, the only solution is to study harder still. I see students going off to the library every night after dinner and coming back when it closes at midnight. I wish they would sometimes forget about their peers and go to a movie. I hear the clacking of typewriters in the hours before dawn. I see the tension in their eyes when exams are approaching and papers are due: *"Will I get everything done?"*

Probably they won't. They will get sick. They will get "blocked." They will sleep. They will oversleep. They will bug out. *Hey Carlos, help!*

Part of the problem is that they do more than they are expected to do. A professor will assign five-page papers. Several students will start writing ten-page papers to impress him. Then more students will write ten-page papers, and a few will raise the ante to fifteen. Pity the poor student who is still just doing the assignment.

"Once you have twenty or thirty percent of the student population deliberately overexerting," one dean points out, "it's bad for everybody. When a teacher gets more and more effort from his class, the student who is doing normal work can be perceived as not doing well. The tactic works, psychologically."

Why can't the professor just cut back and not accept longer papers? He can, and he probably will. But by then the term will be half over and the damage done. Grade fever is highly contagious and not easily reversed. Besides, the professor's main concern is with his course. He knows his students only in relation to the course and doesn't know that they are also overexerting in their other courses. Nor is it really his business. He didn't sign up for dealing with the student as a whole person and with all the emotional baggage the student brought along from home. That's what deans, masters, chaplains, and psychiatrists are for.

To some extent this is nothing new: a certain number of professors have always been self-contained islands of scholarship and shyness, more comfortable with books than with people. But the new pauperism has widened the gap still further, for professors who actually like to spend time with students don't have as much time to spend. They also are overexerting. If they are young, they are busy trying to publish in order not to perish, hanging by their fingernails onto a shrinking profession. If they are old and tenured, they are buried under the duties of administering departments—as departmental chairmen or members of committees—that have been thinned out by the budgetary axe.   30

Ultimately it will be the students' own business to break the circles in which they are trapped. They are too young to be prisoners of their parents' dreams and their classmates' fears. They must be jolted into believing in themselves as unique men and women who have the power to shape their own future.

"Violence is being done to the undergraduate experience," says Carlos Hortas. "College should be open-ended: at the end it should open many, many roads. Instead, students are choosing their goal in advance, and their choices narrow as they go along. It's almost as if they think that the country has been codified in the type of jobs that exist—that they've got to fit into certain slots. Therefore, fit into the best-paying slot.

"They ought to take chances. Not taking chances will lead to a life of colorless mediocrity. They'll be comfortable. But something in the spirit will be missing."

I have painted too drab a portrait of today's students, making them seem a solemn lot. That is only half of their story; if they were so dreary I wouldn't so thoroughly enjoy their company. The other half is that they are easy to like. They are quick to laugh and to offer friendship. They are not introverts. They are unusually kind and are more considerate of one another than any student generation I have known.

Nor are they so obsessed with their studies that they avoid sports and extracurricular activities. On the contrary, they juggle their crowded hours to play on a variety of teams, perform with musical and dramatic groups, and write for campus publications. But this in turn is one more cause of anxiety. There are too many choices. Academically, they have 1,300 courses to select from; outside class they have to decide how much spare time they can spare and how to spend it.   35

This means that they engage in fewer extracurricular pursuits than their predecessors did. If they want to row on the crew and play in the symphony they will eliminate one; in the '60s they would have done both. They also tend to choose activities that are self-limiting. Drama, for instance, is flourishing in all twelve of Yale's residential colleges as it never has before. Students hurl themselves into these productions—as actors, directors, carpenters, and technicians—with a dedication to create the best possible play, knowing that the day will come when the run will end and they can get back to their studies.

They also can't afford to be the willing slave of organizations like the *Yale Daily News*. Last spring at the one-hundredth anniversary banquet of that paper—whose past chairmen include such once and future kings as Potter Stewart, Kingman Brewster, and William F. Buckley, Jr.—much was made of the fact that the editorial staff used to be small and totally committed and that "newsies" routinely worked fifty hours a week. In effect they belonged to a club; Newsies is how they defined themselves at Yale. Today's student will write one or two articles a week, when he can, and he defines himself as a student. I've never heard the word Newsie except at the banquet.

If I have described the modern undergraduate primarily as a driven creature who is largely ignoring the blithe spirit inside who keeps trying to come out and play, it's because that's where the crunch is, not only at Yale but throughout American education. It's why I think we should all be worried about the values that are nurturing a generation so fearful of risk and so goal-obsessed at such an early age.

I tell students that there is no one "right" way to get ahead—that each of them is a different person, starting from a different point and bound for a different destination. I tell them that change is a tonic and that all the slots are not codified nor the frontiers closed. One of my ways of telling them is to invite men and women who have achieved success outside the academic world to come and talk informally with my students during the year. They are heads of companies or ad agencies, editors of magazines, politicians, public officials, television magnates, labor leaders, business executives, Broadway producers, artists, writers, economists, photographers, scientists, historians—a mixed bag of achievers.

40 I ask them to say a few words about how they got started. The students assume that they started in their present profession and knew all along that it was what they wanted to do. Luckily for me, most of them got into their field by a circuitous route, to their surprise, after many detours. The students are startled. They can hardly conceive of a career that was not pre-planned. They can hardly imagine allowing the hand of God or chance to nudge them down some unforeseen trail.

MLA CITATION

Zinsser, William. "College Pressures." *The Norton Reader: An Anthology of Nonfiction*, edited by Melissa A. Goldthwaite et al., 16th ed., W. W. Norton, 2024, pp. 595–600.

QUESTIONS

1. William Zinsser's essay includes statistics from when he wrote it (paragraphs 9, 12, and 13). Update the essay by annotating it with contemporary numbers.

2. What are the four kinds of pressure Zinsser describes for the 1970s? Are they the same kinds of pressure that trouble students today, or have new ones taken their place?

3. Compare Zinsser's description of college with Tara Westover's account of her experience in "From *Educated*" (pp. 592–94). What pressure might Westover add to Zinsser's list?

4. Write an essay in which you explain how you have experienced and handled the pressures of college (or school).

10 NATURE AND THE ENVIRONMENT

> The majesty of nature is not restricted to canyons and mountains.
> It can be found in the wilds of perception. . . . Wilderness is not
> distant. We are continually immersed in it. It is there for us to
> imagine, to savor and to protect.
>
> —ED YONG

The selections in this chapter celebrate connections between human life and our natural world, and call our attention to the consequences of disconnection. Although some of the selections consider the environmental impact of human activity (so great in scale that a new geological epoch has been proposed: the Anthropocene), many of the pieces show the sheer pleasure of being attentive to particular places and wildlife. The writers in this chapter draw us closer to nature by traveling through what science journalist Ed Yong calls the "wilds of perception." All the writers share the conviction that we best serve the earth by understanding it; they use poetic, anthropological, personal, scientific, and historical language to describe and analyze what they see and where they are.

Some of the essays focus on particular animals, often revealing as much about human nature as they do about the species itself. The chapter begins with hummingbirds and ends with fireflies. Brian Doyle's lyric essay "Joyas Voladoras" poetically explores a common feature of humans and animals—hearts—from the tiny, fast-beating hearts of hummingbirds to the room-sized hearts of whales to the torn and repaired hearts of humans. The chapter ends with Aimee Nezhukumatathil sharing how her family instilled in her a love of nature on childhood evenings spent wondering in a field of fireflies. Animals with sharp teeth populate this chapter, too. Through stories of how Kenyan farmers adjudicate a hyena attack or how Indonesian villagers understand crocodiles who kill people, Cormac Cullinan and coauthors Anna Lowenhaupt Tsing and Nils Bubandt illustrate new ways of thinking about the violence enacted by humans and beasts.

It's not difficult to imagine why many humans feel connected to cute baby animals or beautiful places. Other connections, though, may surprise some readers. John Muir, instead of taking shelter during a violent windstorm in the forest, goes outside; he describes the sound of the wind in the trees as music and even climbs a tall tree as it "flapped and swished in the passionate torrent." Colson Whitehead also writes, both lovingly and grudgingly, about the rain, using a series of vignettes to describe a downpour in New York City. Although Edward Abbey in "The Great American Desert" proclaims his love for the Utah desert, he uses a hyperbolic and acerbic tone to warn others away by listing the hazards they might encounter, such as kissing bugs as "quiet as . . . assassin[s]." Terry Tempest Williams claims her place in "The Clan of One-Breasted Women" and

writes of a lineage of women—impacted by nuclear testing in the Utah desert—
marching, singing, and protesting to protect their lives and the sacred land.

As these nature essays illustrate, not all places worth writing about feature colorful wild-
flowers, towering mountains, and glorious sunsets. Nature isn't just the idealized and filtered images that appear on Nature Conservancy calendars and *Instagram* feeds. William
Cronon asks us to rethink our assumption that wilderness is something apart from humans.
In "Collards Are Just as Good as Kale," Heather McTeer Toney extends the argument,
showing us the long connection between Black people and the land, arguing that this
knowledge, too, is environmentalism. Robin Wall Kimmerer, an Indigenous environmental
scientist and botanist, writes about her lifetime of learning to entwine her training in
botany and her emotional tie to the beauty and bounty of the earth. Again and again,
these essays show us that nature, culture, history, and humans are intricately connected.

As you write about nature and the environment, consider the places you feel most connected to: a backyard, a city park, a garden, a stream. You may need to visit that place to
write about it, describing the sights, sounds, smells, and other sensory features. What kind
of wildlife inhabits that place? Look up the names of trees and birds and flowers and weeds.
Why do you feel connected to that place? What memories of it do you have? How have
humans shaped that place? Is there anything that threatens it or its inhabitants? Who is
seeking to protect that place, if anyone? What happened there in the past? What hopes
do you have for its future?

BRIAN DOYLE

Joyas Voladoras

CONSIDER THE HUMMINGBIRD for a long moment. A hummingbird's
heart beats ten times a second. A hummingbird's heart is the size
of a pencil eraser. A hummingbird's heart is a lot of the hummingbird. *Joyas voladoras*, flying jewels, the first white explorers
in the Americas called them, and the white men had never seen
such creatures, for hummingbirds came into the world only in the
Americas, nowhere else in the universe, more than three hundred species of
them whirring and zooming and nectaring in hummer time zones nine times
removed from ours, their hearts hammering faster than we could clearly hear
if we pressed our elephantine ears to their infinitesimal chests.

Each one visits a thousand flowers a day. They can dive at sixty miles an
hour. They can fly backward. They can fly more than five hundred miles without
pausing to rest. But when they rest they come close to death: on frigid nights,
or when they are starving, they retreat into torpor, their metabolic rate slowing
to a fifteenth of their normal sleep rate, their hearts sludging nearly to a halt,
barely beating, and if they are not soon warmed, if they do not soon find that

First published in the American Scholar *(2004), a magazine published by the Phi Beta Kappa
Society, and later chosen for inclusion in* The Best American Essays *(2005).*

which is sweet, their hearts grow cold, and they cease to be. Consider for a moment those hummingbirds who did not open their eyes again today, this very day, in the Americas: bearded helmetcrests and booted racket-tails, violet-tailed sylphs and violet-capped woodnymphs, crimson topazes and purple-crowned fairies, red-tailed comets and amethyst woodstars, rainbow-bearded thornbills and glittering-bellied emeralds, velvet-purple coronets and golden-bellied star-frontlets, fiery-tailed awlbills and Andean hillstars, spatuletails and pufflegs, each the most amazing thing you have never seen, each thunderous wild heart the size of an infant's fingernail, each mad heart silent, a brilliant music stilled.

Hummingbirds, like all flying birds but more so, have incredible enormous immense ferocious metabolisms. To drive those metabolisms they have race-car hearts that eat oxygen at an eye-popping rate. Their hearts are built of thinner, leaner fibers than ours. Their arteries are stiffer and more taut. They have more mitochondria in their heart muscles—anything to gulp more oxygen. Their hearts are stripped to the skin for the war against gravity and inertia, the mad search for food, the insane idea of flight. The price of their ambition is a life closer to death; they suffer more heart attacks and aneurysms and ruptures than any other living creature. It's expensive to fly. You burn out. You fry the machine. You melt the engine. Every creature on earth has approximately two billion heartbeats to spend in a lifetime. You can spend them slowly, like a tortoise, and live to be two hundred years old, or you can spend them fast, like a hummingbird, and live to be two years old.

The biggest heart in the world is inside the blue whale. It weighs more than seven tons. It's as big as a room. It *is* a room, with four chambers. A child could walk around in it, head high, bending only to step through the valves. The valves are as big as the swinging doors in a saloon. This house of a heart drives a creature a hundred feet long. When this creature is born it is twenty feet long and weighs four tons. It is waaaaay bigger than your car. It drinks a hundred gallons of milk from its mama every day and gains two hundred pounds a day, and when it is seven or eight years old it endures an unimaginable puberty and then it essentially disappears from human ken, for next to nothing is known of the mating habits, travel patterns, diet, social life, language, social structure, diseases, spirituality, wars, stories, despairs, and arts of the blue whale. There are perhaps ten thousand blue whales in the world, living in every ocean on earth, and of the largest mammal who ever lived we know nearly nothing. But we know this: the animals with the largest hearts in the world generally travel in pairs, and their penetrating moaning cries, their piercing yearning tongue, can be heard underwater for miles and miles.

5   Mammals and birds have hearts with four chambers. Reptiles and turtles have hearts with three chambers. Fish have hearts with two chambers. Insects and mollusks have hearts with one chamber. Worms have hearts with one chamber, although they may have as many as eleven single-chambered hearts. Unicellular bacteria have no hearts at all; but even they have fluid eternally in motion, washing from one side of the cell to the other, swirling and whirling. No living being is without interior liquid motion. We all churn inside.

So much held in a heart in a lifetime. So much held in a heart in a day, an hour, a moment. We are utterly open with no one, in the end—not mother and father, not wife or husband, not lover, not child, not friend. We open windows to each but we live alone in the house of the heart. Perhaps we must. Perhaps we could not bear to be so naked, for fear of a constantly harrowed heart. When young we think there will come one person who will savor and sustain us always; when we are older we know this is the dream of a child, that all hearts finally are bruised and scarred, scored and torn, repaired by time and will, patched by force of character, yet fragile and rickety forevermore, no matter how ferocious the defense and how many bricks you bring to the wall. You can brick up your heart as stout and tight and hard and cold and impregnable as you possibly can and down it comes in an instant, felled by a woman's second glance, a child's apple breath, the shatter of glass in the road, the words "I have something to tell you," a cat with a broken spine dragging itself into the forest to die, the brush of your mother's papery ancient hand in the thicket of your hair, the memory of your father's voice early in the morning echoing from the kitchen where he is making pancakes for his children.

MLA CITATION

Doyle, Brian. "Joyas Voladoras." *The Norton Reader: An Anthology of Nonfiction*, edited by Melissa A. Goldthwaite et al., 16th ed., W. W. Norton, 2024, pp. 603–5.

QUESTIONS

1. Brian Doyle considers the hearts of hummingbirds (paragraphs 1–3), blue whales (paragraph 4), and humans (paragraph 6) in this lyric essay, which uses poetic features such as metaphor, contrast, and repetition. What is his purpose in doing so? How does he make a transition from a focus on animals to a focus on humans?

2. Doyle incorporates several lists into this essay. Trace his use of lists throughout. Which one do you find most effective? Why?

3. Write a lyric essay in which you closely consider some element of human and animal nature. Consider using some of the poetic features identified in the first question.

4. Create or search for three or four illustrations to accompany this essay. Then write a brief artist's statement about the illustrations, noting reasons for their style and their subject matter.

JOHN MUIR

A Wind-Storm in the Forests

THE MOUNTAIN WINDS, like the dew and rain, sunshine and snow, are measured and bestowed with love on the forests to develop their strength and beauty. However restricted the scope of other forest influences, that of the winds is universal. The snow bends and trims the upper forests every winter, the lightning strikes a single tree here and there, while avalanches mow down thousands at a swoop as a gardener trims out a bed of flowers. But the winds go to every tree, fingering every leaf and branch and furrowed bole; not one is forgotten; the Mountain Pine towering with outstretched arms on the rugged buttresses of the icy peaks, the lowliest and most retiring tenant of the dells; they seek and find them all, caressing them tenderly, bending them in lusty exercise, stimulating their growth, plucking off a leaf or limb as required, or removing an entire tree or grove, now whispering and cooing through the branches like a sleepy child, now roaring like the ocean; the winds blessing the forests, the forests the winds, with ineffable beauty and harmony as the sure result.

After one has seen pines six feet in diameter bending like grasses before a mountain gale, and ever and anon some giant falling with a crash that shakes the hills, it seems astonishing that any, save the lowest thickset trees, could ever have found a period sufficiently stormless to establish themselves; or, once established, that they should not, sooner or later, have been blown down. But when the storm is over, and we behold the same forests tranquil again, towering fresh and unscathed in erect majesty, and consider what centuries of storms have fallen upon them since they were first planted,—hail, to break the tender seedlings; lightning, to scorch and shatter; snow, winds, and avalanches, to crush and overwhelm,—while the manifest result of all this wild storm-culture is the glorious perfection we behold; then faith in Nature's forestry is established, and we cease to deplore the violence of her most destructive gales, or of any other storm-implement whatsoever.

There are two trees in the Sierra forests that are never blown down, so long as they continue in sound health. These are the Juniper and the Dwarf Pine of the summit peaks. Their stiff, crooked roots grip the storm-beaten ledges like eagles' claws, while their lithe, cord-like branches bend round compliantly, offering but slight holds for winds, however violent. The other alpine conifers—the Needle Pine, Mountain Pine, Two-leaved Pine, and Hemlock Spruce—are never thinned out by this agent to any destructive extent, on account of their admirable toughness and the closeness of their growth. In general the same is true of the giants of the lower zones. The kingly Sugar Pine, towering aloft to a height of more than 200 feet, offers a fine mark to storm-winds: but it is not densely foliaged, and its long, horizontal arms swing round compliantly in the

From John Muir's The Mountains of California *(1894), a book of scientific observation and personal memoir.*

A wind-storm in the California forests (after a sketch by the author).

blast, like tresses of green, fluent algæ in a brook; while the Silver Firs in most places keep their ranks well together in united strength. The Yellow or Silver Pine is more frequently overturned than any other tree on the Sierra, because its leaves and branches form a larger mass in proportion to its height, while in many places it is planted sparsely, leaving open lanes through which storms may enter with full force. Furthermore, because it is distributed along the lower portion of the range, which was the first to be left bare on the breaking up of the ice-sheet at the close of the glacial winter, the soil it is growing upon has been longer exposed to post-glacial weathering, and consequently is in a more crumbling, decayed condition than the fresher soils farther up the range, and therefore offers a less secure anchorage for the roots.

While exploring the forest zones of Mount Shasta, I discovered the path of a hurricane strewn with thousands of pines of this species. Great and small had been uprooted or wrenched off by sheer force, making a clean gap, like that made by a snow avalanche. But hurricanes capable of doing this class of work are rare in the Sierra, and when we have explored the forests from one extremity of the range to the other, we are compelled to believe that they are the most beautiful on the face of the earth, however we may regard the agents that have made them so.

There is always something deeply exciting, not only in the sounds of winds in the woods, which exert more or less influence over every mind, but in their varied waterlike flow as manifested by the movements of the trees, especially those of the conifers. By no other trees are they rendered so extensively and impressively visible, not even by the lordly tropic palms or tree-ferns responsive to the gentlest breeze. The waving of a forest of the giant Sequoias is indescribably impressive and sublime, but the pines seem to me the best interpreters of winds. They are mighty waving goldenrods, ever in tune, singing and writing wind-music all their long century lives. Little, however, of this noble tree-waving and tree-music will you see or hear in the strictly alpine portion of the forests. The burly Juniper, whose girth sometimes more than equals its height, is about as rigid as the rocks on which it grows. The slender lash-like sprays of the Dwarf Pine stream out in wavering ripples, but the tallest and slenderest are far too unyielding to wave even in the heaviest gales. They only shake in quick, short vibrations.

5

The Hemlock Spruce, however, and the Mountain Pine, and some of the tallest thickets of the Two-leaved species bow in storms with considerable scope and gracefulness. But it is only in the lower and middle zones that the meeting of winds and woods is to be seen in all its grandeur.

One of the most beautiful and exhilarating storms I ever enjoyed in the Sierra occurred in December, 1874, when I happened to be exploring one of the tributary valleys of the Yuba River. The sky and the ground and the trees had been thoroughly rain-washed and were dry again. The day was intensely pure, one of those incomparable bits of California winter, warm and balmy and full of white sparkling sunshine, redolent of all the purest influences of the spring, and at the same time enlivened with one of the most bracing wind-storms conceivable. Instead of camping out, as I usually do, I then chanced to be stopping at the house of a friend. But when the storm began to sound, I lost no time in pushing out into the woods to enjoy it. For on such occasions Nature has always something rare to show us, and the danger to life and limb is hardly greater than one would experience crouching deprecatingly beneath a roof.

It was still early morning when I found myself fairly adrift. Delicious sunshine came pouring over the hills, lighting the tops of the pines, and setting free a stream of summery fragrance that contrasted strangely with the wild tones of the storm. The air was mottled with pine-tassels and bright green plumes, that went flashing past in the sunlight like birds pursued. But there was not the slightest dustiness, nothing less pure than leaves, and ripe pollen, and flecks of withered bracken and moss. I heard trees falling for hours at the rate of one every two or three minutes; some uprooted, partly on account of the loose, water-soaked condition of the ground; others broken straight across, where some weakness caused by fire had determined the spot. The gestures of the various trees made a delightful study. Young Sugar Pines, light and feathery as squirrel-tails, were bowing almost to the ground; while the grand old patriarchs, whose massive boles had been tried in a hundred storms, waved solemnly above them, their long, arching branches streaming fluently on the gale, and every needle thrilling and ringing and shedding off keen lances of light like a diamond. The Douglas Spruces,[1] with long sprays drawn out in level tresses, and needles massed in a gray, shimmering glow, presented a most striking appearance as they stood in bold relief along the hilltops. The madroños[2] in the dells, with their red bark and large glossy leaves tilted every way, reflected the sunshine in throbbing spangles like those one so often sees on the rippled surface of a glacier lake. But the Silver Pines were now the most impressively beautiful of all. Colossal spires 200 feet in height waved like supple goldenrods chanting and bowing low as if in worship, while the whole mass of their long, tremulous foliage was kindled into one continuous blaze of white sun-fire. The force of the gale was such that the most steadfast monarch of them all rocked down to its roots with a motion plainly perceptible when one leaned against it. Nature was holding high festival, and every fiber of the most rigid giants thrilled with glad excitement.

1. Another name for Douglas firs.
2. Type of evergreen trees.

I drifted on through the midst of this passionate music and motion, across many a glen, from ridge to ridge; often halting in the lee of a rock for shelter, or to gaze and listen. Even when the grand anthem had swelled to its highest pitch, I could distinctly hear the varying tones of individual trees,—Spruce, and Fir, and Pine, and leafless Oak—and even the infinitely gentle rustle of the withered grasses at my feet. Each was expressing itself in its own way,— singing its own song, and making its own peculiar gestures,—manifesting a richness of variety to be found in no other forest I have yet seen. The coniferous woods of Canada, and the Carolinas, and Florida, are made up of trees that resemble one another about as nearly as blades of grass, and grow close together in much the same way. Coniferous trees, in general, seldom possess individual character, such as is manifest among Oaks and Elms. But the California forests are made up of a greater number of distinct species than any other in the world. And in them we find, not only a marked differentiation into special groups, but also a marked individuality in almost every tree, giving rise to storm effects indescribably glorious.

Toward midday, after a long, tingling scramble through copses of hazel and ceanothus,[3] I gained the summit of the highest ridge in the neighborhood; and then it occurred to me that it would be a fine thing to climb one of the trees to obtain a wider outlook and get my ear close to the Æolian music[4] of its topmost needles. But under the circumstances the choice of a tree was a serious matter. One whose instep was not very strong seemed in danger of being blown down, or of being struck by others in case they should fall; another was branchless to a considerable height above the ground, and at the same time too large to be grasped with arms and legs in climbing; while others were not favorably situated for clear views. After cautiously casting about, I made choice of the tallest of a group of Douglas Spruces that were growing close together like a tuft of grass, no one of which seemed likely to fall unless all the rest fell with it. Though comparatively young, they were about 100 feet high, and their lithe, brushy tops were rocking and swirling in wild ecstasy. Being accustomed to climb trees in making botanical studies, I experienced no difficulty in reaching the top of this one, and never before did I enjoy so noble an exhilaration of motion. The slender tops fairly flapped and swished in the passionate torrent, bending and swirling backward and forward, round and round, tracing indescribable combinations of vertical and horizontal curves, while I clung with muscles firm braced, like a bobolink on a reed.

In its widest sweeps my tree-top described an arc of from twenty to thirty degrees, but I felt sure of its elastic temper, having seen others of the same species still more severely tried—bent almost to the ground indeed, in heavy snows— without breaking a fiber. I was therefore safe, and free to take the wind into my pulses and enjoy the excited forest from my superb outlook. The view from here must be extremely beautiful in any weather. Now my eye roved over the piny hills

10

3. Type of evergreen shrubs.
4. Music made by the wind. From Aeolus, the Greek god of the winds, the strings of whose harp were sounded by the wind.

and dales as over fields of waving grain, and felt the light running in ripples and broad swelling undulations across the valleys from ridge to ridge, as the shining foliage was stirred by corresponding waves of air. Oftentimes these waves of reflected light would break up suddenly into a kind of beaten foam, and again, after chasing one another in regular order, they would seem to bend forward in concentric curves, and disappear on some hillside, like sea-waves on a shelving shore. The quantity of light reflected from the bent needles was so great as to make whole groves appear as if covered with snow, while the black shadows beneath the trees greatly enhanced the effect of the silvery splendor.

Excepting only the shadows there was nothing somber in all this wild sea of pines. On the contrary, notwithstanding this was the winter season, the colors were remarkably beautiful. The shafts of the pine and libocedrus[5] were brown and purple, and most of the foliage was well tinged with yellow; the laurel groves, with the pale undersides of their leaves turned upward, made masses of gray; and then there was many a dash of chocolate color from clumps of manzanita,[6] and jet of vivid crimson from the bark of the madroños, while the ground on the hillsides, appearing here and there through openings between the groves, displayed masses of pale purple and brown.

The sounds of the storm corresponded gloriously with this wild exuberance of light and motion. The profound bass of the naked branches and boles booming like waterfalls; the quick, tense vibrations of the pine-needles, now rising to a shrill, whistling hiss, now falling to a silky murmur; the rustling of laurel groves in the dells, and the keen metallic click of leaf on leaf—all this was heard in easy analysis when the attention was calmly bent.

The varied gestures of the multitude were seen to fine advantage, so that one could recognize the different species at a distance of several miles by this means alone, as well as by their forms and colors, and the way they reflected the light. All seemed strong and comfortable, as if really enjoying the storm, while responding to its most enthusiastic greetings. We hear much nowadays concerning the universal struggle for existence, but no struggle in the common meaning of the word was manifest here; no recognition of danger by any tree; no deprecation; but rather an invincible gladness as remote from exultation as from fear.

I kept my lofty perch for hours, frequently closing my eyes to enjoy the music by itself, or to feast quietly on the delicious fragrance that was streaming past. The fragrance of the woods was less marked than that produced during warm rain, when so many balsamic buds and leaves are steeped like tea; but, from the chafing of resiny branches against each other, and the incessant attrition of myriads of needles, the gale was spiced to a very tonic degree. And besides the fragrance from these local sources there were traces of scents brought from afar. For this wind came first from the sea, rubbing against its fresh, briny waves, then distilled through the redwoods, threading rich ferny gulches, and spreading itself in broad undulating currents over many a flower-enameled ridge of the coast

5. Genus of cedar trees. In the Sierra Nevada, *Libocedrus decurrens* often reaches a height of 150 feet.

6. Type of evergreen shrubs.

mountains, then across the golden plains, up the purple foot-hills, and into these piny woods with the varied incense gathered by the way.

Winds are advertisements of all they touch, however much or little we may be able to read them; telling their wanderings even by their scents alone. Mariners detect the flowery perfume of land-winds far at sea, and sea-winds carry the fragrance of dulse and tangle far inland, where it is quickly recognized, though mingled with the scents of a thousand land-flowers. As an illustration of this, I may tell here that I breathed sea-air on the Firth of Forth, in Scotland, while a boy; then was taken to Wisconsin, where I remained nineteen years; then, without in all this time having breathed one breath of the sea, I walked quietly, alone, from the middle of the Mississippi Valley to the Gulf of Mexico, on a botanical excursion, and while in Florida, far from the coast, my attention wholly bent on the splendid tropical vegetation about me, I suddenly recognized a sea-breeze, as it came sifting through the palmettos and blooming vine-tangles, which at once awakened and set free a thousand dormant associations, and made me a boy again in Scotland, as if all the intervening years had been annihilated.

Most people like to look at mountain rivers, and bear them in mind; but few care to look at the winds, though far more beautiful and sublime, and though they become at times about as visible as flowing water. When the north winds in winter are making upward sweeps over the curving summits of the High Sierra, the fact is sometimes published with flying snow-banners a mile long. Those portions of the winds thus embodied can scarce be wholly invisible, even to the darkest imagination. And when we look around over an agitated forest, we may see something of the wind that stirs it, by its effects upon the trees. Yonder it descends in a rush of water-like ripples, and sweeps over the bending pines from hill to hill. Nearer, we see detached plumes and leaves, now speeding by on level currents, now whirling in eddies, or, escaping over the edges of the whirls, soaring aloft on grand, upswelling domes of air, or tossing on flame-like crests. Smooth, deep currents, cascades, falls, and swirling eddies, sing around every tree and leaf, and over all the varied topography of the region with telling changes of form, like mountain rivers conforming to the features of their channels.

After tracing the Sierra streams from their fountains to the plains, marking where they bloom white in falls, glide in crystal plumes, surge gray and foam-filled in boulder-choked gorges, and slip through the woods in long, tranquil reaches—after thus learning their language and forms in detail, we may at length hear them chanting all together in one grand anthem, and comprehend them all in clear inner vision, covering the range like lace. But even this spectacle is far less sublime and not a whit more substantial than what we may behold of these storm-streams of air in the mountain woods.

We all travel the milky way together, trees and men; but it never occurred to me until this stormday, while swinging in the wind, that trees are travelers, in the ordinary sense. They make many journeys, not extensive ones, it is true; but our own little journeys, away and back again, are only little more than tree-wavings—many of them not so much. ✸

When the storm began to abate, I dismounted and sauntered down through the calming woods. The storm-tones died away, and, turning toward the east, I beheld the countless hosts of the forests hushed and tranquil, towering above one another on the slopes of the hills like a devout audience. The setting sun filled them with amber light, and seemed to say, while they listened, "My peace I give unto you."

20   As I gazed on the impressive scene, all the so-called ruin of the storm was forgotten, and never before did these noble woods appear so fresh, so joyous, so immortal.

MLA CITATION

Muir, John. "A Wind-Storm in the Forests." *The Norton Reader: An Anthology of Nonfiction*, edited by Melissa A. Goldthwaite et al., 16th ed., W. W. Norton, 2024, pp. 606–12.

QUESTIONS

1. Research two or three of the species of trees mentioned in this essay and annotate the essay with additional details about them. What does it add to your understanding to know more about the differences among types of trees?

2. What preconceptions might a reader bring to John Muir's title "A Wind-Storm in the Forests"? Does the opening sentence—indeed, the entire opening paragraph—suggest a different perspective? How so?

3. The central adventure in this essay occurs when Muir climbs a Douglas Spruce (paragraph 9). Why does Muir undertake this climb? What does he wish to experience?

4. Write about an experience you have had in nature, whether dramatic, as in Muir's essay, or more quiet.

COLSON WHITEHEAD
Rain

UT ON the street they hardly notice the clouds before it starts raining. The rain comes down in sheets. Drenched all at once, not drop by drop. The first drop is the pistol at the start of the race and at that crack people move for shelter, any ragtag thing, they huddle under ripped awnings, the doorway of the diner, suddenly an appetite for coffee. Pressed up against buildings

Colson Whitehead (b. 1969) won the Pulitzer Prize for his novel The Underground Railroad *(2016). This essay comes from his 2003 essay collection* The Colossus of New York: A City in Thirteen Parts.

as if on the lam. Little sprints and dashes between horizontal cover. Dry here. Surely it will stop soon, they think. They can wait it out. It cannot last forever.

SUSPECTING such an eventuality, the umbrella salesmen emerge to make deals. They wait all week for this and have ample supply of one-dollar bills. The virtues of their merchandise are self-evident. She carries an umbrella every day no matter what the news says because you can never tell and is vindicated by moisture. It pops open. The doused press down on reluctant buttons and the mechanisms pop open. Underneath their personal domes, they are separated from the peasants. To be this easily isolated from all worry. The silver tips dart and jab for eye sockets. Probability says many are blinded by pointy umbrella spokes and you are surely the next victim. At the corner he wrestles with a ghost for the soul of his umbrella. The gust gains the upper hand as he waits for the light to change and the umbrella is ripped inverse. Many are lost. The wounded, the fallen in this struggle, poke out of trash cans, abandoned, black fabric rippling against split chrome ribs. This is their lot. Either in the trash can or forgotten in the restaurant, the movie theater, the friend's foyer, spreading their slow puddles across floors. Forming an attachment to an umbrella is the shortest route to heartbreak in this town. Any true accounting would reveal that there are only twenty umbrellas in this city, in constant movement from palm to palm. Bunch of Lotharios.[1] So do we learn loss from umbrellas.

THE NEW RIVERS along curbs shove newspaper and grit to gutters. Too big to squeeze through grates the garbage bobs in place like the unstylish waiting for night-club doors to open. The liquid sinks below. The alligators don't mind. Eventually a clog sends a puddle advancing. A sliver of moon, the surface of the puddle is tormented by brief craters. Each drop explodes and extends the surface of the puddle. Doing their part for the water cycle, the bus wheels return the puddle to air again. Complacent beneath her umbrella she is thoroughly soaked when she stands too close to the curb. The enemy came from below. The metropolitan transit authority reinforces old lessons: every puddle wants to hug you. If not heavy motor vehicles then it is the children in their bright red boots detonating puddles on people. Knock it off.

IT FINDS the nape of your neck easily. It traces the length of your spine greedily. The long list of errands shrinks into what people can do in the least amount of water. So much for the dry cleaning. All over town the available number of cabs shrinks as thin fingers tilt and quiver at the edges of traffic. The bastard one block upriver gets it before you can stick a hand out, just as you are someone else's bastard one block downriver. Epithets are tossed against the flow of traffic, upon the unbeknownst. Everybody just wants to get home, so they make calculations and jockey. What's a better block for a cab. East or west, up a street or down. Schemes multiply and divide the longer you stand there. The super-

---

1. Lothario, a man who shamelessly seduces women, from the name of a character in Miguel de Cervantes's novel *Don Quixote* (1605).

computer of cab-catching. Sixth Avenue is uptown and Seventh is down, important variables. The time of day, the direction and force of the wind, sun spots,
that Pacific typhoon, all important considerations in the acquisition of a cab.
She hailed it because she thought it was empty, but it speeds by with smug fares
in the backseat who do not even notice her. Day like this all it takes is a little
cab fare in your pocket to become royalty.

5   COUPLES FORCED into doorways kiss, coached by the cinema. One of them says one
two three and they make a break out of the latest slim refuge. They are reminded
after a few steps of how cold the rain is. They stop at the next outpost to catch their
breath and forget how cold the rain is. This is the start of her long illness. The
wrapping would be ruined by the water so he holds the present under his coat,
lending to his belly the contours of an absurd pregnancy. She hides in the bus
stand. She hasn't taken the bus in years and feels a secret terror. Pressed up against
other people: what's the point of money. In shelter they make plans. He doesn't
know where he is supposed to be because the paper got wet and now the address is
a smudge. Lost at intersections. Look at all the trenchcoats—it is the detectives'
convention come at last to take care of all our loose ends. Up in all the windows,
leaning on the sills, the dry people look down on the street and think, Glad I'm not
out in that. As if they are without problems. Open half an inch, the window in the
next room is still open wide enough to get the floor wet before they notice.

A MAN of liberal convictions, he got this umbrella by pledging money to public
radio. It sends the message that he supports public radio. Has a matching tote
bag. Now no one will suspect she has been crying. After a block it is evident
that they both will not fit under the compact umbrella and one must make do
with a dry shoulder. Is this the end of their love. The weekend outdoorsman
strides through in his appropriate gear, this is no cliff face or ravine, and he is
well equipped. Her glasses are too wet to see through so she takes them off
and squints through precipitation. When she gets inside she'll use up napkins.
Unable to decide which side of the bed is more comfortable, the windshield
wipers toss and turn. Sleepless like rivers. How swiftly the newspaper becomes
a sodden brick over his head. It doesn't keep him dry at all despite clichés. From
street level as he looks up into the clouds each advancing drop is elongated, a
comet, until it hits his cheek and crashes. On his lips it doesn't taste so bad.
One drop hits his eye and stings more than mere water should. He blinks. Sooty
streaks trail under windowsills. Every building a coquette, a face powdered by
industry. This so-called cleansing leaves behind more than it washes away. But
then few things are as advertised.

NEW SOCKS tint soaked toes blue. The shoes take forever to dry. Last time it
rained he put them under the radiator and hours later they were warped and
twisted, as if it were agony to let the water go. Next time he will remember the
water repellent spray. It is available at local pharmacies. Secure in her foresight,
she wonders about the etymology of the word galoshes. Of course it is a ridiculous thing to walk around with plastic bags tied over your shoes, but do you know

how much these things cost. The puddle at the curb is deeper than it looks, an ancient loch. Trying to jump over it you fall short and the lagoon spills into your shoes. Tonight the bunched balls of his socks will dry and stiffen into dingy fists, and roll under the bureau, where they will hide for months and foment.

HE CLIMBS UP the steps and realizes that while he was in the subway the whole world changed. It's all gray. Pull lapels tight. Only the gargoyles seem happy, up there on the roofs. If you're lucky when you die, you become one and get to hang out here forever. He says, You think the money they get paid, the weathermen would get it right for a change. Remembering only disasters. The stock boy rips up cardboard boxes to lay down in the entrance of the store. All our vain gestures. It makes the boss happy, it's how they did it in the old days. The newspaper vendor takes all these wet bills in stride. But no one wants to buy a wet newspaper. The stacks got wet before he could cover them up. In the competing store across the street the news piles up underneath a transparent tarp. Survival of the fittest, but of course he is not saddled with an idiot nephew. In the phone booth preparing for the next sortie. Lay all that money out for the hairdresser and now this. They will drag their feet across doormats and track floors nonetheless. Identical twins wear identical yellow slickers, out of which identical noses poke. What's this in the raincoat pocket. Apparently the last time it rained he saw a romantic comedy.

AT THE CORNER it's worse, thrown into their faces like needles or proof. The wind whips it around. Once they find a parking space they decide to wait it out and make out, tilting the car seats back to uncomfortable angles. A nipple gives against a thumb. Once the engine is off they can make out the rain's true incantation on the roof of the car and clench each other tighter. Safe here. The talk always comes around to the weather. Underneath the scaffolding the conversations among strangers range from grunts to bona fide connections. Quite serendipitous. It leaks. From block to block the people display an assortment of strides, every station between a walk and a run. Each has a personal strategy of how best to move in this. The best of them gave up long ago. The best of them cease stooping, stand up straight, stop dodging, take it as it comes. Apparently they are supposed to get wet, so they give in. It is like letting go of something and a small miracle wrung from accident. Walking slowly and naturally in this downpour, they are avoided by the more sensible, who walk swiftly around them, unsettled by these strange creatures. Citizens of a better city.

IT STOPS. From the river you can see the clouds haunch over adjacent boroughs. 10 What transpired is a problem for sewers now, out of sight and out of mind. Snapping the umbrella open and closed as if it will scare the water off. It pulsates like a jellyfish in bleak fathoms. She tries to button the strap on her umbrella but keeps losing the snap in the folds. Now her hands are all wet. Some people think it's a trick and keep their umbrellas open for blocks just in case. They walk out of the movie theater and say to each other, Did it rain, pointing at puddles. Yes, they are sure of it, something happened and they missed it.

MLA CITATION

Whitehead, Colson. "Rain." *The Norton Reader: An Anthology of Nonfiction*, edited by
    Melissa A. Goldthwaite et al., 16th ed., W. W. Norton, 2024, pp. 612–15.

QUESTIONS

1. In paragraph 2, Colson Whitehead personifies umbrellas. What kind of personality does he give them? What surprises you about these descriptions? Do you imagine umbrellas as having a different personality—or any personality at all?

2. Whitehead jokes that "the alligators don't mind" (paragraph 3), referring to an
urban legend that alligators live in the city sewers. What is the effect of that joke
on the tone of the piece overall? Where else do you find humor in the essay?

3. This essay is organized organically through the evolution of a rainstorm, from
the first drops to the moment an umbrella is no longer needed. Go through the essay
again and name the phases of a rainstorm, according to Whitehead. Add some categories of your own.

4. There is a narrative voice in this essay, but the narrator does not describe himself. What clues does the narrator offer as to his personality?

5. Write an essay about how a place that you know well changes when the weather
suddenly changes.

ROBIN WALL KIMMERER
Goldenrod and Asters: My Life with Plants

I LIKE TO IMAGINE that they were the first flowers I saw, over my mother's
shoulder, as the pink blanket slipped away from my face and their
colors flooded my consciousness. I've heard that early experience can
attune the brain to certain stimuli, so that they are processed with
greater speed and certainty, so that they can be used again and again,
so that we remember. Love at first sight. Through cloudy newborn eyes
their radiance formed the first botanical synapses in my wide-awake brain,
which until then had encountered only the blurry gentleness of pink faces. I'm
guessing all eyes were on me, a little round baby all swaddled in bunting, but
mine were on goldenrod and asters. I was born to these flowers and they came
back for my birthday every year, weaving me into our mutual celebration.

People flock to our hills for the fiery suite of October but they often miss
the sublime prelude of September fields. As if harvest time were not enough—

Published in its current form in Commons: A Gathering of Stories & Culture, *a publication of Blue Mountain Center, which offers residencies and retreats for writers, artists, and
those working for social justice. This piece, in a slightly different form, also appears in the
chapter "Asters and Goldenrod" from Robin Wall Kimmerer's* Braiding Sweetgrass: Indigenous Wisdom, Scientific Knowledge, and the Teachings of Plants *(2013).*

peaches, grapes, sweet corn, squash—the fields are also embroidered with drifts of golden yellow and pools of deepest purple, a masterpiece.

I wanted to make a good first impression. There were hardly any women at the forestry school in those days and certainly none who looked like me. For the freshman intake interview, I wore my new red plaid shirt, a hallmark of foresters, so I'd fit right in. My new faculty adviser peered at me over his glasses and said, "So, Miss Wall, why do you want to major in botany?" His pencil was poised over the registrar's form, twitching, while portraits of Linnaeus and Asa Gray[1] looked on from his walls.

How could I answer, how could I tell him that I was born a botanist, that I had shoeboxes of seeds and piles of pressed leaves under my bed, that plants colored my dreams, that the plants had chosen me?

So I told him the truth. I was proud of my well-planned answer, its fresh-   5
man sophistication apparent to anyone, revealing what I hoped was a deep knowledge of plants. I told him that I chose botany because I wanted to learn about why asters and goldenrod looked so beautiful together. I'm sure I was smiling then, in my new red plaid shirt.

But he was not. He laid down his pencil as if there was no need to record what I had said. "Miss Wall," he said, fixing me with a disappointed smile, "I must tell you that that is not science. Beauty is not the sort of thing with which botanists concern themselves." I tried again: I'd like to learn why plants make medicines, why willow bends for baskets and why strawberries are sweeter in the shade. "Also not science," he said and he ought to know, sitting in his laboratory, a learned professor of botany. "And if you want to study beauty, you should go to art school."

I had no rejoinder; I had made a mistake. I did not have the words for resistance, only embarrassment at my error. But he promised to put me right. "I'll enroll you in General Botany so you can learn what it is." And so it began.

I didn't think about it at the time, the echo of my grandfather's first day at the Carlisle Indian school, when he was ordered to leave everything—language, culture, family—behind. But they did not cut my hair.

If a fountain could jet bouquets of chrome yellow in dazzling arches of chrysanthemum fireworks, that would be Canada goldenrod. Each three-foot stem is a geyser of tiny gold daisies, ladylike in miniature, exuberant en masse. Where the soil is damp enough, they stand side by side with their perfect counterpart, New England asters. Not the pale domesticates of the perennial border, the weak sauce of lavender or sky blue, but full-on royal purple that would make a violet shrink. The daisy-like fringe of purple petals surrounds a disc as bright as the sun at high noon, a golden-orange pool, just a tantalizing shade darker than the surrounding goldenrod. Alone, each is a botanical superlative. Together, the visual effect is stunning. Purple and gold, the heraldic colors of

1. Carl Linnaeus (1717–1778), Swedish botanist known as the "father of modern taxonomy"; Gray (1810–1888), American botanist and author of *Manual of the Botany of the Northern United States, from New England to Wisconsin and South to Ohio and Pennsylvania Inclusive* (1848), which is now referred to as Gray's *Manual*.

the king and queen of the meadow, a regal procession in complementary colors. I just wanted to know why.

10   Why do they stand beside each other when they could grow alone? There are plenty of pinks and whites and blues dotting the fields, so is it only happenstance that the magnificence of purple and gold end up side by side? Einstein himself said that "God doesn't play dice with the universe." Why is the world so beautiful? It seemed like a good question to me.

In moving from a childhood in the woods to the university I had unknowingly shifted between worldviews, from a natural history of experience, in which I knew plants as teachers and companions into the realm of science. The questions scientists raised were not "Who are you?" but "What is it?" No one asked plants "What can you tell us?" The primary question was "How does it work?" The botany I was taught was reductionist, mechanistic. Plants were reduced to objects; they were no longer subjects. The way botany was conceived and taught didn't seem to leave much room for a person who thought the way I did. The only way I could make sense of it was to conclude that the things I had always believed about plants must not be true after all.

That first plant science class was almost a disaster. I barely scraped by with a C and could not muster much enthusiasm for memorizing the concentrations of essential plant nutrients. There were times when I wanted to quit, but the more I learned, the more fascinated I became with the intricate structures that made up a leaf and the alchemy of photosynthesis. Companionship between asters and goldenrod was never mentioned, but I memorized botanical Latin as if it was poetry, eagerly tossing aside the name "goldenrod" for *Solidago canadensis*.

I scarcely doubted the primacy of scientific thought. Following the path of science trained me to separate, to distinguish perception from physical reality, to atomize complexity into its smallest components, to honor the chain of evidence and logic, to discern one thing from another, to savor the pleasure of precision. The more I did this, the better I got at it. A master's degree, a PhD followed. No doubt on the strength of the letter of recommendation from that freshman adviser, which read, "She's done remarkably well for an Indian girl."

I am grateful for the knowledge that was shared with me and deeply privileged to carry the powerful tools of science as a way of engaging the world. I remember feeling, as a new professor, as if I finally understood plants. I too began to teach the mechanics of botany, emulating the approach that I had been taught. And yet there was always something tapping at my shoulder, willing me to turn around.

15   To walk the science path I had stepped off the path of indigenous knowledge. But the world has a way of guiding your steps. Seemingly out of the blue came an invitation to a small gathering of Native elders, to talk about traditional knowledge of plants. One teacher I will never forget—a Navajo woman without a day of university botany training—spoke for hours and I hung on every word. One by one, name by name, she told of the plants in her valley. Where each one lived, when it bloomed, who it liked to live near and all its relationships, who ate it, who lined their nests with its fibers, what kind of medicine it offered. She also

shared the stories held by those plants, their origin myths, how they got their names, and what they have to tell us. She spoke of beauty.

Her words were like smelling salts for me—I was suddenly newborn wide awake—and profoundly humbled in the shallowness of my own understanding. Her knowledge was so much deeper and wider and engaged all the human ways of knowing. She could have explained asters and goldenrod. It was the beginning of my reclaiming that other way of knowing that I had helplessly let science supplant. I felt like a malnourished refugee invited to a feast, the dishes scented with the herbs of home.

I circled right back to where I had begun, to the question of beauty. Back to the questions that science does not ask, not because they aren't important, but because science as a way of knowing is too narrow for the task. Had my adviser been a better scholar, he would have celebrated my questions, not dismissed them. He offered me only the cliché that beauty is in the eye of the beholder, and since science separates the observer and the observed, by definition beauty could not be a valid scientific question. I should have been told that my questions were bigger than science could touch.

He was right about beauty being in the eye of the beholder, especially when it comes to purple and yellow. Color perception in humans relies on banks of specialized receptor cells, the rods and cones in the retina. The job of the cone cells is to absorb light of different wavelengths and pass it on to the brain's visual cortex, where it can be interpreted. The visible light spectrum, the rainbow of colors, is broad, so the most effective means of discerning color is not one generalized jack-of-all-trades cone cell, but rather an array of specialists, each perfectly tuned to absorb certain wavelengths. The human eye has three kinds. One type excels at detecting red and associated wavelengths. There is one for blue and the last one optimally perceives light of two colors: purple and yellow.

The human eye is superbly equipped to detect these colors and send a signal pulsing to the brain. This doesn't explain why I perceive them as beautiful, but it does explain why that combination gets my undivided attention. I asked my artist friends about the power of purple and gold, and they sent me right to the color wheel: these two are complementary colors, as different in nature as could be. In composing a palette, putting them together makes each more vivid; just a touch of one will bring out the other. Purple and yellow are a reciprocal pair.

Our eyes are so sensitive to these wavelengths that the cones can get oversaturated and the stimulus pours over onto the other cells. A printmaker I know showed me that if you stare for a long time at a block of yellow and then shift your gaze to a white sheet of paper, you will see it, for a moment, as violet. This phenomenon—the colored afterimage—occurs because there is energetic reciprocity between purple and yellow pigments, which goldenrod and asters knew well before we did.

The real beholder whose eye they hope to catch is a bee bent on pollination. As it turns out, goldenrod and asters appear very similarly to bee eyes and human eyes. Their striking contrast when they grow together makes them the

20

most attractive target in the whole meadow. Growing together, both receive more pollinator visits than they would if they were growing alone.

It's a testable hypothesis; it's a question of science, a question of art, and a question of beauty. Why are they beautiful together? It is a phenomenon simultaneously material and spiritual, for which we need all wavelengths of knowledge. When I stare too long at the world with science eyes, I see an afterimage of indigenous knowledge. Might science and traditional knowledge be purple and yellow to one another? We see the world more fully when we use both.

The question of goldenrod and asters was of course just emblematic of what I really wanted to know. It was an architecture of relationships that I yearned to understand. I wanted to see the shimmering threads that hold it all together and why the most ordinary scrap of meadow can rock us back on our heels in awe. And I wanted to know why we love the world.

There was a time when I teetered precariously with an awkward foot in each of two worlds: the scientific and the indigenous. But then I learned to fly. It was the bees that showed me how to move between different flowers—to drink the nectar and gather pollen from both. It is this dance of cross-pollination that can produce a new species of knowledge, a new way of being in the world. After all, there aren't two worlds, there is just this one good green earth.

25   That September pairing of purple and gold is lived reciprocity; its wisdom is that the beauty of one is illuminated by the radiance of the other. Science and art, matter and spirit, indigenous knowledge and Western science—can they be goldenrod and asters for each other? When I am in their presence, their beauty asks me for reciprocity, to be the complementary color, to make something beautiful in response.

MLA CITATION

Kimmerer, Robin Wall. "Goldenrod and Asters: My Life with Plants." *The Norton Reader: An Anthology of Nonfiction*, edited by Melissa A. Goldthwaite et al., 16th ed., W. W. Norton, 2024, pp. 616–20.

QUESTIONS

1. Robin Wall Kimmerer describes a time when she "teetered precariously with an awkward foot in each of two worlds" (paragraph 24), but she learned to bring scientific and Indigenous knowledge together. What does she value from each of those worlds? How do those areas of knowledge complement each other?

2. Beauty is a theme in Kimmerer's essay. What disciplines does she draw from to discuss beauty?

3. Choose two disciplines or areas of knowledge that interest you. What distinguishes these disciplines? How might you bring these areas of knowledge together? Write a proposal for an interdisciplinary project that looks at a specific question through the lenses of two disciplines.

ANNA LOWENHAUPT TSING AND NILS BUBANDT
Swimming with Crocodiles

L EARNING OFTEN TAKES circuitous, vortexlike routes. Certainly it did for us. We had set out to the Raja Ampat islands of West Papua to study sea cucumbers, which, since the 1990s, have been one of the most important elements to the local economy, boiled and dried and exported to China. Perhaps we should have been suspicious about this ostensibly straightforward task from the beginning. Perhaps we should not have been surprised when the sea cucumbers gave way to a larger story, one that would change our understanding of this time of heedless human influence on the earth's environment.

Our plan was to stop in every Indonesian city along the way to the islands and inquire of marine-product merchants about the sea cucumber trade, which we assumed would be buzzing, but the merchants largely put us off. When we arrived in Raja Ampat, the villagers were too busy with the tourist trade to care about sea cucumbers. We were told to visit Mayalibit Bay, where it was said that sea cucumbers remain an important livelihood, but when we got there, we learned that no one was harvesting sea cucumbers anymore. Too many people had died from attacks by crocodiles.

The first indication of this came from Mister Rodeo, an old man so named for the large cowboy hat he sported. Mister Rodeo was a spirit quester who had spent many months living with the occult beings that dwell in the mountains of Waigeo. We were sheltering from a heavy downpour in his house one afternoon when he told us about the recent shift in crocodile behavior. "Crocodiles were never evil in the past," he said, using the Indonesian word *jahat*, which means "evil" and "demonic" as well as "criminal." But in the last ten years, there had been half a dozen attacks in the region. What might have caused the crocodiles to turn into demons?

There are twenty-three extant crocodilian species, all descended from a lineage a quarter-billion years old, predating the fifth mass extinction and surviving the dinosaurs. They maintain healthy bodies, well defended against disease. Their blood coagulates almost immediately in response to flesh wounds or even amputations. At full stature, a crocodile has no enemies to fear—except humans.

For citizens in Southeast Asia, the "Great Acceleration" that characterized   5
the twentieth century brought about cheap, accessible water transportation via outboard motors known as "Johnsons" (after the American company that supplied them as war machines during the US-Indochina War). Increased transportation has led to increased coastal development, destroying crocodile habitats. Those creatures not maimed by passing boats are caused crippling pain by the shriek of motors.

Originally published in Orion *(2020), a quarterly, advertisement-free, nonprofit magazine focused on nature, culture, and place through a lens of ecological awareness.*

The sudden encroachment of humans over crocodiles gave way to a rapid boost in the crocodile skin trade. Saltwater crocodiles, whose scales are less obstructive to the creation of leather fashion goods, were in particularly high demand. By the 1970s, the populations of all species of crocodile were crashing on a global scale. Concerned about the decline but failing to see a full stop to the trade, conservationists began to encourage crocodile ranching, a practice in which wild crocodile eggs are gathered and raised in captivity for the leather industry.

When the bottom fell out of the crocodile skin market in the 1990s and the ranches ceased their turnover, crocodile populations slowly began to recover. Where hunters had once killed off all adults, mature crocodiles were now reemerging across Southeast Asia, larger and more hostile than ever before. Were they seeking revenge? We thought of the work of the philosopher Isabelle Stengers, who refers to the biogeology of the planet as Gaia. In her book *In Catastrophic Times*, she suggests that Gaia is striking back against environmental insults. The world she depicts is one in which we no longer can assume passivity of the landscape. Might crocodiles be among the agents of this movement?

As we traveled to villages where crocodile attacks had occurred, we found ourselves embroiled in further mysteries. Beyond the narrative of hungry and dangerous crocodiles were those of crocodiles as guardian spirits, sorcerers, enactors of God's will. Through them all was a constant refrain: "There's no proof." There is something unknowable about these encounters, we were told. Perhaps crocodiles attack because they are commandeered by spirits, by sorcery, by ancestral anger. Or perhaps because they are hungry? One can guess the reasons, but the true cause remains hidden in the same way a crocodile hides in a murky estuary.

Traditional beliefs, so we often tell ourselves in the West, provided certainty to villagers in simpler times before modernity sent our world awry. In Raja Ampat we found no such firm beliefs to pin down the crocodile attacks. Unable to hold fast to the imagined clarity of modern research, we fell under the spell of uncertainty. Doubt entered our way of knowing alongside danger: another feature of the Anthropocene.[1] When Gaia strikes back against anthropogenic design, we are left with designs undone and gone astray. And when the best-laid plans for the mastery of the earth prove unrealizable, neatness itself becomes suspicious, and we suddenly return to what we once imagined as archaic fears: what of the beast lurking just below the surface?

10   In the dream of modernity, human ways were separated from nonhuman ones so that the former could conquer the latter. But how irrelevant the match seems to someone sitting in a small boat at night amid the phosphorescence of a tropical sea. There is no Man versus Nature toss-up to prepare for, no prize to seek; instead, there is only the possibility of something out there surrounding you. Perhaps there are no crocodiles at all, or perhaps one is right under

1. The proposed name for the time during which human activities have impacted the environment enough to constitute a distinct geological change.

the boat. Even if your flashlight catches two red eyes, who knows what it is in a world where both witches and crocodiles have shining red eyes?

Piecing through our own morass of doubts, the best we can do is offer a report on what we learned while inquiring about crocodile attacks in Raja Ampat. The stories we heard formed a thickening cascade, as one attack followed another. The following dates are the years in which the attacks are reported to have occurred. All people involved have been given pseudonyms and place-names obscured, but the reports are as true as we know how to make them.

Mayalibit Bay is a great expanse of brackish water embraced by the nickel-and-limestone arms of the island of Waigeo. Sediments run down the sharp slopes, especially where industrial logging has left skeletal landscapes of tangled vines. Caught in the twining roots of mangroves, mud piles up in plains and estuaries reaching into the water, which sometimes is so dark and thick that underwater one can barely see a meter ahead. This is not a good distance to watch for crocodiles.

Pilu, 2014

A man, let's call him Ali, went out to hunt birds in the mountains. Ali paddled across the bay and took his boat into the mouth of a muddy creek. Tying the boat to a tree, he might have proceeded into the forest on foot. He might have come back later. No one knows because no one ever saw him again. Ali's boat was found tied neatly where he left it, with the white cockatoo that he used as a lure still perched on its wooden pole.

A fellow villager heard someone cry out. Search parties went out to look for him, and offerings of cigarettes and betel nut were made, but Ali was never found. In the next few days, help was called in from surrounding villages. Pilu villagers sought out Pak Johannes, an elder from Garuwa. Many believe that Pak Johannes can speak to crocodiles, but he insists that he speaks only to God and the ancestors. In fact, he resents the implication that he speaks to crocodiles; only witches speak animal language, he says. Then Pak Johannes fixes us with an intense stare: "For all I know, it is you Westerners who speak the language of crocodiles." For the descendant of a population ravaged for centuries by Dutch-sponsored raids, this possibility is not farfetched. Maybe Westerners are the real witches?

Warwar, 2014

A few months later, an incident happened near the village of Warwar. Eager to make some money, a teenaged boy named Rudy went to dive for sea cucumbers at Serpent Point. It was night, the time when sea cucumbers are most active and easiest to find. By morning he hadn't returned. Offerings were made on the village pier. A few days later, Rudy's body was found in the creek at Serpent Point. The intestines were out of the body; the legs and feet were fractured and gnawed. Strangely, in response to the offerings, the crocodile had presented the body standing up with its feet in the mud. The head of the corpse stared out above the waterline.

15

Pak Riady, the village leader, could not comprehend the incident. Crocodiles, he mused, are traditional enemies of wild boar as well as dogs, but they had never before indulged in human flesh. He had heard the idea that once a crocodile tastes human flesh, it won't stop, but the recent attacks were distributed widely, impossible to attribute to an individual crocodile. He wondered if crocodiles who have found a good food source invite each other to dinner—just as humans do. Perhaps this crocodile had been a guest of one such gathering and had there acquired a taste for humans.

But why pick Rudy, a young man so full of life? Here Pak Riady, a pious Muslim, could only refer us to the will of God. Rudy's allotted time was over.

Garuwa, circa 2010

Before the deaths began, several people had been hurt, but not killed, by crocodiles. One couple, Maria and Darius, told us they were working in their garden, which lay at some distance from their village house. Heading home that evening, Darius suggested that they gather clams for dinner. Maria wanted to go straight home, but Darius insisted, and so they stopped to look for clams. Maria was washing her feet in the stream when a crocodile grabbed her leg. She cried out and Darius ran over, grabbed her, and attempted to pry her out of the crocodile's grasp, which tore the flesh off her leg. Then Darius heard a bird call to him in a human voice: "Yell!" it instructed him. So Darius yelled, and at once the crocodile let go.

Maria was transported to the hospital. Her foot is still deformed from the bite, but she gets along well despite it. The attack actually seems to have drawn husband and wife together in affection and generous regard. Darius recalls the

incident with a sense of both bewilderment and blessing. And what was that bird with the human voice? Darius believes it was God. Perhaps the crocodile had been "sent" by sorcery, he says, as a result of Maria's troubles with her siblings over their land. One never can tell with crocodiles.

Even the bodies of crocodiles are uncannily unknowable, almost human-like in their strangeness. Crocodiles attack not with their mouths but with their hands, the villagers explained to us. They use their hands to pull their victim into the water, hold them in a tight embrace, and roll around until the victim has drowned. Then they place the body on their back, as a villager might carry garden produce home in woven baskets.

To Western science, this explanation does not gel with natural history. The limbs of the saltwater crocodile are almost vestigial compared to other crocodiles, so well adapted are they to swimming. Crocodiles therefore must grab with their teeth. Even so, it's hard to ignore the sense of crocodile-human connection the Raja Ampat stories offer. Most animals are said only to have feet, after all, not hands. This resemblance brought our interlocutors closest to thinking with the crocodile: "Perhaps he was hungry," people said, distancing themselves from the more personal motivations for the attack.

Markan, 2015

Just a few months after the attack at Warwar, a young man named Hanson was taken near Markan. He too had gone out to dive for sea cucumbers at night. He was with two friends, both of whom took the land side of the boat, while he took the deepwater side. The friends heard him cry out for help, and at first they thought they could indeed help, because they saw him rise up from the water, fighting the crocodile. But then the crocodile dove, bringing Hanson under. The friends could only get back into the boat and go home to report his fate.

People from nearby villages came to ask the crocodile to return the body. A group found something along a muddy stream amid the mangroves—the crocodile, pulling the corpse back into the water. (We were told that crocodiles stash their victims for a few days until the meat softens.) Pak Johannes, the elder from Garuwa, prepared offerings, casting them into the water, and he prayed for assistance. In half an hour, the corpse came floating up from the bottom of the river. The crocodile had surrendered the body.

Why had Hanson been attacked? Several theories circulated. Hanson had quarreled with his parents, who had forbidden him from diving, but he went anyway. Many people thought that this quarrel had inadvertently angered the family's ancestors, and that is what put him in harm's way. But a second observation pushed the event in a different direction. A monitoring boat from the nongovernmental organization Conservation International had stopped by the day before Hanson's dive. The boat was patrolling the marine protected area that had been established in the bay in 2007. On their patrol they had spotted several crocodiles. "Watch out, there are crocodiles around here," the conservation monitor remembers telling Hanson. But Hanson replied boldly, "How can a crocodile eat a crocodile?" Did his comment suggest that he had been playing with black magic and now perceived himself as a crocodile? Or was it just boyish bravado, a joke?

25   Many people suggested that a crocodile would not attack someone at random. "There are three reasons a crocodile might attack a human," said Pak Abraham, a village elder. "It could be the will of God. It could be that the person trespassed against traditional custom and law. Or it could be that the crocodile was sent by a sorcerer." In the case of Hanson, the village consensus was that it was the second of these. Besides the fight with his parents, Hanson had been a harsh critic of the no-take zone established in the bay in an environmentalist-brokered conservation compact between Christian and Muslim villages. The compact was put into place through ecumenical offerings to place-based *mon* spirits. Some speculated that Hanson may have offended those spirits in his search for sea cucumbers. Perhaps environmentalism itself, in its alliance with local spirits, had claimed him.

Even as crocodiles respond to trespasses, they are also sentient animals. Pak Abraham took us back to his parents' and grandparents' time. Even though crocodiles were plenty then, Pak Abraham does not remember any attacks on humans. Crocodiles could often be seen coasting the waters of the bay, seemingly oblivious to humans. Then, when he was a teenager, crocodile hunting began in earnest. The crocodile population dwindled until there were only small ones to harvest. Crocodiles became wary, disappearing as soon as humans came into view.

Pak Abraham remembers going out at night with a friend, one paddling and one standing ready with a spear. You could find the crocodiles' eyes shining red when hit by a flashlight, he said. On a good night, you might kill two. On land, the skin was dried with salt, rolled up, and carried to the city of Sorong, where the merchants were.

Since the crash of the crocodile skin market in the 1990s, the people of Markan have increasingly turned to sea cucumbers. *Teripang gosok* is one of the most coveted of sea cucumbers. Known as "sandfish" in English, *teripang gosok* is the primary source for the dried bêche-de-mer, fetching good prices in the global commodity supply chains that end in China. Labeled as endangered on the International Union for Conservation of Nature (IUCN) Red List, sandfish are easily gathered at night when they come out to forage on the mud and sand of the bay. Hanson was the first person in the village to be attacked by a crocodile while searching for sea cucumbers, but since his death no one wants to go out. Meanwhile, crocodiles have grown braver and more numerous. They have eaten a number of village dogs. Crocodiles lunge at dogs when they stand on shore, dragging them to their death.

Pak Abraham's stories were as close as we were able to get to Indigenous natural histories. We were disappointed at first; we had hoped for more guidance on crocodile behavior. But the crocodile is an elusive creature, rarely available for close observation. It's a pool of fear, a guess within murky waters. People wondered, speculated, but explained that they did not know. One person suggested that the eggs were twisted into mangrove roots, where few people ventured. Others suggested that crocodiles must give birth to live young, because they had never seen their eggs. In the end, people told us, crocodiles are a mystery. They would turn the conversation to the question that seemed most pressing: why that victim was taken at that time. Had something been done to bring on the attack?

Housing Block 300, 2013

Mayalibit Bay has had more than its fair share of crocodile attacks, but it has not been the exclusive site for them. As we glided along Waigeo's outer coast, not far from the mouth of the bay, our friend Pak Salmon pointed to a sheltered cove: that's where the boat of the first man killed by a crocodile was found, he said. The victim lived in Housing Block 300, a new complex of houses. He had gone night diving for sea cucumbers and had never returned. His torso was found nearby. Then his head turned up to the west, near the regency capital, quite a distance away. Later, his legs were observed along the coast to the east, past the mouth of the bay.

    Saltwater crocodiles are known for their long-distance swimming, as well as for their tendency to follow coastlines. Male saltwater crocodiles swim up to thirty kilometers a day over several consecutive days, covering distances of up to four hundred kilometers in one stretch. As mobile as the Western tourists who visit the area, crocodiles from the Mayalibit Bay may reach any of the remote islands in Raja Ampat, carrying in tow whatever fragments of food they have yet to consume.

Interlude with Shape-Shifters, 2017

Following limestone coastlines with bright glittering coral reefs, we found ourselves among Beser-speaking people, migrants from Biak (off the north coast of Papua), known for their entrepreneurial ambitions and millennial dreams. Our first conversationalist on crocodile lives was Markus. We asked Markus if crocodiles can be sent by sorcery. Yes, he said, and he mimed the way a request such as that can be sent, blowing onto his lifted hand. When we asked for examples, Markus told us about spirits of the land who can appear as crocodiles. If you kill those crocodiles, the spirit, which lives in a tree, does not die. He saw two crocodiles in Waisai, the regency capital, one in the main harbor with all the boats and the other blithely crossing a city street. Both were killed as soon as people saw them. But what exactly was seen? When you see a crocodile, it's not immediately clear what it is: sorcerer, spirit, or perhaps ordinary animal? Even after they're killed, it's impossible to say.

Walimu, 2016

Crossing the water but still following coasts, we arrived at the island where a Russian tourist whom we will call Dimitri was attacked by a crocodile. He had been living most of the previous month at a homestay, swimming and diving in the day. How could such a thing have happened? It was not just decades but centuries since the villagers had heard of anything like this. For hundreds of years, they said, there have been no crocodile attacks on humans in that area.

After his death, Dimitri grew larger in the memory of his host family. He could free-dive to thirty meters, they said, visiting the depths "where the manta rays sleep." They turned him into a navy captain, one who could swim around the whole island of Walimu (unlike the other European at the homestay, Nick, a poor swimmer). Every day after his swim, Dimitri would eat pastries the family prepared for him. He spoke no Indonesian, so communication was difficult, but the family said he thrived on the island. When he first arrived, he was skinny, but he filled out during his stay. They'll remember him in the late afternoon, happily gobbling doughnuts.

35   Dimitri's vacation was to have ended the day before his death; he and Nick were planning to check out and return to Europe together. At the last minute, Dimitri decided to stay one more day, the family recalled, and he convinced Nick to stay too. Nick spent the day, as usual, on the beachfront reef. But Dimitri set out into the jungle with his snorkeling gear to another, more deserted place, and never came back. Nick left the next day with tears running down his face.

The family brought in the police, who looked for Dimitri for several days. Four days after his death, the search-and-rescue team found his body in a bay on the other side of the island, with one arm missing, one leg broken, and wounds to the torso, but otherwise intact. A crocodile was seen near the body, seemingly guarding it. The police took the body away to be returned to Dimitri's home country, but to the family, Dimitri's spirit, his *nín* or "shadow," seemed stuck on the island. In late afternoons, they could hear his characteristic cough in the place where they once served him doughnuts. A bad death can leave a spook.

The family went to the place where his corpse was discovered to retrieve his spirit, and they made a grave right in the middle of the tourist cottages. They poured a bottle of water out, thinking it might make the drowned spirit comfortable by clearing its airways. With stones and shells surrounding it, the grave became a kind of memorial. Dimitri was still very much there. "I never really spoke to him while he was alive, for he knew no Indonesian and only one or two words in English," said Pak Amos, the father in the family. "But now he even speaks our local language, Beser, fluently. Dimitri is my friend. I speak to him every night." Pak Amos sleeps in the nipa leaf hut next to Dimitri's memorial and often confers with him before undertaking difficult endeavors. Dimitri has become an ancestor spirit, what Beser speakers call a *rúr*.

The bay where Dimitri's body was found, where he had apparently gone snorkeling, was not an ordinary place. It was the kind of bay that local people—using the Dutch word—call a *hol*, a deep concave bay, usually deserted, and that still carries some of its additional Dutch meanings: a hollow place, a den, a lair. It was the site of the first village on Walimu, and was still guarded by five *ípon*, ancestral spirits that come out if you offend the land, for example, by logging or mining without permission. They are known to take the form of crocodiles.

Pak Lukas is the ritual expert for this ancestral place. A circumspect man, Pak Lukas does not speak carelessly about the ancestors and was initially reluctant to talk to us. And anyway, he said, his older brother, recently deceased, was really in charge of the offerings; he had only just come into this role. Slowly, he loosened up and began talking more freely. Yes, Dimitri had apparently offended the rúr spirits. Spirits are sensitive. Once Pak Lukas had gone to cut down some trees, but he had forgotten to bring betel nut for the land spirits. He immediately became sick. His whole body hurt. He started up his chain saw, but it would not cut the wood. The spirits had been offended. Only later, after he brought them a yellow rice offering, did he begin to feel better.

Pak Lukas had checked the ritual plates at the hol and found one missing. The plate that Dimitri seems to have taken was made of a powerful ancient porcelain and was known to be full of magical potential. Immensely valuable, it was a necessary component of making ritual offerings. It was also invisible and as big as a house. But how could a Western person have seen a giant invisible plate that typically only a local ritual expert could spot? Had Dimitri been an ancestor spirit all along? If ancestors can assume many forms, had they now assumed that of a Western tourist? Somehow the mystery of those "who came before" and those who come from far away had collided in a fatal crocodile attack, motivated perhaps by the mystery of crocodiles themselves.

40

SORONG, 2017

We left Raja Ampat through the city of Sorong, a raw-edged frontier town that illustrates just how much fossil fuel, sweat, compliance, and coercion it takes to create a space without crocodiles—except in cement enclosures. At our hotel, air conditioners struggled fitfully and unsuccessfully to keep out the moist, hot air. We were back in the Anthropocene as aspiration, rather than Anthropocene as warning.

We decided to cap our trip with a visit to a crocodile ranching operation we had heard about in the islands. Indonesia exports between three thousand and seven thousand skins from captive ranched saltwater crocodiles every year, mainly from farms in the province of Papua. At least there we might see an actual crocodile, rather than just hear about their mysterious presence. It was August 17, Indonesia's national birthday, and the official celebration was punctuated by the grumbling disquiet of freedom-seeking Papuans. Schoolchildren wore their formal uniforms in the morning, but hurried to take them off for the rest of the free day. We splurged on a taxi and spent the morning winding through peri-urban neighborhoods, looking for our destination. At last we found the place, a giant junkyard near the coast. Enormous earth-moving machines took up the largest space, some rusty and some still clean. Beyond them, mud and weeds: a saltwater marsh of anthropogenic abandonment. Balancing on sticks across muddy ditches, we wandered to the middle of the mess. There, indeed, was a room-size cement-and-board enclosure around a mud hole.

When conservationists started worrying about crocodiles in the late 1970s, they came up with a plan: flood the market for crocodile skins with skins from ranches. Then, they believed, there would be no need to harvest wild crocodiles. It was the kind of plan governments and development organizations love, one that offered opportunities for businessmen to take resources once common and show how they could be privatized to concentrate profits for the elite. Ranching was a modern Anthropocene dream: the idea that one could only encourage the growth of nature by *mastering* it.

Sorong became a regional center for crocodile ranching and a model for the nation. The forestry department sponsored one ranch; others were private. Sorong Motors, which owned the muddy junkyard in which we found ourselves, once had more than a thousand crocodiles in a system of interlinked cement-enclosed ponds. Now the crocodile industry had moved on to other places, and this business sat in abandonment. Pak Natu, the caretaker, showed us what was left.

45   Once, he said, the operation was vast. Now all the crocodiles had died or been sold except one, a lazy beast he estimated as seventy years old. He liked the crocodile, calling him Tuni, after the farm in Bintuni Bay from where it had come. Every week or so, he bought some fish for it. It would come out for him and even feed from his hand, he said. But it was just a remnant. The once vast ponds were now muddy swamp; the enclosures had been scavenged for their materials and were now a bit shaky. In a flood, the crocodile escaped, and it had taken fourteen men with chains to bring it back, Pak Natu recalled. But lately it didn't do anything but nap.

Pak Natu and our taxi driver threw rocks at the pool to see if they could get the crocodile's attention. It came up, looked around, saw no food, and submerged. Pak Natu kept calling for it, and, every now and again, it would surface, look around, and sink once more. We asked the taxi driver to go to a local market to buy a tuna. When Pak Natu waved a fish at the crocodile, it finally took notice, swallowing the snack in a single gulp. The crocodile then lay quietly at the surface, digesting before us. Such a patient survivor. As modernist dreams turn to mud, those of us privileged enough to survive will sit in our cement enclosures, hoping that someone will come along to throw us a fish.

There was a time when people in this area of the world nurtured their relations with crocodiles. Children could safely bathe in the bay, protected by their crocodile kin. People often developed close relations with a particular one. Indeed, we talked to members of one clan in Mayalibit Bay whose ancestors had been crocodile shape-shifters, offering protection in exchange for tobacco and betel nut. But what kinship we once enjoyed with crocodiles came to a halt with the colonial order. Viewed from this distance, the colonial separation of humans and beasts appears with its own exoticism: we call it Anthropocene. It has been a strange time, and now it forces us into a new wariness. Other natures beckon, whether of land spirits or animal kin. As dangers reemerge around us, human and not human, we find ourselves, again, swimming with crocodiles.

MLA CITATION

Tsing, Anna Lowenhaupt, and Nils Bubandt. "Swimming with Crocodiles." *The Norton Reader: An Anthology of Nonfiction*, edited by Melissa A. Goldthwaite et al., 16th ed., W. W. Norton, 2024, pp. 621–30.

Questions

1. Create an annotated map of the places where the crocodile attacks mentioned in this essay occurred. If possible, look up photos of those locations and add them to your map. What new insights can you gain from visualizing the places written about here?

2. Anna Lowenhaupt Tsing and Nils Bubandt present a range of explanations for the cause of increased crocodile attacks. What types of causes do people hypothesize as catalyzing or explaining the attacks (e.g., environmental, religious, personal, etc.)? Annotate the essay, marking and analyzing the places where explanations are offered.

3. Of the plan to farm crocodiles and harvest their skins, Tsing and Bubandt write, "It was the kind of plan governments and development organizations love" (paragraph 43). What do they mean by this, and how does the way they express it leave room for multiple opinions about the plan? What do you think of the plan?

4. This essay is coauthored. With a partner, write a brief response to "Swimming with Crocodiles," summarizing the essay's conclusions on crocodiles in Indonesia and adding your suggestions for what humans should do to repair our relationship with them. After finishing your response, discuss with your partner about what was harder and easier about working with a coauthor.

Cormac Cullinan
If Nature Had Rights

IT WAS THE SUDDEN RUSH of the goats' bodies against the side of the *boma*[1] that woke him. Picking up a spear and stick, the Kenyan farmer slipped out into the warm night and crept toward the pen. All he could see was the spotted, sloping hindquarters of the animal trying to force itself between the poles to get at the goats—but it was enough. He drove his spear deep into the hyena.

The elders who gathered under the meeting tree to deliberate on the matter were clearly unhappy with the farmer's explanation. A man appointed by the traditional court to represent the interests of the hyena had testified that his careful examination of the body had revealed that the deceased was a female who was still suckling pups. He argued that given the prevailing drought and the hyena's need to nourish her young, her behavior in attempting to scavenge food from human settlements was reasonable and that it was wrong to have killed her. The elders then cross-examined the farmer carefully. Did he appreciate, they asked, that such killings were contrary to customary law? Had he considered the hyena's situation and whether or not she had caused harm? Could he not have simply driven her away? Eventually

Originally published in Orion *(2008), a quarterly, advertisement-free, nonprofit magazine focused on nature, culture, and place through a lens of ecological awareness.*

1. Swahili for "a hut or enclosure."

the elders ordered the man's clan to pay compensation for the harm done by driving more than one hundred of their goats (a fortune in that community) into the bush, where they could be eaten by the hyenas and other wild carnivores.

The story, told to me by a Kenyan friend, illustrates African customary law's concern with restorative justice rather than retribution. Wrongdoing is seen as a symptom of a breakdown in relationships within the wider community, and the elders seek to restore the damaged relationship rather than focusing on identifying and punishing the wrongdoer.

The verdict of a traditional African court regarding hyenacide may seem of mere anthropological interest to contemporary Americans. In most of today's legal systems, decisions that harm ecological communities have to be challenged primarily on the basis of whether or not the correct procedures have been followed. Yet consider how much greater the prospects of survival would be for most of life on Earth if mechanisms existed for imposing collective responsibility and liability on human communities and for restoring damaged relations with the larger natural community. Imagine if we had elders with a deep understanding of the lore of the wild who spoke for the Earth as well as for humans. If we did, how might they order us to compensate for, say, the anticipated destruction of the entire Arctic ecosystem because of global climate change, to restore relations with the polar bears and other people and creatures who depend on that ecosystem? How many polluting power plants and vehicles would it be fair to sacrifice to make amends?

5   "So what would a radically different law-driven consciousness look like?" The question was posed over three decades ago by a University of Southern California law professor as his lecture drew to a close. "One in which Nature had rights," he continued. "Yes, rivers, lakes, trees. . . . How could such a posture in law affect a community's view of itself?" Professor Christopher Stone may as well have announced that he was an alien life form. Rivers and trees are objects, not subjects, in the eyes of the law and are by definition incapable of holding rights. His speculations created an uproar.

Stone stepped away from that lecture a little dazed by the response from the class but determined to back up his argument. He realized that for nature to have rights the law would have to be changed so that, first, a suit could be brought in the name of an aspect of nature, such as a river; second, a polluter could be held liable for harming a river; and third, judgments could be made that would benefit a river. Stone quickly identified a pending appeal to the United States Supreme Court against a decision of the Ninth Circuit that raised these issues. The Ninth Circuit Court of Appeals had found that the Sierra Club Legal Defense Fund was not "aggrieved" or "adversely affected" by the proposed development of the Mineral King Valley in the Sierra Nevada Mountains by Walt Disney Enterprises, Inc. This decision meant that the Sierra Club did not have "standing" so the court didn't need to consider the merits of the matter. Clearly, if the Mineral King Valley itself had been recognized as having rights, it would have been an adversely affected party and would have had the necessary standing.

Fortuitously, Supreme Court Justice William O. Douglas was writing a preface to the next edition of the *Southern California Law Review*. Stone's seminal "Should Trees Have Standing? Toward Legal Rights for Natural Objects" ("Trees") was hurriedly squeezed into the journal and read by Justice Douglas before the Court issued its judgment. In "Trees," Stone argued that courts should grant legal standing to guardians to represent the rights of nature, in much the same way as guardians are appointed to represent the rights of infants. In order to do so, the law would have to recognize that nature was not just a conglomeration of objects that could be owned, but was a subject that itself had legal rights and the standing to be represented in the courts to enforce those rights. The article eventually formed the basis for a famous dissenting judgment by Justice Douglas in the 1972 case of *Sierra Club v. Morton* in which he expressed the opinion that "contemporary public concern for protecting nature's ecological equilibrium should lead to the conferral of standing upon environmental objects to sue for their own preservation."

Perhaps one of the most important things about "Trees" is that it ventured beyond the accepted boundaries of law as we know it and argued that the conceptual framework for law in the United States (and by analogy, elsewhere) required further evolution and expansion. Stone began by addressing the initial reaction that such ideas are outlandish. Throughout legal history, as he pointed out, each extension of legal rights had previously been unthinkable. The emancipation of slaves and the extension of civil rights to African Americans, women, and children were once rejected as absurd or dangerous by authorities. The Founding Fathers, after all, were hardly conscious of the hypocrisy inherent in proclaiming the inalienable rights of all men while simultaneously denying basic rights to children, women, and to African and Native Americans.

"Trees" has since become a classic for students of environmental law, but after three decades its impact on law in the United States has been limited. After it was written, the courts made it somewhat easier for citizens to litigate on behalf of other species and the environment by expanding the powers and responsibilities of authorities to act as trustees of areas used by the public (e.g., navigable waters, beaches, and parks). Unfortunately, these gains have been followed in more recent years by judicial attempts to restrict the legal standing of environmental groups. Damages for harm to the environment are now recoverable in some cases and are sometimes applied for the benefit of the environment. However, these changes fall far short of what Stone advocated for in "Trees." The courts still have not recognized that nature has directly enforceable rights.

Communities have always used laws to express the ideals to which they aspire   10
and to regulate how power is exercised. Law is also a social tool that is usually shaped and wielded most effectively by the powerful. Consequently, law tends to entrench a society's fundamental idea of itself and of how the world works. So, for example, even when American society began to regard slavery as morally abhorrent, it was not able to peaceably end the practice because the fundamental concept that slaves were property had been hard-wired into the legal system. The abolition of slavery required not only that the enfranchised recognize that slaves

were entitled to the same rights as other humans, but also a political effort to change the laws that denied those rights. It took both the Civil War and the Thirteenth Amendment to outlaw slavery. The Thirteenth Amendment, in turn, played a role in changing American society's idea of what was acceptable, thereby providing the bedrock for the subsequent civil rights movement.

In the eyes of American law today, most of the community of life on Earth remains mere property, natural "resources" to be exploited, bought, and sold just as slaves were. This means that environmentalists are seldom seen as activists fighting to uphold fundamental rights, but rather as criminals who infringe upon the property rights of others. It also means that actions that damage the ecosystems and the natural processes on which life depends, such as Earth's climate, are poorly regulated. Climate change is an obvious and dramatic symptom of the failure of human government to regulate human behavior in a manner that takes account of the fact that human welfare is directly dependent on the health of our planet and cannot be achieved at its expense.

In the scientific world there has been more progress. It's been almost forty years since James Lovelock first proposed the "Gaia hypothesis": a theory that Earth regulates itself in a manner that keeps the composition of the atmosphere and average temperatures within a range conducive to life. Derided or dismissed by most people at the time, the Gaia hypothesis is now accepted by many as scientific theory. In 2001, more than a thousand scientists signed a declaration that begins "The Earth is a self-regulating system made up from all life, including humans, and from the oceans, the atmosphere and the surface rocks," a statement that would have been unthinkable for most scientists when "Trees" was written.

The acceptance of Lovelock's hypothesis can be understood as part of a drift in the scientific world away from a mechanistic understanding of the universe toward the realization that no aspect of nature can be understood without looking at it within the context of the systems of which it forms a part. Unfortunately, this insight has been slow to penetrate the world of law and politics.

But what if we were to imagine a society in which our purpose was to act as good citizens of the Earth as a whole?

15   What might a governance system look like if it were established to protect the rights of all members of a particular biological community, instead of only humans? Cicero[2] pointed out that each of our rights and freedoms must be limited in order that others may be free. It is far past time that we should consider limiting the rights of humans so they cannot unjustifiably prevent non-human members of a community from playing their part. Any legal system designed to give effect to modern scientific understandings (or, indeed, to many cultures' ancient understandings) of how the universe functions would have to prohibit humans from driving other species to extinction or deliberately destroying the functioning of major ecosystems. In the absence of such regulatory mechanisms, an oppressive and self-destructive regime will inevitably emerge. As indeed it has.

2. Marcus Tullius Cicero (106–43 BCE), Roman orator, philosopher, politican, and lawyer.

In particular, we should examine the fact that, in the eyes of the law, corporations are considered people and entitled to civil rights. We often forget that corporations are only a few centuries old and have been continually evolving since their inception. Imagine what could be done if we changed the fiduciary responsibilities of directors to include obligations not only to profitability but also to the whole natural world, and if we imposed collective personal liability on corporate managers and stockholders to restore any damage that they cause to natural communities. Imagine if landowners who abused and degraded land lost the right to use it. In an Earth-centered community, all institutions through which humans act collectively would be designed to require behavior that is socially responsible from the perspective of the whole community. A society whose concern is to maintain the integrity or wholeness of the Earth must also refine its ideas about what is "right" and "wrong." We may find it more useful to condone or disapprove of human conduct by considering the extent to which an action increases or decreases the health of the whole community and the quality or intimacy of the relationships between its members. As Aldo Leopold's[3] famous land ethic states, "a thing is right when it tends to preserve the integrity, stability, and beauty of the biotic community. It is wrong when it tends otherwise." From this perspective, individual and collective human rights must be contextualized within, and balanced against, the rights of the other members and communities of Earth.

On September 19, 2006, the Tamaqua Borough of Schuylkill County, Pennsylvania, passed a sewage sludge ordinance that recognizes natural communities and ecosystems within the borough as legal persons for the purposes of enforcing civil rights. It also strips corporations that engage in the land application of sludge of their rights to be treated as "persons" and consequently of their civil rights. One of its effects is that the borough or any of its residents may file a lawsuit on behalf of an ecosystem to recover compensatory and punitive damages for any harm done by the land application of sewage sludge. Damages recovered in this way must be paid to the borough and used to restore those ecosystems and natural communities.

According to Thomas Linzey, the lawyer from the Community Environmental Legal Defense Fund who assisted Tamaqua Borough, this ordinance marks the first time in the history of municipalities in the United States that something like this has happened. Coming after more than 150 years of judicially sanctioned expansion of the legal powers of corporations in the US, this ordinance is more than extraordinary—it is revolutionary. In a world where the corporation is king and all forms of life other than humans are objects in the eyes of the law, this is a small community's Boston tea party.[4]

In Africa, nongovernmental organizations in eleven countries are also asserting local community rights in order to promote the conservation of bio-

3. American writer, scientist, and naturalist (1887–1948), author of *A Sand County Almanac* (1949), which includes his essay "The Land Ethic."
4. American colonist protest (1773) against the British-imposed Tea Act.

diversity and sustainable development. Members of the African Biodiversity Network (ABN) have coined the term "cultural biodiversity" to emphasize that knowledge and practices that support biodiversity are embedded in cultural tradition. The ABN works with rural communities and schools to recover and spread traditional knowledge and practices.

20   This is part of a wider effort to build local communities, protect the environment by encouraging those communities to value, retain, and build on traditional African cosmologies, and to govern themselves as part of a wider Earth community.

These small examples, emerging shoots of what might be termed "Earth democracy," are pressing upward despite the odds. It may well be that Earth-centered legal systems will have to grow organically out of human-scale communities, and communities of communities, that understand that they must function as integrated parts of wider natural communities. In the face of climate change and other enormous environmental challenges, our future as a species depends on those people who are creating the legal and political spaces within which our connection to the rest of our community here on Earth is recognized. The day will come when the failure of our laws to recognize the right of a river to flow, to prohibit acts that destabilize Earth's climate, or to impose a duty to respect the intrinsic value and right to exist of all life will be as reprehensible as allowing people to be bought and sold. We will only flourish by changing these systems and claiming our identity, as well as assuming our responsibilities, as members of the Earth community.

MLA CITATION

Cullinan, Cormac. "If Nature Had Rights." *The Norton Reader: An Anthology of Nonfiction*, edited by Melissa A. Goldthwaite et al., 16th ed., W. W. Norton, 2024, pp. 631–36.

QUESTIONS

1. Annotate the moments in which Cormac Cullinan makes an analogy between extending rights to nature and extending rights to enslaved people, women, and children. Explain the logic behind these analogies. How can a tree or an animal be like a person or a class of persons? When does it make sense to use the law in this way? When might it be a bad idea?

2. Cullinan asks, "What might a governance system look like if it were established to protect the rights of all members of a particular biological community, instead of only humans?" (paragraph 15). What are the features of that system for Cullinan? Point to passages that support your answer.

3. Cullinan often references slavery in his argument. Explain the comparisons he makes. Do you find these comparisons compelling? Why or why not?

4. Write an argument either for or against giving legal rights to elements of nature. If you argue for such rights, use evidence beyond what Cullinan provides.

WILLIAM CRONON

The Trouble with Wilderness

P RESERVING WILDERNESS has for decades been a fundamental tenet—indeed, a passion—of the environmental movement, especially in the United States. For many Americans, wilderness stands as the last place where civilization, that all-too-human disease, has not fully infected the earth. It is an island in the polluted sea of urban-industrial modernity, a refuge we must somehow recover to save the planet. As Henry David Thoreau famously declared, "In Wildness is the preservation of the World."

But is it? The more one knows of its peculiar history, the more one realizes that wilderness is not quite what it seems. Far from being the one place on earth that stands apart from humanity, it is quite profoundly a human creation—indeed, the creation of very particular human cultures at very particular moments in human history. It is not a pristine sanctuary where the last remnant of an endangered but still transcendent nature can be encountered without the contaminating taint of civilization. Instead, it is a product of that civilization. As we gaze into the mirror it holds up for us, we too easily imagine that what we behold is nature when in fact we see the reflection of our own longings and desires. Wilderness can hardly be the solution to our culture's problematic relationship with the nonhuman world, for wilderness is itself a part of the problem.

To assert the unnaturalness of so natural a place may seem perverse: we can all conjure up images and sensations that seem all the more hauntingly real for having engraved themselves so indelibly on our memories. Remember this? The torrents of mist shooting out from the base of a great waterfall in the depths of a Sierra Nevada canyon, the droplets cooling your face as you listen to the roar of the water and gaze toward the sky through a rainbow that hovers just out of reach. Or this: Looking out across a desert canyon in the evening air, the only sound a lone raven calling in the distance, the rock walls dropping away into a chasm so deep that its bottom all but vanishes as you squint into the amber light of the setting sun. Remember the feelings of such moments, and you will know as well as I do that you were in the presence of something irreducibly nonhuman, something profoundly Other than yourself. Wilderness is made of that too.

And yet: what brought each of us to the places where such memories became possible is entirely a cultural invention.

For the Americans who first celebrated it, wilderness was tied to the myth of the frontier. The historian Frederick Jackson Turner wrote the classic academic statement of this myth in 1893, but it had been part of American thought for well over a century. As Turner described the process, Easterners and European immigrants, in moving to the wild lands of the frontier, shed the

5

William Cronon published a number of versions of this essay, each aimed at a different audience. This version comes from the New York Times *(1995); another appears as the introduction to a book Cronon edited,* Uncommon Ground: Toward Reinventing Nature *(1995), a collection of essays on the environment.*

trappings of civilization and thereby gained an energy, an independence and a creativity that were the sources of American democracy and national character. Seen this way, wilderness became a place of religious redemption and national renewal, the quintessential location for experiencing what it meant to be an American.

Those who celebrate the frontier almost always look backward, mourning an older, simpler world that has disappeared forever. That world and all its attractions, Turner said, depended on free land—on wilderness. It is no accident that the movement to set aside national parks and wilderness areas gained real momentum just as laments about the vanishing frontier reached their peak. To protect wilderness was to protect the nation's most sacred myth of origin.

The decades following the Civil War saw more and more of the nation's wealthiest citizens seeking out wilderness for themselves. The passion for wild land took many forms: enormous estates in the Adirondacks and elsewhere (disingenuously called "camps" despite their many servants and amenities); cattle ranches for would-be roughriders on the Great Plains; guided big-game hunting trips in the Rockies. Wilderness suddenly emerged as the landscape of choice for elite tourists. For them, it was a place of recreation.

In just this way, wilderness came to embody the frontier myth, standing for the wild freedom of America's past and seeming to represent a highly attractive natural alternative to the ugly artificiality of modern civilization. The irony, of course, was that in the process wilderness came to reflect the very civilization its devotees sought to escape. Ever since the nineteenth century, celebrating wilderness has been an activity mainly for well-to-do city folks. Country people generally know far too much about working the land to regard unworked land as their ideal.

There were other ironies as well. The movement to set aside national parks and wilderness areas followed hard on the heels of the final Indian wars, in which the prior human inhabitants of these regions were rounded up and moved onto reservations so that tourists could safely enjoy the illusion that they were seeing their nation in its pristine, original state—in the new morning of God's own creation. Meanwhile, its original inhabitants were kept out by dint of force, their earlier uses of the land redefined as inappropriate or even illegal. To this day, for instance, the Blackfeet continue to be accused of "poaching" on the lands of Glacier National Park, in Montana, that originally belonged to them and that were ceded by treaty only with the proviso that they be permitted to hunt there.

10   The removal of Indians to create an "uninhabited wilderness" reminds us just how invented and how constructed the American wilderness really is. One of the most striking proofs of the cultural invention of wilderness is its thoroughgoing erasure of the history from which it sprang. In virtually all its manifestations, wilderness represents a flight from history. Seen as the original garden, it is a place outside time, from which human beings had to be ejected before the fallen world of history could properly begin.[1] Seen as the frontier, it

---

1. Reference to the biblical story of Adam and Eve, who were ejected from the Garden of Eden for disobeying God's command.

is a savage world at the dawn of civilization, whose transformation represents the very beginning of the national historical epic. Seen as sacred nature, it is the home of a God who transcends history, untouched by time's arrow. No matter what the angle from which we regard it, wilderness offers us the illusion that we can escape the cares and troubles of the world in which our past has ensnared us. It is the natural, unfallen antithesis of an unnatural civilization that has lost its soul, the place where we can see the world as it really is, and so know ourselves as we really are—or ought to be.

The trouble with wilderness is that it reproduces the very values its devotees seek to reject. It offers the illusion that we can somehow wipe clean the slate of our past and return to the tabula rasa[2] that supposedly existed before we began to leave our marks on the world. The dream of an unworked natural landscape is very much the fantasy of people who have never themselves had to work the land to make a living—urban folk for whom food comes from a supermarket or a restaurant instead of a field, and for whom the wooden houses in which they live and work apparently have no meaningful connection to the forests in which trees grow and die. Only people whose relation to the land was already alienated could hold up wilderness as a model for human life in nature, for the romantic ideology of wilderness leaves no place in which human beings can actually make their living from the land.

We live in an urban-industrial civilization, but too often pretend to ourselves that our real home is in the wilderness. We work our nine-to-five jobs, we drive our cars (not least to reach the wilderness), we benefit from the intricate and all too invisible networks with which society shelters us, all the while pretending that these things are not an essential part of who we are. By imagining that our true home is in the wilderness, we forgive ourselves for the homes we actually inhabit. In its flight from history, in its siren song[3] of escape, in its reproduction of the dangerous dualism that sets human beings somehow outside nature—in all these ways, wilderness poses a threat to responsible environmentalism at the end of the twentieth century.

Do not misunderstand me. What I criticize here is not wild nature, but the alienated way we often think of ourselves in relation to it. Wilderness can still teach lessons that are hard to learn anywhere else. When we visit wild places, we find ourselves surrounded by plants and animals and landscapes whose otherness compels our attention. In forcing us to acknowledge that they are not of our making, that they have little or no need for humanity, they recall for us a creation far greater than our own. In wilderness, we need no reminder that a tree has its own reasons for being, quite apart from us—proof that ours is not the only presence in the universe.

We get into trouble only if we see the tree in the garden as wholly artificial and the tree in the wilderness as wholly natural. Both trees in some ultimate sense are wild; both in a practical sense now require our care. We need to rec-

2. Latin for "clean slate."

3. An alluring but deceptive appeal. In Homer's *Odyssey*, the Sirens use irresistible songs to tempt Odysseus and his crew to steer their ship toward destruction.

oncile them, to see a natural landscape that is also cultural, in which city, suburb, countryside and wilderness each has its own place. We need to discover a middle ground in which all these things, from city to wilderness, can somehow be encompassed in the word "home." Home, after all, is the place where we live. It is the place for which we take responsibility, the place we try to sustain so we can pass on what is best in it (and in ourselves) to our children.

15   Learning to honor the wild—learning to acknowledge the autonomy of the other—means striving for critical self-consciousness in all our actions. It means that reflection and respect must accompany each act of use, and means we must always consider the possibility of nonuse. It means looking at the part of nature we intend to turn toward our own ends and asking whether we can use it again and again and again—sustainably—without diminishing it in the process. Most of all, it means practicing remembrance and gratitude for the nature, culture and history that have come together to make the world as we know it. If wildness can stop being (just) out there and start being (also) in here, if it can start being as humane as it is natural, then perhaps we can get on with the unending task of struggling to live rightly in the world—not just in the garden, not just in the wilderness, but in the home that encompasses them both.

MLA CITATION

Cronon, William. "The Trouble with Wilderness." *The Norton Reader: An Anthology of Nonfiction*, edited by Melissa A. Goldthwaite et al., 16th ed., W. W. Norton, 2024, pp. 637–40.

QUESTIONS

1. In paragraph 12, William Cronon writes, "We live in an urban-industrial civilization, but too often pretend to ourselves that our real home is in the wilderness." Cronon gives no examples. What examples might back up Cronon's statement? Can you think of counterexamples as well?

2. Who is Cronon's "we" throughout his essay? Why does he use "we" so frequently?

3. Cronon raises the issue of whether wilderness provides us with a "mirror" (paragraph 2). Look through the essay for similar visual imagery; then explain the role that such imagery plays.

4. If you found significant counterexamples in response to question 1, write an essay in which you interrogate or object to one or more aspects of Cronon's argument.

EDWARD ABBEY
The Great American Desert

I N MY CASE IT WAS LOVE AT FIRST SIGHT. This desert, all deserts, any desert. No matter where my head and feet may go, my heart and my entrails stay behind, here on the clean, true, comfortable rock, under the black sun of God's forsaken country. When I take on my next incarnation, my bones will remain bleaching nicely in a stone gulch under the rim of some faraway plateau, way out there in the back of beyond. An unrequited and excessive love, inhuman no doubt but painful anyhow, especially when I see my desert under attack. "The one death I cannot bear," said the Sonoran-Arizonan poet Richard Shelton. The kind of love that makes a man selfish, possessive, irritable. If you're thinking of a visit, my natural reaction is like a rattlesnake's—to warn you off. What I want to say goes something like this.

Survival Hint #1: Stay out of there. Don't go. Stay home and read a good book, this one for example. The Great American Desert is an awful place. People get hurt, get sick, get lost out there. Even if you survive, which is not certain, you will have a miserable time. The desert is for movies and God-intoxicated mystics, not for family recreation.

Let me enumerate the hazards. First the Walapai tiger, also known as cone-nose kissing bug. *Triatoma protracta* is a true bug, black as sin, and it flies through the night quiet as an assassin. It does not attack directly like a mosquito or deerfly, but alights at a discreet distance, undetected, and creeps upon you, its hairy little feet making not the slightest noise. The kissing bug is fond of warmth and like Dracula requires mammalian blood for sustenance. When it reaches you the bug crawls onto your skin so gently, so softly that unless your senses are hyperacute you feel nothing. Selecting a tender point, the bug slips its conical proboscis into your flesh, injecting a poisonous anesthetic. If you are asleep you will feel nothing. If you happen to be awake you may notice the faintest of pinpricks, hardly more than a brief ticklish sensation, which you will probably disregard. But the bug is already at work. Having numbed the nerves near the point of entry the bug proceeds (with a sigh of satisfaction, no doubt) to withdraw blood. When its belly is filled, it pulls out, backs off, and waddles away, so drunk and gorged it cannot fly.

At about this time the victim awakes, scratching at a furious itch. If you recognize the symptoms at once, you can sometimes find the bug in your vicinity and destroy it. But revenge will be your only satisfaction. Your night is ruined. If you are of average sensitivity to a kissing bug's poison, your entire body breaks out in hives, skin aflame from head to toe. Some people become seriously ill, in many cases requiring hospitalization. Others recover fully after five or six hours except for a hard and itchy swelling, which may endure for a week.

Solicited in 1973 for the hiking book Sierra Club Naturalist's Guide to the Deserts of the Southwest *(1977), this essay was, in revised form, also collected in Edward Abbey's* The Journey Home: Some Words in Defense of the American West *(1977).*

5   After the kissing bug, you should beware of rattlesnakes; we have half a
dozen species, all offensive and dangerous, plus centipedes, millipedes, taran-
tulas, black widows, brown recluses, Gila monsters, the deadly poisonous coral
snakes, and giant hairy desert scorpions. Plus an immense variety and near-
infinite number of ants, midges, gnats, bloodsucking flies, and blood-guzzling
mosquitoes. (You might think the desert would be spared at least mosquitoes?
Not so. Peer in any water hole by day: swarming with mosquito larvae. Venture
out on a summer's eve: The air vibrates with their mournful keening.) Finally,
where the desert meets the sea, as on the coasts of Sonora and Baja California, we have the usual assortment of obnoxious marine life: sandflies, ghost
crabs, stingrays, electric jellyfish, spiny sea urchins, man-eating sharks, and
other creatures so distasteful one prefers not even to name them.
           It has been said, and truly, that everything in the desert either stings, stabs,
stinks, or sticks. You will find the flora here as venomous, hooked, barbed,
thorny, prickly, needled, saw-toothed, hairy, stickered, mean, bitter, sharp, wiry,
and fierce as the animals. Something about the desert inclines all living things
to harshness and acerbity. The soft evolve out. Except for sleek and oily growths
like the poison ivy—oh yes, indeed—that flourish in sinister profusion on the
dank walls above the quicksand down in those corridors of gloom and labyrin-
thine monotony that men call canyons.
           We come now to the third major hazard, which is sunshine. Too much of
a good thing can be fatal. Sunstroke, heatstroke, and dehydration are common
misfortunes in the bright American Southwest. If you can avoid the insects,
reptiles, and arachnids, the cactus and the ivy, the smog of the southwestern
cities, and the lung fungus of the desert valleys (carried by dust in the air), you
cannot escape the desert sun. Too much exposure to it eventually causes, quite
literally, not merely sunburn but skin cancer.
           Much sun, little rain also means an arid climate. Compared with the high
humidity of more hospitable regions, the dry heat of the desert seems at first not
terribly uncomfortable—sometimes even pleasant. But that sensation of comfort is false, a deception, and therefore all the more dangerous, for it induces
overexertion and an insufficient consumption of water, even when water is available. This leads to various internal complications, some immediate—sunstroke,
for example—and some not apparent until much later. Mild but prolonged dehydration, continued over a span of months or years, leads to the crystallization of
mineral solutions in the urinary tract, that is, to what urologists call urinary
calculi or kidney stones. A disability common in all the world's arid regions.
Kidney stones, in case you haven't met one, come in many shapes and sizes,
from pellets smooth as BB shot to highly irregular calcifications resembling
asteroids, Vietcong shrapnel, and crown-of-thorns starfish. Some of these
objects may be "passed" naturally; others can be removed only by means of the
Davis stone basket or by surgery. Me—I was lucky; I passed mine with only a
groan, my forehead pressed against the wall of a pissoir in the rear of a Tucson
bar that I cannot recommend.
           You may be getting the impression by now that the desert is not the most
suitable of environments for human habitation. Correct. Of all the Earth's

climatic zones, excepting only the Antarctic, the deserts are the least inhabited, the least "developed," for reasons that should now be clear.

You may wish to ask, Yes, okay, but among North American deserts which   10
is the *worst*? A good question—and I am happy to attempt an answer.

Geographers generally divide the North American desert—what was once
termed "the Great American Desert"—into four distinct regions or subdeserts.
These are the Sonoran Desert, which comprises southern Arizona, Baja California, and the state of Sonora in Mexico; the Chihuahuan Desert, which
includes west Texas, southern New Mexico, and the states of Chihuahua and
Coahuila in Mexico; the Mojave Desert, which includes southeastern California
and small portions of Nevada, Utah, and Arizona; and the Great Basin Desert,
which includes most of Utah and Nevada, northern Arizona, northwestern
New Mexico, and much of Idaho and eastern Oregon.

Privately, I prefer my own categories. Up north in Utah somewhere is the
canyon country—places like Zeke's Hole, Death Hollow, Pucker Pass, Buck-
skin Gulch, Nausea Crick, Wolf Hole, Mollie's Nipple, Dirty Devil River, Horse
Canyon, Horseshoe Canyon, Lost Horse Canyon, Horsethief Canyon, and
Horseshit Canyon, to name only the more classic places. Down in Arizona and
Sonora there's the cactus country; if you have nothing better to do, you might
take a look at High Tanks, Salome Creek, Tortilla Flat, Esperero ("Hoper") Canyon, Holy Joe Peak, Depression Canyon, Painted Cave, Hell Hole Canyon,
Hell's Half Acre, Iceberg Canyon, Tiburon (Shark) Island, Pinacate Peak, Infernal Valley, Sykes Crater, Montezuma's Head, Gu Oidak, Kuakatch, Pisinimo,
and Baboquivari Mountain, for example.

Then there's The Canyon. *The* Canyon. The Grand. That's one world. And
North Rim—that's another. And Death Valley, still another, where I lived one
winter near Furnace Creek and climbed the Funeral Mountains, tasted Badwa-
ter, looked into the Devil's Hole, hollered up Echo Canyon, searched for and
never did find Seldom Seen Slim.[1] Looked for *satori*[2] near Vana, Nevada, and
found a ghost town named Bonnie Claire. Never made it to Winnemucca.
Drove through the Smoke Creek Desert and down through Big Pine and Lone
Pine and home across the Panamints to Death Valley[3] again—home sweet home
that winter.

And which of these deserts is the worst? I find it hard to judge. They're all
bad—not half bad but all bad. In the Sonoran Desert, Phoenix will get you if the
sun, snakes, bugs, and arthropods don't. In the Mojave Desert, it's Las Vegas,
more sickening by far than the Glauber's salt in the Death Valley sinkholes. Go to
Chihuahua and you're liable to get busted in El Paso and sandbagged in Ciudad
Juárez—where all old whores go to die. Up north in the Great Basin Desert, on

1. Nickname for Charles Ferge (1889–1968), prospector and sole resident of Ballarat
ghost town.
2. Buddhist term for "understanding or enlightenment."
3. Winnemucca . . . Death Valley, desert towns in Nevada and California. Throughout
the essay, Abbey uses local as well as official names to convey a feel for desert places.

the Plateau Province, in the canyon country, your heart will break, seeing the strip mines open up and the power plants rise where only cowboys and Indians and J. Wesley Powell ever roamed before.

15   Nevertheless, all is not lost; much remains, and I welcome the prospect of an army of lug-soled hiker's boots on the desert trails. To save what wilderness is left in the American Southwest—and in the American Southwest only the wilderness is worth saving—we are going to need all the recruits we can get. All the hands, heads, bodies, time, money, effort we can find. Presumably—and the Sierra Club, the Wilderness Society, the Friends of the Earth, the Audubon Society, the Defenders of Wildlife[4] operate on this theory—those who learn to love what is spare, rough, wild, undeveloped, and unbroken will be willing to fight for it, will help resist the strip miners, highway builders, land developers, weapons testers, power producers, tree chainers, clear cutters, oil drillers, dam beavers, subdividers—the list goes on and on—before that zinc-hearted, termite-brained, squint-eyed, near-sighted, greedy crew succeeds in completely californicating what still survives of the Great American Desert.

So much for the Good Cause. Now what about desert hiking itself, you may ask. I'm glad you asked that question. I firmly believe that one should never—I repeat *never*—go out into that formidable wasteland of cactus, heat, serpents, rock, scrub, and thorn without careful planning, thorough and cautious preparation, and complete—never mind the expense!—*complete* equipment. My motto is: Be Prepared.

That is my belief and that is my motto. My practice, however, is a little different. I tend to go off in a more or less random direction myself, half-baked, half-assed, half-cocked, and half-ripped. Why? Well, because I have an indolent and melancholy nature and don't care to be bothered getting all those *things* together—all that bloody *gear*—maps, compass, binoculars, poncho, pup tent, shoes, first-aid kit, rope, flashlight, inspirational poetry, water, food—and because anyhow I approach nature with a certain surly ill-will, daring Her to make trouble. Later when I'm deep into Natural Bridges Natural Moneymint or Zion National Parkinglot or say General Shithead National Forest Land of Many Abuses why then, of course, when it's a bit late, then I may wish I had packed that something extra: matches perhaps, to mention one useful item, or maybe a spoon to eat my gruel with.

If I hike with another person it's usually the same; most of my friends have indolent and melancholy natures too. A cursed lot, all of them. I think of my comrade John De Puy,[5] for example, sloping along for mile after mile like a goddamned camel—indefatigable—with those J. C. Penny [sic] hightops on his feet and that plastic pack on his back he got with five books of Green Stamps and nothing inside it but a sketchbook, some homemade jerky and a few cans of

4. Sierra Club . . . Defenders of Wildlife, organizations founded—from 1892 to 1969—to protect wilderness habitat and its plants and animals.

5. Painter (1927–2023) living in Taos, New Mexico, who met Abbey when Abbey was editing the Taos newspaper *El Crepusculo*.

green chiles. Or Douglas Peacock,[6] ex–Green Beret, just the opposite. Built like a buffalo, he loads a ninety-pound canvas pannier on his back at trailhead, loaded with guns, ammunition, bayonet, pitons and carabiners, cameras, field books, a 150-foot rope, geologist's sledge, rock samples, assay kit,[7] field glasses, two gallons of water in steel canteens, jungle boots, a case of C-rations, rope hammock, pharmaceuticals in a pig-iron box, raincoat, overcoat, two-man mountain tent, Dutch oven, hibachi, shovel, ax, inflatable boat, and near the top of the load and distributed through side and back pockets, easily accessible, a case of beer. Not because he enjoys or needs all that weight—he may never get to the bottom of that cargo on a ten-day outing—but simply because Douglas uses his packbag for general storage both at home and on the trail and prefers not to have to rearrange everything from time to time merely for the purposes of a hike. Thus my friends De Puy and Peacock; you may wish to avoid such extremes.

A few tips on desert etiquette:

1. Carry a cooking stove, if you must cook. Do not burn desert wood, which is rare and beautiful and required ages for its creation (an ironwood tree lives for over 1,000 years and juniper almost as long).
2. If you must, out of need, build a fire, then for God's sake allow it to burn itself out before you leave—do not bury it, as Boy Scouts and Campfire Girls do, under a heap of mud or sand. Scatter the ashes; replace any rocks you may have used in constructing a fireplace; do all you can to obliterate the evidence that you camped here. (The Search & Rescue Team may be looking for you.)
3. Do not bury garbage—the wildlife will only dig it up again. Burn what will burn and pack out the rest. The same goes for toilet paper: Don't bury it, *burn it*.
4. Do not bathe in desert pools, natural tanks, *tinajas*, potholes. Drink what water you need, take what you need, and leave the rest for the next hiker and more important for the bees, birds, and animals—bighorn sheep, coyotes, lions, foxes, badgers, deer, wild pigs, wild horses—whose *lives* depend on that water.
5. Always remove and destroy survey stakes, flagging, advertising signboards, mining claim markers, animal traps, poisoned bait, seismic exploration geophones, and other such artifacts of industrialism. The men who put those things there are up to no good and it is our duty to confound them. Keep America Beautiful. Grow a Beard. Take a Bath. Burn a Billboard.

Anyway—why go into the desert? Really, why do it? That sun, roaring at you all day long. The fetid, tepid, vapid little water holes slowly evaporating under a scum of grease, full of cannibal beetles, spotted toads, horsehair worms, liver flukes, and down at the bottom, inevitably, the pale cadaver of a ten-inch centipede. Those pink rattlesnakes down in The Canyon, those diamondback monsters   20

---

6. Vietnam veteran and author (b. 1942) best known for his writing about grizzly bears and wilderness.

7. Used to test water purity.

thick as a truck driver's wrist that lurk in shady places along the trail, those unpleasant solpugids and unnecessary Jerusalem crickets that scurry on dirty claws across your face at night. Why? The rain that comes down like lead shot and wrecks the trail, those sudden rockfalls of obscure origin that crash like thunder ten feet behind you in the heart of a dead-still afternoon. The ubiquitous buzzard, so patient—but only so patient. The sullen and hostile Indians, all on welfare. The ragweed, the tumbleweed, the Jimson weed, the snakeweed. The scorpion in your shoe at dawn. The dreary wind that blows all spring, the psychedelic Joshua trees waving their arms at you on moonlight nights. Sand in the soup du jour. Halazone tablets[8] in your canteen. The barren hills that always go up, which is bad, or down, which is worse. Those canyons like catacombs with quicksand lapping at your crotch. Hollow, mummified horses with forelegs casually crossed, dead for ten years, leaning against the corner of a barbed-wire fence. Packhorses at night, iron-shod, clattering over the slick-rock through your camp. The last tin of tuna, two flat tires, not enough water and a forty-mile trek to Tule Well. An osprey on a cardón cactus, snatching the head off a living fish—always the best part first. The hawk sailing by at 200 feet, a squirming snake in its talons. Salt in the drinking water. Salt, selenium, arsenic, radon and radium in the water, in the gravel, in your bones. Water so hard it bends light, drills holes in rock and chokes up your radiator. Why go there? Those places with the hardcase names: Starvation Creek, Poverty Knoll, Hungry Valley, Bitter Springs, Last Chance Canyon, Dungeon Canyon, Whipsaw Flat, Dead Horse Point, Scorpion Flat, Dead Man Draw, Stinking Spring, Camino del Diablo, Jornado del Muerto . . . Death Valley.

Well then, why indeed go walking into the desert, that grim ground, that bleak and lonesome land where, as Genghis Khan[9] said of India, "the heat is bad and the water makes men sick"?

Why the desert, when you could be strolling along the golden beaches of California? Camping by a stream of pure Rocky Mountain spring water in colorful Colorado? Loafing through a laurel slick in the misty hills of North Carolina? Or getting your head mashed in the greasy alley behind the Elysium Bar and Grill in Hoboken, New Jersey? Why the desert, given a world of such splendor and variety?

A friend and I took a walk around the base of a mountain up beyond Coconino County, Arizona. This was a mountain we'd been planning to circumambulate for years. Finally we put on our walking shoes and did it. About halfway around this mountain, on the third or fourth day, we paused for a while—two days—by the side of a stream, which the Navajos call Nasja because of the amber color of the water. (Caused perhaps by juniper roots—the water seems safe enough to drink.) On our second day there I walked down the stream, alone, to look at the canyon beyond. I entered the canyon and followed it for half the afternoon, for three or four miles, maybe, until it became a gorge so deep, narrow and dark, full of water and the inevitable quagmires of quicksand,

8. For disinfecting water.
9. Founder and ruler of the Mongol empire (c. 1162–1227).

that I turned around and looked for a way out. A route other than the way I'd come, which was crooked and uncomfortable and buried—I wanted to see what was up on top of this world. I found a sort of chimney flue on the east wall, which looked plausible, and sweated and cursed my way up through that until I reached a point where I could walk upright, like a human being. Another 300 feet of scrambling brought me to the rim of the canyon. No one, I felt certain, had ever before departed Nasja Canyon by that route.

But someone had. Near the summit I found an arrow sign, three feet long, formed of stones and pointing off into the north toward those same old purple vistas, so grand, immense, and mysterious, of more canyons, more mesas and plateaus, more mountains, more cloud-dappled sun-spangled leagues of desert sand and desert rock, under the same old wide and aching sky.

The arrow pointed into the north. But what was it pointing *at*? I looked at the 25 sign closely and saw that those dark, desert-varnished stones had been in place for a long, long time; they rested in compacted dust. They must have been there for a century at least. I followed the direction indicated and came promptly to the rim of another canyon and a drop-off straight down of a good 500 feet. Not that way, surely. Across this canyon was nothing of any unusual interest that I could see—only the familiar sun-blasted sandstone, a few scrubby clumps of black-brush and prickly pear, a few acres of nothing where only a lizard could graze, surrounded by a few square miles of more nothingness interesting chiefly to horned toads. I returned to the arrow and checked again, this time with field glasses, looking away for as far as my aided eyes could see toward the north, for ten, twenty, forty miles into the distance. I studied the scene with care, looking for an ancient Indian ruin, a significant cairn, perhaps an abandoned mine, a hidden treasure of some inconceivable wealth, the mother of all mother lodes. . . .

But there was nothing out there. Nothing at all. Nothing but the desert. Nothing but the silent world.

That's why.

MLA CITATION

Abbey, Edward. "The Great American Desert." *The Norton Reader: An Anthology of Nonfiction*, edited by Melissa A. Goldthwaite et al., 16th ed., W. W. Norton, 2024, pp. 641–47.

QUESTIONS

1. Edward Abbey loves the desert, as he states in the first sentence. Why, then, does he enumerate all of its negative features? What is his strategy?

2. Many paragraphs in this essay use lists. Choose one list, analyze its structure (if there is one), and explain what the arrangement of details achieves.

3. How do you explain the ending of this essay—both what Abbey discovers and how he uses it to convey his point?

4. Write an essay about a place you love, detailing its negative features as Abbey does.

TERRY TEMPEST WILLIAMS
The Clan of One-Breasted Women

I BELONG TO a Clan of One-breasted Women. My mother, my grand-mothers, and six aunts have all had mastectomies. Seven are dead. The two who survive have just completed rounds of chemotherapy and radiation.

I've had my own problems: two biopsies for breast cancer and a small tumor between my ribs diagnosed as "a border-line malignancy."

This is my family history.

Most statistics tell us breast cancer is genetic, hereditary, with rising percentages attached to fatty diets, childlessness, or becoming pregnant after thirty. What they don't say is living in Utah may be the greatest hazard of all.

5   We are a Mormon family with roots in Utah since 1847. The word-of-wisdom, a religious doctrine of health, kept the women in my family aligned with good foods: no coffee, no tea, tobacco, or alcohol. For the most part, these women were finished having their babies by the time they were thirty. And only one faced breast cancer prior to 1960. Traditionally, as a group of people, Mormons have a low rate of cancer.

Is our family a cultural anomaly? The truth is we didn't think about it. Those who did, usually the men, simply said, "bad genes." The women's attitude was stoic. Cancer was part of life. On February 16, 1971, the eve before my mother's surgery, I accidently picked up the telephone and overheard her ask my grandmother what she could expect.

"Diane, it is one of the most spiritual experiences you will ever encounter."

I quietly put down the receiver.

Two days later, my father took my three brothers and me to the hospital to visit her. She met us in the lobby in a wheelchair. No bandages were visible. I'll never forget her radiance, the way she held herself in a purple velour robe and how she gathered us around her.

10   "Children, I am fine. I want you to know I felt the arms of God around me."

We believed her. My father cried. Our mother, his wife, was thirty-eight years old.

Two years ago, after my mother's death from cancer, my father and I were having dinner together. He had just returned from St. George where his construction company was putting in natural gas lines for towns in southern Utah. He spoke of his love for the country: the sandstoned landscape, bare-boned and beautiful. He had just finished hiking the Kolob trail in Zion National Park. We got caught up in reminiscing, recalling with fondness our walk up Angel's

From The Witness *(1989), a small-circulation journal that called itself "a feisty, independent, provocative, intelligent, feminist voice of Christian social conscience"; later included in* Refuge: An Unnatural History of Family and Place *(1991). All notes in this piece were written by the author unless indicated otherwise.*

Landing on his fiftieth birthday and the years our family had vacationed there. This was a remembered landscape where we had been raised.

Over dessert, I shared a recurring dream of mine. I told my father that for years, as long as I could remember, I saw this flash of light in the night in the desert. That this image had so permeated my being, I could not venture south without seeing it again, on the horizon, illuminating buttes and mesas.

"You did see it," he said.

"Saw what?" I asked, a bit tentative.   15

"The bomb. The cloud. We were driving home from Riverside, California. You were sitting on your mother's lap. She was pregnant. In fact, I remember the date, September 7, 1957. We had just gotten out of the Service. We were driving north, past Las Vegas. It was an hour or so before dawn, when this explosion went off. We not only heard it, but felt it. I thought the oil tanker in front of us had blown up. We pulled over and suddenly, rising from the desert floor, we saw it, clearly, this golden-stemmed cloud, the mushroom. The sky seemed to vibrate with an eerie pink glow. Within a few minutes, a light ash was raining on the car."

I stared at my father. This was new information to me.

"I thought you knew that," my father said. "It was a common occurrence in the fifties."

It was at this moment I realized the deceit I had been living under. Children growing up in the American Southwest, drinking contaminated milk from contaminated cows, even from the contaminated breasts of their mother, my mother—members, years later, of the Clan of One-breasted Women.

It is a well-known story in the Desert West, "The Day We Bombed Utah," or   20
perhaps, "The Years We Bombed Utah."[1] Above ground atomic testing in Nevada took place from January 27, 1951, through July 11, 1962. Not only were the winds blowing north, covering "low use segments of the population" with fallout and leaving sheep dead in their tracks, but the climate was right.[2] The United States of the 1950s was red, white, and blue. The Korean War was raging. McCarthyism was rampant. Ike was it and the Cold War was hot.[3] If you were against nuclear testing, you were for a Communist regime.

Much has been written about this "American nuclear tragedy." Public health was secondary to national security. The Atomic Energy Commissioner,

1. Fuller, John G., *The Day We Bombed Utah* (New York: New American Library, 1984).

2. Discussion on March 14, 1988, with Carole Gallagher, photographer and author, *American Ground Zero: The Secret Nuclear War*, published by Random House, 1994.

3. Events and figures of the 1950s: the Korean War (1950–53), a conflict that pitted the combined forces of the Republic of Korea and the United Nations (primarily the United States) against the invading armies of communist North Korea; McCarthyism, named after Republican Senator Joseph S. McCarthy, the communist "witch hunt" led by the senator; Ike, the nickname of Dwight D. Eisenhower, president from 1953 to 1961; the Cold War, the power struggle between the Western powers and the communist bloc that began at the end of World War II [Editor's note].

Thomas Murray, said, "Gentlemen, we must not let anything interfere with this series of tests, nothing."[4]

Again and again, the American public was told by its government, in spite of burns, blisters, and nausea, "It has been found that the tests may be conducted with adequate assurance of safety under conditions prevailing at the bombing reservations."[5] Assuaging public fears was simply a matter of public relations. "Your best action," an Atomic Energy Commission booklet read, "is not to be worried about fallout." A news release typical of the times stated, "We find no basis for concluding that harm to any individual has resulted from radioactive fallout."[6]

On August 30, 1979, during Jimmy Carter's presidency, a suit was filed entitled *Irene Allen vs. the United States of America.* Mrs. Allen was the first to be alphabetically listed with twenty-four test cases, representative of nearly 1,200 plaintiffs seeking compensation from the United States government for cancers caused from nuclear testing in Nevada.

Irene Allen lived in Hurricane, Utah. She was the mother of five children and had been widowed twice. Her first husband with their two oldest boys had watched the tests from the roof of the local high school. He died of leukemia in 1956. Her second husband died of pancreatic cancer in 1978.

25   In a town meeting conducted by Utah Senator Orrin Hatch, shortly before the suit was filed, Mrs. Allen said, "I am not blaming the government, I want you to know that, Senator Hatch. But I thought if my testimony could help in any way so this wouldn't happen again to any of the generations coming up after us . . . I am really happy to be here this day to bear testimony of this."[7]

God-fearing people. This is just one story in an anthology of thousands.

On May 10, 1984, Judge Bruce S. Jenkins handed down his opinion. Ten of the plaintiffs were awarded damages. It was the first time a federal court had determined that nuclear tests had been the cause of cancers. For the remaining fourteen test cases, the proof of causation was not sufficient. In spite of the split decision, it was considered a landmark ruling.[8] It was not to remain so for long.

In April, 1987, the 10th Circuit Court of Appeals overturned Judge Jenkins' ruling on the basis that the United States was protected from suit by the legal doctrine of sovereign immunity, the centuries-old idea from England in the days of absolute monarchs.[9]

4. Szasz, Ferenc M., "Downwind from the Bomb," *Nevada Historical Society Quarterly*, Fall 1987, Vol. XXX, No. 3, p. 185.

5. Fradkin, Philip L., *Fallout* (Tucson: University of Arizona Press, 1989), 98.

6. Ibid., 109.

7. Town meeting held by Senator Orrin Hatch in St. George, Utah, April 17, 1979, transcript, 26–28.

8. Fradkin, *Fallout*, 228.

9. US v. Allen, 816 Federal Reporter, 2d/1417 (10th Circuit Court 1987), cert. denied, 108 S. Ct. 694 (1988).

In January, 1988, the Supreme Court refused to review the Appeals Court decision. To our court system, it does not matter whether the United States Government was irresponsible, whether it lied to its citizens or even that citizens died from the fallout of nuclear testing. What matters is that our government is immune. "The King can do no wrong."

In Mormon culture, authority is respected, obedience is revered, and independent thinking is not. I was taught as a young girl not to "make waves" or "rock the boat."   30

"Just let it go—" my mother would say. "You know how you feel, that's what counts."

For many years, I did just that—listened, observed, and quietly formed my own opinions within a culture that rarely asked questions because they had all the answers. But one by one, I watched the women in my family die common, heroic deaths. We sat in waiting rooms hoping for good news, always receiving the bad. I cared for them, bathed their scarred bodies and kept their secrets. I watched beautiful women become bald as cytoxan, cisplatin and adriamycin were injected into their veins. I held their foreheads as they vomited green-black bile and I shot them with morphine when the pain became inhuman. In the end, I witnessed their last peaceful breaths, becoming a midwife to the rebirth of their souls. But the price of obedience became too high.

The fear and inability to question authority that ultimately killed rural communities in Utah during atmospheric testing of atomic weapons was the same fear I saw being held in my mother's body. Sheep. Dead sheep. The evidence is buried.

I cannot prove that my mother, Diane Dixon Tempest, or my grandmothers, Lettie Romney Dixon and Kathryn Blackett Tempest, along with my aunts contracted cancer from nuclear fallout in Utah. But I can't prove they didn't.

My father's memory was correct, the September blast we drove through in 1957 was part of Operation Plumbbob, one of the most intensive series of bomb   35
tests to be initiated. The flash of light in the night in the desert I had always thought was a dream developed into a family nightmare. It took fourteen years, from 1957 to 1971, for cancer to show up in my mother—the same time, Howard L. Andrews, an authority on radioactive fallout at the National Institutes of Health, says radiation cancer requires to become evident.[10] The more I learn about what it means to be a "downwinder," the more questions I drown in.

What I do know, however, is that as a Mormon woman of the fifth generation of "Latter-Day-Saints," I must question everything, even if it means losing my faith, even if it means becoming a member of a border tribe among my own people. Tolerating blind obedience in the name of patriotism or religion ultimately takes our lives.

When the Atomic Energy Commission described the country north of the Nevada Test Site as "virtually uninhabited desert terrain," my family members were some of the "virtual uninhabitants."

10. Fradkin, Op. cit., 116.

One night, I dreamed women from all over the world circling a blazing fire in the desert. They spoke of change, of how they hold the moon in their bellies and wax and wane with its phases. They mocked at the presumption of even-tempered beings and made promises that they would never fear the witch inside themselves. The women danced wildly as sparks broke away from the flames and entered the night sky as stars.

And they sang a song given to them by Shoshoni grandmothers:

Ah ne nah, nah
nin nah nah—
Ah ne nah, nah
nin nah nah—
Nyaga mutzi
oh ne nay—
Nyaga mutzi
oh ne nay—[11]

40   The women danced and drummed and sang for weeks, preparing themselves for what was to come. They would reclaim the desert for the sake of their children, for the sake of the land.

A few miles downwind from the fire circle, bombs were being tested. Rabbits felt the tremors. Their soft leather pads on paws and feet recognized the shaking sands while the roots of mesquite and sage were smoldering. Rocks were hot from the inside out and dust devils hummed unnaturally. And each time there was another nuclear test, ravens watched the desert heave. Stretch marks appeared. The land was losing its muscle.

The women couldn't bear it any longer. They were mothers. They had suffered labor pains but always under the promise of birth. The red hot pains beneath the desert promised death only as each bomb became a stillborn. A contract had been broken between human beings and the land. A new contract was being drawn by the women who understood the fate of the earth as their own.

Under the cover of darkness, ten women slipped under the barbed wire fence and entered the contaminated country. They were trespassing. They walked toward the town of Mercury in moonlight, taking their cues from coyote, kit fox, antelope squirrel, and quail. They moved quietly and deliberately through the maze of Joshua trees. When a hint of daylight appeared they rested, drinking tea and sharing their rations of food. The women closed their eyes. The time had come to protest with the heart, that to deny one's genealogy with the earth was to commit treason against one's soul.

At dawn, the women draped themselves in mylar, wrapping long streamers of silver plastic around their arms to blow in the breeze. They wore clear masks

11. This song was sung by the Western Shoshone women as they crossed the line at the Nevada Test Site on March 18, 1988, as part of their "Reclaim the Land" action. The translation they gave was: "Consider the rabbits how gently they walk on the earth. Consider the rabbits how gently they walk on the earth. We remember them. We can walk gently also. We remember them. We can walk gently also."

that became the faces of humanity. And when they arrived on the edge of Mercury, they carried all the butterflies of a summer day in their wombs. They paused to allow their courage to settle.

The town which forbids pregnant women and children to enter because of   45
radiation risks to their health was asleep. The women moved through the streets as winged messengers, twirling around each other in slow motion, peeking inside homes and watching the easy sleep of men and women. They were astonished by such stillness and periodically would utter a shrill note or low cry just to verify life.

The residents finally awoke to what appeared as strange apparitions. Some simply stared. Others called authorities, and in time, the women were apprehended by wary soldiers dressed in desert fatigues. They were taken to a white, square building on the other edge of Mercury. When asked who they were and why they were there, the women replied, "We are mothers and we have come to reclaim the desert for our children."

The soldiers arrested them. As the ten women were blindfolded and handcuffed, they began singing:

> You can't forbid us everything
> You can't forbid us to think—
> You can't forbid our tears to flow
> And you can't stop the songs that we sing.

The women continued to sing louder and louder, until they heard the voices of their sisters moving across the mesa.

> Ah ne nah, nah
> nin nah nah—
> Ah ne nah, nah
> nin nah nah—
> Nyaga mutzi
> oh ne nay—
> Nyaga mutzi
> oh ne nay—

"Call for re-enforcement," one soldier said.

"We have," interrupted one woman. "We have—and you have no idea of our   50
numbers."

On March 18, 1988, I crossed the line at the Nevada Test Site and was arrested with nine other Utahns for trespassing on military lands. They are still conducting nuclear tests in the desert. Ours was an act of civil disobedience. But as I walked toward the town of Mercury, it was more than a gesture of peace. It was a gesture on behalf of the Clan of One-breasted Women.

As one officer cinched the handcuffs around my wrists, another frisked my body. She found a pen and a pad of paper tucked inside my left boot.

"And these?" she asked sternly.

"Weapons," I replied.

55   Our eyes met. I smiled. She pulled the leg of my trousers back over my boot.

"Step forward, please," she said as she took my arm.

We were booked under an afternoon sun and bussed to Tonapah, Nevada. It was a two-hour ride. This was familiar country to me. The Joshua trees standing their ground had been named by my ancestors who believed they looked like prophets pointing west to the promised land. These were the same trees that bloomed each spring, flowers appearing like white flames in the Mojave. And I recalled a full moon in May when my mother and I had walked among them, flushing out mourning doves and owls.

The bus stopped short of town. We were released. The officials thought it was a cruel joke to leave us stranded in the desert with no way to get home. What they didn't realize is that we were home, soul-centered and strong, women who recognized the sweet smell of sage as fuel for our spirits.

MLA CITATION

Williams, Terry Tempest. "The Clan of One-Breasted Women." *The Norton Reader: An Anthology of Nonfiction*, edited by Melissa A. Goldthwaite et al., 16th ed., W. W. Norton, 2024, pp. 648–54.

QUESTIONS

1. Terry Tempest Williams uses a variety of evidence in this essay, including personal memory, family history, government documents, and other sources. List the evidence and the order in which she uses it. Why might Williams present her material in this order?

2. The essay begins with a description of what Williams later calls a "family nightmare" (paragraph 35) and ends with a dreamlike encounter. What is the rhetorical effect of this interactive opening and closing?

3. What do you think Williams means by the statement "I must question everything" (paragraph 36)?

4. Conduct some research on an environmental issue that affects you, your friends, or your family, and, using Williams as a model, write an essay that combines both your personal experience and research.

HEATHER MCTEER TONEY
Collards Are Just as Good as Kale

ANY PEOPLE THINK of "environmentalists" as White people hugging trees, and of "the environment" as the forest or jungle as opposed to their own backyard. My relationship with the natural world, my people's relationship, is a swirl of gratitude, trauma, and spiritual connection. My Black, southern, rural ancestors connected to land and soil in ways that are both good and bad but almost always, and most of all, powerful.

Black folks have always had a deep and physical connection to the environment. The land that our ancestors were forced to work was the very same space where they lived. The field where our mothers toiled was often the place where they also gave birth. Our history has entwined us with the land in a profound way, and our connection to the land is as symbiotic as bees to flowers. Yet our voices are constantly ignored on matters concerning climate impacts and environmental protections.

Mainstream America ignores hard-learned lessons from a people who, enslaved and forced to travel across the Atlantic under unimaginable conditions, to work a land they did not know, figured out how to make things thrive and grow using their wisdom of nature and spirit. As we all face a climate crisis that threatens our very existence, the ability of my ancestors to adapt to wholly new environments offers wisdom to embrace.

I'm from an agrarian part of the country. The Mississippi Delta is home to some of the world's most fertile soil. My hometown, Greenville, Mississippi, sits midway up the state, bordered on one side by the powerful Mississippi River. Growing up, nature was a part of everything we did, whether we knew it or not. I knew when deer season started and ended, not because my family hunted but because our neighbors would take weeks to prepare and ready themselves for opening day. I could tell when the cotton and soybeans had been planted, not because I was a farmer but because of the constant roar of crop dusters overhead, spraying pesticides from small planes. I knew that dark leafy greens came during the fall, squash in the spring, and tomatoes in summer—not because I studied horticulture but because my godmother, Mrs. Loubirtha Irvin, kept a garden visible from her kitchen windows. I chuckle thinking of American society's recent lovefest with kale—and how people are still in the dark about collard greens, which have been around just as long and are just as good (better, if you ask me). From homegrown vegetables and pecan picking in the fall to knowing full well that mild winters meant the mosquitoes would be relentless in the summer, everywhere I turned I was surrounded by the interweaving of nature with Black culture, poverty, and the rural South.

From All We Can Save *(2020), a collection of essays and poems by over sixty women climate activists.*

5   It is the Black part of American culture that is especially precious to me but largely missing from the public conversation around environment and climate solutions. Environmental justice is a fundamental civil rights issue, and the rural South is plagued with so many critical needs and civil rights concerns that it's hard to keep up.

In 1969 my father came to Mississippi straight out of law school to help establish voting rights for people of the Delta, and my mother accompanied him to teach school. The conditions they embraced upon their arrival still exist today. In addition to the extreme poverty that has plagued the Delta for generations, the rights of poor people were being trampled—voter intimidation, racial discrimination, and educational disparities. People wanted to believe the promise of jobs and economic security peddled by big companies, but their operations yielded polluted land and water. The land became increasingly toxic; food insecurity was rife. In some ways, little has changed in the intervening decades. Our local elected leaders remain overwhelmed and underfunded as they face the struggles of maintaining basic infrastructure like streets and sewers, all while living with the knowledge that they need to somehow build resilience in order to survive worsening storms and other climate impacts.

When I look back at my evolution within environmental work, it has emerged from understanding that all of this—ancestry, nature, faith, and civil rights—is about community. Community is the lens so often left out of the environmental discussion, but it's vital for identifying real solutions.

My community spoke the language of faith. That's what kept us believing that things would turn around someday. Whether it be Jesus, a job, or a young Black girl known for being smart, adventurous, and a bit sassy, empowerment would come. You will not find a place filled with more love, resilience, and faith than Black communities in the Delta.

The same faith that was evident in my childhood continues to be relevant in the work of climate and, particularly, climate justice. Of all the scripture I heard growing up, the one passage I will never forget comes from the book of Hebrews:

> Now faith is assurance of things hoped for, a conviction of things not seen. . . .
> By faith we understand that the worlds have been framed by the word of God,
> so that what is seen hath not been made out of things which appear.

10   We repeated these words almost every Sunday at Agape Storge Christian Center, the nondenominational church where I was raised. There I learned not only of God's grace and mercy but also of his expectation of humanity to love all of creation and to care for it as God cares for us. As a Christian, I was taught that this was the only way to enact my faith, and with faith, nothing is impossible.

But there is an important accompaniment to this scripture that we often forget:

> For as the body apart from the spirit is dead, even so faith apart from works
> is dead.

In other words, as our pastor's wife would often lovingly say:

> You can pray and believe all you want, but without action, "ain't nothing about to happen." You just wasting the Lord's sweet, precious time.

We can plant seeds, but without watering and tending the garden, nothing grows. We can talk about how awful our elected officials are on issues of climate justice and civil rights, but if we don't go vote . . .

So where was the faith for our environment? Unbeknownst to some, you can believe in Jesus and accept the reality of climate science at the same time. Throughout my journey, my faith has made it more and more evident that it is my responsibility as a Christian to take care of what God has blessed me with, including my place on this Earth. We've done a disservice to the environmental movement by couching Christianity as dominionism (the idea that God has given us dominion or rulership over the Earth) as opposed to creation care (the understanding that God has charged us with the care and stewardship of creation, and that its prosperity is tied to our own). This is often a point of difference between conservative evangelical (and typically White) Christian theology and a more progressive understanding of the Bible often found in the Black church. The tenets of my faith require that we "tend and keep" God's creation. The idea of salvation is an idea of freedom that carries with it the sense of responsibility to care for all things, to care for one another better.

During my time as mayor of Greenville, Mississippi, 2004–2012, I had to display and use that faith more than ever. I grew from seeing nature and the environment as just part of life to respecting my responsibility to care for and protect it. While well aware of the environmental injustices that have plagued Black communities for years, I did not foresee the dramatic climate impacts my state would face during my term. Lisa Jackson, then administrator of the US Environmental Protection Agency (EPA), visited my community and later asked me to serve as chairwoman for the EPA's Local Government Advisory Committee.

Two weeks after I accepted the appointment, the BP oil spill occurred. Talk about a trial by fire—I was charged with convening local elected officials across the Gulf Coast and providing advice to the EPA on coastal cleanup from a local perspective. All this as southern cities and towns, not quite ready to accept the reality of climate change, were increasingly experiencing its effects. Over the course of my eight years as mayor, Greenville also experienced two historic flood events. Not since the great flood of 1927, when the levees broke and both lives and land were lost, had our town seen such water. Now, though, this has become a relatively common occurrence. We weren't waiting for climate change; climate change had come.

Despite hearing the Republican rhetoric of "climate change ain't real," 15 people knew that something more than a rising river was changing and amiss. The river waters were coming faster and stronger from the increased snow up north. (Heavier wintertime precipitation is yet another outcome of rising global temperatures.) Each time Chicago, Minneapolis, and other midwestern cities got strong winter storms, the snow melted into streams that eventually made their way to the Mississippi Delta. Deer and duck seasons weren't the same as in years past. Cotton and soybean crop yields were different. Increased heat, droughts, and floods meant more pests. Meanwhile, it felt like no one was listening to the voices of the poor, of rural folks, of southerners.

I was later selected to lead the EPA's Southeast Region, which includes eight states and six federally recognized tribes. My new boss, then administrator Gina McCarthy, made it clear: She didn't need shy and demure. She needed leadership that had local people in mind and could listen with an ear to help. We immediately got to work meeting with mayors and community leaders and addressing the region's toughest issues. It wasn't easy, but I had pulled together a strong team. My immediate office consisted of four attorneys, two financial specialists, three community leaders, and experts in everything from Indigenous communities to particulate matter in the air.

This team was also 90 percent Black women. All too often I secretly wished for a hidden camera to take a picture of the faces around our conference room table when a guest realized that *we* were the leadership team. And while our team was not perfect, we agreed that elevating and empowering the voices of the community was our priority. We would create seats at the table—even give up our own if need be. The issues around environmental justice and climate solutions would take each one of us, and there was no room for petty division.

At the end of 2015, I became pregnant with my first child. I was excited and fearful of what it meant. Children are especially susceptible to things like heat, asthma, allergies, and insect-borne diseases, which are all made worse by extreme weather and emissions. Behavioral and mental health challenges have also been directly linked to a worsening climate. Studies even connect climate change to violent crime. Today's evidence of hot weather being linked to increased shootings is a tragic "I told you so."

Being pregnant brought me closer to other issues too. The idea that my unborn son could suffer harm from something like the Zika virus, a disease made worse by climate change, made every insect an enemy. I listened with new ears when talking with mothers who were farm workers in Florida. Their fear of working around pesticides, and the pains they took to make sure they didn't bring home harmful chemicals on their clothes, took on new meaning. My heart ached for the mothers of Flint, Michigan, dealing with an ongoing water crisis. My environmental work was no longer simply to develop and implement sound science policy and good governance—it was to save lives and ensure our planet is habitable for kids in the years to come.

20   My fear became my focus. After leaving the EPA at the end of the Obama administration, I joined Moms Clean Air Force. We engage parents in work to move cities and towns to create municipal climate action plans and build support for clean energy and green spaces. Our community of more than 1.2 million moms and dads across the country is dedicated to reducing air pollution and protecting all children from the climate crisis we're facing. We are demanding 100 percent clean energy and no additional climate pollution in the United States as soon as possible. We are combating the draconian funding cuts and

regulatory weakening that harm children's health. We protested right alongside our own children as they marched for climate action in strikes across America on September 20, 2019. Through every effort and every channel, we are encouraging more and more parents to get involved.

My faith keeps me focused. And through it all, I know: Climate change is a threat to Black life.

African Americans, Black women—particularly southern Black women—are no strangers to environmental activism. Don't believe the contrary stereotypes. Many of us live in communities with polluted air and water. Many work in industries from housekeeping to hairdressing where we are surrounded by toxic chemicals. We live in food deserts with limited healthy food options, and the options we do have are often laden with pesticides and growth hormones not intended for our well-being.

Caring about climate change is not a bougie Black thing. Who exactly do you think is on the front lines every single day, fighting to keep our communities safe from industries, polluters, and those seeking to harm our kids? Who do you think is fighting that filthy incinerator at the end of the neighborhood block, that coal-ash pile on the way to work, or that cement plant next door to the church? Who do you think has to take care of children who are made sick on their own playgrounds but can't afford to rush to emergency rooms?

We live in pollution, play around it, work for it, and pray against it. Hell, we even sing about it. Black women are everyday environmentalists; we are climate leaders. We just don't get the headlines too often.

Rarely do we see or hear Black voices as part of national conversations   25
about climate policy, the green economy, or clean energy—even though 57 percent of Black Americans are concerned or alarmed about climate change, compared to 49 percent of White folks. We're relegated to providing an official comment on environmental justice issues like the water crisis in Flint, or we're the faces in the photos when candidates need to show that they're inclusive. Fortunately, this is slowly changing as more and more women of color step loudly up to the table and make their expertise known in climate justice and culturally competent, solution-based thinking.

For decades Dr. Beverly Wright, a professor of sociology, has been training leaders from our country's historically Black colleges and universities (HBCUs) through the Deep South Center for Environmental Justice. Her students have assisted Hurricane Katrina victims, researched climate impacts on vulnerable communities, and taken their brilliance to places like the United Nations climate negotiations in Paris. Dr. Wright is truly a sage teacher of the environmental justice movement.

Catherine Garcia Flowers fled her native New Orleans during Hurricane Katrina, only to arrive in Houston, Texas, and get bombarded by a storm once more. Instead of moving again, she became involved in climate advocacy. Catherine ran for city council in 2019 and, though she lost, her campaign elevated the issues of climate change among people in her district. A first-generation woman of both African American and Honduran heritage, she works tirelessly as the Houston-area team lead for Moms Clean Air Force and reminds me constantly that "common sense isn't common." She sees her role as "creative problem solver" and helps leaders realize that sometimes cultural solutions are found simply by validating the trauma and feelings of the underserved and harmed.

Dr. Mildred McClain is whom I picture when I imagine a matriarch of the environmental justice movement. Arrayed in colorful skirts and beautiful wraps, her presence speaks of strength, struggle, and perseverance. It's for good reason: For three decades Dr. McClain has been the voice of resilience throughout the Savannah, Georgia, community. When the air was thick with pollution from the shipping channels in the Savannah port, Dr. McClain convened community meetings so that people were part of the solution. She encouraged African Americans in her community to become certified in environmental fields like hazardous-waste removal, soil remediation, and air monitoring. Not only is she an environmental justice leader, but she is our environmental justice griot, the holder of stories past and instructor of how to survive what is to come.

In 2019 I attended the Woman's Auxiliary meeting of the National Baptist Convention in Jackson, Mississippi. A group of us from Moms Clean Air Force had produced a climate-focused Bible study, including scriptures, lessons, and ways to activate communities on climate. Each lesson offered actions that members could take either individually or collectively as a congregation—from simple nature walks with a Sunday-school class to calculating your ecological footprint to discussing air pollution and asthma.

30   The content was on point, but we'd made a miscalculation. Over 350 women leaders of Black churches showed up for our session. We quickly ran out of the fifty Bible study books we had on hand.

"Look, baby, stick this in your bra." I looked over as a stout lady with a serious-looking smile leaned over to my colleague and handed her a small piece of folded paper with her name and address written inside. We laughed, as we knew exactly what she meant.

Only items of precious value and importance are kept in a Black woman's bra. Be it a twenty-dollar bill, the phone number of a special person, or numbers to be played in the lottery, there is no more secure place on this planet. To be given a note to put in one's bra, close to the heart, is an unspoken message of trust, and this dear lady was communicating it clearly. My friend stuck the paper in her bosom. She'd make sure the woman got her book.

Across the country, women of all colors and creeds are not waiting for anyone to tell us what we should do about the climate crisis. We're giving directions, demanding action, and riding into battle to save our children and our country from the impending destruction we know may result if there is not a drastic reduction in greenhouse gas emissions and a cessation of global temperature rise. We know we don't have time to sit around and wait for someone else to make decisions. Instead, we are simply finding ways in our communities to effect change. We are sitting on sustainability boards and commissions, studying the science, galvanizing our friends and neighbors, and teaching

Sunday-school classes. We're finding every foothold of action available because our communities, our mothers, and our daughters are depending on us, and because our ancestors are watching. We shall make them all proud.

MLA CITATION

Toney, Heather McTeer. "Collards Are Just as Good as Kale." *The Norton Reader: An Anthology of Nonfiction*, edited by Melissa A. Goldthwaite et al., 16th ed., W. W. Norton, 2024, pp. 655–61.

QUESTIONS

1. Annotate this essay by researching and offering a few sentences of biographical information and professional achievement for some of the Black women environmentalists that Heather McTeer Toney names.

2. Toney makes a case for the importance of Black voices in the environmental movement. What reasons does she offer for this conviction?

3. In paragraph 12 and elsewhere, Toney describes how her faith lives alongside her environmental commitments. When does religion help (or hinder) work to protect the earth?

4. Research a hyperlocal environmental problem in your community, such as a polluted creek or a neglected playground, and write a memo describing both the problem and some steps people should take to address it.

AIMEE NEZHUKUMATATHIL
Firefly

HEN THE FIRST GLIMMER-POP of firefly light appears on a summer night, I always want to call my mother just to say hello. The bibliography of the firefly is a tender and electric dress, a small flame sputtering in the ditches along a highway, and the elytra covering the hind wings of the firefly lift like a light leather, suppler than any other beetle's. In flight, it is like a loud laugh, the kind that only appears in summer, with the stink of meats sizzling somewhere down the street, and the mouths of neighborhood children stained with popsicle juice and hinging open with the excitement of a ball game or tag.

I used to see fireflies as we drove home from family vacations, back to rural western New York. My father loved to commute through the night, to avoid the summer glare and heat. My sister and I would be wrapped in blankets, separated by a giant ice chest in the back seat, and I'd fall in and out of a sleep made all the more delicious by hearing the pleasant murmurings of my parents

From World of Wonders: In Praise of Fireflies, Whale Sharks, and Other Astonishments *(2020), a collection of short essays on nature by Aimee Nezhukumatathil.*

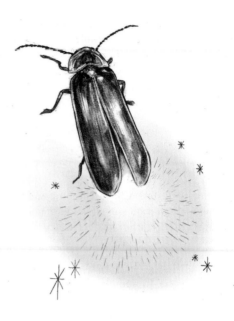

in the front. Sometimes I tried to listen, but looking out the car window, I'd always get distracted by the erratic flashes of light blurring past us.

For a couple of weeks every June, in the Great Smoky Mountains, the only species of synchronous firefly in North America converges for a flashy display. Years ago, my family stopped in this area during one of our epic road trips. My father knew to park our car away from the side of an impossibly verdant hill that plunged into a wide valley full of trillium, pin cherry, and hobblebush. He knew to cover our one flashlight with a red bag, so as not to disturb the fireflies, and to only point it at the ground as he led his wife and semi-aloof teenage daughters through the navy blue pause just moments after twilight. I confess, at first I wanted to be back in the air-conditioned hotel room—anywhere but on an isolated gravel path with the odd bullfrog clamor interrupting the dark. But now I think of my sister and I scattered in different homes as adults and am so grateful for all of those family vacations where we could be outdoors together, walking this earth.

My mother's temper was always frazzled by vacation's end, but I know each day off from work and spent with her family was something sweet and rare. How I crave those slow vacation days and even slower nights, her taking her time to select our frilled nightclothes, to laugh about the day's sightseeing and the cheap trinkets I'd bought. She'd pull a coverlet to my chin. Her gorgeous, dark and wavy hair tickled when she leaned over to kiss me good-night, smelling of Oil of Olay and spearmint gum. Only on those trips would I know such a degree of tenderness, the quiet reassurances a mother can give a daughter, while she stroked my bangs to the side of my face. No rush in the mornings to get me and my sister shuffled onto a school bus and herself off to work. When my mother is no longer here, I know I will cling to that lovely fragrance of mint and a moisturizer I'll always associate with beauty and love. I will cling to those summer nights we raced—and yet didn't race—home. I will try to bang myself back to that Oldsmobile like the lacewings that argue nightly with my porch light bulb, to what my small family was then, not even big enough to call a swarm: one sister, two parents.

5   I grew up near scientists who worked with indigo buntings. There is no other blue like that of these birds, no feather more electric. They navigate by following the North Star, and these scientists were trying to trick them into following a

false star in a darkened room. But most of these buntings don't fall for the ruse. When released, they find their way home the same as always. The buntings know the North Star by heart, learn to look for it in their first summer of life, storing this knowledge to use years later when they first learn to migrate. How they must have spent hours gazing at the star during those nestling nights, peeking out from under their mother. What shines so strong holds them steady.

Where the buntings remain steadfast, fireflies are more easily deceived. They lose their light rhythm for a few minutes after a single car's headlights pass. Sometimes it takes hours for them to recalibrate their blinking patterns. What gets lost in the radio silence? What connections are translated incorrectly or missed entirely? Porch lights, trucks, buildings, and the harsh glow of streetlamps all complicate matters and discourage fireflies from sending out their love-light signals—meaning fewer firefly larvae are born the next year.

Scientists can't agree on how or why these fireflies achieve synchronicity. Perhaps it is a competition between males, who all want to be the first to send their signals across the valleys and manna grass. Perhaps if they all flash at once, the females can better determine whose glow is most radiant. Whatever the reason—and in spite of, or rather, because of, all the guided tours that now pop up in the Smokies—fireflies don't glow in sync all night long anymore. The patterns sometimes occur in short flashes, then abruptly end in haunting periods of darkness. The fireflies are still out there, but they fly or rest on grass blades in visual silence. Perhaps a visitor forgot to dim a flashlight or left their car lights on for too long, and this is the firefly's protest.

Firefly eggs and larvae are bioluminescent, and the larvae themselves hunt for prey. They can detect a slime trail from a slug or snail and follow it all the way to the juicy, unsuspecting source. Whole groups of larvae have been known to track relatively large prey, such as an earthworm—like a macabre, candlelit chase right out of an old B-movie, to the edge of a soupy pond, the larvae pulsing light as they devour a still-wriggling worm. Some firefly larvae live completely underwater, their lights fevering just under the surface as they capture and devour aquatic snails.

For a beetle, fireflies live long and full lives—around two years—though most of it is spent underground, gloriously eating and sleeping to their hearts' content. When we see these beacons flashing their lights, they usually have only one or two weeks left to live. Learning this as a child—I could often be found walking slowly around untrimmed lawns, stalling and not quite ready to go inside for dinner—made me melancholy, even in the face of their brilliance. I couldn't believe something so full of light would be gone so soon.

I know I will search for fireflies all the rest of my days, even though they dwindle a little bit more each year. I can't help it. They blink on and off, a lime glow to the summer night air, as if to say: *I am still here, you are still here, I am still here, you are still here, I am, you are*, over and over again. Perhaps I can will it to be true. Perhaps I can keep those summer nights with my family inside an empty jam jar, with holes poked in the lid, a twig and a few strands of grass tucked inside. And for those unimaginable nights in the future, when I know I'll miss my mother the most, I will let that jar's sweet glow serve as a night-light to cool and cut the air for me.

MLA CITATION

Nezhukumatathil, Aimee. "Firefly." *The Norton Reader: An Anthology of Nonfiction*, edited by Melissa A. Goldthwaite et al., 16th ed., W. W. Norton, 2024, pp. 661–64.

QUESTIONS

1. "Firefly" includes many different modes of writing. Go back through and annotate the essay, marking the mode of each paragraph—personal narrative, scientific observation, poetic observation, and more. Are there some modes you prefer to others? Is there a transition that seems especially effective to you?

2. Aimee Nezhukumatathil contrasts how indigo buntings navigate with how fireflies do (paragraphs 5–7). What do you already know about migratory animals? Research the movement patterns of another migratory animal. How does it find its way? Are human actions endangering its migration?

3. Write an essay about an animal—whether a wild animal or the family pet—that draws to mind one of your family members the way that fireflies conjure Nezhukumatathil's childhood with her parents and sister. Describe your or your family member's love for that animal and consider, as Nezhukumatathil does, what that love has taught you.

11 Declarations

We hold these truths to be self-evident.

—Thomas Jefferson

The United States began with a declaration. Declarations make things happen; they change the world. The truths that Thomas Jefferson and the founders declared to be self-evident did not match the reality of their world, but in declaring their allegiance to these truths, they worked to make a dramatic and consequential political change: A new nation was born. Over seventy years later, Elizabeth Cady Stanton added "and women" to Jefferson's second clause, declaring it self-evident "that all men *and women* are created equal," a declaration yet to be realized even today. The essays in this chapter have force and make demands. Some of them helped to create the world we now inhabit; others conjure a future we have yet to achieve; all help us imagine a future better than the authors' present.

Many of these declarations make claims on behalf of the extension of civil rights—to colonized subjects, to women, and to racially marginalized people, especially Black people (Sojourner Truth, Audre Lorde, Imani Perry). Others address climate change (Greta Thunberg) and the future of our nation (Abraham Lincoln, John F. Kennedy). There are two winners of the Nobel Peace Prize: Martin Luther King Jr. and Malala Yousafzai. Yousafzai was only seventeen when she won in 2014, making her the youngest recipient of the prize. In 1948, the prize was not awarded in deference to Mohandas Gandhi's recent death by an assassin's bullet. Gandhi's speech in this chapter, given at trial for protesting British colonial violence, connects his faith and his doctrine of nonviolent resistance. Thunberg and Yousafzai wrote their pieces as teenagers; their courage to speak out, rather than waiting for adults to give them permission, can inspire you to be brave and hopeful about how to use your voice and why it might matter.

To make a declaration is to take a clear stand. Declarations are bold. Here you will find lists of demands and indictments of kings, corporations, and other powerful entities. You will also find descriptions of hopes for the future, defenses of finding joy in the present despite the ongoing struggle. Writing classes often emphasize making fine distinctions and nuanced claims over bold declarations. This chapter is an opportunity, as well as an invitation, to exercise a different set of writing muscles: Be bold!

GRETA THUNBERG
There Is Hope

 YEAR AND A HALF AGO I didn't speak to anyone unless I really had to. But then I found a reason to speak. Since then I've given many speeches, and learnt that when you talk in public you should start with something personal or emotional to get everyone's attention. Say things like our house is on fire, I want you to panic or how dare you.

But today I will not do that. Because then those phrases are all that people focus on. They don't remember the facts, the very reason why I say those things in the first place. We no longer have time to leave out the science. For about a year I've been constantly talking about our rapidly declining carbon budgets. Over and over again. But since that is still being ignored, I will just keep repeating it.

In chapter 2, on page 108 in the SR1.5 IPCC report[1] that came out last year, it says that if we are to have a 67 percent chance of limiting the global temperature rise to below 1.5°C, we had, on January 1, 2018, about 420 gigatonnes of CO_2 left to emit in that carbon dioxide budget. And of course that number is much lower today. As we emit about 42 gigatonnes of CO_2 every year, including land use.

With today's emissions levels, that remaining budget will be gone within eight years.

5   These numbers aren't anyone's opinions or political views. This is the current best available science. Though many scientists suggest these figures are too moderate, these are the ones that have been accepted through the IPCC.

And please note that these figures are global and therefore do not say anything about the aspect of equity, which is absolutely necessary to make the Paris Agreement work on a global scale.

That means that richer countries need to do their fair share and get down to "real zero" emissions much faster, and then help poorer countries do the same, so that people in less fortunate parts of the world can raise their living standards.

The numbers also don't include most feedback loops, nonlinear tipping points and additional warming hidden by toxic air pollution. Most models, however, assume that future generations will somehow be able to suck hundreds of billions of tonnes of CO_2 out of the air with technologies that do not exist in the scale required and maybe never will. The approximate 67 percent chance

This speech, from the United Nations Climate Change Conference (COP25) in Madrid, 2019, was published in the expanded edition of No One Is Too Small to Make a Difference *(2019), a collection of Greta Thunberg's works.*

1. *Global Warming of 1.5°C* (SR15), a report detailing the impacts of global warming of 1.5°C above preindustrial levels and related global greenhouse gas emissions. It was published by the Intergovernmental Panel on Climate Change (IPCC), the United Nations body for assessing the science related to climate change, on October 8, 2018.

budget is the one with the highest odds given by the IPCC. And now we have less than 340 gigatonnes of CO_2 left to emit in that budget to share fairly.

And why is it so important to stay below 1.5°C? Because even at 1°C people are dying from climate change and ecosystems are collapsing. Because that is what the united science calls for to avoid destabilizing the climate—so that we have the best possible chance to avoid setting off irreversible chain reactions such as melting glaciers, polar ice and thawing permafrost. Every fraction of a degree matters.

So there it is again. This is my message. This is what I want you to focus on.   10
So please tell me, how do you react to these numbers without feeling at least some level of panic? How do you respond to the fact that basically nothing is being done about this, without feeling the slightest bit of anger? And how do you communicate this without sounding alarmist? I would really like to know.

Since the Paris Agreement global banks have invested 1.9 trillion dollars in fossil fuels.

One hundred companies are responsible for 71 percent of global emissions. The G20[2] countries account for almost 80 percent of total emissions.

The richest 10 percent of the world's population produce half of our CO_2 emissions while the poorest 50 percent account for just one tenth.

We indeed have some work to do, but some more than others.

Recently a handful of rich countries pledged to reduce their emissions of   15
greenhouse gases by so and so many percent and by this or that date. Or to become "climate neutral" or "net zero" in so and so many years.

This may sound impressive at first glance. But even though the intentions may be good, this is not leadership. This is not leading, this is misleading. Because most of these pledges do not include aviation, shipping, and imported and exported consumption. They do, however, include the possibility for countries to "offset" their emissions elsewhere.

These pledges don't include the immediate yearly reduction rates needed for wealthy countries—which is necessary to stay within the tiny remaining budget. Zero in 2050 means nothing. If high emissions continue even for a few years, then the remaining budget will be gone.

Without seeing the full picture, we will not solve this crisis. Finding holistic solutions is what the COP[3] should be all about. But instead it seems to have turned into an opportunity for countries to negotiate loopholes and avoid raising their ambition.

Countries are finding clever ways around having to take real action. Like double counting emissions reductions. And moving their emissions overseas. And walking back on their promises to enhance ambition.

And refusing to pay for solutions or loss and damage.   20

2. An international governing body composed of nineteen countries and the European Union.

3. Conference of the Parties, a term in international relations to denote a committee that is created after an international treaty is signed, tasked with making decisions about how that treaty is implemented.

This has to stop. What we need is real, drastic emission cuts at the source. But of course just reducing emissions is not enough. Our greenhouse gas emissions have to stop. To stay below 1.5°C we need to keep the carbon in the ground.

Only setting up distant dates, and saying things which give the impression that action is under way will most likely do more harm than good—because the changes required are still nowhere in sight. The politics needed do not exist today despite all the fancy words you might hear from world leaders.

And I still believe the biggest danger is not inaction. The real danger is when politicians and CEOs are making it look like real action is happening, when in fact almost nothing is being done, apart from clever accounting and creative PR.

I have been fortunate enough to be able to travel around the world. And my experience is that the lack of awareness is the same everywhere. Not the least amongst those elected to lead us.

25   There is no sense of urgency whatsoever. Our leaders are not behaving as if we were in an emergency. In an emergency, you change your behavior.

If there is a child standing in the middle of the road, and cars are coming at full speed, you don't look away because it is too uncomfortable. You immediately run out and rescue that child.

And without that sense of urgency, how can we, the people, understand that we are facing a real crisis? And if the people are not fully aware of what is going on, then they will not put pressure on their elected leaders to act. And without pressure from the people, our leaders can get away with doing basically nothing. Which is where we are now. And around and around it goes.

In just three weeks we will enter a new decade. A decade that will define our future. Right now we are desperate for any sign of hope.

Well, I am telling you there is hope. I have seen it. But it does not come from governments or corporations. It comes from the people.

30   The people who have been unaware of the climate and environmental emergency but are now starting to wake up. And once we become aware, we change. People can change. People are ready for change. And that is the hope because we have democracy.

And democracy is happening all the time, not just on election day but every second and every hour. It is public opinion that runs the free world. In fact, every great change throughout history has come from the people. We do not have to wait. We can start the change right now. We, the people.

MLA CITATION

Thunberg, Greta. "There Is Hope." *The Norton Reader: An Anthology of Nonfiction*, edited by Melissa A. Goldthwaite et al., 16th ed., W. W. Norton, 2024, pp. 666–68.

QUESTIONS

1. We often think of facts as dry and incontrovertible, but Greta Thunberg insists that her anger comes from facing the facts. What is the role of outrage in making

an argument? What does Thunberg herself say about how she balances facts and anger when she speaks about climate change?

2. The hypocrisy of large nations and corporations that Thunberg exposes is called "greenwashing." Research an example of greenwashing and write a response explaining how companies get away with this behavior and what should be done about it.

3. For Thunberg, hope lies in the grassroots actions of individuals and small groups. Find and interview a local climate activist in your community. Write an editorial that shares the news of the activist's work more widely.

MALALA YOUSAFZAI
Nobel Lecture

B ISMILLAH HIR RAHMAN IR RAHIM. In the name of God, the most merciful, the most beneficent.

Your Majesties, Your Royal Highnesses, distinguished members of the Norweigan Nobel Committee,

Dear sisters and brothers, today is a day of great happiness for me. I am humbled that the Nobel Committee has selected me for this precious award.

Thank you to everyone for your continued support and love. Thank you for the letters and cards that I still receive from all around the world. Your kind and encouraging words strengthen and inspire me.

I would like to thank my parents for their unconditional love. Thank you   5
to my father for not clipping my wings and for letting me fly. Thank you to my mother for inspiring me to be patient and to always speak the truth—which we strongly believe is the true message of Islam. And also thank you to all my wonderful teachers, who inspired me to believe in myself and be brave.

I am proud, well in fact, I am very proud to be the first Pashtun, the first Pakistani, and the youngest person to receive this award. Along with that, I am pretty certain that I am also the first recipient of the Nobel Peace Prize who still fights with her younger brothers. I want there to be peace everywhere, but my brothers and I are still working on that.

I am also honoured to receive this award together with Kailash Satyarthi, who has been a champion for children's rights for a long time. Twice as long, in fact, than I have been alive. I am proud that we can work together, we can work together and show the world that an Indian and a Pakistani can work together and achieve their goals of children's rights.

Dear brothers and sisters, I was named after the inspirational Malalai of Maiwand who is the Pashtun Joan of Arc. The word *Malala* means "grief stricken," "sad," but in order to lend some happiness to it, my grandfather would always call me "Malala—The happiest girl in the world" and today I am very happy that we are together fighting for an important cause.

Malala Yousafzai delivered this lecture when presented with the Nobel Peace Prize in 2014.

This award is not just for me. It is for those forgotten children who want an education. It is for those frightened children who want peace. It is for those voiceless children who want change.

10   I am here to stand up for their rights, to raise their voice . . . it is not time to pity them. It is time to take action so it becomes the last time that we see a child deprived of education.

I have found that people describe me in many different ways.

Some people call me the girl who was shot by the Taliban.

And some, the girl who fought for her rights.

Some people call me a "Nobel Laureate" now.

15   However, my brothers still call me that annoying bossy sister. As far as I know, I am just a committed and even stubborn person who wants to see every child getting quality education, who wants to see women having equal rights and who wants peace in every corner of the world.

Education is one of the blessings of life—and one of its necessities. That has been my experience during the 17 years of my life. In my paradise home, Swat, I always loved learning and discovering new things. I remember when my friends and I would decorate our hands with henna on special occasions. And instead of drawing flowers and patterns we would paint our hands with mathematical formulas and equations.

We had a thirst for education, because our future was right there in that classroom. We would sit and learn and read together. We loved to wear neat and tidy school uniforms and we would sit there with big dreams in our eyes. We wanted to make our parents proud and prove that we could also excel in our studies and achieve those goals, which some people think only boys can.

But things did not remain the same. When I was in Swat, which was a place of tourism and beauty, it suddenly changed into a place of terrorism. I was just ten when more than 400 schools were destroyed. Women were flogged. People were killed. And our beautiful dreams turned into nightmares.

Education went from being a right to being a crime.

20   Girls were stopped from going to school.

When my world suddenly changed, my priorities changed too.

I had two options. One was to remain silent and wait to be killed. And the second was to speak up and then be killed.

I chose the second one. I decided to speak up.

We could not just stand by and see those injustices of the terrorists denying our rights, ruthlessly killing people and misusing the name of Islam. We decided to raise our voice and tell them: Have you not learnt, have you not learnt that in the Holy Quran Allah says: if you kill one person it is as if you kill all of humanity?

25   *Do you not know that Mohammad, peace be upon him, the prophet of mercy, he says, "do not harm yourself or others."*

And do you not know that the very first word of the Holy Quran is the word *Iqra*, which means "read"?

The terrorists tried to stop us and attacked me and my friends who are here today, on our school bus in 2012, but neither their ideas nor their bullets could win.

We survived. And since that day, our voices have grown louder and louder.

I tell my story, not because it is unique, but because it is not.

It is the story of many girls. 30

Today, I tell their stories too. I have brought with me some of my sisters from Pakistan, from Nigeria and from Syria, who share this story. My brave sisters Shazia and Kainat who were also shot that day on our school bus. But they have not stopped learning. And my brave sister Kainat Soomro who went through severe abuse and extreme violence; even her brother was killed, but she did not succumb.

Also my sisters here, whom I have met during my Malala Fund campaign. My 16-year-old courageous sister, Mezon from Syria, who now lives in Jordan as a refugee and goes from tent to tent encouraging girls and boys to learn. And my sister Amina, from the North of Nigeria, where Boko Haram threatens, and stops girls and even kidnaps girls, just for wanting to go to school.

Though I appear as one girl, one person, who is 5 foot 2 inches tall, if you include my high heels (it means I am 5 foot only), I am not a lone voice, I am many.

I am Malala. But I am also Shazia.

I am Kainat. 35

I am Kainat Soomro.

I am Mezon.

I am Amina. I am those 66 million girls who are deprived of education. And today I am not raising my voice, it is the voice of those 66 million girls.

Sometimes people like to ask me why should girls go to school, why is it important for them. But I think the more important question is why shouldn't they? Why shouldn't they have this right to go to school?

Dear sisters and brothers, today, in half of the world, we see rapid progress 40 and development. However, there are many countries where millions still suffer from the very old problems of war, poverty and injustice.

We still see conflicts in which innocent people lose their lives and children become orphans. We see many people becoming refugees in Syria, Gaza and Iraq. In Afghanistan, we see families being killed in suicide attacks and bomb blasts.

Many children in Africa do not have access to education because of poverty. And as I said, we still see girls who have no freedom to go to school in the north of Nigeria.

Many children in countries like Pakistan and India, as Kailash Satyarthi mentioned, especially in India and Pakistan, are deprived of their right to education because of social taboos, or they have been forced into child marriage or into child labour.

One of my very good school friends, the same age as me, who had always been a bold and confident girl, dreamed of becoming a doctor. But her dream remained a dream. At the age of 12, she was forced to get married. And then

45

soon she had a son. She had a child when she herself was still a child—only 14. I know that she could have been a very good doctor.

But she couldn't . . . because she was a girl.

Her story is why I dedicate the Nobel Peace Prize money to the Malala Fund, to help give girls quality education, everywhere, anywhere in the world and to raise their voices. The first place this funding will go to is where my heart is, to build schools in Pakistan—especially in my home of Swat and Shangla.

In my own village, there is still no secondary school for girls. And it is my wish and my commitment, and now my challenge to build one so that my friends and my sisters can go to school there and get a quality education and get this opportunity to fulfill their dreams.

This where I will begin, but it is not where I will stop. I will continue this fight until I see every child in school.

Dear brothers and sisters, great people who brought change, like Martin Luther King and Nelson Mandela, Mother Teresa and Aung San Suu Kyi, once stood here on this stage. I hope the steps that Kailash Satyarthi and I have taken so far and will take on this journey will also bring change—lasting change.

50   My great hope is that this will be *the last time* we must fight for education. Let's solve this once and for all.

We have already taken many steps. Now it is time to take a leap.

It is not time to tell the world leaders to realise how important education is—they already know it and their own children are in good schools. Now it is time to call them to take action for the rest of the world's children.

We ask the world leaders to unite and make education their top priority.

Fifteen years ago, world leaders decided on a set of global goals, the Millennium Development Goals. In the years that have followed, we have seen some progress. The number of children out of school has been halved, as Kailash Satyarthi said. However, the world focused only on primary education, and progress did not reach everyone.

55   During 2015, representatives from all around the world will meet at the United Nations to set the next set of goals, the Sustainable Development Goals. This will set the world's ambition for the next generations.

The world can no longer accept that basic education is enough. Why do leaders accept that for children in developing countries, only basic literacy is sufficient, when their own children do homework in Algebra, Mathematics, Science and Physics?

Leaders must seize this opportunity to guarantee a free, quality, primary *and* secondary education for every child.

Some will say this is impractical, or too expensive, or too hard. Or maybe even impossible. But it is time the world thinks bigger.

Dear sisters and brothers, the so-called world of adults may understand it, but we children don't. Why is it that countries which we call "strong" are so powerful in creating wars but are so weak in bringing peace? Why is it that giving guns is so easy but giving books is so hard? Why is it that making tanks is so easy, but building schools is so hard?

We are living in the modern age and we believe that nothing is impossible. 60 We reached the moon 45 years ago and maybe we will soon land on Mars. Then, in this 21st century, we must be able to give every child quality education.

Dear sisters and brothers, dear fellow children, we must work . . . not wait. Not just the politicians and the world leaders, we all need to contribute. Me. You. We. It is our duty.

Let us become *the first* generation that decides to be *the last* that sees empty classrooms, lost childhoods and wasted potentials.

Let this be the **last time** that a girl or a boy spends their childhood in a factory.

Let this be the last time that a girl is forced into early child marriage.

Let this be the last time that a child loses life in war. 65

Let this be the last time that we see a child out of school.

Let this end with us.

Let's begin this ending . . . together . . . today . . . right here, right now. Let's begin this ending now.

Thank you so much.

MLA CITATION

Yousafzai, Malala. "Nobel Lecture." *The Norton Reader: An Anthology of Nonfiction*, edited by Melissa A. Goldthwaite et al., 16th ed., W. W. Norton, 2024, pp. 669–73.

QUESTIONS

1. Malala Yousafzai jokes about still fighting with her brothers despite winning the Nobel Peace Prize. How does humor contribute to her tone? How does she fulfill and subvert your expectations of what a Nobel Peace Prize speech should be?

2. Why does education matter to you? How does hearing about others who struggle for the right to become educated affect your commitment to your own education?

3. Annotate this speech, noting the reasons Yousafzai gives for supporting girls' education. Which are most persuasive to you and why?

4. Research the story of Yousafzai's fight to stay in school or the story of one of the other girls she mentions. Do a written, video, or audio essay sharing her story with others and arguing for the importance of education.

THOMAS JEFFERSON AND OTHERS
The Declaration of Independence

ORIGINAL DRAFT

A Declaration of the Representatives of the UNITED STATES
OF AMERICA, in General Congress Assembled.

W HEN IN THE COURSE OF HUMAN EVENTS it becomes necessary for a people to advance from that subordination in which they have hitherto remained, & to assume among the powers of the earth the equal & independant station to which the laws of nature & of nature's god entitle them, a decent respect to the opinions of mankind requires that they should declare the causes which impel them to the change.

We hold these truths to be sacred & undeniable; that all men are created equal & independant, that from that equal creation they derive rights inherent & inalienable, among which are the preservation of life, & liberty, & the pursuit of happiness; that to secure these ends, governments are instituted among men, deriving their just powers from the consent of the governed; that whenever any form of government shall become destructive of these ends, it is the right of the people to alter or to abolish it, & to institute new government, laying it's foundation on such principles & organising its powers in such form, as to them shall seem most likely to effect their safety & happiness. Prudence indeed will dictate that governments long established should not be changed for light & transient causes: and accordingly all experience hath shewn that mankind are more disposed to suffer while evils are sufferable, than to right themselves by abolishing the forms to which they are accustomed. but when a long train of abuses & usurpations, begun at a distinguished period, & pursuing invariably the same object, evinces a design to subject them to arbitrary power, it is their right, it is their duty, to throw off such government & to provide new guards for their future security. such has been the patient sufferance of these colonies; & such is now the necessity which constrains them to expunge their former systems of government. The history of his present majesty, is a history of unremitting injuries and usurpations, among which no one fact stands single or solitary to contradict the uniform tenor of the rest, all of which have in direct object the establishment of an absolute tyranny over these states. to prove this, let facts be submitted to a candid world, for the truth of which we pledge a faith yet unsullied by falsehood.

On June 11, 1776, Thomas Jefferson was elected by the Second Continental Congress to join John Adams, Benjamin Franklin, Robert Livingston, and Roger Sherman in drafting a declaration of independence. The draft presented to Congress on June 28 was primarily the work of Jefferson. The final version resulted from revisions made to Jefferson's original draft by members of the committee, including Adams and Franklin, and by members of the Continental Congress.

he has refused his assent to laws the most wholesome and necessary for the public good:

he has forbidden his governors to pass laws of immediate & pressing importance, unless suspended in their operation till his assent should be obtained; and when so suspended, he has neglected utterly to attend to them.

he has refused to pass other laws for the accommodation of large districts of people unless those people would relinquish the right of representation, a right inestimable to them, & formidable to tyrants alone:[1]

he has dissolved Representative houses repeatedly & continually, for opposing with manly firmness his invasions on the rights of the people:

he has refused for a long space of time to cause others to be elected, whereby the legislative powers, incapable of annihilation, have returned to the people at large for their exercise, the state remaining in the mean time exposed to all the dangers of invasion from without, &, convulsions within:

he has suffered the administration of justice totally to cease in some of these colonies, refusing his assent to laws for establishing judiciary powers:

he has made our judges dependant on his will alone, for the tenure of their offices, and amount of their salaries:

he has erected a multitude of new offices by a self-assumed power, & sent hither swarms of officers to harrass our people & eat out their substance: he has kept among us in times of peace standing armies & ships of war:

he has affected[2] to render the military, independent of & superior to the civil power:

he has combined with others to subject us to a jurisdiction foreign to our constitutions and unacknowledged by our laws; giving his assent to their pretended acts of legislation, for quartering large bodies of armed troops among us; for protecting them by a mock-trial from punishment for any murders they should commit on the inhabitants of these states;

for cutting off our trade with all parts of the world;

for imposing taxes on us without our consent;

for depriving us of the benefits of trial by jury

he has endeavored to prevent the population of these states; for that purpose obstructing the laws for naturalization of foreigners; refusing to pass others to encourage their migrations hither; & raising the conditions of new appropriations of lands;

for transporting us beyond seas to be tried for pretended offences:

for taking away our charters & altering fundamentally the forms of our governments;

for suspending our own legislatures & declaring themselves invested with power to legislate for us in all cases whatsoever:

he has abdicated government here, withdrawing his governors, & declaring us out of his allegiance & protection:

he has plundered our seas, ravaged our coasts, burnt our towns & destroyed the lives of our people:

---

1. At this point in the manuscript, a strip containing the following clause is inserted: "he called together legislative bodies at places unusual, unco[mfortable, & distant from] the depository of their public records for the sole purpose of fatiguing [them into compliance] with his measures." Missing parts in the Library of Congress text are supplied from the copy made by Jefferson for George Wythe. This copy is in the New York Public Library. The fact that this passage was omitted from John Adams's transcript suggests that it was not a part of Jefferson's original draft.

2. Tried.

he is at this time transporting large armies of foreign mercenaries to compleat the works of death, desolation & tyranny, already begun with circumstances of cruelty & perfidy unworthy the head of a civilized nation:

he has endeavored to bring on the inhabitants of our frontiers the merciless Indian savages, whose known rule of warfare is an undistinguished destruction of all ages, sexes, & conditions of existence:

he has incited treasonable insurrections of our fellow-citizens, with the allurements of forfeiture & confiscation of our property:

he has waged cruel war against human nature itself, violating it's most sacred rights of life & liberty in the persons of a distant people who never offended him, captivating & carrying them into slavery in another hemisphere, or to incur miserable death in their transportation thither. this piratical warfare, the opprobrium of *infidel* powers, is the warfare of the CHRISTIAN king of Great Britain. determined to keep open a market where MEN should be bought & sold; he has prostituted his negative for suppressing every legislative attempt to prohibit or to restrain this execrable commerce: and that this assemblage of horrors might want no fact of distinguished die, he is now exciting those very people to rise in arms among us, and to purchase that liberty of which *he* has deprived them, by murdering the people upon whom *he* also obtruded them; thus paying off former crimes committed against the *liberties* of one people, with crimes which he urges them to commit against the *lives* of another.

20   in every stage of these oppressions we have petitioned for redress in the most humble terms; our repeated petitions have been answered by repeated injury. a prince whose character is thus marked by every act which may define a tyrant, is unfit to be the ruler of a people who mean to be free. future ages will scarce believe that the hardiness of one man, adventured within the short compass of twelve years only, on so many acts of tyranny without a mask, over a people fostered & fixed in principles of liberty.

Nor have we been wanting in attentions to our British brethren. we have warned them from time to time of attempts by their legislature to extend a jurisdiction over these our states. we have reminded them of the circumstances of our emigration & settlement here, no one of which could warrant so strange a pretension: that these were effected at the expence of our own blood & treasure, unassisted by the wealth or the strength of Great Britain: that in constituting indeed our several forms of government, we had adopted one common king, thereby laying a foundation for perpetual league & amity with them; but that submission to their [Parliament, was no Part of our Constitution, nor ever in Idea, if History may be][3] credited: and we appealed to their native justice & magnanimity, as to the ties of our common kindred to disavow these usurpations which were likely to interrupt our correspondence & connection. they too have been deaf to the voice of justice & of consanguinity, & when occasions have been given them, by the regular course of their laws, of removing from their councils the disturbers of our harmony, they have by their free election re-established them in power. at this very time too they are permitting their chief magistrate to send over not only soldiers of our common blood, but Scotch & foreign mercenaries to invade &

3. Passage illegible in the original. It is supplied here from Adams's transcription.

deluge us in blood. these facts have given the last stab to agonizing affection, and manly spirit bids us to renounce for ever these unfeeling brethren. we must endeavor to forget our former love for them, and to hold them as we hold the rest of mankind, enemies in war, in peace friends. we might have been a free & a great people together; but a communication of grandeur & of freedom it seems is below their dignity. be it so, since they will have it: the road to glory & happiness is open to us too; we will climb it in a separate state, and acquiesce in the necessity which pronounces our everlasting Adieu!

We therefore the representatives of the United States of America in General Congress assembled do, in the name & by authority of the good people of these states, reject and renounce all allegiance & subjection to the kings of Great Britain & all others who may hereafter claim by, through, or under them; we utterly dissolve & break off all political connection which may have heretofore subsisted between us & the people or parliament of Great Britain; and finally we do assert and declare these colonies to be free and independant states, and that as free & independant states they shall hereafter have power to levy war, conclude peace, contract alliances, establish commerce, & to do all other acts and things which independent states may of right do. And for the support of this declaration we mutually pledge to each other our lives, our fortunes, & our sacred honour.

FINAL DRAFT

In Congress, July 4, 1776
The unanimous Declaration of the
Thirteen United States of America

W HEN IN THE COURSE OF HUMAN EVENTS it becomes necessary for one people to dissolve the political bands which have connected them with another, and to assume among the powers of the earth, the separate and equal station to which the Laws of Nature and of Nature's God entitle them, a decent respect to the opinions of mankind requires that they should declare the causes which impel them to the separation.

We hold these truths to be self-evident, that all men are created equal, that they are endowed by their Creator with certain unalienable Rights, that among these are Life, Liberty and the pursuit of Happiness. That to secure these rights, Governments are instituted among Men, deriving their just powers from the consent of the governed. That whenever any Form of Government becomes destructive of these ends, it is the Right of the People to alter or to abolish it, and to institute new Government, laying its foundation on such principles and organizing its powers in such form, as to them shall seem most likely to effect their Safety and Happiness. Prudence, indeed, will dictate that Governments long established should not be changed for light and transient causes; and accordingly all experience hath shewn that mankind are more disposed to suffer, while evils are sufferable, than to right themselves by abolishing the forms to which they are accustomed. But when a long train of abuses and usurpations, pursuing invariably the same Object evinces a design to reduce them under absolute Despotism, it is their right, it is their duty, to throw off such Government, and to provide new Guards for their future security. Such has been the patient sufferance of these Colonies; and such is now the necessity which constrains them to alter their former Systems of Government. The history of the present King of Great Britain is a history of repeated injuries and usurpations, all having in direct object the establishment of an absolute Tyranny over these States. To prove this, let Facts be submitted to a candid world.

He has refused his Assent to Laws, the most wholesome and necessary for the public good.

He has forbidden his Government to pass laws of immediate and pressing importance, unless suspended in their operation till his Assent should be obtained; and when so suspended, he has utterly neglected to attend to them.

5   He has refused to pass other Laws for the accommodation of large districts of people, unless those people would relinquish the right of Representation in the Legislature, a right inestimable to them and formidable to tyrants only.

He has called together legislative bodies at places unusual, uncomfortable, and distant from the depository of their Public Records, for the sole purpose of fatiguing them into compliance with his measures.

He has dissolved Representative Houses repeatedly, for opposing with manly firmness his invasions on the rights of the people.

He has refused for a long time, after such dissolutions, to cause others to be elected; whereby the Legislative Powers, incapable of Annihilation, have returned to the People at large for their exercise; the State remaining in the mean time exposed to all the dangers of invasion from without, and convulsions within.

He has endeavored to prevent the population of these States; for that purpose obstructing the Laws for Naturalization of Foreigners; refusing to pass others to encourage their migration hither, and raising the conditions of new Appropriations of Lands.

10   He has obstructed the Administration of Justice, by refusing his Assent to Laws for establishing Judiciary Powers.

He has made Judges dependent on his Will alone, for the tenure of their offices, and the amount and payment of their salaries.

He has erected a multitude of New Offices, and sent hither swarms of Officers to harass our people, and eat out their substance.

He has kept among us, in times of peace, Standing Armies without the Consent of our legislatures.

He has affected to render the Military independent of and superior to the Civil Power.

15   He has combined with others to subject us to a jurisdiction foreign to our constitution, and unacknowledged by our laws; giving his Assent to their Acts of pretended Legislation: For quartering large bodies of armed troops among us: For protecting them, by a mock Trial, from punishment for any Murders which they should commit on the Inhabitants of these States: For cutting off our Trade with all parts of the world: For imposing Taxes on us without our Consent: For depriving us in many cases, of the benefits of Trial by Jury: For transporting us

beyond Seas to be tried for pretended offenses: For abolishing the free System of English Laws in a neighboring Province, establishing therein an Arbitrary government, and enlarging its Boundaries so as to render it at once an example and fit instrument for introducing the same absolute rule into these Colonies: For taking away our Charters, abolishing our most valuable Laws, and altering fundamentally the Forms of our Governments: For suspending our own Legislatures, and declaring themselves invested with power to legislate for us in all cases whatsoever.

He has abdicated Government here, by declaring us out of his Protection and waging War against us.

He has plundered our seas, ravaged our Coasts, burnt our towns, and destroyed the lives of our people.

He is at this time transporting large Armies of foreign Mercenaries to complete the works of death, desolation and tyranny, already begun with circumstances of Cruelty & Perfidy scarcely paralleled in the most barbarous ages, and totally unworthy the Head of a civilized nation.

He has constrained our fellow Citizens taken Captive on the high Seas to bear Arms against their Country, to become the executioners of their friends and Brethren, or to fall themselves by their Hands.

He has excited domestic insurrections amongst us, and has endeavored to   20
bring on the inhabitants of our frontiers, the merciless Indian Savages, whose known rule of warfare, is an undistinguished destruction of all ages, sexes, and conditions.

In every stage of these Oppressions We have Petitioned for Redress in the most humble terms: Our repeated Petitions have been answered only by repeated injury. A Prince, whose character is thus marked by every act which may define a Tyrant, is unfit to be the ruler of a free people.

Nor have We been wanting in attention to our British brethren. We have warned them from time to time of attempts by their legislature to extend an unwarrantable jurisdiction over us. We have reminded them of the circumstances of our emigration and settlement here. We have appealed to their native justice and magnanimity, and we have conjured them by the ties of our common kindred to disavow these usurpations, which would inevitably interrupt our connections and correspondence. They too have been deaf to the voice of justice and of consanguinity. We must, therefore, acquiesce in the necessity, which denounces our Separation, and hold them, as we hold the rest of mankind, Enemies in War, in Peace Friends.

We, THEREFORE the Representatives of the UNITED STATES OF AMERICA, in General Congress, Assembled, appealing to the Supreme Judge of the world for the rectitude of our intentions, do, in the Name, and by Authority of the good People of these Colonies, solemnly publish and declare, That these United Colonies are, and of Right ought to be FREE AND INDEPENDENT STATES; that they are Absolved from all Allegiance to the British Crown, and that all political connection between them and the State of Great Britain, is and ought to be totally dissolved; and that as Free and Independent States, they have full Power to levy War, conclude Peace, contract Alliances, establish Commerce, and to do all other Acts and Things which Independent States may of right do. And for the support of this Declaration, with a firm reliance on the protection of Divine Providence, we mutually pledge to each other our Lives, our Fortunes, and our sacred Honor.

MLA CITATION

Jefferson, Thomas, et al. "The Declaration of Independence." *The Norton Reader: An Anthology of Nonfiction*, edited by Melissa A. Goldthwaite et al., 16th ed., W. W. Norton, 2024, pp. 674–80.

QUESTIONS

1. The Declaration of Independence is an example of deductive argument: Thomas Jefferson sets up general principles, details particular instances, and then draws conclusions. In both the original and final drafts, locate the three sections of the Declaration that use deduction. Explain how they work as arguments.

2. Locate the general principles (or "truths") that Jefferson sets up in the first section of both the original and final drafts. Mark the language he uses to describe them: For example, he calls them "sacred & undeniable" (paragraph 2) in the original draft and "self-evident" (paragraph 2) in the final draft. What kinds of authority does his language appeal to in each draft? Why might he or others have revised the language?

3. Note the stylistic differences (including choices of grammar and punctuation) between the original and final drafts of the Declaration of Independence. What effect do those differences have?

4. In an essay, choose one or two significant revisions that Jefferson made between the original and final draft of the Declaration and explain why they are significant.

5. Study Jefferson's list of the wrongs of the king and make a list (in written, oral, or video form), serious or satirical, in which you lay out your own list of wrongs against someone who has some authority over you (e.g., a parent or a manager at work).

ELIZABETH CADY STANTON
Declaration of Sentiments and Resolutions

HEN, IN THE COURSE OF HUMAN EVENTS, it becomes necessary for one portion of the family of man to assume among the people of the earth a position different from that which they have hitherto occupied, but one to which the laws of nature and of nature's God entitle them, a decent respect to

Written and presented at the first US women's rights convention in Seneca Falls, New York, in 1848. Elizabeth Cady Stanton published this version in History of Woman Suffrage *(1881), edited by herself, Susan B. Anthony, and Matilda Joslyn Gage, all prominent leaders of the American women's movement.*

the opinions of mankind requires that they should declare the causes that impel them to such a course.

We hold these truths to be self-evident: that all men and women are created equal; that they are endowed by their Creator with certain inalienable rights; that among these are life, liberty, and the pursuit of happiness; that to secure these rights governments are instituted, deriving their just powers from the consent of the governed. Whenever any form of government becomes destructive of these ends, it is the right of those who suffer from it to refuse allegiance to it, and to insist upon the institution of a new government, laying its foundation on such principles, and organizing its powers in such form, as to them shall seem most likely to effect their safety and happiness. Prudence indeed, will dictate that governments long established should not be changed for light and transient causes; and accordingly all experience hath shown that mankind are more disposed to suffer, while evils are sufferable, than to right themselves by abolishing the forms to which they were accustomed. But when a long train of abuses and usurpations, pursuing invariably the same object evinces a design to reduce them under absolute despotism, it is their duty to throw off such government, and to provide new guards for their future security. Such has been the patient sufferance of the women under this government, and such is now the necessity which constrains them to demand the equal station to which they are entitled.

The history of mankind is a history of repeated injuries and usurpations on the part of man toward woman, having in direct object the establishment of an absolute tyranny over her. To prove this, let facts be submitted to a candid world.

He has never permitted her to exercise her inalienable right to the elective franchise.

He has compelled her to submit to laws, in the formation of which she had   5
no voice.

He has withheld from her rights which are given to the most ignorant and degraded men—both natives and foreigners.

Having deprived her of this first right of a citizen, the elective franchise, thereby leaving her without representation in the halls of legislation, he has oppressed her on all sides.

He has made her, if married, in the eye of the law, civilly dead.

He has taken from her all right in property, even to the wages she earns.

He has made her, morally, an irresponsible being, as she can commit many   10
crimes with impunity, provided they be done in the presence of her husband. In the covenant of marriage, she is compelled to promise obedience to her husband, he becoming, to all intents and purposes, her master—the law giving him power to deprive her of her liberty, and to administer chastisement.

He has so framed the laws of divorce, as to what shall be the proper causes, and in case of separation, to whom the guardianship of the children shall be given, as to be wholly regardless of the happiness of women—the law, in all cases, going upon a false supposition of the supremacy of man, and giving all power into his hands.

After depriving her of all rights as a married woman, if single, and the owner of property, he has taxed her to support a government which recognizes her only when her property can be made profitable to it.

He has monopolized nearly all the profitable employments, and from those she is permitted to follow, she receives but a scanty remuneration. He closes against her all the avenues to wealth and distinction which he considers most honorable to himself. As a teacher of theology, medicine, or law, she is not known.

He has denied her the facilities for obtaining a thorough education, all colleges being closed against her.

15   He allows her in Church, as well as State, but a subordinate position, claiming Apostolic authority for her exclusion from the ministry, and, with some exceptions, from any public participation in the affairs of the Church.

He has created a false public sentiment by giving to the world a different code of morals for men and women, by which moral delinquencies which exclude women from society, are not only tolerated, but deemed of little account in man.

He has usurped the prerogative of Jehovah himself, claiming it as his right to assign for her a sphere of action, when that belongs to her conscience and to her God.

He has endeavored, in every way that he could, to destroy her confidence in her own powers, to lessen her self-respect, and to make her willing to lead a dependent and abject life.

Now, in view of this entire disfranchisement of one-half the people of this country, their social and religious degradation—in view of the unjust laws above mentioned, and because women do feel themselves aggrieved, oppressed, and fraudulently deprived of their most sacred rights, we insist that they have immediate admission to all the rights and privileges which belong to them as citizens of the United States.

20   In entering upon the great work before us, we anticipate no small amount of misconception, misrepresentation, and ridicule; but we shall use every instrumentality within our power to effect our object. We shall employ agents, circulate tracts, petition the State and National legislatures, and endeavor to enlist the pulpit and the press in our behalf. We hope this Convention will be followed by a series of Conventions embracing every part of the country.

MLA CITATION

Stanton, Elizabeth Cady. "Declaration of Sentiments and Resolutions." *The Norton Reader: An Anthology of Nonfiction*, edited by Melissa A. Goldthwaite et al., 16th ed., W. W. Norton, 2024, pp. 680–82.

QUESTIONS

1. Elizabeth Cady Stanton imitates both the argument and the style of the Declaration of Independence. Where does her declaration diverge from Thomas Jefferson's in "The Declaration of Independence" (pp. 674–80)? For what purpose?

2. Annotate a few items from Stanton's list of wrongs that women have suffered at the hands of men. Note the extent to which this list is applicable to the world we live in—in other words, which wrongs have been righted, and which persist?

3. Stanton's declaration was presented at the first conference on women's rights in Seneca Falls, New York, in 1848. Using books or web resources, do research on this conference; then use your research to explain the political aims of one of the resolutions.

4. Write your own "declaration" of political, educational, or social rights, using the declarations of Jefferson and Stanton as models.

SOJOURNER TRUTH
Ain't I a Woman?

1851 VERSION

I WANT TO SAY A FEW WORDS about this matter. I am a woman's rights [sic]. I have as much muscle as any man, and can do as much work as any man. I have plowed and reaped and husked and chopped and mowed, and can any man do more than that? I have heard much about the sexes being equal. I can carry as much as any man, and can eat as much too, if I can get it. I am as strong as any man that is now. As for intellect, all I can say is, if a woman have a pint, and a man a quart—why can't she have her little pint full? You need not be afraid to give us our rights for fear we will take too much,—for we can't take more than our pint'll hold. The poor men seems to be all in confusion, and don't know what to do. Why children, if you have woman's rights, give it to her and you will feel better. You will have your own rights, and they won't be so much trouble. I can't read, but I can hear. I have heard the Bible and have learned that Eve caused man to sin. Well, if woman upset the world, do give her a chance to set it right side up again. The Lady has spoken about Jesus, how he never spurned woman from him, and she was right. When Lazarus died, Mary and Martha came to him with faith and love and besought him to raise their brother. And Jesus wept and Lazarus came forth. And how came Jesus into the world? Through God who created him and the

Sojourner Truth (c. 1797–1883), born Isabella Baumfree, was a Black abolitionist and women's rights activist. On May 28, 1851, at the Women's Rights Convention in Akron, Ohio, Truth delivered an extemporaneous speech that is most often titled "Ain't I a Woman?" Since what was passed down is a reported version of what Truth said, the speech is a composite of her words and the recollections of two individuals who witnessed it. Two versions appear here—the first recorded version of the speech reported by editor Marius Robinson in the Anti-Slavery Bugle *in 1851 and another, more famous version published by the abolitionist, writer, and speaker Frances Dana Gage in the* National Anti-Slavery Standard *on May 2, 1863.*

woman who bore him. Man, where was your part? But the women are coming up blessed be God and a few of the men are coming up with them. But man is in a tight place, the poor slave is on him, woman is coming on him, he is surely between a hawk and a buzzard.

MLA CITATION

Truth, Sojourner. "Ain't I a Woman?" 1851. *The Norton Reader: An Anthology of Nonfiction*, edited by Melissa A. Goldthwaite et al., 16th ed., W. W. Norton, 2024, pp. 683–84.

1863 VERSION

 ELL, CHILDREN, WHERE THERE IS SO MUCH RACKET there must be something out of kilter. I think that 'twixt the negroes of the South and the women at the North, all talking about rights, the white men will be in a fix pretty soon. But what's all this here talking about?

That man over there says that women need to be helped into carriages, and lifted over ditches, and to have the best place everywhere. Nobody ever helps me into carriages, or over mud-puddles, or gives me any best place! And ain't I a woman? Look at me! Look at my arm! I have ploughed and planted, and gathered into barns, and no man could head me! And ain't I a woman? I could work as much and eat as much as a man—when I could get it—and bear the lash as well! And ain't I a woman? I have borne thirteen children, and seen most all sold off to slavery, and when I cried out with my mother's grief, none but Jesus heard me! And ain't I a woman?

Then they talk about this thing in the head; what's this they call it? [member of audience whispers, "intellect"] That's it, honey. What's that got to do with women's rights or negroes' rights? If my cup won't hold but a pint, and yours holds a quart, wouldn't you be mean not to let me have my little half measure full?

Then that little man in black there, he says women can't have as much rights as men, 'cause Christ wasn't a woman! Where did your Christ come from? Where did your Christ come from? From God and a woman! Man had nothing to do with Him.

5   If the first woman God ever made was strong enough to turn the world upside down all alone, these women together ought to be able to turn it back, and get it right side up again! And now they is asking to do it, the men better let them.

Obliged to you for hearing me, and now old Sojourner ain't got nothing more to say.

MLA CITATION

Truth, Sojourner. "Ain't I a Woman?" 1863. *The Norton Reader: An Anthology of Nonfiction*, edited by Melissa A. Goldthwaite et al., 16th ed., W. W. Norton, 2024, p. 684.

QUESTIONS

1. Sojourner Truth uses both comparison and contrast to develop her speech. How does she compare herself to a man? In what ways does she believe she is not like a man? What do these similarities and differences tell us about how she understands gender?

2. Discuss Truth's use of the Bible to challenge the limitations others try to impose on her. How does her use of biblical allusions support her argument?

3. When Truth notes that white gender norms of the time (such as helping white women in and out of carriages) do not apply to her, as a Black woman, she invokes what legal scholar Kimberlé Crenshaw has since called "intersectionality," the idea that many of us inhabit multiple identities at once (e.g., both Black and female). How does intersectionality help you understand Truth's argument?

4. Write an essay comparing the two versions of Truth's speech. What do they have in common, and how do they differ? Which version do you think would have been more persuasive to its original audience? Which version is more persuasive to you?

ABRAHAM LINCOLN
Second Inaugural Address

A T THIS SECOND appearing to take the oath of the presidential office, there is less occasion for an extended address than there was at the first. Then a statement, somewhat in detail, of a course to be pursued, seemed fitting and proper. Now, at the expiration of four years, during which public declarations have been constantly called forth on every point and phase of the great contest which still absorbs the attention, and engrosses the energies of the nation, little that is new could be presented. The progress of our arms, upon which all else chiefly depends, is as well known to the public as to myself; and it is, I trust, reasonably satisfactory and encouraging to all. With high hope for the future, no prediction in regard to it is ventured.

On the occasion corresponding to this four years ago, all thoughts were anxiously directed to an impending civil war. All dreaded it—all sought to avert it. While the inaugural address was being delivered from this place, devoted altogether to *saving* the Union without war, insurgent agents were in the city seeking to *destroy* it without war—seeking to dissolve the Union, and divide effects, by negotiation. Both parties deprecated war; but one of them would *make* war rather than let the nation survive; and the other would *accept* war rather than let it perish. And the war came.

Delivered on March 4, 1865, as Abraham Lincoln took office for a second term as America's sixteenth president. In the nineteenth century, US presidents took office in March, not in January as they do today.

One-eighth of the whole population were colored slaves, not distributed generally over the Union, but localized in the Southern part of it. These slaves constituted a peculiar and powerful interest. All knew that this interest was, somehow, the cause of the war. To strengthen, perpetuate, and extend this interest was the object for which the insurgents would rend the Union, even by war; while the government claimed no right to do more than to restrict the territorial enlargement of it. Neither party expected for the war, the magnitude, or the duration, which it has already attained. Neither anticipated that the *cause* of the conflict might cease with, or even before, the conflict itself should cease. Each looked for an easier triumph, and a result less fundamental and astounding. Both read the same Bible, and pray to the same God; and each invokes His aid against the other. It may seem strange that any men should dare to ask a just God's assistance in wringing their bread from the sweat of other men's faces; but let us judge not that we be not judged.[1] The prayers of both could not be answered; that of neither has been answered fully. The Almighty has His own purposes. "Woe unto the world because of offenses! for it must needs be that offenses come; but woe to that man by whom the offense cometh!"[2] If we shall suppose that American slavery is one of those offenses which, in the providence of God, must needs come, but which, having continued through His appointed time, He now wills to remove, and that He gives to both North and South, this terrible war, as the woe due to those by whom the offense came, shall we discern therein any departure from those divine attributes which the believers in a Living God always ascribe to Him? Fondly do we hope—fervently do we pray—that this mighty scourge of war may speedily pass away. Yet, if God wills that it continue, until all the wealth piled by the bondman's two hundred and fifty years of unrequited toil shall be sunk, and until every drop of blood drawn with the lash, shall be paid by another drawn with the sword, as was said three thousand years ago, so still it must be said "the judgments of the Lord are true and righteous altogether."[3]

With malice toward none; with charity for all; with firmness in the right, as God gives us to see the right, let us strive on to finish the work we are in; to bind up the nation's wounds; to care for him who shall have borne the battle, and for his widow, and his orphan—to do all which may achieve and cherish a just, and a lasting peace, among ourselves, and with all nations.

MLA CITATION

Lincoln, Abraham. "Second Inaugural Address." *The Norton Reader: An Anthology of Nonfiction*, edited by Melissa A. Goldthwaite et al., 16th ed., W. W. Norton, 2024, pp. 685–86.

1. Lincoln alludes to Jesus's statement in the Sermon on the Mount—"Judge not, that ye be not judged" (Matthew 7:1)—and to God's curse on Adam—"In the sweat of thy face shalt thou eat bread, till thou return unto the ground" (Genesis 3:19).
2. From Jesus's speech to his disciples (Matthew 18:7).
3. Psalms 19:9.

QUESTIONS

1. Abraham Lincoln's speech includes both allusions to and direct quotations from the Bible. What argument do these references support? Why might biblical references be important as a persuasive technique for Lincoln's audience?

2. In paragraphs 1 and 2, Lincoln reflects on his first inaugural address in order to set the stage for his present speech. Find a copy of the first inaugural address online or in the library. In what ways does that thirty-five-paragraph speech help inform this four-paragraph speech? What aspects of the "Second Inaugural Address" does it clarify?

3. Read the text of a more recent presidential address and compare or contrast it to Lincoln's address. (See, for example, John F. Kennedy's "Inaugural Address" [pp. 691–94]; others can be found online.) Does the more recent address use a similar style, language, or set of allusions? How does it differ?

MOHANDAS GANDHI
Nonviolence Is the First Article of My Faith

I WANTED TO AVOID VIOLENCE, I want to avoid violence. Nonviolence is the first article of my faith. It is also the last article of my creed. But I had to make my choice. I had either to submit to a system which I considered had done an irreparable harm to my country, or incur the risk of the mad fury of my people bursting forth, when they understood the truth from my lips. I know that my people have sometimes gone mad. I am deeply sorry for it, and I am therefore here to submit not to a light penalty but to the highest penalty. I do not ask for mercy. I do not plead any extenuating act. I am here, therefore, to invite and cheerfully submit to the highest penalty that can be inflicted upon me for what in law is a deliberate crime and what appears to me to be the highest duty of a citizen. The only course open to you, the judge, is, as I am just going to say in my statement, either to resign your post or inflict on me the severest penalty, if you believe that the system and law you are assisting to administer are good for the people. I do not expect that kind of conversation, but by the time I have finished with my statement, you will perhaps have a glimpse of what is raging within my breast to run this maddest risk which a sane man can run.

I owe it perhaps to the Indian public and to the public in England to placate which this prosecution is mainly taken up that I should explain why from a staunch loyalist and cooperator I have become an uncompromising disaffectionist and non-cooperator. To the court too I should say why I plead guilty to

Mohandas Gandhi gave this speech at his 1922 trial for speaking out and writing against the repressive Rowlatt Acts, which the colonizing British government used to imprison Indians who protested colonization. He was convicted and sentenced to six years in prison; he served a two-year term.

the charge of promoting disaffection toward the government established by law in India.

My public life began in 1893 in South Africa in troubled weather. My first contact with British authority in that country was not of a happy character. I discovered that as a man and as an Indian I had no rights. More correctly, I discovered that I had no rights as a man because I was an Indian.

But I was baffled. I thought that this treatment of Indians was an excrescence upon a system that was intrinsically and mainly good. I gave the government my voluntary and hearty cooperation, criticizing it freely where I felt it was faulty but never wishing its destruction.

5 Consequently, when the existence of the empire was threatened in 1899 by the Boer challenge, I offered my services to it, raised a volunteer ambulance corps, and served at several actions that took place for the relief of Ladysmith. Similarly in 1906, at the time of the Zulu revolt, I raised a stretcher-bearer party and served till the end of the "rebellion." On both these occasions I received medals and was even mentioned in dispatches. For my work in South Africa I was given by Lord Hardinge a Kaiser-i-Hind Gold Medal. When the war broke out in 1914 between England and Germany, I raised a volunteer ambulance corps in London consisting of the then-resident Indians in London, chiefly students. Its work was acknowledged by the authorities to be valuable. Lastly, in India, when a special appeal was made at the War Conference in Delhi in 1918 by Lord Chelmsford for recruits, I struggled at the cost of my health to raise a corps in Kheda, and the response was being made when the hostilities ceased and orders were received that no more recruits were wanted. In all these efforts at service I was actuated by the belief that it was possible by such services to gain a status of full equality in the empire for my countrymen.

The first shock came in the shape of the Rowlatt Act, a law designed to rob the people of all real freedom. I felt called upon to lead an intensive agitation against it. Then followed the Punjab horrors beginning with the massacre at Jallianwala Bagh and culminating in crawling orders, public floggings, and other indescribable humiliations. I discovered too that the plighted word of the prime minister to the Mussulmans of India regarding the integrity of Turkey and the holy places of Islam was not likely to be fulfilled. But in spite of the forebodings and the grave warnings of friends, at the Amritsar Congress in 1919, I fought for cooperation and working with the Montagu-Chelmsford reforms, hoping that the prime minister would redeem his promise to the Indian Mussulmans, that the Punjab wound would be healed, and that the reforms, inadequate and unsatisfactory though they were, marked a new era of hope in the life of India.[1]

---

1. The 1919 Montagu-Chelmsford Reforms were a moderate, largely inadequate response to the demands of Gandhi and others for greater self-governance. "Mussulman" is an archaic term for a Muslim person. The Punjab region is a Muslim-majority area. A province during British control, it became the state of West Punjab upon independence, and later, when India partitioned into East and West Pakistan (later, Bangladesh and Pakistan), part of Punjab joined Pakistan.

But all that hope was shattered. The Khilafat promise was not to be redeemed.[2] The Punjab crime was whitewashed, and most culprits went not only unpunished but remained in service and in some cases continued to draw pensions from the Indian revenue, and in some cases were even rewarded. I saw too that not only did the reforms not mark a change of heart, but they were only a method of further draining India of her wealth and of prolonging her servitude.

I came reluctantly to the conclusion that the British connection had made India more helpless than she ever was before, politically and economically. A disarmed India has no power of resistance against any aggressor if she wanted to engage in an armed conflict with him. So much is this the case that some of our best men consider that India must take generations before she can achieve the dominion status. She has become so poor that she has little power of resisting famines. Before the British advent, India spun and wove in her millions of cottages just the supplement she needed for adding to her meager agricultural resources. This cottage industry, so vital for India's existence, has been ruined by incredibly heartless and inhuman processes as described by English witnesses. Little do town dwellers know how the semi-starved masses of India are slowly sinking to lifelessness. Little do they know that their miserable comfort represents the brokerage they get for the work they do for the foreign exploiter, that the profits and the brokerage are sucked from the masses. Little do they realize that the government established by law in British India is carried on for this exploitation of the masses. No sophistry, no jugglery in figures can explain away the evidence that the skeletons in many villages present to the naked eye. I have no doubt whatsoever that both England and the town dwellers of India will have to answer, if there is a God above, for this crime against humanity which is perhaps unequaled in history. The law itself in this country has been used to serve the foreign exploiter. My unbiased examination of the Punjab Martial Law cases has led me to believe that at least 95 percent of convictions were wholly bad. My experience of political cases in India leads me to the conclusion that in nine out of every ten the condemned men were totally innocent. Their crime consisted in the love of their country. In ninety-nine cases out of a hundred justice has been denied to Indians as against Europeans in the courts of India. This is not an exaggerated picture. It is the experience of almost every Indian who has had anything to do with such cases. In my opinion, the administration of the law is thus prostituted consciously or unconsciously for the benefit of the exploiter.

The greater misfortune is that Englishmen and their Indian associates in the administration of the country do not know that they are engaged in the crime I have attempted to describe. I am satisfied that many Englishmen and Indian officials honestly believe that they are administering one of the best

2. Gandhi and other leaders of the Indian National Congress, mostly Hindu, joined with the Muslim-majority leaders of the Khilafat movement to engage in acts of civil disobedience against British rule. After some initially promising successes, the colonial government soon arrested Gandhi and other leaders.

systems devised in the world and that India is making steady though slow progress. They do not know that a subtle but effective system of terrorism and an organized display of force, on the one hand, and the deprivation of all powers of retaliation or self-defense, on the other, have emasculated the people and induced in them the habit of simulation. This awful habit has added to the ignorance and the self-deception of the administrators. Section 124-A, under which I am happily charged, is perhaps the prince among the political sections of the Indian Penal Code designed to suppress the liberty of the citizen. Affection cannot be manufactured or regulated by law. If one has an affection for a person or system, one should be free to give the fullest expression to his disaffection, so long as he does not contemplate, promote, or incite to violence. But the section under which Mr. Banker [a colleague in nonviolence] and I are charged is one under which mere promotion of disaffection is a crime. I have studied some of the cases tried under it, and I know that some of the most loved of India's patriots have been convicted under it. I consider it a privilege, therefore, to be charged under that section. I have endeavored to give in their briefest outline the reasons for my disaffection. I have no personal ill will against any single administrator; much less can I have any disaffection toward the king's person. But I hold it to be a virtue to be disaffected toward a government which in its totality has done more harm to India than any previous system. India is less manly under the British rule than she ever was before. Holding such a belief, I consider it to be a sin to have affection for the system. And it has been a precious privilege for me to be able to write what I have in the various articles, tendered in evidence against me.

10   In fact, I believe that I have rendered a service to India and England by showing in non-cooperation the way out of the unnatural state in which both are living. In my humble opinion, non-cooperation with evil is as much a duty as is cooperation with good. But in the past, non-cooperation has been deliberately expressed in violence to the evildoer. I am endeavoring to show to my countrymen that violent non-cooperation only multiplies evil and that as evil can only be sustained by violence, withdrawal of support of evil requires complete abstention from violence. Nonviolence implies voluntary submission to the penalty for non-cooperation with evil. I am here, therefore, to invite and submit cheerfully to the highest penalty that can be inflicted upon me for what in law is a deliberate crime and what appears to me to be the highest duty of a citizen. The only course open to you, the judge, is either to resign your post, and thus dissociate yourself from evil if you feel that the law you are called upon to administer is an evil and that in reality I am innocent, or to inflict on me the severest penalty if you believe that the system and the law you are assisting to administer are good for the people of this country and that my activity is therefore injurious to the public weal.

MLA CITATION

Gandhi, Mohandas. "Nonviolence Is the First Article of My Faith." *The Norton Reader: An Anthology of Nonfiction*, edited by Melissa A. Goldthwaite et al., 16th ed., W. W. Norton, 2024, pp. 687–90.

QUESTIONS

1. Mohandas Gandhi challenges the judge in the very opening paragraph—either impose the harshest sentence on him or have him resign his post. What is his reasoning for this challenge, and how do you imagine the judge, who would have been a white, British colonial officer, heard that challenge?

2. Gandhi was a lawyer. Where do you see his legal training and expertise in this piece? How do you think that affected his ability to persuade his audience?

3. In paragraph 10, Gandhi avers that "non-cooperation with evil is as much a duty as is cooperation with good." Explain what he means and how it fits into his larger vision of nonviolent civil disobedience. How does his vision compare with Martin Luther King Jr.'s in "Letter from Birmingham Jail" (pp. 695–707)?

4. Following Gandhi's example in paragraph 8, describe, using as much detail as possible, a situation you find unjust or unfair that you suspect the authorities aren't aware of, don't understand, or aren't addressing.

JOHN F. KENNEDY
Inaugural Address

E OBSERVE TODAY not a victory of a party but a celebration of freedom—symbolizing an end as well as a beginning—signifying renewal as well as change. For I have sworn before you and Almighty God the same solemn oath our forebears prescribed nearly a century and three-quarters ago.

The world is very different now. For man holds in his mortal hands the power to abolish all forms of human poverty and all forms of human life. And yet the same revolutionary beliefs for which our forebears fought are still at issue around the globe—the belief that the rights of man come not from the generosity of the state but from the hand of God.

We dare not forget today that we are the heirs of that first revolution. Let the word go forth from this time and place, to friend and foe alike, that the torch has been passed to a new generation of Americans—born in this century, tempered by war, disciplined by a hard and bitter peace, proud of our ancient heritage—and unwilling to witness or permit the slow undoing of those human rights to which this nation has always been committed, and to which we are committed today at home and around the world.

Let every nation know, whether it wishes us well or ill, that we shall pay any price, bear any burden, meet any hardship, support any friend, oppose any foe to assure the survival and success of liberty.

This much we pledge—and more. 5

Inaugural address of John F. Kennedy (1917–1963), America's thirty-fifth president, delivered on January 20, 1961.

To those old allies whose cultural and spiritual origins we share, we pledge the loyalty of faithful friends. United, there is little we cannot do in a host of cooperative ventures. Divided, there is little we can do—for we dare not meet a powerful challenge at odds and split asunder.

To those new states whom we welcome to the ranks of the free, we pledge our word that one form of colonial control shall not have passed away merely to be replaced by a far more iron tyranny. We shall not always expect to find them supporting our view. But we shall always hope to find them strongly supporting their own freedom—and to remember that, in the past, those who foolishly sought power by riding the back of the tiger ended up inside.

To those peoples in the huts and villages of half the globe struggling to break the bonds of mass misery, we pledge our best efforts to help them help themselves, for whatever period is required—not because the Communists may be doing it, not because we seek their votes, but because it is right. If a free society cannot help the many who are poor, it cannot save the few who are rich.

To our sister republics south of our border,[1] we offer a special pledge—to convert our good words into good deeds—in a new alliance for progress—to assist free men and free governments in casting off the chains of poverty. But this peaceful revolution of hope cannot become the prey of hostile powers. Let all our neighbors know that we shall join with them to oppose aggression or subversion anywhere in the Americas. And let every other power know that this hemisphere intends to remain the master of its own house.

10   To that world assembly of sovereign states, the United Nations, our last best hope in an age where the instruments of war have far outpaced the instruments of peace, we renew our pledge of support—to prevent it from becoming merely a forum for invective—to strengthen its shield of the new and the weak—and to enlarge the area in which its writ may run.

Finally, to those nations who would make themselves our adversary, we offer not a pledge but a request: that both sides begin anew the quest for peace, before the dark powers of destruction unleashed by science[2] engulf all humanity in planned or accidental self-destruction.

We dare not tempt them with weakness. For only when our arms are sufficient beyond doubt can we be certain beyond doubt that they will never be employed.

But neither can two great and powerful groups of nations take comfort from our present course—both sides overburdened by the cost of modern weapons, both rightly alarmed by the steady spread of the deadly atom, yet both racing to alter that uncertain balance of terror that stays the hand of mankind's final war.

So let us begin anew—remembering on both sides that civility is not a sign of weakness, and sincerity is always subject to proof. Let us never negotiate out of fear. But let us never fear to negotiate.

---

1. In this paragraph, Kennedy makes many references to Cuba, which by 1961 had turned to communism under Fidel Castro and had allied itself with the Soviet Union.

2. Reference to atomic weapons.

Let both sides explore what problems unite us instead of belaboring those   15
problems which divide us. Let both sides, for the first time, formulate serious and
precise proposals for the inspection and control of arms—and bring the absolute
power to destroy other nations under the absolute control of all nations.

Let both sides seek to invoke the wonders of science instead of its terrors.
Together let us explore the stars, conquer the deserts, eradicate disease, tap
the ocean depths, and encourage the arts and commerce.

Let both sides unite to heed in all corners of the earth the command of
Isaiah—to "undo the heavy burdens and to let the oppressed go free."[3]

And if a beachhead of cooperation may push back the jungle of suspicion,
let both sides join in creating a new endeavor—not a new balance of power but
a new world of law, where the strong are just and the weak secure and the peace
preserved.

All this will not be finished in the first one hundred days. Nor will it be
finished in the first one thousand days, nor in the life of this administration,
nor even perhaps in our lifetime on this planet. But let us begin.

In your hands, my fellow citizens, more than mine, will rest the final suc-   20
cess or failure of our course. Since this country was founded, each generation
of Americans has been summoned to give testimony to its national loyalty.

3. Isaiah 58:6.

The graves of young Americans who answered the call to service surround the globe.

Now the trumpet summons us again—not as a call to bear arms, though arms we need—not as a call to battle, though embattled we are—but a call to bear the burden of a long twilight struggle, year in and year out, "rejoicing in hope, patient in tribulation"[4]—a struggle against the common enemies of man: tyranny, poverty, disease, and war itself.

Can we forge against these enemies a grand and global alliance, North and South, East and West, that can assure a more fruitful life for all mankind? Will you join in that historic effort?

In the long history of the world, only a few generations have been granted the role of defending freedom in its hour of maximum danger. I do not shrink from this responsibility—I welcome it. I do not believe that any of us would exchange places with any other people or any other generation. The energy, the faith, the devotion which we bring to this endeavor will light our country and all who serve it—and the glow from that fire can truly light the world.

And so, my fellow Americans, ask not what your country can do for you— ask what you can do for your country.

25   My fellow citizens of the world, ask not what America will do for you, but what together we can do for the freedom of man.

Finally, whether you are citizens of America or citizens of the world, ask of us here the same high standards of strength and sacrifice which we ask of you. With a good conscience our only sure reward, with history the final judge of our deeds, let us go forth to lead the land we love, asking His blessing and His help, but knowing that here on earth God's work must truly be our own.

MLA CITATION

Kennedy, John F. "Inaugural Address." *The Norton Reader: An Anthology of Nonfiction*, edited by Melissa A. Goldthwaite et al., 16th ed., W. W. Norton, 2024, pp. 691–94.

QUESTIONS

1. Choose a prominent rhetorical device (for example: repetition, allusion, lists, or juxtaposition) that John F. Kennedy uses in his speech and identify where it occurs. For the device you have identified, read it to yourself and then out loud. Why is it effective?

2. On what level of generality is Kennedy operating? When does he get specific?

3. Consider and deepen your answer to question 1 by writing an analysis of Kennedy's speech. Make a claim about the significance of one or more rhetorical devices used in the speech; support your thesis with specific examples from the text.

---

4. Romans 12:12.

MARTIN LUTHER KING JR.
Letter from Birmingham Jail[1]

MY DEAR FELLOW CLERGYMEN:

While confined here in the Birmingham city jail, I came across your recent statement calling my present activities "unwise and untimely." Seldom do I pause to answer criticism of my work and ideas. If I sought to answer all the criticisms that cross my desk, my secretaries would have little time for anything other than such correspondence in the course of the day, and I would have no time for constructive work. But since I feel that you are men of genuine good will and that your criticisms are sincerely set forth, I want to try to answer your statement in what I hope will be patient and reasonable terms.

I think I should indicate why I am here in Birmingham, since you have been influenced by the view which argues against "outsiders coming in." I have the honor of serving as president of the Southern Christian Leadership Conference, an organization operating in every southern state, with headquarters in Atlanta, Georgia. We have some eighty-five affiliated organizations across the South, and one of them is the Alabama Christian Movement for Human Rights. Frequently we share staff, educational, and financial resources with our affiliates. Several months ago the affiliate here in Birmingham asked us to be on call to engage in a nonviolent direct-action program if such were deemed necessary. We readily consented, and when the hour came we lived up to our promise. So I, along with several members of my staff, am here because I was invited here. I am here because I have organizational ties here.

But more basically, I am in Birmingham because injustice is here. Just as the prophets of the eighth century BC left their villages and carried their "thus saith the Lord" far beyond the boundaries of their home towns, and just as the Apostle Paul left his village of Tarsus and carried the gospel of Jesus Christ to the far corners of the Greco-Roman world, so am I compelled to carry the gospel of freedom beyond my own home town. Like Paul, I must constantly respond to the Macedonian call for aid.

Written on April 16, 1963, while Martin Luther King Jr. was jailed for civil disobedience; subsequently published in Why We Can't Wait *(1964), King's book on nonviolent resistance to segregation in America.*

1. This response to a published statement by eight fellow clergymen from Alabama (Bishop C. C. J. Carpenter, Bishop Joseph A. Durick, Rabbi Milton L. Grafman, Bishop Paul Hardin, Bishop Nolan B. Harmon, the Reverend George M. Murray, the Reverend Edward V. Ramage and the Reverend Earl Stallings) was composed under somewhat constricting circumstances. Begun on the margins of the newspaper in which the statement appeared while I was in jail, the letter was continued on scraps of writing paper supplied by a friendly Negro trusty, and concluded on a pad my attorneys were eventually permitted to leave me. Although the text remains in substance unaltered, I have indulged in the author's prerogative of polishing it for publication [Author's note].

Moreover, I am cognizant of the interrelatedness of all communities and states. I cannot sit idly by in Atlanta and not be concerned about what happens in Birmingham. Injustice anywhere is a threat to justice everywhere. We are caught in an inescapable network of mutuality, tied in a single garment of destiny. Whatever affects one directly, affects all indirectly. Never again can we afford to live with the narrow, provincial "outside agitator" idea. Anyone who lives inside the United States can never be considered an outsider anywhere within its bounds.

5   You deplore the demonstrations taking place in Birmingham. But your statement, I am sorry to say, fails to express a similar concern for the conditions that brought about the demonstrations. I am sure that none of you would want to rest content with the superficial kind of social analysis that deals merely with effects and does not grapple with underlying causes. It is unfortunate that demonstrations are taking place in Birmingham, but it is even more unfortunate that the city's white power structure left the Negro community with no alternative.

In any nonviolent campaign there are four basic steps: collection of the facts to determine whether injustices exist; negotiation; self-purification; and direct action. We have gone through all these steps in Birmingham. There can be no gainsaying the fact that racial injustice engulfs this community. Birmingham is probably the most thoroughly segregated city in the United States. Its ugly record of brutality is widely known. Negroes have experienced grossly unjust treatment in the courts. There have been more unsolved bombings of Negro homes and churches in Birmingham than in any other city in the nation. These are the hard, brutal facts of the case. On the basis of these conditions, Negro leaders sought to negotiate with the city fathers. But the latter consistently refused to engage in good-faith negotiation.

Then, last September, came the opportunity to talk with leaders of Birmingham's economic community. In the course of the negotiations, certain promises were made by the merchants—for example, to remove the stores' humiliating racial signs. On the basis of these promises, the Reverend Fred Shuttlesworth and the leaders of the Alabama Christian Movement for Human Rights agreed to a moratorium on all demonstrations. As the weeks and months went by, we realized that we were the victims of a broken promise. A few signs, briefly removed, returned; the others remained.

As in so many past experiences, our hopes had been blasted, and the shadow of deep disappointment settled upon us. We had no alternative except to prepare for direct action, whereby we would present our very bodies as a means of laying our case before the conscience of the local and the national community. Mindful of the difficulties involved, we decided to undertake a process of self-purification. We began a series of workshops on nonviolence, and we repeatedly asked ourselves: "Are you able to accept blows without retaliating?" "Are you able to endure the ordeal of jail?" We decided to schedule our direct-action program for the Easter season, realizing that except for Christmas, this is the main shopping period of the year. Knowing that a strong economic-withdrawal program would be the by-product of direct action, we felt that this would be the best time to bring pressure to bear on the merchants for the needed change.

Then it occurred to us that Birmingham's mayoral election was coming up in March, and we speedily decided to postpone action until after election day. When we discovered that the Commissioner of Public Safety, Eugene "Bull" Connor, had piled up enough votes to be in the run-off, we decided again to postpone action until the day after the run-off so that the demonstrations could not be used to cloud the issues. Like many others, we wanted to see Mr. Connor defeated, and to this end we endured postponement after postponement. Having aided in this community need, we felt that our direct-action program could be delayed no longer.

You may well ask, "Why direct action? Why sit-ins, marches, and so forth? Isn't negotiation a better path?" You are quite right in calling for negotiation. Indeed, this is the very purpose of direct action. Nonviolent direct action seeks to create such a crisis and foster such a tension that a community which has constantly refused to negotiate is forced to confront the issue. It seeks so to dramatize the issue that it can no longer be ignored. My citing the creation of tension as part of the work of the nonviolent-resister may sound rather shocking. But I must confess that I am not afraid of the word "tension." I have earnestly opposed violent tension, but there is a type of constructive, nonviolent tension which is necessary for growth. Just as Socrates felt that it was necessary to create a tension in the mind so that individuals could rise from the bondage of myths and half-truths to the unfettered realm of creative analysis and objective appraisal, so must we see the need for nonviolent gadflies to create the kind of tension in society that will help men rise from the dark depths of prejudice and racism to the majestic heights of understanding and brotherhood. 10

The purpose of our direct-action program is to create a situation so crisis-packed that it will inevitably open the door to negotiation. I therefore concur with you in your call for negotiation. Too long has our beloved Southland been bogged down in a tragic effort to live in monologue rather than dialogue.

One of the basic points in your statement is that the action that I and my associates have taken in Birmingham is untimely. Some have asked: "Why didn't you give the new city administration time to act?" The only answer that I can give to this query is that the new Birmingham administration must be prodded about as much as the outgoing one, before it will act. We are sadly mistaken if we feel that the election of Albert Boutwell as mayor will bring the millennium to Birmingham. While Mr. Boutwell is a much more gentle person than Mr. Connor, they are both segregationists, dedicated to maintenance of the status quo. I have hoped that Mr. Boutwell will be reasonable enough to see the futility of massive resistance to desegregation. But he will not see this without pressure from devotees of civil rights. My friends, I must say to you that we have not made a single gain in civil rights without determined legal and nonviolent pressure. Lamentably, it is an historical fact that privileged groups seldom give up their privileges voluntarily. Individuals may see the moral light and voluntarily give up their unjust posture; but, as Reinhold Niebuhr[2] has reminded us, groups tend to be more immoral than individuals.

2. American Protestant theologian (1892–1971).

We know through painful experience that freedom is never voluntarily given by the oppressor; it must be demanded by the oppressed. Frankly, I have yet to engage in a direct-action campaign that was "well timed" in the view of those who have not suffered unduly from the disease of segregation. For years now I have heard the word "Wait!" It rings in the ear of every Negro with piercing familiarity. This "Wait" has almost always meant "Never." We must come to see, with one of our distinguished jurists, that "justice too long delayed is justice denied."

We have waited for more than 340 years for our constitutional and God-given rights. The nations of Asia and Africa are moving with jetlike speed toward gaining political independence, but we still creep at horse-and-buggy pace toward gaining a cup of coffee at a lunch counter. Perhaps it is easy for those who have never felt the stinging darts of segregation to say, "Wait." But when you have seen vicious mobs lynch your mothers and fathers at will and drown your sisters and brothers at whim; when you have seen hate-filled policemen curse, kick, and even kill your black brothers and sisters; when you see the vast majority of your twenty million Negro brothers smothering in an airtight cage of poverty in the midst of an affluent society; when you suddenly find your tongue twisted and your speech stammering as you seek to explain to your six-year-old daughter why she can't go to the public amusement park that has just been advertised on television, and see tears welling up in her eyes when she is told that Funtown is closed to colored children, and see ominous clouds of inferiority beginning to form in her little mental sky, and see her beginning to distort her personality by developing an unconscious bitterness toward white people; when you have to concoct an answer for a five-year-old son who is asking, "Daddy, why do white people treat colored people so mean?"; when you take a cross-country drive and find it necessary to sleep night after night in the uncomfortable corners of your automobile because no motel will accept you; when you are humiliated day in and day out by nagging signs reading "white" and "colored"; when your first name becomes "nigger," your middle name becomes "boy" (however old you are) and your last name becomes "John," and your wife and mother are never given the respected title "Mrs."; when you are harried by day and haunted by night by the fact that you are a Negro, living constantly at tiptoe stance, never quite knowing what to expect next, and are plagued with inner fears and outer resentments; when you are forever fighting a degenerating sense of "nobodiness"—then you will understand why we find it difficult to wait. There comes a time when the cup of endurance runs over, and men are no longer willing to be plunged into the abyss of despair. I hope, sirs, you can understand our legitimate and unavoidable impatience.

15　　　You express a great deal of anxiety over our willingness to break laws. This is certainly a legitimate concern. Since we so diligently urge people to obey the Supreme Court's decision of 1954 outlawing segregation in the public schools, at first glance it may seem rather paradoxical for us consciously to break laws. One may well ask: "How can you advocate breaking some laws and obeying others?" The answer lies in the fact that there are two types of laws: just and unjust. I would be the first to advocate obeying just laws. One has not only a legal but a moral responsibility to obey just laws. Conversely, one has a moral responsibility to disobey unjust laws. I would agree with St. Augustine[3] that "an unjust law is no law at all."

Now, what is the difference between the two? How does one determine whether a law is just or unjust? A just law is a man-made code that squares with the moral law or the law of God. An unjust law is a code that is out of harmony with the moral law. To put it in the terms of St. Thomas Aquinas:[4] An unjust law is a human law that is not rooted in eternal law and natural law. Any law that uplifts human personality is just. Any law that degrades human personality is unjust. All segregation statutes are unjust because segregation distorts the soul and damages the personality. It gives the segregator a false sense of superiority and the segregated a false sense of inferiority. Segregation, to use the terminology of the Jewish philosopher Martin Buber,[5] substitutes an "I-it" relationship for an "I-thou" relationship and ends up relegating persons to the status of things. Hence segregation is not only politically, economically, and sociologically unsound, it is morally wrong and sinful. Paul Tillich[6] has said that sin is separation. Is not segregation an existential expression of man's tragic separation, his awful estrangement, his terrible sinfulness? Thus it is that I can urge men to obey the 1954 decision of the Supreme Court, for it is morally right; and I can urge them to disobey segregation ordinances, for they are morally wrong.

Let us consider a more concrete example of just and unjust laws. An unjust law is a code that a numerical or power majority group compels a minority group to obey but does not make binding on itself. This is *difference* made legal. By the same token, a just law is a code that a majority compels a minority to follow and that it is willing to follow itself. This is *sameness* made legal.

Let me give another explanation. A law is unjust if it is inflicted on a minority that, as a result of being denied the right to vote, had no part in enacting or devising the law. Who can say that the legislature of Alabama which set up that state's segregation laws was democratically elected? Throughout Alabama all sorts of devious methods are used to prevent Negroes from becoming registered voters, and there are some counties in which, even though Negroes constitute a majority of the population, not a single Negro is registered. Can any law enacted under such circumstances be considered democratically structured?

Sometimes a law is just on its face and unjust in its application. For instance, I have been arrested on a charge of parading without a permit. Now, there is nothing wrong in having an ordinance which requires a permit for a parade. But such an ordinance becomes unjust when it is used to maintain segregation and to deny citizens the First-Amendment privilege of peaceful assembly and protest.

I hope you are able to see the distinction I am trying to point out. In no sense do I advocate evading or defying the law, as would the rabid segregationist. That would lead to anarchy. One who breaks an unjust law must do so openly, lovingly,   20

3. Early Christian church father (354–430).
4. Christian philosopher and theologian (1225–1274).
5. Austrian-born Israeli philosopher (1878–1965).
6. German-born American Protestant theologian (1886–1965).

and with a willingness to accept the penalty. I submit that an individual who breaks a law that conscience tells him is unjust, and who willingly accepts the penalty of imprisonment in order to arouse the conscience of the community over its injustice, is in reality expressing the highest respect for law.

Of course, there is nothing new about this kind of civil disobedience. It was evidenced sublimely in the refusal of Shadrach, Meshach, and Abednego to obey the laws of Nebuchadnezzar,[7] on the ground that a higher moral law was at stake. It was practiced superbly by the early Christians, who were willing to face hungry lions and the excruciating pain of chopping blocks rather than submit to certain unjust laws of the Roman Empire. To a degree, academic freedom is a reality today because Socrates practiced civil disobedience.[8] In our own nation, the Boston Tea Party represented a massive act of civil disobedience.

We should never forget that everything Adolf Hitler did in Germany was "legal" and everything the Hungarian freedom fighters[9] did in Hungary was "illegal." It was "illegal" to aid and comfort a Jew in Hitler's Germany. Even so, I am sure that, had I lived in Germany at the time, I would have aided and comforted my Jewish brothers. If today I lived in a Communist country where certain principles dear to the Christian faith are suppressed, I would openly advocate disobeying that country's anti-religious laws.

I must make two honest confessions to you, my Christian and Jewish brothers. First, I must confess that over the past few years I have been gravely disappointed with the white moderate. I have almost reached the regrettable conclusion that the Negro's great stumbling block in his stride toward freedom is not the White Citizen's Counciler or the Ku Klux Klanner, but the white moderate, who is more devoted to "order" than to justice; who prefers a negative peace which is the absence of tension to a positive peace which is the presence of justice; who constantly says, "I agree with you in the goal you seek, but I cannot agree with your methods of direct action"; who paternalistically believes he can set the timetable for another man's freedom; who lives by a mythical concept of time and who constantly advises the Negro to wait for a "more convenient season." Shallow understanding from people of good will is more frustrating than absolute misunderstanding from people of ill will. Lukewarm acceptance is much more bewildering than outright rejection.

I had hoped that the white moderate would understand that law and order exist for the purpose of establishing justice and that when they fail in this purpose they become the dangerously structured dams that block the flow of social progress. I had hoped that the white moderate would understand that the present tension in the South is a necessary phase of the transition from an obnoxious negative peace, in which the Negro passively accepted his unjust plight, to

---

7. Their story is told in Daniel 3.

8. Socrates, the ancient Greek philosopher, was tried by the Athenians for corrupting their youth through his skeptical, questioning manner of teaching. He refused to change his ways and was condemned to death.

9. In the anti-communist revolution of 1956, which was quickly put down by the Soviet army.

a substantive and positive peace, in which all men will respect the dignity and worth of human personality. Actually, we who engage in nonviolent direct action are not the creators of tension. We merely bring to the surface the hidden tension that is already alive. We bring it out in the open, where it can be seen and dealt with. Like a boil that can never be cured so long as it is covered up but must be opened with all its ugliness to the natural medicines of air and light, injustice must be exposed, with all the tension its exposure creates, to the light of human conscience and the air of national opinion, before it can be cured.

In your statement you assert that our actions, even though peaceful, must   25
be condemned because they precipitate violence. But is this a logical assertion? Isn't this like condemning a robbed man because his possession of money precipitated the evil act of robbery? Isn't this like condemning Socrates because his unswerving commitment to truth and his philosophical inquiries precipitated the act by the misguided populace in which they made him drink hemlock? Isn't this like condemning Jesus because his unique God-consciousness and never-ceasing devotion to God's will precipitated the evil act of crucifixion? We must come to see that, as the federal courts have consistently affirmed, it is wrong to urge an individual to cease his efforts to gain his basic constitutional rights because the quest may precipitate violence. Society must protect the robbed and punish the robber.

I had also hoped that the white moderate would reject the myth concerning time in relation to the struggle for freedom. I have just received a letter from a white brother in Texas. He writes: "All Christians know that the colored people will receive equal rights eventually, but it is possible that you are in too great a religious hurry. It has taken Christianity almost two thousand years to accomplish what it has. The teachings of Christ take time to come to earth." Such an attitude stems from a tragic misconception of time, from the strangely irrational notion that there is something in the very flow of time that will inevitably cure all ills. Actually, time itself is neutral; it can be used either destructively or constructively. More and more I feel that the people of ill will have used time much more effectively than have the people of good will. We will have to repent in this generation not merely for the hateful words and actions of the bad people, but for the appalling silence of the good people. Human progress never rolls in on wheels of inevitability; it comes through the tireless efforts of men willing to be co-workers with God, and without this hard work, time itself becomes an ally of the forces of social stagnation. We must use time creatively, in the knowledge that the time is always ripe to do right. Now is the time to make real the promise of democracy and transform our pending national elegy into a creative psalm of brotherhood. Now is the time to lift our national policy from the quicksand of racial injustice to the solid rock of human dignity.

You speak of our activity in Birmingham as extreme. At first I was rather disappointed that fellow clergymen would see my nonviolent efforts as those of an extremist. I began thinking about the fact that I stand in the middle of two opposing forces in the Negro community. One is a force of complacency, made up in part of Negroes who, as a result of long years of oppression, are so drained of self-respect and a sense of "somebodiness" that they have adjusted to segregation; and in part of a few middle-class Negroes who, because of a degree of academic and economic security and because in some ways they profit by segregation, have become insensitive to the problems of the masses. The other force is one of bitterness and hatred, and it comes perilously close to advocating violence. It is expressed in the various black nationalist groups that are springing up across the nation, the largest and best-known being Elijah Muhammad's Muslim movement.[10] Nourished by the Negro's frustration over the continued existence of racial discrimination, this movement is made up of people who have lost faith in America, who have absolutely repudiated Christianity, and who have concluded that the white man is an incorrigible "devil."

I have tried to stand between these two forces, saying that we need emulate neither the "do-nothingism" of the complacent nor the hatred and despair of the black nationalist. For there is the more excellent way of love and nonviolent protest. I am grateful to God that, through the influence of the Negro church, the way of nonviolence became an integral part of our struggle.

If this philosophy had not emerged, by now many streets of the South would, I am convinced, be flowing with blood. And I am further convinced that if our white brothers dismiss as "rabblerousers" and "outside agitators" those of us who employ nonviolent direct action, and if they refuse to support our nonviolent efforts, millions of Negroes will, out of frustration and despair, seek solace and security in black-nationalist ideologies—a development that would inevitably lead to a frightening racial nightmare.

30   Oppressed people cannot remain oppressed forever. The yearning for freedom eventually manifests itself, and that is what has happened to the American Negro. Something within has reminded him of his birthright of freedom, and something without has reminded him that it can be gained. Consciously or unconsciously, he has been caught up by the *Zeitgeist*,[11] and with his black brothers of Africa and his brown and yellow brothers of Asia, South America, and the Caribbean, the United States Negro is moving with a sense of great urgency toward the promised land of racial justice. If one recognizes this vital urge that has engulfed the Negro community, one should readily understand why public demonstrations are taking place. The Negro has many pent-up resentments and latent frustrations, and he must release them. So let him march; let him make prayer pilgrimages to the city hall; let him go on freedom rides—and try to understand why he must do so. If his repressed emotions are not released in nonviolent ways, they will seek expression through violence; this is not a threat but a fact of history. So I have not said to my people, "Get rid of your discontent." Rather, I have tried to say that this normal and healthy discontent can be channeled into the creative outlet of nonviolent direct action. And now this approach is being termed extremist.

But though I was initially disappointed at being categorized as an extremist, as I continued to think about the matter I gradually gained a measure of satisfaction from the label. Was not Jesus an extremist for love: "Love your enemies, bless

10. Muhammad (1897–1975) succeeded to the leadership of the Nation of Islam in 1934.
11. Spirit of the times.

them that curse you, do good to them that hate you, and pray for them which despitefully use you, and persecute you." Was not Amos an extremist for justice: "Let justice roll down like waters and righteousness like an ever-flowing stream." Was not Paul an extremist for the Christian gospel: "I bear in my body the marks of the Lord Jesus." Was not Martin Luther an extremist: "Here I stand; I cannot do otherwise, so help me God." And John Bunyan:[12] "I will stay in jail to the end of my days before I make a butchery of my conscience." And Abraham Lincoln: "This nation cannot survive half slave and half free." And Thomas Jefferson: "We hold these truths to be self-evident, that all men are created equal. . . ." So the question is not whether we will be extremists, but what kind of extremists we will be. Will we be extremists for hate or for love? Will we be extremists for the preservation of injustice or for the extension of justice? In that dramatic scene on Calvary's hill three men were crucified. We must never forget that all three were crucified for the same crime—the crime of extremism. Two were extremists for immorality, and thus fell below their environment. The other, Jesus Christ, was an extremist for love, truth, and goodness, and thereby rose above his environment. Perhaps the South, the nation, and the world are in dire need of creative extremists.

I had hoped that the white moderate would see this need. Perhaps I was too optimistic; perhaps I expected too much. I suppose I should have realized that few members of the oppressor race can understand the deep groans and passionate yearnings of the oppressed race, and still fewer have the vision to see that injustice must be rooted out by strong, persistent, and determined action. I am thankful, however, that some of our white brothers in the South have grasped the meaning of this social revolution and committed themselves to it. They are still all too few in quantity, but they are big in quality. Some—such as Ralph McGill, Lillian Smith, Harry Golden, James McBridge Dabbs, Ann Braden, and Sarah Patton Boyle—have written about our struggle in eloquent and prophetic terms. Others have marched with us down nameless streets of the South. They have languished in filthy, roach-infested jails, suffering the abuse and brutality of policemen who view them as "dirty nigger-lovers." Unlike so many of their moderate brothers and sisters, they have recognized the urgency of the moment and sensed the need for powerful "action" antidotes to combat the disease of segregation.

Let me take note of my other major disappointment. I have been so greatly disappointed with the white church and its leadership. Of course, there are some notable exceptions. I am not unmindful of the fact that each of you has taken some significant stands on this issue. I commend you, Reverend Stallings, for your Christian stand on this past Sunday, in welcoming Negroes to your worship service on a nonsegregated basis. I commend the Catholic leaders of this state for integrating Spring Hill College several years ago.

But despite these notable exceptions, I must honestly reiterate that I have been disappointed with the church. I do not say this as one of those negative

12. Amos, Old Testament prophet; Paul, New Testament apostle; Luther (1483–1546), German Protestant reformer; Bunyan (1628–1688), English preacher and author.

critics who can always find something wrong with the church. I say this as a minister of the gospel, who loves the church; who was nurtured in its bosom; who has been sustained by its spiritual blessings and who will remain true to it as long as the cord of life shall lengthen.

35   When I was suddenly catapulted into the leadership of the bus protest in Montgomery, Alabama, a few years ago,[13] I felt we would be supported by the white church. I felt that the white ministers, priests, and rabbis of the South would be among our strongest allies. Instead, some have been outright opponents, refusing to understand the freedom movement and misrepresenting its leaders; all too many others have been more cautious than courageous and have remained silent behind the anesthetizing security of stained-glass windows.

In spite of my shattered dreams, I came to Birmingham with the hope that the white religious leadership of this community would see the justice of our cause and, with deep moral concern, would serve as the channel through which our just grievances could reach the power structure. I had hoped that each of you would understand. But again I have been disappointed.

I have heard numerous southern religious leaders admonish their worshipers to comply with a desegregation decision because it is the law, but I have longed to hear white ministers declare: "Follow this decree because integration is morally right and because the Negro is your brother." In the midst of blatant injustices inflicted upon the Negro, I have watched white churchmen stand on the sideline and mouth pious irrelevancies and sanctimonious trivialities. In the midst of a mighty struggle to rid our nation of racial and economic injustice, I have heard many ministers say: "Those are social issues, with which the gospel has no real concern." And I have watched many churches commit themselves to a completely otherworldly religion which makes a strange, un-Biblical distinction between body and soul, between the sacred and the secular.

I have traveled the length and breadth of Alabama, Mississippi, and all the other southern states. On sweltering summer days and crisp autumn mornings I have looked at the South's beautiful churches with their lofty spires pointing heavenward. I have beheld the impressive outlines of her massive religious-education buildings. Over and over I have found myself asking: "What kind of people worship here? Who is their God? Where were their voices when the lips of Governor Barnett dripped with words of interposition and nullification? Where were they when Governor Wallace[14] gave a clarion call for defiance and hatred? Where were their voices of support when bruised and weary Negro men and women decided to rise from the dark dungeons of complacency to the bright hills of creative protest?"

Yes, these questions are still in my mind. In deep disappointment I have wept over the laxity of the church. But be assured that my tears have been tears of love. There can be no deep disappointment where there is not deep love. Yes,

13. In December 1955, when Rosa Parks refused to move to the back of a bus.

14. Ross Barnett (1898–1987), governor of Mississippi, opposed James Meredith's admission to the University of Mississippi; George Wallace (1919–1998), governor of Alabama, opposed admission of several Black students to the University of Alabama.

I love the church. How could I do otherwise? I am in the rather unique position of being the son, the grandson, and the great-grandson of preachers. Yes, I see the church as the body of Christ. But, oh! How we have blemished and scarred that body through social neglect and through fear of being nonconformists.

There was a time when the church was very powerful—in the time when the early Christians rejoiced at being deemed worthy to suffer for what they believed. In those days the church was not merely a thermometer that recorded the ideas and principles of popular opinion; it was a thermostat that transformed the mores of society. Whenever the early Christians entered a town, the people in power became disturbed and immediately sought to convict the Christians for being "disturbers of the peace" and "outside agitators." But the Christians pressed on, in the conviction that they were "a colony of heaven," called to obey God rather than man. Small in number, they were big in commitment. They were too God-intoxicated to be "astronomically intimidated." By their effort and example they brought an end to such ancient evils as infanticide and gladiatorial contests.

Things are different now. So often the contemporary church is a weak, ineffectual voice with an uncertain sound. So often it is an archdefender of the status quo. Far from being disturbed by the presence of the church, the power structure of the average community is consoled by the church's silent—and often even vocal—sanction of things as they are.

But the judgment of God is upon the church as never before. If today's church does not recapture the sacrificial spirit of the early church, it will lose its authenticity, forfeit the loyalty of millions, and be dismissed as an irrelevant social club with no meaning for the twentieth century. Every day I meet young people whose disappointment with the church has turned into outright disgust.

Perhaps I have once again been too optimistic. Is organized religion too inextricably bound to the status quo to save our nation and the world? Perhaps I must turn my faith to the inner spiritual church, the church within the church, as the true *ekklesia*[15] and the hope of the world. But again I am thankful to God that some noble souls from the ranks of organized religion have broken loose from the paralyzing chains of conformity and joined us as active partners in the struggle for freedom. They have left their secure congregations and walked the streets of Albany, Georgia, with us. They have gone down the highways of the South on tortuous rides for freedom. Yes, they have gone to jail with us. Some have been dismissed from their churches, have lost the support of their bishops and fellow ministers. But they have acted in the faith that right defeated is stronger than evil triumphant. Their witness has been the spiritual salt that has preserved the true meaning of the gospel in these troubled times. They have carved a tunnel of hope through the dark mountain of disappointment.

I hope the church as a whole will meet the challenge of this decisive hour. But even if the church does not come to the aid of justice, I have no despair about the future. I have no fear about the outcome of our struggle in Birmingham, even if our motives are at present misunderstood. We will reach the goal

15. Greek New Testament word for "the early Christian church."

of freedom in Birmingham and all over the nation, because the goal of America is freedom. Abused and scorned though we may be, our destiny is tied up with America's destiny. Before the pilgrims landed at Plymouth, we were here. Before the pen of Jefferson etched the majestic words of the Declaration of Independence across the pages of history, we were here. For more than two centuries our forebears labored in this country without wages; they made cotton king; they built the homes of their masters while suffering gross injustice and shameful humiliation—and yet out of a bottomless vitality they continued to thrive and develop. If the inexpressible cruelties of slavery could not stop us, the opposition we now face will surely fail. We will win our freedom because the sacred heritage of our nation and the eternal will of God are embodied in our echoing demands.

45   Before closing I feel impelled to mention one other point in your statement that has troubled me profoundly. You warmly commended the Birmingham police force for keeping "order" and "preventing violence." I doubt that you would have so warmly commended the police force if you had seen its dogs sinking their teeth into unarmed, nonviolent Negroes. I doubt that you would so quickly commend the policemen if you were to observe their ugly and inhumane treatment of Negroes here in the city jail; if you were to watch them push and curse old Negro women and young Negro girls; if you were to see them slap and kick old Negro men and young boys; if you were to observe them, as they did on two occasions, refuse to give us food because we wanted to sing our grace together. I cannot join you in your praise of the Birmingham police department.

It is true that the police have exercised a degree of discipline in handling the demonstrators. In this sense they have conducted themselves rather "nonviolently" in public. But for what purpose? To preserve the evil system of segregation. Over the past few years I have consistently preached that nonviolence demands that the means we use must be as pure as the ends we seek. I have tried to make clear that it is wrong to use immoral means to attain moral ends. But now I must affirm that it is just as wrong, or perhaps even more so, to use moral means to preserve immoral ends. Perhaps Mr. Connor and his policemen have been rather nonviolent in public, as was Chief Pritchett in Albany, Georgia, but they have used the moral means of nonviolence to maintain the immoral end of racial injustice. As T. S. Eliot[16] has said, "The last temptation is the greatest treason: To do the right deed for the wrong reason."

I wish you had commended the Negro sit-inners and demonstrators of Birmingham for their sublime courage, their willingness to suffer, and their amazing discipline in the midst of great provocation. One day the South will recognize its real heroes. They will be the James Merediths,[17] with the noble sense of purpose that enables them to face jeering and hostile mobs, and with the agonizing loneliness that characterizes the life of the pioneer. They will be

16. American-born English poet (1888–1965). The lines are from his play *Murder in the Cathedral*.

17. Meredith (b. 1933), the first Black student to enroll at the University of Mississippi.

old, oppressed, battered Negro women, symbolized in a seventy-two-year-old woman[18] in Montgomery, Alabama, who rose up with a sense of dignity and with her people decided not to ride segregated buses, and who responded with ungrammatical profundity to one who inquired about her weariness: "My feets is tired, but my soul is at rest." They will be the young high school and college students, the young ministers of the gospel and a host of their elders, coura-geously and nonviolently sitting in at lunch counters and willingly going to jail for conscience sake. One day the South will know that when these disinher-ited children of God sat down at lunch counters, they were in reality standing up for what is best in the American dream and for the most sacred values in our Judaeo-Christian heritage, thereby bringing our nation back to those great wells of democracy which were dug deep by the founding fathers in their formulation of the Constitution and the Declaration of Independence.

Never before have I written so long a letter. I'm afraid it is much too long to take your precious time. I can assure you that it would have been much shorter if I had been writing from a comfortable desk, but what else can one do when he is alone in a narrow jail cell, other than write long letters, think long thoughts, and pray long prayers?

If I have said anything in this letter that overstates the truth and indicates an unreasonable impatience, I beg you to forgive me. If I have said anything that understates the truth and indicates my having a patience that allows me to settle for anything less than brotherhood, I beg God to forgive me.

I hope this letter finds you strong in the faith. I also hope that circum-   50
stances will soon make it possible for me to meet each of you, not as an integra-tionist or a civil-rights leader but as a fellow clergyman and a Christian brother. Let us all hope that the dark clouds of racial prejudice will soon pass away and the deep fog of misunderstanding will be lifted from our fear-drenched commu-nities, and in some not too distant tomorrow the radiant stars of love and broth-erhood will shine over our great nation with all their scintillating beauty.

Yours for the cause of Peace and Brotherhood,
MARTIN LUTHER KING JR.

MLA CITATION

King, Martin Luther, Jr. "Letter from Birmingham Jail." *The Norton Reader: An Anthology of Nonfiction*, edited by Melissa A. Goldthwaite et al., 16th ed., W. W. Norton, 2024, pp. 695–707.

QUESTIONS

1. Martin Luther King Jr. addressed "Letter from Birmingham Jail" to eight fellow clergy members who had written a statement criticizing his activities (see note 1). Where and how, in the course of the "Letter," does he attempt to make common cause with them?

---

18. King is referring to Rosa Parks (1913–2005).

2. King was trained in oral composition, that is, in composing and delivering sermons. One device he uses is prediction: He announces, in advance, the organization of what he is about to say. Locate examples of prediction in the "Letter."

3. Summarize the theory of nonviolent resistance that King presents in this essay.

4. Imagine an unjust law that, to you, would justify civil disobedience. In an essay, describe the law, the form your resistance would take, and the penalties you would expect to incur.

AUDRE LORDE
Uses of Anger: Women Responding to Racism

R ACISM. The belief in the inherent superiority of one race over all others and thereby the right to dominance, manifest and implied. WOMEN RESPOND TO RACISM. My response to racism is anger. I have lived with that anger, ignoring it, feeding upon it, learning to use it before it laid my visions to waste, for most of my life. Once I did it in silence, afraid of the weight. My fear of anger taught me nothing. Your fear of that anger will teach you nothing, also.

Women responding to racism means women responding to anger; the anger of exclusion, of unquestioned privilege, of racial distortions, of silence, ill-use, stereotyping, defensiveness, misnaming, betrayal and co-option.

My anger is a response to racist attitudes and to the actions and presumptions that arise out of those attitudes. If your dealings with other women reflect those attitudes, then my anger and your attendant fears are spotlights that can be used for growth in the same way I have used learning to express anger for my growth. But for corrective surgery, not guilt. Guilt and defensiveness are bricks in a wall against which we all flounder; they serve none of our futures.

5   Because I do not want this to become a theoretical discussion, I am going to give a few examples of interchanges between women that illustrate these points. In the interest of time, I am going to cut them short. I want you to know there were many more.

For example:

I speak out of direct and particular anger at an academic conference, and a white woman says, "Tell me how you feel but don't say it too harshly or I cannot hear you." But is it my manner that keeps her from hearing, or the threat of a message that her life may change?

The women's studies programme of a southern university invites a Black woman to read following a week-long forum on Black and white women. "What has this week given to you?" I ask. The most vocal white woman says, "I think

Audre Lorde delivered this speech at the National Women's Studies Association Conference in Storrs, Connecticut, in 1981. It was later published in The Master's Tools Will Never Dismantle the Master's House *(2017).*

I've gotten a lot. I feel Black women really understand me a lot better now; they have a better idea of where I'm coming from." As if understanding her lay at the core of the racist problem.

After fifteen years of a women's movement which professes to address the life concerns and possible futures of all women, I still hear, on campus after campus, "How can we address the issues of racism? No women of colour attended." Or, the other side of that statement, "We have no one in our department equipped to teach their work." In other words, racism is a Black women's problem, a problem of women of colour, and only we can discuss it.

After I read from my work entitled "A Poem for Women in Rage" a white   10
woman asks me: "Are you going to do anything with how we can deal directly with *our* anger? I feel it's so important." I ask, "How do you use *your* rage?" And then I have to turn away from the blank look in her eyes, before she can invite me to participate in her own annihilation. I do not exist to feel her anger for her.

White women are beginning to examine their relationships to Black women, yet often I hear them wanting only to deal with little coloured children across the roads of childhood, the beloved nursemaid, the occasional second-grade classmate—those tender memories of what was once mysterious and intriguing or neutral. You avoid the childhood assumptions formed by the raucous laughter at Rastus and Alfalfa,[1] the acute message of your mommy's handkerchief spread upon the park bench because I had just been sitting there, the indelible and dehumanizing portraits of *Amos 'n' Andy* and your daddy's humorous bedtime stories.

I wheel my two-year-old daughter in a shopping cart through a supermarket in Eastchester in 1967, and a little white girl riding past in her mother's cart calls out excitedly, "Oh look, mommy, a baby maid!" And your mother shushes you, but she does not correct you. And so fifteen years later, at a conference on racism, you can still find that story humorous. But I hear your laughter is full of terror and disease.

A white academic welcomes the appearance of a collection by non-Black women of colour. "It allows me to deal with racism without dealing with the harshness of Black women," she says to me.

At an international cultural gathering of women, a well-known white american woman poet interrupts the reading of the work of women of colour to read her own poem, and then dashes off to an "important panel."

If women in the academy truly want a dialogue about racism, it will require   15
recognizing the needs and the living contexts of other women. When an academic woman says, "I can't afford it," she may mean she is making a choice about how to spend her available money. But when a woman on welfare says "I can't afford it" she means she is surviving on an amount of money that was barely subsistence in 1972, and she often does not have enough to eat. Yet the National Women's Studies Association here in 1981 holds a conference in which

1. Black characters from popular culture who played to racist stereotypes for comic effect.

it commits itself to responding to racism, yet refuses to waive the registration fee for poor women and women of colour who wished to present and conduct workshops. This has made it impossible for many women of colour—for instance, Wilmette Brown, of Black Women for Wages for Housework—to participate in this conference.

Is this to be merely another case of the academy discussing life within the closed circuits of the academy?

To the white women present who recognize these attitudes as familiar, but most of all, to all my sisters of colour who live and survive thousands of such encounters—to my sisters of colour who like me still tremble their rage under harness or who sometimes question the expression of our rage as useless and disruptive (the two most popular accusations)—I want to speak about anger, my anger, and what I have learned from my travels through its dominions.

> everything can be used
> except what is wasteful
> (you will need
> to remember this when you are accused of destruction.)
> from "For Each of You"

Every woman has a well-stocked arsenal of anger potentially useful against those oppressions, personal and institutional, which brought that anger into being. Focused with precision it can become a powerful source of energy serving progress and change. And when I speak of change, I do not mean a simple switch of positions or a temporary lessening of tensions, nor the ability to smile or feel good. I am speaking of a basic and radical alteration in those assumptions underlining our lives.

I have seen situations where white women hear a racist remark, resent what has been said, become filled with fury, and remain silent because they are afraid. That unexpressed anger lies within them like an undetonated device, usually to be hurled at the first woman of colour who talks about racism.

But anger expressed and translated into action in the service of our vision and our future is a liberating and strengthening act of clarification, for it is in the painful process of this translation that we identify who are our allies with whom we have grave differences, and who are our genuine enemies.

20   Anger is loaded with information and energy. When I speak of women of colour, I do not only mean Black women. The woman of colour who is not Black and who charges me with rendering her invisible by assuming that her struggles with racism are identical with my own has something to tell me that I had better learn from, lest we both waste ourselves fighting the truths between us. If I participate, knowingly or otherwise, in my sister's oppression and she calls me on it, to answer her anger with my own only blankets the substance of our exchange with reaction. It wastes energy. And yes, it is very difficult to stand still and to listen to another woman's voice delineate an agony I do not share, or one to which I myself have contributed.

In this place we speak removed from the more blatant reminders of our embattlement as women. This need not blind us to the size and complexities of the forces mounting against us and all that is most human within our environment. We are not here as women examining racism in a political and social vacuum. We operate in the teeth of a system for which racism and sexism are primary, established, and necessary props of profit. Women responding to racism is a topic so dangerous that when the local media attempt to discredit this conference they choose to focus upon the provision of lesbian housing as a diversionary device—as if the *Hartford Courant* dare not mention the topic chosen for discussion here, racism, lest it become apparent that women are in fact attempting to examine and to alter all the repressive conditions of our lives.

Mainstream communication does not want women, particularly white women, responding to racism. It wants racism to be accepted as an immutable given in the fabric of your existence, like evening time or the common cold.

So we are working in a context of opposition and threat, the cause of which is certainly not the angers which lie between us, but rather that virulent hatred levelled against all women, people of colour, lesbians and gay men, poor people, against all of us who are seeking to examine the particulars of our lives as we resist our oppressions, moving towards coalition and effective action.

Any discussion among women about racism must include the recognition and the use of anger. This discussion must be direct and creative because it is crucial. We cannot allow our fear of anger to deflect us nor seduce us into settling for anything less than the hard work of excavating honesty; we must be quite serious about the choice of this topic and the angers entwined within it because, rest assured, our opponents are quite serious about their hatred of us and of what we are trying to do here.

And while we scrutinize the often painful face of each other's anger, please remember that it is not our anger which makes me caution you to lock your doors at night and not to wander the streets of Hartford[2] alone. It is the hatred which lurks in those streets, that urge to destroy us all if we truly work for change rather than merely indulge in academic rhetoric.   25

This hatred and our anger are very different. Hatred is the fury of those who do not share our goals, and its object is death and destruction. Anger is a grief of distortions between peers, and its object is change. But our time is getting shorter. We have been raised to view any difference other than sex as a reason for destruction, and for Black women and white women to face each other's angers without denial or immobility or silence or guilt is in itself a heretical and generative idea. It implies peers meeting upon a common basis to examine difference, and to alter those distortions which history has created around our difference. For it is those distortions which separate us. And we must ask ourselves: Who profits from all this?

Women of colour in america have grown up within a symphony of anger, at being silenced, at being unchosen, at knowing that when we survive, it is in spite of a world that takes for granted our lack of humanness, and which hates

2. A large city near the conference center.

our very existence outside of its service. And I say *symphony* rather than *cacophony* because we have had to learn to orchestrate those furies so that they do not tear us apart. We have had to learn to move through them and use them for strength and force and insight within our daily lives. Those of us who did not learn this difficult lesson did not survive. And part of my anger is always libation for my fallen sisters.

Anger is an appropriate reaction to racist attitudes, as is fury when the actions arising from those attitudes do not change. To those women here who fear the anger of women of colour more than their own unscrutinized racist attitudes, I ask: Is the anger of women of colour more threatening than the woman hatred that tinges all aspects of our lives?

It is not the anger of other women that will destroy us but our refusals to stand still, to listen to its rhythms, to learn within it, to move beyond the manner of presentation to the substance, to tap that anger as an important source of empowerment.

30   I cannot hide my anger to spare you guilt, nor hurt feelings, nor answering anger; for to do so insults and trivializes all our efforts. Guilt is not a response to anger; it is a response to one's own actions or lack of action. If it leads to change then it can be useful, since it is then no longer guilt but the beginning of knowledge. Yet all too often, guilt is just another name for impotence, for defensiveness destructive of communication; it becomes a device to protect ignorance and the continuation of things the way they are, the ultimate protection for changelessness.

Most women have not developed tools for facing anger constructively. Consciousness-raising groups in the past, largely white, dealt with how to express anger, usually at the world of men. And these groups were made up of white women who shared the terms of their oppressions. There was usually little attempt to articulate the genuine differences between women, such as those of race, colour, age, class, and sexual identity. There was no apparent need at that time to examine the contradictions of self, woman as oppressor. There was work on expressing anger, but very little on anger directed against each other. No tools were developed to deal with other women's anger except to avoid it, deflect it, or flee from it under a blanket of guilt.

I have no creative use for guilt, yours or my own. Guilt is only another way of avoiding informed action, of buying time out of the pressing need to make clear choices, out of the approaching storm that can feed the earth as well as bend the trees. If I speak to you in anger, at least I have spoken to you: I have not put a gun to your head and shot you down in the street; I have not looked at your bleeding sister's body and asked, "What did she do to deserve it?" This was the reaction of two white women to Mary Church Terrell's telling of the lynching of a pregnant Black woman whose baby was then torn from her body. That was in 1921, and Alice Paul had just refused to publicly endorse the enforcement of the Nineteenth Amendment for all women—by refusing to endorse the inclusion of women of colour, although we had worked to help bring about that amendment.

The angers between women will not kill us if we can articulate them with precision, if we listen to the content of what is said with at least as much intensity as we defend ourselves against the manner of saying. When we turn from anger we turn from insight, saying we will accept only the designs already known, deadly and safely familiar. I have tried to learn my anger's usefulness to me, as well as its limitations.

For women raised to fear, too often anger threatens annihilation. In the male construct of brute force, we were taught that our lives depended upon the goodwill of patriarchal power. The anger of others was to be avoided at all costs because there was nothing to be learned from it but pain, a judgment that we had been bad girls, come up lacking, not done what we were supposed to do. And if we accept our powerlessness, then of course any anger can destroy us.

But the strength of women lies in recognizing differences between us as   35 creative, and in standing up to those distortions which we inherited without blame, but which are now ours to alter. The angers of women can transform difference through insight into power. For anger between peers births change, not destruction, and the discomfort and sense of loss it often causes is not fatal, but a sign of growth.

My response to racism is anger. That anger has eaten clefts into my living only when it remained unspoken, useless to anyone. It has also served me in classrooms without light or learning, where the work and history of Black women was less than a vapour. It has served me as fire in the ice zone of uncomprehending eyes of white women who see in my experience and the experience of my people only new reasons for fear or guilt. And my anger is no excuse for not dealing with your blindness, no reason to withdraw from the results of your own actions.

When women of colour speak out of the anger that laces so many of our contacts with white women, we are often told that we are "creating a mood of hopelessness," "preventing white women from getting past guilt," or "standing in the way of trusting communication and action." All these quotes come directly from letters to me from members of this organization within the last two years. One woman wrote, "Because you are Black and Lesbian, you seem to speak with the moral authority of suffering." Yes, I am Black and lesbian, and what you hear in my voice is fury, not suffering. Anger, not moral authority. There is a difference.

To turn aside from the anger of Black women with excuses or the pretexts of intimidation is to award no one power—it is merely another way of preserving racial blindness, the power of unaddressed privilege, unbreached, intact. Guilt is only another form of objectification. Oppressed peoples are always being asked to stretch a little more, to bridge the gap between blindness and humanity. Black women are expected to use our anger only in the service of other people's salvation or learning. But that time is over. My anger has meant pain to me but it has also meant survival, and before I give it up I'm going to be sure that there is something at least as powerful to replace it on the road to clarity.

What woman here is so enamoured of her own oppression that she cannot see her heel print upon another woman's face? What woman's terms of oppression have become precious and necessary to her as a ticket into the fold of the righteous, away from the cold winds of self-scrutiny?

40   I am a lesbian woman of colour whose children eat regularly because I work in a university. If their full bellies make me fail to recognize my commonality with a woman of colour whose children do not eat because she cannot find work, or who has no children because her insides are rotted from home abortions and sterilization; if I fail to recognize the lesbian who chooses not to have children, the woman who remains closeted because her homophobic community is her only life support, the woman who chooses silence instead of another death, the woman who is terrified lest my anger trigger the explosion of hers; if I fail to recognize them as other faces of myself, then I am contributing not only to each of their oppressions but also to my own, and the anger which stands between us then must be used for clarity and mutual empowerment, not for evasion by guilt or for further separation. I am not free while any woman is unfree, even when her shackles are very different from my own. And I am not free as long as one person of colour remains chained. Nor is any one of you.

I speak here as a woman of colour who is not bent upon destruction, but upon survival. No woman is responsible for altering the psyche of her oppressor, even when that psyche is embodied in another woman. I have suckled the wolf's lip of anger and I have used it for illumination, laughter, protection, fire in places where there was no light, no food, no sisters, no quarter. We are not goddesses or matriarchs or edifices of divine forgiveness; we are not fiery fingers of judgment or instruments of flagellation; we are women forced back always upon our woman's power. We have learned to use anger as we have learned to use the dead flesh of animals, and bruised, battered, and changing, we have survived and grown and, in Angela Wilson's words, we *are* moving on. With or without uncoloured women. We use whatever strengths we have fought for, including anger, to help define and fashion a world where all our sisters can grow, where our children can love, and where the power of touching and meeting another woman's difference and wonder will eventually transcend the need for destruction.

For it is not the anger of Black women which is dripping down over this globe like a diseased liquid. It is not my anger that launches rockets, spends more than sixty thousand dollars a second on missiles and other agents of war and death, slaughters children in cities, stockpiles nerve gas and chemical bombs, sodomizes our daughters and our earth. It is not the anger of Black women which corrodes into blind, dehumanizing power, bent upon the annihilation of us all unless we meet it with what we have, our power to examine and to redefine the terms upon which we will live and work; our power to envision and to reconstruct, anger by painful anger, stone upon heavy stone, a future of pollinating difference and the earth to support our choices.

We welcome all women who can meet us, face to face, beyond objectification and beyond guilt.

MLA CITATION

Lorde, Audre. "Uses of Anger: Women Responding to Racism." *The Norton Reader: An Anthology of Nonfiction*, edited by Melissa A. Goldthwaite et al., 16th ed., W. W. Norton, 2024, pp. 708–14.

QUESTIONS

1. Audre Lorde often makes her argument through anecdotes. Which of these anecdotes are most effective? What are the advantages and pitfalls of anecdotes as evidence? What guidance would you give an author wanting to use an anecdote to make a point?

2. In paragraph 12, Lorde tells the story, many years later, of her toddler being called a "'baby maid'" by a white child from both her own perspective and that of the child's mother. How do these perspectives differ, and what does Lorde want us to understand from that difference?

3. Anger and guilt are both perceived as negative emotions, but Lorde believes in the value of anger (paragraphs 19–20 and 28) while rejecting the value of guilt (paragraph 32). What is the basis for her position? To what extent do you agree or disagree with her assessment?

4. Following Lorde's example, gather three or four instances of using anger (as opposed to logic or coolheadedness) in the face of injustice. Shape these stories into a larger project on the value of emotionality in fighting for a more just world.

IMANI PERRY

Racism Is Terrible. Blackness Is Not.

A LOT OF KIND STATEMENTS about black people are coming from the pens and minds of white people now. That's good thing. But sometimes, it is frankly hard to tell the difference between expressions of solidarity and gestures of absolution (*See, I'm not a racist, I said you matter!*) Among the most difficult to swallow are social-media posts and notes that I and others have received expressing sorrow and implying that blackness is the most terrible of fates. Their worrisome chorus: "I cannot imagine . . . How do you . . . My heart breaks for you . . . I know you are hurting . . . You may not think you matter but you matter to me." Let me be clear: I certainly know I matter. Racism is terrible. Blackness is not.

I cannot remember a time in my life when I wasn't earnestly happy about the fact of my blackness. When my cousins and I were small, we would crowd in front of the mirrors in my grandmother's house, admiring our shining brown faces, the puffiness of our hair.

My elders taught me that I belonged to a tradition of resilience, of music that resonates across the globe, of spoken and written language that sings. If you've had the good fortune to experience a holiday with a large black American

First published in the Atlantic *(2020), a magazine covering literature, culture, and politics, where Imani Perry is a contributing writer. Perry also serves as a professor of African American studies at Princeton University.*

family, you have witnessed the masterful art of storytelling, the vitality of our laughter, and the everyday poetry of our experience. The narrative boils down quite simply to this: "We are still here! Praise life, after everything, we are still here!" So many people taught us to be more than the hatred heaped upon us, to cultivate a deep self-regard no matter what others may think, say, or do. Many of us have absorbed that lesson and revel in it.

One of the classic texts in African American studies is Zora Neale Hurston's[1] 1928 essay "How It Feels to Be Colored Me." Her playful yet profound articulation resonates for me now. She wrote, "I am not tragically colored. There is no great sorrow dammed up in my soul, nor lurking behind my eyes. I do not mind at all. I do not belong to the sobbing school of Negrohood who hold that nature somehow has given them a lowdown dirty deal and whose feelings are all but about it . . . No, I do not weep at the world—I am too busy sharpening my oyster knife."

5   Some of her words, I must admit, are too hopeful, at least for me right now. In fact, I *do* weep at the world; I am, in a sense, part of the sobbing school; and I am skeptical that my lone oyster knife can cut any of the rot out of this nation. But, like Hurston, I refuse to see the story of who I am as a tragedy.

Joy is not found in the absence of pain and suffering. It exists through it. The scourges of racism, poverty, incarceration, medical discrimination, and so much more shape black life. We live with the vestiges of slavery and Jim Crow, and with the new creative tides of anti-blackness directed toward us and our children. We know the wail of a dying man calling for his mama, and it echoes into the distant past and cuts into our deepest wounds. The injustice is inescapable. So yes, I want the world to recognize our suffering. But I do not want pity from a single soul. Sin and shame are found in neither my body nor my

---

1. Major Black novelist, folklorist, and anthropologist (1891–1960); see pp. 286–89.

identity. Blackness is an immense and defiant joy. As the poet Sonia Sanchez wrote in a haiku about her power—and her struggles:

> Come windless invader
> I am a carnival of
> stars a poem of blood

People of all walks of life are protesting the violent deaths handed out by police officers.[2] This is extraordinary both because the victims were black—and when does black death elicit such a response?—and because Americans in general have a hard time dealing with death. Think about how uncomfortable many Americans are with grief. You are supposed to meet it with a hidden shamefulness, tuck yourself away respectably for a season, and then return whole and recovered. But that is not at all how grief courses through life. It is emetic, peripatetic; it shakes you and stops you and sometimes disappears only to come barreling back to knock the wind out of you.

Black Americans right now are experiencing a collective grief, one that unfolds publicly. And we are unable to tuck it away. I do think Hurston would have to admit this too, were she around today. She wrote her essay before *Brown v. Board of Education*, the Montgomery bus boycott, the Birmingham crusade, the March on Washington, Freedom Summer, the Voting Rights Act, the Civil Rights Acts, the rise of black mayors, the first black governor, the first black president. She wrote her essay before we understood how tightly this nation would grasp onto its original sin even after legions of black people came with razor-sharp oyster knives and hands full of pearls.

Black Americans continue to die prematurely—whether under the knee of a police officer, or struggling for breath on a respirator, or along the stretch of the Mississippi River known as Cancer Alley, or in the shadow of Superfund sites, or in one of the countless other ways we are caught in the spokes. The trauma is repetitive. We weep. But we are still, even in our most anguished seasons, not reducible to the fact of our grief. Rather, the capacity to access joy is a testament to the grace of living as a protest—described by Lorraine Hansberry, who, as one of the greatest playwrights in the history of American theater, wrote *A Raisin in the Sun*. Whenever she recounted the story of black America in lectures or discussions, she pointed to the extraordinary achievements we attained under obscene degradation. "Isn't it rather remarkable that we can talk about a people who were publishing newspapers while they were still in slavery in 1827, you see?" she said during a speech in 1964.

Some of us who comment on racial inequality these days are averse to such accounts of black history, thinking them romantic and not frank enough about the ravages of racism. So I hope that no one is confused by my words. American racism is unquestionably rapacious. To identify the achievement and exhilaration in black life is not to mute or minimize racism, but to shame racism, to

10

---

2. Reference to the widespread #BlackLivesMatter protests that erupted in response to the brutal police killing of George Floyd in Minneapolis, Minnesota, on May 25, 2020.

damn it to hell. The masters were wrong in the antebellum South, when they described the body-shaking, delighted chuckle of an enslaved person as simplemindedness. No, that laugh—like our music, like our language, like our movement—was a testimony that refused the terms of our degradation. In the footage of the protests over the past several weeks, we have seen black people dancing, chanting, singing. Do not misunderstand. This is not an absence of grief or rage, or a distraction. It is insistence.

And so, I must turn the pitying gaze back upon any who offer it to me, because they cannot understand the spiritual majesty of joy in suffering. But my rejection of their account also comes with an invitation. If you join us, you might feel not only our pain but also the beauty of being human.

MLA CITATION

Perry, Imani. "Racism Is Terrible. Blackness Is Not." *The Norton Reader: An Anthology of Nonfiction*, edited by Melissa A. Goldthwaite et al., 16th ed., W. W. Norton, 2024, pp. 715–18.

QUESTIONS

1. Annotate the proper names in Imani Perry's article, adding context for the historical figures she cites and the events she mentions. How does your preliminary research enhance your understanding of the text?

2. In your own words, explain the distinction Perry makes in her title between racism and Blackness.

3. What case does Perry make for Black joy? Why is joy important even when racism and injustice still exist?

12 LIVING VALUES

Open your arms to change, but don't let go of your values.
—THE DALAI LAMA

Some of our values we inherit from our families, religions, communities, and cultures; others we choose for ourselves. But however we acquire them, our values define who we are and how we relate to the world. The title of this chapter can be interpreted in at least two ways. First, living our values, or trying to, is what gives our lives purpose and meaning. Second, our values themselves are living, in that they can evolve and change as we ourselves learn, grow, and experience life. The readings in this chapter explore "living values" in both senses. They show their authors wrestling not only with what they believe and why but also how to put their values into action.

The chapter begins with a pair of essays that state and reflect the values by which their respective authors live or lived their lives: nineteenth-century American essayist and philosopher Henry David Thoreau's "Where I Lived, and What I Lived For," the second chapter of his 1854 book *Walden*, and the contemporary writer and teacher Scott Russell Sanders's reflection on his own reading (and rereading) of *Walden* over the course of his life. The chapter continues with two essays that consider, in general terms, the relationship of thought and perception to ethical action. In "Thoughts on Peace in an Air Raid," written during the Blitz, Germany's bombing of Great Britain during World War II, modernist writer Virginia Woolf considers the nature of war and what people—women especially—might do to bring about peace. In "Sight into Insight," essayist Annie Dillard ponders the challenge and importance of truly seeing, of looking hard at the world.

The last half of the chapter offers a series of essays that make values-based arguments about contemporary social and political questions. Margaret Renkl, in "Christmas Isn't Coming to Death Row," insists that those who regard themselves as "pro-life" ought to oppose the death penalty. Political philosopher Teresa M. Bejan, in "The Two Clashing Meanings of 'Free Speech,'" frames contemporary debates over the nature and limits of this foundational political value as a conflict between two distinct understandings of it, which she terms *isegoria* and *parrhesia*. In his brief essay "Be Nice," Matt Dinan extends arguments offered by Bejan and others for the importance of civility in political and social discourse to present the imperative of his title as a means of furthering social justice. In "Definitions," a chapter from his book *How to Be an Antiracist*, the historian and activist Ibram X. Kendi outlines a program for combating racism grounded in the value of racial equity. The chapter's final selection, a speech by the farmer and activist Leah Penniman, offers an approach to ethical food production rooted in traditional African and Indigenous agricultural practices.

As you read these essays, follow the example of their authors in considering not only what values you hold and why but also what actions those values demand from you. How can you be sure your values are the right ones? What kind of society do your values imply? How can you live your values in everyday life?

Henry David Thoreau
Where I Lived, and What I Lived For

WHEN I FIRST took up my abode in the woods, that is, began to spend my nights as well as days there, which, by accident, was on Independence day, or the fourth of July, 1845, my house was not finished for winter, but was merely a defence against the rain, without plastering or chimney, the walls being of rough weather-stained boards, with wide chinks, which made it cool at night. The upright white hewn studs and freshly planed door and window casings gave it a clean and airy look, especially in the morning, when its timbers were saturated with dew, so that I fancied that by noon some sweet gum would exude from them. To my imagination it retained throughout the day more or less of this auroral character, reminding me of a certain house on a mountain which I had visited the year before. This was an airy and unplastered cabin, fit to entertain a travelling god, and where a goddess might trail her garments. The winds which passed over my dwelling were such as sweep over the ridges of mountains, bearing the broken strains, or celestial parts only, of terrestrial music. The morning wind forever blows, the poem of creation is uninterrupted; but few are the ears that hear it. Olympus[1] is but the outside of the earth every where.

The only house I had been the owner of before, if I except a boat, was a tent, which I used occasionally when making excursions in the summer, and this is still rolled up in my garret; but the boat, after passing from hand to hand, has gone down the stream of time. With this more substantial shelter about me, I had made some progress toward settling in the world. This frame, so slightly clad, was a sort of crystallization around me, and reacted on the builder. It was suggestive somewhat as a picture in outlines. I did not need to go out doors to take the air, for the atmosphere within had lost none of its freshness. It was not so much within doors as behind a door where I sat, even in the rainiest weather. The *Harivansa*[2] says, "An abode without birds is like a meat without seasoning." Such was not my abode, for I found myself suddenly neighbor

---

From Henry David Thoreau's book Walden *(1854), an account of his life in a small cabin on Walden Pond, outside the village of Concord, Massachusetts; in* Walden, *Thoreau not only describes his life in the woods but also develops a philosophy for living.*

1. Mountain where the Greek gods dwell.
2. Fifth-century epic poem about the Hindu god Krishna.

to the birds; not by having imprisoned one, but having caged myself near them. I was not only nearer to some of those which commonly frequent the garden and the orchard, but to those wilder and more thrilling songsters of the forest which never, or rarely, serenade a villager,—the wood-thrush, the veery, the scarlet tanager, the field-sparrow, the whippoorwill, and many others.

I was seated by the shore of a small pond, about a mile and a half south of the village of Concord and somewhat higher than it, in the midst of an extensive wood between that town and Lincoln, and about two miles south of that our only field known to fame, Concord Battle Ground;[3] but I was so low in the woods that the opposite shore, half a mile off, like the rest, covered with wood, was my most distant horizon. For the first week, whenever I looked out on the pond it impressed me like a tarn high up on the side of a mountain, its bottom far above the surface of other lakes, and, as the sun arose, I saw it throwing off its nightly clothing of mist, and here and there, by degrees, its soft ripples or its smooth reflecting surface was revealed, while the mists, like ghosts, were stealthily withdrawing in every direction into the woods, as at the breaking up of some nocturnal conventicle. The very dew seemed to hang upon the trees later into the day than usual, as on the sides of mountains.

This small lake was of most value as a neighbor in the intervals of a gentle rain storm in August, when, both air and water being perfectly still, but the sky overcast, mid-afternoon had all the serenity of evening, and the wood-thrush sang around, and was heard from shore to shore. A lake like this is never smoother than at such a time; and the clear portion of the air above it being shallow and darkened by clouds, the water, full of light and reflections, becomes a lower heaven itself so much the more important. From a hill top near by, where the wood had been recently cut off, there was a pleasing vista southward across the pond, through a wide indentation in the hills which form the shore there, where their opposite sides sloping toward each other suggested a stream flowing out in that direction through a wooded valley, but stream there was none. That way I looked between and over the near green hills to some distant and higher ones in the horizon, tinged with blue. Indeed, by standing on tiptoe I could catch a glimpse of some of the peaks of the still bluer and more distant mountain ranges in the north-west, those true-blue coins from heaven's own mint, and also of some portion of the village. But in other directions, even from this point, I could not see over or beyond the woods which surrounded me. It is well to have some water in your neighborhood, to give buoyancy to and float the earth. One value even of the smallest well is, that when you look into it you see that earth is not continent but insular. This is as important as that it keeps butter cool. When I looked across the pond from this peak toward the Sudbury meadows, which in time of flood I distinguished elevated perhaps by a mirage in their seething valley, like a coin in a basin, all the earth beyond the pond appeared like a thin crust insulated and floated even by this small sheet of intervening water, and I was reminded that this on which I dwelt was but *dry land*.

3. Site of the famous Battle of Concord, April 19, 1775, considered the start of the American Revolution.

5   Though the view from my door was still more contracted, I did not feel
crowded or confined in the least. There was pasture enough for my imagination. The low shrub-oak plateau to which the opposite shore arose, stretched
away toward the prairies of the West and the steppes of Tartary,[4] affording
ample room for all the roving families of men. "There are none happy in the
world but beings who enjoy freely a vast horizon,"—said Damodara,[5] when his
herds required new and larger pastures.

Both place and time were changed, and I dwelt nearer to those parts of
the universe and to those eras in history which had most attracted me. Where
I lived was as far off as many a region viewed nightly by astronomers. We are
wont to imagine rare and delectable places in some remote and more celestial
corner of the system, behind the constellation of Cassiopeia's Chair, far from
noise and disturbance. I discovered that my house actually had its site in such
a withdrawn, but forever new and unprofaned, part of the universe. If it were
worth the while to settle in those parts near to the Pleiades or the Hyades, to
Aldebaran or Altair,[6] then I was really there, or at an equal remoteness from
the life which I had left behind, dwindled and twinkling with as fine a ray to
my nearest neighbor, and to be seen only in moonless nights by him. Such was
that part of creation where I had squatted;—

> "There was a shepherd that did live,
>   And held his thoughts as high
> As were the mounts whereon his flocks
>   Did hourly feed him by."[7]

What should we think of the shepherd's life if his flocks always wandered to
higher pastures than his thoughts?

Every morning was a cheerful invitation to make my life of equal simplicity, and I may say innocence, with Nature herself. I have been as sincere a wor-
shipper of Aurora[8] as the Greeks. I got up early and bathed in the pond; that
was a religious exercise, and one of the best things which I did. They say that
characters were engraven on the bathing tub of king Tching-thang[9] to this
effect: "Renew thyself completely each day; do it again, and again, and forever
again." I can understand that. Morning brings back the heroic ages. I was as
much affected by the faint hum of a mosquito making its invisible and unimaginable tour through my apartment at earliest dawn, when I was sitting with
door and windows open, as I could be by any trumpet that ever sang of fame.

---

4. Region that includes what is today northern Pakistan.

5. One of the many names of Krishna, the Hindu god.

6. Cassiopeia's Chair, the Pleiades, and the Hyades are constellations; Aldebaran and
Altair are stars.

7. Lines from "The Shepherd's Love for Philladay" from Thomas Evans's *Old Ballads*
(1810).

8. Goddess of dawn.

9. Confucius (551–479 BCE), Chinese philosopher.

It was Homer's[10] requiem; itself an *Iliad* and *Odyssey* in the air, singing its own wrath and wanderings. There was something cosmical about it; a standing advertisement, till forbidden, of the everlasting vigor and fertility of the world. The morning, which is the most memorable season of the day, is the awakening hour. Then there is least somnolence in us; and for an hour, at least, some part of us awakes which slumbers all the rest of the day and night. Little is to be expected of that day, if it can be called a day, to which we are not awakened by our Genius, but by the mechanical nudgings of some servitor, are not awakened by our own newly-acquired force and aspirations from within, accompanied by the undulations of celestial music, instead of factory bells, and a fragrance filling the air—to a higher life than we fell asleep from; and thus the darkness bear its fruit, and prove itself to be good, no less than the light. That man who does not believe that each day contains an earlier, more sacred, and auroral hour than he has yet profaned, has despaired of life, and is pursuing a descending and darkening way. After a partial cessation of his sensuous life, the soul of man, or its organs rather, are reinvigorated each day, and his Genius tries again what noble life it can make. All memorable events, I should say, transpire in morning time and in a morning atmosphere. The Vedas[11] say, "All intelligences awake with the morning." Poetry and art, and the fairest and most memorable of the actions of men, date from such an hour. All poets and heroes, like Memnon,[12] are the children of Aurora, and emit their music at sunrise. To him whose elastic and vigorous thought keeps pace with the sun, the day is a perpetual morning. It matters not what the clocks say or the attitudes and labors of men. Morning is when I am awake and there is a dawn in me. Moral reform is the effort to throw off sleep. Why is it that men give so poor an account of their day if they have not been slumbering? They are not such poor calculators. If they had not been overcome with drowsiness they would have performed something. The millions are awake enough for physical labor; but only one in a million is awake enough for effective intellectual exertion, only one in a hundred millions to a poetic or divine life. To be awake is to be alive. I have never yet met a man who was quite awake. How could I have looked him in the face?

We must learn to reawaken and keep ourselves awake, not by mechanical aids, but by an infinite expectation of the dawn, which does not forsake us in our soundest sleep. I know of no more encouraging fact than the unquestionable ability of man to elevate his life by a conscious endeavor. It is something to be able to paint a particular picture, or to carve a statue, and so to make a few objects beautiful; but it is far more glorious to carve and paint the very atmosphere and medium through which we look, which morally we can do. To affect the quality of the day, that is the highest of arts. Every man is tasked to make his life, even in its details, worthy of the contemplation of his most elevated and

10. Greek epic poet (eighth century BCE), author of the *Odyssey* and the *Iliad*.

11. Sacred texts from ancient India that contain hymns, incantations, and rituals.

12. Son of Aurora, the goddess of dawn, and a mortal, Memnon was king of the Ethiopians. He was slain by Achilles while fighting the Greeks in Troy. When he died, his mother's tears formed the morning dew.

critical hour. If we refused, or rather used up, such paltry information as we get, the oracles would distinctly inform us how this might be done.

I went to the woods because I wished to live deliberately, to front only the essential facts of life, and see if I could not learn what it had to teach, and not, when I came to die, discover that I had not lived. I did not wish to live what was not life, living is so dear, nor did I wish to practise resignation, unless it was quite necessary. I wanted to live deep and suck out all the marrow of life, to live so sturdily and Spartan-like as to put to rout all that was not life, to cut a broad swath and shave close, to drive life into a corner, and reduce it to its lowest terms, and, if it proved to be mean, why then to get the whole and genuine meanness of it, and publish its meanness to the world; or if it were sublime, to know it by experience, and be able to give a true account of it in my next excursion. For most men, it appears to me, are in a strange uncertainty about it, whether it is of the devil or of God, and have *somewhat hastily* concluded that it is the chief end of man here to "glorify God and enjoy him forever."

10   Still we live meanly, like ants; though the fable tells us that we were long ago changed into men;[13] like pygmies we fight with cranes;[14] it is error upon error, and clout upon clout, and our best virtue has for its occasion a superfluous and evitable wretchedness. Our life is frittered away by detail. An honest man has hardly need to count more than his ten fingers, or in extreme cases he may add his ten toes, and lump the rest. Simplicity, simplicity, simplicity! I say, let your affairs be as two or three, and not a hundred or a thousand; instead of a million count half a dozen, and keep your accounts on your thumb nail. In the midst of this chopping sea of civilized life, such are the clouds and storms and quicksands and thousand-and-one items to be allowed for, that a man has to live, if he would not founder and go to the bottom and not make his port at all, by dead reckoning, and he must be a great calculator indeed who succeeds. Simplify, simplify. Instead of three meals a day, if it be necessary eat but one; instead of a hundred dishes, five; and reduce other things in proportion. Our life is like a German Confederacy,[15] made up of petty states, with its boundary forever fluctuating, so that even a German cannot tell you how it is bounded at any moment. The nation itself, with all its so called internal improvements, which, by the way, are all external and superficial, is just such an unwieldy and overgrown establishment, cluttered with furniture and tripped up by its own traps, ruined by luxury and heedless expense, by want of calculation and a worthy aim, as the million households in the land; and the only cure for it as for them is in a rigid economy, a stern and more than Spartan[16] simplicity of life and elevation of purpose. It lives too fast. Men think that it is essential that the *Nation* have commerce, and export ice, and talk through a telegraph, and ride thirty miles an hour, without a

13. In a Greek fable, Aeacus asks Zeus to increase a scanty population by turning ants into men.

14. From the *Iliad* by Homer, in which the Trojans are represented as cranes.

15. A group of thirty-nine Central European states created in 1815 by the Congress of Vienna after the collapse of the Holy Roman Empire.

16. Referring to the militaristic ancient Greek city-state.

doubt, whether *they* do or not; but whether we should live like baboons or like men, is a little uncertain. If we do not get our sleepers, and forge rails, and devote days and nights to the work, but go to tinkering upon our *lives* to improve *them*, who will build railroads? And if railroads are not built, how shall we get to heaven in season? But if we stay at home and mind our business, who will want railroads? We do not ride on the railroad; it rides upon us. Did you ever think what those sleepers are that underlie the railroad? Each one is a man, an Irishman, or a Yankee man. The rails are laid on them, and they are covered with sand, and the cars run smoothly over them. They are sound sleepers, I assure you. And every few years a new lot is laid down and run over; so that, if some have the pleasure of riding on a rail, others have the misfortune to be ridden upon. And when they run over a man that is walking in his sleep, a supernumerary sleeper in the wrong position, and wake him up, they suddenly stop the cars, and make a hue and cry about it, as if this were an exception. I am glad to know that it takes a gang of men for every five miles to keep the sleepers down and level in their beds as it is, for this is a sign that they may sometime get up again.

Why should we live with such hurry and waste of life? We are determined to be starved before we are hungry. Men say that a stitch in time saves nine, and so they take a thousand stitches to-day to save nine to-morrow. As for *work*, we haven't any of any consequence. We have the Saint Vitus' dance,[17] and cannot possibly keep our heads still. If I should only give a few pulls at the parish bell-rope, as for a fire, that is, without setting the bell, there is hardly a man on his farm in the outskirts of Concord, notwithstanding that press of engagements which was his excuse so many times this morning, nor a boy, nor a woman, I might almost say, but would forsake all and follow that sound, not mainly to save property from the flames, but, if we will confess the truth, much more to see it burn, since burn it must, and we, be it known, did not set it on fire,—or to see it put out, and have a hand in it, if that is done as handsomely; yes, even if it were the parish church itself. Hardly a man takes a half hour's nap after dinner, but when he wakes he holds up his head and asks, "What's the news?" as if the rest of mankind had stood his sentinels. Some give directions to be waked every half hour, doubtless for no other purpose; and then, to pay for it, they tell what they have dreamed. After a night's sleep the news is as indispensable as the breakfast. "Pray tell me any thing new that has happened to a man any where on this globe,"—and he reads it over his coffee and rolls, that a man has had his eyes gouged out this morning on the Wachito River;[18] never dreaming the while that he lives in the dark unfathomed mammoth cave of this world, and has but the rudiment of an eye himself.

For my part, I could easily do without the post-office. I think that there are very few important communications made through it. To speak critically, I never received more than one or two letters in my life—I wrote this some years ago—that were worth the postage. The penny-post is, commonly, an institution

17. Nervous disorder marked by jerky, spasmodic movements that occurs in cases of rheumatic fever involving the connective tissue of the brain.

18. In southern Arkansas.

through which you seriously offer a man that penny for his thoughts which is so often safely offered in jest. And I am sure that I never read any memorable news in a newspaper. If we read of one man robbed, or murdered, or killed by accident, or one house burned, or one vessel wrecked, or one steamboat blown up, or one cow run over on the Western Railroad, or one mad dog killed, or one lot of grasshoppers in the winter,—we never need read of another. One is enough. If you are acquainted with the principle, what do you care for a myriad instances and applications? To a philosopher all *news*, as it is called, is gossip, and they who edit and read it are old women over their tea. Yet not a few are greedy after this gossip. There was such a rush, as I hear, the other day at one of the offices to learn the foreign news by the last arrival, that several large squares of plate glass belonging to the establishment were broken by the pressure,—news which I seriously think a ready wit might write a twelvemonth or twelve years beforehand with sufficient accuracy. As for Spain, for instance, if you know how to throw in Don Carlos and the Infanta, and Don Pedro and Seville and Granada, from time to time in the right proportions,—they may have changed the names a little since I saw the papers,—and serve up a bull-fight when other entertainments fail, it will be true to the letter, and give us as good an idea of the exact state of ruin of things in Spain as the most succinct and lucid reports under this head in the newspapers: and as for England, almost the last significant scrap of news from that quarter was the revolution of 1649; and if you have learned the history of her crops for an average year, you never need attend to that thing again, unless your speculations are of a merely pecuniary character. If one may judge who rarely looks into the newspapers, nothing new does ever happen in foreign parts, a French revolution not excepted.

What news! how much more important to know what that is which was never old! "Kieou-he-yu (great dignitary of the state of Wei) sent a man to Khoung-tseu to know his news. Khoung-tseu caused the messenger to be seated near him, and questioned him in these terms: What is your master doing? The messenger answered with respect: My master desires to diminish the number of his faults, but he cannot come to the end of them. The messenger being gone, the philosopher remarked: What a worthy messenger! What a worthy messenger!" The preacher, instead of vexing the ears of drowsy farmers on their day of rest at the end of the week,—for Sunday is the fit conclusion of an ill-spent week, and not the fresh and brave beginning of a new one,—with this one other draggle-tail of a sermon, should shout with thundering voice,—"Pause! Avast! Why so seeming fast, but deadly slow?"

Shams and delusions are esteemed for soundest truths, while reality is fabulous. If men would steadily observe realities only, and not allow themselves to be deluded, life, to compare it with such things as we know, would be like a fairy tale and the *Arabian Nights' Entertainments*. If we respected only what is inevitable and has a right to be, music and poetry would resound along the streets. When we are unhurried and wise, we perceive that only great and worthy things have any permanent and absolute existence,—that petty fears and petty pleasures are but the shadow of the reality. This is always exhilarating and sublime. By closing the eyes and slumbering, and consenting to be deceived by shows, men establish and confirm their daily life of routine and habit every where, which still is built on purely illusory foundations. Children, who play life, discern its true law and relations more clearly than men, who fail to live it worthily, but who think that they are wiser by experience, that is, by failure. I have read in a Hindoo book, that "There was a king's son, who, being expelled in infancy from his native city, was brought up by a forester, and, growing up to maturity in that state, imagined himself to belong to the barbarous race with which he lived. One of his father's ministers having discovered him, revealed to him what he was, and the misconception of his character was removed, and he knew himself to be a prince. So soul," continues the Hindoo philosopher, "from the circumstances in which it is placed, mistakes its own character, until the truth is revealed to it by some holy teacher, and then it knows itself to be *Brahme*."[19] I perceive that we inhabitants of New England live this mean life that we do because our vision does not penetrate the surface of things. We think that that *is* which *appears* to be. If a man should walk through this town and see only the reality, where, think you, would the "Mill-dam"[20] go to? If he should give us an account of the realities he beheld there, we should not recognize the place in his description. Look at a meeting-house, or a court-house, or a jail, or a shop, or a dwelling-house, and say what that thing really is before a true gaze, and they would all go to pieces in your account of them. Men esteem truth remote, in the outskirts of the system, behind the farthest star, before Adam and after the last man. In eternity there is indeed something true and sublime. But all these times and places and occasions are now and here. God himself culminates in the present moment, and will never be more divine in the lapse of all the ages. And we are enabled to apprehend at all what is sublime and noble only by the perpetual instilling and drenching of the reality that surrounds us. The universe constantly and obediently answers to our conceptions; whether we travel fast or slow, the track is laid for us. Let us spend our lives in conceiving then. The poet or the artist never yet had so fair and noble a design but some of his posterity at least could accomplish it.

Let us spend one day as deliberately as Nature, and not be thrown off the track by every nutshell and mosquito's wing that falls on the rails. Let us rise early and fast, or break fast, gently and without perturbation; let company come and let company go, let the bells ring and the children cry,—determined to make a day of it. Why should we knock under and go with the stream? Let us not be upset and overwhelmed in that terrible rapid and whirlpool called a dinner, situated in the meridian shallows. Weather this danger and you are safe, for the rest of the way is down hill. With unrelaxed nerves, with morning vigor, sail by it, looking another way, tied to the mast like Ulysses. If the engine whistles, let it whistle till it is hoarse for its pains. If the bell rings, why should we run? We will consider what kind of music they are like. Let us settle ourselves, and work and wedge our feet downward through the mud and slush of opinion, and prejudice, and tradition, and delusion, and appearance, that alluvion which

15

19. Supreme soul, the essence of all being, in Hinduism.
20. Dam built in 1635 in the town of Concord on the site of an Indigenous fishing weir.

covers the globe, through Paris and London, through New York and Boston and Concord, through church and state, through poetry and philosophy and religion, till we come to a hard bottom and rocks in place, which we can call *reality*, and say, This is, and no mistake; and then begin, having a *point d'appui*,[21] below freshet and frost and fire, a place where you might found a wall or a state, or set a lamp-post safely, or perhaps a gauge, not a Nilometer,[22] but a Realometer, that future ages might know how deep a freshet of shams and appearances had gathered from time to time. If you stand right fronting and face to face to a fact, you will see the sun glimmer on both its surfaces, as if it were a cimeter,[23] and feel its sweet edge dividing you through the heart and marrow, and so you will happily conclude your mortal career. Be it life or death, we crave only reality. If we are really dying, let us hear the rattle in our throats and feel cold in the extremities; if we are alive, let us go about our business.

Time is but the stream I go a-fishing in. I drink at it; but while I drink I see the sandy bottom and detect how shallow it is. Its thin current slides away, but eternity remains. I would drink deeper; fish in the sky, whose bottom is pebbly with stars. I cannot count one. I know not the first letter of the alphabet. I have always been regretting that I was not as wise as the day I was born. The intellect is a cleaver; it discerns and rifts its way into the secret of things. I do not wish to be any more busy with my hands than is necessary. My head is hands and feet. I feel all my best faculties concentrated in it. My instinct tells me that my head is an organ for burrowing, as some creatures use their snout and fore-paws, and with it I would mine and burrow my way through these hills. I think that the richest vein is somewhere hereabouts; so by the divining rod and thin rising vapors I judge; and here I will begin to mine.

MLA CITATION

Thoreau, Henry David. "Where I Lived, and What I Lived For." *The Norton Reader: An Anthology of Nonfiction*, edited by Melissa A. Goldthwaite et al., 16th ed., W. W. Norton, 2024, pp. 720–28.

QUESTIONS

1. Henry David Thoreau's title "Where I Lived, and What I Lived For" identifies his essay as a statement about values. What values does Thoreau embrace? How are those values reflected in the way he lived?

2. Throughout this essay, Thoreau poses questions—for example, "Why is it that men give so poor an account of their day if they have not been slumbering?" (paragraph 7), or "Why should we live with such hurry and waste of life?" (paragraph 11). To what extent does he answer these questions? Why might he leave some unanswered or only partially answered?

---

21. Reference point.
22. Gauge placed in the Nile River in ancient times to measure the rise of the water.
23. Saber with a curved blade, usually spelled *scimitar*.

3. Thoreau is known for his aphorisms (short, witty nuggets of wisdom). Find one you like and explain its relevance for living today.

4. If you have ever chosen to live unconventionally at some point in your life, write about your decision, including the reasons and the consequences.

SCOTT RUSSELL SANDERS
Hooks Baited with Darkness

I FIRST READ *WALDEN* when I was seventeen, the summer before starting college, at the urging of a high school teacher who sensed that my adolescent mind, brimming with questions, would benefit from grappling with a truly radical thinker. Much of the book baffled me. The tone shifted unpredictably from conversational to prophetic, from jokey to stern, from earthy to mystical. I was bewildered by some of the lengthy sentences, which zigzagged among ideas and images, and I was stumped by the cryptic short ones, which seemed to compress whole paragraphs of meaning into a few words. Not yet having made any big decisions about how to lead my life, I couldn't figure out what was troubling this Henry David Thoreau. So what if his neighbors thought he should use his Harvard degree to land a job and a wife, and then proceed to have kids, buy a house, get rich, and distribute alms to the poor? Couldn't he just ignore the scolds and go his own way? Not yet having lost a loved one to accident, illness, or old age, I only dimly understood his brooding about that amoral process we call nature. So what if armies of red ants and black ants slaughtered one another, herons gobbled tadpoles, a dead horse stank up the woods, or a thousand seeds perished for each one that took root? What did all that mayhem and waste have to do with us, the owners of souls aiming at heaven?

At seventeen, still a believer in souls and heaven, I didn't know which parts of the book were supposed to be wise and which parts cranky, so I read it all with an open mind. While missing much, I was sufficiently intrigued by the story of Thoreau's sojourn in the woods and sufficiently engaged by his cocky, inquisitive manner to keep reading. His brashness was evident from the opening paragraphs, where he announces that he will write in the first person, thus breaking one of the cardinal rules of composition I had learned in school, and he places himself at the center of his book without apology: "I should not talk so much about myself if there were any body else whom I knew as well. Unfortunately, I am confined to this theme by the narrowness of my experience."[1] As

Originally appeared in Daedalus (2014), *the quarterly journal of the American Academy of Arts and Sciences. All notes in this piece were written by the author.*

1. Henry David Thoreau, *Walden*, ed. Jeffrey S. Cramer (New Haven, Conn.: Yale University Press, 2004), 2. Originally published in 1854 under the title *Walden: or, Life in the Woods*, Thoreau's most famous book has gone through many editions. Cramer's

a boy from the back roads of Ohio, untraveled and unsophisticated, wondering what to make of my own narrow experience, I felt Thoreau was speaking to me, an impression confirmed a few lines later: "Perhaps these pages are more particularly addressed to poor students" (2). While I was a good student academically, I was a poor one financially, able to enroll in an Ivy League college that fall only thanks to a full scholarship.

Short of cash, I was long on country skills. My parents and neighbors, all of them frugal, taught me how to hunt, fish, garden, can, fence a pasture, care for livestock, fell trees, fix machines, repair a house, run electrical wiring, and sew on buttons. That summer of my first *Walden* reading I spent as an apprentice carpenter, learning to frame, hang drywall, install trim, and shingle roofs. So I took seriously Thoreau's suggestion that the students at Harvard, instead of paying rent, could have saved money and gained practical knowledge by building their own dormitories. I was fascinated by his detailed account of the cabin construction, from the digging of a cellar hole and the laying up of a chimney to the plastering of walls. Because I enjoyed such work, I understood why he would ask: "Shall we forever resign the pleasure of construction to the carpenter? What does architecture amount to in the experience of the mass of men? I never in all my walks came across a man engaged in so simple and natural an occupation as building his house" (48). Since I had cobbled together treehouses in the backyard maples, forts in the meadow, and brush huts in the woods, and since I had helped frame homes for strangers, I expected to build my own house one day.

Here was a philosopher with dirt under his fingernails and calluses on his palms. Here was a man famous for his ideas who could say, "To be a philosopher is not merely to have subtle thoughts, nor even to found a school, but so to love wisdom as to live according to its dictates, a life of simplicity, independence, magnanimity, and trust. It is to solve some of the problems of life, not only theoretically, but practically" (14). The thrifty, resourceful people among whom I grew up prepared me to admire Thoreau's effort to provide some of the necessities of life with his own hands: not only by constructing a cabin, but also by sawing and splitting fallen trees for the stove (from Emerson's woodlot), by hauling water from the pond (still safe to drink in his day), and by hoeing beans (he made it only partway through his seven miles of rows and resolved to plant fewer the following year).

5   I did not yet appreciate, however, why he took such pains to distinguish between the necessities of life and luxuries, between enough and too much. When I packed for college that summer, everything I owned—clothes, books, towel, toiletries, clock radio, slide rule—fitted into my grandfather's sea trunk, which I could carry on my shoulder. I did not feel encumbered by property. Nor

edition, with an introduction by Denis Donoghue, is the most authoritative currently available: it has the additional virtue of being inexpensive and well suited to classroom use. All subsequent quotations from *Walden* will be taken from this edition, and the page numbers will be shown within parentheses following the quotation. All italics within quotations are in the original.

did I feel, with a radio as my only electronic device and without a car, that technology was forcing me to live at a faster and faster pace, and thus I could not grasp why Thoreau fretted about the accelerating influence of railroads, factories, and telegraph. Likewise, in that limbo between high school and college, without bills to pay or appointments to keep, with no occupations aside from carpentry, reading, meals, and sleep, I felt no need to simplify my life.

While my upbringing enabled me to follow the practical side of what Thoreau called his "experiment" in simple living, my youth prevented me from fully understanding the philosophy that accompanied it.[2] My difficulty had as much to do with his style as with his ideas. I puzzled over his paradoxes: "We do not ride on the railroad; it rides upon us" (98–99). I resisted his exaggerations: "I have lived some thirty years on this planet, and I have yet to hear the first syllable of valuable or even earnest advice from my seniors" (8). Well, I found myself asking, who had taught him to build houses, grow beans, or tie his shoes? If people older than thirty had nothing to teach him, why did he read all those ancient—and presumably elderly—sages from India and China and Greece? I bridled at his boastful claims: "There is a certain class of unbelievers who sometimes ask me such questions as, if I think that I can live on vegetable food alone; and to strike at the root of the matter at once—for the root is faith—I am accustomed to answer such, that I can live on board nails" (69). Really? Would those be the nails he salvaged from the Irishman's shanty? Would he scrape off the rust before devouring them? Such faith, as he called it, reminded me of certain implausible beliefs I was beginning to question in church.

Thoreau often seemed to hide his meaning in riddles, like a Shakespearean fool wary of offending the king. (I had read *King Lear* at the urging of the same high school teacher.) What did he mean, for instance, by saying "I have a great deal of company in my house; especially in the morning, when nobody calls" (147–148)? Or what did he mean by saying of the men who came to fish in the pond at night that "they plainly fished much more in the Walden Pond of their own natures, and baited their hooks with darkness" (141)? It was far from plain to me. Baiting with worms or crickets, sure. But darkness? Or when he claims, "It is a surprising and memorable, as well as valuable experience, to be lost in the woods any time," how does he arrive, a few lines later, at his grand conclusion: "Not till we are lost, in other words, not till we have lost the world, do we begin to find ourselves, and realize where we are and the infinite extent of our relations" (186–187)? Getting lost in the woods I could imagine, but I could not see how this might lead to finding one's place in infinity.

2. The words *experiment, experiments*, and *experimentalists* appear seventeen times in *Walden*, a sign of Thoreau's respect for the methods and prestige of science. By calling his stay at Walden Pond an experiment, he may also have wished to present it as a one-man alternative to the communal experiments—most of them, like Brook Farm and Fruitlands, short-lived—that were springing up across the United States and Europe in the 1840s and 1850s.

Time and again, *Walden* makes such dizzying leaps from the literal to the symbolic. Consider one further example, from a passage on carpentry, a subject I was less ignorant of than most other things:

> I would not be one of those who will foolishly drive a nail into mere lath and plastering; such a deed would keep me awake nights. Give me a hammer, and let me feel for the furring. Do not depend on the putty. Drive a nail home and clinch it so faithfully that you can wake up in the night and think of your work with satisfaction—a work at which you would not be ashamed to invoke the Muse. So will help you God, and so only. Every nail driven should be as another rivet in the machine of the universe, you carrying on the work. (358–359)

I knew about lath, plaster, putty, and furring; I knew about the satisfaction of driving a nail home with two or three blows. So I followed this passage easily enough until I came to the Muse and God, and then I scratched my head, wondering how they entered the picture, and wondering even more how a well-driven nail and the person who hammered it could be useful to the universe.

10   Even where the style posed no problems, I often balked at the philosophy. Take the chapter grandly entitled "Higher Laws." In the opening lines, Thoreau confesses an urge to kill and devour a woodchuck raw, an impulse that stirs him to reflect: "I found in myself, and still find, an instinct toward a higher, or, as it is named, spiritual life, as do most men, and another toward a primitive rank and savage one, and I reverence them both" (229). Thus far I stayed with him, for I felt simultaneously the allure of science and girls, of books and basketball, and I was glad to think that both of these instincts deserved respect. But then Thoreau spends several pages elevating "purity" and denigrating everything "primitive rank and savage" about human life, from the eating of meat and the drinking of tea to "sensuality" of every kind, especially the "generative energy, which, when we are loose, dissipates and makes us unclean, when we are continent invigorates and inspires us" (239–240). Lest readers miss the allusion to sex, he goes on to insist that "Chastity is the flowering of man" (240), sounding less like a dissident thinker than like a Scoutmaster or high school nurse. Having begun by claiming to "reverence" the body's urges, Thoreau ends by declaring, "He is blessed who is assured that the animal is dying out in him day by day, and the divine being established" (240)—advice that could have come from St. Paul, the chief source of shame in my childhood.

Somewhere between hungering after a woodchuck and repudiating sex, Thoreau provoked me to say no. I could not have fully explained the grounds of my objection, neither at this point in my reading nor at any other point where I disagreed with him, but the fact of my disagreement, and the force of it, was exhilarating. I sensed that to question his philosophy, to test his ideas and opinions against my own reason and experience, was wholly in keeping with the philosophy itself.

Despite my reservations and confusions, what came through to me from *Walden*, and what most excited me, was Thoreau's desire to lead a meaningful life. The very title of the second chapter—"Where I Lived, and What I Lived For"—thrilled me. The "where" concerned me less than the "what for." At seventeen, I imagined that life must have a purpose beyond mere survival and the passing on of genes, beyond piling up money and possessions, beyond auditioning for paradise. But what might that purpose be? How could one discover it? And if life did have a purpose beyond those dictated by religion, economics, or biology, what then? How should one live in light of it?

I was haunted by such questions, yet my friends never spoke of them, and the adults I knew seemed to have resigned themselves to one or another conventional answer. So it was heartening to find Thoreau asking these very questions, in a passage I would later discover to be among the most celebrated in the book:

> I went to the woods because I wished to live deliberately, to front only the essential facts of life, and see if I could not learn what it had to teach, and not, when I came to die, discover that I had not lived. I did not wish to live what was not life, living is so dear; nor did I wish to practise resignation, unless it was quite necessary. I wanted to live deep and suck out all the marrow of life, to live so sturdily and Spartan-like as to put to rout all that was not life, to cut a broad swath and shave close, to drive life into a corner, and reduce it to its lowest terms, and, if it proved to be mean, why then to get the whole and genuine meanness of it, and publish its meanness to the world; or if it were sublime, to know it by experience, and be able to give a true account of it in my next excursion. For most men, it appears to me, are in a strange uncertainty about it, whether it is of the devil or of God, and have *somewhat hastily* concluded that it is the chief end of man here to "glorify God and enjoy him forever." (97)

Behind the bravado, I could hear his longing to find a true path, a way of spending his time and talents that would be worthy of the precious, fleeting gift of life. I shared that longing, as I shared his wariness about otherworldly philosophies. I did not recognize the source of his quotation in the last line—the Westminster Shorter Catechism, which opens with the declaration that "Man's chief end is to glorify God and to enjoy him forever"—but I had heard such pieties often, in sermons that discounted the value of life here and now except as preparation for life hereafter. What appealed to me most deeply in that first reading of *Walden* was Thoreau's determination to observe and enjoy the marvels of Earth, to be fully awake and alive, right here, right now.

Today, fifty years and many rereadings later, *Walden* is quite a different book for me: less bewildering, since I have made my share of difficult choices and suffered my share of losses, and also more challenging, since I have come to recognize more clearly my own limitations as well as those of the book. 15

Although I have renovated the old house in which my wife and I reared our children, and in which we now entertain our grandchildren, I realize, at age sixty-seven, I will never build a house from scratch. Although I remain cautious about technology—agreeing with Thoreau that many of our inventions merely offer "improved means to an unimproved end" (55)—my life depends on electricity and petroleum and the devices they power, as well as on the global networks that supply them. I try to minimize my possessions, giving away whatever I don't use, yet I keep acquiring new ones, which must be paid for, stored, insured, cleaned, repaired, and eventually replaced, thus demonstrating the truth of Thoreau's dictum that "the cost of a thing is the amount of . . . life which is required to be exchanged for it, immediately or in the long run" (32). I would rather not think about money, yet I spend hours keeping track of its coming and going, mainly to satisfy the IRS, merchants, and banks. As a husband, father, and now a grandfather, as a teacher for the past four decades, and as a citizen engaged in numerous causes, I bear responsibilities that I could not have imagined at the age of seventeen. No matter how I strive to simplify my life, it remains stubbornly complex. In short, I have failed to become the unencumbered, self-reliant, perpetually awake person I had envisioned in my youth.

Neither, I discovered, was Thoreau as unencumbered as he appeared to be on my first reading of *Walden*. During his sojourn in the woods, he frequently visited the village, saw friends, ate meals with his family, helped in the family pencil business, earned money from surveying and other jobs, carried on correspondence, gave lectures, and took trips. He revealed only part of himself on the page, which is all that even the most personal book can do. On the other hand, he presented far more of his thoughts and observations than actually occurred during the twenty-six months he spent living in the woods. The chronicle of his experiment at Walden Pond draws on material recorded in his journal from a period beginning years before and extending years after his time at the cabin. As a result, many passages in the book seem overstuffed, as if he felt compelled to include every anecdote, aphorism, witticism, image, and insight that had ever come to him concerning a given topic. Having worked with many young writers in my classes, and having once been a young writer myself, I recognize this tendency to excess as a common sign of ambition. Better overdo it than leave out something valuable.[3] I am more tolerant now of this and other stylistic quirks in *Walden*. The bluster and bragging are more than compensated for by the vigor and candor. For every showy allusion to classical literature or mythology, there is a burst of gritty American vernacular. For every willful obscurity in the prose, there are a dozen brilliant clarities.

While I am less inclined to quarrel with the style of *Walden*, I am more inclined to question some of the postures and opinions of the brash narrator. Thoreau's portrait of a solitary, self-sufficient life in the woods now appears to me as excessively, if unconsciously, male. His radical individualism, however necessary in his day as a bulwark against demands for conformity from church and society, now appears too narrow, rejecting as it does all responsibility of the self toward others. His opposition of spirit and flesh strikes me today as an expression of the dualism at the root of our ecological crisis, a dualism that sets mind against matter, culture against wildness. Thus our patron saint of environmentalism

3. Such an encyclopedic ambition has resulted in many a bloated, shapeless tome, of course, but it also gave us *Moby-Dick* and *Leaves of Grass*, which were published, respectively, three years before and one year after *Walden*.

can declare: "Nature is hard to be overcome, but she must be overcome" (241). Recognizing such misgivings does not diminish my appreciation for the book's many strengths, or my gratitude for all that it has taught me.

When I compare my current reading of *Walden* with impressions from that first reading, I am reminded of Italo Calvino's remark that books read in youth can be "formative, in the sense that they give a form to future experiences, providing models, terms of comparison, schemes for classification, scales of value, exemplars of beauty. . . . If we reread the book at a mature age, we are likely to rediscover these constants, which by this time are part of our inner mechanisms, but whose origins we have long forgotten."[4] My experience differs from Calvino's description only in that I have not forgotten the source of those "inner mechanisms." The example of Thoreau's life and the challenge of his thought remain potent influences for me, as they have been potent influences for generations of readers.

Of all his writings, *Walden* has had the broadest impact, moving count-   20
less people to seek a way of life that is close to nature, materially simple, purposeful, and reflective. His vision has been transmitted and transmuted through a lineage of American writers, from John Muir and Aldo Leopold and Rachel Carson to Wendell Berry and Terry Tempest Williams and Bill McKibben, all of them striving to harmonize human behavior with the constraints and patterns of our planetary home. We are far from achieving such a harmony—as witness climate disruption, for example, or the accelerated extinction of species—but we would be farther still without the questioning and imagining Thoreau inspired. We have him to thank, as much as anyone, for the shift in consciousness that led to the creation of America's national parks, designated wilderness areas, and laws aimed at protecting air and water and soil. We still need his cautionary, curmudgeonly voice, because in our day the craving for more—more stuff, more money, more power—no longer merely enslaves individuals; it degrades the conditions for life on Earth.

Great books read us as surely as we read them, revealing, by the aspects of our character and personal history they illuminate, who we are. Today when I revisit *Walden* it is usually in the company of my students, whose reactions remind me of my own early bafflement, resistance, and exhilaration. When they protest, as they often do, that they have no taste for Thoreau's experiment in simple living, I draw their attention to his disclaimer: "I would not have any one adopt *my* mode of living on any account; for, beside that before he has fairly learned it I may have found out another for myself, I desire that there may be as many different persons in the world as possible; but I would have each one be very careful to find out and pursue *his own* way, and not his father's or his mother's or his neighbor's instead" (75). Finding out and pursuing one's own way, while learning all one can about the ways that others have found, is the essential task not merely of education but of life.

4. Italo Calvino, *The Uses of Literature*, trans. Patrick Creagh (New York: Harcourt Brace Jovanovich, 1986), 127.

Thoreau continued his search after moving from the cabin back into town, a search that would lead to his public denunciation of slavery, to inventions that improved the making of pencils and the refining of graphite, to meticulous natural history studies, to research on Native Americans, to essays and journals and travel accounts that would fill a shelf of books published after his death. Wanting my students to bear in mind that ongoing life, beyond the confines of *Walden*, I draw their attention to another passage, this one from the final chapter: "I left the woods for as good a reason as I went there. Perhaps it seemed to me that I had several more lives to live, and could not spare any more time for that one. It is remarkable how easily and insensibly we fall into a particular route, and make a beaten track for ourselves" (351). What he sought for himself and urged for his readers was the freedom to keep thinking, keep experimenting, keep striking out afresh.

We commonly imagine Thoreau outdoors, chasing loons on the pond, watching frozen mud thaw, identifying wild-flowers, plucking wild fruits. But those excursions were informed and interpreted during countless hours he spent indoors, reading and writing. The chapter of *Walden* called "Reading" is a hymn to books, as eloquent as any of his tributes to nature. "Books are the treasured wealth of the world and the fit inheritance of generations and nations," he declares, recommending to us not just any books, but the great ones, the classics, those "we have to stand on tip-toe to read and devote our most alert and wakeful hours to" (110, 112). Such effort, he promises, will be abundantly repaid:

> There are probably words addressed to our condition exactly, which, if we could really hear and understand, would be more salutary than the morning or the spring to our lives, and possibly put a new aspect on the face of things for us. How many a man has dated a new era in his life from the reading of a book. The book exists for us perchance which will explain our miracles and reveal new ones. The at present unutterable things we may find somewhere uttered. These same questions that disturb and puzzle and confound us have in their turn occurred to all the wise men; not one has been omitted; and each has answered them, according to his ability, by his words and his life. (115–116)

Besieged as we are by advertisements and the cult of consumerism, racing to keep up with our gadgets, rushing from one sensation to the next, we need more than ever to ask the questions posed in *Walden*: What is life for? What are the necessities of a good life? How much is enough? Do we own our devices or do they own us? What is our place in nature? How do we balance individual freedom with social responsibility? How should we spend our days? Whether or not *Walden* speaks to your condition, I tell my students, there are other books that will do so, giving voice to what you have felt but have not been able to say, asking your deepest questions, stirring you to more intense life.

MLA CITATION

Sanders, Scott Russell. "Hooks Baited with Darkness." *The Norton Reader: An Anthology of Nonfiction*, edited by Melissa A. Goldthwaite et al., 16th ed., W. W. Norton, 2024, pp. 729–36.

QUESTIONS

1. How did Scott Russell Sanders's experience working with his hands inform his reading of *Walden*?

2. Sanders observes that at sixty-seven, he finds *Walden* both "less bewildering" and "more challenging" than he did in his youth (paragraph 15). What aspects of the book puzzled him as a teenager? What challenges does it pose to him as an older man?

3. Sanders writes, "While I am less inclined to quarrel with the style of *Walden*, I am more inclined to question some of the postures and opinions of the brash narrator" (paragraph 18). How do Sanders's opinions or values differ from Henry David Thoreau's, in "Where I Lived, and What I Lived For" (pp. 720–28), either as presented by Sanders or as you understand them from your reading of Thoreau's essay?

4. Following Sanders's model, write an honest essay in which you detail what you admire, dislike, and do not yet understand about a celebrated text.

VIRGINIA WOOLF
Thoughts on Peace in an Air Raid

THE GERMANS WERE OVER this house last night and the night before that. Here they are again. It is a queer experience, lying in the dark and listening to the zoom of a hornet which may at any moment sting you to death. It is a sound that interrupts cool and consecutive thinking about peace. Yet it is a sound—far more than prayers and anthems—that should compel one to think about peace. Unless we can think peace into existence we—not this one body in this one bed but millions of bodies yet to be born—will lie in the same darkness and hear the same death rattle overhead. Let us think what we can do to create the only efficient air-raid shelter while the guns on the hill go pop pop pop and the searchlights finger the clouds and now and then, sometimes close at hand, sometimes far away a bomb drops.

Up there in the sky young Englishmen and German men are fighting each other. The defenders are men, the attackers are men. Arms are not given to Englishwomen either to fight the enemy or to defend herself. She must lie weaponless tonight. Yet if she believes that the fight going on up in the sky is a fight by the English to protect freedom, by the Germans to destroy freedom, she must fight, so far as she can, on the side of the English. How far can she fight for freedom without firearms? By making arms, or clothes or food. But there is another way of fighting for freedom without arms; we can fight with the mind.

Published in the New Republic *(1940), an American magazine founded in 1914 to "bring liberalism into the modern era."*

We can make ideas that will help the young Englishman who is fighting up in the sky to defeat the enemy.

But to make ideas effective, we must be able to fire them off. We must put them into action. And the hornet in the sky rouses another hornet in the mind. There was one zooming in the *Times*[1] this morning—a woman's voice saying, "Women have not a word to say in politics." There is no woman in the Cabinet; nor in any responsible post. All the idea makers who are in a position to make ideas effective are men. That is a thought that damps thinking, and encourages irresponsibility. Why not bury the head in the pillow, plug the ears, and cease this futile activity of idea making? Because there are other tables besides officer tables and conference tables. Are we not leaving the young Englishman without a weapon that might be of value to him if we give up private thinking, tea-table thinking, because it seems useless? Are we not stressing our disability because our ability exposes us perhaps to abuse, perhaps to contempt? "I will not cease from mental fight," Blake[2] wrote. Mental fight means thinking against the current, not with it.

The current flows fast and furious. It issues in a spate of words from the loudspeakers and the politicians. Every day they tell us that we are a free people, fighting to defend freedom. That is the current that has whirled the young air-

1. Venerable British newspaper of record that is moderately conservative in its political orientation.
2. William Blake (1757–1827), British artist and poet.

man up into the sky and keeps him circling there among the clouds. Down here, with a roof to cover us and a gas mask handy, it is our business to puncture gas bags and discover seeds of truth. It is not true that we are free. We are both prisoners tonight—he boxed up in his machine with a gun handy; we lying in the dark with a gas mask handy. If we were free we should be out in the open, dancing, at the play, or sitting at the window talking together. What is it that prevents us? "Hitler!" the loudspeakers cry with one voice. Who is Hitler? What is he? Aggressiveness, tyranny, the insane love of power made manifest, they reply. Destroy that, and you will be free.

The drone of the planes is now like the sawing of a branch overhead. Round   5 and round it goes, sawing and sawing at a branch directly above the house. Another sound begins sawing its way into the brain. "Women of ability"—it was Lady Astor[3] speaking in the *Times* this morning—"are held down because of a subconscious Hitlerism in the hearts of men." Certainly we are held down. We are equally prisoners tonight—the Englishmen in their planes, the Englishwomen in their beds. But if he stops to think he may be killed; and we too. So let us think for him. Let us try to drag up into consciousness the sub-conscious Hitlerism that holds us down. It is the desire for aggression; the desire to dominate and enslave. Even in the darkness we can see that made visible. We can see shop windows blazing; and women gazing; painted women; dressed-up women; women with crimson lips and crimson fingernails. They are slaves who are trying to enslave. If we could free ourselves from slavery we should free men from tyranny. Hitlers are bred by slaves.

A bomb drops. All the windows rattle. The anti-aircraft guns are getting active. Up there on the hill under a net tagged with strips of green and brown stuff to imitate the hues of autumn leaves guns are concealed. Now they all fire at once. On the nine o'clock radio we shall be told "Forty-four enemy planes were shot down during the night, ten of them by anti-aircraft fire." And one of the terms of peace, the loudspeakers say, is to be disarmament. There are to be no more guns, no army, no navy, no air force in the future. No more young men will be trained to fight with arms. That rouses another mind-hornet in the chambers of the brain—another quotation. "To fight against a real enemy, to earn undying honor and glory by shooting total strangers, and to come home with my breast covered with medals and decorations, that was the summit of my hope. . . . It was for this that my whole life so far had been dedicated, my education, training, everything. . . ."

Those were the words of a young Englishman who fought in the last war.[4] In the face of them, do the current thinkers honestly believe that by writing "Disarmament" on a sheet of paper at a conference table they will have done all that is needful? Othello's[5] occupation will be gone; but he will remain

---

3. Nancy Witcher Astor, Viscountess Astor (1879–1964), first female member of Parliament.

4. World War I, known as the Great War (1914–18).

5. Referring to the title character in William Shakespeare's tragedy *Othello, the Moor of Venice* (1603), a Black general serving the city of Venice.

Othello. The young airman up in the sky is driven not only by the voices of loudspeakers; he is driven by voices in himself—ancient instincts, instincts fostered and cherished by education and tradition. Is he to be blamed for these instincts? Could we switch off the maternal instinct at the command of a table full of politicians? Suppose that imperative among the peace terms was: "Childbearing is to be restricted to a very small class of specially selected women," would we submit? Should we not say, "The maternal instinct is a woman's glory, It was for this that my whole life has been dedicated, my education, training, everything." . . . But if it were necessary for the sake of humanity, for the peace of the world, that childbearing should be restricted, the maternal instinct subdued, women would attempt it. Men would help them. They would honor them for their refusal to bear children. They would give them other openings for their creative power. That too must make part of our fight for freedom. We must help the young Englishmen to root out from themselves the love of medals and decorations. We must create more honorable activities for those who try to conquer in themselves their fighting instinct, their subconscious Hitlerism. We must compensate the man for the loss of his gun.

The sound of sawing overhead has increased. All the searchlights are erect. They point at a spot exactly above this roof. At any moment a bomb may fall on this very room. One, two, three, four, five, six . . . the seconds pass. The bomb did not fall. But during those seconds of suspense all thinking stopped. All feeling, save one dull dread, ceased. A nail fixed the whole being to one hard board. The emotion of fear and of hate is therefore sterile, unfertile. Directly that fear passes, the mind reaches out and instinctively revives itself by trying to create. Since the room is dark it can create only from memory. It reaches out to the memory of other Augusts—in Bayreuth, listening to Wagner; in Rome, walking over the Campagna;[6] in London. Friends' voices come back. Scraps of poetry return. Each of those thoughts, even in memory, was far more positive, reviving, healing and creative than the dull dread made of fear and hate. Therefore if we are to compensate the young man for the loss of his glory and of his gun, we must give him access to the creative feelings. We must make happiness. We must free him from the machine. We must bring him out of his prison into the open air. But what is the use of freeing the young Englishman if the young German and the young Italian remain slaves?

The searchlights, wavering across the flat, have picked up the plane now. From this window one can see a little silver insect turning and twisting in the light. The guns go pop pop pop. Then they cease. Probably the raider was brought down behind the hill. One of the pilots landed safe in a field near here the other day. He said to his captors, speaking fairly good English, "How glad I am that the fight is over!" Then an Englishman gave him a cigarette, and an English woman made him a cup of tea. That would seem to show that if you

---

6. Wilhelm Richard Wagner (1813–1883), German composer; Campagna, rustic region outside of Rome, Italy.

can free the man from the machine, the seed does not fall upon altogether stony ground. The seed may be fertile.

At last all the guns have stopped firing. All the searchlights have been 10 extinguished. The natural darkness of a summer's night returns. The innocent sounds of the country are heard again. An apple thuds to the ground. An owl hoots, winging its way from tree to tree. And some half-forgotten words of an old English writer come to mind: "The huntsmen are up in America. . . ."[7] Let us send these fragmentary notes to the huntsmen who are up in America, to the men and women whose sleep has not yet been broken by machine-gun fire, in the belief that they will rethink them generously and charitably, perhaps shape them into something serviceable. And now, in the shadowed half of the world, to sleep.

MLA CITATION

Woolf, Virginia. "Thoughts on Peace in an Air Raid." *The Norton Reader: An Anthology of Nonfiction*, edited by Melissa A. Goldthwaite et al., 16th ed., W. W. Norton, 2024, pp. 737–41.

QUESTIONS

1. Virginia Woolf's title "Thoughts on Peace in an Air Raid" marks her piece as an *occasional essay* (that is, something written on or for a specific occasion) and gestures toward her theme: the crucial importance of human thought in bringing about real peace. Woolf wrote this essay from London for an American magazine during the Blitz, Germany's eight-month bombing campaign of Great Britain that began in September 1940, to American women who had asked her how they might help the war effort. Why does this context matter? According to Woolf, how does the bombing hinder thinking, and how can thinking foster peace?

2. Why does Woolf see men as responsible for war? What does she see as the necessary role of women in bringing about peace? How does her conception of men and women, or of gender more generally, compare to how we conceive of gender today? Why or why not? Annotate the essay, marking your reactions to her ideas.

3. What does Woolf mean by "'subconscious Hitlerism'" (paragraph 5), and how, according to Woolf, can it be resisted? Do you find her prescription realistic? Why or why not?

4. Imagine that Woolf were alive today and that you have been invited to interview her about a major social or political issue facing our world. What questions would you ask her? What do you think she would say? Write that dialogue.

---

7. From *The Garden of Cyrus* (1658), a prose discourse by Sir Thomas Browne (1605–1682).

Sight into Insight

W HEN I WAS SIX OR SEVEN YEARS OLD, growing up in Pittsburgh, I used to take a penny of my own and hide it for someone else to find. It was a curious compulsion; sadly, I've never been seized by it since. For some reason I always "hid" the penny along the same stretch of sidewalk up the street. I'd cradle it at the roots of a maple, say, or in a hole left by a chipped-off piece of sidewalk. Then I'd take a piece of chalk and, starting at either end of the block, draw huge arrows leading up to the penny from both directions. After I learned to write I labeled the arrows "SURPRISE AHEAD" or "MONEY THIS WAY." I was greatly excited, during all this arrowdrawing, at the thought of the first lucky passerby who would receive in this way, regardless of merit, a free gift from the universe. But I never lurked about. I'd go straight home and not give the matter another thought, until, some months later, I would be gripped by the impulse to hide another penny.

There are lots of things to see, unwrapped gifts and free surprises. The world is fairly studded and strewn with pennies cast broadside from a generous hand. But—and this is the point—who gets excited by a mere penny? If you follow one arrow, if you crouch motionless on a bank to watch a tremulous ripple thrill on the water, and are rewarded by the sight of a muskrat kit paddling from its den, will you count that sight a chip of copper only, and go your rueful way? It is very dire poverty indeed for a man to be so malnourished and fatigued that he won't stoop to pick up a penny. But if you cultivate a healthy poverty and simplicity, so that finding a penny will make your day, then, since the world is in fact planted in pennies, you have with your poverty bought a lifetime of days. What you see is what you get.

Unfortunately, nature is very much a now-you-see-it, now-you-don't affair. A fish flashes, then dissolves in the water before my eyes like so much salt. Deer apparently ascend bodily into heaven; the brightest oriole fades into leaves. These disappearances stun me into stillness and concentration; they say of nature that it conceals with a grand nonchalance, and they say of vision that it is a deliberate gift, the revelation of a dancer who for my eyes only flings away her seven veils.[1]

For nature does reveal as well as conceal: now-you-don't-see-it, now-you-do. For a week this September migrating red-winged blackbirds were feeding heavily down by Tinker Creek at the back of the house. One day I went out to investigate the racket; I walked up to a tree, an Osage orange, and a hundred birds flew away. They simply materialized out of the tree. I saw a tree, then a whisk

Originally published in Harper's Magazine *(1974), an American monthly covering politics, society, culture, and the environment, this piece was included in Annie Dillard's Pulitzer Prize–winning book* Pilgrim at Tinker Creek *(1974).*

1. Allusion to the biblical story of Salome dancing for Herod, her uncle and stepfather.

of color, then a tree again. I walked closer and another hundred blackbirds took flight. Not a branch, not a twig budged: the birds were apparently weightless as well as invisible. Or, it was as if the leaves of the Osage orange had been freed from a spell in the form of red-winged blackbirds; they flew from the tree, caught my eye in the sky, and vanished. When I looked again at the tree, the leaves had reassembled as if nothing had happened. Finally I walked directly to the trunk of the tree and a final hundred, the real diehards, appeared, spread, and vanished. How could so many hide in the tree without my seeing them? The Osage orange, unruffled, looked just as it had looked from the house, when three hundred red-winged blackbirds cried from its crown. I looked upstream where they flew, and they were gone. Searching, I couldn't spot one. I wandered upstream to force them to play their hand, but they'd crossed the creek and scattered. One show to a customer. These appearances catch at my throat; they are the free gifts, the bright coppers at the roots of trees.

It's all a matter of keeping my eyes open. Nature is like one of those line drawings that are puzzles for children: Can you find hidden in the tree a duck, a house, a boy, a bucket, a giraffe, and a boot? Specialists can find the most incredibly hidden things. A book I read when I was young recommended an easy way to find caterpillars: you simply find some fresh caterpillar droppings, look up, and there's your caterpillar. More recently an author advised me to set my mind at ease about those piles of cut stems on the ground in grassy fields. Field mice make them; they cut the grass down by degrees to reach the seeds at the head. It seems that when the grass is tightly packed, as in a field of ripe grain, the blade won't topple at a single cut through the stem; instead, the cut stem simply drops vertically, held in the crush of grain. The mouse severs the bottom again and again, the stem keeps dropping an inch at a time, and finally the head is low enough for the mouse to reach the seeds. Meanwhile the mouse is positively littering the field with its little piles of cut stems into which, presumably, the author is constantly stumbling.

   If I can't see these minutiae, I still try to keep my eyes open. I'm always on the lookout for ant lion traps in sandy soil, monarch pupae near milkweed, skipper larvae in locust leaves. These things are utterly common, and I've not seen one. I bang on hollow trees near water, but so far no flying squirrels have appeared. In flat country I watch every sunset in hopes of seeing the green ray. The green ray is a seldom-seen streak of light that rises from the sun like a spurting fountain at the moment of sunset; it throbs into the sky for two seconds and disappears. One more reason to keep my eyes open. A photography professor at the University of Florida just happened to see a bird die in midflight; it jerked, died, dropped, and smashed on the ground.

   I squint at the wind because I read Stewart Edward White:[2] "I have always maintained that if you looked closely enough you could *see* the wind—the dim, hardly-made-out, fine débris fleeing high in the air." White was an excellent

2. Prolific American writer (1873–1946) of travel literature and adventure fiction who also wrote books of spiritualism later in his life.

observer, and devoted an entire chapter of *The Mountains* to the subject of seeing deer: "As soon as you can forget the naturally obvious and construct an artificial obvious, then you too will see deer."

But the artificial obvious is hard to see. My eyes account for less than 1 percent of the weight of my head; I'm bony and dense; I see what I expect. I once spent a full three minutes looking at a bullfrog that was so unexpectedly large I couldn't see it even though a dozen enthusiastic campers were shouting directions. Finally I asked, "What color am I looking for?" and a fellow said, "Green." When at last I picked out the frog, I saw what painters are up against: the thing wasn't green at all, but the color of wet hickory bark.

The lover can see, and the knowledgeable. I visited an aunt and uncle at a quarter-horse ranch in Cody, Wyoming. I couldn't do much of anything useful, but I could, I thought, draw. So, as we all sat around the kitchen table after supper, I produced a sheet of paper and drew a horse. "That's one lame horse," my aunt volunteered. The rest of the family joined in: "Only place to saddle that one is his neck"; "Looks like we better shoot the poor thing, on account of those terrible growths." Meekly, I slid the pencil and paper down the table. Everyone in that family, including my three young cousins, could draw a horse. Beautifully. When the paper came back it looked as though five shining, real quarter horses had been corraled by mistake with a papier-mâché moose; the real horses seemed to gaze at the monster with a steady, puzzled air. I stay away from horses now, but I can do a creditable goldfish. The point is that I just don't know what the lover knows; I just can't see the artificial obvious that those in the know construct. The herpetologist asks the native, "Are there snakes in that ravine?" "Nosir." And the herpetologist comes home with, yessir, three bags full. Are there butterflies on that mountain? Are the bluets in bloom, are there arrowheads here, or fossil shells in the shale?

10   Peeping through my keyhole I see within the range of only about 30 percent of the light that comes from the sun; the rest is infrared and some little ultraviolet, perfectly apparent to many animals, but invisible to me. A nightmare network of ganglia, charged and firing without my knowledge, cuts and splices what I do see, editing it for my brain. Donald E. Carr[3] points out that the sense impressions of one-celled animals are *not* edited for the brain: "This is philosophically interesting in a rather mournful way, since it means that only the simplest animals perceive the universe as it is."

A fog that won't burn away drifts and flows across my field of vision. When you see fog move against a backdrop of deep pines, you don't see the fog itself, but streaks of clearness floating across the air in dark shreds. So I see only tatters of clearness through a pervading obscurity. I can't distinguish the fog from the overcast sky; I can't be sure if the light is direct or reflected. Everywhere darkness and the presence of the unseen appalls. We estimate now that only one atom dances alone in every cubic meter of intergalactic space. I blink and squint. What planet or power yanks Halley's Comet out of orbit? We haven't seen it yet; it's a question of distance, density, and the pallor of reflected light.

3. American research chemist and science journalist (1903–1986).

We rock, cradled in the swaddling band of darkness. Even the simple darkness of night whispers suggestions to the mind. This summer, in August, I stayed at the creek too late.

Where Tinker Creek flows under the sycamore log bridge to the tear-shaped island, it is slow and shallow, fringed thinly in cattail marsh. At this spot an astonishing bloom of life supports vast breeding populations of insects, fish, reptiles, birds, and mammals. On windless summer evenings I stalk along the creek bank or straddle the sycamore log in absolute stillness, watching for muskrats. The night I stayed too late I was hunched on the log staring spellbound at spreading, reflected stains of lilac on the water. A cloud in the sky suddenly lighted as if turned on by a switch; its reflection just as suddenly materialized on the water upstream, flat and floating, so that I couldn't see the creek bottom, or life in the water under the cloud. Downstream, away from the cloud on the water, water turtles smooth as beans were gliding down with the current in a series of easy, weightless push-offs, as men bound on the moon. I didn't know whether to trace the progress of one turtle I was sure of, risking sticking my face in one of the bridge's spider webs made invisible by the gathering dark, or take a chance on seeing the carp, or scan the mudbank in hope of seeing a muskrat, or follow the last of the swallows who caught at my heart and trailed it after them like streamers as they appeared from directly below, under the log, flying upstream with their tails forked, so fast.

But shadows spread and deepened and stayed. After thousands of years we're still strangers to darkness, fearful aliens in an enemy camp with our arms crossed over our chests. I stirred. A land turtle on the bank, startled, hissed the air from its lungs and withdrew to its shell. An uneasy pink here, an unfathomable blue there, gave great suggestion of lurking beings. Things were going on. I couldn't see whether that rustle I heard was a distant rattlesnake, slit-eyed, or a nearby sparrow kicking in the dry flood debris slung at the foot of a willow. Tremendous action roiled the water everywhere I looked, big action, inexplicable. A tremor welled up beside a gaping muskrat burrow in the bank and I caught my breath, but no muskrat appeared. The ripples continued to fan upstream with a steady, powerful thrust. Night was knitting an eyeless mask over my face, and I still sat transfixed. A distant airplane, a delta wing out of nightmare, made a gliding shadow on the creek's bottom that looked like a stingray cruising upstream. At once a black fin slit the pink cloud on the water, shearing it in two. The two halves merged together and seemed to dissolve before my eyes. Darkness pooled in the cleft of the creek and rose, as water collects in a well. Untamed, dreaming lights flickered over the sky. I saw hints of hulking underwater shadows, two pale splashes out of the water, and round ripples rolling close together from a blackened center.

At last I stared upstream where only the deepest violet remained of the cloud, a cloud so high its underbelly still glowed, its feeble color reflected from a hidden sky lighted in turn by a sun halfway to China. And out of that violet, a sudden enormous black body arced over the water. Head and tail, if there was a head and tail, were both submerged in cloud. I saw only one ebony fling, a headlong dive to darkness; then the waters closed, and the lights went out.

15   I walked home in a shivering daze, up hill and down. Later I lay open-mouthed in bed, my arms flung wide at my sides to steady the whirling darkness. At this latitude I'm spinning 836 miles an hour round the earth's axis; I feel my sweeping fall as a breakneck arc like the dive of dolphins, and the hollow rushing of wind raises the hairs on my neck and the side of my face. In orbit around the sun I'm moving 64,800 miles an hour. The solar system as a whole, like a merry-go-round unhinged, spins, bobs, and blinks at the speed of 43,200 miles an hour along a course set east of Hercules. Someone has piped, and we are dancing a tarantella until the sweat pours. I open my eyes and I see dark, muscled forms curl out of water, with flapping gills and flattened eyes. I close my eyes and I see stars, deep stars giving way to deeper stars, deeper stars bowing to deepest stars at the crown of an infinite cone.

"Still," wrote Van Gogh[4] in a letter, "a great deal of light falls on everything." If we are blinded by darkness, we are also blinded by light. Sometimes here in Virginia at sunset low clouds on the southern or northern horizon are completely invisible in the lighted sky. I only know one is there because I can see its reflection in still water. The first time I discovered this mystery I looked from cloud to no-cloud in bewilderment, checking my bearings over and over, thinking maybe the ark of the covenant[5] was just passing by south of Dead Man Mountain. Only much later did I learn the explanation: polarized light from the sky is very much weakened by reflection, but the light in clouds isn't polarized. So invisible clouds pass among visible clouds, till all slide over the mountains; so a greater light extinguishes a lesser as though it didn't exist.

   In the great meteor shower of August, the Perseid, I wail all day for the shooting stars I miss. They're out there showering down committing hara-kiri in a flame of fatal attraction, and hissing perhaps at last into the ocean. But at dawn what looks like a blue dome clamps down over me like a lid on a pot. The stars and planets could smash and I'd never know. Only a piece of ashen moon occasionally climbs up or down the inside of the dome, and our local star without surcease explodes on our heads. We have really only that one light, one source for all power, and yet we must turn away from it by universal decree. Nobody here on the planet seems aware of this strange, powerful taboo, that we all walk about carefully averting our faces, this way and that, lest our eyes be blasted forever.

   Darkness appalls and light dazzles; the scrap of visible light that doesn't hurt my eyes hurts my brain. What I see sets me swaying. Size and distance and the sudden swelling of meanings confuse me, bowl me over. I straddle the sycamore log bridge over Tinker Creek in the summer. I look at the lighted creek bottom: snail tracks tunnel the mud in quavering curves. A crayfish jerks, but by the time I absorb what has happened, he's gone in a billowing smoke screen of silt. I look at the water; minnows and shiners. If I'm thinking minnows, a carp will fill my brain till I scream. I look at the water's surface: skaters, bubbles,

4. Vincent van Gogh (1853–1890), Dutch Postimpressionist painter.
5. Repository for the stone tablets of the Ten Commandments carried by the ancient Israelites during their desert wanderings.

and leaves sliding down. Suddenly, my own face, reflected, startles me witless. Those snails have been tracking my face! Finally, with a shuddering wrench of the will, I see clouds, cirrus clouds. I'm dizzy, I fall in.

This looking business is risky. Once I stood on a humped rock on nearby Purgatory Mountain, watching through binoculars the great autumn hawk migration below, until I discovered that I was in danger of joining the hawks on a vertical migration of my own. I was used to binoculars, but not, apparently, to balancing on humped rocks while looking through them. I reeled. Everything advanced and receded by turns; the world was full of unexplained foreshortenings and depths. A distant huge object, a hawk the size of an elephant, turned out to be the browned bough of a nearby loblolly pine. I followed a sharp-shinned hawk against a featureless sky, rotating my head unawares as it flew, and when I lowered the glass a glimpse of my own looming shoulder sent me staggering. What prevents the men at Palomar[6] from falling, voiceless and blinded, from their tiny, vaulted chairs?

I reel in confusion: I don't understand what I see. With the naked eye I can see two million light-years to the Andromeda galaxy. Often I slop some creek water in a jar, and when I get home I dump it in a white china bowl. After the silt settles I return and see tracings of minute snails on the bottom, a planarian or two winding round the rim of water, roundworms shimmying, frantically, and finally, when my eyes have adjusted to these dimensions, amoebae. At first the amoebae look like *muscae volitantes*, those curled moving spots you seem to see in your eyes when you stare at a distant wall. Then I see the amoebae as drops of water congealed, bluish, translucent, like chips of sky in the bowl. At length I choose one individual and give myself over to its idea of an evening. I see it dribble a grainy foot before it on its wet, unfathomable way. Do its unedited sense impressions include the fierce focus of my eyes? Shall I take it outside and show it Andromeda, and blow its little endoplasm? I stir the water with a finger, in case it's running out of oxygen. Maybe I should get a tropical aquarium with motorized bubblers and lights, and keep this one for a pet. Yes, it would tell its fissioned descendants, the universe is two feet by five, and if you listen closely you can hear the buzzing music of the spheres.

Oh, it's mysterious, lamplit evenings here in the galaxy, one after the other. It's one of those nights when I wander from window to window, looking for a sign. But I can't see. Terror and a beauty insoluble are a riband of blue woven into the fringe of garments of things both great and small. No culture explains, no bivouac offers real haven or rest. But it could be that we are not seeing something. Galileo[7] thought comets were an optical illusion. This is fertile ground: since we are certain that they're not, we can look at what our scientists have been saying with fresh hope. What if there are *really* gleaming, castellated cities hung up-side-down over the desert sand? What limpid lakes and cool date palms have our caravans always passed untried? Until, one by one, by the blindest of leaps, we light on the road to these places, we must stumble in darkness and

20

6. Astronomical observatory in California.
7. Galileo Galilei (1564–1642), Italian astronomer and mathematician.

hunger. I turn from the window. I'm blind as a bat, sensing only from every direction the echo of my own thin cries.

I chanced on a wonderful book called *Space and Sight*, by Marius Von Senden. When Western surgeons discovered how to perform safe cataract operations, they ranged across Europe and America operating on dozens of men and women of all ages who had been blinded by cataracts since birth. Von Senden collected accounts of such cases; the histories are fascinating. Many doctors had tested their patients' sense perceptions and ideas of space both before and after the operations. The vast majority of patients, of both sexes and all ages, had, in Von Senden's opinion, no idea of space whatsoever. Form, distance, and size were so many meaningless syllables. A patient "had no idea of depth, confusing it with roundness." Before the operation a doctor would give a blind patient a cube and a sphere; the patient would tongue it or feel it with his hands, and name it correctly. After the operation the doctor would show the same objects to the patient without letting him touch them; now he had no clue whatsoever to what he was seeing. One patient called lemonade "square" because it pricked on his tongue as a square shape pricked on the touch of his hands. Of another post-operative patient the doctor writes, "I have found in her no notion of size, for example, not even within the narrow limits which she might have encompassed with the aid of touch. Thus when I asked her to show me how big her mother was, she did not stretch out her hands, but set her two index fingers a few inches apart."

For the newly sighted, vision is pure sensation unencumbered by meaning. When a newly sighted girl saw photographs and paintings, she asked, "'Why do they put those dark marks all over them?' 'Those aren't dark marks,' her mother explained, 'those are shadows. That is one of the ways the eye knows that things have shape. If it were not for shadows, many things would look flat.' 'Well, that's how things do look,' Joan answered. 'Everything looks flat with dark patches.'"

In general the newly sighted see the world as a dazzle of "color-patches." They are pleased by the sensation of color, and learn quickly to name the colors, but the rest of seeing is tormentingly difficult. Soon after his operation a patient "generally bumps into one of these color-patches and observes them to be substantial, since they resist him as tactual objects do. In walking about it also strikes him—or can if he pays attention—that he is continually passing in between the colors he sees, that he can go past a visual object, that a part of it then steadily disappears from view; and that in spite of this, however he twists and turns—whether entering the room from the door, for example, or returning back to it—he always has a visual space in front of him. Thus he gradually comes to realize that there is also a space behind him, which he does not see."

25   The mental effort involved in these reasonings proves overwhelming for many patients. It oppresses them to realize that they have been visible to people all along, perhaps unattractively so, without their knowledge or consent. A disheartening number of them refuse to use their new vision, continuing to go over objects with their tongues, and lapsing into apathy and despair.

On the other hand, many newly sighted people speak well of the world, and teach us how dull our own vision is. To one patient, a human hand, unrecognized, is "something bright and then holes." Shown a bunch of grapes, a boy calls out, "It is dark, blue and shiny. . . . It isn't smooth, it has bumps and hollows." A little girl visits a garden. "She is greatly astonished, and can scarcely be persuaded to answer, stands speechless in front of the tree, which she only names on taking hold of it, and then as 'the tree with the lights in it.'" Another patient, a twenty-two-year-old girl, was dazzled by the world's brightness and kept her eyes shut for two weeks. When at the end of that time she opened her eyes again, she did not recognize any objects, but "the more she now directed her gaze upon everything about her, the more it could be seen how an expression of gratification and astonishment overspread her features; she repeatedly exclaimed: 'Oh God! How beautiful!'"

I saw color-patches for weeks after I read this wonderful book. It was summer; the peaches were ripe in the valley orchards. When I woke in the morning, color-patches wrapped round my eyes, intricately, leaving not one unfilled spot. All day long I walked among shifting color-patches that parted before me like the Red Sea and closed again in silence,[8] transfigured, wherever I looked back. Some patches swelled and loomed, while others vanished utterly, and dark marks flitted at random over the whole dazzling sweep. But I couldn't sustain the illusion of flatness. I've been around for too long. Form is condemned to an eternal danse macabre with meaning: I couldn't unpeach the peaches. Nor can I remember ever having seen without understanding; the color-patches of infancy are lost. My brain then must have been smooth as any balloon. I'm told I reached for the moon; many babies do. But the color-patches of infancy swelled as meaning filled them; they arrayed themselves in solemn ranks down distance which unrolled and stretched before me like a plain. The moon rocketed away. I live now in a world of shadows that shape and distance color, a world where space makes a kind of terrible sense. What Gnosticism[9] is this, and what physics? The fluttering patch I saw in my nursery window—silver and green and shape-shifting blue—is gone; a row of Lombardy poplars takes its place, mute, across the distant lawn. That humming oblong creature pale as light that stole along the walls of my room at night, stretching exhilaratingly around the corners, is gone, too, gone the night I ate of the bittersweet fruit, put two and two together and puckered forever my brain. Martin Buber[10] tells this tale: "Rabbi Mendel once boasted to his teacher Rabbi Elimelekh that evenings he saw the angel who rolls away the light before the darkness, and mornings the angel who rolls away the darkness before the light. 'Yes,' said Rabbi Elimelekh, 'in my youth I saw that too. Later on you don't see these things anymore.'"

Why didn't someone hand those newly sighted people paints and brushes from the start, when they still didn't know what anything was? Then maybe we all could see color-patches too, the world unraveled from reason, Eden before

8. According to the book of Exodus in the Bible, the Red Sea parted for the Israelites and closed over the Egyptians pursuing them.

9. Promise of secret knowledge of the divine.

10. Austrian-born Israeli philosopher (1878–1965).

Adam gave names. The scales would drop from my eyes; I'd see trees like men walking; I'd run down the road against all orders, hallooing and leaping.

Seeing is of course very much a matter of verbalization. Unless I call my attention to what passes before my eyes, I simply won't see it. If Tinker Mountain erupted, I'd be likely to notice. But if I want to notice the lesser cataclysms of valley life, I have to maintain in my head a running description of the present. It's not that I'm observant; it's just that I talk too much. Otherwise, especially in a strange place, I'll never know what's happening. Like a blind man at the ball game, I need a radio.

30   When I see this way I analyze and pry. I hurl over logs and roll away stones; I study the bank a square foot at a time, probing and tilting my head. Some days when a mist covers the mountains, when the muskrats won't show and the microscope's mirror shatters, I want to climb up the blank blue dome as a man would storm the inside of a circus tent, wildly, dangling, and with a steel knife claw a rent in the top, peep, and, if I must, fall.

But there is another kind of seeing that involves a letting go. When I see this way I sway transfixed and emptied. The difference between the two ways of seeing is the difference between walking with and without a camera. When I walk with a camera I walk from shot to shot, reading the light on a calibrated meter. When I walk without a camera, my own shutter opens, and the moment's light prints on my own silver gut. When I see this second way I am above all an unscrupulous observer.

It was sunny one evening last summer at Tinker Creek; the sun was low in the sky, upstream. I was sitting on the sycamore log bridge with the sunset at my back, watching the shiners the size of minnows who were feeding over the muddy sand in skittery schools. Again and again, one fish, then another, turned for a split second across the current and flash! the sun shot out from its silver side. I couldn't watch for it. It was always just happening somewhere else, and it drew my vision just as it disappeared: flash! like a sudden dazzle of the thinnest blade, a sparking over a dun and olive ground at chance intervals from every direction. Then I noticed white specks, some sort of pale petals, small, floating from under my feet on the creek's surface, very slow and steady. So I blurred my eyes and gazed toward the brim of my hat and saw a new world. I saw the pale white circles roll up, roll up, like the world's turning, mute and perfect, and I saw the linear flashes, gleaming silver, like stars being born at random down a rolling scroll of time. Something broke and something opened. I filled up like a new wineskin. I breathed an air like light; I saw a light like water. I was the lip of a fountain the creek filled forever; I was ether, the leaf in the zephyr; I was flesh-flake, feather, bone.

When I see this way I see truly. As Thoreau[11] says, I return to my senses. I am the man who watches the baseball game in silence in an empty stadium. I see the game purely; I'm abstracted and dazed. When it's all over and the

11. Henry David Thoreau (1817–1862), American transcendentalist; see "Where I Lived, and What I Lived For" (pp. 720–28).

white-suited players lope off the green field to their shadowed dugouts, I leap to my feet, I cheer and cheer.

But I can't go out and try to see this way. I'll fail, I'll go mad. All I can do is try to gag the commentator, to hush the noise of useless interior babble that keeps me from seeing just as surely as a newspaper dangled before my eyes. The effort is really a discipline requiring a lifetime of dedicated struggle; it marks the literature of saints and monks of every order east and west, under every rule and no rule, discalced[12] and shod. The world's spiritual geniuses seem to discover universally that the mind's muddy river, this ceaseless flow of trivia and trash, cannot be dammed, and that trying to dam it is a waste of effort that might lead to madness. Instead you must allow the muddy river to flow unheeded in the dim channels of consciousness; you raise your sights; you look along it, mildly, acknowledging its presence without interest and gazing beyond it into the realm of the real where subjects and objects act and rest purely, without utterance. "Launch into the deep," says Jacques Ellul,[13] "and you shall see."

The secret of seeing, then, is the pearl of great price. If I thought he could teach me to find it and keep it forever I would stagger barefoot across a hundred deserts after any lunatic at all. But although the pearl may be found, it may not be sought. The literature of illumination reveals this above all: although it comes to those who wait for it, it is always, even to the most practiced and adept, a gift and a total surprise. I return from one walk knowing where the killdeer nests in the field by the creek and the hour the laurel blooms. I return from the same walk a day later scarcely knowing my own name. Litanies hum in my ears; my tongue flaps in my mouth, *Alim non*, alleluia! I cannot cause light; the most I can do is try to put myself in the path of its beam. It is possible, in deep space, to sail on solar wind. Light, be it particle or wave, has force: you rig a giant sail and go. The secret of seeing is to sail on solar wind. Hone and spread your spirit till you yourself are a sail, whetted, translucent, broadside to the merest puff.

When her doctor took her bandages off and led her into the garden, the girl who was no longer blind saw "the tree with the lights in it." It was for this tree I searched through the peach orchards of summer, in the forests of fall and down winter and spring for years. Then one day I was walking along Tinker Creek thinking of nothing at all and I saw the tree with the lights in it. I saw the backyard cedar where the mourning doves roost charged and transfigured, each cell buzzing with flame. I stood on the grass with the lights in it, grass that was wholly fire, utterly focused and utterly dreamed. It was less like seeing than like being for the first time seen, knocked breathless by a powerful glance. The flood of fire abated, but I'm still spending the power. Gradually the lights went out in the cedar, the colors died, the cells unflamed and disappeared. I was still ringing. I had been my whole life a bell, and never knew it until at that moment I was lifted and struck. I have since only very rarely seen the tree with the lights in it. The vision comes and goes, mostly goes, but I live

35

12. Shoeless, as in the order of the Discalced Carmelites.
13. French Protestant theologian and critic of technology (1912–1994).

for it, for the moment when the mountains open and a new light roars in spate through the crack, and the mountains slam.

MLA CITATION

Dillard, Annie. "Sight into Insight." *The Norton Reader: An Anthology of Nonfiction,* edited by Melissa A. Goldthwaite et al., 16th ed., W. W. Norton, 2024, pp. 742–52.

QUESTIONS

1. Annie Dillard is concerned with seeing, but the kind of seeing she considers at the end of her essay differs from the kind she describes at its beginning. How?

2. Dillard often uses several examples to support a general claim. In paragraph 3, for instance, she writes, "nature is very much a now-you-see-it, now-you-don't affair" and follows with "[a] fish flashes, then dissolves" and "the brightest oriole fades into leaves." Locate other examples of this technique, marking the general statements and examples that accompany them. What purpose does this technique serve? In what kinds of writing is it appropriate? inappropriate?

3. Take one of Dillard's general statements and come up with supporting examples of your own.

4. Dillard writes, "I see what I expect" (paragraph 8) but also, "Specialists can find the most incredibly hidden things" (paragraph 5). Pick something that you have seen repeatedly but have not regarded as remarkable. Look at it carefully and write a detailed description of it. Then learn something more about the thing you picked, either through your own research or by talking to an expert, and write a second description. How did your newfound knowledge change what you saw?

MARGARET RENKL
Christmas Isn't Coming to Death Row

When it comes to the death penalty, guilt or innocence shouldn't really matter to Christians.

U NTIL AUGUST, Tennessee had not put a prisoner to death in nearly a decade. Last Thursday, it performed its third execution in four months.

This was not a surprising turn of events. In each case, recourse to the courts had been exhausted. In each case, Governor Bill Haslam, a Republican, declined to intervene, though there were many reasons to justify intervening. Billy Ray Irick suffered from psychotic episodes that

Originally published as an op-ed in the New York Times *on December 10, 2018, under the title "There's a Lot of Killing in Thou-Shalt-Not-Kill States" and reprinted in Margaret Renkl's 2021 collection* Graceland, At Last: Notes on Hope and Heartache from the American South.

raised profound doubts about his ability to distinguish right from wrong. Edmund Zagorski's behavior in prison was so exemplary that even the warden pleaded for his life. David Earl Miller also suffered from mental illness and was a survivor of child abuse so horrific that he tried to kill himself when he was six years old.

Questions about the humanity of Tennessee's lethal-injection protocol were so pervasive following the execution of Mr. Irick that both Mr. Zagorski and Mr. Miller elected to die in Tennessee's electric chair, which was first used in 1916. (The state spruced it up in 1989.) Their choice says something very clear about Tennessee's three-drug execution cocktail, as Justice Sonia Sotomayor noted in a dissenting opinion to the Supreme Court's decision not to hear Mr. Miller's case: "Both so chose even though electrocution can be a dreadful way to die," she wrote. "They did so against the backdrop of credible scientific evidence that lethal injection as currently practiced in Tennessee may well be even worse." Electrocution might not be any more humane than death by lethal injection, in other words, but at least it offers a speedier hideous death.

Presumably this is the same thinking behind the position taken by fifty-one death row prisoners in Alabama who want to die in an untested nitrogen gas chamber rather than by either the electric chair or lethal injection.

Nitrogen gas. That's where we are in the whole ungodly machinery of capital punishment: human beings are choosing to die by nitrogen gas.   5

Here in red-state America, the death penalty is supported by 73 percent of white evangelical Christians and by a solid majority of Catholics—53 percent, despite official church teaching to the contrary—according to a Pew Research Center survey released in June.

The three men Tennessee most recently executed were all convicted of especially brutal murders—in Mr. Irick's case, the rape and murder of a little girl left in his care; in Mr. Miller's, the murder of his girlfriend, a young woman with cognitive disabilities. Mr. Zagorski murdered two men who were meeting him to buy a hundred pounds of marijuana with cash. Death row inmates are not sympathetic figures. Not that being sincerely remorseful and using your time in prison for genuine transformation gets you very far here in Execution Alley. In 1998, Texas executed a woman who became a born-again Christian while in prison. In 2015, Georgia executed a woman who had earned a theology degree on death row.

It's hard not to notice that all these inmates, rehabilitated or not, were killed in the Bible Belt, in states where a sizable portion of the population believes they live—or at least believes they should live—in a Christian nation. Mr. Miller was the second inmate in the South to be executed last week, and two more—one in Texas and one in Florida—will die at state hands by Thursday. That's a lot of killing for the thou-shalt-not-kill states and at a time of year that's particularly ironic. What is Advent,[1] after all, but a time of waiting for the birth of a baby who will grow up to be executed himself?

For many anti-abortion Christians, there's no contradiction between taking a "pro-life" position against allowing a woman to choose whether to continue a

1. In Western Christian traditions, a period of preparation encompassing the four Sundays preceding Christmas.

pregnancy and taking a "tough on crime" position whose centerpiece is capital punishment. An unborn fetus, they argue, is innocent, while a prisoner on death row is by definition guilty.

10   But for a true "pro-life" Christian, guilt or innocence really shouldn't be the point. Cute and cuddly or brutish and unrepentant, human life is human life. It doesn't matter whether you like the human life involved. If you truly believe that human life is sacred, right down to an invisible diploid cell, then you have no business letting the state put people to death in your name, even if those people have committed hideous crimes.

There are numerous pragmatic reasons to abolish the death penalty. It doesn't deter crime. It doesn't save the state money. It risks ending an innocent life. (The Death Penalty Information Center lists the names of 164 innocent people who have been exonerated after serving years on death row. The most recent, Clemente Javier Aguirre-Jarquin, was released from a Florida prison just last month.) It is applied in a haphazard and irrational manner that disproportionately targets people of color. It puts prison staff in the position of executing a human being they know personally and often truly care for. But the real problem with the death penalty can't be summed up by setting pros and cons on different sides of a balance to see which carries more weight. The real problem of the death penalty is its human face.

A person on death row is a person. No matter how ungrieved he may be once he is gone, he is still a human being. And it is not our right to take his life any more than it was his right to take another's.

MLA CITATION

Renkl, Margaret. "Christmas Isn't Coming to Death Row." *The Norton Reader: An Anthology of Nonfiction*, edited by Melissa A. Goldthwaite et al., 16th ed., W. W. Norton, 2024, pp. 752–54.

QUESTIONS

1. Margaret Renkl challenges the notion that "a true 'pro-life' Christian" (paragraph 10) can oppose abortion while supporting the death penalty. What is her argument, and how might someone who disagrees with her respond?

2. Renkl begins her piece not by stating her main point (although she does encapsulate it in her opening statement) but by humanizing the three men executed by Tennessee and by emphasizing the inhumane nature of contemporary means of capital punishment: lethal injection, electrocution, and asphyxiation by nitrogen gas. Why?

3. Why does Renkl consider it "particularly ironic" (paragraph 8) that so many executions happen in the Bible Belt during the Christmas season? More generally, how would you describe Renkl's tone throughout her piece? Annotate the text to note how she evokes it.

4. Write an opinion piece of your own in which you take a stance against a policy or practice you find morally wrong.

TERESA M. BEJAN

The Two Clashing Meanings of "Free Speech"

ITTLE DISTINGUISHES DEMOCRACY IN AMERICA more sharply from Europe than the primacy—and permissiveness—of our commitment to free speech. Yet ongoing controversies at American universities suggest that free speech is becoming a partisan issue. While conservative students defend the importance of inviting controversial speakers to campus and giving offense, many self-identified liberals are engaged in increasingly disruptive, even violent, efforts to shut them down. Free speech for some, they argue, serves only to silence and exclude others. Denying hateful or historically "privileged" voices a platform is thus necessary to make *equality* effective, so that the marginalized and vulnerable can finally speak up—and be heard.

The reason that appeals to the First Amendment cannot decide these campus controversies is because there is a more fundamental conflict between two, very different concepts of free speech at stake. The conflict between what the ancient Greeks called *isegoria*, on the one hand, and *parrhesia*, on the other, is as old as democracy itself. Today, both terms are often translated as "freedom of speech," but their meanings were and are importantly distinct. In ancient Athens, *isegoria* described the equal right of citizens to participate in public debate in the democratic assembly; *parrhesia*, the license to say what one pleased, how and when one pleased, and to whom.

When it comes to private universities, businesses, or social media, the would-be censors are our fellow-citizens, not the state. Private entities like *Facebook* or *Twitter*, not to mention Yale or Middlebury, have broad rights to regulate and exclude the speech of their members. Likewise, online mobs are made up of outraged individuals exercising their own right to speak freely. To invoke the First Amendment in such cases is not a knock-down argument, it's a non sequitur.[1]

John Stuart Mill[2] argued that the chief threat to free speech in democracies was not the state, but the "social tyranny" of one's fellow citizens. And yet today, the civil libertarians who style themselves as Mill's inheritors have for the most part failed to refute, or even address, the arguments about free speech and equality that their opponents are making.

The two ancient concepts of free speech came to shape our modern liberal democratic notions in fascinating and forgotten ways. But more importantly, understanding that there is not one, but *two* concepts of freedom of speech,   5

Published in the Atlantic *(2017), a magazine covering literature, culture, and politics.* Teresa M. Bejan *is the author of* Mere Civility: Disagreement and the Limits of Toleration *(2017).*

1. Latin for "does not follow," a logically invalid argument.
2. British utilitarian philosopher, economist, and political theorist (1806–1873); author of *On Liberty* (1859).

and that these are often in tension if not outright conflict, helps explain the frustrating shape of contemporary debates, both in the US and in Europe—and why it so often feels as though we are talking past each other when it comes to the things that matter most.

Of the two ancient concepts of free speech, *isegoria* is the older. The term dates back to the fifth century BCE, although historians disagree as to when the democratic practice of permitting any citizen who wanted to address the assembly actually began. Despite the common translation "freedom of speech," the Greek literally means something more like "equal speech in public." The verb *agoreuein*, from which it derives, shares a root with the word *agora* or marketplace—that is, a public place where people, including philosophers like Socrates,[3] would gather together and talk.

In the democracy of Athens, this idea of addressing an informal gathering in the *agora* carried over into the more formal setting of the *ekklesia* or political assembly. The herald would ask, "Who will address the assemblymen?" and then the volunteer would ascend the *bema*, or speaker's platform. In theory, *isegoria* meant that any Athenian citizen in good standing had the right to participate in debate and try to persuade his fellow citizens. In practice, the number of participants was fairly small, limited to the practiced rhetoricians and elder statesmen seated near the front. (Disqualifying offenses included prostitution and taking bribes.)

Although Athens was not the only democracy in the ancient world, from the beginning the Athenian principle of *isegoria* was seen as something special. The historian Herodotus[4] even described the form of government at Athens not as *demokratia*, but as *isegoria* itself. According to the fourth-century orator and patriot Demosthenes, the Athenian constitution was based on speeches (*politeia en logois*) and its citizens had chosen *isegoria* as a way of life. But for its critics, this was a bug, as well as a feature. One critic, the so-called "Old Oligarch,"[5] complained that even slaves and foreigners enjoyed *isegoria* at Athens, hence one could not beat them as one might elsewhere.

Critics like the Old Oligarch may have been exaggerating for comic effect, but they also had a point: as its etymology suggests, *isegoria* was fundamentally about equality, not freedom. As such, it would become the hallmark of Athenian democracy, which distinguished itself from the other Greek city-states *not* because it excluded slaves and women from citizenship (as did every society in the history of humankind until quite recently), but rather because it *included the poor*. Athens even took positive steps to render this equality of public speech effective by introducing pay for the poorest citizens to attend the assembly and to serve as jurors in the courts.

3. Greek philosopher (470–399 BCE).

4. Greek historian (484–c. 420 BCE) whose *History* documents the Greco-Persian Wars (492–449 BCE).

5. Unknown author of the political treatise "Constitution of the Athenians."

As a form of free speech then, *isegoria* was essentially political. Its competitor, *parrhesia*, was more expansive. Here again, the common English translation "freedom of speech" can be deceptive. The Greek means something like "all saying" and comes closer to the idea of speaking freely or "frankly." *Parrhesia* thus implied openness, honesty, and the courage to tell the truth, even when it meant causing offense. The practitioner of *parrhesia* (or *parrhesiastes*) was, quite literally, a "say-it-all."

Parrhesia could have a political aspect. Demosthenes and other orators stressed the duty of those exercising *isegoria* in the assembly to speak their minds. But the concept applied more often outside of the *ekklesia* in more and less informal settings. In the theater, *parrhesiastic* playwrights like Aristophanes offended all and sundry by skewering their fellow citizens, including Socrates, by name. But the paradigmatic *parrhesiastes* in the ancient world were the Philosophers, self-styled "lovers of wisdom" like Socrates himself who would confront their fellow citizens in the *agora* and tell them whatever hard truths they least liked to hear. Among these was Diogenes the Cynic,[6] who famously lived in a barrel, masturbated in public, and told Alexander the Great[7] to get out of his light—all, so he said, to reveal the truth to his fellow Greeks about the arbitrariness of their customs.

The danger intrinsic in *parrhesia*'s offensiveness to the power-that-be—be they monarchs like Alexander or the democratic majority—fascinated Michel Foucault, who made it the subject of a series of lectures at Berkeley (home of the original campus Free Speech Movement[8]) in the 1980s. Foucault noticed that the practice of *parrhesia* necessarily entailed an asymmetry of power, hence a "contract" between the audience (whether one or many), who pledged to tolerate any offense, and the speaker, who agreed to tell them the truth and risk the consequences.

If *isegoria* was fundamentally about equality, then, *parrhesia* was about liberty in the sense of *license*—not a right, but rather an unstable privilege enjoyed at the pleasure of the powerful. In Athenian democracy, that usually meant the majority of one's fellow citizens, who were known to shout down or even drag speakers they disliked (including Plato's[9] brother, Glaucon) off the *bema*. This ancient version of "no-platforming" speakers who offended popular sensibilities could have deadly consequences—as the trial and death of Socrates,[10] Plato's friend and teacher, attests.

Noting the lack of success that Plato's loved ones enjoyed with both *isegoria* and *parrhesia* during his lifetime may help explain why the father of

6. Greek philosopher (unknown–c. 320 BCE).

7. King of Macedonia (356–323 BCE) whose conquests resulted in a vast empire stretching from Greece to India.

8. Foucault (1926–1984), French philosopher, historian, and political theorist; Free Speech Movement, student-led protest movement in the 1960s.

9. Greek philosopher (c. 429–347 BCE).

10. Socrates was condemned to death for the crime of corrupting Athenian youth.

Western philosophy didn't set great store by either concept in his works. Plato no doubt would have noticed that, despite their differences, *neither* concept relied upon the most famous and distinctively Greek understanding of speech as *logos*—that is, reason or logical argument. Plato's student, Aristotle,[11] would identify *logos* as the capacity that made human beings essentially *political* animals in the first place. And yet neither *isegoria* nor *parrhesia* identified the reasoned speech and arguments of *logos* as uniquely deserving of equal liberty *or* license. Which seems to have been Plato's point—how was it that a democratic city that prided itself on free speech, in all of its forms, put to death the one Athenian ruled by *logos* for speaking it?

15   Unsurprisingly perhaps, *parrhesia* survived the demise of Athenian democracy more easily than *isegoria*. As Greek democratic institutions were crushed by the Macedonian empire,[12] then the Roman, *parrhesia* persisted as a rhetorical trope. A thousand years after the fall of Rome, Renaissance humanists[13] would revive *parrhesia* as the distinctive virtue of the counselor speaking to a powerful prince in need of frank advice. While often couched in apologetics, this *parrhesia* retained its capacity to shock. The hard truths presented by Machiavelli and Hobbes[14] to their would-be sovereigns would inspire generations of "libertine" thinkers to come.

Still, there was another adaptation of the *parrhesiastic* tradition of speaking truth to power available to early modern Europeans. The early Christians took a page from Diogenes's book in spreading the "good news" of the Gospel throughout the Greco-Roman world—news that may not have sounded all that great to the Roman authorities. Many of the Christians who styled themselves as "Protestants" after the Reformation thought that a return to an authentically *parrhesiastic* and deliberately offensive form of evangelism was necessary to restore the Church to the purity of "primitive" Christianity. The early Quakers, for example, were known to interrupt Anglican[15] services by shouting down the minister and to go naked in public "for a sign."

Isegoria, too, had its early modern inheritors. But in the absence of democratic institutions like the Athenian *ekklesia*, it necessarily took a different form. The 1689 English Bill of Rights secured "the freedom of speech and debates in Parliament," and so applied to members of Parliament only, and only when they were present in the chamber. For the many who lacked access to formal political participation, the idea of *isegoria* as an equal right of public speech belonging

11. Greek philosopher (384–322 BCE).

12. Created by Alexander the Great.

13. Fall of Rome, traditionally dated to 476 CE; Renaissance humanism, early modern European intellectual and cultural movement valuing classical learning and individual thought and expression.

14. Niccolò Machiavelli (1469–1527), Florentine statesman and political philosopher; Thomas Hobbes (1588–1679), English political philosopher.

15. Quakers, dissenting Protestant group that emerged in England in the 1600s; Anglicanism, the official Church of England.

to all citizens would eventually migrate from the concrete public forum to the virtual public sphere.

For philosophers like Spinoza and Immanuel Kant,[16] "free speech" meant primarily the intellectual freedom to participate in the public exchange of arguments. In 1784, five years before the French Revolution,[17] Kant would insist that "the freedom to make public use of one's reason" was the fundamental and equal right of any human being or citizen. Similarly, when Mill wrote *On Liberty* less than a century later, he did not defend the freedom of speech as such, but rather the individual "freedom of thought and discussion" in the collective pursuit of truth. While the equal liberty of *isegoria* remained essential for these thinkers, they shifted focus from actual *speech*—that is, the physical act of addressing others and participating in debate—to the mental exercise of *reason* and the exchange of ideas and arguments, very often in print. And so, over the course of two millennia, the Enlightenment finally united *isegoria* and *logos* in an idealized concept of free speech as freedom only for *reasoned* speech and rational deliberation that would have made Plato proud.

This logo-centric Enlightenment ideal remains central to the European understanding of free speech today. Efforts in Europe to criminalize hate speech owe an obvious debt to Kant, who described the freedom of (reasoned) speech in public as "the most harmless" of all. The same could never be said of ancient or early modern *parrhesia*, which was always threatening to speakers and listeners alike. Indeed, it was the obvious harm caused by their *parrhesiastic* evangelism to their neighbors' religious sensibilities that led so many evangelical Protestants to flee prosecution (or persecution, as they saw it) in Europe for the greater liberty—or license—of the New World. American exceptionalism can thus be traced all the way back to the seventeenth and eighteenth centuries: while America got the evangelicals and libertines, Europe kept the philosophers.

Debates about free speech on American campuses today suggest that the rival concepts of *isegoria* and *parrhesia* are alive and well. When student protesters claim that they are silencing certain voices—via no-platforming, social pressure, or outright censorship—in the name of free speech itself, it may be tempting to dismiss them as insincere, or at best confused. As I witnessed at an event at Kenyon College in September, when confronted with such arguments the response from gray-bearded free-speech fundamentalists like myself is to continue to preach to the converted about the First Amendment, but with an undercurrent of solidaristic despair about "kids these days" and their failure to understand the fundamentals of liberal democracy.

No wonder the "kids" are unpersuaded. While trigger warnings, safe spaces, and no-platforming grab headlines, poll after poll suggests that a more subtle, shift in mores is afoot. To a generation convinced that hateful speech is itself a form of violence or "silencing," pleading the First Amendment is to miss the

20

---

16. Benedict de Spinoza (1632–1677), Dutch Jewish philosopher; Kant (1724–1804), German philosopher.

17. Revolution resulting in the end of the *ancien régime*, or "old order."

point. Most of these students do not see themselves as standing against free speech at all. What they care about is the *equal right* to speech, and equal access to a public forum in which the historically marginalized and excluded can be heard and count equally with the privileged. This is a claim to *isegoria*, and once one recognizes it as such, much else becomes clear—including the contrasting appeal to *parrhesia* by their opponents, who sometimes seem determined to reduce "free speech" to a license to offend.

Recognizing the ancient ideas at work in these modern arguments puts those of us committed to America's *parrhesiastic* tradition of speaking truth to power in a better position to defend it. It suggests that to defeat the modern proponents of *isegoria*—and remind the modern *parrhesiastes* what they are fighting for—one must go beyond the First Amendment to the other, orienting principle of American democracy behind it, namely *equality*. After all, the genius of the First Amendment lies in bringing *isegoria* and *parrhesia* together, by securing the equal right and liberty of citizens not simply to "exercise their reason" but to speak their minds. It does so because the alternative is to allow the powers-that-happen-to-be to grant that liberty as a *license* to some individuals while denying it to others.

In contexts where the Constitution does not apply, like a private university, this opposition to arbitrariness is a matter of culture, not law, but it is no less pressing and important for that. As the evangelicals, protesters, and provocateurs who founded America's *parrhesiastic* tradition knew well: When the rights of all become the privilege of a few, neither liberty nor equality can last.

MLA CITATION

Bejan, Teresa M. "The Two Clashing Meanings of 'Free Speech.'" *The Norton Reader: An Anthology of Nonfiction*, edited by Melissa A. Goldthwaite et al., 16th ed., W. W. Norton, 2024, pp. 755–60.

QUESTIONS

1. In this essay, Teresa M. Bejan argues that conflicts over "free speech" on campuses today have their roots in two competing concepts of "free speech" from ancient Athens: *isegoria* and *parrhesia*. How would you explain these concepts to a peer who has not read Bejan's essay? Why is it important to recover them? (Couldn't Bejan simply have noted that people today understand "free speech" in two conflicting ways?)

2. Throughout the essay, Bejan distinguishes between social and legal constraints on speech. Why does this distinction matter?

3. Most of Bejan's essay is devoted to developing the claim she makes at the end of her introduction, that recognizing that "free speech" has two competing meanings can help to explain why present-day debates over "free speech" seem so intractable (paragraph 5). She waits until the conclusion of her essay to acknowledge her own views. Why does Bejan value "free speech," and how does her perspective differ

from that of today's students? How does her distinction between *isegoria* and *parrhesia* help her find common ground with them?

4. Use Bejan's distinction between *isegoria* and *parrhesia* to analyze a specific instance of conflict over "free speech" on campus.

MATT DINAN
Be Nice

ROWING UP, I NEVER CONSIDERED MYSELF to be particularly nice, perhaps because I'm from a rural part of New Brunswick, one of Canada's Maritime Provinces—the conspicuously "nicest" region in a self-consciously nice country. My parents are nice in a way that almost beggars belief—my mother's tact is such that the strongest condemnation in her arsenal is "Well, I wouldn't say I don't like it, per se . . ." As for me, teenage eye-rolls gave way to undergraduate seriousness, which gave way to graduate-student irony. I thought of Atlantic Canadian nice as a convenient way to avoid telling the truth about the way things are—a disingenuous evasion of the nasty truth about the world. Even the word *nice* seems the moral equivalent of "uninteresting"—anodyne, tedious, otiose.

That's why I remember being a bit shocked when my colleagues at my first job in Massachusetts kept informing me that I was "too nice" to share my opinion about something or someone. Didn't they know they were speaking to a percipient and courageous truth-teller? Maybe it was my harrowing stint as a commuter in Worcester—why won't these people on the MassPike in fact *use* their "blinkahs"?[1]—or maybe becoming a dad softened me up, but I have, initially with some dismay, found myself increasingly enjoying trying to be nice.

But my newfound appreciation for niceness may have come too late: Niceness has fallen on hard times. Even bare civility has become the target of a serious theoretical critique. As Tavia Nyong'o and Kyla Wazana Tompkins[2] bracingly put it in a recent online article, "Eleven Theses on Civility," "Civility is not care, but it pretends to be." By masking the violence of unjust social systems with complaints about discursive violence, "calls for civility seek to evade . . . calls for change."

This essay first appeared in the Hedgehog Review *(2018), a journal of cultural studies published by the University of Virginia's Institute for Advanced Studies in Culture.*

1. The Mass Pike, Interstate 90, runs across Massachusetts; "blinkahs," a mimic of a stereotypical Boston accent in which "er" is pronounced "ah."
2. Nyong'o (b. 1974), professor of African American studies, American studies, and theater and performance studies at Yale University; Tompkins (b. 1968), professor of English and gender and women's studies at Pomona College.

Doubtless, these and other criticisms are partly, even mostly, true about the way civility is often deployed in political argument. But as Teresa Bejan[3] shows so well in her book *Mere Civility*, civility doesn't necessarily mean being nice or polite, and it's more than a set of procedural rules for public argument. Civility, rather, means engaging with those with whom one fundamentally disagrees, and so a curious feature of these latest skirmishes in the civility war is the basic civility of civility's critics. In observing that the entire civility game—usually identified as "tone policing"—is often marshaled to constrain political discussion within certain parameters, civility's critics are doing the heavy lifting of civil discourse.

5   One strength of *Mere Civility* is Bejan's insistence that civility is actually a sort of conversational virtue, though not a particularly nice one. So one defense of civility would consist of contrasting it with a milquetoast quality like "niceness." But can we push things just a little further and actually defend being, for lack of a better word, *nice*? Even *online*? Could being nice be a virtue, and can it be a virtue even in the struggle for social justice?

When it comes to virtue, it's difficult to find a better guide than Aristotle.[4] While there is no description of the virtue of civility or niceness in his most famous account of the good life, the *Nicomachean Ethics*,[5] he *does* present an array of seemingly minor virtues pertaining to common life that cover similar ground. Ranging from gentleness and honesty to wit or tact, the social virtues seem like a decided step down after the memorable peak of his discussion of moral virtue in greatness of soul. But it is precisely in contrast to greatness of soul that the social virtues emerge as so important.

Aristotle initially presents greatness of soul as the ordered whole of moral virtue—an ornament for the *megalopsychos*, the person with complete virtue, that makes the rest of the virtues shine that much brighter. This person is truly great, and knows it. Greatness of soul is presented as virtue that governs one's relationship to the greatest honors and thus to the esteem of the community, but it turns out that the only person whose judgment the *megalopsychos* ultimately consults is himself. The great-souled one cares little for the world outside himself, even to the point of lacking wonder (*thaumastikos*), which in the *Metaphysics*[6] Aristotle says comes naturally to human beings. It perhaps goes without saying that the person with greatness of soul is not a great party guest: He is unusually direct in his evaluations of others, and "disposed to feeling contempt for others." He refuses most honors and requests for aid, fails to remember boons or evils done him by others, and is incapable of living with consideration of another (unless it is a friend). Aristotle's description of the *megalopsychos* culminates in an almost comic portrayal of a man (of course it's a man) with a low voice and a slow gait, who can hardly be bothered to interact

---

3. Professor of political theory (b. 1984) at Oriel College, Oxford; see "The Two Clashing Meanings of 'Free Speech'" (pp. 755–60).

4. Greek philosopher (c. 384–322 BCE).

5. Aristotle's principal treatise on ethics written in 350 BCE.

6. Treatise by Aristotle on what he termed "first philosophy."

with those around him. The great-souled person is thus the image of perfect self-sufficiency. As a result, he isn't very civil and definitely isn't nice.

From a certain vantage point, Aristotle at first blush seems to condone the apparent haughtiness of the great-souled person, since it's justified. But since greatness of soul seems to abstract so completely from human dependence on others, the inclusion of such attributes as gentleness, friendliness, and wit in his catalogue of virtues directly after his characterization of the *megalopsychos* seems like an invitation to consider what it might mean to flourish alongside others. Since the great-souled individual cares little for the affairs of others, it's impossible to imagine him possessing a virtue like friendliness. Friendliness, we learn, differs from friendship per se because it arises not from passion but "as a result of being the sort of person one is" in order to give pleasure to others. A friendly person therefore acts similarly toward people she knows and people she doesn't—she is discriminately indiscriminate in her pleasantness.

Aristotle enumerates yet another similar virtue at the very end of his description of the moral virtues, variously called wit or tact. Wit or tact is what the friendly person displays in times of relaxation—not only being funny, but doing so in the right way and listening to others. It's not clear what precisely makes one tactful from Aristotle's perspective, although it's necessarily situational (and what could be worse than defining what it means to be funny?). But the comparison here seems not just to what might be amusing, but to the ways in which wit differs from the other major image of excellence in the *Ethics*. When Aristotle emphasizes the lightness and motion of the character of the tactful or witty person, we cannot help but see it as a counterpoint to the inactivity of greatness of soul. Aristotle even makes an Aristotle joke in his account of wit, saying that the *eutrapelos* (witty person) is etymologically related to *eutropos*, a word meaning dexterity, versatility, or being "good at turning." Wit may not be as grand as greatness of soul, but its seeming motion and life are themselves winsome.

Aristotle bestows unusually high praise on this humble virtue, noting that the tactful person is "a sort of law unto [himself]"; in thinking of the other, we learn how to most fully govern ourselves. But the irruptive character of laughter— the fact that it is always surprising and unbidden (which is probably why "lol" is the preeminent surviving Internet shorthand from the *AOL* Messenger[7] days)— demonstrates our lack of self-sufficiency. Wit and tact thereby allow for a certain independence or self-governance by helping us say the right things so as not to offend, while also reminding us that we are limited, relational beings.

So "being nice" can be more than cynically smoothing over differences. Niceness's concern for pleasing others, *and* its affirmation of our dependence and limitation, paints a fuller picture of what it means to be human. The great-souled person, who is both right and good, is in danger of losing this insight, and perhaps those who would jettison civility in the interest of justice run a parallel risk in a way that might be inimical to solidarity. If the goal of social justice is in part to help us understand the full extent to which solidarity is an ethical necessity, then cultivating the virtue of being nice is not a barrier to justice, but a path toward it.

7. One of the first internet messaging applications developed in the late 1990s.

MLA CITATION

Dinan, Matt. "Be Nice." *The Norton Reader: An Anthology of Nonfiction*, edited by
    Melissa A. Goldthwaite et al., 16th ed., W. W. Norton, 2024, pp. 761–63.

QUESTIONS

1. Matt Dinan's essay is an argument for the imperative in its title: "Be Nice." What
is Dinan's thesis or main point, and where in his essay does he state it most fully
and directly? How does the structure of Dinan's essay reflect his thesis?

2. Dinan cites several sources in his essay: Tavia Nyong'o and Kyla Wazana Tompkins's "Eleven Theses on Civility," Teresa M. Bejan's *Mere Civility*, and Aristotle's
Nicomachean Ethics and *Metaphysics*. How does he use each of these to further
his argument? What do you imagine the authors of these other sources might say
back to Dinan?

3. Using Dinan's essay as a model, write an essay of your own that recuperates a
virtue that, like niceness, "has fallen on hard times" (paragraph 3).

IBRAM X. KENDI
Definitions

> **RACIST:** One who is supporting a racist policy through their actions or inac-
> tion or expressing a racist idea.
>
> **ANTIRACIST:** One who is supporting an antiracist policy through their
> actions or expressing an antiracist idea.

SOUL LIBERATION SWAYED onstage at the University of Illinois arena,
rocking colorful dashikis and Afros that shot up like balled fists—
an amazing sight to behold for the eleven thousand college students in the audience. Soul Liberation appeared nothing like the
White ensembles in suits who'd been sounding hymns for nearly
two days after Jesus's birthday in 1970.

Black students had succeeded in pushing the InterVarsity Christian Fellowship, the US evangelical movement's premier college organizer, to devote
the second night of the conference to Black theology. More than five hundred
Black attendees from across the country were on hand as Soul Liberation began
to perform. Two of those Black students were my parents.

They were not sitting together. Days earlier, they had ridden on the same
bus for twenty-four hours that felt like forty-two, from Manhattan through
Pennsylvania, Ohio, and Indiana, before arriving in central Illinois. One hundred Black New Yorkers converged on InterVarsity's Urbana '70.

Published as the first chapter of Ibram X. Kendi's How to Be an Antiracist *(2019). All notes
in this piece were written by the author.*

My mother and father had met during the Thanksgiving break weeks earlier when Larry, an accounting student at Manhattan's Baruch College, co-organized a recruiting event for Urbana '70 at his church in Jamaica, Queens. Carol was one of the thirty people who showed up—she had come home to Queens from Nyack College, a small Christian school about forty-five miles north of her parents' home in Far Rockaway. The first meeting was uneventful, but Carol noticed Larry, an overly serious student with a towering Afro, his face hidden behind a forest of facial hair, and Larry noticed Carol, a petite nineteen-year-old with dark freckles sprayed over her caramel complexion, even if all they did was exchange small talk. They'd independently decided to go to Urbana '70 when they heard that Tom Skinner would be preaching and Soul Liberation would be performing. At twenty-eight years old, Skinner was growing famous[1] as a young evangelist of Black liberation theology. A former gang member and son of a Baptist preacher, he reached thousands via his weekly radio show and tours, where he delivered sermons at packed iconic venues like the Apollo Theater in his native Harlem. In 1970, Skinner published his third and fourth books, *How Black Is the Gospel?* and *Words of Revolution*.[2]

Carol and Larry devoured both books like a James Brown tune, like a   5
Muhammad Ali fight. Carol had discovered Skinner through his younger brother, Johnnie, who was enrolled with her at Nyack. Larry's connection was more ideological. In the spring of 1970, he had enrolled in "The Black Aesthetic,"[3] a class taught by legendary Baruch College literary scholar Addison Gayle Jr. For the first time, Larry read James Baldwin's *The Fire Next Time*, Richard Wright's *Native Son*, Amiri Baraka's wrenching plays, and the banned revolutionary manifesto *The Spook Who Sat by the Door* by Sam Greenlee.[4] It was an awakening. After Gayle's class, Larry started searching for a way to reconcile his faith with his newfound Black consciousness. That search led him to Tom Skinner.

Soul Liberation launched into their popular anthem, "Power to the People."[5] The bodies of the Black students who had surged to the front of the arena

---

1. For explanatory pieces on Skinner's life and influence and role in Urbana '70, see "The Unrepeatable Tom Skinner," *Christianity Today*, September 12, 1994, available at www.christianitytoday.com/ct/1994/september12/4ta011.html; and "A Prophet out of Harlem," *Christianity Today*, September 16, 1996, available at www.christianitytoday .com/ct/1996/september16/6ta036.html.

2. Tom Skinner, *How Black Is the Gospel?* (Philadelphia: Lippincott, 1970); and Tom Skinner, *Words of Revolution: A Call to Involvement in the Real Revolution* (Grand Rapids, MI: Zondervan, 1970).

3. For the lessons Addison Gayle shared in this course, see his landmark book *The Black Aesthetic* (Garden City, NY: Doubleday, 1971).

4. James Baldwin, *The Fire Next Time* (New York: Dial, 1963); Richard Wright, *Native Son* (New York: Harper, 1940); Amiri Baraka (LeRoi Jones), *Dutchman and the Slave: Two Plays* (New York: William Morrow, 1964); and Sam Greenlee, *The Spook Who Sat by the Door* (New York: Baron, 1969).

5. For a remembrance of this evening with Soul Liberation playing and Tom Skinner preaching that is consistent with my parents' memories, see Edward Gilbreath,

started moving almost in unison with the sounds of booming drums and heavy bass that, along with the syncopated claps, generated the rhythm and blues of a rural Southern revival.

The wave of rhythm then rushed through the thousands of White bodies in the arena. Before long, they, too, were on their feet, swaying and singing along to the soulful sounds of Black power.

Every chord from Soul Liberation seemed to build up anticipation for the keynote speaker to come. When the music ended, it was time:[6] Tom Skinner, dark-suited with a red tie, stepped behind the podium, his voice serious as he began his history lesson.

"The evangelical church . . . supported the status quo. It supported slavery; it supported segregation; it preached against any attempt of the Black man to stand on his own two feet."

10   Skinner shared how he came to worship an elite White Jesus Christ, who cleaned people up through "rules and regulations," a savior who prefigured Richard Nixon's vision of law and order. But one day, Skinner realized that he'd gotten Jesus wrong. Jesus wasn't in the Rotary Club and he wasn't a policeman. Jesus was a "radical revolutionary, with hair on his chest and dirt under his fingernails." Skinner's new idea of Jesus was born of and committed to a new reading of the gospel. "Any gospel that does not . . . speak to the issue of enslavement" and "injustice" and "inequality—any gospel that does not want to go where people are hungry and poverty-stricken and set them free in the name of Jesus Christ—is not the gospel."

Back in the days of Jesus, "there was a system working just like today," Skinner declared. But "Jesus was dangerous. He was dangerous because he was changing the system." The Romans locked up this "revolutionary" and "nailed him to a cross" and killed and buried him. But three days later, Jesus Christ "got up out of the grave" to bear witness to us today. "Proclaim liberation to the captives, preach sight to the blind" and "go into the world and tell men who are bound mentally, spiritually, and physically, 'The liberator has come!'"

The last line pulsated through the crowd. "The liberator has come!" Students practically leapt out of their seats in an ovation—taking on the mantle of this fresh gospel. The liberators had come.

My parents were profoundly receptive to Skinner's call for evangelical liberators and attended a series of Black caucuses over the week of the conference that reinforced his call every night. At Urbana '70, Ma and Dad found themselves leaving the civilizing and conserving and racist church they realized they'd been part of. They were saved into Black liberation theology[7] and

---

Reconciliation Blues: A Black Evangelical's Inside View of White Christianity (Downers Grove, IL: InterVarsity Press, 2006), 66–69.

6. For the audio and text of Tom Skinner's sermon at Urbana '70 entitled "Racism and World Evangelism," see urbana.org/message/us-racial-crisis-and-world-evangelism.

7. For a good book on the philosophy of Black theology, see James H. Cone, *Risks of Faith: The Emergence of a Black Theology of Liberation, 1968–1998* (Boston: Beacon Press, 2000).

joined the churchless church of the Black Power movement.[8] Born in the days of Malcolm X, Fannie Lou Hamer, Stokely Carmichael, and other antiracists who confronted segregationists and assimilationists in the 1950s and 1960s, the movement for Black solidarity, Black cultural pride, and Black economic and political self-determination had enraptured the entire Black world. And now, in 1970, Black power had enraptured my parents. They stopped thinking about saving Black people and started thinking about liberating Black people.

In the spring of 1971, Ma returned to Nyack College and helped form a Black student union, an organization that challenged racist theology, the Confederate flags on dorm-room doors, and the paucity of Black students and programming. She started wearing African-print dresses and wrapped her growing Afro in African-print ties. She dreamed of traveling to the motherland as a missionary.

Dad returned to his church and quit its famed youth choir. He began [15] organizing programs that asked provocative questions: "Is Christianity the White man's religion?" "Is the Black church relevant to the Black community?" He began reading the work of James Cone, the scholarly father of Black liberation theology and author of the influential *Black Theology & Black Power*[9] in 1969.

One day in the spring of 1971, Dad struck up the nerve to go up to Harlem and attend Cone's class at Union Theological Seminary. Cone lectured on his new book, *A Black Theology of Liberation*.[10] After class, Dad approached the professor.

"What is your definition of a Christian?" Dad asked in his deeply earnest way.

Cone looked at Dad with equal seriousness and responded: "A Christian is one who is striving for liberation."

James Cone's working definition of a Christian described a Christianity of the enslaved, not the Christianity of the slaveholders. Receiving this definition was a revelatory moment in Dad's life. Ma had her own similar revelation in her Black student union—that Christianity was about struggle and liberation. My parents now had, separately, arrived at a creed with which to shape their lives, to be the type of Christians that Jesus the revolutionary inspired them to be. This new definition of a word that they'd already chosen as their core identity naturally transformed them.

My own, still-ongoing journey toward being an antiracist began at Urbana '70. [20] What changed Ma and Dad led to a changing of their two unborn sons—this new definition of the Christian life became the creed that grounded my parents' lives and the lives of their children. I cannot disconnect my parents' religious strivings to be Christian from my secular strivings to be an antiracist. And the key act for both of us was defining our terms so that we could begin to

8. For a good overview of Black Power, see Peniel E. Joseph, *Waiting 'Til the Midnight Hour: A Narrative History of Black Power in America* (New York: Henry Holt, 2007).

9. James H. Cone, *Black Theology & Black Power* (New York: Seabury, 1969).

10. James H. Cone, *A Black Theology of Liberation* (Philadelphia: Lippincott, 1970).

describe the world and our place in it. Definitions anchor us in principles. This is not a light point: If we don't do the basic work of defining the kind of people we want to be in language that is stable and consistent, we can't work toward stable, consistent goals. Some of my most consequential steps toward being an antiracist have been the moments when I arrived at basic definitions. To be an antiracist is to set lucid definitions of racism/antiracism, racist/antiracist policies, racist/antiracist ideas, racist/antiracist people. To be a racist is to constantly redefine racist in a way that exonerates one's changing policies, ideas, and personhood.

So let's set some definitions. What is racism? Racism is a marriage of racist policies and racist ideas that produces and normalizes racial inequities. Okay, so what are racist policies and ideas? We have to define them separately to understand why they are married and why they interact so well together. In fact, let's take one step back and consider the definition of another important phrase: racial inequity.

Racial inequity is when two or more racial groups are not standing on approximately equal footing. Here's an example of racial inequity: 71 percent of White families lived in owner-occupied homes in 2014, compared to 45 percent of Latinx families and 41 percent of Black families.[11] Racial equity is when two or more racial groups are standing on a relatively equal footing. An example of racial equity would be if there were relatively equitable percentages of all three racial groups living in owner-occupied homes in the forties, seventies, or, better, nineties.

A racist policy is any measure that produces or sustains racial inequity between racial groups. An antiracist policy is any measure that produces or sustains racial equity between racial groups. By policy, I mean written and unwritten laws, rules, procedures, processes, regulations, and guidelines that govern people. There is no such thing as a nonracist or race-neutral policy. Every policy in every institution in every community in every nation is producing or sustaining either racial inequity or equity between racial groups.

Racist policies have been described by other terms: "institutional racism," "structural racism," and "systemic racism," for instance. But those are vaguer terms than "racist policy." When I use them I find myself having to immediately explain what they mean. "Racist policy" is more tangible and exacting, and more likely to be immediately understood by people, including its victims, who may not have the benefit of extensive fluency in racial terms. "Racist policy" says exactly what the problem is and where the problem is. "Institutional racism" and "structural racism" and "systemic racism" are redundant. Racism itself is institutional, structural, and systemic.

25   "Racist policy" also cuts to the core of racism better than "racial discrimination," another common phrase. "Racial discrimination" is an immediate and

11. These figures can be found in Matthew Desmond, "Housing," *Pathways: A Magazine on Poverty, Inequality, and Social Policy*, Special Issue, 2017, 16–17, available at inequality.stanford.edu/publications/pathway/state-union-2017. This essay is part of the Stanford Center on Poverty & Inequality's State of the Union 2017.

visible manifestation of an underlying racial policy. When someone discriminates against a person in a racial group, they are carrying out a policy or taking advantage of the lack of a protective policy. We all have the power to discriminate. Only an exclusive few have the power to make policy. Focusing on "racial discrimination" takes our eyes off the central agents of racism: racist policy and racist policymakers, or what I call racist power.

Since the 1960s, racist power has commandeered the term "racial discrimination," transforming the act of discriminating on the basis of race into an inherently racist act. But if racial discrimination is defined as treating, considering, or making a distinction in favor or against an individual based on that person's race, then racial discrimination is not inherently racist. The defining question is whether the discrimination is creating equity or inequity. If discrimination is creating equity, then it is antiracist. If discrimination is creating inequity, then it is racist. Someone reproducing inequity through permanently assisting an overrepresented racial group into wealth and power is entirely different than someone challenging that inequity by temporarily assisting an underrepresented racial group into relative wealth and power until equity is reached.

The only remedy to racist discrimination is antiracist discrimination. The only remedy to past discrimination is present discrimination. The only remedy to present discrimination is future discrimination. As President Lyndon B. Johnson said in 1965, "You do not take a person who, for years, has been hobbled by chains and liberate him, bring him up to the starting line of a race and then say, 'You are free to compete with all the others,' and still justly believe that you have been completely fair."[12] As US Supreme Court Justice Harry Blackmun wrote in 1978, "In order to get beyond racism, we must first take account of race. There is no other way. And in order to treat some persons equally, we must treat them differently."[13]

The racist champions of racist discrimination engineered to maintain racial inequities before the 1960s are now the racist opponents of antiracist discrimination engineered to dismantle those racial inequities. The most threatening racist movement is not the alt right's unlikely drive for a White ethnostate but the regular American's drive for a "race-neutral" one. The construct of race neutrality actually feeds White nationalist victimhood by positing the notion that any policy protecting or advancing non-White Americans toward equity is "reverse discrimination."

That is how racist power can call affirmative action policies that succeed in reducing racial inequities "race conscious" and standardized tests that produce racial inequities "race neutral." That is how they can blame the behavior of entire

12. For a full video of President Johnson's speech at Howard, see "Commencement Speech at Howard University, 6/4/65," The LBJ Library, available at www.youtube.com/watch?v=vcfAuodA2x8.

13. For his full dissent, see Harry Blackmun, Dissenting Opinion, *Regents of the Univ. of Cal. v. Bakke, 1978,* C-SPAN Landmark Cases, available at landmarkcases.c-span.org/Case/27/Regents-Univ-Cal-v-Bakke.

racial groups for the inequities between different racial groups and still say their ideas are "not racist." But there is no such thing as a not-racist idea, only racist ideas and antiracist ideas.[14]

30   So what is a racist idea? A racist idea is any idea that suggests one racial group is inferior or superior to another racial group in any way. Racist ideas argue that the inferiorities and superiorities of racial groups explain racial inequities in society. As Thomas Jefferson suspected a decade after declaring White American independence: "The blacks, whether originally a distinct race, or made distinct by time and circumstances, are inferior to the whites in the endowments both of body and mind."[15]

An antiracist idea is any idea that suggests the racial groups are equals in all their apparent differences—that there is nothing right or wrong with any racial group. Antiracist ideas argue that racist policies are the cause of racial inequities.

Understanding the differences between racist policies and antiracist policies, between racist ideas and antiracist ideas, allows us to return to our fundamental definitions. Racism is a powerful collection of racist policies that lead to racial inequity and are substantiated by racist ideas. Antiracism is a powerful collection of antiracist policies that lead to racial equity and are substantiated by antiracist ideas.

Once we have a solid definition of racism and antiracism, we can start to make sense of the racialized world around us, before us. My maternal grandparents, Mary Ann and Alvin, moved their family to New York City in the 1950s on the final leg of the Great Migration,[16] happy to get their children away from violent Georgia segregationists and the work of picking cotton under the increasingly hot Georgia sun.

To think, they were also moving their family away from the effects of climate change. Do-nothing climate policy is racist policy, since the predominantly non-White global south is being victimized by climate change more than the Whiter global north, even as the Whiter global north is contributing more to its acceleration.[17] Land is sinking and temperatures are rising from Florida to Bangladesh. Droughts and food scarcity are ravishing bodies in Eastern and Southern Africa, a region already containing 25 percent of the world's malnourished population. Human-made environmental catastrophes disproportionately harming bodies of color are not unusual; for instance, nearly four

---

14. See Ibram X. Kendi, *Stamped from the Beginning: The Definitive History of Racist Ideas in America* (New York: Nation Books, 2016).

15. Thomas Jefferson, *Notes on the State of Virginia* (Boston: Lilly and Wait, 1832), 150.

16. For the best book on the Great Migration, see Isabel Wilkerson, *The Warmth of Other Suns: The Epic Story of America's Great Migration* (New York: Vintage Books, 2011).

17. See "Climate Change Will Hit Poor Countries Hardest, Study Shows," the *Guardian*, September 27, 2013, available at www.theguardian.com/global-development/2013/sep/27/climate-change-poor-countries-ipcc.

thousand US areas—mostly poor and non-White—have higher lead poisoning rates than Flint, Michigan.[18]

I am one generation removed from picking cotton for pocket change under   35
the warming climate in Guyton, outside Savannah. That's where we buried my grandmother in 1993. Memories of her comforting calmness, her dark green thumb, and her large trash bags of Christmas gifts lived on as we drove back to New York from her funeral. The next day, my father ventured up to Flushing, Queens, to see his single mother, also named Mary Ann. She had the clearest dark-brown skin, a smile that hugged you, and a wit that smacked you.

When my father opened the door of her apartment, he smelled the fumes coming from the stove she'd left on, and some other fumes. His mother nowhere in sight, he rushed down the hallway and into her back bedroom. That's where he found his mother, as if sleeping, but dead. Her struggle with Alzheimer's, a disease more prevalent among African Americans, was over.[19]

There may be no more consequential White privilege than life itself. White lives matter to the tune of 3.5 additional years[20] over Black lives in the United States, which is just the most glaring of a host of health disparities, starting from infancy, where Black infants die at twice the rate of White infants.[21] But at least my grandmothers and I met, we shared, we loved. I never met my paternal grandfather. I never met my maternal grandfather, Alvin, killed by cancer three years before my birth. In the United States, African Americans are 25 percent more likely to die of cancer than Whites.[22] My father survived prostate cancer, which kills twice as many Black men as it does White men. Breast cancer disproportionately kills Black women.[23]

18. See "Reuters Finds 3,810 U.S. Areas with Lead Poisoning Double Flint's," Reuters, November 14, 2017, available at www.reuters.com/article/us-usa-lead-map/reuters-finds-3810-u-s-areas-with-lead-poisoning-double-flints-idUSKBN1DE1H2.

19. For an excellent essay on African Americans and Alzheimer's, see "African Americans Are More Likely than Whites to Develop Alzheimer's. Why?," the *Washington Post Magazine*, June 1, 2017, available at www.washingtonpost.com/lifestyle/magazine/why-are-african-americans-so-much-more-likely-than-whites-to-develop-alzheimers/2017/05/31/9bfbcccc-3132-11e7-8674-437ddb6e813e_story.html.

20. For a summary of this data, see "Life Expectancy Improves for Blacks, and the Racial Gap Is Closing, CDC Reports," the *Washington Post*, May 2, 2017, available at www.washingtonpost.com/news/to-your-health/wp/2017/05/02/cdc-life-expectancy-up-for-blacks-and-the-racial-gap-is-closing.

21. "Why America's Black Mothers and Babies Are in a Life-or-Death Crisis," the *New York Times Magazine*, April 11, 2018, available at www.nytimes.com/2018/04/11/magazine/black-mothers-babies-death-maternal-mortality.html.

22. For this disparity and other disparities in this paragraph, see "Examples of Cancer Health Disparities," National Cancer Institute, National Institutes of Health, available at www.cancer.gov/about-nci/organization/crchd/about-health-disparities/examples.

23. "Breast Cancer Disparities: Black Women More Likely than White Women to Die from Breast Cancer in the US," ABC News, October 16, 2018, available at www.abcnews.go.com/beta-story-container/GMA/Wellness/breast-cancer-disparities-black-women-white-women-die/story?id=58494016.

Three million African Americans and four million Latinx secured health insurance through the Affordable Care Act,[24] dropping uninsured rates for both groups to around 11 percent before President Barack Obama left office. But a staggering 28.5 million Americans remained uninsured, a number primed for growth after Congress repealed the individual mandate in 2017.[25] And it is becoming harder for people of color to vote out of office the politicians crafting these policies designed to shorten their lives. Racist voting policy has evolved from disenfranchising by Jim Crow voting laws to disenfranchising by mass incarceration and voter-ID laws.[26] Sometimes these efforts are so blatant that they are struck down: North Carolina enacted one of these targeted voter-ID laws, but in July 2016 the Court of Appeals for the Fourth Circuit struck it down, ruling that its various provisions "target African Americans with almost surgical precision."[27] But others have remained and been successful. Wisconsin's strict voter-ID law suppressed approximately two hundred thousand votes—again primarily targeting voters of color—in the 2016 election. Donald Trump won that critical swing state by 22,748 votes.[28]

We are surrounded by racial inequity, as visible as the law, as hidden as our private thoughts. The question for each of us is: What side of history will we stand on? A racist is someone who is supporting a racist policy by their actions or inaction or expressing a racist idea. An antiracist is someone who is supporting an antiracist policy by their actions or expressing an antiracist idea. "Racist" and "antiracist" are like peelable name tags that are placed and replaced based on what someone is doing or not doing, supporting or expressing in each moment. These are not permanent tattoos. No one becomes a racist or antiracist. We can only strive to be one or the other. We can unknowingly strive to be a racist. We can knowingly strive to be an antiracist. Like fighting an addiction,

24. Namrata Uberoi, Kenneth Finegold, and Emily Gee, "Health Insurance Coverage and the Affordable Care Act, 2010–2016," ASPE Issue Brief, Department of Health & Human Services, March 3, 2016, available at aspe.hhs.gov/system/files/pdf/187551 /ACA2010-2016.pdf.

25. "Since Obamacare Became Law, 20 Million More Americans Have Gained Health Insurance," *Fortune*, November 15, 2018, available at fortune.com/2018/11/15/Obamacare -americans-with-health-insurance-uninsured.

26. For three recent studies on voter suppression, see Carol Anderson, *One Person, No Vote: How Voter Suppression Is Destroying Our Democracy* (New York: Bloomsbury, 2018); Allan J. Lichtman, *The Embattled Vote in America: From the Founding to the Present* (Cambridge, MA: Harvard University Press, 2018); and Ari Berman, *Give Us the Ballot: The Modern Struggle for Voting Rights in America* (New York: Farrar, Straus & Giroux, 2015).

27. "The 'Smoking Gun' Proving North Carolina Republicans Tried to Disenfranchise Black Voters," the *Washington Post*, July 29, 2016, available at www.washingtonpost .com/news/wonk/wp/2016/07/29/the-smoking-gun-proving-north-carolina-republicans -tried-to-disenfranchise-black-voters/.

28. "Wisconsin's Voter-ID Law Suppressed 200,000 Votes in 2016 (Trump Won by 22,748)," the *Nation*, May 9, 2017, available at www.thenation.com/article/wisconsins -voter-id-law-suppressed-200000-votes-trump-won-by-23000/.

being an antiracist requires persistent self-awareness, constant self-criticism, and regular self-examination.

Racist ideas have defined our society since its beginning and can feel so   40
natural and obvious as to be banal, but antiracist ideas remain difficult to comprehend, in part because they go against the flow of this country's history. As Audre Lorde said in 1980, "We have all been programmed to respond to the human differences between us with fear and loathing and to handle that difference in one of three ways: ignore it, and if that is not possible, copy it if we think it is dominant, or destroy it if we think it is subordinate. But we have no patterns for relating across our human differences as equals."[29] To be an antiracist is a radical choice in the face of this history, requiring a radical reorientation of our consciousness.

MLA CITATION

Kendi, Ibram X. "Definitions." *The Norton Reader: An Anthology of Nonfiction*, edited by Melissa A. Goldthwaite et al., 16th ed., W. W. Norton, 2024, pp. 764–73.

QUESTIONS

1. Why are definitions of terms so important to Ibram X. Kendi?

2. Kendi's essay falls into two roughly equal parts: his account of his parents' meeting and their investment in Black liberation theology (paragraphs 1–19) and his explanation of his key terms (paragraphs 20–40). How does his parents' story contribute to his persona and argument?

3. Kendi asserts, "There is no such thing as a nonracist or race-neutral policy" (paragraph 23). Do you agree? Why is Kendi so insistent on this point? What challenge is he posing to his readers?

4. Near the end of his essay, Kendi notes, "'Racist' and 'antiracist' are like peelable name tags that are placed and replaced based on what someone is doing or not doing, supporting or expressing in each moment. These are not permanent tattoos" (paragraph 39). What misunderstanding is he trying to forestall?

5. Kendi writes, "A racist policy is any measure that produces or sustains racial inequity between racial groups. An antiracist policy is any measure that produces or sustains racial equity between racial groups" (paragraph 23). Apply Kendi's principles to assess a policy in your own school or community. Do a project documenting that policy's effects and then in a letter to your school's administration or community leaders, endorse the policy or propose a change.

---

29. Audre Lorde, "Age, Race, Class, and Sex: Women Redefining Difference," in *Sister Outsider: Essays and Speeches* (Freedom, CA: Crossing Press, 1984), 115.

LEAH PENNIMAN

An Afro-Indigenous Approach to Agriculture and Food Security

MY ANCESTRAL GRANDMOTHERS in West Africa braided seeds of okra, molokhia, and levant cotton into their hair before being forced to board Transatlantic slave ships. They hid sesame, black-eyed peas, rice, and melon seeds in their locks. They stashed away amara kale, gourds, sorrel, basil, tamarind, and cola in their tresses. The seed was their most precious legacy, and they believed against odds in a future of tilling and reaping the earth; they believed that we—their descendants—would exist and that we would receive and honor the gift of the seed.

With the seed, our grandmothers also braided their eco-systemic and cultural knowledge. They braided the wisdom of sharing land, labor, and wealth. They braided the wisdom of caring for the sacred Earth, with practices such as building the dark earth compost of Ghana, the raised beds of the Ovambo people,[1] and the polycultures of Nigeria.

But when our ancestors arrived on this continent, they encountered a very different system of relating to land and food. Here, the land was not shared but stolen and privatized. Led by the white Christian Doctrine of Discovery,[2] settlers murdered millions of Indigenous people, displaced those who survived, and laid claim to their land.

Our African ancestors learned that even when they tried to own land, they were punished. Despite the broken promise of 40 acres and a mule after emancipation,[3] Black farmers purchased nearly 16 million acres of land. Almost all of that land is now gone. Not only did white supremacist groups like the Ku Klux Klan and the White Caps murder over 4,000 Black land owners, but the US Department of Agriculture also systematically discriminated against Black farmers, leading to foreclosures and evictions. Today, approximately 95 percent of the agricultural land in the US is white-owned.

5   When they arrived, our ancestors found that it was not just land that was exploited—it was also people. Millions of agricultural experts were kidnapped from their homes across Africa, forced into bondage to build the wealth of

Adapted from a keynote talk given at the 2020 Bioneers Conference, which is dedicated to identifying "visionary and practical solutions" to the ecological and social challenges of today's world. This version appeared in Civil Eats, *a news source for "critical thought about the American food system."*

1. Southern African ethnic group, also called Ambo.

2. Doctrine originating in a series of fifteenth-century papal bulls that lands inhabited by non-Christians could be "discovered" and claimed by European nations.

3. A promise to freed people by US General William Tecumseh Sherman (1820–1891) toward the end of the American Civil War, later reversed by President Andrew Johnson (1808–1875).

Dr. George Washington Carver.

this nation. Even after chattel slavery officially ended, the exploitation of labor morphed into new forms, such as convict leasing. Southerners created new laws called the "Black Codes," which criminalized loitering and unemployment and, as a result, filled prisons with Black people who were rented back to plantations—a system that continues to this day.

The Black people who were not forced onto the plantation through incarceration were trapped there as sharecroppers in a perpetual cycle of debt and poverty. Even today, farmworkers are not protected by basic labor laws and do not have the right to a day off, overtime pay, collective bargaining, or other protections. Approximately 85 percent of farm labor is performed by people of color, often undocumented. Today, farm ownership is one of the whitest professions in the US, while farm work is among the brownest.

Our ancestors learned that the food system here was not about honoring the earth, but rather about extracting her resources. Industrial agriculture had burned up 50 percent of the soil carbon, catalyzing climate change and devastating biodiversity.

Despite the heartbreak and terror that those ancestors experienced, there were those in every generation who remembered the seeds they had inherited and the wisdom carried in those seeds. Fannie Lou Hamer[4] remembered cooperative land ownership and cooperative labor when she created the Freedom Farm in Mississippi with other sharecroppers. So did Charles and Shirley Sherrod[5] when they created the first ever community land trust in Georgia.

Dr. George Washington Carver, one of the founders of the regenerative and organic agriculture movements, remembered right relationship with land. So did Booker T. Whatley,[6] one of the progenitors of the farm-to-table movement and diversified small farms. Carver spread the word about caring for soil and community through the first extension agency out of Tuskegee University, inspiring a whole generation of organic farmers in the late 1800s and early 1900s.

10   The Black Panther Party[7] remembered right relationship to our human communities when they fed 20,000 children free breakfasts every morning, catalyzing the public school food programs. And so did the Federation of Southern Cooperatives, the National Black Farmers Association, and the Land Loss Prevention Project,[8] as they fought for the rights of Black farmers and farmworkers who have struggled to save their land over the years.

When I started farming over 24 years ago, I began to wonder: How could I honor the legacy of the seeds braided into my ancestors' hair? Could I help create a farm based on the wisdom carried in those seeds?

In 2010, Soul Fire Farm was born with a mission to reclaim our ancestral belonging to land and to end racism and exploitation in the food system. What began as a small family farm is now a community organization committed to this systemic and ancestral change. And we pray that the words from our mouths, the meditations in our hearts, and the work of our hands are all acceptable to our grandmothers who passed us these seeds.

4. Mississippi civil rights leader and champion of women's rights and voting rights (1917–1977). She founded Freedom Farm in 1969.

5. Among other accomplishments, civil rights leaders Charles Sherrod (1937–2022) and Shirley Sherrod (b. 1948) founded the Georgia farm collective New Communities in 1969.

6. Carver (1864–1943) and Whatley (1915–2005) were professors of agriculture at the Tuskegee Institute (renamed Tuskegee University in 1985), a historically Black academic institution in Alabama.

7. Left-wing political organization embracing armed self-defense and Black Power that was founded in Oakland, California, in 1966.

8. Organizations protecting Black farming and land ownership that were founded in 1967, 1995, and 1982, respectively.

We got to work regenerating 80 acres of land through Afro-Indigenous farming and forestry practices, we began sharing the harvest at no cost for people impacted by state violence, and we have been supporting families in building their own self-sufficiency gardens. We got to work equipping the next generation of Black and Brown farmers through training, mentorship, and connection to resources. We got to work using the land as a tool, to heal from the trauma of centuries of land-based oppression, recognizing that, for many of us, the land was the scene of the crime, even though she wasn't the criminal. We got to work creating natural buildings using straw bales, cob, solar energy, cluster development, and energy efficient design. We put the land into a cooperative, giving nature rights and a vote on the council, and returning land rights to the Mohican people[9] through a cultural respect easement.

We wondered if one small farm could help make a big change, and we are excited by the progress we've made using the regenerative farming practices that we inherited from Carver, Hamer, and the Ovambo people, and the progress in the larger movement.

We have restored the soil here on this mountainside to its pre-colonial levels of organic matter, and increased native biodiversity. We have witnessed neighbors across the capital region of New York pitching in to cover the cost of vegetable deliveries to those in need, allowing hundreds of people to receive a weekly share of fresh food. We have seen the power of small, localized food systems—which were able to turn on a dime when COVID hit—to keep people fed. We have seen thousands of new Indigenous, Black, and Brown farmers and food justice activists get trained in 35 states, and the majority of them go on to make powerful waves in the food system. And, for the first time since the early 1900s, the ag census recorded a small increase in the number of Indigenous farmers.

Our alumni even catalyzed the creation of a new land trust to share land back with people who've been dispossessed, as well as a reparations map to return stolen wealth to Earth stewards for their crucial work. And we're building powerful networks with Black Farmers United New York, HEAL Food Alliance, and the National Black Food and Justice Alliance to get at the root cause of exploitation of the Earth and those who tend and care for her. Together with these regional, national, and international networks, we're changing the conversation about food and land.

And folks are finally listening. From presidential candidates to major media outlets, society is waking up to the fact that we cannot have a healthy food system if we ignore racial justice or if we ignore the health of the land. We are in the midst of an uprising and we have entered a portal to something ancient and new.

But the question is: Are you willing to carry on the seeds of sovereignty and fight for the rights of all people to carry on those seeds? Or will you let

15

---

9. Algonquian-speaking Native American people who historically inhabited areas of upstate New York, western Connecticut and Massachusetts, and southern Vermont.

them die out? Beyond the great unraveling, what will you do to weave a world anew?

My daughter, Nashima, talks about the food system as everything it takes to get sunshine onto your plate. Every aspect of that system—land, labor, capital, ecology, food itself—needs to be infused with justice. And the good news with such a wide arc of possibility is that there are so many ways to engage. For some of us, the right answer is reparations; it's giving back resources to those who've been dispossessed. For others it might be returning land to Indigenous people, handing deeds over to tribal governments and Native organizations. Others might advocate for policy, like the Justice for Black Farmers Act or the Fairness for Farm Workers Act.[10] And others who run or work for institutions with purchasing power might be sourcing food from Black, Indigenous, and people of color producers, or transferring our institutional resources, power, and dignity to Black, Indigenous, and people of color leadership.

20   A powerful story illustrates this from the Haudenosaunee[11] community. The people of the Long House were dropping from hunger in the long winter months. Three sisters arrived at their door. One of them was dressed in green, another in yellow, and another in orange. Disguised as beggars, they asked the people for food. And because they were generous of heart, the people handed over the last scrapings of their bowls to feed these strangers. Touched by that generosity, the sisters revealed themselves as corn, beans, and squash—the basis of the three sisters milpa garden. The corn grows tall and provides starch and niacin for the people, the bean sister winds around her older sister and provides nitrogen for the soil and protein for the people, and squash, laying low on the grounds, shades out weeds and provides vitamins and fats in the seeds so the people would never go hungry again.

The powerful thing is that Indigenous folks of Turtle Island[12] shared these seeds, these three sisters, widely, with settlers who did not have their interests at heart, and did not understand the covenant with the sisters. Now corn, or maize, has been pulled apart from squash and beans to be grown in monocultures. This 8,700-year-old synergy of teosinte[13] and Mayan hands has been weaponized, turned into industrial animal feed and corn syrup, fueling diabetes in our communities, and driving climate change. They appropriated and scandalized our seed heritage, commodified our sacred foods, violated the law of sharing, and ripped her away from her sisters.

My belief is that the work of this moment is to return maize, both literally and metaphorically, to her sisters—to restore the covenant, restore the polyculture, and put carbon back in the soil while honoring our ancient and powerful ways.

10. US bills introduced in 2020 and 2021, respectively.

11. Meaning "people of the long house," the Indigenous name for the Iroquois Confederacy (French) or League of Five Nations (English).

12. Indigenous name for North America.

13. A wild grass native to Mexico; the ancestor of corn.

In the words of Pablo Neruda:[14] "Pardon me if when I want to tell the story of my life, it's the land I talk about. This is the land. It grows in your blood, and you grow. If it dies in your blood, you die out."

MLA CITATION

Penniman, Leah. "An Afro-Indigenous Approach to Agriculture and Food Security." *The Norton Reader: An Anthology of Nonfiction*, edited by Melissa A. Goldthwaite et al., 16th ed., W. W. Norton, 2024, pp. 774–79.

QUESTIONS

1. What values inform Leah Penniman's approach to agriculture as manifested in Soul Fire Farm (paragraph 12)?

2. Why does Penniman situate Soul Fire Farm within a lineage that extends from her "ancestral grandmothers" (paragraph 1) who brought seeds with them from Africa on slave ships to contemporary organizations working to promote Black farming and land ownership?

3. This essay is adapted from a talk Penniman delivered at a 2020 conference. How do you think she wanted her audience to respond? How do you know?

4. Have you been motivated by your own social or ethical commitments to undertake a project in your school or community? Write an account of that project that explains how it emerges from and reflects your personal values and history. Alternatively, write a letter to Penniman explaining how her essay affected you.

---

14. Chilean poet and diplomat (1904–1973) who received the 1971 Nobel Prize for Literature.

AUTHOR BIOGRAPHIES

Edward Abbey (1927–1989)

American essayist, novelist, and self-described "agrarian anarchist." Born in Pennsylvania, Abbey lived in the Southwest from 1948, when he began his studies at the University of New Mexico, until his death. He took as his most pervasive theme the beauty of the Southwestern desert and the ways it has been despoiled by government, business, and tourism. Abbey's novels include *Fire on the Mountain* (1963), *Good News* (1980), and *The Monkey Wrench Gang* (1975), which is credited with helping to inspire the radical environmentalist movement. He published several collections of essays, among them *Abbey's Road* (1979), *Beyond the Wall: Essays from the Outside* (1984), *One Life at a Time, Please* (1988), and, most famously, *Desert Solitaire: A Season in the Wilderness* (1968), drawing on his years as a ranger in the national parks of southern Utah. *Hayduke Lives!*, a sequel to *The Monkey Wrench Gang*, was published posthumously in 1990. *Confessions of a Barbarian: Selections from the Journals of Edward Abbey 1951–1989*, edited by David Petersen, was published in 1994. See also abbeyweb.net.

Hanif Abdurraqib (b. 1983)

American poet, essayist, and cultural critic. Born in Columbus, Ohio, Abdurraqib graduated from Beechcroft High School. His poetry has been published in numerous journals. His essays and music criticism have been published in *Pitchfork*, the *New Yorker*, and the *New York Times*. He has published several poetry collections. His first, *The Crown Ain't Worth Much*, was a finalist for the Hoffer Book Prize. His second, *A Fortune for Your Disaster* (2019), won the Lenore Marshall Prize. His first collection of essays *They Can't Kill Us Until They Kill Us* (2017) was named a book of the year by numerous publications and media outlets. The collection of essays *Go Ahead in the Rain: Notes to a Tribe Called Quest* (2019) became a *New York Times* bestseller. In 2021, *A Little Devil in America* was a finalist for several awards, including the National Book Award. The book won the 2022 Andrew Carnegie Medal for Excellence in Nonfiction and the Gordon Burn Prize. In 2021, Abdurraqib was awarded a MacArthur Fellowship. See also abdurraqib.com.

Diana Abu-Jaber (b. 1960)

American author and teacher. The daughter of a Jordanian father and an American mother, Abu-Jaber was born in Syracuse, New York, and she grew up in both Jordan and Upstate New York, eventually earning a PhD in English and creative writing from the State University of New York at Binghamton. The six award-winning books she has written since then, including the novels *Crescent* (2003), *Origin* (2007), and *Birds of Paradise* (2011), as well as her memoirs *The Language of Baklava* (2005) and *Life Without a Recipe* (2016), explore her Arab American identity and the Arab culture she knows firsthand, with a particular focus on the outsize role played by food as a cultural centerpiece. A young adult novel, *Silverworld*, was published in the spring of 2020. She currently teaches creative writing at Portland State University. See also dianaabujaber.com.

Asam Ahmad (b. 1993)

Canadian essayist, poet, journalist, cultural critic, and community activist. Ahmad describes his dwelling place as Treaty 13 land in Tkaranto, the original Mohawk name for Toronto, Ontario. Ahmad's work—criticism, opinion, and poetry—has appeared in several publications, including *CounterPunch*, *Black Girl Dangerous*, *Briarpatch*, *Youngist*, *Colorlines*, and, in 2021, *The Nation*. He writes, determinedly, with a voice for those who, like himself, are poor and working class. Ahmad participated in a CBC radio broadcast and online panel on call-out culture in 2019.

Elizabeth Alexander (b. 1962)

American poet, educator, scholar, and cultural advocate. Alexander was born in Harlem, New York, and raised in Washington, DC. Since 2018, she has served as the president of the Mellon

Foundation, the largest funder of arts and culture, and humanities in higher education in the United States. Before her Mellon appointment, Alexander taught on the faculties of Columbia University, Yale University (her alma mater), Smith College, and the University of Chicago, among other institutions. After attending Yale, she received an MA from Boston University, where she studied poetry writing with Derek Walcott. She earned a PhD from the University of Pennsylvania. She has won numerous awards for her poetry and was selected twice as a finalist for the Pulitzer Prize for poetry and biography. She is chancellor emeritus of the Academy of American Poets. In addition to her academic degrees, she also holds honorary degrees from several universities and colleges. In 2009, she was invited to become only the fourth poet, until then, asked to read at the inauguration of an American president, namely Barack Obama. In addition to these honors, she has won numerous awards, citations, and prizes for her written oeuvre. See also elizabethalexander.net.

Maya Angelou (1928–2014)
American memoirist, poet, essayist, and playwright. Born Marguerite Annie Johnson in St. Louis, Missouri, Angelou attended public schools in Arkansas and California before studying music and dance. In her lifetime, she worked as a cook, streetcar conductor, singer, actress, dancer, teacher, and director, with her debut film *Down in the Delta* (1998). Author of numerous volumes of poetry (her *Complete Collected Poems* was published in 1994) and ten plays (stage, screen, and television), Angelou may be best known for *I Know Why the Caged Bird Sings* (1969), the first volume of her autobiography and one of the most influential accounts of a Black woman's experience in contemporary literature. Angelou published the seventh and final volume of her autobiography, *Mom & Me & Mom*, in 2013. See also mayaangelou.com.

Gloria Anzaldúa (1942–2004)
American poet and writer. Anzaldúa was born to Mexican American parents and worked on the family ranch in southern Texas until attending Pan American University as the first woman from her family to enter college. She received an MA in English from the University of Texas, Austin, and embarked on a career

as a writer, college instructor, independent scholar, and social activist. Her most ambitious work, *Borderlands / La Frontera: The New Mestiza* (1987), examines "border women" like herself who grew up estranged from both their Mexican Indian heritage and the Anglo-American society that considers them outsiders. Her other works include the anthology *This Bridge Called My Back* (coedited with Cherríe Moraga, 1981); *Making Face, Making Soul / Haciendo Caras* (1990); and "La Prieta" (1997), an autobiographical essay written in her characteristic Spanglish, a mixture of Spanish and English. See also poetryfoundation.org/bio/gloria-e-anzaldua.

Kwame Anthony Appiah (b. 1954)
Ghanaian British philosopher, scholar, and novelist. The son of a prominent Ghanaian politician father and an English novelist mother, Appiah was educated in both Ghana and England before earning his BA and then his PhD in philosophy at Cambridge University. He has taught at many of the world's leading universities; currently he is a professor of philosophy and law at New York University. His first book, *In My Father's House* (1992), examined the roots of contemporary African culture. Since then his many publications have included three novels and such scholarly works as *Color Conscious: The Political Morality of Race*, coauthored with Amy Gutmann (1996), *The Ethics of Identity* (2005), *Cosmopolitanism: Ethics in a World of Strangers* (2006), and *The Honor Code: How Moral Revolutions Happen* (2010). Appiah was general editor of the Global Ethics Series, published by W. W. Norton. In 2015, he began to write the weekly Ethicist column for the *New York Times Magazine*. See also appiah.net.

Margaret Atwood (b. 1939)
Canadian novelist, poet, and essayist. Atwood was born in Ottawa, grew up in Ontario and Québec, earned her BA at Victoria College, part of the University of Toronto, and earned her MA from Harvard University. The author of more than forty books, Atwood has long been a literary superstar and feminist icon. She was only twenty-two when she published her first book, *Double Persephone* (1961), an award-winning collection of poems. Since then her prodigious output has included *The Edible Woman* (1969), her first novel; *Surfacing* (1972), a novel exploring gender identities and sexual politics; and *Survival: A Thematic*

Guide to Canadian Literature (1972), her first foray into nonfiction. Her tenth novel, *The Blind Assassin*, won England's prestigious Booker Prize in 2000. Many of her works have been adapted for film and television, most notably *The Handmaid's Tale* (1985), her dystopian novel depicting a harsh patriarchal theocracy. A sequel to *The Handmaid's Tale*, entitled *The Testaments*, was published in 2019 and was cowinner of the Booker Prize for that year. Her latest book *Old Babes in the Wood*, a collection of short stories—her first in nearly a decade—was published in 2023. See also margaretatwood.ca.

James Baldwin (1924–1987)

American essayist, novelist, and social activist. Baldwin was born in Harlem, became a minister at fourteen, and grew to maturity in an America plagued by racism and homophobia. He moved to Paris in 1948 believing that only outside the United States could he be read as "not merely a Negro; or, even, merely a Negro writer." His first published novel, *Go Tell It on the Mountain* (1953), and his first play, *The Amen Corner* (1954), are autobiographical explorations of race and identity. Although he would write other plays, Baldwin concentrated his energies on essays and on novels such as *Giovanni's Room* (1956) and *Another Country* (1962). His stories are collected in *Going to Meet the Man* (1965); his essay collections, including *Notes of a Native Son* (1955) and *The Fire Next Time* (1963), demonstrate Baldwin's skills as a social critic. His work, both published and unfinished, is treasured as the basis for new interpretations and adaptations. His incomplete manuscript *Remember This House* was expanded and adapted as a documentary feature in 2016, *I Am Not Your Negro*, which was nominated for an Academy Award. In 2018, his novel *If Beale Street Could Talk* was adapted as a feature film of the same title and won nominations and awards in several categories of the Academy Awards and Golden Globes; it was also named one of the top ten films of 2018 by the American Film Institute. See also "James Baldwin, The Art of Fiction" at parisreview.org.

Lynda Barry (b. 1956)

American cartoonist and author. Born in Wisconsin, Barry grew up in Seattle and attended The Evergreen State College in Olympia, Washington, where she began to draw comic strips. Without her knowledge, a friend and fellow cartoonist, Matt Groening (creator of *The Simpsons*), launched her career by publishing Barry's strips in the *University of Washington Daily*. Since then her weekly comic strip, *Ernie Pook's Comeek*, has appeared in more than fifty publications; her many books include such collections as *The Fun House* (1987) and *Down the Street* (1988); the illustrated novels *The Good Times Are Killing Me* (1988) and *Cruddy* (1999); and *What It Is* (2008), a graphic novel that is part memoir and part how-to guide for creating graphic novels. Barry's most recent work is *Making Comics* (2019). She teaches interdisciplinary creativity at the University of Wisconsin–Madison, where she is associate professor of art and Discovery Fellow. See also drawnandquarterly.com/author/lynda-barry.

Teresa M. Bejan (b. 1984)

American political theorist and author. Bejan earned degrees at both the University of Chicago and the University of Cambridge before receiving her PhD in political science from Yale University in 2013. Much of her subsequent career in academia has been devoted to the study of the way civility, as a fundamental aspect of any political system, has evolved historically. She has published widely in academic journals as well as the *Atlantic* and the *New York Times*; her first book, *Mere Civility: Disagreement and the Limits of Toleration* (2017; paperback, 2019), has made Bejan a familiar presence in television and radio debates about the meaning of civility in our contentious political era. She is presently working on a book, under contract with Harvard University Press, on the history of equality before modern egalitarianism took root. In addition to teaching and conducting research at Oriel College, Oxford, Bejan also writes regularly for popular outlets, including the *New York Times* and the *Atlantic*. Her 2018 TED Talk "Is Civility a Sham?" has garnered over 1.7 million views. See also teresabejan.com.

Eula Biss (b. 1977)

American nonfiction writer. Upon graduating from Hampshire College, Biss moved to New York City, where she taught in public schools for several years before leaving to earn an MFA degree in the University of Iowa's nonfiction writing program. Since then she has published four books, including: *The Balloonists* (2002), a collection of autobiographical prose poems; *Notes from No Man's Land* (2009), a volume of essays about race in America; *On Immunity: An Inoculation* (2014), an exploration of vaccination, vampires, and the value we place on health; and *Having and Being Had*, an exploration of the value system behind American home ownership, which was a *New York Times* editor's choice and a *Time* best book of 2020. Acknowledging the influence of poets Adrienne Rich and Sylvia Plath, Biss has written: "I count that as one of the reasons why I tend to think of personal narrative—particularly when it concerns the body or domesticity—as a perfectly viable space for intellectual exploration." Currently Biss teaches nonfiction for the Bennington Writer Seminars. See also eulabiss.net.

Molly McCully Brown (b. 1991)
American poet and essayist. Brown was born in Virginia and grew up on the campus of Sweet Briar College. She graduated from Bard College at Simon's Rock and earned a BA from Stanford University. Brown was a John and Renée Grisham Fellow at the University of Mississippi, where she received her MFA in Poetry. Her poetry collection *The Virginia State Colony for Epileptics and Feebleminded* (2017) won the 2016 Lexi Rudnitsky First Book Prize and was named a *New York Times* critics' top book of 2017. Brown has received the Amy Lowell Poetry Traveling Scholarship, a United States Artists Fellowship, a Civitella Ranieri Foundation Fellowship, and the Jeff Baskin Writers Fellowship from the Oxford American magazine. Her poems and essays have appeared in the *Paris Review*, *Tin House*, the *Guardian*, the *Virginia Quarterly Review*, *Vogue*, the *New York Times*, *Crazyhorse*, the *Yale Review*, and elsewhere. She is the coauthor, with Susannah Nevison, of the poetry collection *In the Field between Us* (2020). Brown's essay collection *Places I've Taken My Body* was published in 2020. She teaches at Kenyon College, where she is the Kenyon Review Fellow in Poetry. See also mollymccullybrown.com.

Nils Bubandt (b. 1966)
Danish anthropologist, scholar, and academic. A professor at the Aarhus University of Denmark, Bubandt earned a BA there in 1989. He has an MA from the University of Melbourne and a PhD from the Australian National University. In 2016, he was the first person at Arhaus

University to be awarded a higher doctoral degree in anthropology (Dr.scient.anth.). He has been published widely in scholarly journals, with numerous citations since the start of his professional career. His research includes the anthropology of religion, magic and witchcraft, politics and sovereignty, and environmentalism. Bubandt has written several books, including *The Empty Seashell: Witchcraft and Doubt on an Indonesian Island* (2014), which won the Gregory Bateson Prize from the Society for Cultural Anthropology. He has coauthored several works with Anna Lowenhaupt Tsing, including the book *Arts of Living on a Damaged Planet: Ghosts and Monsters of the Anthropocene* (2017). Bubandt's awards include a Guggenheim in 2018 and the Danish National Research Foundation's EliteForsk Prize in 2016. A member of the Royal Danish Academy of Sciences and Letters, Bubandt has held visiting professorships at universities around the world.

Garnette Cadogan (b. 1971)
American essayist, scholar, and editor. But, if pressed, Cadogan would describe himself as a wanderer. His belief that walking opens up the world and draws one closer to it regularly leads him to look for opportunities to wander. Most of his meandering is done in cities, and so his work often focuses on cities, particularly the great challenge of pluralism—how do we coexist? He holds and has held fellowships or appointments at the Department of Urban Studies and Planning at Massachusetts Institute of Technology, the Institute for Advanced Studies in Culture at the University of Virginia, the Institute for Public Knowledge at New York University, and the Yale School of Art. He is editor-at-large for *Nonstop Metropolis: A New York City Atlas* (coedited by Rebecca Solnit and Joshua Jelly-Schapiro) and, to no one's surprise, is at work on a book on walking, excerpts from which have appeared in literary journals, like *Freeman's*. See also lithub.com/the-future-of-new-writing-garnette-cadogan.

Joy Castro (b. 1967)
American memoirist, novelist, and essayist. Castro was born in Miami and strictly raised as a Jehovah's Witness in London and West Virginia. After her parents divorced, her mother married a man who turned violently abusive. At fourteen, she ran away to live with her father and eventually graduated from Trinity University

in Texas. Allowed as a child to read only religious literature, in adulthood she has blossomed into an eclectic writer of both fiction and nonfiction. Her best-known books are her memoirs, *The Truth Book: Escaping a Childhood of Abuse among Jehovah's Witnesses* (2005) and *Island of Bones* (2012). Her novels *Hell or High Water* (2012) and *Nearer Home* (2013) are mysteries set in New Orleans after the catastrophic flooding caused by Hurricane Katrina in 2005. Her most recent book is *One Brilliant Flame* (2023), a novel set in Key West, Florida, in 1866. See also joycastro.com.

Victoria Chang (b. 1970)
American poet, writer, and editor. Born and raised in Detroit, Chang has received degrees from the University of Michigan, Harvard University, and Stanford University, as well as an MFA from Warren Wilson College. She received a 2017 Guggenheim Fellowship and other awards. Chang serves as a contributing editor for *On the Seawall* and as a poet-editor of the *New York Times Magazine* Poem column. She is the program chair of Antioch University's low-residency MFA program. Chang has published several books of poetry, including *The Trees Witness Everything* (2022) and *Obit* (2020), which was named a *New York Times* notable book and received the *Los Angeles Times* Book Prize, the Anisfield-Wolf Book Award, and the PEN/Voelcker Award. A book of nonfiction, *Dear Memory*, was published in 2021, and a book of poems, *With My Back to the World*, has been announced for 2024. She has also published several books for young readers. She lives in Los Angeles with her family. See also victoriachangpoet.com.

Judith Ortiz Cofer (1952–2016)
American novelist, poet, and essayist. Born in Hormigueros, Puerto Rico, Cofer spent much of her childhood traveling between her Puerto Rican home and Paterson, New Jersey. Educated at Augusta College, Florida Atlantic University, and Oxford University, Cofer was a longtime professor of English and creative writing at the University of Georgia. *Silent Dancing: A Partial Remembrance of a Puerto Rican Childhood* (1990) reflects her lifelong efforts to explore her bicultural and bilingual roots as a member of what she calls "the Puerto Rican diaspora." Her other books include *The Latin Deli: Prose and Poetry* (1993), *Woman in Front of the Sun: On Becoming a Writer* (2000), *The Meaning of Consuelo* (2003), the young

adult novel *Call Me María* (2004), and *A Love Story Beginning in Spanish: Poems* (2005). See also georgiaencyclopedia.org; search for "Cofer."

Teju Cole (b. 1975)
American writer, photographer, and art historian. Born to Nigerian parents in Kalamazoo, Michigan, Cole grew up in Lagos, Nigeria, and returned to the United States at age seventeen to pursue his education. He earned a BA at Kalamazoo College, then cut medical studies short and turned to art history, eventually receiving a PhD at Columbia University. His essays and fiction have appeared in the *New York Times*, the *New Yorker, Granta, Brick*, and many other periodicals; his "On Photography" column in the *New York Times Magazine* was a finalist for a 2016 National Magazine Award. In addition to a book of his own photographs and writings, *Blind Spot* (2017), Cole has authored an autobiographical novella, *Every Day Is for the Thief* (2007); a novel, *Open City* (2011); and a collection of essays, *Known and Strange Things* (2016). His more recent work consists of five books that often combine photography (by Cole, other practitioners, or both) and text. *Black Paper* (2021) is a collection of thematically unified essays on the senses, photography, darkness, and ethics. Currently Cole teaches as the Gore Vidal Professor of the Practice of Creative Writing at Harvard University. See also tejucole.com.

William Cronon (b. 1954)
American environmental historian. Born in Connecticut and raised in Wisconsin, Cronon was a double major in history and English at the University of Wisconsin–Madison. After winning a Rhodes scholarship and completing a degree at Oxford University, in 1985 Cronon was granted a MacArthur Fellowship. He earned a PhD in 1990 from Yale University, where he taught for over a decade. Cronon later returned to the University of Wisconsin–Madison, where he taught American environmental history and the history of the American West. After retiring as the university's Vilas Research Professor in 2020, he became emeritus professor. His books, all of which concern the way humans shape the natural world and are in turn shaped by it, include *Changes in the Land: Indians, Colonists, and the Ecology of New England* (1983); *Nature's Metropolis: Chicago and the Great West* (1991);

Under an Open Sky: Rethinking America's Western Past (1992); and *Uncommon Ground: Rethinking the Human Place in Nature* (1995). Currently he is working on a book entitled *The Making of the American Landscape*. See also williamcronon.net.

Cormac Cullinan (b. 1962)
South African environmental attorney and author. Cullinan grew up wandering the hills near Pietermaritzburg, South Africa, with a keen sense that modern "monoculture" has disordered our relationship with nature. He received his legal education at the University of Natal and King's College London. Since 1992, the former anti-apartheid activist has turned his legal expertise to the drafting of a broad range of environmental treaties, laws, and policies in more than twenty countries. Cullinan's clients have included national and municipal governments, businesses, and NGOs such as Greenpeace Africa. A founding member of the executive committee of the Global Alliance for Rights of Nature, he oversaw the establishment of the International Tribunal on the Rights of Nature and was the presiding judge at the tribunal hearings in December 2015 in Paris. Cullinan's *Wild Law: A Manifesto for Earth Justice* (2nd ed., 2011) provides a blueprint for what he calls Earth Jurisprudence. In 2018, he received the Enviropaedia Ecologic lifetime achievement award. In 2021, he was awarded the Nick Steele Environmentalist of the Year Award. See also orionmagazine.org/contributor/cormac-cullinan/.

James Densley (b. 1982)
British American sociologist. Densley is professor of criminal justice at Metropolitan State University. A graduate of the University of Northampton, he also has a degree and a teacher's license from Pace University. He received a DPhil in sociology from Oxford University's Extra-Legal Governance Institute. Densley and Jillian Peterson are cofounders of the Violence Project, a nonprofit organization that maintains a comprehensive database of mass shootings, mass shooters, and related characteristics. They are also coauthors of the best-selling book *The Violence Project: How to Stop a Mass Shooting Epidemic* (2021). Densley and Peterson are highly sought-after experts and speakers on how to contain, reduce, and prevent the growth in mass killings. See also jamesdensley.com.

Anita Diamant (b. 1951)
American novelist and blogger. Born in Brooklyn, Diamant grew up in Newark, New Jersey, and Denver, Colorado. She earned her BA at Washington University in St. Louis, Missouri, and her MA in American literature at the State University of New York at Binghamton. She embarked on her writing career as a journalist in Boston before publishing feature articles—about everything from medical ethics to pet ownership—in such national publications as *Self*, *McCall's*, and *Ms*. Her first book, *The New Jewish Wedding* (1985), has been followed by a number of other Jewish guidebooks, including *The New Jewish Baby Book* (1988). The first of Diamant's five historical novels, *The Red Tent* (1997), gave life to an obscure biblical figure named Dinah; the book was adapted into a television miniseries in 2014. Diamant's most recent novel is *The Boston Girl* (2014), depicting the struggles of immigrant life in the early twentieth century. Her latest book of nonfiction, published in 2021, is *Period. End of Sentence.: A New Chapter in the Fight for Menstrual Justice*, a collection of essays whose title derives from the Academy Award–winning documentary on the same subject. See also anitadiamant.com.

Joan Didion (1934–2021)
American novelist, essayist, and screenwriter. A native Californian, Didion studied at the University of California, Berkeley. After winning *Vogue* magazine's Prix de Paris contest for excellence in writing, she worked for the magazine until 1963, the year her first novel, *Run River*, was published. Since then she has written five more novels, most recently *The Last Thing He Wanted* (1996). The essays collected in *Slouching Towards Bethlehem* (1968) and *The White Album* (1979) captured the spirit of the 1960s and 1970s, respectively, and put Didion in the forefront of American essayists. Later works of nonfiction include *Fixed Ideas: America since 9.11* (2003), *The Year of Magical Thinking* (2005 winner of the National Book Award), and *South and West: From a Notebook* (2017). *We Tell Ourselves Stories in Order to Live* (2006) collects her first seven volumes of nonfiction. *Let Me Tell You What I Mean* (2021) is a collection of

essays written between 1967 and 2000. See also thejoandidion.com.

Annie Dillard (b. 1945)
American nature writer, poet, and novelist. Born in Pittsburgh, Pennsylvania, Dillard received her BA and MA in English from Hollins College. She has published books that range from the poetry of her first book, *Tickets for a Prayer Wheel* (1974), to the nature meditation *Holy the Firm* (1977), the memoir *An American Childhood* (1987), the literary theory in *Living by Fiction* (1982), the essay collections *Teaching a Stone to Talk* (1982) and *The Abundance: Narrative Essays Old & New* (2016), and the novels *The Living* (1992) and *The Maytrees* (2007). In her Pulitzer Prize–winning nonfiction narrative *Pilgrim at Tinker Creek* (1974), Dillard recounts years she spent living in seclusion in the natural world, much like Henry David Thoreau. In *The Writing Life* (1989) she muses on her life's work—"to examine all things intensely and relentlessly." See also anniedillard.com.

Matt Dinan (b. 1984)
Canadian scholar and essayist. Dinan grew up in Miramichi, New Brunswick, and earned his BA in Great Ideas at St. Thomas University in Fredericton, New Brunswick. After receiving his PhD in political theory at Baylor University in Waco, Texas, in 2012, he taught for three years at the College of the Holy Cross in Worcester, Massachusetts, before returning to St. Thomas University, where, as associate professor with tenure, he teaches in the Great Books program and conducts research in ancient and contemporary political thought. "I study and teach about Aristotle," he writes, noting that Aristotle "rates the social virtues and friendship as especially important for a happy human life"—elements of life he finds to be understudied in academia and underappreciated in the culture more broadly. In 2021, he coedited *Politics, Literature, and Film in Conversation: Essays in Honor of Mary P. Nichols*. See also mattdinan.ca.

Frederick Douglass (1817–1895)
American abolitionist, orator, journalist, and memoirist. Born enslaved in Maryland, Douglass learned at a young age how to read and write, even though it was against the law to teach literacy to an enslaved person. In 1836, he escaped from his master and fled to the North with Anna Murray, also formerly enslaved, whom he later married. Douglass soon became an important orator in the abolitionist movement and, with the publication of his first autobiography, *Narrative of the Life of Frederick Douglass, an American Slave, Written by Himself* (1845), an international spokesman for freedom. Douglass founded the antislavery newspaper the *North Star* in 1847 and actively recruited Black soldiers to join the Union Army at the outbreak of the Civil War. He continued his autobiography in *My Bondage and My Freedom* (1855) and *Life and Times of Frederick Douglass* (1881, rev. 1892). See also docsouth.unc .edu/neh/douglass/bio.html.

Brian Doyle (1956–2017)
American novelist, essayist, and editor. Born in New York City, Doyle received his BA from the University of Notre Dame in 1978. He worked on various magazines and newspapers in Chicago and Boston, and for twenty-six years edited the University of Portland's *Portland Magazine*. A passionate storyteller and a prolific writer of essays, stories, and the prose poems he called "proems," Doyle published sixteen books, including the essay collection *Spirited Men* (2004), about male musicians and writers, and *The Wet Engine* (2005), about "hearts and how they work and do not work and get repaired and patched, for a while." As his life neared its end, Doyle produced a flurry of award-winning novels: *Mink River* (2010), *The Plover* (2014), *Martin Marten* (2015), and *The Adventures of John Carson in Several Quarters of the World* (2017). In 2019, Little, Brown and Company posthumously published a collection of spiritual essays by Doyle, *One Long River of Song: Notes on Wonder and the Spiritual and Nonspiritual Alike*. See also opb.org/artsandlife/article/brian -doyle-oregon-author-books.

Jennifer L. Eberhardt (b. 1965)
American social psychologist and scholar. Eberhardt grew up in Cleveland, Ohio, and earned her BA at the University of Cincinnati. After receiving her PhD in psychology from Harvard University and then teaching for several years at Yale University, she joined the faculty at Stanford University, where, as a professor in the Department of Psychology, she teaches, conducts research, and acts as co-director of SPARQ (Social Psychological Answers to Real-World Questions). Much of her work centers on the psychological underpinnings of racial

consciousness and racial bias, especially as they play out in economic inequality and the criminal justice system. Her first book, *Biased: Uncovering the Hidden Prejudice That Shapes What We, See, Think, and Do*, was published in 2019. In 2014, she received a MacArthur Fellowship, and in that same year she was recognized in *Foreign Policy* magazine's list of "100 Leading Global Thinkers." She has also been elected to the National Academy of Sciences and the American Academy of Arts and Sciences. See also stanford.edu/~eberhard.

Nora Ephron (1941–2012)
American journalist, director, and screenwriter. Born in New York City, Ephron grew up in Beverly Hills, California, the daughter of two screenwriters. Soon after graduating from Wellesley College in 1962, she began writing for the *New York Post, Esquire*, the *New York Times Magazine*, and *New York* magazine. In the mid-1970s, she turned from journalism to screenplays and was nominated for three Academy Awards for best original screenplay, for *Silkwood* (1983), *When Harry Met Sally* (1989), and *Sleepless in Seattle* (1993). In the 1990s, she began directing films, including *You've Got Mail* (1998), *Lucky Numbers* (2000), and *Julie & Julia* (2009). Her books include the novel *Heartburn* (1983) and the essay collections *Wallflower at the Orgy* (1970); *Crazy Salad* (1975); *Scribble, Scribble: Notes on the Media* (1978); and *I Remember Nothing: And Other Reflections* (2010). See also longreads.com; search for "Ephron."

June Eric-Udorie (b. 1998)
British essayist and feminist campaigner of Nigerian descent. Eric-Udorie is a journalist and blogger for the *Guardian, Fusion*, the *Independent*, and the *New Statesman*. Her bona fides as a feminist activist include executing a campaign when she was eighteen years old to overturn the British government's intention to remove the study of feminism from the A-level politics curriculum. Eric-Udorie was named *Elle* magazine's 2017 "Female Activist of the Year." In 2021, she graduated from Duke University, six years after a period of homelessness and sleeping on friends' bedroom floors. She has worked for Random House as a trainee editor and is listed in the Penguin Random House Speakers Bureau. See also prhspeakers.com/speaker/june-eric-udorie.

Rhea Ewing (b. 1990)
American graphic novelist, illustrator, and fine artist. Ewing grew up in Kentucky and attended the University of Wisconsin–Madison, graduating with a BFA in drawing and printmaking. Now based in California, they published *Fine: A Comic about Gender* in 2022. The book was named one of the ten best graphic novels of the year by the *Washington Post* and appears on several other ten-best lists of graphic novels. *Fine* not only is a detailed and compelling examination through first-person accounts of dozens of subjects grappling with the question of their own gender identity, it also chronicles Ewing's own trials during a wrenching childhood in rural Kentucky, with the added challenge of confronting their own questions of personal identity in adolescence. Ewing found answers in their training as a graphic artist and developing their talent as a storyteller. See also rheaewing.com.

Kathy Fish (b. 1960)
American short-story writer. Born in Waterloo, Iowa, Fish earned a BA in psychology at the University of Northern Iowa in Cedar Falls. She is a master of the so-called short short story—also called flash fiction—and her work has been called prose poetry: minimalist, dreamlike stories ("Strong Tongue") or, sometimes, steel-trap mini-essays of astonishing power ("Collective Nouns for Humans in the Wild"). A frequent award winner in the literary subgenre of flash fiction, she has published her work in *Guernica*, the *Indiana Review*, the *Mississippi Review, Quick Fiction*, the *Denver Quarterly*, and many others, especially online. Her stories have been collected in five volumes, including her first, *Together We Can Bury It* (2012), and, most recently, *Wild Life: Collected Works from 2003–2018* (2018). Fish teaches fiction and mentors students in the Mile High MFA program at Denver's Regis University. She continues to write and publish short works of fiction, at least four in 2022, which continue to win nominations for significant awards. A 2021 story, "Some Hard, Hot Places," was selected for the 2022 W. W. Norton collection *Flash Fiction America*. See also kathy-fish.com.

Joey Franklin (b. 1980)
American essayist. Franklin grew up in Beaverton, Oregon, and after a two-year stint as a Mormon missionary in Japan he

earned a BA in English at Brigham Young University, an MA in creative nonfiction at Ohio University, and a PhD in literature and creative writing from Texas Tech University. A specialist in creative nonfiction, Franklin professes an interest in "memory, identity, and self-representation." His essays have appeared in *American Literary Review*, *Gettysburg Review*, and the *Writer's Chronicle*; many of these are collected in his first book, *My Wife Wants You to Know I'm Happily Married* (2015). A second collection of his essays, *Delusions of Grandeur*, was published in 2020. In 2022, Bloomsbury published his *The Writer's Hustle*, a comprehensive guide to all the things successful writers do when not at their keyboards. Franklin is an associate professor of English, teaching creative writing at Brigham Young University. See also joeyfranklin.com.

Ian Frazier (b. 1951)
American essayist, humorist, and novelist. Born in Cleveland and raised in Hudson, Ohio, Frazier studied at Western Reserve Academy and Harvard University, where he worked at the satirical *Harvard Lampoon*. Since then he has written over a dozen books. Many of the humorous pieces he has published in the *New Yorker* have been collected in such volumes as *Dating Your Mom* (1986), *Coyote v. Acme* (1996), and *Lamentations of the Father* (2000). Frazier's best-known work of nonfiction, *Great Plains* (1989), like *Family* (1994) and *On the Rez* (2000), is based on both extensive research and his own experiences after moving to Montana in 1982. Since relocating to the East Coast he has published *Gone to New York: Adventures in the City* (2005), the best-selling *Travels in Siberia* (2010), *The Cursing Mommy's Book of Days* (2012), and *Hogs Wild: Selected Reporting Pieces* (2016). His most recent book is a collection of humor pieces, *Cranial Fracking* (2021). See also newyorker.com/contributors/ian-frazier.

Mohandas Gandhi (1869–1948)
Indian lawyer, politician, social activist, and writer. Often referred to by the title Mahatma, Gandhi led the nationalist movement that eventually saw the separation of India from British rule and the establishment of a sovereign nation. His work as an activist and proponent of nonviolent advocacy and resistance to promote civil rights and freedom throughout the world began at the age of twenty-four in South Africa. He worked

and campaigned in that country for twenty-one years. In 1915, he returned to his native India to organize peasants and urban laborers, and in 1921, when he became leader of the Indian National Congress, he led many nationwide campaigns to ease poverty, expand women's rights, end racism, but above all to establish self-rule for India. His support for these principles was unswerving, even if it meant opposing the participation of native Indians in the Allied participation in World War II. He was assassinated in January 1948 by a gunman, a member of a right-wing Hindu nationalist organization that opposed Gandhi's conciliatory and accommodating views toward Muslims. Gandhi died, but not before he realized his goal, the independence of India, which occurred just months before his death. His writing, teaching, and political advocacy led eventually to being perceived as the martyred father of his country and a folk hero. See also britannica.com/biography/Mahatma-Gandhi.

Henry Louis Gates Jr. (b. 1950)
American scholar and literary critic. Born and raised in West Virginia, Gates was educated at both Yale and Cambridge universities. Now a professor at Harvard University, Gates edits African American literature, composes literary criticism, and writes for general audiences. He has created a number of television documentaries, including *African American Lives* (2006) and *Finding Your Roots* (2012); his essays have appeared in the *New Yorker*, *Newsweek*, *Sports Illustrated*, and the *New York Times*. Gates's many books include *Figures in Black: Words, Signs, and the "Racial" Self* (1987); *The Signifying Monkey* (1988), winner of the National Book Award; *Colored People* (1994), his best-selling autobiography; *The Henry Louis Gates Jr. Reader* (2012), a collection of his writings; and, most recently, *Stony the Road: Reconstruction, White Supremacy, and the Rise of Jim Crow* (2019). Gates is the general coeditor of *The Norton Anthology of African American Literature* (3rd ed., 2014). He was named editor in chief of the *Oxford Dictionary of African American English* in 2022. Since 2019, Gates has received a large number of awards and prizes in recognition of his lifelong of achievements and contributions to the understanding of culture and enlightenment on matters of race, scholarship, and literature.

See also aaas.fas.harvard.edu/people/henry-louis-gates-jr.

Atul Gawande (b. 1965)
American surgeon, teacher, essayist, and public health official. Born in Brooklyn to Indian immigrant parents, Gawande grew up in Athens, Ohio. He earned his BA at Stanford University, studied at Oxford University as a Rhodes Scholar, and then earned his MD from Harvard Medical School. He was named a MacArthur Fellow in 2006. In addition to scholarly studies published in the *New England Journal of Medicine*, his articles about health care and the medical profession have appeared frequently in *Slate* and the *New Yorker*, where he has served as a staff writer. Gawande's four books, including *Complications: A Surgeon's Notes on an Imperfect Science* (2002) and *The Checklist Manifesto: How to Get Things Right* (2009), have been widely praised for the clarity with which they illuminate a complex technical subject for a general readership. His most recent book is *Being Mortal: Medicine and What Matters in the End* (2014). In 2022, Gawande was appointed assistant administrator for global health at USAID by President Biden. See also gawande.com.

Ross Gay (b. 1974)
American poet, essayist, and professor. Gay earned degrees from Lafayette College (BA), Sarah Lawrence College (MFA), and Temple University (PhD in English). He has been honored with fellowships from the Guggenheim Foundation, Cave Canem Workshop, and the Bread Loaf Writer's Conference. He teaches at Indiana University. Bloomington, and in Drew University's low-residency MFA program. He has published several books of poetry. *Catalog of Unabashed Gratitude* (2015) won the Kingsley Tufts Poetry Award and the National Book Critics Circle Award for poetry. He coauthored two books: a chapbook, with Aimee Nezhukamatathil, and *River*, with Richard Wehrenberg Jr. His collection of essays *The Book of Delights* (2019) celebrates the world for its ordinary delights. *Inciting Joy: Essays* was released in 2022. See also rossgay.net.

Roxane Gay (b. 1974)
American writer and commentator. Born in Omaha, Nebraska, Gay earned an MA at the University of Nebraska at Lincoln and a PhD in rhetoric and technical communications from Michigan Technological University. She has taught at Eastern Illinois University; Purdue University, where she was an associate professor of English; and Yale University, where she was a Presidential Fellow. She is currently an endowed professor of media, culture, and feminist studies at Rutgers University. Her short stories and essays have appeared in such publications as *Time*, *McSweeney's*, and the *Nation*, as well as in a broad range of anthologies, from *Best Sex Writing* (2012) to *Best American Mystery Stories* (2014). Her books include *Ayiti* (2011), a short-story collection; *An Untamed State* (2014), a novel; *Bad Feminist* (2014), a volume of essays that discusses the difficulties of being a woman in a world without perfect role models; *Difficult Women* (2017), a story collection; and *Hunger* (2017), a memoir. Her most recent book *Opinions* was published in 2023. Gay is also the founder of Tiny Hardcore Press and the editor of the online *Gay Mag*. See also roxanegay.com.

A. Bartlett Giamatti (1938–1989)
American scholar and author. Born in Boston and raised in South Hadley, Massachusetts, Giamatti spent much of his life at Yale University. There he earned his BA and PhD, was a professor of English, and, in 1978, began his tenure as Yale's youngest-ever president. Eight years later he left Yale and turned to his first love: baseball. Giamatti was named president of the National League in 1986 and commissioner of Major League Baseball in 1989. Just five months after assuming his dream job, he died suddenly of a heart attack at the age of fifty-one. Author of eight books, Giamatti published influential scholarly volumes such as *Play of Double Senses: Spenser's Faerie Queene* (1975) and books about academia's role in American culture like *The University and the Public Interest* (1981). His lyrical essays about baseball are collected in *A Great and Glorious Game* (1998). See also mlb.com/official-information/commissioners/giamatti.

Malcolm Gladwell (b. 1963)
Canadian journalist and essayist. Born in England and raised in Canada, Gladwell graduated from the University of Toronto in 1984 and soon began his career as a journalist, writing for various publications including the *Washington Post*. Since joining the staff of the *New Yorker* in 1996, he has contributed articles on a wide array of topics, from the "science of shopping" to highway safety

to mammography to the SAT. His books, all international bestsellers, include *The Tipping Point: How Little Things Can Make a Big Difference* (2000); *Blink: The Power of Thinking without Thinking* (2005); *Outliers: The Story of Success* (2008); *What the Dog Saw* (2009); *David and Goliath: Underdogs, Misfits, and the Art of Battling Giants* (2013); *Talking to Strangers: What We Should Know about the People We Don't Know* (2019); and *The Bomber Mafia: A Dream, a Temptation, and the Longest Night of the Second World War* (2021). See also gladwellbooks.com.

Emily Fox Gordon (b. 1948)
American author and teacher. Gordon's works include two memoirs, a novel, and a collection of essays, *Book of Days*. Her essays appear in a variety of journals and other publications, including *Ploughshares*, the *New York Times*, *Salmagundi*, and *Southwest Review*. "At Sixty Five" was selected for *Best American Essays 2014*. She has earned two Pushcart Prizes and was named a Guggenheim Fellow in 2014. She teaches workshops on the personal essay at several institutions around the country, including Columbia University, Rutgers University, Rice University, and the University of Wyoming. See also emilyfoxgordon.com.

Annette Gordon-Reed (b. 1958)
American historian, law professor, and author. Gordon-Reed is the Carl M. Loeb University Professor at Harvard University and Charles Warren Professor of American Legal History at Harvard Law School. She has won sixteen book prizes, including the Pulitzer Prize in History and the National Book Award. Her list of honors includes a Guggenheim Fellowship, a MacArthur Fellowship, the National Humanities Medal, the Frederick Douglass Book Prize, and the George Washington Book Prize. Her career spans a lifetime of study of law and justice in American history, with a particular interest in the role of race on that history. She has written extensively on a broad range of topics, but with specific attention to the life of Thomas Jefferson and his relationship with, as her book title defines, *The Hemingses of Monticello: An American Family*. Her book *On Juneteenth* examines the received wisdom concerning national and Texas history regarding emancipation. Gordon-Reed colors her rendition with her reflections as a native Texan. See also annettegordonreed.com.

Stephen Jay Gould (1941–2002)
American paleontologist, essayist, and educator. Raised in New York City, Gould graduated from Antioch College and received a PhD from Columbia University in 1967. He then joined the faculty of Harvard University as a professor of geology and zoology and taught courses in paleontology, biology, and the history of science. Gould demystified science for lay readers in the essays he wrote for a regular column in *Natural History* magazine; many of these were collected in *Ever Since Darwin* (1977), *Hen's Teeth and Horse's Toes* (1983), and *Eight Little Piggies* (1993). Gould's *The Mismeasure of Man* (1981), which questioned traditional ways of testing intelligence, won the National Book Critics Circle Award for essays and criticism. In broader recognition of his achievements, Gould was named a MacArthur Fellow, class of 1981. A renowned neo-Darwinian, Gould championed the theory of evolution throughout his career; his last book on this subject, *The Structure of Evolutionary Theory*, appeared in 2002. See also amnh.org/science/bios/gould.

John Green (b. 1977)
American writer, content creator, podcaster, and philanthropist. Green was born in Indiana and raised in Florida, graduating from Kenyon College in 2000. While studying, Green served as a student chaplain, an experience that later inspired his young adult novel *The Fault in Our Stars* (2012). Despite publishing two best-selling novels prior to its release, the success of *The Fault in Our Stars* allowed Green to pursue other endeavors. His earlier novels also won prestigious awards, including the Printz Award from the American Library Association. From 2007 to 2010, he published three novels on his own and a fourth with a coauthor. *The Fault in Our Stars* remained a *New York Times* best-seller for an extended period. In 2017, he released another novel and, in 2021, a critically acclaimed volume of essays, *The Anthropocene Reviewed*. Much of his work has been anthologized or adapted for other media. Since 2007, he has collaborated with his brother and wife on various podcast and video productions. His commercial successes have enabled

him to support numerous charitable and NGO efforts focused on health and education. See also johngreenbooks.com.

Jessica Grose (b. 1982)
American journalist, editor, and novelist. Born, raised, and schooled in New York City, Grose attended Brown University and graduated in 2004. She began her journalism career as associate editor of the blog *Jezebel*, owned by Gawker Media. Later Greene started her own popular blog *Postcards from Yo Momma*, collaborating with Doree Shafrir. That effort was the basis of a 2009 book. That same year Greene became managing editor of *Slate*'s website for women, *Double X*, and cohosted a podcast associated with the site. In the years following, she published her debut novel *Sad Desk Salad* and served as deputy editor of *Vulture*, the culture blog of *New York* magazine. She joined the staff of the *New York Times* in 2021 as an opinion writer. In addition to two previous books—one a novel, the other nonfiction—she published *Screaming on the Inside: The Unsustainability of American Motherhood* (2022). She lives with her two daughters and her husband in Brooklyn, New York. See also jessicagrose.com.

Michael Hamad (b. 1972)
American music critic, podcast producer, and visual artist. Hamad holds an MA in music theory from the Hartt School and a PhD in musicology from Brandeis University. As a staff music writer and senior journalist for the *Hartford Courant* from 2013 to 2021, he covered popular music, jazz, "and whatever else sounds interesting." Hamad is also a guitarist and a visual artist who has devised a unique way of visually reimagining music in the form of "schematics"— assemblages of words and symbols, created in real time, that graph his aural experience in two or even three dimensions. Hamad's artwork has appeared in the *Village Voice*, the *Believer*, and the *New York Times*; he is currently consulting in communications for EASTCONN, a nonprofit Regional Education Service Center. See also setlistschematics.tumblr.com.

Daisy Hernández (b. 1975)
American journalist, author, and social activist. Daughter of a Colombian mother and a Cuban father, Hernández grew up in New Jersey and earned an MA at New York University's school of journalism and an MFA from the University of Miami. She has reported for the *New York Times*, the *Atlantic*, and *Slate*; her essays and fiction have appeared in the *Bellingham Review, Fourth Genre, Rumpus*, and many other journals. She taught at several institutions of higher learning, including Vanderbilt University and the University of North Carolina at Chapel Hill. An ardent feminist, she has been a columnist for *Ms.* magazine and was a coeditor of *Colonize This! Young Women of Color on Today's Feminism* (2002). Hernández is the author of *A Cup of Water under My Bed* (2014), her coming-of-age memoir of "learning about feminism, queer identity, race, and immigration in the Americas." *The Kissing Bug* (2021) won the PEN / Jean Stein Book Award and was named one of *Time*'s ten best nonfiction books of the year. She currently teaches at Northwestern University as associate professor of creative writing. See also daisyhernandez.com.

Zora Neale Hurston (1891–1960)
American anthropologist, folklorist, and writer. A central figure of the Harlem Renaissance of the 1920s and 1930s, Hurston was born in Notasulga, Alabama, and grew up in Eatonville, Florida, the daughter of a Baptist preacher and a seamstress. She attended Howard University and in 1928 received a BA from Barnard College, where she studied anthropology and developed an interest in Black folk traditions and in oral history. Hurston's writing draws on her knowledge of folklore and uses a vigorous, rhythmical, direct prose style that influenced many later American writers. Her works include the play *Mule Bone: A Comedy of Negro Life in Three Acts* (1931), written with Langston Hughes; the novel *Their Eyes Were Watching God* (1937); her autobiography *Dust Tracks on a Road* (1942); and her *Collected Stories* (1995) and *Collected Plays* (2008). Her nonfiction work, compiled as *You Don't Know Us Negroes and Other Essays*, originally published in the first decades of the twentieth century, has been reissued in a continuing series under the aegis of Henry Louis Gates Jr. as coeditor by the publishing house Amistad, an imprint of HarperCollins, which keeps many of her classic works of fiction in print. See also zoranealehurston.com.

Ursula Murray Husted (b. 1980)
Minneapolis-based American artist and graphic novelist. Husted has an MFA from Minneapolis College of Art and a

PhD in design communication and visual ethnography from the University of Minnesota. Husted formerly was a tenured associate professor at the University of Wisconsin–Stout but now devotes her full-time professional efforts to writing and drawing. Husted has published both graphic novels and illustrated short fiction. She has also published a book about professional practices in the creation of comics, with various exercises and tips. In 2020, she published *A Cat Story*, a graphic novel set in Malta. She has a work in progress, with the working title of *Botticelli's Apprentice*, a graphic novel, which, like her others, is inspired in part by her expertise in art history. Her graphic texts have been mainly aimed at young adults and middle-grade readers. See also ursulamurrayhusted.com.

Lauren Michele Jackson (b. 1991)
American essayist and scholar. A native of Batavia, Illinois, Jackson graduated from the University of Illinois at Urbana-Champaign in 2013 and received her PhD in English language and literature from the University of Chicago. Much of her criticism, which has appeared in a broad range of publications including the *Atlantic*, the *Paris Review*, *Rolling Stone*, and the *New Yorker*, investigates racial aesthetics in contemporary American culture. Her first book, an essay collection, is *White Negroes: When Cornrows Were in Vogue . . . and Other Thoughts on Cultural Appropriation* (2019). Her second book *Back* will be published by Amistad. Jackson is an assistant professor on the faculty of both English and African American Studies departments at Northwestern University. See also laurjackson.com.

Leslie Jamison (b. 1983)
American novelist and essayist. Jamison was born in Washington, DC, and raised in Los Angeles. In addition to winning accolades for work produced as a student, her earliest published works won significant critical acclaim, as well as significant commercial success. She has degrees from Harvard University, the Iowa Writers Workshop, and a PhD from Yale University in English literature, with a dissertation that examined the theme of addiction recovery as depicted in twentieth-century American literature—a theme pursued in her creative and memoir writing. Her notable publications include the novel *The Gin Closet* (2014) and several volumes of essays,

including the best-selling *The Empathy Exams* (2014) and *Make It Scream, Make It Burn* (2019). During the winter of 2022–23, she was contracted by Little, Brown and Company to write two volumes, a novel, and a memoir about single motherhood. She is associate professor of writing on the faculty of the Columbia University School of the Arts. See also lesliejamison.com.

Thomas Jefferson (1743–1826)
American lawyer, architect, and writer; governor of Virginia (1779–81), secretary of state to George Washington (1790–93), vice president to John Adams (1797–1801), and third president of the United States (1801–9). A learned man of significant accomplishments in many fields, Jefferson became a lawyer and was elected to Virginia's House of Burgesses, where he argued the cause of American independence. After completing his second term as president of the United States, he founded the University of Virginia, designing both the buildings and the curriculum. A fluent prose stylist, Jefferson authored Virginia's Statute of Religious Freedom and wrote books on science, religion, architecture, and even Anglo-Saxon grammar. He is best known for writing the Declaration of Independence; his preliminary drafts were edited by a committee that included Benjamin Franklin and John Adams before Jefferson prepared the final revision. See also monticello.org.

Rachel Pieh Jones (b. 1978)
American author and blogger. Born and raised in Minnesota, Jones and her husband, an English professor, settled in Djibouti in 2004. A few years later she started her blog *Djibouti Jones* with the mission "to help you live the best expatriate life possible." Soon her articles began to appear in periodicals such as the *New York Times*, *Christianity Today*, and even *Runner's World* (she's an avid runner). Her cookbook, *Djiboutilicious* (2006), features recipes from the Horn of Africa. A practicing Christian living in a Muslim country, Jones writes with respect and insight about spirituality and religion, calling herself a witness: "I aim to observe beautiful, creative aspects of our world and call out the good in them." In 2019, she published *Stronger than Death: How Annalena Tonelli Defied Terror and Tuberculosis in the Horn of Africa*. Her memoir *Pillars: How Muslim Friends Led Me Closer to Jesus* (2022) won a Gold Medal

from the Independent Publisher Book Awards. See also rachelpiehjones.com.

David Joy (b. 1983)
American author of fiction and nonfiction. Born in Charlotte, North Carolina, Joy holds a BA from Western Carolina University. He debuted with a memoir, *Growing Gills: A Fly Fisherman's Journey* (2011). His first novel, *Where All Light Tends to Go* (2015), is set in the hardscrabble Appalachia of western North Carolina; it was a finalist for the Edgar Award for best first novel by an American and was long-listed for the International Dublin Literary Award. Joy followed with two more novels: *The Weight of This World* (2017) and *The Line That Held Us* (2018). Joy coedited *Gather at the River: Twenty-Five Authors on Fishing* (2019). More recently he published the novels *When These Mountains Burn* (2020) and *Those We Thought We Knew* (2023). His short stories and essays have appeared in numerous periodicals, including *Drafthorse*, *Smoky Mountain Living*, *Time*, and the *New York Times Magazine*. He lives in Webster, North Carolina. See also david-joy.com.

Joan Naviyuk Kane (b. 1977)
Inupiaq American poet and teacher of writing in higher education. Born Joan Marie Kane in Alaska, Kane has served in a succession of distinguished appointments as chair of writing, fellow, and faculty member in creative writing and Native and Indigenous studies at various institutions, including Harvard College, Tufts University, Brown University, the Bread Loaf School of Writing, and Scripps College. She attended Harvard College, graduating in 2000, and received an MFA in poetry writing from Columbia University in 2006. She straddles the disparate worlds of her roots and early upbringing, centering on Uguivak (King Island), Alaska, the Bering Sea, and the world of academia, in which she received her extensive formal training, mainly on the East Coast. She has published poems, essays, and short stories in many publications, including the *Guardian*, *Orion*, the *Boston Review*, the *Colorado Review*, *Poetry International*, and *Poetry* magazine. Since 2009, she has published eight volumes of poetry, including *Dark Traffic* (2021). Her work has received many awards and prizes. See also poetryfoundation.org/poets/joan-kane.

Ibram X. Kendi (b. 1982)
American professor, author, anti-racist activist, and historian. Born Ibram Henry Rogers, Kendi received his primary and most of his secondary education in Queens, New York, moving to Manassas, Virginia, with his family while still in high school. Florida A&M University gave him tandem BS degrees in African American studies and sports journalism (2004). Subsequently, Temple University granted Kendi an MA and then a PhD (2010) in African American studies. He taught at several institutions of higher learning, attaining a full professorship at age thirty-four. In 2020, he was appointed to the endowed Andrew W. Mellon Professorship at Boston University (BU). During his initial tenure, he cofounded the BU Center for Antiracist Research. Among a long list of achievements, Kendi won the National Book Award for nonfiction in 2016 for *Stamped from the Beginning: The Definitive History of Racist Ideas in America*. He has written numerous articles and books and has won diverse awards and fellowships, including, in 2021, a MacArthur Fellowship. These honors are largely in recognition of his growing body of theory and scholarship on new strategies to more successfully combat racism. His books are tailored to address these questions for audiences ranging from children to adults. See also ibramxkendi.com.

John F. Kennedy (1917–1963)
American author, politician, and thirty-fifth president of the United States. Born in Brookline, Massachusetts, Kennedy graduated from Harvard University and developed his senior thesis into the best-selling *Why England Slept* (1940). He received the Navy and Marine Corps Medal for his service in World War II. At twenty-nine Kennedy was elected to the US House of Representatives; six years later he narrowly won a seat in the US Senate, representing Massachusetts. His book *Profiles in Courage* (1956), detailing notable instances of political integrity by US senators, won the Pulitzer Prize for biography and added to his growing fame. In 1960, his eloquence and poise in televised debates against Richard Nixon helped Kennedy win the presidency. His inaugural address, call-

ing for all citizens' participation in the affairs of their nation, is one of the best-known speeches in American history. On November 22, 1963, Kennedy was assassinated in Dallas, Texas. See also jfklibrary.org.

Philip Kennicott (b. 1966)
American music, art, and architecture critic. Kennicott grew up in Schenectady, New York, attended Deep Springs College, and graduated summa cum laude from Yale University with a degree in philosophy. He began his career in journalism as the classical music critic for the *Detroit News* before moving on to the *St. Louis Post-Dispatch* and then the *Washington Post*, where he now serves as chief art and architecture critic. His articles about classical music have appeared in the *New Republic*, *Gramophone*, and *Opera News*. In addition to music, he has written on a broad array of topics, including gun control, Abraham Lincoln, and the US Holocaust Memorial Museum. His essay "Smuggler," first published in the *Virginia Quarterly Review*, was selected for *Best American Essays* (2015). In 2013, Kennicott was awarded the Pulitzer Prize for criticism in recognition of "his eloquent and passionate essays on art and the social forces that underlie it." His first book *Counterpoint: A Memoir of Bach and Mourning* (2020) has won significant critical acclaim. See also philipkennicott.com.

Robin Wall Kimmerer (b. 1953)
American botanist and ecologist. Kimmerer was born in Upstate New York to parents of both European and Native American ancestry. She earned her BS in botany at the State University of New York's College of Environmental Science and Forestry in Syracuse, and her MS and PhD at the University of Wisconsin. She has devoted her career to combining two ways of understanding the natural world—through the lens of modern science and through a broader view incorporating traditional and cultural knowledge. In 2002, she cofounded the Traditional Ecological Knowledge section of the Ecological Society of America. An expert on mosses, she has authored two award-winning books: *Gathering Moss: A Natural and Cultural History of Mosses* (2003) and *Braiding Sweetgrass: Indigenous Wisdom, Scientific Knowledge, and the Teachings of Plants* (2013). Kimmerer is director of the Center for Native Peoples and the

Environment at SUNY-ESF. See also robinwallkimmerer.com.

Martin Luther King Jr. (1929–1968)
American clergyman and civil rights leader. By the age of twenty-six, the Atlanta-born King had completed his undergraduate education, finished divinity school, and received a PhD in religion from Boston University. In 1956 King took a public stand to support Blacks boycotting segregated buses in Montgomery, Alabama, marking his entry into the struggle for equality. Soon he became a major figure in the civil rights movement, advocating nonviolent protest in the spirit of Jesus's teachings and Mahatma Gandhi's principles of passive resistance. In 1963, Birmingham, Alabama, one of the most segregated cities in the South, became the focal point for violent racial confrontations: Over 2,400 civil rights workers, King among them, were jailed, occasioning his now-famous "Letter from Birmingham Jail." In 1964, at thirty-five, he became the youngest recipient of the Nobel Peace Prize. King was assassinated on April 4, 1968, in Memphis, Tennessee. See also thekingcenter.org.

Stephen King (b. 1947)
American fiction writer. Born in Portland, Maine, King grew up fascinated with horror comics and began writing macabre tales while still a teenager. Not long after graduating with a BA in English from the University of Maine in 1970, he began writing short stories, one of which he threw away but then developed—on the advice of his wife Tabitha—into his first published novel, *Carrie* (1973). This bestselling supernatural thriller was soon followed by *Salem's Lot* (1975), *The Shining* (1977), and the serialized fantasy *The Dark Tower: The Gunslinger* (1977–81). Today King is a publishing phenomenon; upwards of sixty novels, six nonfiction books, and ten collections of short stories have sold more than 350 million copies worldwide. Even after sustaining severe injuries in a 1999 road accident, he has managed to fulfill his daily quota of 2,000 words. See also stephenking.com.

Tim Kreider (b. 1967)
American essayist and cartoonist. Kreider grew up in Baltimore, where he went to public schools before attending Johns Hopkins University's Writing Seminars program. For twelve years his satirical cartoons ran in the *Baltimore City Paper*

and other alternative weeklies; these have been collected in three volumes as *The Pain—When Will It End?* (2004), *Why Do They Kill Me?* (2005), and *Twilight of the Assholes* (2011). His cartoons and essays—about politics, books, movies, and life in general—have appeared in many periodicals, including *Men's Journal*, the *Comics Journal*, and the *New York Times*. Kreider's most recent books are collections of essays: *We Learn Nothing* (2012) and *I Wrote This Book Because I Love You* (2018). Through 2020, he wrote a regular column for the web portal *Medium*. See also timkreider.com.

J. Drew Lanham (b. 1965)
American professor, author, poet, and wildlife biologist. Lanham is a native of Edgefield and Aiken, South Carolina, and attended Clemson University for his entire career in higher education. He attained two degrees in zoology and a PhD in forest resources. He is tenured at Clemson University, holding an endowed chair as an Alumni Distinguished Professor (of wildlife). His 2017 bestseller *The Home Place: Memoirs of a Colored Man's Love Affair with Nature* also won a number of awards and was chosen as one of the eleven best scholarly books of the 2010s by the *Chronicle of Higher Education*. Lanham's CV boasts a lengthy bibliography of scholarly articles in his specialized fields of wildlife study, including ornithology and the flora and fauna of forest resources. He is also an award-winning poet. In 2022, he became a MacArthur Fellow. For more information see jdlanham.wixsite.com/blackbirder. See also clemson.edu/cafls/faculty_staff/profiles/lanhamj.

Kiese Laymon (b. 1974)
American professor, essayist, novelist, and poet. Laymon is the Libby Shearn Moody Professor of English and Creative Writing at Rice University. He has taught on the faculties of Vassar College and the University of Mississippi. His book *Long Division* won the 2022 NAACP Image Award for fiction, and the second iteration of his memoir / essay collection *How to Slowly Kill Yourself and Others in America* (originally 2013) was named a notable book in 2021 by the *New York Times*. Born and raised in Mississippi, Laymon graduated from Oberlin and holds an MFA from Indiana University, Bloomington. See also kieselaymon.com.

Abraham Lincoln (1809–1865)
American lawyer, orator, legislator, and sixteenth president of the United States. Born in Kentucky, Lincoln was largely self-made and self-taught. In 1830, his family moved to Illinois, where Lincoln prepared himself for a career in law. In 1834, he was elected to the first of four terms in the Illinois state legislature, and in 1847, to the US Congress. Elected president in 1860, Lincoln guided the Union through the Civil War while pressing for passage of the Thirteenth Amendment (1865), which outlawed slavery "everywhere and forever" in the United States. His most famous speech, the Gettysburg Address (1863), was delivered at the site of one of the Civil War's bloodiest battles. Shortly after his reelection and with the war drawing to a close, Lincoln gave his second inaugural address (1865), an eloquent appeal for reconciliation and peace. He was assassinated a little more than a month later. See also whitehouse.gov/1600/presidents/abraham-lincoln.

Audre Lorde (1934–1992)
American writer, professor, womanist, feminist, civil rights activist, and, more emphatically, by Lorde's own description, a "black, lesbian, mother, warrior, poet." She was born and raised in New York City, attending Catholic schools until she graduated Hunter High School. She published her first poem in *Seventeen* magazine while still a student there. Her career in higher education began as a student at National University of Mexico, during a self-described period of affirmation and self-renewal. She returned to New York and eventually graduated from Hunter College. She also earned an MS in library science in 1961 from Columbia University. Lorde is perceived as a pioneer and major pillar of several universal progressive movements that saw significant growth during the last half of the twentieth century, a period that coincided with the entirety of Lorde's adult life. Her contributions, particularly as a spokeswoman and activist in several dimensions, are recognized as establishing women's liberation, Black equality, and sexual and gender identity as issues of primary importance on a global basis. See also poetryfoundation.org/poets/audre-lorde.

Teresa Lust (b. 1964)
American chef, food writer, and editor. Lust grew up in Yakima, Washington, and earned a BS in biology at Washington

State University before earning her MA in liberal studies at Dartmouth College. Her first book *Pass the Polenta: And Other Writings from the Kitchen, with Recipes* (1998) is a blend of memoir, thoughts about food and its meaning in our lives, and the recipes of her Italian immigrant grandmother, for whom food was family, love, and life itself. *The Bread of Kings* (2015) traces the surprisingly rich history of *grissini*—Italian breadsticks. A professional chef and an Italian teacher, Lust is also the translator of Italian author Alessandra Lavagnino's novel *Librarians of Alexandria: A Tale of Two Sisters* (2006). In 2020, she published *A Blissful Feast: Culinary Adventures in Italy's Piedmont, Maremma, and Le Marche*, which continues her personal creative mission. See also teresalust.com.

Nancy Mairs (1943–2016)
American poet and essayist. Mairs was born in Long Beach, California, and grew up in Boston. Married at nineteen, she completed her BA at Wheaton College, had a child, and earned MFA and PhD degrees from the University of Arizona. The personal difficulties that inform her writing include a near-suicidal bout of agoraphobia and anorexia and the later discovery, at age twenty-eight, that she was afflicted with multiple sclerosis. She found salvation both in writing and in Roman Catholicism, to which she converted in her thirties. Her first book was a collection of poems, *In All the Rooms in the Yellow House* (1984). Her eight books of essays and memoirs include *Plaintext: Deciphering a Woman's Life* (1986), *Carnal Acts* (1990), *Voice Lessons: On Becoming a (Woman) Writer* (1994), *Waist-High in the World: A Life among the Nondisabled* (1996), and *A Dynamic God: Living an Unconventional Catholic Faith* (2007). See also nytimes.com/2016/12/07/books/nancy-mairs-dead-author.html.

John McWhorter (b. 1965)
American professor, linguist, writer, and cultural critic. Born and raised in Philadelphia, McWhorter attended Friends Select School and Simon's Rock College. He graduated from Rutgers University (1985) and received advanced degrees from New York University (MA) and Stanford University (PhD in linguistics). He is on the faculty at Columbia University, teaching in diverse disciplines and writing frequently on many subjects, including linguistics, American studies, philosophy, and music history. As the lin-

guistics program is housed under the Department of Slavic Languages, including a newly revived major in the subject, McWhorter is an associate professor in that department, teaching courses that include the study of Native American languages, Creole (his original field of specialization), Black English—which he views as a viable and complete language—and American Sign Language. In addition to his contributions to many national publications, both major news outlets and magazines of general interest, McWhorter is a regular opinion columnist for the *New York Times* and a contributing editor of the *Atlantic*. See also americanstudies.columbia.edu/people/john-h-mcwhorter.

John Muir (1838–1914)
American naturalist, preservationist, and writer. Muir's family emigrated from Scotland to the United States in 1849 and settled in Wisconsin; he became a naturalized US citizen in 1903. An avid student of nature, Muir studied geology and botany at the University of Wisconsin, though he left without taking a degree. As a young man, Muir traveled widely in the western United States to study its flora and fauna. He became a vocal advocate for what was then called "preservationism," cofounding the Sierra Club in 1892 to promote the protection of wilderness areas from development. Muir's efforts are largely responsible for the creation of Yosemite National Park; in 1976, the California Historical Society voted him "The Greatest Californian." His writings, which celebrate wilderness and extol the natural beauty of the American West, include such classics as *The Mountains of California* (1894) and *My First Summer in the Sierra* (1911). See also vault.sierraclub.org/john_muir_exhibit/life.

Aimee Nezhukumatathil (b. 1974)
American poet, essayist, and scholar. Born in Chicago, Illinois, to a Filipina mother and a Malayali father, Nezhukumatathil is a professor of English, teaching environmental literature and poetry writing in the MFA program at the University of Mississippi. Her poetry often explores the intersection of her multiple cultural roots combined with her American upbringing. Her poems appear in several anthologized collections of Asian American writers. She has published four collections of poetry, often added to the curricula of high school and college courses in writing and literature. Her *New York Times* best-selling book of essays

World of Wonders: In Praise of Fireflies, Whale Sharks, and Other Astonishments (2020) was a finalist for the Kirkus Prize in nonfiction and named the Barnes and Noble book of the year. In 2020, she was named a Guggenheim Fellow in poetry. See also aimeenez.net.

Ngũgĩ wa Thiong'o (b. 1938)
Kenyan novelist, playwright, and social critic. Born in what was then British East Africa, Ngũgĩ grew up amid colonialism, revolution, and the emergence of independent Kenya in 1963. His first novel, *Weep Not, Child* (1964), and his second, *A Grain of Wheat* (1967), depict the Mau Mau Uprising against the British. His 1977 play *Ngaahika Ndeenda*, written in his native Gĩkũyũ and translated by the author as *I Will Marry When I Want* (1982), was critical of the Kenyan government, resulting in Ngũgĩ's yearlong imprisonment. He has since lived in self-imposed exile in the United States and is currently a professor of comparative literature at the University of California, Irvine. His books include *Decolonizing the Mind* (1986), which argues for the use of native languages; his masterpiece *Wizard of the Crow* (2006), a novel; and *Dreams in a Time of War: A Childhood Memoir* (2010). His fiction is well regarded, and he has spent recent years writing nonfiction that recall his struggles as an artist or address the larger questions and challenges facing Africans, particularly in his native Kenya. In 2016, he published *Secure the Base: Making Africa Visible in the Globe* and a memoir, *Birth of a Dream Weaver: A Writer's Awakening*. His prison memoir *Wrestling with the Devil* (2018) is written entirely in flashback recalling his punitive year spent in Kenya's Kamiti Maximum Security Prison in 1978. His novel, written in Gĩkũyũ as an epic poem and recounting the origin myth of his people, was translated into English and published in 2020 with the title *The Perfect Nine*. In 2021, it was long listed for the International Booker Prize, the first work written in an indigenous African language to receive this recognition, making Ngũgĩ the first nominee as both author and translator of the same book. See also ngugiwathiongo.com.

Viet Thanh Nguyen (b. 1971)
American professor and author of fiction and nonfiction. Born in Vietnam, at the age of four Nguyen and his family fled the communist takeover of South Vietnam and eventually found refuge in San Jose,

California. Nguyen holds two BA degrees, in English and ethnic studies, and a PhD in English from the University of California, Berkeley. He had already distinguished himself as a professor at the University of Southern California when, in 2015, his first novel, *The Sympathizer*, was published to great acclaim, becoming a number-one bestseller and winner of the Pulitzer Prize for fiction. His follow-up, the nonfiction *Nothing Ever Dies: Vietnam and the Memory of War* (2016), was a finalist for the National Book Award. *The Refugees*, a short-story collection, appeared in 2017. Nguyen coedited *The Displaced: Refugee Writers on Refugee Lives* (2018). He is the recipient of both Guggenheim and MacArthur fellowships. His second novel *The Committed* (2021) continues the story of *The Sympathizer*. Nguyen continues to teach at the University of Southern California as University Professor, Aerol Arnold Chair of English, and professor of English and American studies and ethnicity and comparative literature. See also vietnguyen.info.

George Orwell (1903–1950)
Pen name of Eric Blair, English journalist, essayist, novelist, and social critic. Born in India and educated in England, Orwell was an officer in the Indian Imperial Police in Burma, an experience he later recounted in the novel *Burmese Days* (1934). In 1927, he went to Europe to pursue his career as a writer. His first book *Down and Out in Paris and London* (1933) depicts his years of poverty and struggle while working as a dishwasher and day laborer. Orwell's experiences fighting in the Spanish Civil War are the subject of the memoir *Homage to Catalonia* (1938). Of his seven novels, the satiric *Animal Farm* (1945) and the dystopian *Nineteen Eighty-Four* (1949), both indictments of totalitarianism, have become classics. Orwell, one of the most polished and respected stylists in the English language, published five collections of essays, including *Shooting an Elephant and Other Essays* (1950). See also george-orwell.org.

Joseph Osmundson (b. 1983)
American biophysicist and writer. Osmundson is a clinical assistant professor of biology at New York University, and he serves on the associate faculty of the Brooklyn Institute for Social Research. Writing not only on subjects of clinical and research interest, Osmundson is the author of several books that examine the subject areas of bodies, queerness, race,

and geography. Osmundson's third book *Virology* (2022) is a collection of essays that focus on the impact of viruses on society and the perspectives of the scientific community, including the continuing efforts of HIV/AIDS activism. See also as.nyu.edu/faculty/joseph-osmundson.

Ann Patchett (b. 1963)
American novelist. Born in Los Angeles, Patchett grew up from the age of six in Nashville, Tennessee, which she has made her home. She published her first work of fiction in the *Paris Review* while still an undergraduate at Sarah Lawrence College, her alma mater. Her first novel was published in 1992. She has since published several novels and has written shorter pieces for a wide assortment of general interest magazines of major stature, including the *New Yorker*, *Elle*, *GQ*, the *New York Times Magazine*, and others. Patchett's fourth novel *Bel Canto* (2001) won the PEN/Faulkner Award and was a National Book Critics Award finalist. She published a memoir, *Truth and Beauty: A Friendship* (2007), about her lifelong friendship with writer Lucy Grealy (who died in 2002 of a drug overdose). Her novel *State of Wonder* (2011) was short listed for the Orange Prize. Her first children's book was released in 2019, and her novel *The Dutch House* was a finalist for the 2020 Pulitzer Prize for fiction. The essay collection *These Precious Days* (2021) was described by Patchett as "the sequel" to *This Is the Story of a Happy Marriage* (2013), an earlier collection of essays. See also annpatchett.com.

Matt de la Peña (b. 1973)
American author of books for children and young adults. De la Peña grew up in San Diego, California, and attended the University of the Pacific on a basketball scholarship before earning an MFA from San Diego State University. His first book, the young adult novel *Ball Don't Lie* (2005), was made into a movie starring Ludacris. His next book, *Mexican White-Boy* (2008), was banned from classrooms in Tucson, Arizona, because it was alleged to contain "critical race theory"; in 2017, a court ruled that this was a violation of the constitutional rights of Mexican American students. In 2016, de la Peña's picture book *Last Stop on Market Street* (illustrated by Christian Robinson) won the Newbery Medal for the year's "most distinguished contribution to American literature for children," and the

National Council of Teachers of English honored de la Peña with its National Intellectual Freedom Award. In 2019, he was awarded an honorary doctorate by the University of the Pacific. In 2022, he published *Patchwork*, a children's book about the power of human potential. As of 2023, he is living in Southern California and teaching creative writing at San Diego State University. See also mattdelapena.com.

Leah Penniman (b. 1980)
American farmer, writer, and activist. Born in Massachusetts of African/Haitian American and Caucasian parentage, Penniman and her siblings were raised in the Worcester area. She graduated from Clark University in 2002, where she also received an MAT degree in 2003. She taught as a high school biology and environmental science teacher for seventeen years, while founding and developing Soul Fire Farm in 2010 with her husband. The farm is in Grafton, New York, near Albany, and was established with the mission of ending "racism in the food system and [to] reclaim our ancestral connection to land," recalling her own African and Creole descent. Farm-training programs are tailored specifically for Black and Brown people. She has published two books relating, in practical terms, the fruits of her experiences in farming and food distribution. *Soul Fire Farm's Practical Guide to Liberation on the Land* appeared in 2018, and *Black Earth Wisdom: Soulful Conversations with Black Environmentalists* in 2023. See also soulfirefarm.org/leah-penniman.

Imani Perry (b. 1972)
American scholar of interdisciplinary studies and author of scholarly texts and creative nonfiction. Born in Birmingham, Alabama, and raised in Cambridge, Massachusetts, Perry has degrees from Yale University (BA), Harvard University (JD and PhD), and Georgetown University Law Center (LLM). She has published seven books, each of which has won or been a finalist for a variety of awards and prizes for works of scholarship or nonfiction. Her latest book *South to America: A Journey below the Mason-Dixon to Understand the Soul of a Nation* (2022) won the National Book Award for nonfiction. Projects she has planned or is in the process of creating include an examination of African American theories of law and justice and a meditation on the color blue in Black culture. She is

the Hughes-Rogers Professor of African American Studies at Princeton University and a faculty associate with the programs in law and public affairs, gender and sexuality studies, and jazz studies. See also aas.princeton.edu/people/imani-perry.

Jillian Peterson (b. 1980)
American psychologist, criminologist, and media commentator. A St. Paul, Minnesota, native, Peterson holds a BA from Grinnell College and graduate degrees in psychology and social behavior from the University of California, Irvine. She is an associate professor of criminology and criminal justice and director of the Forensic Psychology Program at Hamline University. Prior to teaching, Peterson worked as a special investigator for the New York Capital Defenders Office, where she researched life histories of men facing the death penalty. Peterson and James Densley are the cofounders of the Violence Project, a nonprofit organization that maintains a comprehensive database of mass shootings, mass shooters, and related characteristics. They are also coauthors of the best-selling book *The Violence Project: How to Stop a Mass Shooting Epidemic* (2021). Peterson and Densley are highly sought-after experts on how to contain, reduce, and prevent the growth in mass killings. See also jillianpeterson.com.

Claudia Rankine (b. 1963)
American poet, playwright, and essayist. Born in Kingston, Jamaica, Rankine holds a BA from Williams College and an MFA from Columbia University. Her poems have been published in five collections, including *Nothing in Nature Is Private* (1994) and *Don't Let Me Be Lonely: An American Lyric* (2004). Her best-known book *Citizen: An American Lyric* (2014), combining poetry, prose, and visual images, was a finalist for the National Book Award; not only did it win the National Book Critics Circle Award for poetry, but it was the first book ever to be named a finalist in both the poetry and criticism categories. She has coedited a number of books, most recently *The Racial Imaginary: Writers on Race in the Life of the Mind* (2014). Rankine teaches poetry at Yale University. With the money she won as a MacArthur Fellow, in 2017 she established the Racial Imaginary Institute. In 2020, Rankine published *Just Us: An American Conversation*, which, like *Citizen*, combines a mélange of genres, including poetry, essays, visual content, and other literary instruments of inquiry, to examine the challenges and conflicts faced by Americans as we progress through a divisive period in history. Rankine joined the New York University Creative Writing Program as a tenured professor in the fall of 2021. See also claudiarankine.com.

Margaret Renkl (b. 1961)
American poet and writer. A native of Alabama, Renkl writes poetry and nonfiction and is a contributing opinion writer for the *New York Times*. She lives in Tennessee and is a graduate of Auburn University. During her brief stint in the PhD program at the University of Pennsylvania, she found the northern climate was not to her temperament and the emphasis on critical theory incompatible with her poetic aspirations and dropped out. She graduated from the University of South Carolina with an MFA in creative writing. Renkl taught high school English for ten years at a private school in Nashville. She then devoted her time to writing for several publications. In 2009, she became founding editor of *Chapter 16*, an online literary magazine featuring Tennessee and Tennessee-adjacent writers, from which she stepped down in 2019. She was appointed contributing opinion writer to the *New York Times* in 2021. She has focused on writing prose after fifteen years of writing poetry. Her first book of essays *Late Migrations: A Natural History of Love and Loss* (2019) was a finalist for the Southern Book Prize and won several best book awards. Her 2021 collection *Graceland, At Last: On Hope and Heartache from the American South* won the Southern Book Prize and the 2022 PEN America Award for the Art of the Essay. See also margaretrenkl.com.

Jason Reynolds (b. 1983)
American author of fiction and poetry for young adults and middle-grade audiences. Nevertheless, many of Reynolds's works resonate with readers of all ages. He was born in Washington, DC, in 1983. Inspired by rap, he published several collections of poetry before his first novel *When I Was the Greatest* (2014), which won the Coretta Scott King / John Steptoe Award for New Talent. Reynolds has published over a dozen books, including *The Boy in the Black Suit* and

All American Boys, which he coauthored with Brendan Kiely. He is also the author of the *New York Times* best-selling Track series about a group of young runners. Individual titles in this series have won national awards, and *Ghost* (2016) was a National Book Award for Young Readers finalist. In addition to his writing, Reynolds is an advocate for literacy and reading. He has served as a national ambassador for young people's literature and has spoken at numerous events and conferences about the importance of reading and storytelling. Other awards for his work include the NAACP Image Award for Outstanding Literary Work and the Michael L. Printz Award. See also jasonwritesbooks.com.

Alexandra Robbins (b. 1976)
American author, lecturer, and journalist. Robbins has published a variety of nonfiction books that focus on young adults, education, nursing, and modern college life. Five of her books have appeared on the *New York Times* bestseller list. Raised in Maryland, she attended Yale University and graduated summa cum laude in 1998. She has written for several publications of national distribution, from newspapers of record to major news and business periodicals, as well as magazines for general interest in cultural matters, like the *Atlantic* and *Vanity Fair*. She appears in the media regularly and has made appearances on hundreds of shows. See also alexandrarobbins.com.

Mike Rose (1944–2021)
American educator and author. Born to Italian immigrant parents in Altoona, Pennsylvania, Rose grew up in Los Angeles. In high school, he was wrongly placed on the "vocational track" for academic underachievers; a teacher discovered the error, and Rose went on to excel as a student, earning his BA from Loyola University and a PhD in education from the University of California, Los Angeles (UCLA), as well as two MA degrees. Rose has made a career of championing the academic potential of the poor and underprivileged. A longtime teacher, he was a professor at the UCLA Graduate School of Education and Information Studies. His books include *Lives on the Boundary* (1989), which argues that poor preparation, not lack of intelligence, hampers most underachieving students; *The Mind at Work: Valuing the Intelli-*

gence of the American Worker (2004); *Why School? Reclaiming Education for All of Us* (2009); and *Back to School: Why Everyone Deserves a Second Chance at Education* (2012). See also newyorker.com/culture/postscript/the-teacher-who-changed-how-we-teach-writing.

Scott Russell Sanders (b. 1945)
American novelist, essayist, and teacher. Born in Memphis, Tennessee, and educated at both Brown and Cambridge universities, Sanders has spent his teaching career at Indiana University at Bloomington, where he is professor of English. The author of four novels, three short-story collections, and seven children's books, he is best known for his nature writing and his personal essays. Among his many books are *Wilderness Plots: Tales about the Settlement of the American Land* (1983, 2007); *The Paradise of Bombs* (1987), a collection of essays about violence in the United States; *Staying Put: Making a Home in a Restless World* (1993); *The Force of Spirit* (2000), a collection of meditations on family and the passage of time; *A Private History of Awe* (2006), a spiritual memoir; *A Conservationist Manifesto* (2009); *Earth Works: Selected Essays* (2012); and the novels *Divine Animal* (2014) and *The Engineer of Beasts* (2019). *Small Marvels: Stories* was published in 2022. See also scottrussellsanders.com.

David Sedaris (b. 1956)
American humorist, writer, and raconteur. Born in New York and raised from childhood in Raleigh, North Carolina, Sedaris is the second oldest of six children. He attended three institutions of higher learning before getting a degree from the School of the Art Institute of Chicago in 1987. A devoted diarist since the 1970s, Sedaris engaged in an itinerant career of odd jobs in Raleigh, Chicago, and New York, including performing as a humorist in clubs, reading from his own work. Ira Glass, a radio host and producer, asked Sedaris to perform on his show *The Wild Room*. This proved to be the launch of a successful lifelong arc as an author and a raconteur of his pieces in live performance and in broadcast. Readings from his "Santaland Diaries" on NPR in 1992 got national attention. He has since published fourteen books, mainly story and essay collections and excerpts

from the initial fifteen-year course of his diaries. He has also written several plays, all produced in collaboration with his sister Amy. Sedaris was elected to the American Academy of Arts and Letters in 2019. See also davidsedarisbooks.com.

Amy Sequenzia (b. 1983)
American poet, essayist, and disability and human rights activist. Born Autistic, with epilepsy and cerebral palsy, Florida native Sequenzia grew up being labeled "low-functioning" and even "retarded." Because she does not speak, it wasn't until she learned to type that she found her voice and was able to become a fierce advocate for herself and for neurodiversity in general. "Today," she writes, "I cannot imagine being silenced again." Her poem "Being Proudly Autistic" begins: "Being proudly Autistic. / Being proudly Disabled. / Being me. / . . . / I define myself." Coeditor of *Typed Words, Loud Voices* (2015), a book about typed communication, Sequenzia currently serves on the board of directors of the Autistic Self-Advocacy Network (ASAN). See also peoplepill.com/people/amy-sequenzia.

David Shields (b. 1956)
American author and filmmaker. Born in Los Angeles, Shields holds a BA in English from Brown University and an MFA from the University of Iowa Writers' Workshop. His first two books, *Heroes* (1984) and *Dead Languages* (1989), were both more or less traditional literary novels; since then he's written another twenty books, many of them genre-blurring, "self-deconstructing nonfiction" such as *Remote: Reflections on Life in the Shadow of Celebrity* (1996), *Reality Hunger* (2010), and *How Literature Saved My Life* (2013). His most recent books are *Nobody Hates Trump More than Trump: An Intervention* (2018) and *The Trouble with Men: Reflections on Sex, Love, Marriage, Porn, and Power* (2019). Shields is also a documentary filmmaker; his latest film is *Lynch: A History* (2018), about the pro football player Marshawn Lynch. Shields teaches at the University of Washington as professor of English and Warren Wilson College. In 2022, Shields collected and transcribed every interview he had given over the previous forty years. The results were published as *The Very Last Interview*. See also davidshields.com.

Rebecca Skloot (b. 1972)
American science journalist and author. Skloot grew up in Portland, Oregon, and attended Portland Community College to become a veterinary technician; she then earned a BS in biology from Colorado State University and an MFA in creative nonfiction from the University of Pittsburgh. Her more than 200 feature articles and essays have appeared in such publications as *Discover*, *O: The Oprah Magazine*; the *New York Times Magazine*; and *Popular Science*, where she is a contributing editor. Skloot's first book *The Immortal Life of Henrietta Lacks* (2010), the story of a line of cells taken from an unwitting subject and used in revolutionary biological research, is a case study in social class, race relations, and modern science. A publishing phenomenon, the book took ten years to research and write, was a number-one *New York Times* bestseller, and has been translated into more than twenty-five languages. She has a book in progress, inspired by her experiences over more than a decade as a veterinary technician in a variety of venues for the treatment and care of animals. It examines the practices and ethics of the bond between humans and animals. See also rebeccaskloot.com.

s.e. smith
American journalist, essayist, and editor. Based in Northern California, smith writes on disability, culture, and social attitudes. Their work has appeared in publications such as the *Washington Post*, *Time*, the *Guardian*, *Rolling Stone*, *Esquire*, and *Vice*, in addition to several anthologies, most recently *Body Language* (2022). They received a National Magazine Award in 2020 for their work in *Catapult*. See also realsesmith.com.

Rebecca Solnit (b. 1961)
American essayist and author. Born in Bridgeport, Connecticut, Solnit grew up in Novato, California, and received all of her formal education in California public schools, even through college—San Francisco State University—and graduate school—the University of California, Berkeley, where she earned an MA in journalism. She has combined activism in an array of environmental and human rights causes with writing that has appeared in many periodicals, most notably *Harper's Magazine*, where she is a regular columnist, and in twenty-three books. *A Paradise Built in Hell: The Extraordinary Communities That Arise in Disaster* (2009) explores people's resilience in the face of catastrophe. *Savage Dreams* (2014) argues that the suppres-

sion of American Indians has never stopped. The essays in her collections *Men Explain Things to Me* (2014) and *The Mother of All Questions* (2017) provide a feminist take on intergender communication. The six titles published between 2019 and 2022 explore a broad array of issues and themes via the diverse genres Solnit has mastered throughout her career. She continues her activism by contributing critical opinions to major media outlets online and in print. See also rebeccasolnit.net.

Kory Stamper (b. 1975)
American lexicographer and author. Stamper grew up in Colorado, but it was at Smith College that she found her calling—languages. A course on medieval Icelandic family sagas led her to a study of Latin, Greek, Norse, Old English, and Middle English. For twenty years she worked as a lexicographer for Merriam-Webster where, in addition to her editorial duties, she also presented "Ask the Editor" videos that discuss words and the way they're used. Since 2018, she has served as executive director of the Dictionary Society of North America. Stamper keeps up a blog, *Harmless Drudgery: Defining the Words that Define Us*, and she provides commentary on language for the *Chicago Tribune*. She is acclaimed as the author of *Word by Word: The Secret Life of Dictionaries* (2017) and is at work on a book about the words we use for colors. In 2021, she appeared in every episode of a six-part series on *Netflix* titled *History of Swear Words*, wherein Stamper gamely upheld her expert status commenting on the linguistic histories of obscene terms. See also korystamper.wordpress.com.

Elizabeth Cady Stanton (1815–1902)
American abolitionist and women's rights activist. Born in Johnstown, New York, Stanton excelled academically at Johnstown Academy but, because of her sex, was barred from nearby Union College. She married the prominent abolitionist Henry B. Stanton, and the two spent their honeymoon at the World's Anti-Slavery Convention in London. In 1848, Stanton joined Lucretia Mott and others to organize the first American convention for women's rights, held in Seneca Falls, New York, where Stanton presented her draft of the "Declaration of Sentiments and Resolutions," now seen as a founding document of modern feminism. Three years later she was introduced to Susan B.

Anthony, who became her lifelong friend and colleague; together they founded the National Woman Suffrage Association in 1869. Stanton spent the rest of her life campaigning for women's suffrage and legislation that would make divorce laws more favorable to women. See also nps .gov; search for "Stanton."

Sandra Steingraber (b. 1959)
American activist, biologist, author, and cancer survivor. Steingraber was raised from infancy by adoptive parents, spending most of her childhood in Tazewell County, Illinois. She had a significant lifelong interest in sustainable development and organic agriculture instilled in her from childhood by her parents, who were heavily influenced by the philosophy and outlook of naturalist writer Rachel Carson. Steingraber herself became a devotee of Carson's work while engaged in her research in the late 1990s. Steingraber entered college and while studying was diagnosed with bladder cancer, the treatment for which was disruptive. Finally, in remission, she finished her degree in biology from Illinois Wesleyan University—the beginning of a career-long advocacy on the impact of environmental factors on reproductive health. She subsequently received a PhD in biology from the University of Michigan, as well as an MA in English from Illinois State University. Her book *Living Downstream* (1997) recounts the relationship between the environment and the incidence and etiology of cancer, using narratives of industrial and agricultural pollution, buttressed by scientific and medical data. In addition to being a distinguished visiting scholar at Ithaca College, she is an ongoing activist, with a particular focus on the negative effects of fracking and, more generally, the impact of various forms of chemical pollution on the incidence of breast cancers. As an activist she has been arrested several times and, rather than pay fines, served brief stints in jail as further protest and provocation. She has published several books on the foregoing subjects, in addition to *Living Downstream*, and has won many awards and other accolades to recognize her energetic advocacy. See also steingraber.com.

Cheryl Strayed (b. 1968)
American writer and podcaster. Strayed graduated magna cum laude in 1991, with a BA in English and women's

studies. While she was still a senior, her mother, at age forty-five, died suddenly of cancer. This marked the onset of a long-lived grief, which she calls her "genesis story." A tailspin culminated for a while in heroin addiction. She has written about her mother's death and her own grief in several books. In 2002, she received an MFA in fiction writing from Syracuse University. Strayed has published books of both fiction and non-fiction. Her book *Wild*, an account of the story surrounding her hike the length of the 1,100-mile Pacific Coast Trail in 1995, appeared in 2012 and subsequently topped the *New York Times* bestseller list for seven weeks. It was also selected as the first book on Oprah's Book Club 2.0. Separately, Strayed has had significant recognition as an essay writer, with three pieces selected for individual editions of *Best American Essays* in 2000, 2003, and 2015. She won the Pushcart Prize for an essay based on receiving a letter from Alice Munro when Strayed was still a young writer. Starting in 2010, she wrote an advice column, "Dear Sugar," for the website *The Rumpus*. This column eventually led to spin-off productions, including a popular podcast series for the *New York Times*. Strayed's book *Tiny Beautiful Things*, also based on the "Dear Sugar" advice column, was a bestseller. The book was adapted for the stage and appeared twice at the Public Theater in New York and is successfully being produced in several other American cities. See also cherylstrayed.com.

Jonathan Swift (1667–1745)
Anglo-Irish poet, satirist, and cleric. Born to English parents who resided in Ireland, Swift studied at Trinity College, Dublin, and then moved to London in 1689. There he became part of the literary and political worlds, beginning his career by writing political pamphlets in support first of the Whigs, then the Tories. Swift earned an MA at Oxford University before returning to Ireland. Ordained in the Church of Ireland in 1695, he was appointed dean of St. Patrick's Cathedral, Dublin, in 1713 and held the post until his death. One of the master satirists of the English language, he wrote several scathing attacks on extremism and anti-Irish bigotry, including *The Battle of the Books* (1704), *A Tale of a Tub* (1704), and *A Modest Proposal* (1729), but he is probably best known for the imaginative worlds he cre-

ated in *Gulliver's Travels* (1726). See also poetryfoundation.org/poets/jonathan-swift.

Nicholas Tampio (b. 1973)
American professor of political science and author. After growing up in the Washington, DC, area, Tampio earned his BA at New College of Florida, his MA at Indiana University, and his PhD at Johns Hopkins University; since then his career has been devoted to research in the history of political thought, contemporary political theory, and education policy. His first book *Kantian Courage* (2012) explores the continuing influence of eighteenth-century philosopher Immanuel Kant on political thinking. His second book *Deleuze's Political Vision* (2015) is a reconsideration of the political theories of French philosopher Gilles Deleuze. Two of Tampio's three most recent books, *Common Core: National Education Standards and the Threat to Democracy* (2018) and *Learning versus the Common Core* (2019), argue against the "common core" standards that dominate much of American educational policy today. His most recent book *Teaching Political Theory: A Pluralistic Approach* (2022) expands on these arguments. Since 2008, Tampio has taught political theory at Fordham University, where he is a professor of political science. See also faculty.fordham.edu/tampio.

Henry David Thoreau (1817–1862)
American philosopher, essayist, naturalist, and poet. A graduate of Harvard University, Thoreau worked at a number of jobs—schoolmaster, house painter, employee in his father's pencil factory—before becoming a writer. He befriended Emerson and joined the Transcendental Club, contributing frequently to its journal, the *Dial*. Drawn to the natural world, he wrote his first book *A Week on the Concord and Merrimack Rivers* (1849) about a canoe trip with his brother. Thoreau's abolitionist stance against slavery led to his arrest for refusing to pay the Massachusetts poll tax (an act of protest against the Mexican War, which he viewed as serving the interests of slaveholders). His essay defending this act, "Civil Disobedience" (1849), his book on the solitary life, *Walden* (1854), and his speech "A Plea for Captain John Brown" (1859) are classics of American literature. See also thoreausociety.org.

Greta Thunberg (b. 2003)

Swedish environmental activist. Thunberg is a globally recognized leader and commentator for her generation, calling for universal and immediate climate change mitigation. She first came to the attention of the news media for appearing regularly outside the Swedish national parliament in public protests and calling for a "school strike for climate." Notice was taken of her youth, age fifteen at the time, and her singularly open and blunt speaking manner. Thunberg's concept of universal school strikes was inspired by American public-school students refusing to return to class after a cluster of school shootings in February 2018. The teenage activists who organized protests to support gun control provided Thunberg with motivation to initiate her own movement. After her first day as a solitary striker, Thunberg was joined by others, and then the demonstrations grew to spread internationally. From this first appearance in the public eye, Thunberg has demonstrated her fearlessness and willingness to confront the highest ranks of power with her universal concern. The watershed moment in her growing influence was an invitation to speak to the plenary session of the United Nations Climate Action Summit in New York City in 2019. While speaking she famously admonished all those assembled, "How dare you?," a phrase and sentiment that became a watchcry for the movement and was later set to music. Even though Thunberg was impeded for nearly two years in logistical terms because of the imposition of lockdown protocols due to the COVID-19 pandemic, the influence of Thunberg's calls to action has grown. Her own activities have also continued, including the publication of her speeches and interviews, as well as her book *Our House Is on Fire*, coauthored with the members of her family. See also thegretathunbergfoundation.org.

Jia Tolentino (b. 1988)

American writer and editor. Born in Toronto, Ontario, to Filipino parents, Tolentino moved to Houston, Texas, with her family when she was six. Tolentino entered high school early and graduated as class salutatorian. She entered the University of Virginia in 2005 and graduated in 2009 with a BA. She serves as a staff writer for the *New Yorker*. Previously she was a deputy editor of *Jezebel* and then a contributing editor of *Hairpin*. She also wrote occasionally for the *New York Times Magazine* and *Pitchfork*. Her book of essays *Trick Mirror* was published in 2019. Its critical and commercial success (published in at least a dozen languages) includes being named a best book of the year by the *New York Times* and the New York Public Library. Like much of her work in periodicals and online, her book consists of essays of social and cultural critique. She combines this emphasis with personal insights, especially in terms of how her life is affected by ongoing phenomena and news events. She received a National Magazine Award in 2023. See also jia.blog.

Heather McTeer Toney (b. 1975)

American environmental activist, speaker, attorney, and author. Born and raised in Greenville, Mississippi, Toney is the daughter of a civil rights attorney and a public-school teacher. She was elected as Greenville's first Black and first woman mayor, serving two terms from 2004 to 2012. When she took office at age twenty-seven, she was the youngest mayor in the history of the city. After her second term she was appointed by President Obama in 2014 to serve as regional administrator for the Environmental Protection Agency's (EPA) Southeast Region, headquartered in Atlanta, Georgia. Toney has a BA in sociology from Spelman College in Atlanta and earned a JD from the Tulane University School of Law. After her tenure as an EPA administrator, Toney has served as an environmental justice organizer. See also heathermcteertoney.com/about.

Sojourner Truth (c. 1797–1883)

American abolitionist and women's rights activist. Born into slavery as Isabella Baumfree in New York, Truth escaped to freedom with her infant daughter in 1826, just a year before slavery was abolished in New York State, and then won a court battle to free one of her sons—the first such legal victory of a Black woman over a white man. In 1843, declaring that "the Spirit calls me, and I must go," she adopted the name Sojourner Truth and became an itinerant preacher, condemning the institution of slavery. The famed abolitionist William Lloyd Garrison encouraged her to dictate her memoirs, which he then published as *The Narrative of Sojourner Truth: A Northern Slave* in 1850. A year later, while attending the Women's Rights Convention in Akron, Ohio, she extemporaneously delivered the speech that became known as "Ain't I a Woman?" See also sojournertruth.org.

Anna Lowenhaupt Tsing (b. 1952)
American anthropologist, academic, and scholar. Tsing is on the faculty of anthropology at the University of California, Santa Cruz. She has also held appointments at the University of Colorado and the University of Massachusetts. Tsing is the author of over forty articles in prominent scholarly journals. Among other accolades, she has won the Henry J. Benda Prize for her book *In the Realm of the Diamond Queen* (1994) and the Senior Book Award for *Friction: An Ethnography of Global Connection* (2005). Tsing's other awards include the 2016 Gregory Bateson Prize of the Society for Cultural Anthropology and the 2016 Victor Turner Prize of the Society for Humanistic Anthropology. She has coauthored works with Nils Bubandt, including *Arts of Living on a Damaged Planet* (2017), which explores the ways in which different cultures understand and respond to environmental change in the modern era. Her book *The Mushroom at the End of the World. On the Possibility of Life in Capitalist Ruins* (2021), which examines "the relation between capitalist destruction and collaborative survival within multispecies landscapes," has received significant critical attention. See also gf.org/fellows/anna-lowenhaupt-tsing.

Sherry Turkle (b. 1948)
American sociologist and author. Turkle grew up in Brooklyn and earned her BA degree at Radcliffe College; she received her MA as well as a joint PhD degree in sociology and personal psychology at Harvard University. Much of her work has centered on the relationship between people and technology. Her nine books include *The Second Self: Computers and the Human Spirit* (1984) and *Life on the Screen: Identity in the Age of the Internet* (1995); both explore the transformative effect of computers on our lives today. *Alone Together: Why We Expect More from Technology and Less from Each Other* (2011) and *Reclaiming Conversation: The Power of Talk in a Digital Age* (2015) are cautionary examinations of what is lost when we communicate through digital intermediaries. She published *The Empathy Diaries: A Memoir* in 2019. Turkle is a licensed clinical psychologist; she teaches as the Abby Mauzé Rockefeller Professor of the Social Studies of Science and Technology at the Massa-chusetts Institute of Technology. See also sherryturkle.mit.edu.

Jose Antonio Vargas (b. 1981)
American journalist, filmmaker, and author. Born in the Philippines, as a twelve-year-old Vargas was sent to live with his grandparents in California, where he learned English, excelled in school, and then, at age sixteen, discovered that his identity documents were false—he was "illegal." His life since then has had two phases. While living in the shadows he graduated from San Francisco State University and established himself as a journalist, even winning a Pulitzer Prize for breaking news reporting as a member of a *Washington Post* team. Then, in 2011, he published his life story in the *New York Times Magazine*. Since then he has become the public face of the undocumented in America, founding the advocacy organization Define American for those who "just don't have the right papers." He has told his story in the 2013 film *Documented* and in his memoir *Dear America: Notes of an Undocumented Citizen* (2018). His second book *White Is Not a Country* is forthcoming. See also joseantoniovargas.com.

Frans de Waal (b. 1948)
Dutch American primatologist and ethologist. De Waal is the Charles Howard Candler Professor Emeritus of Primate Behavior and former director of the Living Links Center at Emory University. He is a member of the United States National Academy of Sciences and the Royal Netherlands Academy of Arts and Sciences. De Waal is known for his academic findings and major scholarly texts, in addition to being a best-selling author in lay book markets, including the *New York Times* bestseller list. *Mama's Last Hug* was adapted by HBO into a popular video. His book *Difference* (2022) addresses questions of gender in terms of biology and behavior in primates, including humans. He retired in 2019, though he continues to write. See also fransdewaal.com.

Rafael Walker (b. 1984)
American professor, scholar, and essayist. Walker attended Washington University in Saint Louis and received his AB degree in English. He attended the University of Pennsylvania as a graduate student in English and received an MA

and PhD in 2013. He specializes in several fields, including nineteenth- and twentieth-century American literature, African American and ethnic American literature, African American cultural studies, gender and sexuality studies, modernism and modernity, and transatlantic studies. He has published scholarly studies extensively in these areas. Walker has regularly contributed opinion pieces on issues in academia and pedagogy related to the impact of racism and inequities in society at large. He maintains an active presence in academic social media. Forthcoming are two works: one a monograph tentatively titled "Realism after Liberalism: Women, Desire, and the Modern American Novel" and the other on biracialism in American literature and culture. See also english.upenn.edu/people/rafael-walker.

Taté Walker (b. 1983)
Two Spirit storyteller and Indigenous rights activist. A citizen of the Cheyenne River Sioux Tribe of South Dakota, Walker is Mniconjou Lakota and an award-winning writer, photographer, and videographer for outlets like *Native Peoples* magazine, *Everyday Feminism*, *Indian Country Today*, and more. Their work can also be found in *FIERCE: Essays by and about Dauntless Women* (2018); their first book *Thunder Thighs & Trickster Vibes* appeared in the fall of 2020. Walker uses their fifteen years of experience working for news media, social justice organizations, and tribal education systems to organize students and professionals around issues of critical cultural competency, anti-racism/anti-bias, and inclusive community building. Their book *The Trickster Riots: An Illustrated Poetry Book* was published in 2022, with illustrations by their child Ohíya Walker. See also jtatewalker.com.

Esmé Weijun Wang (b. 1983)
American novelist and essayist. Wang was born in Michigan to Taiwanese immigrant parents. She attended Yale University, then transferred to Stanford University, from which she graduated with a BA in 2006. She has an MFA in fiction writing from the University of Michigan. In her first novel *The Border of Paradise* (2016), Wang explores the themes of mental illness, family, and migration. She was named in 2017 one of the best young American novelists by *Granta* magazine in a decen-

nial compilation. In 2018, she won the Whiting Award. In 2013, she was diagnosed with schizoaffective disorder, and in 2015 with late-stage Lyme disease. While waiting for her book to come to market, she began writing about her afflictions in the form of essays. With a degree in writing fiction and one novel to her credit, Wang "had never planned to write a nonfiction book," yet her collection of essays *The Collected Schizophrenias* was published in 2019 and won her publisher's Greywolf Prize for nonfiction. She continues to write short works, both essays and fiction, and operates an online writing school, which features live workshops and seminars in which she participates. See also esmewang.com.

Elissa Washuta (b. 1985)
American author. Washuta is a member of the Cowlitz Indian Tribe of Washington State and a nonfiction writer. Her parents met while in college in the Seattle area and subsequently moved to New Jersey, where Washuta graduated from high school (Hackettstown, New Jersey) in 2003. She holds a BA degree in English from the University of Maryland (2007). Her MFA from the University of Washington (2009) is in fiction writing. She has taught at the Ohio State University in the Department of English since 2017 and is an associate professor of creative writing. She has published four books, all nonfiction, including, in 2021, *White Magic*, which was a finalist for the PEN / Open Book Award and was named a best book of 2021 by *Time*, NPR, and the New York Public Library. Her published work largely surveys the subjugation and inequitable treatment of the Native American peoples, both historically and to the present day. Washuta relates stories about her own upbringing and trials as a result of misdiagnosed mental and emotional difficulties and, in particular, her relationship with food and consumption, manifested as body dysmorphia and eating disorders. Her young adulthood is the subject of two memoirs, *My Body Is a Book of Rules* (2014) and *Starvation Mode* (2015). She continues to write essays that appear in many publications. See also english.osu.edu/people/washuta.2.

Ellen Wayland-Smith (b. 1966)
American professor, scholar, and writer. Descended in part from John Humphrey Noyes, the founder of the experimental

nineteenth-century utopian community of Oneida, in Upstate New York, Wayland-Smith spent holidays and summers during her childhood on the ancestral estate. She eventually wrote about the history of the family and its philosophically radical forebear Noyes. She attended Amherst College (BA, 1989) and Princeton University, for comparative literature (MA, 1994; PhD, 1999). She is an associate professor of writing at the University of Southern California. Her book *Oneida: From Free Love Utopia to the Well-Set Table* was published in 2016. Another history with significant biographical dimensions, *The Angel in the Marketplace: Adwoman Jean Wade Rindlaub and the Selling of America* was published in 2020 by the University of Chicago Press. She has also published essays, which appear in such publications as *Guernica*, *Catapult*, the *New Republic*, and the *Los Angeles Review of Books*. She lives in Los Angeles with her family. See also ellenwaylandsmith.com.

Tara Westover (b. 1986)
American historian and memoirist. Born the youngest of seven children in a fundamentalist Mormon family in Clifton, Idaho, Westover was homeschooled by her survivalist family and was seventeen years old the first time she entered a formal classroom. She soon realized the deficits in her knowledge of the world and determined to teach herself enough about grammar and mathematics to get into college. Ten years later, after graduating magna cum laude from Brigham Young University, earning an MA as a scholarship student at Cambridge University, and spending a year as a teaching fellow at Harvard University, she received a PhD in history from Cambridge. Her remarkable memoir *Educated* created an immediate sensation when it was published in 2018, becoming a number-one *New York Times* bestseller. Writing in *Time*, Bill Gates included her in a list of the one hundred most influential people of 2019. See also tarawestover.com.

E. B. White (1899–1985)
American poet, journalist, editor, and essayist. Elwyn Brooks White was born in Mount Vernon, New York. Just three years after graduating from Cornell University in 1921, he began a sixty-year career on the staff of the *New Yorker*, contributing poems and articles and serving as a discreet and helpful editor. Among his many books, three written

for children earned him lasting fame: *Stuart Little* (1945), *Charlotte's Web* (1952), and *The Trumpet of the Swan* (1970). Renowned for his graceful prose, White revised and edited William Strunk's text *The Elements of Style* (1919, 1959), a classic guide to writing still widely known as "Strunk and White." The collection *Essays of E. B. White* was published in 1977; a year later White was awarded a Pulitzer Prize for a lifetime of literary achievement. See also britannica.com/biography/E-B-White.

Colson Whitehead (b. 1969)
American novelist. Born in New York City, Whitehead grew up as a dedicated bookworm in Manhattan before earning his BA in English at Harvard University. He began his career writing movie and record reviews for the *Village Voice*. *The Intuitionist* (1999), his first novel, was a critical and commercial success and was soon followed by his second, *John Henry Days* (2001), about the "steel-drivin' man" of folklore. The five novels he has written since then include *The Underground Railroad* (2016), winner of both the National Book Award and the Pulitzer Prize for fiction, and *Nickel Boys* (2019), about a hellish "reform school" in Florida. *The Colossus of New York* (2003) is a collection of essays; *The Noble Hustle* (2014) is an account of the 2011 World Series of Poker. In 2002, Whitehead was awarded a MacArthur Fellowship. Whitehead began his Harlem Trilogy with the release of *Harlem Shuffle* in the fall of 2021. The second book, entitled *Crook Manifesto*, is scheduled for publication in 2023. Whitehead's *The Underground Railroad* was adapted as a major streaming miniseries, directed by Academy Award winner Barry Jenkins, and released to critical acclaim in 2021. See also colsonwhitehead.com.

Chris Wiewiora (b. 1987)
American writer. Born in Buckhannon, West Virginia, Wiewiora grew up first in Warsaw, Poland, where his parents were missionaries, and then in Orlando, Florida. He earned his BA in English with honors at the University of Central Florida, where he served as an editor at the *Florida Review*. His essay "The Gift of Nothing" led to his acceptance into Iowa State University's Creative Writing and Environment Program, where he was managing editor of *Flyway*; the essay, first published in *Stymie*, has since been cited as "Notable" in *Best American Sports*

Writing (2012). Wiewiora has held a variety of jobs; his stint as a pizza maker led to his essay "This Is Tossing," which was published in the literary magazine *MAKE* as well as the anthology *Best Food Writing* (2013). Many of his essays have appeared on *The Good Men Project*, an online review. Wiewiora's website features an astonishing list of the books he reads—nearly a hundred each year. His chapbook *The Distance Is More Than an Ocean: A Travelogue Memoir* (2020) is an account of his return as a child to the United States from Poland and a subsequent visit as an adult to Poland, no longer behind the Iron Curtain. See also chriswiewiora.com.

Florence Williams (b. 1967)
American journalist and author. Williams grew up in New York City, spending her summers camping in the West and Canada. "From an early age," she recalls, "I learned that forests and rivers and big landscapes provided fun and excitement, as well as peace and reflection." She graduated from both Yale University and the University of Montana, where she earned an MFA degree. Always an avid outdoorswoman, she has been a staff writer for *High Country News* and is presently a contributing editor for *Outside* magazine; her feature journalism has also appeared in *National Geographic*, *Slate*, *Mother Jones*, *Bicycling*, and the *New York Times Magazine*. Her first book *Breasts: A Natural and Unnatural History* (2012) won the *Los Angeles Times* Book Prize in science and technology. In 2017, Williams published *The Nature Fix: Why Nature Makes Us Happier, Healthier, and More Creative* Her memoir *Heartbreak: A Personal and Scientific Journey* (2022) records the devastating impact on her physical and mental well-being after a sudden request from her husband for divorce after twenty-five years of marriage. See also florencewilliams.com.

Terry Tempest Williams (b. 1955)
American poet, nature writer, and environmental activist. Born to a Mormon family in Corona, California, Williams grew up surrounded by the vast desert landscape of Utah; she holds a BA in English and an MA in environmental education from the University of Utah. Her book *Pieces of White Shell: A Journey to Navajoland* (1984) is a personal exploration of Native American myths; her much-reprinted essay "The Clan of One-Breasted Women" became the final section of the autobiographical *Refuge: An Unnatural History of Family and Place* (1991). Her subsequent books include *Red: Passion and Patience in the Desert* (2001), *The Open Space of Democracy* (2004), *When Women Were Birds* (2012), and *The Hour of Land: A Personal Topography of America's National Parks* (2016). Since then Williams has published a collection of essays on the subject that gives the book its title, *Erosion: Essays of Undoing* (2019), and *The Moon Is Behind Us* (2021), for which she provides the text to accompany photos by Fazal Sheikh. Williams is a frequent contributor to publications such as the *New York Times*, the *New Yorker*, and *Orion*. She is a columnist at the *Progressive*. See also coyoteclan.com.

Emily Wilson (b. 1971)
English classicist, writer, and translator. Born and raised in Oxford, England, Wilson attended Oxford University, where her mother, who came from a long line of academics, taught English literature. Wilson received two degrees, a BA in classics and an MPhil in English literature (1500–1660). She has a PhD from Yale University in classics and comparative literature. She is a professor of classical studies and chair of the Program in Comparative Literature and Literary Theory at the University of Pennsylvania. Her three books derive from studies of classical authors—the first text, though, is more of an overview of the motifs of tragedy in works from Sophocles to Milton. She has also published many chapters and articles on the reception of classical literature in English literature. Wilson is the classics editor of *The Norton Anthology of World Literature* and *The Norton Anthology of Western Literature*. The stature of her scholarly efforts is buttressed by the publication, in 2017, of her translation in verse of Homer's *Odyssey*. Her version is the first published form of the epic in English translated by a woman. Wilson lives in Philadelphia with her family. See also english.upenn.edu/people/emily-wilson.

Virginia Woolf (1882–1941)
English writer. Woolf was born and raised, including homeschooling from an early age, in London. She attended the Ladies' Department of King's College London from 1897 to1902, studying classics and history. It was also while at King's College that she was introduced to early reformers of women's higher

education and proponents of the women's rights movement. In 1900, she began her career as a professional writer. She formed the literary and artistic Bloomsbury Group, named for the district of London to which her family had moved in 1904. She married Leonard Woolf, a political theorist, author, and publisher, in 1912. In 1917, she and her husband formed the Hogarth Press, which became the publisher of much of her work. They lived in Sussex, moving there permanently in 1940, after renting a home there for many years. Writing in many forms, Woolf has become best known for her novels, especially *Mrs. Dalloway*, *To the Lighthouse*, and *Orlando*. The novels comprise a long experiment in stylistic variation that in the aggregate are considered a milestone in the definition of the modernist sensibility in writing. More generally, their collective interior and intuitive, random approach to narrative, one aspect of which is labeled "stream of consciousness," went far in shaping the course of the genre in the hands of subsequent writers through the twentieth and twenty-first centuries.

Sungjoo Yoon (b. 2005)
American writer, debater, and athlete. A first-generation Korean American, Yoon emigrated to this country with his family. On arrival in the United States, he knew not a word of English. Yoon is a senior and a varsity athlete, as well as a champion debater, at Burbank High School. As chair of the Burbank Youth Board, he is the youngest person to serve on the Burbank City Commission. He is a member of the 2022–23 USA Debate Team of the National Speech and Debate Association. He is a speechwriter for US Congressman Brad Sherman and the editor in chief of the Burbank High newspaper. He enters Stanford University as a member of the class of 2027. Yoon's opinions and work focusing on classroom rights and youth politics have been featured in the *New York Times*, ABC News, the *Chicago Tribune*, Fox News, *Newsweek*, the National Coalition against Censorship, the *Los Angeles Times*, and more.

Malala Yousafzai (b. 1997)
Pakistani women's and children's education rights activist and the 2014 Nobel Peace laureate. Yousafzai was born and raised in Swat, a district of Pakistan with a significant Pashtun (ethnic Irani-Afghani) population, considered out-

casts by the Pakistani Taliban, which has long subjugated the native residents with terrorist and repressive actions. Starting at age eleven, when she pseudonymously posted a blog for BBS Urdu describing life in Swat under Taliban occupation, Yousafzai has been fearlessly outspoken in her criticism and activist views, especially on behalf of women's education. She was targeted for her activities, and in October 2012 a Taliban assassin fired a gun point-blank at her head. Rendered comatose, she was in critical condition for some time but improved while being treated at a national military hospital in the Punjab region, later being transferred to facilities in England for more advanced care. Her ordeal and subsequent recovery elicited worldwide attention and recognition, culminating in Yousafzai's appointment as corecipient of the Nobel Peace Prize with Kailish Satyarthi of India. She thereby, at age seventeen, became the youngest recipient of this award in history. She continues her work, having cofounded the Malala Fund, a nonprofit organization that advocates for girls' education. See also malala.org.

Michelle Zauner (b. 1989)
Korean American musician and author. Born in South Korea to a Korean mother and a Jewish American father and raised in Eugene, Oregon, Zauner is well known as lead vocalist of her band Japanese Breakfast. She went to Bryn Mawr College and graduated in 2011. She then formed a Philadelphia-based emo band, Little Big League, with three other musicians, one of whom she had met as a student at Bryn Mawr when she also recorded some of her first musical output. While still a member of Little Big League, Zauner began to release music in 2013 under the name Japanese Breakfast, an identity and brand she retains. She left Little Big League in 2014 after the release of their second album to care for her cancer-stricken mother in Eugene. In 2016, after her mother's death, she released the debut album of Japanese Breakfast, *Psychopomp*. Although she is best known as a musician and vocalist, her essay writing has appeared in *Glamour*, the *New Yorker*, and *Harper's Bazaar*. Her first book *Crying in H Mart: A Memoir* was published in 2021 and received significant critical approbation, in addition to landing on the *New York Times* bestseller list. See also michellezauner.com.

William Zinsser (1922–2015)

American journalist, writer, editor, and educator. Born in New York City, Zinsser graduated from Princeton University and then served in the army for two years at the end of World War II. In 1946, he joined the staff of the *New York Herald Tribune*, eventually becoming an editorial writer. A freelancer throughout the 1960s, Zinsser contributed to periodicals such as *Life*, *Look*, and the *New York Times Magazine*. In the 1970s, he joined the English faculty at Yale University, where he taught nonfiction writing and edited the alumni magazine. Zinsser's nineteen books range in subject from travel to jazz to baseball, but he is best known for *On Writing Well* (1976, 1998), a classic guide to clear, economical nonfiction writing, as well as the memoir *Writing Places: The Life Journey of a Writer and Teacher* (2009). His award-winning columns from the *American Scholar* have been collected in *The Writer Who Stayed* (2012). See also williamzinsserwriter.com.

CREDITS

PHOTOS:

Page 7: Artwork by Andrea Mongia; p. 31: Illustration by Ben Giles, frame and queen by 20th Century Fox Film Corporation / Everett Collection; p. 46: Photo courtesy of Sandra Steingraber with permission for painting by artist, Robert Shetterly; p. 93: US National Archives (NAID: 182778372); p. 98: Go Nakamura / Stringer / Getty Images; p. 117: Taté Walker, Mniconjou Lakota; p. 118: Taté Walker, Mniconjou Lakota; p. 119: Taté Walker, Mniconjou Lakota; p. 120: Taté Walker, Mniconjou Lakota; p. 121: Taté Walker, Mniconjou Lakota; p. 150: CPA Media Pte Ltd / Alamy Stock Photo; p. 156: REUTERS / Alamy Stock Photo; pp. 226–27: Copyright © Deborah Luster; courtesy of the artist and Jack Shainman Gallery, New York; p. 229: jackie sumell; p. 386: Gemma Winston / iStock / Getty Images; p. 405: REUTERS / Alamy Stock Photo; p. 431: Illustrissimo; p. 436: StanelyFormanPhotos.com, Pulitzer Prize 1976; p. 437: StanelyFormanPhotos.com, Pulitzer Prize 1976; p. 438: StanelyFormanPhotos.com, Pulitzer Prize 1976; p. 441: Eleanor Davis; p. 462: Dmitry Orlov / Alamy Stock Photo; p. 497: Pictorial Press Ltd / Alamy Stock Photo; p. 518: Photos by Mike Rose; courtesy of Foundation for the Los Angeles Community Colleges; p. 521: Photos by Mike Rose; courtesy of Foundation for the Los Angeles Community Colleges; p. 536: bpk Bildagentur / Städel Museum / Art Resource, NY; p. 554: Allie Sullberg; p. 574: Matt Eich Photography; p. 575: Matt Eich Photography; p. 607: Public domain; p. 624: Waterframe / Alamy Stock Photo; p. 662: Firefly illustration by Fumi Mini Nakamura; reprinted with the permission of The Permissions Company, LLC on behalf of Milkweed Editions, milkweed.org; p. 672: PA Images / Alamy Stock Photo; p. 693: American Photo Archive / Alamy Stock Photo; p. 716 (left): Copyright © Paolo Pellegrin / Magnum Photos; p. 716 (center): Copyright © Alex Majoli / Magnum Photos; p. 716 (right): Copyright © Alex Majoli / Magnum Photos; p. 738: Archive PL / Alamy Stock Photo; p. 775: GRANGER.

CHRONOLOGICAL INDEX

GENRES INDEX

Evaluation and Review

Graphic Memoir

Humor and Satire

Literacy Narratives

NATURE WRITING

OP-EDS

Profile of a Person

Profile of a Place

Proposals

Reportage

RHETORICAL MODES INDEX

Cause/Effect Analysis

Classifying and Dividing

Comparison and Contrast

Definition

DESCRIPTION

EVALUATION

EXEMPLIFICATION

EXPLAINING A PROCESS

NARRATION

Thematic Index

HEALTH AND MEDICINE

HISTORY

HUMAN NATURE

LANGUAGE AND COMMUNICATION

LAW AND JUSTICE

Life and Death

Literature and the Arts

MEDIA

MENTAL HEALTH

NATURE AND THE ENVIRONMENT

PEOPLE AND PLACES

POLITICS

POP CULTURE

RACE AND ETHNICITY

Religion and Spirituality

Self and Society

INDEX

ABOUT THE AUTHORS

Melissa A. Goldthwaite (PhD, The Ohio State University), General Editor, is professor of English at Saint Joseph's University, where she teaches composition, creative writing, and rhetorical theory. She has edited, coedited, or coauthored many books, including *Good Eats: 32 Writers on Eating Ethically* (New York University Press, 2024); *Food, Feminisms, Rhetorics* (Southern Illinois University Press, 2017); *Books That Cook: The Making of a Literary Meal* (New York University Press, 2014); *The Norton Pocketbook of Writing by Students* (2010); *Surveying the Literary Landscapes of Terry Tempest Williams* (University of Utah Press, 2003); and *The St. Martin's Guide to Teaching Writing* (2003, 2008, 2014).

Joseph Bizup (PhD, Indiana University) is associate professor of English at Boston University. He previously served as director of Boston University's College of Arts & Sciences Writing Program and also of writing programs at Yale University and Columbia University in New York City. He is the author of *Manufacturing Culture: Vindications of Early Victorian Industry* (University of Virginia Press, 2003). He revised Joseph M. Williams's *Style: Lessons in Clarity and Grace* (Pearson; 2014, 2017, 2020) and *Style: The Basics of Clarity and Grace* (Pearson, 2015). He is also co-revisor of *The Craft of Research* (University of Chicago Press; 2016, 2024); *A Manual for Writers of Research Papers, Theses, and Dissertations* (University of Chicago Press, 2018); and *Student's Guide to Writing College Papers* (University of Chicago Press, 2019). His scholarly interests include nineteenth-century literature, especially nonfiction prose, and writing studies, especially genre, style, and argumentation.

Anne E. Fernald (PhD, Yale University) is professor of English and women's, gender, and sexuality studies at Fordham University. She is the editor of *The Norton Critical Edition of* Mrs. Dalloway (2021) and *The Oxford Handbook of Virginia Woolf* (2021), and she is the author of *Virginia Woolf: Feminism and the Reader* (Palgrave Macmillan, 2006) as well as articles and reviews on Woolf and feminist modernism. At Fordham, she has worked as the director of first-year writing at Fordham's Lincoln Center campus; cochaired the university council on diversity, equity, and inclusion; and spearheaded university-wide faculty development during the COVID-19 pandemic. She is at work on a book on modernist women writers.